INHERITANCE ACT CLAIMS

TRUSTS, WILLS AND PROBATE LIBRARY

INHERITANCE ACT CLAIMS

FOURTH EDITION

SIDNEY ROSS, B.A. (Open), LL.B., Ph.D (London),
FCIArb, TEP
Barrister of Middle Temple and Lincoln's Inn

SWEET & MAXWELL

 THOMSON REUTERS

(1993) By Sidney Ross
(2000) By Sidney Ross
(2011) By Sidney Ross
(2017) By Sidney Ross

Published in 2017 by Thomson Reuters,
trading as Sweet & Maxwell. Registered in England & Wales, Company No.1679046.
Registered Office and address for service: 5 Canada Square, Canary Wharf, London,
E14 5AQ. For further information on our products and services, visit
http://www.sweetandmaxwell.co.uk.

Typeset by YHT, London.
Printed and bound by CPI Group (UK) Ltd,
Croydon, CR0 4YY.

No natural forests were destroyed to make this product: only farmed timber was used
and replanted.

A CIP catalogue record for this book is available from the British Library.

ISBN 978-0-414-06081-4

FOREWORD BY LORD JUSTICE HENDERSON

It gives me the greatest pleasure to welcome this fourth edition of Sidney Ross's distinguished textbook on Inheritance Act Claims, some 24 years after its first appearance (in a different format) in 1993.

The benefits of the author's close involvement over such a long period with the law and practice of family provision claims are apparent throughout the book. His experience as a barrister in practice at the Chancery Bar, combined with his academic background, ideally qualify him to analyse, explain and comment on the deceptively simple looking provisions of the 1975 Act, and the steady stream of case law to which they have given rise for more than four decades. That stream has, of course, recently culminated in the first case under the Act to reach the Supreme Court (or, previously, the House of Lords), *Ilott v Mitson (No. 2)*, which was heard by a panel of seven justices in December 2016 and judgment in which was delivered on 15 March 2017. This timing could hardly have been more serendipitous, enabling Mr Ross to deal fully with the judgments and integrate them into his text at the appropriate places, while avoiding every legal author's nightmare of finding his cherished handiwork overtaken by the appearance of a landmark case shortly before the date of publication.

In the event, I suspect that many will agree with the author's measured comments on the significance of *Ilott*, while perhaps also sharing some of the frustrations expressed by Lady Hale in her judgment about the lack of statutory guidance on how to evaluate the numerous factors which have to be taken into account in deciding whether a claim by an adult child of the deceased should succeed, and (if so) how the court should determine "such financial provision as it would be reasonable in all the circumstances of the case for the applicant to receive for his maintenance". It is, indeed, a striking feature of the 1975 Act that, in a given factual situation, there is often room for a wide divergence of legitimate views about the value judgments which have to be made under the Act. In advising clients on these matters, and in bringing, defending and (where possible) compromising claims under the Act, busy practitioners need all the assistance they can get. They will find this book an invaluable companion and resource, not least for its very full and user-friendly treatment of the case law. Of particular value, in my view, are the detailed case summaries in Appendix 6, which are grouped by subject and include references to articles and case notes relating to individual cases.

If I may be forgiven a personal reminiscence, the first case which I heard as a deputy High Court judge in 2001 was a claim in the Chancery Division by a widow under the 1975 Act: *McNulty v McNulty*. The case is duly noted at a number of points in the text, and it is included in section A of the case summaries dealing with claims by surviving spouses and civil partners. It features in the author's discussion of the difficult "notional divorce" criterion in s.3(2), which has now received some welcome clarification by an amendment which came into force in 2014. That amendment, and others which resulted from the Law Commission's 2011 Report on *Intestacy and Family Provision Claims on Death*, are fully treated by the author in the comprehensive work of revision and updating which he has performed since the appearance of the third edition of this work in 2011.

Another striking feature of claims under the Act is the way in which they sometimes require the skills of an expert family lawyer, sometimes the skills of a Chancery practitioner, and not infrequently a combination of both. No doubt for that reason, claims under the Act may be brought (in the High Court) in either the Chancery or the Family Divisions. At a time when the work of the Chancery Division is about to be subsumed under the umbrella of the blandly named Business and Property Courts of England and Wales, it is opportune to reflect on the very significant contribution which Chancery judges and practitioners have made over the years to the jurisprudence and literature on family provision claims, and to express the hope that they will continue to form a flourishing part of the wide range of work undertaken by the Chancery Bar.

Mr Ross's book has long played an important role in that illustrious tradition, and I have every confidence that it will continue to do so.

Launcelot Henderson
1 September 2017

PREFACE TO THE FOURTH EDITION

The second decade of the twenty-first century has been, to date, an important period in the development of the law of family provision. The Law Commission Report No.331, *Intestacy and Family Provision Claims on Death*, was published in December 2011, the month after the previous edition of this work. The recommendations of the report were to be implemented by the draft Inheritance and Trustees' Powers Bill (Appendix A), implementing the recommendations of Pts 2–7 of the report, and the Inheritance (Cohabitation) Bill (Appendix B), implementing those of Pt 8. The first of those bills received Royal Assent on 15 May 2014 and the Inheritance and Trustees' Powers Act 2014 ("the 2014 Act") came into force on 1 October 2014. It had always been intended that this would be the first of the two Bills to be enacted but, as discussed in Appendix 2 (Inheritance Rights for Cohabitants), it is increasingly unlikely that its companion Bill will reach the statute book in the foreseeable future.

The 1975 Act was amended by s.6 and Schs 2 and 3 of the 2014 Act, and the majority of the amendments were directed towards reform of aspects of the 1975 Act where either its interpretation was uncertain or experience had shown that the application of its provisions as originally enacted had resulted, or had the potential to result, in unsatisfactory outcomes. These amendments are all fully discussed in the main text but, broadly speaking, the amendments to s.3(2) (the "notional divorce") and s.3(4) (assumption of responsibility) fall into the first category and those to s.1(1)(d) (new definition of the class of eligible claimant), and ss.4 (time limit) and 23 (date when representation was first taken out) are in the second. The amendments to s.1(3) which does away with the "balance–sheet approach" (as the Law Commission termed it) and to s.9 (treating severable share of jointly owned property as part of the net estate) address both types of difficulty which have been experienced with the original provisions. However, one major feature of the Bill did not survive the legislative process. Dissatisfaction with domicile as the jurisdictional gateway led to the recommendation for an alternative precondition, permitting the making of an application if the deceased's estate included, or was treated as including, certain property to which the domestic succession law of England and Wales applied. This recommendation proved unacceptable to the Government, and the further consultation initiated by the Ministry of Justice in March 2013 showed little enthusiasm by the consultees for any of the alternatives proposed. In the result, it remains necessary for the deceased to have died domiciled in England and Wales for the court to entertain a claim under the 1975 Act.

This legislative activity and the developments in the case-law which are discussed in the three following paragraphs have not led to any major alteration in the structure of this book, though there has been some internal reorganisation. The increasing amount of accessible material has made it possible to approach some aspects of the law in a more systematic manner than before; examples are the treatment of "Obligations of the Deceased" and of "Other matters, including conduct" in Ch.4, and of reasonable provision in successful claims by adult children, in Ch.6. The author is aware, both from his previous academic and his present professional career, of the tendency which affects all textbook writers, to impose patterns where they may not, in reality, exist. Necessary or desirable as this may be for the purposes of exposition, it is not intended to suggest that the classifications devised for this work are immutable and that all relevant cases must be somehow forced into one of them; indeed the allocation of a separate sub-section of Ch.6 to *Ilott v Mitson* illustrates the need to acknowledge that a particular case may be *sui generis* and incapable of accommodation within an existing framework.

The recent landscape of case-law has of course been dominated by *Ilott v Mitson*, which in its various stages from 29 May 2007 to 15 March 2017 occupied the attention of a district judge, two High Court judges of the Family Division, the Court of Appeal (twice), at least one Lord Justice of Appeal on an application for permission to appeal, and a seven-member Supreme Court which turned the judicial wheel full circle and restored the award made to Mrs Ilott by the District Judge in 2007. It has been the author's view throughout that *Ilott v Mitson* was not the existential threat to testamentary freedom that some commentators perceived and was simply (although not falling within any category of his own classification) an application of perfectly well-known principles which had been established in the early years of the currency of the 1975 Act; and in that regard we may note that the cases to which the Supreme Court gave the most consideration in forming its judgment were *Coventry* (1980), *Dennis* (1981), *Jennings* (1994), *Hancock* (1998), and one comparative newcomer, *Myers* (2005).

However, the thirty-eight cases decided in and after 2011 and added to Appendix 6 (case summaries) include a number of important decisions both on provision for specific classes of applicant and on other provisions of the Act. Particularly noteworthy are *Lilleyman v Lilleyman* [2013] Ch. 225 (a short-marriage, big money claim by a surviving spouse), *Lewis v Warner* [2016] W.T.L.R. 1399 (an unusual award, made in a claim by a cohabitant), *Wright v Waters* [2015] W.T.L.R 353 (the first reported case in which an otherwise viable claim was totally defeated by the claimant's conduct) and *King v Dubrey* [2015] W.T.L.R 1225 (a claim by a dependant, where the importance lay in the detailed consideration given by the Court of Appeal to the law of *donatio mortis causa*). In relation to specific provisions of the Act there were important decisions on s.4 (*Berger v Berger* [2014] W.T.L.R. 35), s.8(1) (*Goenka v Goenka* [2016] Ch. 267), s.9 (*Lim v Walia* [2015] Ch. 375), s.10 (a transcript of interlocutory proceedings in *Dellal v Dellal* [2015] EWHC 907 (Fam)) and s.15 (*Chekov v Fryer* [2015] EWHC 1642 (Ch)), while s.5 made its first appearance in a reported case (*Smith v Smith* [2012] 2 F.L.R. 230) and s.6 made its debut with *Taylor v Bell*, though that case has not been fully reported. *Holliday v Musa,* a claim by a dependant, shared with *Ilott v Mitson* the distinction of reaching the Court of Appeal twice, but with the claimant achieving a perfect score, winning on both domicile (*Holliday v Musa* [2010] 2 F.L.R. 702) and the substantive issue at first instance and on appeal (*Musa v Holliday* [2013] 1 F.L.R. 806).

Reports of separate judgments on costs have begun to appear and the costs judgments in *Lilleyman v Lilleyman* [2012] 1 W.L.R. 2801 and *Wooldridge v Wooldridge* [2016] 3 Costs L.O. 531 illustrate the damaging consequences of taking up unrealistic negotiating positions and making unfounded allegations of misconduct by the other party. Those two cases have been added to the "to do and not to do" list at the end of Ch.1, so that the "ten frequent errors" first identified in the Practitioner Series version of this work (2006) and to which one was added in the 2011 edition now stand at thirteen. The author would ask whether, in view of the steady growth of family provision litigation, it is not time for consideration to be given to more specific training in this area for practitioners, because it is not one which fits comfortably into such more generally recognised areas of practice such as general litigation, probate or matrimonial cases.

Because cases are increasingly being heard at first instance by Masters and District Judges, and by Circuit Judges in the County Court and in district registries, it is becoming more difficult for practitioners to keep up with developments in the case-law through the medium of reports. Wills and Trusts Law Reports has now become, in the author's view, an indispensable resource for that purpose, and the Family Law Reports, together with the case comments in Family Law, continue to provide valuable coverage. However, for the cases which do not appear in those reports, access to LexisNexis, or Westlaw, or (ideally) both is now essential, though BAILII, which has the advantage of being free, is also a useful source of unreported High Court and Court of Appeal cases.

Because of the circumstances in which this edition of the book has been written, the acknowledgments take a slightly different form from those in previous versions of this work. I had committed to the task of preparing a new edition in the autumn of 2015, shortly before the chambers of which I had been a member for thirty-one years dissolved. My first expression of gratitude, therefore, is to my new colleagues at 10 Old Square for welcoming me into their number and for their general support and interest in the progress of this work. My membership of 10 Old Square has greatly facilitated its production, and Keith Plowman and his clerking team have managed my practice with great efficiency during the seven months of almost full-time work which has been devoted to it. Martyn Frost, well known to many practitioners in this field, kindly agreed to read the manuscript and I am greatly indebted to him for his perceptive comments, for drawing my attention to some cases which I might otherwise have missed, and for bringing to my attention a number of practical points from his own professional experience. Finally, it is a great pleasure to thank Richard Hepton at Sweet & Maxwell for his continued enthusiasm for this niche-market product and all his team for their contribution to its production. As on the occasion of the publication of previous editions, all whom I have mentioned are entitled to share in the credit should it prove successful; for any errors and infelicities, the responsibility is mine alone.

I have endeavoured to state the law as it is at 1 June 2017.

Q.E.F.

Sidney Ross
Ten Old Square Chambers
Lincoln's Inn
30 June 2017

CONTENTS

TABLE OF ABBREVIATIONS

ENTRIES MARKED WITH AN ASTERISK INDICATE REPORTS
WHICH FORM PART OF THE ENGLISH REPORTS

A.C.	Appeal Cases
All E.R.	All England Reports
App.Cas	Appeal Cases (1875–1890)
A.T.C.	Annotated Tax Cases
Beav.	Beavan*
B.C.L.C.	Butterworth's Company Law Cases
C.A.T.	Court of Appeal transcript
C.F.L.Q.	Child and Family Law Quarterly
Ch.	Chancery
Ch. App. Cas.	Chancery Appeal Cases (1865–1875)
Ch.D.	Chancery Division (1875–1890)
Ch. Div. (NI)	Chancery Division (Northern Ireland)
C.L.J.	Cambridge Law Journal
C.L.Y.	Current Law Yearbook
C.O.D.	Crown Office Digest
Conv.	The Conveyancer and Property Lawyer
Cox Eq Cas	Cox's Equity Cases*
Cr. App. R.	Criminal Appeal Reports
C.T.P.	Capital Tax Planning
Denning L.J.	Denning Law Journal
D.L.R.	Dominion Law Reports
E.C.A.	Elderly Client Adviser
E.G.	Estates Gazette
E.R.	English Reports
Eld. L.J.	Elder Law Journal
EWCA Civ	England & Wales Court of Appeal, Civil Division
EWHC	England & Wales High Court
Fam.	Family Division
Fam. Law	Family Law
F.L.J.	Family Law Journal
Fam. M.	Family Matters
F.C.R.	Family Court Reports

F.L.R.	Family Law Reports
F.L.T.	Family Law Today
Hag. Con.	Haggard (Consistory)*
H.L.C.	House of Lords Cases*
H.L.R.	Housing Law Reports
H. & C.	Hurlstone and Coltman*
H. & N.	Hurlstone and Norman*
I.C.L.Q.	International Comparative Law Quarterly
I.C.R.	Industrial Cases Reports
I.H.L.	In-House Lawyer
J.P.	Justice of the Peace
J.P.N.	Justice of the Peace Journal
Jur.	The Jurist
Jur. N.S.	The Jurist (new series)
K.B.	King's Bench
L. Ex.	Legal Executive
L.G.R.	Local Government Reports
Lit.	Litigation
L.J.	Law Journal
L.J.Ch.	Law Journal, Chancery
L.J.K.B.	Law Journal, King's Bench
L.J.P.C.	Law Journal, Privy Council
L.J.P.	Law Journal, Probate
L.J.Q.B.	Law Journal, Queen's Bench
L.J.R.	Law Journal Reports
Lloyds Rep.	Lloyd's Reports
L.R. P. & D.	Law Reports, Probate and Divorce cases (1865–75)
L.S. Gaz.	Law Society Gazette
L.T.	Law Times
L.T.J.	Law Times Journal
L.T.O.S.	Law Times (old series)
M.L.B.	Manx Law Bulletin
M.L.R.	Modern Law Review
Mod.	Modern Reports*
M. & W.	Meeson & Welsby*
New L.J.	New Law Journal
N.I.	Northern Ireland Law Reports
N.I.J.B.	Northern Ireland Judgments Bulletin
Nott. L.J.	Nottingham Law Journal
N.Z.L.R.	New Zealand Law Reports
O.J.L.S.	Oxford Journal of Legal Studies
P	Probate
P.C.B.	Private Client Business
P. & C.R.	Property and Compensation Reports
P.I.L.J.	Personal Injury Law Journal
P.N.	Professional Negligence
Q.B.	Queen's Bench

Q.B.D.	Queen's Bench Division (1875–1890)
R. & I.T.	Rating and Income Tax Reports
R.V.R.	Rating and Valuation Reporter
S.J.	Solicitors' Journal
S.T.C.	Simon's Tax Cases
T.C.	Tax Cases
T.E.L.J.	Trusts and Estates Law Journal
T.E.L. & T.J.	Trusts and Estates Law and Tax Journal
T.L.I.	Trust Law International
T.L.R.	Times Law Reports
T.Q.R.	Trust Quarterly Review
T.R.	Times Reports
Tr. & Est.	Trusts and Estates
UKHL	United Kingdom, House of Lords
UKSC	United Kingdom, Senior Court
Ves.	Vesey*
V.R.	Victorian Reports
W.L.R.	Weekly Law Reports
W.N.	Weekly Notes
W.R.	Weekly Reports
W.T.L.R.	Wills and Trusts Law Reports
W.W.R. (NS)	Western Weekly Reports (new series)
Y & CCC	Yonge and Collier's Chancery Cases*

SHORT TITLES OF BOOKS AND REPORTS

In each chapter, the books and reports listed here are referred to by their full titles in the first citation, and by their short titles thereafter.

BOOKS

Chamberlain and Whitehouse
E. Chamberlain OBE and C. Whitehouse, *Trust Taxation,* 4th edn (London: Sweet & Maxwell, 2014)

Cook on Costs
S. Middleton and J. Rowley (eds), *Cook on Costs 2017* (London: LexisNexis Butterworths, 2017)

CPAG Handbook
Child Poverty Action Group, *Welfare Benefits and Tax Credits Handbook,* 19th edn (London: CPAG, 2017)

Dicey, Morris and Collins
Lord Collins of Mapesbury, J. Harris, A. Dickinson, D. McClean, P. McEleavy, C. McLachan, R. Aikens, V. Ruiz Abou-Nigm, F. Toube QC

(eds), *Dicey, Morris and Collins on the Conflict of Laws,* 15th edn (London: Sweet & Maxwell, 2012)

Foskett
The Hon. Mr Justice Foskett, *The Law and Practice of Compromise*, 8th edn (London: Sweet & Maxwell, 2015)

Francis
A. Francis, *Inheritance Act Claims—Law, Practice and Procedure* (London: LexisNexis Butterworths)

Lewin
L. Tucker, N. Le Poidevin QC and J. Brightwell, *Lewin on Trusts,* 19th edn (London: Sweet & Maxwell, 2015)

McCutcheon
Withers LLP, A. Nathan and M. Lemos, *McCutcheon on Inheritance Tax*, 7th edn (London: Sweet & Maxwell, 2016)

Snell
J. McGhee QC (ed), *Snell's Equity*, 33rd edn (London: Sweet & Maxwell, 2015)

Theobald
J. R. Martyn, A. Learmonth, J. E. Gordon, C. Ford and T. Fletcher, *Theobald on Wills*, 18th edn (London: Sweet & Maxwell, 2016)

Tristram and Coote
P. Teverson, R. d'Costa and T. Synak, *Tristram and Coote's Probate Practice*, 31st edn (London: LexisNexis Butterworths, 2015)

Tyler
E.L.G. Tyler and R.D. Oughton, *Tyler's Family Provision*, 3rd edn (London: LexisNexis Butterworths, 1997)

Williams on Wills
R. F. D. Barlow, R. A. Wallington, S. L. Meadway, J. A. D. MacDougald, *Williams on Wills*, 10th edn (London: LexisNexis Butterworths, 2014)

REPORTS

Jackson Report
Right Honourable Lord Justice Jackson, *Review of Civil Litigation Costs: Final Report* (The Stationery Office, 2009)

Law Com WP 42
Law Commission Working Paper No.42, *Family Property Law* (1971)

Law Com LC 61
Law Commission Report No.61, *Family Law: Second Report on Family Property: Family Provision on Death* (1974)

Law Com LC 187
Law Commission Report No.187, *Family Law: Distribution on Intestacy* (1989)

Law Com CP 191
Law Commission Consultation Paper No.191, *Intestacy and Family Provision Claims on Death* (2009)

Law Com LC 295
Law Commission Report No.295, *The Forfeiture Rule and the Law of Succession* (2005)

Law Com LC 307
Law Commission Report No.307, *Cohabitation: the financial consequences of relationship breakdown* (2007)

Law Com LC 331
Law Commission Report No.331, *Intestacy and Family Provision Claims on Death* (2011)

MoJ CP6
Ministry of Justice Consultation Paper CP6/2013, *Draft Inheritance and Trustees' Powers Bill* (March 2013)

MoJ CP6, response
Ministry of Justice Response to Consultation CP6/2013 (July 2013)

TRANSCRIPTS OF UNREPORTED CASES

There is a substantial amount of case-law which has not been reported but which may be of value in considering the circumstances of any particular claim. It may be helpful to practitioners to know where the transcripts of these unreported decisions can be found and the two-part list which follows provides that information.

There are two main sources of transcripts. LexisNexis holds transcripts of almost all the unreported cases from 1980 to 1997 cited in this work. These cases, which are Court of Appeal decisions unless otherwise indicated, are listed in Part I. This Part also includes some transcripts of cases referred to by their neutral citations

Where a case is referred to by its neutral citation but is unreported, the transcript may, alternatively, be found on Westlaw, which is also a source of transcripts of cases decided in district registries and County Courts. These are listed in Part II

Part I

Barnsley v Ward	8 January 1980
Capocci v Cooke	2 February 1996
Clark v Jones	2 December 1985
Clifford v Tanner	10 June 1986
Cumming-Burns v Burns	4 July 1985
Dixit v Dixit	23 June 1988
Eeles v Evans	6 July 1989
Hedy v Firth	15 August 1989
Hocking v Hocking	12 July 1997
Ilott v Mitson (permission to appeal)	[2010] EWCA Civ 1426
Jevdjovic v Milenko	12 March 1990
J (a minor), Re	9 December 1991
Legat v Ryder (Ch.D., Dillon J)	2 May 1980
Lewis v Lynch	13 March 1980
Moody v Haselgrove	16 November 1987
Palmer v Lawrence (Birmingham, HH Judge Purle QC)	[2011] EWHC 3961 (Ch)
Patel v Vigh	[2013] EWHC 3403 (Ch)
Patel v Vigh (permission to appeal)	[2014] EWCA Civ 1825
Perry v Horlick	19 November 1987
Polackova v Sobolewski (Executor of A. Pichlak, Deceased)	28 October 1985
Portt, Re, Allcorn v Harvey and Woodcock	25 March 1980
Rhodes v Dean	28 March 1996
Riggs v Lloyds Bank	27 November 1992
Roberts v Fresco	[2017] EWHC 283 (Ch)
Smith v Loosely	18 June 1986
Stephens v Stephens	1 July 1985
Taylor v Bell (Leeds County Court)	[2015] All E.R. (D) 208
Tibbs v Beresford-Webb	18 December 1997
Walker v Walker	10 May 1980
Wallace v Thorburn	9 October 1987
Winfield v Billington	30 July 1990

Part II
Note: Where the claim was heard in a County Court or district registry, the location is given

Ames v Jones (Central London)	16 August 2016
Burnard v Burnard	[2014] EWHC 340 (Ch)
D v D	[2010] EWHC 138 (Fam)
J v J	[2009] EWHC 2654 (Fam)
Lewis v Warner (costs)	[2016] EWHC 1787 (Ch)
Martin v Williams	[2017] EWHC 491 (Ch)

TABLE OF CASES

TABLE OF STATUTES

TABLE OF STATUTORY INSTRUMENTS

CHAPTER 1

WHAT CLAIMS MAY BE MADE ON DEATH

1.—INTRODUCTION

(a) General

Although this is a book about claims under the Inheritance (Provision for **1–001** Family and Dependants) Act 1975 ("the 1975 Act"), its scope must necessarily extend to the other types of claim which may arise on the death of the person out of whose estate financial provision is being claimed under that Act. The 1975 Act has been further amended in relation to deaths after 1 October 2014 by the Inheritance and Trustees' Powers Act 2014 ("the 2014 Act") ss.6 and 12, and Sch.2. All practitioners who deal with 1975 Act claims will appreciate that, in addition to providing the occasion for such a claim, the death of the deceased may also give rise to one or more other claims. Some of those claims may be based wholly on facts, and raise issues, which are quite separate from those arising in the 1975 Act claim, and some will involve facts and issues in common, to a greater or lesser extent, with those of the 1975 Act claim. The reported cases show an increasing tendency to advance multiple claims. Claims which raise issues separate from those of the 1975 Act claim include challenges to the will, resulting in a probate action,[1] claims for rectification of the will under s.20 of the Administration of Justice Act 1982,[2] claims in professional negligence, and an unusual case in which the 1975 Act claim was an alternative to a claim for a declaration that property had been transferred to the claimant by way of *donatio mortis causa*.[3] Those based on facts or raising issues in common with the 1975 Act claim may include claims under the Trusts of Land and Appointment of Trustees Act 1996 (TLATA) asserting a beneficial interest in the estate or some specified asset of it[4]; claims based on proprietary estoppel,[5] and claims by the personal representatives for possession of land occupied by the prospective claimant.[6]

1–002   It is essential for anyone conducting a 1975 Act claim to be aware of these possibilities and to consider, should any of them arise, the way in which the claims will interact, the roles of the parties in the various claims, and the manner in which the proceedings will have to be constituted as a result of their having arisen. These matters are dealt with more fully in Ch.7,[7] but it is as well to have them in mind from the outset.

(b) Territorial Scope of the 1975 Act

1–003   The 1975 Act applies in England and Wales. The corresponding legislation in Northern Ireland is the Inheritance (Provision for Family and Dependants) (Northern Ireland) Order 1979,[8,9] and in the Isle of Man, the Inheritance (Provision for Family and Dependants) Act 1982. In both cases the provisions of the legislation closely follow the 1975 Act. In all three of those jurisdictions, a claim may be made only if the deceased had died

---

[1] *Baker v Baker* [2008] 2 F.L.R. 767; [2008] W.T.L.R. 565; *Pinnock v Rochester* [2011] EWHC 4049 (Ch); *Watts v Watts* [2014] EWHC 668 (Ch).

[2] *Grattan v McNaughton* [2001] W.T.L.R. 1305, in which the 1975 Act claim had also been preceded by an unsuccessful claim in professional negligence.

[3] *King v Dubrey* [2016] Ch 221.

[4] *Churchill v Roach* [2003] W.T.L.R. 779, where there were also claims based on constructive trust and proprietary estoppel; *Baker v Baker* [2008] 2 F.L.R. 767; [2008] W.T.L.R. 565; *Negus v Bahouse* [2008] 1 F.L.R. 381. In *Seals v Williams* [2015] W.T.L.R. 1265, the 1975 Act claim had been preceded by a dispute about title to land involving the same parties; see *Williams v Seals* [2015] W.T.L.R. 339.

[5] *Bye v Colvin-Scott* [2010] W.T.L.R. 1; *Wright v Waters* [2015] W.T.L.R. 353.

[6] *Moody v. Stevenson* [1992] Ch 486; *Negus v Bahouse* [2008] 1 F.L.R. 381; *Bye v Colvin-Scott* [2010] W.T.L.R. 1; *Lewis v Warner* [2016] 3 W.L.R. 1545.

[7] See s.2, "Claims Relating to the Estates of Deceased Persons", in particular s.2(g), "Multiple Claims; An Overview".

[8] The 2014 Act does not apply to Northern Ireland except for the minor and consequential amendments effected by Sch.4 to that Act.

[9] For a useful comparison of the succession regimes in these jurisdictions and in Scotland, see Hilary Hiram, "New Developments in UK Succession Law", Vol.10.3, Electronic Journal of Comparative Law (December 2006 *https://www.ejcl.org/103/abs103-7.html* [Accessed 6 July 2017].

domiciled within the jurisdiction.[10] In Hong Kong, the Inheritance (Provision for Family and Dependants) Ordinance 1981 was modelled on the 1975 Act, but is more complex in many respects because of the variety of family relationships recognised in that jurisdiction. The Hong Kong legislation permits applications by an eligible person if the deceased had been resident within the jurisdiction at any time in the three years immediately before their death.

The 1975 Act does not apply to Scotland, which has no corresponding   **1–004** legislation of its own. Statutory provision for dependants is achieved in Scotland, as also in Jersey and in many European countries, by a system of forced heirship, though the fixed rights of inheritance in Scotland are restricted to the prior rights of the spouse in an intestate estate (not confined to Scottish domiciliaries) and to the legal rights of spouse and issue in the moveable property of the deceased if the deceased died domiciled in Scotland. The Succession (Scotland) Act 2016, which came into force on 4 March 2016, but whose provisions have not all, at the time of writing, taken effect, does not affect the legal and prior rights in estates of deceased persons conferred by the Succession (Scotland) Act 1964.

(c) The Family Provision Case-law and the Development of the Legislation

The history of the legislation was dealt with at some length in the two   **1–005** previous editions of this text, in which the pre-1975 Act case law was also considered in detail. This was because relatively few cases had been reported during the earlier years of the 1975 Act. Further, Oliver J had referred, in *Re Coventry*,[11] to the pre-1975 Act law as forming a continuum with the law under the new regime; in consequence, the principles by which cases under the Inheritance (Family Provision) Act 1938 ("the 1938 Act") had been decided were still applicable notwithstanding the expansion of the class of potential applicants. Although, for the reasons discussed below, much of the pre-1975 Act case-law has become irrelevant to the present-day practitioner, the cases from which the principles that are still applicable derive are identified and discussed as and when appropriate.

Under the 1938 legislation, the Chancery Division of the High Court had   **1–006** exclusive jurisdiction except in cases where the net estate was below the limit specified from time to time by the Lord Chancellor. There is little, if any, trace of decisions under the then existing matrimonial legislation influencing the way in which Chancery judges dealt with applications under the family provision legislation. The present interaction between the family provision and the matrimonial case-law has its origins in the 1971 Law Commission working paper on family property law, which resulted in the pronounced similarities between s.3 of the 1975 Act and s.25 of the Matrimonial Causes Act 1973. These provisions specify, respectively, the matters to which the court is to have regard in exercising its powers under s.2 of the 1975 Act and ss.23, 24 and 24A of the Matrimonial Causes Act 1973.

---

[10] The relevant aspects of the law of domicile are discussed in the first part of Ch.2.
[11] *Re Coventry* [1980] Ch 461, CA.

1–007   The Law Commission had the interests of surviving spouses very much at heart, since one of its particular concerns was whether the court should be given a wide discretionary power to rewrite a will by giving the surviving spouse "a fair share of the family assets, over and above her strict maintenance needs". Although this solution was not adopted, the outcome of claims by surviving spouses has (as is discussed in Ch.6) been increasingly influenced by the matrimonial case-law, beginning with the decision of the House of Lords in *White v White*[12] in which judges were urged to test their tentative views against the yardstick of equal division and, subsequently, with the approach based on considerations of needs, sharing and compensation, developed in the high-value matrimonial cases of *Miller v Miller, McFarlane v McFarlane*[13] and *Charman v Charman (No.4)*,[14] which was adopted in *Lilleyman v Lilleyman*.[15]

(d) The 1975 Act as Originally Enacted

1–008   The eligibility of a prospective claimant under the 1975 Act is treated in detail in Ch.2, but it is appropriate at this stage to summarise the manner in which the 1975 Act widened the pool of potential claimants, and differentiated between surviving spouses and other classes of claimant. Former spouses who had not remarried and whose right to apply for provision out of the estate of their deceased spouses had previously arisen from the matrimonial legislation were brought within the ambit of the 1975 Act by s.1(1)(b). Children of the deceased, of whatever age, and whether or not suffering from disability, became eligible under s.1(1)(c), as did step-children, if they came within the description of a person (not a child of the deceased) who:

> "...in the case of any marriage to which the deceased was a party, was treated by the deceased as a child of the family in relation to the marriage",

under s.1(1)(d). Finally, s.1(1)(e) brought in persons wholly or partly maintained by the deceased immediately before their death, thereby raising a violent but short-lived storm both in Parliament and in the press, of luridly expressed moral indignation.

1–009   The special position accorded to the surviving spouse by the 1975 Act rendered the bulk of the previous case-law, in relation to such applicants, irrelevant. The higher standard of maintenance specified by s.1(2)(a) of the 1975 Act meant the court was no longer to consider what was reasonable for the applicant's maintenance, but what it was reasonable for the applicant to have in all the circumstances, whether or not that provision was required for his or her maintenance. Further, s.3(2) required the court to take into

---

[12] *White v White* [2001] 1 A.C. 596. For the yardstick of equality, see Lord Nicholls at 605G.
[13] *Miller v Miller, McFarlane v McFarlane* [2006] 2 A.C. 618 (HL).
[14] *Charman v Charman (No.4)* [2007] 1 F.L.R. 1246, CA.
[15] *Lilleyman v Lilleyman* [2013] Ch 225.

account what the surviving spouse might reasonably expect to have received if, on the date when the deceased died, the marriage had instead of being terminated by death, been terminated by a decree of divorce. Judges have differed strongly as to whether that provision should be the starting point for consideration of applications by surviving spouses, or whether it is simply a factor to which no special status should be accorded.[16] The only other area of the 1975 Act case-law which has excited such differing judicial views is the manner in which applications by adult children who were able to earn their own living should be dealt with.

(e) Extensions to the Scope of the 1975 Act

In 1989 a Law Commission report was published which made proposals for an amendment to the 1975 Act.[17] The report was designed to deal with the law relating to intestacy, and the Law Commission appreciated that this proposal went over the boundary of intestacy, since the 1975 Act also applies to testate succession. The question arose because of the view expressed in the public opinion survey that the intestacy rules should automatically apply to cohabitants. The Law Commission rejected that view, mainly on the grounds that the provisions for division of an estate between, say, a surviving spouse and a cohabitant would be complex, and factual disputes would arise as to whether the prospective beneficiary was a cohabitant.[18] Their preferred solution was to create a new class of persons eligible to apply, namely, those cohabitants who satisfied the conditions of eligibility specified by s.1(3)(b) of the Fatal Accidents Act 1976.   **1–010**

That solution was implemented by the Law Reform (Succession) Act 1995, for applications under the 1975 Act where the deceased died on or after 1 January 1996. A new para.1(ba) was inserted into the 1975 Act, bringing within its scope any person (other than a surviving spouse or a former spouse who has not remarried) who has, during the whole of the period of two years immediately before the death of the deceased, been living: **1–011**

    (a) in the same household as the deceased; and
    (b) as the husband or wife of the deceased.

The corresponding Northern Ireland legislation has been amended in an identical fashion by the Succession (Northern Ireland) Order 1996.

Section 71 of the Civil Partnership Act 2004 (CPA), which came into force on 5 December 2005, provides that Sch.4 amends enactments relating to wills, administration of estates and family provision so that they apply in relation to civil partnerships as they apply in relation to marriage. The relevant provisions of the Schedule, which are discussed in more detail in   **1–012**

---

[16] See Ch.6, s.5(e): "The 'Notional Divorce'".
[17] Law Commission Report No.187, *Family Law: Distribution on Intestacy* (1989).
[18] Law Commission Consultation Paper No.91, *Intestacy and Family Provision Claims on Death* (2009), discussed at para.1–013.

Ch.2, are paras 15–27. In outline, the right to claim reasonable provision out of the deceased's estate is accorded to:

(a) a surviving civil partner of the deceased, who will, by analogy with a surviving spouse, be entitled to receive "what it would be reasonable for a civil partner to receive whether or not that provision is required for his or her maintenance" under s.1(2)(a) as amended);

(b) a same-sex cohabitant who has lived, for the requisite period, in the same household as the deceased, and as the civil partner of the deceased;

(c) a former civil partner of the deceased who has not subsequently married or registered a civil partnership; and

(d) a person (not being a child of the deceased) who in the case of any civil partnership to which the deceased was a party, was treated by the deceased as a child of the family in relation to the civil partnership.

There have so far been very few reported cases to provide guidance on the questions whether the indicia of living together as civil partners should differ (and, if so, how) from the indicia of living together as husband and wife. At the time of writing, only two claims by surviving civil partners have been reported, and both of them failed.[19] In one other case the question whether the claimant was eligible under s.1(1A) of the Act was tried as a preliminary issue and the report contains some judicial guidance as to what amounts to "living together in the same household as husband or wife".[20]

(f) Further Reform of the 1975 Act

1–013   In its consultation paper published in October 2009, the Law Commission, while noting the amendments introduced by the Law Reform (Succession) Act 1995 and the Civil Partnership Act 2004, observed that the 1975 Act had not been subject to a fundamental review since it was enacted.[21] It had by then published a report entitled "Cohabitation: the financial consequences of relationship breakdown".[22] Both in England and Wales and in Scotland, public attitudes had by then become markedly more favourable to an amelioration of the position of cohabitants on the death of their partners, and the consultation paper contained a number of proposals designed to have that effect in relation to the law of intestacy and the law of family provision. The recommendations of the subsequent Law Commission

---

[19] *Saunders v Garrett* [2005] W.T.L.R. 49, and *Baynes v Hedger* [2008] 2 F.L.R. 1805; [2008] W.T.L.R. 1719. The latter case went to appeal but the party who claimed as a cohabitant and failed at first instance did not appeal.

[20] *Lindop v Agus* [2009] W.T.L.R. 1175. See also *Baynes v Hedger*, n.17.

[21] Law Com. CP 191, para.1.18.

[22] Law Commission Report No.307, *Cohabitation: the financial consequences of relationship breakdown* (2007).

Report[23] were expressed in the two draft bills appended to it. The draft Inheritance and Trustees' Powers Bill[24] (Appendix A) embodying the recommendations of Pts 2–7 of the Report underwent substantial amendment before the legislation received the Royal Assent on 14 May 2014. Except for the amendment of s.1(1)(d) which widens the class of persons entitled to apply as persons having been treated as a child of the family, there is no extension to the range of eligible claimants. Parties to same-sex relationships, either as a married couple or a couple living together as a married couple are brought within the scope of the 1975 Act not by amendment of that Act but by the interpretation provisions of the Marriage (Same-Sex Couples) Act 2013.[25] The individual amendments are referred to in the subsequent chapters where the amended provisions are discussed. The draft Inheritance (Cohabitation) Bill (Appendix B) which was intended to embody the recommendations of Pt 8 of the Report and introduced as the Cohabitation Rights Bill[26] did not progress beyond its second reading in the House of Lords during the term of office of the coalition government. On its re-introduction in the subsequent Parliament it received its first reading on 4 June 2015 but has not progressed further. Appendix 2 of this work contains the text of the Bill in so far as it relates to family provision and other succession issues, and discusses the Law Commission's recommendations and the Parliamentary debates following its introduction.

2.—THE CONDUCT OF FAMILY PROVISION LITIGATION

(a) General Approach and Compliance with Protocols

This section provides an overview of the matters which have to be considered when planning the conduct of the litigation, irrespective of whether the client is the claimant or the defendant, and whether they are party to the proceedings in a personal or a representative capacity, or both. Chapter 7 contains more detailed discussion of pre-action conduct, protocols, alternative dispute resolution, offers of settlement and costs.   **1–014**

For a number of reasons, family provision litigation often displays a much greater degree of complexity than other civil litigation. As mentioned above, other claims may arise on the death of the deceased. The procedure applicable to each type of claim is discussed in more detail in Ch.7, but, if other claims are to be brought or defended, the practitioner will be faced, at an early stage, with the task of ensuring that the substance of each claim is communicated clearly to the prospective defendants; that each claim is properly conducted according to its own procedure; and that proper consideration is given to the question how the case embracing those claims can   **1–015**

---

[23] Law Commission Report No.331, *Intestacy and Family Provision Claims on Death* (2011).

[24] The Inheritance and Trustees' Powers Act 2014 (c.16), came into force on 1 October 2014.

[25] Marriage (Same-Sex Couples) Act 2013 Sch.3, Interpretation of Legislation Pt 1, Existing England and Wales legislation paras 1 and 2, in force from 13 March 2014.

[26] Appendix 2 contains the text of the draft bill and a summary of the relevant Law Commission recommendations.

be most efficiently and economically managed. This is vitally important in view of the substantial costs which are incurred under the CPR regime at a relatively early stage in the litigation.

1–016   The Practice Direction on pre-action protocols,[27] which now applies to disputes where there is no applicable pre-action protocol (PAP) approved by the Master of the Rolls, has been substantially amended following the criticisms contained in Lord Justice Jackson's report.[28] Paragraphs 3–6 address the objectives of PAPs, proportionality and steps to be taken before issuing a claim, and para.8, which deals with settlement and ADR, precedes its exposition of the available methods by stating that litigation is a last resort. The section on compliance at paras 13–15 emphasises that if the dispute proceeds to litigation, the court will expect the parties to have complied with the relevant PAP or practice direction, identifies conduct which the court may regard as non-compliant, and states the sanctions for non-compliance. *Civil Procedure 2017* does not contain any officially approved protocol letter for use in 1975 Act claims. However, a draft pre-action protocol was published in the April 2001 edition (no.24) of the newsletter of the Association of Contentious Trust and Probate Specialists (ACTAPS).[29] It was intended to apply to the resolution of trust and probate disputes and contains an annex setting out a letter of claim in a form recommended for intimating a claim under the 1975 Act for reasonable financial provision out of the estate of the deceased.

1–017   The basic elements of the ACTAPS draft pre-action protocol are that:

(a)   as soon as there is sufficient information to substantiate a claim, the claimant should send a letter of claim to the personal representatives and to each of the persons likely to be adversely affected by the claim (referred to as "the proposed defendants"). The letter should contain a clear summary of the claim and should, so far as possible, address the matters referred to in ss.3(1) and whichever of 3(2), (2A), (3) and (4) of the Act applies to the claimant. Copies of documents on which the claimant or any other party is likely to rely should be enclosed with the letter of claim;

(b)   each of the proposed defendants should respond to the letter of claim within 21 days stating whether they admit or deny the claim, responding in outline to the matters of fact relied on by the claimant and setting out the matters of fact on which they rely. Again, the letter should address, so far as possible, the matters under s.3(1) and any other applicable subsection of s.3, and relevant documents should be enclosed. If a proposed defendant intends to make a claim on their own behalf, the letter of response should contain the same information and documents as a letter of claim in respect of a Pt 20 claim. If they are unable to respond within the

---

[27] *Civil Procedure 2017*, Vol.1, section C.
[28] Right Honourable Lord Justice Jackson, *Review of Civil Litigation Costs* (The Stationery Office, December 2009), Ch.35, section 6, p.353.
[29] Reproduced, with permission, in Appendix 3.

time limit on any particular matter they should explain why and indicate when a response will be available.

The draft pre-action protocol recognises that, as events unfold, matters **1-018** may come to light which will alter the basis on which a party wishes to put their case. Consequently, letters of claim and of response do not have the same status as statements of case. The authors of the draft protocol express the view that it would not be consistent with the spirit of the protocol for a party to complain about the difference between the case as set out in the letter of claim (or response) and the case as eventually pleaded provided that there was no indication of any attempt to mislead.

(b) Compromises

The CPR regime encourages compromise and, through the provisions of Pts **1-019** 36 and 44, provides for costs penalties of varying severity to be visited on parties who fail to achieve better terms than were available to them by way of compromise or who conduct their cases unreasonably. What is unreasonable will vary from case to case,[30] but it is prudent to assume that it will include failure to set out the case clearly in a letter before action, unwillingness to compromise and, if a compromise is offered, failure to explain adequately to the offeree the basis on which the terms offered in the compromise have been arrived at.

However desirable it is to compromise, practitioners may often find it **1-020** difficult to set any effective negotiating process in train. A compromise of either family provision or probate litigation may affect a substantial number of parties with differing interests in the deceased's estate, and some of these parties may be under a disability (that is, either children or patients), unascertained or unborn, in which case the compromise must be approved by the Court in accordance with CPR r.21.10. When the interests of a substantial number of beneficiaries (particularly when some of them are under a disability) stand to be adversely affected, the negotiating process can become unwieldy and protracted.

Additionally, family provision litigation differs from probate litigation in **1-021** that, in probate litigation, the disputed will is almost always set aside or upheld as a whole, so the parties know from the start how the success or failure of the claim will affect their respective positions. Again, where there is a claim to a beneficial interest, it will at least be known whose position will be affected, although it may not be easy to quantify the claim. In such circumstances it may be relatively simple to formulate terms of compromise which can sensibly be offered or accepted.

In contrast, unless the dispositions on death are such that the bulk of the **1-022** estate passes to one person, it is often uncertain whose interests will be adversely affected if a family provision claim succeeds. Since s.2(4) of the 1975 Act gives the court very wide powers to determine how the burden of

---

[30] Section 6 of this chapter, "To do and not to do" gives some examples from cases decided since the publication of the previous edition (2011) of this work.

the award in favour of a successful claimant is to be borne among the beneficiaries of the deceased's estate, the effect on the individual beneficiaries' interests may be virtually unpredictable, particularly when the estate passes mainly by way of specific or pecuniary legacies. In such a case it may be difficult, if not impossible, to dispose of the claim by way of compromise unless express power to compromise without the consent of, and at the expense of, legatees and residuary beneficiaries is conferred on the executors by the will. The position of the personal representatives in relation to compromise negotiations is discussed in s.4(c), below.

(c) Alternative Dispute Resolution

1–023   While there is no requirement for parties to consider alternative dispute resolution (ADR), a refusal to do so, or to engage in ADR, may be considered unreasonable. The Court of Appeal held, in *Halsey v Milton Keynes General NHS Trust, Joy v Steel*,[31] that the court could not compel parties to engage in mediation, but it also stated that all members of the legal profession who conduct litigation should now routinely consider with their clients whether disputes are suitable for ADR; and may give their clients robust advice in that regard.[32] However, it is still not settled whether the court has power to direct ADR. In *Halsey* the court took the view that CPR r.1.4(2)(e) did not expressly permit the court to direct that such procedures should be used, but may merely encourage and facilitate their use,[33] and said that it was likely that compulsory ADR would constitute a violation of Art.6 of the European Convention on Human Rights as an unreasonable constraint on access to the courts.[34] Judicial debate on the question continues, one position being that the court has power to direct ADR under the existing rules,[35] and another is that the court can direct the parties to consider whether the case is capable of being resolved by ADR, and can require a party who considers it unsuitable to justify their position, with the possibility of a costs sanction should the judge determine otherwise. Broadly speaking, the position in practice appears to be that the court will not compel parties to engage in mediation (or any other form of ADR) but will

---

[31] *Halsey v Milton Keynes General NHS Trust, Joy v Steel* [2004] 1 W.L.R. 3002, CA. *Halsey* has been repeatedly followed but was distinguished in *Vale of Glamorgan Council v Roberts* [2008] EWHC 2911 (Ch) where the claimant local authority was largely successful in a boundary dispute but the defendant contended that a costs order should not be made in their favour. This contention was rejected as none of his own offers had positively suggested mediation, so that there was no actual refusal to mediate, and it would be going too far to disallow their costs because they had not initiated the mediation process.

[32] *Civil Procedure 2017*, Vol.2, para.14–8.

[33] For facilitation and encouragement of ADR procedures by case management, see *Civil Procedure 2017*, Vol.2, paras 14–12 and 14–13 (which set out the "Ungley Order" and a variation of it requiring a more immediate statement of parties' intentions concerning ADR).

[34] *Halsey*, [9].

[35] *Civil Procedure 2017*, Vol.2, para.14–9 provides a survey of judicial speeches on the power to direct ADR. Sir Anthony Clarke, the then Master of the Rolls, considered that the court had such powers via the combined effect of r.1.4(2)(e) (encouraging the parties to use an ADR procedure) and r.3.1(2)(m) (which enables the court to take any step in managing a case to further the overriding objective).

manage cases in a manner which puts parties who refuse to engage in ADR at a high risk of incurring costs sanctions. Chapter 7 contains a more detailed discussion of the decision in *Halsey* and the subsequent case law.[36]

3.—CONDUCT OF LITIGATION ON BEHALF OF A CLAIMANT

(a) Where the Claimant is Acting Only in Their Personal Capacity

It is of paramount importance to elicit from the claimant as much infor- **1–024** mation as possible relating to the matters set out in s.3(1) of the 1975 Act, which specifies the matters to which the court is directed to have regard in all cases, and to those in s.3(2) to which the court must have regard in considering claims by particular classes of claimant. Questionnaire QP in Appendix 4 has been compiled for that specific purpose. It also includes questions relating to other claims which might be brought.

In the normal course of events, the claimant will have little or no infor- **1–025** mation about a number of the matters listed in s.3(1); in particular, the financial needs and resources of other applicants or beneficiaries, see ss.3(1)(b) and (c) respectively. They may have little or no information about the nature and extent of the net estate (s.3(1)(e)), but this has to be supplied by the defendant personal representatives within 21 days of service of the claim on them, so that deficiency is, usually, quickly remedied.

It is vital to obtain full details of the claimant's financial needs and **1–026** resources, see s.3(1)(a); and s.3(6) requires their earning capacity to be taken into account. If the claimant is suffering from any disability, see s.3(1)(f), it is likely that medical evidence will be required as to its effect on their ability to work and their life expectancy. They should be asked to supply any correspondence with the Benefits Agency relating to benefits received in respect of disability. Many claimants who are in need of financial provision are in receipt of means-tested State benefits. When considering the merits of a 1975 Act claim, it is necessary to be aware of the effect which receipt of either a lump sum (which is by far the most usual type of award) or periodical payments will have on the claimant's entitlement to means-tested benefits. Working tax credit and child tax credit are not affected by receipt of a lump sum award, but are subject to gross income thresholds and would be affected by receipt of periodical payments.

Questions of obligation[37] appear from the reported cases to arise most **1–027** commonly in applications by adult children. It is clear from the Court of Appeal decision in *Re Jennings, Harlow v National Westminster Bank*,[38] that in order to be taken into account, the obligation must be one which is still subsisting at the date of the deceased's death. It is not always easy to decide whether a particular incident or train of events should be regarded as

---

[36] Ch.7, s.5, "Disposal of Claims by ADR".
[37] See s.3(1)(d) of the 1975 Act, which directs the court to have regard to the responsibilities and obligations which the deceased had towards applicants and beneficiaries.
[38] *Re Jennings, Harlow v National Westminster Bank* [1994] Ch. 286, CA.

creating an obligation for the purposes of s.3(1)(d) or as "any other relevant matter, including the conduct of the applicant or any other person", under s.3(1)(g). There may also be an overlap with s.3(1)(f), when the obligation arises out of the claimant's disability, as in *Re Debenham*[39] and *Hanbury v Hanbury*.[40]

1–028 Sometimes the decision is clear cut, as when the deceased has made a promise (not necessarily to the claimant) to leave certain assets to the claimant. Such promises were held by the Court of Appeal to create an obligation in *Goodchild v Goodchild*[41] and *Espinosa v Bourke*.[42] Conduct by the claimant which disadvantages them but benefits the deceased, as, for example, caring for the deceased (given as an example in *Re Coventry*) or working for low wages in the deceased's business (as in *Re Abram*[43] and *Re Pearce*[44]) may fall to be considered under either heading, and in practice it makes little, if any difference, which. Conduct by persons other than the claimant will generally come under s.3(1)(g).

1–029 It is very often the case, in practice, that the claimant's desire to bring a 1975 Act claim originates from, or is heavily influenced by, matters of conduct. However, it is important to realise that issues of conduct[45] do not often have a significant effect on the outcome of the claim. At the time of writing, *Wright v Waters*[46] is the only reported case in which an otherwise viable claim failed because of the conduct of the claimant, which involved verbal abuse leading to permanent estrangement and financial abuse, though *Re Snoek*[47] (in which the claimant widow's conduct included physical violence towards the deceased) came near to failure. In *Espinosa v Bourke*[48] an adult daughter's claim was dismissed at first instance, principally on the ground of the claimant's conduct towards the deceased, but the Court of Appeal reversed that decision and held, in awarding the claimant £60,000, that too much emphasis had been placed on her conduct and that the judge had failed to give proper consideration to her financial position, which was of paramount importance. Practitioners should therefore take care to ensure that the claimant's financial position is set out in the witness statement as fully and clearly as possible, and that matters of conduct are not given undue prominence.

1–030 For a number of reasons, it is highly desirable to ascertain from the claimant what particular type of provision is desired. If a specified objective is clearly in mind, that helps to focus the drafting of the witness statement,

---

[39] *Re Debenham* [1986] 1 F.L.R. 404.
[40] *Hanbury v Hanbury* [1999] 2 F.L.R. 255.
[41] *Goodchild v Goodchild* [1997] 3 All E.R. 63, CA.
[42] *Espinosa v Bourke* [1999] 1 F.L.R. 747, CA.
[43] *Re Abram* [1996] 2 F.L.R. 379.
[44] *Re Pearce* [1998] 2 F.L.R. 705.
[45] The types of conduct which have had significant effects are discussed more fully in Ch.4, ss.6(a) (conduct of the claimant) and 6(c) (conduct of the deceased).
[46] *Wright v Waters* [2015] W.T.L.R. 353.
[47] *Re Snoek* (1983) 13 Fam. Law 19. Wood J described her conduct towards the deceased as "atrocious and vicious" but took into account her role in bringing up the children of the marriage during its earlier years. She was awarded £5,000 out of an estate of £40,000.
[48] *Espinosa v Bourke* [1999] 1 F.L.R. 747, CA.

and also provides a basis on which negotiations can be usefully started. It may also assist when advising the client as to the prospects of success.

Finally, it is essential that the claimant be warned about the costs risk. It must be clearly understood that, whether it stands alone or is combined with other claims, a 1975 Act claim is, as between the claimant and the beneficiaries whose interests will be adversely affected, hostile litigation, and is subject to the normal costs regime which governs hostile litigation. There is no reason to suppose that an unsuccessful claimant will be allowed to recover their costs out of the estate; indeed, the practice of making such costs orders was deprecated by the Court of Appeal in *Re Fullard*.[49]   **1–031**

(b) Where the Claimant is Also a Personal Representative

In general, it is perfectly in order for a claimant under the 1975 Act to act as personal representative, and this situation can arise in a number of ways. It most commonly occurs when the surviving spouse is either appointed executor by the will or has the right to a grant on the deceased's death intestate, and is in competition with the deceased's children, whether by that or an earlier marriage. It could also come about where the claim involves an application under s.9 of the 1975 Act for the deceased's severable share of jointly owned property (particularly the matrimonial home) to be treated as part of the net estate.   **1–032**

While it may be natural to assume that a personal representative in such a situation ought to renounce, that is not so. There is no need for a claimant named as executor or having a right to administration to renounce. Making a 1975 Act claim is in no way inconsistent with the claimant's role as personal representative; they are not, by doing so, challenging the will, nor are they making a claim adverse to the estate, as they would be if (for example) they were claiming a beneficial interest in an asset which the deceased had purported to dispose of by their will. They are merely seeking a redistribution of the estate at the expense of the existing beneficiaries.   **1–033**

Everything which has been said in subs.(a) above, applies equally to a claimant who is also a personal representative. In their representative capacity their only role is to assist the court, and for this purpose they are not required by CPR r.57.16 to make a statement about the matters specified in the Practice Direction supplementing the rule. Only a *defendant* who is a personal representative is required to do so. The claimant may, of course, wish to include those matters, so far as they are aware of them, in the witness statement in support of their claim. It is, however, unlikely that they will have occasion to do anything, purely in their representative capacity, in the course of the proceedings, though for such acts they would be entitled to recover their costs out of the estate.   **1–034**

---

[49] *Re Fullard* [1982] Fam. 42, CA. The position under the CPR costs regime is discussed in Ch.7, s.9(b).

4.—Conduct of Litigation on Behalf of a Defendant

(a) Where the Defendant is Acting Only in Their Personal Capacity

1–035   In principle, such litigation should be conducted along the same lines as it would be on behalf of a claimant; and a defendant beneficiary is exposed to the same costs risk as a claimant.

1–036   1975 Act claims must be conducted in accordance with the Pt 8 procedure; therefore there is no requirement to file and serve a defence. Further, a defendant, in their capacity as beneficiary, is not obliged by CPR Pt 57 to serve any evidence. However, a beneficiary who either intends to contest the claim, or, while accepting that the claim has some merit, wishes to guard (so far as possible) against having to bear a disproportionate share of the burden of any award, would be well advised to make a witness statement which deals with any relevant matters to which the court is directed to have regard and, in particular, their financial needs and resources.[50]

1–037   Failure to do so (and, in particular, failure to provide the court with financial information) is likely to cause the court to conclude that the beneficiary's resources are amply sufficient to support their current way of living without recourse to the benefits that they stand to obtain under the deceased's will or intestacy or otherwise.[51] A beneficiary who does not want to reveal their financial circumstances to the claimant may, therefore, have a difficult decision to make. In *Lilleyman v Lilleyman*[52] the sons of the deceased's first marriage, who were the defendants to the widow's claim, declined to reveal their financial positions, and it was evident that their father had made significant financial provision for them during his lifetime. Briggs J (as he then was) went on to say:

> "Nonetheless it is apparent that the future careers and financial security of the defendants, and the financial security of their families, may well be dependent, to an extent, which the court cannot precisely measure, on preserving the three companies, whose shares constitute the most valuable assets in the estate, from undue attrition by the consequences of any award made in Mrs Lilleyman's favour."

In the result, the award to Mrs Lilleyman was funded entirely out of other assets; the only impingement on the companies was that £250,000, being that part of their increased value due to Mr Lilleyman's activities rather than passive economic growth, was included in the calculation of the value of the matrimonial property for the purpose of the divorce cross-check.

---

[50] See s.3(1)(c).
[51] For example, in the form of property that could be treated as part of the net estate under ss.8 or 9, or benefits payable following the death of the deceased which are not caught by s.8(2).
[52] *Lilleyman v Lilleyman* [2013] Ch 225, [66], [78].

(b) Where a Defendant Beneficiary is Also a Personal Representative

This is an extremely common situation. An obvious example is a surviving **1–038** spouse who has been appointed executor and benefits substantially under the will, or has taken a grant of administration on the death of the deceased intestate. There is no substance in the assertion that such a person cannot be represented by the same solicitor in both capacities. The role of the personal representative is one of strict neutrality and there is no conflict of interest.

It is most important that defendants in such a position keep their roles **1–039** separate. The function of the personal representative is to assist the court, and the most important aspect of that function is compliance with CPR r.57.16(5), which requires filing and service of the evidence specified in para.16 of the Practice Direction. The rule provides that a personal representative who is a defendant must, within 21 days of service of the claim form on them, file with the court a witness statement in answer to the claim which states, to the best of their ability:

(a) full particulars of the deceased's net estate, as defined by s.25(1) of the 1975 Act;
(b) the persons or classes of persons beneficially interested in the estate, giving the names and (in the case of those not already parties) the addresses of all living beneficiaries, and the value of their interests so far as ascertained;
(c) if it be the case, that any living beneficiary is a child or a or a person who lacks capacity within the meaning of the Mental Capacity Act 2005[53]; and
(d) any facts known to them which might affect the exercise of the Court's powers under the Act.

Unlike the former RSC Ord.99, CPR Pt 57 is silent on the question of **1–040** whether a personal representative is obliged to make any enquiries or investigations in order to ascertain or confirm any matters within the 21-day period; under the former regime the obligation was only to state the facts known to them at the time when they made the statement. In practice it may well be that a personal representative would continue with inquiries to obtain accurate values of the assets and liabilities of the estate, even after issue of the grant if appropriate. Keeping all parties informed of progress in that respect would no doubt further the overriding objective. It is suggested here that the proper course is to make such inquiries as are reasonable in respect of (a)–(c) above and in respect of (d) in so far as there is reason to doubt the claimant's eligibility, as discussed in the next paragraph.

Although the defendant should not, in their representative capacity, **1–041** attempt to defeat the claim on the merits, it is perfectly proper to draw the

---

[53] The Mental Capacity Act 2005 s.1(2) provides that a person must be assumed to have capacity unless it is established that they lack capacity. The test of capacity is set out in s.2. Lack of capacity involves the inability to make a decision and that aspect of incapacity is dealt with in s.3.

attention of the court to any facts which might raise doubt about the claimant's eligibility. The questions of eligibility which usually arise are whether:

(i)   the deceased died domiciled in England and Wales;
(ii) a claimant under s.1(1)(e) was being maintained by the deceased;
(iii) a claimant under s.1(1)(ba) had lived with the deceased as husband and wife or, as the case may be, the civil partner of the deceased and, if so, in the same household and/or for the requisite period[54];
(iv) a claimant under s.1(1)(c) is the child of the deceased;

and, less frequently, whether:

(v)   a claimant under s.1(1)(d) was treated as a child of the family. Such a claimant is not ineligible simply because they are an adult; see *Re Callaghan*[55] and *Leach v Lindemann*[56];
(vi) a surviving or former spouse was validly married to the deceased.

On the whole it is not desirable for the statement made by the personal representative to deal in any detail with matters of conduct, since it is difficult, if not impossible, to do so while maintaining the neutral attitude appropriate to a personal representative. To the limited extent that they are likely to assist in defeating the claim on the merits, these matters are best dealt with in a separate statement made by the defendant in their personal capacity.

(c) Where the Defendant is Acting Only as a Personal Representative

1–042   Where such a defendant is a professional executor, one can expect (though the expectation is not always fulfilled) an absence of partisanship. Family friends are more likely to want to take sides, since they may well be acquainted with personal matters which lead them to form views on the merits of a claim. Expressions of such views should, at any rate in witness statements, be firmly discouraged.

1–043   Personal representatives (including defendant beneficiaries acting in their representative capacity) are at no risk on costs provided that they confine themselves to assisting the court as explained above. They are entitled to their costs of rendering such assistance out of the estate.

(d) Compromises

1–044   Because they are seen as being above the conflict, it is not unusual for personal representatives to become involved in negotiations for the settlement of 1975 Act claims. There are sound practical reasons for such

---

[54] See subss.1(1A) and 1(1B).
[55] *Re Callaghan* [1985] Fam. 1.
[56] *Leach v Lindemann* [1986] Ch. 226, CA.

involvement, at any rate if there is a professional personal representative, since it should reduce the possibility of errors and unworkable terms in the formulation of the compromise, ensure that proper attention is paid to fiscal matters such as capital tax and SDLT liabilities, and the effect of the terms on state benefits, and provide a clear basis for assessing the incidence of costs. Section 15(f) of the Trustee Act 1925 provides that a personal representative may, as they think fit:

> "...compromise, compound, abandon, submit to arbitration or other-
> wise settle any debt, account, claim or thing whatever relating to the
> testator's or intestate's estate; and for those purposes may enter into,
> give, execute and do such agreements, instruments of composition or
> arrangement, releases and other things as seem to him expedient,
> without being responsible for any loss occasioned by any act or thing so
> done by him in good faith."

It was initially doubted whether this power extended to compromises of **1–045** 1975 Act claims, because such claims are not claims against the estate but claims for it to be distributed in a manner not provided for under the will or intestacy. That view may derive from the following passage of the judgment of Megarry V-C in *In Re Earl of Strafford, deceased*[57]:

> "I think that it has to be borne in mind that section 15 is concerned
> with what may be called external disputes, or cases in which there is
> some issue between the trustees on behalf of the trust as a whole and the
> outside world. It is not concerned with internal disputes, where one
> beneficiary under the trusts is at issue with another beneficiary under
> the trusts."

On a literal reading of s.15(f), a 1975 Act claim is "a claim ... relating to **1–046** the testator's or the intestate's estate". However, the position is correctly stated in the following passage from *The Law and Practice of Compromise*[58]:

> "The settlement of disputed claims arising under the [1975] Act should
> be seen against the background of the general proposition that such
> claims are claims against the individual rights of the beneficiaries of the
> estate and not against the estate as a whole. The consequence is that the
> personal representatives have no power to compromise claims under
> the Act pursuant to s.15 of the Trustee Act without reference to the
> beneficiaries. The appropriate course for the personal representatives to
> adopt (if the beneficiaries wish them to assume that role) is to seek to
> negotiate a compromise with the authority of the beneficiaries (with
> suitable indemnities as to costs) and (if any children or protected per-

---

[57] *In Re Earl of Strafford, deceased* [1980] Ch. 28 at 28H.
[58] The Hon. Mr Justice Foskett, *The Law and Practice of Compromise* (London: Sweet & Maxwell, 8th edn, 2015), para.25-01.

sons are affected or if any real doubt exists as to the propriety of the compromise) for the personal representatives to apply to the court for its approval to any resulting compromise using the procedure available under para.1A of PD 64A—Estates, Trusts and Charities."

Personal representatives, of course, have no power to vary wills, though they will have to be parties to the variation if additional tax becomes due as a result of it.[59]

1–047   Personal representatives should be aware that the exercise of the power of compromise is now subject to the statutory duty of care under the Trustee Act 2000. Section 1(1) provides that, whenever the duty of care applies to a trustee, they must exercise such care and skill as is reasonable in the circumstances, having regard in particular:

(a)   to any special knowledge or experience that they have or hold themselves out as having; and

(b)   if they act as a trustee in the course of a business or profession, to any knowledge or experience that it is reasonable to expect of a person acting in the course of that business or profession.

Schedule 1 para.4 applies the duty of care to a trustee when exercising power under s.15 of the Trustee Act 1925 to do any of the things referred to in that section. The effect of s.35(1) of the Trustee Act 2000 is that that Act applies to personal representatives administering an estate as it does to trustees carrying out a trust.

5.—OTHER PROCEEDINGS POTENTIALLY AFFECTING THE OUTCOME OF THE 1975 ACT CLAIM

(a) Can the Court Determine Other Claims Within the 1975 Act Proceedings?

1–048   Anecdotal evidence suggests the existence of some doubt as to what questions a court hearing a 1975 Act claim has jurisdiction to determine. In particular it appears to be thought in some quarters that there is jurisdiction to determine, in the course of a 1975 Act claim, whether a particular item of property is an asset of the estate. For example, in *Re Krubert*,[60] the applicant widow had contributed to the purchase price of the matrimonial home. One of the grounds of appeal against the decision at first instance (in the Caernarvon County Court) was that the judge had not quantified the beneficial interest to which she was entitled by reason of that contribution. The Court of Appeal held that, because the applicant had paid for the plot on which the matrimonial home was built, she had a small beneficial interest, but did not find it necessary to quantify it in deciding what amounted to reasonable provision for her. Logically, it is entirely appropriate for the

---

[59] Inheritance Tax Act 1984 s.142(2A)(b).
[60] *Re Krubert* [1997] Ch. 97, CA.

nature and extent of the net estate to be determined before considering whether and in what manner its distribution should be varied, but the Act does not give the court jurisdiction to do so. The practical solution is for the court to direct the claims to be tried consecutively on the same occasion,[61] the claim to the beneficial interest being tried first. However, as discussed in para.(c), below, this may not always be the most appropriate direction.

(b) Probate Claims

During the currency of the Inheritance (Family Provision) Act 1938, exclusive jurisdiction to hear and determine applications under that Act was vested in the Chancery Division of the High Court. As probate claims were also dealt with exclusively by the Chancery Division, it appears to have been thought that matters of testamentary validity could be determined in the course of claims under the 1938 Act. However, it has been held that allegations of testamentary incapacity and undue influence should not be raised within family provision proceedings; see *Re Blanch*,[62] and *Williams v Johns*,[63] where it was said that the allegation of undue influence should have been made in another court at an earlier stage. The same must logically apply to any other challenge to the validity of a will.

1–049

Whereas the Chancery and Family Divisions have concurrent jurisdiction over 1975 Act claims, and the County Court also has unlimited financial jurisdiction in such claims,[64] probate claims, which are also dealt with in accordance with CPR Pt 57, must be commenced either in the High Court, a County Court hearing centre which is also a Chancery District Registry,[65] or the County Court at Central London.[66] It is relatively unusual for a probate claim and a 1975 Act claim to be tried on the same occasion, though the court has power under CPR r.3.1(2)(h) to direct that this be done. In *Watts v Watts*[67] the deceased had purportedly made a will in 2011 leaving her entire estate to her adopted son, superseding her 1999 will which had divided her estate equally between him and her adopted daughter. The daughter challenged the 2011 will on the ground that it had not been duly executed and also made a 1975 Act claim. The result of the four-day trial was that the challenge to the 2011 will succeeded, so no order was made on the 1975 Act claim; however, it was also found that, had the 2011 will not been set aside, it would have failed to make reasonable provision for the daughter.

1–050

---

[61] Which it has power to do under CPR r.3.1(2)(h).

[62] *Re Blanch* [1967] 1 W.L.R. 987.

[63] *Williams v Johns* [1988] 2 F.L.R. 475 at 488.

[64] For the jurisdiction of the County Court to hear and determine 1975 Act claims, see s.25 of the County Courts Act 1984, as amended by the Crime and Courts Act 2013 Sch.9 para.10(1), with effect from 22 April 2014.

[65] Those registries are listed in para.57APD.2.3. At the time of writing, 57APD had not been amended to reflect the repeal of s.32 of the County Courts Act 1984 (relating to the contentious probate jurisdiction of the County Court) by the Crime and Courts Act 2013; see Sch.9 para.10(3).

[66] CPR r.57.2(3).

[67] *Watts v Watts* [2014] EWHC 668 (Ch).

(c) Claims to Beneficial Interests

1–051 Except for claims relating to the ownership of personal chattels, it is suggested that directions should be sought for the claim to be tried on the same occasion as the 1975 Act claim. The extremely robust judgment of Waite J in *Hammond v Mitchell*[68] makes it clear that every effort should be made to dispose of such claims without recourse to litigation.

1–052 In the unreported case of *Perry v Horlick*,[69] the applicant under the 1975 Act also claimed a declaration that he had an equitable interest in a house asserted by the personal representative to be an asset of the estate. The Court of Appeal (which was hearing an application for permission to commence proceedings out of time, not the substantive claim) expressed the view that it would be unfortunate if the two claims were not before the court at the same time. The order in which the claims should be heard may depend on the nature of the property in which the beneficial interest is claimed by the applicant and the nature of the provision which he is seeking.

1–053 It is suggested that unless the property in question is a house in which the claimant both claims a beneficial interest and seeks for financial provision which includes such an interest, the claim to the beneficial interest should be tried first as the nature and extent of the net estate will have been determined for the purpose of the 1975 Act proceedings. However, if the dispute centres around a house in the way described above, it may be more effective to try the 1975 Act application first, because the debate as to the beneficial ownership may then become irrelevant.

(d) Possession Claims

1–054 Where the applicant is occupying a property which is undisputedly an asset of the estate, it may, again, be preferable to try the 1975 Act proceedings first. In *Moody v Stevenson*[70] the former matrimonial home was the only substantial asset of the estate. In the County Court proceedings the executor applied for possession of the house and the surviving spouse made a cross-application under the 1975 Act. The claim for possession succeeded and the 1975 Act application was dismissed. The appeal against the dismissal of the 1975 Act claim succeeded, it being clear that the wrong test of reasonableness of provision had been applied. Had the relevant authorities been before the County Court Judge and the 1975 Act claim been tried first, it should have succeeded, in which case the possession proceedings would have been rendered unnecessary.

---

[68] *Hammond v Mitchell* [1992] 2 All E.R. 109. A useful general survey of this rather neglected topic is in Ann Stanyer, *Personal Chattels: Law, Practice and Tax with Precedents* (London: Sweet & Maxwell, 2009).

[69] *Perry v Horlick* unreported 16 November 1987, CA.

[70] *Moody v Stevenson* [1992] Ch. 486, CA.

6.—To Do and Not To Do

(a) Illustrative Cases

There are two cases of which every practitioner who is handling a 1975 Act   **1–055**
claim should be aware. They are the Court of Appeal decision in *Hannigan v
Hannigan*,[71] and the judgment of HH Judge Langan in *Parnall v Hurst*.[72]
Between them, they identify a staggering list of instances of inappropriate
conduct of such cases, some relatively trivial, some serious and fundamentally misconceived. The judgments make clear that solicitors should be ready
to co-operate in resolving minor (or even quite substantial) technical disputes on terms as to costs, rather than litigating with the object of getting
the claim dismissed on such grounds; such a sanction may well be (and was,
in both the cases referred to) found to be wholly disproportionate to the
gravity of the technical breaches. A similar view was taken by Briggs J in
Nesheim v Kosa,[73] where the procedural issue was the failure to serve proceedings out of the jurisdiction within the six-month time limit prescribed by
rules of court.[74] His judgment carefully analyses the principles relevant to a
grant of retrospective permission so as to remedy defective service, and
emphasises, by permitting the case to proceed on its merits in spite of the
procedural irregularity, the importance of the overriding objective of dealing
with cases justly.

Notwithstanding that neither in *Hannigan* (despite the multiplicity of   **1–056**
errors in that case) nor *Parnall* (where, apart from the general conduct of the
case, the breach of the rules was a serious one) was the claim struck out,
practitioners should not assume that either the claim will survive, or that
they will escape unscathed, if they conduct 1975 Act litigation in the manner
in which those cases were conducted. As Brooke LJ said in *Hannigan*, his
judgment was not to be taken as a green light for sloppy and inefficient
practices in solicitors' offices.

The judgments discussed in the two previous paragraphs must now be   **1–057**
considered in the light of the decision of the Court of Appeal in *Denton v
T.H.White*.[75] That case is concerned with applications under CPR r.3.9(1)
for relief from sanctions for failure to comply with case management
directions. The Court of Appeal was concerned to provide guidance in that
respect as a result of differing judicial approaches to the application of
Mitchell v News Group Newspapers,[76] of which the approaches adopted at

---

[71] *Hannigan v Hannigan* [2000] F.C.R. 650; [2006] W.T.L.R. 597, CA.
[72] *Parnall v Hurst* [2003] W.T.L.R. 997.
[73] *Nesheim v Kosa* [2007] W.T.L.R. 149.
[74] At the time, the relevant rule was CPR r.7.5(3), but the rule was substantially changed with
effect from 1 October 2008; see the commentary in *Civil Procedure 2017* Vol.1, para.7.5.1.
Service out of the jurisdiction is now regulated by CPR rr.6.30–6.47 and Practice Direction
6B.
[75] *Denton v T.H. White Ltd (De Laval Ltd (Pt 20 defendant))* [2014] 1 W.L.R. 3926. Relevant
paragraphs of the judgment are indicated by numbers in square brackets.
[76] *Mitchell v News Group Newspapers* [2014] 1 W.L.R. 795, CA.

first instance in *Denton* and in the two other cases which they considered in their judgment are examples.[77] *The White Book* provides a very extensive and detailed commentary to the rule,[78] but the following points from the judgment of Lord Dyson MR and Vos LJ[79] should be particularly noted.

(i) A judge should address an application for relief from sanctions under CPR r.3.9.1 in three stages, which are:

    (a)   identification and assessment of the seriousness and significance of the failure to comply with any rule, practice direction or court order which engages that rule;

    (b)   consideration of why the default occurred; and

    (c)   evaluation of all the circumstances of the case so as to enable the court to deal justly with the application including the factors in sub-paragraphs (a) and (b)[80] [24].

If a judge concludes that a breach is not serious or significant, relief from sanctions will usually be granted and it will usually be unnecessary to spend much time on the second or third stages. If the court decides that the breach is serious or significant, the second and third stages assume greater importance [28].

(ii) The important misunderstanding[81] that has occurred is that, if (i) there is a non-trivial (now referred to as "serious or significant") breach and (ii) there is no good reason for the breach, the application for relief from sanctions will automatically fail. That is not so and is not what the court said in the *Mitchell* case [31, 38].

(iii) Parties who opportunistically and unreasonably oppose applications for relief from sanctions take up court time and act in breach of [the obligation to help the court to further the overriding objective] [40]; [t]he court will be more ready in the future to penalise opportunism [43].[82]

(iv) ... [I]t is wholly inappropriate for litigants or their lawyers to take advantage of mistakes made by opposing parties in the hope that relief from sanctions will be denied and that they will obtain a windfall strike out or other litigation advantage. In a case where (a) the failure can be seen to be neither serious nor significant, (b) where a good reason is demonstrated, or (c) where it is otherwise obvious that relief from sanctions is appropriate, parties should agree that relief from sanctions be granted without the need for further costs to be expended in satellite

---

[77] *Decadent Vapours Ltd v Bevan* and *Utilise TDS v Davies* [2014] 1 W.L.R. 3926 at, respectively, [58–66] and [67–80].

[78] See the commentary in *Civil Procedure 2017*, Vol.1 to CPR r.3.9 (relief from sanctions) at paras 3.9.1–3.9.13 and, in particular, para.3.9.3, "Formulation of the rule since April 2013".

[79] Jackson LJ delivered a separate judgment [83–99] which discusses the construction of r.3.9 and the approach to the third stage of its application at [84]–[88].

[80] That is, the need (a) for litigation to be conducted efficiently and at proportionate cost; and (b) to enforce compliance with rules, practice directions and orders.

[81] That is, of what was said in *Mitchell* in relation to (iii).

[82] This paragraph gives an overview of the range of sanctions that might be imposed.

litigation. The parties should in any event be ready to agree limited but reasonable extensions of time up to 28 days as envisaged by the new CPR r.3.8(4)[83] [41].

(v) It seems that some judges have ignored the fact that it is necessary in every case to consider all the circumstances of the case (what we have characterised as the third stage). This may be the reason for the decisions in *Decadent* and *Utilise*. But other judges have adopted what might be said to be the traditional approach of giving pre-eminence to the need to decide the claim on the merits, an approach which should have disappeared following the Woolf reforms. There is certainly no room for it in the post-Jackson era [81].

It may well be, particularly in view of (v) above, that if the circumstances   **1–058** of the illustrative cases were to recur, the outcome would be significantly less favourable to the defaulting parties. However, it should be kept in mind that the guidance relates to applications for relief from sanctions under CPR r.3.9 and that it does not require the court to alter its established approach to applications under s.4 of the 1975 Act for permission to commence proceedings out of time. As Megarry J held in *Re Salmon*,[84] the section is a substantive, not a procedural provision, and the approach to those applications, based on *Re Salmon* and *Re Dennis*,[85] will continue to require consideration of the merits.

(b) Thirteen Serious Errors

Entering a caveat in order to prevent time running against a prospective   **1–059** claimant. Although s.4 has now been amended so as to permit claims to be commenced before a grant of representation is taken out,[86] it is still wrong to enter a caveat for that purpose. The Law Commission's reasons for recommending the amendment[87] are not directed towards giving encouragement for that course of action, but towards facilitating the making of a claim in circumstances where the claimant may be prejudiced by the inactivity of those who are entitled to a grant. That inactivity may be due to inertia; but it may be that the deceased's only significant assets pass outside the estate (an interest in jointly owned property, for example, or benefits under a pension scheme) so that there is little need or incentive to obtain a grant of representation. Problems can also arise in the common situation where the person who intends to make a claim against the estate is also the person with priority to take a grant. A new para.3A inserted into CPR r.57.16 provides that, where no grant has been obtained, the claimant may

---

[83] Which regulates the parties' ability to extend time for compliance by prior written agreement.
[84] *Re Salmon* [1981] Ch 167.
[85] *Re Dennis (deceased)* [1981] 2 All E.R. 140.
[86] Inheritance and Trustees' Powers Act 2014 s.6 and Sch.2 para.6, which adds to s.4 as originally enacted the words (but nothing prevents the making of an application before a grant is taken out).
[87] Law Com LC 331, paras 7.47–7.49.

make a claim without naming a defendant and may apply for directions[88] as to the representation of the estate. Their written evidence must explain the reason why it has not been possible for a grant to be obtained. In order to keep a check on whether a grant has been issued, apply for a standing search as provided by r.43 of the Non-Contentious Probate Rules 1987.

1–060   Attempting to defeat the claim otherwise than on its merits. In the previous edition of this work the view was expressed that courts would be unlikely to be receptive to strike out applications on technical grounds if there is a reasonable case on the merits. In the light of the decision of the Court of Appeal in *Denton v T.H. White Ltd*[89] that is no longer the position. However, caution should still be exercised before deciding to take preliminary points about the claimant's eligibility. It may be worth applying to strike out the claim when the preliminary point is one which can be decided in isolation and without going into the merits, such as the validity of a marriage, or paternity, or domicile. It is generally bad tactics if the point at issue is whether the claimant satisfies the conditions of s.1(1)(ba) or s.1(1)(e). The cases of *Jelley v Iliffe*[90] and *Bishop v Plumley*[91] dramatically illustrate the potential hazards of this approach. There is useful guidance on the conditions required to establish a claim as a cohabitant in *Re Watson*,[92] *Baynes v Hedger*[93] and *Lindop v Agus*,[94] and on whether the claimant was being maintained by the deceased immediately before his death in *Churchill v Roach*[95] and *Gully v Dix*.[96]

1–061   Failing to issue the proceedings within the six-month limit. Even if an application to commence proceedings out of time succeeds (as in the cases noted in the following paragraph), unnecessary costs will have been incurred in making it. However, long delay may well be fatal even where there is an arguable case on the merits. In *Berger v Berger*,[97] the applicant widow had an arguable case and the estate, which had not been fully distributed, was likely to be sufficient to fund any award that might be made to her. It was understandable that up till the time of her application she had not wished to litigate with her family, but there was no satisfactory explanation for delaying the commencement of the proceedings until six years after the expiry of the time limit. The Court of Appeal, while critical of the trial judge's approach in certain respects, upheld the refusal of permission to commence proceedings out of time. However, one disadvantage of failure to

---

[88] CPR r.57.16(3B) gives the court power to make directions when a claim has been commenced under para.3A, as to the parties to the claim and the representation of the estate, either on the claimant's application or its own initiative. At the time of writing, 57APD.18 (production of the grant) has not been amended to deal with the situation where the grant is not available at the hearing of the claim.

[89] *Denton v T.H. White Ltd (De Laval Ltd (Pt 20 defendant))* [2014] 1 W.L.R. 3926.

[90] *Jelley v Iliffe* [1981] Fam. 128, CA.

[91] *Bishop v Plumley* [1991] 1 All E.R. 236, CA.

[92] *Re Watson* [1999] 1 F.L.R. 878.

[93] *Baynes v Hedger* [2008] 2 F.L.R. 1805.

[94] *Lindop v Agus* [2009] W.T.L.R. 1175.

[95] *Churchill v Roach* [2004] 2 F.L.R. 989.

[96] *Gully v Dix* [2004] 1 W.L.R. 139.

[97] *Berger v Berger* [2014] W.T.L.R 35, CA.

apply within the six-month period has ceased to exist. As a result of the amendment to s.9, it is no longer the case that the claimant will have lost the opportunity to apply for an order that the deceased's severable share of any joint property be treated as part of the net estate.[98]

Assuming that failure to issue the proceedings within the six-month limit is fatal to the claim. Courts may be readier than was formerly the case to give permission, even after very long delays, provided there is a reasonable claim on the merits; see *Stock v Brown*[99] and *Re C (Deceased)*.[100]   **1–062**

Failing to serve the claimant's written evidence with the claim form. This is, potentially, a very serious error since, under CPR r.8.6, the court can refuse to permit the evidence to be given at the hearing, with the effect that the claim has, for all practical purposes, been struck out; see *Parnall v Hurst*, referred to in para.1–055. Again, the decision in *Denton v T.H. White Ltd*[101] may have the effect of encouraging courts to take such a course.   **1–063**

Failing to ensure that the claimant's written evidence deals adequately with their financial resources and needs, including earning capacity. Remember, in this context, to take into account assets which the claimant may receive on the death of the deceased, other than under the will or intestacy (e.g. proceeds of insurance policies written in trust, or property passing by survivorship). In theory there may be no matter to which the court should ascribe more weight than any other, but in practice this is almost without exception the most important aspect of the claimant's evidence.   **1–064**

Failing to appreciate the impact of an award on the claimant's present and (to the extent that it is ascertainable) future entitlement to means-tested benefits. The circumstances may be such that the claimant's position would not be improved by a successful claim. The case of *Ilott v Mitson*, both in regard to the question whether the will made reasonable provision for the claimant[102] and the manner in which and the extent to which the court should exercise its discretion in her favour,[103] illustrates the difficulties created by failure to provide full and accurate information about benefits subject to capital restrictions and tax credits subject to an income threshold.   **1–065**

Assuming, when considering the merits of a claim, that it is bound to succeed either because: **1–066**

---

[98] Inheritance and Trustees' Powers Act 2014 Sch.2 para.7. The Law Commission was of the view that the protection afforded to joint tenants by s.9 as it then stood was more illusory than real; see Law Com. LC 331, paras 7.75–7.80 and 7.83.

[99] *Stock v Brown* [1994] 1 F.L.R. 840.

[100] *Re C, Deceased* [1995] 2 F.L.R. 24.

[101] *Denton v T.H. White Ltd* [2014] 1 W.L.R. 3926, CA.

[102] *Ilott v Mitson* [2012] 2 F.L.R 170, CA. The district judge had decided this issue in favour of the claimant and the Court of Appeal reversed the decision of Eleanor King J setting aside the district judge's order. The parties were strongly encouraged to reach agreement on quantum but that issue has been fought all the way up to the Supreme Court.

[103] *Ilott v Mitson* [2017] UKSC 17, setting aside the order of the Court of Appeal ([2016] 1 All E.R. 932; [2015] 2 F.L.R. 1409, CA) and restoring the order of the district judge.

   (i)   the net estate is large, or the beneficiaries are well off, or both; see *Re Bunning*[104] and *Re Clarke*[105]; or

   (ii) no provision has been made for the claimant. There are several reported cases in which the court has found that it was reasonable to make no provision; see, for instance, *Cameron v Treasury Solicitor*[106]; *Re Fullard*[107]; *Re Coventry*[108]; *Aston v Aston*[109] where the claimant was a surviving spouse and *Hope v Knight*,[110] where the claimants were a surviving spouse and an adult daughter.

1–067   Assuming, conversely, that a claim against a small estate is bound to fail; see *Re Clayton*,[111] a 1938 Act case which is still relevant, and the judgment of Goff LJ in *Re Coventry*,[112] which, although emphasising the possibility that the costs may become wholly disproportionate to the end in view, made it plain that the small size of the estate was no bar either to the making of an application or due consideration of the application on its merits.

1–068   Adopting the stance, in a surviving spouse claim, that the claimant is entitled to at least half the net estate. The cases of *P v G, P and P (Family Provision: Relevance of Divorce Provision)*[113] and *Cunliffe v Fielden*[114] had already made it absolutely clear that there was no presumption of equal division. The exercise of "checking ... against the yardstick of equality" does not have to, and very rarely does, result in an award of 50 per cent to the surviving spouse; as the cases show, it may be greater or smaller, according to the circumstances of the individual claim. The position has now been clarified by the amendment of s.3(2) which adds to the "notional divorce" provision and to the corresponding provision relating to surviving civil partners the words:

   "...but nothing requires the court to treat such provision as setting an upper or a lower limit to the provision which may be made by an order under s.2."[115]

1–069   Failing to give the lay client realistic advice as to the likely cost of the litigation and to the costs risks to which they may be personally exposed. As the case of *Aston v Aston*[116] makes clear, family provision claims are

---

[104] *Re Bunning* [1984] Ch. 480.
[105] *Re Clarke* [1991] 21 Fam. Law 364.
[106] *Cameron v Treasury Solicitor* [1996] 2 F.L.R. 716, CA.
[107] *Re Fullard* [1982] Fam. 42, CA.
[108] *Re Coventry* [1980] Ch. 461, CA.
[109] *Aston v Aston* [2007] W.T.L.R. 1349.
[110] *Hope v Knight* [2011] W.T.L.R. 583.
[111] *Re Clayton* [1966] 1 W.L.R. 969.
[112] *Re Coventry* [1980] Ch. 461 at 486F.
[113] *P v G, P and P (Family Provision: Relevance of Divorce Provision)* [2006] 1 F.L.R. 431; also reported as *P v E* [2007] W.T.L.R. 691.
[114] *Cunliffe v Fielden* [2006] Ch. 361, CA, also reported as *Fielden v Cunliffe* [2006] 1 F.L.R. 745; [2006] W.T.L.R. 29. In both cases the surviving spouse was awarded less than 50 per cent of the net estate.
[115] Inheritance and Trustees' Powers Act 2014 Sch.2 para.5(2).
[116] *Aston v Aston* [2007] W.T.L.R. 1349.

adversarial litigation to which the normal principles as set out in CPR Pt 44 apply,[117] except as regards a personal representative who remains neutral. Never assume (whatever may be said about "the usual order") that all parties' costs will be ordered to be paid out of the estate.

Taking up an unreasonable or unrealistic position prior to or at trial. In **1–070** *Lilleyman v Lilleyman*[118] (although there had been protracted but ultimately unsuccessful attempts at settlement) the defendants' case was opened on the basis that the will made reasonable provision for the claimant, and that unrealistic assertion[119] was not abandoned until early on in the closing submissions. This had costs consequences. In a separate judgment on costs,[120] the application of CPR r.36.14(2) fell to be considered, as the claimant failed to obtain an award more advantageous than a Pt 36 offer made by the defendants in July 2011, some eight months before the trial. Briggs J was critical of the "no holds barred" approach of both parties which, in his judgment, was not at all appropriate in Inheritance Act claims. He concluded that it would be unjust if the strict application of r.36.14(2) were to prevent the court from signifying its disapprobation of the "no holds barred" approach and, after considering both parties' conduct of the case, disallowed 20 per cent of the costs to which the defendants would have been entitled by reason of the claimant's failure to beat the Pt 36 offer made in July 2011.

Another aspect of unreasonable conduct of a case is the making of **1–071** exaggerated and unsubstantiated claims. In *Wooldridge v Wooldridge*[121] (also a surviving spouse case) the claimant asserted that she and her husband had enjoyed the life of the "super-rich" and that she required a further annual income of £372,000 to support it; that assertion was not in accord with evidence of the deceased's declared income. Unusually for a surviving spouse, her claim was dismissed. In a subsequent judgment on costs,[122] the question arose whether she should pay the costs of the defendant beneficiaries, as well as those of the executors, on the indemnity basis. While it is not a basis for awarding indemnity costs merely that one party lost resoundingly or that the case was unlikely to succeed or failed in fact, the claim fell within the principle identified in *Fiona Trust & Holding Corporation v Yuri Privalov*[123] by Andrew Smith J that a claim which is "thin", "far-fetched" and "irreconcilable with the contemporaneous documents" is one where indemnity costs should be ordered. Her claim was outside the norm because of its weakness and the manner in which it was conducted. It

---

[117] Except where that regime is displaced by the making of a Pt 36 offer.

[118] *Lilleyman v Lilleyman* [2013] Ch. 225.

[119] As Briggs J described it at [83]. He also found considerable force (at [87]) in the submission that the award of £1.5 million contended for on behalf of the claimant was too high; while £128,000 together with a life interest in the matrimonial home, as contended for on behalf of the defendant was too little. The eventual award was in the region of £500,000.

[120] *Lilleyman v Lilleyman (Costs)* [2012] 1 W.L.R. 2801. For the criticisms referred to, see [17], [23].

[121] *Wooldridge v Wooldridge* unreported 12 February 2016, County Court at Central London.

[122] For the subsequent judgment on costs, see *Wooldridge v Wooldridge* [2016] 3 Costs L.O. 531.

[123] *Fiona Trust & Holding Corporation v Yuri Privalov* [2011] EWHC 664 (Comm).

had been exaggerated with respect to her lifestyle and her financial needs. As to conduct, she had failed to deal with sensible offers to settle in the way that they ought to be dealt with and had raised allegations of financial impropriety and tax evasion without evidence that would withstand scrutiny to support them. Accordingly, she was ordered to pay the costs of the defendant beneficiaries on the indemnity basis.

1–072   Finally, it is by no means the case that, even if all the above errors are avoided, the conduct of the litigation will be plain sailing.

CHAPTER 2

PERSONS WHO MAY APPLY

1.—DOMICILE OF THE DECEASED

(a) The Concept of Domicile

Notwithstanding that domicile was described in 1964 as "a superannuated **2–001** concept",[1] s.1(1) of the 1975 Act begins with the words "Where after the commencement of this Act a person dies domiciled in England and Wales ...". Thus, if the deceased dies domiciled elsewhere, there is no jurisdiction to entertain an application under the 1975 Act. The domicile of the applicant is irrelevant. Section 27(2) of the 1975 Act provides that it shall not extend to

---

[1] Neither the English nor the Scottish Law Commission regarded domicile as a "super-annuated concept" (see *Law of Domicile*, (1987) Law Com. No.168, Scot Law Com. No.107), but their recommendations for changes in the law of domicile have not been implemented.

Scotland and Northern Ireland. The legislation applicable to Northern Ireland is the Inheritance (Provision for Family and Dependants) Act (Northern Ireland) Order 1979,[2] the provisions of which closely resemble the 1975 Act. An application for provision under the Order can be made only if the deceased died domiciled in Northern Ireland.[3] Similarly, the Manx statute[4] requires the deceased to have died domiciled in the Island.

2–002   In its 2009 consultation paper,[5] the Law Commission reviewed the criticisms made of the requirement ("the domicile precondition") that, in order for a claim to be entertained, the deceased must have died domiciled in England and Wales. Although it was suggested in the case of *Cyganik v Agulian*[6] that the "somewhat antiquated"[7] concept of domicile might be replaced by "habitual residence" as a precondition, the Law Commission was unenthusiastic about that proposal, but was attracted to the idea of a reform of the current law that would enable applications under the 1975 Act to be made whenever the distribution of any property left by the deceased is governed by English succession law.[65] Following consultation, the Law Commission recommended that a 1975 Act claim should be possible in any case where either the deceased was domiciled in England and Wales, or English domestic succession law applied to any part of the estate.[8] In 2013 the Ministry of Justice issued a consultation paper on the draft Bill[9] in which consultees were invited to consider four options.[10] The conclusion in the response paper published on 30 July 2013[11] was that the additional ground of jurisdiction should be that, at the time of death, the applicant was

---

[2] Inheritance (Provision for Family and Dependants) Act (Northern Ireland) Order 1979 (SI 1979/924).

[3] Inheritance (Provision for Family and Dependants) Act (Northern Ireland) Order 1979 (SI 1979/924 art.3(1)).

[4] Inheritance (Provision for Family and Dependants) Act 1975 s.1(1).

[5] Law Commission Consultation Paper No.191, *Intestacy and Family Provision Claims on Death* (2009) paras 7.40–7.56.

[6] The case, although often referred to as *Cyganik v Agulian is* reported at the appellate level as *Agulian v Cygani* [2006] 1 F.C.R. 406; [2006] W.L.R. 565, CA, reversing [2005] W.T.L.R. 1049.

[7] Longmore LJ, agreeing (without enthusiasm) with the conclusion reached in the leading judgment given by Mummery LJ, quoted the observation of Dr J.H.C. Morris in the third edition (1984) of his book on *Conflict of Laws* (not to be confused with the work of the same name now known as *Dicey, Morris and Collins on the Conflict of Laws* which had at that time reached its 10th edition, the last of which Dr Morris was the sole editor): "Originally it was a good idea; but a once simple concept has been so overloaded by a multitude of cases that it has been transmuted into something further and further removed from the practicalities of life" [58].

[8] Law Commission Report No.331, *Intestacy and Family Provision Claims on Death* (2011) at [7.37], and Sch.2 para.2 of the draft Inheritance and Trustees' Powers Bill (App.A to the Report).

[9] Ministry of Justice Consultation Paper CP6/2013, *Draft Inheritance and Trustees' Powers Bill* (March 2013).

[10] The options were: 1. applicable succession law (as recommended by the Law Commission); 2. option 1 with the added condition that provision could be made only out of property within the jurisdiction of England and Wales; 3. that the deceased's net estate included property within the jurisdiction (alternatively, immovable property within the jurisdiction); and 4. habitual residence of the applicant within the jurisdiction.

[11] Ministry of Justice Response to Consultation CP6/2013 (July 2013).

habitually resident in England and Wales.[12] The draft Bill as introduced into the House of Lords on 31 July 2013 amended clause 1(1) of the 1975 Act by permitting applications to be made either when a person died domiciled in England and Wales and was survived by an eligible person[13] or when a person died and was survived by an eligible person who was, at the time of death, habitually resident in England and Wales. However, at the Committee stage, an amendment deleting this extension to the jurisdiction was moved.[14] Concerns had been raised about possible effects that it might have on inheritance rights under Scots law, and it was also acknowledged that the provision was at variance both with the Law Commission's recommendation and the majority[15] view of the consultees who responded to the Ministry of Justice consultation paper. The "domicile precondition" therefore remains as the sole jurisdictional gateway.

Domicile is a concept of law designed to establish a connection between an individual and the legal system of the territory with which they either: **2–003**

(a)   have the closest connection in fact; or
(b)   are considered to have the closest connection in law, by reason of their dependence on some other person.

In *Whicker v Hume*[16] it was said that:

"By domicile we mean home, the permanent home; and if you do not understand your permanent home, I am afraid that no illustration drawn from foreign writers or foreign languages will very much help you to it."

However, as the learned editors of *Dicey, Morris and Collins, Conflict of Laws* demonstrate,[17] this pronouncement has limited value:

"While the notion of a permanent home can be explained largely in the light of common-sense principles, the same is not true of domicile. Domicile is an 'idea of law' which diverges from the notion of permanent home in two respects. In the first place, the elements which are required for the acquisition of a domicile go far beyond those required for the acquisition of a permanent home ... Secondly, domicile differs from permanent home in that the law in some cases says that a person is

---

[12] MoJ CP6 response at paras 2.55, 2.56.
[13] The classes of eligible persons remained unchanged apart from the amendment of para.1(1)(d) (person treated as a child of the family) for which see s.2(g), para.2–071.
[14] *Hansard*, 22 October 2013, cols GC 339–40.
[15] There was in fact no majority view; of the 22 responses, the most favoured option was option 3, which had seven supporters.
[16] *Whicker v Hume* (1858) 7 H.L. Cas. 124 at 160.
[17] *Dicey, Morris and Collins, The Conflict of Laws*, 15th edn (London: Sweet & Maxwell, 2012) at para.6–005.

domiciled in a country whether or not he has his permanent home in it."[18]

In a survey of selected cases drawn from over a century of case law,[19] Scarman J adopted the principle, stated in *Henderson v Henderson*,[20] that domicile is:

"...that legal relationship between a person ... and a territory subject to a distinctive legal system which invokes the system as [his] personal law."[21]

Domicile, as the link between an individual and their personal law, is an important concept in the context of that individual's illegal presence in the territory in which it is claimed that they have acquired a domicile of choice, particularly in relation to their position under the matrimonial law[22] and the law of succession[23] of that territory.

(b) Types of Domicile

2–004   Two general principles of the law of domicile are that no person can be without a domicile[24] and that no person can at the same time and for the same purpose have more than one domicile.[25] Domicile may be of three types, namely, of origin, of choice, and of dependency. A person ("A") may die domiciled in England and Wales because:

(1)   their domicile of origin is there and either:

(a)   they have never acquired any other domicile; or

(b)   they have acquired another domicile but subsequent to that their domicile of origin has revived;

(2)   their domicile of dependency is there and on becoming independent they have acquired that domicile as a domicile of choice;

(3)   neither their domicile of origin nor their domicile of dependency was there, but they have acquired a domicile of choice there.

(i) Domicile of origin

2–005   Every person receives at birth a domicile of origin, in accordance with the following rules:[26]

---

[18] For example, children under 16 and mentally disordered persons.

[19] *In the estate of Fuld (No.3)*, *Hartley v Fuld* [1968] P. 675 at 682–86. In addition to the 17 cases referred to in the judgment, a further 62 were cited in argument.

[20] *Henderson v Henderson* [1967] P. 77 at 79.

[21] Cf. the Second American Restatement, which defines domicile as "the place, generally the home, which the law assigns a person for certain legal purposes".

[22] See *Mark v Mark* [2006] 1 A.C. 98 on jurisdiction to entertain a petition for divorce.

[23] See *Witkowska v Kaminski* [2006] W.T.L.R. 1293 on whether W was precluded from making a claim under the 1975 Act because her presence in England was illegal.

[24] *Dicey, Morris and Collins*, r.5, para.6R–011.

[25] *Dicey, Morris and Collins*, r.6, para.6R–013.

[26] *Dicey, Morris and Collins*, r.9(1), para.6R–025.

(a) if A is legitimate and born within his father's lifetime, A's domicile of origin is that of his father at A's birth;

(b) if A is either legitimate and born after his father's death, or illegitimate, A's domicile of origin is that of his mother at A's birth;

(c) if A is a foundling, his domicile of origin is in the country where he was found.

If A is a minor child, his domicile of origin may be changed[27] as a result of either adoption, because he is treated in law[28] as born to his adoptive parents in wedlock, or by a parental order under the Human Fertilisation and Embryology Act 2008.[29] However, if he is legitimated, or his parents acquire a new domicile, the domicile which he acquires as a result is a domicile of dependency; see *Henderson v Henderson*.[30]

(ii) Domicile of dependency

This is, in general, the same as, and changes (if at all) with the domicile of the person on whom the dependant is, as regards their domicile, legally dependent.[31] Since the coming into force, on 1 January 1974, of the Domicile and Matrimonial Proceedings Act 1973, the only dependent persons are children under 16 and unmarried, and mentally disordered persons. Before that, all infants and all married women were dependent for that purpose; a married woman who was an infant being dependent on her husband, not her father.   **2–006**

A married woman who had her husband's domicile of dependency before that date[32] is treated as retaining that domicile as a domicile of choice (if it is not also her domicile of origin) unless and until it is changed by acquisition or revival of another domicile on or after that date. A child, on reaching the age of 16, will usually retain the domicile of the parent on whom they were for that purpose dependent, as a domicile of choice. They may now acquire a domicile of choice, independently of their parent, on attaining the age of 16 or marrying under that age. Section 4 of the Domicile and Matrimonial Proceedings Act 1973 provides for a child (defined in that Act as a person incapable of having an independent domicile) to take their mother's domicile where the spouses are living apart and the child makes their home with their mother.   **2–007**

On ceasing to be dependent, a person often continues to be domiciled in the country of their domicile of dependency. A child, on reaching the age of 16, will usually retain the domicile of the appropriate parent as a domicile of   **2–008**

---

[27] *Dicey, Morris and Collins*, r.9(2), para.6R–025.

[28] Adoption and Children Act 2002 s.67.

[29] Under s.54, a court may make a parental order on the application of two people ("applicants") providing for the child to be treated in law as the child of the applicants. S.54(2) provides that the applicants must be (a) husband or wife; or (b) civil partners of each other; or (c) two persons who are living as partners in an enduring family relationship and are not within prohibited degrees of relationship in relation to each other.

[30] *Henderson v Henderson* [1967] P. 77.

[31] *Dicey, Morris and Collins*, r.14, para.6R–078.

[32] *Dicey, Morris and Collins*, paras 6–084–6–085.

choice, as discussed above. But, on reaching that age, they have the normal capacity to change their domicile, and such a change may result from acts done during the period of their dependency.[33]

(iii) Domicile of choice

2–009 In general, every independent person can acquire a domicile of choice by the combination of residence (*factum*) and intention of permanent or indefinite residence (*animus manendi*), but not otherwise.[34] In determining whether a domicile of choice has been acquired, any circumstance which is evidence of a person's residence or of their intention to reside permanently or indefinitely in a country must be considered.[35]

2–010 In *Fuld (No.3)*,[36] Scarman J held that:

> "...a domicile of choice is acquired when a man fixes voluntarily his sole or chief residence in a particular place with an intention of continuing to reside there for an unlimited time."

Subject to one qualification, this was followed by Buckley LJ in *IRC v Bullock*.[37] In his judgment, the intention to make a home in the new country did not need to be irrevocable; the true test was whether:

> "...he intends to make his home in the new country until the end of his days, unless and until something happens to make him change his mind."

2–011 Scarman J's judgment was considered in detail by the Court of Appeal in *Agulian v Cyganik*,[38] a 1975 Act claim in which the question was whether the deceased, Mr Nathanael, who was born in Cyprus, died domiciled in England and Wales. It was Ms Cyganik's case that she and the deceased (whom she had then known for about seven years) agreed in 1999 to marry, and that preparations made during 2002 would have culminated in a marriage at Easter 2003 had he not died in February of that year. The trial judge found that to be so, but the Court of Appeal, while upholding that finding, differed as to what inference could be legitimately drawn from it. In the course of his exposition of the legal principles relating to domicile, Mummery LJ referred to Scarman J's judgment as being in terms that the Court of Appeal should expressly approve. Although words suggestive of a higher standard of proof have often been used, Scarman J's judgment makes it clear that the standard of proof is the civil, not the criminal, standard.[39] This was considered in

---

[33] *Dicey, Morris and Collins*, para.6–086.
[34] *Dicey, Morris and Collins*, r.10, para.6R–033.
[35] *Dicey, Morris and Collins*, r.11, para.6R–046.
[36] *Fuld (No.3)* [1968] P. 675. at p.682E.
[37] *IRC v Bullock* [1976] 1 W.L.R. 1178, CA.
[38] *Agulian v Cyganik* [2006] W.T.L.R. 565, CA, reversing the decision in *Cyganik v Agulian* [2005] W.T.L.R. 1049.
[39] *Fuld (No.3)* [1968] P. 675 at pp.685F–686D.

some detail by Arden LJ in *Barlow Clowes International Ltd (in liquidation) v Henwood*.[40] There is a longstanding line of authority, exemplified by *Winans v Attorney-General*[41] that domicile of origin is tenacious but, as she made clear, this does not import a higher standard of proof; the powerful phrases used in the case-law were a warning against reaching too facile a conclusion upon a too superficial investigation or assessment of the facts of a particular case. They emphasise the nature and quality of the intention that has to be proved as much as the standard of proof.

Mummery LJ held that:

2–012

(1) in order to decide whether the deceased had acquired a domicile of choice at the date of their death, the court had to look at "the whole of [his] life,[42] at what he had done with his life, at what life had done to him, and at what were his inferred intentions ..."; and

(2) special care must be taken in the analysis of evidence about isolating individual factors present over time and treating a particular factor as decisive. In that regard, the authorities support the proposition that if H with a domicile of origin in country A marries W with a domicile in country B and lives with her in B after the marriage, H does not as a matter of law thereby acquire a domicile of choice in country B and abandon his domicile of origin.

He had earlier observed that, in a case of proof of the subjective intentions of a person who has died, little weight is attached to direct or indirect evidence of statements or declarations of intention by that person.[43] Subjective inferences had to be ascertained by the court as a fact by a process of inference from all the available evidence about that person's life. He concluded that had the judge taken into account all the connecting factors with Cyprus and England over the whole of the deceased's life, he would have found that the evidence was not sufficiently cogent and convincing to establish such a serious matter as a change of domicile.

2–013

As Longmore LJ put it in his analysis of the trial judge's judgment, the question was not so much whether the deceased intended to return per-

2–014

---

[40] *Henwood v Barlow Clowes International Ltd (In Liquidation)* [2008] EWCA (Civ) 577, at [85]–[88].

[41] *Winans v Attorney-General* [1904] A.C. 287, HL, at 290.

[42] In carrying out that exercise, "there is no act, no circumstance in a man's life, however trivial it may be in itself, which ought to be left out of consideration in trying the question whether there was an intention to change the domicile. A trivial act might possibly be of more weight with regard to determining this question than an act which was of more importance to a man in his lifetime"; *Drevon v Drevon* (1864) 34 L.J.(Ch) 129, at 133.

[43] As in other aspects of 1975 Act claims, such as statements by the testator made for the purpose of justifying their testamentary dispositions (see, e.g., *Singer v Isaac* [2001] W.T.L.R. 1045), the court may regard them as self-serving and attach little weight to them. Thus in *Barlow Clowes International Ltd (in liquidation) v Henwood* [2008] EWCA (Civ) 577, it was in Mr Henwood's interest to establish that he had acquired a domicile of choice in Mauritius. Arden LJ, giving the leading judgment, stated at [39] that she read the trial judge's adverse comments on Mr Henwood's evidence as meaning that he did not accept any documents created by Mr Henwood or on his instructions.

manently to Cyprus, as whether it had been shown that, by the date of his death, he had formed the intention permanently to reside in England. The crucial point was that he had a domicile of origin in Cyprus until it was proved that he intended to reside permanently or indefinitely in England.

2–015   In *Holliday v Musa*,[44] again a trial of the preliminary issue of domicile, the only question was whether it could properly be inferred that, at any time during his residence in England for various periods between 1958 and 2006, the deceased had formed the intention to reside in England indefinitely and abandon his domicile of origin.[45] Before setting out a lengthy chronology of relevant facts,[46] Waller LJ said:

> "In considering whether [the deceased] had at some stage an intention to reside permanently and indefinitely in England, long residence in England is of course a starting point. It is furthermore important that the residence in England was the home of his family ... It is common sense that the longer the residence and the more it is home, the more likely the inference that there is the intention to reside permanently and indefinitely. But at any stage when it might be proper to make that inference, it is important to place in the balance any continued connections with Cyprus so as to be able to be clear whether his intention has become one of settling finally in England, abandoning Cyprus. One must further be satisfied that the situation is not one in which [he] has simply not finally made up his mind because ... in such a situation the domicile of origin is retained."[47]

2–016   A domicile of choice is abandoned if both residing there (*factum*) and intention to reside there permanently or indefinitely (*animus manendi*) cease, in which case, unless a new domicile of choice is acquired, the domicile of origin revives.[48] In *Re Shaffer, Morgan v Cilento*[49] the issue was whether the late Anthony Shaffer, whose domicile of origin was in England and Wales, had at any time established a domicile of choice in Queensland and, if so, whether he had subsequently abandoned it. This was relevant both to the extent of the IHT liability and to the jurisdiction of the court to entertain a 1975 Act claim by one of the defendants. Lewison J considered that, in order for a domicile of choice to be lost, it must be shown that:

> (1)   the *propositus* had ceased to reside in the territory in which they had a domicile of choice;[50] and

---

[44] *Holliday v Musa* [2010] 2 F.L.R. 702, CA.
[45] The decision at first instance, although upheld in the result, was criticised on account of the judge not having kept in mind that this was the only real issue.
[46] *Holliday v Musa* [2010] 2 F.L.R. 702, CA at [25]–[64].
[47] *Holliday v Musa* [2010] 2 F.L.R. 702, CA at [23].
[48] *Dicey, Morris and Collins*, r.13, para.6R–074.
[49] *Re Shaffer, Morgan v Cilento* [2004] W.T.L.R. 457.
[50] The facts on the basis of which he found that the deceased had acquired a domicile of choice in Queensland are set out at para.73 of the judgment.

(2)   they had no intention to return to reside there (as opposed to an intention not to return).[51]

(iv) Illegal presence

The question whether a person is debarred by illegality from acquiring a   **2–017**
domicile of choice in England and Wales or from claiming to be habitually
resident in the jurisdiction has been considered by the House of Lords in
Mark v Mark.[52] The context in which the question arose was whether the
courts of England and Wales had jurisdiction, based either on habitual
residence or domicile, to entertain a petition for divorce when the presence
of the petitioner in the jurisdiction was unlawful due to her being an
overstayer.

At first instance Hughes J held that the petitioner wife could not rely on   **2–018**
her illegal residence in England in order to establish that she had been
habitually resident within the jurisdiction for the required period of one
year,[53] but that her illegal presence did not prevent her from having acquired
a domicile of choice in England and Wales.[54] This was inconsistent with an
English case decided in 1980[55] and with the law as stated in the then current
edition of *Dicey and Morris*.[56, 57] Hughes J concluded that that statement
must rest on the rule of public policy that a person cannot acquire a benefit
from their own criminal conduct; however, he observed that domicile
regulated wide areas besides the divorce jurisdiction and was capable of
operating as much to the disadvantage as to the advantage of the *propositus*.
He stated that:

> "...the concept of domicile is not that of a benefit to the *propositus*.
> Rather, it is a neutral rule of law for determining that system of per-
> sonal law with which the individual has the appropriate connection, so
> that it shall govern his personal status and questions relating to him
> and his affairs."[58]

---

[51] Permission to appeal in relation to that direction of law was given in *Re Shaffer* [2004] EWCA Civ 631. Ward LJ considered that the questions which arose were (1) whether the first limb of the test should have included the words "permanently or indefinitely"; and (2) whether the parenthesis at the end of the second limb implied a more stringent test than that considered in *Re Flynn* [1968] 1 W.L.R. 103. It does not appear that this appeal was pursued.
[52] *Mark v Mark* [2006] 1 A.C. 98, affirming the decision of the Court of Appeal [2005] Fam. 267.
[53] Domicile and Matrimonial Proceedings Act 1973 s.5(2)(b).
[54] Thus conferring jurisdiction on the court to entertain the petition, under s.5(2)(a).
[55] *Puttick v Attorney General* [1980] Fam. 1. Commonwealth authority to the contrary is to be found in *Jablonowski v Jablonowski* (1972) 28 D.L.R. (3d) 440 and in the unreported Australian case of *Bashir* referred to by Thorpe LJ in *Mark v Mark* [2005] Fam. 275 at [44].
[56] *Dicey and Morris on the Conflict of Laws*, 9th edn (London: Stevens & Sons, 1973), p.96.
[57] See also M.P. Pilkington, *Illegal Residence and the Acquisition of a Domicile of Choice* (1984) 33 I.C.L.Q. 885, where it is concluded that the public interest could be adequately protected without recourse to a rule whereby illegal presence automatically vitiated domicile.
[58] Cited by Baroness Hale of Richmond in *Mark v Mark* [2006] 1 A.C. 98 at [44].

2–019   Latham LJ observed that all three members of the Court of Appeal were uncomfortable with a solution which treated illegality of presence differently in relation to habitual residence and to domicile.[59] It seemed to him that there were stronger grounds for concluding that domicile required the further element of lawfulness than existed when considering habitual residence. Nevertheless, he was content to adopt the analysis of Thorpe and Waller LJJ. Thorpe LJ expressed the view that:

> "...the imperative to prevent the acquisition by illegal conduct of what might be described as public law benefits such as residence, income support, income-based jobseekers allowance, housing benefit, council tax benefit, housing assistance, has driven, unnecessarily, the adoption of an absolute rule which in the context of private law rights is very difficult to explain or justify."[60]

He favoured an approach which gave the court a margin of discretion in determining whether an element of illegality tainting the entry or staying within the jurisdiction of a party precluded the acquisition of a domicile of choice. Waller LJ referred to Hughes J's observation that domicile of choice should be a neutral concept which connected a person with a system of law. In his view, the acquisition of a domicile of choice should not be treated as the obtaining of a benefit by reference to which the public policy principle must be applied.

2–020   In the result, therefore, the Court of Appeal held that there was no rule of public policy that precluded a person who was unlawfully resident in a country from acquiring a domicile of choice there, but that the fact of such unlawful residence was relevant to the question whether the necessary domicile and residence had been established; and that, in the circumstances, the wife had acquired a domicile of choice in England. Hughes J's decision was reversed to the extent that, despite her illegal presence, the wife was also held to have been habitually resident in England for the requisite period.

2–021   In the House of Lords, Lord Hope and Baroness Hale, who gave the only substantive judgments, each considered the authorities and other material which had been before the Court of Appeal. Neither of them found support there for the proposition that illegal presence in a country was a bar to the acquisition of a domicile of choice there. For Lord Hope, illegality was relevant to the question whether the person intended to reside in a country with the intention to reside there permanently or indefinitely, but not to the question whether the person was present there. If the court found that the requisite intention had been established by reliable and credible evidence, it would seem contrary to principle to decline to give effect to it by recognising that a domicile of choice had been acquired.

2–022   Baroness Hale concluded that the authorities did not disclose a long-standing and consistent approach to the issue such that there should be

---

[59] *Mark v Mark* [2005] Fam. 267, CA at [85].
[60] *Mark v Mark* [2005] Fam. 267, CA at [45].

reluctance to depart from it. Citing the passage of the judgment of Hughes J, set out at para.2–018 above, she said that recognising that connection, despite the illegality of the presence of the *propositus,* does not offend against any general principle that a person cannot be permitted to acquire a benefit from their own criminal conduct. Indeed, were the state to have any particular interest, it would probably lie in accepting that those who intend to remain here permanently have acquired a domicile here, whatever their immigration status. Like Lord Hope, she considered the legality of a person's presence to be relevant to intention, but that was a question of fact, not of law. Nor was it a question of discretion or of the court being "hostile" to the assertion of a domicile of choice by an illegal entrant or resident.[61] A person either acquired a domicile of choice in this country, or did not. If the former, it was not to be denied because the court considered the case to be unmeritorious or tainted with moral or legal turpitude. If the latter, it was not to be granted because the claimant was virtuous. It was a matter of fact whether the intention existed at the relevant time.

In *Witkowska v Kaminski*[62] the court was concerned not with whether it   **2–023** had jurisdiction to entertain a claim under the 1975 Act, but whether the claimant was eligible to make one. W's claim for provision out of the deceased's intestate estate was on the alternative bases that she was a cohabitant, within subss.1(1)(ba) and 1(1A), or a dependant, within subs.1(1)(e). The question arose whether her claim could succeed having regard to her illegal presence in England during the period of her alleged cohabitation and/or dependency.

Rather unusually, permission was given both for W, who succeeded at   **2–024** trial, to appeal, and for K to cross-appeal. Permission was given to W on the basis that the trial judge had recognised that the award which he had made was inadequate to meet her needs if she were to continue to live in England, where she had, by the date of the hearing, been living for eight years. He was also attracted by a point (which he called "the underlying EU point") raised in relation to Art.12 of the EC Treaty. K was given permission to cross-appeal in relation to the question whether W was precluded from making a claim under the 1975 Act because her presence in the United Kingdom was illegal.

---

[61] See *Mark v Mark* at [60], disapproving of a statement to that effect in *Rayden and Jackson on Divorce and Family Matters,* 17th edn (London: LexisNexis, 1998) at para.2.16. Nevertheless, *Rayden and Jackson on Relationship Breakdown, Finances and Children* (London: LexisNexis UK, 2016) states at para.1.219, that "illegal entry and residence would clearly make a court hostile to an assertion that the illegal immigrant had thereby acquired a domicile of choice" and cites *Shah v Barnet London Borough Council* [1983] 2 A.C. 309. Baroness Hale also questioned, at [57], whether it could be said that that legality is an essential element in residence (as appeared to her to be the view expressed in the then current (13th) edition of *Dicey and Morris*). The current (15th) edition states that: "Although there is some Commonwealth authority and one English dictum supporting the proposition that a domicile of choice cannot be acquired on the basis of residence which is illegal, it is now settled that in English law the illegality of residence is no bar to the acquisition of a domicile of choice in England"; see *Mark v Mark* [2006] 1 A.C. 98, per Lord Hope at [11] and Baroness Hale at [44].
[62] *Witkowska v Kaminski* [2006] W.T.L.R. 1293; [2006] EWHC 1940 (Ch).

2–025   Article 12 provides that:

> "Within the scope of application of this treaty and without prejudice to special provisions therein any discrimination on the grounds of nationality shall be prohibited."

It was submitted for W that by limiting the award to what was sufficient to maintain her in Poland, the judge was effectively forcing her to return there. Rejecting this submission, Blackburne J said that the award was not conditional on her returning to Poland; she remained free, subject to immigration law, to remain in this country as she had done for most of the time since the deceased's death. He also accepted the submission on behalf of K that Art.12 operated only within the scope of the treaty and had no application to the substantive law of succession to a deceased's estate or to the jurisdiction conferred by the 1975 Act to alter the manner in which a will or intestacy would otherwise operate in respect of a deceased person's estate.

2–026   Blackburne J also held that Art.14 of the European Convention of Human Rights had no application. This provides, so far as was relevant, that:

> "...the enjoyment of rights and freedoms set forth in this Convention shall be secured without discrimination on any ground such as ... national ... origin."

Further, Art.2 of the Fourth Protocol to the Convention is to the effect that:

> "...everyone within the territory of a State shall, within that territory, have the right to liberty of movement and freedom to choose his residence."

In relation to this, Blackburne J held that there was no substance to the suggestion that the Art.14 right had been infringed. In any event, Art.14 was not a freestanding guarantee of equal treatment, but related to substantive rights and freedoms set out elsewhere in the Convention. In addition, Art.2 of the Fourth Protocol was not one of the Convention rights to which the Human Rights Act 1998 applied, since the Fourth Protocol had never been ratified by the United Kingdom.

2–027   W's immigration status was raised by both parties on the appeal. For W, it was contended that the trial judge had failed to have regard to subs.3(5) of the 1975 Act, which requires the court to have regard to the facts at the date of the hearing. It was submitted that he had failed to assess W's reasonable needs by reference to the state of affairs at the date of trial when she was lawfully entitled to live in the United Kingdom, as opposed to the state of affairs at the date of death, when she was an illegal overstayer.

2–028   It then emerged (as had not been previously realised) that in all probability W's residence was still unlawful, notwithstanding Poland's accession to the European Union on 1 May 2004. The effect of the relevant regulations[63] was that, for a period of five years from the date of accession, nationals of (inter alia) Poland were permitted to reside in the United Kingdom without leave only if the person in question:

(a) had sufficient resources to avoid becoming a burden on the social assistance system of the United Kingdom; and

(b) was covered by sickness insurance in respect of all risks in the United Kingdom.

It was not suggested on behalf of W that she met those requirements.

In the result, both the appeal and the cross-appeal failed. On W's appeal, **2–029** Blackburne J did not accept that the decision as to the level of maintenance assumed that W's residence in England continued to be unlawful. On the cross-appeal, he rejected the argument that her unlawful presence in England during the period while she was being maintained by and/or cohabiting with the deceased barred her from making a 1975 Act claim.

(c) Evidence of Change of Domicile

(i) Burden and standard of proof

In general, the burden of proof lies on the party asserting that a change of **2–030** domicile has taken place; the standard of proof is the balance of probabilities, subject to the principle that so serious a matter as the acquisition or abandonment of a domicile of choice is not to be lightly inferred from slight indications or casual words.[64] In 1975 Act cases, the applicant bears the burden of proof that the deceased died domiciled in England and Wales. Thus, in *Mastaka v Midland Bank Executor and Trustee Company*,[65] the testatrix had married a Russian husband who was in England at the time of the marriage, but whose whereabouts at his death were unknown. At that time, the law was such that the testatrix, on marriage, acquired the domicile of her husband; there was no evidence that he had either died or acquired an English domicile. The primary ground on which Farwell J held that the application failed was that s.1(1) of the 1938 Act required an applicant to prove that the deceased died domiciled in England. He also found, apart from that, that since the applicant had been left in the care of another woman from an early age, had never requested or received any assistance from the deceased throughout her lifetime, and therefore the ordinary relationship between mother and daughter had ceased to exist, so that there

---

[63] Immigration (European Economic Area) Regulations (as amended) 2000 (SI 2016/1052) regs 5, 14 and 21(3) and the Accession (Immigration and Worker Registration) (as amended) Regulations 2004 (SI 2004/1219).

[64] *Barlow Clowes International Ltd (in liquidation) v Henwood* [2008] EWCA (Civ) 577, at [85]–[88], discussed at para.2–13 above; *Agulian v Cyganik* [2006] W.T.L.R. 565 per Longmore LJ at [53]: "all the cases state that a domicile of origin can only be replaced by clear cogent and compelling evidence that the relevant person intended to settle permanently and indefinitely in the alleged domicile of choice."

[65] *Mastaka v Midland Bank Executor and Trustee Company* [1941] Ch. 192.

was no obligation for the testatrix to have provided for the applicant by her will.

2–031 In that case, no assertion was made, on behalf of the defendants, about the domicile of the testatrix; there was simply no evidence. However, where it is asserted that the deceased, who had an English domicile of origin, had acquired a foreign domicile of choice, the question arises, in connection with claims under the 1975 Act, whether it is for the applicant to prove that they are entitled to make a claim (as held by Farwell J in *Mastaka*) and thus to prove that no foreign domicile was acquired; or for those asserting that the deceased had acquired a foreign domicile of choice to prove it, in accordance with the normal rule that the burden of proving a change of domicile lies on the person who asserts it.

2–032 In *Bheekhun v Williams*,[66] the deceased was born in 1931 in Mauritius, then a Crown Colony. In 1960 he moved to England, followed by his wife, with whom he had undergone a ceremony of marriage in 1956. The couple set up home in England, buying their own property in 1968. When Mauritius became independent in that year, they chose to retain British nationality. The marriage relationship broke down in 1975 and the wife left the husband and commenced divorce proceedings in 1977, but these were dismissed by consent in 1989. A decree nisi was pronounced in her subsequent divorce proceedings but had not been made absolute at the date of the husband's death. The judge at first instance found that in 1960 Mr Bheekhun came to England with the intention of seeking a permanent home there, but that that intention was conditional on his finding work and a place to live. He then reviewed the events which took place between then and 1968, and summarised them under the three headings of: employment and a place to live; nationality and passports; and visits to Mauritius and the establishment of a business there. Chadwick LJ considered that the judge had directed himself correctly and was entitled to reach the conclusion that by mid-1968 the deceased had come to regard England as his permanent home. He said:[67]

> "He was correct to regard the decision, taken at the time when Mauritius became independent, to obtain a British passport and to take British nationality, as a clear pointer to the deceased's intention, at that time, that he would make his home in England. The decision coincided with plans to buy a house in London. There was no need for the deceased to obtain a British passport in order to have a valid travel document. He already had the Mauritian passport which he had renewed in 1965 for a further period of 5 years. The correct inference, it seems to me, is that he decided to obtain a British passport because he wanted to cement his relationship with the country in which he was then living."

[66] *Bheekhun v Williams* [1999] 2 F.L.R. 229, CA.
[67] *Bheekhun v Williams*, at 239B–C.

If (as the trial judge found) Mr Bheekhun had acquired an English domicile of choice in 1968, it would have been for the personal representatives to establish that, when he later went to live in Mauritius (where he spent the period from April 1991 to January 1992) he had ceased to reside in England without having the intention of returning there. There was, in the view of the Court of Appeal, no evidence on which the judge could have arrived at that conclusion.

Two subsequent cases in which the deceased had strong ties with two jurisdictions are *Sylvester v Sylvester* [68] and *Kebbeh v Farmer*.[69] These cases illustrate the importance of adopting the approach to determining questions of domicile stated by Mummery LJ,[70] which requires examination of the entire course of the deceased's life and not giving undue importance to any individual matter. In *Sylvester*, the claimant was one of the adult children of the deceased (S), who was born in Carriacou, a dependency of Grenada, in 1925, and was married in Trinidad in 1953. S came to live in England, where her husband (Sh) had already obtained employment, in 1957, and she also obtained employment, continuing to work until about the time when Sh retired, in 1986. Their two younger children were born in London, in 1959 and 1965, respectively. They purchased a house in Kilburn in 1962 and occupied it as the matrimonial home and both became naturalised as British citizens, but also maintained their citizenship of Grenada and had a substantial property built in Carriacou, to which they moved some of their personal possessions in 1989. S thereafter spent much of her time in Carriacou but made frequent visits to London for medical treatment; in September 2006 she was diagnosed with renal failure. In 2001 her husband was diagnosed with terminal cancer and they returned to the Kilburn property, where they lived until his death in 2004, and where she continued to live, save for two brief visits to Carriacou in 2004 and early 2006, until her death in 2008. It was held that S was not in a position to make a choice during the period of her husband's illness but that after his death, she could have returned to her substantial home in Carriacou and remained there, but she chose to return to London. Her return was not forced upon her by her illness;[71] she had the resources to obtain medical treatment in Carriacou. The requisite intention to remain permanently in England and Wales for the rest of her life had been formed by early 2006 at latest. Accordingly, the court had jurisdiction to entertain the claim, but there is no report of its outcome.

2–033

In *Kebbeh v Farmer,* the claimant (K) was the widow of the deceased's second marriage, for whom his will made no provision. The deceased (M) had a domicile of origin in England and Wales, but moved to Gambia in 1994 where he built himself a "rather splendid" home, and died there in 2011. There was much evidence from those who were close to him that he had expressed the intention to live indefinitely or permanently in Gambia,

2–034

---

[68] *Sylvester v Sylvester* [2014] W.T.L.R. 127.
[69] *Kebbeh v Farmer* [2016] W.T.L.R. 1011.
[70] *Cyganik v Agulian* [2006] W.T.L.R. 565, CA; see para.2–011, above.
[71] For the importance of this, see *Udny v Udny* [1869] L.R.1 Sc. and Div. 441.

and the desire to be buried there. It was not decisive that he did not obtain Gambian citizenship or that he retained a number of connections with England; these included the child of his second marriage (J) being born in England, where he lived for a short time before returning to Gambia, with J, in 2003. Also, he had business interests in England, he had made a will in English form with an English executor and beneficiaries in 2006, and had purchased two investment properties in England in 2010 or 2011. These matters were held to be unimportant in determining his domicile. It was held that M had acquired a domicile of choice in Gambia and K's claim therefore failed.

2–035 The necessity to connect a person with a system of law by which their legal relationships can be regulated leads to the two rules[72] that no person can be without a domicile, and that no person can at the same time for the same purpose have more than one domicile. It has been suggested that a person can have different domiciles for different purposes;[73] thus, in *Lawrence v Lawrence*,[74] Purchas LJ envisaged the possibility that "domicile" might have a different meaning according to the purpose for which it was used.[75] However, in *Mark v Mark*,[76] Waller LJ took a contrary view, emphasising the importance of "unity of domicile".

2–036 A person may have a deemed domicile for some purposes, and the reasons (particularly if they include a long period of residence) for which they have been deemed to have that domicile might also be evidence in favour of their having acquired the deemed domicile as a domicile of choice. Some English tax legislation treats persons who are not domiciled in the United Kingdom as though they are domiciled there; thus, s.267(1)(b) of the Inheritance Tax Act 1984 provides that a person who is not domiciled in the United Kingdom at the relevant time shall be treated as if they were so domiciled if they were resident in the United Kingdom in not less than 17 of the 20 years of assessment, ending with the year of assessment in which the relevant time falls. That, however, is not the same as providing that those persons have a separate United Kingdom domicile for tax purposes.[77]

(ii) Declarations relating to domicile

2–037 Written declarations by the deceased as to their domicile are admissible but not conclusive. As with any other form of hearsay evidence, the court should, in estimating the weight (if any) to be given to it, have regard to any circumstances from which inferences may reasonably be drawn as to the reliability or otherwise of such evidence.[78] The list of circumstances to which

---

[72] *Dicey, Morris and Collins*, rr.5 and 6, paras 6R–011 and 6R–013.

[73] *Dicey, Morris and Collins*, para.6–015.

[74] *Lawrence v Lawrence* [1985] Fam. 106 at 132–33.

[75] Citing Bramwell B in *Attorney General v Rowe* (1862) 1 Hurl and C. 31 at 45; 158 E.R. 789 at 795.

[76] *Mark v Mark* [2005] Fam. 267, CA, where Waller LJ said at [75]: "It is not possible for a person to have a domicile of choice for one purpose."

[77] *Tristram and Coote's Probate Practice* (London: LexisNexis, 2015) at para.4.176. The notional domicile assumed for those purposes is irrelevant for probate purposes.

[78] Civil Evidence Act 1995 s.4(1).

regard may be had, in particular, includes "whether any person involved had any motive to conceal or misrepresent matters".[79] This may be relevant in relation to the concern expressed by the Law Commission that a change of domicile might be effected as a means of eliminating the possibility of a 1975 Act claim.[80] In any event, a declaration is simply one of the facts to be considered, and the other relevant circumstances may be found to be consistent with the declaration, as in *Re Lloyd Evans*[81] where the deceased temporarily left Belgium, the country of his acquired domicile of choice, when it was invaded by Germany in 1940, but declared himself to be a citizen of, and domiciled in, Belgium; or inconsistent, as in *Re Liddell-Grainger's Will Trusts*[82] where the deceased declared in his will that he had not relinquished, and did not intend to relinquish, his English domicile, but the judge found that he had acquired a Scottish domicile of choice by 38 years' residence and by other acts which manifested an intention to live permanently in Scotland.

The purpose for which the declaration was made will also be relevant. In **2-038** *Holliday v Musa*[83] the deceased was born in Cyprus in 1932, but left there in 1958 and subsequently married and brought up a family in England. However, he visited Cyprus, purchased land there and was involved in politics, standing for election in 1998, the same year in which he bought property in Cyprus. He then announced his intention to stand for the Presidency of Cyprus in 2000. In the early 1990s the Revenue took an interest in his affairs and he declared himself to be domiciled in Cyprus and stated that he intended to return there; in 1997 he signed a DOM 1 form to that effect. He did make visits to Cyprus in almost every year from 1996 to 2006, and he died in Cyprus in November 2006. As Waller LJ said, his declarations to the Revenue must be treated with some caution, but they could not be ignored when they were consistent with the facts. He observed that:[84]

"...where someone had clearly set up his home for a very long time in a country, has had a family there, and does not have a home elsewhere, that must provide a strong starting point. Having expressed to the Inland Revenue[85] an intention to retire to Cyprus, it is worth pointing out that at the age of 74 he still had not done so ... Then there are his declarations to the Revenue. But it seems to me that the declarations were consistent with what [the deceased] wished the facts to be. He wished to achieve a non-dom status. But his expressed intention to retire to Cyprus was of that vague variety in which he could still be

---

[79] Civil Evidence Act 1995 s.4(2)(d). Five other matters are listed in s.4(2).
[80] Law Com. CP 191 at para.7.41; Law Com. LC 331 at para.7.14.
[81] *Re Lloyd Evans, National Provincial Bank v Evans* [1947] 1 Ch. 695.
[82] *Liddell-Grainger's Will Trusts* [1936] 3 All E.R. 173.
[83] *Holliday v Musa* [2010] W.T.L.R. 839, CA. See also *Barlow Clowes International Ltd (in liquidation) v Henwood* [2008] EWCA (Civ) 577, where, if Mr Henwood had been able to establish that he was domiciled in Mauritius on the relevant date, the courts of England and Wales would have had no jurisdiction to make a bankruptcy order against him.
[84] *Holliday v Musa* [2010] W.T.L.R. 839, CA at paras 67, 69.
[85] In 1991–93 and in 1997 (nine years before his death).

intending to reside permanently in England in order to achieve a domicile of choice in England."

In the result, the Court of Appeal upheld the finding of the trial judge that the deceased had died domiciled in England, though on rather different grounds.

(iii) Public documents containing statements relating to domicile

2–039   Section 1(3) of the Civil Evidence Act 1995 provides that nothing in that Act affects the admissibility of evidence which is admissible apart from s.1, so the Act does not affect statutory provisions making hearsay admissible. Section 7(2) of that Act provides that the common law rules effectively preserved by ss.9(1) and 9(2)(b)–(d) of the Civil Evidence Act 1968 shall continue to have effect. Thus, the rule of law whereby public documents (for example, public registers) are admissible as evidence of the facts stated in them, continues to have effect. Where exceptions are preserved by s.7, the hearsay contained in the documents is admissible apart from s.1 of the Act, so the notice provisions in ss.2–6 do not apply. Thus, a certified copy of an entry in the register of births or deaths is admissible as evidence of the facts stated therein.[86] Evidence must be adduced that the applicant is the person to whom the entry in the register of births relates.

2–040   In the case of a marriage, proof is required that a ceremony of marriage was celebrated and that the persons named in the certificate are the persons whose marriage is to be proved. Where a marriage was celebrated in England and Wales, the certificate is evidence of the marriage to which it relates.[87] In *Re Peete*,[88] the applicant claimed provision out of the estate of the deceased under the 1938 Act on the basis that she was his surviving spouse, she having married him on 23 June 1919, as the marriage certificate showed. She had been married previously, but believed that her husband had been killed in an accident in 1916 and that she was free to remarry. However, she was unable to produce a death certificate. Roxburgh J observed that s.36 of the Marriage Act 1836 empowered the registrar to ask the parties for the particulars required to be registered, but created no obligation to satisfy himself that they were true; her statement that she was a widow was uncorroborated. It was held that as there was evidence which put in issue the death of her first husband, the certificate of the second marriage, though describing her as "widow", could not be regarded as evidence that she had the capacity to marry.

2–041   That case was distinguished in *Re Watkins*,[89] where the applicant went through a ceremony of marriage in 1948, believing that her husband had died in 1942 and not having heard from him since 1922, although she had been in touch with his close relatives from 1922 to 1937. Harman J took the

---

[86] Births and Deaths Registration Act 1953 s.34.
[87] Marriage Act 1949 s.65.
[88] *Re Peete* [1952] 2 All E.R. 599.
[89] *Re Watkins* [1953] 1 W.L.R. 1323.

view that, notwithstanding the applicant had made no search or inquiry for her first husband, it was permissible to infer after that lapse of time that he was dead and that, therefore, her second marriage was valid. Note that, although a grant of representation to the estate of the deceased may state that the deceased died domiciled in England and Wales, such a statement is not conclusive.

2.—ELIGIBILITY

(a) Claimants in General

It is for the applicant to prove that they fall within the relevant class. So far as applicants claiming to be spouses, former spouses who have not remarried or children are concerned, documentary evidence in the form of the appropriate birth, marriage or death certificates may normally be expected to be available and, in appropriate cases, reference may be made to the record of previous divorce or nullity proceedings. **2–042**

As to civil partners, the Civil Partnership Act 2004 provides that a civil partnership is formed when two people have signed a civil partnership document in the presence of each other, the registrar and two witnesses, all of whom must also sign. Unless the special procedure requiring the issue of a Registrar-General's licence is used, the document will be a civil partnership schedule.[90] The Registrar-General is required to provide a system for keeping records that relate to civil partnerships.[91] **2–043**

The amendment of enactments relating to wills, administration of estates and family provision was implemented by s.71 and Sch.4 of the Civil Partnership Act so that they apply in relation to civil partnerships as they apply in relation to marriage. The amendments to the 1975 Act are contained in paras 15–27 of the Schedule. The effect of para.15 is that the classes of persons who may make a claim under the 1975 Act are extended by the insertion, into subss.1(a), 1(b), 1(ba) and 1(d), of provisions referring to civil partnerships which mirror the existing provisions referring to marriage or living together as husband and wife. The Marriage (Same-Sex Couples) Act 2013[92] does not amend the 1975 Act, but provides that in existing England and Wales legislation: **2–044**

- (a) a reference to a marriage is to be read as including a reference to a marriage of a same-sex couple;
- (b) a reference to a married couple is to be read as including a reference to a married same-sex couple; and
- (c) a reference to a person who is married is to be read as including a reference to a person who is married to a person of the same sex.

---

[90] Civil Partnership Act 2004 s.14.
[91] Civil Partnership Act 2004 s.30.
[92] Marriage (Same-Sex Couples) Act 2013 Sch.3 Pt 1 para.1.

In what follows, the amendments are considered in relation to each of the classes defined by subss.1(1)(a), (b), (ba) and (d).

(b) Spouses

2–045   Except in three cases, the evidential requirements should be straightforward. The exceptions concern:

    (i)   parties to foreign marriages;
    (ii)   survivors of void[93] marriages entered into in good faith; and
    (iii) parties who have been judicially separated.

(i) Parties to foreign marriages

2–046   A surviving party to a marriage celebrated outside England and Wales has the status of a spouse for the purposes of the 1975 Act if the English courts recognise the marriage. Among the marriages so recognised are those where the marriage is celebrated in a form required by the law of the country where the marriage was celebrated. If a polygamous marriage is recognised by the English courts, a partner in such a marriage is a spouse for the purposes of s.1(1)(a) of the 1975 Act. Prior to the coming into force of the Matrimonial Proceedings (Polygamous Marriages) Act 1972 (now incorporated into the Matrimonial Causes Act 1973 as s.47), parties to polygamous marriages could not obtain matrimonial relief in the English Courts. In *Re Sehota*,[94] it was held that a claim under the 1975 Act was a matter of succession, not a matrimonial claim, but even if it were a claim for matrimonial relief, s.1(1)(a) of the 1975 Act was to be construed in the light of the matrimonial legislation referred to above. The circumstances of *Re Sehota* have not recurred in any reported case, but it was cited in *Official Solicitor v Yemoh*[95] in which it was held that on the death intestate of the husband of a polygamous marriage, who had died domiciled in Ghana, those of the surviving wives who were validly married according to the law of his domicile[96] together constituted the surviving spouse for the purposes of s.46 of the Administration of Estates Act 1925 and were entitled to share one statutory legacy between them.

(ii) Survivors of void marriages entered into in good faith

2–047   By s.25(4) of the 1975 Act, any reference to a spouse is treated as including a reference to a person who entered *in good faith* into a void marriage with the

---

[93] If the marriage is voidable (see Matrimonial Causes Act 1973 s.12; grounds include, for example, non-consummation or absence of valid consent) it is a subsisting marriage until it has been avoided by the grant of a decree of nullity but the marriage is treated as valid and subsisting up till the grant of the decree. A survivor of such a marriage would be eligible to claim under s.1(1)(b) if they had not remarried.
[94] *Re Sehota* [1978] 3 All E.R. 385.
[95] *Official Solicitor v Yemoh* [2011] 1 W.L.R. 1450.
[96] There was a question whether one of the eight surviving wives had been validly married according to Ghanaian customary law.

deceased, unless either the marriage was dissolved or annulled or the survivor remarried. Thus, all survivors of void marriages who entered into the marriage with the deceased in good faith are within the ambit of the provision. It would have covered the applicant in *Re Peete*,[97] as well as a person who believes that they are free to remarry in the interval between the granting of a decree nisi and a decree absolute. The decision of the Court of Appeal in *Re Seaford*[98] makes it clear that such a belief is mistaken; the parties remain married until the decree is made absolute.

In *Gandhi v Patel*[99] the claimant had entered into a Hindu marriage **2–048** ceremony with the deceased but had never entered into an English marriage ceremony with him. The deceased had previously married another woman, whom he had never divorced. The claimant accepted that, because of the bigamy, she was not the wife of the deceased, but sought to invoke subs.25(4). The claim failed on two grounds: First, the term "void marriage" had the same meaning as it had in s.11 of the Matrimonial Causes Act 1973. If a ceremony which took place in England was to create a relationship which English law would recognise as a marriage, it at least had to purport to comply with the formal requirements of English law, mainly contained in the Marriages Acts. The ceremony on which the claimant relied to establish that relationship did not comply or purport to comply with those requirements and was not a void marriage; it was not a marriage at all.[100] Secondly, it was found as a fact that on the balance of probabilities, the claimant knew that the deceased was still married at the time of the ceremony on which she relied and thus could not have entered into it in good faith.

By s.25(5) of the 1975 Act, a reference to a remarriage or to a person who **2–049** has remarried includes a reference to a marriage which is by law void or voidable[101] or, as the case may be, to a person who has entered into such a marriage. Thus, a former spouse whose first marriage was valid and who subsequently enters into a void or voidable marriage has remarried, for the purposes of the 1975 Act, and is barred from relief. The same subsection also provides that a marriage shall be treated as a remarriage, in relation to

---

[97] *Re Peete* [1952] 2 All E.R. 599 referred to at para.2–038.
[98] *Re Seaford* [1968] P. 53, CA. The litigation came about because it was not known, at the time when the wife's (W) notice of application to make the decree absolute was filed, that the husband (H) was already dead. Her interest was that, since H had died intestate, she would be the person entitled to administration of his estate. Had the marriage been dissolved, H's mother (M), as next of kin, would have been entitled. The judge at first instance had ruled in favour of M, holding that the legal fiction known as the doctrine of relation back of a judicial act applied. The Court of Appeal held unanimously in favour of W; the purported dissolution of the marriage was a nullity. Russell LJ (at pp.73–74) declined to import into the law of England the equation "Nullity + Fiction = Reality". As he pithily expressed the position: "...when the judicial act was purported to be performed, so as to determine the plaintiff's marriage to the deceased by decree absolute, the marriage had ceased to exist, and the ability of the court to determine it was equally non-existent, whether the court knew or was ignorant of that situation. Whom God had put asunder, no man could join together, even for the purpose of putting them asunder again."
[99] *Gandhi v Patel* [2002] 1 F.L.R. 603.
[100] The distinction was analysed at length by Park J in *Gandhi v Patel* at [34]–[49], particular reliance being placed on the decision of Hughes J in *A-M v A-M (Divorce: Jurisdiction, Validity of Marriages)* [2001] 2 F.L.R. 6.
[101] See, respectively, Matrimonial Causes Act 1973 ss.11 and 12.

any party thereto, notwithstanding that the previous marriage of that party was void or voidable. It should be noted that a decree of nullity granted in respect of a voidable marriage operates to annul the marriage only from the time when the decree has been made absolute, and the marriage is treated as having existed until that time.

(iii) Judicially separated spouses

2–050   Although a judicially separated spouse is within the definition of a wife or husband, such a surviving spouse is specifically barred by s.1(2)(a) of the 1975 Act from receiving the higher standard of maintenance if the decree was in force and the separation was continuing at the date of death of the deceased.

(c) Parties to Registered Civil Partnerships

2–051   Such persons were brought within the scope of the 1975 Act by the amendment of subs.1(1)(a) so as to read, "the spouse or civil partner of the deceased".[102] Their position in relation to the standard of provision was aligned with that of surviving spouses by the insertion of subs.1(2)(aa),[103] whose effect was to entitle survivors of civil partnerships to the higher standard of maintenance afforded to surviving spouses. Subsections 25(4A) and 25(5A)[104] relate, respectively, to persons in good faith forming a void civil partnership and the effect of formation of a subsequent civil partnership.

(d) Former Spouses Who Have Not Remarried and Former Parties to Civil Partnerships Who Have Not Formed a Subsequent Civil Partnership

2–052   Under the 1975 Act as originally enacted, a former spouse was a person whose marriage with the deceased was dissolved or annulled during the lifetime of the deceased by a decree of divorce or nullity under the Matrimonial Causes Act 1973. This meant that no relief under s.1(1)(b) was available to a former spouse whose marriage had been dissolved in another jurisdiction, though such a person might have qualified as a dependant under s.1(1)(e). However, s.25(1) of the 1975 Act was amended by s.25 of the Matrimonial and Family Proceedings Act 1984 so as to put persons whose marriages had been terminated outside the British Isles in a manner recognised as valid by the law of England and Wales on the same footing as those whose marriages were terminated within the jurisdiction. This extension is, of course, subject to the deceased having died domiciled in England and Wales. Practitioners dealing with such claims, which have become increasingly rare, should take care to ascertain whether any order has been

---

[102] Civil Partnership Act 2004 Sch.4 para.15(2). This sub-paragraph also amended subs.1(1)(b) of the 1975 Act so as to read, "a former spouse or civil partner of the deceased but not one who has formed a subsequent marriage or civil partnership".

[103] Civil Partnership Act 2004 Sch.4 para.15(6).

[104] Which mirror the provisions of subss.25(4) and 25(5) relating to marriages.

made under ss.15(1) or 15ZA(1) debarring the surviving party to the dissolved marriage or civil partnership party from applying for an order under s.2 of the 1975 Act.

(e) Cohabitants

(i) Opposite-sex cohabitants

The Law Reform (Succession) Act 1995 ("the 1995 Act") entitled cohabitants who satisfied certain conditions to apply for provision under the 1975 Act without the need to show dependence on the deceased. Those conditions are based on, but not identical with, the conditions determining entitlement to bring claims as dependants under the Fatal Accidents Act 1976. Under that Act, persons were eligible who were living with the deceased in the same household immediately before the date of death, had been doing so for a period of two years immediately before the date of death, and had been living during the whole of that period as the husband or wife of the deceased.   **2–053**

The effect of ss.1(1)(ba) and 1(1A) of the 1975 Act, as amended by the   **2–054**
1995 Act is to permit persons (other than surviving spouses or former spouses who have not remarried), to claim, provided that the deceased died on or after 1 January 1996 and, during the whole of the period of two years ending immediately before the deceased died, the claimant was living (a) in the same household as the deceased, and (b) as the husband or wife of the deceased. In *Re Watson*,[105] the first reported claim under s.1(1)(ba), "immediately" was given the same broad meaning as in the dependency cases discussed below. Neuberger J held that, as a matter of ordinary language, the fact that someone is in hospital, possibly for a long period, at the end of which they die, does not mean that, before their death, they ceased to be part of the household of which they were part until they were forced by illness to go to hospital, and to which they would have returned had they not died. This interpretation has also been adopted where there had been a temporary breakdown in the relationship during the two-year period, and even though the parties were not living together at the date of the deceased's death. In such cases it is necessary to look beyond the two-year period in order to ascertain the nature of the established relationship.

The effect of a temporary break in the relationship was considered by the   **2–055**
Court of Appeal as a preliminary issue in *Gully v Dix*.[106] The relevant facts were that the claimant and the deceased, who was an alcoholic, had lived together for some 27 years before his death in 2001. He had suffered serious head injuries in a fall and was incontinent. On a number of occasions the

---

[105] *Re Watson* [1999] 1 F.L.R. 878.
[106] *Gully v Dix* [2004] 1 F.L.R. 918, CA. See also *Kaur v Dhaliwal* [2014] W.T.L.R. 1381, a claim under s.1(1)(ba), in which it was held that it was possible for the parties to be living together in the same household at the moment of the deceased's death even if they had been living separately at that moment. The claim succeeded even though there was an eight-month gap in the two-year period for which it was not possible to identify any address at which the parties had lived together.

claimant had left him for a short time because of the extreme squalor of their living conditions, but she invariably returned to him when he apologised and promised to reform. However, some three months before his death, she found the situation intolerable and left to live with her daughter, taking only a few clothes with her. The deceased telephoned on a number of occasions but the daughter never passed on any of the messages to her. He died intestate leaving an estate worth £170,000 which passed to his brother. The claimant claimed reasonable provision both as a cohabitant under s.1(1)(ba) and as a dependant under s.1(1)(e). For the brother it was contended that as she had left to live with her daughter some three months before his death, the claimant had neither lived in the same household as the deceased as man and wife for the period of two years immediately before his death, nor was she being wholly or partly maintained by him immediately before his death.

2–056   The trial judge declared that the claimant satisfied both of those conditions but gave permission to appeal as the claim had raised a question of interpretation of the Act. He found that the element of maintenance was satisfied by the fact that, up until the time she left him, the deceased was providing living accommodation for the claimant in his house for less than full valuable consideration. As to the word "immediately", he held that he was not confined to considering only the period of two years ending with the death of the deceased, but was required to look also at the preceding period, if necessary, so as to discover the nature of the established relationship. He found as a fact that the relationship had not come to an end and that she would have once more returned to him had he promised her that he would reform, and the fact that her daughter had concealed the telephone calls from her made it clear that she would have gone back to him if asked to do so. He also found that the deceased did (contrary to the contention of the brother) want her to come back to him. The Court of Appeal considered the judge to have approached the matter correctly and not to have erred in law or in fact.

2–057   What amounts to "living as husband and wife" is not easy to define. As is demonstrated by the cases now discussed, the phrase can cover so many fact situations that (as the courts have tacitly recognised) a universally applicable definition cannot be formulated. *Adeoso (otherwise Ametepe) v Adeoso*[107] was a case in which the Court of Appeal had to consider the construction of s.1(2) of the Domestic Violence and Matrimonial Proceedings Act 1976, which applies to a man and a woman who are living together in the same household as husband and wife as it applied to parties to a marriage. Ormrod LJ said in that case:

> "...to anyone looking at them from the outside, there can be no doubt whatever that they were and are apparently living together as husband and wife";

---

[107]   *Adeoso v Adeoso, Ametepe v Adeoso* [1981] 1 All E.R. 107, CA.

and it was held that they were "living together as husband and wife" since they were occupying the same small flat, though there was no contact or communication between them.

In 1975 Act claims the question is likely to be resolved by applying that **2–058** type of test, rather than the more mechanical "check-list" approach which is found in the social security cases of *Crake v Supplementary Benefit Commissioners, Butterworth v Supplementary Benefit Commissioners.*[108] There, the factors considered relevant were (a) whether the parties live together; (b) the stability of the relationship; (c) financial support; (d) the existence of a sexual relationship; (e) caring for a child of the relationship; and (f) public acknowledgment. While any or all of those matters might be relevant in any given case, the "check-list" approach has no place in the determination of family provision claims. Its dangers were referred to in *Kimber v Kimber.*[109] In the course of analysing the factors to be considered, HH Judge Tyrer said that "living together in the same household" generally meant that the parties lived under the same roof, illness, holidays, work and other periodic absences apart.[110]

In *Re Watson*, it seemed to Neuberger J that, when considering the **2–059** question, the court should ask itself whether, in the opinion of a reasonable person with normal perceptions, it could be said that the two people in question were living together as husband and wife; but that the multifarious nature of marital relationships should not be ignored. The applicant said in evidence that, to the rest of the world, she and the deceased were as man and wife; and, notwithstanding the absence of any sexual relationship during the last ten years of their living together, the court (rightly, it is submitted) reached that conclusion. As *Re Watson* shows, once it is established that there has been a relationship of husband and wife, it may be a permissible inference that the relationship is continuing even though some of its original features no longer exist.

Since *Watson*, the question whether two persons had been living together **2–060** in the same household as husband and wife has been considered in the context of the 1975 Act and of landlord and tenant law. In *Churchill v Roach*,[111] where the 1975 Act claim was made on the alternative bases of cohabitation and dependency, the judge had no doubt that from 14 December 1998 until the death of the deceased on 15 April 2000, the claimant and the deceased lived together in the same household as husband and wife. However, on the evidence of the state of the relationship between them before that time, he concluded that they were maintaining not only two separate properties (which would not by itself have been fatal to the claim) but (notwithstanding the time they spent together at weekends) two separate

---

[108] *Crake v Supplementary Benefit Commissioners, Butterworth v Supplementary Benefit Commissioners* [1982] 1 All E.R. 498.
[109] *Kimber v Kimber* [2000] 1 F.L.R. 383. The "check-list" approach has continued to be found useful in cases under the Fatal Accidents Act 1976; see, e.g., *Kotke v Saffarini* [2005] 2 F.L.R. 878.
[110] *Kimber v Kimber* [2000] 1 F.L.R. 383 at 391.
[111] *Churchill v Roach* [2004] 2 F.L.R. 989. There was a claim to a beneficial interest (which failed) as well as the 1975 Act claims.

establishments with two separate domestic economies. The claim as a cohabitant thus failed[112] as they had not lived together in the same household for the whole of the two years immediately[113] before the death of the deceased.

2–061   In *Nutting v Southern Housing Group*[114] the question arose whether the survivor of a same-sex relationship was entitled to succeed to a tenancy pursuant to s.17(4) of the Housing Act 1988.[115] The judge at first instance set out a test based on four indicia of "living together as husband and wife"[116] and found that the claimant had failed to satisfy that test. On appeal, Evans-Lombe J, though critical of certain aspects of the test, upheld the finding. He held that a test of whether there existed an emotional relationship of mutual lifetime commitment openly and unequivocally presented to the outside world[117] was an entirely adequate test and one which was consistent with the authorities. He also found that the judge at first instance had been entitled to conclude that the claimant had failed to demonstrate a relationship of sufficient permanence.

2–062   The requirement of open and unequivocal presentation of the relationship to the outside world would, as a matter of ordinary language, appear to add a further element to the test as originally formulated in *Watson*; instead of simply conveying the impression, by their ordinary behaviour, of acting like husband and wife, the parties may in future be required to engage in some overt act which demonstrates (or could be seen as demonstrating) commitment. However, in *Swetenham v Walkley*[118] the requirements were described in more general terms; there had to be a tie of mutual society both privately between the parties and for others to witness. There was evidence that they were perceived as a married couple, but there was no particular factor which was regarded as utterly determinative of whether the relationship of living together as husband and wife existed.

2–063   In *Lindop v Agus*,[119] where the issue of open demonstration of commitment came to the fore, HH Judge Behrens described the test approved by Evans-Lombe J as a more stringent test. *Lindop v Agus* was the trial of the preliminary issue whether the claimant was eligible to bring a claim either as a cohabitant or as a dependant. The defendant executors accepted that there was a relationship between the claimant and the deceased but did not accept either that they were living together in the same household as husband and

---

[112] The claim as a dependant succeeded.

[113] "Immediately" is construed in the same way as in cases under s.1(1)(e) (for which, see paras 2–075 to 2–077), that is to say, one looks at the settled state of affairs over the relevant period. Thus, for instance, if the deceased died in a hospital or nursing home, that would not prevent the two-year condition from being met; see *Re Watson* [1999] 1 F.L.R. 878. The same would apply if the deceased died during a temporary breakdown of the cohabitation relationship; see *Gully v Dix* [2004] 1 F.L.R. 918, CA.

[114] *Nutting v Southern Housing Group* [2005] 2 P. & C.R. 14 p.254.

[115] Which provides that, for the purposes of s.17, a person who was living with the tenant as their wife or husband should be treated as the tenant's spouse.

[116] *Nutting v Southern Housing Group* [2005] 2 P. & C.R. 14 p.257 at paras 36–37.

[117] Items (b) and (c) of the four indicia.

[118] *Swetenham v Walkley* [2014] W.T.L.R. 845.

[119] *Lindop v Agus* [2009] W.T.L.R. 1175 at [38].

wife or that the deceased had been maintaining her other than for full valuable consideration. At trial, attention was drawn to a considerable amount of documentary evidence showing that during the period of alleged cohabitation, the claimant had been registered at her father's address on the electoral register and that her bank statements, P60s and other official documents were sent to her there. Although there was also some documentary evidence of her living at the deceased's address, it was argued that the relationship failed to satisfy the test of being "openly and unequivocally displayed to the outside world", since the "outside world" included public authorities. HH Judge Behrens saw the submission to be not without force, but the weight of the evidence of those who had observed the relationship pointed to their living openly together and displaying that to the outside world. Consequently, L was entitled to claim under s.1(1A) of the 1975 Act.

(ii) Same-sex cohabitants

The 21st century has seen a radical alteration in the status of same-sex   **2–064**
cohabitants, both under the 1975 Act and under the law generally.[120] The extension of the 1975 Act by the Law Reform (Succession) Act 1995 did not bring them within its ambit. Same-sex cohabitants could claim only under s.1(1)(e), in which case the court had to be satisfied that they were being maintained (as that term is defined in s.1(3) of the Act) by the deceased immediately before their death. Nor did developments in other areas of the law give encouragement to the view that parties to same-sex relationships should be treated for any purpose as if they were husband and wife. Thus, in *Fitzpatrick v Sterling Housing Association*,[121] the House of Lords rejected the submission that "spouse", for the purposes of para.2(2) of Sch.1 to the Rent Act 1977, was to be interpreted as including two persons of the same sex intimately linked in a relationship which was not merely transient and had all the indicia of a marriage save that the parties could not have children. It was held unanimously that the extended definition of "spouse" was gender-specific, connoting a relationship between a man and a woman.

However, two developments, one general and one specific, affected the   **2–065**
status of same-sex cohabitants. The general development was in the field of human rights. In *Karner v Austria*,[122] K, who was the survivor of a homosexual relationship with W, claimed to have been a victim of discrimination

---

[120] The Marriage (Same-Sex Couples) Act 2013 Sch.3 Pt 1 para.2 provides that, in the interpretation of existing England and Wales legislation, (a) a reference to persons who are not married but are living together as a married couple is to be read as including a reference to a same-sex couple who are not married but are living together as a married couple and (b) a reference to a person who is living with another person as if they were married is to be read as including a reference to a person who is living with another person of the same sex as if they were married.

[121] *Fitzpatrick v Sterling Housing Association* [2001] 1 A.C. 27.

[122] *Karner v Austria* [2003] 2 F.L.R. 623.

on the ground of his sexual orientation in that the Austrian Supreme Court had denied him the status of "life companion" within the meaning of s.14(3) of the Rent Act 1974.[123] He invoked Art.14[124] together with Art.8.[125] The European Court of Human Rights held that Art.14 applied since, had it not been for his sexual orientation, K could have been accepted as a "life companion" to succeed to the lease pursuant to the statute. The Government's narrow interpretation of the statute had not been justified[126] and there had been a violation of Art.14 taken together with Art.8.

2–066   In *Ghaidan v Godin-Mendoza*,[127] shortly after the decision in *Karner*,[128] the House of Lords held that s.3 of the Human Rights Act 1998 compelled them to read the corresponding provision of the Rent Act 1977[129] as though the survivor of a same-sex relationship was the surviving spouse of the other party. It thus became apparent that the passing reference by Lord Hobhouse in *Fitzpatrick*[130] to the reasoning in *Re Watson* as "wholly inconsistent with extending the category (as defined by s.1(1)(ba) of the 1975 Act) beyond heterosexual relationships" was out of date.

2–067   The scope of the 1975 Act was extended to same-sex cohabitants[131] by the Civil Partnership Act 2004, which came into force on 5 December 2005, so that *Saunders v Garrett*,[132] a 1975 Act claim by a same-sex cohabitant, in which judgment had been given some 10 months before, was overtaken by events. There were two aspects of Mr Saunders' claim; one was for a sum of money to enable him to rectify the defects in his home, and the other was for provision to meet his income shortfall and to provide a fund for contingencies. As a matter of construction of the 1975 Act as it then was, Master Bowles, following the decision of the House of Lords in *Fitzpatrick v Sterling Housing Association*,[133] held that the words "husband" and "wife" were gender-specific and that, as a matter of conventional construction, subss.1(1)(ba) and 1(1A) applied only where a man and a woman had lived together in the same household for the requisite period.

2–068   On considering the question whether, pursuant to s.3 of the Human Rights Act 1998, an extended construction could and should be imposed on those provisions, he concluded that:

---

[123] The district and regional courts had each decided this question in K's favour. The Supreme Court reversed those decisions on the basis that the Act had to be interpreted as at the time it had been enacted and the legislature had not, at that time, intended to afford that status to persons of the same sex.

[124] "The enjoyment of the rights and freedoms set forth in the Convention shall be secured without discrimination on any ground..."

[125] "Everyone has the right to respect for his private and family life [and] his home..."

[126] The Vienna Regional Court had found that the provision in issue protected persons who had been living together for a long time without being married against sudden homelessness and applied to homosexuals as well as heterosexuals.

[127] *Ghaidan v Godin-Mendoza* [2004] 2 A.C. 557, 21 June 2004 affirming the decision of the Court of Appeal [2003] Ch. 380.

[128] Made on 24 July 2003.

[129] Sch.1 to the Rent Act 1977 para.2(2).

[130] *Fitzpatrick* [2001] 1 A.C. 27 at 69.

[131] Civil Partnership Act 2004 Sch.4 para.15(3).

[132] *Saunders v Garrett* [2005] W.T.L.R. 749. Judgment was given on 7 February 2005.

[133] *Fitzpatrick v Sterling Housing Association* [2001] 1 A.C. 27.

(1) subs.1(1)(ba) and 1(1A) of the 1975 Act as then in force did dis-
     criminate against Mr Saunders on the ground of his sexual
     orientation and in a way which was not justified on the basis of
     some legitimate aim. Article 14 of the European Convention on
     Human Rights therefore came into play such that his engaged
     rights should be secured to him without discrimination. Conse-
     quently, the court should exercise its powers under s.3 of the
     Human Rights Act 1988 to "read up" those provisions of the 1975
     Act so as to render them Convention-compliant;

(2) Art.8 of the First Protocol, which provides that "Every person has
     the right to respect for his private and family life, his home and his
     correspondence" was not engaged by the claim for capital to effect
     the rectification of defects in his home, but was engaged in the
     claim for a fund to meet his income shortfall and to provide a fund
     for contingencies. In effect that was a claim to protect his current
     occupancy of his home and fell within the ambit of his right to
     respect for his home;

(3) rights of inheritance and succession as between those in a family
     relationship (including a single-sex relationship) were an aspect of
     family life; thus the right to make a 1975 Act claim was within the
     ambit of inheritance and succession rights and, therefore, of his
     Art.8 right to respect for his family life;

(4) Art.1, which is concerned with entitlement to peaceful enjoyment
     of possessions, was not engaged. Neither the right to make a 1975
     Act claim, nor a legitimate expectation of such a right, fell within
     the concept of "possessions" in Art.1.

In the result, however, the claim failed on the merits, it being found that the
provision made for Mr Saunders by the deceased's will was reasonable in all
the circumstances.

Subsection 1(1)(ba) was amended so as to read "any person (not being a   **2–069**
person included in paragraph (a) or (b) above)[134] to whom subsection 1(1A)
or 1(1B) applies" and the new section 1(1B) is expressed to apply to a person
who, for the whole of the period of two years immediately before the death
of the deceased was living (a) in the same household as the deceased, and (b)
as the civil partner of the deceased.[135] The question whether a claimant was
living as the civil partner of the deceased has been addressed in the case of
Baynes v Hedger.[136]

In that case, claims for financial provision out of the estate of Mary   **2–070**
Spencer Watson (Mary), who died on 7 March 2006, aged 92, were made by
two parties, only one of whom (Margot) claimed under s.1(1B). As the
proceedings were constituted, she was a defendant, the original claimant

---

[134] Civil Partnership Act 2004 Sch.4 para.15(3).
[135] Civil Partnership Act 2004 Sch.4 para.15(5).
[136] *Baynes v Hedger* [2008] 2 F.L.R. 1805; [2008] W.T.L.R. 1719. There was an appeal, but not
     on the issue whether the claimant satisfied the conditions of subs.1(1B) of the 1975 Act and
     was thus eligible to make a claim under.s.1(1)(ba).

being one of her daughters (Hetty). Both Margot and Hetty claimed as dependants under s.1(1)(e). The connection between the parties originated from a lease of Mary's family home, Dunshay Manor, being granted to a Mr Baynes in 1955; Mary continued to live on the estate in which Dunshay Manor was comprised. At that time, Mr Baynes was married to Margot and they had four children; Hetty was born in 1956. An intimate relationship between Mary and Margot soon developed, Mr Baynes left Dunshay Manor and eventually he and Margot were divorced. Mary became a quasi-parental figure and a dominant influence in the lives of the Baynes children, was generous to them financially in their younger days, and continued to be generous, particularly to Hetty and Margot.

2–071   From 1965 until the late 1970s, Mary, Margot and Hetty were living in the same household (at first, with other members of the Baynes family) and during that period Mary and Margot shared a bedroom and were seen as a couple. There was evidence that, from the 1990s onwards, when Margot was living in Kingston-on-Thames, Mary was regularly seen there and would stay for a weekend and sometimes for a couple of weeks. This would happen every month or two. Margot would also go to stay with Mary at Dunshay every three months for a weekend or a week, but these visits became less frequent as Margot's health deteriorated due to Alzheimer's syndrome, which was diagnosed in 2000. Mary, however, continued to visit Margot at weekends and Christmas, and Margot's carer from October 2005 onwards gave evidence that Mary would come for a weekend every other week and stay for three or four days. Each had a room in the other's house where she kept clothes and other possessions.

2–072   Lewison J approached the issue of Margot's eligibility under subs.1(1B) by reference to the decisions in *Ghaidan v Godin-Mendoza*[137] and *Nutting v Southern Housing Group*,[138] both of which concerned the question whether the survivor of a same-sex relationship was entitled to succeed to a tenancy. He found as facts that since the late 1970s, the settled pattern of residence was that Margot's main residence was in Kingston and Mary's at Dunshay, and that Mary regarded the Kingston property as Margot's home, not a joint home or one in joint names; similarly, she regarded Dunshay as her home, not as the (or a) joint home of theirs. Her 1977 will left Dunshay unconditionally to charity and she never consulted Margot about her dispositions of it. For at least the last 20 years, they did not in any real sense live under the same roof; and in the last two years of Mary's life, the relevant statutory period, Margot's need for 24-hour care made it impracticable for her to go to Dunshay, while Mary was never more than a visitor to King-

---

[137] *Ghaidan v Godin-Mendoza* [2004] 2 A.C. 557; see para.2–062. The decision of the House of Lords in *Ghaidan* had by then been given statutory force by the insertion of a provision in Sch.1 para.2(2) of the Rent Act 1977 that a person who was living with the original tenant as if they were civil partners shall be treated as the civil partner of the original tenant; see Sch.8 to the Civil Partnership Act 2004 para.13(3).

[138] *Nutting v Southern Housing Group* [2005] 2 P. & C.R. 14, discussed above at para.2–057.

ston. As found in *Churchill v Roach*,[139] there were two separate establishments and two separate domestic economies.

In Lewison J's view, as marriage and civil partnership were publicly **2–073** acknowledged relationships, the open and unequivocal display to the outside world of a relationship in which the parties lived together as if they were civil partners was essential.[140] The existence of two separate establishments and two separate domestic economies would have been sufficient to dispose of Margot's claim under s.1(1B), but, additionally, the true nature of the relationship between them was never acknowledged to the outside world. In his judgment it was not possible to establish that two people lived together as civil partners unless their relationship as a couple was an openly acknowledged one.

(f) Children

Section 25(1) of the 1975 Act defines "child" as including an illegitimate **2–074** child and a child *en ventre sa mere* at the death of the deceased; there is no specific reference to adopted children. Notwithstanding the reference in s.3(3) to the manner in which the applicant was being or in which they might expect to be educated or trained, "child" is not synonymous with "minor".[141] The provisions relating to the status of adopted children[142] were considered in *Re Collins*.[143] C had two children, an illegitimate daughter, (D), and a son, (S), by her marriage to the defendant. Although C had obtained a decree nisi less than two years after her marriage to the defendant, it had not been made absolute when C died, and her estate being about £27,000, he would take it all on her intestacy. S, having been taken into care, was adopted on 19 March 1987. Letters of administration having been granted to the Official Solicitor on 6 February 1987, applications under the 1975 Act were made on 3 June 1987 on behalf of both D and S. Hollings J accepted the submissions on behalf of the Official Solicitor that the effect of s.39(2) of the Adoption Act 1976 was to bar any claim by S. It provided that:

> "An adopted child, subject to subsection 3[144] shall be treated in law as if he were not the child of any person other than the adopters or the adopter."

He rejected the submission that the claim was saved by s.42(4), which read:

---

[139] *Churchill v Roach* [2004] 2 F.L.R. 989. See para.2–056.
[140] *Baynes v Hedger* [2008] 2 F.L.R. 1805; [2008] W.T.L.R. 1719 at [125].
[141] An argument to that effect was decisively rejected in *Re Callaghan* [1985] Fam. 1.
[142] At that time, Pt IV of the Adoption Act 1976. The relevant statute at the time of writing is the Adoption and Children Act 2002 Ch.4 of which contains the provisions relating to the status of adopted children.
[143] *Re Collins* [1990] Fam. 56.
[144] Which was not relevant in that case.

"Section 39(2) does not prejudice any interest vested in possession in the adopted child before the adoption, or any interest expectant (whether immediately or not) upon an interest so vested."

It was argued that S's right to make a claim under the 1975 Act, before he was adopted, was an interest expectant, but it was held that this was a mere hope, not an interest expectant. In *Whytte v Ticehurst*[145] it had been held that, where a wife had died before the hearing of an application under the 1975 Act, there was no cause of action within the meaning of the Law Reform (Miscellaneous Provisions) Act 1934 which could survive for the benefit of her estate. Hollings J relied on that case as indicating that S had no cause of action before he was adopted.

(g) Persons Treated as Children of the Family

2–075   Section 1(1)(d) of the 1975 Act introduced a new class of potential applicants by providing that an application may be made by any person (not being a child of the deceased) who, in the case of any marriage to which the deceased was at any time a party, was treated by the deceased as a child of the family in relation to that marriage. The class has been extended by inserting the words "or civil partnership" after "marriage" in the two places where the word "marriage" occurs.[146] In accordance with the Law Commission recommendation,[147] the amended definition of the eligible claimant is now:

"Any person (not being a child of the deceased) who in relation to any marriage or civil partnership to which the deceased was at any time a party, or otherwise in relation to any family in which the deceased at any time stood in the role of a parent, was treated as a child of the family."

The amendment[148] reflects a view, which proved on consultation to be widely held, that s.1(1)(d) as originally enacted creates an anomalous situation, in that applicants having the same quality of relationship with the deceased would not all be treated in the same way; those who were treated as a child by the deceased alone or in the context of a cohabitation were ineligible. The Law Commission therefore considered it appropriate that the factor defining eligibility should be the assumption of a parental role[149] by the deceased, not the relationship (if any) within which that role was assumed. Consistently with that view, para.3 of the draft Inheritance and Trustees' Powers Bill inserted a new subs.(2A) to make it clear that a family for these purposes may be a "single parent family" composed only of the deceased and

---

[145] *Whytte v Ticehurst* [1986] Fam. 64, applied in *Re Bramwell, Campbell v Tobin* [1988] 2 F.L.R. 263.
[146] Civil Partnership Act 2004 Sch.4 para.15(4).
[147] Law Com. LC 331 at para.6.41.
[148] Inheritance and Trustees' Powers Act 2014 s.6 and Sch.2 para.2.
[149] The word "role" (rather than "responsibility") is used so as to avoid confusion with "parental responsibility" resulting from the making of a parental responsibility order under Pt I of the Children Act 1989.

the applicant. This has been implemented by the insertion into the 1975 Act of a new s.1(2A) which provides that:

"The reference in subsection 1(1)(d) above to a family in which the deceased stood in the role of a parent includes a family of which the deceased was the only member (apart from the applicant)."[150]

The expression "child of the family" as defined in s.52(1) of the Matri-   **2–076**
monial Causes Act 1973 in relation to the parties to a marriage includes:

(a) a child of both those parties; and
(b) any other child, not being a child who has been boarded out with those parties by a local authority or voluntary organisation, who has been treated by both of those parties as a child of the family.

For the purpose of both s.1(1)(d) of the 1975 Act and s.52(1)(b) of MCA 1973, the same two questions have to be addressed, namely, whether there is a family, and whether the child has been treated as a child of the family. As a result of the amendment to s.1(1)(d), it can no longer be the case that there is no "family" for the purpose of that provision until the parties have married or, as the case may be, formed a civil partnership. If one of those two relationships has been formed, the fact that the parties remain in it is not conclusive of the question whether there is a "family" during the whole or any period of the relationship.

These questions arose in *M v M*,[151] a case decided some five years before   **2–077**
the first reported application under s.1(1)(d) of the 1975 Act. In *M v M*, the parties married in September 1970, separated in April 1971, a child was born to the wife in 1972, and it was accepted that the husband was not the father of the child. Between 1971 and 1977 they lived entirely separate lives and, although the husband had visited the wife from time to time, cohabitation had not been resumed. It was held (reversing the trial judgment) that at no time during the child's lifetime had there been any family of which he was a part. Whether a child has been treated as a child of the family is a question of fact to be judged objectively by looking at and considering carefully what the party did and how he behaved towards the child. It was held that, for that purpose, the court should look at the question broadly and answer it broadly, trying to reach the conclusion that any ordinary, sensible citizen would reach if they asked the question.

In *Re Callaghan*,[152] Booth J held that "child" had the same meaning in   **2–078**
subs.1(1)(c) and (d); thus an independent adult who had been treated as a child of the family could apply. She also held that the duty laid down in s.3(3) of the 1975 Act to have regard to certain matters which were referable to minor or dependent children did not limit the scope of the Act to such children. Fol-

---

[150] Inheritance and Trustees' Powers Act 2014 Sch.2 para.2(3).
[151] *M v M* (1981) 2 F.L.R. 39, CA, also reported as *Re M (a minor)* (1980) 10 Fam. Law 184, CA.
[152] *Re Callaghan* [1985] Fam. 1.

lowing the decision in *Leach v Lindeman*,[153] conduct towards the applicant which took place prior to the marriage in respect of which the applicant was treated as a child of the family was held to be relevant. These two cases remain, at the time of writing, the only reported cases under s.1(1)(d).

(h) Dependants

(i) The statutory conditions; general

2–079 There are three conditions specific to applicants under this heading, and all of them, as contained in the 1975 Act as originally enacted, have given rise to difficulties of construction which the amendments effected by the Inheritance and Trustees' Powers Act 2014 are intended to eliminate. In order to qualify as a dependant, the claimant has to satisfy the condition in s.1(1)(e) of having been, *immediately* before the death of the deceased, maintained either wholly or partly by the deceased. As the cases discussed under the heading "immediately" show, it was quickly established that the word was not to be given its literal meaning but construed as a reference to the settled state of affairs existing before and up to the death of the deceased, so that temporary cessation of maintenance did not constitute an automatic bar to an application under that provision. However, the problems created by the other two conditions were not so easily resolved, with the consequence that the Law Commission recommended that s.1(3) and s.3(4) should be amended.[154]

(ii) Section 1(3)

2–080 Section 1(3), as originally enacted, provided that:

> "...a person shall be treated as being maintained by the deceased if the deceased, otherwise than for full valuable consideration, was making a substantial contribution in money or money's worth to the reasonable needs of that person."

This was in accordance with the recommendation of the Law Commission.[155] In the earliest reported case,[156] the applicant was the 68-year-old sister of the deceased, with whom she had lived for seven years, doing some housework and cooking but not making any financial contribution to the

---

[153] *Re Leach, Leach v Lindeman* [1986] Ch. 226.
[154] Law Com. LC 331 at paras 6.76 (relating to s.1(3)) and 6.59 (relating to s.3(4)).
[155] Law Commission Report No.61, *Family Law: Second Report on Family Property, Family Provision on Death*, (1974) at para.98. This paragraph identified some of the situations envisaged, but left open the question whether (for example) a widowed sister receiving board and lodging at the expense of the deceased but making a cash contribution to the household expenses was being "wholly or partly maintained" by the deceased within the meaning of s.1(3). It expressed the belief that such questions could be resolved by the courts on common-sense lines.
[156] *Re Wilkinson, Neale v Newell* [1978] Fam 22, in which Sir John Arnold P affirmed the registrar's decision that the claimant was entitled under s.1(1)(e) to apply for financial provision out of the deceased's estate.

household expenses. It was held that it was irrelevant whether there was a contract under which those services were provided and (with considerable uncertainty) that they did not amount to full valuable consideration for the benefits received. The court did not (and, indeed, could not) attempt to quantify the value of the applicant's services; the report of the case does not reveal the existence of any evidence which would have served as a basis for such quantification.

In any event, it became apparent that if the commercial value of an **2–081** applicant's services were to be weighed in the balance against (say) the provision of rent-free accommodation by the deceased, the paradox arose that the more the applicant did for the deceased, the more likely it became that the application would fail because they had given full valuable consideration for the benefits received. On the other hand, the unabashed sponger who did nothing at all in return for free board and lodging would be completely free of that risk. These uncomfortable and counter-intuitive outcomes could only be avoided by leaving the commercial value of the services (if any) rendered by the applicant out of the equation altogether, as the cases discussed under the heading "Otherwise than for full valuable consideration" show. The Law Commission found this to be an unsatisfactory state of affairs and recommended that:

"...it should not be necessary for a person claiming family provision as a dependant under the Inheritance (Provision for Family and Dependants) Act 1975 to show that the deceased contributed more to the parties' relationship than did the applicant";

in other words, the abolition of what it described as "the balance-sheet approach".[157] That recommendation has been implemented by the following amendment to s.1(3),[158] which now reads:

"For the purposes of s.1(1)(e), a person shall be treated as having been maintained by the deceased (either wholly or partly, as the case may be), only if the deceased was making a substantial contribution in money or money's worth towards the reasonable needs of that person other than a contribution made for full valuable consideration pursuant to an arrangement of a commercial nature."

The provision, as amended, thus excludes claims by carers and providers of domestic services rendered under normal contractual terms. It also recognises claims based on "interdependency", that is, where two people who can sustain a comfortable lifestyle together, which they could not manage separately, are in a real sense dependent on the continuance of their relationship.

---

[157] Law Com. LC 331 at paras 6.66–6.76.
[158] Inheritance and Trustees' Powers Act 2014 s.6 and Sch.2 para.3.

(iii) Section 3(4)

2–082   Finally, s.3(4), as originally enacted, directed the court, in relation to
applications under s.1(1)(e), to have regard to the extent to which, and the
basis on which, the deceased assumed responsibility for the maintenance of
the applicant, and the length of time for which they discharged that
responsibility. This has proved to be the most problematical of the three
conditions. The section does not say what "assumption of responsibility"
means, nor indeed whether it is (as the courts have taken it to be) a separate
concept from maintenance itself. Treating "assumption of responsibility" as
a separate concept led to its judicial interpretation as a necessary condition
of any claim as a dependant, additional to the fact of maintenance. The
contrary view could have been adopted, since the structure of the Act
appears to be that threshold conditions are laid down by s.1 and that s.3 is
concerned with matters to which the court should have regard when it was
satisfied (if there was any dispute about eligibility) that the applicant had
crossed the threshold.[159] However, judicial interpretation did not take that
course,[160] and in order to avoid requiring the applicant to demonstrate the
requisite assumption of responsibility in every case, the courts have adopted
what the Law Commission euphemistically termed a "workaround": it will
usually be presumed from the fact that the deceased maintained the applicant. That presumption is rebuttable by evidence that the deceased did not
intend to assume such responsibility.

2–083   The Law Commission criticised that workaround as complex and unsatisfactory and drew attention to *Bouette v Rose*,[161] where the applicant was
claiming against the estate of her daughter, for whom she had been a full-
time carer. The deceased had not been capable of actually assuming
responsibility for anyone; she was only 14 when she died and suffered from
severe mental disability. However, the court found that the assumption of
responsibility could be presumed from the mother's reliance on funds held
for the daughter by the Court. It described the process of circumventing the
requirement for assumption of responsibility by presuming it from the fact
of maintenance as "tortuous" reasoning and referred to the uncertainty and
complexity which may discourage potentially meritorious applicants from
bringing family provision claims. It therefore recommended that:

> (1)   a person who was being maintained by the deceased immediately
> before the death should be eligible to apply for family provision as

---

[159] The Law Commission was sympathetic to the view that the statute itself does not create
such a threshold requirement but decided that the necessary clarification could best be
achieved by legislative reform; Law Com LC 331 at paras 6.57–6.59.

[160] *Re Beaumont (Deceased); Martin v Midland Bank Trust Co.* [1980] Ch. 444 was the first case
in which assumption of responsibility was treated as a necessary condition, and the Court of
Appeal did so in *Jelley v Iliffe* [1981] Fam. 128 and *Baynes v Hedger* [2009] 2 F.L.R. 767,
though in the latter case it was conceded. The application in *Beaumont* was dismissed, it
being held that the applicant was not being maintained by the deceased but that they were
two persons of independent means who had chosen to live together and pool their resources
without either undertaking responsibility for the maintenance of the other.

[161] *Bouette v Rose* (also reported *sub nom Re B, deceased*) [2000] Ch. 662, CA.

a dependant under the Inheritance (Provision for Family and Dependants) Act 1975 whether or not, beyond the fact of providing maintenance, the deceased assumed responsibility for that person's maintenance; and

(2) the question of whether or not there was such an assumption of responsibility, and its extent, should be taken into account as a factor in assessing whether there was a failure to make reasonable provision for the applicant and considering the exercise of the court's powers.

The amended s.3(4)[162] now directs the court to have regard to:

(a) the length of time for which and basis on which the deceased maintained the applicant and to the extent of the contribution made by way of maintenance; and

(b) to whether and, if so, to what extent, the deceased assumed responsibility for the maintenance of the applicant.

(iv) Persons found not to have been dependants

The eligibility of claimants under s.1(1)(e) may be disputed by way of either **2–084** an application to strike out the proceedings, or at the substantive hearing. However, there are disadvantages to the defendant in proceeding by way of an application to strike out. If an initial decision to strike out is reversed, the case will be remitted to the court of first instance for a hearing on the merits, resulting, if the initial application is fought all the way to the Court of Appeal, in the possibility of four hearings. The Court of Appeal in *Jelley v Iliffe*,[163] where the net estate was £17,304, was markedly unsympathetic to the plight of the beneficiaries brought about by adopting this course. Stephenson LJ said:

"It is only in plain cases that this drastic jurisdiction should be exercised, even where a doubtful dependant seeks the statutory provision out of a small estate. To invoke the jurisdiction in cases which are not plain is not to save costs but to increase them."

Griffiths LJ reached the conclusion that the appeal must succeed with some reluctance, since he appreciated how undesirable it was that a small estate should be eaten up by the cost of litigation. However, he went on to say:

"But the beneficiaries under the deceased's will have brought it on themselves by moving to strike out the appellant's claim rather than meeting it and seeking to defeat it on the merits."

---

[162] Inheritance and Trustees' Powers Act 2014 s.6 and Sch.2 para.5(4).
[163] *Jelley v Iliffe* [1981] Fam. 128, CA.

Not only, then, is the estate liable to be depleted by costs to a greater extent than would be the case if the matter were fought on its merits, but the defendant assumes a burden of proof which he would not otherwise have. It was pointed out in *Re Kirby*[164] that, in a situation where the deceased and the applicant had been mutually interdependent on each other for a long time, the contribution of each to the maintenance of the other must necessarily be substantial. In such a situation, a defendant, in order to succeed in striking out a claim, must show that there is no triable issue, which in turn involves showing that the contributions were equally balanced or that, on balance, the deceased was dependent on the applicant. As that had not been shown, it was right to refuse to strike out the application, and the appeal against the Registrar's decision refusing to strike it out failed. Had the action been fought on the merits, it would, as has been said above, have been for the applicant to show that they were dependent on the deceased.

2–085   The dispute will usually be based on one of the following contentions:

    (i)   the deceased was not maintaining the applicant *immediately* before their death, as in *Kourgky v Lusher*[165] or at all, as found by Lewison J in relation to Margot's claim[166] and by the Court of Appeal in relation to Hetty's claim, in *Baynes v Hedger*;[167]

    (ii)   the deceased was not making a substantial contribution to the reasonable needs of the applicant;[168]

    (iii) the applicant was giving full valuable consideration for any such contribution[169]; or

    (iv) the deceased and the applicant were merely living together and pooling their resources, neither having assumed responsibility for the maintenance of the other.[170]

In cases of types (iii) and (iv) the position has been altered with effect from 1 October 2014 by the amendments to s.1(3) and s.3(4), respectively.

2–086   In *Kourgky v Lusher,* the applicant had been the mistress of the deceased intermittently between 1969 and 1979. Over that period he contributed to her maintenance from time to time but was reluctant to engage in any long-term financial commitment. In 1977 he helped her to buy a flat, by assuming responsibility for the mortgage; but when the applicant wished to move into larger and more elegant accommodation, he refused to enter into another mortgage, though he was content for the proceeds of sale of the flat, in which he had a 38 per cent interest, to be applied in the purchase of the new accommodation. About three months before he died he had arranged to go

---

[164]   *Re Kirby* (1982) 3 F.L.R. 269.
[165]   *Kourgky v Lusher* (1983) 4 F.L.R. 65.
[166]   *Baynes v Hedger* [2008] 2 F.L.R. 1805.
[167]   *Baynes v Hedger* [2009] 2 F.L.R. 767, CA.
[168]   *Re Watson* [1999] 1 F.L.R. 878. *McIntosh v McIntosh* [2013] W.T.L.R. 1565.
[169]   In *Wilkinson dec'd* [1978] Fam. 22, Arnold J decided this question, with some hesitation, in favour of the applicant.
[170]   *Re Beaumont, Martin v Midland Bank Trust Co* [1980] Ch. 444.

on holiday with his wife, and did so on 14 July 1979. The applicant moved into the new house on 19 July; the deceased returned from holiday on 29 July and he saw the applicant once more before his death on 7 August 1979. It was found that there was a general arrangement for the maintenance of the applicant up until 14 July 1979 but that the deceased abandoned his responsibility in that respect when he returned from holiday; accordingly, she was not a person being maintained by the deceased immediately before his death. As these facts show, a claim may be defeated where maintenance ceases only shortly before the deceased's death, provided that the evidence showing that assumption of responsibility for the claimant's maintenance has ceased is sufficiently clear.

In *Baynes v Hedger* the crucial issue in Margot's claim as a dependant was **2–087** whether, although the deceased (Mary) was the original source of the benefits which she was receiving, she was being maintained by Mary immediately before her death. The two initial gifts to Margot were in 1972, when Mary settled £15,000 upon trust for Margot for life, remainder to Hetty for life and then to Hetty's children, and 1978, when Mary bought her a house. From 1996/97 to 2003/04 she received income of £2,000–£3,000 per year from the 1972 settlement, and payments of about £8,000 per year in total for home help and grocery bills which also ceased in 2003/04, when capital was advanced to Margot from the trust fund. On 24 August 2003, Mary consented to the capital of the trust being advanced to Margot to pay for her care. Thereafter there were two one-off payments totalling £1,600 and a contribution of £50 per month which did little more than cover the cost of her own visits to Margot. There was no evidence of Mary providing in any other way for Margot's care thereafter.

Lewison J rejected the argument that either the purchase of the house or **2–088** the capital advances from the settlement constituted maintenance. He drew attention to the use of the words "was making a substantial contribution" in s.1(3) of the Act and considered that this suggested a continuing action on the part of the donor, not a one-off, completed act. Providing rent-free accommodation or allowing someone to live in one's property at a concessionary rent could be a continuous provision, but an outright gift of a house 30 years previously was not. That contribution towards Margot's reasonable needs was made when the gift was made and the house became Margot's house to do as she pleased with. As to the advances out of the settlement, once the money had been settled it ceased to be Mary's money. The fact that Mary was a trustee of the settlement and thus a party to the exercise of the power of advancement did not alter that. Those contributions to Margot's maintenance came from the settlement, not from Mary. Accordingly, none of the benefits conferred on Margot by Mary could be regarded as "maintenance" for the purposes of the 1975 Act, so her claim as a dependant failed.

In Hetty's case, there was a continuous history from 1986 until shortly **2–089** before Mary's death of her getting into financial difficulties and Mary rescuing her, sometimes with gifts, and at other times with loans which were to be repaid on various terms. The loans made between 1986 and 1999 were repaid in 2000, but later that year Hetty was in difficulties again. Mary borrowed money from her bank in 2001 and twice more in 2003; before the second of those payments was made to Hetty, a meeting took place at which Mary's accountant was present and at which Mary made plain to Hetty that this was the last time she would assist her. She did make a series of small cash payments to her in late 2005, which she referred to as "stop-gap" payments. In January 2006 Mary made it clear both in writing and orally that she no longer considered herself to have any responsibility for supporting Hetty, and despite further pressure from Hetty she did not provide her with any more money.

2–090   On this issue, Lewison J considered the contributions Mary was making towards Hetty's reasonable needs immediately before her death, whether they were substantial and whether they were made otherwise than for full valuable consideration. He identified payments of £3,000 plus a generous Christmas present in 2004, and about £8,200 in 2005, part of which was the "stop-gap" payments which were expected to be repaid. He concluded that, by a narrow margin, these payments were "substantial". The payment of Hetty's mortgage for six months in 2005 was an arrangement strictly limited in time; it ceased in January 2006 and did not count as maintenance. He was also persuaded that, in so far as the sums paid by Mary were loans to Hetty, they were "soft" loans; that is, they were interest-free, would not be enforced, did not have to be repaid and were in fact unlikely to be repaid. They were therefore made for less than full valuable consideration and qualified as maintenance. Hetty was therefore eligible to make a claim as having been partly maintained by Mary immediately before her death.

2–091   In determining whether the will failed to make reasonable provision for Hetty, Lewison J considered Hetty's financial position; whether and, if so, what obligations Mary had to her, Margot and the other beneficiaries, and Hetty's conduct. Two particular aspects of that conduct were the way in which she had dealt with the substantial assets that Mary had given her over the years, and the pressure which she was exerting on Mary towards the end of her life to make further financial support available to her. He concluded that in all the circumstances the will did not fail to make reasonable provision for her, and her claim therefore failed. Hetty appealed and the defendant charity cross-appealed on the further ground that she was not a person who had been maintained by the deceased immediately before her death.

2–092   On appeal it was accepted[171] on behalf of Hetty that an assumption of responsibility for the claimant's maintenance was an essential ingredient in the qualification of a person entitled to make a claim under s.1(1)(e). However, since the decision of the Court of Appeal in *Jelley v Iliffe*,[172] it has generally been held that if the deceased was in fact maintaining the claimant,

---

[171] The author has serious doubts, expressed in "Inheritance Act Claims by Dependants" (2010) Fam. Law, 490–99, whether that proposition should have been accepted, having regard to Robert Walker LJ's analysis of s.3(4) in *Bouette v Rose* (reported as *In Re B, Dec'd* [2000] Ch. 662, CA at 672H–673E).

[172] *Jelley v Iliffe* [1981] Fam. 128, CA.

there was at least a rebuttable presumption that he had assumed responsibility for doing so.[173]

Sir Andrew Morritt's analysis of this question was that Lewison J could **2–093** not have concluded (as he did) that Hetty was being maintained by Mary immediately before her death without considering whether Mary had assumed responsibility for Hetty's maintenance; but the facts which he found did not support such a conclusion. Lewison J had emphasised that Mary's primary concern in the period before her death was to pay off Hetty's existing debts. He said:

"The payment of those debts is not 'maintenance' for the purposes of Hetty's claim. Mary had disclaimed any responsibility for Hetty's continuing support or providing Hetty with a home, and Hetty knew it."

Therefore, in Sir Andrew Morritt's judgment, Hetty was not being partly maintained by Mary; thus she failed to satisfy the requirements of s.1(3) and was not eligible to make a claim, so the question whether the will failed to make reasonable provision for her did not arise. He did, however, hold that if it had been necessary to decide that question, he would have agreed with Lewison J's finding that it did not.

In *Re Beaumont*[174] the basic facts were that the applicant and the deceased **2–094** had lived together, except for some separations during and soon after the war, as man and wife for 36 years; she died, having made a will just under three years before her death, in which she left her estate of £17,000 to her three sisters. They lived in a bungalow which belonged to her; he paid her a weekly amount for his accommodation, even when she was in hospital in the last few months of her life, and contributed towards the household expenses. He also owned, and paid most of the running expenses of, the car in which they went about. She paid most of the outgoings of the house and did the cooking and housework, while he did some work in the garden.

It was found, on those facts, that the whole picture was one of:

"...two people, each with their own earnings and, latterly, their own pensions, who chose to pool such of their individual resources as were needed for them to be able to live with each other without either undertaking any responsibility for maintaining the other. Each paid his or her own way, and there is nothing to suggest that any change in this state of affairs was even contemplated."

In the absence of any evidence that the deceased had assumed responsibility for the applicant's maintenance, the originating summons was struck out

---

[173] See *Williams v Roberts* [1986] 1 F.L.R. 349; *Rees v Newbery and the Institute of Cancer Research* [1998] 1 F.L.R. 1041; *Churchill v Roach* [2004] 2 F.L.R. 989.
[174] *Re Beaumont* [1980] Ch. 444.

under the inherent jurisdiction of the court. The burden of proof of that assumption of responsibility was on the applicant.

(i) Words and phrases

(i) "Immediately"

2–095 On the literal meaning of the word, an applicant would be disqualified if maintenance had ceased the week or even the day before the death of the deceased. In *Re Beaumont*[175] that construction was rejected. It was held that the court had to consider "something more substantial and enduring" than the de facto state or balance of maintenance at or near the moment of death. The "something" was characterised as a settled basis or arrangement between the parties as regards maintenance.

2–096 In *Re Kirby*[176] it was said that the court:

> "...must look to see whether a settled pattern had been established between the parties involved, ignoring any transitory interruptions owing to changes of circumstances occurring immediately before the death and possibly in anticipation of it."

In *Re Dymott*,[177] the "norm of the relationship" during the four years of its subsistence was viewed as one of mutual independence. The only period during which the deceased maintained the applicant was one of five months which ended almost a year before his death; during that time he paid her £10 per week. At first instance it was held that such payments constituted a substantial contribution but that the applicant was not being maintained by the deceased immediately prior to his death. By contrast, in *Kourgky v Lusher*,[178] although there had been a pattern of maintenance (albeit intermittently) for several years, it was found that, by acts committed shortly before his death, he had abandoned responsibility for the maintenance of the applicant.

(ii) "Otherwise than for full valuable consideration"

2–097 Section 25(1) of the 1975 Act provides that "valuable consideration" does not include marriage or a promise of marriage. The phrase is not confined to consideration arising under a contract.[179] In practice, the question rarely arises, since the most common fact situation is one in which one party is maintaining the other by providing rent-free accommodation to the other, who takes on some or all of the domestic work, which may include caring for the provider of the accommodation. The courts have moved away from the attempt to quantify the value of such services in deciding whether full

---

[175] *Re Beaumont* [1980] Ch. 444.
[176] *Re Kirby, Hirons v Rolfe* (1982) 3 F.L.R. 249.
[177] *Re Dymott, Spooner v Carroll* unreported 15 December 1980, CA.
[178] *Kourgky v Lusher* (1983) 4 F.L.R. 65.
[179] *Re Wilkinson* [1978] Fam. 22, referred to in the passage quoted from *Jelley v Iliffe* (see para.2–079, above); *Re C, CA v CC* (1979) 123 S.J. 35.

valuable consideration has been given. As Stephenson LJ said in *Jelley v Iliffe*:[180]

> "...the balancing of imponderables like companionship and other services, on which the court has to put a financial value, against contributions of money and accommodation, is a hard task."

Similarly, Griffiths LJ said that it could not be "an exact exercise of evaluating services in pounds and pence".[181] Both in *Jelley v Iliffe* and in *Bishop v Plumley*[182] the attempt to strike that balance resulted in the failure of the claim at first instance, the dismissal of the subsequent appeal, and the reversal of that dismissal by the Court of Appeal.

In *Bishop v Plumley*, Butler-Sloss LJ was conscious of the paradox that in a situation where one party was providing accommodation and receiving care and support from the other, the introduction of the commercial value of that care and support into the equation would put the conscientious and devoted carer in a worse position than one who did less in those respects, and she did not accept that Parliament could have intended that result.[183] However, it is by no means obvious that the words in which she criticised the decisions below provide clear guidance to the proper analysis of such fact situations. She said:[184]   **2–098**

> "In my view, both the registrar and the judge fell into error in their approach to the test to be applied under s.1(3). Neither referred to or appeared to take into account the passage from the judgment of Griffiths LJ to which I have just referred. If [they] had approached the factual analysis of substantial contribution and full valuable consideration by including the mutual love and support of the couple, demonstrated as it was by the applicant in the devotion she gave him in the final years of their cohabitation,[185] it is inconceivable that either would have excluded the applicant from advancing to the second stage to be resolved by ss.2 and 3 of the Act."

---

[180] *Jelley v Iliffe* [1981] Fam. 128, CA, at 138E. At 140D he ventured the opinion that what the plaintiff did for the deceased by way of domestic services was "perhaps enough to equal" what she did for him, including the provision of rent-free accommodation.

[181] *Jelley v Iliffe* [1981] Fam. 128, CA at 141E. The passage from which those words were taken is quoted at length by Butler-Sloss LJ in *Bishop v Plumley* [1991] 1 W.L.R. 582, CA at 587C–E.

[182] *Bishop v Plumley* [1991] 1 W.L.R. 582, CA.

[183] *Bishop v Plumley*, at 587H–588A.

[184] *Bishop v Plumley*, at 588B–C.

[185] At that time it was not possible to claim as a cohabitant per se, so a cohabitant who could not satisfy the court that they were being maintained by the deceased in accordance with s.1(3) had no remedy under the Act. As a matter of historical interest, the opposition to the extension of the legislation which enabled persons who were being maintained by the deceased to apply for provision was largely fuelled by the perception that it would encourage what were then thought of as "irregular unions"; the article at [1980] Conv. 46 about s.1(1)(e) was entitled "A Mistresses' Charter", while a well-known textbook referred to the legislation as permitting "successful claims by a well-paid prostitute".

2–099   The reference to the speech of Griffiths LJ presumably is principally to the passage in which he considered the situation where a man who was living with a woman as his wife had provided the house and all the money for the living expenses; she would clearly be dependent on him, but it would not be right to deprive her of her claim by arguing that she was in fact performing the services that a housekeeper would perform and it would cost more to employ a housekeeper than was spent on her. As a matter of justice between individuals that is right; but one can avoid the paradox identified by Butler-Sloss LJ only by ignoring altogether the commercial value of the services provided by the dependent party. However, now that both same and opposite sex cohabitants are eligible, there will be few, if any, claims[186] in which this paradox needs to be addressed.

(iii) "Reasonable needs"

2–100   In *Malone v Harrison*[187] Hollings J said, in relation to the phrase "financial needs" in s.3(1)(a) of the 1975 Act, "She needs enough to maintain herself reasonably in her present flat". That was true in the context of the particular relationship, but the circumstances of the reported cases are so varied that it is not possible to formulate any general approach to the quantification of what is reasonable for the claimant to have in all the circumstances. The approach adopted by Hollings J which involved quantifying the dependency and calculating its capitalised equivalent, taking into account the applicant's own resources including her own earning capacity, was not generally adopted at that time.[188]

2–101   In *Harrington v Gill*[189] it was held that the words "need" or "needs" in that section and in s.1(3), meant "reasonable requirements", taking into account factors such as age, health and standard of living, as was decided in relation to the word "need" in the Matrimonial Causes Act 1973,[190] but the concept of "reasonable requirements" is itself now obsolete.

2–102   It is clear from *Jelley v Iliffe* and *Bishop v Plumley* that provision of secure accommodation, rent-free, is a contribution to the reasonable needs of the person for whom it is provided, but the question which arose in *Rees v Newbery and the Institute of Cancer Research*[191] was whether the letting of a flat to the applicant at substantially below the market rent also constituted such a contribution. In that case, the applicant, an impecunious actor, and the deceased, a property owner who had taken up acting, became close friends. They first met in 1980, and in 1988 the applicant moved into a flat in

---

[186] An elderly relative acting as a housekeeper and/or general factotum in return for board and lodging might be such a claimant.
[187] *Malone v Harrison* [1979] 1 W.L.R. 1353.
[188] Many judges were reluctant to accept actuarial calculations or to explain how they arrived at the awards which they made. The multiplier-multiplicand method used by Hollings J is of historical interest only and has been superseded by Duxbury and, to a lesser extent, Ogden calculations in capitalising annual income needs. See Ch.6, s.4, "Methods of Capitalisation".
[189] *Harrington v Gill* (1983) 4 F.L.R. 265, CA.
[190] See *O'D v O'D* [1976] Fam. 83; *Page v Page* (1981) 2 F.L.R. 198.
[191] *Rees v Newbery, Re Lankesheer* [1998] 1 F.L.R. 1041.

premises owned and occupied by the deceased, at a rent of £200 per month. No written tenancy agreement was ever entered into and there was no evidence that the deceased had asked the applicant to sign one. In October 1993 the deceased gave instructions for a will to be drawn up whereby the premises were to be devised to the Royal Opera House Covent Garden Benevolent Fund subject to the applicant's right to remain in the flat during his lifetime at the same rent adjusted to take account of inflation; the residue was to go to four named charities. The deceased died before the new will was drawn up and his earlier will, by which his entire estate was left to various charities, was proved. In the proceedings under the 1975 Act, the applicant sought to be allowed to remain in the flat as the deceased had intended; the first defendant, who was the executor, counterclaimed for possession of the flat.

It was held that, on the facts, the deceased had a settled intention that, **2–103** after his death, the applicant should continue to occupy the flat at a rent well below the market rent for as long as he wished. That, together with the fact he had so occupied it for some five years immediately before the death of the deceased, led to the conclusions that he was being maintained by the deceased immediately before his death; that the deceased was making a substantial contribution towards his reasonable needs otherwise than for full valuable consideration; and that the deceased (albeit not formally) had assumed responsibility for his maintenance. The fact that there was a formal legal relationship under which the applicant was paying an agreed rent did not detract from that last conclusion; the relationship was not simply one of landlord and tenant. In the learned Judge's view, the deceased recognised a moral obligation to make provision for the applicant when giving instructions for a new will. It was a recognition of the claims of friendship and of the fact that the applicant could not afford to pay the full market rent for the home in which he had been living for the past five years. In the result, a possession order was made so that the estate could be realised for the benefit of the residuary beneficiaries, but the applicant was awarded a lump sum to cover his living expenses.

"Reasonable needs" was also considered in *Re Watson*, where the **2–104** applicant claimed under s.1(1)(ba) and, in the alternative, under s.1(1)(e). Although the alternative did not need to be considered, as her claim succeeded under s.1(1)(ba), Neuberger J did so as it had been fully argued. Two points were raised in relation to that issue: the first was that, as the applicant owned a house during the last few years of the deceased's life, the provision of a home for her by the deceased did not constitute a substantial contribution to her reasonable needs. The second was that she gave full valuable consideration, by providing domestic services, for the maintenance which she received. On the first point Neuberger J concluded that, since the applicant owned an empty house in the same town as that in which she was being housed by the deceased, and that the "needs" referred to in s.1(3) are the applicant's needs at, and perhaps shortly before, the death of the deceased, the first argument succeeded and the applicant was not within s.1(1)(e) of the Act. This rendered the determination of the second point doubly unnecessary and it was not dealt with. In subsequent cases where the claimant was a cohabitant, courts have taken account of the standard of living which the claimant had enjoyed during the relationship, and made awards which have put the claimant into a roughly similar position. Thus in *Negus v Bahouse*[192] the court considered it to be not unreasonable that the claimant should have a modest long leasehold or freehold flat similar to that which she and the deceased had occupied as their home and the award was calculated accordingly. Refusing permission to appeal,[193] Mummery LJ said that the statement in *Re Dennis* of what was connoted by "maintenance"[194] seemed to him:

> "...to allow regard to be had to the fact that some people have a much more expensive or extravagant way of life than others. Having regard to what standard of living is appropriate to him means that one does not apply some objective standard of what is reasonable for everybody; it is a standard which has to be flexible to suit the circumstances of the case. It is what is appropriate to the case, and that means looking at what style of life the claimant was accustomed to live with the deceased during his lifetime";

and Munby J endorsed this, it being perfectly plain to him that:

> "...in assessing in any particular case what is or what is not reasonable maintenance, the court must have regard to the nature and quality of the lifestyle previously enjoyed by the applicant and the deceased."

In the same vein, in *Webster v Webster*[195] the award was such as to fund the claimant's present way of living "other than holidays and the like".

2–105   The Law Commission recognised this judicial approach to claims by cohabitants (referring specifically to *Negus v Bahouse*)[196] but the amendment to the 1975 Act included in the draft Inheritance (Cohabitation) Bill did not provide for cohabitants to be entitled to the higher standard of provision applicable to surviving spouses and civil partners. In so far as the position of cohabitants on the death of the other party to the relationship was ameliorated, that was to be achieved by reform of the law relating to intestacy. However, the legislation, under the title "Cohabitation Rights Bill 2014" which was introduced into the House of Lords during the term of office of the coalition government and reached its second reading, included an amendment to s.1(2) of the 1975 Act which did afford the higher standard of

---

[192] *Negus v Bahouse* [2008] 1 F.L.R. 381.
[193] *Negus v Bahouse* [2012] W.T.L.R. 1117, CA at [12] per Mummery LJ and at [24] per Munby J.
[194] *Re Dennis* [1981] 2 All E.R. 140 at 145, per Browne-Wilkinson J: "in my judgment the word 'maintenance' connotes only payments which directly or indirectly enable the applicant in the future to discharge the cost of his daily living at whatever standard of living is appropriate to him."
[195] *Webster v Webster* [2009] 1 F.L.R. 1240.
[196] Law Com LC 331 at para.8.8.

reasonable provision to surviving cohabitants.[197] At the time of writing it has not made any further progress since its re-introduction on 4 June 2016 and it has, of course, been lost again following the dissolution of Parliament in 2017. Appendix 2 of this work includes the text of the Bill, in so far as it relates to the law of intestacy and family provision,[198] as re-introduced.

(iv) "Substantial"

Now that the "balance-sheet approach" has been discarded as a result of the amendment of s.1(3), there is no room for the differing views formerly expressed about whether it is the contribution made by the deceased, or the difference between the contribution made by the deceased and the consideration received by the deceased, or both, which has to be substantial. In relation to arrangements other than those of a commercial nature, the amended s.1(3) provides that a person is being wholly or partly maintained by the deceased only if the deceased was making a substantial contribution to their reasonable needs.[199] As Purchas LJ observed in *Re Kirby*:[200]   **2–106**

> "Where two people have been mutually interdependent upon each other during a long period of association of the nature of marriage, the contribution one way or the other must be 'substantial', not least because it has persisted for a long time and in its aggregate must be of very considerable value either in money or money's worth."

It remains to be seen whether courts will attempt to quantify the net benefit to the claimant for the purpose of assessing the extent of the dependency on the deceased, but it is submitted that such a judicial development of the law is unlikely. There is no reported case in which an attempt has been made to determine the value of the services provided by the claimant and it is probable that the cost of such an exercise would be disproportionate to its effect on the outcome of the claim. It is true that the extent of dependency has occasionally been found relevant; thus in *Rhodes v Dean*[201] the claim was dismissed partly on the ground that the deceased had provided her with free accommodation but not with support for her way of living. However, that did not involve quantification, but only the qualitative identification of the extent to which he had assumed responsibility for her maintenance.

---

[197] By inserting a new para.1(2)(ab) in terms corresponding to those of paras 1(2)(a) and 1(2)(aa).

[198] Cohabitation Rights Bill (HL): to provide certain protections for persons who live together as a couple or have lived together as a couple; and to make provision about the property of deceased persons who are survived by a cohabitant; and for connected purposes. See ss.19–20 (intestacy of cohabitant), 21–22 (financial provisions for cohabitant from deceased's estate) and Sch.2 (Amendments: Financial Provision on a cohabitant's death).

[199] In *McIntosh v McIntosh* [2013] W.T.L.R. 1565, the £200 per month paid by the deceased to the claimant which he spent on drinking, smoking, socialising and petrol, was not considered by the court to be a substantial contribution to his reasonable needs. It is interesting to speculate whether the court might have taken a different view had the claimant been leading a godly, righteous and sober life.

[200] *Re Kirby* (1982) 3 F.L.R. 249, CA.

[201] *Rhodes v Dean* unreported 26 March 1996, CA.

(v) "Assumption of responsibility"

2–107 The law in this area had developed in a somewhat confusing manner as a result of the failure to keep in mind the structure of the 1975 Act and to differentiate between conditions which govern eligibility and matters to which the court must have regard when determining whether reasonable provision has been made for the claimant and, if so, whether to exercise its discretion accordingly. The origin of that confusion was identified in the section of the Law Commission's consultation paper[202] headed "Assumption of responsibility", which began with the words:

> "According to the case law, it is a prerequisite for a claim by a dependant that there was an 'assumption of responsibility' by the deceased."

That was a paraphrase of the passage from *Re Beaumont*[203] which reads:

> "But section 3(4) assumes that in any case within paragraph (e) of section 1(1) which reaches that stage there has in fact been an assumption of responsibility, and so I think excludes from the Act any case where there has been no such assumption of responsibility."

There is no longer any need to consider the subsequent developments in the law relating to claims by dependants. Section 3(4) has been firmly confined to its proper function of identifying the matters, specific to claims by dependants, to which the court must have regard in determining whether the dispositions on the deceased's death were such as to make reasonable provision and, if not, how the court should exercise its discretion.

2–108 A person who is maintaining another can, by words or conduct, show that they do not assume, or intend to abandon, responsibility for maintaining another, as was held to be the case in *Kourgky v Lusher*, while in *Re Viner*,[204] the court took account of the fact that the testator had grudgingly maintained the applicant during his lifetime. Interestingly, in the context of assumption of responsibility, attention has been paid not only to the indicia of such an assumption, but also to methods of denying it. Thus it has been suggested that a testator wishing to preserve their estate from claims under s.1(1)(e) should carry out an overt act for the purpose of demonstrating that they had not assumed any such responsibility.[205] Some courses of action which have been suggested for the testator are to (a) declare in the presence of witnesses that they are not assuming responsibility for the maintenance of the potential applicant; (b) obtain a written acknowledgment to that effect; or (c) write to the potential applicant and/or make a statement in, or to be

---

[202] Law Com CP 191 at paras 6.12–6.17.
[203] *Re Beaumont, Martin v Midland Bank Trust Co* [1980] Ch. 444 at 455E.
[204] *Re Viner* [1978] C.L.Y. 3091.
[205] See C.E. Cadwaller, "Inheritance Act Applications by Financial Dependants—A Loophole" (1981) 125 S.J. 1175; J.G. Ross Martyn, "The Inheritance (Provision for Family and Dependants) Act 1975—Precautions and Pitfalls" (1986) 83 L.S. Gaz. 3571.

kept with their will, to that effect. It is clear from *Re Beaumont* at 458D–G
that Sir Robert Megarry had in mind the expression of the Law Commission's views[206] and, consonantly with those views, suggested that:

> "...would-be benefactors who wish to protect their families ought to
> obtain from anyone to whose maintenance they propose to contribute
> an acknowledgment that they are undertaking no responsibility for his
> or her maintenance."

There is yet to be a reported case in which the efficacy of any of these devices
has been tested, but it may well be that such statements would be treated as
self-serving or that such acknowledgments viewed as having been obtained
by pressure (whether or not amounting to coercion), and thus afforded
relatively little weight.

---

[206] Law Com LC 61 at paras 89–91.

CHAPTER 3

PROPERTY AVAILABLE FOR FINANCIAL PROVISION

1.—INTRODUCTION: THE NET ESTATE

The court has power to make orders under s.2 of the 1975 Act that reasonable financial provision shall be made for the applicant out of the net estate of the deceased. The Act provides a complicated regime for determining what property is available for financial provision. Before the 1975 Act came into force, "net estate"[1] was taken simply to mean: **3–001**

> "...all the property of which the deceased had power to dispose by his will (otherwise than by virtue of a special power of appointment) less the amount of his funeral, testamentary and administration expenses, debts and liabilities, and estate duty payable out of his estate on his death."

Thus, there was no power to make provision out of any property which had been the subject of a death-bed gift (*donatio mortis causa*), or which had passed by survivorship. Nor were there any anti-avoidance provisions which enabled the court to adjust the effect of transactions entered into by the deceased during his lifetime.

The scope of the 1975 Act in this respect has been greatly extended, since   **3–002**
the definition of "net estate" in s.25 now embraces five categories of property. The first is the net estate as originally defined. In the majority of cases, there is no property in any of the other four categories.

The second is defined by s.25 as: **3–003**

---

[1] Inheritance (Family Provision) Act 1938 s.5(1).

"...any property in respect of which the deceased held a general power of appointment (not being a power exercisable by will) which has not been exercised."

There has not, at the time of writing, been any reported case in which the net estate has included property of this description.

3–004   The remaining three categories are defined by reference to other sections of the Act. However, the Act does not operate in the same way in relation to each of these three categories. Where property has been nominated and falls within the description in s.8(1), or was the subject of a *donatio mortis causa* (s.8(2)), then the value of that property at the date of the deceased's death, less any inheritance tax payable in respect of it, is automatically treated as part of the net estate. Where property was held on a beneficial joint tenancy immediately before the death of the deceased, the court has a discretion to treat it as part of the net estate, but an application under s.9 must be made in order for that discretion to be exercised.

3–005   The position is different again in relation to transactions caught by the anti-avoidance provisions contained in ss.10 and 11. If an application is made under these provisions the court has power, if it is satisfied that the necessary conditions are met, to order the person who has benefited from the transaction to provide a sum of money (not exceeding the value of the property which they received as a result of the transaction, and after deduction of any inheritance tax payable in respect of it), for the purpose of making financial provision for the claimant. The transaction itself is not set aside.

3–006   The definition of "net estate" makes no reference to the situation of the property. Under the 1975 Act, jurisdiction to make an order depends on the domicile of the deceased, not on the situation of the property. The courts of England and Wales are therefore able to make orders in respect of property forming part of the net estate of a person who died domiciled within the jurisdiction, except for immovable property situated outside the jurisdiction. All rights over or in relation to such property are governed by the *lex situs*, which also determines whether the property in question is movable or immovable.[2]

2.—PROPERTY TREATED BY SECTION 8 AS PART OF THE NET ESTATE

(a) Nominations

3–007   Section 8(1) of the 1975 Act treats, as part of the net estate, any sum of money or other property (less any inheritance tax payable thereon) which any person has been nominated to receive, provided that the nomination is:

---

[2] *Dicey, Morris and Collins, The Conflict of Laws,* 15th edn (London: Sweet & Maxwell, 2012), r.128, para.22R–001. The qualifications to that general rule which are expressed in rr.130 and 131 are extremely unlikely to be of any relevance in the context of a 1975 Act claim.

    (a)   in force at the time of the deceased's death; and

    (b)   in accordance with the provisions of any enactment.

Statutory nominations can be made in writing by persons who have attained the age of 16 years, in respect of limited amounts of money in accounts with friendly societies or industrial and provident societies, and trade unions.[3] This method of disposition on death was formerly available in respect of money in the Trustee Savings Bank,[4] or in the National Savings Bank or invested in National Savings Certificates.[5] The amount, which can be paid without a grant, has been periodically altered by statutory instrument.[6] The legislation provides for the manner in which nominations shall be made and revoked, and governs the effect of marriage and subsequent wills on a nomination.

Complex questions would arise in the event of a nomination under a   **3–008** foreign enactment. *Tyler's Family Provision*[7] states that, on general principles, the law governing statutory nominations will be the law of the enactment creating the right to nominate; thus:

> "...a person who acquires title to property by a nomination under the provisions of an English enactment will have such title respected by English law and such nominated property will not form part of the estate of the deceased."

A number of cases[8] are cited which illustrate the longstanding general principle that the validity of a transfer of movables is governed by the *lex situs* and if under that law the transferee acquires a valid title, an English court would recognise it.[9] *Francis*[10] draws attention to the well-known principle of the law of England and Wales that the court will not make an order which would be ineffective because it would not be recognised by the state in which the property is situated, even though the property in that state fell within the definition of the net estate. It may be, as stated in *Francis*[11]

---

[3] Friendly Societies Act 1974 ss.66, 67; Industrial and Provident Societies Act 1965 ss.23, 24; Trade Union (Nominations) Regulations 1977 (SI 1977/789).

[4] Trustee Savings Banks Regulations (SI 1972/764), amended by SI 1979/259. The facility ceased with effect from 1 May 1979.

[5] National Savings Bank Regulations (SI 1972/764), amended by SI 1981/484; Savings Certificates Regulations (SI 1972/641), amended by SI 1981/486. These facilities were withdrawn with effect from 1 May 1981.

[6] See Sch.2 to the Administration of Estates (Small Payments) Act 1965 and the Administration of Estates (Small Payments) Orders (SI 1984/539). The present limit is £5,000.

[7] *Tyler's Family Provision*, 3rd edn (London: LexisNexis Butterworths, 1997), p.58.

[8] e.g., *Winkworth v Christie Manson & Woods* [1980] Ch. 496 (sale of chattels in market overt held to give good title to the buyer as against the person from whom they were stolen), *Tyler*, p.58, n.15.

[9] *Cammell v Sewell* (1858) 3 Hurl. & N. 617 at 638; (1858) 157 E.R. 615 at 638; approved, (1860) 5 Hurl. & N. 728 at 744; (1860) 157 E.R. 1371 at 1378.

[10] A. Francis, *Inheritance Act Claims—Law, Practice and Procedure* (London: LexisNexis), para.9–19(b).

[11] *Francis*, para.9–19(e), commenting on the judgment of Chadwick LJ in *Bheekhun v Williams* [1999] 2 F.L.R. 229 at 242.

that a court would order a personal representative subject to the jurisdiction to take certain actions that lay within their power in order for reasonable provision to be made for the claimant, but nominated property could not be brought in by such an order, since it would not have devolved on the personal representative.

(b) Occupational Pension Schemes

3–009   The question here is whether s.8(1) applies to benefits under an occupational pension scheme. If the benefits are to be paid to the deceased's personal representatives under the terms of the scheme, they are part of the net estate independently of the provisions of s.8. If, on the other hand, they are payable under the terms of the scheme to some person (for example, a surviving spouse), or if the employee has no power to nominate and their destination is entirely under the control of the trustees, they are not part of the net estate.

3–010   However, most pension schemes empower the employee to nominate the beneficiary. A nomination may bind the scheme trustees or merely take effect as a request to them. The Law Commission did not consider specifically amending s.8(1) in any way but addressed the wider question whether the 1975 Act should be reformed so as to make pension benefits available for distribution in response to a claim for family provision.[12] In the result, no formal recommendation was made in relation to pension benefits, and in particular, it was accepted, following consultation, that it was not realistic to adapt the legislative mechanism for pension sharing provided by the Matrimonial Causes Act 1973. The position continues to be that pension benefits can be made available towards satisfying 1975 Act claims only if they are caught by s.8(1) or are settlements which can be varied under s.2(1)(f) or (g) as ante-nuptial or post-nuptial settlements or their equivalent in relation to a civil partnership.

3–011   If there is a power to nominate, s.8(1) will apply provided the scheme is contained in an enactment. Private sector occupational pension schemes will not be contained in enactments, and thus fall outside the ambit of s.8. Public sector pension schemes are often set up by way of statutory instrument rather than under the provisions of an Act. It was held in *Rathbone v Bundock*[13] that the decision whether or not statutory regulations constitute an enactment depends on the context. That case was considered in *Re Cairnes deceased*.[14] There, the deceased (C) was a member of a private pension scheme, his employers being the airline, TWA. Under the scheme, the employee had to nominate a beneficiary, who should be either his wife or

---

[12] Law Commission Report No.331, *Intestacy and Family Provision Claims on Death* (2011) at [7.99]–[7.120]. No formal recommendation was made about any aspect of the current occupational pension regime.

[13] *Rathbone v Bundock* [1962] 2 Q.B. 260, CA.

[14] *Re Cairnes deceased, Howard v Cairnes* (1983) 4 F.L.R. 225. At 232A, referring to *Rathbone v Bundock*, the judgment in *Cairnes* reads "it was made clear that the word 'enactment' did not even include statutory regulations". That is not an accurate summary of the relevant passage in *Rathbone v Bundock*; see para.3–012, below.

a person dependent on him in a specified manner. Both nominations and cancellations by the employee had to receive the trustees' consent. C divorced his wife (W) but continued to maintain her voluntarily, and began to cohabit with H, though he lived with W on and off. On C's death, H applied for an order under s.2 of the 1975 Act. The financial resources, apart from the death benefit, were meagre. On a preliminary point it was held (i) that the nomination in favour of W was still effective, since she was a dependant for the purposes of the scheme at his death, and (ii) that the death benefit was not part of C's net estate. It was not property of which he could dispose by will under s.25(1)(a), nor was it money which W had been nominated to receive in accordance with the provisions of any enactment. Anthony Lincoln J accepted that, had the rules of the pension fund been made in accordance with some statute, the condition in s.8(1) would have been satisfied, but this was not so when the rules were simply contained in a trust deed.

Goenka v Goenka[15] is the first reported 1975 Act case in which the question   **3–012** whether a nomination made pursuant to a statutory regulation is "a nomination made in accordance with any enactment" has been raised in relation to benefits under a public sector occupational pension scheme. In *Goenka*, the deceased (G) was a consultant endocrinologist employed by the National Health Service. G nominated his father to receive the lump sum death in service benefit payable under the National Health Service Pension Scheme Regulations 1995,[16] which were made under the Superannuation Act 1972.[17] Those regulations are not primary legislation and, so it was argued on behalf of the estate, they were not, strictly speaking, "enacted". It was argued on behalf of the claimant widow that s.8(1) applied to the lump sum death in service benefit so that it was included in G's net estate. *Bennion on Statutory Interpretation*[18] recognises that "enactment" can be used with reference to the whole or part of an item of delegated legislation and also that in some Acts the context may indicate that references to an "enactment" do not include subordinate legislation; *Rathbone v Bundock* illustrates the latter position. In that case Ashworth J, giving the leading judgment said:

> "In some cases the word 'enactment' may include not only a statute but also a statutory regulation, but, as it seems to me, the word does not have that wide meaning in the [Road Traffic] Act of 1960. On the contrary, the language used in a number of instances suggests that in this particular Act the draftsman was deliberately distinguishing between a statute and a statutory regulation."

---

[15] *Goenka v Goenka* [2016] Ch. 267.
[16] National Health Service Pension Scheme Regulations 1995 (SI 1995/300).
[17] Superannuation Act 1972 ss.10(1)–(3), 12(1)–(2) and Sch.3.
[18] *Bennion on Statutory Interpretation*, 6th edn (London: LexisNexis, 2013), pp.379–80.

Conversely, in *Allsop v North Tyneside Metropolitan Borough Council*[19] the court found that a statement in s.111(1) of the Local Government Act 1972, that the local authority's powers were subject to any other "enactment" included regulations made under ss.7 and 24 of the Superannuation Act 1972. That was said to be because the reference to the powers being subject to any "enactment" passed before or after the Act would be meaningless unless it was permissible to look at what the regulations made pursuant to those powers provided.

3–013   As HH Judge Hodge QC acknowledged in *Goenka*, it was possible to give meaning and content to s.8(1) of the 1975 Act by construing the reference to "any enactment" as limited to primary legislation by way of Act of Parliament, but he saw no good reason for doing so. There was nothing in the 1975 Act which would justify that limitation. The nomination was made pursuant to rules made by way of statutory instrument which was itself made under a power conferred by a statute and should, within the meaning of the 1975 Act, be regarded as "a nomination made in accordance with the provisions of any enactment". That conclusion was also consistent with the judgment of Anthony Lincoln J in *Re Cairnes*.

3–014   Section 10 of the 1975 Act, which is discussed in s.4 of this chapter, is concerned with dispositions intended to defeat applications for financial provision. If a non-statutory nomination can be considered a "disposition" for the purposes of s.10(7) of the Act, the benefit or some part of it might be brought into the net estate under the anti-avoidance provisions,[20] but there are practical difficulties in proving the necessary intention[21] and in identifying the property disposed of.

(c) Insurance Policies

3–015   The section does not apply to life insurance policies. If the insured created no trust of the policy, the proceeds form part of their net estate under s.25(1)(a). If they created a trust of the policy, they do not. However, it may be that whether or not a trust of the policy was created, the payment of any premium could be attacked under the anti-avoidance provisions of s.10.

(d) Donationes Mortis Causa

3–016   *Donationes mortis causa*[22] are gifts which, by s.8(2) of the 1975 Act, are automatically included in the net estate to the extent of their value at the date of death less any inheritance tax payable thereon. The requirements which a gift must satisfy in order to be an effective *donatio mortis causa* are:

---

[19] *Allsop v North Tyneside Metropolitan Borough Council* [1991] R.V.R. 209.
[20] See para.3–050, below.
[21] Inheritance (Provision for Family and Dependants) Act 1975 s.10. See paras 3–071—3–074.
[22] See *Snell's Equity*, 33rd edn (London: Sweet & Maxwell, 2015), paras 24–016–24–024 and second cumulative supplement (updated to 1 October 2016). A. Borkowski, *Deathbed Gifts—The Law of Donatio Mortis Causa*, (London: Blackstone Press, 1999) provides a general survey of what its author describes in the preface as "one of the fascinating byways of the law of property".

(a) it must have been made when the donor was contemplating their impending death in the near future for a specific reason;

(b) it must be made upon condition that it becomes absolute and complete on the death of the donor;

(c) the donor must have made a delivery of the subject matter of the gift, or some means of accessing it, or documents evidencing an entitlement to possess it.

The law relating to the first three of those requirements was compre- 3–017
hensively reviewed at first instance in *Sen v Headley*,[23] though the decision itself was reversed on appeal.[24] The Court of Appeal held that a house passed as a *donatio mortis causa* by delivery to the donee of the only key to the locked box in which the title deeds to the house were kept. Whether the same result would have been reached if the title to the house had been registered is unclear.[25] Borkowski[26] has expressed the view that it would be an intolerable anomaly if that were not the case, but recognises the difficulty of identifying the essential indicia of title, it being arguable that the land certificate does not meet that description.[27]

In *Woodard v Woodard*[28] the property in question was a motor-car and the 3–018
question was whether the deceased (L) had made either an outright gift or a *donatio mortis causa* of the car to his son (B), or whether it passed to his wife (M), the sole personal representative and beneficiary of his estate. The facts were that L was admitted to hospital, and at that time B was in possession of L's car and a set of keys. The following day L told B, in the presence of M, that he could keep the keys as he (L) would not be driving the car any more. Three days later, L died. There had been a similar incident some four months earlier, but on that occasion L recovered and did resume driving the car. At first instance it was held that there had been an outright gift of the car by L to B; no claim to a *donatio mortis causa* was pleaded.

In the Court of Appeal, the argument turned on whether the subject 3–019
matter of the gift had been delivered. It was argued that the delivery only of one set of keys (there may possibly have been another set) and the non-delivery of any documents relating to the car was not sufficient to show the intent to part with dominion. In *Re Craven's Estate, Lloyds Bank v*

[23] *Sen v Headley* [1990] Ch. 728.
[24] *Sen v Headley* [1991] Ch. 425, CA.
[25] For the extension of the principles to registered land, see N. Roberts, "*Donationes mortis causa* in a dematerialised world" (2013) 2 Conv. 113
[26] Borkowski, *Deathbed Gifts*, 1999 at para.7.4.9.
[27] The question of what constitutes the "essential indicia of title" was considered in *Birch v Treasury Solicitor* [1951] Ch. 298.
[28] *Woodard v Woodard* [1995] 3 All E.R. 980 CA.

Cockburn,[29] Farwell J expressed the view that, where it was known that there were two keys to a box and the donor had handed over only one, it would probably not be held to be a sufficient parting with dominion over the box because the donor would have retained dominion by retaining the power to open the box, even though it might be in the possession of the donee. However, in *Woodard*, Dillon LJ, giving the leading judgment, considered that the handing over, or not, of the documents would be a matter of evidence as to intention to make a gift, but they were not things which needed to be handed over to give the donee dominion over the car. He also said that, in the circumstances of the case, which included the fact that B already had possession and use of the car, it would be unreal to conclude that dominion had not been given to B simply because there was, or might be, another set of keys which L could not use unless he recovered, in which case the gift would be revoked.

3–020   Two more recent cases, each involving an alleged *donatio mortis causa* of a house, are *Vallee v Birchwood*[30] and *King v Dubrey*.[31] In *Vallee v Birchwood* the claimant, who was then living with her two daughters in France, visited her elderly father, Mr Bogusz, at his home in Reading in August 2003. He was unwell at the time. She planned to visit him again at Christmas and he replied that he did not expect to live very much longer and might not be alive by then. He said that he wanted her to have the house when he died and gave her the deeds and a key, as well as some personal memorabilia. She did not see him again before returning to France and was informed on or about 11 December 2003 that he had died, the cause of death being bronchopneumonia and chronic obstructive pulmonary disease. He died intestate and, as the claimant had been adopted by another couple when she was about 13, she was not entitled to take on his intestacy. Initially it was unclear whether Mr Bogusz, who was born in the Ukraine, had any living relatives, though it was later discovered that he had a brother living and that there were four children of another, deceased, brother. Both the Treasury Solicitor and, subsequently, the administrator who had taken an attorney grant for the use and benefit of the surviving brother, rejected Mrs Vallee's claim to the house, but her claim succeeded before the judge in the Oxford County Court. He found that the donor was in poor health and not expecting to live much longer, the gift had been made in contemplation of death, that he handed over the deeds and the key on the basis that the house was to be hers when he died, and that by doing so he had parted with

---

[29] *Re Craven's Estate, Lloyds Bank v Cockburn* [1937] Ch. 423. The case involved a *donatio mortis causa* of movable property situated in Monaco. See *Dicey, Morris and Collins*, para.24–014, n.41, where the case is contrasted with *Re Korvine's Trusts* [1921] 1 Ch. 343. The learned editors comment in that footnote that *Re Craven's Estate* was better reported at 53 T.L.R. 694 and also that it was treated, wrongly it would seem, as a matter of administration. *Re Korvine's Trust* was cited in argument but no cases were referred to in the judgment.

[30] *Vallee v Birchwood* [2014] Ch. 271.

[31] *King v Dubrey* [2014] W.T.L.R 1411, *revsd.*, as to the decision on the validity of the *donatio mortis causa*, [2016] Ch. 221, CA, *sub nom. King v Chiltern Dog Rescue* [2015] W.T.L.R. 1225, CA.

dominion over the subject matter of the gift. On appeal to the High Court it was argued that the interval of four months between the gift and the death showed that it was not made in contemplation of impending death. In the deputy judge's view, that missed the point; he said:

> "The question was not whether the donor had good grounds to anticipate his imminent demise or whether his demise proved to be as speedy as he had feared but whether the motive for the gift was that he subjectively contemplated the possibility of death in the near future."

He then considered whether a valid *donatio mortis causa* of land required that the donor should give exclusive physical possession of the land and held that it did not, and that the handing over of the title deeds and the key was a sufficient delivery of dominion. Accordingly, the appeal was dismissed.

In *King v Dubrey*, the circumstances in which the *donatio mortis causa* was alleged to have been made were somewhat similar to those in *Vallee v Birchwood*. In 2007 the claimant (K) came to live with his aunt, who was then 78, on the basis that he would care for her and she would provide him with board and lodging. She died on 10 April 2011 and K brought proceedings for a declaration that she had made a valid *donatio mortis causa*, and, alternatively, for reasonable financial provision to be made for him out of her net estate. The claimant's account of the relevant events was that the deceased, who was his aunt, had said to him, some four to six months before her death, that "this will be yours when I go" and presented him with the title deeds to her property (which was unregistered land), and that her tone of voice and appearance indicated to him that she knew that her health was failing and death was approaching. The property, worth some £350,000, was the major asset of her estate. Under her last will, made in 1998, her residuary estate passed to seven animal charities; she was well known to be fond of animals and a supporter of such charities. Some time after handing over the title deeds to the claimant she signed a form of will purporting to leave her residuary estate to the claimant, in the hope that he would care for her dogs and cats, but that document was not witnessed. The charities contested both the claim for a declaration and the 1975 Act claim.

At first instance,[32] both claims succeeded. K's account of the relevant   **3–022** events was accepted, albeit with some circumspection. The validity of the *donatio mortis causa* was challenged both on the basis that the deceased did not have capacity to make it and that the necessary conditions (in particular, the requirement that the gift be made in contemplation of impending death) had not been satisfied. There was no evidence to justify a finding of lack of capacity. As to the necessary conditions, the trial judge, following *Vallee v Birchwood*, found that the gift had been made in contemplation of impending death and, applying *Birch v Treasury Solicitor*,[33] found that the

3–021

---

[32] *King v Dubrey* [2014] W.T.L.R 1411.

[33] *Birch v Treasury Solicitor* [1951] Ch 298. Although (unlike the facts of *Sen v Headley*) the title deeds remained in the deceased's home, that being where K was living, he put them in a wardrobe in a place known to, and used exclusively by him.

deceased had parted with dominion over the subject matter of the gift. He also found that the gift had not been revoked by the subsequent ineffective will. He then went on to consider the 1975 Act claim and concluded that, had he not declared in favour of the validity of the *donatio mortis causa,* he would have awarded K the sum of £75,000 by way of reasonable financial provision. The charities appealed in relation to the outcomes of both claims and K cross-appealed, contending that the award should have been £350,000.

3–023   On appeal, the leading judgment was given by Jackson LJ. At the end of a comprehensive survey of the doctrine of *donatio mortis causa* from the time of Justinian to the present day,[34] he emphasised the importance of keeping the doctrine within its proper bounds and urged courts to resist the temptation to extend it to an ever widening range of situations. In identifying those bounds he stated the meaning of the requirement of contemplation of impending death as being that the donor (D) should be contemplating death in the near future for a specific reason. The operation of the doctrine was not limited to cases where D was on his death-bed, but it was clear on the authorities[35] that D must have good reason to anticipate death in the near future from an identified cause. However, it was also clear that death need not be inevitable.[36] Following those authorities, Jackson LJ's crucial finding was that the gift had not been made in contemplation of impending death. The conversation on which K relied had taken place four to six months before his aunt's death. There was no evidence of her suffering from any specific illness; she had not visited a doctor for some time. It could not be said that she was contemplating her impending death in the sense in which that phrase was used in the authorities cited. She was not suffering from a fatal illness, nor about to undergo a dangerous operation or embark on a hazardous journey. Accordingly, on that issue alone, the charities' appeal must succeed and, while he did not criticise the trial judge for concluding differently, it was now clear that *Vallee v Birchwood* had been wrongly decided.[37] Both the charities' appeal and K's cross-appeal on the 1975 Act award were dismissed.

3–024   Both subss.8(1) and 8(2) contain a provision exempting from liability any person who pays a sum of money or transfers property in order to give effect to the nomination or the *donatio mortis causa*, as the case may be.

---

[34] *King v Dubrey* [2016] Ch. 221, CA, *sub nom. King v Chiltern Dog Rescue* [2015] W.T.L.R. 1225, CA at [34]–[53].

[35] *In Re Beaumont* [1902] 1 Ch 889 (D seriously ill in hospital); *Wilkes v Allington* [1931] 2 Ch. 104 (D had an incurable disease and knew that he had not long to live); *In Re Craven's Estate* [1937] 1 Ch. 423 (D about to undergo an operation which might be, and proved to be, fatal); *Birch v Treasury Solicitor* [1951] Ch. 298 (D was a frail elderly woman in hospital after a serious accident); *Sen v Headley* [1991] Ch. 425 (D in hospital suffering from incurable pancreatic cancer).

[36] *In Re Craven's Estate* [1937] 1 Ch. 423 (D might have recovered from the operation).

[37] *King v Dubrey* [2016] Ch. 221, CA, *sub nom. King v Chiltern Dog Rescue* [2015] W.T.L.R. 1225, CA at [67]–[70]. See also the short judgment of Patten LJ on that issue, at [89]–[96] and, in particular, his conclusion that the deceased's attempts to make subsequent wills were strong evidence that she did not believe that she had already given him the property. Jackson LJ upheld the alternative award of £75,000 in respect of the 1975 Act claim; see [77]–[82].

A *donatio mortis causa* of tangible movable property will be treated, for   **3–025**
the purpose of conflict of laws, as an inter vivos transfer and not a matter of
succession; therefore its validity and effect on proprietary rights are governed by the law of the country where the movable is at the time of transfer.[38] In *Re Korvine's Trust*[39] a domiciled Russian, who died intestate in
England, made a *donatio mortis causa* to a donee in England of chattels and
cash situated in England. It was held that the validity of the gift was governed by English law.

Tyler[40] has noted the anomaly created by the domestic legislation where   **3–026**
the donor dies domiciled within the jurisdiction having effected the *donatio
mortis causa* elsewhere. In this situation the property has passed according
to the law of the country where it was situated and will not form part of the
net estate under s.8(2).

3.—Property Which May, Under Section 9, be Treated as Part of the Net Estate

Under the pre–1975 legislation there was no power to make provision out of   **3–027**
property which passed by survivorship. In its 1974 report, the Law Commission felt it to be unacceptable that the availability of resources out of
which to make provision might depend on the accident of whether the
parties to a marriage held the beneficial interest in the matrimonial home as
joint tenants or tenants in common. However, they also considered that
surviving joint tenants ought, in justice, to know with the least possible
delay what their position was in relation to jointly owned property.[41] For
this reason, s.9(1), as originally enacted, provided that if an application for
an order under s.2 of the 1975 Act was made within the six-month statutory
period, the court, for the purpose of facilitating the making of financial
provision for the applicant, may order that the deceased's severable share of
any jointly held property, at its value immediately before their death, be
treated, to the extent the court thinks just, as part of their net estate. The
extension of time which the court has discretion to grant under s.4 was not
available for applications under s.9.

When the Law Commission addressed this topic in 2009,[42] the results of   **3–028**
the consultation showed considerable support for a change in the law that
would give the court discretion in an appropriate case to exercise its powers
under s.9 of the 1975 Act even where the application for family provision
was brought more than six months after the grant of representation. Its
report expressed the view that the protection afforded to joint tenants under

---

[38] *Dicey, Morris and Collins*, r.133, para.24R–001; and see the exception relating to movables in
transit, para.24E–016.
[39] *Re Korvine's Trust* [1921] 1 Ch. 343.
[40] *Tyler*, pp.59–60.
[41] Law Commission *Second Report on Family Property: Family Provision on Death* (1974), Law
Com. No.61, at paras 137–142.
[42] Law Commission Consultation Paper No.191, *Intestacy and Family Provision Claims on
Death* (2009), at paras 7.61–7.65.

s.9 as it currently stood was seen as perhaps more illusory than real. Time runs from the grant of representation, which (as happened in the much discussed case of *Dingmar v Dingmar*)[43] may not be obtained for some years after the death. If the strict time limit was intended to avoid prolonged uncertainty for surviving joint tenants, it had not achieved that aim. That view was implemented by the amended s.9(1),[44] which omits the words:

"...before the end of the period of six months from the date on which representation to the estate of the deceased was first taken out..."

and provides that:

"Where a deceased person was immediately before his death beneficially entitled to a joint tenancy then, if an application is made for an order under section 2 of this Act the court, for the purpose of facilitating the making of financial provision for the applicant under this Act may order that the deceased's severable share of that property[45] shall, to such extent as appears to the court to be just in all the circumstances, be treated for the purpose of this Act as part of the net estate of the deceased."

3–029   In determining the extent to which any severable share is to be treated as part of the net estate, the court must have regard, by s.9(2), to any inheritance tax payable thereon. A person's share of property held by them in either form of co-ownership is part of their estate for inheritance tax purposes. Section 171(2) of the Inheritance Tax Act (IHTA) 1984 provides that the termination on death of any interest or the passing of any interest by survivorship are not changes in the value of any person's estate which are to be taken into account as if they had occurred immediately before his death. Apart from that, ss.3–5 of IHTA 1984 apply to property held on a beneficial joint tenancy as they do generally.

3–030   Section 9(3) protects, for instance, a bank which pays out money in a joint bank account to the survivor from being liable to account for it in proceedings under the 1975 Act; but the money can still be made the subject of an order. The effect of s.9(4) of the 1975 Act is that a chose in action may be made subject to an order under s.9(1).

3–031   The commentary which follows relates to the cases in which there was some analysis of the provisions of s.9.[46] At the time of writing, there is no

---

[43] *Dingmar v Dingmar* [2007] Ch. 109, CA.

[44] Inheritance and Trustees' Powers Act 2014 s.6 and Sch.2 paras 7(1) and 7(2).

[45] The omission of the words "at the value thereof immediately before his death" is discussed in relation to the decision of the Court of Appeal in *Dingmar v Dingmar* [2007] Ch. 109, at paras 3–036–3–040, below.

[46] In two surviving spouse cases, orders were made under s.9 but there was no analysis of that provision. Both of them are discussed in Ch.6 ("Reasonable financial provision"). *Jevdjovic v Milenko* unreported 12 March 1990, Court of Appeal, is also mentioned in Ch.5, s.2(b) ("Transfers, settlements and acquisition of property") and *Re Jessop* [1992] 1 F.L.R. 591, CA in Ch.4, ss.3(b) ("Financial needs and resources") and 7(a) ("Matters specific to surviving spouses").

reported case which was decided after 1 October 2014, when the amendments to the 1975 Act made by the Inheritance and Trustees' Powers Act 2014 took effect.[47] The first reported case in which s.9 was considered is *Kourgky v Lusher*.[48] This case was largely concerned with the question whether the applicant was a person maintained by the deceased immediately prior to his death, but an issue also arose as to whether, if any order were made, the deceased's severable share of the matrimonial home should be treated as part of his net estate. In that case Wood J looked at the report of the Law Commission to discover the mischief at which the provision was aimed. Such reference is not constrained in the way that reference to parliamentary debates is constrained.[49] Having done so, he held that any question to be decided under the various paragraphs of the definition of net estate in s.25, (thus including questions arising under ss.8–11) should be considered before the net estate is assessed. The claim failed, it being found that the deceased had ceased to maintain the applicant before his death and that she had failed to show that his will (under which she did not benefit) failed to make reasonable provision for her.

In *Re Crawford*[50] it was contended by the plaintiff (the former spouse of   **3–032**
the deceased), and accepted by the defendants (his second wife and the children of that marriage), that a lump sum order under s.2(1)(b) should be made. Three issues which arose for consideration were:

    (i)   whether the court should take into account financial benefits to the beneficiaries under the will of the deceased which did not form part of the net estate;

    (ii) what principles applied to the exercise of the power under s.9 in relation to property held on a joint tenancy;

    (iii) if an order under s.9 was made, whether the property subject to the order should be treated differently from any other property in his net estate.

The property in question was the deceased's severable share of a bank account and a building society account, each in the joint names of himself and his second wife, the source of the monies therein being a lump sum of £69,727.21 paid to him by his employers on his taking premature retirement. The sums paid by the trustees of his former employers' pension fund to his widow (that is, his second wife) and to her two children did not form part of his net estate, but they fell to be taken into account under s.3(1)(c). Eastham J considered that the first question was answered by s.3(1)(c), which directs the court to have regard to the financial needs and resources of any bene-

---

[47] The most recent case, at the time of writing, is *Lim v Walia* [2015] Ch. 375, CA, in which the deceased died in March 2011 and the judgment of the Court of Appeal was given on 29 July 2014.

[48] *Kourgky v Lusher* (1983) 4 F.L.R. 65.

[49] *Black-Clawson International v Papierwerke Waldhof-Aschaffenburg AG* [1975] A.C. 591, HL.

[50] *Re Crawford* (1983) 4 F.L.R. 273. The first marriage, of which there was one child, had taken place in 1943 and had been terminated by divorce in 1968.

ficiary. As to the other two issues, he held that there were no specific principles to be applied since s.9 contained the appropriate guidance and that property which is the subject of an order under s.9 should be treated on the same footing as other property forming part of the net estate. He awarded the plaintiff a lump sum sufficient to provide an annuity of about £4,000 per annum, bringing in the deceased's severable share of the joint accounts to the extent required[51] in order to make that provision.

3–033   In the Northern Ireland case of *Re Patton*,[52] the applicants were the two illegitimate children of the deceased, both of whom were minors. Among the assets of his estate was the sum of £10,000 in a bank account in the Isle of Man, held in the joint names of the deceased and a nephew (DT) of his, who was one of the six residuary beneficiaries. The court did not concern itself with the ownership of this money during the lifetime of the deceased, or whether it should be regarded as subject to a resulting trust in favour of the deceased. The dictum of Wood J in *Kourgky v Lusher* was followed, so that the exercise of the discretion to treat the deceased's severable share of jointly owned property as part of his net estate was exercised at the stage of deciding whether reasonable provision had been made, not merely at the stage of making the order. On the assumption that there was no resulting trust, and that DT took the monies in the joint account by survivorship, it was ordered that one-half of those monies should be treated as part of the net estate of the deceased for the purpose of making provision for the applicants.

3–034   In *Powell v Osbourne*,[53] the deceased, Mr Powell, was married; a decree nisi had been pronounced, but not made absolute. For the last two years of his life he lived with a Mrs Osbourne. Two months before his death, he and Mrs Osbourne purchased a house, of which they were legal and beneficial joint tenants, with the aid of a mortgage advance of £85,000. Mrs Powell made a claim (which included a claim under s.9) for provision out of her husband's estate. At first instance it was considered that the only asset of the estate was the equity in the house. There was also a life policy on the joint lives of Mr Powell and Mrs Osbourne which supported the mortgage, the minimum benefit on death of the first to die being £85,000. Awarding Mrs Powell £5,750, this being almost the entire equity of redemption in the house, the trial judge indicated that, had he been able to regard the house as free of mortgage, he would have awarded her £15,000. He had taken the view that the effective value of the policy of insurance immediately before the death of the deceased was zero. It had no surrender value, nor did it realistically have any sale value. However, the Court of Appeal did not consider that to be decisive. Section 9 of the Act provides for property held on a beneficial joint tenancy to be treated as part of the net estate at its value

---

[51] Inheritance (Provision for Family and Dependants) Act 1975 s.9(1) enables the court to order that: "the deceased's severable share ... shall, to such extent as appears to the court to be just in all the circumstances of the case, be treated ... as part of the net estate of the deceased."

[52] *Re Patton, McElween v Patton* [1986] N.I. 45.

[53] *Powell v Osbourne* [1993] 1 F.L.R. 1001, CA.

immediately before death; not, as in s.8, at its value at the date of death. The difference in the wording of the two provisions is explicable if one considers that the moment immediately before death is the last moment at which severance is possible, and for the purposes of s.9 it is the severable share which is to be valued; no such consideration applies to s.8. On that basis, the value of the deceased's net estate was held to include the value of a half-share in the policy monies, and the provision for the applicant was increased to £15,000.

In *Hanbury v Hanbury*[54] the applicant, who was aged 45 at the date of the   **3–035** hearing, was the daughter of the deceased by his first marriage. She was physically disabled and had a mental age of about 12. That marriage broke down when the applicant was about four years of age, and the deceased had not had any contact with her since that time; that was his own decision. He paid the sum of £600 per year for her maintenance; this amount was increased to £900 in 1980, and, by his will, he left her a legacy of £10,000. He remarried shortly after the termination of his first marriage and the second marriage, which lasted 38 years, was still subsisting at the time of his death in 1995. During the course of his second marriage he and his second wife (W2) engaged in a number of transactions whereby his assets were transferred to accounts in their joint names, and assets were purchased from those joint accounts in W2's sole name. These included eight investment trust holdings whose value at the date of the deceased's death was £100,601.25. In consequence, the estate passing under his will was reduced to £11,981, whereas W2's capital assets amounted to £268,477. The judge found that there was a joint scheme to reduce the husband's assets so that there would be no money in the estate to answer a claim by the applicant under the 1975 Act. Having reviewed the evidence, he said:

> "In my judgment, since the eight investment trust holdings were paid for out of the joint account, even when they (or some of them) might have been paid for by Mrs Hanbury, in the light of her evidence that everything was joint and since, when shares were sold, the proceeds went back into the joint account, and in the light of the joint purpose of ostensibly stripping Mr Hanbury's assets, the correct inference is to conclude that the parties intended that the holding should be held beneficially as joint tenants."

He therefore applied s.9 to the husband's half of the investment trust holding valued as at his death and to the balance of £1,300 in the account out of which they were purchased. The net estate was thus increased to about £63,000. In considering the matrimonial home and its contents, he held that it would not be just to treat the husband's severable share in the home, nor any chattels derived from the parties' parents, or personal items, as part of the net estate. There was insufficient evidence to decide which were the chattels jointly acquired by purchase after the intention to defeat the

---

[54] *Hanbury v Hanbury* [1999] 2 F.L.R. 255.

applicant's claim was formed; but, as the net estate including the severable half-share of the investment trust holdings was sufficient to meet the applicant's claim, it was not necessary to go further into that matter. In the result it was ordered that the sum of £39,000 be settled on the applicant on discretionary trusts.

3–036   The meaning of the words "at the value thereof immediately before his death"[55] has also been considered in relation to the value of the deceased's severable share of the matrimonial home. In *Dingmar v Dingmar*[56] the facts were that the deceased (H) bought a house in joint names with his first wife (W1). There were two children of the marriage, one of whom, a son (S) was the defendant to the claim. After W1's death, H put the house into the joint names of himself and S by way of gift, and shortly afterwards married W2. When the house passed by survivorship to S on H's death in 1997, W2 continued to live there with the children of the first marriage, who were at that time 13 and 11. H had died intestate but his estate contained no assets of any value, so no grant of administration was made at the time. In 2004 S claimed possession of the house. As a necessary preliminary to her claim under the 1975 Act, W2 obtained letters of administration. Since the estate contained no other assets, she applied under s.9 for an order that H's severable share of the house be treated as an asset of his net estate. It was agreed that the value of the house was £40,000 at the date of H's death and £95,000 at the date of the hearing. The judge at trial found that reasonable financial provision had not been made for W2, and that reasonable provision would be a half-share of the house. However, he held that under s.9 the provision which could be made for her was limited to the value of the severable share at H's death. In effect, he awarded her an equitable charge over the property for £20,000.

3–037   That decision gave rise to two questions on W2's appeal, viz.:

(i)   could the award have been in the form of a beneficial interest rather than a lump sum; and

(ii) whichever type of award was made, was the quantum limited by the value of the property at H's death?

It may be, as Lloyd LJ surmised, that Parliament had never considered the type of situation that arose in *Dingmar*. An order under s.9 could, at that time, be made only if a claim under s.2 was commenced within the period of six months from the date when representation is first taken out. Thus, provided a grant was applied for reasonably soon after death, a significant increase in value of the severable share between the date of death and the date of hearing would have been unlikely. In *Dingmar*, a grant was not

---

[55] This has been discussed at some length owing to the division of opinion between the judges who heard the case (Ward and Jacob LJJ prevailing over Lloyd LJ and the trial judge) and the recognition, by the Law Commission, that the law on this point was in need of reform; see Law Com. CP 191 at paras 7.61–7.65 and Law Com. LC 331 at paras 7.74–7.83 (the six-month time limit) and 7.86–7.96 (date of valuation of the severable share).

[56] *Dingmar v Dingmar* [2007] Ch. 109, CA.

required for the administration of H's estate, the value of which was negligible, but as a preliminary to W2's 1975 Act claim, which was itself prompted by S's commencement of possession proceedings, seven years after H's death.

Lloyd LJ (with whom the other members of the court agreed on this   **3–038** point) held that an order giving W2 a beneficial interest in the house could have been made under s.2(1)(c), which gives the court power to order a transfer of such property comprised in the estate as is specified; however, in his dissenting judgment, he held that the award was limited by the words "at the value thereof immediately before his death", and therefore the share to be transferred could not exceed 21 per cent, that figure being the percentage of the value of the house at the date of the hearing (£90,000) represented by the value of the half-share at death (£20,000). It seems that, like the trial judge, he reached this conclusion with some regret, but, in his judgment, to hold otherwise would have involved treating those words as having no effect. However, for somewhat differing reasons, Jacob and Ward LJJ felt able to decide, on the basis of a more purposive approach[57] that the words did not prevent the court from awarding W2 a half-share of the property, not limited by its value at the date of death. Jacob LJ prayed in aid the specific purpose expressed in the Law Commission's *Second Report on Family Property* :

> "We think that justice requires that in all cases where property whether real or personal was held by the deceased on a beneficial joint tenancy, the interest which passes by right under survivorship should be available for family provision."[58]

His solution was:

> "One takes the proportionate share of the property which would have belonged to the deceased if there had been severance of joint ownership and treats that proportion of the property as the share of the property which the court is empowered to treat as part of the estate."[59]

In the instant case, that would give a half-share.

Like Jacob LJ, Ward LJ emphasised that the court was dealing with the   **3–039** severable share of the property itself, not its monetary value.[60] Each of them expressed the view that, because it was so irrational, Parliament could not have intended to arrive at the result reached by the trial judge and Lloyd

---

[57] See the case comment by Rebecca Bailey-Harris in *Dingmar* [2006] Fam. Law 1025, where she describes Jacob and Ward LJJ as having adopted the teleological approach to statutory construction.

[58] Law Com. LC 61 at para.140.

[59] *Dingmar v Dingmar* [2007] Ch. 109, CA at [59(iii)].

[60] *Dingmar v Dingmar* [2007] Ch. 109, CA at [65]–[69], [83]–[87], respectively.

LJ[61] Ward LJ drew attention to s.3(5), which directs the court to take into account the facts as known to the court at the date of the hearing. As he observed, that provision gave effect to the Law Commission's recommendation that:

"...it be made clear that the relevant circumstances for the court to consider are those existing at the date of the hearing and not those existing at the date of death."[62]

The trial judge's order was varied to the effect that S should hold the property upon trust for himself and W2 as tenants in common in equal shares.

3–040   On considering how s.9 might best be amended in relation to the valuation issues, the Law Commission concluded that the wording of the statute should make it clear that there was no restriction to the value of the deceased's interest in jointly owned property at the date of death.[63] The facts of *Dingmar v Dingmar* showed that such a limit could arbitrarily prejudice a family provision claim where the deceased's only significant asset was their share of the family home. It took into account the variety of circumstances that might affect the value of the property between the date of death and the date of hearing of the claim and concluded that it was not appropriate to change the date of valuation to either the date of the application or the date of the hearing, but that the court should have discretion to adopt whichever valuation date was appropriate in the circumstances.

3–041   Accordingly, s.9 has been amended by the insertion of a new subs.9(1A)[64] which provides that:

"Where an order is made under subsection (1) the value of the deceased's severable share of the property concerned is taken for the purposes of the Act to be the value that the share would have had at the date of the hearing of the application for the order under s.2 had the share been severed immediately before the deceased's death, unless the court orders that the share is to be valued at a different date."

3–042   *Lim v Walia*[65] was the trial of a preliminary issue concerning the right to a death benefit payable under a joint lives insurance policy. Jocelyn (J) and the

---

[61] If one studies the history of the passage of the 1975 Act through Parliament (for a survey of which, see *Tyler*, pp.78–79 and 81–84), it becomes apparent that Parliament devoted relatively little time to considering its provisions, and it can hardly be said that, in relation to the majority of them, Parliament evinced any intentions whatever. In particular, it would seem improbable that Parliament gave any thought to the anomaly which arose in *Dingmar*, because if, as s.9(1) envisaged, an application under that section could be made only if the claim under s.2 was brought within the six-month period, it would be rare for the value of the property to have appreciated substantially between the date of death and the date of the hearing.
[62] Law Com. LC 61 at para.104.
[63] Law Com. LC 331 at paras 7.89–7.96.
[64] Inheritance and Trustees' Powers Act 2014 s.6 and Sch.2 paras.7(1), 7(3).
[65] *Lim v Walia* [2015] Ch 375, CA.

defendant, Mr Walia (W) purchased a fixed-term life insurance policy on 21 May 2002. They married on 18 July 2003 and their daughter (Emma-Kaur) was born on 8 November 2004. The death benefit was payable on the death of the first of the lives insured, but there was also a right to have the death benefit brought forward on proof, to the insurer's satisfaction, that one of the lives insured was suffering from a terminal illness. The insurer required that terminal illness claims be notified within three months of the occurrence of the insured event and at least 18 months before the expiration of the policy. Only one sum was payable under the policy. Following their separation, J went to live in the Philippines and formed a relationship with a Mr Lim (L), and a son Philip, was born on 20 July 2009. J was diagnosed with terminal cancer in February 2011 and died, intestate, on 25 March of that year. No claim to bring forward the death benefit was made before J's death. W received the entire estate on her intestacy, together with £113,000 under the life policy. Claims under the 1975 Act were made initially on behalf of Philip (the claimant in the reported case) and subsequently by L and on behalf of Emma.

The preliminary issue was formulated as follows: **3–043**

    (i)   was J, immediately before her death, beneficially entitled to a joint tenancy of the right under the policy to benefit from her death before the death of W; and/or

   (ii)   was J, immediately before her death, beneficially entitled to a joint tenancy of the right under the policy to benefit from her (assumed)[66] terminal illness before her death?

The trial judge ordered that the issue be determined on the footing that J had the right set out in (ii) and that W should pay one-half of the death benefit into court. He gave W permission to appeal. On appeal, the appeal was allowed by a majority (Arden and McFarlane LJJ, McCombe LJ dissenting). Giving the first of the two majority judgments, Arden LJ held that the trial judge had determined, correctly, that W had a severable interest in the terminal illness benefit, but that he had not determined the value of that interest in accordance with the decisions of the Court of Appeal in *Powell v Osbourne*[67] and *Dingmar v Dingmar*.[68] Both the dissenting and the majority judgments cited *Murphy v Murphy*.[69] In that case, it was claimed that the deceased (H) had a severable share in monies paid out to his estranged wife (W) on his death under the terms of a life policy. The policy provided for benefit to be paid out either on the death of the first of H and W to die or the terminal illness of one of them. The Court of Appeal held by a majority (Thomas and Pill LJJ) that the death benefit was to be paid to the survivor

---

[66] That is, it was assumed for the purpose of argument that J would be able to establish that she had a terminal illness.

[67] *Powell v Osbourne* [1993] 1 F.L.R. 1001.

[68] *Dingmar v Dingmar* [2007] Ch. 109, CA.

[69] *Murphy v Holland* [2003] EWCA (Civ) 1862, reported *sub nom Murphy v Murphy* [2004] 1 F.C.R. 1; [2004] W.L.T.R. 239.

(in that case, W) and therefore, the claimant's claim failed. The death benefit could be distinguished from the terminal illness benefit because the policy provided that the terminal illness benefit was to be paid to H and W jointly. Although, as both parties accepted, the terminal illness benefit belonged to H and W jointly, it did not follow that (as the claimant contended) the death benefit did so. Chadwick LJ, although dissenting on the question whether H had a severable interest in the death benefit immediately prior to death, accepted that if no claim was made for the terminal illness benefit and the death benefit was paid out, no terminal illness benefit would exist. In Arden LJ's judgment,[70] *Powell* established that where the value of an interest depended on death, as was the case with a life policy, the value immediately before death would be the same as the value on death, and *Dingmar* confirmed that the curtain did not come down on death but that the valuation must take into account events occurring after the date at which the valuation is to be taken. As she observed, the preliminary issue, as formulated, did not require the judge to determine the value of the severable interest, and he did not do so. He was wrong to order W to pay half the death benefit into court; the value of the severable interest in the terminal illness benefit was nil, because no claim for payment of the benefit had been made, as required by the terms of the policy. Her death terminated the contingent right to have the benefit brought forward and there was, therefore, no interest of any value to be treated as part of the estate.

3–044   Whether an order can be made under s.9 in respect of foreign property depends on the nature of the property in question and on how, in the case of tangible movables, the effect of survivorship is characterised. Rights in foreign immovables are regulated by the *lex situs*[71]; rights in choses in action by the law of the country where they are properly recoverable or can be enforced[72]; and rights in foreign tangible movables either (if treated as an inter vivos disposition) by the *lex situs*, or (if the matter is treated as an aspect of the law of succession) by the *lex domicilii* of the deceased.[73] Only in the last case will the English court be able to make an order under s.9.

4.—ANTI-AVOIDANCE PROVISIONS: SECTIONS 10–13

(a) General

3–045   The principle underlying the provisions of ss.10 and 11 is that a person who has received money or other property from the deceased during their life-

---

[70] *Lim v Walia* [2015] Ch 375, CA, at [47].

[71] *Dicey, Morris and Collins*, r.132, para.23R–062 which is subject to an exception referring to contracts with regard to an immovable (para.23E–080). The lex situs determines whether the thing is to be considered an immovable or a movable, and whether any right, obligation or document connected with the thing is considered to be an immovable or a moveable.

[72] *Dicey, Morris and Collins*, r.129(1) (situs of choses in action), para.22R–023 and the commentary at 22–025ff. For interests in unadministered estates and under trusts, see the commentary to r.129 at paras 22–047 and 22–048 respectively.

[73] *Dicey, Morris and Collins*, rr.149, paras 27R–010–27R–012 and 151, paras 27R–023–27R–024.

time may be ordered by the court to provide money or property for the purpose of facilitating the making of financial provision under the 1975 Act. They differ in one important aspect; there is a six-year time bar in relation to dispositions intended to defeat applications for financial provision (s.10), but none in relation to contracts to leave property by will (s.11). The court has power to review such contracts whenever made. The reason for making the distinction between inter vivos dispositions and contracts to leave property by will is apparently that, in the former case, the donor divests themselves of property altogether, which they might be reluctant to do, while, in the latter, they retain the enjoyment of the property during their lifetime, which is a more attractive alternative and therefore requires sterner discouragement. It remains to be seen whether this distinction was worth making; at the time of writing, there is no reported case under s.11.

It should be understood that these provisions affect the donee or their **3–046** estate, not the property given to the donee. The remedy provided is not a tracing remedy. Section 10(2) renders it immaterial that the donee may have disposed of the actual property given to them. Section 12(4) enables an application under s.10 to be made or continued against their estate, though no order can be made which affects property already distributed by their personal representatives, nor are they liable for having distributed any property before they had notice of an application under s.10 or s.11 on the ground that they should have taken into account the possibility of such an application being made. The donee (or, if they are dead, their personal representatives) may challenge any other disposition which the deceased has made that comes within the conditions stated in ss.10(5)(a) and (b), which are, in summary:

(a) the making of a disposition within six years before death with intent to defeat a claim for financial provision; and
(b) that full valuable consideration was not given for the disposition.

Essentially they are the same as those of ss.10(2)(a) and (b).

The effect of ss.10(3) and 10(4) is that, if the court makes an order under **3–047** s.10(2) against the donee, they cannot be ordered to provide money or property exceeding, in amount or value, the amount of the payment made to them or, as the case may be, the value, at the date of death, of the property transferred to them by the deceased after deducting any inheritance tax borne by them in respect of that payment. Therefore, if property transferred to the donee increases in value after the death of the deceased, the donee can keep the increase; but if its value falls, they will have to make up the deficit. There is no provision specifically dealing with the situation where the value of the property transferred falls because it is, by its nature, a wasting asset rather than (as may have been envisaged) because of fluctuations in market value. Section 10(4) provides that, if the donee disposes of property transferred to them, the maximum sum which they may be ordered to pay is the value of the property at the date of the disposal, less any inheritance tax which they have paid in respect of the transfer of the property to them by the deceased.

3–048   On an application under s.6 for variation or discharge of an order for periodical payments, the court cannot make any order under ss.10 or 11. The claimant can apply for an order under ss.10 or 11 only in proceedings for an order under s.2; there appears to be no room for the court to make such an order of its own motion.

3–049   Section 10(7) defines "disposition" first by excluding transactions whose subject matter is already available to meet a claim, since it remains part of the net estate. Thus, by subs.(a), *donationes mortis causa* and such nominated property as is referred to in s.8(1) are excluded, as are all dispositions by will. Additionally, subs.(b) excludes transactions whose subject matter is property which was never part of the deceased's net estate, that is, property subject to a special power of appointment which has been disposed of inter vivos. This leaves, as the subject matter of reviewable transactions, property which would, but for the transaction, have formed part of the net estate.

3–050   Such transactions are defined, by s.10(7), as including any payment of money, including the payment of a premium under a policy of assurance; and any conveyance, assurance, appointment or gift of any property, whether made by an instrument or otherwise. At first glance that definition would appear to include contracts to leave property by will, but presumably contracts to which s.11 applies are meant to be excluded. Since, in the circumstances defined in s.12(2), there is a presumption that the contract was made with the intention of defeating a claim for financial provision, whereas no such presumption applies to a disposition within s.10, some clarification is desirable. However that may be, there seems no doubt that "disposition" includes a settlement or an assignment pursuant to a deed of family arrangement. It may be that a disclaimer is not caught, since as a matter of ordinary language X cannot "dispose" of something which they have never had; however, it is arguable that a disclaimer by X is a transaction whereby they have disposed of property which would have formed part of their net estate.

3–051   There is no time limit within which an application for an order under s.10 must be made. The section merely permits the claimant to apply for an order under s.10(2) "where an application is made to the court under s.2 of this Act". Thus, where the court exercises its discretion under s.4 to allow an application out of time, an application can be made for an order under s.10. Such an application was made in *Clifford v Tanner*,[74] where the application was refused at first instance because the substantive application was considered to be practically hopeless. In the particular circumstances of that case, the substantive application under s.2 could succeed only if an order was made under s.10, so the Court of Appeal had to decide whether there was an arguable case for making such an order. The Court of Appeal decision is discussed in the next two paragraphs.

---

[74] *Clifford v Tanner* [1987] C.L.Y. 3881, CA, per Nicholls LJ.

(b) Cases on the Anti-Avoidance Provisions

The relevant facts of *Clifford v Tanner* are that the deceased, Mr Clifford,   **3–052**
made a will in April 1977, under which he gave his wife, the applicant, the
right to live in the matrimonial home, which he had purchased some 15
years before their marriage, until she should remarry. Shortly afterwards he
executed a deed of gift in favour of his daughter, Mrs Tanner, who entered
into a covenant to permit Mr and Mrs Clifford and the survivor of them to
live in the property, from which covenant she was expressly released in the
event of the applicant remarrying after the death of the deceased. In 1979
the deed was varied so as to release the covenant if Mrs Clifford let or shared
possession of the property. In June 1983 Mr Clifford started divorce proceedings and, on July 6 of that year, he executed a homemade will leaving
his entire estate to his daughter. On advice from his solicitors he executed a
deed nine days later, releasing Mrs Tanner from her covenant to allow the
applicant to remain in the house after his death. At this time he was 78,
confined to a wheelchair and living in a nursing home. He died two months
later.

The Court of Appeal considered that, on these facts, there was a triable   **3–053**
issue as to the deceased's intention, and also rejected the argument that the
1983 deed was not a disposition. That argument was based on the proposition that, in order to be a disposition within the meaning of s.10(7), the
transaction had to be such as would take out of the estate property which
would otherwise have been available for making financial provision for the
applicant. Nicholls LJ held that prior to his death, the deceased was pos-
sessed of the benefit of the covenant as to occupation, which, until released,
was enforceable by an order for specific performance. The covenant was an
asset of the estate and it had some value. Its existence was a serious fetter on
the respondent's rights in and of enjoyment of the property, it substantially
depreciated its value in her hands, and she could have been expected to pay
the estate of the deceased for its release. It was therefore an asset with a
realisable value and its release was a disposition for the purposes of s.10 of
the Act. This appears to be the only case in which the meaning of "disposition" for the purposes of s.10 has been considered.

Kennedy v Official Solicitor,[75] although a decision of a County Court   **3–054**
judge, is now discussed, as there are very few reported cases under s.10. The
deceased and the applicant (A) had been married for 29 years when he
deserted her and went to live with M. Some seven years later, on 29 March
1977, the deceased transferred his leasehold house to M in consideration of
natural love and affection. He later made a will leaving her his entire estate.
On 21 April 1977, A filed a petition for divorce on the ground of five years'
separation, and indicated her intention to apply for financial relief under the
Matrimonial Causes Act 1973. The deceased died before a decree nisi was
granted, and M died intestate a few months later. A's application for an
order under s.10 was dismissed. It was held that it was not essential to show

---

[75] *Kennedy v Official Solicitor* [1980] C.L.Y. 2820, HH Judge Willis (in Shoreditch County
Court).

that the Act or its provisions were present to the mind of the deceased when he entered into the impugned transaction, but there had to be evidence that he intended to defeat a claim made against his estate.

3–055   In *Dawkins v Judd*,[76] Bush J had no difficulty in concluding that such evidence existed. The applicant and the deceased had each been married before; the applicant had two sons, and the deceased a daughter, by their respective earlier marriages. During their marriage, they lived in the deceased's house, and some 15 months later he made a will leaving her £8,000 and a life interest in the house. He later transferred the house to his daughter for £100. There would have been nothing in the estate with which to satisfy the legacy to the applicant; but, shortly before his death, he made a will leaving his entire estate to his daughter. The applicant claimed under s.10 for a payment out of the proceeds of sale of the matrimonial home. Bush J was satisfied that the sale of the house to the daughter was made with the intention, if not the sole intention, of defeating a claim under the 1975 Act.

3–056   The application of s.10 was considered in *Hanbury v Hanbury*.[77] In that case, it was found that, over a period of some 16 years before his death, the deceased and his second wife had participated in a scheme whose object was to reduce his estate so that there would be no assets in it to answer a claim under the 1975 Act. HH Judge Bromley QC made an order under s.9 which had the effect of increasing the estate by some £51,000, but he said that, were he wrong in his conclusions and in applying s.9, he would apply s.10 but subject to the limit under s.10(3). He further concluded that one other transaction was tainted by the deceased's continued intention to defeat the applicant's claim and thus fell within s.10(2)(a) and (b) but, as the amount involved was only £1,961.57 and the effect of applying s.9 was sufficient to ensure that the estate was adequate for reasonable provision to be made, a s.10 order in respect of that sum could not be made as it would not facilitate the making of financial provision for the applicant; see s.10(2)(c).

3–057   There are two Northern Ireland cases in which orders were made under art.12 of the 1979 Order, which corresponds to s.10 of the 1975 Act. In *Weir v Davey*[78] JCW died while estranged from his wife (MW), who took no benefit under his will, and who applied for reasonable financial provision from his estate. The net estate amounted to £78,552. He left specific gifts to M, with whom he had been living after leaving his wife, and the residue of his estate to J, the daughter of his marriage, who was aged 15 at the date of the hearing. Some days before he died, he bought a TSB investment bond for £16,535, which was written in trust for the benefit of his mother on his death. At the date of the hearing its value was £23,607. Evidence was given by M that JCW had telephoned her on the day before his death to the effect that he had managed to hide the money away from his wife's claim in divorce proceedings. There was also evidence that he avoided paying

---

[76] *Dawkins v Judd* [1986] 2 F.L.R. 360.
[77] *Hanbury v Hanbury* [1999] 2 F.L.R. 255; see para.3–029, above, for the s.9 aspect of this case.
[78] *Weir v Davey* [1993] 2 N.I.J.B. 45.

maintenance to his wife. It was found that the purchase of the bond in his mother's favour was a disposition intended to defeat an application for financial provision. MW was awarded £13,000 and it was ordered that this be paid to her out of the proceeds of the bond.

Morrow v Morrow[79] was also an application by a surviving spouse, not only for reasonable financial provision out of the estate of the deceased under art.3 of the 1979 Order, but for an order under art.12 setting aside the transfer of his farm to their son. The deceased had made a series of wills but, by his last will dated 30 November 1992, he gave some specific legacies of chattels to various beneficiaries, and his residuary estate (the value of which was under £10,000) to his wife absolutely. However, by an agreement of the same date, which was referred to in the will, he agreed to transfer his farm land, livestock, machinery and tools to his son (S) in consideration of certain undertakings given and payments to be made by him. Thus, if the estate were to be taken as being confined to the property vesting in the deceased's executor, it was impossible to say that reasonable provision had not been made, because the deceased had left his entire residuary estate to the applicant. However, that would not be so if the property transferred by the agreement was taken into consideration. It was found that the deceased, in entering into the agreement, did have the intention to defeat a claim for financial provision, though that was not his sole intention; that full valuable consideration had not been given by S; and that the making of an order under art.12 would facilitate the making of reasonable provision. It was ordered that two fields (valued at £35,000) representing about one-fifth of the acreage of the farm be transferred to her and that she should receive an annuity of £2,500 per year charged on the remainder of the farm land.

3–058

The most recent reported case involving consideration of s.10 is *Dellal v Dellal*.[80] That case is a claim by the widow of the property dealer Jack Dellal,[81] who died on 28 October 2012, survived also by six adult children, now middle-aged. They, together with a sister and a grandchild (aged, respectively, at the date of the hearing, 96 and 31), are the defendants to the claim. His will, dated 15 November 2006, to all intents and purposes left his entire estate to the claimant; his disclosed assets, which included very little cash and no income-producing assets, amounted to £15.4 million. The claimant's case was that the true scale of his personal wealth was much greater and if his estate had been reduced to such an extent, that must have been because, unknown to her, he had given most of it away to the defendants.

3–059

The hearing, which took place on 19 and 20 March 2015, was concerned with a number of interlocutory applications, but the discussion which follows is concerned only with the defendants' application for an order summarily terminating the s.10 application without a trial, either by an order striking it out pursuant to CPR r.3.4(2) or by summary judgment under

3–060

---

[79] *Morrow v Morrow* [1995] N.I.J.B. 46.
[80] *Dellal v Dellal* [2015] W.T.L.R. 1137; [2015] Fam. Law 1042.
[81] Referred to as "Jack" in Mostyn J's judgment and in the excerpts quoted here.

CPR r.24.2. The substantive claim, as explained by Mostyn J,[82] was for provision out of the net estate, defined by s.25 of the 1975 Act as including:

> "...any sum of money or other property which is, by reason of a disposition ... made by the deceased, ordered under s.10 ... of the Act to be provided for the purpose of the making of financial provision under this Act."

He referred to the decision of Campbell J in the Northern Ireland case of *Morrow v Morrow*[83] which showed that, while uncommon, the fact that a claimant stands to inherit whatever may fall into the actual death estate did not preclude an order being made under Arts 3 and 12 (the equivalents, in the Northern Ireland legislation, of ss.2 and 10 of the 1975 Act) in her favour. Her substantive claim in the proceedings was under ss.10 and 13.[84]

3–061   The period during which a disposition caught by s.10 can be reviewed is six years from the date of death; consequently, no payment could be ordered in respect of any dispositions made before 28 October 2006. Mostyn J stated that if the claimant was to succeed in her application under s.10 she would have to show at trial the following as against each separate defendant:

(i)   at least one disposition was made by Jack in favour of the defendant in question after 28 October 2006;

(ii)   for these purposes a disposition is an outright transfer of the beneficial ownership of the transferred thing done otherwise than for full valuable consideration. A transfer to a person to hold the thing as agent or nominee or bare trustee is not within the section. A transfer to a person as trustee presupposes that the trust is more than just a bare trust;

(iii) where it is said that the disposition was to a trustee, that the trustee actually holds some money or property deriving from the disposition;

(iv)   the disposition was done by Jack with the intention of defeating the claimant's claim for financial provision under s.2 of the 1975 Act. The motive does not have to be the dominant motive in the transaction; if it is a subsidiary (but material) motive then that will suffice[85];

(v)   a payment order would facilitate the making of an award for financial provision under the 1975 Act in favour of the claimant;

(vi)   where the defendant is out of the jurisdiction that the order for payment would be enforceable in the foreign land[86];

---

[82] *Dellal*, at [6], [7].

[83] *Morrow v Morrow* [1995] N.I.J.B. 46.

[84] Section 13 specifies the powers of the court in relation to trustees where an application is made for an order under ss.10 or 11.

[85] *Kemmis v Kemmis (Welland and Others Intervening); Lazard Brothers and Co (Jersey) Ltd v Norah Holdings Ltd* [1988] 1 W.L.R. 1307, CA.

[86] *Hamlin v Hamlin* [1986] Fam. 11, CA, per Kerr LJ. In *Dellal,* one of the children was resident in the state of New York and the 96-year-old sister was resident in Switzerland.

(vii) the court should exercise its discretion to make an order for a payment to the estate.

Mostyn J first considered the strike-out route.[87] He was critical of the language of CPR PD3A,[88] as suggesting that a strike-out application could be made where a party believes that his opponent's case has no real prospect of success on the facts. He saw this as very odd, as a dismissal of a case in such circumstances was precisely what CPR r.24.2 was for. He considered the equivalent provision in the Family Procedure Rules (FPR)[89] and the similar criticism voiced by Lord Wilson in *Vince v Wyatt*.[90] He adopted the view of Lord Wilson in holding that under CPR r.3.4(2)(a), arguments about real prospect of success can only arise in a literal sense, viz., that a claim which is legally unrecognisable has no prospects of success. He also rejected the argument that the claim should be struck out under CPR r.3.4(2)(b) for failure to comply with a rule (r.8(2)(b)) in that the claim form did not specify with sufficient particularity what the claimant was seeking or the legal basis for it.[91]   **3–062**

For the defendants (other than the seventh defendant) it was argued that the claim should be struck out or summarily dismissed because[92]:   **3–063**

    (i)   the claimant had not identified any disposition in favour of a defendant that took place between October 2006 and October 2012;

    (ii)   she had not identified any matters which could prove the necessary motive; and

    (iii) having regard to the scale of her assets, she had no prospects of success at trial in persuading the court to exercise the discretion under s.10 in her favour.[93] The fact that she might have lost some of their value by mismanagement could not avail her.

Mostyn J concluded that the strike-out application did not in any respect meet the standards required by CPR r.3.4(2)(a) or (b) and dismissed it.[94]

In relation to the application for summary judgment he set out the law as   **3–064**

---

[87] *Dellal* at [14]–[21].

[88] CPR PD3A paras 1.5, 1.7.

[89] FDR PD4A para.2.4, which, in Lord Wilson's judgment, was to be construed without reference to "real prospects of success". CPR PD3A gives, as an example of a claim that can be struck out under r.3.4(2)(a), claims which contain a coherent set of facts but those facts, even if true, do not disclose any legally recognisable claim against the defendant.

[90] *Vince v Wyatt* [2015] UKSC 14; [2015] 1 W.L.R. 1228.

[91] *Dellal*, at [55]. The argument relied on *Hytrac Conveyors Ltd v Conveyors International Limited* [1983] 1 W.L.R. 44 at 47G–48, as to which Mostyn J remarked that, as he had shown, we have moved on a long way since 1983.

[92] *Dellal*, at [32].

[93] *Dellal*, at [72], sets out a list of assets consisting mainly of real property and chattels, with a total net value of £41,490,000.

[94] *Dellal*, at [65].

it has developed since *Tanfern v Cameron-MacDonald*[95] in considerable detail.[96] While that and subsequent cases emphasise the distinction between "real" and "fanciful" prospects of success, the possibility exists that evidence might yet emerge which could turn a fanciful prospect of success into a real one; as Lord Hobhouse observed in *Three Rivers D.C. v Bank of England*[97]:

> "The difficulty in the application of the criterion used by Part 24 is that it requires an assessment to be made in advance of a full trial as to what the outcome of such a trial would be."

In Mostyn J's judgment, the claimant had a strong prima facie case that at his death, Jack had access to very considerable assets, but the evidence that he had made outright dispositions to any of the defendants during the six-year period was thin indeed. The claimant's case in that regard was almost entirely inferential and was that if he was very rich, and his estate had mysteriously shrunk, then the money could only have gone to his blood relations, there being no other candidates. While he decisively rejected the strike-out application, he took a different view of the summary judgment application. He did not go so far as to say that the claimant's case was merely a speculative punt, and considered it appropriate to follow the course mapped out in the *Arsenal*[98] case. The application for summary judgment should be adjourned with liberty to restore and there should be specific disclosure pursuant to CPR r.31.12.[99] The documents disclosed would enable everyone to determine if the claimant had a real prospect of making good her s.10 claim or whether it was hopeless. His overarching conclusion was that it would be fundamentally unjust to terminate the application at this stage before there has been a scrutiny of the underlying documents which would prove conclusively whether or not the averrals by each of the defendants that there have been no relevant dispositions in their favour are true or false.

(c) Foreign Dispositions

3-065   The powers of the court in relation to dispositions taking place outside the jurisdiction and made with the requisite intent are not clear. The nature of the relief available under s.10 is, according to *Tyler,* best described as restitutionary.[100] Before the coming into force of the Rome II Regulation,[101] the

---

[95] *Tanfern Ltd v Cameron-MacDonald (Practice Note)* [2000] 1 W.L.R. 1311 at [21]; *Swain v Hillman* [2001] 1 All E.R. 91.

[96] For the discussion of the law, see *Dellal* at [22]–[31].

[97] *Three Rivers D.C. v Bank of England* [2003] 2 A.C. 1, at [160].

[98] *Arsenal Football Club Plc v Elite Sports Distribution Limited* [2002] EWHC 3057 (Ch); [2003] F.S.R. 26, per Geoffrey Vos QC (as he then was), paras [35], [40], quoted in *Dellal*, at [29].

[99] *Dellal*, at [51]–[52], [65]–[69].

[100] *Tyler*, p.60.

[101] For the current choice of law rules for obligations arising out of unjust enrichment, see *Dicey, Morris and Collins*, r.257 (1)–(5), paras 36R–001, 36–003—36–007.

position was as follows.[102] The relevant choice of law rule was that the obligation to restore the benefit of an enrichment gained at another's expense is governed by the proper law of the obligation and, if the obligation arose otherwise than in connection with a contract or a transaction concerning land, that law is the law of the country where the enrichment occurs. However, if the "closest and most relevant connection" test were applied in order to determine the proper law of the obligation in such circumstances, it might well be that the law of the country where the loss was sustained is more appropriate.[103] In almost all cases, that is likely to be England and Wales.

5.—COMPARISON WITH THE CORRESPONDING MATRIMONIAL LEGISLATION

Unlike the matrimonial legislation, the family provision legislation before 1975 did not take into account the possibility that property might be disposed of inter vivos so as to defeat a defendant's claims and, indeed, methods of doing so were discussed in standard textbooks.[104] The Law Commission did not consider s.37 of the Matrimonial Causes Act 1973 to be altogether satisfactory as a model for the anti-avoidance provisions of the 1975 Act,[105] but in view of the scarcity of reported cases on the 1975 Act provisions,[106] a comparison with the matrimonial legislation may be of some value.   **3–066**

The three principal differences between s.10 of the 1975 Act and s.37 of the Matrimonial Causes Act 1973 are in the mode of dealing with the transaction,[107] the incidence of the burden of proof, and the existence of a time bar. In summary: **3–067**

---

[102] *Dicey, Morris and Collins*, para.36–008.

[103] *Dicey, Morris and Collins*, Ch.36, s.1, "Choice of law rules for obligations arising out of unjust enrichment".

[104] See, e.g. the precedent entitled "Settlement on Mistress and Illegitimate Child for the Purpose of Evading the Provisions of the Act", in Albery, *The Inheritance (Family Provision) Act 1938* (London: Sweet & Maxwell, 1950) at App.D.

[105] Law Com. No.61 at paras 189–246, particularly 198 and 227, where the basic schemes of ss.10 and 11, respectively, are set out.

[106] Sherrin, "Defeating the Dependants" [1978] Conv. 13 noted that there had been, up until then, very few reported cases concerning the anti-avoidance provisions of the matrimonial legislation; such provisions had been enacted some years before the coming into force of the Matrimonial Causes Act 1973. Until *Dellal*, where the hearing was concerned with interlocutory matters, there had been no reported case on s.10 of the 1975 Act since *Hanbury v Hanbury* [1999] 2 F.L.R. 255 (where the provision was not invoked) and no reported case at all on s.11 in the 41 years (at the time of writing) since the 1975 Act came into force.

[107] For a recent comment on this aspect of the difference between the anti-avoidance provisions of MCA 1973 (s.37) and the 1975 Act (s.10), see *AC v DC (Financial Remedy: Effect of s.37 Avoidance Order) (No.1)* [2012] EWHC 2032 (Fam); [2013] 2 F.L.R. 1483 at [15] where Mostyn J said: "In my judgment, a transaction caught by s.37 is plainly a voidable transaction. By contrast, and by design of the draftsman, a transaction caught by [the 1975 Act] s.10 is not a voidable transaction but rather, a fully valid transaction, which, on proof of similar facts to those required by s.37, can, in the exercise of discretion, give rise to an obligation to repay."

    (i)   s.37(2) provides that the court may set aside a transaction in matrimonial proceedings if it is satisfied that the transaction was made with the intention of defeating a claim for financial relief and, if it were set aside, financial relief or different financial relief would be granted to the applicant;

    (ii) s.37(5) provides that where an application is made within three years of such a transaction, or in respect of a transaction which is about to take place, and the court is satisfied that the transaction has (or, as the case may be, would have) the effect of defeating the applicant's claim for financial relief, it shall be presumed, unless the contrary is shown, that the person who entered or is about to enter into the transaction in question did so or is about to do so, with the intention of defeating such claim;

    (iii) there is no time limit barring a transaction from being set aside under s.37.

3–068   "Disposition" is defined by s.37(6) as not including any provision contained in a will or codicil, but, with that exception, includes any conveyance, assurance or gift of property of any description, whether made by an instrument or otherwise. In *Woodley v Woodley*[108] it had been held at first instance that the presentation of a petition by a husband, for a bankruptcy order against himself, was a disposition of property within the meaning of s.37. However, in *Woodley v Woodley (No.2)*,[109] the Court of Appeal disagreed, expressing the view that if the presentation of a petition was a fraudulent device intended to defeat a claim in matrimonial proceedings, it could be countered by annulment of the bankruptcy order under s.282(1)(a) of the Insolvency Act 1986.

3–069   The "setting aside" method implemented by s.37(2) of the Matrimonial Causes Act 1973 was not adopted in s.10 of the 1975 Act, due to anticipated difficulties should the property come into the hands of third or subsequent parties. The case of *National Provincial Bank Ltd v Ainsworth*[110] illustrates the problems which may arise. In consequence, the 1975 Act treats these transactions differently. By s.10(2), the court must be satisfied that:

    (a)   the deceased, less than six years before their death, made a disposition with intent to defeat an application for financial provision under the Act; and

---

[108] *Woodley v Woodley* [1992] 2 F.L.R. 427.
[109] *Woodley v Woodley (No.2)* [1993] 4 All E.R. 1010, CA.
[110] *National Provincial Bank Ltd v Ainsworth* [1965] A.C. 1175; the "deserted wife's equity" case. At the date of the possession hearing at first instance (reported as *National Provincial Bank Ltd v Hastings Car Mart* [1964] Ch. 9), there was an application by the wife under s.2 of the Matrimonial Causes (Property and Maintenance) Act 1958 for an order setting aside the conveyance of the matrimonial home as having been made with the intention of defeating her claims against him for financial relief. Cross J held that her claim, as a deserted wife in actual occupation, to occupy the property, was not an overriding interest. That decision was reversed by a majority of the Court of Appeal (Denning MR, Donovan LJ) in *National Provincial Bank Ltd v Hastings Car Mart* [1964] Ch. 665), but restored by the unanimous decision of the House of Lords.

(b) full valuable consideration was not given by the person to whom or for whose benefit the disposition was made ("the donee"), or by any other person; and

(c) the making of an order under the section would facilitate the making of financial provision for an applicant under the Act.

The court can then order the donee to provide such sum of money or other property as is specified, provided that the sum of money or value of property does not exceed the amount or value disposed of by the deceased after deducting any inheritance tax paid by the donee.

As to presumptions and the burden of proof in relation to applications **3–070** under ss.10 and 11 of the 1975 Act, the original view was that the scheme of s.37 should be followed. However, s.12(1) of the 1975 Act provides that the necessary intention is established where the court is of the opinion, on the balance of probabilities, that, in making the disposition, it was the sole intention of the deceased, or a substantial part of their intention, to defeat a claim for family provision wholly or in part. Section 12(2) is the only provision for a presumption; the necessary intention is presumed in the case where there is a contract to leave property by will and *no* valuable consideration has been given or promised. If consideration was given or promised but it is alleged that it was less than full valuable consideration, the burden of proof of that allegation is on the applicant. "Valuable consideration" as defined in s.25(1) does not include marriage or a promise of marriage.

6.—EVIDENCE OF INTENTION

There are a few reported cases under the matrimonial legislation which deal **3–071** with the question of what has to be demonstrated in order for the court to be satisfied that a disposition was made with the intention of defeating a claim. In *Jordan v Jordan*,[111] it was held that it was not sufficient for the maker of the disposition to prove the mere absence of direct purpose, malignancy or spite. The word "intention" did not, in the context, import an element of purpose or design. The meaning of the word "satisfied" in s.37(2) of the Matrimonial Causes Act 1973 was considered at some length in *K v K*,[112] where Ormrod LJ said:

"...the question the judge has to ask himself is 'Am I satisfied that [the disposition] was made with the intention of defeating the wife's future claim?'"

Both he and Dunn LJ said that it was not helpful to import notions which are relevant to the setting aside of fraudulent conveyances. Reviewing the

[111] *Jordan v Jordan* (1965) 129 S.J. 353.
[112] *K v K* (1983) 4 F.L.R. 31, CA.

authorities, he concluded that "satisfied" meant just what it said and that no synonyms or additions would clarify its meaning.

3–072   In *Kemmis v Kemmis*[113] the Court of Appeal considered what was meant by the word "intention" in s.37(2). Acknowledging that the more one seeks to analyse that meaning, the harder it becomes, Lloyd LJ concluded that:

> (i)   the court was concerned with the disponor's intention in a sub-jective sense; it was his state of mind, not what he had done, which was being investigated;
>
> (ii) the court would usually be thrown back on inference, since that state of mind would rarely be declared in advance, and, even if it were, it would not be conclusive, or even very persuasive, unless his declaration was against interest; and
>
> (iii) in determining whether the disponor had the requisite state of mind, the court could have regard to the natural consequences of his acts.[114]

3–073   In *Kemmis*, Nourse LJ agreed with the first proposition, expressing the opinion that it was clear that the intention to defeat the claim did not have to be the sole or dominant intention; it was enough if it played a substantial part in their intentions as a whole. The nature of the test to be applied under the 1975 Act is expressed in very similar language by s.12(1), which also lays down the standard as being that of the balance of probabilities. He rejected the submission that any higher standard applied under s.37 of the Matrimonial Causes Act 1973, though he agreed that, if a dishonest or fraudulent intention was alleged, the evidence required to tip the balance would have to be correspondingly more convincing.

3–074   The accepted principles regarding the use of out-of-court acts and statements for establishing intention may be summarised as follows:

> (i)   where a person's state of mind is material in relation to a trans-action, all facts and declarations from which that state of mind may be inferred are, generally speaking, admissible evidence either for or against them;
>
> (ii) proof of the intention with which an act was done may be by declarations at or before the time of the act, or, where the act is of a continuous nature, by declarations made at any time during its currency;
>
> (iii) oral or written declarations made by deceased persons as to facts within their personal knowledge and consciously against their proprietary or pecuniary interests are admissible in proof of the matters stated;

---

[113] *Kemmis v Kemmis (Welland and Others Intervening); Lazard Brothers and Co (Jersey) Ltd v Norah Holdings Ltd* [1988] 1 W.L.R. 1307, CA.

[114] See *Phipson on Evidence*, 18th edn (London: Sweet & Maxwell, 2013), Ch.16, s.3 "Proof of states of mind and body", subs.(c)(i), para.16–10. "Intention-when in issue, or relevant."

(iv) in connection with the presumption of advancement,[115] acts and declarations of the parties at the time of the transaction are admissible whether for or against the party doing or making them, but subsequent acts and declarations are admissible only against the doer or maker.

---

[115] Abolished by s.199 of the Equality Act 2010; however, this and the other provisions of Pt 15 (Family Property) were not in force at the time of writing. S.216(2) of the Equality Act provides that the provisions of Pt 15 shall come into force on such day as the Lord Chancellor may appoint.

CHAPTER 4

WHAT THE COURT MUST CONSIDER

1.—GENERAL

Section 3 of the 1975 Act directs the court to have regard to certain matters **4–001** both in determining whether the disposition of the deceased's estate is such as to make reasonable provision for the claimant, and, if it considers that reasonable provision has not been made, whether and in what manner to exercise its discretion in favour of the claimant. The matters relevant to claims by any class of claimant are listed in subs.3(1). Those specific to particular classes of claimant are contained in subss.3(2) (surviving spouses and civil partners,[1] former spouses who have not remarried, and former civil partners who have not formed a subsequent civil partnership), 3(2A) (cohabitants[2] as defined by ss.1(1A) and 1(1B)), 3(3) (children of the deceased, and persons other than children of the deceased who were treated by the deceased as children of the family) and 3(4) (persons other than those in the categories already specified, who were being maintained by the deceased immediately before their death). The scheme of this chapter is to consider first, the matters of general application, beginning with financial matters and then going on to personal matters, and then the matters specific to the various classes of applicant. Section 3(5) directs the court to take into account the facts known to it at the date of the hearing.

4–002   Section 3 of the 1975 Act does not establish any hierarchy among the matters to which the court must have regard. Generally speaking, however, the size and nature of the net estate and the current and foreseeable needs and resources of the claimant are likely to be the most influential factors in the court's assessment of whether there has been a failure to make reasonable provision for the claimant and, if so, whether and to what extent the court should exercise its discretion in the claimant's favour. The one exception to that generalisation is to be found in the cases on claims by surviving spouses. Ever since *Re Besterman*[3] there has been a lack of judicial consensus about the weight to be given to those words of s.3(2) which direct the court to have regard to the provision which the claimant might reasonably have expected to receive had the marriage been terminated on the date of the deceased's death by a decree of divorce, though valuable guidance has since been provided by the judgments of Black J in *P v G, P and P (Relevance of Divorce Provision)*[4] and of the Court of Appeal in *Cunliffe v Fielden*.[5] Further, the amendment of s.3(2) by the addition of the words:

> "...but nothing requires the court to treat such provision as setting an upper or lower limit on the provision which may be made by such an order under s.2"[6]

provides some welcome clarification. The present position is discussed in s.7(a)(iii) of this chapter, under the heading "The 'Notional Divorce'".

---

[1] Inheritance (Provision for Family and Dependants) Act 1975 s.3(2) was amended by s.17 of the Civil Partnership Act 2004 so as to include references to surviving civil partners and former civil partners who have not formed a subsequent civil partnership.

[2] Inheritance (Provision for Family and Dependants) Act 1975 s.3(2A) was amended by s.18 of the Civil Partnership Act 2004 to include references to a person who has been living as a civil partner of the deceased, i.e. same-sex cohabitants. The conditions of eligibility to claim as a member of this class are contained in s.1(1B) of the 1975 Act.

[3] *Re Besterman* [1984] Ch. 458, varying the order made at first instance by HH Judge Mervyn Davies (1982) 3 F.L.R. 255.

[4] *P v G, P and P (Relevance of Divorce Provision)* [2006] 1 F.L.R. 431 .

[5] *Cunliffe v Fielden* [2006] Ch. 361, CA.

[6] Inheritance and Trustees' Powers Act 2014 s.6 and Sch.2 paras 5(1), 5(2).

2.—THE NET ESTATE

(a) Size of the Estate

It has been said in a number of cases that applications for financial provi-   **4–003**
sion out of small estates are to be discouraged, as are appeals to the Court of
Appeal in such circumstances, since it is undesirable that the estate should
be substantially depleted by costs. It still remains to be seen whether, and to
what extent, the parties may be found to have conducted their cases
unreasonably or incurred disproportionate costs for the purpose of the CPR
costs regime,[7] by bringing or, as the case may be, resisting a 1975 Act claim
when the estate is a small one.[8] In *Piglowska v Piglowski*[9] Lord Hoffman
referred to:

> "...the principle of proportionality between the amount at stake and the
> legal resources of the parties and the community which it is appropriate
> to spend on resolving the dispute."

None the less, the 1975 Act, like the 1938 Act, contains no provision   **4–004**
restricting the right to make a claim by reference to the size of the estate, and
the words of Ungoed-Thomas J in *Re Clayton*[10] are equally applicable to
claims under the 1975 Act. He said:

> "Dependants of a dead person, including husbands, have the right to
> make a claim against that person's estate, however small it may be ...
> However small the estate, all the relevant circumstances have to be
> considered before the court's decision is made. The smallness of the
> estate excludes neither jurisdiction nor full consideration. Smallness of
> the estate, however, is significant in relation to (i) the availability of
> State aid for the claimant; (ii) the extent to which the estate can
> effectively contribute towards the claimant's maintenance, and (iii) the
> costs which are necessarily involved in the application."

[7] See CPR r.44.3(1), (2) and (5), r.44.4 and the commentary at paras 44.3.3–44.4.4.
[8] It was said in *Brill v Proud* (1984) 14 Fam. Law, CA, where the estate was worth £12,000 but,
after the costs of all the proceedings had been paid out of the estate, only some £2,800 would
remain, caution should have been exercised before an appeal was embarked on. That
observation (which is nevertheless of general application) was made in relation to a practitioner's duty towards the Law Society in publicly funded cases. That context no longer exists
since, under s.9(1)(a) of the Legal Aid, Sentencing and Punishment of Offenders Act 2012
(LASPO), civil legal services are available to an individual only in the cases specified in Sch.1
Pt 1, which does not include family provision claims. Also, the provisions of ss.49 and 50,
under which applications can be made for legal services orders, do not apply to claims under
the 1975 Act.
[9] *Piglowska v Piglowski* [1999] 1 W.L.R. 1360 at 1373. See also *Civil Procedure* (2017), Vol.1,
para.1.4.10 under the heading "Cost-Benefits of Taking a Particular Step", which can be
regarded as an aspect of proportionality; for this, see Vol.2, para.11–10.
[10] *Re Clayton* [1966] 2 All E.R. 370.

In *Re Coventry*,[11] all three judges of the Court of Appeal referred to the inadvisability of burdening small estates (in that case, some £7,000) with the costs of such proceedings. Goff LJ did, however, go on to say:

> "...of course that does not mean that an application cannot be made in a small estate, nor that when made it should not be duly considered on its merits."

4-005   Another difficulty which will almost inevitably arise with small estates such as that in *Re Coventry*[12] is the insufficiency of assets to satisfy all the competing claims. Several such cases reached the Court of Appeal in the 1980s; see, for example, the case summaries of *Re Portt*[13] (adult daughter competing with granddaughter, net estate £12,000), *Walker v Walker*[14] (first and second wives, net estate £22,000) and *Wallace v Thorburn*[15] (former wife and woman friend who was not a cohabitant, net estate £17,855), but now that permission is required to appeal at all levels, it is unlikely that many such appeals will be permitted, or succeed if they are permitted, on the ground that the judge at first instance did not weigh the competing obligations correctly. In a frequently cited judgment relating to the exercise of the court's discretion when making an order under s.25 of the Matrimonial Causes Act 1973[16] Lord Hoffman, having observed that that Act did not lay down any hierarchy among the matters which the court had to consider, said:

> "It is one of the functions of the Court of Appeal, in appropriate cases, to lay down general guidelines on the relative weights to be given to various factors in different circumstances. These guidelines, not expressly stated by Parliament, are derived by the courts from values about family life which it considers would be widely accepted in the community. But there are many cases which involve value judgments on which there are no such generally held views ... [There] are value judgments on which reasonable people may differ. Since judges are also people, this means that some degree of diversity in their application is inevitable and, within limits, an acceptable price to pay for the flexibility of the discretion conferred by the 1973 Act."

---

[11] *Re Coventry* [1980] Ch. 461.
[12] The value of the estate at the death of the deceased in June 1976, after adjustment for the effect of inflation at the time of writing, would increase by a factor of about seven.
[13] *Re Portt, Allcorn v Harvey and Woodcock*. unreported 25 March 1980, CA.
[14] *Walker v Walker* unreported 10 May 1988, CA.
[15] *Wallace v Thorburn* unreported 9 October 1987, CA.
[16] *Piglowska v Piglowski* [1999] 1 W.L.R. 1360 at 1372, where Lord Hoffman considered, in some detail, the principles on which an appellate court should act where the exercise of discretion in the court below was being called in question.

Given their common origin in the work of the Law Commission in the 1970s[17] and the structural resemblance between the relevant provisions of the two Acts, that passage is equally applicable to the exercise of discretion under the 1975 Act.

It is not the case that, because the estate is comparatively large, a claimant   **4-006** is entitled to any, or any further provision. Judges have reiterated the principle of testamentary freedom, though with the gloss, in surviving spouse cases, that that principle is subject to the statutory duty of a husband to provide for his wife, and, in a more recent remarkable judicial testament to gender equality, the obligation of a wife to provide for her husband. In *Barron v Woodhead*,[18] HH Judge Behrens held that:

> "It remains the law that a deceased spouse who leaves a widower is entitled to leave her estate to whomsoever she pleases. Her only obligation is to make reasonable provision for her widower."

This mirrors the observation of Wall LJ in *Cunliffe v Fielden*[19] that:

> "In cases under the 1975 Act a deceased spouse who leaves a widow is entitled to leave his estate to whomsoever she pleases; his only statutory[20] obligation is to make reasonable provision for his widow."

The principle of testamentary freedom was invoked by Eleanor King J in   **4-007** *Ilott v Mitson*,[21] a claim by an adult daughter of the deceased, who had made no provision for her in her will. This case reached the High Court by way of

---

[17] Law Commission Working Paper No.42, *Family Property* (1971); Law Commission Report No.52, *First Report on Family Property—a new approach* (1973); Law Commission Report No.61, *Second Report on Family Property: Family Provision on Death* (1974).

[18] *Barron v Woodhead* [2009] 1 F.L.R. 747; [2008] W.T.L.R. 1675 at [14].

[19] *Cunliffe v Fielden* [2006] Ch. 361 at [21].

[20] It is worth noting that the common law duty of a husband to maintain his wife is expressly abolished by s.198 of the Equality Act 2009, though at the time of writing this provision is not yet in force. Under s.199, the same fate awaits the presumption of advancement, but its abolition will not be retrospective.

[21] This case is generally referred to as *Ilott v Mitson*, though it was originally reported *sub nom. H v J's Personal Representatives, Blue Cross, RSPB and RSPCA* [2010] 1 F.L.R. 1613; [2010] Fam. Law 343 (case comment); and as *H v M* [2010] 1 W.T.L.R. 1. That decision was overruled by the Court of Appeal in *Ilott v Mitson* [2012] 2 F.L.R. 170 which attracted a substantial amount of comment because of the perception that it erodes or subverts the principle of testamentary freedom. The second series of hearings on the issue of quantum (*Ilott v Mitson* [2015] EWCA (Civ) 797; [2015] 2 F.L.R. 1409, CA, reversing the decision of Parker J, [2015] 1 F.L.R. 291, not to interfere with the award of quantum originally made by the District Judge) has prompted further academic comment; see L. Tattersall "On the road to the Supreme Court; the practical applications of *Ilott v Mitson*" (2016) T & T 22(7), 787–793; B. Sloan, "The 'disinherited' daughter and the disapproving mother" (2016) C.L.J.75(1), 31–34; S. Douglas, "Estranged children and their inheritance" (2016) L.Q.R. 132 (Jan) 20–25. None of those commentators regards the principle of testamentary freedom as being under threat as a result of the Court of Appeal decision on quantum. On 18 March 2017, the Supreme Court unanimously set aside the order of the Court of Appeal (*Ilott v Mitson* [2017] UKSC 17) and restored the order of the District Judge following the hearing on 29 and 30 May 2007 (though the order was not perfected until 17 December of that year).

an appeal by the claimant, who contended that the award made to her by the
district judge was insufficient. The charities then cross-appealed on the
ground that he had failed to apply the law correctly and that, had he done
so, he would have found that no provision was reasonable provision.
Having said that "it would be a severe court indeed that did not have a
measure of sympathy for the daughter" and commented on the view of the
district judge that the deceased's treatment of her daughter was unreasonable, Eleanor King J continued[22]:

> "The fact remains that unless one or more of the other of the factors set
> out in s.3 of the 1975 Act serve to tip the balance in favour of such
> interference, then for so long as the laws of England and Wales reject
> the concept of forced heirship, its courts will decline to step in and
> interfere with the validly expressed intention of the testator in relation
> to his or her adult children, albeit in necessitous circumstances."

4-008   The principle of testamentary freedom will not be overridden merely
because the beneficiaries have not made out a positive case for retention of
the benefits which they stand to receive,[23] nor, in a case where the applicant
has sufficient financial resources and no financial needs, simply because the
estate is a large one.[24] There may be circumstances where the amount of
provision made, although very small compared with the value of the net
estate, may be considered reasonable. Thus, in *Rowlands v Rowlands*,[25]
where the deceased had excluded his widow from all benefit under his will,
and the trial judge had awarded her £3,000 out of an estate worth almost
£100,000, the Court of Appeal rejected a submission that an award which
was so palpably low could not amount to reasonable provision.

4-009   It is rare for there to be a substantial increase in the net estate between the
date of death and the date of the hearing,[26] but in such a case the effect of
s.3(5) of the 1975 Act may be dramatic. In *Re Hancock Deceased*[27] the
deceased died in 1985 leaving a widow and seven children, of whom the
applicant was one. His estate at the date of his death consisted of the
matrimonial home, a plot of land worth £100,000, and money and chattels
to the value of £80,000, which was left to his wife. He expressed a wish that
she should provide in her will for their daughters (the applicant and her
sister). The wife died in 1986, leaving the applicant £1,000. In 1989, the land
was sold for a net figure of £663,000. For reasons which did not reflect
adversely on the applicant, the application was not heard until 1996. At first
instance it was found that (i) on the facts as they were at the date of death, it
was not unreasonable for the will to have made no provision for the

---

[22] *H v J's Personal Representatives, Blue Cross, RSPB and RSPCA* [2010] 1 F.L.R. 1613 at [70].
[23] *Re Clarke* [1991] Fam. Law 364.
[24] *Gold v Curtis* [2005] W.T.L.R. 673.
[25] *Rowlands v Rowlands* [1984] F.L.R. 813, CA.
[26] In *Dingmar v Dingmar* [2007] Ch. 109, CA, the value of the matrimonial home, in relation to
which there was an application under s.9, increased substantially between the date of death
and the date of the hearing.
[27] *Re Hancock Deceased* [1998] 2 F.L.R. 346, CA.

applicant and (ii) that she had failed to demonstrate any moral obligation owed to her, or special circumstances, but (iii) assessing the relevant matters at the date of the hearing, her resources fell short of what was required for her reasonable maintenance. It was ordered that she be paid £3,000 per year out of the estate. On appeal it was held that the change in the size of the estate, up or down, was clearly a relevant fact for the court at the date of the hearing, and the judge had not erred in taking it into account.

(b) Nature of the Estate

Section 1(5) of the 1938 Act provided that the court should not order any provision to be made which would necessitate a realisation that would be improvident having regard to the interests of the deceased's dependants and of the persons who, apart from the order, would be interested in the property. There is no such provision in the 1975 Act. However, situations may arise where it is desirable to keep an asset in being, no matter that there is entitlement to it in specie, because realisation might seriously diminish its value or break up a going concern on whose existence family members depended.   **4–010**

The position in relation to the breaking up of a going concern has been addressed in a number of cases in the field of ancillary relief, where the question has frequently arisen. Indeed, the break-up of the family farming business was a major issue in the paradigm case of *White v White*.[28] The observations made in the ancillary relief cases are equally applicable to 1975 Act claims. The following statement of Coleridge J in *N v N (Financial Provision: Sale of Company)*[29] was quoted with approval by Munby J in *P v P (Inherited Property)*[30]:   **4–011**

> "There is no longer any taboo against selling the goose that lays the golden egg, but if it is essential to sell her, it is essential that her condition be such that her egg-laying qualities are damaged as little as possible in the process."

In *P v P*, Munby J considered that the proper approach was to make an award based on the wife's reasonable needs for accommodation and income. In the circumstances which he summarised, giving her more than she reasonably needed for accommodation and income would tip the balance unfairly against the husband, particularly since any other approach would compel a sale of the farm with devastating consequences for him. These two cases were cited with approval in *Miller v Miller, McFarlane v McFarlane*.[31]

---

[28] *White v White* [2001] 1 A.C. 596 (HL).
[29] *N v N (Financial Provision: Sale of Company)* [2001] 2 F.L.R. 69 at 80.
[30] *P v P (Inherited Property)* [2005] 1 F.L.R. 576.
[31] *Miller v Miller, McFarlane v McFarlane* [2006] 2 A.C. 618, at [148]. *P v P (Inherited Property)* was also considered in *D v D* [2010] EWHC 138 (Fam), where Charles J in analysing the approach to needs and sharing, treated the strong argument that the husband should, if reasonably possible, be permitted to continue farming through the family company (which had been in existence for almost 60 years), as a magnetic factor, and the award reflected that approach.

4–012   Comparable situations have arisen in a number of 1975 Act cases where the major asset of the estate is a working farm or some other established family business. Thus in *Rowlands v Rowlands*,[32] the major asset of the estate, whose value was £96,000, was farm land which had been in the family for some 50 years and was being worked by one of the testator's sons. In making an award of £3,000 to the applicant widow, the trial judge considered it relevant that the estate consisted of farm land and that the intention of the testator was to keep it together to inure for the benefit of his children and succeeding generations. Although he had adverted to the difficulty of realisation, he had recognised that an appropriate lump sum could be raised on mortgage or by sale of part of the land. The appeal failed. The 1975 Act does not in terms require the court to have regard to the testator's intentions but, given the emphasis placed on the principle of testamentary freedom from *Re Coventry*[33] onwards, those intentions can properly be regarded as relevant matters under s.3(1)(g). Statements of his reasons for making or not making any disposition were formerly expressly admissible under s.21 of the 1975 Act. They are now admissible under the hearsay provisions of the Civil Evidence Act 1995, subs.4(1) of which provides that in estimating the weight (if any) to be given to hearsay evidence, the court shall have regard to any circumstances from which any inference can reasonably be drawn as to the reliability or otherwise of the evidence. Among the matters to which the court may have particular regard are whether any person had any motive to conceal or misrepresent matters and whether the statement was made for a particular purpose.[34]

4–013   *Rowlands* was cited in *McGuigan v McGuigan*,[35] a Northern Ireland case where the bulk of the deceased's estate consisted of two farms with associated buildings. It was argued that regard should be had to the desirability of keeping the farms together as one unit. However, in *McGuigan* the deceased had made a series of wills which, when reviewed, did not warrant any belief that he had an intention to keep the farms together; nor was there any evidence that the farming business would be adversely affected if the farm lands were not kept together. Although, in the result, the applicant was given a life interest in all the farm land, it is clear from the judgment that this was not a factor in the decision. In another Northern Ireland farm case, *Morrow v Morrow*,[36] the court considered whether a reduction in the size of a farm in order to provide a capital sum for the applicant would have a serious effect on the business undertaking and found that it would not.

4–014   In *Lilleyman v Lilleyman*[37] the value of the net estate was approximately £6 million, of which £5.085 million was represented by the value of the estate's shareholding in three family companies. The deceased was engaged in the steel stockholding business and the companies had been formed or

---

[32] *Rowlands v Rowlands* [1984] F.L.R. 813.
[33] *Re Coventry* [1980] Ch. 461, per Oliver J at 474G.
[34] Civil Evidence Act 1995 s.4(2)(d), (e).
[35] *McGuigan v McGuigan* [1996] N.I.J.B. 47.
[36] *Morrow v Morrow* [1995] N.I.J.B. 46.
[37] *Lilleyman v Lilleyman* [2013] 1 F.L.R. 47.

acquired in 1982, 1990 and 2004, thus, all pre-dating the relationship between the deceased and the claimant. Both of the deceased's sons by his first marriage worked in the family business. They did not disclose their own financial positions, but it was apparent from the evidence that their future careers and the financial security of themselves and their families might well be dependent, to an extent which could not be precisely measured, on preserving the companies from undue attrition by any award made to the claimant.[38] In considering the divorce cross-check, an issue arose whether the increase in value of one of the companies during the marriage should be attributed to the deceased's activities (in which case the increase would be treated as matrimonial property) or passive economic growth.[39] In the event the value of the award to the claimant was £500,000 (roughly 35 per cent of the total matrimonial property, thereby reflecting the shortness of the relationship[40]), so the question of attrition of the value of the companies did not arise in practice.

Difficulties have arisen where the estate consists mainly of a house and the testator's dispositions are such that the applicant is given the right to reside in the house during their lifetime, but cannot afford to live in it[41] and is unable to sell or lease it. A former method of dealing with this was to order that the property be vested in the applicant as tenant for life under the Settled Land Act 1925[42] but, following the coming into force of the Trusts of Land and Appointment of Trustees Act 1996, the creation of a strict settlement is no longer an option. However, the court has power under s.2(4)(b) of the 1975 Act to direct the settlement, for the benefit of the applicant, of such property comprised in the estate as may be specified; see,

4–015

---

[38] *Lilleyman*, at [66].

[39] *Lilleyman*, at [76]–[79]. In the result, £250,000 of the £550,000 increase in value was included in the value of the matrimonial property, giving a total value of approximately £1,475,000.

[40] The parties, both of whom had previously been married, had a relationship lasting somewhat more than four years, but were married for only two-and-a-quarter years before the death of the deceased.

[41] An early example of this is *Re Inns, Inns v Wallace* [1947] Ch. 576. Under her husband's will the applicant widow received the income of £85,000 and the right to reside in the matrimonial home for life or until remarriage, on either of which events it was to be offered to the local authority (whose consent, as well as her own, was required for a sale during her lifetime). Her claim for financial provision was on the ground that her income did not provide her with the means to live in the house as the testator had intended her to do. Wynn-Parry J dismissed the application, holding that that did not make the provision under the will unreasonable.

[42] See *Re Mason* (1975) 5 Fam. Law 124; *Lewis v Lynch* unreported 13 March 1980, CA. In the latter case, the testator made a will in 1971 empowering his trustees to lay out £10,000 in the purchase of a house for occupation by his widow during her widowhood. He also provided for an annuity of £2,000 per year to be purchased for her. After his death in 1974, his trustees, due to inflation, were unable to purchase a suitable house for £10,000 and ultimately they spent £18,000. Her application for financial provision out of his estate was heard in 1979 and on the hearing of that application the house purchased for her occupation was ordered to be vested in her as tenant for life under the Settled Land Act. On her appeal, the Court concluded that, while the award at trial had recognised the consequences of inflation in relation to the house purchase, it had not done so in respect of income provision. The annuity of £2,000, together with her other resources, was insufficient to meet her reasonable needs and she was awarded a further £10,000.

for example, *Harrington v Gill*.[43] In that case the applicant and the deceased had lived together in the deceased's house for some eight years prior to his death. At first instance, she was ordered to vacate the house and she was awarded a lump sum of £5,000 and the income from a further £5,000. On appeal, the applicant contended that the award was inadequate as it did not provide for her accommodation. The Court of Appeal considered that a reasonable man would have wished her to remain in the house for her life and ordered that the house be vested in trustees for sale on trust for the applicant for life, and the remainder to the daughter of the deceased who had been the sole beneficiary.

4–016   In *Moody v Haselgrove*[44] the appellant wife had been left a life interest in the bulk of the estate, with the remainder to his three cousins. The judge at first instance had held that the provision was not reasonable, as it left her with the right to occupy a house but without resources to maintain it. He ordered that, subject to a mortgage out of which (inter alia) immediate pecuniary legacies should be provided for the three cousins, the house should be held on trust for her absolutely. The Court of Appeal, dismissing the wife's appeal,[45] held that the judge was entitled to make an order which did not entirely defeat the testator's intentions.

4–017   In *Iqbal v Ahmed*[46] the claimant (W) was the widow of the deceased (D) and the defendant (S) was his son from a previous marriage. D's net estate, which was sworn for probate as not exceeding £178,000, included the matrimonial home ("the property"), valued at £115,000, and £28,000 in cash. By his will dated 28 January 2009 he appointed S as the sole executor and S and a friend (H) as trustees. He gave W a legacy of £8,000 and the right to occupy the property rent-free, but subject to a liability to pay for "outgoings insurance repair decoration and other matters as the Property Trustees shall from time to time consider reasonable". The trial judge found that the will did not make reasonable provision for W; her right of occupation was precarious because she did not have the resources to fund the repair costs and the trustees were not obliged to fund them. If the property became uninhabitable she would have no resources to put towards the purchase or rental of a property for her occupation. She had no share in its ownership to allow her to obtain a secured loan to cover the cost of repair. She was awarded the whole of the residuary estate and a life interest in the property, which would be subject to a trust for sale, postponed during W's lifetime or until her agreement to a sale. There would also be an agreement by S to pay half the cost of insurance and structural repairs to the property. The proceeds of sale would be held upon trust for W and S in equal shares. Permission to appeal was granted, limited to the point whether the judge failed to consider adequately or at all if reasonable provision would have

---

[43] *Harrington v Gill* (1983) 4 F.L.R. 265, CA.
[44] *Moody v Haselgrove* unreported 16 November 1987, CA.
[45] The trial judge's order was, however, varied in two respects; the sum ordered to be raised on mortgage was increased from £12,000 to £15,000, and the legacies were ordered to be charged on the house not, as originally ordered, on residue.
[46] *Iqbal v Ahmed* [2012] 1 F.L.R. 31, CA.

been made by awarding W a life interest in the property and its proceeds of sale and otherwise making the same orders. On appeal, the court identified three reasons why the award of a life interest was inappropriate. The governing reality was the small size of the estate. A life interest would be inadequate to fund the repairs and permit W to maintain herself; an award of a beneficial interest was appropriate where there had been a long marriage (22 years) and that outweighed the fact that D had owned the property before his marriage to W; and the level of hostility between the parties dictated a clean break. The appeal was dismissed.

Another possibility is to order the sale of the property and award the   **4–018** applicant a lump sum, to be paid out of the proceeds of sale; see *Re Parkinson*[47] and *Stephens v Stephens*.[48] However, having regard to the more than six-fold rise in average property prices since the 1980s, this may be a less satisfactory solution than it was then.[49] One of the reasons why the Court of Appeal varied the order made at first instance in *Stephens* was that, in awarding the applicant widow the entire net estate, the judge had paid insufficient attention to the testator's expressed wish that there should be nothing which his widow could pass on to her son by her previous marriage. Balcombe LJ, giving the only substantive judgment, said:

> "We have not yet in this country abolished the right of free testamentary disposition—the Inheritance (Provision for Family and Dependants) Act 1975 is of course an encroachment on it-but, subject to a will not making reasonable provision for a dependant, the order which the court ought to make is to make proper provision for a dependant, bearing in mind the proper weight which should be given to the deceased's reasons for doing what he did."

The order was varied so that the matrimonial home be sold and that she should receive 60 per cent of the net estate.

3.—FINANCIAL CIRCUMSTANCES

(a) General

The scheme of s.3(1) makes it clear that the court will frequently have to   **4–019** weigh up competing interests. Although there are relatively few reported cases of applications on behalf of two or more persons, the court will, save for the exceptional cases where the estate is large enough to satisfy all claims, have to strike a balance between the claims of applicants and bene-

---

[47] *Re Parkinson, The Times*, 3 October 1975.
[48] *Stephens v Stephens* unreported 1 July 1985, CA.
[49] Taking the House Price Index as 100 in 1983, then for all houses in the UK the HPI in 2015 (the latest year given) is 648.4; see the House Price Index module in @AGlance (FLBA, 2016–17). At the end of successive decades it was 223.2 (1990), 275.1 (2000) and 540.0 (2010).

ficiaries. Section 2(4) of the 1975 Act gives the court power to include in any order:

> "...such consequential provisions as it thinks necessary or expedient ... for the purpose of securing that the order operates fairly as between one beneficiary ... and another."[50]

This is not a licence to the court to vary the dispositions in a manner which would be considered fair as between the claimant and the beneficiaries; its purpose is to give the court power to ensure that the burden of the award is shared fairly among those who stand to be adversely affected by it.

4–020   That may be quite a complex exercise where the estate has been disposed of among a large number of specific or pecuniary legatees, or where it falls to be divided among a large number of relatives on intestacy. One solution where there are several such legatees is to order that the burden of the award be borne by the specific legatee who stands to benefit to the greatest extent under the will; this was done in *Malone v Harrison*.[51] There is no reported case in which specific legacies were ordered to abate rateably. An example of the situation arising out of intestacy is *Clarke v Roberts*.[52] Mr Clarke made a will leaving a pecuniary legacy of £1,000 to his wife and the rest of his estate, of value roughly £23,000, to his mother. Less than three months after his death, his mother in turn died, having left her entire estate to him. As that gift had lapsed, Mr Clarke's estate passed as on his mother's intestacy and fell to be distributed among some 40 cousins and their issue. The applicant widow was awarded half the income of the residuary estate for life or until re-marriage so, in effect, the burden of the award was shared equally per stirpes.

(b) Financial Needs and Resources

4–021   The first three subsections of s.3(1) direct the court to have regard to the financial needs and resources of, respectively, the applicant, any other applicant, and any beneficiary. Section 3(6) directs the court to take into account the earning capacity of any person when considering their financial resources, and their financial obligations and responsibilities when considering their needs. Financial resources include income and capital of whatever nature and from whatever source, whether present or prospective, though in the latter case the court must take into account the likelihood of those resources being acquired.

4–022   It is important to realise that, in considering the financial needs and resources of any person, the court may take into account, for the purposes of applications under both s.2 and s.9, assets received by any applicant or beneficiary to which there can be no recourse because they do not form part

---

[50] Inheritance (Provision for Family and Dependants) Act 1975 s.2(4).
[51] *Malone v Harrison* [1979] 1 W.L.R. 1353.
[52] *Clarke v Roberts* [1968] 1 All E.R. 451.

of the net estate. Thus, in *Re Jessop*[53] the Court of Appeal restored an order made by the Registrar, whereby he directed that the deceased's severable share of a house worth £42,000 be treated, to the extent of £10,000, as part of his net estate for the purpose of facilitating the making of reasonable financial provision for the appellant wife. The judge, when discharging the Registrar's order, had failed to take into account that the beneficiary had, in accordance with the deceased's wishes, been paid a lump sum of nearly £40,000 by the trustees of the deceased's pension fund, such sum not being part of his net estate within the scope of s.8.

As regards the acquisition of financial resources, the 1975 Act gives no guidance on the degree of probability fitting the description "likely to", or the length of time which might be considered to lie "within the foreseeable future". The phrase "likely to have in the foreseeable future" also occurs in s.25(2)(a) of the Matrimonial Causes Act 1973, and the meaning of both "likely to" and "in the foreseeable future" has been considered in a number of cases under the matrimonial legislation. From those cases[54] one can collect that "likely to" means "likely to on the balance of probabilities", and that that standard would not be met if the acquisition of the resource in question were to depend on decisions of third parties over which the potential acquirer had no control. In *Michael v Michael*,[55] a matrimonial case, Nourse LJ considered the words "likely to have in the foreseeable future", citing a number of cases[56] involving property in which a party to the marriage had a vested or contingent interest, albeit of an uncertain nature; such property fell within that description. He further held that the words were not confined to property in which there were interests which recognisably bore "the sober uniforms of property law" but:

4-023

> "...could extend to something which in the language of that law is a mere expectancy or *spes successionis*, for example an interest which might be taken under the will of a living person."[57]

He expanded on this as follows[58]:

---

[53] *Re Jessop* [1992] 1 F.L.R. 992, CA.

[54] *Calder v Calder* (1976) 6 Fam. Law, CA; *Priest v Priest* (1980) 1 F.L.R. 189 CA; *Re Clayton* [1966] 2 All E.R. 370 (a 1938 Act case); *Milne v Milne* (1981) 2 F.L.R. 286.

[55] *Michael v Michael* [1986] 2 F.L.R. 389, CA. The passage from the judgment at p.396E was cited with approval by Munby J in *C v C (Ancillary Relief: Trust Fund)* [2010] 1 F.L.R. 337 at [37]. In that case, Munby J held that a husband's reversionary interest in trust property was a financial interest which he was likely to have in the foreseeable future, notwithstanding that the amount likely to accrue to him could not be ascertained and was unlikely to be realized for a further 15 years.

[56] *Morris v Morris* (1977) 7 Fam. Law 244; *Priest v Priest* (1980) 1 F.L.R. 280 (both cases of a serving soldier who would qualify for a gratuity on discharge if he served beyond a specified year); *Milne v Milne* (1981) 2 F.L.R. 286 (occupational pension scheme; contingent interest in retirement benefit and vested but defeasible interest in lump sum death in service benefit); *Davies v Davies* [1986] 1 F.L.R. 497 (vested interest in surplus, if any, after dissolution of farming partnership).

[57] *Michael* [1986] 2 F.L.R. 389 at 395F–G.

[58] *Michael* [1986] 2 F.L.R. 389 at 396C–E.

"I have already expressed the view that section 25(2)(a) of the Act of 1973 as amended could in certain circumstances extend to an interest which might be taken under the will of a living person. Suppose, for example, a case where there was clear evidence first, that the respondent's father was suffering from a terminal illness; secondly, that his will left property of a substantial but uncertain value to the respondent; and, third, that it was highly unlikely that he could or would revoke it. In such a case it could hardly be doubted that the property was property which the respondent was likely to have in the foreseeable future ... However, those facts, being extremely rare, demonstrate that the occasions on which such an interest will fall within section 25(2)(a) of the Act of 1973 are likely to be rare. In the normal case uncertainties in both the fact of inheritance and the time at which it will occur will make it impossible to hold that the property is property which is likely to be had in the foreseeable future."

4–024   It has become increasingly important, in an age of many and varied state benefits, both means-tested and non-means-tested, of tax credits and of occupational and private pension plans, to ascertain not only what benefits a claimant (or, as the case may be, a defendant beneficiary) is receiving, but what benefits that person is likely to receive. It should be a matter of normal practice to obtain a benefit forecast. A lump sum award (which is by far the commonest type of award) will have a profound effect on the party's eligibility for means-tested benefits.

4–025   It has been said that the treatment of state benefits in family provision applications has not been happy. It is certainly true that there has been no settled approach to the questions whether, and, if so, to what extent, state benefits which are available to the applicant should be taken into account in deciding whether reasonable financial provision has been made. However, although such questions cannot be ignored, it is doubtful whether they can usefully be considered in isolation. The earlier cases showed, on the whole, that where an applicant receiving state benefits had been unsuccessful, it was because the estate was small, or the competitor was even worse off than the applicant, or both.

4–026   The nearest approach to a statement of principle was in *E v E*[59] where it was said that it was reasonable to make no provision where the estate was small and the only effect of making provision would be pro tanto to relieve the National Assistance Fund, whereas there was no reason not to make provision out of a large estate even if the claimant was able to obtain National Assistance. It was applied in *Millward v Shenton*,[60] an application under the 1938 Act by the 54-year-old disabled son of the deceased whose income was derived entirely from state benefits. He was awarded eleven-twelfths of the estate, which had been left entirely to charity. It has also been

[59]   *E v E* [1966] 2 All E.R. 244.
[60]   *Millward v Shenton* [1972] 2 All E.R. 1025; [1972] 1 W.L.R. 711; (1972) 116 S.J. 335.

considered in a number of 1975 Act cases[61] and applied in *Re Collins*.[62] In that case the applicant, the adult daughter of the deceased, was in receipt of social security benefits; it was held that that fact was not relevant to the question whether the law of intestacy had made reasonable financial provision for her. In *Moore v Holdsworth*,[63] it seemed to Kitchin J overwhelmingly likely that, if the claimant, who suffered from multiple sclerosis and might require long-term residential care, were awarded an absolute interest in the family property, a large part of the estate would be used up in paying for her care, a situation which both she and the deceased had wished to avoid. For that and other reasons, he considered it appropriate to award her only a life interest in her deceased husband's beneficial share as tenant in common.

The case of *Ilott v Mitson* is fully discussed in all its aspects in Ch.6[64] and is mentioned here only in relation to state benefits. In that case, where some 65 per cent of the family income was derived from state benefits in the form of housing benefit and tax credits, Arden LJ said in her judgment on the issue whether the will had made reasonable provision for the claimant, "The fact that the state makes provision for financial hardship does not mean that it is reasonable for a testatrix to make no provision for an adult child".[65] To similar effect, Ryder LJ said, in the second appeal on quantum:

    4–027

> "As a matter of public policy, the court was not constrained to treat a person's reasonable financial provision as being limited by their existing State benefits, nor is the court's discretion substituted for by any assessment of benefits undertaken by the state."[66]

(c) Competing Needs

As the Supreme Court has acknowledged, there will be cases in which the competing claims of others may inhibit the practicability of wholly meeting the needs of the claimant, however reasonable.[67] In several cases under the 1975 Act a balancing exercise between the positions of the applicant and the beneficiaries has been carried out in some detail. It was held in *Re Portt*[68] that the mere existence of a financial disparity between the applicant and the beneficiary is not, without more, a reason for interfering with the testamentary dispositions of the deceased. In *Gold v Curtis*,[69] where the claim succeeded, the court acknowledged that the award still left the claimant substantially worse off than the defendant beneficiary, but observed that the

    4–028

---

[61] *Re Coventry* [1980] Ch. 458; *Negus v Bahouse* [2008] 1 F.L.R. 381; *Webster v Webster* [2009] 1 F.L.R. 1240.
[62] *Re Collins* [1990] Fam. 56.
[63] *Moore v Holdsworth* [2010] W.T.L.R. 1213.
[64] Ch.6, s.8(e)(ii), paras 6–160–6–191 is entirely devoted to *Ilott v Mitson*.
[65] *Ilott v Mitson* [2012] 2 F.L.R. 170, CA at [65].
[66] *Ilott v Mitson* [2015] 2 F.L.R. 1409, CA, at [69].
[67] *Ilott v Mitson* [2017] UKSC 17, reported *sub nom Ilott v Blue Cross* [2017] 2 W.L.R 979, at [22].
[68] *Re Portt, Allcorn v Harvey and Woodcock* unreported 25 March 1980, CA.
[69] *Gold v Curtis* [2005] W.T.L.R. 673.

purpose of the Act was to make reasonable financial provision, not to procure equality between the parties.

4–029 The balancing exercise usually involves consideration, not only of the relative financial positions of the persons involved, but the obligations of the deceased to each of them, a matter to which the court's attention is specifically directed by s.3(1)(d) of the 1975 Act. In the early years of that legislation, many of those cases reached the Court of Appeal, the ground of appeal being that the trial judge had exercised his discretion wrongly in carrying out the balancing exercise and making the resulting award. Such cases appear to have become less frequent in recent years. A case in point was *Eeles v Evans*[70] where the competitors were the widow and the daughter of the deceased, the latter being the sole beneficiary. It was common ground that reasonable provision had not been made for the widow. The main ground of appeal against the award at first instance was that proper regard had not been paid to the 73-year-old applicant's needs in respect of the cost of providing future nursing care or nursing home accommodation. Giving the judgment of the Court of Appeal dismissing the appeal, Dillon LJ cited the following passage from the judgment of Asquith LJ in *Bellenden v Satterthwaite*[71]:

> "It is, of course, not enough for the wife to establish that this court would, or might, have made a different order. We are here concerned with a judicial discretion, and it is of the essence of such discretion that on the same evidence two different minds might reach widely different decisions without either being appealable. It is only where the decision exceeds the generous ambit within which reasonable disagreement is possible, and is, in fact, plainly wrong, that an appellate body is entitled to interfere."

In *Re Crawford*[72] the three issues which arose for consideration were:

(1) whether the court should take into account financial benefits to the beneficiaries under the will of the deceased which did not form part of the net estate;

(2) what principles applied to the exercise of the power under s.9 in relation to property held on a joint tenancy;

(3) if an order under s.9 was made, whether the property subject to the order should be treated differently from any other property in his net estate.

4–030 The property in question was the deceased's severable share of a bank account and a building society account, each in the joint names of himself

---

[70] *Eeles v Evans* unreported 6 July 1989, CA. This case is of interest as being the only accessible case in which an order has been made under s.14 of the 1975 Act.

[71] *Bellenden v Satterthwaite* [1948] 1 All E.R. 343, CA. See also the quotation at para.4–005 from the judgment of Lord Hoffman in *Piglowska v Piglowski* [1999] 1 W.L.R. 1360, HL.

[72] *Re Crawford* (1983) 4 F.L.R. 273.

and his second wife, the source of the monies therein being a lump sum of £69,727.21 paid to him by his employers on his taking premature retirement. The sums paid by the trustees of his former employers' pension fund to his widow (that is, his second wife) and to her two children did not form part of his net estate, but they fell to be taken into account under s.3(1)(c). Eastham J considered that the first question was answered by s.3(1)(c), which directs the court to have regard to the financial needs and resources of any beneficiary. As to the other two issues, he held that there were no specific principles to be applied, since s.9 contained the appropriate guidance, and that property the subject of an order under s.9 should be treated on the same footing as other property forming part of the net estate. He awarded the plaintiff a lump sum sufficient to provide an annuity of about £4,000 per annum, bringing in the deceased's severable share of the joint accounts for the purpose of making that provision.

Cumming-Burns v Burns[73] illustrates the interaction between competing needs and competing obligations. In that case, the deceased's first marriage had been terminated by divorce after 40 years, though the parties had separated long before that event. The deceased made provision for the applicant during his lifetime, but his second wife was the sole beneficiary under his will. Although the applicant was in a worse financial position than the beneficiary, the judge at first instance took into account that the deceased's estate derived very largely from gifts made to him by his second wife and that he had depended on her for practically everything which he had. His moral obligation to his second wife was the stronger of the two and tipped the scale in her favour. The Court of Appeal upheld that decision.

4–031

The case of *Dixit v Dixit*[74] involved a particularly complex exercise, the parties involved being the four children of the deceased's first marriage, who were the only beneficiaries under the will, and the widow and the two infant children of the second marriage, who were beneficiaries under a trust declared by the deceased and the widow. The objectives which the judge at first instance sought to achieve were:

4–032

(i) to provide secure accommodation for the widow and children of the second marriage;
(ii) that that accommodation should be, if possible, in the home which they at that time occupied; and
(iii) that the accommodation problem should be solved in a manner which struck a fair balance between the moral claims of the applicants under the 1975 Act and the adult daughters of his first marriage for whom he had felt a moral obligation to provide.

However, the solution reached at first instance could not stand as its Capital Gains Tax implications had not been put before the judge and were not

[73] *Cumming-Burns v Burns* unreported 4 July 1985, CA.
[74] *Dixit v Dixit* unreported 23 June 1988, CA. This is another case which is of interest as it is the only one of its type, the unique feature being the attempt to achieve reasonable provision by means of an order under s.2(1)(f).

present to his mind. His discretion had, therefore, been exercised on a basis which was wrong, and, as discussed elsewhere,[75] that is one of the situations in which an appellate court will exercise its own discretion.

4–033   In *Re J (A minor)*[76] the deceased left his entire estate, amounting to some £30,000, to his second wife, by whom he had a daughter, aged five at the time of the hearing. At first instance the applicant, his 16-year-old daughter by his first marriage, was awarded one-fourth of the net estate. This order was varied on appeal on the grounds that:

(i)   the process by which that result was arrived at could not readily be followed; and
(ii)   the widow had the greater claim.

The award was subsequently reduced to £5,000. In *Wallace v Thorburn*[77] the competing needs were those of the former spouse and a woman friend of the testator. The award made at first instance in favour of the former spouse was increased by the Court of Appeal, May LJ saying that the exercise of the judge's discretion was:

"...susceptible to valid challenge in that [the] ultimate figure was arrived at either by an approach, the nature of which one cannot discern, or alternatively by an approach which on its face was wholly wrong."

This observation was made because the trial judge did not explain how he arrived at the conclusion that if an award of £7,200 were made to the applicant, he would be satisfied that, taking into account her own assets, she would be able to buy a house.

4–034   In *Ames v Jones*,[78] the testator died in 2013, survived by the 63-year-old widow (E) of his second marriage, who was the sole beneficiary of his will, and the 41-year-old daughter (D) of his first marriage, who would have benefited if E had predeceased him. On the hearing of D's claim for reasonable financial provision, it was found that the estate was not large enough to support both D and E. Whereas E was past working age and in poor health, though the financial consequences of her poor health were not clearly established, D was capable of working and had failed to discharge the burden of proving that she was unable to obtain work; thus, her lack of employment was a lifestyle choice. E had at most a modest surplus of income over expenditure and required the entire capital of the estate to meet her reasonable needs, while D had not satisfied the court as to her own financial needs and resources. Her claim was dismissed.

---

[75] Ch.7, s.13(b): "Circumstances in which an appeal might be entertained".
[76] *Re J (A Minor)* unreported 9 December 1991, CA.
[77] *Wallace v Thorburn* unreported 9 October 1987, CA.
[78] *Ames v Jones* unreported 19 August 2016, Central London County Court.

4.—OBLIGATIONS OF THE DECEASED

The relevant provision of the 1975 Act is s.3(1)(d), which directs the court to   **4–035**
have regard to any obligations or responsibilities which the deceased had
towards any applicant for an order under s.2 of the Act or towards any
beneficiary of the estate of the deceased. It has been considered most often in
two types of case, namely, those where the question is whether the deceased
had any obligation at all to the applicant, and those in which obligations
owed to more than one person had to be weighed against each other. This is
particularly likely to be the case where the deceased is survived by members
of families from two relationships or where there are several adult children.
The provision does not differentiate between legal and moral obligations
and responsibilities, but in *Espinosa v Bourke*[79] Butler-Sloss LJ, having
comprehensively reviewed the use of the words "moral duty", moral claim"
and "moral obligation"[80] in family provision cases both before[81] and after
the coming into force of the 1975 Act, said in relation to s.3(1)(d):

> "Plainly those obligations and responsibilities extend beyond legal
> obligations and responsibilities and that is why, in my view, the word
> 'moral' has been used to underline and explain that the deceased's
> obligations and responsibilities were not to be narrowly construed as
> legal obligations but to be taken into account in a broad sense of
> obligation and responsibility. Any other meaning of 'moral' (such as
> the distinction between right and wrong) would more appropriately be
> considered under [s.3(1)](g)".

(a) Is There an Obligation?

Re Jennings, Harlow v National Westminster Bank[82] is authority for the   **4–036**
proposition that the obligation must be subsisting immediately before the
death of the deceased. The case concerned the question whether, and in what
circumstances, the court should take into account the failure of a parent to
discharge their responsibilities towards a child. The applicant was an adult
son, aged 49 at the date of the hearing, claiming for financial provision out
of the estate of his father. The judge at first instance had held that the
deceased's failure to honour moral and financial obligations to the applicant
during his minority brought the case within the provisions of ss.3(1)(d) and

---

[79] *Espinosa v Bourke* [1999] 1 F.L.R. 749, CA.
[80] *Espinosa*, at 752D–755D.
[81] The first case which she cited was *Re Ducksbury* [1966] 1 W.L.R. 1226, where Buckley J
referred, at 1231, to the deceased as owing a moral duty to make some provision for his
daughter, and said at 1233 "...for the reasons I have indicated I think he was under a moral
obligation to make some provision for her". The applicant was the 34-year-old unmarried
daughter of the deceased by his first marriage, who became estranged from him and whose
subsequent attempts at reconciliation were unavailing. Buckley J held that the deceased's
primary duty was to provide for his second wife, to whom he had been married for 11 years
at his death but he gave effect to the moral obligation by awarding the daughter £2 per week
for life or until she married.
[82] *Re Jennings, Harlow v National Westminster Bank* [1994] Ch. 286, CA.

(g) of the 1975 Act. The Court of Appeal emphatically disagreed with that view. The judge had construed s.3(1)(d):

"...so as to include legal obligations and responsibilities which the deceased had, but failed to discharge, during the child's minority, albeit they were long spent and would have been incapable of founding a claim against him immediately before his death. In my respectful opinion that is an impossible construction of s.3(1)(d). While it is true that it requires regard to be had to obligations and responsibilities which the deceased 'had', that cannot mean 'had at any time in the past'. At all events as a general rule, that provision can only refer to obligations and responsibilities which the deceased had immediately before his death. An Act intended to facilitate the making of reasonable financial provision cannot have been intended to revive defunct obligations and responsibilities as a basis for making it. Nor, if they do not fall within a specific provision such as section 3(1)(d), can they be prayed in aid under a general provision such as section 3(1)(g)."[83]

4–037   Although the above proposition is not in doubt, *Re Jennings* was distinguished in *Re Pearce*,[84] another application by an adult son which involved the conduct of the deceased towards the applicant in his childhood and earlier adult life. In *Re Pearce*, in which the applicant had done a substantial amount of work on the deceased's farm and had repeated promises made to him that he would inherit the farm, it was held at first instance that the deceased had a continuing moral obligation towards him which did not cease on the sale of the farm and was still subsisting at the date of his death a year or two later. The Court of Appeal upheld that judgment both as to the existence of the moral obligation and the quantification of the award.

(b) Obligations Owed to the Claimant

4–038   The question has arisen, in a number of cases whether the deceased had any obligation towards an applicant who was a former spouse who had not remarried, or a spouse who had not divorced but who had been separated from the deceased for a substantial period. The former spouse cases are becoming increasingly rare due to the almost invariable inclusion of a s.15 order[85] in the settlement achieved on divorce. In *Re Crawford*[86] the applicant and the deceased were divorced after a marriage lasting 24 years; he lived for

---

[83] *Re Jennings* [1994] Ch. 286, CA, per Nourse LJ at 296C–E; see also Henry LJ at 301D.
[84] *Re Pearce* [1998] 2 F.L.R. 705, CA, at 711G where Nourse LJ quoted the findings of the trial judge (HH Judge Behrens) on the issue of moral obligation. The relevant passage is: "It was a moral obligation which continued right up to the time of the plaintiff's father's death and therefore this case is distinguishable from *Re Jennings*, where the only obligation which was pointed to was an obligation to maintain him which ended at the age of 16."
[85] Before the amendment brought about by s.8(1) of the Matrimonial and Family Proceedings Act 1984, with effect from 12 October 1984, the court could make such an order only if the parties to the marriage agreed.
[86] *Re Crawford* (1983) 4 F.L.R. 273.

a further 12 years. It was held that the deceased had a moral obligation to the applicant, taking into consideration the length of the marriage, her contribution to the welfare of the family by bringing up the only child and the fact that she was never expected to work. As demonstrated by *Legat v Ryder*[87] and *Barrass v Harding*,[88] separations for a substantial length of time may be a factor in refusing provision. In the latter case, the parties married in 1939 and were divorced in 1964. The husband remarried, but his second wife predeceased him, and by his last will he left his estate to his wife's sister. At first instance the applicant, who was 79 at the date of the hearing and in poor financial circumstances, was awarded £30,000 out of an estate of £200,000, but this was reversed by the Court of Appeal. In the absence of any rapprochement between the deceased and the applicant, or of any indication that he might provide for her in such circumstances, there was no basis for making any provision for her.

Cameron v Treasury Solicitor[89] is another former spouse case in which there was a long interval between the breakdown of the marriage and the death of the deceased ex-husband (R). There, the parties had been married for almost 15 years, and there were no children of the marriage. In the ancillary relief proceedings in 1981, a "clean break" order was made under which the wife (C) received £8,000, but there was no s.15 order. R died intestate in 1990 leaving net estate £7,677, which passed to the Crown as bona vacantia. C, who was aged 64 at the date of the hearing in the county court, was in poor health and difficult financial circumstances, and she was awarded the entire estate. On appeal that order was set aside. It was held that (1) the principles laid down by *Re Coventry*[90] were equally applicable to former spouse cases, and on applying them, C's poor health and difficult financial circumstances did not found a moral obligation, and (2) the fact that the estate would devolve on the Crown was neutral.

4-039

The last of this series of cases is *Parish v Sharman*.[91] There, the parties had been married for about 18 years before the marriage broke down. A decree nisi was pronounced but never made absolute, and the wife never made any application for ancillary relief. The husband began to cohabit with another person and left the bulk of his estate to her. He died 11 years later and the wife's claim failed at first instance. It did not appear, having regard to the extent of her own resources, that the will failed to make reasonable provision for her. The trial judge found that if the marriage had been terminated by divorce on the day of the husband's death, no capital provision would have been made for her; by never applying for ancillary relief the wife had lulled the husband into a false sense of security that their financial affairs had been settled once and for all. The Court of Appeal affirmed the decision

4-040

---

[87] *Legat v Ryder* unreported 2 May 1980, Ch.D. Dillon J considered that, in the circumstances which existed after the breakdown of the marriage, the deceased was not under any obligation to provide for the applicant by his will.

[88] *Barrass v Harding* [2001] 1 F.L.R. 138, CA.

[89] *Cameron v Treasury Solicitor* [1996] 2 F.L.R. 716, CA.

[90] *Re Coventry* [1980] Ch 461, CA. Those principles, and the adult child cases in which they were applied, are discussed at paras 4-041-4-045, below.

[91] *Parish v Sharman* [2001] W.T.L.R. 593, CA.

on that ground and also due to the unreliability of her evidence on a number of matters. It is unlikely that today the courts would follow the cases under the Inheritance (Family Provision) Act 1938 in which provision was awarded to a former spouse who had not remarried and there had been a long interval between the divorce (or, in the case of a still subsisting marriage between separated spouses, the time of the separation) and the former husband's death.[92]

4–041 The question whether the deceased owed any obligation to the applicant is a prominent feature in applications for provision by adult children, and the landmark decision under the 1975 Act is *Re Coventry*.[93] The starting point is, in general, that the existence of a blood relationship coupled with the precarious financial position of the applicant will be insufficient to justify the making of any provision, even though resources are available for the purpose.[94] This reasoning was adopted by the Court of Appeal in affirming the decision at first instance.

4–042 In the course of reviewing the facts of that case Oliver J observed that the plaintiff was not in any sense dependant on the deceased and continued[95]:

"An application under such circumstances would not have been possible at all before April 1, 1976, but the Act of 1975 now enables a child of the deceased to apply for provision, even though that child is male, of full age, and suffering from no disability. Nevertheless, applications under the Act of 1975 for maintenance by able-bodied and comparatively young men in employment and able to maintain themselves must be relatively rare and need to be approached, I should have thought, with a degree of circumspection."

At the close of his review of the facts he said[96]:

"Obviously the plaintiff's financial situation is such that any assistance which he can get in maintaining himself will be welcome and the more so because he now finds himself in a position in which he may be forced to leave the house which he occupied under the arrangement with his

---

[92] See, e.g., *Re Sanderson, The Times*, 2 November 1963. The parties were separated but not divorced. The applicant wife was successful, in spite of a separation of over 30 years, during all but the last two years of which the deceased had been making payments under a deed of separation. In *Re W, deceased* (1975) 119 S.J. 439, the parties were divorced and during the 29 years before the death of the deceased no maintenance was paid or applied for. The applicant wife was awarded £11,000 out of an estate of £28,000 in spite of the strong moral claims of the two beneficiaries.

[93] *Re Coventry* [1980] Ch. 461, CA. For the general principles, see Ch.6, s.8(d), "Adult children able to support themselves", paras 6–135–6–140 and s.8(f), "Unsuccessful claims", paras 6–192–6–195.

[94] *Re Coventry* [1980] Ch. 461, CA per Oliver J at 475C, quoted with approval by Goff LJ at 488A.

[95] *Re Coventry* [1980] Ch. 461, CA at 465F–G. He also referred, at 472H, to the fact that under the 1938 Act the only class of adult male who could apply for provision was a surviving husband and to the caution, as exemplified by *Re Sylvester* [1941] Ch. 87 and *Re Styler* [1942] Ch. 387, with which the court approached such applications.

[96] *Re Coventry* [1980] Ch. 461, CA, at 468.

father. But, I ask myself, is this the sort of case in which it was the intention of Parliament that the court should interfere to upset the dispositions which the deceased has made or the dispositions which, if he dies intestate, the legislature has made on his behalf?"

After considering a number of cases under the previous legislation[97] and the report of the Law Commission,[98] he reached the following conclusion,[99] which has given rise to so much judicial debate:

"[T]here must, as it seems to me, be established some moral claim by the applicant to be maintained by the deceased or at the expense of the estate beyond the mere fact of a blood relationship, some reason why it can be said that, in the circumstances, it was unreasonable that no, or no greater provision was made";

and he quoted, with approval, from the judgment of Buckley J[100] in *Re Ducksbury*, who had held in that case that the testator was under a moral obligation to make some provision for his daughter.

The appeal in *Re Coventry* rested on three main grounds, two of which **4–043** were concerned with "moral obligation". One was that Oliver J had made the existence of a moral obligation a pre-condition to the success of a 1975 Act application; the other, that he was wrong in finding that the deceased did not owe his son a moral obligation. Goff LJ, giving the leading judgment, emphatically rejected the argument that Oliver J had made the existence of a moral obligation a prerequisite to the success of the claim. The reference to a need for a moral obligation was confined to the facts of the particular case because, in the absence of a moral obligation there was no other circumstance which made it unreasonable for the deceased to have made no provision for the plaintiff.[101] He also accepted the reasoning which underlay the finding of fact that there was no moral obligation, citing[102] the passage which ended with the following:

"No doubt it could be thought that reasonable family affection might have prompted a father to make some provision for a son who, although earning an adequate living, was clearly not well-to-do; but there is no question of the plaintiff having given up work and disabled

[97] *Re Sylvester* [1941] Ch. 87; *Re Styler* [1942] Ch. 387 (noting the subsequent criticism directed at the subjective approach adopted in that case); *Re Ducksbury* [1966] 1 W.L.R. 1226.
[98] He considered *Wachtel v Wachtel* [1973] Fam. 72, CA, and *Black Clawson Ltd v Papierwerke-Waldhof-Aschaffenburg AG* [1975] A.C. 591 and held that those decisions rendered the Law Commission Report (Law Com. LC 61) admissible not as a direct aid to interpretation but as a means of identifying the mischief which subsequent legislation, passed as a result of the report, was intended to remedy.
[99] *Re Coventry* [1980] Ch. 461, CA, at 475G–H.
[100] Who had by then been elevated to the Court of Appeal and, together with Goff and Geoffrey Lane LJJ, upheld his judgment.
[101] *Re Coventry*, at 487H, citing Oliver J's judgment at 475C–D and 478B–D.
[102] *Re Coventry* at 489G–490A; the complete passage from Oliver J's judgment is at 476G–477D.

himself from earning an adequate living in order to devote himself to his father and I cannot see anything in the history of the relationship between them which could be said to impose any sort of moral duty on the father to provide for his son's maintenance, either during his lifetime or after his death."

4–044 The same principles were applied in *Williams v Johns*,[103] an application by an adult daughter for provision out of her mother's estate. Under the 1938 Act, an adult daughter who was not rendered incapable of maintaining herself due to mental or physical disability could apply only if she had not been married. The applicant would not have been eligible under the 1938 Act, as she was capable of earning her own living, had been independent of her mother for some years, and also had been married, though subsequently divorced. The judge, adopting the words of Oliver J in *Re Coventry*, quoted above, and also applying the test articulated in *Re Dennis*,[104] said:

"...it seems to me the cases say that, although she is unemployed and necessitous, that is not enough; she has to show something in the nature of an obligation. It has been called 'a moral obligation'; some reason why it would be reasonable for the testatrix, her mother, to make some provision for her, and she has put forward no affirmative reason here."

In *Re Jennings, Harlow v National Westminster Bank*,[105] Nourse LJ said:

"It was established by the decisions of Oliver J and this court in *Re Coventry* that, on an application by an adult son of the deceased who is able to earn, and earns his own living that there must be some special circumstance, typically a moral obligation of the deceased towards him before the first question[106] can be determined in his favour. Although the decisions were in terms confined to the case of a son, the principle of them is applicable no less to the case of a daughter and, with developments in the structure of society, instances of its application in such cases may become more common."

This was indeed prophetic, since *Re Hancock*[107] and *Espinosa v Bourke*,[108] which followed soon afterwards, were both successful claims by adult daughters in which the Court of Appeal made it clear that there was no

---

[103] *Williams v Johns* [1988] 2 F.L.R. 475.
[104] *Re Dennis* [1981] 2 All E.R. 140 at 145b–c, per Browne-Wilkinson J: "A son is in the same position as all other able-bodied applicants. A person who is physically capable of earning a living faces a difficult task in getting provision made, because the Court is inclined to ask 'Why should anybody else make provision for you if you are capable of maintaining yourself?'"
[105] *Re Jennings, Harlow v National Westminster Bank* [1994] Ch. 286, CA.
[106] That is, whether the dispositions on death were such as to make reasonable financial provision for the applicant.
[107] *Re Hancock* [1998] 2 F.L.R. 346, CA.
[108] *Espinosa v Bourke* [1999] 1 F.L.R. 747, CA, where an obligation arose from a promise made by the deceased to the claimant's mother.

general principle requiring the existence of a moral obligation or special circumstances as a prerequisite to the success of a claim by an adult child. In *Hancock*, all three judges rejected the argument that there was any such principle.[109] The trial judge had expressly found that there was no moral obligation owed to the applicant. The facts which weighed in her favour were that, by the time the matter came on for hearing, she was 69 years of age, had long retired and had no hope of improving her financial position, and that the estate out of which she was claiming provision had substantially increased in value between the deceased's death and the date of the hearing.

The case-law since *Re Coventry* was again extensively reviewed by Sir **4–045** Nicholas Wall P in *Ilott v Mitson*.[110] It is a testament to the uncertainty which continues to exist in this area of the law that he should have said at the very beginning of his review that *Re Coventry*:

> "...bears careful examination for what it says and, as importantly, for what it is believed to say, but does in fact not say";

and in reiterating that dictum shortly afterwards, adding that it was equally important, in his judgment "to resist the temptation to impose judicial glosses on the statute". The case which he found to be of greatest assistance was *Espinosa v Bourke*,[111] both for its analysis of s.3(1)(d)[112] and in relation to "maintenance", where the formulation in *Re Dennis*[113] was adopted. He also quoted, with approval, the observations of Aldous LJ in *Espinosa v Bourke* relating to the trial judge's failure to arrive at the correct value judgment and which included Oliver J's caution that the case:

> "...should not be approached upon a preconceived notion that there was a heavy burden on applicants of full age. In these days where persons without qualifications find it difficult to obtain employment, the court should not approach the question of what is the appropriate maintenance with any preconceived view."[114]

His judgment also contains a generally applicable warning about the dangers of over-analysis. In relation to the balancing exercise one of Eleanor King J's criticisms of the district judge was that:

---

[109] *Re Hancock*, per Butler-Sloss L.L. at 351F, Judge LJ at 355E, Sir John Knox at 357F–H, adding that: "Of course there has to be a reason justifying a court's conclusion that there has been a failure to make reasonable financial provision, but the use of the phrase 'special circumstances' does not advance the argument. The word 'special' means nothing more than what is necessary to overcome the factors in the opposite scale."

[110] *Ilott v Mitson* [2012] 2 F.L.R. 170, CA, at p.[16]–[35]. The dicta quoted at para.4–045 are at [16], [19].

[111] *Espinosa v Bourke* [1999] 1 F.L.R. 747, CA.

[112] Taken by Butler-Sloss LJ from her own judgment in *Re Hancock* [1998] 2 F.L.R. 346, CA.

[113] *Re Dennis* [1981] 2 All E.R. 140, at 145.

[114] *Ilott v Mitson*, at [36]. The passage quoted by Aldous LJ in *Espinosa v Bourke*, [60], is taken from *Re Coventry* at 474.

"...he erred in his balancing of the s.3 factors with the consequence that he was plainly wrong in concluding that the deceased had failed to make provision for his [sic] daughter."

Disagreeing with that criticism, Wall P said that the district judge was not required to carry out the balancing exercise *at that stage*[115] (that is, the stage at which he made the value judgment), but that, although he did not need to do it, that was what he did. He amplified this as follows:

"There is, moreover, plainly an overlap between the value judgment that the provision is unreasonable and the exercise of the discretion in making an award. I would not wish to be too prescriptive about which element falls into which stage. What matters is that the decision, taken as a whole, explains why the judge or the district judge has reached the conclusion he or she has."

The Supreme Court commented, in *Ilott v Mitson*,[116] that it had become conventional to treat the consideration of a 1975 Act claim as a two-stage process, and recognised that the first stage was best described as a value judgment and the second, an exercise of discretion. Nevertheless, in many cases there was a large degree of overlap between the two stages. There might be cases in which it would be convenient to separate the question whether reasonable provision had been made from the question whether and if so, to what extent, the court should exercise its discretion, but in many cases the same conclusions would answer both questions. There could be nothing wrong, in such cases, with the judge simply setting out the facts as they found them and addressing both questions arising under the Act without repeating them. Further, Goff LJ's observations[117] should not be taken to mean that there should be any difference in the approach of an appeal court as to the two parts of the process. In referring to the particularly apposite observations of Lord Hoffmann in *Piglowska v Piglowski*[118] on the role of the appellate court the Supreme Court said:

"It is to 'kill the parties with kindness' to permit marginal appeals in cases which are essentially individual value judgments such as those under the 1975 Act should be. The present case, as it happens, is an example of much to be regretted prolongation, and presumably expensive prolongation, of the forensic process."

[115] Emphasis as in the judgment, at [49].
[116] *Ilott v Mitson* [2017] UKSC 17, at [23]–[24].
[117] *Re Coventry* [1980] Ch. 461, CA at 486–87, quoting Oliver J's judgment at 469G in relation to the two-stage process and observing that in this case, the plaintiff had failed to get over the first hurdle; he had not satisfied the judge that reasonable provision had not been made for him.
[118] *Piglowska v Piglowski* [1999] 1 W.L.R. 1360, at 1373–74.

The basis on which the making of provision may be justified in any given **4–046** case is discussed in detail in Ch.6.[119] In summary, the matters which have persuaded the court that able-bodied and comparatively young claimants, able to maintain themselves, have made out an arguable case, arc:

(i) a promise by the deceased, to someone other than the claimant, that the claimant will benefit in some way on their death, in circumstances in which it would be unconscionable for them not to fulfil the promise; the nature of the promise in two important cases is summarised in the next paragraph;

(ii) where the claimant has acted to their own disadvantage or for the deceased's benefit, either without expectation of gaining any benefit by so doing, or due to encouragement by the deceased of a belief that they would benefit on the deceased's death[120];

(iii) an obligation of the deceased to maintain the claimant, which was subsisting at the time of his death. One situation of this nature occurred in *Hocking v Hocking*,[121] where the daughters of the deceased by his first marriage, aged 22 and 18 at the time of his death, had both embarked on further education or training. The deceased had remarried and on his death intestate in 1994 his entire estate of £107,850 passed to his second wife. The daughters were awarded £4,000 and £8,000 respectively, the larger award to the younger daughter reflecting the fact that she would require support for a longer period.

The two important cases referred to in the previous paragraph are *Re* **4–047** *Goodchild*[122] and *Espinosa v Bourke*.[123] In *Goodchild*, where the parties to a marriage had made simultaneous wills in similar form, in favour of the claimant, it was found that the wills were not mutual wills but that the wife (J) had made her will on the understanding that her husband (D) would give effect to what she believed were their shared intentions. After J's death, D remarried and made a new will in favour of his second wife. It was held at first instance that the circumstances in which D and J made their wills gave rise to a moral obligation on D, and the claimant was eventually awarded £185,000 out of an estate of £450,000. On appeal, the judgment was described as not only sensible, but unimpeachable.[124] Whereas in *Goodchild* there was no agreement between the parties as to the dispositions made by their wills, in *Espinosa v Bourke* the testator had made a promise to the

---

[119] Ch.6, s.8(e)(i), "Successful Claims-classes of case", paras 6–141–6–159.
[120] Those cases are discussed in subs.6(a) of this chapter under the heading "Conduct of the claimant".
[121] *Hocking v Hocking* unreported 12 July 1997, Court of Appeal. The award was made at first instance and the appeal by the daughters for an increased award was dismissed.
[122] *Re Goodchild* [1997] 1 W.L.R. 1216, CA, affirming [1996] 1 W.L.R. 664. The claimant was 51 at the date of the hearing.
[123] *Espinosa v Bourke* [1999] 1 F.L.R. 747, CA, reversing the judgment at first instance. The claimant was 55 at the date of the hearing.
[124] *Re Goodchild* [1997] 1 W.L.R. 1216, CA, per Leggatt LJ at 1229.

claimant's mother that if she did not change the will which she had made in his favour, he would see that her estate, which included an interest in a portfolio of shares, would be left to the claimant in his will. In the event, he made a will leaving his estate of about £196,000 to his grandson. The promise was held to have created a moral obligation which had not (contrary to the decision at first instance) been discharged by the claimant's conduct towards the deceased. She was awarded £60,000, to clear her accumulated indebtedness and provide a small amount for immediate needs.

(c) Competing Obligations

4–048 In this type of case, the balancing of financial circumstances and the comparison of obligations are usually interlinked to a degree which makes it difficult to identify either matter as being decisive. However, competition between applicants who can establish some obligation and beneficiaries who would take on intestacy is often resolved in favour of the former. In both *Re Callaghan*[125] and *Re Leach*,[126] the applicant was a middle-aged person who had been treated as a child of the family, and in both cases the applicant succeeded at the expense of the siblings of the testator who would have taken on intestacy.

4–049   Infant children and those who are responsible for their upbringing are generally considered to have strong claims in comparison with other persons. In the unreported case of *Re Cohen*,[127] the infant son of the testator's mistress benefited at the expense of his widow; the 1938 Act case of *Re Bateman*,[128] where the competition was between the infant daughter and the widow, had a similar outcome. In *Dixit v Dixit*[129] the court acknowledged the existence of a moral obligation towards the four adult children of the testator's first marriage, but considered the obligation towards the widow and two infant children of the second marriage to be the most important. Again, in *Re J (A minor)*,[130] the widow of the testator's second marriage, who had a child aged five, was considered to have a far stronger claim than the 16-year-old daughter of his first marriage. In the Northern Ireland case of *Re Patton*,[131] the claims of the deceased's illegitimate twin children were judged to have priority over those of any of the beneficiaries under the will, viz., their mother (for whom some other provision had been made) and six nephews and nieces.

---

[125] *Re Callaghan* [1985] Fam. 1.
[126] *Re Leach* [1986] Ch. 226.
[127] *Re Cohen* unreported 23 February 1979, John Mills QC. This was a 1938 Act case and was summarised in the first two editions (1993 and 2000) of this work; see also *Tyler,* pp.201, 208.
[128] *Re Bateman* (1941) 85 S.J. 454.
[129] *Dixit v Dixit* unreported 23 June 1988, CA.
[130] *Re J (A Minor)* unreported 12 December 1991, CA.
[131] *Re Patton, McElween v Patton* [1986] N.I. 45.

5.—MENTAL OR PHYSICAL DISABILITY

Under the 1938 Act the existence of such disability determined whether an   **4–050**
adult son, or a daughter who had been married, was a dependant as defined
by s.1(1). As the scope of the 1975 Act extends to all children of the
deceased, mental or physical disability is not a qualification, but simply one
of the many matters to which the court must have regard in determining
whether, and in what manner, to exercise its powers under the Act.

Although most of the material relating to the 1938 Act cases which   **4–051**
appeared in earlier editions has been omitted, some of them are discussed
since they may still provide some useful guidance. In *Re Watkins*[132] the
applicant, a daughter who had been previously married and had been an
inmate of a private mental hospital, failed in her application. The testator
was held to be entitled to distribute his estate in accordance with his previously announced intention to make no further contribution to her upkeep
once the National Health Service Act 1946 had come into operation. In *Re
Pringle*[133] the applicant, who was 43 years old and an inmate of a mental
hospital, was the only son of the testatrix. She left her entire estate to two
friends as her son was being maintained by the state. It was held that, as he
had some ability to enjoy "comforts", and it was well known that state
hospitals were somewhat lacking in the smaller pleasures of life, a small
periodical payment for their provision was appropriate.

In *Re Andrews*,[134] the applicant was the 69-year-old daughter of the tes-   **4–052**
tator; she had left home when aged 25 and subsequently had six children by
a man to whom she was not married, and who, in fact, was married to
someone else. She was, by reason of physical disability, incapable of
maintaining herself. She thus qualified under the 1938 Act both as an
unmarried daughter and as a disabled person, but her application failed, it
being held that, from the time when she left home to live permanently with a
married man, her father had no moral obligation to maintain her. It was
held in that case that she could not be successful on either of those two
grounds:

"...unless it is demonstrated that in all the circumstances the testator
was under some moral obligation to her with the result that, by
excluding her from his will, as he did in this case, that he has failed to
make reasonable provision for her maintenance."

However, as *Re Hancock*[135] makes plain, the absence of a moral obligation is
not fatal to a claim by a person who is unable, by reason of age or infirmity,
to maintain themselves.

In *Millward v Shenton*[136] the testatrix left her entire estate to charity in   **4–053**

---

[132] *Re Watkins* [1949] 1 All E.R. 695.
[133] *Re Pringle, The Times*, 2 February 1956; [1956] C.L.Y. 9248.
[134] *Re Andrews* [1955] 1 W.L.R. 1105.
[135] *Re Hancock* [1998] 2 F.L.R. 346, CA.
[136] *Millward v Shenton* [1972] 2 All E.R. 1025, CA.

order to prevent her six children from quarrelling over it. The applicant was her 52-year-old son who suffered from muscular dystrophy and had been unable to do anything for himself for the previous six years. This case is of particular interest in that it marks a change in judicial approach to the determination of the question whether reasonable provision had been made. Up until 1969, it was generally thought that the test was whether the testator had acted reasonably; but after Megarry J had held in *Re Goodwin*[137] that the test was whether the provision made was objectively reasonable, that interpretation gradually gained acceptance. While Lord Denning MR embraced this formulation with enthusiasm, his fellow appellate judges were more non-committal.[138] Both Megaw and Stamp LJJ were content to rest their agreement in the result on the plain facts of the case which showed that reasonable provision had not been made. The appeal from the County Court judge was allowed and the applicant was awarded eleven-twelfths of the estate after provision for administration costs and the costs below.

4–054   In cases under the 1938 Act, advancing age was not, of itself, viewed as a disability, though, when combined with a disability not requiring confinement in a hospital or mental institution, it often attracted the sympathy of the court. The oldest applicant reported to have been successful[139] was aged 91 at the time of hearing, though in holding that a legacy to him of £100 out of an estate of £6,000 was manifestly unreasonable, Buckley J did not place any emphasis on his age. He was awarded £4 per week until death or remarriage, "the latter provision being necessary as a matter of form, however unlikely the contingency".

4–055   There are several 1975 Act cases in which physical or mental disability has been an important factor in the outcome. Where the claimant is unable, or finds it difficult, to maintain themselves due to age, illness or disability, that, without more, may be considered as justifying the making of provision even though, as was found at first instance in *Re Hancock*[140] there was no subsisting obligation to make provision for the applicant daughter at the date of the testator's death. Thus, the fact that the 52-year-old applicant in *Re Debenham*[141] was severely disabled by epilepsy was crucial to the decision of

---

[137] *Re Goodwin* [1969] Ch. 283 at 287; approved by Winn LJ in *Re Gregory, Gregory v Goodenough* [1970] 1 W.L.R. 1455, CA.

[138] To Megaw LJ "whatever may be the true view of certain perhaps sometimes subtle matters of construction which have been debated before us, there can be no doubt" that reasonable provision had not been made. Stamp LJ was quite satisfied that that was so, "whether you apply the objective or the subjective test" as to which he did not think it necessary to express an opinion.

[139] *Re Wilson, Wilson v Powell* (1969) 113 S.J. 794. The oldest successful female applicant so far is the wife in *Re Rowlands* (1984) F.L.R. 813, who was 90 at the date of the hearing.

[140] *Re Hancock* [1999] 2 F.L.R. 346, CA. The applicant was 58 at the date of her father's death, but 69 when her claim was heard. The trial judge found that during that period, her needs had increased and her prospects had become worse. Owing to a massive increase in the value of the estate in that period, resources became available out of which provision could be made for her.

[141] *Re Debenham* [1986] 1 F.L.R. 404.

Ewbank J to award her provision out of her mother's estate. In *Gold v Curtis*[142] the fact that the applicant suffered from a severe depressive condition was material to the success of his claim. In *Swetenham v Walkley*,[143] a successful claim by a cohabitant, the claimant (S) was not financially dependent on the deceased; he had never given her any money and had frequently stayed at her house, where he had his own bedroom and kept his clothes and she did his washing and ironing. S, who was 80 years of age, had a genuine claim for financial support from the estate. In the light of her "multi-difficulties" and the definition of "disability" given in s.1 of the Disability Discrimination Act 1995,[144] she was a person who could properly be described as physically disabled. The support she required consisted of funding for an appropriate health care plan and a capital cushion of £3,500 per year over the nine-and-a-half year period of her actuarial life expectancy; taking her own available resources into account, the total provision required amounted to £201,219, which was approximately one-third of the net estate. In contrast, the mere fact of independence from the deceased, even where the applicant suffers from a disability, may be a reason for denying a claim; thus, in *Rowlands v Rowlands*,[145] the claim by the younger adult daughter, who had been independent of the deceased for many years, was living on supplementary benefit and was an epileptic, but found not to be severely disabled by that condition, was unsuccessful. It was also held in that case that, while the voluntary acceptance of a low standard of living would not negate the making of an award if the will did not make reasonable provision,[146] the duration of the separation and the estrangement would operate to diminish, substantially, the provision ordered.

The cases under the 1975 Act generally view the age of the claimant as an indication of future earning capacity[147] and, perhaps surprisingly in view of increasing life expectancy, show a tendency to place the cessation of a claimant's significant earning capacity at an increasingly lower age. As an

4–056

---

[142] *Gold v Curtis* [2005] W.T.L.R. 673, a case where there had been a fractious relationship between the testatrix and her son, the claimant; both were argumentative and all attempts at reconciliation had failed. The summary of principles at [36] provides a useful basic guide and is noteworthy for principle 8, which states that: "The Act is not intended to be a charter for spendthrifts or wastrels, but nowhere in the Act or in authority is there any suggestion that lack of filial piety is necessarily an overwhelming consideration for the court."

[143] *Swetenham v Walkley* [2014] W.T.L.R. 845

[144] For the purposes of the Disability Discrimination Act 1995, a person was defined by s.1(1) as having a disability if he had a physical or mental impairment which had a substantial or long-term adverse effect on his ability to carry out normal day-to-day activities. That Act was repealed by the Equality Act 2010 Sch.27 with effect from 5 April 2011.

[145] *Rowlands v Rowlands* [1984] F.L.R. 813.

[146] As demonstrated by *Re Borthwick (No.2)* [1949] Ch. 395.

[147] There was no specific provision in the 1938 Act which required the court to have regard to earning capacity; s.1(6) provided that the court should have regard to "any past, present or future capital or income from any source of the dependant to whom the application relates". In *Talbot v Talbot* [1962] 3 All E.R. 174, the reasons for holding that the second wife's needs outweighed the claim of the applicant (a former spouse who had not remarried, such persons being entitled to apply under s.3 of the Matrimonial Causes and Property Act 1958) included the fact that the second wife had no earning capacity due to anaemia and asthma.

illustration, the award to the 38-year-old claimant in *Malone v Harrison*,[148] who had not worked for the previous 12 years, was calculated on the basis that she would be able to find a job and work until she was 60, whereas in *Negus v Bahouse*[149] the trial judge considered it unjust to assume that the 50-year-old claimant, who had not worked for 8 to 10 years, would find employment at her age and with such experience as she had.

4-057   In *Hanbury v Hanbury*[150] the applicant, who was the 45-year-old daughter of the deceased by his first marriage, had been born prematurely and was both physically and mentally disabled. Her mental age was 12, but her physical disabilities were not such as to decrease her actuarial life expectancy, which was 35.56 years. At the time of the hearing she was being cared for by her mother, who was 71 with a life expectancy of 13.8 years, and it was therefore estimated that she would need institutional care for 22 years after her mother's death and anticipated that such a need might arise sooner. The court concluded that provision for a placement in a private residential home would be appropriate, that the local authority would fund it and that it would not be right to determine the provision at a level which would fully meet the cost of that accommodation. The need for maintenance was considered in relation to three periods, which were:

(1) while she was living at home with her mother, which would require provision of a car;
(2) while she was in residential care during her mother's lifetime; and
(3) while she was in care after her mother's death.

Having regard to the legacy of £10,000 which she would receive under the deceased's will, and assuming that she stood to inherit a share of her mother's estate amounting to £12,000, it was ordered that £39,000 be settled on her on discretionary trusts.

4-058   More recent cases have shown that substantial disabilities will not necessarily be sufficient to secure a favourable outcome for the claimant. Thus in *Christofides v Seddon*,[151] where the claimant's mother (M) had left her residuary estate to the claimant, his two sisters and the daughter of one of the sisters in equal shares, the claimant, who was 53 at the date of the hearing and needed 24-hour care, as he suffered from serious health problems including diabetes, chronic kidney disease, high blood pressure and bronchial asthma; his medical records described him as morbidly obese. He had been living in M's house but wished to purchase accommodation for himself that would be smaller and easier to manage. All three of the other beneficiaries were in financial difficulty. It was held that M had discharged her obligations and responsibilities to her adult children by giving them each an equal share and that, although she knew that the claimant was unwell, she plainly did not regard the provision of accommodation for him as her

148 *Malone v Harrison* [1979] 1 W.L.R. 1353.
149 *Negus v Bahouse* [2008] 1 F.L.R. 381.
150 *Hanbury v Hanbury* [1999] 2 F.L.R. 255.
151 *Christofides v Seddon* [2014] W.T.L.R. 215.

obligation or responsibility. While the test of whether reasonable provision had been made was an objective test, the deceased's wishes should count for quite a lot where there was a modest estate. In *McIntosh v McIntosh*,[152] a claim under s.1(1)(e), the claimant suffered from a major, but treatable, depressive disorder, but had never undergone treatment for it. His claim failed as it was found that the sums of money which he received from the deceased from time to time were not contributions towards his reasonable needs,[153] nor had he satisfied the court that the deceased had assumed any responsibility for his maintenance or that there was a relationship of dependence accepted by him and the deceased.[154] The case of *Wright v Waters*,[155] in which the serious disabilities from which the claimant suffered were outweighed by her conduct towards the deceased, is discussed in the next part of this chapter.

6.—OTHER MATTERS, INCLUDING CONDUCT

Under both the present Act and its predecessor,[156] the courts have taken account of the conduct of the applicant towards the deceased and, less frequently, of the deceased towards the applicant. Section 3(1)(g) of the 1975 Act directs the court to have regard to:

4-059

> "...any other matter, including the conduct of the applicant or any other person, which in the circumstances of the case the court might consider relevant."

Two areas of what could, in ordinary language, be described as conduct, are the subject of more specific provisions. An obligation or responsibility of the deceased towards any applicant or beneficiary which arose from conduct would be considered under s.3(1)(d); a distinction between such matters and conduct in a more general sense was drawn by Butler-Sloss LJ in *Espinosa v Bourke*.[157] The other area is the contribution of the applicant to the welfare of the family of the deceased, including any contribution made by looking after the home or caring for the family.[158] The provisions directing the court to have regard to that matter are expressed to apply without prejudice to the generality of s.3(1)(g) and are contained in s.3(2), which relates to applications by surviving spouses, surviving civil partners and in s.3(2A) where the applicant is a cohabitant.

---

[152] *McIntosh v McIntosh* [2013] W.T.L.R. 1565.
[153] He spent the money on drinking, smoking, petrol and socialising.
[154] Applying *Baynes v Hedger* [2008] 2 F.L.R. 1805.
[155] *Wright v Waters* [2015] W.T.L.R. 353.
[156] Inheritance (Family Provision) Act 1938 s.1(6), as amended, directed the court to have regard to "the conduct of the applicant in relation to the deceased and otherwise...".
[157] *Espinosa v Bourke* [1999] 1 F.L.R. 747, CA, at 755.
[158] Under the 1938 Act there was no specific requirement to consider such matters, and *Re Sylvester* [1941] Ch. 87, discussed at para.4–062 below, is the only reported case in which it was a significant factor.

4–060　It is frequently the case that matters of conduct are powerful factors in a decision to bring, or to contest, 1975 Act claims. It is important not to overestimate the significance of conduct, because the weight that a court might afford to such matters is difficult to predict. That unpredictability can lead to serious costs consequences, as it is hard to gauge whether the likely cost of raising the issue will be proportionate, which may result in costs being disallowed even if the party raising the issue has been successful.[159] Even more seriously, a party making allegations of bad conduct which are not substantiated at trial may, as was the case in *Wooldridge v Wooldridge*,[160] be ordered to pay the costs of the parties against whom they were made on the indemnity basis. Further, there are relatively few reported cases in which conduct has substantially affected the outcome. Issues of conduct played a significant part in less than five per cent of the cases summarised in Appendix 6 and, of those, there is only one where conduct has outweighed all the other factors in the claimant's favour, so that an otherwise viable claim has failed,[161] and only one in which a claim succeeded because of matters favourable to the claimant which outweighed very serious misconduct on their part.[162] Conduct may, of course, conduce to either a favourable or an unfavourable outcome for the claimant, and the discussion of conduct of the claimant which follows is organised accordingly.

(a) Conduct of the Claimant

(i) Conduct actually or potentially favourable to the outcome for the claimant

4–061　Although judges have from time to time made laudatory comments on the conduct of persons who have applied successfully, for instance the comment in the 1938 Act case of *Millward v Shenton* that "the relationship between the [applicant] son and the mother had been a normal affectionate one" and the dictum of Oliver J in *Re Besterman*[163] that:

---

[159] In his judgment on costs in *Lilleyman v Lilleyman* [2013] 1 F.L.R. 69, Briggs J expressed his disapproval of the "no holds barred" approach to the conduct of the case by both parties and considered disallowing some part of both parties' costs. He found that the defendants were initially responsible for the introduction of irrelevant matters of personal criticism, to which the claimant responded (but which were not persisted in at the trial) and, in the result, disallowed 20 per cent of the costs to which the defendants were entitled by reason of the successful claimant having failed to beat the defendants' Pt 36 offer.

[160] *Wooldridge v Wooldridge* [2016] 3 Costs L.O. 531. The official transcript of the substantive judgment is available on Westlaw. It is one of the very few 1975 Act cases in which a claim by a surviving spouse has been dismissed.

[161] *Wright v Waters* [2015] W.T.L.R. 353 which involved financial abuse by the claimant and rejection by her of the relationship with her mother; see para.4–080.

[162] *Land v Land's Estate* [2007] 1 W.L.R. 1009, where the claimant was convicted of causing his mother's death, apparently by gross negligence manslaughter.

[163] *Re Besterman* [1984] Ch. 458. More recently, see *Adams v Lewis* [2001] W.T.L.R. 493, where the claimant was eulogised as a good wife for over 50 years and a good mother to her children; cf. *Re Morris, The Times*, 4 April 1967 where, in dismissing the application, the court took into account that the applicant had not been a good and loving wife. In *Cunliffe v Fielden* [2006] Ch. 361, CA, Wall LJ said at para.77 that *Re Besterman* remained authority for the proposition that the blameless widow of a wealthy man is entitled to look forward to financial security throughout her remaining lifetime and that reasonable financial provision, which was not limited to maintenance, must be viewed accordingly.

"...the wholly blameless widow of a wealthy man is entitled to look forward to financial security for the whole of her lifetime",

a passage quoted with approval by Wall P.in *Cunliffe v Fielden*.[164] Nevertheless it should be borne in mind that, as Oliver J said in *Re Coventry*[165] when emphasising freedom of testamentary disposition, "it is not the purpose of the [1975] Act to provide legacies or rewards for meritorious conduct".[166] Therefore, while virtuous conduct towards the deceased may favour the claimant, it by no means guarantees the success of a claim. In *Ilott v Mitson*, the Supreme Court, commenting on the significance of the long estrangement between mother and daughter and their respective responsibilities for it, expanded on Oliver J's dictum by warning that care must be taken to avoid making awards under the 1975 Act primarily rewards for good behaviour on the part of the claimant or penalties for bad behaviour on the part of the deceased.

In applications by surviving or former spouses, under the 1938 Act, there **4–062** were no specific provisions such as subss.3(2) and 3(2A) of the 1975 Act requiring the court to have regard to the applicant's contribution to the welfare of the family of the deceased, including looking after the home or caring for the family. The applicant spouse's domestic virtues or lack of them were sometimes taken into account, but assistance in the conduct of the deceased's business was also considered.[167] An unusual surviving spouse case under the 1938 Act was *Re Sylvester*,[168] where the applicant husband gave up his employment at the wife's request, and thereafter did the housework and looked after her when she was ill. However, the fact that the applicant has performed domestic duties for the deceased is not, without more, a factor in their favour; in *Re Styler*,[169] as in *Re Sylvester*, the applicant husband gave up work at his wife's request so that he could be at home constantly, but his application was dismissed on the grounds that he had a sufficient income to keep himself, and his wife's estate, which was small, had been substantially derived from her previous husband. In other cases, there has been a correlative benefit to the applicant for providing the domestic services[170] or an obligation to perform them.[171]

---

[164] *Cunliffe v Fielden* [2006] Ch. 361, CA.
[165] *Re Coventry* [1980] Ch. 461, CA at 474G.
[166] This dictum was acknowledged as a correct statement of the law in *Re Abram* [1996] 2 F.L.R. 379.
[167] *Re Lawes*, [1946] 90 S.J. 200; cf. *Re Brownbridge* [1942] 193 L.T.J 185, where the assistance rendered in the testator's business by the beneficiary of his will was a factor in the dismissal of the applicant spouse's claim.
[168] *Re Sylvester* [1941] Ch. 87.
[169] *Re Styler* [1942] Ch. 38
[170] *Re Coventry* [1980] Ch. 461, CA at 467, 476 (claimant living in the deceased's house rent-free, looking after the deceased and contributing to the cost of food and outgoings).
[171] *Re Rowlands* [1984] F.L.R. 813, CA (testator owed some small moral obligation to his wife in view of her age and infirmity and contribution to the welfare of the family, despite the long separation); *Espinosa v Bourke* [1999] 1 F.L.R. 747, CA (claimant had an obligation to care for the deceased, employing resources provided by him, which she did not fulfill).

4–063   In *Re Coventry*,[172] in the course of analysing the facts of the case, Oliver J said, in relation to the domestic arrangements, that there was:

> "...no question of the plaintiff having given up work and disabled himself from earning a living in order to devote himself to his father",

which suggests that, had he done so, his application might have been viewed in a more favourable light. Care given to a parent has contributed to a favourable outcome even where claimants have not disabled themselves from earning a living in consequence but have added the burden of care to other domestic responsibilities. Thus in the Northern Ireland case (in which jurisdiction the relevant legislation[173] is modelled on and is very substantially identical with the 1975 Act) of *Re McGarrell*,[174] a married daughter was held to have established a moral claim for provision out of her father's estate, particularly by caring for him during the last year of his life, when he came to live in her house, thus adding substantially to her domestic responsibilities which included the upbringing of her four adolescent children. Another successful Northern Ireland case of a similar nature is *McGuigan v McGuigan*[175] where both her work on the family farm and her care for the deceased was taken into account in evaluating the contribution of the applicant widow to the welfare of the family.

4–064   Helping in the family business for little or no reward was taken into account in favour of the claimant in *Re Abram*,[176] where the claimant (A), who was the 52-year-old son of the deceased, had worked in the family business for 17 years in the expectation that he would inherit it, but left as a result of the way in which his mother had treated him. She then made a will disinheriting him but did not make a new will after the subsequent reconciliation. Both the family business and A's business failed; A later entered into an individual voluntary arrangement, his total indebtedness being £200,000. His claim succeeded as a result of those special circumstances and provision was made for him by way of a settlement of half the estate on protective trusts. There are also four Northern Ireland cases involving long periods of work in family businesses; in three of these[177] the business was a farm and in one, a shoe business.[178]

---

[172]   *Re Coventry* [1980] Ch. 461, at 477.
[173]   Inheritance (Provision for Family and Dependants) (Northern Ireland) Order 1979.
[174]   *Re McGarrell* [1983] N.I.J.B. 8.
[175]   *McGuigan v McGuigan* [1996] N.I.J.B. 47.
[176]   *Re Abram* [1996] 2 F.L.R. 379.
[177]   *Re Campbell* [1983] N.I. 10 (son, 53, working on the family farm since age of 15); *McGuigan v McGuigan* [1996] N.I.J.B. 47 (surviving spouse, aged 81, married for 65 years, working on family farm as well as providing care for the deceased); similarly, *Morrow v Morrow* [1995] N.I.J.B. 47 (surviving spouse aged 75, married for 52 years).
[178]   *Re Creeney* [1984] N.I. 10 (son, aged 57, working in the family shoe business for low pay in expectation of succeeding to it, but leaving after a falling out. Unlike *Re Abram,* there was no subsequent reconciliation; father made will leaving entire estate to daughter).

(ii) Conduct actually or potentially damaging to the outcome for the claimant

The majority of the reported cases in which conduct has significantly **4–065** affected the outcome, or has had potential to do so, are of this type, though in some of those cases there are countervailing factors sufficient to persuade the court to make some provision for the claimant. There is a very wide spectrum of such conduct which may for the purpose of exposition be divided into three broad categories,[179] though in any given case where conduct is in issue, there may be instances of conduct falling within more than one category. At the least damaging end of the spectrum there is relatively passive conduct such as indifference to the deceased's welfare, or estrangement due to cessation of contact either over a period of time, so that the relationship becomes attenuated to the point of non-existence, or by a single act resulting in a clean break. Another type of passive conduct, seen in surviving spouse cases, is acquiescence in a deceased husband's failure to discharge his duty to maintain his wife adequately or at all. A second category includes conduct which is not specifically directed at the deceased but may be persisted in, even in the knowledge that it will excite their disapproval, such as the adoption of a particular way of life or general mode of behaviour. Improvident behaviour may be either a factor in such conduct or may, without more, be damaging to the claimant. At the extreme limit of the spectrum there is conduct actively directed at the deceased. This category includes financially abusive conduct designed to secure an advantage for the claimant at the deceased's expense, verbally or physically abusive conduct, whether or not it is intended to disrupt or terminate the relationship, and extreme neglect of the deceased.

(1) Passive conduct

The underlying feature common to such cases is that the claimant has, by **4–066** words or conduct or both, abandoned the relationship or acquiesced in its abandonment and not thereafter made any claim for support during the lifetime of the other party to it, whether on the basis of a legal or moral obligation or otherwise, for a substantial period before the death of that other party. Two applications under the 1938 Act by surviving spouses, in which there were such circumstances, are *Re Borthwick*[180] and *Re Gregory*.[181] In *Borthwick*, the testator left the major asset of his estate of £130,000 to his executors, a legacy to the woman with whom he had been living, his residuary estate to charities to be selected by the executors, and left his wife, from whom he had lived apart for many years and to whom he had never given more than £3 per week during that period, an annuity of £250. He also left £1,000 on trust for his second daughter and her issue. Both the wife and the daughter applied for provision and the individuals interested under the

---

[179] One might visualise these three categories, in relation to the spectrum as blue (passive), green (active but not directed at the deceased) and red (actively directed at the deceased).
[180] *Re Borthwick, Borthwick v Beauvais (No.2)* [1949] Ch. 395.
[181] *Re Gregory, Gregory v Goodenough* [1970] 1 W.L.R. 1455, CA.

will supported their applications. The only opposition came from counsel instructed on behalf of the Attorney General. Harman J said:

> "It is said here on behalf of the Crown, who are here as protectors of the charities who take residue ... that ... [the wife] did manage to live for 20 years or so on this miserable pittance of £3 per week. She never complained about it, and therefore £250 per year, which is more than that, is a reasonable provision for the testator to have made by his will. In other words it is said that the worse a man treats his wife during his lifetime, the less he need leave her when he is dead. I cannot accept such a cynical conclusion."

He increased the provision for the wife to £1,000 per year and for the daughter to £100 per year while her mother was alive and she remained unmarried.

4-067   In *Gregory*, the testator (H) and the applicant (R) married in 1916. There was one child of the marriage, a daughter born in 1926. That year, the testator left the applicant to live with another woman (M). He did not pay the applicant any maintenance after 1927, nor did she ask for any; she supported herself, her daughter and her mother by her own efforts. There was no contact between them for 20 years thereafter, when H offered her some money which she declined to accept while he was living with M. After M's death he asked R to return to him, but she refused. She went to Chile to visit their daughter and H engaged a housekeeper. After a brief visit to England she returned to Chile to live with the daughter and remained there permanently. H made a series of wills under which R would have benefited and there was correspondence between them, but her responses were not to his liking. When making his last will in 1966 he told the draftsman that she had lost interest in him and he was leaving her nothing. His estate of £2,500 went to members of his family and friends. The trial judge dismissed R's application and the Court of Appeal affirmed his decision, holding that (notwithstanding H's responsibility for the breakdown of the marriage)[182] he had no responsibility or obligation towards R, and that the trial judge had exercised his discretion correctly. In relation to the passage from Winn LJ's judgment set out in n.182, it is worth noting that s.1(6) of the 1938 Act directed the court to have regard to:

> "...the conduct of the dependant towards the deceased and otherwise and to any other matter or thing which in the circumstances of the case

---

[182] *Re Gregory*, at 1462, per Winn LJ. Having acknowledged that R was guiltless in relation to the breakdown of the marriage, he continued: "On the other hand, her conduct towards him provided him with no comfort, no assistance, no company, from 1926 onwards. It may be that that was entirely his fault, but that is not the relevant question. The court is directed to have regard to the conduct of the applicant towards the deceased, not whether the fault, as between the two of them rested with the one or the other. It is whether, when he died, he owed her any and if so what degree of obligation for what she had done for him as wife, *qua* wife, and in the present case that must be answered that, albeit it was his fault, she had done nothing for him for 40 years and he had derived nothing from her."

the court may consider relevant or material in relation to that dependant...",

so there was nothing to prevent him from considering H's conduct had he thought it relevant. The 1975 Act is more explicit, since s.3(1)(g) directs the court to have regard to:

"...any other matter, including the conduct of the applicant or any other person, which in the circumstances of the case the court may consider relevant."

It is submitted that, were a case comparable to *Re Gregory* to occur nowadays, the court would certainly take into account where the responsibility for the breakdown of the marriage lay and would attach to that fact such weight as was appropriate, rather than regarding it as irrelevant.

In *Re Rowlands*,[183] an application by a widow (M) and two adult   **4–068**
daughters (W and E), the testator, who was survived by four of the five children of the marriage, died in 1981. His net estate, valued at approximately £96,000, was mainly represented by his interest in the farmland near Welshpool which he held jointly with the widow of another son who had died in 1962 and which was worked partly by them and partly by one of his sons. His will made no provision for M; he gave legacies of £1,000 to each of the children and residue to his two sons. He had married M in 1919 and they separated in 1938; M went to live and work in Hampshire. She returned in the early 1950s and thereafter lived in one of the two cottages on the farm together with W and her husband and disabled son. By then she was subject to asthma attacks and could not work. The trial judge described the marital relationship as follows:

"...the relationship between the testator and his wife had grown completely cold. Geographically they were close to each other but there was little else to suggest that they felt anything other than a degree of friendliness. There was no apparent animosity between them but there was certainly no love and no relationship at all during this long period of separation."

The cottage, which was rented to the household at £13 per year, provided an appallingly low standard of accommodation but, as the judge observed:

"...neither the occupants themselves nor the testator nor the son seemed seem to have been in the least enthusiastic about doing anything about the standard of the accommodation."

[183] *Re Rowlands* [1984] 5 F.L.R. 813, CA. The quoted passage is from the judgment of Anthony Lincoln J at 816 C–D.

He concluded his judgment in relation to the s.3(1) factors as follows[184]:

> "Finally, as to her conduct and all the other circumstances of this case.
> In my view, while the voluntary acceptance of a low standard of living
> of an applicant should not deprive her of a reasonable provision, if it is
> considered that there is no reasonable provision in the will, the duration
> of the separation and the estrangement must diminish the figure which
> would otherwise be awarded and must diminish it, in my judgment,
> substantially."

The applications by the two adult daughters were dismissed. In W's case,
having regard to the low rent paid for the accommodation, the absence of
any relationship with her father and her household's resources, she had
failed to show that the will did not make reasonable provision for her. E's
claim was dismissed as wholly without merit. The circumstances of her case
somewhat resembled those in the 1938 Act case of *Re Andrews*,[185] which was
referred to in the judgment. She had left home, been married and divorced,
and was living with another man, over whose status in her household there
was, in the judge's words, a justifiable question mark. She was epileptic but
not severely disabled by the condition; her income derived entirely from
supplementary benefits and she did not need any more money.

(2) Conduct not directed at the deceased

4–069 Improvident conduct by the claimant would normally fall into this category,
and where it has been relevant, it is not because the deceased disapproved of
it but because the court has concluded that had resources been used more
prudently, the claimant would not be in financial difficulty, and that the
dispositions on the death of the deceased, even if the claimant does not
benefit at all from them, do not fail to make reasonable provision. Thus in
Rhodes v Dean,[186] the testator (D) died in 1989, by which time he had been
living with the applicant (R) for about four years. By his will, made in 1986,
he had divided his estate between members of his family; R received nothing. She was substantially dependent on D before his death, enjoying a high
standard of living; at the time of his death, she had capital of £35,869 in a

---

[184] *Re Rowlands*, at 819A.
[185] *Re Andrews* [1955] 1 W.L.R. 1105; [1955] 3 All E.R. 248 (this citation is incorrectly given in
the report of *Re Rowlands*, at 820B, as [1953] 3 All E.R. 248). In *Andrews*, the applicant, the
unmarried daughter of the deceased, had left home in 1911 to live with a married man (P) by
whom she had six children. At the date of the hearing she was 69 years of age, unable to
maintain herself because of physical disability and living on National Assistance. There had
been a reconciliation with her father, but the relationship broke down again after a quarrel
in 1951, two years before his death. Wynn-Parry J held that his moral obligation to
maintain her ceased once she left the parental home and entered into the relationship with P,
which was still subsisting at her father's death.
[186] *Rhodes v Dean* unreported 28 March 1996, Court of Appeal. The testator died before the
coming into force of the Law Reform (Succession) Act 1995, so the claim had to be made
under s.1(1)(e), on the basis that R was being maintained by him immediately before his
death. Had she been able to claim as a cohabitant, the court would not have been required
to consider whether and to what extent he had assumed responsibility for her maintenance.

joint account with him and a pension of £26.60 per week. She was not in a position to earn her own living. At first instance it was found that D had assumed responsibility for providing accommodation for R but not for keeping up that standard of living. By about a year after R's death she had spent about three-quarters of the money in the joint account. That money could have been used either to provide her with accommodation suitable to her needs or to enhance her income. The Court of Appeal affirmed the trial judge's finding that in those circumstances it was reasonable for D to have made no provision for her out of the estate.

In *Robinson v Bird*,[187] the claimant (V) was the adult daughter of the **4–070** deceased, and benefited equally with a grandson under her mother's will. Following her mother's admission to a nursing home, her house was sold and a lifetime gift of its proceeds of sale made to V. She invested £165,000 of this in medium to high-risk investments in order to provide a higher income but after some three years that sum had fallen to less than half its value. Her claim was dismissed because substantial provision had been made for her during her mother's lifetime, she could have invested that money more prudently and still, taking into account her other financial resources, have enjoyed an annual income of some £24,000, but she had chosen to adopt a riskier investment strategy to support a way of life in which her expenditure exceeded her income. *Garland v Morris*[188] is somewhat similar. The claimant (Y) was one of the two daughters of her father's first marriage. She received nothing under his will and codicil, almost the whole of the estate of £284,631 passing to her sister (B). Y, who was unmarried and had three children aged 21, 9 and 3, had no capital resources except for her own house, which she had bought with money inherited from her mother, and which was in a bad state of repair. Her claim at trial was for approximately £34,000 plus VAT for works of repair and conversion to the house. It was found that although Y was in financial need and lived in sub-standard housing, she had failed to establish that the will did not make reasonable provision for her. She had inherited the whole of her mother's estate. She had been estranged from her father, whereas B had maintained a close relationship with him. The poor condition of the house was largely her own fault, and the judge also considered there to be some truth in the suggestion made by B that Y was the architect of her own misfortunes, having had three children by a man who, she must have realised, would never make any effort to contribute to their maintenance.[189]

---

[187] *Robinson v Bird* [2003] W.T.L.R. 1535. The proceedings in the Court of Appeal, which are concerned with the question whether the judgment below was vitiated by a procedural irregularity, are reported *sub nom. Robinson v Fernsby* [2004] W.T.L.R. 257. In his draft judgment the judge had awarded V £60,000 but changed his mind after receiving written submissions which he had invited counsel to provide. It was held not merely that there was no procedural irregularity or error of law but that if on further consideration he concluded that his draft judgment was erroneous, he had a positive duty to amend it.

[188] *Garland v Morris* [2007] 2 F.L.R. 528.

[189] For these observations, see [42], [54]–[55] and [58]. The words "second defendant" in line 2 of [58] are clearly incorrect and should be replaced by "claimant".

4–071   One other case in which the applicant was in financial difficulty owing to expenditure on a house is *Re Farrow*,[190] an application by a former spouse who had not remarried. In the divorce proceedings she was awarded £50,000, £20,000 of which was to buy, repair and refurnish a house in which she was then living and did not own and £30,000 as an income-producing capital sum, together with periodic payments of £5,500 per year. Her husband died intestate less than a year afterwards and no periodical payments were made after his death except for £1,300 in 1985. In the event she spent more than had been intended on the house and also had to draw on the lump sum for living expenses. Hollings J considered that although she was to some extent responsible for her situation,[191] continuing periodical payments should be made to her, together with a lump sum to compensate to some extent for the periodical payments which she had not received, but not fully, because her own improvidence was a contributory factor. She was awarded £5,000 per year and a lump sum of £15,000.

4–072   A rather odd case which does not fit easily into the sequence of discussion is *Gandhi v Patel*,[192] where the claimant invoked s.25(4) of the 1975 Act, which provides that "wife" includes a person who in good faith enters into a void marriage. Park J held that the ceremony in which the claimant (H) had taken part did not lead to a marriage but to a relationship which English law did not recognise, and doubted also whether it had been entered into in good faith. There was not a marriage, void or valid; it was a "non-marriage". The conclusion of his judgment is to the effect that if H had been an eligible claimant, he would have considered that the will did not make reasonable provision for her but that there was evidence relating to H's conduct (which he did not need to explore in view of his conclusion on the s.25(4) point) which left open the possibility that he would have reduced the provision which he would otherwise have thought it right to make for H.

4–073   In *Myers v Myers*[193] the claimant (B), who was 60 years of age, was one of the deceased's two children by his first marriage. By his will he left his estate, valued at £8,356,400, to his second wife and the three children of that marriage. B had always had a poor relationship with her father (G), who had provided her with a much more limited education than her brother. That restricted her employment opportunities, and her career was further hampered by mental fragility and ill health, including a nervous breakdown in 1970. G displayed considerable antipathy to B, asserting that she had not made the most of the opportunities she had been given, and in a witness statement her behaviour towards him was described as "deplorable" and her lifestyle as "indolent".[194] In 1989 he instructed the trustees of a discretionary

---

[190] *Re Farrow* [1987] 1 F.L.R. 205.
[191] He referred to her as having "dissipated" the £50,000; see *Farrow* at 215D.
[192] *Gandhi v Patel* [2002] 1 F.L.R. 603.
[193] *Myers v Myers* [2005] W.T.L.R. 851
[194] *Myers*, at [68], p.879 D—F. This was the statement of the first defendant, G's elder son by his second marriage, and the word "indolent" is his, not G's, though Munby J accepted, at [69], 880D, that it accurately reflected G's feelings towards B.

settlement created by him to appoint 17,500[195] shares in Unilever, which would have been worth some £310,000 at the time of his death, to B absolutely, and considered that his obligations to her were thereby fully discharged. In considering the s.3(1) factors, Munby J said:

> "The deceased owed the claimant the ordinary obligations of a father to an adult and fully emancipated daughter.[196] He did not owe her any special obligations or have any particular responsibilities towards her except arising out of what he knew or ought to have known of her financial, personal and medical circumstances at the time he made his last will."[197]

Munby J concluded that the will did not make reasonable provision for B.[198] She had received substantial provision from G during his lifetime; she had made much less of her life than many others in her position might have done, and she had been to some extent responsible for her own misfortune. As against that, she was living in circumstances of great financial stringency, her failure to achieve more in her life was not due to indolence but to her awkward personality and mental fragility which hampered her ability to make a more successful career; she had not behaved nearly as badly towards the deceased as he seemed to have believed, and there was more than enough to go round.

Until *Myers v Myers*, there had been no reported case in which a child of **4–074** the testator had been disinherited because of disapproval of their lifestyle generally, but there had been cases in which it had resulted from a marriage[199] or extra-marital relationship[200] disapproved of by the parent. In *Debenham*, the applicant (S) was the 58-year-old daughter of the first of the testatrix's four marriages. Her mother did not want her and never acknowledged her, and she was brought up in South Africa by her father's parents. She visited her mother in 1948 but did not return permanently to England until 1953. Between then and 1973, during which period she had settled in Bradford, she had occasional contact with her mother, who made a will in 1973 leaving her £500 and some jewellery which had belonged to her own mother. S married in 1978 and when her mother heard of this, she reduced the legacy to £200, which so upset S that she refused to accept it when she heard of it. The bulk of the estate of £172,000 was left to six

---

[195] It had originally contained 3,500 shares worth some £93,800 when the settlement was created in 1976 but there had subsequently been a five-for-one split. By the date of the hearing in 2004 B had realised some of the shares and the value of the remainder was about £200,000.

[196] Neither in this case, nor in *Ilott v Mitson*, where the district judge referred at para.51 of his judgment to "the ordinary family obligations of a mother towards her only child who was an independent adult", was the nature of such obligations explained. His observation was quoted by Eleanor King J in *Ilott v Mitson* (reported *sub nom. H v J's personal representatives, Blue Cross, RSPB and RSPCA* [2010] 1 F.L.R. at [50].

[197] *Myers* [78], at 883 G.

[198] *Myers* at [84]–[87], 884D–885H.

[199] *Re Debenham* [1986] 1 F.L.R. 404.

[200] *Re Andrews* [1955] 1 W.L.R. 1105, cited in *Re Rowlands* [1984] 5 F.L.R. 813, CA.

charities. S was unable to work due to her epilepsy and bad eyesight, and could no longer be supported by her husband, who was a year older than her and had been made redundant, so that they were reduced to living on National Assistance. As Ewbank J said, allowing the application[201]:

> "When her daughter became epileptic, one might have thought that any mother, however aloof, might feel some obligation to support her daughter."

4-075 The marriage which excited maternal disapproval in *Ilott v Mitson* (reported under a variety of names) originated in very different circumstances. It showed a range of conduct by the claimant; initially, a relationship entered into in disregard of her mother's wishes, then a series of intermittent but ultimately unsuccessful attempts at reconciliation, and final acceptance of the position. The history of the case, a summary of the relevant facts and the conclusions reached in the various judgments[202, 203] delivered between 7 August 2007 by District Judge Million in the Watford County Court, awarding her £50,000, and by the seven-member Supreme Court (upholding his award) on 15 March 2017, are set out in Ch.6, at paras 6–160 to 6–191.

4-076 The two cases next discussed are on the borderline between this and the most extreme category; both involved quarrels with the testatrix but there was other conduct not specifically directed at her. In *Re Portt, Allcorn v Harvey and Woodcock*[204] the testatrix died in 1977 aged 90. By her will, made in 1969, she left her residuary estate, valued at about £11,000, to her granddaughter and excluded her daughter altogether. Evidence was given that the will was made after what was described as "a blazing row" between mother and daughter. The daughter, aged 71, had a history of litigious behaviour and was a combative individual who quarrelled with her mother on several occasions. Neither the daughter nor the granddaughter were in affluent circumstances, nor were either of them in actual want. Taking into account the daughter's conduct, and the financial positions of the parties, the trial judge dismissed the application and his decision was affirmed by the

---

[201] S was awarded a lump sum of £3,000 for immediate necessities, which would avoid the need to backdate the order. £6,000 per year would have been enough to provide reasonable maintenance for her and her husband, but considering her needs alone, the appropriate sum was £4,500.

[202] On whether the will made reasonable provision for the claimant: *H v J's Personal Representatives, Blue Cross, RSPB and RSPCA* [2010] 1 F.L.R. 1613; [2010] Fam Law 343 and also as *H v M* [2010] W.T.L.R. 193 (Eleanor King J), setting aside the order of the district judge; *Ilott v Mitson* [2012] 2 F.L.R. 170, CA, reversing the decision of Eleanor King J and restoring the order of the District Judge.

[203] On quantum; *Ilott v Mitson* (sometimes referred to as *Ilott v Mitson (No.2)* [2015] 1 F.L.R. 291 (Parker J, declining to allow the appeal against quantum); *Ilott v Mitson* [2015] 2 F.L.R. 1409, CA, setting aside the order of the district judge and awarding greatly increased provision; *Ilott v Mitson* [2017] UKSC 17, reported as *Ilott v Blue Cross* [2017] 2 W.L.R. 979, reversing the decision of the Court of Appeal and restoring the order of the District Judge.

[204] *Re Portt, Allcorn v Harvey and Woodcock* unreported 25 March 1980, CA.

Court of Appeal. In *Williams v Johns*,[205] the applicant (W) was the deceased's adopted daughter, aged 43. The mother died in 1985 having made a will in 1979 leaving her residuary estate to her son. With the will there was a statement made some five years later that she had made provision for W beyond any reasonable expectation, that she had never received from her the response and affection which she had hoped for, and that she felt no moral obligation towards her. W had a history of juvenile delinquency and drug-taking,[206] causing her mother shame and distress.[207] The will was made after a quarrel between them, though it did not lead to a permanent estrangement. Although unemployed and having no income, she was capable of working and had been independent of her mother for some years. Applying *Re Coventry*[208] and *Re Dennis*,[209] it was held that she had failed to show that the will did not make reasonable provision for her.

(iii) Conduct directed at the deceased

In *Bye v Colvin-Scott*,[210] there was financial abuse of the deceased (S). The **4–077** claimant was her daughter (E). The only gift to E in S's will was a diamond ring, the rest of her estate being left to her brother and sisters. The brother, as executor, claimed possession of the flat owned by S in which E had been living with S, and E counterclaimed on a number of grounds[211] which included a 1975 Act claim. In finding that the will had not failed to make reasonable provision for E, the judge referred to E's abusive treatment of S, including taking her to a solicitor to make a new will and execute an enduring power of attorney, neither of which S had wished to do, and obtaining her signature to a document purporting to give her a right of occupation of the flat. S had not wished to maintain E by allowing her to live in the flat and would have preferred it to be sold so that she could purchase sheltered accommodation. These matters, together with evidence that E was able to support herself, were material to the dismissal of her claim.

In *Wright v Waters*,[212] there was financial and emotional abuse. The **4–078** claimant (P) was the 64-year-old daughter of the deceased (M). P, who was a widow, had a daughter and two grandchildren and neither she nor they

---

[205] *Williams v Johns* [1988] 2 F.L.R. 478.

[206] In 1984, when W was aged 42, she was convicted and fined for growing cannabis in her window box, though the judge accepted her evidence that her mother had made light of that episode, and also that there was a continuing relationship; see 481D and 488D.

[207] That was held to be a matter which the court was entitled to take into account; see 488G.

[208] *Re Coventry* [1980] Ch 461, at 474–75 per Oliver J, and 484, 488 per Goff LJ, who stated, in the latter citation, that "an express reason for rejecting the applicant is a different matter [from a wish that a particular person should benefit] and may be very relevant to the problem".

[209] *Re Dennis* [1981] 2 All E.R. 140, at 145B, posing the question to a person capable of earning their own living "Why should anybody else make provision for you if you are capable of maintaining yourself?"

[210] *Bye v Colvin-Scott* [2010] W.T.L.R. 1.

[211] Claims based on proprietary estoppel and on the document purporting to give her a right of occupation also failed.

[212] *Wright v Waters* [2015] W.T.L.R. 353.

benefited under M's will. In a letter written on the same day as the will, made some 15 months before her death, M explained that this was because P had already taken £10,000 of her savings,[213] she had been a constant source of trouble to her for many years, there had been no contact between them for nine years and P had shown no interest in her welfare. The estrangement had occurred in 2001 when P wrote a letter to M disowning her as her mother, stating that she was not fit to call herself that, and concluding by wishing her dead; those words were never retracted. There were many factors in P's favour, apart from the blood relationship. She had worked for a time in the family shop,[214] she was in difficult financial circumstances, she suffered from ill health to the extent that she was wheelchair bound, and no other beneficiary had demonstrated a need for M's bounty. Taking all those factors into account, the value judgment was that her conduct outweighed all the factors in her favour and it was objectively reasonable that the will made no provision for her.

4–079   A case involving physical and emotional abuse is *Re Snoek*,[215] in which the applicant was the second wife of the testator. After about 11 years, the marriage began to fall apart owing to the applicant's uncontrollable temper and outbursts of violence. Between 1976, when the testator had obtained, inter alia, a non-molestation injunction against the applicant, and 1980 when he died, she subjected him to further violence and denied him access to the youngest child of the marriage. She was left nothing in his will. Wood J saw no reason why conduct under s.3(1)(g) of the 1975 Act should be viewed any differently from conduct under s.25 of the Matrimonial Causes Act 1973. In deciding whether the will had made reasonable financial provision for the applicant, he was minded to think that a reasonable man, in view of the applicant's atrocious and vicious behaviour over the latter part of the marriage, would say that the deceased had not failed to make reasonable provision for the applicant by giving her nothing. However, this did not take into account her conduct during the early part of the marriage, when she had managed the home and brought up the four children of the marriage. With some hesitation, he awarded her £5,000 out of an estate of £40,000.

4–080   In *Espinosa v Bourke*[216] the applicant, who was the deceased's daughter, had failed to fulfil the terms of an arrangement with him. The trial judge identified two obligations which the deceased had had towards the applicant, one arising from a promise which he had made to her mother to leave certain shares to her (the "promise" obligation), and the other from an arrangement under which she would look after him, using resources provided by him (the "conduct" obligation), on which she defaulted. It was that default, coupled with his disapproval of her personal life (which included

---

[213] The £10,000 was part of the proceeds of sale of a villa in Spain, which M had entrusted to P to invest on her behalf. P paid M only one year's interest on the investment and refused to return the capital when asked to do so.

[214] Her claim to an interest in the shop based on proprietary estoppel also failed on the grounds that there were no sufficiently clear representations on which she could reasonably have relied.

[215] *Re Snoek* (1983) 13 Fam. Law 19.

[216] *Espinosa v Bourke* [1999] 1 F.L.R. 747.

bringing young men home and sharing her bedroom with them) that prompted him to make a will leaving his entire estate to his grandson. At first instance her conduct towards him was held to discharge or vitiate any obligation which he had towards her, with the result that her application failed at that stage. The Court of Appeal considered that, while the "conduct" obligation owed by the deceased might have been discharged by the applicant's failure to keep to her part of the arrangement, the "promise" obligation had not. Her conduct was not considered by the Court of Appeal to outweigh her obvious need for maintenance arising from her precarious financial position (including her virtually non-existent earning capacity).

The final case in this sequence is *In re Land (deceased)*.[217] The claimant **4–081** (DL) was the executor and sole beneficiary under the will, dated 2 April 1996, of his mother (ML). DL had lived at home all his life and had a series of labouring jobs, the last of which he gave up in 2002 at ML's request so that he could look after her. He did this as best he could, but after ML suffered a fall in September 2003 and refused either to go to hospital or to permit a doctor to see her, he gradually became less able to cope. However, he did not seek any professional help until 4 January 2004, when she lost consciousness and he called an ambulance. She died two days later and DL was charged with manslaughter,[218] to which he pleaded guilty on 27 April 2004. On 21 May 2004 he was sentenced to four years' imprisonment. On 2 August 2004 he made a claim under s.2 of the Forfeiture Act 1982, which was four days out of time. His legal representatives then successfully applied to amend the claim, seeking a declaration that the forfeiture rule did not apply, or alternatively an order under s.2 of the 1975 Act for reasonable provision out of ML's estate. In the event his claim under the 1975 Act succeeded, it being held that the public interest would not be served by depriving DL of all benefit; the judicial analysis leading to that outcome is set out in the section on the law of forfeiture which follows.

(b) The Law of Forfeiture

There is a longstanding rule of public policy, first considered in detail in **4–082** *Cleaver v Mutual Reserve Fund Life Association*,[219] that one (K) who unlawfully kills another (V) is not entitled to any property which he would have acquired as a result of V's death. Concerns expressed about the inflexibility of the rule of public policy and the harshness with which it operated where the unlawful killing involved a low degree of moral culpability, provided the impetus for legislative intervention. Section 1(1) of the Forfeiture Act 1982 ("the 1982 Act") defines the forfeiture rule as:

---

[217] *In re Land (deceased)* [2007] 1 W.L.R. 1009, also reported *sub nom. Land v Land's Estate* [2006] W.T.L.R. 1447.
[218] The judgment sets out the relevant events at paras [2]–[8]. At [7] it is stated that the basis of the charge must have been manslaughter by gross negligence founded on indifference to an obvious risk of injury to health.
[219] *Cleaver v Mutual Reserve Fund Life Association* [1892] 1 Q.B. 147, CA.

"...the rule of public policy which in certain circumstances precludes a person who has unlawfully killed another from acquiring a benefit in consequence of the killing."

4–083   The court has power under subs.2(1) to make an order modifying the effect of the rule, but subs.2(2) provides that the court shall not make such an order unless it is satisfied that, having regard to the conduct of the offender and the deceased, and to such other circumstances as appear to be material, the justice of the case requires the effect of the rule to be so modified in that case. Further, subs.2(3) provides that no such order shall be made unless proceedings are brought before the expiry of the period of three months beginning with the conviction. The court has no jurisdiction to extend that period.

4–084   The effect of ss.3(1) and 3(2)(a) of the 1982 Act is that the forfeiture rule does not preclude any person from making any application under the 1975 Act, or the making of any order on such an application. In *Re Royse*,[220] W was convicted, in 1979, of the manslaughter of her husband (H), with a finding of diminished responsibility. Under his last will, she was the sole executrix and trustee and, subject to her surviving him for a specified period, the sole beneficiary of his net estate. In 1982, some six months before the 1982 Act came into force, she made an application under the 1975 Act for financial provision out of H's estate. Her application was struck out as disclosing no reasonable cause of action and she appealed. Affirming the decision at first instance, the Court of Appeal held that:

(a)   she was not entitled to apply under the 1975 Act because reasonable provision had been made for her by the will;

(b)   the rule that no-one could benefit by a crime applied to the 1975 Act, and therefore the court had no discretion to make an order under it; and

(c)   even if the Forfeiture Act were capable of applying retrospectively, an application under s.2 for an order modifying the effect of the forfeiture rule would be time-barred by s.2(3) as it had not been made within three months of her conviction for manslaughter.

4–085   *Re Royse* was referred to in *Re K*,[221] where Vinelott J said:

"It is clear, I think, that the relative financial position of a person claiming relief under the [Forfeiture] Act and of others with claims under the testator's will or intestacy are circumstances which the court is entitled to take into account in the exercise of its discretion ... In *re Royse* ... the Court of Appeal held that a person for whom reasonable [financial] provision is made by the deceased's will but who forfeits the benefits conferred cannot make a claim under the Act of 1975 ...

---

[220]   *Re Royse* [1985] Ch. 22, CA.
[221]   *Re K* [1985] Ch. 85; affirmed [1986] Ch. 180, CA.

because he or she cannot satisfy the precondition in section 2(1) of the Act of 1975 (viz., that the court is satisfied that the disposition of the deceased's estate ... is not such as to make reasonable financial provision for the applicant). Such a person can therefore claim, if at all, only under section 2 [of the Forfeiture Act]. But in entertaining a claim by a person who apart from the interest forfeited would have had a claim under the joint effect of the Act of 1975 and of section 3 of the Act of 1982 the court must, I think, be entitled to have regard to the principles and the considerations set out in the Act of 1975. Such a person cannot be in a worse position than one for whom no provision is made in the deceased's will or by virtue of his intestacy and who accordingly can only claim under the Act of 1975 as applied by section 3 of the Act of 1982."

Notwithstanding indications by the courts, both before and after the coming into force of the 1982 Act, that not all cases of manslaughter involve the consequence that K forfeits all rights of inheritance from V, the position is now settled, unless and until it is altered by legislation[222] by the decision of the Court of Appeal in *Dunbar v Plant*,[223] followed in *Dalton v Latham*.[224] In *Dunbar v Plant*, K was the survivor of a suicide pact. Phillips LJ analysed the law relating to manslaughter cases and concluded that there was no discernible logical basis for not applying the forfeiture rule to all cases of manslaughter; it applied whenever anyone had caused the death of another by criminal conduct. While the harshness of applying it inflexibly to all cases of manslaughter in all circumstances was such that the rule probably could not survive unvaried, there was no need for judicial modification of the rule. The powers given to the court by the 1982 Act enabled the appropriate course to be taken when the application of the rule appeared to conflict with the ends of justice.   **4–086**

In Re Land's Estate[225] is the first reported 1975 Act case in which the court has had to consider the effect of s.3 of the Forfeiture Act 1982.[226] In that case, the claimant was charged with manslaughter, to which he pleaded guilty on 27 April 2004. His claim under s.2 of the 1982 Act was made on 2 August 2004 and was therefore four days out of time. His legal representatives then successfully applied to amend the claim, seeking a declaration that the forfeiture rule did not apply, or alternatively an order under s.2 of the 1975 Act for reasonable provision out of ML's estate. Adopting the reasoning of the majority of the Court of Appeal in *Dunbar v Plant*[227] which   **4–087**

---

[222] The purpose of the legislation enacted following the Law Commission report on *The Forfeiture Rule and the Law of Succession* (2005), Law Com. No.295 is discussed at para.4–091, below. It is not in any way concerned with the issues that arose in *Dunbar v Plant* and the cases in which it has been followed.

[223] *Dunbar v Plant* [1998] Ch. 412.

[224] *Dalton v Latham, Re Murphy* [2003] EWHC 796 (Ch); [2003] W.T.L.R. 687.

[225] *In Re Land's Estate* [2007] 1 W.L.R. 1009.

[226] See para.4–081, above, for a summary of the basic facts.

[227] *Dunbar v Plant* [1998] Ch. 412 at 435E–436H; on this point, see *In Re Land's Estate* at [12]–[13].

he regarded as part of the ratio of the majority decision, HH Judge Norris QC (as he then was) considered himself unable to declare that the forfeiture rule did not apply to the offence to which the claimant had pleaded guilty.

4–088   In considering the 1975 Act claim, the judge concluded that he was not bound by any direct decision, but had to approach the meaning of s.3 of the 1982 Act in the light of current rules of construction. The court was required by s.3 of the Human Rights Act 1998 to read and give effect to primary legislation in a way compatible with Convention rights. Article 8 of the First Protocol to the ECHR provided that no-one should be deprived of his possessions except in the public interest and subject to the conditions provided for by the law. The right to inherit property under a will was a "possession" for that purpose, but following the decision in *Dunbar* the claimant would be deprived of it whether or not it was in the public interest, unless either relief under s.2 of the 1982 Act was available, or, if not s.3 was read as meaning that the forfeiture rule did not preclude the making of an order under the 1975 Act. That provision was to be read, so far as permissible, in a manner which enabled the court to deprive the wrongdoer of benefit when it was in the public interest to do so, but, in its discretion, to mitigate the harshness of the forfeiture rule when it was not.

4–089   He then considered the policy underlying s.3. Was it to afford relief only to unlawful killers (K) for whom reasonable provision was not made under V's will or intestacy, or to the presumably much larger class of those for whom V had made provision or would take under his intestacy? The latter seemed the far more likely policy, and s.3 should be read so as to give the fullest effect to its words and as not precluding the making of an order in favour of K under the 1975 Act, notwithstanding that it was the forfeiture rule and not the terms of V's will or the devolution of his estate on intestacy which meant that no provision was made for the claimant.[228] He then found, on the facts of the case, that the public interest would not be served by depriving the claimant of all benefit. For an adult son, the standard of provision was what was reasonable, in all the circumstances, for his maintenance. The deceased's house was ordered to be transferred to him outright and he was also awarded a legacy of £1,000 to meet his immediate financial needs. The balance of the cash in the estate would pass to those entitled on intestacy.

4–090   The Estates of Deceased Persons (Forfeiture Rule and Law of Succession) Act 2011, which came into force on 1 February 2012, implements the recommendations of the Law Commission report,[229] which were aimed at meeting the criticisms of the law of forfeiture arising from the decision of the Court of Appeal in *Re DWS (Deceased)*.[230] In that case, an only son, who was illegitimate, murdered both his parents (S and Mrs S), who had not made wills. The result of the automatic disinheritance of the killer (R) was that his son (T) could not benefit from S's estate (as he could have done, had

---

[228] *Re Royse* [1985] Ch. 22 per Ackner LJ at 27F–G, Slade LJ at 30G–31A; followed by Vinelott J in *Re K* [1985] Ch. 85 at 101E–F; see *In Re Land's Estate* at [14]–[17].
[229] Law Commission Report No.295, *The Forfeiture Rule and the Law of Succession* (2005).
[230] *Re DWS (Deceased)* [2001] Ch. 568, CA.

R predeceased S) and in the result the estate passed to the collateral relatives living at the date of the murder (in this case, S's sister W who subsequently died, so the contest was effectively between T and W's executors).[231] The Law Commission's criticisms of this result were that it was unfair for grandchildren to suffer for the sins of a parent; that it was more likely that the deceased would have wished to benefit the grandchild than his other relatives; and that the general policy of intestacy law is to benefit descendants rather than collaterals. The effect of the 2011 Act, whose provisions are implemented by way of amendments to ss.46 and 47 of the Administration of Estates Act 1925 and s.33 of the Wills Act 1837, is to introduce a rule of "deemed predecease" where an interest in residue on intestacy or a devise or bequest under a will is disclaimed or forfeited. The provisions of the Act do not affect the power of the court under s.2 of the Forfeiture Act 1982 to modify the effect of the forfeiture rule. It also contains provisions designed to ensure that a killer cannot benefit, directly or indirectly, from an inheritance to which a minor child becomes entitled.

(c) Conduct of the Deceased

There are relatively few cases in which the conduct of the deceased has had a **4–091** significant effect on the outcome of a family provision claim, and most of those are 1938 Act claims by surviving spouses who had left their husbands, and where behaviour which caused or contributed to the breakdown of the marriage was found to be relevant.[232] In *Thornley v Palmer*,[233] after 10 years of a fairly uneventful marriage, the deceased formed a liaison with another woman (P) and began to treat his wife with great violence when he had been drinking. After four years she left him and he treated P, who lived with him for four years after that, in the same way. Out of a net estate of £16,000 he left the applicant an annuity of £8 per week and the rest of his estate to P. Increasing the award made to her at first instance, Edmund Davies LJ held that the deceased's moral obligation to his widow was much greater than that owed to P, having regard to the length of the marriage and her considerable contribution in work and money to the success of the business, as well as the treatment she had suffered from him. *Barron v Woodhead*[234] also featured incidents of domestic violence, both parties being heavy drinkers, but that did not affect the outcome of the proceedings.

---

[231] This was the view of the majority (Simon Brown and Aldous LJJ). Sedley LJ, dissenting, held that it passed to the Crown as bona vacantia, though the Treasury Solicitor, taking the view that the Crown had no interest, declined to take part in the proceedings.

[232] See *Re Carter* (1968) 112 S.J. 136 (deceased was largely responsible for the break up of the marriage); *Re Clarke* [1968] 1 All E.R. 451 (husband mis-stating the facts in giving his reasons for not providing for his wife); *Re Lavender* (1964) 108 S.J. 879 (wife justified in leaving deceased after a relatively short marriage, although her own conduct had not been entirely satisfactory); *Re Gregory* [1971] 1 All E.R. 497, CA (deceased leaving wife immediately after the child of the marriage was born; he never offered to pay, nor did she apply for, any maintenance). All except the applicant in *Re Gregory* succeeded and in that case, the small size of the estate (£2,500) was a factor.

[233] *Thornley v Palmer* [1969] 3 All E.R. 31, CA.

[234] *Barron v Woodhead* [2009] 1 F.L.R. 747.

4-092   The Supreme Court, in discussing the objective standard of reasonable
provision required by the 1975 Act, observed that the court cannot make an
order on the basis that the deceased is adjudged to have acted unreasonably;
that is an objective test, but it is not the test laid down by the Act. Nevertheless, it acknowledged that the unreasonableness of the deceased's decision were undoubtedly capable of being a factor for consideration within
s.3(1)(g) and possibly within s.3(1)(d).[235] In cases such as those discussed
above under the heading "passive conduct", the extent to which the
deceased was responsible for the state of the relationship at the time of death
is part of the factual matrix, but has not been a weighty factor in the
determination of the outcome. In *Ilott v Mitson*[236] the Supreme Court noted
that the district judge had held that both sides were responsible for the
continuation of the estrangement, with the deceased bearing the greater
responsibility. While the estrangement was a highly significant factor, there
is no indication that the apportionment of fault between the parties was
itself particularly significant. More importance may be attached to failure by
the deceased to honour an obligation owed to the claimant, provided that it
is subsisting at the date of death.[237] However, the Court of Appeal in *Re
Jennings*[238] rejected a submission that failure to honour obligations owed to
the applicant (aged 50 at the date of the hearing) during his childhood was
relevant conduct for the purpose of s.3(1)(g). Henry LJ said that:

> "It is not the purpose of the 1975 Act to punish or redress past bad or
> unfeeling parental behaviour where that behaviour does not still
> impinge on the applicant's financial situation."

(d) Statements Made by the Deceased

4-093   By s.1(7) of the 1938 Act, the court was directed to have regard to the
testator's reasons for making, or not making, any provision or further
provision for a dependant; and it provided for the reception of any evidence
of the deceased's reasons, including a written statement, signed by the
deceased and dated, regarding those matters. However, not only statements
of reasons, but facts from which those reasons could be inferred, were held
admissible.[239] In estimating the weight to be attached to such statements, the
court was directed to have regard to "all the circumstances from which any
inference can reasonably be drawn as to the accuracy of the statement". In
Pugh v Pugh[240] it was held that statements of the testator's intentions, as
distinct from statements of their reasons, were not admissible.

4-094   Section 21 of the 1975 Act, as originally enacted, provided for any
statement made by the deceased, however made, to be admissible as evi-

---

[235] *Ilott v Mitson* [2017] UKSC 17 at [16]–[17].
[236] *Ilott v Mitson* [2017] UKSC 17 at [47].
[237] As in *Re Goodchild* [1997] 1 W.L.R 1216, CA, affirming [1966] 1 W.L.R. 664 and *Espinosa v
        Bourke* [1999] 1 F.L.R. 747, CA.
[238] *Re Jennings, Harlow v National Westminster Bank plc* [1994] Ch. 286, at 301D.
[239] *Re Smallwood* [1951] Ch. 369.
[240] *Pugh v Pugh* [1943] Ch. 187.

dence of any fact stated therein under s.2 of the Civil Evidence Act 1968 as if the statement fell within s.2(1) of that Act. There was no specific requirement to have regard to the testator's reasons for making, or not making, any particular disposition.

That provision was repealed by the Civil Evidence Act 1995 ("the 1995 **4–095** Act"), which abolished the hearsay rule in civil proceedings. In contrast to the 1968 Act, which was concerned with the conditions under which hearsay evidence is admissible, rather than the weight to be attributed to it s.4(1) of the 1995 Act lays down the general principle that, in estimating the weight to be given to hearsay evidence in civil proceedings, the court shall have regard to any circumstance from which any inference can reasonably be drawn as to the reliability or otherwise of the evidence. These words are very similar to the words of s.1(7) of the 1938 Act; however, the 1995 Act goes further in that s.4(2) sets out a number of circumstances to which the court may have particular regard in attributing the appropriate weight to hearsay evidence. Those circumstances need to be considered carefully if (as is by no means uncommon) a testator wishes to include in their will or in a letter to their executors a statement explaining why they are making no provision, or no greater provision, for any specified person. In that context, the circumstances most likely to require consideration are whether the original statement was made contemporaneously with the occurrence or existence of the matters stated[241]; whether any person involved had any motive to conceal or misrepresent matters[242]; and whether the original statement was made for a particular purpose.[243]

Where the testator's reason for excluding or making little provision for a **4–096** person is that they have during their lifetime made provision for that person, that reason will, in most cases, be highly relevant. However, it is for the court to decide whether the provision, if any, stated to have been made is of such a nature or extent that the dispositions of the will fail to amount to reasonable financial provision. Thus, in *Gold v Curtis*,[244] the court did not accept the testatrix's statement that the claimant had "had enough from his parents during their lifetime".

Courts may well find that, where the stated reason for not making pro- **4–097** vision is unacceptable conduct on the part of the claimant or a breakdown in the relationship between the deceased and the claimant, the deceased's expressed view of the position is, in the light of all the other evidence, inaccurate or over-critical, and thus attach little or no weight to it. A particularly striking illustration is *Singer v Isaac*,[245] a claim by the widow of the deceased's second marriage, the major beneficiaries being the adult children of the deceased's first marriage. The parties married in 1988 but by 1994 the marriage was under considerable strain. On 11 May 1994 the deceased made his will and signed the first of four memoranda setting out his perception of

---

[241] Civil Evidence Act 1995 s.4(2)(b).
[242] Civil Evidence Act 1995 s.4(2)(d).
[243] Civil Evidence Act 1995 s.4(2)(e).
[244] *Gold v Curtis* [2005] W.T.L.R. 673.
[245] *Singer v Isaac* [2001] W.T.L.R. 1045.

the state of the marriage and his reasons for making the dispositions which
he had made. Divorce proceedings were started but later abandoned. The
last of the four memoranda was signed on 17 August 1999, 10 days before
his death, when he also executed his last will.

4–098   In the Master's judgment, the memoranda were indisputably admissible
to the extent that they were relevant, and the questions which had to be
considered were their relevance and their weight. As to their weight, he
regarded them, particularly as they had manifestly been prepared with the
benefit of legal advice, with some scepticism. They were in a real sense self-
serving documents, being justificatory of the deceased's conduct in making
the testamentary provision which he did make. The very fact of their existence could be seen as recognising that, subject to the explanation or reasons
which they gave, reasonable financial provision had not been made. As to
relevance, the exercise which had to be carried out was objective, and the
question was, therefore, whether reasonable provision had been made, not
whether the deceased believed that he had made reasonable provision. The
most relevant fact contained in the deceased's memoranda was that the
marriage had been unhappy for a long time. The Master accepted that that
was the deceased's true perception of the state of affairs and that, from his
point of view, there was never a true reconciliation. However, he also
accepted the claimant's evidence that she genuinely believed that there had
been a reconciliation, and the deceased had not disabused her of that belief.
Thus his obligations had to be viewed in the light of the appearances he gave
to her, namely that they had been reconciled, rather than by reference to his
reservations which he did not explain to her. Consequently, the matters set
out in the memoranda did not persuade the court that reasonable financial
provision had been made.

4–099   More recently, in *Myers v Myers*,[246] Munby J found that the claimant had
not behaved as badly to the deceased as he seemed to have thought, and that
her situation was due to her mental fragility and awkward personality rather
than to the indolence which the deceased had attributed to her. This finding
was significant in his conclusion that, taking into account the provision
which the deceased had made for her during his lifetime, and his very
substantial wealth, reasonable provision had not been made for her by his
will.

(e) Forfeiture Clauses in the Deceased's Will

4–100   Occasionally, testators seek to head off Inheritance Act claims by the
insertion of a clause in their wills (sometimes referred to as a "no-contest"
clause) designed to exclude from benefit anyone who contests the will.[247] An

---

[246] *Myers v Myers* [2005] W.T.L.R. 851.
[247] See S. Ross, "Forfeiture Clauses in Wills", [2003] T.Q.R 1(1), pp.7–17.

example of such a clause is the precedent (F14e) contained in *Practical Will Precedents*.[248] That precedent avoids the argument whether a claim under the Inheritance Act is a contest or dispute of the will by specifically providing that the clause shall have effect if such a claim is made. The commentary at F14–001[249] draws attention to the very general nature of the precedent and gives the sound advice that:

"...where the testator is able to identify more specifically the evil that the clause is intended to address, e.g. by reference to a particular beneficiary or particular cause of action, it would be preferable to do so."

The effectiveness of such a clause was considered in *Nathan v Leonard*.[250] **4–101** In accordance with two Commonwealth decisions where wills contained "no contest" clauses and applications for provision were made under the corresponding legislation, viz. *In the Will of Gaynor*,[251] an application under Pt IV of the Administration and Probate Act 1958 (Victoria), and *Re Kent*,[252] an application under the Wills Variation Act 1979 (British Columbia), it was held that a beneficiary who brought an application for provision out of the deceased's estate under the relevant family provision legislation had thereby disputed the will and triggered the operation of the forfeiture clause. It was also held in *Nathan v Leonard* that such clauses were not void as contrary to public policy. It is true that there is 19th-century authority[253] for the proposition that forfeiture clauses are not, in general, contrary to public policy. However, that authority requires further consideration in view of the changes in social and economic conditions and the legislative developments which have since taken place.[254]

The question of public policy which was not considered in *Nathan v* **4–102** *Leonard* is whether the state should, in effect, permit persons to make their own private law by excluding or hindering others from availing themselves of their statutory rights. That question arose in *Hyman v Hyman*[255] in

---

[248] *Practical Will Precedents* (London: Sweet & Maxwell), precedent F14e at para.F14–111. There is also commentary on Inheritance Act claims at F16–004 relating to precedents F16d (a declaration that no provision is made because provision was made during the testator's lifetime) and F16e (provision not made because the specified individual has greater financial security than other beneficiaries for whom the testator wishes to provide). For another, more general form of "no-contest" clause, see Kessler, *Drafting Trusts and Will Trusts*, 13th edn (London: Sweet & Maxwell, 2016), para.29–14. See also *Williams on Wills*, 10th edn (London: LexisNexis, 2014), vol.2, form B.19, para.219.35 (forfeiture on contesting the will or attempting to intermeddle).

[249] Under the heading "Construction and exclusion clauses".

[250] *Nathan v Leonard* [2003] 1 W.L.R. 827.

[251] *In the Will of Gaynor* [1960] V.R. 640.

[252] *Re Kent* (1982) D.L.R. (d) 382.

[253] *Cooke v Turner* (1847) 15 M. & W. 727; (1846) 153 E.R. 1044, approved by the Judicial Committee of the Privy Council in the case of *Evanturel v Evanturel* (1874) L.R. 6 P.C. 1.

[254] For recent commentary, see Kessler, *Drafting Trusts and Will Trusts*, 13th edn, paras 29–07–29–11; *Lewin on Trusts*, 19th edn (London: Sweet & Maxwell, 2015), paras 5–003, 5–006–5–010; *Theobald on Wills*, 18th edn (London: Sweet & Maxwell, 2016), para.27–041; *Williams on Wills*, 10th edn (London: LexisNexis, 2014) at paras 35 and 38.

[255] *Hyman v Hyman* [1929] A.C. 601.

connection with the court's power to make orders for maintenance. There, a wife had covenanted, in a deed of separation, not to take proceedings against her husband to allow her alimony or maintenance beyond the provisions of the deed. She later obtained a decree of divorce on the grounds of his adultery, and the House of Lords held that she was not precluded by the covenant from taking such proceedings. The reasoning was firmly based on public policy grounds. Lord Atkin said:

> "In my opinion the statutory powers ... were granted partly in the public interest to provide a substitute for the husband's duty of maintenance and to prevent the wife from being thrown on public support. If this be true, the powers of the Court cannot be restricted by the private agreement between the parties ... the wife's right to future maintenance is a matter of public concern, which she cannot barter away."[256]

4–103   Section 34(1) of the Matrimonial Causes Act 1973 provides that if a maintenance agreement includes a provision purporting to restrict any right to apply to a court for an order containing financial arrangements, then (a) that provision shall be void; but (b) any other financial arrangements contained in the agreement shall not thereby be rendered void or unenforceable and shall, unless they are void or unenforceable for any other reason, be (subject to ss.35[257] and 36[258]) binding on the parties to the agreement.

4–104   The Law Commission had public policy in mind when compiling the report which led to the enactment of the 1975 Act, and s.15(1) of the Act (which applies on the grant of a decree of divorce, nullity or judicial separation) permits the parties to apply for an order (which the court may make if it thinks just to do so) that neither of them, on the death of the other, shall be entitled to apply for an order under s.2 of the Act.[259] Although aware of the position both at common law[260] and by statute,[261] the Law Commission was of the view that, since they proposed that contracting out would be subject to the overriding discretion of the court, that discretion would be a sufficient safeguard. In fact, courts have from the early years of the operation of the 1975 Act been disinclined to make awards to former spouses who have not remarried.[262] In *Re Fullard*,[263] the first reported case of

---

[256] *Hyman v Hyman* [1929] A.C. 601, at 629.
[257] Alteration of agreements by the court during the lives of the parties.
[258] Alteration of agreements by the court after the death of one party.
[259] Law Com. LC 61 at paras 185–188.
[260] *Hyman v Hyman* [1929] A.C. 601.
[261] Matrimonial Causes Act 1973 s.34.
[262] The last reported case involving a claim under s.1(1)(b) in which there was a substantive outcome is *Barrass v Harding* [2001] 1 F.L.R. 138, CA, where the Court of Appeal set aside the trial judge's order awarding the claimant £30,000 out of an estate of £200,000. *Parnall v Hurst* [2003] W.T.L.R. 987 reports an application to strike out a claim for breach of procedural rules. HH Judge Langan QC held that the claim had sufficient merit to be allowed to proceed, but there is no report of its outcome.
[263] *Re Fullard* [1982] Fam. 42, CA at 49B.

application by a former spouse who had not remarried, Ormrod LJ posed the question whether, in all the circumstances, it was unreasonable for the deceased to have made no provision by his will for his former wife. He observed that the deceased thought he and the plaintiff had sorted out their financial claims as between each other when they reached the agreement about the house. He went on to say:

> "On one view it might be said that the court, and legal advisers acting in these cases, might be well advised to remember section 15 and, if they can persuade the other side to agree,[264] to write into an order the appropriate provision. I regard section 15 as a form of insuring against applications under the Inheritance (Provision for Family and Dependants) Act 1975 which some people may very reasonably wish to do having made financial provision ... for the former spouse."

So far have s.15 orders become the norm that in *Cameron v Treasury Solicitor*,[265] Thorpe LJ expressed the view that the absence of a s.15 order from a "clean break" ancillary relief order would be so irregular as to suggest a fundamental error in drafting. This statutory contracting out is, therefore, in accord with public policy since its intended result is that the financial arrangements between the parties are settled once for all at the time of the decree. It is in the author's view strongly arguable that any other mode of contracting out of the right to make a 1975 Act claim is against public policy and that it is equally against public policy for an otherwise eligible claimant to be prevented or deterred from exercising that right by a unilateral act.   **4–105**

However that may be, the practical utility of inserting a clause in a will which disinherits a beneficiary who brings a 1975 Act claim is in any event limited, since it is uncommon for a 1975 Act claim to be made by a beneficiary who stands to take any significant benefit under the will. In the previous edition of this work it was suggested that the most likely claimant of that type would be a surviving spouse who has taken less than half the net estate under the will and whose argument[266] is that *White v White*[267] ought to be applied so that she receives a greater share of the net estate, but since s.3(2) of the 1975 Act has now been amended to the effect that nothing requires the court to treat the provision which would have been made on the "notional divorce" as setting an upper or a lower limit to the provision   **4–106**

---

[264] *Re Fullard* was heard in the Court of Appeal on 30 January 1981. It was not until October 1984, when s.15(1) was amended by s.8 of the Matrimonial and Family Proceedings Act 1984, that the court was given power to make such an order on the application of either party.

[265] *Cameron v Treasury Solicitor* [1996] 2 F.L.R. 716, CA.

[266] Notwithstanding the firm statements by the Court of Appeal in *Cunliffe v Fielden* [2006] Ch. 361 and Black J in *P v G, P and P (Relevance of Divorce Provision)* [2006] 1 F.L.R. 431 that there is no presumption of equal division.

[267] *White v White* [2001] A.C. 596.

which might be made by an order under s.2,[268] it is now unlikely that a claim would be advanced on such a basis.

(f) Inter Vivos Gifts Made by the Deceased

4–107 It will generally be relevant that the claimant has received money or property from the deceased during their lifetime, whether or not the deceased has made any statement to the effect that the claimant has been sufficiently provided for by them in his lifetime. Such cases include *Robinson v Bird*,[269] where the claimant had anticipated a substantial part of her inheritance during her mother's lifetime, *Gold v Curtis*,[270] where the court did not accept the statement in the will of the testatrix that he had "had enough from his parents in his lifetime" and *Re Myers*,[271] where, notwithstanding the provision made by the claimant's father during her lifetime, his will was found not to have made reasonable provision for her. In the 1938 Act case of *Re Carter*,[272] the fact that the deceased had given property to someone else during his lifetime was held to be relevant. The testator, who died in 1966, left nothing to his wife, from whom he had separated in 1942. He left his entire estate of £7,400 to two friends, one of whom had received shares worth £3,000 from him three months earlier. Buckley J held that the inter vivos gift satisfied the testator's moral obligation to his friends and that the whole of the estate should go to the applicant. In *Iqbal v Ahmed*[273] the beneficiaries of the deceased's will were the widow of the deceased and his son by a previous marriage. The estate was sworn for probate as not exceeding £178,000 and it was considered relevant that the son had received a lifetime gift of £21,500 from the deceased.

7.—MATTERS SPECIFIC TO VARIOUS CLASSES OF CLAIMANT

(a) Surviving Spouses and Civil Partners

(i) Age and duration of relationship and contribution to the welfare of the family

4–108 There are, at the time of writing, no reported cases involving claims by surviving civil partners. The courts have found little difficulty in taking into account the matters referred to in s.3(2)(a) and (b) of the 1975 Act, that is to say, (a) the age of the applicant and the duration of the marriage, and (b) the contribution made by the applicant to the welfare of the family of the deceased, including any contribution made by looking after the home or caring for the family. Long marriages and substantial contributions to the welfare of the family may be expressly acknowledged by the court as factors

---

[268] Inheritance and Trustees' Powers Act 2014 s.6 and Sch.2 para.5(2).
[269] *Robinson v Bird* [2003] W.T.L.R. 1535.
[270] *Gold v Curtis* [2005] W.T.L.R. 673.
[271] *Re Myers* [2005] W.T.L.R. 851.
[272] *Re Carter* (1968) 112 S.J. 136.
[273] *Iqbal v Ahmed* [2012] 1 F.L.R 31, CA.

in the applicant's favour.[274] They may outweigh other factors which are adverse to the applicant; see *Re Rowlands*,[275] where the applicant succeeded although she had been separated from the deceased for the last 44 years before his death. Her contribution to the welfare of the family by looking after the home and bringing up the family during the marriage, which had lasted for 18 years, was material to the success of her application. Conversely, a short marriage may lead to a lower award being made. In *Cunliffe v Fielden*[276] the applicant widow was awarded £800,000 out of an estate of £1.4 million. The executors appealed and the award was reduced to £600,000. The shortness of the marriage and the limited contribution of the applicant towards it were held to justify the departure from equality which appeared on carrying out a *White v White* cross-check, though the departure was not substantial. The parties were married for a year and two weeks and the award to Mrs Cunliffe represented 43 per cent of the residuary estate. The shortness of the marriage was also highly relevant in *Lilleyman v Lilleyman*,[277] where the duration of the relationship, including cohabitation before the marriage, was four years. Out of an estate of approximately £6 million, of which just over £5 million was represented by the value of the family business created by the deceased, the widow was awarded assets to the value of approximately £500,000.

Provision may also be reduced, or denied altogether, where the marriage **4–109** has broken down some time before the death of the deceased. In *Parish v Sharman*[278] the parties had been separated for some 11 years before the death of the husband. A decree nisi was pronounced but never made absolute, and the wife never made an application for ancillary relief. The trial judge found that, in effect, the parties had gone their separate ways and the husband had been led to believe, by her inactivity, that their financial affairs had been settled once and for all at the time of the separation. Her claim was dismissed and that decision was upheld on appeal.[279]

In *Aston v Aston*[280] the parties married in 1985 but the marriage had a **4–110** troubled history. The deceased had instructed solicitors to issue divorce proceedings in August 2001, but his final illness became apparent in 2002 and he did not pursue them. It was found that, by the time he died in November 2004 the marriage was in practice extinct and there was no prospect of reviving it. Analysing the claimant's financial position, the judge found that it was better than it would have been on a divorce; she had half the equity in the former matrimonial home, the proceeds of an insurance policy, and a widow's pension from the deceased's employers; she also had a

---

[274] As in *Re Crawford* (1983) 4 F.L.R. 273 and *Re Bunning* [1984] Ch. 480.
[275] *Re Rowlands* (1984) F.L.R. 813, CA.
[276] *Cunliffe v Fielden* [2006] Ch. 361, CA, also reported *sub nom. Fielden v Cunliffe* [2006] 1 F.L.R. 747; see the judgments of Wall LJ, at [33]–[39], [70]–[75] and Mummery LJ at [110].
[277] *Lilleyman v Lilleyman* [2013] 1 F.L.R. 47.
[278] *Parish v Sharman* [2001] W.T.L.R. 593, CA.
[279] For the effect of long delay on applications for financial relief under the matrimonial jurisdiction, see *Lamagni v Lamagni* [1995] 2 F.L.R. 452, CA, and *Rossi v Rossi* [2007] 1 F.L.R. 790.
[280] *Aston v Aston* [2007] W.T.L.R. 1349.

job and no dependants. Her claim failed. In *Barron v Woodhead*[281] the
parties had cohabited for about seven years before marrying; the marriage,
which was marred by domestic violence, broke down in 2001 and the parties
separated, but were not divorced when the wife died in 2003. She had made
no provision for her husband in her will. The judge found it very difficult to
assess what provision might have been made for him on divorce in such
circumstances but concluded that he would have been provided with a roof
over his head and a small lump sum, and ordered provision accordingly.

4–111   In neither of the two cases discussed in the previous paragraph does it
appear that the claimant had made a substantial contribution to the welfare
of the family. However, even when that is the case, the contribution may be
outweighed by other relevant matters. Thus in *Re Snoek*[282] Wood J, while
taking into account the wife's contribution to the welfare of the family in the
earlier part of the marriage where she had managed the home and brought
up the four children, considered that her subsequent conduct[283] towards the
deceased was such that it was reasonable to make no provision for her. She
was awarded £5,000 out of a net estate of £40,000.

(ii) The "notional divorce"

4–112   Considerable attention has been paid to the part of s.3(2) which reads:

> "...the court shall also ... have regard to the provision which the
> applicant might reasonably have expected to receive if on the day the
> deceased died the marriage, instead of having been terminated by
> death, had been terminated by a decree of divorce."

There have been three types of judicial approach to this provision. One was
to discount it as being difficult or impossible to apply, on the facts of the
case, or to perceive its application as being purposeless in the circumstances.
Thus in *Re Rowlands*,[284] where the applicant wife had been separated for 44
years, it was said to be a curious exercise in the circumstances for the court
to engage in. The difficulty of carrying it out was referred to in *Dawkins v
Judd*,[285] where the problem was that, with so little capital involved, it could
not be known precisely what a court would have done on divorce to provide
each of the parties with a home in which to live; further, the situation at the
date of the hearing was quite different, since the applicant's needs were not
for a home but for a capital sum to provide the comforts of life. In *Eeles v
Evans*,[286] Dillon LJ considered the question to be highly artificial in the
circumstances of the case and unhelpful in providing the answer to the

---

[281] *Barron v Woodhead* [2009] 1 F.L.R. 747.
[282] *Re Snoek* (1983) 13 Fam. Law 19.
[283] Involving a campaign of violence towards and denigration of him, such that he obtained
various non-molestation orders against her.
[284] *Re Rowlands* (1984) F.L.R. 813.
[285] *Dawkins v Judd* [1986] 2 F.L.R. 360.
[286] *Eeles v Evans* unreported 6 July 1989, CA.

question of what constituted reasonable financial provision. In *Winfield v Billington*[287] it was considered irrelevant. In that case, the dispute centred on the destination of the beneficial interests in the matrimonial home. The judge at first instance took the view that in divorce proceedings, the destination of the matrimonial home would depend on the nature of the order relating to custody of the children of the marriage.

Those cases all pre-date the introduction of the *White v White* cross-check   **4–113**
into the law of family provision, but cases continue to occur in which the exercise is not carried out. In *Grattan v McNaughton*,[288] the judge accepted the submission that the spouse's entitlement on the "notional divorce" was unlikely to be decisive, because of the limited resources available[289]; consequently, there was no scope for the application of *White v White*. In *Stephanides v Cohen*,[290] the award to the widow was based on her perceived need for housing and not on the outcome of the "notional divorce" exercise. In two Northern Ireland cases,[291] the assets of the estate were of such a nature that preservation of the property in specie was considered to be appropriate, regardless of the outcome of the "notional divorce". More recently, the nature and amount of the award to the surviving spouse in *Iqbal v Ahmed*[292] was determined by her need for secure housing and a capital cushion to provide for contingencies, while in *Palmer v Lawrence*[293] the divorce cross-check was not considered to be particularly helpful in the circumstances and the court was not persuaded that it would have yielded a better outcome for the claimant widow.

The second approach was to carry out the exercise and then arrive at an   **4–114**
answer which might or might not reflect the outcome of the "notional divorce" exercise, so that either greater or lesser provision was made for the surviving spouse than the outcome of that exercise would have suggested. The limits to the extent to which that exercise should be taken have been formulated in *P v G, P and P (Family Provision: Relevance of Divorce Provision)*[294] by Black J as follows:

> "Ultimately I have concluded that what the statute contemplates in a case such as this is not that the entire fictional ancillary relief case should be played out within the Inheritance Act claim but that the court should simply reach sufficient of a conclusion about how it would

---

[287] *Winfield v Billington* unreported 30 July 1990, CA.
[288] *Grattan v McNaughton* [2001] W.T.L.R. 1307.
[289] The net estate was approximately £80,000.
[290] *Stephanides v Cohen* [2002] W.T.L.R. 1373.
[291] *Re Moorhead* [2002] N.I.J.B. 83 (farmland); *O'Neill v McPhillimy* [2004] N.I. Ch. 4 (estate included three heavily mortgaged public houses).
[292] *Iqbal v Ahmed* [2012] 1 F.L.R. 31, CA. The widow was awarded the residuary estate and a 50 per cent interest in the matrimonial home.
[293] *Palmer v Lawrence* [2011] EWHC 3961 (Ch). This is one of the very few cases where a claim by a surviving spouse has failed; it was found that the will had made reasonable provision for her.
[294] *P v G, P and P (Family Provision: Relevance of Divorce Provision)* [2006] 1 F.L.R. 431, at [236]. She was comforted by Oliver LJ's "not particularly precise" approach to the divorce exercise in *Re Besterman*.

have been resolved to take that factor into account in considering what would be reasonable provision under the 1975 Act."

4–115 In *Re Besterman*[295] the matrimonial legislation and case-law was considered in detail. It was contended on behalf of the applicant that £350,000 out of an estate of over £1.5 million would have been appropriate on divorce, and a fortiori a larger sum would be appropriate on death. Oliver LJ said, of that estimate of provision on divorce, that while it was a matter of speculation, he would not seriously quarrel with the suggestion that an overall sum of £350,000 could not be considered excessive, but rejected the argument that the provision on death must necessarily be greater. He also observed that the two Acts were not directed towards obtaining the same result. In the event, the applicant was awarded £378,000, an increase of £119,000 over the award made at first instance. In *Re Bunning*,[296] Vinelott J did not derive any assistance from the cases cited to him which dealt with applications under the corresponding provisions in the matrimonial legislation. For the applicant it was contended that on divorce the wife would have received £90,000. Vinelott J concluded that the court might well have regarded £36,000 as the maximum which the wife should receive on divorce, but he awarded her £60,000. Again, in *Kusminow v Barclays Bank*[297] Sir Stephen Brown P said that if the court had been dealing with the matter as if it were considering financial provision following the dissolution of the marriage by divorce it would have taken into account the fact of a long marriage in which the wife had worked hard for the benefit of both parties and, in the circumstances of the plaintiff, it would have calculated that she was entitled at any rate to a half-share in the family assets of £120,000; but he actually awarded her £45,000. *McNulty v McNulty*[298] is a post-*White* case in which the cross-check was carried out and the applicant widow awarded more than half of the net estate.

4–116 The third approach was to carry out the exercise prescribed by s.3(2) and to treat it, so far as possible, as determinative of the outcome. *Re Moody, Moody v Stevenson*[299] was such a case. It was an appeal against the dismissal, by the County Court judge, of an application by a surviving husband, aged 81, for reasonable provision out of his late wife's estate. Waite J, giving the judgment of the Court of Appeal, said:

> "Although this last requirement has been criticised because of the mental gymnastics which it is liable to impose on the court, the underlying purpose of Parliament seems plain enough. The objective is that the acceptable minimum posthumous provision for a surviving spouse should correspond as closely as possible to the inchoate rights enjoyed by that spouse in the deceased's lifetime by virtue of his or her

---

[295] *Re Besterman* [1984] Ch. 458, CA.
[296] *Re Bunning* [1984] Ch. 480.
[297] *Kusminow v Barclays Bank* (1989) 19 Fam. Law 66.
[298] *McNulty v McNulty* [2002] W.T.L.R. 357.
[299] *Re Moody, Moody v Stevenson* [1992] Ch. 486, CA.

prospective entitlement under the matrimonial law. There will, of course, be occasions when that objective turns out to be unattainable."

After setting out some situations in which that might be the case, the judgment continues:

"Nevertheless it is the court's duty, in our judgment, to do its best to see that that objective is fulfilled whenever it is feasible to do so. The Act does not, in laying down the lengthy catalogue of matters to which the judge is bound by section 3 to have regard, specify in which order he should tackle them. Nevertheless, in cases where the applicant is a surviving spouse, the logical starting point, as it seems to us, would be an appraisal of the claimant's notional entitlement under [the amended] sections 25 and 25A of the Matrimonial Causes Act 1973, assuming there has been a decree of divorce at the date of death (section 3(2)) and treating the assets in the deceased's estate as if they had been matrimonial assets valued as at the date of the hearing (section 3(5))."

However, as far as can be seen from the subsequent reported cases, this **4–117** approach has not been favoured. In *Re Krubert*,[300] which was the next surviving spouse case to reach the Law Reports, the Court of Appeal took a different view. The judge at first instance had directed himself in accordance with the observations of the Court of Appeal in *Re Moody*, particularly those emphasising the situation on the "notional divorce" as the starting point for consideration of what would constitute reasonable financial provision. However, there was by that time a line of authority[301] favouring the view that no greater prominence was to be given to the applicant's expectation on the "notional divorce" than to any of the other matters to which the 1975 Act directs the court to have regard. The Court of Appeal thus took the view that there was a conflict between *Re Besterman* and *Re Moody*, and remarked that there was anecdotal evidence that the approach adopted in *Re Moody* was causing confusion among district and circuit judges, especially in cases of small estates. The court considered the approach of Oliver LJ in *Re Besterman* to be preferable, being more in accordance with the intention of the 1975 Act when read as a whole. Both judgments adverted to the circumstance that, whereas on a divorce there are two parties to be provided for, on an application under the 1975 Act there is only one; and identified it as a reason why the *Moody* approach may be less than satisfactory in small estate cases. As discussed in Ch.6, the judgments in the two subsequent leading cases which address this point have come

---

[300] *Re Krubert* [1997] Ch. 97, CA.
[301] *Besterman v Besterman* [1984] Ch. 458, CA; *Re Bunning* [1984] Ch. 480; *Re Jessop* [1992] 1 F.L.R. 591, CA.

down decisively in favour of the *Besterman* approach.[302] Superimposed on this judicial difference of opinion is the question whether, and if so in what circumstances and to what extent, the surviving spouse's reasonable expectations on the "notional divorce", as considered by the House of Lords in *White v White*[303] and subsequent high-value matrimonial cases[304] should be taken into account in 1975 Act applications by surviving spouses. At the time of writing, the only such case is *Lilleyman v Lilleyman*,[305] where the net estate was approximately £6 million.

(b) Former Spouses Who Have Not Remarried and Former Civil Partners Who Have Not Entered Into a Subsequent Civil Partnership

4–118   There are relatively few such cases, as the combined effect of the judgment in *Re Fullard*[306] which restricts the situations in which such an application might have a prospect of success, and the routine inclusion of s.15 orders in ancillary relief settlements once the requirement for the parties to agree to such an order ceased to exist, leaves very few viable claims.

4–119   In the few accessible cases, the matters specified in s.3(2) have not played a significant part in the outcome. In *Legat v Ryder*,[307] Dillon J observed that the Court was not concerned simply to reward the applicant for meritorious conduct in that she was the deceased's wife for 11 years, had worked in his business for five years and contributed to the household expenses from her own resources; the application failed. Although it would have been reasonable for the deceased to have made provision for her, it did not follow that he was under any obligation to do so. He found, in effect that, having regard to her own financial circumstances, reasonable provision was nil.

4–120   Where applications under s.1(1)(b) have succeeded, the decisive factor appears to have been the existence, at the time of the deceased's death, of an obligation on his part to maintain the applicant. Thus, in *Re Farrow*,[308] an award was made to compensate the applicant for periodical payments which had not been made; and in *Parnall v Hurst*,[309] where the claim might well have been struck out because of the numerous procedural irregularities, it was considered that the claim had sufficient merit to be allowed to proceed. There had been a final settlement in the divorce proceedings but, at the date of the deceased's death, there was an ongoing periodical payments order, and without that financial support the claimant would have had no

---

[302]   *P v G, P and P (Family Provision: Relevance of Divorce Provision)* [2006] 1 F.L.R. 431; also reported as *P v E* [2007] W.T.L.R. 691 per Black J at paras [223]–[226, [237]–[247]; *Cunliffe v Fielden* [2006] Ch. 361, CA, also reported as *Fielden v Cunliffe* [2006] W.T.L.R. 29; [2006] 1 F.L.R. 745, CA, per Wall LJ at paras [19]–[21], [95]–[99].
[303]   *White v White* [2001] 1 A.C. 596.
[304]   *Miller v Miller, McFarlane v McFarlane* [2006] 2 A.C. 618 HL; *Charman v Charman (No.4)* [2007] 1 F.L.R. 1246, CA. See S. Ross, "1975 Act Claims by Surviving Spouses—The Impact of *Miller* and *Charman*" (2007) 5 T.Q.R. 4, p.35.
[305]   *Lilleyman v Lilleyman* [2013] 1 F.L.R. 47.
[306]   *Re Fullard* [1982] Fam. 42 (CA), at 49E–F per Ormrod LJ and 52E–G per Purchas LJ.
[307]   *Legat v Ryder* unreported 2 May 1980 (Ch.D).
[308]   *Re Farrow* [1987] 1 F.L.R. 205.
[309]   *Parnall v Hurst* [2003] W.T.L.R. 987.

resources other than the state pension. There is no report of the outcome of the substantive claim.

(c) Cohabitants

Subsection 3(2A) reads: **4–121**

"Without prejudice to the generality of paragraph (g) of subsection (1) above, where an application is made by virtue of section 1(1)(ba) of this Act, the court shall, in addition to the matters specifically mentioned in paragraphs (a) to (f) of that subsection, have regard to:

    (a)   the age of the applicant and the length of the period during which the applicant lived as the husband or wife of the deceased and in the same household as the deceased;

    (b)   the contribution made by the applicant to the welfare of the family of the deceased, including any contribution made by looking after the home or caring for the family."

These provisions mirror those of s.3(2) which apply to surviving spouses and former spouses who have not remarried.

In *Re Watson*[310] the court appears to have taken into account not only the   **4–122** 10 years during which the parties actually met the co-habitation requirements of s.1(1A), but the fact that the relationship had subsisted for a total of 30 years; they began to co-habit only when neither of them had elderly parents to care for. In *Negus v Bahouse*[311] the relationship between the parties began in 1995, but cohabitation did not begin until 1997 when the claimant moved into the deceased's flat, gave up her job at his request and became a full-time housewife in all but name. The deceased developed diabetes and became severely depressed in August 2004, when the relationship became strained, but the trial judge found that she had no intention of leaving him and that they continued to love and care for each other. The deceased committed suicide in March 2005. Provision was made for the claimant on the basis that she should have a modest flat and an income which enabled her to maintain a way of life which bore some resemblance to that which she had enjoyed during the relationship. In other recent reported cases there has been a question whether, as a fact, the parties were cohabiting within the meaning of s.1(1A)[312] or 1(1B),[313] as the case may be.

---

[310] *Re Watson* [1999] 1 F.L.R. 878.
[311] *Negus v Bahouse* [2008] W.T.L.R. 97.
[312] *Churchill v Roach* [2004] 2 F.L.R. 989 (parties had not cohabited for the full two years, but claim in the alternative under s.1(1)(e) succeeded); *Gully v Dix* [2004] 1 F.L.R. 918, CA (relationship lasting 27 years but claimant left deceased some three months before his death; there was a settled relationship which had not come to an end); *Lindop v Agus* [2009] W.T.L.R. 1175 (preliminary issue whether the cohabitation amounted to "living together as husband and wife"). In the latter two cases the claimant would also have succeeded under s.1(1)(e).
[313] *Baynes v Hedger* [2008] 2 F.L.R. 767 (cohabitation found to have ceased many years before the deceased's death, but the claim would have failed in any event as their relationship as a couple was never openly acknowledged).

4–123   In *Swetenham v Walkley*[314] there was a long-term relationship between the deceased (B) and the claimant (S) displaying a number of features which were relied on by the defendants as evidence that the relationship was merely one of friendship or companionship. It was held that although individual features of their relationship might be characteristic of friendship or companionship, no one factor was utterly determinative. In the instant case, what was determinative was a combination of all that they has done for each other during the 30 years of their relationship and, particularly, its exclusivity. Although B owned and used other properties, during the relationship he lived his life with S and not elsewhere.

4–124   In *Kaur v Dhaliwal*[315] the question was whether the parties had been living together in the same household for the required period. The claimant (K) had first met the deceased (H) in May 2005 and they became engaged during the following month. It was common ground that H was living in the same household as K and as his wife from July to September 2006 and for the period of one year and 49 weeks from the beginning of July 2007 until H's death on 7 June 2009. A submission that the claim must fail due to the gap between the two periods of cohabitation was rejected. Barling J held that "household" was a word essentially referring to people held together by a particular kind of tie, even if temporarily separated.[316] It was sufficient to ask whether either party has demonstrated a settled acceptance or recognition that the relationship is at an end. If the relationship has irretrievably broken down the parties no longer live in the same household and the Act is not satisfied. If the interruption is transitory but the relationship is still recognised to be subsisting, then they would be living in the same household and the claim would lie.

(d) Children and Persons Treated as Children of the Family

4–125   Section 3(3) requires the court to have regard, in respect of both classes of applicant, to the manner in which the applicant was being or might have expected to be educated or trained. Where the claimant is a person (not being a child of the deceased) who in relation to any marriage or civil partnership to which the deceased was at any time a party, or otherwise in relation to any family in which the deceased at any time stood in the role of a parent was treated by the deceased as a child of the family, regard must also be had to the matters set out in ss.3(3)(a), (b) and (c) which are concerned with the deceased's responsibility for the claimant's maintenance and the liability of any other person to maintain the claimant.

4–126   There have been few applications in which the education or training of the applicant has been considered, though this factor may be expected to feature more frequently as the proportion of children going on to higher education, with the concomitant burden of tuition fees and student loans, increases. In

---

[314] *Swetenham v Walkley* [2014] W.T.L.R. 845.
[315] *Kaur v Dhaliwal* [2014] W.T.L.R 1381.
[316] *Re Santos* [1972] Fam 247, CA, per Sachs LJ at 263.

Re Chatterton[317] where the application was made on behalf of the six-year-old daughter of the deceased, it was said that the court, in considering what was reasonable provision, must have regard to the walk of life in which the parents were and the sort of life that the applicant would have had if the father had lived until she became 18; there was no reference, in terms, to her prospective education or training.

The Court of Appeal in *Dixit v Dixit*,[318] when balancing the claims of the applicants, who were the widow and two infant daughters of the deceased's second marriage, against those of the beneficiaries, who were the four adult daughters of his first marriage, took into account that the older daughter of the second marriage, who was at that time 16, was hoping shortly to take A-levels and then go on to university. In *Re J (A minor)*[319] the judge at first instance referred to the possibility that the 16-year-old applicant might go to college, but it does not appear from the report of the proceedings in the Court of Appeal that this affected the decision at any stage. In *Re Hocking*[320] the Court of Appeal upheld an award to two daughters of the deceased by way of capital sums representing commuted maintenance payments over the period during which they would be undergoing further or higher education.

4-127

In *Re Callaghan*,[321] where the applicant was a man aged 47, it was unsuccessfully argued that the inclusion in s.3 of the factors set out in s.3(3)(a)–(c) required the words "treated by the deceased as a child of the family" in s.1(1)(d) to be construed as referring to a minor or dependent child. In rejecting this argument, Booth J pointed out that no such limitation could apply in the case of an applicant under s.1(1)(c) and held that the word "child" was to do with the relationship between the deceased and the applicant, and "treatment" did not mean treatment as a minor or dependent child. There was no express consideration of the matters set out in s.3(3)(a)–(c).

4-128

A similar submission was unsuccessfully advanced in *Re Leach, Leach v Lindemann*,[322] where the applicant was the 55-year-old step-daughter of the deceased. Whereas the definition of "child" in s.25(1)(a) of the 1975 Act includes an illegitimate child or a child *en ventre sa mere* at the death of the deceased, it does not include a step-child, and such a person could at that time apply only if they had been treated by the deceased as a child of the family in relation to that marriage. It was submitted that such a person could apply only if they had been treated by the deceased as an "unfledged person", in the sense that there had been an assumption by the deceased of parental responsibility, care and control. This submission was founded not only on the provisions of s.3(3)(a)–(c) but on the judgment of Templeman LJ in *D v D*,[323] which was concerned with the question whether a step-

4-129

[317] *Re Chatterton* unreported 11 November 1978, CA.
[318] *Dixit v Dixit*, unreported 23 June 1988, CA.
[319] *Re J (A Minor)* unreported 9 December 1991, CA.
[320] *Re Hocking* unreported 12 June 1997, CA.
[321] *Re Callaghan* [1985] Fam. 1.
[322] *Re Leach, Leach v Lindemann* [1986] Ch. 226, CA.
[323] *D v D* (1981) 2 F.L.R. 93.

daughter had, between the ages of 10 and 14, been treated as a child of the family as defined by s.52(1) of the Matrimonial Causes Act 1973. Following *Callaghan*, it was rejected. Another unsuccessful submission was based on the failure of the trial judge to make express mention of the matters set out in s.3(3) in the part of his judgment which dealt with the question whether the intestacy of the deceased had made reasonable provision for the applicant. The Court of Appeal was satisfied that the trial judge had sufficiently taken into account the obvious fact that the deceased had never assumed responsibility for the maintenance of the applicant.[324]

4–130   Section 3(3)(b) of the 1975 Act directs the court to have regard to whether, in assuming and discharging the responsibility of treating the applicant as a child of the family, the deceased did so knowing that the applicant was not his child. It should be understood that the question whether the deceased knew that the applicant was not his own child is irrelevant to whether the applicant was treated as a child of the family. It may go to the question in s.3(3)(a) of whether, to what extent and on what basis the deceased assumed that responsibility, but there is no case-law on the point.

(e) Persons Being Maintained by the Deceased Immediately Before Their Death

4–131   Section 3(4), as originally enacted, directs the court, when considering applications by persons claiming to be within s.1(1)(e), to have regard to the extent to which and the basis upon which the deceased assumed responsibility for the maintenance of the applicant and the length of time for which the deceased discharged that responsibility. In formulating that provision, the Law Commission had regard to the possibility of cases occurring in which the deceased had evinced an intention that maintenance should cease on their death, and considered that the formulation was widely enough expressed to deal with that possibility.[325] It is therefore unsurprising that the attitude of the deceased towards the person whom they were maintaining immediately before their death is sometimes relevant, and s.3(4), both in its original form and as amended[326] provides statutory recognition of that factor. It now requires the court to have regard to:

(a)   the length of time for which and basis on which the deceased maintained the applicant and to the extent of the contribution made by way of maintenance; and

(b)   to whether and, if so, to what extent, the deceased assumed responsibility for the maintenance of the applicant.

---

[324] *Leach v Lindemann* (1984) 5 F.L.R. 590, Michael Wheeler QC.
[325] Law Com. LC 61, paras 96(a), 97.
[326] Inheritance and Trustees' Powers Act 2014 s.6 and Sch.2 para.5(4). As originally enacted, it required the court to have regard to the extent to which and the basis upon which the deceased assumed responsibility for the maintenance of the applicant and to the length of time for which he discharged that responsibility.

In *Re Viner*,[327] the court took account of the fact that the testator had   **4–132**
maintained the applicant grudgingly and held, for that reason, that provision should be restricted to what she had received during the testator's
lifetime. In *Re Kirby*,[328] an unsuccessful appeal against a decision of the
district registrar refusing to strike out an application under s.1(1)(e), s.3(4)
was considered and it was found that the responsibility assumed by both the
parties (that is, the applicant and the deceased) could not for practical
purposes be distinguished from those accepted by a married couple towards
each other. True it was that they were not formal obligations, but they were
none the less effective for that.

In the previous edition of this work, the question whether it is necessary   **4–133**
for the deceased to have assumed responsibility for the claimant's maintenance in order for a claim to be entertained was addressed at some
length.[329] The Law Commission's 2009 consultation paper on the law of
intestacy and family provision remarked on the state of the case-law.[330] The
Law Commission in its 2011 report made it clear that the present state of the
law in that regard was unsatisfactory and that legislative amendment was
appropriate.[331] As a result of the amendment of s.3(4),[332] the discussion of
that question is now of historical interest only and is no longer included.

While assumption of responsibility is no longer to be regarded as a   **4–134**
threshold condition, it is still necessary to consider whether, and if so, to
what extent the deceased assumed responsibility for the maintenance of the
claimant. Assumption of responsibility is clearly demonstrated in the two
recent reported cases now discussed. In *Wright-Gordon v Legister*[333] the
settled arrangement subsisting at the date of the deceased's death was found
to be that he had been providing the claimant (A) with rent-free accommodation, and the household tasks including cooking, cleaning and washing
carried out by A as a member of the household, quasi-family member and
friend did not amount to full valuable consideration. His provision of free,
or cheap, accommodation for A for an extended time also demonstrated his
assumption of responsibility, and on that footing he was held to owe an

---

[327] *Re Viner* [1978] C.L.Y. 3091.
[328] *Re Kirby* (1982) 3 F.L.R. 249.
[329] Ross, *Inheritance Act Claims*, 3rd edn (London: Sweet & Maxwell, 2011), paras 4–102, 103.
[330] Law Com. CP 191 at paras 6.12–6.17. It summarised the position in the following words:
"According to the case law, it is a prerequisite for a claim by a dependant that there was an
'assumption of responsibility' by the deceased". See *Baynes v Hedger* [2009] 2 F.L.R. 767,
CA at [40] where Sir Andrew Morritt C said, "Counsel for the appellant did not dispute that
as a matter of law an assumption of responsibility by the deceased for the maintenance of
the claimant was an essential ingredient to the qualification of a person entitled to make a
claim under s.1(1)(e)"and cited *Jelley v Iliffe* [1981] Fam. 128, CA as authority for the
proposition.
[331] Law Com. LC 331 at paras 6.56–6.59.
[332] See para.4–131, above.
[333] *Wright-Gordon v Legister*, reported *sub nom. Gordon v Legister* [2014] W.T.L.R. 1675.

obligation to A to ensure that, after his death, she was sufficiently provided for to resettle herself in suitable accommodation. In *King v Dubrey*[334] the claimant (K) moved into his aunt (J)'s house in 2007 for the purpose of caring for her, which he did until her death in 2011 and, in return, he received board and lodging, expenses and small sums of money. That arrangement was held to involve an assumption of responsibility on both sides. In *McIntosh v McIntosh*[335] the payments made to the claimant (B) by the deceased were found not to be contributions to his reasonable needs and therefore B failed to satisfy the court that the deceased had assumed responsibility for his maintenance or that there was a relationship of dependency accepted by him and the deceased.

---

[334] *King v Dubrey* [2014] W.T.L.R. 1411. In that case there was also a claim that the deceased had made a valid *donatio mortis causa* to the claimant (K). The first instance decision in K's favour on that claim was reversed by the Court of Appeal, but the trial judge's award to K under his 1975 Act claim was upheld; see *King v Dubrey* [2016] Ch 221, *sub nom. King v The Chiltern Dog Rescue* [2015] W.T.L.R. 1225, CA.

[335] *McIntosh v McIntosh* [2013] W.T.L.R. 1565.

CHAPTER 5

ORDERS WHICH THE COURT CAN MAKE

1.—THE SCHEME OF THE 1975 ACT

The 1975 Act is divided into five parts. The first part (ss.1–7) is concerned **5–001** with the making of financial provision, and the principal powers of the court to make orders are conferred by s.2. Section 4, which is considered separately from the other provisions of this part, provides that an application for an order under s.2 shall not, without the permission of the court, be made after the end of the period of six months from the date on which representation is first taken out, which is defined by s.23. The amendments to these provisions brought into effect by the Inheritance and Trustees' Powers Act 2014[1] are discussed in s.4 of this chapter. Since the merits of the substantive claim are a highly relevant factor in the decision whether to give permission, it is usual, when seeking to commence proceedings out of time, to include an application for permission under s.4 in the substantive claim rather than to make a freestanding application under s.4. However, the court may decide to determine the application to commence proceedings out of time as a preliminary issue. Ancillary powers are contained in s.5 (power to make interim orders) s.6 (variation and discharge of orders for periodical payments) and s.7 (power to order payment of lump sums by instalments). Subss.6(3) and 6(10) have been amended[2] by inserting, where subsequent marriages are referred to, words relating to the formation of a subsequent civil partnership.

The second part (ss.8–9) is concerned with property available for financial **5–002**

---

[1] Inheritance and Trustees' Powers Act 2014 s.6 and Sch.2 para.6 (s.4); Sch.3 para.2 (s.23).
[2] Civil Partnership Act 2004 s.71 and Sch.4 para.19.

provision.[3] The two sections operate in different ways. Whereas s.8 simply defines certain classes of property which are automatically treated as part of the net estate s.9 confers on the court the power to order that the deceased's severable share of any property held on a joint tenancy immediately before their death may, in whole or in part, be treated as part of the net estate for the purpose of facilitating the making of financial provision. The effect of the amendment to s.9(1) by the Inheritance and Trustees' Powers Act 2014[4] is that a claim for an order under s.9 can now be brought whether or not the claim for an order under s.2 was commenced within the six-month period specified by s.4.

5–003   The Law Commission[5] was concerned about the fact that, if the matrimonial home were to pass by survivorship, no part of its value would be available for the purpose of making provision for children or other dependants of the deceased.[6] The requirements of justice were thought to demand that property passing by survivorship[7] should be so available, but also that the person who held the property jointly with the deceased should know with certainty how their rights are going to be affected with the least possible delay; consequently, it was thought desirable that an interest which passed by right of survivorship should only be made available for family provision where the application for such provision is made promptly after the death. However, in the report which led to the enactment of the Inheritance and Trustees' Powers Act 2014, the Law Commission expressed the view that the protection afforded to joint tenants by s.9 as originally enacted might be seen as more illusory than real.[8] One situation where it fails to achieve the desired certainty as to their rights for the surviving joint tenant occurs when the grant is not taken out until long after the death of the deceased joint tenant.[9] Another is when the grant is issued fairly soon after the death of the deceased and the application for an order under s.2 is made within the six-month period, but a further application under s.9 is made during the course of the proceedings.

5–004   Sections 10–13 are concerned with anti-avoidance provisions. Applications for orders under ss.10 and 11 cannot be made as freestanding claims, but only within the substantive claim for an order under s.2. Sections 12 and 13 contain provisions supplementary to ss.10 and 11.

---

[3] This area of the Act is the subject of Ch.3.

[4] Inheritance and Trustees' Powers Act 2014 s.6 and Sch.2 para.7.

[5] Law Commission, Report No. 61, *Second Report on Family Property: Family Provision on Death* (1974), paras 137–142.

[6] In practice, as is discussed in considerable detail in *Tyler's Family Provision*, 3rd edn (London: LexisNexis Butterworths, 1997), pp.297–301, it is the converse situation which arises; viz., that the court will be less ready to make an order under s.9 if the property in question is a dwelling occupied by the survivor

[7] Jointly owned bank accounts were discussed at para.142.

[8] Law Commission, Report No.331, *Report on Intestacy and Family Provision Claims on Death* (2011), at paras 7.75–7.83.

[9] As in *Dingmar v Dingmar* [2007] Ch. 109 where the deceased died on 28 June 1997 and a grant of administration was not obtained until 8 July 2005. There were no assets of any significant value in the estate and there would have been no need for the widow to have taken out a grant had it not been for the commencement, in 2004, of a claim for possession of the matrimonial home by the surviving co-owner, a son of the deceased.

Sections 14–18 contain provisions which relate to cases of divorce and **5–005** separation. The Civil Partnership Act 2004 has made substantial additions to those provisions.[10] Section 14 is concerned with the position of former spouses and judicially separated spouses whose financial position had not been dealt with in matrimonial proceedings, either because no application had been made under ss.23 or 24 of the Matrimonial Causes Act 1973 (MCA 1973), or because it had been made, but not finally disposed of, before the death of the deceased. Broadly speaking, the effect of s.14A is to put a surviving civil partner whose partner has died within 12 months of the termination of the civil partnership in the same position as a surviving spouse whose spouse has died within 12 months of the termination of the marriage. In either case the court has power to treat the claimant as if the relationship was still subsisting at the date of death of the deceased.

Section 15ZA imposes the like restrictions, in the case of proceedings for **5–006** the dissolution of civil partnerships, as are imposed by s.15 in the case of divorce proceedings. In each case the court has power to order, on the application of either party to the relationship, that the other party shall not, on the death of the applicant, be entitled to apply for an order under s.2 of the Act. In the same way that it is now standard practice to include such a provision in consent orders made on applications for financial relief in divorce proceedings, the like provision should be included where the application is made in proceedings for the dissolution of a civil partnership.

Section 15A of the 1975 Act imposed similar restrictions in proceedings **5–007** where an order is made under s.17 of the Matrimonial and Family Proceedings Act 1984 (orders for financial provision and property adjustment following overseas divorces, etc.). Section 15B contains the like restrictions in relation to proceedings under Sch.7 to the Civil Partnership Act 2004. The schedule, which implements s.72(4) of that Act, relates to financial relief in England and Wales in cases where the civil partnership has been terminated, or the partners have been legally separated, by proceedings in an overseas country which are recognised as valid by the courts of England and Wales.

Where a claim is made under s.2 of the 1975 Act by a person who was, at **5–008** the time of death of the deceased, entitled to payment from the deceased under a secured periodical payments order made under the MCA 1973 or Sch.5 to the Civil Partnership Act 2004, s.16(1) of the 1975 Act as amended[11] gives the court power to vary or discharge such an order if an application is made by either the claimant under the 1975 Act or the personal representative of the deceased. Section 17 confers on a court seised of a family provision application the power to revoke or vary maintenance arrangements made by the deceased with their spouse or former spouse. The minor amendments introduced into ss.16(1) and 17(4) of the 1975 Act have the effect of extending the power to vary or discharge orders for secured periodical payments under the MCA 1973 to the like orders made under Sch.5 to the Civil Partnership Act, and the power to vary or revoke maintenance

---

[10] Civil Partnership Act 2004 s.71, Sch.4 paras 20–25.
[11] Civil Partnership Act 2004 s.71, Sch.4 paras 23(a) and (b).

agreements between the deceased and any person with whom they entered into a marriage is extended to maintenance agreements between the deceased and any party with whom they entered into a civil partnership.

5–009 Section 18 of the 1975 Act was enacted in order to deal with the possibility that an applicant for a variation of a secured periodical payments order under s.31 of the MCA 1973 might, if the person liable to make the payment had died, find that the court's power to vary the order had been defeated by a disposition of a nature which might have been successfully challenged under the anti-avoidance provisions of the 1975 Act. The section provides that in the circumstances described in s.18(1), the court shall have power to direct that an application under ss.31(6) or 36(1) of the MCA 1973 shall be deemed to have been accompanied by an application under s.2 of the 1975 Act. The new s.18A gives the court the same powers in relation to applications under paras 60 (relating to secured periodical payments) and 73 (relating to maintenance agreements) of Sch.5 to the Civil Partnership Act as it has by virtue of s.18 in respect of applications under ss.31(6) and 36(1) of the MCA 1973.

5–010 The miscellaneous and supplementary provisions contained in ss.19, 20 and 23–27 do not include any powers for the court to make orders. Section 19, which is concerned with the effect, duration and form of orders, was amended[12] so as to refer to civil partners and partnerships as it refers to spouses and marriage. Section 19(3) provides for any order made under the Act, other than an order under s.15(1), to be endorsed on or permanently annexed to the probate or letters of administration under which the estate is being administered; it is therefore necessary for the original of the grant to be produced at the hearing of the claim or when a consent or Tomlin order is submitted. Section 25 of the Act is amended[13] so as to include a definition of "former civil partner" and to replace references to "husband" and "wife" by references to spouses and civil partners.

2.—THE CASE LAW ON ORDERS UNDER SECTION 2

(a) Sections 2(1)(a) and (b): Periodical or Lump Sum Payment

5–011 The great majority of monetary awards made in 1975 Act cases are lump sum awards.[14] This is generally considered desirable in the interests of finality. However, the 1975 Act contains no provision for varying a lump sum award, and in *Re Besterman*[15] Oliver J expressed the view that greater account should be taken of contingencies and inflation when making an award for payment of a lump sum than if a periodical payments order were made. He considered that reasonable provision for the applicant widow

---

[12] Civil Partnership Act 2004 s.71, Sch.4 para.26.

[13] Civil Partnership Act 2004 s.71, Sch.4 para.27.

[14] Cases in which lump sum awards were made in order to facilitate provision for housing needs are discussed in the next section, which is concerned with transfers, settlements and acquisition of property.

[15] *Re Besterman* [1984] Ch. 458 at 478F–H.

should be, in addition to the secure roof over her head, a sum which would provide an adequate income and a cushion in the form of available capital which would enable her to meet all reasonably foreseeable emergencies; but in *Cunliffe v Fielden*[16] Wall LJ observed that such a "cushion" was no longer considered a proper approach to financial proceedings following divorce. It was no longer the case (as it had been when *Besterman* was decided) that the court was required to exercise its powers so as to put the parties in the financial positions in which they would have been if the marriage had not irretrievably broken down and each had properly discharged their financial obligations and responsibilities towards the other.[17]

The relatively few cases in which a periodical payments order was made,   **5–012**
or consideration was given to making such an order, display no common factors. In *Re Debenham*,[18] the applicant was the 58-year-old daughter of the testatrix. She was epileptic and thereby disabled from working. Ewbank J considered that, in view of her age and life expectancy, a lump sum payment was not appropriate, except for a relatively small amount to meet immediate needs. Financial provision for the applicant was awarded by way of periodical payments, which were to be reduced when she became eligible for an old-age pension. In *Stead v Stead*[19] the 82-year-old applicant widow received, under the will, a life interest in the matrimonial home and a lump sum of £6,000 out of the £34,000 representing the rest of the estate. She was awarded a further £2,500 and periodical payments of £1,500 per year. The report throws no light on the reason for making that type of award; it is concerned with her unsuccessful appeal on the ground that insufficient weight had been given to the matters specified in s.3(2) of the 1975 Act. In *Re Farrow, Deceased*[20] the 59-year-old applicant had, following her divorce, been entitled to receive a lump sum of £50,000 and periodical payments of £5,500 per year; these were considerably in arrear at the time of the deceased's death. She was awarded a lump sum of £15,000 by way of compensation for having to draw on the original capital provision to make up for the lapsed periodical payments order, and periodical payments of £5,000 per year. In *Re Collins*,[21] the 19-year-old applicant was awarded a lump sum of £5,000 out of an estate of £27,000. A periodical payments order was considered inappropriate because finality was desirable and also because of her age and the modest size of the estate.

(b) Sections 2(1)(c), (d) and (e): Transfers, Settlements and Acquisition of Property

Orders of this nature have been made in a substantial number of cases under   **5–013**
the 1975 Act, though applications for such relief have quite often failed. The majority of such cases were claims by surviving spouses, but more recently

---

[16] *Cunliffe v Fielden* [2006] Ch. 361, [76]–[77] ("the *Besterman* cushion"), and [83].
[17] Matrimonial Causes Act 1973 s.25(1) as originally enacted.
[18] *Re Debenham* [1986] 1 F.L.R. 404.
[19] *Stead v Stead* [1985] F.L.R. 16, CA.
[20] *Re Farrow, Deceased* [1987] 1 F.L.R. 205.
[21] *Re Collins* [1990] Fam. 56.

orders of this nature have been made in claims by cohabitants and dependants. However, the first reported case in which a transfer of property order was made was *Re Christie*,[22] where the applicant was the adult son of the testatrix. She had made a will leaving him her interest in a house in Essex. This house was later sold, the testatrix purchasing another house; the gift to the son therefore lapsed under the doctrine of ademption. He applied for, and obtained, an order by which, inter alia, the replacement house was transferred to him. That decision soon attracted considerable criticism, being perceived as giving an overly broad view of what was meant by "maintenance". In *Re Coventry*,[23] Oliver J said that the very broad view of maintenance expressed in *Re Christie* seemed to him to come dangerously near to equating it simply with "well-being" or "benefit". Giving the leading judgment on the appeal, Goff LJ amplified this; "maintenance" did not mean just enough to enable a person to get by, but on the other hand it did not mean anything which might be regarded as reasonably desirable for their general benefit or welfare.[24]

5–014   In several subsequent cases, the question has arisen whether the housing needs of an applicant should be met by awarding a life interest or an absolute interest in the property made available for that purpose. The Supreme Court has recently addressed that question in *Ilott v Mitson*.[25] While acknowledging that it had been envisaged (obiter) in *Re Dennis*[26] that there was no reason why housing should not be maintenance in some cases, the judgment emphasises the necessity to remember that the statutory power is to provide maintenance, not to confer capital on the claimant. If housing was provided by way of maintenance, it would be likely more often to be provided by such a life interest rather than by a capital sum.[27] While the order of the Court of Appeal was set aside because the district judge had not made either of the two fundamental errors attributed to him,[28] the Supreme Court was also critical of some of the terms of the order,[29] saying, of the £143,000 awarded to the claimant so that she could buy the house (rented from the Housing Association) in which the family was living, that:

> "Plainly some judges might legitimately have concluded that this was a case in which reasonable financial provision should be made by way of housing, even though the actual benefit of doing so would be much reduced by loss of housing benefit. In the absence of error of principle

---

[22] *Re Christie* [1979] Ch. 168. "Maintenance" is discussed in detail in Ch.6, s.2.

[23] *Re Coventry* [1980] Ch. 461 at 471, quoting the passage in *Re Christie*, at 174.

[24] *Re Coventry*, at 485.

[25] *Ilott v Mitson* [2017] UKSC 17, reported *sub nom. Ilott v Blue Cross* [2017] 2 W.L.R. 979, setting aside the order of the Court of Appeal [2015] 2 F.L.R. 1409, CA.

[26] *Re Dennis* [1981] 2 All E.R. 140.

[27] *Ilott v Mitson*, at [15], commending the approach of Munby J in *Re Myers* [2005] W.T.L.R. 851, a claim by the 60-year-old daughter of the deceased, where the provision ordered, which included housing, was made by way of a life interest in a trust fund with power to advance capital if needed to fund care for the claimant in old age.

[28] *Ilott v Mitson*, at [32]–[42].

[29] *Ilott v Mitson*, [44]–[47]. The order itself is set out at [31] and appears in the judgment of Arden LJ at [2015] 2 F.L.R. 1409, at [60]–[64].

by the district judge the occasion for the Court of Appeal to say what its own order might have been did not of course arise. But even if it had arisen, the right order would be likely to have been a life interest in the necessary sum, rather than an outright payment of it. There was no discussion of this question in the judgment."

It may be that, had the district judge made the errors of principle attributed to him by the Court of Appeal, so that his order could be set aside, Mrs Ilott's housing needs could have been met by a life interest in the necessary sum, but as he did not, it was not necessary to work out how that might have been achieved.

The following review of the cases in which provision has been made for   **5–015** housing needs shows that there would have been considerable room for discussion of the nature of the housing provision for Mrs Ilott and that, for a variety of reasons, the appropriate provision in any given case may properly be an award of an absolute interest in property, in a fund to be applied towards the purchase of a property, or the transfer of the estate's interest in jointly owned property. It is, for instance, apparent that circumstances may exist in which the need for a clean break is the (or a) "magnetic" factor in assessing what constitutes reasonable provision. It is as well to remember that the frequently quoted and regularly applied passage in *Re Dennis* is not a statutory definition. While "maintenance" may normally connote provision for daily income needs or a lump sum whose effect is to release income to meet those needs, there is nothing in the legislation which prevents the making of an award which has the effect of conferring capital on the claimant. One can of course distinguish between claims by surviving spouses[30] and claims by other classes of claimant, because provision for surviving spouses is not restricted to maintenance, and it may be reasonable in all the circumstances for an award to be made which will confer capital on a surviving spouse. Nevertheless there are several reported cases in which absolute interests in property, or in a fund awarded to enable property to be purchased, for the claimant's occupation, have been awarded to claimants for whom financial provision is restricted to maintenance. In what follows, the surviving spouse cases are discussed first.

In the earlier years of the legislation, it was more common to award life   **5–016** interests, even to surviving spouses. An early case under the 1975 Act is *Re Lewis*,[31] where the testator had directed his trustees to expend £10,000 on the purchase of a house for occupation by the applicant during widowhood. At first instance it was ordered that she be constituted as the Settled Land Act tenant for life; on appeal the order was varied on the ground that the income provision made for her did not take inflation into account. In *Re Moody*[32] the testatrix left her estate of some £40,000, represented almost entirely by her house, to her step-daughter. She expressly declared that she had made

---

[30] There are, at the time of writing, no reported cases involving claims by others entitled to the higher standard of provision.
[31] *Re Lewis, Lewis v Lynch* unreported 13 March 1980, CA.
[32] *Re Moody, Moody v Stevenson* [1992] Ch. 486, CA.

no provision for her husband as she considered that he had adequate resources of his own. These consisted of savings of about £6,000. If he had to give up possession of the house, he would have nowhere else to live. The only order that could sensibly be made, in the circumstances, was to give him a continued right of occupation of the property. Unsuccessful applications were made for, respectively, the transfer of a further share, and of the whole of, the matrimonial home, in *Winfield v Billington*[33] and *Davis v Davis*.[34] In *Jevdjovic v Milenko*[35] it was held that the outright transfer of the matrimonial home ordered at first instance was excessive and ordered that the property be sold and the applicant receive £50,000 from the net proceeds of sale. While she had some need for capital, reasonable provision did not require that she should have the entire interest in the only valuable asset of the estate.

5–017   *Re Krubert*[36] was also an application by a surviving spouse in which the order of the County Court judge was appealed and, again, the disposition of the matrimonial home was an important issue. In that case, the deceased and the applicant had been married for 44 years, the marriage being childless; he was 83 years of age at his death and the applicant was 89 at the time of the Court of Appeal hearing. Two years after the marriage, the deceased bought a plot of land in his own name for £200, provided entirely by the applicant; and built a house on it in which they lived until his death. By his will he gave £10,000 and most of his chattels to the applicant, and permitted her to live in the house for so long as she wished to do so and, subject to that interest, he devised the house to trustees upon trust for sale to pay the income to the applicant during her life and then to hold it for the benefit of his brother and sister in equal shares. On her application for reasonable provision, the judge at first instance ordered the house to be transferred to her absolutely and that the rest of his will should take effect as if he had given legacies of £7,000 each to his brother and sister and the rest of his estate to the applicant absolutely. The Court of Appeal considered that, although the applicant needed the house to live in and would need the additional income generated by the reinvested proceeds of sale if she had to move, she had no financial need for an absolute interest in it, and that the judge had erred in principle in awarding her such an interest. The order made was that she should have an absolute interest in the whole estate save for the house and certain specified chattels; and a life interest in the house with remainder to the deceased's brother and sister in equal shares. In making that order the court acknowledged that she had a measurable beneficial interest in the house itself. In *Grattan v McNaughton*[37] the widow's right of occupation of the matrimonial home was not enlarged to an absolute interest, but its terms were made less stringent; her right to occupy was no longer to terminate on marriage or cohabitation, while on her

[33] *Winfield v Billington* unreported 30 July 1990, CA.
[34] *Davis v Davis* [1993] 1 F.L.R. 54, CA.
[35] *Jevdjovic v Milenko* unreported 12 March 1990, CA.
[36] *Re Krubert* [1997] Ch. 97, CA.
[37] *Grattan v McNaughton* [2001] W.T.L.R. 1305.

ceasing to reside in the property another property could be purchased for her occupation out of the proceeds of sale. The provision made for the 73-year-old applicant widower in *Barron v Woodhead*[38] was a sum of £100,000 to be applied to the purchase of a house or flat for occupation rent free for his lifetime with him paying the outgoings. Any surplus was to be invested to maximise the income, which was also to be paid to him for life.

There are several cases in which the surviving spouse was awarded an   **5–018** absolute interest in the matrimonial home or in the fund provided to meet their housing needs, albeit, in the first two cases mentioned, the property was charged with pecuniary legacies to other family members. In *Rajabally v Rajabally*,[39] the matrimonial home was ordered to be transferred to the applicant subject to a legacy to her oldest son charged on it, and a similar course was adopted at first instance in *Moody v Haselgrove*,[40] where, unusually, the Court of Appeal used the powers under s.2(4) to vary the trial judge's order. In *Adams v Lewis*[41] the widow was awarded the matrimonial home absolutely. In *P v G, P and P*[42] the widow's interest in the former matrimonial home under her husband's will terminated on her death or remarriage; this was enlarged to an absolute interest and she was also awarded a lump sum. In *Cunliffe v Fielden*[43] the lump sum award to the widow was to meet both her housing and income needs and it was left to her to apportion the sum between them. In *Lilleyman v Lilleyman*,[44] it was ordered that the estate's interest in two residential properties, or its cash equivalent be transferred to the widow outright. In *Iqbal v Ahmed*,[45] the applicant widow was awarded an absolute interest in the estate's share of the property which she was occupying at the time of the deceased's death. The Court of Appeal held that a life interest was not an appropriate form of provision as it would not provide a capital cushion (which might have been necessary to fund essential repairs to the property) and also, that the hostile relations between her and the deceased's son, who was one of the trustees of the property, made a clean break essential.

There is a similar spectrum of outcomes in cases where the lower standard   **5–019** of reasonable financial provision applies. In *Harrington v Gill*[46] the applicant and the deceased, who died intestate, had lived together for six years prior to his death. After his death she continued to live in his house but retained, for some three years after his death, the tenancy of the council flat in which she

---

[38] *Barron v Woodhead* [2009] 1 F.L.R. 747.
[39] *Rajabally v Rajabally* [1987] 2 F.L.R. 390, CA.
[40] *Moody v Haselgrove* unreported 16 November 1987, CA.
[41] *Adams v Lewis* [2001] W.T.L.R. 493. The provision under the will was that out of the residuary estate the trustees should provide and keep up a residence for her.
[42] *P v G, P and P* [2006] 1 F.L.R. 431.
[43] *Cunliffe v Fielden* [2006] Ch. 361, CA.
[44] *Lilleyman v Lilleyman* [2013] 1 F.L.R. 47.
[45] *Iqbal v Ahmed* [2012] 1 F.L.R. 32, CA, affirming the decision of the trial judge.
[46] *Harrington v Gill* (1983) 4 F.L.R. 265, CA.

had previously been living. On appeal, the house was ordered to be settled on her for life, in addition to the provision ordered at first instance. In *Baker v Baker*,[47] where the claimant was a cohabitant, the provisional order was made that the claimant should have a life interest in the property and its proceeds of sale, which might be applied towards the purchase of another property for her occupation.

5–020　　In both *Re Haig*,[48] where the applicant was a dependant, and *Wallace v Thorburn*,[49] where she was a former spouse who had not remarried, provision for housing was made by way of a sum to be applied in the purchase of a house. In *Re Haig* the applicant had been living with the testator in his house for some years before his death, but the alternative of transferring it to her was not considered appropriate as she was on bad terms with his son, who lived nearby. The lump sum provision ordered in *Re Callaghan*[50] is an example of the type of maintenance identified in *Re Dennis*[51] as that which releases income and thus enables the applicant to meet other daily living expenses. The lump sum award of £14,000 in *Re Leach*[52] was also made on the basis that it would enable the applicant to pay off mortgage liabilities and personal indebtedness to the co-owner of her house, thus releasing additional income which would be available for her maintenance. Two more recent cases in which a non-spouse applicant was awarded an absolute interest in property are *Negus v Bahouse*,[53] in which the claimant was a cohabitant and the award included a transfer to her, free of mortgage, of the property in which she and the deceased had been living immediately before his death, and *Musa v Holliday*,[54] a claim by a dependant in which the Court of Appeal upheld the trial judge's decision to meet her housing needs (and those of her 13-year-old son by the deceased) by the outright transfer to her of the house in which she had been living at the death of the deceased. There was ample evidence of the hostility between her and the deceased's adult

---

[47] [2008] 2 F.L.R. 767. No grant of probate had yet been made, but the parties agreed that the deputy judge should consider and rule on the 1975 Act claim on the material before him. There were also unsuccessful claims to set aside the deceased's will and to establish a right to the property in which they had been living on the basis of proprietary estoppel.

[48] *Re Haig* (1979) 129 N.L.J. 420.

[49] *Wallace v Thorburn* unreported 9 October 1987, CA (estate left to cohabitant; provision made to assist in purchase of house for former wife who had not remarried).

[50] *Re Callaghan* [1985] Fam. 1 (adult male treated as child of the family; provision to purchase his home outright instead of having to buy it with the aid of a mortgage, thus freeing income for general living expenses).

[51] *Re Dennis* [1981] 2 All E.R. 140, where Browne-Wilkinson J said at 144–45: "The provision can be by way of a lump sum, for example, to buy a house in which the applicant can be housed, thereby relieving him *pro tanto* of income expenditure. Nor am I suggesting that there may not be cases in which the payment of existing debts may not be appropriate as a maintenance payment; for example, to pay the debts of an applicant in order to enable him to continue to carry on a profit-making business sor profession may well be for his maintenance."

[52] *Re Leach, Leach v Lindemann* [1986] Ch. 226, CA, varying the amount of the award made at first instance (this being necessary due to an incorrect value of the net estate having been used initially), but otherwise affirming the judgment.

[53] *Negus v Bahouse* [2008] 1 F.L.R. 381.

[54] *Musa v Holliday* [2013] 1 F.L.R. 816, CA, at [26]–[27].

children. Sir Nicholas Wall P said that, if the judge came to the conclusion that the transfer of the house was needed in order to meet the statutory objective, there could be no objection in principle to such an order. It was clearly not the case for a life interest; the case cried out for a clean break. In *Williams v Martin*,[55] the deceased (N) had been separated from his wife for many years, but had never changed the will which he had made in 1986 leaving all his estate to her. The claimant (J) cohabited with him for a long period, the last three years of which were spent living together in a house (20 Coburg Road) which they had bought jointly. Her claim was specifically for provision by way of the transfer of N's half share of that property to her. The trial judge held that, taking into account the long cohabitation, the claimant's age (69) and financial position, and her contribution to the welfare of the family, it was appropriate to vest N's half share in 20 Coburg Road in her absolutely. However, that decision was successfully appealed[56] on three grounds, one of which was that the trial judge had wrongly disregarded J's 50 per cent interest in another property as an asset available to meet her needs and it was found that the award of a life interest in N's share of 20 Coburg Road would constitute reasonable financial provision for her.

In *Re Abram (Deceased)*[57] the applicant was the adult son of the testatrix,   **5–021** under whose will he received no benefit. He had been in business, which had failed, and he had entered into an individual voluntary arrangement with his creditors under which any sums which he recovered from the 1975 Act proceedings would go to his creditors. It was found that the will did not make reasonable financial provision for him. The court considered that maintenance could best be provided for him by directing a settlement for his benefit pursuant to s.2(1)(d) of the 1975 Act. It was ordered that 50 per cent of the estate net of everything except inheritance tax be settled on protective trusts for him for life with remainder on the trusts of his will.

(c) Section 2(1)(f), (g) and (h): Variation of Settlements

Section 2(1)(f) empowers the court to make an order varying any ante-   **5–022** nuptial or post-nuptial settlement made on the parties to a marriage to which the deceased was one of the parties, the variation being for the benefit of the surviving party to the marriage, a child of the marriage, or a person who was treated by the deceased as a child of the family in relation to that marriage. The essential features of such a settlement for the purposes of the 1975 Act are:

(a) it should be in some way referable to the parties' capacity as a married couple[58]; and

(b) it must be a settlement in relation to a marriage of the deceased.

---

[55] *Williams v Martin* [2016] W.T.L.R. 1075.
[56] *Martin (Deceased), Re* [2017] EWHC 491 (Ch), Marcus Smith J.
[57] *Re Abram, Deceased* [1996] 2 F.L.R. 379.
[58] See *Hargreaves v Hargreaves* [1926] P. 42 at 45 where it was defined as: "a settlement made in contemplation of, or because of, marriage and with reference to the interests of married people, or their children."

Section 2(1)(g)[59] confers on the court power to make an order varying any settlement made:

(a) during the subsistence of a civil partnership formed by the deceased; or

(b) in anticipation of the formation of a civil partnership by the deceased;

on the civil partners (including such a settlement made by will), the settlement being for the benefit of the surviving civil partner or any child of both the civil partners, or any person who was treated as a child of the family in relation to that civil partnership.

5–023   A settlement involving co-owned residential property has sufficient reference to the marriage to be an ante-nuptial or post-nuptial settlement,[60] even in a case where although both parties had contributed to the purchase of the matrimonial home, it had been conveyed into the sole name of the husband. In *Cook v Cook*[61] it was held that the effect of that transaction was to confer an equitable right on each spouse to an undivided share of the house, a settlement being constituted by the purchase of the house as a joint enterprise, each spouse contributing to the cost. That created a trust for sale and, pending sale, an equitable tenancy in common. Affirming the judgment of Phillimore J that a post-nuptial settlement had been created, Willmer LJ concluded that each spouse enjoyed the benefits attributable to both parties' contributions and that that resulted in continuing provision being made for each spouse in their character as a spouse. In *N v N*,[62] a company, of which the trust was the sole shareholder, purchased a property for occupation, as the matrimonial home, by the parties to a contemplated marriage, and they occupied it both before and after the marriage. At that time the husband was the sole beneficiary of the trust. It was envisaged that the parties would occupy the property on the terms of a tenancy agreement between the company and themselves. The agreement, which created an assured short-hold tenancy, was not executed until some three-and-a-half years after the purchase, and the marriage broke down shortly afterwards, the wife vacating the property. Coleridge J held that the creation of the tenancy did not undermine the fundamental relationship of trustee and beneficiary,

---

[59] Inserted by Sch.4 to the Civil Partnership Act 2004 para.16.

[60] *Brown v Brown* [1959] P. 86, CA. In that case it was said, citing *Bosworthick v Bosworthick* [1927] P. 64, that a deed vesting property in trustees and creating successive legal or beneficial interests so as to have the attributes of a settlement familiar to conveyancers was a settlement for the purposes of s.25 of the MCA 1950.

[61] *Cook v Cook* [1962] P. 235, CA. Unlike *Brown v Brown*, there was no vesting deed or other document which established in terms that there was a settlement, but the argument that there could be no settlement without such a document was rejected.

[62] *N v N* [2006] 1 F.L.R. 856, where the law relating to anti[sic]-nuptial and post-nuptial trusts, from the mid-19th century up to *Brooks v Brooks* [1996] A.C. 375, is reviewed at [22]–[30] of the judgment.

between the husband and the trustees, and the arrangement was an ante-nuptial settlement which the court had power to vary.

By the time that *N v N* was decided, it had already been recognised that a   **5–024**
nuptial settlement could lose its nuptial character.[63] Since then, there has been a series of cases in which the question whether an originally non-nuptial settlement could, in whole or part, acquire a nuptial character.[64] The debate as to the circumstances in which an originally non-nuptial trust can or has become nuptialised continues apace,[65] but, given the paucity of 1975 Act cases in which the power to vary nuptial settlements has been exercised, it seems improbable that the outcome of that debate will be of much significance in the field of family provision claims.

At the time of writing s.2(1)(f) has only once received detailed judicial   **5–025**
consideration. In the unreported case of *Dixit v Dixit*,[66] the order made in the first instance was set aside on appeal because no consideration had been given to the Capital Gains Tax consequences of making it. In consequence it was not decided whether the order, which involved "switching" the trusts of two properties so that each was to be held on the trusts on which the other was originally held, was one that could be made under s.2(1)(f). It may be, however, that judicial attention will be directed towards s.2(1)(f) more frequently following the extensive consideration given to pre-nuptial contracts in *Radmacher v Granatino*[67] and the recent Law Commission consultation on marital property agreements.[68] The Supreme Court[69] reaffirmed the rule laid down in *Hyman v Hyman*[70] that the jurisdiction of the courts in financial remedy (ancillary relief) matters cannot be ousted, but held that:

"The court should give effect to a nuptial agreement that is freely entered into by each party with a full appreciation of its implications

---

[63] *Prescott v Fellowes* [1958] P. 260, CA. (no "property settled" at the date of the decree absolute); *C v C (Ancillary relief: Nuptial settlements)* [2005] Fam. 250 (discretionary trust, nuptial when created, capable of losing its nuptial character, though on the facts the exercise by the trustees of a revocable power to remove beneficiaries had not deprived it of its nuptial character).

[64] *N v N* is such a case, since the matrimonial home comprised in the originally non-nuptial Fermain Trust was held by Coleridge J to be subject to an ante-nuptial settlement.

[65] See, for example, the differing views of Coleridge J in *Quan v Bray* [2015] 2 F.L.R. 546, at [58]–[60], [66], [69] and Sir Peter Singer in *Joy v Joy-Morancho* [2016] 1 F.L.R. 815, [104]–[113], the "telescoping" approach adopted by Mostyn J in *Hope v Krejci* [2013] 1 F.L.R. 182, and the "piercing of the corporate veil" also considered in that case and further analysed by Lord Sumption in *Prest v Petrodel Resources* [2013] 2 A.C. 415, at [27]–[28], [37].

[66] *Dixit v Dixit* unreported 23 June 1988, CA.

[67] *Radmacher v Granatino* [2011] 1 A.C. 534 (SC), dismissing (by a majority of 8–1) the appeal from the Court of Appeal [2009] 2 F.L.R. 1181, which allowed the wife's appeal from the decision at first instance [2009] 1 F.L.R. 1478.

[68] Law Commission, Consultation Paper 198, *Marital Property Agreement* (2011). The interaction between binding marital property agreements and the 1975 Act is considered at [7.77]–[7.89] and particular attention is devoted to the question whether it would be appropriate for them to contain a provision equivalent to a s.15 order.

[69] *Radmacher v Granatino* [2011] 1 A.C. 534 (SC), at [25].

[70] *Hyman v Hyman* [1929] A.C. 601.

unless, in the circumstances prevailing, it would not be fair to hold the parties to their agreement."

5–026   Section 2(1)(f) has not yet been invoked in relation to a personal pension scheme,[71] and the Law Commission considered the possibility of making pension benefits as a source of provision.[72] It initially took the view that the legislative mechanism of the pension sharing provisions within the MCA 1973 could be adapted for use in the family provision context,[73] but was persuaded by the consultation responses that that was not realistic.[74] The position therefore remains that pension benefits are available as a source of financial provision only if they are caught by s.8(1) of the 1975 Act or by the exercise of the court's powers under s.2(1)(f) or, where the claimant is a surviving civil partner s.2(1)(g), analogous to the power under the MCA 1973 to make orders varying ante-nuptial and post-nuptial settlements.[75] The MCA 1973 also contains a provision[76] directing the court to have regard, when deciding to exercise its powers under (inter alia) s.24, to the value, to each of the parties to the marriage, of any benefit, including a pension which, by reason of the dissolution or annulment of the marriage, that party will lose the chance of acquiring.

5–027   These provisions were considered by the House of Lords in *Brooks v Brooks*.[77] In ancillary relief proceedings, District Judge Plumstead (as she then was) held that a company pension fund set up by Mr Brooks was a post-nuptial settlement and that, as under the rules of the pension scheme he could elect to provide out of the funds a pension for a spouse, the court had power under s.24(1)(c) of the MCA 1973 to vary it. This decision was affirmed at first instance,[78] then by the majority of the Court of Appeal.[79] Waite and Neill LJJ took the view that where a pension scheme is entered into after marriage, a sufficient nexus can be shown between the married state and the pension scheme that the scheme can be regarded as a post-nuptial settlement if the wife has an interest in the scheme or some prospect

---

[71] In *P v G, P and P (Family Provision: Relevance of Divorce Provision)* [2006] 1 F.L.R. 431, the claimant widow was a beneficiary of a small self-administered company pension scheme (the C pension scheme), in which her entitlement as widow was £3,453,000 (see [130]–[38]). There were doubts about the security of the scheme (see [143]–[144]) She wished to sever her connection with the scheme in its existing format (see [248]) as to which Black J was willing to make a *Brooks* type order if required. The judgment does not in terms refer to s.2(1)(f).

[72] In Law Com. CP 191, consultees were asked (paras 7.82 and 7.83) whether they favoured reform of the 1975 Act so as to make benefits from pension funds available as a source of provision, and what, if any, legal or practical difficulties they foresaw.

[73] Law Com. CP 191, at para.7.79.

[74] Law Com. LC 331, at para.7.112. Although there was considerable support for such a reform (see [7.105]), the Law Commission did not recommend it; the scale of the problem created by the unavailability of pension benefits did not warrant the administrative complexities which the reform would inevitably engender; see paras 7.106–7.112.

[75] MCA 1973 s.24(1)(c).

[76] MCA 1973 s.25(2)(b).

[77] *Brooks v Brooks* [1996] A.C. 375.

[78] By Ewbank J in *Brooks v Brooks* [1993] Fam. 322.

[79] *Brooks v Brooks* [1995] Fam. 70, CA.

of obtaining an interest in it in her capacity as wife. Hoffman LJ dissented; his analysis was that a settlement was post-nuptial if:

"...it conferred benefits on the husband in his capacity as a husband, or the wife in her capacity as wife, or both of them in their capacity as husband and wife."[80]

The scheme conferred benefits on Mr Brooks in his capacity as an employee, though arguably it gave him power to create a post-nuptial settlement.

The House of Lords' decision in *Brooks* turned on two rules of the   **5–028** scheme. Rule 1(e) entitled Mr Brooks to elect, on his retirement, to give up a portion of his pension to provide, from the date of his death, a deferred pension for life for his spouse or anyone else financially dependent on him. Rule 2(c) provided that if he died while still employed by the company, the scheme trustees had discretion to pay the benefits to a class including Mr Brooks' spouse, parents, grandparents, children, or the issue of any of them. In Lord Nicholls' opinion, the presence of those rules placed the scheme within the matrimonial legislation and the court had power to vary it. It thus follows that assets of a private pension scheme which pass to the deceased's personal representatives and form part of the net estate on death may, if the terms of the scheme are such as to bring it within the description of a post-nuptial settlement, be made the subject of an order under s.2(1)(f) of the 1975 Act.

It was brought to the attention of the Law Commission[81] that, although   **5–029** the court has power to order the settlement, for the benefit of the applicant, of property comprised in the net estate, it lacks the power to vary, for the benefit of the applicant, trusts which have arisen under the deceased's will or by operation of the intestacy rules. It does have power to vary these trusts for the purpose of giving effect to an order or for the purpose of securing that any such order operates fairly as between one beneficiary of the estate and another, but that power is only ancillary to the powers in s.2(1) and cannot be used under that subsection to satisfy the applicant's claim.[82] The desired result may be achieved by resettling on new trusts property that is held on existing trusts, which the court has power to do under s.2(1)(d) of the 1975 Act, but that might be a disproportionate and unwieldy approach which could be avoided if it were possible simply to vary an existing trust. The Law Commission concluded that that power should be available in all cases and its availability should be clear on the face of the Act. In accordance with its recommendation, a new s.2(1)(h) was added,[83] giving the court power to make:

---

[80] *Prinsep v Prinsep* [1929] P. 225.
[81] Law Com. LC 331 at paras 7.121–7.126.
[82] A. Francis, *Inheritance Act Claims: Law, Practice and Procedure* at para.13[5].
[83] Inheritance and Trustees' Powers Act 2014 s.6 and Sch.2 paras 4(1), 4(3).

"(h) an order varying for the applicant's benefit the trusts on which the deceased's estate is held (whether arising under the will, or the law relating to intestacy, or both)."

(d) Section 2(4): Consequential Directions

5–030　　The consequential directions which can be given under s.2(4) include the apportionment of the burden of an award so that the order operates fairly as between one beneficiary of the estate of the deceased and another.[84] This is implicit in the requirements in s.3(1)(c) to consider the financial needs and resources of any beneficiary of the estate, in ss.3(1)(d) and (f) which refer to any applicant for an order and any beneficiary of the estate, and 3(1)(g) which refers to the conduct of the applicant or any other person. It is usually, but not invariably, the case that the burden of the award is borne by residue[85]; minor pecuniary and specific legacies are very unlikely to be depleted for that purpose. In *Re Bunning*,[86] Vinelott J ordered that the provision made for the wife fall primarily on the gift of residue to Cambridge University and then rateably on the pecuniary legacies to the University and the Royal Society for the Protection of Birds. In *Malone v Harrison*,[87] where residue was exhausted by the liability to capital transfer tax and there had to be an abatement of the specific legacies, the provision made for the applicant was ordered to be paid entirely out of the share of the major beneficiary. Section 2(4) was not explicitly considered in either case.

5–031　　However s.2(4) was considered by Morritt LJ in *Re Goodchild*[88] in relation to the order made by Carnwath J at first instance when the case was restored for further argument as to the amount of the award and the manner in which it was to be provided. Under the will of the applicant's father (D), his entire estate was left to his second wife (E). At trial, the applicant (G) was awarded £185,000 and the matter was then adjourned to give the parties the opportunity, as Carnwath J put it, "to arrive at a sensible financial arrangement which meets their respective needs and would be tax-efficient". This they were unable to do and the matter was restored for further argument, after which an order was drawn up. The order provided that the will should have effect and be deemed always to have had effect as if D had bequeathed a legacy of £185,000 to trustees to hold the same upon trust to pay the income to E until her death or until 1 March 1996, whichever was the sooner, and thereafter to the applicant (G) absolutely. The purpose of inserting the life interest in favour of E was to obtain the spouse exemption under s.18 of the Inheritance Tax Act 1984. This would, of course, create a

---

[84] Provisions with the same effect in the pre-1975 Act legislation were contained in s.3(2) of the 1938 Act and in s.28(3) of the MCA 1965.

[85] See *Re Simson* [1950] Ch. 38 at 40, where Vaisey J said: "it is an illusion all too prevalent that these provisions are normally or primarily made out of residue", but at 44, when explaining why two-thirds of the burden is to be borne by the pecuniary legacies and one-third by residue, he said "Of course, residue is the normal and obvious place from which provision is made."

[86] *Re Bunning* [1984] Ch. 480.

[87] *Malone v Harrison* [1979] 1 W.L.R. 1353.

[88] *Re Goodchild* [1997] 3 All E.R. 63, CA.

prospective liability on the death of E, but, because of the "taper relief" provision[89] this would reduce as time went on and, because the transfer was a potentially exempt transfer[90] it might never mature. It was not possible to eliminate the liability by agreement between E and G because, by the time the order was made, more than two years had elapsed since the death of D, with the consequence that a variation of the deceased's will would not have been effective for IHT purposes.[91] The only way of doing so was by an order of the court pursuant to s.2 of the 1975 Act.[92]

Morritt LJ then said, in relation to s.2(4)(b) of the 1975 Act: 5–032

> "If the order made is properly within the jurisdiction of the court, the fact that it was sought with the motive of seeking to achieve a better tax position is usually irrelevant. But where the effect of the order is to confer a substantial advantage on the parties at the expense of the revenue it is in my view important that the court should be satisfied that the order is not only within its jurisdiction but also one which may properly be made."

After observing that there was no challenge to the manner in which provision had been made, it being in both parties' interests that the order made, if any, should be in that form, he continued:

> "We have heard no argument on whether the order was or was not warranted by the terms of subsection (4); that would be a matter for the Revenue. However, I think it is important for the future that if an order such as this is to be made the grounds on which it is thought to be authorised by subsection (4) should be clearly demonstrated, for the consent and wishes of the parties is not enough."

In the Northern Ireland case of *Re Campbell*,[93] the deceased (a widow)   5–033 died intestate leaving ten surviving children and two grandchildren (MH and SC) who were the children of a son who had predeceased her. The question arose whether the court had power under art.4 of the 1979 Order (corresponding to s.2 of the 1975 Act) to increase the share of a non-applicant beneficiary of the estate. It was held, rightly, that it did not; it could only treat the non-applicant more favourably by relieving them, in whole or in part, from the burden of contributing towards such provision as was ordered for the applicants: see *Re Preston, Preston v Hoggarth*.[94] An increase in the share taken by a non-applicant could not be regarded as something which was consequential upon or supplemental to the provision made for the applicant by the order, and it would open the door to the

---

[89] Inheritance Tax Act (IHTA) 1984 s.7.
[90] IHTA 1984 s.3A.
[91] IHTA 1984 s.142.
[92] IHTA 1984 s.146.
[93] *Re Campbell* [1983] N.I. 10.
[94] *Re Preston, Preston v Hoggarth* [1969] 1 W.L.R. 317.

possibility of embarking on a general review of the position of other beneficiaries.

3.—Sections 5, 6 and 7: Interim Orders and Variation of Orders

5–034　There is very little case-law on these provisions. In *Barnsley v Ward*[95] the
Court of Appeal warned against appealing interim orders. Templeman LJ
said, in that case:

> "Speaking for myself, I deprecate appeals against orders made under
> section 5, because where a judge comes to the conclusion that an
> applicant is in need of immediate financial assistance, his conclusion
> and his order can be almost completely frustrated by an appeal",

and Ormrod LJ spoke in similar terms. The power to make interim orders is
restricted to ordering the payment to the applicant of such sum or sums at
such intervals as the court thinks reasonable. Interim payments may not
continue beyond the date on which the order under s.2 is made or, as the
case may be, the date on which the court decides not to exercise its powers
under the section. It is normal for orders under s.5 to be expressed to run
until judgment in the action or further order. In *Re Besterman*[96] an interim
award was made for payment to the applicant of a lump sum of £75,000 and
income of £11,500 per year. The purpose of the capital provision was to
enable her to buy another house and to vacate the matrimonial home so that
it could be sold. Provision was also made for the upkeep of the matrimonial
home pending the hearing of the action.

5–035　In the Northern Ireland case of *O'Reilly v Mallon*,[97] the surviving spouse
was one of two applicants for financial provision out of the estate of the
deceased. She was entitled to an annuity of £5,000 under the will of the
deceased. Under art.7 of the 1979 Order (corresponding to s.5 of the 1975
Act) she applied for interim relief and it was ordered that the executor pay
to her such sums as might appear reasonable in respect of accounts for rates,
telephone, oil, and the services of a home help and a night nurse.

5–036　Section 5 does not provide for interim relief by way of allowing an
applicant to occupy any property pending the hearing of the action.[98] In
Smith v Smith[99] the claimant widow had married the deceased (T) in 1991,
but the marriage broke down and in 2003 she returned to her native country,
Russia, where she had a flat, and thereafter returned to England only for
short periods, during which she stayed with T in the property which had

---

[95] *Barnsley v Ward*, unreported 8 January 1980, CA.

[96] *Re Besterman* (1982) 3 F.L.R. 255, at first instance (HH Judge Mervyn Davies QC).

[97] *O'Reilly v Mallon* [1995] NI Ch. 1.

[98] Family Law Act 1996 Pt IV ss.30–43; a surviving spouse may, in certain circumstances, be
entitled to home rights and a surviving spouse or cohabitant may be able to apply for an
occupation order in relation to the matrimonial home.

[99] *Smith v Smith* [2012] 2 F.L.R. 230.

been the matrimonial home ("the Property"). T died in 2009 and some 18 months later the widow made a claim for interim relief, seeking a payment of £25,000 so that she could repay loans made to her by friends, and an order that she be permitted to live in the Property. Dismissing the claim, Mann J held that she had failed to meet the requirement laid down by s.5(1)(a) of showing that she was in immediate financial need. She had no family in England and there was no evidence that she wanted to move away from her family and social circle in Russia or make her home in the Property. The section does not provide any power to preserve property, or include any provision analogous to s.37 of the MCA 1973, which enables orders to be made for the purpose of restraining acts by the person against whom the proceedings are brought from dealing with property with a view to defeating a claim for financial relief. These matters are discussed more fully in Ch.7.

Section 6 confers the power to vary orders for periodical payments, and if such orders have been varied under s.6(1), they may be further varied under s.6(4). Section 6(6) of the 1975 Act defines "relevant property", and provides that an order under the section can affect only relevant property. This provision was considered in *Fricker v Personal Representatives of Fricker*.[100] In 1977, a consent order had been made under s.26 of the MCA 1965, under which the applicant was permitted to live in a house purchased by the trustees of the estate of her deceased husband. In 1981 she applied for a variation of the order under s.6 of the 1975 Act, transferring the property to her so that she might sell it subject to her right of occupation. The trustees took the point that the house was not "relevant property" as defined by s.6(6), viz., property the income of which was applicable wholly or in part for the maintenance of, or the making of periodical payments to, the applicant. French J held that, as the applicant had not derived any actual income from the property, it was not relevant property. Neither her occupation of the property, nor the notional income which she might in some circumstances be deemed to have derived from that occupation, constituted periodical payments to her or income applicable for her maintenance.

5–037

A variation of the original order under s.6 may be by way of increasing or decreasing a periodical payments order, and altering the conditions attached thereto; it can also provide for the payment of a lump sum out of any relevant property or for a transfer of the relevant property, or a specified part of it, to any person who has applied or who would, but for s.4 of the Act, be entitled to apply. There is no power to order a settlement of property, the acquisition of property out of property comprised in the estate, or a variation of a settlement, nor can any order be made under ss.9, 10 or 11; see s.6(9). There is no reported case under the 1975 Act of an application for a variation being made by anyone other than the original applicant.

5–038

The persons permitted to apply under s.6 are specified in s.6(5). They include persons who would benefit from a downward variation or discharge

5–039

---

[100] *Fricker v Personal Representatives of Fricker* (1982) 3 F.L.R. 228.

of a periodical payments order. In this context, the term "beneficiaries" includes:

(a) persons who are beneficially interested in the estate of the deceased under their will or intestacy, or would be so interested if an order had not been made under the Act; and

(b) persons who have received any sum of money or other property which by virtue of s.8(1) or 8(2) of the Act is treated as part of the net estate, or would have received that sum or other property if an order had not been made under the Act.

However, neither survivors of joint tenants where the deceased's severable share has been treated as part of the net estate, nor persons interested in dispositions in respect of which an order has been made under ss.10 or 11, are beneficiaries within the meaning of s.6(5).

5–040   Section 6(7) directs the court to have regard, when exercising its powers to vary an order, to all the circumstances of the case, including any change in any of the matters to which the court was required to have regard when making the order which is sought to be varied. These circumstances would presumably include changes in the financial position of the applicant, any other applicant, or any beneficiary, and the occurrence of or recovery from any mental or physical disability affecting any such person. The case of *Taylor v Bell*[101] is one in which such a change of circumstances occurred.

5–041   Mr Taylor's father died in 2006, leaving net estate of approximately £2 million. No provision was made for him in the will and he was not included as a beneficiary of the discretionary trust created on the same day as the will, to which the residuary estate was an accretion. His claim for reasonable financial provision out of his father's estate was compromised, the terms being embodied in a consent order made by HH Judge Langan QC on or about 27 May 2008. The purpose of the order was to make reasonable financial provision for his maintenance during his sixth form college and university studies. The maximum amount payable was £210,000, which was to be kept in a separate bank account, and payments were to cease on 31 August 2014.[102] Mr Taylor was a keen and talented singer and wished to pursue a career as an opera singer. Unfortunately his education did not go according to plan, partly because of a severe accident which he suffered in April 2008, requiring treatment over a period of some four months and partly because of learning difficulties which affected his memory, information processing speed and ability to manage his time and organise his work. In the event he did not finish his university education by 31 August 2014 and it was anticipated that he would not do so until the summer of 2015.[103] He also wished to pursue a postgraduate course of two years' duration either at the Royal College of Music or the Guildhall School of Music and he sought

---

[101] *Taylor v Bell* [2015] All E.R. (D) 208.
[102] The order is set out in detail at [13]–[14].
[103] That is, several months after the judgment, which was handed down on 15 February 2015.

to have the order varied so as to extend the funding both for the remainder of the undergraduate course and the whole of the postgraduate course. At the time of his application he had received £112,443.71, which was £97,556.79 less than the maximum sum payable under the order. However, at the date of the application there was only £38,479 in the estate account.

The executors opposed the application on several grounds. Mr Taylor had **5-042** not yet been accepted on either of the courses, as the necessary auditions were not due until after the hearing. They contended initially that he did not have the musical talent to undergo the course, but in the event they accepted the expert evidence to the contrary on both sides.[104] The principal legal argument was based on the case of *Barder v Caluori*[105] though neither that nor the other authorities cited[106] were found to be of any assistance.[107] *Barder v Caluori* is a divorce case in which an order was set aside at first instance as being vitiated by mistake, that judgment being finally upheld in the House of Lords after reversal by the Court of Appeal. Lord Brandon held that the conditions necessary for a court to exercise its discretion to grant leave to appeal out of time from an order for financial provision or property transfer made after divorce, on the ground of new events, were:

(a)   the new event invalidates the basis or fundamental assumption on which the order was made;
(b)   the new event occurred after a relatively short time;
(c)   the application was made promptly; and
(d)   the grant of leave must not prejudice third parties.

It was submitted that there was a heavy onus on Mr Taylor in seeking to set aside the consent order and that he could not meet those conditions. However, HH Judge Behrens did not accept those submissions. Mr Taylor's application was not of that nature; it was an in-time application to vary an order for periodical payments made under s.2(1)(a) of the 1975 Act. Section 6(3) permitted such applications to be made within six months of the expiry of the order and conditions (b) and (c) were inconsistent with that provision. Nor was the jurisdiction under s.6 circumscribed in the manner stated in condition (a). There were no specific hurdles to be overcome before the jurisdiction under s.6 could be exercised. There was nothing in the order purporting to exclude the statutory power conferred by s.6 and indeed it was not apparent that it could be excluded. Subsection 6(10) made it clear that

---

[104]   The judge was critical of the costs incurred by the executors on investigating this and Mr Taylor's financial position, regarding it as both unfortunate and, having regard to the sums remaining in the estate account, disproportionate. The total costs incurred in defending the application were £23,268. Further criticism was expressed at [44]–[47] and the judge's provisional view was that the executors should be allowed costs of £15,000 including VAT and disbursements out of the estate.

[105]   *Barder v Caluori* [1988] A.C. 20, HL, per Lord Brandon at 43B–E.

[106]   *X v X* [2002] 1 F.L.R. 508; *Edgar v Edgar* [1980] 1 W.L.R 1410; (considered in *X v X*, both cases being divorce cases); *Brennan v Bolt Burdon* [2005] Q.B. 303 (concerned with the extent of mistake necessary to invalidate a compromise agreement in a personal injury claim and held to be of no assistance as there was no mistake).

[107]   See the judgment at [32]–[38].

the court had power to extend the periodical payments beyond the period provided for in the original order. The expressed purpose of the order was to provide maintenance for Mr Taylor until the end of his postgraduate studies. The timetable envisaged had not been met and the reasons for that did not reflect adversely on him. The sum limited by the order had not been fully expended and Mr Taylor was in need of further maintenance. There was no evidence of need or any other compelling evidence by any other beneficiary. The appropriate award was £6,500 to meet his needs during the remainder of the current academic year and £7,500 for each of the two following years, conditional on his attending a full-time post-graduate course of training.

5–043   There is no reported case of an application to vary a lump sum under s.7. Lump sum provision may be made by way of an original order under s.2(1)(b) or a variation under s.6(2)(b), and either type of order may provide for the amount awarded to be paid by instalments. The terms which may be varied are the amount, number and date of payment of instalments; the persons who may apply are the person to whom the sum is payable, the personal representatives of the deceased, and the trustees of the property out of which the lump sum is payable.

4.—TIME LIMITS: SECTIONS 4 AND 23

(a) Case-law on Section 4

5–044   The two earliest reported cases are still among the most important on this topic, though there are several more, reported and unreported, from which useful guidance can be obtained. The first of the two major cases is *Re Salmon*,[108] which does not refer to any of the cases decided under the 1938 Act except for *Re Ruttie*[109] and *Re Gonin*.[110] In *Re Salmon*, Megarry VC referred to what Ungoed-Thomas J had said in *Re Ruttie* and disclaimed any intention to lay down principles. However, he collected from that case that:

(1)   the judicial discretion to extend time was unfettered, and was to be exercised judicially and in accordance with what is just and proper; and

(2)   the onus of taking the case out of the general rule lies on the applicant, and the rule is substantive, not procedural; thus the applicant must make out a substantial case for being allowed an extension of time.

---

[108]   *Re Salmon* [1981] Ch. 167.
[109]   *Re Ruttie* [1969] 3 All E.R. 1633.
[110]   *Re Gonin* [1979] Ch. 16; [1977] 2 All E.R. 720. There were two consolidated actions. One was a claim to the deceased's house and furniture, the other was an application under the 1938 Act, brought over two years out of time. The outcome of the application under the 1938 Act is reported only at [1977] 2 All E.R. 720, at 736–737.

The remaining guidelines were not derived from the then decided cases, though *Re Gonin* was mentioned in connection with the last of them. They are:

(3) how promptly and in what circumstances the applicant has sought the permission of the court after the time limit has expired. This is not simply a question of how much delay there has been. The reasons for delay are to be looked at, as is the promptitude with which notice of the intended claim was given, by letter before action or otherwise;

(4) whether negotiations had been commenced within the time limit;

(5) whether the estate has been distributed before a claim has been made or notified. In relation to this, it is relevant that s.20(1) of the 1975 Act provides statutory protection for a personal representative who distributes after the end of the six-month period, although without prejudice to any power to recover, by reason of an order under the Act, any part of the estate so distributed; and

(6) whether the refusal of an extension of time would leave the applicant without a remedy against anyone.

In *Re Salmon*, the statutory period had expired on 15 June 1979, and the originating summons was issued on 27 November, five-and-a-half months late. Before the expiry of the period, a request had been made to the executors (National Westminster Bank) for an ex gratia payment, but that was rejected in a letter which left it to the applicant to take such action as she might be advised, and, as no action was taken, the estate was distributed on the expiry of the six-month period. The executors were not informed of a possible claim until 11 November. It is therefore unsurprising, having regard to guidelines (3), (4) and (5), that the application was refused.

In *Re Gonin*, to which Megarry VC referred in formulating this last   **5–045** guideline, the reason given for the delay of two-and-a-half years that the applicant had received wrong advice from her solicitors. In refusing permission to apply out of time, Walton J emphasised that she had known from the outset that her claim to her mother's house and furniture (which was consolidated with the 1938 Act claim[111]) was disputed, because that was stated in her estate duty affidavit. She therefore knew what her position might be in the end and, whoever was at fault, no application was made until nearly two-and-a-half years after it should have been made. In such circumstances, when (as he put it) all the vital dates were under her control from start to finish, time should not be extended.[112] In considering the

---

[111] The deceased died intestate in 1968. The applicant took out letters of administration on 22 September 1970, and issued the summons under the 1938 Act on 4 September 1973. She claimed to have been advised that she could only apply if she were disabled, which, as Walton J said, was plainly wrong, if such advice had been given. Unmarried daughters were eligible applicants whether disabled or not.

[112] In relation to the contention that there would be no prejudice to the defendants if time were to be extended, Walton J said that it was always prejudicial to anyone not to receive money to which they were entitled at the earliest opportunity.

relevance of the existence of a remedy against the applicant's solicitors, Megarry J referred to the approach suggested by the cases on dismissal for want of prosecution.[113] Even where the fault was not that of the plaintiff, the solicitors' delays must be treated as the plaintiff's delays; but the injustice to the plaintiff would often be avoided by the existence of the plaintiff's right to sue the solicitors in negligence.

5–046   The guidelines taken from *Re Salmon* were also considered in *Re Dennis*,[114] an application by an adult son of the deceased. Probate was granted on 17 January 1978 and the application for leave to bring proceedings out of time was issued on 22 February 1980. Of the guidelines in *Re Salmon*, the facts relating to the third and fifth were considered in some detail. As to these, the long delay was held to be partly excusable, in that initially the applicant had received incorrect advice from his mother's solicitors, but the rest of the delay was not excusable. It was considered that the beneficiaries would not be prejudiced by the delay, because the estate had been complicated to administer and had not yet been distributed. The guidelines formulated in *Re Salmon* had not been put forward as a comprehensive list of matters to be considered. No reference had been made in *Re Salmon* to *Re Stone*,[115] where the Court of Appeal had held, by analogy with RSC Ord.14 proceedings[116] that leave should be given if the applicant had an arguable case, that is, if there was a triable issue. In *Re Dennis*, there were two factors which made it very unlikely that the applicant would succeed in the substantive action. The first was that he was an able-bodied person of 38. In his judgment, Browne-Wilkinson J observed that a person physically capable of earning their own living faced a difficult task in getting provision made for them, since the court was inclined to ask: "Why should anybody else make provision for you if you are capable of maintaining yourself?"[117] The second was the purpose for which the provision was said to be required, namely, in order to pay the capital transfer tax on an inter vivos gift from his father. It was held, departing from the decision in *Re Christie*,[118] that "maintenance" connoted only payments which, directly or indirectly, enabled the applicant to discharge the cost of his daily living at whatever standard was appropriate to him. While there were circumstances in which payment to discharge a debt might be regarded as maintenance, that was not the case here. Thus, the long delay in applying, coupled with the lack of an arguable case on the merits, resulted in the dismissal of the application.

5–047   Both of the above cases had been decided by the time the case of *Re Adams*[119] reached the Court of Appeal. In that case, leave to appeal was

---

[113] He referred to *Alfred McAlpine & Sons Ltd* [1968] 2 Q.B. 229, CA, per Diplock LJ at 256–57.

[114] *Re Dennis* [1981] 2 All E.R. 140.

[115] *Re Stone* (1970) 114 S.J. 36.

[116] The provision in the former RSC relating to applications for summary judgment.

[117] *Re Dennis* [1981] 2 All E.R. 140 at 145c.

[118] Browne-Wilkinson J observed that *Re Christie* had been disapproved both at first instance and on appeal by Goff LJ in *Re Coventry* [1980] Ch. 458.

[119] *Re Adams*, unreported 22 July 1981, CA. The case has been subsequently reported as *Adams v Schofield* [2004] W.T.L.R. 1049.

sought in respect of an order by Reeve J, dismissing an appeal from the decision of the District Registrar whereby he refused an application for leave to commence proceedings out of time. Probate had been granted on 22 August 1980, and the originating summons was issued on 12 March 1981, 19 days late. Proceedings had been issued on 3 March, but they were in the wrong form. The executors' solicitors were aware that a claim would be made under the Act, and the applicant's solicitor was aware that any application for an extension of time would be strenuously resisted. It was clear that the delay was wholly due to the conduct of the applicant's solicitor. The trial judge considered all the guidelines laid down in *Re Salmon*, and, on the first five, did not come to any conclusion adverse to the applicant. However, in regard to the last, he said:

> "In this case the executors through their solicitors have done all they could to have the matter brought in the proper way: and even after time expired they were trying by making an *ex gratia* offer to protect and preserve the estate being anxious to avoid proceedings and costs. They have not put a foot wrong, as opposed to the solicitors representing—I use the words almost in inverted commas—the applicants. In trying to keep the balance between these two parties, I have come clearly to the conclusion that I should exercise my discretion in favour of the defendants and dismiss this application. In doing so I am in a sense doing an injustice to the applicants, but I remind myself of the sixth consideration [as laid down in *Re Salmon*] ... Mrs. Adams has a clear case in negligence against her former solicitors, and I bear in mind that she may duly be able to recover damages from them. The injustice she suffers will to that extent be mitigated."[120]

Allowing the appeal, the Court of Appeal stated the principle that, in applications under s.4, there was an unfettered discretion which had to be exercised judicially. The weight to be attached to the availability of a remedy against the applicant's solicitor would depend on all the circumstances. Dunn LJ said: **5–048**

> "It may be that, in a particular case, the fact that the plaintiff has a cast iron and easily computable remedy against the solicitor may be a factor to which some weight could be attached",

and Ormrod LJ said:

> "...when it comes to considering what is the weight to be given to the existence of a claim for damages against solicitors in these cases, it seems to me that the right approach is to consider the justice of the case as between the parties, first of all, and to take into account all the matters set out very helpfully by the Vice-Chancellor in *Re Salmon*. It is

---

[120] *Adams v Schofield* [2004] W.T.L.R. 1049.

only if, having done that computation, one finds that the plaintiff on the one hand has suffered severe prejudice, and the defendant on the other hand has suffered severe prejudice, or will if the limitation period is extended, that the claim for damages against the plaintiff's solicitors becomes relevant."

Further, he said that, where the only disadvantage to the defendants was the purely formal disadvantage that they had lost the protection of s.4, the existence of the claim for damages would be of little weight; it would be a bonus to them, in that a possibly substantial claim against them would be transferred to the solicitors' insurers, unnecessarily and contrary to the justice of the case. Moreover, situations might well arise (as in the instant case) where the damages would be very difficult to quantify, and cause confusion as to the interests of the beneficiaries under the disposition which was being challenged.

5–049   In contrast, *Escritt v Escritt*[121] was a case in which solicitors correctly advised the applicant widow that she had a good claim under the 1975 Act, but, for fear of causing dissension within the family, she did not make it. Subsequently her health and financial position both deteriorated and in 1981, some three years out of time, she applied for leave to issue proceedings. At the time of her application, certain shares which were the subject of a specific bequest had been transferred to the beneficiary, but, apart from that, there had been no distribution. The case was therefore one in which the *Re Salmon* guidelines had very little relevance. Sir John Arnold P came to the conclusion that, where a person entitled to apply failed to do so within the time limit, and then repented of that decision and sought to apply out of time, and the only point in her favour was there had been no distribution, the grounds were not sufficiently strong for the time limit to be waived. The appeal from his judgment was dismissed.

5–050   The relevance of the availability of a remedy against negligent solicitors was also considered in *Re Longley*.[122] In that case, the deceased, who left a widow (W), also had a mistress (A) by whom he had an illegitimate daughter (B). He made a will appointing A his executor and leaving to her the house in which she was living; the remainder of his property was not disposed of by the will and devolved on W as on his intestacy. A renounced probate in favour of W so that she could make a claim on behalf of herself and B under the 1975 Act; letters of administration were thereupon granted to W. There was some correspondence between the parties' solicitors, though no offer of settlement was made. A's solicitors failed to make a claim within the time limit, therefore the estate was administered and a distribution made to W; the cash of the estate was in an identifiable fund in a building society account and was available as a source of provision. A took further advice

---

[121] *Escritt v Escritt* (1982) 3 F.L.R. 280.
[122] *Re Longley, Longley v Longley* [1981] C.L.Y. 2885. For comment on this case and on *Re Adams*, above, in connection with the relevance of the remedy against negligent solicitors, see also the articles by Prime, "Time Limits in Family Provision Cases" (1985) 129 S.J. 659 and by Borkowski (1987) 3 P.N. 161.

and, some 14 months after the distribution to W, proceedings were issued on her behalf. A's application for leave to issue proceedings out of time was dismissed; the claim had not been formulated till long after the expiry of the time limit, and B had a good claim against her solicitors. It was not the duty of the court to protect negligent solicitors.

There are several cases dating from the 1980s which have not been fully **5–051** reported but merit some discussion, as they deal with a variety of circumstances which have occurred where applications have been made for permission to commence proceedings out of time. The first of these was *Polackova v Sobolewski*,[123] an appeal against the decision of the deputy Vice Chancellor to give leave to the applicant to bring proceedings out of time, thereby reversing the decision of the Registrar. In that case, the testator and the applicant (P) were married in 1951. The parties separated in 1963; in 1965 the testator made a will by which he left nothing to P, and in that year he began divorce proceedings. The marriage was terminated by decree absolute of divorce on 1 July 1968. There was no claim by P for alimony or maintenance either in, or subsequent to, the divorce proceedings. The testator died on 10 December 1982, by which time the parties had been separated for some 19 years, though P deposed in her affidavit in support of her application under the 1975 Act that association between them had been resumed shortly before the testator's death. On 6 January 1983 P discovered that her former husband had died and consulted solicitors. They inquired of the executor's solicitors what the position was, but received no reply. Probate was granted on 6 June 1983, but P did not know this when she consulted other solicitors on 9 August 1983. They were informed on 12 August by the executor's solicitors, that those solicitors acted in the administration of the estate, that the assets had not all been got in, and that no distribution was envisaged at that stage. The Court of Appeal considered that 12 August was a date on which it would be reasonable to suppose that steps would be taken to institute proceedings. In fact, nothing was done until 13 March 1984, so the application was three months out of time. For the respondent it was argued that there was no good reason for the delay, which had caused prejudice owing to the inability of the personal representatives to distribute the estate, and also that P had no arguable case. In support of this argument, reliance was placed on P's failure to take advantage of r.68(2) of the Matrimonial Causes Rules 1977 (SI 1977/344), by virtue of which she could have applied to the court for ancillary relief notwithstanding the absence of such a claim in her cross-prayer, and it was contended that, had she made such an application, it would have had no chance of succeeding. Rejecting this argument, Anthony Lincoln J said that r.68(2) was irrelevant; under s.3(5) of the 1975 Act, the court had to take into account the circumstances prevailing at the time of the hearing. If the matters alleged in P's affidavit were true, she was in a much worse position than she had been in 1968. There were also other matters alleged which could not have been taken into

---

[123] *Polackova v Sobolewski (Executor of A. Pichlak, Deceased)* unreported 28 October 1985, CA.

account at an earlier time. There was clearly an arguable case and the appeal would be dismissed.

5–052   In *Clifford v Tanner*[124] a circumstance not within the *Re Salmon* guidelines fell to be considered, namely, whether any delay on the part of the applicant was due to failure to provide information, or the provision of misleading information, by the personal representatives. The substantive application made by the deceased's widow was for an order under s.2 and under s.10. The s.10 application related to a deed of release executed by the deceased in July 1983, shortly after he had made his last will. The effect of the deed was to deprive his wife of the right to continue living in the matrimonial home after his death. The estate was otherwise almost valueless, and there would be no property out of which financial provision could be made unless the deed of release could be avoided under s.10 of the 1975 Act. At first instance doubts were expressed whether the deed of release was a disposition within the meaning of the section, or whether there was sufficient evidence that the deceased executed it with the necessary intention; the application under s.4 was dismissed on the ground that there was not an arguable case. On appeal it was accepted that, if the applicant did have an arguable case for an order under s.10, leave should not be refused solely on the ground of the eight-month delay. The Court of Appeal held that as:

(i)   the respondent had always known that the applicant was claiming the house or the right to live in it;

(ii)   there had been no distribution made in reliance on the absence of proceedings within the time limit; and

(iii)   no copy of the crucial 1983 deed had been provided by the respondent's solicitors until after the statutory time limit had expired, after which the application had proceeded with reasonable expedition;

leave to bring the proceedings out of time should be granted. The deed was held to be a disposition within s.10, and the surrounding circumstances were sufficient to raise a triable issue on the subject of the deceased's intention. Accordingly, leave to apply out of time under s.2, which application would involve and include an application under s.10, was given.

5–053   *Smith v Loosely*[125] was an appeal against a decision allowing proceedings to be brought out of time; in that case, the judge had upheld the registrar's decision. The applicant was the widow of the deceased, whose will was proved on 19 April 1985. By that will she was given a life interest in the deceased's personal chattels and his residuary estate; the remainder interest went to a nephew, his wife and their two children. It appeared that she did not fully understand what was meant by a life interest and there was a dispute between her and one of the beneficiaries as to whether she could give things away. She finally consulted a solicitor in October 1985 but the claim

---

[124] *Clifford v Tanner* [1987] C.L.Y. 3881; unreported 10 June 1986, CA.
[125] *Smith v Loosely* unreported 18 June 1986, CA.

was only notified to the executors the day before the time limit expired. The originating summons was issued on 4 December 1985 and proceedings were therefore seven weeks out of time. Dismissing the appeal, the Court of Appeal held that it was not necessary for the applicant to give a satisfactory explanation why the application is being brought before one proceeds further to see whether or not the application should be entertained. The reason why the application was being brought out of time was a relevant matter but it would be more important in some cases than in others. The question was whether the applicant had an arguable case and, if that was so, the court was not to express any view about the strength or weakness of the case.

The appeal in *Perry v Horlick*[126] was against a refusal by the judge at first **5–054** instance to allow proceedings to be brought out of time. The applicant had been living with the deceased for some 24 years as a lodger, and he alleged that during the last four years of her life he maintained the house and met the outgoings, but was allowed to live there rent free. On that basis he claimed to be a person who was wholly or partly maintained by the deceased immediately before her death, within the meaning of s.1(1)(e) of the Act. The deceased died intestate on 12 March 1984 and the applicant consulted solicitors on 11 April. Solicitors for the son of the deceased, who was the person entitled to take on her intestacy, replied the next day to the effect that he was considering the position with regard to the house; this was, in effect, the entire estate. The applicant applied for legal aid to bring proceedings for a declaration that he had an equitable interest in the house, but this was refused on financial grounds. Nothing then happened until 18 January 1985, when the solicitors for the son informed the applicant's solicitors that Mr Horlick (now described as the administrator of the deceased's estate, whereas in the initial correspondence he had been referred to as "the proposed administrator") intended to put the house on the market, and by the same letter terminated the applicant's licence to occupy the property. It was not stated (as was the case) that letters of administration had been granted on 3 September 1984, that is, four months earlier, and the applicant did not know of that fact until 15 April 1985, six weeks after the time limit had expired. By this time the applicant had again applied for legal aid in respect of the proposed proceedings for a declaration, and legal aid was granted limited to obtaining counsel's opinion. The possibility of a claim under the 1975 Act was notified to the administrator's solicitors on 31 May 1985 and the proceedings were issued on 6 September 1985.

In refusing leave to issue the proceedings out of time, the judge took into **5–055** account the extent to which difficulties over legal aid had contributed to the delay, concluded (rightly in the opinion of the Court of Appeal) that the applicant had no redress against his solicitors, and held that, although the estate had not been administered, there would be prejudice to the personal representatives by being burdened with a second action (since the 1975 Act proceedings would, as the Court of Appeal put it, run in parallel with the claim for an equitable interest in the house). The Master of the Rolls, giving

---

[126] *Perry v Horlick* unreported 19 November 1987, CA.

the leading judgment, considered first that the judge had not given sufficient weight to the fact that the estate was unadministered and that the applicant was living in the house which was virtually its sole asset; he was there as an obstacle to its administration throughout. More importantly, he had not contemplated the situation which might well arise that in trying the claim for a declaration, the judge might conclude that, while it failed, there was a strong case under the 1975 Act—though the latter conclusion would be obiter. It would be unfortunate, in such circumstances, if the 1975 Act claim was not also before the court. It would add very little to the costs or to any delay in the administration of the estate. On that basis he held that the judge had misdirected himself as to the weight to be attached to those matters, and the appeal was allowed.

5–056   In *McNulty v McNulty*,[127] a claim by a surviving spouse, the statutory period had expired in September 1995 but the claim was not issued until April 1999. The judge[128] took the slightly unusual step of considering the case on its merits before deciding whether to permit the claim to proceed out of time. He concluded that the will had not made reasonable provision for the claimant and calculated the appropriate award as £175,000. Two factors in her favour were that the estate had not been distributed and that there would be no prejudice to the other beneficiaries if the claim were allowed to proceed. He found as a fact that before June 1998 (when a claim would have been nearly two years out of time) she had no idea of the value of the only substantial asset of the estate ("the Denby Land"), and at that time the value of her husband's share in the family business had been certified for probate as a negative value. However, he rejected as irrelevant the submission that the question of permission had not been taken as a preliminary issue:

> "...betokened the acceptance by the Defendant that the real substance of this part of the case lies in entitlement to provision and/or quantum, not permission."

If the claimant had acted promptly when she got to know of the value of the Denby Land in June 1998 he would have granted permission without hesitation, but the subsequent delay between then and April 1999 was inexcusable. Had any identifiable prejudice been caused to the defendants by that delay, he would have considered refusing permission, leaving the claimant to such remedies as she might have had against her legal advisers. However, there had been no such prejudice; the time limit should not be regarded as a disciplinary provision which should be enforced for its own sake, but as a measure of protection for personal representatives and of certainty for the beneficiaries, enabling the estate to be distributed when the period had elapsed.

---

[127] *McNulty v McNulty* [2002] W.T.L.R. 737. There was also a dispute between the same parties as to the administration of the estate but it had ceased to be of significance by the time of the hearing in late 2001.

[128] Launcelot Henderson QC (as he then was), sitting as a deputy judge of the High Court.

The decisions in two subsequent cases, in which applications were made **5–057** very substantially out of time, show the importance attached to the substantive merits of the applicant's case in considering whether to grant leave under s.4 of the 1975 Act.[129] In *Stock v Brown*,[130] the applicant was the 90-year-old widow of the deceased. Probate was granted in 1987; she had had no independent legal advice about the implications of the will or of her right to challenge it and did not take any action until 1993, when her financial position had seriously deteriorated. Thorpe J affirmed the decision of the district judge to give leave to issue the proceedings out of time. He recognised that the burden on the applicant was a very heavy one when the proceedings were sought to be brought over five years after the time limit had expired, but took the view that the application was necessitated by extraneous circumstances beyond the applicant's control, viz., the dramatic fall in interest rates in 1992 which reduced her income to half its former amount.

The other case, variously reported as *Re C (Deceased)*[131] and *Re W (A* **5–058** *minor)*[132] concerned an infant, aged eight at the time of the application. W was born in 1986 after a brief relationship between her mother (M) and the deceased (C). C died in 1990 and probate was granted in January 1992. M did not take legal advice until April 1993 and the application, which was issued in January 1994, was dismissed by the district judge. On appeal, Wilson J found that W had a very strong case on the merits. Although M's delay had not been satisfactorily explained, it was important to remember that it was W not M, who was the applicant. The case of *Escritt v Escritt*[133] referred to by the district judge as being "quite close to this case", was not analogous. It was relevant that, by contrast with the provisions of the Limitation Act 1980, Parliament had not made any distinction between the position of a person under disability and one who was sui juris. In *Re Salmon* it had been held that a relevant factor was whether the refusal of leave would leave the applicant without a remedy against anyone. As to this, Wilson J said:

"If the adult claimant who has only herself to blame for the delay is more likely to obtain permission than the adult claimant who can, for instance, blame her solicitors, the minor claimant who is personally blameless but who has no redress against a third party should be in an even stronger position. Although some criticism can be made of the child's former legal advisers in this case, there is no question of any actionable negligence; nor could the child in my view sue the mother, who is in any case without means."

---

[129] This was also an important factor in *Parnall v Hurst* [2003] W.T.L.R. 987 where the numerous procedural errors might well have led to the striking out of the claim, though it was issued and served in time.

[130] *Stock v Brown* [1994] 1 F.L.R. 840.

[131] *Re C (Deceased)* [1995] 2 F.L.R. 24.

[132] *In the Estate of the Right Honourable Simon George, Earl of Craven, W (A minor) v Ironside-Smith* [1995] 2 F.C.R. 689.

[133] *Escritt v Escritt* (1982) 3 F.L.R. 280.

It was argued that, notwithstanding there had been no distribution of the estate other than interim distributions of income, there would be prejudice to the estate because there might be argument (requiring to be resolved at extra expense) between the beneficiaries as to where the burden of the provision might fall. It was accepted that this contention had some force, but given the size of the estate, it was not considered that it would be an intractable problem. Realistically, it was clear that an order for substantial provision for W out of the estate was inevitable; there were no reported cases referred to in which the prospects of substantial success were so clear. Leave to apply out of time was granted.

5–059   In a Northern Ireland case[134] in which A brought a claim for provision out of the estate of her former partner (D), by whom she had a son (AD), D had died on 27 October 2007 and her solicitors wrote to C, mentioning an endowment policy which was understood to have been in the joint names of A and D, but not intimating a claim for provision out of D's estate. This was not pursued; administration was taken out on or about 14 March 2008 and, although a further letter on her behalf was written in December 2008, the application for permission to issue proceedings out of time was not made until 10 July 2009. On the facts it appears that she was not in actual need; she was married and in employment, and had received £35,000 under the policy. Additionally, there was no obvious excuse for her failure to pursue the claim promptly. It was also relevant that she would have been in competition with her son for provision out of the estate. He, however, was found to be in a different position. He was still a minor, D had been paying maintenance for him until a few weeks before his death and he could not be blamed for any lack of activity on the part of A or anyone else. Accordingly, permission was given for the claim on his behalf to be commenced out of time, but refused in respect of A's claim on her own behalf.

5–060   In *Berger v Berger*,[135] a claim by a surviving spouse, the husband died in June 2005 and probate was granted on 27 January 2006. Within a few months the widow was expressing dissatisfaction about the inadequacy of the income she was receiving from the trust created by the will; the income-producing assets of the trust were properties managed by the sons of her husband's first marriage. She consulted a series of solicitors, but it does not appear that she was ever advised at that time about the existence of the 1975 Act or of any possible claims which she might have under it, and she is recorded at that time as wishing to avoid litigation or disputes with other family members or the executors. She did not seek any further advice until about August 2011 and had not entirely overcome her reluctance to take proceedings by the end of March 2012. There was then a delay because she had a heart attack at the beginning of April and proceedings under the 1975 Act were finally brought on 15 June 2012, almost six years out of time. Of the *Re Salmon* guidelines, the only one in her favour was that the estate had

---

[134] *A on behalf of AD and on her own behalf v C (Executor of the estate of D, Deceased)* [2009] N.I. Ch. 10.
[135] *Berger v Berger* [2014] W.T.L.R. 35, CA.

not been fully distributed and the residue would have been sufficient to fund any provision that might have been made for her had she had (contrary to the trial judge's view) an arguable case on the merits. The factor pointing inexorably to the dismissal of the claim was the lengthy delay without any good reason. On appeal, it was held that the judge's conclusion on the merits of the claim was vitiated by his approach to the material question of what she might reasonably have expected to receive on divorce, but he was right to focus on the very significant delay in commencing proceedings. Not only the length of the delay, but the history of the claim, was relevant. The claim had not been brought about by a particular unexpected event[136]; the claimant had shown from the outset that she was capable of pursuing her interests but took no steps to do so. In such circumstances it would not be appropriate to permit her to commence proceedings out of time.

Zarrinkhat v Kamal[137] was a claim by the 51-year-old daughter (H) of the **5–061** deceased (T), who died in 2009 leaving net estate £573,000. During her lifetime T had given H £16,000 and by her will she left her a pecuniary legacy of £50,000. Probate was granted on 11 March 2011 and H's claim was issued on 20 June 2012, some nine months out of time. She had disinstructed her first solicitors (who did not advise her of the possibility of making a 1975 Act claim) in January 2010 and had not instructed her current solicitors until August or September 2011. Master Marsh found that, although English was not her first language, the limitations of her English language skills had not put her at a significant disadvantage in taking advice about a claim or bringing a claim. There was no satisfactory explanation of the delay in instructing new solicitors, and although there had been conversations between her and one of the residuary beneficiaries, they could not be characterised as negotiations. She had failed to show sufficient grounds for the delay and her claim would not have succeeded on the merits. In practice it was not possible to separate the s.4 application from the substantive claim, because the strength of the claim was relevant to the s.4 application, which was therefore refused, and her claim was dismissed.

It is not easy to collect coherent principles from a body of case-law **5–062** embracing applications made in a wide variety of circumstances. Nevertheless it is submitted that, from those cases, the following conclusions may be drawn:

(1) the stronger the case on its merits, the more readily will a delay be excused; conversely, delay is less likely to be excused even if some of the *Re Salmon* guidelines pointed in favour of permitting the claim to proceed;

---

[136] Compare *Stock v Brown* [1994] 1 F.L.R. 840, where a dramatic fall in interest rates had halved the claimant widow's income; she was allowed to commence proceedings five years out of time, and *McNulty v McNulty* [2002] W.T.L.R. 737 (claimant unaware of the value of the estate until almost two years after the expiry of the six-month period).

[137] *Zarrinkhat v Kamal* [2013] W.T.L.R. 1477.

(2)   in particular, the fact that the estate has not been distributed, or
       fully distributed, will not assist the applicant if granting permis-
       sion will prejudice other parties;

(3)   the wish to avoid dissension within the family is very unlikely to be
       accepted as an excuse for long delay;

(4)   the length of the delay is not, by itself, decisive one way or the
       other, but must be considered together with the circumstances
       giving rise to the delay and the conduct of the case to date; and

(5)   the existence of a remedy against the applicant's solicitors is not
       decisive against the applicant, but it may be an important factor in
       cases where the defendant will suffer substantial prejudice if the
       proceedings are allowed to be brought out of time.

5–063   While it has always been clear that an extension of time will be refused if
the substantive claim has no prospect of success on the merits, the decided
cases do not give a clear indication of the degree of likelihood of success
required to be demonstrated in order for the application to succeed. In *Re
Dennis*[138] it was held that the applicant had to satisfy the court that he had
an arguable case that he was entitled to reasonable financial provision, and
that in approaching that matter, the approach of the court would be rather
similar to that adopted in deciding whether a defendant should have leave to
defend proceedings for summary judgment. The standard set by CPR r.24.2
is that the party has no real prospect of succeeding on the claim or issue or,
as the case may be, the defendant has no real prospect of successfully
defending the claim or issue. The commentary to the rule states that the
inclusion of the word "real" means that the court is to disregard prospects
which are false, fanciful or imaginary, and that the respondent has to have a
case which is better than merely arguable, but is not required to show that
their case will probably succeed at trial.[139]

5–064   However, quite apart from the merits of the case, there is a question
whether, in all the circumstances, refusing permission to commence proceedings out of time would be a disproportionate response to the errors
which contributed to the failure to commence the claim in time. This
question was considered in *Nesheim v Kosa*,[140] a 1975 Act claim in which the
claim form had been issued very shortly before the expiry of the six-month
period, but permission was required to serve the claim form out of the
jurisdiction, and that permission was not obtained within the prescribed
time limit. The claimant was granted retrospective permission to serve out of
the jurisdiction and the defendant appealed against that decision. In that
case, Briggs J identified a tension between two competing principles. An
important purpose of the overriding objective was to avoid long and costly

---

[138]   *Re Dennis* [1981] 2 All E.R. 140, 144j–145a. The then current rule, RSC Ord.14 r.3(1) stated
        that the court should refuse an application for summary judgment against a defendant
        where the defendant satisfied the court that there was an issue which ought to be tried or
        whether for some other reason there ought to be a trial.
[139]   *Civil Procedure 2017*, Vol.1, para.24.2.3.
[140]   *Nesheim v Kosa* [2007] W.T.L.R. 149.

procedural disputes and to cause the parties to focus on the real issues in dispute between them; however, it was also a principle that rules as to the commencement and service of proceedings were there to be obeyed and were likely to be strictly enforced. He referred to the application of the first of those principles by the Court of Appeal in *Hannigan v Hannigan*,[141] an appeal against a decision striking out a 1975 Act claim on account of the numerous procedural errors made in the course of the proceedings. Brooke LJ held that it would be the antithesis of justice to allow the claim to be struck out in its infancy without any investigation into its merits. Despite the large number of technical errors and the fact that the claimant's solicitors had no good reason for making them, the scales were tipped overwhelmingly in her favour by the interests of the administration of justice and the fact that to strike out the claim in the circumstances would be a totally disproportionate response to the errors made.

Dismissing the appeal, Briggs J referred to the nature of the time limit **5–065** under the 1975 Act. It was:

"...both of a special type in that it confers on the court a discretionary power to permit a claim to be made out of time on well settled principles and it exists for a particular purpose, namely to avoid the unnecessary delay in the administration of estates to be caused by the tardy bringing of proceedings under the Act and to avoid the difficulties which might be occasioned if distributions of an estate are made before proceedings were brought, requiring possible recoveries from beneficiaries if those proceedings once brought are successful."[142]

He concluded that permission to serve out of the jurisdiction would have been granted had it been applied for in time. The last of the factors which militated against the grant of that relief was the prejudice occasioned to the defendant by the loss of the right to insist that the 1975 Act claim against her was statute barred, but, in his judgment, that supposed prejudice should be assessed at a very low level. It would be inevitable, if he allowed the appeal and refused to grant retrospective permission, that there would be an application to commence a fresh claim out of time and that, applying the *Re Salmon* guidelines, the applicant would have a very considerable prospect of success in that application. The only factor pointing in the other direction was the likelihood that he would have a remedy against his solicitors but that purely financial remedy would be at the highest, an unsatisfactory approximation to the relief sought in the claim.[143] He had an arguable case that, in principle, ought to be tried if it could not be compromised and (following *Hannigan v Hannigan*) to refuse retrospective permission in a clear case for the English court assuming jurisdiction would be to put the

---

[141] *Hannigan v Hannigan* [2002] 2 F.C.R. 650, CA at [38]. A similar approach was adopted in *Parnall v Hurst* [2003] W.T.L.R. 997.
[142] *Nesheim v Kosa*, at [26].
[143] The claimant sought a transfer to him of his deceased wife's share in the house where he had lived for many years, or a life interest in it.

need for disciplining lawyers for a genuine mistake[144] ahead of the clear interests of doing justice between the parties.

(b) When is the Grant of Representation First Taken Out?

5–066 Following the recommendations made by the Law Commission,[145] both s.4[146] and s.23 have been amended. The impetus for the amendment of s.4 so as to permit claims to be commenced before a grant of representation had been taken out stemmed from a widespread perception that there were circumstances in which an applicant for family provision might be prejudiced by the inactivity of those who are entitled to a grant.[147] In addition, it remained uncertain whether *Re McBroom*,[148] in which it was held that a claim could not be commenced before a grant of representation had been taken out, was rightly decided. It continued to be argued that the 1938 Act case of *Re Searle*[149] was authority for the proposition that a claim could be commenced before a grant of representation had been taken out. The amendment to s.4 has rendered that debate otiose. Finally it should be noted that, while the Law Commission's reasons for recommending the amendment did not include the facilitation of the widely criticised practice of entering a caveat to prevent time running against a prospective claimant,[150] an unintended consequence of the amendment is that nothing prevents a claimant from entering a caveat and commencing a claim while it remains in force. It is submitted that the entry of a caveat is inappropriate; there is no reason why a prospective claimant seeking an order under the 1975 Act should wish or need to oppose the grant.[151] It remains to be seen how the courts will ensure compliance with the requirements of PD57A paras 16

---

[144] They had mistakenly believed that the claim could be served in Norway under the Lugano Convention without the permission of the court, but claims under the Inheritance Act are outside the scope of the Convention.

[145] Law Com, LC 331 at paras 7.49 (s.4) and 7.68 (s.23).

[146] Inheritance and Trustees' Powers Act 2014 s.6 and Sch.2 para.6, which adds to s.4 as originally enacted the words (but nothing prevents the making of an application before a grant is taken out).

[147] The report mentioned the observation of the Association of Her Majesty's District Judges that "others involved may, for their own motives and self-interest, deliberately delay in applying for a grant."

[148] *Re McBroom, Deceased* [1992] 2 F.L.R. 49. As in *Re Searle*, the decision rested largely on procedural grounds, which included the requirement in s.19 of the 1975 Act for a copy of every order under the Act to be endorsed on or permanently annexed to the probate or letters of administration under which the estate is being administered, and RSC Ord.99 r.3 (the rule of court then applicable), which provided that there should be lodged with the court an affidavit by the applicant in support of the summons, exhibiting an official copy of the grant of representation of the deceased's estate.

[149] *Re Searle, Searle v Siems* [1949] Ch. 73; [1948] 2 All E.R. 426. Under the former Ord.54F r.7, there was no requirement for a copy of the grant to be exhibited to the affidavit in support of the application; r.13 provided that the personal representative was to produce the probate or letters of administration in court. Roxburgh J held that, as the matter had proceeded to a hearing without the point having been taken, and as there had been a grant issued by the time of the hearing, the irregularity had been waived.

[150] See Ch.1, s.6, "To do and not to do".

[151] See *Tristram and Coote's Probate Practice*, 31st edn (London: LexisNexis, 2015) at paras 23–05 (purposes) and 23.67 (caveator having no contrary interest).

(evidence to be given by personal representatives who are defendants) and 18 (production of the grant) in such circumstances.

Section 23 of the 1975 Act, as originally enacted, provided that: **5–067**

> "In considering for the purposes of this Act when representation with respect to the estate of a deceased person was first taken out, a grant limited to settled land or trust property shall be left out of account and a grant limited to real estate or to personal estate shall be left out of account unless a grant to the remainder of the estate has been previously made or is made at the same time."

There has been very little case-law on that provision. In *Re Freeman*,[152]   **5–068** the deceased died in 1978 leaving a will which made provision both for the applicant, a woman with whom he had been living for some 10 years, and his mother. Probate was granted on 17 September 1979 but was revoked on 16 May 1983 on the ground that the will had not been properly executed. Under the resulting intestacy the mother became entitled to the whole of the estate, and letters of administration were granted to her on 23 August 1983. On the question of construction of the phrase, "six months from the date on which representation with respect to the estate of the deceased is first taken out", it was held that "representation" meant "effective or valid representation"; otherwise a situation would arise whereby the applicant, though perfectly satisfied with the disposition under the will, would have to bring an action within six months of probate of that will being granted, in order to protect her position in case the grant should later be revoked.

In *Re Johnson (Paul Anthony), Deceased*,[153] a grant had been issued in   **5–069** 1983, limited to pursuing negligence claims in relation to the road accident in which the testator died. Probate of his will was granted in 1987. It was held that the first effective grant of representation was the grant of probate, as the earlier grant merely enabled a particular thing to be done and did not enable distribution to take place.

The Law Commission perceived an inconsistency in s.23 as originally   **5–070** enacted,[154] in that certain grants which limited the type of property which can be distributed were left out of account, while grants limited to special purposes which do not enable the administrator to distribute any property appear to start time running for these purposes. They considered that a grant which does not permit any property to be distributed should therefore be left out of account for the purposes of s.4 of the 1975 Act and that it should also be put beyond doubt that a foreign grant did not start time running for these purposes. The personal representatives (or their equivalent in the jurisdiction where the grant was obtained) would not be in a position to distribute the part of the estate governed by English succession law. It

---

[152] *Re Freeman* [1984] 3 All E.R. 906.
[153] *Re Johnson (Paul Anthony), Deceased* [1987] C.L.Y. 3882; case analysis is available on Westlaw.
[154] Law Com. LC 331 at paras 7.66–7.68. The section as originally enacted continues to apply to deaths before 1 October 2014.

might also not be obvious to a potential family provision applicant when a foreign grant had been made.

5–071   Accordingly, the amended s.23[155] provides that:

"(1) The following are to be left out of account when considering for the purposes of this Act when representation with respect to the estate of a deceased person was first taken out:

(a) a grant limited to settled land or trust property,

(b) any other grant that does not permit any of the estate to be distributed

(c) a grant limited to real estate or to personal estate, unless a grant to the remainder of the estate has been previously made or is made at the same time,

(d) a grant, or its equivalent, made outside the United Kingdom (but see subsection (2) below).

(2) A grant under s.2 of the Colonial Probates Act 1892 counts as a UK grant for the purposes of this Act but is taken to be dated at the date of sealing."

5.—SPECIAL PROVISIONS RELATING TO DIVORCE AND SEPARATION: SECTIONS 14–18

5–072   The general effect of these provisions and the manner in which they have been amended by the Civil Partnership Act 2004 has been summarised in s.1 of this chapter. There is at the time of writing, no case-law on the provisions introduced into this part of the 1975 Act by the Civil Partnership Act, but one can expect the case law on the 1975 Act provisions to be applied in the same manner in the context of civil partnerships.

5–073   Section 14 of the 1975 Act[156] is concerned with a problem which is peculiar to former spouses who have not remarried and spouses who were judicially separated from the deceased at the time of death of the deceased. If certain conditions exist, s.14(1) gives the court discretion to treat such persons as if the decree of divorce or nullity had not been made absolute, or, as the case may be, the decree of judicial separation had not been granted. Those conditions are that:

"...if, within 12 months of the decree of divorce or nullity having been made absolute, or the decree of judicial separation having been granted, one party to the marriage dies, and either:

---

[155] Inheritance and Trustees' Powers Act 2014 s.6 and Sch.3 para.2.
[156] Section 14A is the corresponding provision relating to cases where no financial relief was granted on the dissolution of a civil partnership.

(a) the other party has not made an application for a financial provision order under s.23, or a property adjustment order under s.24, of the Matrimonial Causes Act 1973; or

(b) such an application has been made but the proceedings have not been determined at the time of the death of the deceased."

Additionally s.14(2) provides, in the case of judicially separated spouses, that the decree must be in force and the separation must be continuing at the time of the deceased's death.

The effect of these provisions is to treat the spouse in whose favour they are applied as if they were a surviving spouse and thus make provision according to the higher standard prescribed by s.1(2)(a) of the 1975 Act. The power is discretionary and examples have been given of situations in which it might not be appropriate to exercise it; as when the applicant had been guilty of unjustified delay in making an application under the relevant provisions of the MCA 1973.   5–074

The purpose and origin of s.14 was considered in *Harb v King Fahd Abdul Aziz (No.2)*.[157] Mrs Harb had issued an originating application against the King under s.27 of MCA 1973.[158] The proceedings were challenged on the ground of sovereign immunity and the challenge was upheld at first instance. The Court of Appeal granted permission to appeal but the King died before the hearing of the appeal. The right to apply under s.27 is available to "either party to the marriage" and is against "the other party to the marriage". The relevant provisions therefore apply only during the joint lives of the parties. On the other hand, ss.33(1) and (3) and ss.36(1) and (2) of MCA 1973 expressly permit applications beyond joint lives. That contrast reinforced the view of the Court of Appeal that the remedy provided by s.27 was available during joint lives only. Thorpe LJ then drew attention to the possibility that the death of the respondent during the dependency of an application under ss.23 or 24 of MCA 1973[159] might cause injustice to the applicant and he referred to s.14 of the 1975 Act as recognising and safeguarding against that possibility. However, no such safeguard was necessary where the application was under s.27 terminated by judgment prior to the death of the respondent since the applicant spouse could obtain relief under the 1975 Act. In the event, the question whether to exercise the s.14 jurisdiction in her favour never arose because the King had not died domiciled in England and Wales.   5–075

In *Harb*, Wall LJ viewed the 1975 Act as part of: 5–076

---

[157] *Harb v King Fahd Abdul Aziz (No.2) (Department of Constitutional Affairs, intervening)* [2006] 1 W.L.R. 578, CA.
[158] Financial provision orders, etc., in case of neglect by party to marriage to maintain other party or child of the marriage.
[159] Respectively, financial provision orders in connection with divorce proceedings, etc., and property adjustment orders in connection with divorce proceedings, etc.

"...an extensive and exclusive statutory code whereby spouses and former spouses can make applications for financial provision and property adjustment orders against each other."[160]

In emphasising the importance of s.14 he accepted the argument for the King that if the applicant's claim under s.27 of MCA 1973 did not abate on death, s.14 would be unnecessary. The Law Commission, in considering the situation of former spouses and judicially separated spouses whose financial position had not been dealt with in matrimonial proceedings,[161] was sympathetic to those who had not had the opportunity to seek a share of the family assets because the death of the other party had supervened before the court had made an order in the matrimonial proceedings, and considered that special provision should be made for such a spouse who, without fault on her part, had been placed in such a position. However, it felt that such spouses should not automatically be entitled to the higher standard of reasonable provision and recommended, in the interests of certainty and finality, that the discretion to treat such spouses as if they were surviving spouses should be limited to cases where the deceased had died within 12 months of the grant of the decree of divorce, nullity or judicial separation. Such cases are extremely rare, the only accessible case being *Eeles v Evans*,[162] in which the judge at first instance exercised the discretion where a decree absolute was pronounced on 14 May 1981 and the deceased died on 14 January 1982. The widow, who was 73, nevertheless contended that the award was inadequate,[163] and appealed. For Dillon LJ, who gave the only substantive judgment, the crux of the matter was whether the award made sufficient provision for the foreseeable costs of her nursing care and/or care accommodation. He concluded that the award was not generous but not so plainly wrong as to justify interference.

5–077   The rights of the parties to a marriage to contract out of the 1975 Act are regulated entirely by s.15 of that statute, as amended by s.8(1) of the Matrimonial and Family Proceedings Act 1984.[164] Subsection (1), as originally enacted, provided that on or after the time when a decree of divorce, nullity or judicial separation is granted, the court may, if it seems just and the parties to the marriage agree, order that either party shall not, on the death of the other, be entitled to apply for an order under s.2 of the 1975 Act. The amendment to the subsection enabled the court to make such an order on the application of either party. The effect of subs.(2) is that, if such

---

[160] *Harb v King Fahd Abdul Aziz (No.2) (Department of Constitutional Affairs, intervening)* [2006] 1 W.L.R. 578, C.A, [59]–[65].

[161] Law Com. LC 61, at paras 59–63.

[162] *Eeles v Evans* unreported 6 July 1989, CA.

[163] Out of £330,000 available for distribution he awarded her a lump sum of £5,000 and ordered £85,000 to be settled on her for life, the trustees having power to advance up to half the capital. Based on then current nursing-home costs and interest rates, the income of that sum, together with her pension, would have left her an annual income surplus of over £1,000.

[164] Section 15A of the 1975 Act (restrictions imposed in proceedings under the MFPA 1984) was inserted by s.25(3) of that Act.

an order is made before the decree of divorce or nullity is made absolute, it shall not take effect until the decree is made absolute. Once the court has made such an order, it no longer has jurisdiction to entertain an application by one party on the death of the other. Section 15ZA, which is the corresponding provision relating to dissolution of civil partnerships, was inserted by the Civil Partnership Act 2004.[165]

Section 15 was first considered in *Re Fullard*.[166] The deceased married the applicant in 1939 and they were divorced in 1977. The financial arrangements agreed between them were that the applicant would pay the deceased £4,500 and he would transfer his interest in the former matrimonial home to her. The deceased then moved out and went to live with a woman friend; he died in January 1978 having left all his estate, worth about £7,100 to her. The former wife's application was dismissed at first instance and in the Court of Appeal. So far as s.15 was concerned, Ormrod LJ considered that, in cases such as this, the court and legal advisers might be well advised to remember s.15, and, if they could persuade the other side to agree, to write into the order an appropriate provision. He regarded s.15 as the form of insuring against applications under the 1975 Act, which some people might very reasonably wish to do, having made capital provision for the former spouse. Circumstances where a former spouse might have some prospect of success in an application under the 1975 Act could include:

    5–078

(a)   the passage of a long period of time since the dissolution of the marriage, where a continuing obligation had been established by an order of the court (whether by consent or otherwise) under which periodical payments have been, and continue to be, made up until death; or

(b)   the unlocking of a substantial capital asset of which the testator should have been aware and from which, had they made a will at a time immediately before their death, they ought to have made some provision.

In *Whiting v Whiting*,[167] the parties married in 1961 and the marriage was dissolved in 1975. By consent, periodical payments were ordered in favour of the wife and the three children of the marriage, and the matrimonial home was to be held by the husband and wife on trust for sale as tenants in common in equal shares, the wife to reside there until the first to occur of her death, her remarriage or the youngest child reaching the age of 18. In 1979 the periodical payments order in favour of the wife was reduced to a nominal sum. In 1983 the husband was made redundant and the periodical payments in favour of the youngest child fell into arrears. In May 1986 he applied for relief under s.31(7) of the MCA 1973 and also for an order under s.15(1) of the 1975 Act, that the wife should not be entitled, on his death, to

    5–079

---

[165] Civil Partnership Act 2004 s.71, Sch.4 Pt 2 para.21. S.15B (restrictions imposed in proceedings under Sch.7 to the Civil Partnership Act 2004 was inserted by para.22 of Sch.4 Pt 2.
[166] *Re Fullard* [1982] Fam. 42, CA.
[167] *Whiting v Whiting* [1988] 2 F.L.R. 189.

make any application for provision out of his estate. Balcombe LJ, with whom Stocker and Slade LJJ agreed on this point, said:

"For the court to make an order under s.15(1), it must consider it just to do so. In my judgment, before the court can consider it just to make an order depriving a divorced spouse of any opportunity to claim financial provision from the estate of the other spouse, it should be given some indication of what that estate is likely to consist of and some details of the persons whom the applicant considers to have a prior claim on his estate in the event of his decease."

He went on to say that the husband had not made out a case to support his application under s.15. The appeal against the judge's refusal to make an order under s.15 of the 1975 Act was dismissed.

5–080   In *Hedy v Firth*[168] the parties came to an agreement in relation to financial matters in 1979, whereby the husband was to accept £10,000 in satisfaction of all his claims and consent to them being dismissed. That agreement was never carried out, but on 5 November 1987 a consent order was made whereby on his agreement to accept £8,000 in full and final settlement of his claim for periodical payments, his claim would stand dismissed. He would not be entitled to make any further application under s.23(19)(a) or (b) of the MCA 1973, and neither party would be entitled, on the death of the other, to apply for an order under s.2 of the 1975 Act. On 21 February 1989 he was refused leave to appeal out of time against that order. In dismissing his appeal against that decision, Balcombe LJ said that one of the cardinal principles on which courts acted was that orders should not be disturbed without very strong grounds, particularly when they had been made by consent and had stood for a long time.

5–081   An order for secured periodical payments under the MCA 1973 may continue to have effect after the death of the person against whom it was made, but s.31 of that Act gives the court power to vary or discharge such an order. It has been held that an order for secured maintenance should not properly be treated as predetermining what a survivor is to receive after the death of the spouse, though it is an important factor to be considered.[169] In *Re Crawford*[170] attention was drawn to the difference between what the court was required to do under s.25 of the 1973 Act and under s.1(2)(b) of the 1975 Act. At that time s.25 of the 1973 Act required the court, so far as was practicable, to put the parties in the same position as they would have been in, had the marriage not broken down, whereas s.1(2)(b) of the 1975 Act defined reasonable financial provision as that which was reasonable, in all the circumstances, for her maintenance. Thus, it could not be assumed that reasonable financial provision under the 1975 Act could be equated to periodical payments awarded during her lifetime under s.25 of the 1973 Act.

[168] *Hedy v Firth* unreported 15 August 1989, CA.
[169] *Eyre v Eyre* [1968] 1 All E.R. 968.
[170] *Re Crawford* (1983) 4 F.L.R. 273.

Section 16 of the 1975 Act gives the court power to vary or discharge a **5–082** periodical payments order when an application is made for an order under s.2 of the 1975 Act. Either the person entitled to receive the payments or the personal representative of the deceased may apply for the order to be varied or discharged. Where no proceedings under the 1975 Act are on foot, or the person entitled to the payments is barred by s.15 of the 1975 Act from commencing such proceedings, the application to vary or discharge may still be made under s.31 of the MCA 1973. Section 16(2) of the 1975 Act, which sets out the matters to which the court must have regard in considering an application under s.16(1), corresponds to s.31(7) of the 1973 Act.

Section 17 of the 1975 Act is concerned with the variation and revocation **5–083** of maintenance agreements. Maintenance agreements which provide for a person to receive payments after the death of the deceased may be varied or revoked. Under both s.36 of the MCA 1973 and s.17(1) of the 1975 Act the court has power, on the application of the person who benefits under the agreement or the personal representatives of the deceased, to vary or revoke the agreement. As with s.16 of the 1975 Act, it will be necessary for the applicant to proceed under the 1973 Act if there is a s.15 order against him or there are no s.2 proceedings on foot. Subsections 2, 3 and 4 deal, respectively, with the matters to which the court must have regard in considering an application, the consequences of varying the agreement, and the definition of the term "maintenance agreement".

Section 18(1) gives the court power to direct that, where an application is **5–084** made under either s.31(6) or s.36(1) of the MCA 1973, it shall be deemed to have been accompanied by an application under s.2 of the 1975 Act; but s.18(3) provides that, if the applicant is subject to an order under s.15, no order can be made under s.18(1). The principal purpose of s.18 is to confer on applicants the benefit of the anti-avoidance provisions contained in ss.10–13 of the 1975 Act; s.18(2) enables the court to give such consequential directions as are necessary for the exercise of those powers. There is a corresponding provision in relation to the availability of the court's powers in applications under paras 60 and 73 of Sch.5 to the Civil Partnership Act 2004.[171]

---

[171] Section 18A, inserted by the Civil Partnership Act 2004 s.71, Sch.4 Pt 2 para.25.

CHAPTER 6

REASONABLE FINANCIAL PROVISION

1.—THE STANDARD OF PROVISION

(a) Reasonable Provision

6–001   Under the 1938 Act, both as originally enacted and as subsequently amended, there was one standard of provision which applied to all dependants. The court was empowered, if it considered that the disposition on death was not such as to make reasonable provision for the maintenance of the dependant, to order that such reasonable provision as it thought fit be made out of the deceased's estate for the maintenance of that dependant; and it could order such provision to be made either by way of periodical payments or lump sum. The power to vary such orders was very restricted.

6–002   The 1975 Act implemented a radical change to the statutory definition of reasonable provision by placing surviving spouses in a more favourable position than other applicants. Reasonable provision for surviving spouses was no longer limited to what was reasonable for their maintenance. Section 1(2) of the 1975 Act provides that "reasonable financial provision":

(a)   in the case of an application made by virtue of subs.1(a) by the husband or wife of the deceased (except where the marriage with the deceased was the subject of a decree of judicial separation and at the date of the death the decree was in force and the separation was still continuing), means such financial provision as it would be reasonable in all the circumstances of the case for a husband or wife to receive, whether or not that provision is required for his or her maintenance; or

(b)   in the case of any other application made by virtue of subs.(1), means such financial provision as it would be reasonable in all the circumstances of the case for the applicant to receive for his maintenance.

The 1975 Act has been amended by the insertion of a new subpara.(aa) into subs.1(2) which mirrors para.(a) of the subsection and applies the higher standard of provision to surviving civil partners.[1] Surviving civil partners who have in good faith entered into a void civil partnership with the deceased are put on the same footing as surviving spouses who have in good faith entered into a void marriage with the deceased by the amendments to subss.25(4) and (5) of the 1975 Act.[2]

6–003   Many of the earlier cases were decided on the basis that the test of whether reasonable provision had been made was whether the testator had acted unreasonably. Although an objective test had been formulated as early as 1968 by Megarry J in *Re Goodwin*[3] and approved two years later by the

---

[1]   Civil Partnership Act 2004 s.71 and Sch.4 para.15(6). The amendments effected by that Act came into force on 5 December 2005.
[2]   Civil Partnership Act 2004 s.71 and Sch.4 paras 27(4), (5).
[3]   *Re Goodwin* [1969] Ch. 283; [1968] 3 W.L.R. 558.

Court of Appeal in *Re Gregory*,[4] a number of the reported cases from the 1980s show that the dictum of Morton J in *Re Styler*[5] propounding the subjective view was not finally discarded until 1992. The Court of Appeal then held, in *Moody v Stevenson*[6] that, notwithstanding the continued inclusion of *Re Styler* in the notes to the Act in the County Court Practice, the test was an objective one, not the subjective test based on Morton J's dictum in that case. Formulating the now accepted test, Megarry J said:

"The statutory language is thus wholly impersonal. The question is simply whether the will or the disposition has made reasonable provision, and not whether it was unreasonable on the part of the deceased to have made no provision or no larger provision for the dependant. A testator may have acted entirely reasonably; he may have taken skilled advice on the drafting of his will, intending to make a fully reasonable provision; and yet through some blunder of the draftsman (perhaps as to the incidence of estate duty) or by some change of circumstance unknown to the testator in his lifetime, the provision may in fact have been wholly unreasonable. Conversely, the testator may have acted wholly unreasonably in deciding what provisions to insert in the will, but by some happy accident, such as the lapse of a share of residue which then passed to the widow on intestacy, the provision in fact may be entirely reasonable. In my judgment the question is not subjective but objective. It is not whether the testator stands convicted of unreasonableness but whether the provision made is in fact reasonable."

"Reasonableness" in both contexts has been very fully considered in the case-law; most recently, at the time of writing, by the Supreme Court in *Ilott v Mitso*.[7] There, the objective nature of the test was emphasised, and the Court observed that it was possible to ask the wrong objective question; the Act did not permit the court to make an order when it judged that the testator had acted unreasonably. Nevertheless, the reasonableness of the deceased's decisions were capable of being a factor for consideration within s.3(1)(g), and possibly s.3(1)(d) also. The outcome might on some, but not all, occasions not differ significantly whether the right or the wrong question was asked. The question had already been considered by the Court of Appeal[8] when addressing the question of whether the deceased's will had made reasonable provision for the claimant, and at other stages of the judicial process. Because of the previously unheard-of length of the proceedings, and the multiplicity of judicial views expressed in the judgments on

6–004

[4] *Re Gregory* [1970] 1 W.L.R 1455, CA.
[5] *Re Styler* [1942] Ch. 387.
[6] *Moody v Stevenson* [1992] Ch. 486, CA.
[7] *Ilott v Mitson* [2017] UKSC 17, reported as *Ilott v Blue Cross* [2017] 2 W.L.R. 979.
[8] *Ilott v Mitson* [2012] 2 F.L.R. 170, CA.

whether the will made reasonable provision for Mrs Ilott and the quantum of the award, a complete subsection of this chapter[9] has been devoted to *Ilott v Mitson*, and it is not discussed further at this stage.

(b) Testamentary Freedom

6–005   As now discussed, the case-law on the 1975 Act is replete with references to testamentary freedom. It is therefore appropriate to recall that complete freedom of testation existed in English law only during the 47-year period between the enactment of the Mortmain and Charitable Uses Act 1891 and the coming into force of the Inheritance (Family Provision) Act 1938.[10] In *Re Coventry*,[11] Oliver J said:

> "Subject to the Court's powers under the Act and to fiscal demands, an Englishman remains at liberty at his death to dispose of his own property in whatever way he pleases or, if he chooses to do so, to leave that disposition to be regulated by the laws of intestate succession."

This has also been expressed in terms that the court should start from the position that the provisions of the will should be upheld except to the extent that they are displaced by the obligation to maintain the widow[12] during her lifetime.[13] In *Re Bunning*,[14] Vinelott J made a similar pronouncement, though he referred to the fact that the husband had largely built up his assets by his own efforts before the marriage. More recently, Wall LJ said in *Cunliffe v Fielden*[15] that a deceased spouse who leaves a widow is entitled to bequeath his estate to whomever he pleases; his only statutory obligation is to make provision for his widow, while in *Barron v Woodhead*,[16] where the husband was the surviving spouse, HH Judge Behrens expressed the position of the testatrix who left a widower in corresponding terms. Testamentary freedom was also addressed in the judgment in *Ilott v Mitson* written by Baroness Hale of Richmond, with which Lord Kerr of Tonaghmore and Lord Wilson agreed,[17] and that judgment is discussed at

---

[9] Subsection 8(e)(ii); "Children of the Deceased"; (e) "Successful Claims", (ii) "*Ilott v Mitson*".

[10] Michael Albery, *The Inheritance (Family Provision) Act 1938* (London: Sweet & Maxwell, 1950), pp.1–2.

[11] *Re Coventry* [1980] Ch. 461 at 474G.

[12] This principle has held to be applicable to widowers; see *Barron v Woodhead* [2009] 1 F.L.R. 747, at [14(1)] and should, logically, extend to the survivor of any marriage or civil partnership.

[13] *Re Besterman* (1982) 3 F.L.R. 255 at 266F, per Judge Mervyn Davies QC, referred to by Oliver J on appeal in *Re Besterman* [1984] Ch. 458 at 477H. Oliver J was critical of this approach in that it was directed towards providing a sum for the applicant which would buy her an appropriate annuity.

[14] *Re Bunning* [1984] Ch. 480 at 499B.

[15] *Cunliffe v Fielden* [2006] Ch. 361, [21].

[16] *Barron v Woodhead* [2009] 1 F.L.R. 747, at [14(1)].

[17] *Ilott v Mitson* [2017] UKSC 17, reported *sub nom. Ilott v The Blue Cross* [2017] 2 W.L.R 979, at [49]–[66].

the end of the subsection of this chapter which deals with successful claims by adult children.[18]

2.—MAINTENANCE

(a) General

"Maintenance" has never been defined in the family provision legislation, **6–006** and many of the judicial dicta which have been applied are more illuminating as to what "maintenance" is not, rather than what it is. From quite an early stage, there was general agreement that "maintenance" meant more than mere subsistence. In *Re Borthwick*,[19] it was unsuccessfully argued that, as the widow had been living on a very small allowance during the testator's lifetime, an award of a similar sum would amount to reasonable maintenance after his death. From the decisions in that case and in a number of others, it is clear that there is no hard and fast rule that the level of maintenance appropriate for a claimant should correspond to that which they received during the testator's lifetime. Thus in *Re Elliott*[20] it was unsuccessfully argued that the surviving widow should receive nothing as she was, by reason of having become entitled to a pension, better off than she had been in her husband's lifetime; contrast *Re Inns*,[21] where it was held that the testator's omission to ensure that the widow had the means to live in the matrimonial home as he had intended her to do did not mean that the provision for her was not reasonable maintenance. Two more recent claims by cohabitants provide a similar contrast. In *Negus v Bahouse*,[22] the financial provision awarded included a transfer to the claimant of the flat in which she had been living with the deceased immediately before his death, while in *Cattle v Evans*[23] it was found that the claimant did not need a home of the size and value that she had occupied while living with the deceased.

In the Ontario case of *Re Duranceau*,[24] "maintenance" was said to be **6–007** provision which was:

> "...sufficient to enable the dependant to live neither luxuriously nor miserably, but decently and comfortably according to his or her station in life."

This was quoted with approval by the Court of Appeal in *Re Coventry*.[25] In *Re E*,[26] the purpose of the 1938 Act was described as:

---

[18] Subsection 8(e); see (ii)(5), "Reflections on the judgments of the Supreme Court", paras 6–184 to 6–191.
[19] *Re Borthwick* [1949] Ch. 395.
[20] *Re Elliott* [1956] C.L.Y. 9249.
[21] *Re Inns* [1947] Ch. 576.
[22] *Negus v Bahouse* [2008] 1 F.L.R. 381.
[23] *Cattle v Evans* [2011] 2 F.L.R. 843.
[24] *Re Duranceau* [1952] 3 D.L.R. 714.
[25] *Re Coventry* [1980] 461 at 485C per Goff LJ.
[26] *Re E* [1966] 2 All E.R. 44.

"...not to require a deceased to keep the dependants there specified above the breadline[27] but to ensure that reasonable provision is made for them having regard to all the circumstances of the case."

6–008   There never has been any rule that reasonable provision must or should be equated or related to any measure of state provision, and in *Ilott v Mitson*[28] Ryder LJ said that, as a matter of public policy, the court was not constrained to treat a person's reasonable financial provision as being limited by their existing state benefits, nor was the court's function substituted for by any assessment of benefits undertaken by the state. That must surely be correct, even though the judgment of the Court of Appeal of which it formed a part was reversed by the Supreme Court. The same is true of the applicant's entitlement on intestacy. Indeed, when the operation of the 1938 Act was extended to cases where the deceased had died intestate, it was provided by s.1(8) (inserted by the Intestates' Estates Act 1952) that, in considering whether the disposition made reasonable provision for the dependant, the court should not be bound to assume that the law relating to intestacy makes reasonable provision in all cases. There is at the time of writing no reported case under the 1975 Act in which an application by a surviving spouse has failed on the ground that the provision made by the law of intestacy amounted to reasonable provision.

6–009   The decision in *Re Christie*[29] that "maintenance", for the purpose of s.1(2)(b) of the 1975 Act, referred to:

"...the applicant's way of life and well-being, his health, financial security and allied matters such as the life, well-being and security of his immediate family for whom he was responsible",

is generally regarded as anomalous and has not been followed. It was considered by Oliver J[30] to be very broad and dangerously near to equating "maintenance" with "wellbeing" or "benefit". The third of the unsuccessful applicant's nine grounds of appeal in *Re Coventry* was that the construction placed on the word "maintenance" by Oliver J was unduly restrictive, but that criticism was rejected by the Court of Appeal. It was common ground that, in line with the 1938 Act cases, something more than mere subsistence was meant; but, as Goff LJ put it, "it does not mean anything which may be regarded as reasonably desirable for [the applicant's] general benefit or welfare". In the Northern Ireland case of *Re McGarrell*[31] one of the grounds on which an application by a married adult daughter of the deceased was resisted was that, since the applicant was being maintained by her husband, any payment to her out of her father's estate would be a bonus or enrichment, rather than maintenance. This argument was rejected, the court

---

[27] More accurately described, suggested Goff LJ, as "subsistence level".
[28] *Ilott v Mitson* [2015] 2 F.L.R. 1409, CA, at [69].
[29] *Re Christie* [1979] Ch. 168.
[30] *Re Coventry* [1980] Ch. 461 at 471E–F.
[31] *Re McGarrell* [1983] N.I.J.B. 8.

holding that in her difficult financial circumstances, a payment to her out of her father's estate would constitute maintenance as that term was understood in *Re Coventry* and the cases cited therein.

In *Re Dennis*,[32] the applicant (an adult child) who was applying for permission to commence proceedings out of time, specifically claimed a lump sum with which to pay the capital transfer tax on a gift of £90,000 left to him by the deceased. While Browne-Wilkinson J declined to define the exact meaning of "maintenance", he expressed the view that the word connoted only: **6-010**

> "...payments which, directly or indirectly, enable the applicant in the future to discharge the cost of his daily living at whatever standard of living is appropriate to him. The provision that is to be made is to meet recurring expenses, being expenses of living of an income nature. This does not mean that the provision need be by way of income payments. The provision can be by way of a lump sum, for example, to buy a house in which the applicant can be housed, thereby relieving him *pro tanto* of income expenditure. Nor am I suggesting that there may not be cases in which payment of existing debts may not be appropriate as a maintenance payment, for example, to pay the debts of an applicant in order to enable him to carry on a profit-making business or profession may well be for his maintenance."

The Supreme Court in *Ilott v Mitson*[33] acknowledged that that summary had been often cited with approval. Having identified a number of other forms of provision which might be made by way of lump sum payments,[34] the judgment continues by referring to the necessity to remember that the statutory power was to provide for maintenance, rather to confer capital on the claimant. The approach of Munby J in *Re Myers*[35] in making housing provision by way of a life interest in a capital sum with a power to advance capital to cater for the possibility of care expenses in advanced old age was commended, and it was said to be likely that if housing was provided by way of maintenance, it would by way of such a life interest rather than a capital sum. As will be seen, the reported cases to date do not altogether bear out that view and it remains to be seen whether it will be adopted as a default position (effectively creating a presumption that the interest awarded should be a life interest) or the question is treated as open-ended.

In the decision of the Court of Appeal on quantum in *Ilott v Mitson*,[36] Ryder LJ commented that in so far as there was a debate about how maintenance ought to be construed for the purpose of s.1(2) of the 1975 Act, **6-011**

[32] *Re Dennis* [1981] 2 All E.R. 140.
[33] *Ilott v Mitson* [2017] UKSC 17, reported *sub nom. Ilott v The Blue Cross* [2017] 2 W.L.R 979, at [14].
[34] Provision of a vehicle to enable the applicant to get to work was given as an example.
[35] *Re Myers* [2005] W.T.L.R. 851.
[36] *Ilott v Mitson* (cited as [2016] 1 All E.R. 932 in *Lewis v Warner*), [2015] 2 F.L.R. 1409, CA, at [68].

it could await a case in which the circumstances permitted of a broader discussion. *Lewis v Warner*[37] is such a case, as, most unusually, the provision made was by way of an option to acquire the house in which the claimant had been living, and which was the principal asset of the deceased's estate, at an agreed market value. This raises the question whether "maintenance" can be provided in a manner which involves no transfer of value from the estate to the claimant.

(b) Freeing Income by Discharging Debts

6–012   Whether or not that broader discussion takes place, there is no doubt that maintenance can be provided by way of a lump sum for that purpose. This is clearly contemplated by *Re Dennis*, and has been the basis for the provision of maintenance in a number of cases where the claimant was an adult child or a person treated as a child of the family; the relevant cases are discussed in the sections relating to the relevant class of claimant. The adult child claimant was successful in *Re Pearce*,[38] *Espinosa v Bourke*[39] and *Re Abram, Deceased*,[40] but not in *Re Jennings*,[41] where the trial judge had found that the applicant (an adult son of the deceased) reasonably required an amount which would enable him to discharge the mortgage on his house, and awarded him £40,000, but his decision was reversed by the Court of Appeal. Provision of that nature had previously been made in *Re Callaghan*,[42] where the applicant (a 47-year-old man who had been treated as a child of the family) was awarded a lump sum of £15,000 to enable him to buy the council house in which he and his family were living.

(c) Provision for Meeting Obligations to Others

6–013   In *Riggs v Lloyds Bank*[43] the applicant was the married daughter of the deceased, with two children aged 14 and 10. At first instance she was awarded a sum of £20,000, payable in two instalments and expressed by the judge to be "not a legacy to Mrs Riggs, but a commuted sum for maintenance while her children are still dependent". The Court of Appeal allowed the appeal on that issue. The need to provide for her children had not been part of her case; it was a claim that had been devised by the judge himself. The applicant's own case had been, in effect, that the deceased had a moral obligation towards her, and it was unfair that the whole estate, which had considerable development value, should pass to her brother. There was no evidence that she was generally in need of maintenance; the sum awarded

---

[37] *Lewis v Warner* [2017] Ch. 13. The judgment of Newey J, dismissing the appeal from the order of Mr Recorder Gardner QC made on 11 November 2015, was handed down on 18 July 2016. At the time of writing there is an appeal outstanding. The case is discussed in detail at paras 6–114 to 6–119, below.

[38] *Re Pearce* [1998] 2 F.L.R. 705, CA (lump sum for investment in his business premises and improvements to his house).

[39] *Espinosa v Bourke* [1999] 1 F.L.R. 747, CA (lump sum to pay off debts).

[40] *Re Abram* [1996] 2 F.L.R. 379 (settlement on protective trusts to relieve the applicant from the consequences of his indebtedness).

[41] *Re Jennings* [1994] Ch. 286, CA.

[42] *Re Callaghan* [1985] Fam. 1.

[43] *Riggs v Lloyds Bank* unreported 27 November 1992, CA.

could not be justified as being for her maintenance and the judge had erred in principle in trying to turn it into maintenance by expressing a general view that it was for the benefit of her children. However, it is submitted that the judge did not err in principle. In having regard to the applicant's financial needs, as s.3(1)(a) directs, the judge was required by s.3(6) to take into account her financial obligations and responsibilities, which included her legal obligation to maintain her children. The fact that her case was put on a different basis was no doubt relevant, but the question to be determined was whether, objectively, the will had made reasonable provision for her.

The case bears some resemblance to the 1938 Act case of *Re Goard*,[44] **6–014** which was not cited. That was an application by a surviving spouse who had had a daughter by the testator before they were married, the daughter (aged 15 at the time of the hearing) having been legitimated by the subsequent marriage. Its relevance is that, although the application was solely by the widow, the situation of the infant daughter was considered. Although she was not a party to the application, she could not be ignored. It was held that, if the daughter was not to be considered, the mother's claim would fail; but as she was, the mother was entitled to be paid something in respect of her.

(d) The Claimant's Standard of Living Before the Death of the Deceased

This section is not concerned with claims by surviving spouses, because **6–015** provision for them is not limited to what is required for their maintenance. The claims in question are mentioned briefly here and, as with those mentioned in s.(b), above,[45] are discussed more fully in the sections of this chapter relating to the relevant class of applicant. They are claims by dependants who were unable to claim as cohabitants in the then state of the law, and by dependants and cohabitants since the extension of the 1975 Act by the Law Reform (Succession) Act 1995. In claims by dependants, the court is directed by s.3(4) to have regard to, inter alia, the extent to which the deceased assumed responsibility for the maintenance of the applicant.

In *Malone v Harrison*[46] Hollings J took the applicant's standard of living **6–016** into account to the extent that:

> "...as he was generous to her in his lifetime, so within the limits set by the statute should the court be in deciding what if any order to make",

and that she would need enough to maintain herself reasonably in her present or a similar flat and to keep herself in a reasonable but not extravagant style. The unreported case of *Rhodes v Dean*[47] is another in which the claim was made under s.1(1)(e), but the applicant had been cohabiting with the deceased.[48] At first instance it was found that the deceased had assumed

---

[44] *Re Goard* (1962) 106 S.J. 721.
[45] Section 2(b), Freeing Income by Discharging Debts, para.6–012.
[46] *Malone v Harrison* [1979] 1 W.L.R. 1353, at 1364B and 1365G.
[47] *Rhodes v Dean* unreported 26 March 1996, CA.
[48] He had died on 1989, so she could only claim as a dependant. The hearing at first instance took place on 13 September 1994.

responsibility for providing her with accommodation, but not for all her maintenance needs, and that he had discharged that responsibility for some two years and two months, but had not assumed responsibility for maintaining the standard of living which she claimed to have enjoyed. Her application was dismissed at first instance and that decision was affirmed on appeal.

6–017   The position of cohabitants is different, as s.3(2A) is concerned with the nature and duration of the relationship and not with the benefit (if any) provided by the deceased to the claimant, though it will normally be the case that the claimant was dependent on the deceased to some extent. The standard of living which the claimant enjoyed during the joint lives of the parties is obviously capable of being a relevant matter within the meaning of s.3(1)(g). It was considered in some detail in *Negus v Bahouse*[49] where the claimant's case was, in essence, that she had enjoyed a very comfortable lifestyle for the eight years of cohabitation, in which she wanted for nothing, had a secure roof over her head and had given up work at the request of the deceased so that she could look after him and the home. Her needs were for continued security in her home and an income which would at least to some extent reflect her standard of living during the relationship. One feature of the assessment of her needs was the rejection by the trial judge of the argument that she could return to the type of accommodation that she had before the relationship with the deceased and his finding that it was not unreasonable that she should have a modest long leasehold or freehold flat or apartment similar to the one in which she had been living with the deceased at the date of his death. On the application for permission to appeal, the Court of Appeal decisively rejected the contention that the trial judge erred in taking into account what counsel for the appellant described as the claimant's previous "lavish lifestyle".[50] The claimant's standard of living was also a relevant consideration in *Webster v Webster*,[51] where it was found that the couple had enjoyed a comfortable lifestyle during their cohabitation. The order made would enable the claimant to fund her existing lifestyle with the exception of holidays, entertainment and the like which could be funded from her savings. Although it was acknowledged in *Negus v Bahouse* that some people have more expensive lifestyles than others, the line was drawn at the "unmerited extravagance" in which the claimant in *Cattle v Evans*[52] was found to have indulged. In particular, it was found that reasonable provision for her housing did not require the transfer to her of a property of the size and value of the property in which she had been living with the deceased at the date of his death; a life interest in a smaller property would be sufficient.

---

[49] *Negus v Bahouse* [2008] 1 F.L.R. 381.
[50] *Negus v Bahouse* [2012] W.T.L.R. 1117, CA, per Munby J, at [21].
[51] *Webster v Webster* [2009] 1 F.L.R. 1240, [35], citing *Negus v Bahouse* [84]–[88].
[52] *Cattle v Evans* [2011] 2 F.L.R 843. The 1975 Act claim was tried together with a claim to the quasi-matrimonial home based on constructive trust, which failed; see [32]–[41].

3.—Types of Provision

(a) Monetary Awards

Under the 1975 Act, monetary awards may be made either by way of per-   **6–018**
iodical payments (s.2(1)(a)) or lump sum payments (s.2(1)(b)). Section 2(2)
specifies the payment conditions which an order under s.2(1)(a) may contain. The case-law shows that lump sums are awarded much more frequently
than periodical payments.[53] This is generally desirable in the interests both
of the personal representatives, who do not have to keep a fund in being to
provide income payments, and the parties, so as to facilitate a clean break.
However, if those considerations are not important, and maintenance is
needed only for a relatively short defined period, an order for periodic
payments may be appropriate. In *Taylor v Bell*,[54] the claimant had been
excluded from his father's will and his 1975 Act claim was compromised.
Under the terms of the consent order made in 2008, the trustees were to set
aside a fund out of which payments would be made from time to time for his
maintenance during the remainder of his education. The order specified the
maximum payments that were to be made and that no further payments
were to be made after 31 August 2014. In the event, due to unforeseen
circumstances, the completion of his further education was delayed and, on
an application under s.6 to vary the payments specified by the consent
order[55] he was awarded further periodical payments to cover the final year
of his undergraduate studies and for two years of postgraduate training,
conditional on his attending a full-time course.

Where an order for payment of a lump sum has been made under either   **6–019**
s.2(1)(b) or, by way of variation of a periodical payments order under
s.6(2)(b), and the order provides for the payment of the lump sum by
instalments s.7(2) provides for the order to be varied by varying the number
of instalments payable, the amount of any instalment and the date on which
the instalment becomes payable. There is no power to vary the total amount
payable. Provision by way of lump sum thus necessarily involves the
applicant forgoing the right to come back to the court for further provision.
It was this feature of the legislation which caused Oliver J to introduce into
his assessment of reasonable provision what came to be known as the
"*Besterman* cushion".[56] The more recent cases in which the *Besterman*
cushion has been held to be no longer appropriate are considered in s.5 of
this chapter which deals with provision for surviving spouses and civil
partners.

---

[53] Among the relatively few such cases are *Re Stead* [1985] F.L.R. 16; *Re Debenham* [1986] 1
F.L.R. 404 and *Re Farrow* [1987] 1 F.L.R. 205.
[54] *Taylor v Bell* [2015] All E.R. (D) 208.
[55] For discussion of the application in *Taylor v Bell* under s.6, see Ch.5, paras 5–041 and 5–042.
[56] *Re Besterman* [1984] Ch. 458 at 476G–477E; referred to by Vinelott J in *Re Bunning* [1984]
Ch. 480 at 495D–F. In *Bunning*, Vinelott J expressed the hope that the award of £60,000
would enable her to buy a property of the type which she wished to acquire together with the
income that she needed and a reserve adequate to provide for exceptional demands and
unforeseen contingencies.

(b) Contingencies and Inflation

6–020   Quite apart from Oliver J's observations in *Re Besterman*, it had been
generally thought at the time when the 1975 Act came into force, and for
some years afterwards, that when formulating a claim for a monetary
award, practitioners should take account of contingencies and inflation. The
need to provide a cushion against contingencies had been recognised in a
number of cases; thus in *Re W*,[57] the 75-year-old applicant was awarded
£11,000, so as to enable her to buy an annuity and be afforded some protection against future uncertainties. The effect of inflation was considered in
some detail in *Lewis v Lewis*,[58] a case decided in a period of severe inflation.[59]
The appeal was on the ground that the trial judge had not considered
whether the applicant's annual income of £3,400 was sufficient, having
regard to the effect of inflation. £2,000 of that income was provided by an
annuity payable under the will of the deceased, which was made in 1971.
£2,000 in February 1979, when the hearing at first instance took place,
would have been worth £1,656 at the time of the Court of Appeal hearing.
£2,000 in March 1971, when the will was made, would have been worth £616
at the date of the appeal hearing. The applicant was awarded a lump sum of
£10,000 with interest from the date of judgment.

6–021   Contingencies may occur which would reduce, rather than increase, the
amount which would be reasonable for the applicant to have. An obvious
example is a future entitlement to a pension. This was taken into account in
Re Debenham,[60] where the periodical payments of £4,500 per year to the 58-
year-old applicant were ordered to be reduced to £3,000 on her becoming
eligible for an old-age pension. Similarly, the likelihood of acquiring
property in the future by way of inheritance or some other form of entitlement following the death of another person would be a relevant matter.

(c) Capitalising Income Needs

6–022   Under the 1938 Act as originally enacted, the orders that could be made
were such that the question of how and when to capitalise income
requirements would rarely arise.[61] In any event, the judges of the Chancery
Division, which at that time had exclusive jurisdiction, were not disposed to
engage in any calculations. Thus, in *Brown v Knowles*,[62] an application by a
surviving spouse, Wynn-Parry J went so far as to say that a judge when
exercising their discretion should do no more than name a figure and should
not condescend to an analytical statement of how they arrived at that figure.

---

[57] *Re W* 1975 (119) S.J. 439. This was an application under the pre-1975 legislation by a former
spouse who had not remarried.
[58] *Lewis v Lewis* unreported 13 March 1980, CA.
[59] RPI (January 1987 = 100) had risen from 52.95 in the month of the trial to 63.93 in the
month of the appeal hearing, 13 months later.
[60] *Re Debenham* [1986] 1 F.L.R. 404.
[61] Subsection 1(2) of the 1938 Act provided that provision for maintenance should be by way of
periodical payments, though subs.1(4) gave the court power to make an order for provision
in whole or in part by way of a lump sum.
[62] *Brown v Knowles* (1955) 105 LJ 169.

The application succeeded, but the reporter appears to have been infected by the judge's reticence, since the report fails to state what award was made.

The question of how to calculate a capital equivalent of a future recurring **6–023** expense or loss of income was not a new one at that time; it had, of course, been a feature of personal injury litigation for many years. Clearly, it would arise when a lump sum award (as was usually the case) was treated as representing commuted maintenance payments over a specified number of years or over the period of the recipient's life expectancy. However, actuarial calculations were regarded with some suspicion by the courts. Thus, Lord Pearson said in *Taylor v O'Connor*[63] that there were too many variables, too many conjectural decisions to be made, and a false appearance of accuracy and precision would result. The experience of practitioners and judges in applying the normal method was the best primary method for making assessments.

The method to which he referred is the multiplier-multiplicand method, **6–024** which was at that time in regular use in personal injury litigation.[64] There is, of course, no reason why the methods used for capitalisation of income needs in other types of claim should not be used in Inheritance Act claims. Indeed, it has been said[65] that there does not seem to be a distinction of fundamental principle between providing for the future needs of plaintiffs in personal injury litigation and applicants in proceedings under the Matrimonial Causes Act 1973 or the Inheritance (Provision for Family and Dependants) Act 1975.

(d) Transfer, Settlement and Acquisition of Property

The case-law shows a wide spectrum of orders designed to provide for the **6–025** housing needs of the applicant, whether by awarding a lump sum out of which a property could be acquired for the applicant's accommodation, or by way of a settlement or transfer of property comprised in the net estate of the deceased. The tendency in the earlier years of the Act was to order that some form of settlement be made in favour of the applicant,[66] but it has become more common in recent years to make orders for an outright transfer, either free from incumbrances or subject to a charge. The order made in *Re Bayliss*[67] was unusual at that time. In that case, the testator had been married twice, and there were legacies to the children of the first marriage which could not be satisfied without resort to the matrimonial home in which the applicant widow was living. By the will she was given

---

[63] *Taylor v O'Connor* [1971] A.C. 115.

[64] See s.4(b) of this chapter, paras 6–032, 6–033.

[65] See the Appendix to *Wells v Wells* at [1997] 1 All E.R. 699–705, prepared by Thorpe LJ, which provides a survey of the then available methods. The observation quoted is at 705c–d.

[66] In the 1938 Act case of *Re Mason* (1975) 5 Fam. Law 124 the net estate was left to the testator's four children in equal shares, but their interest in the matrimonial home was subject to the widow's right to reside there as long as she wished; but she was given no interest in the proceeds of sale. It was held that this did not provide her with sufficient security, and it was ordered that she be given such interest in the home as would constitute her a Settled Land Act tenant for life.

[67] *Re Bayliss* unreported 9 December 1977, CA.

only a life interest in the residuary estate. The Court of Appeal took the view that her interests had priority over those of the grown-up and well-established children of the earlier marriage. A reasonable husband would have left her the entire estate absolutely, and the Court awarded her the matrimonial home absolutely, there being nothing else left in the estate.

6-026   In the earlier years, it appears to have been generally thought that a settlement should be the norm unless either a clean break was deemed to be desirable because of ill-feeling between the applicant and the family of the testator, as in *Re Haig*,[68] or the applicant was the widow of a childless marriage and there were no living potential objects of the testator's bounty to be considered, as in *Re Besterman*[69] and *Re Bunning*.[70] In two cases where the applicant had been awarded an absolute interest at first instance, the order was varied on appeal so as to reduce it to a life interest. In *Jevdjovic v Milenko*[71] the Court of Appeal considered the provision made at first instance to be excessive, while in *Re Krubert*,[72] Nourse LJ accepted that the applicant widow needed the matrimonial home to live in and would need the additional income generated by the reinvested proceeds if she had to move, but concluded that no financial need for an absolute interest had been made out. Similarly, in *Davis v Davis*[73] the Court of Appeal was not persuaded that the appellant widow needed capital provision in the form of an absolute interest in the house in which she had a life interest under the trusts of her husband's will. Other cases in which the applicant has been awarded a limited interest are *Winfield v Billington*,[74] where the husband unsuccessfully applied for the deceased wife's half-share of the former matrimonial home to be transferred to him absolutely; *Capocci v Cooke*,[75] where the applicant husband had been given by the will only a determinable right to live in the matrimonial home, and the decision of the County Court to dismiss his application for an absolute interest was upheld by the Court of Appeal; and *Re Moody, Moody v Stevenson*,[76] where the house was settled on the applicant husband on terms which enabled him to live there as long as he was able and willing to do so.

6-027   As well as orders conferring on the applicant the right to occupy property,[77] rights of occupation granted by the deceased's will have been varied. In *Grattan v McNaughton*[78] the restrictions in the deceased's will on the

---

[68] *Re Haig* (1979) 129 N.L.J. 420.
[69] *Re Besterman* [1984] Ch. 458.
[70] *Re Bunning* [1984] Ch. 480.
[71] *Jevdjovic v Milenko* unreported 12 February 1990, CA.
[72] *Re Krubert* [1997] Ch. 97, CA, at 105E.
[73] *Davis v Davis* [1993] 1 F.L.R. 54, CA.
[74] *Winfield v Billington* unreported 30 July 1990, CA.
[75] *Capocci v Cooke* unreported 2 February 1996, CA.
[76] *Moody v Stevenson* [1992] Ch. 486, CA.
[77] *Re Campbell* [1983] N.I. 10 (non-assignable licence to occupy a dwelling-house on the family farm on which the applicant had worked for many years); *Moody v Stevenson* [1992] Ch. 486 (settlement on terms which enabled the applicant to live in the house for as long as he wished); *Barron v Woodhead* [2009] 1 F.L.R. 747 (right to occupy rent-free for life, but claimant to pay the outgoings of the property).
[78] *Grattan v McNaughton* [2001] W.T.L.R. 1305. Under the will, her right of occupation was to terminate on remarriage, cohabitation or on her ceasing to reside there.

wife's right to occupy the matrimonial home were removed and she was enabled to sell that property and purchase another property for her occupation out of the proceeds of sale. In both *Re Lewis, Lewis v Lynch*,[79] where the applicant was a surviving spouse, and *Harrington v Gill*,[80] where the applicant was a dependant who had been living with the deceased for six years as husband and wife, the house was settled on the applicant for life. In *Myers v Myers*,[81] the award to the 60-year-old daughter of the deceased included the settlement of £275,000 on her to buy a flat. In *Baker v Baker*,[82] the claimant was awarded a life interest in the deceased's house and its proceeds of sale, which could be applied in the purchase of another property or invested to produce income). In *Cattle v Evans*,[83] also a claim by a cohabitant, it was ordered that a sum of not more than £110,000 was to be provided for her from the estate in order to buy a house for her, to be held on trust for her for life or as long as she wished to continue living there, remainder to the two sons of the deceased, and which she was required to keep comprehensively insured to its full value; any property purchased in substitution for it was to be held on the same trusts.

However, it has become more common to make orders for outright   **6–028**
transfer of property, or a beneficial interest in property, and such orders have been made in favour of surviving spouses,[84] cohabitants[85] and dependants.[86] In the two cohabitant cases noted, provision was also made for the discharge of the existing mortgage on the property. The desirability of effecting a clean break between the parties is sometimes a relevant, and occasionally a highly significant consideration. Thus, in *Cunliffe v Fielden*,[87] Wall LJ noted as a subsidiary, but nevertheless relevant factor, that the trial judge had been aiming for a "clean break" settlement. Quite apart from whether it provided accommodation in excess of what was reasonable, the former matrimonial home was a relatively short distance away from the location of the family business and it would be inconsistent with the philosophy of the "clean break" order which was obviously desirable, for her to go on living there. In *Iqbal v Ahmed*,[88] a claim by a surviving spouse, and in *Holliday v Musa*,[89] a claim by a dependant,[90] the high degree of hostility

[79] *Re Lewis, Lewis v Lynch* unreported 13 March 1980, CA.
[80] *Harrington v Gill* (1983) 4 F.L.R. 265.
[81] *Myers v Myers* [2005] W.T.L.R. 851.
[82] *Baker v Baker* [2008] 2 F.L.R. 767.
[83] *Cattle v Evans* [2011] W.T.L.R. 947.
[84] *Adams v Lewis* [2001] W.T.L.R. 493; *P v G, P and P (Family Provision; Relevance of Divorce Provision)* [2006] 1 F.L.R. 431. In *Lilleyman v Lilleyman* [2013] 1 F.L.R. 47, it was left open to the widow to decide whether to take the property awarded to her or its lump sum equivalent.
[85] *Negus v Bahouse* [2008] 1 F.L.R. 381; *Webster v Webster* [2009] 1 F.L.R. 1240.
[86] *Musa v Holliday* [2013] 1 F.L.R. 806, CA, dismissing the appeal from the order made at first instance.
[87] *Cunliffe v Fielden* [2006] Ch. 361, CA, [36]
[88] *Iqbal v Ahmed*, [2012] 1 F.L.R. 31. C.A.
[89] The decision of HH Judge Kushner QC in her judgment dated 11 November 2011, against which leave to appeal was sought, has not been reported. In *Musa v Holliday*, noted above, permission to appeal was granted but the appeal was dismissed.
[90] *Musa v Holliday* [2013] 1 F.L.R. 806, CA.

between the claimant and the beneficiaries was a substantial factor in the decision to make a clean break award. Additionally, in *Iqbal v Ahmed*, the widow's right of occupation under the terms of the will was precarious because of the financial burden imposed on her by the repairing obligations to which that right was subject.

6–029   In *Rajabally v Rajabally*,[91] the transfer of property was ordered subject to a charge. The net estate of the deceased, who had been married twice, was represented almost entirely by a freehold dwelling house worth approximately £55,000. He left his estate to his wife and his three children (one of whom was the mentally disabled son of his first marriage) in equal shares. The Court of Appeal (reversing the judge below) held that reasonable provision required that the widow should have security in the house and awarded it to her absolutely, subject to a legacy of £7,500 to the son to be raised by a charge on the house.

6–030   In *Churchill v Roach*[92] the claimant failed to establish the required period of cohabitation but succeeded on her alternative claim as a dependant. It was found that the claimant's income was sufficient to discharge her normal day-to-day expenses but not to meet her housing needs. Giving her the right to live (until remarriage or permanent cohabitation) in the property recently acquired by the deceased, which was intended to form part of their permanent home[93] was not a solution, as it would involve contact with the deceased's family. Also, as she was much the same age as the deceased's children, they were unlikely to derive much benefit from the reversionary interest in it. It was therefore ordered that the property be transferred to her outright subject to a charge for a sum[94] representing the approximate value of the reversionary interest were she to have been given a life interest terminable on marriage or cohabitation.

4.—METHODS OF CAPITALISATION

(a) General

6–031   Under the 1938 Act as originally enacted, the question of capitalisation did not arise since, except where the value of the estate was less than £2,000, the court had power only to make provision by way of periodical payments. For deaths after 1952, that limit was raised to £5,000. In some cases, a lump sum was awarded outright, but an alternative was to award a sum calculated by reference to the amount required to purchase an annuity. The first reported case in which capitalisation of income needs for that purpose was considered

---

[91] *Rajabally v Rajabally* [1987] 2 F.L.R. 390.
[92] *Churchill v Roach* [2004] 2 F.L.R. 989.
[93] There were two properties which were intended to be converted into one dwelling-house but the two components of the unified property were to be held under separate titles. This arrangement would have been costly to set up and difficult to administer.
[94] The figure of £65,000 also represented an element of interest for the postponement of the estate's entitlement. The deceased had died on 15 April 2000 and the hearing took place on 15–17 July 2002, with judgment being delivered the following day.

was *Re Elliott*.[95] Out of a net estate of £2,670 Danckwerts J awarded the 48-year-old applicant widow such lump sum as, when calculated on the Government annuity tables in accordance with her age, would produce an annuity of 15s per week.[96] This course was occasionally adopted in later years.[97] In *Re Bunning*[98] one of the matters which Vinelott J took into account, when reaching the conclusion that £60,000 was the right award, was the cost of an annuity; he considered that the applicant, then aged 56, would be unwise to buy one at the time but would, if purchased five or ten years later, put her in a position where, combined with her other resources, she would be able to maintain a by no means extravagant lifestyle and have a reasonable but not excessive reserve.

(b) The Multiplier-Multiplicand Method

The multiplier-multiplicand approach, which was conventional in personal injury cases at the time, involved assessment of the income need (the multiplicand) and multiplying it by a factor (the multiplier) roughly equal to half the number of years for which the income need existed.[99] It was first employed in a 1975 Act case in *Malone v Harrison*,[100] an application under s.1(1)(e). The applicant was 38 at the time of the hearing.[101] Hollings J found that:

    6–032

  (i)   the deceased had assumed full responsibility for the applicant's maintenance for a period of 12 years immediately before his death;

  (ii) he had maintained her to the extent of at least £4,000 per year excluding certain non-recurring items and the annual value of the accommodation he had bought for her; and

  (iii) her actuarial life expectancy was 38 years.

---

[95] *Re Elliott*, *The Times*, 18 May 1956.

[96] The Immediate Life Annuity Tables made under SR & O 1934, No.471 and reproduced in J Gilchrist Smith, *Intestacy and Family Provision* (Manchester: Solicitors' Law Stationery Society, 1952) show the price of an immediate annuity of £1 paid quarterly, based on the price of 2 per cent consols. The reader is informed that, having regard to the then price of such stock, only the first 13 tables (covering a price range of £50 to £71.10s per £100 of stock purchased) are reproduced. From those tables one can calculate that an annuity of 15s per week (£39 per year) paid quarterly would have cost £472 17s 6d if the stock was trading at £50 per £100 and £702.19s 6d if it was trading at £70 per £100. Dr Gilchrist Smith was the sole editor of *Emmet on Title*, 12th–15th editions, spanning the years 1930–1967 and the co-editor, with Julian Farrand, of the 16th (1974).

[97] *Re W* [1975] 119 S.J. 439 (award of £11,000 to applicant aged 75, to purchase an annuity and provide some protection against inflation); *Re Crawford* [1983] 4 F.L.R. 273, applicant, then aged 59, awarded £35,000, being a sum sufficient to purchase an annuity of £4,000 per year.

[98] *Re Bunning* [1984] Ch. 480 at 499G.

[99] This way of determining the multiplier equates to assuming net rates of return well in excess of 5 per cent and would thus be extremely unfavourable to present-day claimants.

[100] *Malone v Harrison* [1979] 1 W.L.R. 1353.

[101] The multiplier-multiplicand method was employed in the matrimonial case of *Fournier v Fournier* [1998] 2 F.L.R. 990, where the parties were 37 and 36 respectively and it was considered appropriate to order provision by way of capitalised periodical payments over a period substantially shorter than the wife's life expectancy. The multiplier was assessed at somewhere between 8 and 9.

He assumed that she would be able to work until she was 60 and earn an average of £2,000 per year, and he sought to enable her to have, in income and capital, about £4,000 per year, which would allow her to live in her present flat in a reasonable but not extravagant style. Her income need of £2,000 per year over the 22-year period from age 38 to 60 was capitalised by applying a multiplier of 11, giving a lump sum of £22,000; for the period 60 to 76 her annual income need of £4,000 was capitalised as £20,000, applying a multiplier of 5. From the total of £42,000 he deducted her disposable capital resources of £23,000, and thus awarded her £19,000.

6–033   Subsequently, judicial enthusiasm for this approach has been muted.[102] However, it was resurrected in *Re Pearce*[103] which was heard at first instance in November 1996, when the applicant was awarded £85,000 out of a net estate of £285,000, effectively on the basis that the lump sum was not a commuted maintenance payment but would be expended in a manner which would leave the applicant with an increased income. Having arrived at the figure of £85,000 on that basis, the judge then looked at it in another way, which was that the applicant and his wife had an annual income of between £8,000 and £9,000. An increase of £6,000–£7,000 would give them a maximum of £16,000, which was reasonable for their maintenance, and when one had regard to the age of the plaintiff and the sort of multipliers which would be awarded in a personal injury case, one would arrive at a multiplier of somewhere between 12 and 13. £85,000 represents, roughly, an income need of £6,500 with a multiplier of 13. In the view of the Court of Appeal, it could not be said that the method of capitalising the £6,000 to £7,000 per year was one which the judge could not reasonably have adopted. There was no adequate basis for interfering with his decision, which had achieved substantial justice between the parties.

(c) Duxbury and Ogden Tables

6–034   The multiplier-multiplicand method is generally thought to be a fairly crude way of estimating the immediate capital sum which would reflect the benefit of accelerated receipt of future income and allow for other contingencies. The Ogden tables (*Actuarial Tables with Explanatory Notes for Use in Personal Injury and Fatal Accident Claims*, published by HMSO) provide a somewhat more refined approach. They include tables of multipliers for pecuniary loss for life, up to age 100, for both males and females, and for term certain (1–80 years), for a range of net rates of return calibrated at intervals of 0.5 per cent. In the edition current at the time of writing, the range is from -2.0 per cent to 3.0 per cent; the range in the previous edition

---

[102] See *Re Wood* (1982) 89 L.S. Gaz. 774, where Mervyn Davies J found the calculation along those lines "interesting and instructive" but declined to adopt it; *Clark v Jones* unreported 2 December 1985, CA, where Dillon LJ found the approach of calculating a dependency and a multiplier might be convenient but there was no hard and fast rule; *Williams v Roberts* [1986] 1 F.L.R. 349 where Wood J was referred to the calculations in *Malone v Harrison* but did not find the approach of great assistance.
[103] *Re Pearce* [1998] 2 F.L.R. 705, CA, at 714B–715F, 716H–717B.

had been 0.0–5.0 per cent. For the calculation of damages generally, a very full account is contained in *Kemp and Kemp, The Quantum of Damages*.[104]

The Duxbury tables[105] appear regularly in the annual Family Law Bar **6–035** Association/Class Legal publication, now entitled *At a Glance*.[106] The income need is capitalised on the basis of a net rate of return representing the sum of the percentage income yield and capital growth of the fund, less the rate of inflation. Ideally, the calculated figures would reflect an outcome in which the capital of the fund will be progressively spent, together with the income which the fund produces so that, if the calculation is accurate,[107] the recipient will "expire in the act of drinking the last glass of champagne". The report of *H v H (Periodical Payments: Variation: Clean Break)*[108] quotes a summary of the Duxbury methodology, taken from Table 14 of the 2014–15 edition of *At a Glance*.[109]

The relative merits of Ogden and Duxbury calculations were compared in **6–036** the Appendix (prepared by Thorpe LJ) to the judgment of the Court of Appeal in the personal injury case of *Wells v Wells*.[110] He came down in favour of the Duxbury calculations principally on the ground that the then current (third) edition of the Ogden tables involved assumptions as to the incidence of income tax which were "crude, unrealistic and unduly favourable to plaintiffs". These criticisms have to some extent been addressed in later editions.[111] However, the compilers accepted that, in cases where the impact of personal income tax and CGT is likely to be significant, a more accurate calculation of the value of the payments net of tax might be desirable.

Although not without its defects, *Duxbury* has gained more or less total **6–037** acceptance as the method for capitalising income needs in 1975 Act cases

---

[104] *Kemp and Kemp, The Quantum of Damages* (London: Sweet and Maxwell), a looseleaf publication in four volumes with a separate volume containing tables and indexes. Another useful work of reference is the annual publication *Facts and Figures: Tables for the Calculation of Damages* (London: Sweet and Maxwell), produced by the Professional Negligence Bar Association and edited by Robin de Wilde QC.

[105] *Duxbury v Duxbury* [1990] 2 All E.R. 77, CA.

[106] Formerly *Tables At a Glance*.

[107] See D. Philpotts and S. Bruce, "An Alternative View of Duxbury" [2010] Fam. Law 161, discussed at para.6–046. The article suggested that the rates of return employed were unrealistically high, that the capital sum calculated on a Duxbury basis might be insufficient in practice to provide the required income, and that a purchased life annuity may be a more satisfactory solution. For a contrary view, see L. Marks QC, "An Alternative View of Duxbury: A Reply" [2010] Fam. Law 614 in which he states that there are very good reasons (not for rehearsal there) why the annuity route has not been adopted in ancillary relief cases.

[108] *H v H (Periodical Payments: Variation: Clean Break)* [2015] 2. F.L.R. 447, CA, per Ryder LJ, at [30].

[109] The summary is at Table 9 of the 2017–18 edition. There is an electronic version of this publication (@eGlance), and the Capitalise programme, also available from Class Legal, permits more sophisticated calculations to be carried out.

[110] *Wells v Wells* [1997] 1 All E.R. 673, CA, at 699–705.

[111] The current (seventh) edition was published in October 2011 and Tables 27 (discounting factors for term certain) and 28 (multipliers for pecuniary loss for term certain have been supplemented by calculations for a rate of -0.75 per cent following the fixing of that figure as the discount rate under the Damages Act 1996 by the Lord Chancellor as from 27 February 2017.

since its introduction into that field in 1994,[112] when an income need of
£29,000 per year for an applicant with a life expectancy of 25 years was
quantified at £325,000 on a Duxbury basis with an assumed net rate of
return of 4.25 per cent.[113] The tables current at the time of writing are based
on a net rate of return of 3.75 per cent. Although the use of the method in
ancillary relief proceedings made it an obvious choice in surviving spouse
claims under the 1975 Act, it has become generally accepted for use in claims
by all classes of applicant, for example, *Re Myers*[114] (adult child) and *Negus
v Bahouse*[115] (cohabitant).

6–038   Notwithstanding its general acceptance, other methods are not (despite
judicial dicta to that effect) excluded from use. Those dicta appear to have
originated through a misunderstanding of what Holman J meant by the
words "industry standard" in *F v F (Duxbury Calculation: Rate of
Return)*[116] when he said:

> "In my view it is important that there should indeed be 'an industry
> standard' for the purpose of the Duxbury approach and in my
> experience that standard has already settled at around 4.25%."

A contemporary commentator, Woelke,[117] had understood this correctly,
observing in the aftermath of the Duxbury versus Ogden debate:

> "...an understandable desire on the part of courts and legal advisers to
> have some certainty in the overall uncertainty of a discretionary system.
> It is therefore understandable if the courts advocate 'an industry
> standard' for a rate of return."[118]

An earlier passage in Holman J's judgment makes it clear that he was not
specifying the Duxbury method as an "industry standard" for capitalisation
of income needs in all circumstances. At 846C–D he said:

---

[112] After *Duxbury v Duxbury (Note)* [1992] Fam. 62; also reported as *Duxbury v Duxbury*
[1987] 1 F.L.R. 7, CA.

[113] *Nott v Ward* unreported 12 December 1994 (HH Judge Bromley QC sitting as a High Court
Judge).

[114] *Re Myers* [2005] W.T.L.R. 851.

[115] *Negus v Bahouse* [2008] 1 F.L.R. 381.

[116] *F v F (Duxbury Calculation: Rate of Return)* [1996] 1 F.L.R. 833 at 850A.

[117] Initiated in *Wells v Wells* [1997] 1 All E.R. 673 C.A., in particular the Appendix at p.699
written by Thorpe LJ, revised, [1999] 1 A.C. 345 (HL) at 374D–G, where Lord Lloyd of
Berwick agreed with Thorpe LJ's criticism of the assumptions underlying the way in which
the then current (third) edition of the Ogden tables dealt with income tax. Several articles
were subsequently published in *Family Law* on various aspects of Duxbury; see the Hon Mr
Justice Singer, N. Mostyn QC (as he then was), L. Marks, P. Lobbenberg, T. Lawrence, A.
Gallop, D. Wreford and N. Van Lennep, "Duxbury—The Future" (1998) Fam. Law 562;
T. Lawrence, "Duxbury—Is there a right rate of return?" [1999] Fam. Law 562; A. Woelke,
"Is Duxbury the Answer?" (1999) Fam. Law 766; J. Merron, P. Baxter and M. Bates, "Is
Duxbury Misleading? Yes It Is", (2001) Fam. Law 747; L. Marks QC, "Duxbury—The
Future? Episode II" (2002) Fam. Law 408.

[118] Woelke, "Is Duxbury the Answer?" (1999) Fam. Law 766 at fn.114.

"In particular it is well known that the Duxbury approach can have a very distorting effect both in the case of a relatively young wife after a relatively short marriage and in the case of a relatively old wife after a long marriage. In the former case it produces too high a figure in proportion to the length of the marriage. In the latter case it may well produce a rather low figure which fails to reflect adequately a long marriage."[119]

In fact, this so-called "Duxbury paradox" is not specific to Duxbury type calculations, although Duxbury calculations tend to emphasise it because of the built-in assumption that the claimant is receiving, or will become entitled to receive, a full state retirement pension. To illustrate this point, consider a female claimant aged 80 whose net annual income need is £10,000. The Duxbury tables (based on a net rate of return of 3.75 per cent) give the sum required to fund that need as £33,000. The current Ogden tables, for a net rate of return of 3 per cent, which is the highest rate of return that they cover, give a multiplier of 8.78 for a female aged 80, so the calculated capital sum would be £87,800. But in reality, whatever method of calculation is employed, the paradox is intrinsic to the Act itself. It is a fact of life that (apart from circumstances such as having to fund expensive care or treatment), the sum required to fund a lifetime income shortfall diminishes with age. However, that inevitably militates against giving full recognition to the duration of the marriage. That in turn produces an asymmetry in the way in which s.3(2)(a) is taken into account. A short marriage is, without more, a factor which will decrease the award and result in a departure from equality to the disadvantage of the claimant.[120] Conversely, there is no reported case in which a particularly long marriage has been identified as a factor that by itself justifies a departure from equality in favour of the claimant.[121]

Holman J's nuanced exposition of the limitations of the Duxbury method seems to have been transformed into a broader view of the phrase "industry standard" as a result of the judgment in *Dharamshi v Dharamshi*,[122] where Thorpe LJ said that he saw:

6–039

"...no warrant for introducing the Ogden tables into ancillary relief. The use of the Duxbury tables has had this court's approval for many years."

He continued, in rejecting any need to consider Ogden in preference to Duxbury for ancillary relief capitalisations, by saying that:

"The field of ancillary relief is already sufficiently esoteric without disputing or discarding what was aptly described as 'the industry standard' by Holman J in *F v F (Duxbury Calculation: Rate of Return)*."

---

[119] The so-called "Duxbury paradox", which is acknowledged in Table 9 of *At A Glance 2017–18*.

[120] *Cunliffe v Fielden* [2006] Ch. 361, CA; *Lilleyman v Lilleyman* [2013] 1 F.L.R. 47.

[121] See s.5(c) of this chapter, entitled "Contribution to the Welfare of the Family".

[122] *Dharamshi v Dharamshi* [2001] 1 F.L.R. 736, CA; see the dictum of Thorpe LJ at [11].

That seems to mean that there is, and can be, no other legitimate approach to the capitalisation of income needs in ancillary relief. If that is what those words mean, it is submitted that they are an inaccurate gloss on what Holman J actually said, and should be treated with caution.

6–040   There are, of course, many cases in which Duxbury calculations give as good a starting point for capitalisation of income needs as any other, but uncritical adherence to them (or any other basis of calculation) in all circumstances is liable to lead to unrealistic results. As Wall LJ observed in *Cunliffe v Fielden*[123]:

> "As has been said more than once, the only thing one can be sure about Duxbury is that the figure is likely to be too high or too low. It remains, however, a useful guide."[124]

Those words appear at the beginning of an article in *Family Law* entitled "An alternative view of Duxbury"[125] of which the lead author is a financial planning consultant. A good deal of the article is to do with investment strategies and there is an interesting comparison of a model investment portfolio with an indexed purchased life annuity (PLA). The authors say:

> "One might have thought that the Duxbury figures would broadly follow PLA rates, given that the PLA model mirrors what the Duxbury tables appear to achieve, i.e. a guaranteed income for life, precisely using up the individual's capital and interest over their lifetime, with no balance remaining. However, based on the indicative rates below, it is apparent that in fact the Duxbury tables assume very much higher returns."

They conclude that, for any but the youngest divorcees, any settlement based on the tables is likely to be too low.[126] The compilers of *At A Glance* also acknowledge this[127]; they observe that:

> "The Table shows figures for recipients in the age range 40 to 80, the usefulness of Duxbury calculations for recipients with a life expectancy of less than about 15 years (women over 75 and men over 73) must be questioned ... the proportionate margin of error in relation to life expectancy (in particular) is extremely high, with some recipients living

---

[123] *Cunliffe v Fielden* [2006] Ch. 361, [91]; cf. Ward LJ in *B v B* [1990] 1 F.L.R. 20 "the only certainty is that it will not happen as we have predicted".

[124] For similar judicial dicta as to the extent to which and the purpose for which Duxbury can be relied on, see *A v A (Elderly Applicant: Lump Sum)* [1999] 2 F.L.R. 969; *Harris v Harris* [2001] F.C.R. 68, at [22]; *Pearce v Pearce* [2003] 2 F.L.R. 1144, at [38].

[125] D. Phillips and S. Bruce, "An alternative view of Duxbury" (2010) Fam. Law 161. This article is cited in *At a Glance 2016–17*, Table 11.

[126] They question whether we have to live with the uncertainty inherent in the Duxbury assumptions and whether "a root and branch overhaul involving an annuity or insurance based alternative" is the appropriate solution.

[127] *At a Glance 2017–18*, Table 9.

more than twice longer than expected, not a fate which afflict recipients aged 40, 50 or even 60 years.[128] And the shorter the expectancy the less likely it is that the average returns will return to those historically achievable over longer terms."

The problem of the recipient with relatively short life expectancy arose in *Swetenham v Walkley*,[129] where one of the elements of the award to the 80-year-old claimant was the provision of an annual sum of £3,500 over the period of her actuarial life expectancy of nine-and-a-half years. This was stated in the judgment to require a capital sum of £33,250, which is simply nine-and-a-half times the amount of the income requirement, so no discount for early receipt such as is built into an actuarially based calculation was applied. In fact the discount would be relatively small for a claimant of that age; a Duxbury calculation[130] gives a capital sum of £30,800 (8.8 times the annual income requirement) and the Ogden multiplier for a net rate of return of 3 per cent[131] is 8.78, which would give a capital sum of £30,730.

The Ogden tables have been used in one reported case under the 1975 Act, **6–041** that of *Rees v Newbery and the Institute of Cancer Research*.[132] In that case, it had been held that the deceased was maintaining the applicant by providing him with living accommodation at a rent substantially below the open market value. The income which the court had to capitalise was the difference of £4,656 per year at the date of the hearing, between the open market rent and the rent which the applicant (who was then 50 years of age) was paying. HH Judge Gilliland QC followed the Court of Appeal approach in *Wells* in that he took a yield of 4.5 per cent as the kind of return which a prudent investor would obtain if he had to invest in a mixed portfolio of equities and gilts. The Ogden tables[133] gave the present value of an annual expenditure of £4,650 as £65,565 for a man aged 50.

It remains to be seen whether the methods for capitalisation of income **6–042** needs currently available can be refined so as to address the problems discussed above and whether insurance or annuity-based calculations will supplement or replace them. Given the defects of the available methods, courts will no doubt continue to regard Duxbury or Ogden calculations as no more than approximate guides. Those tables exhibit differing views of long-term net rates of return; whereas the commentary to the 2017–18 Duxbury tables[134] states that "history tells us that average real returns of 3.75% p.a. are over the long term achievable with a cautious investment

---

[128] But see the case of Louise Calment, mentioned in Phillips and Bruce, "An alternative view of Duxbury"; in 1965, at the age of 90, she exchanged the reversionary interest in her apartment for an annual income of one tenth of its value. She died in 1997 aged 122, having outlived the reversioner, who died in 1995 aged 77.

[129] *Swetenham v Walkley* [2014] W.T.L.R. 845, at [47]–[56].

[130] Factoring out the effect of receipt of a state pension (which can be done by setting the pension age to, say, 95); if that is not done, the calculated capital sum would be negative.

[131] This is the highest net rate of return for which the current Ogden tables give multipliers.

[132] *Rees v Newbery and the Institute of Cancer Research* [1998] 1 F.L.R. 1041.

[133] The then current tables were the second edition (1994).

[134] *At A Glance 2017–18*, commentary at p.16 to Table 9.

strategy", the highest net rate of return used in the current edition of the Ogden tables[135] is 3.0 per cent and the tables (unlike those in previous editions) provide for negative net rates of return. If (which is by no means always the case) the figures underlying the claimed income need are realistic, courts will generally be receptive to argument based on such calculations, but there is no guarantee that the provision finally determined by the court will reflect their result. As Holman J said in *F v F (Duxbury Calculation: Rate of Return*,[136] in relation to income needs:

> "Of course, many given figures in a budget can be dismissed as figures taken out of thin air. But at least they provide some calculated and reasoned basis for the overall figure which is even more taken out of thin air.. What should be avoided by lawyers on both sides is an unrealistic attempt to overstate or understate the figures as the case may be."

5.—SURVIVING SPOUSES AND CIVIL PARTNERS

(a) General

6–043 As has already been remarked, the earlier case-law is of limited value, particularly in relation to applications by surviving spouses and civil partners. Nevertheless it is still useful, even in the context of such applications, in that it identifies a number of matters which courts have from time to time taken into account, but to which they were not, and are not now specifically directed to have regard. Section 1(6) of the 1938 Act directed the court to have regard to certain specified matters and also to:

> "...any other matter or thing which in the circumstances of the case the court may consider relevant or material in relation to [the applicant], to persons interested in the estate, or otherwise."

Those matters would nowadays mostly be swept up by the words "any other matter ... which in the circumstances of the case the court may consider relevant" in s.3(1)(g) of the 1975 Act, though some might fall to be considered under s.3(1)(d) or, in the case of surviving spouses s.3(2).

(b) Age and Duration of the Marriage or Civil Partnership

6–044 The mere fact that the applicant is of advanced age may not assist their claim. In *Re Clarke*,[137] the parties, each of whom had been married before, were 78 and 71 at the date of their marriage. There were two children of the husband's previous marriage, but none of the wife's. The husband died aged

---

[135] Seventh edition (2011).
[136] *F v F (Duxbury Calculation: Rate of Return)* [1996] 1 F.L.R. 833, at 845C–E.
[137] *Re Clarke* [1991] 21 Fam. Law 364.

90 and the widow was 86 at the time of the hearing. By his will she received £25,000 and a life interest in the matrimonial home, subject to which his estate was left to his children and grandchildren. They had always kept their finances separate and she had significant capital and income resources. None of the beneficiaries had made out a positive case that they needed the benefits which they took under the will but as, in all the circumstances, reasonable provision had been made for the widow, her claim failed. In *Re Rowlands*,[138] the 90-year-old widow had been awarded £3,000 out of an estate of £96,000; the parties had been married in 1919 and separated in 1938, but they remained married until the husband's death in 1981. Her appeal on quantum failed.

(c) Contribution to the Welfare of the Family

Except in cases such as *Re Rowlands*,[139] where the parties had ceased to live together many years before the death of the testator, a long marriage will generally import a substantial contribution to the welfare of the family, and therefore, as the cases discussed in the next paragraph show, those two matters will normally be considered together. Where the duration of the marriage has been short, the question of the survivor's contribution towards the welfare of the family is unlikely to arise. In *Cunliffe v Fielden*,[140] the shortness of the marriage was a major factor in the decision of the Court of Appeal to reduce the £800,000 awarded by the trial judge to £600,000.   **6–045**

In *Adams v Lewis*[141] the parties had been married for 54 years and there had been 12 children of the marriage. Mr Adams died in 1991 survived by his wife (who was 86 at the date of the hearing) and 11 of the 12 children. Under his will she received £10,000 and the household goods and personal effects, and the trustees had power to apply any part of the residuary estate in providing and keeping up a suitable residence for her. She wished to continue living in the matrimonial home which had been bought by Mr Adams in his sole name. During the marriage she had not been involved in her husband's business but she had had the entire responsibility for the welfare of the family, Mr Adams' role simply being the payment of bills and the provision of housekeeping money. Finding that he owed his widow an obligation of the highest order, the judge awarded Mrs Adams an absolute interest in the matrimonial home, but reduced the legacy to £5,000, to carry interest from the end of the executor's year. This provision amounted to about half the value of the net estate.   **6–046**

In arriving at that result, HH Judge Behrens found himself largely in agreement with the submission that on divorce the applicant would have been awarded half the estate and there was no reason to depart from the principle of equality. He took the view that the provision she would have   **6–047**

---

[138] *Re Rowlands* (1984) 5 F.L.R. 813, CA.
[139] *Re Rowlands* [1984] F.L.R. 813, CA.
[140] *Cunliffe v Fielden* [2006] Ch. 361, CA, at [30]–[35], [38]–[39] per Wall LJ and [108]–[110], where Mummery LJ observed that the shortness of the marriage limited the opportunities of Mrs Cunliffe to make a significant contribution to the welfare of the deceased.
[141] *Adams v Lewis* [2001] W.T.L.R. 493.

received on divorce was a most important factor and that if one concentrated too much on her "needs and resources" there was a danger of
blurring the distinction between ss.1(2)(a) and 1(2)(b) of the Act. He identified the following observations of Lord Nicholls and considered that they
applied equally to 1975 Act cases, viz.:

> (i)   if in their different ways the parties each contributed equally to the
> family then in principle it matters not which of them earned the
> money and built up the assets;
> (ii)   a judge should check any tentative view he forms against the
> yardstick of equal division. As a general guide, equality should
> only be departed if and to the extent that there was a good reason
> for doing so;
> (iii)   the test of "reasonable requirements" was inappropriate;
> (iv)   in principle a wife's wish to have money so that she can pass some
> on to her children is every bit as weighty as a similar wish by the
> husband.

In relation to the last of those points it does not appear that attention was
drawn to the cases of *Whytte v Ticehurst*[142] and *Re Bramwell*.[143] Those cases,
which were followed in *Roberts v Fresco*[144] are authority for the proposition
that the right to make an application under the 1975 Act does not continue
in effect for the benefit of the applicant's estate. Even though reasonable
provision for a surviving spouse is not limited to what is required for their
maintenance, it is not easy to envisage circumstances in which reasonable
provision would include a component for the applicant to pass on to their
children.

(d) Involvement in the Family Business

6–048   Although this is not a matter specified by s.3(2), it is worth separate consideration, because the claimant's contribution to the family business in
addition to her contribution towards the welfare of the family has been
recognised in a number of cases. In *Re Bunning*,[145] the applicant wife, as well
as making a substantial contribution to the welfare of the family, had given
up her employment shortly after marriage and helped her husband in his
fruit and vegetable business both by accompanying him on visits to growers
and markets, as well as doing much of the office work. Vinelott J described
her as "a loyal, dutiful and hard-working wife". In *McNulty v McNulty*[146]

---

[142] *Whytte v Ticehurst* [1985] Fam. 64.
[143] *Re Bramwell* [1988] 2 F.L.R. 263.
[144] *Roberts v Fresco* [2017] EWHC 283 (Ch).
[145] *Re Bunning, Bunning v Salmon* [1984] Ch. 480. Her role is described at 489–90.
[146] *McNulty v McNulty* [2002] W.T.L.R. 737.

the claimant had assisted in the business for the first seven years of the marriage as well as playing a full part in bringing up the family. The *White v White* cross-check[147] was carried out and the award to her exceeded half the value of the estate. Among the Northern Ireland cases in which the widow made a substantial contribution to the family business in the course of a long marriage is *Re Moorhead*[148] in which *Adams v Lewis* was referred to but, as with the other such cases, *White v White* was not applied. In *Re Moorhead*, where the 79-year-old claimant, who had been married to the deceased for 37 years, had given up her own employment to work on the family farm and had cared for the deceased's mother as well as the deceased himself, was awarded a life interest in the farm (worth £400,000) which was the major asset of an estate worth roughly £1 million, an absolute interest in another farm together with livestock and farm equipment (£68,000), and £40,000 out of residue. This case was referred to in *O'Neill v McPhillimy*,[149] where the claimant widow was 66 at the date of the hearing and the marriage had lasted for 36 years. Substantial provision was made for her but neither the equivalent provision to s.3(2) of the 1975 Act[150] nor *White v White* was considered.

A third Northern Ireland case, in which age and contribution to the welfare of the family business was considered in some detail, is *McGuigan v McGuigan*.[151] In that case, the applicant widow and the deceased had been married for 64 years. The principal beneficiary under his will was his grandson, but his wife was given a life interest in part of the estate. There were three children of the marriage and she was 81 at the date of the hearing. Kerr J first compared the obligations and responsibilities of the testator towards his grandson and his wife, of whom he said: **6–049**

> "She had been his faithful spouse for more than 64 years; she had borne his three children and she had, on her own unchallenged account, supported him in his farming activities throughout his life. The obligations and responsibility owed by the testator to the applicant were unquestionable."

In considering art.5(2) he said:

> "On one view, the age of the applicant may be regarded as a factor weighing against making substantial capital provision for her. As

---

[147] This phrase has found its way into the judicial vocabulary as a shorthand for the "application of the statutory provisions to the facts of the individual case with the objective of achieving a result which is fair and non-discriminatory" per Wall LJ in *Cunliffe v Fielden* [2006] Ch. 361, at [19], though at [22] he advised caution when using it in the context of a 1975 Act case.

[148] *Re Moorhead* [2002] N.I.J.B. 83.

[149] *O'Neill v McPhillimy* [2004] N.I. Ch. 4. The family business was a licensed victualing business in which the widow had worked and into which she had put resources of her own.

[150] Inheritance (Provision for Family and Dependants) Order 1979 art.5(2). The provision setting the higher standard for provision for the spouse is art.2(2).

[151] *McGuigan v McGuigan* [1996] N.I.J.B. 47 at 51.

against this, however, the view may be taken that throughout her long marriage she contributed significantly to the success of the farming enterprise and made it possible for the deceased to preserve his ownership of the lands which now form the bulk of the estate. I do not believe that these competing factors can be set against each other in any qualitative[152] way. They are factors to be taken into account for whatever intrinsic influence they may have on the court's overall judgment, rather than as offsetting each other."

He went on to ascribe a limited value to the "notional divorce" provision in the case of such a long marriage as that of the McGuigans, but held that the length of the marriage and her contribution must not be discounted because of her modest capital needs.

(e) The "Notional Divorce"

(i) Its importance relative to other matters

6–050   In the case of a claim by a surviving spouse,[153] s.3(2) directs the court to have regard to:

> "...the provision which the applicant might reasonably expect to have received if on the day on which the deceased died the marriage, instead of being terminated by death, had been terminated by a decree of divorce."

Before the decision in *White v White*,[154] the effects of which are discussed below,[155] there was a spectrum of judicial views, at one end of which was that of Oliver LJ in *Re Besterman*.[156] He drew attention to the two different exercises which the court has to carry out under the matrimonial and the family provision legislation and stated that, in an application under the 1975 Act, the figure resulting from the "notional divorce" exercise was merely one of the factors to which the court must have regard, the overriding consideration was what is reasonable in all the circumstances.

6–051   At the other end was *Moody v Stevenson*,[157] in which *Re Besterman* was not cited. Waite J said that, although that requirement had been criticised because of the mental gymnastics which it is liable to impose on the court, the underlying purpose of Parliament seemed plain enough. The objective was that the acceptable minimum posthumous provision for the surviving spouse should correspond as closely as possible to the inchoate rights enjoyed by that spouse in the deceased's lifetime by virtue of their pro-

---

[152] The author would tentatively suggest that "quantitative" may have been the more appropriate adjective, but that does not detract from the value of the judgment.

[153] Extended to claims by surviving civil partners by the Civil Partnership Act 2004 s.71 and Sch.4 paras 17(4) and (5).

[154] *White v White* [2001] 1 A.C. 596.

[155] See s.5(e)(iii), "*White v White* and equality", paras 6–065 to 6–076.

[156] *Re Besterman* [1984] Ch. 458 at 469F.

[157] *Moody v Stevenson* [1992] Ch. 486, CA, at 498F.

spective entitlement under the matrimonial law. Consequently, the court's logical starting point would be an appraisal of the claimant's notional entitlement under the relevant matrimonial legislation.

In *Re Jessop*,[158] Nourse LJ felt it unnecessary to enter upon any conflict 6–052 between those two decisions, but in *Re Krubert*,[159] he did consider that there was a conflict between them, even if it was only one of emphasis, and preferred the approach of Oliver LJ, which he felt to be more in accordance with the Act when read as a whole. Cazalet J agreed, observing that, particularly in small asset cases, the result of placing too much emphasis on the award which would have been made on the hypothetical divorce was that, where the spouses are living together at the date of death, such an approach might produce financial provision below reasonable financial provision within the meaning of the Act.[160] That would happen because the funds available could not provide satisfactorily for two homes, as opposed to one, and support the couple living apart; but in claims under the 1975 Act the entitlement which the deceased would have obtained or received on divorce could be brought into consideration as potentially available to ensure that reasonable financial provision could be made for applicants under the Act. Despite the problems which had been encountered in various cases, it had become tolerably clear after *Krubert* that Oliver J's view had prevailed. In *Bheekhun v Williams*,[161] the one reported surviving spouse claim between *Krubert* and *White v White*, the application of the "notional divorce" provision was not in issue and the quantum of the award[162] was not challenged. An important case has since made it clear beyond doubt that the view expressed in *Besterman* on this point is to be adopted. In *P v G, P and P (Family Provision: Relevance of Divorce Provision)*,[163] Black J held that in presenting 1975 Act claims to the court, it was inappropriate to replicate the entire fictional ancillary relief process; the court's task was simply to reach a sufficient conclusion as to the outcome of the "notional divorce" and to give due weight to that conclusion, along with the other relevant factors; the "notional divorce" exercise required by subs.3(2) was simply one of the matters to which the court must have regard; see the sections of the judgment headed "Provision on divorce—s.3(2)" and "The Inheritance Act exercise".[164]

---

[158] *Re Jessop* [1992] 1 F.L.R. 591, CA.
[159] *Re Krubert* [1997] Ch. 97, CA, at 104C.
[160] *Re Krubert* [1997] Ch.97, CA, at 106C.
[161] *Bheekhun v Williams* [1999] 2 F.L.R. 229, CA. The issue in the Court of Appeal was whether immovable property situated in Mauritius, which was the deceased's domicile of origin, should be treated as part of the net estate. The decision at first instance, in which it was held that he had by the time of his death acquired an English domicile of choice and that the property should be so treated, was affirmed.
[162] Which represented 44 per cent of what the judge at first instance had held to be the net estate.
[163] *P v G, P v P (Family Provision: Relevance of Divorce Provision)* [2006] 1 F.L.R. 431, at [223]–[236] and [237]–[247], respectively.
[164] *Bheekhun v Williams* [1999] 2 F.L.R. 229, CA.

(ii) Difficulties of the section 3(2) exercise

6–053   Quite apart from any debate as to the weight to be accorded to it, the
"notional divorce" provision has, in a number of cases,[165] attracted comment about the undesirability or difficulty of applying it; a problem also
noted by commentators.[166] Waite J rejected these criticisms, observing, in
Moody v Stevenson,[167] that:

> "Although this requirement has been criticised because of the mental
> gymnastics which it is liable to impose on the court, the underlying
> purpose of Parliament seems to us[168] to be plain enough."

In this context it may be noted that the Working Party[169] had not recommended the inclusion of any such provision, and it is by no means clear why
it was adopted in the Law Commission's report.

6–054   In *Re Bunning*,[170] Vinelott J dealt with the s.3(2) exercise in considerable
detail. Having rejected the submission of counsel for the applicant[171] as to
what Mrs Bunning could have expected to receive on the "notional
divorce", he concluded that she would have received a much lower sum[172]
but did not regard that as limiting the provision which it was reasonable for
her to have. He assessed that provision at £60,000 and, although unable to
demonstrate by any process of deductive reasoning that £60,000 was the
right figure, he felt it to be confirmed in three ways, one of which was that it
would produce a roughly equal division of their combined resources, as
follows.

---

[165] *Re Rowlands* [1984] F.L.R. 813 at 819F ("a curious exercise in the circumstances for the
court to engage in"); *Dawkins v Judd* [1986] 2 F.L.R. 360 ("it is a difficult exercise, with so
little capital involved, to know precisely what a court would have done on any divorce
which provided both a home for the widow and a home for the husband in the event of
divorce"); *Eeles v Evans* unreported 6 July 1989, CA ("highly artificial in the circumstances
of the case and unhelpful in providing the answer to the question of what constituted
reasonable financial provision"). However, in *Stephens v Stephens* unreported 1 July 1985,
CA where the effect of a will was to leave the widow with the right to live in the matrimonial
home but no (or insufficient) income with which to keep it up, the Court of Appeal held that
the trial judge had erred not only in disregarding the testator's wishes, but had also failed to
have proper regard to what the applicant would have received on divorce. It was ordered
that the house be sold and the estate divided as to 60 per cent to the applicant and 40 per
cent to the residuary beneficiary, who was the testator's son by his first marriage.
[166] See *Tyler's Family Provision*, 3rd edn (London: LexisNexis Butterworths, 1997) at p.179
("the mental gymnastics which this requirement dictates have caused judges considerable
problems"). This comment also appeared in the second edition (1984) at p.158, which was
current at the time of Waite J's rejoinder.
[167] *Moody v Stevenson* [1992] Ch. 486 at 498F.
[168] He was sitting with Mustill LJ in a two-judge court.
[169] Law Commission Working Paper No.42 (1971), *Family Property Law*, Pt 3 of which
reviewed the law and practice under the Inheritance (Family Provision) Act 1938 and the
Matrimonial Causes Act 1965. A particular concern was whether the court should be given
a wide discretionary power to rewrite the will by giving the spouse "a fair share of the family
assets, over and above her strict maintenance needs" but this solution was not thought to be
attractive.
[170] *Re Bunning* [1984] Ch. 480.
[171] £90,000.
[172] £36,000.

The "equality" calculation in *Bunning*

Net estate	226,000	
Accrued interest and dividends	11,000	
Costs of litigation		26,000
Available for distribution	211,000	
W's assets (substantially given to her by H)	95,000	
Total	**306,000**	
Half of which is	153,000	
Less W's assets		95,000
Amount required to bring W's assets up to half the total	58,000	
Amount awarded	60,000	

Thus, in doing so, he performed an exercise, not attempted in any other case before *White v White*, which turned out to be very similar to the "*White v White* cross-check" that has now become a feature of the 1975 Act case-law, though its application has been far from straightforward in practice.[173]

(iii) White v White and equality

At the time when their marriage broke down, Mr and Mrs White had been   **6–055** married for 33 years and had raised three children, all of whom were independent by 1996 when Mrs White's application for ancillary relief came before the court. The parties' combined assets were over £4.6 million, a sum considerably in excess of what was needed to provide a home and an income for each of them; a situation which very rarely occurs in 1975 Act claims by surviving spouses. At first instance Mrs White's reasonable requirements, on a clean break basis, were assessed at £980,000. This was to be achieved by a payment to her of £800,000, and her keeping her solely owned assets, but transferring her share of the jointly owned assets to Mr White. The Court of Appeal[174] held that, having regard to the goal of overall fairness, and to the contribution made by Mrs White as wife and mother in addition to her role as partner in the farming business, the provision for her should be increased by £700,000. The result of this was that Mrs White's share of the assets was increased from about 20 per cent to about 40 per cent after allowing for the parties' costs in both courts, which by that stage had reached £310,000.[175]

---

[173] See, e.g., the comment of Professor Rebecca Bailey-Harris in [2006] Fam. Law 178 at 180 on the judgment in *P v G, P and P (Family Provision: Relevance of Divorce Provision)*. She remarks, with masterly understatement, that "it must be accepted that the issues of principle involved in the 'divorce comparison' are not wholly free from difficulty".

[174] *White v White* [1999] Fam. 304, CA.

[175] The parties' untaxed costs of their appeals to the House of Lords were estimated at "the appalling sum of £530,000" per Lord Nicholls *White v White* [2001] A.C. 596 at 612E.

Mrs White appealed, claiming an equal division of the assets, and Mr White cross-appealed, seeking that the original order be restored.

6–056   In the leading speech dismissing both the appeal and the cross-appeal, Lord Nicholls laid down a number of principles relating to the exercise of the court's powers in ancillary relief proceedings, and those which are most frequently invoked in 1975 Act cases are now summarised.[176] First, in seeking to attain a fair outcome, there was no room for discrimination between the parties; if in their different spheres, each contributed equally to the family, then in principle it did not matter who earned the money and built up the assets. It followed that, before making an order providing for an unequal division of the assets, a judge would be well advised to check their tentative views against the yardstick of equality of division and, as a general guide, equality should not be departed from without good reason. However, that did not involve a presumption of equality (for which the statutory language provided no warrant), nor was there a principle that in every case equality would be the starting point in relation to a division of assets.

6–057   In departing from a needs-based approach to the exercise of the court's powers, he stated that a claimant's financial needs, even when interpreted generously and called "reasonable requirements", were not to be treated as determinative, and there was nothing which led to the supposition that the available assets of the respondent husband became irrelevant once the claimant wife's needs were satisfied. While in any given case there might be good reason for limiting the wife to her needs leaving the husband with the much larger balance, mere absence of financial need could not, in itself, be a sufficient reason. If it were, discrimination would be creeping in by the back door; hence the importance of the check against the yardstick of equal division.

6–058   In a valuable survey of the development of that area of the law in Australia,[177] Lord Cooke of Thorndon observed that there might be in the English Act[178] no statutory presumption or prima facie rule, but there was no reason to suppose that in prescribing relevant considerations the legislature had any intention of excluding the development of general judicial practice. While doubting whether the labels "yardstick" or "check" would produce any result different from "guidelines" or starting point", he adopted and underlined what he saw as Lord Nicholls' most important proposition, namely that equality should be departed from only if, and to the extent that, there was good reason for doing so. However, as the following survey of the cases on claims by surviving spouses since *White v White* shows, departures from equality are at least as frequent as adherence to it, and the reasons for those departures are not always articulated.

6–059   Including the cases under the Northern Ireland legislation,[179] which in all material respects is identical with the 1975 Act, there are 22 reported cases

---

[176] *White v White* [2001] 1 A.C. 596 at 605E–608G.
[177] *White v White* [2001] 1 A.C. 596 at 613C–615C.
[178] Matrimonial Causes Act 1973.
[179] Inheritance (Provision for Family and Dependants) (Northern Ireland) Order 1979 (SI 1979/924).

on claims by surviving spouses since *White v White*. Six of these claims were dismissed. In *Gandhi v Patel*[180] it was held that the parties had never undergone a ceremony which would be recognised in English law as a ceremony of marriage. In three cases,[181] the long separation between the parties, without any claim being made by the wife for maintenance during the period of the separation was fatal to the claim. In *Palmer v Lawrence*,[182] it was found that the will did not fail to make reasonable provision for the claimant. The *White v White* cross-check was not seen as being particularly helpful in the circumstances of the case, and the court was not persuaded that the claimant would have done substantially better, on a divorce, than she had done under the will. In *Wooldridge v Wooldridge*[183] the principles of the "deemed divorce check" as explained in *Lilleyman v Lilleyman*[184] were considered, it being noted that, following the amendment to s.3(2) effected by the Inheritance and Trustees' Powers Act 2014,[185] nothing required the court to treat the provision referred to in that section as setting an upper or lower limit on the provision which may be made by an order under s.2 of the 1975 Act. However, the divorce cross-check was not carried out; it was found that the claimant had grossly exaggerated her expenditure and that her own assets were ample to support the luxurious lifestyle that she was enjoying.

In two cases,[186] *Dingmar v Dingmar* and *Iqbal v Ahmed*, the divorce comparison did not arise, the major issue being the interest of the widow in the matrimonial home, and in *Moore v Holdsworth*[187] the determining factor was the need to make provision for the care and medical treatment of the 55-year-old widow, who suffered from multiple sclerosis and had a life expectancy of ten years. In *Singer v Isaac*,[188] it was not applied because, although *White v White* had been decided in the House of Lords by the date of the hearing, the deceased had died 14 months earlier, so the claimant could not reasonably have expected equal division on a divorce at that time, but only a determination based on the then subsisting conventional approach to such cases. In *Barron v Woodhead*[189] it was found that in all the circumstances,

6–060

---

[180] *Gandhi v Patel* [2002] 1 F.L.R. 603.
[181] *Aston v Aston* [2007] W.T.L.R. 1349, where it was found that where it was found that the marriage, although not formally dissolved, was beyond revival at the date of the deceased's death; *Parish v Sharman* [2001] W.T.L.R. 593, CA, where the parties had been separated for 11 years and the wife, on legal advice, had not made any claim for maintenance during that period; *Hope v Knight* [2011] W.T.L.R. 583, 19-year separation without any application for maintenance, *Rossi v Rossi* [2007] 1 F.L.R. 790 applied.
[182] *Palmer v Lawrence* [2011] EWHC 3961 (Ch).
[183] *Wooldridge v Wooldridge* unreported 12 February 2016 (HH Judge Walden-Smith, County Court at Central London). The subsequent costs judgment is reported at [2016] 3 Costs L.O. 531.
[184] *Lilleyman v Lilleyman* [2013] Ch. 225; [2013] 1 F.L.R. 47, at [47], cited in *Wooldridge*, at [54]–[55].
[185] Inheritance and Trustees' Powers Act 2014 s.6 and Sch.2 para.5(2).
[186] *Dingmar v Dingmar* [2007] Ch. 109, CA (value to be attributed to the deceased's severable share of the matrimonial home); *Iqbal v Ahmed*, [2012] 1 F.L.R. 31, CA (nature of the interest in the matrimonial home to be awarded to the widow).
[187] *Moore v Holdsworth* [2010] 2 F.L.R. 1501.
[188] *Singer v Isaac* [2001] W.T.L.R. 1045.
[189] *Barron v Woodhead* [2009] 1 F.L.R. 747.

including the history of the claimant widower's dealings with the matrimonial home, a court would, on divorce, have been concerned to ensure that he had a roof over his head but would have made little, if any more provision for him. The divorce comparison was discussed at some length in *Goenka v Goenka*.[190] In that case, the major issue was whether the death in service benefit payable under the NHS pension scheme of which the deceased was a member was to be treated as part of the net estate in accordance with s.8(1) of the 1975 Act. It was held that they were to be so treated and also that they fell to be taken into account for the purpose of the s.3(2) exercise. However, in the circumstances of the case, the divorce comparison carried little weight. It was considered likely that on divorce there would have been a clean break order, but the award would not have given the claimant as much as she was presently enjoying. The award to the claimant was limited to a sum representing the value of the deceased's savings, which she was to have absolutely rather than at the discretion of the trustees of the will trust.

6–061   In the two cases discussed in this paragraph, *White v White* was not applied but the outcome was one of near equality. In *Stephanides v Cohen*[191] the district judge considered that the circumstances which would have pertained on divorce were so different from those in the case that he could attach very little weight to them. The bulk of the estate[192] was left to the testator's son by his first marriage. The claim was dealt with on the basis that the deceased had a legal obligation to make reasonable provision for his wife, but no legal obligation towards his adult child. The wife's needs were to accommodate herself and to support herself, and the deceased's obligation was, so far as the resources of the estate permitted and so far as was compatible with his son's claims on his bounty, to make such provision as would satisfy those needs. The implementation of that view resulted in the spouse receiving 55 per cent of the estate and the son, 45 per cent. In *Grattan v McNaughton*[193] the judge accepted the submission that the spouse's entitlement on the "notional divorce" was unlikely to be decisive, because of the limited resources available;[194] consequently, there was no scope for the application of *White v White*. The award represented less than 20 per cent of the net estate, but if the benefits to the wife (including the capitalised value of the monthly pension payments) arising by reason of the husband's death were taken into account, she received something over 40 per cent of the assets unlocked by his death.

6–062   In the Northern Ireland case of *Moorhead*,[195] Weatherup J quoted the judgment of Thorpe LJ in the "big money" matrimonial case of *Cowan v*

---

[190] *Goenka v Goenka* [2016] Ch. 267.
[191] *Stephanides v Cohen* [2002] W.T.L.R. 1373.
[192] Net estate £643,500.
[193] *Grattan v McNaughton* [2001] W.T.L.R. 1305.
[194] The net estate was approximately £80,000.
[195] *Moorhead, Deceased* [2002] N.I.J.B. 83.

Cowan and considered the following passage to be applicable to surviving spouse claims[196]:

> "The decision in *White v White* clearly does not introduce a rule of equality. The yardstick of equality is a cross-check against discrimination. Fairness is the rule and in its pursuit the reasons for departure from equality would inevitably prove to be too legion and too varied to permit of classification. They will vary from the substantial to the faint but that range can be reflected in the degree of departure."

Such reasons may derive from the size or the nature of the estate, or both. In *Moorhead*, it was held that, in the circumstances of the case, fairness did not require equal division of the property; such a division would have involved the breaking up of the home farm, a business asset which had been brought into the marriage by the husband. Similar considerations arose in the other Northern Ireland case, that of *O'Neill v McPhillimy*.[197] There, the judge accepted the general proposition enunciated in *Lambert v Lambert*[198] that homemakers were not to be discriminated against in favour of breadwinners, but concentrated his attention on specific adjustments to the distribution of the assets, which consisted mainly of three heavily mortgaged public houses, without reference to the share of the estate that would accrue to the widow as a result.

This leaves only six cases[199] in which the "notional divorce" exercise has been carried out in some depth and has significantly influenced the outcome. Two of these, *P v G, P and P (Family Provision: Relevance of Divorce Provision)* and *Lilleyman v Lilleyman* are, by 1975 Act standards, high-value claims, and are discussed in the following subsection. In *P v G, P and P* the net estate was approximately £5 million on the claimants' case, and just under £4.48 million on the defendants' case. In *Lilleyman*, it was approximately £6 million.

6–063

In *Adams v Lewis*[200] and *McNulty v McNulty*[201] the submission that the court would have awarded the applicant half of the assets on the "notional divorce" was accepted. The table shows the *White v White* cross-check as carried out in *McNulty*. One of the three reasons stated in the judgment as justifying the judge's belief that the award was pitched at about the right level was that, although the cross-check gave an amount significantly lower than the award actually made, the discrepancy was justified because, on death, when there was only one party to provide for, it would often be

6–064

---

[196] *Cowan v Cowan* [2002] 1 F.L.R. 192, CA, at 212.
[197] *O'Neill v McPhillimy* [2004] N.I. Ch. 4.
[198] *Lambert v Lambert* [2003] 4 All E.R. 342.
[199] *Adams v Lewis* [2001] W.T.L.R. 493; *McNulty v McNulty* [2002] W.T.L.R. 357; *P v G, P and P (Family Provision: Relevance of Divorce Provision)* also reported as *P v E* [2006] 1 F.L.R. 431; [2007] W.T.L.R. 691; *Cunliffe v Fielden* [2006] Ch. 361, CA; *Baker v Baker* [2008] 2 F.L.R. 1956 and *Lilleyman v Lilleyman* [2013] Ch. 225; [2013] 1 F.L.R. 47.
[200] *Adams v Lewis* [2001] W.T.L.R. 493.
[201] *McNulty v McNulty* [2002] W.T.L.R. 357.

appropriate under the 1975 Act to make an award greater than would have been made on the "notional divorce".[202]

The *White v White* cross-check in *McNulty*

Net estate	590,000	
Consisting of		
Cash (estimated)	400,000	
Matrimonial home	120,000	
Other jointly owned assets	5,000	
Land comprised in residuary estate	65,000	
Total	590,000	
Half of which is	295,000	
Less wife's assets		190,000
Total required to bring wife's assets up to half the net estate	105,000	
Amount awarded	170,000	

6–065   In *Cunliffe v Fielden*,[203] where *White v White* was applied, and the provision made was for the claimant's housing and income needs, she was awarded £600,000 (42 per cent) out of an estate of approximately £1.4 million, the brevity of the marriage being held to justify the departure from equality. Wall LJ observed, in relation to departure from equality and on the *White v White* cross-check, that:

> "Caution, however, seems to me necessary when considering the *White v White* cross-check in the context of a case under the 1975 Act ... In cases under the 1975 Act a deceased spouse who leaves a widow is entitled to bequeath his estate to whomsoever he pleases; his only statutory obligation is to make reasonable financial provision for his widow. In such a case, depending on the value of the estate, the concept of equality may bear little relation to that provision."

This passage was quoted in *Baker v Baker*,[204] in which the deputy judge checked his award against the yardstick of equality, having taken into account, inter alia, the length of the marriage, Mrs Baker's role as wife and mother and the financial circumstances of all the parties. He acknowledged

---

[202] See also the similar view expressed by Cazalet J in *Re Krubert* [1997] Ch. 97 at 106C–E.
[203] *Cunliffe v Fielden* [2006] Ch. 361, at [19]–[21].
[204] *Baker v Baker* [2008] 2 F.L.R. 1956, at [35].

the deceased's concern to ensure that the business which his sons had devoted time and effort towards building up should continue in operation. The value of the estate was not precisely ascertained but the award of the matrimonial home and a lump sum of £410,000, making a total of £750,000 was, on any footing, over 55 per cent of the net estate.

The author would respectfully agree with Wall LJ's call for caution in the application of the principles laid down in *White v White* to 1975 Act claims. One reason for caution is that the analogy with financial remedy proceedings is imperfect. Despite the common origin of the legislation governing them[205] 1975 Act claims by surviving spouses and financial remedy claims originate in different circumstances, the events which trigger them have different outcomes, and the persons or classes of persons who stand to be affected by those outcomes are not very likely to be identical. The financial needs and resources of the beneficiaries or classes of beneficiary who take on the death of the deceased spouse, to which s.3(1)(c) directs the court to have regard, are not readily to be equated with the needs and resources of the notionally divorced respondent spouse during his (or, occasionally, her) lifetime. The question also arises whether, when checking so as to ensure that provision for the claimant has been assessed in a fair and non-discriminatory manner, the yardstick must necessarily be the yardstick of equality.[206]

6–066

(iv) Departure from equality—a summary

Although it has been said that "the reasons for departure from equality would inevitably prove to be too legion and too varied to permit of classification"[207] and, as with other areas in which the law has developed incrementally, there is no closed list of reasons, it is possible to identify those which occur relatively frequently. First, it may well be the case, and probably is the case in the vast majority of cases which never go to trial, much less get reported, that the resources of the estate are simply insufficient for the "notional divorce" exercise to be sensibly carried out, so the question never arises. Second, as recognised in *Cunliffe v Fielden*, the irreducible minimum provision for a surviving spouse of accommodation of a reasonable standard and an income to discharge the expenses of daily living at whatever rate the court considers appropriate,[208] may absorb the resources of the estate to an extent which renders the question of equal division academic. Third, it is now well settled that a short marriage (including, where relevant, any prior period of cohabitation) justifies a departure from

6–067

---

[205] That is, in Law Com. WP 42 and the subsequent Law Commission Report No.61, *Second Report on Family Property: Family Provision on Death* (1974).

[206] See subs.(v), "High value cases", paras 6–069 to 6–075, the case of *Jones v Jones* [2011] 3 W.L.R. 582 and the article by K. Landells, "*Jones v Jones*, Springboards, Non-Matrimonial Property, Castles and Companies" [2011] Fam. Law 382.

[207] *Cowan v Cowan* [2002] 1 F.L.R. 192, CA, at 212, cited in *Moorhead, Deceased* [2002] N.I.J.B. 83.

[208] Particularly, if regard is had to the higher standard of provision defined by s.1(2)(a) of the 1975 Act.

equality. In addition, it was recognised long before *White v White* that there are cases in which it would be undesirable to break up a going concern in order to make provision for the claimant; the consequence of preserving it is inevitably a departure from equality.

6–068   In *Re Rowlands*[209] the judge at first instance had decided that the estate should not be realised in order to provide the lump sum which he awarded to the applicant, because a sale would have put an end to the farming activities of the family which had been carried on by the testator and his sons for many years. The Court of Appeal considered it to be of major relevance and importance that the estate represented farming assets and that the intention of the testator was to try and keep the farming assets together to inure[210] for the benefit of his family, sons, daughters and the succeeding generation.[211] It has been recognised in the matrimonial jurisdiction[212] that a departure from equality may be justified where the family's wealth consists largely of a family business, such as a farm, though, as envisaged in *N v N (Financial Provision: Sale of Company)*[213] fairness may require that a going concern be realised, albeit due care should be taken not to depreciate its value unduly in the process.

(v) High value cases

6–069   Excluding *Dellal v Dellal*,[214] there are at the time of writing only three reported cases of claims by surviving spouses in which the estate was over £4 million. In the two cases now discussed in detail, the claim succeeded; the third is *Wooldridge v Wooldridge*,[215] where the claim was dismissed. There, the net estate was £6.8 million excluding the value of the matrimonial home, in which the claimant and one of the deceased's sons was living. The claimed annual income need of £372,000 would have required approximately £5.8 million to fund it, thus virtually exhausting the remainder of the estate and necessitating the sale of business assets. That was found to be plainly contrary to the best interests of one of the deceased's two sons and more likely than not to be detrimental to the best interests of the other.

---

[209] *Re Rowlands* [1984] F.L.R. 813, CA.

[210] Per Cumming-Bruce LJ at 824. The *Shorter Oxford Dictionary* states that the spelling "enure" has been replaced by "inure" except in its legal usages which include "to be available; to be applied (to the use of)"; the citation date is 1607.

[211] See also *Baker v Baker* [2008] 2 F.L.R. 1956 (family motor trading and garage business operated by deceased's sons).

[212] *P v P (Inherited Property)* [2005] 1 F.L.R. 576, particularly the analysis at [37]–[48] of what would be fair in the circumstances of that particular case.

[213] *N v N (Financial Provision: Sale of Company)* [2001] 2 F.L.R. 69 at 80.

[214] *Dellal v Dellal* [2015] EWHC 907 (Fam); [2015] W.T.L.R. 1037. The report concerns interlocutory proceedings largely relating to the claimant's application for an order under s.10 of the Act. Her case was that the declared value of £15.4 million for the deceased's estate was far too low and that it had been substantially diminished by lifetime gifts to family trusts and individual family members. At the time of writing there is no report of any proceedings relating to the substantive issues of whether the will had failed to make reasonable provision for her or whether dispositions had been made with the intention to defeat a 1975 Act claim.

[215] *Wooldridge v Wooldridge* unreported 12 February 2016 (HH Judge Walden-Smith, County Court at Central London).

In *P v G, P and P*[216] the claimant (P) and the deceased first met in 1973, at **6–070** which time he had two infant children by his earlier marriage. At that time he was in employment and owned a substantial property (Blackacre) in which there was little equity, as he was heavily in debt. She had no assets. They fairly soon commenced living together, but did not marry until shortly before the birth of their daughter in 1985. By then, he had established two successful businesses which were incorporated, and in which P worked and had a small shareholding. In 1998, divorce was contemplated but the parties continued to live at Blackacre. In July 2000, he retired and began drawing his pension from the company pension fund. In October 2001, P left Blackacre, but they were both unhappy and she moved back in May of the following year. He died on 14 August 2002 having made a Spanish will in favour of his three children and an English will in which he left his residuary estate on discretionary trusts of which P and the three children were the beneficiaries, and Blackacre was left on trust for P during her life or until remarriage, and thereafter on the trusts of the residue. The trustees were requested to have regard to any memorandum of wishes, and such a memorandum was signed on 24 June 1999. On 7 July 2003, the trustees of the company pension fund resolved to pay pensions of £143,057 per year, backdated to 7 October 2002, to each of P and her daughter and to divide the lump sum benefit of £710,220 equally between the three children in accordance with the deceased's nomination. By her claim, P sought to retain her pension entitlement (capitalised at £3,825,000) and to have transferred to her further property worth £3.25 million consisting partly of a cash lump sum and partly of non-pension assets. The defendants offered Blackacre (£900,000) and a lump sum of £100,000. At trial it was found that the "notional divorce" exercise would, on the facts, have resulted in an equal division of assets. In the result, P was awarded £2 million, to include Blackacre.

The following points of general importance appear from the judgment of **6–071** Black J under the headings "Provision on divorce—section 3(2)" and "The Inheritance Act exercise"[217]:

(1) in presenting 1975 Act claims to the court, it was inappropriate to replicate the entire fictional ancillary relief process; the court's task was simply to reach a sufficient conclusion as to the outcome of the "notional divorce" and to give due weight to that conclusion, along with the other relevant factors;

(2) the "notional divorce" exercise required by subs.3(2) was simply one of the matters to which the court must have regard (*Re Besterman* followed)—there is no presumption of equality nor of equal division being a starting point;

---

[216] *P v G, P and P (Family Provision: Relevance of Divorce Provision)* [2006] 1 F.L.R. 431.
[217] *P v G, P and P (Family Provision: Relevance of Divorce Provision)* [2006] 1 F.L.R. 431 at [223]–[236] and [237]–[247], respectively.

(3) it was probable that the difference between the termination of the marriage by death and its dissolution by divorce might often result in greater provision being ordered under the 1975 Act than would have been the case on the "notional divorce" (*Re Krubert* followed).

6–072   In *Lilleyman v Lilleyman*[218] the parties, both of whom had adult children from their first marriages, met in 2004. After becoming engaged, they decided to find a new home rather than to live in either of their own properties and a house (Water Meadows) was purchased originally in Mr Lilleyman's sole name and later transferred into joint names. He later purchased an apartment (Dunhome) in his sole name and it was found that this was purchased as a second home. Including the period of cohabitation before they married in the autumn of 2007, the relationship had lasted approximately four years when Mr Lilleyman died in January 2010. By his will, made in May 2008, Mrs Lilleyman was given his personal chattels not otherwise disposed of,[219] and limited rights of occupation in both properties. In the case of Water Meadows her right of occupation was subject to paying all outgoings and keeping it repaired and insured, and was terminable or remarriage, cohabitation, her ceasing to reside there, or ceasing (in the trustees' view) to perform the repair and insurance obligations. He had also set up a fund under which she received a fixed annuity of £378.72 per month. Subject to her rights of occupation, he gave those two properties, and the remainder of the residuary estate, to his two sons. The major asset of the estate was his 100 per cent shareholding in three steel stockholding companies, its agreed value being £5.085 million. One of the companies had been formed by him in 1982, the second acquired in 1990, and the third formed as a joint venture company with his two sons in 2004. One of his sons had worked full time in the business since 1990 and the other had begun to work part time in 2004 and increased his involvement as his father's health deteriorated. The business also provided employment for other members of the family.

6–073   For the claimants it was submitted that reasonable provision for Mrs Lilleyman should include a substantial share of the matrimonial property in excess of her reasonable needs, in accordance with *Miller v Miller, McFarlane v McFarlane*[220]; for the defendants it was submitted that reasonable provision was to be identified by reference to her housing and income needs, as in *Cunliffe v Fielden*.[221] The main debate centred on the consequences of the requirements to have regard to the divorce cross-check and the short duration of the marriage. In relation to those matters the

---

[218] *Lilleyman v Lilleyman* [2013] Ch. 225.
[219] These included a collection of Dinky toys worth £17,000.
[220] *Miller v Miller, McFarlane v McFarlane* [2006] 2 A.C. 618, HL.
[221] *Cunliffe v Fielden* [2006] Ch. 361 (the case is cited in *Lilleyman* as *Fielden v Cunliffe*). Although that case was referred to in *Lilleyman* (e.g. at [3] and [54]) as a "big money/short marriage case" the net estate was only £1.4 million, and it has not been treated as a high-value case in the present work.

principles relevant to the instant case, as derived from *Miller v Miller, McFarlane v McFarlane* and *Charman v Charman (No.4)*[222] were tentatively summarised as follows:

(1) the fundamental principle is that a marriage is now recognised to be an essentially equal partnership and the division of available property upon breakdown is to be conducted on the basis of fairness and non-discrimination; however, equality of treatment does not necessarily lead to equality of outcome;

(2) the basic concept of equality gives rise to three requirements, financial needs, compensation and sharing. Meeting the divorcing parties' financial needs is the first call on the available property and frequently exhausts it;

(3) compensation addresses prospective economic disparity between the parties arising from the way in which they conducted the marriage;

(4) sharing is applied when those requirements have been satisfied and property remains available and extends in principle to all the parties' property but, to the extent that the property is non-matrimonial, there is likely to be better reason to depart from it. The sharing principle applies as much to short marriages as to long marriages.[223]

The distinction between the Lilleymans' matrimonial and non-matrimo-   **6–074**
nial property[224] was important and the legal principles emerging from and after *Miller v Miller, McFarlane v McFarlane* were summarised as follows:

(1) a person asserting that the property of one or other of the spouses is non-matrimonial bears the burden of proving it;

(2) a matrimonial home is generally to be regarded as matrimonial or family property even if only one person has contributed to it;

(3) property acquired during the marriage other than by inheritance or gift is usually matrimonial property, but may not be family property if it has not been acquired for family use;

(4) conversely, property pre-owned by one of the spouses is usually not so regarded unless it has been committed to family use;

(5) where one spouse brings to the marriage an existing business and develops it during the marriage then its value at the beginning of the marriage may usefully be regarded as non-matrimonial whereas its increase in value during the marriage may be part of

---

[222] *Charman v Charman (No.4)* [2007] 1 F.L.R. 1246, CA, particularly at [66].
[223] *Miller v Miller, McFarlane v McFarlane* [2006] 2 A.C. 618, HL, at [17]–[19], citing *Foster v Foster* [2003] 2 F.L.R. 299, CA, at [19] and disapproving the conclusion in *GW v RW (Financial Provision: Departure from Equality)* [2003] 2 F.L.R. 108 that an entitlement to an equal division only accrued over time.
[224] Or "family and non-family assets"; this distinction was made by Baroness Hale of Richmond in *Miller v Miller, McFarlane v McFarlane*, at [147]–[153]; see *Lilleyman* at [50].

the fruits of the partnership even if wholly derived from the
activities of one of the spouses;

(6)   where one spouse brings to the marriage a pre-existing family
business it may be positively unfair to have recourse to it for the
purpose of equal sharing, in particular if to do so might cripple the
business or deprive it of much of its value.

The extent to which the increase in value of a business brought to the
marriage by one of the spouses may properly be regarded as matrimonial
property was considered in *Jones v Jones*[225] where a distinction was made
between passive economic growth (where the resulting increase in value
might appropriately be excluded from matrimonial property) and growth
resulting from activity "irrespective of whether such is achieved with the
assistance of a springboard already in position". The result of the divorce
cross-check as at Mr Lilleyman's death was that the value of the matrimonial property available for sharing would have been in the region of
£1,475,000[226] including £250,000 of the £550,000 by which one of the companies had increased in value in the region of £500,000 gross, the remaining
increase being attributed to passive economic growth. Taking into account
Mrs Lilleyman's half share in Water Meadows, the amount of the property
adjustment order which would have been made on divorce would have been
£572,500. In the result, it was held that a transfer of value in the region of
£500,000 gross from the estate to Mrs Lilleyman would provide her with
reasonable financial security, including accommodation, and substantially
reflect a fair application of the divorce cross-check. The relative shortness of
the marriage was recognised by excluding almost the entire value of the
family business from sharing. The fairest and most reasonable provision for
her was that both Dunhome[227] and the estate's interest in Water Meadows
be transferred to her outright. A life interest in the estate's share of Water
Meadows was an inherently unattractive means of providing for her housing
needs; it would prevent a clean break between parties who had fallen out
and would be a fetter on her ability to use it as a source of capital if, for
instance, she needed to pay for private care for herself in a residential home.

6–075   *Jones v Jones*, referred to above in relation to the treatment of increase in
the value of a business due to passive economic growth, is also of interest in
the context of the yardstick of equality. In that case, the value of the total
assets at the date of trial was £25 million, and the wife was awarded £5.4

---

[225]   *Jones v Jones* [2011] 3 W.L.R. 582, CA, at [44]–[46].
[226]   There was an alternative computation which took into account the value of a property (Lea
Court) which was acquired during the cohabitation period as a home for one of Mrs
Lilleyman's sons and not, in substance, for family use. Mr and Mrs Lilleyman had agreed
that his financial contribution to its purchase was to be treated as having been repaid.
[227]   Or, at her option, a lump sum of £330,000, representing the agreed market value, in which
case she would be required to give up her right of occupation.

million at first instance.[228] Her claim that she should receive 40 per cent of the total assets was viewed by the trial judge as inappropriate, arbitrary and representing too high a proportion of the total. Having performed the exercise of assessing needs, compensation and sharing, Wilson LJ carried out a "cross-check" in order to ensure a fair result. His instinct at the beginning of the case had been that to award 40 per cent to the wife would be unfair to the husband, and that view had not been displaced in the course of protracted subsequent reflection. He had considered that an award of between 30 and 36 per cent would be fair to both parties; thus the resultant award of 32 per cent (almost equal to the familiar one-third)[229] survived the cross-check.[230] The cross-check, though, was against Wilson LJ's instinctive view of what was fair, not against the yardstick of equality. If cross-checks can be carried out against a standard other than that of equality, without articulation of the reasons for adopting that standard, it would seem that the guidance derived from *White v White* in determining what constitutes reasonable provision for a surviving spouse is not universally applicable.

(f) Other Relevant Circumstances

There are a few surviving spouse cases in which having, or undertaking, responsibility for the deceased's infant children has favoured the applicant. Thus, in *Re Goard*,[231] the testator died in April 1959 leaving a net estate of £2,500, of which £1,000 was readily realisable. By his will, made in 1953, he left his estate to his parents or the survivor of them "in the sure knowledge that they would make adequate provision for my daughter". The applicant and the testator married in 1948. Their daughter had been born in 1947 while the applicant was married to another man. She was legitimated six months after the testator's death. The marriage broke up in 1952 when the testator left the applicant; her application for maintenance was dismissed, it being held that she was responsible for the breakdown of the marriage. The husband paid the applicant £1 per week for the daughter until his death. The applicant was in poor health and could not work much. She and the daughter lived in a boarding-house and the rent of £11 per week was paid by way of National Assistance. Cross J held that if the daughter was not to be considered, the applicant's claim would fail; but, although the daughter was not a party to the application, she could not be ignored. The applicant was entitled to be paid something in respect of the daughter. She was awarded £500 with interest from the date of the order.

6–076

---

[228] For the hearing at first instance, see *J v J* [2009] EWHC 2654 (Fam). The husband's appeal (reported as *Jones v Jones* [2011] 1 F.L.R. 1723, CA), was allowed. See also A. Murray, "A Judicial Safari Tour of Ancillary Relief" (2010) Fam. Law 1111. For a case on the treatment of inherited wealth in ancillary relief proceedings, see *K v L* [2010] 2 F.L.R. 1467. The husband's appeal was dismissed: *K v L* [2012] 1 W.L.R. 306, CA.

[229] *Jones v Jones* per Wall P at [67]: "My own admittedly crude analysis results on the facts of this case and on a cross-check is an old-fashioned third."

[230] *Jones v Jones*, per Wilson LJ at [52].

[231] *Re Goard* (1962) 106 S.J. 721.

6–077   Two Northern Ireland cases of this nature are *Re Morrow*[232] and *Weir v Davey*.[233] In each case the marriage had broken down before the death of the testator but the applicant had made a substantial contribution to the welfare of the family; in *Weir*, the applicant had successfully brought up their child under difficult circumstances; the child was three years old when the marriage broke down and the parties separated. However, where there is competition between an infant child and the child's mother (whether married to the deceased[234] or not[235]) the needs of the child may prevail.

6–078   In a number of cases where the beneficiaries were not closely related to the deceased, the failure to make reasonable provision for the surviving spouse has been remedied at their expense. Thus, the applicant widow succeeded in *Kusminow v Barclays Bank Trust Co, Sokolow and Sitnikova*[236] where the beneficiaries were a niece and nephew of the testator, both living in the Soviet Union, and in *Moody v Haselgrove*,[237] where they were cousins of the testator. In *Re Carter*,[238] where the estate was left to two friends of the deceased, the obligation to the friends was considered to have been satisfied by an inter vivos gift to one of them shortly before the testator's death, and the applicant was awarded the entire estate.

6–079   Charities, however worthy, have not been seen as having a strong claim on the testator's bounty, either under the present or previous[239] family provision legislation. Although the relevant judgments in the 1975 Act cases are not greatly concerned with weighing up competing moral obligations, it was observed of the testator in *Re Besterman*[240] that:

> "Save in the sense that he would, no doubt, have considered that he owed a duty to himself and to posterity to provide for and complete the work of scholarship in which he was passionately interested, it could not be said that he owed the University any duty, much less a duty which could reasonably be thought to override the very real duty which he owed to his wife."

---

[232] *Re Morrow* [1995] N.I.J.B. 46.
[233] *Weir v Davey* [1993] N.I.J.B. 45.
[234] *Re Bateman* (1941) 85 S.J. 454.
[235] *Re Patton, McElveen v Patton* [1986] N.I. 45.
[236] *Kusminow v Barclays Bank Trust Co, Sokolow and Sitnikova* (1989) 19 Fam. Law 66.
[237] *Moody v Haselgrove* unreported 16 November 1987, CA.
[238] *Re Carter* (1968) 112 S.J. 136.
[239] Successful applications by spouses under the 1938 Act include *Re Sylvester* [1941] Ch. 87 (surviving husband who, on marriage, had given up his employment at his wife's request); *Re Lawes* (1946) 90 S.J. 200 (estate of £4,500 left to the RSPCA); per Vaisey J: "Admirable though this cause was, the widow had not fulfilled her moral obligations to her husband"; *Re Bates* [1953] 1 All E.R. 318 (will made no provision for widow and charities did not oppose her application); *Re Greenham, The Times*, 2 December 1964 (entire estate of £137,000 left to Institute of Cancer Research, widow succeeded in spite of 10-year separation); *Re Jackson* [1952] W.N. 352 (bulk of estate of £93,000 left to charities, widow's annuity of £150 under the will increased to £600); *Re Sanderson, The Times*, 2 November 1963 (testator gave his entire estate of £50,000 to charity; applicant was his 80-year-old widow, whom he had left some 40 years earlier).
[240] *Re Besterman* [1984] Ch. 458 at 464–465.

Out of a net estate of some £1.5 million, the testator had left the bulk to Oxford University; to his wife he left his personal chattels and an income of £3,500 per year. Her only other resources consisted of a pension of £400 per year. The award of £239,000 to her at first instance[241] was increased on appeal to £378,000. At the conclusion of his judgment, Oliver LJ sounded the following warning:

> "I desire to emphasise what has been said, no doubt, many times before, that each case in this jurisdiction depends on its own particular facts and I think that it would be a pity if this case should be used as a basis for drawing general deductions of principle to be applied in other and probably quite different cases, whether of large or small estates."

Nevertheless, Oliver LJ's observations were borne in mind by Vinelott J in *Re Bunning*,[242] where the testator had left nothing to his wife (though her capital of £98,000 was mainly derived from gifts by him during their marriage) but had divided his estate between Cambridge University and the Royal Society for the Protection of Birds. She was awarded £60,000 out of a net estate of £237,000.

Under the 1938 Act, there was no list of matters such as that in s.3(1) of **6–080** the 1975 Act, to which the court was directed to have regard; nor were there matters applying to specified classes of applicant such as are contained in the remaining subsections of s.3. The catch-all words of s.1(6)[243] encompassed such matters as the age of the applicant, the duration of the marriage, any physical or mental disability, and the applicant's earning capacity, or lack of it. Where there had been a long marriage and the surviving spouse was either unable to look after himself or was well past the age where he could reasonably be expected to do so, applications have generally succeeded.[244]

The fact that the applicant has resources of their own or is otherwise **6–081** capable of supporting themselves is not necessarily decisive. In *Re Clarke*,[245] the testator left his wife £1,000 out of an estate of £23,000, the rest going to his mother. She died intestate three months after her son, upon which her estate went to her cousins. The marriage had broken down in under a year owing to friction between the applicant and the mother, in whose house the

---

[241] *Re Besterman* (1982) 3 F.L.R. 255, HH Judge Mervyn Davies QC sitting as a High Court judge.

[242] *Re Bunning* [1984] Ch. 480.

[243] Inheritance (Family Provision) Act 1938 s.1(6) "...the court shall have regard ... to any other matter or thing which in the circumstances of the case the court may consider material or relevant ...".

[244] The masculine here, of course, includes the feminine, but it so happens that the cases of this nature under the 1938 Act mainly involved applications by surviving husbands. See *Re Clayton* [1966] 2 All E.R. 370 (applicant was crippled in both legs but still able to work, but there would come a time when he ceased to work and he would be considerably worse off; held, it was unreasonable not to have made provision for him); *Re Pointer* [1941] Ch. 60 (testatrix left her husband in 1893; she died in 1939, when he was over 80); *Re Parry, The Times*, 19 April 1956 (husband aged 84 and blind); *Re Wilson* (1969) 113 S.J. 794 (husband's second marriage, which lasted 27 years; he was 91).

[245] *Re Clarke* [1968] 1 All E.R. 451.

parties were living. It was held that she and the mother were the only persons with moral claims on the testator's bounty, and the fact that she was able to earn her own living did not displace her claim. She was awarded half the income of the estate for life. However, in *Re E, E v E*,[246] where the testator had left his estate to a cohabitant, a factor in the failure of the widow's application was that the estate was a small one, her resources more or less met her needs,[247] and almost the whole of the estate of approximately £1,000 consisted of an occupational death benefit which accrued from his employment during the time that he was cohabiting with the defendant.

6.—FORMER SPOUSES WHO HAVE NOT REMARRIED AND FORMER CIVIL PARTNERS WHO HAVE NOT FORMED ANOTHER CIVIL PARTNERSHIP

(a) General

6-082   Section 1(1)(b) of the 1975 Act extends the scope of the family provision legislation to former spouses who have not remarried,[248] and this provision has been amended[249] so as to apply to former spouses or civil partners who have not formed a subsequent marriage or civil partnership. Former spouses who have not remarried are not, in general, entitled to the higher standard of provision afforded to surviving spouses. However, the court has discretion, in the circumstances defined by s.14(1) of the 1975 Act, to treat such an applicant as if they were a surviving spouse. A new s.14A has been inserted into the 1975 Act which gives the court the same discretion in equivalent circumstances involving former civil partners.[250]

(b) Section 14 Orders

6-083   There is at the time of writing no reported decision on the application of s.14. In *Eeles v Evans*[251] the testator left his entire estate, valued at £159,715, to his 54-year-old daughter, who was the only child of his marriage to the applicant. It was common ground that the will did not make reasonable financial provision for the applicant. The parties were divorced after 45 years of marriage. As the decree was made absolute on 14 May 1981, and the testator died on 16 January 1982, it was open to the judge to exercise his discretion under s.14 of the 1975 Act, and treat the applicant as if the decree had not been made absolute during the deceased's lifetime. The discretion

---

[246] *Re E, E v E* [1966] 2 All E.R. 44.
[247] She had a house worth £3,500, a state pension of £3.7s 6d per week and received £300 per year from letting lodgings in the house.
[248] Before the 1975 Act, such applications were made under the then current matrimonial legislation, i.e. the Matrimonial Causes (Property and Maintenance) Act 1958 s.3, and the Matrimonial Causes Act 1965 s.26. Unlike those statutes, the 1975 Act contains no requirement to satisfy the court that it would have been reasonable for the deceased to make provision for the maintenance of the surviving spouse; the only test is whether reasonable provision has been made.
[249] Civil Partnership Act 2004 s.71 and Sch.4 para.15(2).
[250] Civil Partnership Act 2004 s.71 and Sch.4 para.20.
[251] *Eeles v Evans* unreported 6 July 1989, CA.

was exercised and it enabled the applicant to be treated as if she were a surviving spouse. At the date of hearing, the applicant was 74 and had been living in an old people's home for three years. She was not capable of living on her own or of managing her own affairs. The trial judge awarded her a lump sum of £5,000 and the income of £85,000 for life; this would pay her nursing home expenses and leave £1,200–£1,400 per year for other expenses. Dismissing the applicant's appeal, the Court of Appeal held that the provision ordered, though not generous, was not so plainly wrong that it should be disturbed.

(c) Section 15 Orders

Former spouses who have not remarried may face a difficulty peculiar to   **6–084** that class of applicant. Before s.15 of the 1975 Act was amended by the Matrimonial and Family Proceedings Act 1984, the court could not order that either spouse, on the death of the other, should not make an application under the 1975 Act, unless both parties consented. The amendment gave the court power to make such an order on the application of either party and, as Thorpe LJ said in *Cameron v Treasury Solicitor*[252]:

> "After 12th October 1984, any practitioner or judge of any experience in the field of ancillary relief understood that the inclusion of an Inheritance Act bar was an essential part of any clean break settlement or order ... an order dismissing all claims under the Matrimonial Causes Act 1973 that did not also bar claims under the Inheritance Act would be so irregular as to suggest fundamental error in drafting."

The practical consequence of the amendment is that claims by former spouses who have not remarried (and by former civil partners who have not entered into another civil partnership or married) will be confined to cases where no financial relief was applied for on termination of the marriage or civil partnership, since it is now routine for the order in proceedings for financial relief to provide that claims under the Inheritance Act should be barred. Section 15ZA(1) of the 1975 Act, has the same effect in relation to former civil partners who have not entered into another civil partnership or married, as has s.15(1) in relation to former spouses who have not remarried.[253]

(d) When No Provision May Be Reasonable Provision

There are three types of situation in which the making of no provision has   **6–085** been held to constitute reasonable provision. These are:

(a)   where there has been a "clean break" settlement;

[252] *Cameron v Treasury Solicitor* [1996] 2 F.L.R. 716 at 723.
[253] Civil Partnership Act 2004 s.71 and Sch.4 para.21.

(b) where the estate is insufficient to provide for the former and the surviving spouse; and

(c) where the former spouse has not been dependent on the deceased.

In the first category is *Re Fullard*.[254] After a marriage lasting 37 years the parties divorced. They had both worked throughout their marriage and each had saved about £3,000. Their only asset was the matrimonial home, owned jointly and worth about £9,000. On divorce, the wife bought out the husband's share for £4,500. He went to live with another lady and made a will in which she was the sole beneficiary. He died less than two years later, leaving a net estate of £7,100. The beneficiary and the wife were in similar financial circumstances. Ormrod LJ posed the question:

"Is it reasonable to expect a husband with assets of this kind, who has made arrangements with his former wife that settled their financial affairs, or is it reasonable for the court in his place to make no provision for the wife out of his estate?"

He decided that it was reasonable to make no provision. Having regard to the wide powers which the court has, in matrimonial proceedings, to make property adjustment orders, he considered that very few former wives would be able to "get in within the umbrella of the 1975 Act post-divorce". Two possibilities were visualised:

(i) where a periodical payments order had been going on for a long time and there was a reasonable amount of capital in the estate; or

(ii) where the death of the husband unlocked a substantial capital fund, such as a pension or insurance policies, and (per Purchas J) of which the testator should have been aware and from which, had he made a will immediately before his death, he ought within the criteria of the 1975 Act to have made some provision.

In general, however, his view was that the responsibilities and obligations of a former husband for the maintenance of a former wife are to comply with such orders as the court has made or the parties have agreed between themselves. There is no other legal obligation and, although the word "obligation" in both s.3(1)(d)[255] and s.3(6)[256] has been held to comprehend moral as well as legal obligations, it is difficult to see what moral obligation, over and above the legal obligation, could arise. In *Brill v Proud*[257] it was found that the deceased had no legal or moral obligation to make provision for the applicant in his will and that the divorce and financial settlement had concluded the question of making provision for the applicant.

---

[254] *Re Fullard* [1982] Fam. 42, CA.
[255] *Espinosa v Bourke* [1999] 1 F.L.R. 747, CA, at 752D–755D.
[256] *Lilleyman v Lilleyman* [2013] Ch. 225, at [41]–[43].
[257] *Brill v Proud* (1984) 14 Fam. Law 59, CA.

Those cases were followed in *Cameron v Treasury Solicitor*.[258] There the **6–086** applicant married the deceased in 1956 and the marriage, which was childless, was dissolved in 1971. A "clean break" order under which the deceased was to pay £8,000 to the applicant was made by consent in the ancillary relief proceedings. The deceased died intestate in 1990 and his estate, amounting to £7,677, devolved upon the Crown as bona vacantia. The judge at first instance had held that he was not precluded by the fact of the clean break order from granting her application, and he awarded her the entire estate. The factors which were relied upon by the applicant (respondent) in support of her claim were:

(a) that she remained on friendly terms with the deceased after the divorce and the clean break order;
(b) that she was in need of financial assistance;
(c) that her health was deteriorating; and
(d) that there was no-one, other than the Crown, with an interest in or a claim on the estate.

The first two factors must clearly, in the light of the judgments in *Re Coventry*, be regarded as contributing nothing to the strength of the claim. The other two were not considered to be special circumstances which would justify the making of financial provision.

In rejecting the argument based on point (d), Butler-Sloss LJ said: **6–087**

"In my view the position of the Crown as the ultimate beneficiary does not take it outside the principles set out in *Re Coventry* and reinforced in *Re Fullard* and *Brill v Proud*. The devolution to the Crown cannot enhance the applicant's claim. The applicant's claim under the 1975 Act stands or falls on its own merits and, if there are otherwise no grounds or special circumstances upon which she is able to apply, it cannot be supported or validated by intestacy legislation which provides for the Crown to take the estate in the absence of all others with a prior claim. I agree with Mr Cunningham that this is a neutral factor and not relevant to the criteria to be taken into account under s.3."

The decision to dismiss the appeal was arrived at with regret by one member of the court (Thorpe LJ) and has also been subject to academic criticism on the ground that the cases relied on by the court in *Cameron* all involved competition between persons who by reason of consanguinity, affinity or otherwise had enjoyed some relationship with the deceased, and it was questionable whether the reasoning in those cases should apply where the only competitor is the Crown.

In the author's view, that criticism is well founded. It must, of course, be **6–088** correct that a claim which is otherwise liable to fail cannot succeed merely by reason of the fact that the beneficiary will receive a windfall which they

---

[258] *Cameron v Treasury Solicitor* [1996] 2 F.L.R. 716, CA.

could perfectly well do without. However, it is going well beyond that to say that the fact that the beneficiary is the Crown is neutral and not relevant to the s.3 criteria, particularly since the Crown's entitlement arises by virtue of a statutory default provision[259] of which very few laymen are likely to be aware. Sections 3(1)(c) and (d) must, and s.3(1)(g) may, require consideration of the identity and circumstances of the beneficiaries and their relationship or connection with the deceased. There are, for instance, several reported cases where gifts to charities have been cut down in order to make provision for an applicant and it has been said in the course of the judgment that, although the charity was a worthy cause, the testator owed no moral obligation to it.[260] Further, if s.3(1)(c) is considered, it is obvious that the financial needs and resources of the Crown cannot be perceptibly affected by the destination of the deceased's intestate estate.

6–089   The same result has occurred in cases where children or siblings stood to benefit under either a will[261] or the law of intestacy.[262] In order for the court to override the wishes of the deceased, as expressed by their will, it has to conclude that the applicant has a claim on the deceased which is to be satisfied at the expense of one or more of the beneficiaries. Thus, the identity and the circumstances of the beneficiaries are relevant. If this is so where the deceased has demonstrated an intention to confer a benefit on some relation or some worthy object but their intentions are to be overridden, it must equally be so where the deceased has expressed no intentions in favour of the ultimate recipient at all. There can be few modern testators like Sir Joseph Jekyll (Master of the Rolls 1717–38), who left his fortune to pay the National Debt and whose will was set aside at the instance of his relations "on the grounds of imbecility".[263]

6–090   Although the Crown and the Duchies of Lancaster and Cornwall have power, under s.46(1)(vi) of the Administration of Estates Act 1925 to make ex gratia payments out of intestate estates which they take as bona vacantia, it is doubtful whether persons in positions similar to that of the former Mrs Cameron would fare any better by making an application to the Treasury Solicitor (or as the case may be, the solicitor to the Duchy) for such payment. The persons who may be provided for in this manner are dependants, whether kindred or not, of the intestate, and other persons for whom the intestate might reasonably have been expected to make provision. A former spouse whose claims have been met by way of a "clean break" order in

---

[259] Administration of Estates Act 1925 s.46(3)(vi).
[260] *Milward v Shenton* [1972] 1 W.L.R. 711, CA; *Re Besterman* [1980] Ch. 458; *Re Bunning* [1984] Ch. 480; *Re Debenham* [1986] 1 F.L.R. 404.
[261] See *Re Snoek* [1983] 13 Fam. Law 19; *Williams v Roberts* [1986] 1 F.L.R. 349; and *Re Moody* [1992] Ch. 226, CA.
[262] See *Harrington v Gill* [1983] 4 F.L.R. 265 (CA); *Re Callaghan* [1985] Fam. 1; *Re Leach* [1986] Ch. 226; and *Re Farrow* [1987] 1 F.L.R. 205.
[263] R.E. Megarry, QC, *Miscellany-at-law* (London: Stevens and Sons Ltd, 1955), 171, recounting Lord Mansfield's unsympathetic comment on the bequest that "it was a very foolish one. He might as well have attempted to stop the middle arch of Blackfriars Bridge with his full-bottomed wig".

ancillary relief proceedings is unlikely to be viewed as a person for whom the deceased might reasonably be expected to make provision.

In the second category is *Walker v Walker*,[264] where it was held that the estate was not large enough for the testator to provide maintenance for the widow and the former wife, and he was entitled to choose between them; similarly, in *Cumming-Burns v Burns*,[265] where, again, there was not enough to go round, the greater obligation was held to be owed to the second wife because of the comparative lengths of the marriages and the fact that his estate derived from her gifts to him.

6–091

An early example of the third category is *Legat v Ryder*,[266] where it was found that no moral obligation existed because she had been independent of the deceased for the last 11 years, and she also had substantial capital. A more recent example is *Barrass v Harding*,[267] where the applicant was the first wife of the deceased. The parties were married in 1939 and divorced in 1964; the wife's claims for ancillary relief were later dismissed by consent. The deceased remarried but his second wife predeceased him, and by his last will he left his entire estate to his sister-in-law. Although there was no evidence that the deceased felt any continuing obligation to provide for his first wife, at first instance it was found that two special circumstances existed, namely, the reconciliation between the deceased and the applicant's son (though not with the applicant herself), and the unlocking of the sum of £200,000 represented by the value of the deceased's house. These matters, combined with the fact that the divorce took place before the change in the legislation brought about by the Matrimonial Proceedings and Property Act 1970, were considered sufficient, at first instance, for an award to be made. However, that decision was reversed on appeal. Had the deceased made any sort of rapprochement with her, or given any indication that he thought he ought to be looking after her because she was getting old and was in poor financial circumstances, that would have been a wholly different situation and could have justified the making of an award. As it was, the facts that she was an elderly lady in parlous financial circumstances, that the divorce had taken place under a different regime of matrimonial legislation, and the other matters relied on at first instance did not provide a basis for an award to be made to her.

6–092

(e) Successful Applications

There are not many 1975 Act cases where the former spouse has succeeded. In *Re Crawford*,[268] the applicant former wife had been married to the testator for 25 years and had contributed to the welfare of the family by bringing up the child of the marriage. On divorce, a consent order was made, under which he agreed to pay the applicant one-third of his gross

6–093

---

[264] *Walker v Walker* unreported 10 May 1988, CA.
[265] *Cumming-Burns v Burns* unreported 4 July 1985, CA.
[266] *Legal v Ryder* unreported 2 May 1980 (Dillon J).
[267] *Barrass v Harding* [2001] 1 F.L.R. 138, CA.
[268] *Re Crawford* (1983) 4 F.L.R. 273.

salary less the mortgage and insurance on the matrimonial home; however, he did not keep up the payments. The second wife, to whom he had been married for 12 years at the time of his death, was left life interests in both his share of the matrimonial home and his residuary estate, and benefited substantially from his company pension arrangements, as did the two children of the second marriage. The applicant had no income except for supplementary benefit, and her only capital asset was the house in which she lived. She was aged 59; she had never been expected to work during the marriage and her earning capacity was found to be nil. She was awarded £35,000, a sum sufficient to purchase an annuity of £4,000 per year; this could be found only by treating the deceased's severable share of a joint bank account with a balance of £69,767, in the names of himself and his second wife, as part of his net estate.

6–094   *Re Farrow*[269] was another case in which the applicant brought herself "under the umbrella of the 1975 Act post-divorce". After 19 years of marriage, of which there were two children, the parties separated in 1968. In 1973 a decree nisi based on two years' separation was pronounced, but the ancillary relief proceedings were not heard until 1978. The applicant was awarded £50,000 and periodical payments of £5,500 per year, but the deceased died intestate 11 months later with the result that the applicant received periodical payments of only £4,742 in all, and the deceased's estate, consisting of farm land worth £820,000 (though partly mortgaged and with a Capital Transfer Tax liability in the region of £200,000, of which some £80,000 remained owing) passed to his sons.

6–095   The applicant, at the time of the hearing, had spent the lump sum; the house, which was intended to be bought with £20,000 of it, cost considerably more and there was some extravagance in the way it was furnished. She also had to live off what was left of the capital because she had no income once the periodical payments ceased, though she would shortly become eligible for a state pension of £38.30 per week, and she was getting some support from the man with whom she was living. Hollings J considered that there should be some further provision by way of periodical payments, on the basis that the applicant had received all the capital provision to which she was entitled, but that she ought to be compensated for the difficulties which she encountered as a result of her former husband's death and the cessation of the periodical payments. He rejected the suggestion that the amount should be arrived at by taking the previous award and scaling it up to allow for inflation in the interim. She was awarded £5,000 per year and a lump sum of £15,000, not as a conventional lump sum, but to compensate in part for her not having received any periodical payments between May 1979, when her husband died, and the date of the hearing seven years later. She would not be fully compensated, as her own improvidence was a contributory factor.

6–096   In *Wallace v Thorburn*,[270] the applicant former wife had succeeded at first

---

[269] *Re Farrow* [1987] 1 F.L.R. 205.
[270] *Wallace v Thorburn* unreported 9 October 1987, CA.

instance, but it was concluded on appeal, that either the trial judge had adopted the wrong approach, or his reasoning could not be discerned; in either case, the Court of Appeal could substitute its discretion for that of the judge, and did so by increasing the award to her so that it was adequate to enable her to buy a small house, which was effectively her claim for provision.

Finally, in *Parnall v Hurst*,[271] the course of which was affected by numerous procedural failures, HH Judge Langan QC dismissed the defendants' application to strike out the claim, as he considered it to have merits notwithstanding that there had been a final settlement in the divorce proceedings. The relevant matters were that at the date of the husband's death there was an ongoing order for periodical payments[272] and, without those payments, the claimant's only resources would be her state pension of £92 per week. There is no report of any substantive hearing. **6–097**

The practical lesson to be learnt from the existing case-law for those who wish to guard against claims by former spouses or civil partners is that first, a s.15 provision should be included in any order or settlement made on divorce or separation; second, if that has not been done, steps should be taken to ensure that there are no legal obligations outstanding under the order or settlement at the time of the testator's death; and, finally, nothing should be done to encourage the former spouse or civil partner to believe that further provision for them is likely to be made during the testator's lifetime or by will. **6–098**

7.—COHABITANTS

(a) General

In deciding whether the will of the deceased or, as the case may be, the law of intestacy makes reasonable provision for a cohabitant, the court has to have regard to the matters set out in s.3(2A) of the 1975 Act, as inserted by s.2(4) of the Law Reform (Succession) Act 1995, which has effect for deaths occurring on and after 1 January 1996. This provides that without prejudice to the generality of para.(g) of subs.3(1), where an application for an order under s.2 of the Act is made by virtue of s.1(1)(ba) thereof, the court shall, in addition to the matters specifically mentioned in paras (a)–(f) of subs.3(1), have regard to: **6–099**

---

[271] *Parnall v Hurst* [2003] W.T.L.R. 997. There was a subsequent application, reported at [2005] W.T.L.R. 1241 for withdrawal of the judgment, on which HH Judge Langan QC concluded that he had jurisdiction to do so but declined to exercise it. The parties and the judge were under the common misapprehension that the provisions of the former RSC Ord.99, which governed proceedings commenced before 2 December 2002 (when that Order was revoked), continued to apply when the proceedings were still on foot after that date.
[272] See the discussion of *Re Fullard* at para.6–085.

(a) the age of the applicant and the length of the period during which the applicant lived as the husband or wife of the deceased and in the same household as the deceased; and

(b) the contribution made by the applicant to the welfare of the family of the deceased, including any contribution made by looking after the home or caring for the family.

6–100   Persons living together as civil partners have been brought within the ambit of the 1975 Act by subs.1(1B)[273] though there is one case in which the court entertained a claim by a same-sex cohabitant before that provision became effective.[274] This subsection applies to a person if, for the whole of the period of two years before the date when the deceased died, that person was living:

(a) in the same household as the deceased; and

(b) as the civil partner of the deceased.

The judgment at first instance in *Baynes v Hedger*[275] indicates that (as would be expected) the principles according to which the corresponding conditions in subs.1(1A) have been interpreted will be applied when subs.1(1B) is in issue. The case-law on the interpretation of the statutory conditions is discussed in Chapters 2[276] and 4[277] and is not further addressed in this chapter.

(b) Claiming in the Alternative

6–101   When the 1975 Act first came into force, an applicant who was, in fact, a cohabitant, could claim only as a person being maintained by the deceased immediately before their death. The perception that mistresses were being allowed to claim in the same way as (for example) impecunious sisters[278] and respectable carers or housekeepers[279] provoked considerable moral outrage, and the arguments against the extension of the Act in that manner are rehearsed in *Tyler*.[280] Whatever the merits of those arguments,[281] it is a fact that a substantial number of applicants under s.1(1)(e) in the 20 years before the Act (including the applicant in the first reported case[282]) was extended to permit applications by cohabitants, were in fact cohabitants. This is

---

[273] Civil Partnership Act 2004 s.71 and Sch.4 para.15(5).
[274] *Saunders v Garrett* [2005] W.T.L.R. 749, discussed in Ch.2, s.2(e)(ii), "Same-sex cohabitants".
[275] *Baynes v Hedger* [2009] 2 F.L.R. 1805; see paras 2–070 to 2–073.
[276] Ch.2, s.2(e), Cohabitants; see "(i) Opposite-sex cohabitants", paras 2–053–2–063 and "(ii) Same-sex cohabitants, paras 2–064–2–073.
[277] Ch.4, s.7(c), "Cohabitants", paras 4–121–4–124.
[278] *Re Wilkinson, Neale v Newell* [1978] Fam. 222; *Re Viner, Kreeger v Cooper* [1978] C.L.Y. 3091.
[279] *Re Haig, Powers v Haig* [1979] 129 N.L.J. 420; *Harrington v Gill* (1983) 4 F.L.R. 265, CA.
[280] *Tyler*, pp.100–103.
[281] Although opposition was expressed in milder terms, there was still considerable unease in 2014 about the introduction of legislation to ameliorate the position of cohabitants; see App.2, where the limited progress of the Cohabitation Rights Bill is discussed.
[282] *Malone v Harrison* [1979] 1 W.L.R. 1353.

unsurprising, given that the provision of accommodation rent-free or otherwise for less than full valuable consideration will normally[283] be a substantial contribution to the applicant's reasonable needs.[284] It has nowadays become commonplace for a cohabitant who was living (on whatever terms) in property owned by the deceased to claim also as a dependant.

(c) The Case-law

This section is concerned only with cases in which the applicant has been **6–102** found to satisfy the statutory conditions for eligibility as a cohabitant and the substantive issues have been determined. In *Re Watson*[285] the relationship between the applicant and the deceased had been formed in 1964, but they did not commence living together until 1985, by which time neither of them had their elderly parents to care for. The applicant left her own home unoccupied and went to live with the deceased; she cooked, cleaned and kept house for him but there was no sexual relationship. This state of affairs continued for some 10 years, at which stage the deceased went into hospital. He died there some three weeks later, intestate, and without any known relations, and his estate (which Neuberger J considered, on the evidence before him, to be in the region of £150,000–£200,000), passed to the Crown as bona vacantia.

The claim of the applicant (who was 67 at the time of the hearing) was put **6–103** forward in the alternative, as a dependant within s.1(1)(e) and as a cohabitant within s.1(1)(ba). Having regard to the opening words of s.1(1)(e), viz., "any person not being a person included in the foregoing paragraphs", Neuberger J first had to decide whether the applicant qualified under s.1(1)(ba). He decided that she did, and also that the absence of any provision for her under the deceased's intestacy was not reasonable. Her application under s.1(1)(e) would have failed, as the manner in which she was being maintained was by the provision of rent-free accommodation by the deceased, and she had an empty house of her own, of a similar nature, in the same town. The provision of that accommodation was therefore not a contribution towards her reasonable needs, as is required by s.1(3).

Her financial position was that she had a house of her own and an **6–104** aggregate income of £5,000, which seemed "pretty paltry", though she did manage to live within her means. However, the argument that she was therefore in no need of provision from the deceased's estate, was rejected, particularly on account of her immobility and her deteriorating physical condition, due to the fact that she would be more appropriately accommodated in a bungalow or a ground-floor flat without a garden to look after, and to the location of her own property, which was unsatisfactory and

---

[283] But see *Re Watson*, where Miss Griffiths' occupation of Mr Watson's house was not so regarded, because (inter alia) she had a property of her own in which she could have lived, though because of her physical disability it was not convenient for her to live there.

[284] As, for instance, in *Jelley v Iliffe* [1981] Fam. 128, CA; and *Bishop v Plumley* [1991] 1 All E.R. 236, CA.

[285] *Re Watson* [1999] 1 F.L.R. 878.

would become even more unsatisfactory for her. Her reasonable requirement was considered to be for a further income of £2,500 per year for life,
which was capitalised at £24,000. The evidence relating to the cost of her
purchasing, fitting out, and moving to more suitable accommodation was
not altogether clear, and the application was adjourned to enable the parties
to agree whether:

(i) the Treasury Solicitor would pay £2,500 per year to the applicant
out of the deceased's estate, or whether provision should be made
for her by way of a lump sum of £24,000, or some other appropriate sum, in lieu; and

(ii) what was the appropriate further sum to award her in order to
enable her to purchase, fit out and move into appropriate single-
storey accommodation elsewhere, after taking into account the net
proceeds of sale of her own property.

The point that, because the deceased was in hospital for the last three weeks
of his life, he was not maintaining her immediately before his death was not
taken. It was clear, from the decided cases under s.1(1)(e), that if the court
finds that there was a settled arrangement subsisting in the period before
death, it would not reject the claim because of an interruption of that nature.

6–105   In *Negus v Bahouse*,[286] in addition to the 1975 Act claim, there was also an
unsuccessful claim to a beneficial interest in the property in which the parties
were living at the time of the deceased's death. The claimant (N), who was
then working as a dental receptionist at a salary of £15,000 per year, met the
deceased (B) in 1995. He was a fairly wealthy man who had been married
and divorced twice. On 24 January 1996 B made an English will leaving
£75,000 to each of his three siblings and the residue to G, his only son by his
first marriage. By agreement, the value of the net estate was taken as £2.2
million for the purposes of the 1975 Act claim. B also owned a property in
Spain which was left equally to N and G. In addition, they were nominated
as the beneficiaries of his pension policy, valued at just under £1.15 million.
The relationship between N and B became serious in late 1996; in 1997 she
moved into his flat and shortly afterwards, at his request, gave up her job
and became, in effect, a full-time housewife in all but name. He gave her a
small allowance and they lived an expensive lifestyle with frequent foreign
holidays. On one of these, in 1999, he bought her an expensive ring which N
maintained was an engagement ring, though B's family did not accept that.
In 2000 they began looking for a new home and, after difficulties with one
property (Greenways), B acquired another (Flat 8) on a long lease in his
own name, which became their home until B's death. In August 2004 B, who
had been ill, developed type 2 diabetes, and also became severely depressed.
The relationship became strained but HH Judge Kaye QC was satisfied that

---

[286] *Negus v Bahouse* [2008] 1 F.L.R. 381.

N had no intention of leaving B and that they continued to love and care for each other. On 27 March 2005 B committed suicide.

On the 1975 Act claim, the defendants' case was essentially that N had no **6–106** need for provision out of the net estate; she had received £459,000 from the proceeds of the Scottish Widows policy (of which she had £370,000 left at the date of the hearing), she stood to receive between £110,000 and £200,000 from her half-share of the Spanish property, she was only 50 years of age with no dependants, and could return to work and expect to earn some £15,000 per year. As for her housing needs, she could return to the type of accommodation which she had before she met B. N's case, put shortly, was that she had enjoyed a very comfortable lifestyle for the eight years of cohabitation, in which she wanted for nothing, had a secure roof over her head and had given up work at B's request so that she could look after him and the home. Her needs were for continued security in her home and an income which would at least to some extent reflect her standard of living during the relationship.

The evidence of N's financial position, both during the relationship and **6–107** after B's death, was confusing and contradictory. However, the judge felt able to arrive at a figure of £38,000 per year to meet her reasonable out-goings, other than her housing needs. The remaining proceeds of the Scottish Widows policy, together with the £110,000 which was taken as the minimum value of the Spanish property, could, on a Duxbury basis, fund an income need of just over £25,000. This left an annual shortfall of £13,000 plus her housing needs to be provided for. He did not find it reasonable that she should return to accommodation of the kind which she had occupied before the relationship; although the assurances which B had given her were insufficient to found a claim to a beneficial interest in either Greenways or Flat 8, it was not unreasonable that she should have a modest long leasehold or freehold flat or apartment similar to Flat 8. He also found that it would be unjust to assume that she would be able to return to work at the age of 50 after a break of eight years.[287] He concluded that the will had not made reasonable provision for N and that the correct order was for Flat 8 to be transferred to her free of mortgage (or, if that were not possible, the sum required to pay off the mortgage should be transferred to her) and a lump sum payment of £200,000 to be made to her. That would still leave G with £1.7 million plus his share of the Spanish property and the Scottish Widows policy monies.

The executors sought to appeal against the order as being both too **6–108** generous, and wrong in law. Rimer LJ had refused permission to appeal on paper; in summary, his reasons were that the judge had directed himself

---

[287] Age was obviously a factor; compare *Malone v Harrison* [1979] 1 W.L.R. 1353 where provision for the applicant, who was aged 38 at the date of trial and had not worked for 12 years, was calculated on the basis that she would be able to earn some money up till the age of 60. It may be that the more important factor is whether the claimant has any marketable skill or knowledge; the author recalls a case in which it was found that the male claimant, aged 52, was seriously disadvantaged in the labour market, to the extent of having negligible earning capacity, because he had had little formal education and his manual skills had been rendered obsolete by new technology.

correctly on all relevant questions and that the grounds of appeal amounted to no more than an attempt to re-argue the case on the facts. On the renewed application[288] the Court of Appeal gave judgments upholding Rimer LJ's refusal. In relation to the argument that the judge had approached the question of maintenance incorrectly, and that the award was excessive, Mummery LJ drew attention to the often cited dictum of Browne-Wilkinson J in *Re Dennis*, that:

> "...the word 'maintenance' connotes only payments which, directly or indirectly, enable the applicant in the future to discharge the cost of his daily living at a rate appropriate to him."

In his view, that statement permitted regard to be had to the fact that some people have a more expensive lifestyle than others. Similarly, it was plain to Munby J that in assessing what is reasonable maintenance, the court was not applying some objective standard of what was reasonable for everyone, but a flexible standard whose application required it to look at the style of life to which the claimant was accustomed while living with the deceased.

6–109   *Webster v Webster*[289] is another case in which the 1975 Act claim was accompanied by a claim for a declaration as to the claimant's beneficial interests in property, in this case both in the quasi-matrimonial homes and in a shareholding in a company of which the deceased was a director.[290] The deceased (J) died intestate on 17 December 2004, survived by five children, three from his marriage, which took place in 1972 and broke down in 1977, and two by his relationship with the claimant (A), who had been a friend of his since 1970 and had cohabited with him since 1978. At the date of his death, the house in which J and A were living was in J's sole name, and J also owned 4,000 shares in a company (MKM Building Supplies) for which he worked and of which he was a director. In the proceedings, A claimed a declaration that both the house and the shares were held upon trust for them as beneficial joint tenants, and in the alternative, an order under s.2 of the 1975 Act, and it was common ground that she was eligible either under ss.1(1)(ba) and 1(1A), or s.1(1)(e). J's children accepted that A had some interest in the house but not that she was a beneficial joint tenant of it, or that she had any interest in the shares.

6–110   A was 54 years of age at the date of the trial. Both she and J had worked throughout the relationship and contributed to the family budget. At the time of J's death, he had net annual earnings of £44,000 (£20,000 of which was dividend income from MKM). A's net annual earnings as a care home manager were £13,000 and there was no occupational pension. She received two lump sum payments totalling £148,500 following J's death and at one stage she had savings of £47,000, but by the date of trial these had been

---

[288] *Negus v Bahouse* [2012] W.T.L.R. 1117, CA.
[289] *Webster v Webster* [2009] 1 F.L.R. 1240.
[290] HH Judge Behrens found that A's indirect contributions would found an inference that she had a beneficial interest which he would have put at 33–40 per cent had it been necessary to quantify it. The claim in respect of the shares failed.

reduced to £28,000. For the four years from J's death to the date of trial, A had been paying the mortgage (about £350 per month, making roughly £17,000 over that four-year period) and all other outgoings of the house. Her annual income at the date of trial was £15,609 and her expenditure, excluding holidays, entertainment and hairdressing, but including the mortgage payments, was £20,975. She was not able to show in detail how she had spent her capital over the four years between J's death and the trial, but she said that she had spent some £30,000 on the house and her costs of the proceedings to date were £18,000, some of which she had already paid. J's five children, who would take on his intestacy, were all over 18, in employment and none of them was suffering from any disability. They had not filed any evidence of their own means or of any special need. To the nearest £1, the estate consisted of the house, the equity in which was £148,270, J's minority interest in MKM, which the directors had offered to buy out for £100,000, and a bank account with a credit balance of £19,495. Tax liabilities and administration costs amounted to £11,890 and the parties' costs to date were £42,800. None of the parties wished the house to be sold; if it remained unsold and the mortgage was not discharged, and the directors' offer taken up, there would be some £108,605 to pay such costs as were awarded out of the estate and to be distributed.

It was not seriously disputed that the effect of the intestacy was such as   **6–111** not to make reasonable provision for A. There had been a long period of cohabitation during which two children were born to A and J. She clearly needed a roof over her head. Relations between A and the other three children were not good and a clean break was desirable. Apart from the poor relationship, problems would be created if A wished to effect repairs and improvements or to raise money on the property. It was not a suitable case for giving her a limited interest in the house; it should be transferred to her outright and the only question was whether there should be a further award to cover the outstanding mortgage. If the property were transferred to A free of mortgage, she would have sufficient resources to fund her present way of living other than holidays and the like, and the result of making that further award would be to reduce what remained for the beneficiaries by £2,400 each. They were all in employment and had no demonstrated needs. It was therefore ordered that the house be transferred to her free of mortgage.

Another case involving multiple claims is *Baker v Baker*.[291] In that case,   **6–112** Mr Baker (B) died of liver failure on 27 April 2005, having five days earlier while in intensive care, made a will in which he appointed his brother (R) and Mrs Monica Hazel (H) executors, and left his estate (valued at £257,000) to H if she survived him for 28 days, and if not, to his daughter Cassandra (C) and Mrs Hazel's daughter Nicola (N) in equal shares. C, who was solely entitled to take on B's intestacy, brought a claim that the will

---

[291] *Baker v Baker* [2008] 2 F.L.R. 767 (heard by Paul Girolami QC sitting as a deputy High Court judge of the Chancery Division), not to be confused with the surviving spouse claim *Baker v Baker*, reported at [2008] 2 F.L.R. 1956 (heard by Paul Chaisty QC sitting as a deputy High Court judge of the Chancery Division).

should be set aside on the grounds of lack of testamentary capacity and/or want of knowledge and approval, and for a grant of administration to her. No other will had been found. At trial H claimed a declaration as to her interest in B's house, in which they had been living before he was admitted to hospital on 7 April 2005 with his final illness; and an order under s.2 of the 1975 Act. C's claim to set aside the will succeeded, while H's claim to a beneficial interest failed.

6–113   As no grant of representation had been issued, no order on the 1975 Act claim could be made at that stage. However, the parties agreed that the deputy judge should consider and rule on the claim on the material before him.[292] C disputed H's claim as a cohabitant but was prepared to accept that she had a claim as a dependant. The deputy judge found, applying the test in *Re Watson*,[293] that H and B had been living together in the same household as man and wife for considerably more than two years before his death and H was eligible to claim under s.1(1)(ba), so that there was no need to consider whether H was eligible under s.1(1)(e). He considered that H's principal maintenance needs were for a place to live and access to a reasonable capital sum from which she could supplement her limited income, which derived from part-time work from which she was likely to have to retire on reaching 65, and a monthly pension of £521.76. Her capital amounted to £92,000. The proposed order, which could not be implemented until C (if so entitled) had obtained a grant of administration, was that H should have a life interest in the deceased's house and its proceeds of sale, with the intent that if and when it became appropriate to sell that property, the proceeds might be applied in whole or in part to the purchase of another property, or in being invested to provide further income for H. The balance of the estate would pass to C on B's intestacy.

6–114   In *Cattle v Evans*[294] there was, as well as the 1975 Act claim, a claim (which failed) to an interest in a dwelling-house comprised in the estate by way of constructive trust. In the 1975 Act claim she contended, unsuccessfully, that the obligations and responsibilities of the deceased towards her could only be discharged by the transfer to her of the property in which they were living at the time of his death ("the Cross Hands property") and his pension fund. The net estate was approximately £220,000, of which those assets accounted for £185,000. In assessing what provision was reasonable for her, Kitchin J considered it right to take into account the fact that she had chosen to spend £29,000 on the purchase of a caravan, which seemed to him an unnecessary and inappropriate extravagance and something she could have easily managed without. He also considered that reasonable provision for her housing did not require a property of the size and value of the Cross Hands property and ordered that a property be purchased for her accommodation at a price not exceeding £110,000, to be held on trust for the

---

[292] *Baker v Baker* [2008] 2 F.L.R. 767, at [63].
[293] *Re Watson* [1999] 1 F.L.R. 878.
[294] *Cattle v Evans* [2011] 2 F.L.R. 843. The 1975 Act claim was tried together with a claim to the quasi-matrimonial home based on constructive trust, which failed; see [32]–[41].

deceased's two sons subject to an interest entitling her to live there for as
long as she wished.

Lewis v Warner,[295] in which a second appeal is outstanding at the time of   **6–115**
writing, is a most unusual case. The claimant, Mr Warner, who was 91 at the
date of the hearing before Newey J, had for some 20 years been living with
the deceased, Mrs Blackwell, who was eight-and-a-half years his junior, in
her house (Green Avon) which was situated in the village where he had lived
all his life. Green Avon was the principal asset of her estate. By her will (a
reconstituted version of which was admitted to probate) she appointed her
daughter, Mrs Lewis, as her executor and left her the entire estate. Following her mother's death, Mrs Lewis made a claim for possession of Green
Avon and Mr Warner responded by issuing a claim under the 1975 Act. The
two claims were tried together by the circuit judge.

Mr Warner's evidence in relation to Green Avon had two aspects. As to   **6–116**
its disposition, there was never any understanding that he would have any
interest in Mrs Blackwell's estate, or that he would be able to continue in
occupation, or purchase it, after her death. He did not advance any claim
based on his contributions to the household expenses (including paying for
the oil, which was a major expense), or otherwise. Although he was unhappy
to do so, he had gone so far as to sign a declaration, at the request of Mrs
Lewis and her husband, that he would not make any claim to the house. As
to his wish to remain in Green Avon following Mrs Blackwell's death, he
gave evidence of the distress that a move would cause him both because he
had spent the happiest years of his life there and because he would no longer
have the immediate on-call medical assistance with which his neighbour, a
doctor, was providing him. Mrs Lewis wished to sell Green Avon to the
highest bidder, including Mr Warner, if he was that person. He did have the
means to buy the house but in the event, Mr and Mrs Lewis were unwilling
to accept the £340,000 at which the single joint expert had valued it, and Mr
Warner considered their valuation of £425,000 to be too high. At trial, the
recorder granted permission to introduce a subsequent valuation of
£385,000 obtained by Mr Lewis, and that price was acceptable to Mr
Warner. It was ordered that on payment to the estate of £385,000, Green
Avon should be transferred to Mr Warner.[296] The crucial paragraph of the
judgment reads:

> "Looking at the matter objectively, I am unable to see why the main-
> tenance of a roof over the head of an applicant for 20 years cannot
> come within the definition of 'maintenance' in s.1(2)(b) of the Act. Its
> provision has a financial value because, without it, the applicant would
> have had to rent or buy an alternative roof. Its removal, by there being
> no provision for the continuance of the same in the reconstituted will,

---

[295] *Lewis v Warner* [2016] W.T.L.R. 1399, Newey J, on appeal from the order of Mr Recorder
Gardner QC. For the subsequent judgment on costs, see *Lewis v Warner* [2016] EWHC 1787
(Ch).

[296] For the relevant extracts from the recorder's judgment, see the judgment of Newey J at [12]–
[13].

means, therefore, that it failed to make reasonable financial provision for him and so the first stage is satisfied, enabling the court to proceed to the second, discretionary stage of deciding whether and, if so, what needed to be done about it. Here the court has to balance the interests of the applicant and the beneficiary."

6–117   The next two paragraphs of the judgment show that he weighed the emotional distress and the inconvenience in loss of medical and other care which Mr Warner would suffer if he had to move against the wish of the beneficiary to realise the value of the house. These conflicting considerations were reconcilable by giving Mr Warner an option, for an appropriate period,[297] to have Green Avon transferred to him on payment of £385,000 to the estate. The various grounds on which Mrs Lewis wished to appeal were presented as three main grounds, dealt with by Newey J (and referred to in what follows, using his designations) in the next three paragraphs.

6–118   The s.1(1)(e) point arose from the statement in the recorder's judgment which could be taken as meaning that Mr Warner had been receiving "maintenance" for 20 years and thus created the impression that he was treating the application as having been made under s.1(1)(e), whereas his case had always been put forward under s.1(1)(ba). Newey J read this as meaning that the recorder was making the point that the failure of the will to make any provision for Mr Warner to remain at Green Avon was a failure to make reasonable financial provision for his maintenance, not that he was treating the claim as having been made under s.1(1)(e). This ground of appeal therefore failed.

6–119   The "utterly wrong conclusions" point presented, as a proposition fundamental to the argument, that an Act whose purpose was to enable applicants to ask for reasonable *financial*[298] provision at the expense of the estate[299] imposed on the applicant, as a practical requirement, an obligation to satisfy the court that he had financial needs which were, unreasonably, not met by the will.[300] Mr Warner did not have financial needs. It may have been highly desirable for him to continue in occupation of Green Avon but objectively it was not unreasonable that the terms of the will did not enable him to do so. Newey J referred to the absence of any precise or comprehensive definition of "maintenance" and concluded that, notwithstanding that in the overwhelming majority of cases the provision of maintenance would involve a transfer of value from the estate to the applicant but that, exceptionally, "maintenance" could encompass an arrangement made for

---

[297] Not stated in the judgment.

[298] Emphasis as in the judgment ([21]).

[299] This is, in the author's view, an incorrect statement. Of course a monetary award under s.2(1)(a) or (b) must be at the expense of the estate, but the provisions relating to orders for transfer, settlement or acquisition of property (s.2(1)(c)–(e)) refer to property comprised in the estate and to acquisition *out of* property comprised in the estate of such property as may be so specified. There is no necessary implication that such acquisition cannot be an acquisition for full valuable consideration.

[300] This is, as was subsequently stated as a general proposition in *Ilott v Mitson* [2017] UKSC 17, the wrong question.

full consideration and was not confined to the provision of support for the applicant's cost of daily living. As he put it[301]:

> "If, therefore, a person is in want of a particular thing to sustain a reasonable quality of life, the provision of it could possibly represent 'maintenance' regardless of his financial means. In other words, a person can potentially (albeit only very rarely) be in need of 'financial provision' for his 'maintenance' without being in any way short of money; his money may not be able to secure him what he requires. As a result, there appears to me to be no absolute bar on the provision of something for full consideration representing 'financial provision' for a person's 'maintenance'."

He acknowledged that the circumstances of the case, including the absence of financial need, and the argument that "proper maintenance" did not mean "anything which may be reasonably desirable for [the applicant's] general benefit or welfare" might have persuaded another judge to reach a different conclusion, but it had not been demonstrated to him that the recorder, in reaching his value judgment had made an error of principle or otherwise arrived at an impermissible conclusion. That ground of appeal also failed.

Finally, the "no power" point had two elements. The first was that the court **6–120** had no power to order an asset to be transferred at full market value under the guise (as it was put in argument) of providing for the applicant's maintenance. Newey J considered that this added nothing to the argument on the previous point. If (as he had concluded) the recorder was entitled to decide that, notwithstanding Mr Warner's financial means, the will had not made reasonable provision for him, it must have been open to him to give effect to his view by exercising his powers under s.2 of the Act to compel the transfer of the property. The second element was that the order should have included a requirement that Mr Warner should pay mesne profits for his occupation since Mrs Blackwell's death. There, Newey J observed that the price to be paid for the property was £45,000 more than the valuation given by the joint expert and also that the valuation assumed "exposure to the market of (say) six months", during which the property would not have had a tenant. £385,000 was already quite generous to Mrs Lewis and the recorder was entitled to decide that question as he did. The appeal therefore failed on all grounds.

In *Martin v Williams*,[302] where the original claim was as a cohabitant and, **6–121** in the alternative, as a dependant, the finding at first instance that the claimant qualified as a cohabitant was upheld, but the provision ordered was reduced. Mr Martin died unexpectedly in 2012, survived by his wife from whom he had been separated since 1994 (though they remained in contact and he continued to contribute to the expenses of the former matrimonial home), and the two adult children of their marriage. He moved

---

[301] *Lewis v Warner* [2016] W.T.L.R. 1399, [26].
[302] *Martin v Williams* [2017] EWHC 491 (Ch), allowing the appeal against the order made in *Williams v Martin* [2016] W.T.L.R. 1075 (HH Judge Gerald, County Court at Central London).

out of the matrimonial home which he owned jointly with his wife. Nevertheless, he maintained what was described by Marcus Smith J on appeal as:

> "...an unusually high level of connection with Mrs Martin. Not only did they not divorce, but (for a period at least) they carried on in business together, and maintained the Accounts, into which they both paid and from which they both drew."[303]

He and the claimant, Mrs Williams, then lived together until N's death, the last three years being spent in a property (20 Coburg Road) purchased by them jointly in 2009. He had never changed the will which he had made in 1986 leaving his entire estate to his wife. The claimant, who was 69 at the date of the hearing, claimed on the basis that she was a cohabitant and alternatively as a dependant. M challenged her eligibility in both categories. Her claim was for the transfer to her of the deceased's half share of 20 Coburg Road. She had intended to retire in 2012 but had had to continue working in order to make ends meet. At trial she was awarded an absolute interest in that half-share.

6–122   The appeal succeeded on three of the five grounds on which permission to appeal had been granted. The ground which was crucial to the success of the appeal and was the first of the three to be addressed in the judgment was that the trial judge had wrongly disregarded Mrs Williams' interest in another property, 60 Slade Road, Bristol, as an asset available to Mrs Williams to meet her needs.[304] The property was a three-bedroom house, free of mortgage, which was occupied by Mrs Williams' sister, and the value of Mrs Williams' half-share was £135,000. They had inherited the property in equal shares under their father's will. Marcus Smith J observed that there needed to be good reason to leave that asset out of account and found that there was none. There was no evidence that, as a matter of strict law, she could not enforce her power of sale. In order to make good that contention, she would need to show circumstances that rendered the property "unavailable" as a matter of law[305] and there was no evidence that would have enabled him to make that finding. Indeed, he did not do so; he left that asset out of account essentially because he considered that Mrs Williams ought not to be put in a position where she was forced to evict her sister in order to maintain herself. That gave rise to two questions:

[303] *Martin v Williams* [2017] EWHC 491 (Ch) at [28(iv)].
[304] *Martin v Williams* [2017] EWHC 491 (Ch), at [30]–[40]. The others were that the trial judge wrongly dismissed the evidence of Mrs Martin as to her financial needs in circumstances in which Mrs Martin's evidence was not challenged during cross-examination ([41]–[53]) and that the relief granted was substantially in excess of what was necessary to meet those needs and was a perverse decision ([55]).
[305] Trusts of Land and Appointment of Trustees Act 1996 s.12(1) (Right to occupy) provides that "a beneficiary who is beneficially entitled to an interest in possession in land subject to a trust of land is entitled by reason of his interest to occupy the land, at any time if at that time (a) the purposes of the trust include making the land available for his occupation ... and (b) the land is held by the trustees so as to be so available". The beneficiary has no right of occupation if the land is unavailable for occupation by him; s.12(2).

(i)   as a matter of law under the 1975 Act, is a court entitled to dis-
       regard an asset on such grounds?; and
(ii)   if so, were there sufficient grounds to entitle the judge to do so?

No law was identified that required 60 Slade Road to be treated as a
financial resource available to Mrs Williams whatever the circumstances,
and Marcus Smith J considered that, in an appropriate case, there would be
a discretion to leave a significant asset out of account, but extremely cogent
reasons would be required for that course to be taken in this case, where
Mrs Williams' interest was immediate and of significant value. However, the
evidence was flimsy. In essence it was that Mrs Williams' father had been
strongly of the view that it was to be a roof over her sister's head for her life,
that Mr Martin would look after her but her sister would be more in need of
financial help, and that it was inappropriate, for personal reasons, for her to
live at 60 Slade Road with her sister. In holding that the decision to leave 60
Slade Road out of account was perverse, and could not be justified by any
other facts unstated by the Judge, Marcus Smith J considered that:

(a)   the evidence proceeded very much on the wrong premise. The fact
       was that Mr Martin had left Mrs Williams in the position she was
       in, and it was for her to demonstrate that his testamentary dis-
       positions should be rewritten;
(b)   if necessary, Mrs Williams could have realised and could still
       realise 60 Slade Road. She had agreed, in cross-examination, that
       her sister could easily downsize. There was not enough evidence to
       justify the conclusion that her sister's position would have ren-
       dered this so unreasonable a course of action so as to justify the
       asset being left out of account altogether;
(c)   on the evidence, the choice before the judge was not as stark as
       either:

       (i)   leaving 60 Slade Road out of account altogether; or
       (ii)   forcing Mrs Williams to turf her sister out of her home fol-
              lowing a contentious and acrimonious legal wrangle.

       No consideration appeared to have been given to whether Mrs
       Williams could have used 60 Slade Road to finance her needs
       without requiring her sister to move at all.

The basic premise, that Mrs Williams should not be forced to evict her
sister, was misconceived and wrong and it followed that that ground of
appeal succeeded.

Despite the appeal having succeeded on three grounds, there were sound   **6–123**
reasons to hold that the value judgment should stand.[306] The will did not
make reasonable financial provision for Mrs Williams. Adopting the course

---

[306] *Martin v Williams* [2017] EWCA 491 (Ch), at [57(c)].

taken in *Cunliffe v Fielden*,[307] he revisited the question of reasonable financial provision. It was obvious that that involved ensuring a roof over her head. That could be achieved by using up the remaining equity in 60 Slade Road and Mrs Williams' 50 per cent share in 20 Coburg Road, but that was not reasonable financial provision. She should she be able to reside there rent free, and to choose the terms upon which she left. Although she was considering "downsizing", it was not, given both her emotional attachment to the property and the transaction costs involved in downsizing, a course that should be imposed upon her. A life interest would prevent Mrs Martin from seeking to sell the property over her head, but would not involve the excessive provision that would be the case were Mr. Martin's entire interest to be made over to her. It would also accord with what was reasonable financial provision for Mrs Martin. The argument that animosity between the parties would render the arrangement unworkable was rejected.

8.—CHILDREN OF THE DECEASED

(a) General

6–124   Under the 1938 Act, the only children within the definition of "dependant" were daughters who had not married, infant sons, and any child of the deceased who was, by reason of mental or physical disability, incapable of maintaining themselves. Persons who were not, but had been treated, as children of the deceased were outside the class of dependants. Provision by way of periodical payments could not continue beyond the marriage of the daughter, the majority of the son, or the cesser of the disability, as the case might be. The 1975 Act swept away those restrictions and enabled any child of the deceased to apply.

(b) Infant Children

6–125   Claims of this nature make up a relatively small proportion of the reported or accessible cases. In *Re Chatterton*[308] the testator left one quarter of his residuary estate on trust for his daughter should she reach the age of 18. He had never seen her, and she was about five months old at the time of his death. At first instance her share was increased to one half, contingent on her reaching the age of 18. An appeal seeking a larger share and the deletion of the age contingency was dismissed. In *Re C*,[309] another early case, there were applications on behalf of the testator's mistress (A), and the child of their relationship (C). The testator had left his estate on trust for the son (S) of his earlier marriage, which had been dissolved by decree absolute of divorce. After the testator's death, S returned to his mother, and A continued to look after C. Subject to a legacy to A, the estate was divided

---

[307] *Cunliffe v Fielden* [2006] Ch. 361, CA.
[308] *Re Chatterton* unreported 1 November 1978, CA.
[309] *Re C* (1979) 123 S.J. 35; also reported as *In the estate of McC* (1979) 9 Fam. Law 26; and as *CA v CC, The Times*, November 17, 1978.

equally between the testator's two sons, each to receive his share on attaining the age of 25.

In the Northern Ireland case of *Re Patton*,[310] the applicants were the illegitimate twin children of the deceased, and were aged 13 at the date of the hearing. They received nothing under the will, the bulk of the estate being divided among six of the deceased's nephews and nieces. The deceased had never shown any interest in them during his lifetime, but their mother had obtained a maintenance order against him which was increased on two subsequent applications. It was held that:

(a)   the needs of an infant child rank very high in the order of priorities, and that in the assessment of those priorities they should normally rank well before the needs of other beneficiaries;

(b)   their illegitimacy did not entitle them to lesser consideration than if they had been legitimate; and

(c)   the provision made should not be such as to enable a minor to have a capital sum on attaining his majority; such lump sum payments as may be ordered are really capitalised annual maintenance payments. If the deceased had been making reasonable provision he would have provided a sum which would give them an income in their teens and beyond.

They were awarded £10,000 each, being in the region of one quarter of the net estate discounted to allow for the value of the superannuation payments to which the deceased had contributed for the support of the children until they reached the age of 17.

In *Dixit v Dixit*[311] where the principal application was on behalf of the widow of the testator's second marriage, the provision ordered for the two daughters of that marriage was, contingent on their reaching the age of 18, the remainder interest in the house in which a life interest had been awarded to their mother. The applicant in *Re J (A minor)*[312] was the 16-year-old daughter of the testator's first marriage, who had remained with her mother after her parents divorced. The testator left his estate of about £30,000 to the widow of his second marriage; they had a five-year-old daughter. The award of £7,500 to J at first instance was reduced to £5,000 on appeal, the widow's claims being considered the strongest. Lord Donaldson MR said that the original award would have been correct had the widow not had a young child.

In *Re Collins*,[313] there were two applications for financial provision out of the estate of their deceased mother, who had died intestate and whose estate had passed to her husband—one on behalf of a daughter aged 19 at the date of the hearing[314] and one on behalf of a son aged 10. The son had been

6–126

6–127

6–128

---

[310]   *Re Patton, McElween v Patton* [1986] N.I. 45.
[311]   *Dixit v Dixit* unreported 23 June 1988, CA.
[312]   *Re J (A minor)* unreported 9 December 1991, CA.
[313]   *Re Collins* [1989] Fam. 56.
[314]   See s.8(e) of this chapter, "Successful Claims".

adopted by another family before the application was made. It was successfully argued on behalf of the official solicitor that no claim could be advanced on his behalf. Section 39(2) of the Adoption Act 1976 provides that:

> "An adopted child shall, subject to subsection (3), be treated in law as if he were not the child of any person other than the adopters or adopter."

As to the various arguments advanced against this proposition, it was held that:

(a) the adopted child did not have a cause of action against his mother's estate and, a fortiori, did not have an interest expectant which was capable of being preserved by s.42(4) of the Adoption Act 1976; and

(b) although the applicant might, at the date of the deceased's death, be a member of a class of eligible applicants, they could not apply unless they were qualified to apply at the date of the application.

(c) Disabled Adult Children

6–129   The difficulties identified in *Re Coventry*[315] and *Re Dennis*[316] as standing in the way of a claim by an adult male capable of supporting himself naturally do not apply to claims by disabled adult children. As events have turned out, most of the disabled applicants in the few reported cases were daughters. The first of these was *Re Wood*,[317] where the applicant, who was aged 30 at the date of the hearing, was described as having been born mentally subnormal, with no power of speech and very limited understanding, though she had limited appreciation of some comforts. An award (which was also in satisfaction of her interest under her deceased mother's intestacy) was made to provide additional resources for amenities such as hydrotherapy and occasional outings and holidays.

6–130   In *Re Debenham*[318] the applicant was the child of the first of her mother's four marriages. Her mother never acknowledged her and wanted nothing to do with her, and she was brought up in South Africa by her father's parents. She returned to England in 1953, when she was about 25 and had occasional contact with her mother over the next 20 years. However, after she married in 1977 her mother made a will leaving her £200 out of an estate of £172,000, the residue being divided among six charities. She then developed epilepsy and was made redundant. In 1984, when she heard of the provisions of the will, she wrote to her mother's solicitors refusing the legacy. She was at that time unaware of the provisions of the Act. It is of interest, in view of the

---

[315] *Re Coventry* [1980] Ch. 461.
[316] *Re Dennis* [1981] 2 All E.R. 140.
[317] *Re Wood* (1982) 79 L.S. Gaz. 774.
[318] *Re Debenham* [1986] 1 F.L.R. 404.

decision of the Court of Appeal in *Ilott v Mitson*[319] (to which this case bears a more than superficial resemblance) to note what Ewbank J said on the subject of moral obligation, viz.:

"I then have to have regard to the obligations and responsibilities which the deceased had towards any applicant for an order, or towards any beneficiary. I can say straight away that the deceased had no obligations and responsibilities towards the charities. She decided to give her estate to charities out of her bounty, without obligation or responsibility. The difficult question is whether she owed any obligations and responsibilities to the applicant. She certainly did not owe any legal obligation, because the applicant was a mature woman of more than full age. I have to consider whether she owed any moral obligation or responsibility to the applicant. The circumstances of this case are very unusual. The mother herself never seems to have recognised any obligation to the child from the time of birth onwards. She rejected the child when the child was born. She did not accept any responsibility for the childhood of the child. She repulsed any efforts made by the applicant towards her, and then in later years she seems to have been ashamed of having a daughter at all. Has a mother who takes those views any obligation or responsibility to a grown-up daughter, and particularly one who has married? ... When her daughter became epileptic, it might be thought that any mother, however aloof, might feel some obligation to help her daughter. I have found this a difficult aspect of the case but on the whole I am inclined to the view that there was in the circumstances of this case some obligation to assist the daughter."[320]

Ewbank J rejected the argument that *Re Coventry* applied or that he had to find some special circumstance outside the ambit of s.3 before he could make an order in the applicant's favour. Applying common sense principles, the applicant was not a grown-up man capable of working, but a grown-up woman who was not.[321] The applicant was awarded a lump sum of £3,000 to represent an element of back-dating and to meet current needs, and periodical payments of £4,500 per year, to be reduced *pro tanto*[322] when she became eligible for the state retirement pension.

In *Hanbury v Hanbury*,[323] the applicant was the testator's 45-year-old **6–131** daughter by his first marriage; she was both mentally and physically disabled. Her father had had as little as possible to do with her from the age of four and she had been looked after by her mother ever since, living in her mother's home with assistance from social services. He had provided

[319] *Ilott v Mitson* [2012] 2 F.L.R. 170, CA.
[320] *Re Debenham* [1986] 1 F.L.R. 404, at [409].
[321] The passage from the judgment of Ewbank J which dealt with this aspect of the case was cited in *Ilott v Mitson* by Wall P, [29].
[322] The anticipated reduction would have brought the annual payments down to about £3,000.
[323] *Hanbury v Hanbury* [1999] 2 F.L.R. 255.

maintenance, initially of £600, later of £900 per year, which sum remained unchanged from 1980 until his death in 1995. By his will he left her a legacy of £10,000; and by a series of inter vivos transactions involving his second wife he had reduced the amount passing under his will to £11,981. She had capital of £268,447 and investment and pension income amounting to £27,645 per year. Having considered the applicant's needs over an expected life of just under 40 years, during which she would at first continue to live with her mother, then have to go into residential care during her mother's lifetime (those two periods being expected to span some 12–13 years in total), and finally, remain in residential care for the rest of her life, he concluded that a settlement of £39,000 on discretionary trusts for the applicant would, taking account of her legacy of £10,000, constitute reasonable financial provision.

6–132   In *Challinor v Challinor*,[324] the deceased (G) had been married twice. The claimant (E) was the younger daughter of G's first marriage, which was dissolved in 1974. She was 49 years of age and had been diagnosed as suffering from Down's syndrome at a very early age. After the breakdown of G's marriage E lived with her mother and then with foster parents, but from 1991 onwards she lived in a residential home (Bystock). G remarried in 1974 and in January 1991 he made a will leaving his entire estate to his second wife (S). On G's death in March 2006, E's elder sister, subsequently her litigation friend (A) became concerned that G's will had not made reasonable provision for E. E's care home fees had been paid by a combination of benefits and a local authority top-up, and G and other members of the family contributed to the cost of her other needs. At Bystock, she had a bank account into which her personal spending allowance and cash gifts were paid, and the balance was maintained at about £3,000. She had no other resources. G's net estate was valued at approximately £55,000, but at the date of his death he had assets, jointly owned with S, valued at £531,191, half of which represented the severable share which could be treated as part of his estate under s.9(1). In addition to the assets passing to her by survivorship, S had assets in her own name of some £627,000 and her net income in recent years from employment and dividends had been in the region of £35,000.

6–133   E's needs were assessed by reference to the medical evidence of the deterioration in her condition and the additional care, equipment and facilities which she might reasonably require in consequence. From the medical evidence it was concluded that her life expectancy was unlikely to be much more than 10 years. It was not considered likely that she would have to move from residential to nursing care in the near future and there was no evidence to suggest when, if at all, such a move might be required or, if there was a move, E's local authority funding would be adversely affected. Cooke J concluded that E's reasonable needs could be met by a fund of £100,000, which would include the £15,000 in National Savings Certificates. The fund should be settled on discretionary trusts such that if it was not exhausted at

[324] *Challinor v Challinor* [2009] W.T.L.R. 931.

E's death, the balance should revert to S. G's severable share of the jointly owned assets should be brought into the estate to the extent necessary to make this provision.

In *Christofides v Seddon*,[325] the claimant was the 53-year-old son of the   **6–134**
deceased, who had left her residuary estate[326] equally between him, her two adult daughters and a granddaughter. His health problems included diabetes, chronic kidney disease, high blood pressure and bronchial asthma; his medical records described him as morbidly obese. He had not worked for over 10 years before the hearing and was dependent on state benefits. The budget for his current care plan was £735 per week, which enabled him to pay a full-time carer. He was living in his mother's house in London but wished to purchase accommodation which was smaller, cheaper and easier to run. All the other beneficiaries were in financial difficulty. It was held that the deceased had discharged her obligations and responsibilities towards her children by giving them equal shares of her estate and plainly had not regarded the provision of accommodation for him as her obligation or responsibility.

In *Wright v Waters*[327] the claimant, aged 64, suffered from ill health to the   **6–135**
extent that she was confined to a wheelchair. Her mother's will left her residuary estate, of value £138,000, equally between her son and his wife, and gave pecuniary legacies to each of their children and to two other family members. The claimant and her daughter and granddaughters were all excluded from the will. This was due partly to a long-standing estrangement in the course of which the claimant had written to her mother disowning the relationship and which she had never retracted, and partly to her financially abusive conduct. Although there were factors other than her ill health which would have favoured her claim, her conduct outweighed all of them. It was objectively reasonable that the will made no provision for her and her claim was dismissed.

(c) Adult Children Able to Support Themselves

In the leading case of *Re Coventry*,[328] in which the applicant was 47 years of   **6–136**
age at the date of the hearing, Oliver J expressed the view, on hearing the contentions advanced in his favour, that he had to contain his surprise and look with some care at the circumstances which were said to justify so extreme an application.[329] The applicant had left the Royal Navy at the age

---

[325] *Christofides v Seddon* [2014] W.T.L.R. 215.
[326] It was considered that a realistic estimate of the value of a quarter share of the residuary estate, which included property in Cyprus, would be £125,000.
[327] *Wright v Waters* [2015] W.T.L.R. 353.
[328] *Re Coventry* [1980] Ch. 461, CA.
[329] The judicial surprise is recorded at 465H–466A. The case came before Oliver J on appeal from Master Gowers, who had awarded the applicant £2,000 out of an estate containing about £7,000 in disposable assets. Oliver J heard with some surprise, that the matter had been adjourned to him at the request of the successful plaintiff and, with even more surprise, the contention on his behalf that the entire estate should be awarded to him. How differently might the law have developed if Mr Coventry had been satisfied with Master Gowers' decision?

of 26, after completing a seven-year engagement, and returned to live in his parents' home but was, from then until the death of his father, in full-time employment. Shortly after his return, his mother (who, it was not disputed, had made contributions entitling her to a one-third beneficial interest in the matrimonial home), left and did not return. The mother's statutory legacy on her husband's death intestate would have exhausted the estate.

6–137   *Re Coventry* has been subjected to more judicial exegesis than any other case under the 1975 Act, so much so that Wall P, in the course of his judgment in *Ilott v Mitson*, felt obliged to devote a substantial part of his judgment to a careful examination of the case, not only for what it does say, but, as importantly, for what it is believed to say, but does in fact not say.[330] He quoted at length from the judgment at 474F–475G, in which Oliver J affirmed the principle of testamentary freedom and the right to leave dispositions on death to be regulated by the law of intestate succession. In emphasising that the court had no general power to reform those dispositions, he made it clear that interference by the court was not permissible simply because the testator had acted unreasonably, but must be confined to those cases where the disposition or lack of disposition produced, when viewed objectively, an unreasonable result. In what is, perhaps, the most quoted passage, he said:

> "It cannot be enough to say 'here is a son of the deceased; he is in necessitous circumstances; there is property of the deceased which could be made available to assist him but which is not available if the deceased's dispositions stand; therefore those dispositions do not make reasonable provision for the applicant.' There must, as it seems to me, be established *some sort of moral claim* [author's emphasis] by the applicant to be maintained by the deceased or at the expense of his estate beyond the mere fact of a blood relationship, some reason why it can be said that, in the circumstances, it is unreasonable that no or no greater provision was in fact made."

6–138   This, to put it colloquially, is where the trouble started, and nearly two decades were to pass before the view that there had to be a "moral obligation" or "moral claim" in order for an application by an adult child to succeed received its quietus.[331] The words "moral obligation" seem to have exerted such a strong (if perhaps subliminal) effect on the minds of advocates and judges that the Court of Appeal from time to time felt it necessary to emphasise that the existence of a "moral obligation" was not a requirement but one of a number of "special circumstances" which might tip the balance in the applicant's favour. Those words in their turn were found to be of little assistance; as Sir John Knox said in *Hancock*[332]:

---

[330] *Ilott v Mitson* [2012] 2 F.L.R. 170, CA [16]–[26].
[331] See, in particular, the decisions of the Court of Appeal in *Re Hancock* [1998] 2 F.L.R. 346 and in *Espinosa v Bourke* [1999] 1 F.L.R. 747, both of which were quoted extensively in *Ilott v Mitson*.
[332] *Re Hancock* [1998] 2 F.L.R. 346 at 357H–358A.

"Of course there has to be a reason justifying a court's conclusion that there has been a failure to make reasonable financial provision but the use of the phrase 'special circumstance' does not advance the argument. The word 'special' means no more than what is needed to overcome the factors in the opposite scale."

This debate might well have been unnecessary if these applications had been viewed from the standpoint adopted by Browne-Wilkinson J in *Re Dennis*,[333] when he posed the question, "Why should anybody else make provision for you if you are capable of maintaining yourself?" There would then have been no need to seek for some factor that could be described as a moral obligation, a special circumstance, or in any other way. The relevant circumstance would then have been simply "what(ever) is needed to overcome the factors in the opposite scale", or, on another view, whatever was required over and above kinship, availability of resources and necessitous circumstances[334] to persuade the court that provision should be made.

All of this arose from the fact that, in *Re Coventry*, it had been submitted   **6–139**
at first instance that the deceased owed a moral obligation to the applicant, because he elected to stay at home and go out to work instead of re-enlisting in the Royal Navy. He said that he adopted this course because his father was not accustomed to looking after himself, thereby giving up a career which might have led to his promotion and an early pension on his retirement; and also that he and his wife were, by virtue of the arrangement under which they lived in the house, encouraged not to go and acquire a house for themselves, as they might otherwise have done. On appeal it was submitted that there was a moral obligation and Oliver J had erred in finding that there was not; and also that he had made the existence of a moral obligation a prerequisite to the success of the application, whereas there was no such prerequisite.

Goff LJ agreed with Oliver J that the matters relied on did not create a   **6–140**
moral obligation. He also said, in a much quoted passage[335]:

"Oliver J nowhere said that a moral obligation was a prerequisite of an application under s.1(1)(c); nor did he mean any such thing. It is true he said that a moral obligation was required, but in my view that was on the facts of the case, because he found nothing else sufficient to produce unreasonableness."

Oliver J, prompted by s.3(3),[336] had adverted to one type of situation in which it would be appropriate for an adult capable of earning his own living to seek provision under the Act, that is, where the deceased died whilst his adult son was being supported in the process of acquiring some occupa-

---

[333] *Re Dennis* [1981] 2 All E.R. 140 at 145c.
[334] *Re Coventry* [1980] Ch. 461, CA at 475C.
[335] *Re Coventry* [1980] Ch. 461, CA at 487G; and see the similar view expressed by Buckley LJ at 494H–495A.
[336] *Re Coventry* [1980] Ch. 461, CA at 474E–F.

tional qualification and no provision had been made by the deceased for its completion.[337] It is also clear that another such situation would occur if the applicant had disabled himself from earning an adequate living in order to devote himself to a parent.[338]

6–141   In *Ilott v Mitson*,[339] Black LJ provided a comprehensive survey of the manner in which this aspect of the law of family provision has developed. As she said at the beginning of that survey, the difficulty in articulating how the value judgment is arrived at:

> "...inevitably leads to statements that this or that matter is not enough to found a claim and that this or that matter is required."

However, it does not detract from the value of that insight to point out that, as the case-law demonstrates, almost all successful claims by adult children fall into one of a small group of categories. As with any other area of law which develops incrementally, the list of categories is not closed. It is submitted that, for purposes of exposition and of forming a preliminary view of whether any proposed claim is viable, it is useful to consider the cases in which a claim by an adult child has succeeded in terms of the categories so far identified.

(d) Successful Claims

(i) Classes of case

6–142   From the decided cases, the following categories may be identified:

(i) the deceased had promised someone other than the claimant that the claimant will benefit in some way on their death, in circumstances in which it would be unconscionable for them not to fulfil the promise[340];

(ii) the deceased had encouraged the claimant to believe that they would benefit on the deceased's death, and the claimant had acted to their own disadvantage as a result of that encouragement[341];

(iii) the claimant, without any such encouragement or assurance, had acted in a way which benefited the deceased, and suffered detri-

---

[337]   *Re Hocking* unreported 12 June 1997, CA. The deceased died intestate and provision was made out of his estate for his daughters aged 18 and 22, one of whom was about to embark on higher education and the other had completed a considerable part of hers.

[338]   *Re Coventry* [1980] Ch. 461, CA at 477D.

[339]   *Ilott v Mitson* [2012] 2 F.L.R. 170, CA [89]–[99]. The entire history of this case during the nine-and-a-half years which elapsed between the judgment of District Judge Million in the Watford County Court and the final appeal to the Supreme Court in which his order was unanimously restored is set out in s.8(e)(ii) of this chapter, *"Ilott v Mitson"*, paras 6–160–6–191.

[340]   *Re Goodchild* [1997] 1 W.L.R. 1216, CA, affirming [1996] 1 W.L.R. 694; *Espinosa v Bourke* [1997] 1 F.L.R. 747, CA.

[341]   *Re Pearce* [1998] 2 F.L.R. 705, CA.

ment by so doing. The benefit may have been conferred either by caring for the deceased,[342] or working in the deceased's business, in either case for little or no reward,[343] and perhaps resulting in a partial or total sacrifice of the chance of living an independent life.[344] In these cases the claimant may or may not have expected that they would eventually gain some benefit by their actions;

(iv) the claimant, although not incapacitated, was in some way disadvantaged or vulnerable and, consequently, in need of financial support.[345]

Another possibility, though not so far encountered in claims by adult children, is that the deceased had an obligation (whether legally enforceable or assumed voluntarily) to maintain the claimant which was subsisting at the time of their death.[346] One case not assignable to any of the above categories is *Re Christie*[347]; that decision was criticised in *Re Coventry*[348] and has never been followed. It is noted only for completeness. The four categories of case identified above are now discussed in that order.

The first of the "promise" cases was *Re Goodchild*,[349] in which a husband **6–143** (D) and wife (J) had made simultaneous wills in identical form in favour of the survivor of them and then in favour of their adult son (G). J died and D received all of her estate. D then remarried and made a new will in favour of his second wife (E). On the death of D, proceedings were brought by G and his wife (M) claiming a declaration that E held D's personal estate on trust for G to give effect to the provisions of D's and J's mutual wills and an order for reasonable financial provision to be made for G out of D's estate. At first instance it was found that there was no sufficient evidence of an agreement that the wills should be mutually binding. In relation to the 1975 Act claim it

---

[342] *Re Creeney* [1984] N.I. 397; *Re McGarrell, Heatley v Doherty* [1983] N.I.J.B. 8; *McKernan v McKernan* [2007] N.I. Ch 6; *Donald Land v The Estate of Mary Land* [2007] W.L.R. 1009.

[343] *Re Campbell* [1983] N.I.10; *Re Abram* [1996] 2 F.L.R. 379.

[344] As apparently envisaged in *Re Coventry*, where Oliver J, reviewing the facts, had found that there was no question of the plaintiff having given up work and disabled himself from earning an adequate living in order to devote himself to his father.

[345] *Gold v Curtis* [2005] W.T.L.R. 673 (depressive illness); *Myers v Myers* [2005] W.T.L.R. 851 (mental fragility and awkward personality); *Re Collins* [1990] Fam. 56 (applicant aged 19, support needed during period of unemployment); *Hocking v Hocking* unreported 12 June 1997, CA (applicants aged 22 and 18, support needed during post-secondary education or vocational training); *Re Hancock* [1998] 2 F.L.R. 346, CA (claimant disadvantaged in the labour market; no provision would have been made but for an accretion to the estate after the death of the deceased).

[346] Unfulfilled obligations which are long spent at the date of the deceased's death will not found a claim; see *Re Jennings, Harlow v Westminster Bank* [1994] Ch. 286, CA.

[347] *Re Christie* [1979] Ch.168. By her will his mother devised to her son, the applicant, her interest in a house in Essex as well as leaving him half her residuary estate. After acquiring the whole of the interest in the Essex house she sold it, buying a smaller house out of the proceeds of its sale, so that gift was adeemed. He applied for reasonable financial provision on the basis that that meant the transfer of the replacement house to him in addition to receiving the half share of residue. The application succeeded, it being held that "maintenance" referred to the maintenance of the way of life, wellbeing, health and financial security of him and his family.

[348] *Re Coventry* [1980] Ch. 461, CA; see the judgments of Oliver J at 471 and Goff LJ at 485.

[349] *Re Goodchild* [1997] 1 W.L.R. 1216, CA, affirming [1996] 1 W.L.R. 694.

was found that whereas G's income barely covered his existing requirements, and he was also heavily in debt, E was able to cater for herself;
further, the duration of her marriage to D was short and she had no particular expectations under his will. It was also found that, so far as D's own
share of the property which he had held jointly with J prior to her death was
concerned, D was under neither a legal nor a moral obligation towards G.
However, Carnwath J took a different view in relation to J's share of the
jointly owned property. Although the wills were not mutual wills, he was
satisfied that J made her will on the understanding that D would give effect
to what she believed to be their mutual intentions. The case was, therefore,
an exceptional case and provision should be made for G. He was awarded
£185,000.

6-144   E then appealed against the award and G and M cross-appealed, contending that the judge should have found that the wills were mutually
binding. Both the appeal and the cross-appeal failed. In relation to the 1975
Act appeal, Leggatt LJ said:

> "When the court finds that the testator has been guilty in all the cir-
> cumstances of a breach of a moral obligation owed by a father towards
> his child, leaving the child in straitened financial circumstances, the
> court must ensure that adequate provision is made for the child out of
> the estate, having regard to his need for maintenance and support.
> There was here the plainest possible basis for concluding that, whereas
> D and J had not made a clear agreement for mutual wills, nonetheless
> J's understanding of the effect of the will she had made was such as to
> impose upon D, free though he was from any legal obligation, a moral
> obligation, once G's need for reasonable financial provision was
> established, to devote to his son so much of his mother's estate as
> would have come to him if there had been mutual wills."

6-145   In *Espinosa v Bourke*[350] the judge at first instance took the view that a
moral obligation had been owed by the deceased to the applicant, but that it
had been discharged by his financial support of her during his lifetime and
that, given her behaviour, there was nothing to justify interference with the
terms of the will. By that will, made some nine months before his death, he
left his entire estate, whose value was some £196,000 to his grandson
Andrew, the child of the third of the applicant's five marriages, but who had
been adopted by the applicant and her fourth husband. At the time of the
hearing the applicant was married to her fifth husband and Andrew, then
aged 23, was at university. The moral obligation was said to have arisen in
two ways. One was the care which she had given to him in the period from
1988, when they were living together in her home, until late 1994, from
which time she was absent in Spain for long periods, leaving him to be cared
for by a cleaner and by "meals on wheels", Andrew being out at work. That
obligation, in the judge's view, had been discharged by the financial support

---

[350] *Espinosa v Bourke* [1997] 1 F.L.R. 747, CA.

which the testator had given her, and if that had been the only obligation, her conduct might (as the Court of Appeal accepted) have been sufficient reason for the court not to have interfered with the testator's express wishes.

However, there was a quite separate obligation (referred to in the judg- **6–146** ments of the Court of Appeal as "the promise obligation"). In 1970 the applicant's paternal grandmother died leaving an estate from which she received only £300 but she was told that, on their deaths, she would inherit the portfolio of shares which was divided between her parents. When her mother fell ill in 1987, the disposition of her estate was discussed. By her will she left everything to her husband. The judge, while considering some of the applicant's evidence to be unreliable, accepted that the testator had said that, on his death, her mother's estate would pass to her, and that her mother had said "Do what you want with your share but promise me that my half will go, eventually, to Sandra". The Court of Appeal considered that insufficient regard had been paid to the applicant's financial situation. When the testator died she lost all her sources of income. She had an unencumbered house and, with her unemployed and much younger husband (a Spanish fisherman) she had set up a business, which was not doing well. She was in straitened circumstances and at the age of 55 had no prospect of improving her position other than from the estate. The promise obligation was a weighty one and had not been discharged. If the judge had reached such a conclusion, he based it on inadequate or irrelevant grounds. The applicant was awarded a lump sum of £60,000.

In *Re Pearce*,[351] the applicant was the son of the deceased. He was born in **6–147** 1962 and from the age of six, when his father bought a sheep farm, to the age of 16 he did substantial work on the farm, which his father said on several occasions that he would inherit. The words used were: "It will be yours one day, now you've got to earn it." After he left school, it was made clear to him that he would not be paid to work on the farm and he therefore found other employment. His parents' marriage broke down and the deceased remarried. In 1986 he made a will in favour of his second wife, leaving nothing to the applicant. Four or five years later the farm was sold, realising about £224,000. The deceased died a year or two later in 1992. The net estate at the time of hearing was taken to be £285,900. By then the applicant, aged 34, was married and had five children, the oldest of whom was seven. His house required repairs and improvements and his business profits were being invested in the purchase of plant. He was bringing up his family on £8,000–£10,000 per year and the expense of doing so would be bound to increase for some years to come.

At first instance it was held that by reason of the substantial work he had **6–148** done on the farm and the repeated promises made to him, the deceased had a continuing moral obligation towards him which ended neither with the sale of the farm in 1990 or 1991, nor with his death in 1992. He expressed the view that, in the applicant's financial situation a further income of £6,000–£7,000 per year would not go beyond maintenance, and, when one had

---

[351] *Re Pearce* [1998] 2 F.L.R. 705, CA.

regard to the age of the applicant and the sort of multipliers that would be awarded in a personal injury case, which would be 12–13, then, applying that to the figure for further income, the result was an award of £85,000. The Court of Appeal agreed both as to the existence of the moral obligation and the manner in which the award had been quantified.

6–149   *Re Abram*[352] is a case in which there was no promise or assurance. The successful applicant (M) was the 52-year-old son of the testatrix (T). He had been taken into the family business when he was 17 and lived at home, working long hours and receiving very low wages. In 1969, after some eight years, he married and left home, against strong opposition from T, but continued to work in the business. In 1972, T's marriage collapsed and the parties separated but did not divorce. In that year she made a will leaving substantially the whole of her estate to M. His marriage (of which there were two children) broke down in 1977 and ended in divorce. In 1978 M decided that he could not support his family on the income which he was receiving from the family business and left to go into partnership with another person. T thereupon executed a new will, the effect of which, in the events which occurred, was that M received nothing and the administrator of her estate held the proceeds of sale of her home upon trust to distribute at discretion to charity. Although there was a reconciliation between T and M (who had remarried), she never made another will. Following her death M attempted to keep the family company going, but in 1986 he petitioned to have it wound up as insolvent. His financial circumstances deteriorated and in 1992 he entered into an individual voluntary arrangement (IVA).

6–150   In deciding that the will did not make reasonable provision for M, HH Judge Roger Cooke said:

> "Had the case been (as it might have been) that the plaintiff had worked in the business for many years for a low wage in the expectation that it would one day be his and then while he was still so working, the testatrix died and left her majority shareholding and her home to third parties I would have thought the case for moral obligation or special circumstances would have been overwhelming and the failure to make financial provision wholly unreasonable. In this case the final events turned out differently, because the plaintiff was forced by reasonable circumstances to leave the company and the company ultimately failed. But fundamentally to my mind the special circumstances remain unaltered—it might have been different if his departure had been the result of caprice rather than, as I find, force majeure."

He then considered the effect of the IVA and concluded that the appropriate order would be to direct a settlement, of one half of the estate net of everything except inheritance tax on M for life on protective trusts. The protected life interest imported the statutory trusts under s.33 of the Trustee Act 1925, so that the income would be paid to M for life but, if he sought to

---

[352] *Re Abram* [1996] 2 F.L.R. 379.

alienate his interest, the life interest would be determined and replaced by a discretionary trust for M and his family.

There are also three Northern Ireland cases of this nature. In *Re Cree-* **6–151** *ney,*[353] the testator had two children, a son and a daughter. The son had worked in the family shoe shop for many years at a low wage, in the expectation that he would succeed to the business, though the facts as set out in the judgment do not indicate that he was ever encouraged to believe that that would be so. After some years, he fell out with his father, left the business and obtained employment in England. His father then made a will leaving his entire estate to his daughter. Taking into account the relative financial situations of the parties, the work done by the son and his wife in the family business and, as Carswell J put it "such intangible factors as the conduct of the parties and their relative merits in the affairs of the family" it was ordered that he be paid a lump sum of an amount representing one third of the net estate. In *Re Campbell,*[354] the deceased died intestate survived by 11 children, and the 53-year-old applicant son had been working continuously on the family farm since the age of 15; it does not appear that he had any expectations of inheriting as a result. His intestate share was doubled and he was also granted a non-assignable licence to occupy the farmhouse rent free for life. Finally, in *Re McGarrell*[355] the successful applicant was the daughter of the deceased, a married woman with four adolescent children. Her father had made a will leaving his estate in equal shares to the husbands of two of his nieces and a person taking as trustee of a religious organisation. She had done housework for her father and provided him with general assistance, particularly during the last when he came to live with her and her family. It was held that this gave rise to a moral claim and she was awarded, by consent, one fourth of the net estate.

In the category of claims by adult children who are in some way dis- **6–152** advantaged or vulnerable, though with some capacity to support themselves, there are five decided cases in which the claim succeeded. Two of these were made by claimants who had recently reached the age of majority. In *Re Collins*[356] the application was brought on behalf of two children of the deceased, a daughter and a son aged 19 and 10 respectively at the date of the hearing. Only the younger child was a child of the deceased mother's marriage. The deceased died intestate after two years of marriage; she had obtained a decree nisi some three months before her death but it had not been made absolute. Consequently, her husband was entitled to the whole of her estate of £27,000 on her intestacy. The two children were taken into care

---

[353] *Re Creeney, Creeney v Smyth* [1984] N.I. 397. It later turned out that the award to the applicant could not be given effect unless recourse was had to jointly owned property under art.11 of the 1979 Order (corresponding to s.9 of the 1975 Act). Carswell J held that the court had jurisdiction to amend the order made in the substantive proceedings so that half the jointly owned property was treated as part of the testator's net estate; see *Re Creeney* [1988] 5 N.I.J.B. 47.

[354] *Re Campbell* [1983] N.I. 10. There was also an application by a grandson, who claimed as a person being maintained by the deceased immediately before his death.

[355] *Re McGarrell, Heatley v Doherty* [1983] N.I.J.B. 8, Ch.D.

[356] *Re Collins* [1990] Fam. 56.

and the son was adopted some three months before the proceedings were issued.[357] The daughter had been fostered, had completed her secondary education, obtained a secretarial qualification and attended a YTS course, but was unemployed. She was living in shared accommodation with her boyfriend, and receiving benefits from the DSS, who were also paying the rent. It was held that her receipt of DSS benefit did not preclude consideration of whether the operation of the law of intestacy had resulted in reasonable provision being made for her. It was well established by the matrimonial cases that a person otherwise liable to maintain a wife or child could not excuse himself or herself from that liability on the ground that the claimant was also in receipt of DSS benefits. It was considered that the appropriate order was for a lump sum rather than periodical payments, since it would be difficult to assess an appropriate amount, the estate was relatively small, and there was a need to achieve finality. She was awarded £5,000 for her maintenance in times of unemployment and for her other needs.

6–153   In *Hocking v Hocking*,[358] the deceased died intestate in 1994 at the age of 49, and on his intestacy his estate of £106,000 went to his second wife. On an application by his former wife and the two daughters of his first marriage, the former wife was awarded £18,000. The older daughter, Emma, who was 24 at the time of the hearing, was awarded £4,000 and the younger daughter Lucy, then aged 20, £8,000, the difference reflecting the fact that Lucy would undergo a longer period than Emma, between the date of her father's death and the time when she was able to support herself. On appeal by the daughters only, it was argued that if their father had paid sufficient maintenance to them during his lifetime, they would have been in a better financial position and could have built up fairly substantial savings from their part-time and holiday earnings. The Court rejected this argument as being contrary to the decision in *Re Jennings* and the appeals were dismissed.

6–154   The remaining cases in this category involve middle-aged claimants. In *Gold v Curtis*[359] the deceased, who died aged 80, was survived by a son aged 57 and a daughter aged 60. The entire residuary estate of £870,000 was left to the daughter, who had capital of her own in excess of £1.1 million and income which was ample to cover her expenditure. In her will the deceased stated that she was leaving him nothing "because he had already had enough" but in fact he had received only £1,800 from her during her lifetime. The claimant accepted that he had been estranged from his mother but said that there had been some attempt at reconciliation. In relation to this Master Bowman observed that, while the Act was not intended to be a charter for wastrels and spendthrifts, there was no suggestion in the Act or in authority that lack of filial piety is an overwhelming consideration for the

---

[357] For the outcome of his claim, see subs.(b), "Claims by infant children", para.6–127.
[358] *Hocking v Hocking* unreported 12 June 1997, CA.
[359] *Gold v Curtis* [2005] W.T.L.R. 673.

court. This observation reinforces the comments made elsewhere in this work about the inadvisability of relying heavily on matters of conduct.

The claimant's positive case was that his financial situation was pre- **6–155** carious, depending heavily on his wife's ability to continue working; one of his daughters had been diagnosed as suffering from a psychotic condition and was never likely to be independent, and he himself was suffering from a depressive condition. Reviewing the law, Master Bowman considered that the "special circumstances" which it was thought necessary, since *Re Coventry*, to establish, meant no more than what was necessary to balance the factors in the opposite scale. As to moral obligation, an applicant of working age with a job or capable of obtaining a job might have to identify some very weighty factor to pass the hurdle and that might be some moral obligation, but that phrase meant no more than obligation and responsibility in a broad sense.[360] The claimant was awarded £250,000 of which £30,000 was to provide for capital items requiring replacement. This would still leave him substantially worse off than the defendant, but it was not the task of the court to achieve fairness or equality between the deceased's two children.

In *Re Myers, Myers v Myers*,[361] the deceased died on 28 July 2002 aged 89, **6–156** leaving a net estate of £8,356,400. He had been married twice, the claimant (BM) being one of the children of his first marriage, which had broken down in the early 1950s. He remarried shortly afterwards and was survived by the widow and three children of that marriage. He left his estate to them and their descendants, making no provision for his first wife or the children of that marriage. In 1976 he settled 3,500 shares in Unilever upon trusts for BM under which she was entitled only to the dividend income, but in 1989 the shares, which had by then been split five for one and had a value of £93,800, were released to her. Both before and after the settlement on BM, the deceased wrote a number of memoranda expressing a very low opinion of her, in particular that she was hysterical, she had not taken proper advantage of the education which he had provided for her, and preferred to sponge off others than earn her own living. By the date of the hearing, at which BM was aged 60, she had sold over half of the shares, and the value of the 27,162 which she had retained was £142,600; had she kept the whole portfolio she would (as a result of further splits and consolidations) have had 62,500 with a value of £328,125. She owned no property, she lived mainly in a small rented flat in Paris, and stayed with her mother when she was in England. Her only income other than the dividends from the shares was the state pension of £71 per week.

Balancing the factors for and against the claimant, Munby J concluded **6–157** that the will did not make reasonable provision for her. Against her were the financial provision made for her during the deceased's lifetime and the fact that, as he put it "many of her wounds were self-inflicted"; she had not made the best use of her education and, having obtained a job as an

---

[360] *Gold v Curtis* [2005] W.T.L.R. 673 at 680B.
[361] *Re Myers, Myers v Myers* [2005] W.T.L.R. 851.

established civil servant, threw it up in 1976. In her favour were her severely straitened circumstances, the fact that her situation was due to mental fragility and awkward personality rather than indolence, that she had not behaved as badly to the deceased as he seemed to have thought,[362] and that he had very substantial wealth. Thus, the claimant was entitled to reasonable maintenance, which was not just enough to get by on, but neither did it include anything reasonably desirable for her general benefit or welfare. Provision would be made by way of a settlement on her of a sum sufficient to buy a flat (£275,000), remainder to the deceased, with power for the trustees to apply capital for her maintenance, and a lump sum payment of £241,500 made up of £20,000 to equip her new home, £21,250 representing living costs since the deceased's death, and £200,000 which, together with the capital value of her shares, would provide a fund sufficient to meet a net income requirement of £20,000 per year.

6–158   The last case in this category to be discussed is *Re Hancock*.[363] The applicant was 69 at the date of the hearing at first instance. She had left home at the age of 19 to be married; she was 58 at the date of her father's death, and was living with a man who had no resources save his pension and disability benefits. Under her father's will she received nothing, and under her mother's will, a legacy of £1,000. The judge at first instance held that, on the facts as they were at the testator's death, it was not unreasonable for the will to make no provision for the applicant and that she had failed to demonstrate a moral obligation owed by the deceased towards her or any special circumstances. However, assessing the relevant matters at the date of the hearing, by which time the value of the net estate had increased by over £500,000, the applicant's resources fell short of what was required for her reasonable maintenance, measured by the expectations and way of living adopted by her over the years; and he awarded her periodical payments of £3,000 per year for life.

6–159   On appeal, the court was, not surprisingly, pressed with the decisions in *Re Coventry*[364] and *Re Jennings*.[365] Butler-Sloss LJ did not extract from those decisions the degree of support for the appellants' case that was submitted. It was clear that the Act did not require an adult child to show in all cases a moral obligation or other special circumstances. However, where the facts disclosed that the applicant was in employment, with an earning capacity for the future, it would be unlikely that an application would succeed without

---

[362] Compare *Singer v Isaac* [2001] W.T.L.R. 1045, where Master Bowles found (contrary to the testator's written statements) that there was more than one view about whether there had been a reconciliation between the applicant widow and the deceased. He preferred hers. These cases are a warning against placing too much reliance on the testator's statements, which are of course hearsay and whose weight is to be determined by reference to the guidelines in s.4 of the Civil Evidence Act 1995. Note also that Master Bowman said in *Gold v Curtis* [2005] W.T.L.R. 673 at 679H that while the deceased's express reason for rejecting the applicant as a beneficiary was very relevant, it may be tested by reference to other evidence.

[363] *Re Hancock* [1998] 2 F.L.R. 346, CA.

[364] *Re Coventry* [1980] Ch. 461, CA.

[365] *Re Jennings, Harlow v National Westminster Bank* [1994] Ch. 286, CA. This case is discussed in detail in s.8(f) of this chapter, "Unsuccessful Claims", paras 6–193–6–195.

some special circumstances such as a moral obligation. The trial judge had found:

(a) that there was no moral obligation or responsibility owed by the deceased to the applicant;

(b) that the applicant had been approaching the end of her working life at the time of her father's death, and at the date of the hearing was 69 and long retired;

(c) she no longer had any earning capacity or any hope of improving her condition in life; and

(d) her financial circumstances were stringent.

On such facts the judge was not obliged to find a special circumstance, such as a moral obligation. As to the delay between the time of the death of the deceased and the hearing of the application and, within that range, the important period before the plot of land was sold at its greatly increased value, the judge had concluded that the applicant was not to blame for it and, indeed, had not apportioned the blame for the delay. He had made a value judgment that the provision made for the applicant was not reasonable, and he had not erred in his approach in respect of the increase in the estate nor in the decision to which he came. Rejecting the argument that, in the light of the decisions in *Re Coventry* and *Re Jennings*, an adult child could only succeed in a claim under the Act if it could be shown that the deceased was under some moral obligation or there were other special circumstances. Butler-Sloss LJ said:

"It is clear to me that the 1975 Act does not require, in an application under s.1(1)(c), that an adult child ... has in all cases to show moral obligation or other special circumstance. But on facts similar to those in *Re Coventry* and even more so with the comparatively affluent applicant in *Re Jennings*, if the facts disclose that the adult child is in employment, with an earning capacity for the foreseeable future, it is unlikely that he will succeed in his application without some special circumstance such as a moral obligation."

Although by the time *Hancock* came to be decided, *Re Coventry* had for **6–160** long been the leading case in that area of the law, it is submitted that much of the discussion of it, however valuable in the development of the law in that area, was of little relevance to the outcome of that particular case. On the trial judge's findings as set out above, Miss Hancock was, for all practical purposes, in much the same position as the disabled applicants whose cases are discussed above. Although the evidence did not show that she was physically incapable of working, she was virtually unemployable due to her age and lack of any qualifications or experience. Once the trial judge had decided that the enhanced value of the estate could be taken into account, so that there were resources out of which her reasonable needs could be met, her inability to support herself must, on any rational view, have tipped the scale in her favour.

(ii) Ilott v Mitson

6–161   The last of the successful claims by an adult child to be discussed is the case
reported (in the fullest version of the title) as *Heather Ilott v David Mitson,
Michael Land, The Blue Cross, The Royal Society for the Protection of Birds
and The Royal Society for the Prevention of Cruelty to Animals*[366] (hereafter
referred to, except in footnotes identifying reports under other names, as
Ilott v Mitson). The case does not fit into any of the above categories. Far
from there being any promise or assurance on which she could rely, the
claimant was aware, and acknowledged, that she had no expectation of
benefit under her mother's will. Her precarious financial position was not
due to any circumstances which might have affected her ability to support
herself, but was the consequence of the way of living that she had chosen to
adopt. There was nothing to suggest that she was unemployable had she
attempted to seek work, though there would have been practical difficulties
in finding it and travelling to and from her place of employment.[367] Be that
as it may, her claim succeeded, though it was 13 years after the death of her
mother and almost 10 years after proceedings were commenced, when the
Supreme Court finally upheld the order that the district judge had originally
made.

(1) The history of the proceedings

6–162   The case was first heard by District Judge Million in the Watford County
Court on 29 and 30 May 2007. In a reserved judgment dated 7 August 2007,
he found that her mother's will, which left her entire estate to animal charities, did not make reasonable provision for her, and awarded her £50,000
out of a net estate of £486,000. On appeal, Eleanor King J[368] set aside his
order. Permission to appeal was granted by Wilson LJ,[369] and on appeal her
decision was in turn reversed by the Court of Appeal. All three members of
the court were of the opinion that the district judge was not plainly wrong
and had not committed any error which justified Eleanor King J's exercise
of her appellate jurisdiction to overturn his judgment.[370] Permission to
appeal to the Supreme Court was refused by the Appellate Committee of the
Supreme Court on 27 June 2011. The original order therefore stood,
pending the determination of the claimant's appeal against the district
judge's assessment of quantum, which was remitted to another judge of the
Family Division.

---

[366] *Ilott v Mitson, Land, The Blue Cross, RSPB and RSPCA* [2011] EWCA Civ 346; [2012]
F.L.R. 170; [2011] 2 F.C.R. 1; [2011] W.T.L.R. 779, CA, 31 March 2011.
[367] See the judgment of the district judge at [76]; the section concerned with his assessment of
reasonable provision, at [68]–[80] is reproduced as an appendix to the judgment of Arden
LJ, in *Ilott v Mitson* [2015] 2 F.L.R. 1409, CA.
[368] *H v J's Personal Representatives, Blue Cross, RSPB and RSPCA* [2010] 1 F.L.R. 1613; [2010]
Fam. Law 343, 1 December 2009; also reported as *H v M* [2010] W.T.L.R. 193.
[369] *Heather Ilott v David Robert Mitson (personal representative of Melita Jackson)* [2010]
EWCA (Civ) 1426, 18 November 2010.
[370] *Ilott v Mitson* [2011] 2 F.C.R. 1; [2011] W.T.L.R. 779; [2011] EWCA Civ 346; see [59] per
Wall P, [63] per Arden LJ and [100] per Black LJ.

In the event, the exhortations of the Court of Appeal to settle the issue of **6–163**
quantum proved fruitless.[371] When the matter was remitted to Parker J, she
upheld the order of the district judge and dismissed the appeal.[372] Once
again, however, the Court of Appeal reversed the decision of the Family
Division judge, holding that the district judge had committed errors which
justified the exercise of the appellate jurisdiction. The provision awarded to
Mrs Ilott, principally to enable her to buy her house at a concessionary
price, was some three times as large as the amount of the original award.[373]
From that judgment, permission to appeal to the Supreme Court was
granted in 2016 and the appeal was heard in December of that year. The
judicial process was brought to an end on 15 March 2017, by the judgment
of a seven-member Supreme Court which unanimously reversed the decision
of the Court of Appeal; once again it was held that the judgment of the
district judge[374] was not vitiated by any error justifying the exercise of the
appellate jurisdiction, and for a second time his order was restored.[375] In
what follows, the summary of facts is followed by discussion, first, of the
issue whether the will made reasonable provision for the claimant and then,
of the nature and amount of the provision.

(2) Summary of the facts

The following summary of the facts is taken from the judgment of Eleanor   **6–164**
King J.[376] By her will dated 16 April 2002 the deceased, Melita Jackson made
no provision for the claimant, who was her only child; she left her entire
estate of £486,000 to three charities. With the will was a letter of wishes
explaining her reasons for excluding her daughter from benefit. In early 1978,
when she was aged 17, she had secretly left home to live with the man (N)
whom she later married, in his parents' home. She was reported as missing
but when found, she refused to return. That relationship had been formed in
1977 and Mrs Jackson strongly disapproved of him. As Eleanor King J put

---

[371] As to this Wall P (with whom Arden and Black JJ concurred) urged the parties to consider
carefully whether a further hearing was in anyone's interests. No doubt substantial additional costs would be incurred, and compromise, now that the appellant had won her major
point, must be in the interests of everyone.

[372] *Ilott v Mitson* [2015] 1 F.L.R. 291, 3 March 2014.

[373] *Ilott v Mitson* [2015] 2 F.L.R. 1409, CA, 27 July 2015.

[374] Extracts from his judgment are quoted in the judgment of Eleanor King J, [2010] 1 F.L.R.
1613 at [25] and [49] (on the breakdown of the relationship between mother and daughter
and failure to repair it), at [51]–[53] (obligations of the mother towards the daughter), and
[53]–[54] (the conduct of the parties and the mother's reasons for excluding her daughter
from benefit); in the judgments of the Court of Appeal, [2012] 2 F.L.R. 170, by Wall P at
[44] (unreasonable result) and at [55]–[56] (s.3 factors or elements of the exercise of the
discretion) and by Black LJ ([80]) (unreasonableness of the result). Further, at [81]–[85]
Black LJ discussed paras [65]–[67] of the district judge's judgment, not referred to be
Eleanor King J but which in her opinion showed that he had asked himself the correct
question. The judgment of the Court of Appeal on quantum contains, as an appendix to the
judgment of Arden LJ, paras 67–81 of the judgment of the district judge, which relate to his
assessment of quantum.

[375] *Ilott v Mitson* [2017] UKSC 17; reported at [2017] 2 W.L.R. 979 as *Ilott v The Blue Cross* (on
appeal from *Ilott v Mitson (No.2)*).

[376] *H v J's Personal Representatives, Blue Cross, RSPB and RSPCA* [2010] 1 F.L.R. 1613; see
the section headed "The factual matrix" at paras [12]–[31].

it, the resulting disagreement went far beyond the sort of normal teenage disagreements that occur between adolescent daughters and mothers.

6–165   For the next five years there was no contact between them but, after Mrs Jackson had been told by N's mother in May 1983 that her daughter was pregnant, there was a reconciliation which lasted about a year. However, on 21 March 1984 she made a will in which her daughter was excluded from all benefit and a letter of wishes which referred to her daughter having left her in 1978 and married in 1983. After an unpleasant telephone call from N in May 1984 (in which the claimant was also involved) relations were broken off and there was no contact between mother and daughter until they met accidentally in April 1994. This reconciliation terminated abruptly after a visit to her by her daughter, husband and their four children to on 1 June 1994, the occasion of her 60th birthday. She did not share their view that the day had gone well and wrote a highly critical letter to her daughter the following day. The final attempt in 1999 also occurred as the result of a chance meeting, but in spite of the written apology from her daughter which Mrs Jackson demanded and received, the reconciliation did not last, apparently because she had named her last child after her mother-in-law, whom her mother disliked. After executing the April 2002 will, Mrs Jackson wrote to her daughter to tell her what she had done. In her reply she said "...I have to accept that you have rejected me. It is very upsetting to know this but you obviously have your reasons..." There does not appear to have been any further communication between them before Mrs Jackson's death on 10 July 2004.

(3) Did the will make reasonable provision for the claimant?

6–166   On the initial hearing, District Judge Million found that Mrs Jackson's will did not make reasonable provision for her daughter. In summary,[377] the major factors underlying that finding were the obligation owed to the daughter and the lack of obligation towards the charities who benefited under the will, the conduct of the parties towards each other, and the precarious financial position of her daughter and her family. As to obligations, he said that Mrs Jackson "owed her daughter the ordinary family obligations of a mother towards her only child who was an independent adult", that she had no responsibility or obligation towards anyone else, and that she was aware of the responsibilities and obligations of her daughter (who had very little money) towards her own five children. However, he accepted that she had gone out of her way over a number of years to tell her daughter that she felt no responsibility to her as a daughter, because she left home at 17. In relation to conduct he observed that a daughter was entitled (and indeed would be expected) to make a life with a partner of her own choice and could reasonably hope that a parent would accept that choice and not blame her for it. He found that the 2002 letter of wishes contained many inaccuracies and the overall impression created was unfairly critical of her daughter, though he accepted that she and her husband bore some of the

---

[377] Taken from the judgment of Eleanor King J, *H v J's Personal Representatives, Blue Cross, RSPB and RSPCA,* [2010] 1 F.L.R. 1613, at [49]–[67].

responsibility for the failure to achieve a sustained reconciliation. A crucial part of his judgment was para.64, in which he said:

> "I am satisfied therefore that the rejection by the mother of her only child at the age of 17, and which she then maintained for the rest of her life was unreasonable and that this has led to her unreasonably excluding her daughter from any financial provision in her will, despite her daughter's obviously constrained and needy financial circumstances and her daughter's wish for and attempts at reconciliation."

It was that passage which led Eleanor King J to conclude[378] that he had asked himself the wrong question and thereby erred in law. The question, as emphasised in the authorities, was not whether the deceased had acted unreasonably, but whether on an objective basis, having considered all the factors in s.3, the resulting provision, or lack of it, was unreasonable. A second error was that, despite having looked at all the s.3 factors, he failed thereafter to stand back and assess the impact of them when taken together. That would, in her judgment, have led him to conclude that:

> "...the court was left with a filial relationship and necessitous circumstances with nothing more of sufficient cogency to drive a court to conclude that, in all the circumstances of the case, no provision for the daughter was reasonable provision."

The short judgment of Wilson LJ,[379] granting permission to appeal out of **6–167** time and permission to appeal, has several aspects which repay study. He first explained that it was a second appeal, to which the especially stiff criteria set by CPR r.52.13(2) applied. The relevant rule at the time of writing is CPR r.52.7 (Permission to appeal test—second appeals) and r.52.7(2) provides that:

> "(2) The Court of Appeal will not give permission unless it considers that—
>
> (a) the appeal would—
>   (i) have a real prospect of success; and
>   (ii) raise an important point of principle or practice; or
> (b) there is some other compelling reason for the Court of Appeal to hear it."[380]

---

[378] See her judgment at [58]–[66].

[379] *Heather Ilott v David Robert Mitson (personal representative of Melita Jackson)* [2010] EWCA (Civ) 1426, 18 November 2010. It was given at a hearing at which (for reasons explained in the judgment) none of the parties appeared or was represented.

[380] The commentary in *Civil Procedure 2017*, para.52.7.7 cites the guidance given by Dyson LJ in *Uphill v BRB (Residuary) Ltd* [2005] 1 W.L.R 2070, CA, one limb of which is that there may be circumstances where there is a compelling reason to grant permission to appeal even where the prospects of success are not very high. The commentary goes on to state that the guidance in *Uphill* should not be allowed to ossify into rule.

He then considered the grounds on which Eleanor King J came to her conclusions. On the first of them, he asked why she had not proceeded from para.64 of the district judge's judgment to para.65 where he quoted the relevant part of the judgment of Oliver J, namely, whether the lack of provision produced "an unreasonable result", and 67, where, he concluded the threshold inquiry with the words "In my judgment, all of the above factors has [sic] produced an unreasonable result". He therefore concluded that it was strongly arguable that Eleanor King J was wrong to have discerned an error of law. He then addressed the criticism that the district judge had failed to balance the various factors, particularly the letter written in 2002 which made it clear that the deceased had no intention of making any provision for her daughter, and which Eleanor King J identified as a matter of particular relevance. In summary, his expressed view of the proposed appeal was as follows:

(i)   had the district judge dismissed her claim, it was unlikely that she would have secured a reversal on appeal;

(ii) however, an award had been made and it was highly arguable that the interference with his award was misconceived and also arguable that the subsidiary ground represented no more than an inappropriate attribution of different weight to the factors which he had considered;

(iii) the question was whether one or other of the criteria for a second appeal was met. He was not persuaded that the proposed appeal raised an important point of law or practice;

(iv) however, by the narrowest of margins he concluded that there was some other compelling reason for the court to hear the appeal and it was yielded by his unease about the way in which Eleanor King J had reasoned her reversal of the award to the applicant, which was of such great importance to her and her household, albeit that it was of a modest amount and subject to the appeal on quantum.

6–168   All three members of the Court of Appeal concluded that the district judge had not made any error which justified the exercise of the appellate jurisdiction to overturn his order. The primary argument for the charities[381] was that the case fell squarely within *Re Coventry*; there was simply an impecunious applicant and an estate from which her needs could be met. She was not disabled from working and her precarious financial position was the result of the way in which she had chosen to lead her life. She had no expectation of any benefit from her mother and there was nothing which made it objectively unreasonable for her to receive no provision from the estate, save for her necessitous circumstances, which were insufficient without more. The judge had been entitled and bound to set aside the district judge's judgment; he had overemphasised J's subjective reasons for excluding H from benefit rather than assessing whether the result was

---

[381] *Ilott v Mitson* [2012] 1 F.L.R. 170, CA, at [36]–[40].

objectively reasonable. Wall P rejected that argument for the following reasons:

(i) the district judge had not asked himself the wrong question; he had gone through the s.3 factors and quoted the relevant passage from *Re Coventry*[382] which emphasised that the result must be unreasonable;

(ii) he did not err in the balancing of the s.3 factors. Further, he was not under an obligation to "balance" the s.3 factors or to explain why the combination of those factors led him to conclude that no provision was unreasonable. Having reached the stage at which his discretion fell to be exercised, he explained fully what relief he was minded to award, and why[383];

(iii) he was plainly right to hold:

(1) that the daughter was entitled to make a life with a partner of her choice and have a family of her own, and reasonably to hope that a parent would accept such a choice and not blame her for it; and

(2) that it was reasonable for her to remain at home and that even if she were able to obtain paid work outside the home, she would still be in need and could support herself only "to some limited extent".

Wall P concluded that the case was clearly distinguishable from *Re Coventry* and that the district judge's findings under the s.3 exercise were amply sufficient for him to arrive at the value judgment that the absence of provision was unreasonable. The passage from the judgment of the district judge which underlies that conclusion[384] (and which, as Wilson LJ had noted, Eleanor King J had not gone on to consider) reads:

"In my judgment, all of the above factors *have produced an unreasonable result* in that no provision was made for [H] in her mother's will in circumstances where [H] is in some financial need. However, I accept that [H] has not had any expectancy of any provision for herself. [H and her husband] have managed their lives over many years without any expectancy that [H] would receive anything. That does not mean that *the result is a reasonable one* in the straitened circumstances of the family. But it does mean, in my judgment, that provision must be limited."

As well as commenting on the manner in which value judgments are **6–169** arrived at, the judgment of Arden LJ addresses the important matter of the

---

[382] At 475C–D; the passage is quoted at [2010] 1 F.L.R. 1613, at 1622, para.45. See also *Ilott v Mitson*, at [44]–[45].

[383] *Ilott v Mitson*, at [52]–[53].

[384] *Ilott v Mitson* [2012] 1 F.L.R. 170, CA, quoted by Wall P at [44]; his emphasis added. "[H]" has been substituted for "[appellant]".

claimant's way of life and how it should be regarded. In relation to the process of making the value judgments she said:

> "It is a reality in the twenty-first century that judges are called upon to make judgments of this kind in different cases and in different circumstances. They must do so with such assistance as they can find in existing decided cases. If (as often happens) there are no decided cases, they must decide questions involving value judgments within [the] four corners of the statutory framework and with the benefit of their own awareness and experience of society and social issues, and their own considered view of how such matters ought fairly to be decided in the society in which we live."

This passage, it is submitted, identifies pitfalls for practitioners. The extent of the assistance which might be derived from a value judgment in a decided case would itself have to be evaluated against a possibly different background of society and social issues than that which obtained at the time that the value judgment under consideration was made. Furthermore, *Ilott v Mitson* is a paradigm example of a case in which the "considered view(s) of how such matters ought fairly to be decided in the society in which we live" expressed by the two judges who had previously dealt with it were diametrically opposed. As Arden LJ analysed the district judge's judgment, it contained three value judgments.[385] The third of these was that families such as those of the claimant and her husband "were not all to be blamed for their lack of income which makes a claim for tax credits necessary and possible". This passage from her judgment highlights the importance of not interfering with value judgments unless they are plainly wrong. In effect, the district judge held that her impecuniosity should not weigh against her in the scales because it was the result of the perfectly reasonable way in which she and her husband chose to live their lives. Conversely, Eleanor King J had taken the view that she had to accept the consequences of her "lifestyle choice", even though acknowledging that her constant presence, and her husband's frequent presence around the house was an "inestimable advantage" to the children.[386] Given that both of those views are tenable,[387] the proper exercise of the appellate jurisdiction does not permit the first to be displaced by the second; though, as Arden LJ observed further on in her judgment, the fact that the claimant had chosen that particular way of life would be relevant to quantum; a point which the district judge had also taken.[388]

6–170   The factors that appear to have tipped the balance in the appellant's

---

[385] *Ilott v Mitson* [2012] 1 F.L.R. 170, CA, at [67]–[75]. The passage quoted above is at [68].
[386] *H v J's Personal Representatives, Blue Cross, RSPB and RSPCA* [2010] 1 F.L.R. 1613, at [61(iii)].
[387] As Black LJ said, the conclusion that Eleanor King J reached was meticulously reasoned and well within the ambit of decisions that were open to her and would not be vulnerable to the attentions of this court; *Ilott v Mitson*, at [79].
[388] *Ilott v Mitson* [2012] 2 F.L.R. 170, CA at [73]; and see *H v J's Personal Representatives, Blue Cross, RSPB and RSPCA* [2010] 1 F.L.R. 1613, at [63].

favour are, perhaps, most readily identifiable from the judgment of Black LJ.[389] She observed that the court, on the instant appeal, was concerned only with the "first question"; that is, the question whether the dispositions of the will were such as to make reasonable provision for the claimant. She understood that Eleanor King J would have been troubled by the district judge's focus on what he considered to be the unreasonable conduct of the testatrix. Had his judgment rested there and his conclusion been based on that one circumstance, it would have been rightly overturned; but it did not. After citation of relevant authority, his judgment revealed:

> "...a consideration which is not confined to the unreasonableness (in the District Judge's view) of the deceased's conduct but also extends to 'all of the above factors' which he said[390] (in wording reflecting that used in his earlier quotation from *Re Coventry*) combined to produce 'an unreasonable result' in that no provision at all was made for [the appellant] in her mother's will."

Black LJ went on to provide the following valuable exposition of the way **6–171** in which the law relating to the ascertainment of the answer to "the first question" has developed:

> "A dispassionate study of each of the matters set out in section 3(1) will not provide the answer to the question whether the will makes reasonable financial provision for the applicant, no matter how thorough and careful it is. As Judge LJ said in *Re Hancock* at 355C, section 3 provides no guidance about the relative importance to be attached to each of the relevant criteria. So between the dispassionate study and the answer to the first question lies the value judgment to which the authorities have referred. It seems to me that the jurisprudence reveals a struggle to articulate, for the benefit of the parties in the particular case and of practitioners, how that value judgment has been, or should be, made on a given set of facts. Inevitably, this has led to statements that this or that matter is not enough to found a claim and this or that matter is required."[391]

She then addressed the proposition that financial need cannot of itself ever be enough to make it unreasonable that no provision had been made for the deceased, citing by way of example the statement by Butler-Sloss LJ[392] that "As Oliver J pointed out in *Re Coventry*, necessitous circumstances cannot be in themselves the reason to alter the testator's dispositions". As to this, Black LJ observed that:

---

[389] *Ilott v Mitson* [2012] 2 F.L.R. 170, CA at [80]–[84], [89]–[98].
[390] Which, as Black LJ noted at [84], he had set out at paras [48]–[63] of his judgment.
[391] *Ilott v Mitson* [2012] 2 F.L.R. 170, at [88].
[392] *Espinosa v Bourke* [1999] 1 F.L.R. 747, CA, at 755G.

"A close analysis of the authorities reveals, however, that a bald statement of that kind can be misleading if taken out of context. Necessitous circumstances will never actually be the sole factor from amongst the section 3(1) list to feature in a case."

6–172   Among the other factors which are always to be considered are the size and nature of the net estate and also the position of the beneficiaries. Black LJ had difficulty with the way in which this aspect of the case was approached in *Cameron v Treasury Solicitor*[393] where it was said that the devolution of the estate to the Crown could not enhance the applicant's claim and was a neutral factor, not relevant to the criteria to be taken into account under s.3. However, if the presence of a needy beneficiary had the potential to weaken the applicant's claim (as it must have where the estate is limited), so, in Black LJ's judgment, must the absence of any beneficiary in the conventional sort of need have the potential to assist the applicant. In this case, there was an estate of £486,000 which had been left to charities to which the testatrix had no particular attachment. These were circumstances which, in Black LJ's words, had the potential to assist the applicant. Similarly, in *Debenham*,[394] where the applicant was an only daughter who had married and excited her mother's disapproval by doing so, and almost the entire estate of £172,000 had been left to charity, Ewbank J had observed that the deceased had no obligations or responsibilities to the charities. There, the factor that tipped the balance in the applicant's favour was the obligation which he found that the mother had to assist her daughter who was in difficult financial circumstances and afflicted by epilepsy. In the instant case, the multiplicity of factors, one of which was the perceived unreasonable conduct of the testatrix, combined to produce an unreasonable result.

(4) Quantum

6–173   In his assessment of reasonable provision, the district judge was hampered by lack of information about the effect which any award would have on the tax credits of £8,112 and housing benefit of £5,092 which accounted for roughly two thirds of the family's total income of £20,386 in the years 2006–2007. He rejected the contentions of both parties as to what would constitute reasonable provision. A small sum (£3,000–£5,000) for driving lessons and to help the claimant get back into work was insufficient. The claimant sought provision which would enable her to buy and extend the family home and for a capital sum to fund an annual income shortfall, based on a proposed budget, of £27,776. That capital sum alone would have more than exhausted the estate.

6–174   He accepted that the claimant's continuing obligations and responsibilities to her children[395] made it reasonable for her to wish to remain at

---

[393] *Cameron v Treasury Solicitor* [1996] 2 F.L.R. 716, CA.
[394] *Re Debenham* [1986] 1 F.L.R. 404 at 409E.
[395] Aged, at the date of the hearing in May 2007, 23, 20, 18, 15 and 10.

home rather than seek work or, at any rate, full-time work, but that it would be reasonable to expect her to attempt to support herself by some paid work in the course of the next few years. He made an approximate estimate of what was required for her maintenance by equating it to her notional half share of the tax credits (£4,056) which, in his view, could be said to be an indicated amount which the government accepted as being currently needed to provide her with a reasonable, but basic, standard of living. He arrived at a capitalised sum of £69,200[396] which he reduced to £50,000 on the basis that the claimant ought to eventually be able to find some modest part-time work in order to reduce her dependency. In conclusion he explicitly stated that the figure had a significant degree of approximation but that in the absence of any better method he had had to do the best he could.

By the time of the first appeal on quantum, almost six years after the original hearing, the claimant's circumstances had changed in that only the youngest child, then aged 17, was living at home and the price required for the purchase of the home had fallen to £125,000 (taking into account the discount available to her). The claim was now reduced to £150,000 to meet the purchase price, the costs of the transfer and a modest sum to meet some basic expenses. Parker J declined to allow the appeal.[397] The district judge had found that it was not appropriate to meet the claimant's housing expenses but had made an award intended to provide what Parker J described as "a windfall for her to spend as she liked on improving her circumstances". She could not say that he was manifestly wrong, or even wrong, in taking the view that notwithstanding the claimant and her husband lived in straitened circumstances, the fact that they had done so for many years did not justify an award which improved their circumstances. She rejected the argument which was, in effect, that because there would be no benefit to the claimant unless her housing needs were met, the award must achieve that result. That was the wrong approach and inconsistent with the judge's determination that the award was tempered by the lack of expectancy.   **6–175**

On appeal the leading judgment was given by Arden LJ (with whom the other members of the court agreed) who considered that reasonable financial provision could only be made for the claimant by providing her with the sum that she required to buy her home. She identified two fundamental errors which led her to conclude that the award should be set aside.[398] They were: **6–176**

(i)   the district judge had stated that because of the claimant's lack of expectancy and her ability to live within her means, the award

---

[396] The then current *Tables At A Glance* gave a figure of £173,000 as the capital sum required to meet a net annual income need of £10,000 (the lowest figure for which the Duxbury calculations were made) for a woman aged 46, and the district judge took 40 per cent of that as the amount which would fund an annual need of £4,000.

[397] *Ilott v Mitson* [2015] 1 F.L.R 291, [52]–[54]. The five amended original grounds of appeal [29] are addressed at [42]–[50]. Of the three additional grounds of appeal [30], Parker J held that one could not be raised at that stage since it concerned a matter which there had been ample opportunity to raise in the court below. The others are dealt with at [38]–[50].

[398] *Ilott v Mitson* [2015] 2 F.L.R. 1409, CA, at [34]–[36].

should be limited, but he had not stated how he had limited the award to reflect those matters. It was wrong in law to state that the award had been limited for those reasons without explaining what the award might have otherwise been and to what extent it was limited by the matters in question;

(ii)   he was required to calculate financial provision for the claimant's maintenance but he did not know what effect the award of £50,000 would have had on her state benefits. He made a working assumption that a payment such as he had ordered would disentitle the family to most if not all of those benefits. Failure to verify that assumption undermined the logic of the award.

Having considered all the s.3(1) factors, Arden LJ concluded that the claimant's resources, even with the state benefits, were at such a basic level that they outweighed the importance that would normally be attached to the fact that the claimant was an adult child who had been living independently for many years. The correct test was whether the current living standard was sufficient, and the court should not be motivated by a desire to provide an improved standard of living, as opposed to a desire to meet appropriate living needs; nor was the court bound to limit maintenance to mere subsistence level. Her present income was not reasonable financial provision given the restrictions which she had to impose on her expenditure and the lack of any provision to meet future needs such as those arising from age or ill health.

6–177   Arden LJ then considered how, in those circumstances, the court should set about determining the amount of an award if the effect of the award was to remove state benefits. In her judgment, the court had to balance the claims on the estate fairly. In a passage considered at some length by the Supreme Court, she went on to say:

"There is no doubt that, if the claimant for whom reasonable financial provision needs to be made is elderly or disabled and has extra living costs, consideration would have to be given to meeting these. In my judgment, the same applies to the case where a party has extra financial needs because she relies on state benefits, which must be preserved. Ms Reed submits that the provision of housing would not do this. I disagree. The provision of housing would enable her both to receive a capitalised sum and to keep her tax credits. If those benefits are not preserved then the result is that achieved by DJ Million's order in this case; there is little or no provision for maintenance at all. The claim of the appellant then has to be balanced against that of the Charities but since they do not rely on any competing need they are not prejudiced by what may be a higher award than the court would otherwise need to make."[399]

---

[399]   *Ilott v Mitson* [2015] 2 F.L.R. 1409, CA, at [60]–[61].

The right award, in her judgment was £143,000, being the cost of acquiring the property, the reasonable expenses of acquiring it, together with the option to receive a capital sum not exceeding £20,000 to provide a small amount of income to supplement her state benefits without the need for equity release.

The judgment of the seven-member Supreme Court, delivered by Lord   **6–178**
Hughes, opens with a brief statement of the history and origins of the family provision legislation which ends with the observation that:

> "Some of the factors inevitably dealt with in this judgment may apply also to types of case other than those of adult children living separately from the deceased, but there is no occasion for this court to attempt to meet every difficulty to which claims for family provision may give rise."

Following the review of the facts and of the statutory framework, the judgment addresses the concept of maintenance, drawing attention to the distinction between the paragraphs of s.1(2) which shows that it cannot extend to any or every thing which it would be desirable for the claimant to have[400] and that it must import provision to meet the everyday expenses of living. The level at which maintenance may be provided for is clearly flexible and falls to be assessed on the facts of each case and provision for housing may, as Browne-Wilkinson J envisaged (obiter) in *In re Dennis*,[401] be made in some cases. Families have for generations provided for the maintenance of relatives, and indeed for others such as former employees, by housing them. But it was necessary to remember that the statutory power is to provide for maintenance, not to confer capital on the claimant.[402] If housing were provided by way of maintenance, it would be likely more often to be provided by a life interest rather than by a capital sum.

The words "...reasonable for the claimant to receive" in s.1(2) of the 1975   **6–179**
Act are words of objective standard of financial provision, to be determined by the court. The judgment continues:

> "[16] ... The Act does not say that the court may make an order when it judges that the deceased acted unreasonably. That too would be an objective judgment, but it would not be the one required by the Act.
>
> [17] Nevertheless, the reasonableness of the deceased's decisions are undoubtedly capable of being a factor for consideration within section 3(1)(g), and sometimes section 3(1)(d). Moreover, there may not always be a significant difference in outcome between applying the correct test contained in the Act, and asking the wrong question whether the

---

[400] *In re Jennings, deceased, Harlow v National Westminster Bank* [1994] Ch. 286, CA and *In re Christie (deceased)* [1979] Ch. 168 were referred to as cases in which the provision unsuccessfully sought (in *Jennings*) and awarded (in *Christie*) were cited as examples of provision which was not "maintenance".

[401] *Re Dennis* [1981] 2 All E.R. 140, at 145–46.

[402] *Myers v Myers* [2005] W.T.L.R. 851, at [89]–[90], [99]–[101].

deceased acted reasonably. If the will does not make reasonable
financial provision for the claimant, it may often be because the
deceased acted unreasonably in failing to make it. For this reason it is
very easy to slip into the error of applying the wrong test. It is necessary
for courts to be alert to the danger, because the two tests will by no
means invariably arrive at the same answer. The deceased may have
acted reasonably at the time that his will was made,[403] but the circumstances of the claimant may have altered, for example by supervening chronic illness or incapacity, and the deceased may have been
unaware of the full circumstances, or unable to make a new will in
time."

6–180 Another aspect of reasonable provision is whether, and if so, how, it is
related to the needs of the claimant. However necessitous the circumstances
of the claimant,[404] cases of long estrangement may, according to the judge's
assessment of the particular facts, be an example of the proposition that
needs are not always enough to justify a claim under the Act. It may be, in
any event, that competing claims render it impracticable to satisfy the
claimant's needs, however reasonable, or that the nature or circumstances of
the relationship between the deceased and the claimant may affect what is
the just order to make and whether the claimant's needs are to be satisfied in
full (even if that requires an award of the maximum which the estate can
afford) or in part.

6–181 After a short section summarising the history of the proceedings, the
judgment deals with the decision of the Court of Appeal. As to the first
fundamental error, that is, the failure to explain how the district judge had
limited the award to reflect the matters which caused him to limit it,[405] the
Supreme Court said:

> "[34] The Act requires a single assessment by the judge of what rea-
> sonable financial provision should be made in all the circumstances of
> the case. It does not require the judge to fix some hypothetical standard
> of reasonable provision and then either add to it, or discount from it,
> by percentage points or otherwise, for variable factors. To the contrary,
> the section 3 factors, which are themselves all variables and which are
> likely often to be in tension one with another, are all to be considered so
> far as they are relevant, and in the light of them a single assessment of
> reasonable financial provision is to be made. There is no warrant in the
> Act for requiring a process of the kind suggested by the Court of
> Appeal. If the judge were to arrive at a figure for reasonable financial

---

[403] This extract continues with a reference to *Re Hancock* [1998] 2 F.L.R. 346, CA, where the
change in circumstances was a very substantial increase in the value of the estate after the
death of the testator.

[404] *Cameron v Treasury Solicitor* [1996] 2 F.L.R. 716, CA.

[405] *Ilott v Mitson* [2015] 2 F.L.R. 1409, at [35], referring to para.67 of the district judge's
judgment.

provision without one or more of the relevant facts in the case, he would not be undertaking the assessment required by the Act."

Concluding that he had not made the suggested error or any error, and observing that he had "dutifully worked his way through all the s.3 factors", the Supreme Court approved his reasoning as follows:

"[35] ... The long estrangement was the reason the testator made the will she did. It meant that Mrs Ilott was not only a non-dependent adult child but had made her life entirely separately from her mother, and lacked any expectation of benefit from her estate. Because of these consequences, the estrangement was one of the two dominant factors in this case; the other was Mrs Ilott's very straitened financial position. Some judges might legitimately have concluded that the very long and deep estrangement had meant that the deceased had no remaining obligation to make any provision for her independent adult daughter - as indeed did Eleanor King J when it appeared that she had scope to re-make the decision. As it was, the judge was perfectly entitled to reach the conclusion which he did, namely that there was a failure of reasonable financial provision, but that what reasonable provision would be was coloured by the nature of the relationship between mother and daughter."

Turning to the second fundamental error identified by the Court of Appeal, the Supreme Court considered the real gravamen of that criticism to be: **6–182**

"[39] ... not so much that the District Judge did not 'verify' the benefits rules, but that he produced an award which had little or no value to the claimant because of the impact on benefits."

While acknowledging that the making of such an award might justify the exercise of the appellate jurisdiction, particularly if made in ignorance of the true position, the Supreme Court absolved him in both respects. The award was demonstrably of value to the claimant; it was a central feature of her financial position that although the family was just able to manage on its income, that was at the cost of being unable to maintain the ordinary domestic equipment on which every household depends, and she had produced a list of that equipment; in her case as originally presented she had estimated the cost of replacement and necessary refurbishment at £40,950.[406] She had made a strong case for the necessity of spending a substantial sum on items which could properly be described as necessities for daily living, and expenditure of that nature fitted in perfectly well with the established concept of maintenance. If she spent the bulk of the award in that way so as

---

[406] See para.70(4) of the district judge's judgment; paras 70–75 are quoted in the Supreme Court judgment at [37].

to reduce her capital to below £16,000, she would have retained her entitlement to the means-tested benefits[407] and improved the family's standard of living. It was therefore wrong to describe the award as having little or no value to her. It followed that the district judge did not make the second fundamental error attributed to him. Thus, neither of the grounds on which the Court of Appeal had relied to justify their revisiting of his award[408] had been made out, and in consequence, their order should be set aside and his award should be restored.

6–183   One point in the claimant's case on the appeal which may usefully be discussed here is her contention that the district judge wrongly took the level of tax credits and child benefit (half of which he attributed to her) as a benchmark of basic maintenance income as recognised by the government. This had been the subject of comment by Ryder LJ, who had said:

"As a matter of public policy, the court is not constrained to treat a person's reasonable financial provision as being limited by their existing state benefits nor is the court's function substituted for by any assessment of benefits undertaken by the state."[409]

However, although the district judge had referred to this as an indication of minimum income needs, and checked his figure of £50,000 against the capital sum which would produce an annual £4,000 on a *Duxbury* basis, he had not made his award on that basis. He had considered the cases put before him and concluded that Mrs Ilott's reasonable needs were greater than those put forward by the charities. He had made clear that the award, which met many of her needs for maintenance, was limited to take account of the estrangement, and it was not vitiated by erroneous reliance on the level of income produced by the working tax credits and child benefit. There was nothing in it "outside the generous ambit of judgment available to him".

(5) Reflections on the judgments of the Supreme Court

6–184   What lessons may we learn from the first Inheritance Act claim to reach the Supreme Court? The claim was of an unusual nature; the matters which swayed the balance, in the judgment of the district judge, in favour of the claimant, had not been decisive in any previous reported case and, as was recognised at various stages, the same facts might properly have led another judge to decide the claim differently. In particular, although he had referred to "the ordinary family obligations of a mother towards her only child who was an independent adult",[410] he did not give any indication of the nature of

---

[407] Subject, so long as her capital exceeded £6,000, to the "tariff income" deduction of £1 per week for every £250 above £6,000.
[408] The difficulties with the award which the Court of Appeal had made are discussed at [44]–[47].
[409] *Ilott v Mitson* [2015] 2.F.L.R. 1409, CA, at [69].
[410] *H v J's Personal Representatives, Blue Cross, RSPB and RSPCA* [2010] 1 F.L.R. 1613, at [50], quoting para.51 of his judgment.

those obligations or of why they should be thought to exist in relation to any independent adult, let alone an independent adult who bore a substantial responsibility for the breakdown in the relationship. Nevertheless, it was not held, at any judicial level, that it (or any other matter which was a factor in his decision) was one which he was not entitled to take into account.[411] Of course, if that had been the case, the appellate jurisdiction would plainly have been exercisable. But on the first occasion when his decision was overturned, Eleanor King J did not identify that, or any other matter, as being outside the range of the factors that he was entitled to take into account, but in effect held that he had attached too much weight to those which he found to be in favour of the claimant.[412] On the second occasion, the criticism of the Court of Appeal, which viewed his award as being inadequate, was directed at his failure to quantify the weight that he attached to his reasons for limiting it and what was perceived as the faulty basis on which he arrived at the figure.[413]

Nonetheless, it is submitted that there has been no departure, let alone a radical departure, from established principles but, rather, a reaffirmation of well-established truths. The dictum of Browne-Wilkinson J in *Re Dennis*[414] concerning maintenance was approved and it was held that the inclusion of an element of provision for the improvement of the claimant's domestic circumstances was well within that concept. The test of reasonable provision formulated by Oliver J in *Re Coventry*[415] was approved and the observations of Goff LJ relating to the two-stage approach[416] were explained. On the exercise of the appellate jurisdiction the well-known observations of Lord Hoffmann in *Piglowska v Piglowski*[417] were directly in point. It was to "kill the parties with kindness" to permit marginal appeals in cases which were essentially individual value judgments such as those under the 1975 Act should be.

6–185

In the concluding section of the judgment there is a welcome clarification of the position of charities. The court was informed that the appeal had been brought by the charities largely on principle because of the possible impact of the decision below on other cases, and it is true that successful family provision claims under both the 1938[418] and the 1975 Act[419] have resulted in the depletion of the benefits which charitable beneficiaries stood to receive.

6–186

---

[411] Indeed, it appears that it was tacitly accepted as a matter to be taken into account, though (as argued for the charities) not a moral obligation or special circumstance as found in previous cases, and in any event outweighed by the claimant's status as an independent adult; see *Ilott v Mitson* [2015] 2 F.L.R 1409, CA, at [48]–[49].

[412] *H v J's Personal Representatives, Blue Cross, RSPB and RSPCA* [2010] 1 F.L.R. 1613, at [67].

[413] *Ilott v Mitson* [2015] 2 F.L.R. 1409, CA, at [34]–[36].

[414] *Re Dennis* [1981] 2 All E.R. 140, at 145–46.

[415] *Re Coventry* [1980] Ch. 461, CA, at 474–75.

[416] *Re Coventry* [1980] Ch. 461, CA at 487, referring to Oliver J's judgment at 469 and characterising the determination of the first question as a value judgment and the second as an exercise of discretion.

[417] *Piglowska v Piglowski* [1999] 1 W.L.R. 1360, 1373–1374.

[418] *Millward v Shenton* [1972] 1 W.L.R. 711, CA.

[419] *Re Besterman* [1984] Ch. 458; *Re Bunning* [1984] Ch. 480.

However, in none of those judgments was it said, as it was in *Ilott v Mitson*,[420] that they had no expectation of benefit. In its observations on the order which the Court of Appeal had made, the Supreme Court said:

"[46] ... the order under appeal would give little if any weight to the quarter of a century of estrangement or to the testator's very clear wishes. The Court of Appeal indeed offered the view (at paragraph 51) that these factors counted for little, and that Mrs Ilott's lack of expectation of any benefit from the estate was likewise of little weight, in part because the charities had no expectation of benefit either. Those observations should be treated with caution. The claim of the charities was not on a par with that of Mrs Ilott. True, it was not based on personal need, but charities depend heavily on testamentary bequests for their work, which is by definition of public benefit and in many cases will be for demonstrably humanitarian purposes. More fundamentally, these charities were the chosen beneficiaries of the deceased. They did not have to justify a claim on the basis of need under the 1975 Act, as Mrs Ilott necessarily had to do. The observation, at para 61 of the Court of Appeal judgment, cited above, that, because the charities had no needs to plead, they were not prejudiced by an increased award to Mrs Ilott is, with great respect, also erroneous; their benefit was reduced by any such award. That may be the right outcome in a particular case, but it cannot be ignored that an award under the Act is at the expense of those whom the testator intended to benefit."

6–187   On a practical note, the course which the proceedings took before the district judge and the amount of judicial consideration which had to be devoted to the difficulties that he consequently encountered in formulating his award should remind practitioners of the necessity to consider carefully and identify, where possible, the nature of the award sought, to produce estimates of income need based on realistic assumptions, and, where relevant, to take especial care to ascertain the effect of whatever award might be made on entitlement to means-tested benefits or to credits subject to an income threshold.

6–188   Baroness Hale of Richmond, with whom Lord Kerr of Tonaghmore and Lord Wilson agreed, wrote a further judgment only to demonstrate what, in her view, was the unsatisfactory state of the present law.[421] She drew attention to the profound questions raised by the case, about:

"...the nature of family obligations, the relationship between family obligations and the state, and the relationship between the freedom of property owners to dispose of their property as they see fit and their duty to fulfil their family obligations",

---

[420] *Ilott v Mitson* [2015] 2 F.L.R. 1409, CA, Arden LJ, at [51(ii)].
[421] *Ilott v Mitson*, at [66].

and quoted the following passage from *Albery*[422]:

"The protection of the rights of the family as an essential unit in society is a primary concern of most systems of law. Complete freedom of testation, as enjoyed under English law for a brief period of forty-seven years, is therefore by the standards of comparative jurisprudence an anomaly."

The judgment surveys public attitudes towards testamentary freedom and the wide range of public opinion about the circumstances in which adult descendants ought or ought not to be able to make a claim on an estate which would otherwise go elsewhere. It refers to the Law Commission recommendation to remove the limits imposed by the 1938 Act on claims by adult children, which involved "leaving the court to distinguish between the deserving and the undeserving",[423] but expresses dissatisfaction that the law in its present state provides no guidance as to the factors to be taken into account in deciding whether an adult child is deserving or undeserving and that the Law Commission did not reconsider the fundamental principles underlying such claims when it reported in 2011. The Law Commission[424] expressed the view that:

6–189

"...the limitation of family provision to the 'maintenance' level sets an important practical limit on an adult's claim, because most adults will be supporting themselves. The 1975 Act has been framed so as to be consistent with testamentary freedom; there is no obligation to leave property to a child in one's will, and no principle that a child must inherit solely because of a blood relationship. Testamentary freedom is restricted, so far as one's children are concerned, only where necessary to meet need or some unusual circumstance."

The report went on to note that the Court of Appeal in *Ilott v Mitson*[425] had the opportunity to "conduct a thorough review of the approach to be taken to adult children's claims under the 1975 Act", that the case reinforced the principle that no additional words were to be read into the statute, and that it cast no doubt on the pre-existing case-law. The conclusion drawn was that "it remains the case, therefore, that the expectations of an adult child under the 1975 Act must be quite limited". The report also came down decisively against any legislative reform directed towards giving a greater chance of success to claims by adult children, referring both to the

6–190

---

[422] Michael Albery, *The Inheritance (Family Provision) Act 1938* (London: Sweet & Maxwell, 1950), 1.

[423] Law Com. LC 61, at para.76. That proposal, made in Law Com. WP 42 (1971), was widely supported by those who commented.

[424] Law Commission, *Intestacy and Family Provision on Death* (2011), Law Com. No.331, at para.6.6.

[425] *Ilott v Mitson* [2011] EWCA (Civ) 346; [2011] F.C.R. 1; [2011] W.T.L.R. 779; [2012] 1 F.L.R. 170, per Sir Nicholas Wall P, at [9]. Judgment was given on 31 March 2011; the Law Commission report was ordered to be printed on 13 December 2011.

complexities of the legislation that would be required and the interference with testamentary freedom which would result.[426] It recognised that circumstances could exist in which an adult child could be "deserving" of an inheritance, but commented that:

> "Where the circumstances of a family, or of an individual's lifestyle or conduct, make it appropriate or important that someone receive an inheritance, generally only a will can achieve that."

6–191   It is submitted that that is entirely consistent with Oliver J's much quoted dictum in *Re Coventry*[427] that the purpose of the Act is not to provide legacies or rewards for meritorious conduct. If the testator has failed to recognise that "deserving" conduct, and the adult child is not in need of maintenance, it goes unrewarded. The facts of *Ilott v Mitson* were such as to accentuate that aspect of the case, whose outcome attracted the disapproval of a substantial and vociferous segment of public opinion which viewed the charities as more deserving than the claimant. It was in that sense an extreme case, on the facts of which it was possible to arrive at diametrically opposed value judgments, and it is not easy to see what further guidance in distinguishing between deserving and undeserving claimants (assuming, which is open to doubt, that any such distinction can usefully or properly be made), or what further examination of fundamental principles, could have avoided the situation which Baroness Hale's judgment deplores.

(f) Unsuccessful Claims

6–192   The cases in which applicants have failed are of two main types, which one could call "neutral" and "adverse". The "neutral" cases are those in which there is simply no reason for disturbing the status quo. These include *Re Homer*,[428] where it was held that there was no obligation to provide for a married daughter who had a husband working and running his own business; *Re Rowlands*[429] where it was held that a small moral obligation was owed to the applicant mother, but none to the adult daughters who also applied; and *Wade v Varney*[430] where it was held, in effect, that the law of intestacy had made reasonable provision for the claimant. In that case, the deceased had died intestate on 28 February 2001, and the net estate of £114,731 fell to be divided equally between her son and daughter. The claimant son had been living with his mother in her house, which was the main asset of the estate. He wished to remain in the house and made a claim

---

[426] Law Commission Report No.331, *Intestacy and Family Provision on Death* (2011); see the consultation responses and subsequent discussion, at paras 6.13–6.18 and 6.19–6.26, respectively.

[427] *Re Coventry* [1980] Ch. 461, CA, at 474G.

[428] *Re Homer, Homer v Rann* unreported 6 November 1978, CA.

[429] *Re Rowlands* [1984] F.L.R. 813, CA. The mother was awarded £3,000 having regard to her growing need for improved accommodation; the report of the case acknowledges her contribution to the welfare of the family and the fact that she was 90 years of age and disabled.

[430] *Wade v Varney* [2003] W.T.L.R. 1535.

under the 1975 Act for, in effect, the whole value of the house; the judge concluded that, objectively, there was nothing unreasonable about the estate being equally divided. He applied to appeal out of time and permission was refused by the Court of Appeal. Tuckey LJ said that the question was whether the law of intestacy made reasonable provision. Both parties were adults, both were earning. Equality was the obvious answer; equality was the result of the intestacy. The contrary was almost unarguable. More recently, the adult son's claim in *Christofides v Seddon*[431] failed as it was found that, notwithstanding his disabilities, his mother had discharged her obligations to him by sharing her residuary estate equally between him and the other three beneficiaries. *Hope v Knight*[432] was a claim by a surviving spouse and the daughter of the marriage; the daughter, aged 28, had learning difficulties as a child and was suffering from depression and obsessive compulsive disorder, but was able to earn about £7,600 per year and had some other financial resources. The main reason for the dismissal of both her and her mother's claims appears to have been the finding that the deceased was entitled to take, and reasonably took, the view that the financial arrangements which he made at the time of separation from his wife had satisfied his obligations towards and, although he might have been more generous to his daughter, his death had triggered a pension for her of £2,000 per year for life and a bequest of £45,000 which she otherwise would not have received. In *Ames v Jones*[433] where the claim of the 41-year-old daughter of the deceased's first marriage could have been met only at the expense of the 63-year-old widow of his second marriage, who was the sole beneficiary, it was found that the estate was not large enough to meet the needs of them both. The widow had at most a modest surplus of income over expenditure and required the entire capital of the estate to meet her reasonable needs, whereas the daughter was capable of working and had not satisfied the court as to her own needs and resources.

However, the most important of the "neutral" cases is *Re Jennings*.[434] Its **6–193** importance lies in the formulation of the principle that the failure of the deceased to discharge an obligation owed to the claimant during earlier life is not to be taken into account unless it was subsisting at the time of the deceased's death. In *Jennings*, the applicant (H) was the 50-year-old son of the deceased (J). When H was two years of age, his parents separated and he and his mother went to live with her parents. She and J divorced and she subsequently remarried. H was brought up by his mother and stepfather, and J neither had contact with H nor made any financial provision for him during his upbringing. J left his estate, worth some £300,000, partly to distant relatives and partly to charities. At the time of the hearing, H, who was married with two adult daughters, was able to maintain a comfortable

[431] *Christofides v Seddon* [2014] W.L.T.R. 215.
[432] *Hope v Knight* [2011] W.T.L.R. 583, at [43]–[45]. Both claims were dismissed "with some misgivings".
[433] *Ames v Jones* unreported 16 August 2016 (Mr Recorder Halpern QC, County Court at Central London).
[434] *Re Jennings, Harlow v National Westminster Bank* [1994] Ch. 286, CA.

standard of living. At first instance, it was held that there was no good reason for J to have failed to support H during his minority and he had failed to honour his moral obligations. H was awarded £40,000 in order to enable him to discharge or reduce the mortgage on his house.

6–194 The Court of Appeal reversed this decision, holding that the judge[435] had erred, either in law or in principle, by construing s.3(1)(d) of the 1975 Act as including obligations and responsibilities which J had failed to carry out during H's minority, and that the subsection referred, at any rate as a general rule, to those which the deceased had immediately before his death. In the words of Henry LJ:

> "So the Act of 1975 is limited to situations where reasonable financial provision has not been made. In answering that question it is in my judgment simply irrelevant that this father behaved as he did however much this behaviour may be deplored. It is not the purpose of the Act of 1975 to punish or redress past bad or unfeeling parental behaviour where that behaviour does not still impinge on the applicant's present financial situation."

In the leading judgment, Nourse LJ had said:

> "It was established by the decisions of Oliver J and of this court in *In Re Coventry, decd.* that, on an application by an adult son of the deceased who is able to earn, and earns, his own living, there must be some special circumstance, typically a moral obligation, towards him, before the first question can be determined in his favour. Although the decisions were in terms confined to the case of a son, the principle of them is applicable no less to the case of a daughter and, with developments in the structure of society, instances of its application in such cases may become more common."

Nourse LJ rejected the submission that the failure of the deceased to discharge his legal obligations and responsibilities at the time imposed a continuing moral obligation on him to make financial provision for the applicant at his death, though he did not wish to rule out the possibility, in another case, that circumstances might exist in which that submission would be valid.

6–195 The "adverse" cases, which, curiously, have so far all been claims by adult daughters, are characterised by the applicant having behaved (or having been perceived, by her parent or the court, to have behaved) in an unacceptable manner.[436] This appears to be the area of the law of family pro-

---

[435] Wall J (as he then was) who remarked in *Ilott v Mitson* [2012] 2 F.L.R. 170, at [26] that "We were, initially, spared *Re Jennings, deceased* [1994] Ch. 286, no doubt to spare my blushes, since my decision in that case was reversed by this court".

[436] "How, how, Cordelia, mend your speech a little/Or you may mar your fortunes" (W. Shakespeare, *King Lear*, Act I, scene 1). Lear, as events turned out, had adopted a mistaken view about the relative merits and demerits of his daughters.

vision in which the applicant's conduct assumes the greatest importance, though (as discussed in relation to *Espinosa v Bourke*)[437] care must be taken to avoid unduly emphasising such matters. These cases have been discussed in detail in Ch.4[438] and, for ease of reference, are simply listed here under the relevant heads of conduct, which are improvident conduct,[439] adoption of a way of life exciting disapproval,[440] vexation or distress,[441] financial abuse[442] and emotional abuse.[443]

9.—PERSONS TREATED BY THE DECEASED AS CHILDREN OF THE FAMILY

An eligible claimant under s.1(1)(d) of the 1975 Act was formerly defined as: **6–196**

> "...any person (not being a child of the deceased) who, in the case of any marriage to which the deceased was at any time a party, was treated by the deceased as a child of the family in relation to that marriage."

This provision was amended[444] by the insertion of the words "or civil partnership" after the word "marriage" in the two places in which it occurs. However, it has been further, and more fundamentally, amended by the Inheritance and Trustees' Powers Act 2014. In accordance with the Law Commission recommendation,[445] the amended definition of the eligible claimant is now:

> "Any person (not being a child of the deceased) who in relation to any marriage or civil partnership to which the deceased was at any time a party, or otherwise in relation to any family in which the deceased at any time stood in the role of a parent, was treated as a child of the family."

A further amendment inserts a new s.1(2A) whose purpose is to make clear that a family for these purposes may be a "single parent family" composed only of the deceased and the applicant. There is, at the time of writing, no reported case of an application under the amended provision.

Any comment based on only two reported cases must, at best, be tenta-   **6–197**

---

[437] *Espinosa v Bourke* [1999] 1 F.L.R. 747, paras 6–145, 6–146.
[438] The footnote references which follow identify the relevant paragraphs of Ch.4.
[439] *Robinson v Bird* [2003] W.T.L.R. 1535 (para.4–070); *Garland v Morris* [2007] 2 F.L.R. 528 (para.4–071).
[440] *Myers v Myers* [2005] W.T.L.R. 851 (para.4–073).
[441] *Re Portt, Allcorn v Harvey and Woodcock* unreported 25 March 1980, CA (para.4–078); *Williams v Johns* [1988] 2 F.L.R. 475 (para.4–078).
[442] *Bye v Colvin-Scott* [2010] W.T.L.R. 1 (para.4–079); *Wright v Waters* [2015] W.T.L.R. 353 (para.4–080).
[443] *Wright v Waters* [2015] W.T.L.R. 353 (para.4–080).
[444] Civil Partnership Act 2004 s.71 and Sch.4 para.15(4).
[445] Law Commission Report, *Intestacy and Family Provision Claims on Death*, Law Com. No.331, para.6.41. The reasons for this amendment are discussed in Ch.2(g), para.2–075.

tive; but the judgments in both *Re Callaghan*[446] and *Re Leach*,[447] where the applicants were, respectively, a step-son aged 47 and a step-daughter aged 57, appear to show an approach differing substantially from that which has generally been adopted where the applicant is an adult child of the deceased. There is no suggestion in either judgment that the *Re Coventry* barrier[448] has to be surmounted, and it is not immediately obvious why not. If there is any reason deriving from principle rather than from the facts of the individual cases, it presumably stems from the voluntary assumption of responsibility towards the applicant, on the part of the deceased.

6–198   It so happens that in both cases the deceased died intestate and those who took on the intestacy were siblings; three married sisters in *Re Callaghan*, and a brother and two married sisters in *Re Leach*. Of the competing claims of the applicant and the beneficiaries in *Re Callaghan*, it was said:

> "The obligations and responsibilities which the deceased had to the plaintiff were very considerable indeed; in effect they were the obligations of a widowed parent to a dutiful and responsible only child. The obligations and responsibilities of the deceased towards his sisters were those brought about by the fact of their blood relationship and by the remembrance of that part of their lives which they had shared together in the past. There was nothing to suggest that the deceased was under any other obligation or responsibility towards his sisters, and in that respect their position is very different indeed from that of the plaintiff to whom the deceased was committed."

The fact that the deceased's estate in effect derived from the assets of the plaintiff's mother was also taken into account. The order sought was for a lump sum which would enable the plaintiff to buy his council house without assuming the burden of a mortgage. This was held to be a reasonable requirement for his maintenance, and he was awarded £15,000 out of a net estate of £31,000.

6–199   In *Re Leach* the Court of Appeal enumerated an extensive list of facts which, taken together with the continuous nature of the relationship of mutual affection and trust between the applicant and her stepmother during the relevant period, clearly indicated a relationship in which the deceased assumed the position of a mother towards the applicant, with the attendant responsibilities and privileges. The fact that the deceased had never, during her lifetime contributed to the applicant's maintenance did not disqualify her from seeking relief. A relevant matter, not amounting to an estoppel but nevertheless placing the deceased under some moral obligation to the applicant, was that she had encouraged the applicant to believe that she

---

[446] *Re Callaghan* [1985] Fam. 1.
[447] *Re Leach* [1986] Ch. 286.
[448] A shorthand version of the dictum, applying in the case of adult sons capable of supporting themselves that for the claim to succeed, there must be some factor over and above kinship, necessitous circumstances and availability of assets out of which reasonable provision could be made.

would receive a substantial sum of money on her death, as a result of which she entered into an arrangement with a friend to buy a house jointly on mortgage. Both at first instance and in the Court of Appeal, it was considered that reasonable provision for the applicant's maintenance involved financial assistance with the running expenses of the house, including the mortgage repayments. There was no challenge to the evidence of the applicant's financial position and no evidence that the beneficiaries were in any particular need. Following an adjustment necessitated by an error in the court below as to the size of the net estate, the applicant was awarded £14,000 out of a net estate of £34,000 before deduction of costs, estimated at £7,000.

10.—PERSONS BEING MAINTAINED BY THE DECEASED IMMEDIATELY BEFORE THEIR DEATH

(a) General

When the scope of the family provision legislation was extended by the inclusion, in s.1(1) of the 1975 Act, of this class of applicant, there was a good deal of unfavourable comment both in Parliament and in the press to the effect that immoral relationships would be encouraged as a result. There was also some criticism of a more principled nature, on the basis that dependency was not the appropriate test for inclusion in the class since, the better the applicant had behaved towards the deceased by providing care and attention, the more consideration they would have given for the benefits received, resulting in a greater likelihood that the application would fail. Changing social attitudes have deprived the first type of comment of its force, while, in relation to the other criticism, the courts, as said in the commentary to Re Kirby,[449] "seem to be willing to do their best to ensure that s.1(1)(e) covers those that they consider to be deserving".

6–200

The definition of this category of applicant in s.1(1)(e) of the 1975 Act excludes persons who are included in any of the foregoing paragraphs of subs.1(1), though in practice, cohabitants, who come under para.1(1)(ba), often claim in the alternative as dependants. The definition has to be considered in conjunction with s.1(3) of the Act, which formerly provided that a person:

6–201

> "...shall be treated as being maintained by the deceased, either wholly or partly, as the case may be, if the deceased, otherwise than for full valuable consideration, was making a substantial contribution in money or money's worth, to the reasonable needs of that person."

Claims under s.1(1)(e) have proved a fertile source of dispute about the eligibility of the claimant. The cases in which the claimant has been found

---

[449] *Re Kirby* (1981) 11 Fam. Law 211.

not to be a dependant have been discussed in Ch.2,[450] as have the meanings of the words or phrases "immediately", "otherwise than for full valuable consideration", "reasonable needs" and "substantial" in s.1(3) and "assumption of responsibility" in s.3(4).[451] Those matters are not considered further in this section.

(b) The Balance of Dependency

6–202   The requirement that the contribution must have been made "otherwise than for full valuable consideration", leading to the adoption of what the Law Commission described as "the balance-sheet approach" and considered to have created an unsatisfactory state of affairs,[452] no longer exists except in relation to arrangements of a commercial nature. The amended s.1(3)[453] provides that:

> "For the purposes of s.1(1)(e), a person shall be treated as having been maintained by the deceased (either wholly or partly, as the case may be), only if the deceased was making a substantial contribution in money or money's worth towards the reasonable needs of that person other than a contribution made for full valuable consideration pursuant to an arrangement of a commercial nature."

The discussion which follows is therefore mainly of historical interest.

6–203   In *Re Wilkinson*,[454] the applicant went to live with her sister in 1969; the sister suffered from arthritis which was getting progressively worse. She died in 1976, having made a will leaving £5,000 and various chattels to the applicant and the residue of her estate to a Mr Newell. During the period when they lived together, the applicant acted as a companion to her sister, did some of the cooking and housework (the heavier tasks being beyond her as she herself had a hernia and spinal trouble) and helped to nurse her sister. She received free board and lodging, and the sister paid all the outgoings of the house. Arnold J held, with considerable hesitation, that the companionship provided and services rendered by the applicant did not constitute full valuable requital for the benefits which she had received, and accordingly upheld the registrar's decision that she was a person entitled to apply under s.1(1)(e). Two points which emerge from the judgment are that it is irrelevant whether or not the consideration is provided under a contractual obligation, and that the onus is on the applicant to show that they are entitled to apply under s.1(1)(e).

---

[450] Ch.2, s.2(h)(iv), "Persons Found Not to Have Been Dependants", paras 2–084 to 2–094.

[451] Ch.2, s.2(i), "Words and Phrases", (i–v), at para.2–095 ("immediately"); para.2–097 ("otherwise than for full valuable consideration"); para.2–100 ("reasonable needs"); para.2–106 ("substantial") and para.2–107 ("assumption of responsibility").

[452] Law Com. LC 331, at paras 6.66–6.76. For fuller discussion see Ch.2, s.2(h)(i) "The statutory conditions", paras 2–079–2–081.

[453] Inheritance and Trustees' Powers Act 2014 s.6 and Sch.2 para.3

[454] *Re Wilkinson* [1978] Fam. 22.

In *Re C*,[455] which has already been discussed in relation to the child's   **6–204**
application, there was also an application by C's mother, Miss A. The
submission on behalf of the beneficiary that she was not a dependant within
the meaning of s.1(1)(e), as she had been engaged as a housekeeper and was
in the household as the result of a contractual arrangement, was rejected. Sir
George Baker P took the view that she was a de facto wife. She had had her
own child adopted, and had borne a child to the testator, because that was
what he wanted; it was incumbent on the estate to provide for her and for
the child.

In *Jelley v Iliffe*[456] the applicant was a widower, aged 71, who went to live   **6–205**
in a house which belonged to the widow of his brother-in-law; that house
had been conveyed to her by her children on the understanding that she
would leave it to them on her death, as, in fact, she did, making no provision
for the applicant. They agreed to share the house and pool their incomes,
which included their old-age pensions. The applicant looked after the garden and did some household jobs; he also provided some furniture. The
deceased did the cooking and washing and provided the applicant with rent-
free accommodation. The registrar struck out the application on the ground
that it did not disclose a reasonable cause of action and the judge, presumably following *Re Beaumont*, upheld the registrar's decision on the basis
that the provision of rent-free accommodation for the applicant did not, in
all the circumstances, amount to an assumption of responsibility for his
maintenance.

On this point, the Court of Appeal disagreed with the judgment in *Re*   **6–206**
Beaumont. Megarry VC had held, in that case, that the fact that the
applicant was being maintained by the deceased did not raise a presumption
that the deceased had assumed responsibility for his maintenance. Stephenson and Griffiths LJJ took the contrary view in *Jelley v Iliffe*. They
further held that the provision of rent-free accommodation was a significant
and, in the case of an old-age pensioner, a substantial contribution to his
reasonable needs. As it was not clear beyond doubt, on the applicant's
affidavits, that his contributions had equalled or outweighed the benefit of
rent-free accommodation, there was an arguable case that he was being
maintained by the deceased; the application should not have been struck out
but allowed to go to trial.

Jelley v Iliffe was applied in *Bishop v Plumley*.[457] The applicant and the   **6–207**
deceased cohabited for some 10 years, though during a short period in 1974
when they had separated and were living with their respective families, the
deceased made a will in favour of his son and daughter, leaving nothing to
the applicant. Until the last year of the relationship their circumstances were
broadly similar. They lived together in rented accommodation on their
pooled resources. During the latter part of that period, the deceased
developed angina and received exceptionally devoted care from the appli-

---

[455] *Re C* (1979) 123 S.J. 35.
[456] *Jelley v Iliffe* [1981] Fam. 128, CA.
[457] *Bishop v Plumley* [1991] 1 All E.R. 236, CA.

cant. In early 1984, about 10 months before his death, the deceased, as the
result of becoming entitled to a substantial legacy, bought a house in which
he and the applicant lived until his death. Both the registrar and the judge
appear to have concluded that, up until the end of 1983, the couple were
living together, pooling their modest resources, and, perhaps, that neither
had assumed responsibility for the maintenance of the other. It was found,
in the Court of Appeal, that on those facts, the deceased was not maintaining the applicant prior to the purchase of the house, so it was only the
last nine or ten months of their life together that was relevant. Once the
deceased had bought the house, the situation changed; but the view seems to
have been taken in the lower courts that the benefit which the deceased
conferred on the applicant by providing her with rent-free accommodation
was balanced out by the greatly increased care which the applicant bestowed
on the deceased during the last year of his life.

6–208   In *Jelley v Iliffe* Griffiths LJ had dealt with the question whether the
contribution made by the deceased to the applicant had to be substantially
greater, when measured in money or money's worth, than that made by the
applicant to the deceased, as follows:

> "Only if the balance comes down heavily in favour of the applicant will
> it be shown that the deceased was making 'a substantial contribution in
> money or money's worth towards the reasonable needs' of the appli-
> cant."

However, he qualified this statement. Accepting, as is clearly so, that the
striking of the balance cannot be an exact exercise of evaluating pounds and
pence, he went on to give the following example:

> "...if a man was living with a woman as his wife and providing her the
> house and all the money for their living expenses she would be
> dependent on him, and it would not be right to deprive her of her claim
> by arguing that she was in fact performing the services that a house-
> keeper would perform and it would cost more to employ a housekeeper
> than was spent on her and indeed more than the deceased had available
> to spend on her. Each case will have to be looked at carefully on its own
> facts to see whether common sense leads to the conclusion that the
> applicant can fairly be regarded as a dependant."

6–209   Giving the judgment of the Court of Appeal in *Bishop v Plumley*, Butler-
Sloss LJ said that both the registrar and the judge fell into error in their
approach to the test under s.1(3). Neither had referred to, or taken into
account, the passage from *Jelley v Iliffe* which she cited and the example
from which is set out above.[458] The judgment continues:

---

[458] See the commentary on this judgment by Professor Stephen Cretney at [1991] 21 Fam. Law
62 which includes a passage to the effect that the earlier case-law would seem to support the
view taken in the courts below.

"If the registrar and the judge had approached the factual analysis of substantial contribution and full valuable consideration by including the mutual love and support of the couple, demonstrated as it was by the applicant in the devotion she gave him during the final years of their cohabitation, it is inconceivable that either would have excluded the applicant from advancing to the second stage to be resolved by ss.2 and 3 of the Act."

The factual analysis, as extracted from the judgment, appears to run as follows:

(a) the provision of secure accommodation at the house purchased was a substantial contribution by the deceased; and

(b) either, as the registrar and the judge held, and was argued on behalf of the beneficiaries, the services provided by the applicant were so exceptional as to amount to full valuable consideration; or, as the argument on behalf of the applicant could be expressed, those services should be excluded from the equation as being simply a manifestation, on the part of the applicant, of the mutual love and support flowing from the relationship.

The judgment in favour of the applicant's argument is expressed as follows:

"I do not consider that her evidence that she did everything for him over a period of years can be assessed in isolation from the mutuality of their relationship."

In other words, not only should the applicant not be deprived of her claim by having her services quantified on a commercial basis, or as if they were performed under a contractual obligation; one has to look at the circumstances in which they were rendered before deciding whether to take them into account at all. The above cases, and several of those discussed on the following pages, show that the provision of rent-free accommodation will generally be regarded as a substantial contribution to the reasonable needs of the applicant, though this was not found to be the case in *Re Watson*,[459] where the applicant had a house of her own in which she had chosen not to live.

In *Rees v Newbery*[460] the maintenance was in the form, not of providing **6–210** rent-free accommodation, but letting it to the applicant at substantially less than the market rent. In the mid-1960s, while the testator was working as an actor, he met the applicant, a member of the same profession. The two eventually became close friends and in 1984 the applicant moved into a flat in a building owned and occupied by the testator. There was no written tenancy agreement, but he paid rent of £200 per month. At trial, agreed

---

[459] *Re Watson* [1999] 1 F.L.R. 878.
[460] *Rees v Newbery* [1998] 1 F.L.R. 1041.

evidence was given that, at the date of the deceased's death, the full market rent was £5,640 per year. By his will, which was made in 1979, the testator left his entire estate among three charities (of whom the second defendant was one) and a benevolent fund. In 1993 he gave instructions to his solicitor for a new will; and these included an instruction that the applicant should have the right to remain in occupation of the flat for the rest of his life at a rent which was below the open market rent, though it was apparently decided at some point that it should be adjusted for inflation. However, he died before he was able to consider counsel's draft of the new will and, in consequence, no provision was made for the applicant.

6–211 The applicant, who was 50 years old at the date of the hearing, was earning an average of £8,396 net over the three years immediately before the hearing; he had no capital assets. His case was that the testator had maintained him by renting the flat to him at less than the open market value, and had intended that such an arrangement should continue after his death. It was argued that the testator had not assumed responsibility for the applicant's maintenance and that the relationship between them should be viewed as a commercial relationship of landlord and tenant. However, it was found that the relationship was one of friendship and that the testator had both assumed responsibility for the applicant's maintenance and had made a substantial contribution to his reasonable needs. It was held that the testator had recognised, by the instructions which he gave, a moral obligation to the applicant and that his instructions for the new will were admissible as evidence of his intentions. Therefore, it could properly be said that the applicant had been put in a position of dependency by the deceased and that, the object of the Act being to remedy the injustice of a dependant being deprived of that financial support "by accident or design" (the latter circumstance not being present in the instant case), it was right to make provision for him. Because of the difficulties which would have arisen in satisfying the interests of the beneficiaries under the will if the applicant were allowed to remain in occupation of the flat, he was awarded a pecuniary legacy of £64,000 subject to his paying £200 per month from the date of handing down of the judgment, for his occupation of the flat, which he was to vacate at the expiry of a period of six months from the sealing of the order. This figure was arrived at by capitalising the rental discount using the Ogden tables; this method was considered appropriate since they were addressed directly to the question of what capital sum would be required to meet an anticipated future expenditure.

(c) Unsuccessful Applications by Persons Found to be Dependants

6–212 In *Rhodes v Dean*[461] the applicant was found to be a dependant within the meaning of s.1(1)(e); the deceased had discharged the responsibility for providing accommodation for her over a period of two years and two

---

[461] *Rhodes v Dean* unreported 26 March 1996, CA. The deceased had died on 1989, so Mrs Rhodes could only claim as a dependant. The hearing at first instance took place on 13 September 1994.

months. A crucial factor in the decision of the trial judge that it was reasonable for the deceased to have made no financial provision for her in his will was the fact that, at his death, there was over £36,000 in a joint account. In the 13 months after his death she had dissipated £27,700 of it. He had found that her style of life had dramatically improved since the deceased gave up his business, and indeed that he himself had not enjoyed such a style of life prior to his retirement. She could not reasonably expect to travel and to live off capital in the same way as she had when the deceased had decided to stop working and enjoy the benefit of his labours while life lasted. Accordingly, the judge did not regard her standard of living with him as the measure of her need. If she had to leave the testator's house and was unable to buy another house, that was the result of her own decisions and actions. The testator had made reasonable provision for her in her lifetime and her current situation, objectively regarded, did not lead to the conclusion that she should receive any more maintenance from the estate. The following passage from the judgment at first instance should be noted:

> "The court has to have regard to what has happened since the testator's death and until the date of this hearing. The circumstance that Mrs Rhodes has now dissipated what she received from the testator should not in my judgment lead the court to impose a higher test, or a different test, nor should it lead the court to take the view that what was reasonable at the time of the testator's death is at this stage of the inquiry no longer reasonable."

On appeal, one issue raised was that the judge had erred in not giving any or sufficient weight to the standard of living which the applicant had enjoyed as the benchmark of what was reasonable. Addressing this issue, Ward LJ said:

> "I do not agree with that criticism. It might be appropriate, where one is dealing with a widow's claim, to have express regard to the standard of living enjoyed during the marriage, but here the matter is at large. Here the standard of living is but a matter to which the court has overall regard, and it is a matter which will usually lie within the decision that has to be made as to the extent of the responsibility, the basis of it and the duration of it."

There was nothing wrong with the approach of the trial judge or the way in which he had directed himself, and the appeal must be dismissed.

(d) Successful Applications by Relatives

Of the applications by dependant sisters, *Re Wilkinson* has already been   **6–213**
discussed. In *Re Viner*,[462] where the applicant was the deceased's sister, aged 71, who had been grudgingly maintained by him during his lifetime, it was

---

[462] *Re Viner* [1978] C.L.Y. 3091.

held, for that reason, that she should receive no more than she had in her lifetime; and a lump sum of £2,000 was awarded rather than periodical payments, so as to avoid adverse effects on her rent and rate rebates.

6–214   *Re B, Deceased*[463] was, formally, an application by the mother of the deceased to bring proceedings out of time. However, it raises an important issue of principle as to the extent of the jurisdiction under the Act in claims under s.1(1)(e) and is therefore considered together with other claims by dependants. The facts are most unusual. B and R, who were cohabiting, parted shortly after the birth of their daughter, L, who was born with severe mental and physical disabilities due to medical negligence at birth and in respect of which she was awarded damages of £250,000. R left some eight months after the birth of L and from then until her death in 1994, aged 14, she was cared for by B, who had been appointed by the Court of Protection as her receiver. Part of the award was applied in the purchase of a house (adapted for the special needs of caring for L) where B could live and look after L, the house being held upon trust as to 25 per cent for B absolutely and 75 per cent for L:

> "...when she shall attain the age of 18 years or cease to be a patient under the Mental Health Acts, whichever event shall happen the later."

6–215   While B was caring for L, she received regular payments from the Court of Protection for L's maintenance, but no remuneration or allowance in respect of her own labour in caring for L; and she also received certain other payments either to supplement the income available for, in effect, house-keeping, or for isolated items of expenditure. L died on 14 February 1994 and letters of administration were granted to B on 22 March of that year. Her estate, exclusive of the value of L's interest in the house, amounted to £33,592 plus £2,000 realised from the sale of the van used for transporting L's motorised wheelchair. Although aware that R was entitled to half L's estate, B did not want him to have any of it and she spent it all.

6–216   Her application for leave to bring proceedings out of time was not made until March 1997, some 18 months late, by which time R had commenced an administration action against her. He also made an application to strike out her originating summons, but that was dismissed by the Master, who allowed B's application to bring proceedings out of time and dismissed R's application to strike out. On appeal, R raised the question whether it was possible for L, as a minor of limited mental capacity and all of whose assets and income were available only for her benefit to have assumed responsibility for the maintenance of B within the meaning of s.3(4) of the 1975 Act. The judge had no doubt that the payments made by the Court of Protection to B for the maintenance and benefit of L had the side effect of benefiting B also. Her pre-eminent need was to be housed in suitable accommodation so that B could care for her and meeting that need naturally and inevitably

---

[463] *Re B, Deceased* [2000] Ch. 662, CA; reversing [1999] Ch. 206 (Jonathan Parker J), also reported *sub nom. Bouette v Rose* [2000] 1 F.L.R. 655, CA reversing [1999] 2 F.L.R. 466.

meant that B would indirectly benefit both by the provision of the accommodation and the payments for housekeeping. However, he based his judgment on the following:

(i) the purpose of the payments made by the Court of Protection, as identified by the statutory power which it exercised; and
(ii) the absence, as he saw it, of any assumption of responsibility within s.3(4).

He concluded that B was not being maintained by L, allowed R's appeal and struck out B's application.

On appeal to the Court of Appeal Robert Walker LJ, giving the only 6–217 judgment, accepted the argument on behalf of B that whether a claimant qualified as a dependant under s.1(1)(e) as explained by s.1(3) was a matter of fact, and that s.3(4), as properly understood, did not create a further obstacle. In the instant case, as the judge recognised, L's needs were B's needs; B had to give up her business in order to care for L and had no income other than Social Security benefits; the officials of the Court of Protection who dealt with her case knew of her financial circumstances. There was nothing absurd in the idea of the Court of Protection acting as the conscience of a patient and making provision for those to whom the patient, if of full mental capacity, would have felt a moral obligation.[464] It must have been obvious to those who were taking decisions about L's funds that her funds and her share in the house were to be used in a way that met B's financial and material needs, so that she was enabled to look after L's physical and emotional needs; and that situation was expected to continue throughout L's lifetime. The judge was wrong to attach any weight to the possibility that the payments might be discontinued. For those reasons he concluded that the judge was wrong to hold that he had no jurisdiction. In considering the exercise of the discretion under s.4, he observed that the Master had exercised his discretion in favour of B, and the judge would have done likewise had he not felt driven to decide the jurisdiction issue against her. He was not persuaded that those judgments had gone outside the generous ambit of the decision in *Re Salmon*; the appeal was allowed and the claim restored.

In *King v Dubrey*[465] the claimant, who was the nephew of the deceased, 6–218 claimed a declaration that his aunt had made a valid *donatio mortis causa* of her house to him and, in the alternative, for reasonable financial provision out of her estate, of which the house, worth some £350,000, was the only substantial asset. By her will, made in 1998, she had left the bulk of her estate, including her house, to charities. The first instance decision in his favour on the claim for the *donatio mortis causa* was reversed by the Court of Appeal, but the award of £75,000 which the trial judge would have made

---

[464] See *Re W.J.G.L* [1966] Ch. 135.
[465] *King v Dubrey* [2016] Ch. 221, *sub nom King v The Chiltern Dog Rescue* [2015] W.T.L.R. 1225, CA, affirming. in part [2014] W.T.L.R. 1411.

on the 1975 Act claim had he not granted the declaration, was upheld. In relation to that claim it was found that he was a dependant within the meaning of s.1(1)(e). He had moved into his aunt's house in 2007 for the purpose of caring for her, which he did until her death in 2011 and, in return, he had received board and lodging, expenses and small sums of money. That arrangement involved an assumption of responsibility on both sides. With minor exceptions, he did not work during that period, nor could he realistically could he have done so. He had not worked since his aunt's death and was unable to maintain himself. Applying *Jelley v Iliffe*,[466] there had been maintenance in money and money's worth and the deceased had assumed responsibility for such maintenance. The claimant, aged 58, was unlikely to obtain further employment. He had no significant assets of his own, nor a home, other than his aunt's property. The benefit which he had received over the four years when he was living with his aunt was modest. There were no other claimants under the Act and it was not suggested that the charities had relevant financial needs. On appeal it was argued for the charities that the most that could have been properly awarded was £40,000, representing two years' support, and for the claimant, that an appropriate award would be £150,000, to enable him to purchase a small flat in the area. That argument had been rejected at first instance on the basis that such an award would overstate the dependency, and was rejected again on appeal, where it was held that both parties were wrong and the judge had been right.

(e) Other Successful Applications by Dependants

6-219   Although s.3(4) of the 1975 Act directs the court to have regard to the length of time for which the deceased discharged the responsibility of maintaining the applicant, there is no reported case where the application has failed because the responsibility was discharged for a relatively short time.[467] Successful applications of this nature include *Re Haig*,[468] where the applicant, aged 70, had lived in the deceased's house for three years and looked after him while he was ill; *Re Kozdrach*,[469] in which the 30-year-old applicant was capable of earning her own living, and the relationship lasted for the three to four years immediately before the death of the deceased; *Clark v Jones*,[470] where the applicant had lived with the deceased for three years before his death, and it was possible that they might have married; and *Harrington v Gill*,[471] where there had been an eight-year relationship between the parties, each of whom had been previously married.

6-220   The length of the relationship and the fact that the applicant had cared for the deceased when she became ill were significant factors in *Graham v*

---

[466] *Jelley v Iliffe*, [1981] Fam. 128, CA.
[467] All of these applications were made in cases where the deceased had died before 1 January 1996 and, consequently, none of the applicants could have applied as a cohabitant.
[468] *Re Haig* (1979) 129 N.L.J. 420.
[469] *Re Kozdrach* [1981] Conv. 224.
[470] *Clark v Jones* unreported 2 December 1985, CA.
[471] *Harrington v Gill* (1983) 4 F.L.R. 265.

Murphy.[472] The male applicant (G) claimed reasonable financial provision out of the estate of the female deceased (M), who died intestate in 1994, upon which her estate (which was in the region of £240,000 after discharge of all liabilities) passed to her parents. They were not in any financial need and in fact subsequently assigned their interest in M's estate to their three surviving children. G and M had lived together for some 19 years, and for the last nine years of the relationship they had lived in houses bought in the deceased's sole name. Towards the end of the relationship M's health deteriorated and G cared for her. In view of the provision of that accommodation, and of other substantial benefits received by G, it was found that he was a dependant within the meaning of s.1(1)(e). Having regard to the amount of the net estate, the absence of any dependency or strong moral claim (apart from family ties) on the part of the beneficiaries, the fact that the association of G and M was for a period much longer than that of G's de facto dependency, and his care for her in her illness, it was held that the disposition of her estate under the law relating to intestacy did not make reasonable provision for G, and he was awarded £35,000 in order to enable him to purchase a modest house or flat in an appropriate area.

Williams v Roberts[473] was a case in which the deceased and the applicant **6–221** had met while she was running a guesthouse, at which he eventually went to live. After they had known each other for about two years she bought another guesthouse where they lived together as man and wife. He helped her to run the business, keeping the books and dealing with tax matters, and did various domestic tasks. He paid for his board and lodging as well as other regular periodic sums and occasional, considerably larger, lump sums. It was found that he would have continued these payments had he survived. There was no doubt that the applicant was dependent on him; after taking into account the circumstances of his unmarried twin sisters, aged 64, who, under his will, would have shared his estate of about £110,000 equally, the applicant was awarded a lump sum of £20,000.

Malone v Harrison[474] has been discussed at some length in relation to **6–222** methods of capitalising income needs. The relationship began in 1965, when M was 23. At that time the deceased had been separated from his wife for 26 years and had been living for the last seven years with another woman, who lived in his house with her son and was treated in every way as his wife. He persuaded the applicant to give up her job and did not want her to work, though he gave her a nominal job, at £60 per month less tax, at one of his companies. During the 12 years of their relationship he gave her shares worth £15,000, a flat in Malta and another in England, a car, furs and jewellery. He paid her bills, and gave her small sums in cash from time to time. It was found that, on average, she received about £4,000 per year from him. He told her that he did not intend to leave her anything in his will, and that proved to be the case. However, he did send her a newspaper cutting

[472] *Graham v Murphy* [1997] 1 F.L.R. 860.
[473] *Williams v Roberts* [1986] 1 F.L.R. 349.
[474] *Malone v Harrison* [1979] 1 W.L.R. 1353.

giving details of the 1975 Act, which was going through Parliament at the time.

6–223   Her own earning capacity was slight; she had never been trained to do any work and the deceased, during the 12 years of their relationship, had strongly objected to her working. At his death she was 38, with an actuarial life expectancy of about another 38 years. She had not been a de facto wife, nor claimed to have rendered any particular services in return for his bounty. The findings and the principle on which the assessment proceeded may be summed up in the following passage from the judgment:

> "The deceased, in effect, monopolised the plaintiff for 12 years of her life from the age of 23. He discouraged her from seeking gainful employment. He taught her to rely on him for all her financial needs, but it must be said that she was an apt pupil and was not slow in asking for what she wanted. This does not mean that the deceased through his estate, as it were, should be punished, but as he was generous to her in his lifetime, so within the limits of the statute should the court be in deciding what if any order to make."

6–224   In *Churchill v Roach*[475] the claim was in the alternative and the claimant succeeded in her claim as a dependant; the provision made for her was purely to meet her housing needs, so the question of her general standard of living did not arise. In that case, it was found that the deceased was, and had been for some time before his death, making a substantial contribution to the reasonable needs of the claimant, for less than full valuable consideration. He was providing her with accommodation in the joint home; he paid the larger share of the domestic bills, and made cash advances to her to discharge her more pressing needs. This more than counterbalanced her provision of working facilities to him in her adjoining property. It was in all the circumstances not reasonable to make no financial provision for the claimant. At the time of his death they were both wholly committed to the relationship. Their properties had been physically joined and they were in the process of merging the legal titles. There was by then a common understanding that, on his death, she would be provided for. While her income was sufficient to discharge her reasonable financial needs, it did not meet her need for housing. The proposed solution was to transfer the property to the claimant charged with a payment to the estate of £65,000 before 30 June 2003 (approximately one year after judgment was delivered), that sum being the approximate value of the family's reversionary interest, were the claimant to have been given a life interest terminable on marriage or permanent cohabitation, and including an element of interest for the postponement of the estate's entitlement.

6–225   In *Holliday v Musa*, there were three claimants, Diane Holloway (D), her teenage son, Houssein (H) by her relationship with the deceased, and Kevin, the son of her earlier marriage. The defendants were the deceased's six adult

---

[475] *Churchill v Roach* [2004] 2 F.L.R. 989.

children by his marriage. D had lived with the deceased for some six years but did not claim as a cohabitant; all three claimed only under s.1(1)(e). The deceased, Ramadan Guney, who died intestate in November 2006, was born in Cyprus, but had lived in England since 1958 and had made only occasional visits to Cyprus thereafter. On the trial of the preliminary issue of domicile, that issue was decided in favour of the claimants at first instance and affirmed by the Court of Appeal.[476] On the trial of the substantive issue, all three claims succeeded. The appeal by the deceased's family against the order made in favour of D and H was dismissed.[477]

At the date of the trial of the substantive issue, D was aged 50 and H, 12.   **6–226** She had worked in the family business, that being a company which operated Brookwood Cemetery, but had never earned more than "pin money" and, after, Ramadan's death, she was dismissed by the family members who ran the company. She had had little formal education and had no earning capacity outside the family business. She and the deceased had enjoyed a "more than comfortable" lifestyle, living together in a house in Woking purchased by him in 2003, which she and H continued to occupy after his death. The judge's findings as to her housing and income needs are set out in the judgment of Wall P on the appeal.[478] She concluded that D's income need was £60,000 per year and that her housing need should be met by a transfer to her of the Woking property, free of mortgage. Although it was, in the judge's view, probably a larger property than was absolutely essential, it was entirely reasonable for her not to be expected to uproot herself and her teenage son at that time. Her income need would be met by the transfer of the shares in Brookwood to her, on the footing that she would have to assume the risk of satisfying any outstanding tax liabilities. That provision absorbed the bulk of the net estate in England; the dispositions of the property owned by the deceased in Northern Cyprus remained unaffected.

Following the refusal by the judge of leave to appeal, the Court of Appeal   **6–227** granted leave and dismissed the appeal. The appellants argued that, the judge's approach had been wrong in principle. By assessing her needs at a level which absorbed the bulk of the net estate in England the judge was in effect treating her as if she had been his widow. Rejecting that argument,[479] Wall P held that there had been no error in law or principle. If (which he did not accept) the decision to award her the bulk of the English estate was harsh on the family, they had only themselves to blame for the manner in which they conducted the litigation. If the judge concluded that the transfer of the principal asset (the shares) was necessary to achieve the statutory objective there could be no objection in principle to it. As to the transfer of the Woking property, the case was one which cried out for a clean break and

---

[476] *Holliday v Musa* [2010] 2 F.L.R. 702, CA affirming the first instance decision given on 19 March 2009 by HH Judge Kushner QC sitting as a high court judge.

[477] *Musa v Holliday* [2013] 1 F.L.R. 806, CA, affirming the first instance decision given on 11 November 2011 by HH Judge Kushner QC sitting as a high court judge.

[478] *Musa v Holliday* [2013] 1 F.L.R. 806, CA at [16]–[17] (income) and [14] and [22]–[23] (housing).

[479] *Musa v Holliday* [2013] 1 F.L.R. 806, CA at [26]–[34].

on the facts presented to the judge an outright transfer of the home in which she and their son had lived with the deceased was not an inappropriate decision. It had been common ground that the dispositions on intestacy did not make reasonable provision for them, and the proposition that the court should interfere as little as possible with the deceased's dispositions had to yield to the facts of the case.

6–228   Lloyd LJ addressed the argument that the family home (which, as the trial judge had recognised, was larger than the claimant and her son by the deceased strictly needed) should revert to the estate after her death and that provision for accommodation should be made in a manner analogous to the approach under the Children Act 1989, by way of a settlement on trust with the capital reverting once the child's need for which the father was expected to provide had ended. He did not doubt that suitable trusts could be devised to meet the various eventualities that might occur, but there were two reasons why that would be inappropriate in the present case; either might be sufficient, but the two together were overwhelming. The first was the inadequacy of the estate to provide for what the judge had estimated as D's reasonable needs; the second was that, if ever there were a case for a clean break on an application under the 1975 Act, it was the present case. It would, he said, be:

> "...a recipe for disaster to set up even the best drafted trusts, and even with the most robust and independent of trustees (an exercise which in itself would be expensive to set up and maintain) under which Diane Holliday and the adult family had successive interests in the same property."[480]

6–229   In *Wright-Gordon v Legister*,[481] the claimant had moved into the property which was the principal asset of the deceased's estate, in 2004 and lived there with him until 2008, when she married a Mr G. That marriage broke down in 2010 and the claimant returned to the property and was living with the deceased when he died intestate on 1 February 2012. It was conceded that the relationship did not fulfil the requirements of s.1(1A); her claim was as a dependant under s.1(1)(e); nevertheless the nature of the relationship was relevant when considering whether the deceased had assumed any responsibility for her maintenance. The settled arrangement subsisting at the date of the deceased's death was that he had been providing the claimant with rent-free accommodation, and the household tasks including cooking, cleaning and washing carried out by her did not amount to full valuable consideration. The provision of free, or cheap, accommodation for an extended time also demonstrated his assumption of responsibility. He therefore had an obligation to her, to ensure that she was sufficiently provided for to resettle herself in suitable accommodation, which the disposition of his estate on intestacy did not meet. The measure of provision was

---

[480] *Musa v Holliday* [2013] 1 F.L.R. 806, CA, at [52]–[53].
[481] *Wright-Gordon v Legister*, reported *sub nom. Gordon v Legister* [2014] W.T.L.R. 1675.

the cost to her of living in a shared home, together with some support while she was resettling herself and a modest amount for the expenses occasioned by her having to find a new home. A proper allowance would be two years' rent together with that support and contribution to expenses. She was awarded a lump sum payment of £16,500.

CHAPTER 7

PRACTICE AND PROCEDURE

1.—INTRODUCTION

7–001   This chapter is concerned with the matters which will, or may, arise before, during and after the making of a claim under the 1975 Act. The order in which they are discussed follows, so far as possible, the normal sequence of events within the framework of the proceedings. Consequently, the first topic to be addressed is the nature of the proceedings, if any, which are to be brought. While it may appear, from the instructions given by the prospective claimant (or the defendant making a counterclaim), that their interests might be better served by making some claim other than, or in addition to, a 1975 Act claim, this has rarely proved to be the case in practice.

7–002   The reported cases show that the commonest type of multiple claim is a 1975 Act claim accompanied by a claim of a proprietary nature.[1] In those situations, most of the proprietary claims have failed, though *Suggitt v Suggitt*,[2] where the principal claim was founded on proprietary estoppel, is an exception. The claimant succeeded on that claim both at first instance and on appeal, and the 1975 Act claim did not fall to be considered. The unsuccessful claims brought together with 1975 Act claims have been either claims to beneficial interests under trusts or claims based on proprietary

---

[1] These cases are discussed in more detail in s.2(d), "Claims of a proprietary nature".
[2] *Suggitt v Suggitt* [2012] W.T.L.R. 1667, CA, affirming [2011] 2 F.L.R. 875.

estoppel.[3] In most of those cases, the 1975 Act claim succeeded, and in the two cases where it failed,[4] the claimant's conduct was a significant factor in the outcome. An unusual case relating to a claim to a specific property is *King v Dubrey*[5] in which the 1975 Act claim was brought in the alternative to the primary claim that the deceased had made a valid *donatio mortis causa* of her house in favour of the claimant. The claim relating to the *donatio mortis causa* ultimately failed, but the 1975 Act claim succeeded.

Less frequently, there is a claim relating to some aspect of a will as well as a 1975 Act claim. The claims may have been made in entirely separate proceedings, as in *Grattan v McNaughton*,[6] where the 1975 Act claim was brought after claims for rectification of the will and damages for professional negligence had failed. Generally, in this type of multiple claim, the claims, even if required to be commenced by different procedures, have been tried together. Thus in *Watts v Watts*,[7] the claimant challenged the validity of a will made in 2011 under which she took no benefit, and also made a 1975 Act claim. The 2011 will had been admitted to probate, but at trial it was set aside on the ground that it had not been duly executed. The court pronounced in solemn form in favour of the previous will of the testatrix, made in 1998, which had left a half share in her estate to the claimant. That will was held to have made reasonable provision for her, so the 1975 Act claim fell away. In *Baker v Baker*,[8] the daughter of the deceased was the claimant; she successfully challenged her father's will on the grounds of lack of testamentary capacity and want of knowledge and approval. The defendant, who was the sole beneficiary under the will, had sought by her counterclaim to uphold it and in the alternative she advanced claims in proprietary estoppel (which failed) and under the 1975 Act, as to which it was accepted that the dispositions of the deceased's estate on his intestacy failed to make reasonable provision for her. In the particularly complex case of *Burnard v Burnard*,[9] there was, in addition to the 1975 Act claim and a rectification claim,[10] both of which were out of time, claims contesting the validity of three instruments (a will, a declaration of trust and a transfer of registered land, all of which were held to be valid) and a claim to the

7–003

---

[3] *Churchill v Roach* [2004] 2 F.L.R. 989 (claim to a beneficial joint tenancy, and claims based on constructive trust/proprietary estoppel); *Negus v Bahouse* [2008] 1 F.L.R. 381; *Webster v Webster* [2009] 1 F.L.R. 1240 (both claims for a declaration as to a beneficial interest)); *Cattle v Evans* [2011] W.T.L.R. 947 (constructive trust); *Baker v Baker* [2008] 2 F.L.R. 767; *Bye v Colvin-Scott* [2010] W.T.L.R. 1 (both counterclaims, based on proprietary estoppel); *Wright v Waters* [2015] W.T.L.R. 353 (original claim, based on proprietary estoppel).

[4] *Bye v Colvin-Scott* and *Wright v Waters* (see n.2).

[5] *King v Dubrey* [2016] Ch. 221, *sub nom. King v The Chiltern Dog Rescue* [2015] W.T.L.R. 1225, CA. The Court of Appeal set aside the declaration made at first instance that there had been a valid *donatio mortis causa*, but upheld the award made on the 1975 Act claim.

[6] *Grattan v McNaughton* [2001] W.T.L.R. 1305.

[7] *Watts v Watts* [2014] EWHC 668 (Ch). The official transcript is available on Westlaw.

[8] *Baker v Baker* [2008] 2 F.L.R. 767.

[9] *Burnard v Burnard* [2014] EWHC 340 (Ch).

[10] Time was extended for the 1975 Act claim and the rectification claim, though that was dealt with, at the suggestion of the court, as a matter of construction.

ownership of shares in a company.[11] The 1975 Act claim was not determined in those proceedings.

7–004   *Pinnock v Rochester*[12] is an unusual 1975 Act case also involving the validity of a will. The claimant, who was the son of the deceased, had not attained his majority at the date on which probate of his father's will was granted. His paternity, which was initially disputed, was confirmed by DNA testing. A full and final settlement was achieved by way of a payment of a lump sum and costs, the order being made on 1 April 2008, by which date the claimant had attained his majority. However, during the course of the 1975 Act proceedings, his solicitors had written to the defendant's solicitors stating that, although there had as yet been no challenge to the validity of the will, the claimant reserved his position on that issue. He issued a probate claim on 27 November 2008 and the defendant applied to strike it out on the basis that the doctrine of election[13] operated to preclude him from challenging the validity of the will as he had affirmed it by entering into the consent order and accepting the payment under it. It was therefore inequitable for him to challenge the will subsequently and it was an abuse of process to do so. Those objections were upheld at first instance and the probate claim was struck out.

7–005   Reversing that decision on appeal, Sales J held that a 1975 Act claim was conceptually independent of the existence of a valid will.[14] In his view, there was no illogicality or inconsistency involved in a claimant saying that an existing will was invalid, but that if it was valid, it had failed to make reasonable financial provision for him. In a case such as the present case, where the claimant would have a claim to the estate, or part of the estate, on intestacy, if the will was set aside, he would have to accept that any payment made to him under the 1975 Act would be brought into account in the course of administration. If a claimant accepted that, there was nothing unfair or inequitable in his challenging the will and at the same time making a 1975 Act claim. Sales J also drew attention to the possible risk involved in bringing a challenge to the will after the determination of the 1975 Act claim, of the later claim being found to be an abuse of process within the doctrine of *Henderson v Henderson*,[15] on the ground that there was something vexatious or oppressive in bringing a second claim based on similar

---

[11] *Webster v Webster* [2009] 1 F.L.R. 1240 also involved a claim to the ownership of shares in a company.

[12] *Pinnock v Rochester* [2011] EWHC 4049 (Ch).

[13] The judge at first instance directed himself by reference to *Nexus Communications Group Ltd v Lambert* [2005] EWHC 345 (Ch), at [45] and also relied on the observations of Wynn-Parry J in *Re Pointer* [1946] Ch. 324 on the effect of s.3 of the Inheritance (Family Provision) Act 1938, which is identical to s.19 of the 1975 Act.

[14] It does not appear that the case of *Parnall v Hurst* [2003] W.T.L.R. 997 was drawn to his attention. In that case, HH Judge Langan QC stated at [9] that "to enter a caveat where the caveator's intention is to make an Inheritance Act claim is wholly wrong because first, *ex hypothesi*, the validity of the will is admitted, second, because a delay in the grant of probate entails a corresponding delay in getting the caveator's claim on foot". As to the second point, it is a possibly unintended consequence of the amendment to s.4 of the Act which permits a 1975 Act claim to be commenced even though no grant of representation has been issued that the entry of a caveat no longer precludes the commencement of the claim.

[15] *Henderson v Henderson* (1843) 3 Hare 100.

facts. However, the doctrine operates within narrow limits[16] and did not come into play in the instant case.

Pursuing multiple claims inevitably causes the claimant to incur higher   **7–006** costs, and there is room for doubt whether success under more than one head of claim will lead to an improvement in the outcome which is commensurate with the additional cost.[17] The doubt arises because (to take perhaps the commonest type of multiple claim) success in the claim for a beneficial interest in property, which on the face of it is part of the net estate, will provide the claimant with a resource whose existence the court will have to take into account under s.3(1)(a), thereby diminishing the award under the 1975 Act claim accordingly. Thus, in *Webster v Webster*[18] HH Judge Behrens would have declared, had he found it necessary to do so, that the claimant had acquired a beneficial interest to the value of about 33 to 40 per cent of the property in question; but in the 1975 Act claim he awarded her the entire property outright, free of mortgage.

It may be that the absence of any requirement to specify, in 1975 Act   **7–007** proceedings, the type of order which the claimant wishes the court to make, sometimes results in failure to consider whether the potential advantages of combining it with other claims outweigh the additional costs that are likely to be incurred.[19] Generally, the most economical way of dealing with multiple claims is for the matters in dispute to be tried on the same occasion. The court has power under CPR r.3.1(2)(h) to order this[20] and the commentary to the rule notes that the formulation "on the same occasion" is broad enough to encompass an order either that the claims be tried at the same time, or one immediately after the other, before the same forum. The commentary to CPR Pt 57 states that, as claims under the 1975 Act are required to be made by issuing a Pt 8 claim, they cannot be combined in one claim form with other claims which are likely to involve substantial disputes of fact or for which the Pt 8 procedure is not appropriate or which, as in the case of probate claims, must be commenced using the Pt 7 procedure. An application may instead be made in an appropriate case for a claim under the Act to be tried together with another claim under CPR r.3.1(2)(h).[21] Although the court also has power under CPR r.3.1(2)(g) to consolidate proceedings, it is not suggested that an application for consolidation should be made in such a situation. Indeed, the commentary to that provision states that upon investigation of the question whether consolidation should be ordered it may be recognised that the advantages sought to be achieved by an application for consolidation may be achieved by an order that the

---

[16] *Dexter Limited v Vlieland-Boddy* [2003] EWCA Civ 14.
[17] However, there is possibly a risk for the professional adviser who advises a client to pursue one head of claim only, and that claim fails. The client might allege that the advice was given negligently, on the basis that if a different or an additional head of claim had been pursued, there would have been a better outcome.
[18] *Webster v Webster* [2009] 1 F.L.R. 1240.
[19] See s.2(g), "Multiple Claims—An Overview".
[20] *Civil Procedure 2017*, para.3.1.18.
[21] *Civil Procedure 2017*, para.57.16.2.

several claims be tried on the same occasion and that an order for consolidation is neither desirable nor necessary.[22]

7–008   Where there is more than one claim, some care may need to be exercised
in choosing the forum (that is to say, either the Chancery or the Family
Division of the High Court, or the County Court) in which the 1975 Act
application is to be heard. This should, in practice, be dictated by the nature
and difficulty of the questions raised by such other proceedings as are
contemplated, and their cost implications. In that respect, since the County
Court has unlimited financial jurisdiction in respect of 1975 Act claims,[23]
and the limit of the equity jurisdiction[24] has been raised to £350,000,[25] it is
more frequently possible for multiple claims to be disposed of in the County
Court.

7–009   Probate claims,[26] claims for rectification of wills, claims for the removal or
substitution of personal representatives and claims under the Inheritance
Act are all regulated, procedurally, by CPR Pt 57. Claims for the determination of any question relating to the administration of the estate of a
deceased person are regulated by s.I of CPR Pt 64. Examples of the type of
claim which may be made under r.64.2(a)[27] include:

(1)   a claim for the determination of any question as to who is included
in any class of persons having:

(i)   a claim against the estate of a deceased person;

(ii)   a beneficial interest in the estate of such a person; or

(iii) a beneficial interest in any property subject to a trust.

CPR r.64.3 provides that all claims to which that section applies must be
made by issuing a Pt 8 claim form. There is no mandatory procedure for
commencing claims under s.14 of the Trusts of Land and Appointment of
Trustees Act 1996; choice of the procedure will depend on whether or not
there is likely to be a substantial dispute of fact. Any trustee or person who
has an interest in property subject to a trust of land may apply for an order
under s.14(2)(b) declaring the nature or extent of a person's interest in
property subject to the trust.

[22] *Civil Procedure 2017*, para.3.1.17.

[23] County Courts Act 1984 s.25

[24] The matters specified in s.23 (equity jurisdiction) include (a) proceedings for the administration of the estate of a deceased person and (b)(i) proceedings for the execution of any
trust, or (ii) for a declaration that a trust exists, provided that the estate, or, as the case may
be, the estate or fund subject, or alleged to be subject to the trust, does not exceed the county
court limit.

[25] High Court and County Court Jurisdiction (Amendment) Order 2014 (SI 2014/821) art.3,
with effect from 22 April 2014.

[26] The contentious probate jurisdiction which was formerly exercisable under s.32 of the
County Courts Act 1984 ceased to exist following the repeal of that provision by the Crime
and Courts Act 2013 Sch.9(1), with effect from 22 April 2014.

[27] PD 64A—Estates, Trusts and Charities, Section I, Claims relating to the administration of
trusts and estates.

2.—Claims Relating to the Estates of Deceased Persons

(a) Generally

The title of this section has been chosen in order to draw attention to the **7–010** fundamental distinction between a claim under the 1975 Act and any other claim which may arise following the death of the deceased. A claim under the 1975 Act is a claim by a person who seeks to become a beneficiary, or a larger beneficiary, of the estate; and its object is to bring about a redistribution of the estate between the beneficiaries under the existing disposition (who may include the claimant) and the claimant, if he is not already a beneficiary. It involves neither a challenge to the validity of that disposition nor a claim against the estate, the satisfaction of which would diminish the value of the estate. As is explained in s.4 of this chapter, the role of the personal representatives is quite different in a 1975 Act claim from their role in a probate action or a claim to a beneficial interest.

(b) Probate Claims

A probate claim is defined in CPR r.57.1.(2)(a) as a claim, not being a claim **7–011** which is non-contentious or common-form probate business: (i) for the grant of probate of the will or letters of administration of the estate of a deceased person; (ii) for the revocation of such a grant; or (iii) for a decree pronouncing for or against the validity of an alleged will. The type of probate claim most commonly brought in conjunction with 1975 Act proceedings is a claim for a decree pronouncing for or against the will, which may be brought by an executor or a beneficiary, or a party opposed to the will. A useful summary of the case-law relating to the various grounds on which a will may be challenged is contained in *Tristram and Coote's Probate Practice*.[28] CPR r.57.9 applies where a defendant wishes to counterclaim for any of the remedies mentioned in r.57.1(2)(a) in proceedings other than a probate claim. The rule therefore covers the situation where C makes a claim under the 1975 Act while D wishes to contend that the will is invalid. Probate claims in the High Court are assigned to the Chancery Division. Probate claims in the County Court can be brought only in the County Court at Central London or at a county court hearing centre where there is also a Chancery District Registry.[29]

---

[28] *Tristram and Coote's Probate Practice*, 31st edn (London: LexisNexis, 2015), at Chs 33 (Particulars of Claim) and 34 (Defence and Counterclaim). For forms of pleadings, see App.VI, forms A6.224–A6.260 (CP 14–50).
[29] Birmingham, Bristol, Caernarfon, Cardiff, Leeds, Liverpool, Manchester, Mold, Newcastle-on-Tyne and Preston.

(c) Claims for Rectification of a Will

7–012   There is at the time of writing no decided case[30] in which a claim for rectification of a will has been made in conjunction with a 1975 Act claim, though in *Grattan v McNaughton*[31] there had been unsuccessful claims both for rectification and professional negligence before the 1975 Act claim was heard. However, there is no reason, in principle, why a claim for rectification should not be tried on the same occasion as, and immediately before, a 1975 Act claim.

7–013   Under s.20(1) of the Administration of Justice Act 1982, a court may, if it is satisfied that a will is so expressed that it fails to carry out the testator's intentions in consequence of (a) clerical error[32]; or (b) failure to understand their instructions, order that the will be rectified in order to give effect to their intentions. The provision can apply not only where a clerical error is made by the draftsman or engrosser but by the testator himself; thus, in *Re Williams*[33] the possibility of a testator making a mistake when writing or typing out their own will was referred to.[34] As with 1975 Act claims, the permission of the court is required where a claim for rectification is sought to be made more than six months after the date when a grant of representation is first taken out. It was held in *Chittock v Stevens*[35] that an application for permission to bring a claim for rectification out of time would be determined in accordance with the principles which applied to such applications under the 1975 Act.

(d) Claims of a Proprietary Nature

(i) General

7–014   In what follows, the term "proprietary claim" includes claims arising under a resulting or constructive trust, or under the doctrine of proprietary estoppel. Where there is an express declaration of trust in the conveyance or transfer of land which comprehensively declares the beneficial interests in the property or its proceeds of sale, there is no room for the application of the doctrine of implied, resulting or constructive trusts unless or until the instrument is set aside[36] or rectified.[37] However, the trust-based claims associated with 1975 Act have generally alleged the existence of a common-

---

[30] In *Burnard v Burnard* [2014] EWHC 340 (Ch), referred to above at para.7–003, the rectification claim was dealt with as a matter of construction and the 1975 Act claim was not determined.

[31] *Grattan v McNaughton* [2001] W.T.L.R. 1305.

[32] The meaning of "clerical error" is discussed in depth in *Marley v Rawlings* [2015] A.C. 129.

[33] *Re Williams* [1985] 1 W.L.R. 905.

[34] In *Re Martin, Clarke v Brothwood* [2007] W.T.L.R. 329, a claim for rectification succeeded where the mistake was equally likely to have arisen in one of two ways, either if the draftsman incorrectly recorded the instructions given by the testatrix, or if the testatrix had made an obvious error (which left 60 per cent of her estate undisposed of) in giving the instructions and the draftsman had not applied his mind to the significance of that obvious error.

[35] *Chittock v Stevens* [2000] W.T.L.R. 643.

[36] That is, for fraud or mistake.

[37] *Goodman v Gallant* [1986] Fam. 106, CA, per Slade LJ at 111.

intention constructive trust. As will be seen, claims based on resulting trusts have become increasingly rare in the domestic context, even if, as Lord Neuberger has observed,[38] the decisions of the Court of Appeal both in *Oxley v Hiscock*[39] and *Stack v Dowden*[40] "produced an outcome which would be dictated by a resulting trust solution". If a prospective claimant (C) under the 1975 Act wishes to advance a proprietary claim, it should be determined before the 1975 Act claim is dealt with on its merits, because the existence of an interest under such a claim affects both the size of the net estate and the financial needs and resources of the claimant and of the party or parties otherwise interested in the property in question. The decision whether to pursue a proprietary claim as well as a 1975 Act claim needs careful consideration both of the merits of the two claims and the manner in which, or the extent to which, any award in the 1975 Act proceedings might be reduced if the claim to a proprietary interest is established. There are several specialist works which deal with these aspects of the law in considerable depth[41] and only a brief outline of the current position is given here.

(ii) Resulting trusts

The classical analysis[42] is well expressed in *Maudsley and Burn's Trusts and Trustees,*[43] under the heading "Purchase-money resulting trusts", as follows: **7–015**

> "Where a purchaser buys property in the name of a third party or joins in the purchase of property with another party but in the name of that party only, then subject to the nature of the relationship between the parties, it is presumed that the property is held on resulting trust for the purchaser. That presumption, however, can be rebutted by adducing evidence that the purchase was intended as a gift."

The presumption of a purchase-money resulting trust (such that the parties were beneficially entitled in proportion to their respective contributions) was, classically, rebutted by the presumption of advancement.[44] The com-

---

[38] *Stack v Dowden* [2007] 2 A.C. 432, at [106], [122]. Lord Neuberger dissented in part but delivered a judgment concurring in the result.

[39] *Oxley v Hiscock* [2005] Fam. 211, CA.

[40] *Stack v Dowden* [2005] F.C.R. 739, CA, affirmed on different grounds by *Stack v Dowden* [2007] 2 A.C. 432.

[41] *Snell's Equity*, 33rd edn (London: Sweet & Maxwell, 2015), Chs 12 (Estoppel), 23(8) (Common intention constructive trusts), and 25 (Resulting trusts); *Megarry & Wade, Law of Real Property*, 8th edn (London: Sweet & Maxwell, 2012), Ch.16 (Proprietary estoppel); *Lewin on Trusts*, 19th edn (London: Sweet & Maxwell, 2015), Chs 7 (Trusts arising by operation of law generally) and 9 (Trusts arising in relation to the acquisition of property); G. Thomas and A. Hudson, *The Law of Trusts*, 2nd edn (Oxford: Oxford University Press, 2010), Pt D, "Trusts Implied by Law"; *Underhill and Hayton, Law of Trusts and Trustees*, 18th edn (London: LexisNexis, 2010) Division Three, "Trusts imposed by law".

[42] Expounded in *Dyer v Dyer* (1788) 2 Cox Eq. Cas. 92; 30 E.R. 42.

[43] *Maudsley & Burns Trusts and Trustees*, 7th edn (Oxford: Oxford University Press, 2008), p.260.

[44] Which is abolished by s.199 of the Equality Act 2010, though Pt 15 of that Act, which is concerned with family property has not, at the time of writing, been brought into force.

mon feature of the relationships traditionally giving rise to the presumption of advancement is that C was, or was expected to be, under an equitable obligation to provide for or support D, thus, it would arise where D was C's wife, fiancé, child or person to whom C was in loco parentis. However, the presumption of advancement in favour of a wife has been for some decades thought to be weak. As long ago as 1970 it was observed in *Pettitt v Pettitt*[45] that in modern economic circumstances the force of the presumption as between husband and wife has largely disappeared. In *McGrath v Wallis*[46] where the case turned on whether the presumption applied as between father and child, the Court of Appeal described the presumption, in its application to a house purchased for joint occupation, as a judicial instrument of last resort, and one which could be rebutted by comparatively slight evidence. In any event the presumption of resulting trust can be rebutted by evidence of a common intention that the parties should be entitled in proportions other than the proportions in which they contributed to the purchase price.[47]

7–016   The existence of an interest under a resulting trust may be significant in the context of a 1975 Act claim even though it is not quantified. In *Re Krubert*[48] the major asset of the deceased husband's estate was the matrimonial home, built on a plot of land bought with funds provided by the applicant widow. The Court of Appeal did not attempt to quantify the interest; but, in Nourse LJ's judgment, the fact that she had provided the purchase price of the plot and must therefore be taken to have a measurable beneficial interest in the matrimonial home was an important consideration.

7–017   Since *Stack v Dowden*,[49] there are now relatively few situations in which the quantification of the parties' interests will be determined on resulting trust principles.[50] In relation to the matrimonial or quasi-matrimonial home those principles may operate:

> "...in an updated form which takes account of all significant contributions, whether direct or indirect, and in cash or in kind, happen to be reflected in the parties' common intentions."

However, in a non-domestic context, Lord Neuberger has found room for the resulting trust analysis. In *Laskar v Laskar*,[51] a case in which a mother and daughter had purchased a property primarily for rental income and capital appreciation, he considered that the principles in *Stack v Dowden* did not apply.

---

[45] *Pettitt v Pettitt* [1970] A.C. 777.
[46] *McGrath v Wallis* [1995] 2 F.L.R. 114.
[47] *Gissing v Gissing* [1971] A.C. 886, HL; *Bernard v Josephs* [1982] Ch. 391.
[48] *Re Krubert* [1997] Ch. 97, CA.
[49] *Stack v Dowden* [2007] A.C. 432; see Lord Walker at [31].
[50] See M. Dixon, *Resulting and Constructive Trusts of Land; The Mist Descends and Rises* (2005) Conv. 79, in which he discusses *Curley v Parkes* [2005] 1 P. & C.R. DG 15; [2004] EWCA 1515 and *Oxley v Hiscock* [2005] Fam. 211.
[51] *Laskar v Laskar* [2008] 1 W.L.R. 2695, CA, approving *Adekunle v Ritchie* [2007] W.T.L.R. 1505 (mother purchasing property at a discount with the aid of her son, parties jointly and severally liable under the mortgage raised to provide the balance).

Resulting trust principles have been applied in a number of cases where   **7–018**
the contribution of one party was in the form of a discount to which the
contributor was entitled under the right to buy legislation. In *Marsh v von
Sternberg*[52] it was held, on the facts, that the parties had agreed that the
value of the discount should be taken into account as a contribution, by the
person entitled to the discount, to the purchase of the property. In
Springette v Defoe[53] it was common ground that each of the parties should
have a beneficial interest but there had never been any discussion at the time
of purchase as to the extent of the respective interests. In those circumstances the discount was taken into account as a contribution by the party
entitled to it and the presumption of resulting trust was held not to have
been displaced. However, that decision attracted criticism in *Oxley v Hiscock*[54] and those criticisms were endorsed by the House of Lords in *Stack v
Dowden*.[55] In *Evans v Hayward*[56] Staughton LJ preferred not to regard the
value of the discount as a direct money contribution, but he said that the
facts as to the existence of the discount and the source from which it was
derived were capable of leading to the inference that the parties had made an
agreement as to how the purchase price was provided. The authorities were
considered by the Court of Appeal in *Ashe (Trustee in bankruptcy of
Mumford) v Mumford*,[57] where it was held that there was no principle that
the right to buy discount was to be taken into account as if it were a direct
cash contribution. The presumption of the resulting trust could be displaced
by evidence of some other agreement as to the beneficial interests; or, as was
found in *Ashe v Mumford*, on the ground that the transaction involving the
property in question was a sham.

[52] *Marsh v von Sternberg* [1986] 1 F.L.R. 526.
[53] *Springette v Defoe* [1992] 2 F.L.R. 388, CA.
[54] *Oxley v Hiscock* [2005] Fam. 211 per Chadwick LJ [47]–[48], where he expressed the view that
the reference in *Lloyds Bank v Rosset* [1991] 1 A.C. 107, at 132F, to the need to base "a
finding of an agreement or arrangement to share" on "evidence of express discussion
between the partners" was referring to the primary question whether there was a common
intention that each should have a beneficial interest in the property, and not the secondary
question of their common intention as to the extent of those interests. In *Stack v Dowden*
[2005] F.C.R. 739, CA he said at [24] that: "...properly understood, the authorities before
(and after) *Springette v Defoe* do not support the proposition that, absent discussion between
the parties as to their respective beneficial interests at the time of purchase, it must necessarily follow that the presumption of resulting trust is not displaced and the property is
necessarily held in beneficial shares proportionate to the respective contributions to the
purchase price".
[55] *Stack v Dowden* [2007] A.C. 432, per Baroness Hale of Richmond at [65], agreeing with those
observations. She held that: "the approach to quantification in cases where the home is
conveyed into joint names should certainly be no stricter than the approach to quantification
in cases where it has been conveyed into the name of one only, and that to the extent that
Springette v Defoe and *Huntingford v Hobbs* [1993] 1 F.L.R. 736, C.A. hold otherwise, they
should not be followed."
[56] *Evans v Hayward* [1995] 2 F.L.R. 511.
[57] *Ashe (Trustee in bankruptcy of Mumford) v Mumford* (2001) 33 H.L.R. 67.

7–019   The resulting trust analysis may also apply where the property is acquired on mortgage.[58] In *Huntingford v Hobbs*[59] the parties, who had for some time previously been living together in Mrs Hobbs' former matrimonial home, purchased another property for £63,250 in joint names. The transfer contained no declaration of trust. Mrs Hobbs contributed £38,860 from the proceeds of sale of her property and a joint mortgage for £25,000 was taken out. She had no income and it was anticipated that Mr Huntingford would pay the mortgage instalments. The relationship broke down unexpectedly some three years later, and his actual contribution to the purchase price was assessed at trial as £3,500, made up of the capital instalments which he had paid and the cost of a conservatory. Setting aside the judgment at first instance, the Court of Appeal held the most likely inference from the conduct of the parties to be that they had a common intention at the date of purchase that Mrs Hobbs should be treated as having made her cash contribution, Mr Huntingford as having contributed the whole of the sum borrowed on mortgage and the property should be owned by them in shares proportionate to those contributions. The order reflected that inferred common intention save that Mr Huntingford should be repaid £2,000 representing the cost to him of the conservatory added to the property subsequent to the purchase before division of the net proceeds of sale in those proportions.

(iii) Common-intention constructive trusts

7–020   The general principle underlying the common-intention constructive trust is stated in *Lewin*[60] as follows:

> "A constructive trust arises in connexion with the acquisition by one party of a legal title to property whenever that party has so conducted himself that it would be inequitable to allow him to deny to another party a beneficial interest in the property acquired. This will be so where (i) there was a common intention that both parties should have a beneficial interest either at the date of acquisition or at a later date and (ii) the claimant has acted to his detriment in the belief that by doing so he was acquiring a beneficial interest.[61] Some element of bargain, promise or tacit common intention must be shown in order to establish such a trust."

---

[58] But see *Carlton v Goodman* [2002] 2 F.L.R. 259, CA. There, the defendant had facilitated the purchase of a house by entering into a joint mortgage with the claimant, but had not made any contribution to the purchase price of the property and it was never intended that she should do so. It was held that in those circumstances no resulting trust arose in her favour. For the reasoning leading to that conclusion, see in particular [22], per Mummery LJ and the section entitled "The Resulting Trust Debate" which follows.

[59] *Huntingford v Hobbs* [1993] 1 F.L.R. 736, CA.

[60] *Lewin*, para.9–062.

[61] *Gissing v Gissing* [1971] A.C. 886, H.L. at 905. See also *Grant v Edwards* [1986] Ch. 638, CA, where Nourse LJ said at 648 that the course of conduct must be of a nature on which the claimant could not reasonably have been expected to embark, unless they were to have an interest in the property.

In *Lloyds Bank v Rosset*,[62] Lord Bridge considered the manner in which a   **7–021** common intention to share property beneficially might be established. It was always necessary, independently of any inference to be drawn from the conduct of the parties, to decide whether prior to the acquisition of the property (or, exceptionally, at some later date) there had been any agreement or arrangement entered into, or understanding reached, that the property should be shared beneficially. Such a finding, in his view, could be based only on express discussions between the parties, however imperfectly they may have been remembered and however imprecise their terms may have been. In the absence of any expressed common intention that the beneficial ownership of the property acquired should not follow the legal ownership, the next step is to consider whether such common intention can be inferred. The judgment of Baroness Hale in *Stack v Dowden*[63] provides a survey of the matters to be taken into account for that purpose in cases where the property is held in joint names. Many of these matters will also be relevant in cases where the property is held in a sole name.[64]

In relation to the timing of the agreement, arrangement or understanding,   **7–022** it may be that establishing the common intention by evidence of discussions after the acquisition of the property is not as exceptional as Lord Bridge's statement of the position would suggest. Thus in *Gissing v Gissing*[65] Viscount Dilhorne adverted to the possibility that the spouses might form the intention to share ownership at some time after the acquisition of the property; as, for example, where one spouse takes over from the other the burden of the mortgage payments. In *James v Thomas*[66] it was held that the common intention necessary to found a constructive trust could be formed at any time before, after or during the acquisition of a property and could therefore arise some years after the property had been acquired and registered in the name of one party.

Where there is no evidence of such an agreement, and the court must rely   **7–023** on the conduct of the parties as a basis on which to infer the existence of a common intention to share the property beneficially, the conduct is often that the claimant has made financial contributions referable to the acquisition of the property. However, the view expressed in *Lloyds Bank v Rosset*[67] that it was extremely doubtful whether any conduct other than the making of direct contributions to the purchase price, either initially or by payment of mortgage instalments, would be a sufficient basis for the inference, can no longer be regarded as definitive. In *James v Thomas*,[68] Sir John Chadwick said, in relation to the beneficial interest claimed by Miss James, that it must be determined:

---

[62] *Lloyds Bank v Rosset* [1991] 1 A.C. 107.
[63] *Stack v Dowden* [2007] A.C. 432, at [69].
[64] For a comparison of the position of claimants in sole name and joint name cases, see *Lewin* at para.9–072.
[65] *Gissing v Gissing* [1971] A.C. 886 at 901D–E.
[66] *James v Thomas* [2008] 1 F.L.R. 1598, CA per Sir John Chadwick, at [23]–[25].
[67] *Lloyds Bank v Rosset* [1991] 1 A.C. 107 HL, at 133A.
[68] *James v Thomas* [2008] 1 F.L.R. 1598, at [39].

"...by applying principles of law and equity which (however inadequate to meet the circumstances in which parties live together in the 21st century) must now be taken as well established";

and he went on to cite the observation of Baroness Hale in *Stack v Dowden*[69] that it was:

"...not for the court to abandon the search for the result which reflects what the parties must, in the light of their conduct be taken to have intended, in favour of the result which the court itself considers fair."

In *Abbott v Abbott*[70] the Judicial Committee of the Privy Council held that the task of the court was:

"to ascertain the parties' shared intentions, actual, inferred or imputed, with respect to the property, in the light of their whole course of conduct in relation to it."

While this may be a welcome liberalisation in that it gives greater scope for recognition of the kind of situation in which "the cock can feather the nest because he does not have to spend most of his time sitting on it",[71] it gives no guidance whether any particular form of conduct is likely to be found significant in relation to establishing common intention.[72]

(iv) Claims Based on Proprietary Estoppel

7–024   There is a general rule that a person who incurs expense in improving the property of another has no claim to reimbursement of the expense or a lien over the property[73]; see *Falcke v Scottish Imperial Insurance Co.*[74] However, this rule does not operate in circumstances where the doctrine of proprietary estoppel applies. The doctrine, though mainly concerned with the acquisition of rights and interests in land, may also apply to other types of property.

7–025   In his dissenting speech in *Ramsden v Dyson*,[75] which was a landlord and tenant case, Lord Kingswood made a statement which is accepted as being

---

[69] *Stack v Dowden* [2007] A.C. 432, at [61].
[70] *Abbott v Abbott* [2008] 1 F.L.R. 1451, at [6], where Baroness Hale of Richmond cited her own judgment in *Stack v Dowden* [2007] 2 A.C. 432, at [60].
[71] e.g., one party using their income to meet household expenses so that the other's income is proportionately made available to meet mortgage repayments. The phrase was used by Lord Hodson in *Pettitt v Pettitt* [1970] A.C. 777 at 811 and was attributed by him to Sir Jocelyn Simon, President of the Probate, Divorce and Admiralty Division, speaking extra-judicially.
[72] *Stack v Dowden* [2007] 2 A.C. 432, at [144].
[73] See, generally, *Snell's Equity*, 33rd edn (2015), Ch.12 (Estoppel) which deals with promissory and proprietary estoppel; *Megarry & Wade, The Law of Real Property*, 8th edn (2012), Ch.16 (Proprietary estoppel).
[74] *Falcke v Scottish Imperial Insurance Co* (1886) 34 Ch. D. 234, CA; Snell, para.44–034.
[75] *Ramsden v Dyson* (1866) 1 L.R. (HL) 129 at 140. The principle was expressed in somewhat similar terms by Edward Nugee QC in his judgment in *Re Basham, Deceased* [1986] 1 W.L.R. 1498 at 1503.

of general application in the law of proprietary estoppel and, in that general form, may be expressed as follows:

> "If B, under an expectation created or encouraged by A that B shall have a certain interest in land, takes possession of such land and, with the consent of A, and upon the faith of such expectation and with the knowledge of A and without objection from him, lays out money on the land, a court of equity will compel A to give effect to such expectation."

A broader statement of that principle is found in *Taylor Fashions Ltd v Liverpool Victoria Trustees Co Ltd*[76] where Oliver J said that the approach to it should be towards:

> "...ascertaining whether, in particular individual circumstances, it would be unconscionable for a party to be permitted to deny, that which, knowingly or unknowingly, he has allowed or encouraged another to assume to his detriment, rather than to inquiring whether the circumstances can be fitted within the confines of some preconceived formula serving as a universal yardstick for every form of unconscionable behaviour."[77]

Using the designations above,[78] the elements of proprietary estoppel are that:

(i)   the owner (A) of the property has either actively or passively encouraged the other party (B) to believe that they either have acquired, or will acquire some right over or benefit from that property;

(ii)   B has acted to their detriment in reliance on that belief; and

(iii)   it would be unconscionable thereafter for A to act in such a way as to defeat the expectation which they had encouraged in B.

In relation to those three elements, the following points may be significant   **7–026**
in the context of a claim which is a claim alternative or additional to a 1975 Act claim:

(1) encouragement:

(a)   the right or benefit which B was encouraged to believe that they had, or would acquire must be of a proprietary nature;

---

[76] *Taylor Fashions Ltd v Liverpool Victoria Trustees Co Ltd* [1982] Q.B. 133 at 151.

[77] This can be seen as a warning against the mechanical application of the "five probanda" identified by Fry J in *Willmott v Barber* (1880) 15 Ch. D 96 at 105–106.

[78] Readers of previous editions of this work should note that the designations of the parties have been changed so that A is the owner of the property in question and B is the party claiming under the doctrine of proprietary estoppel. This change has been made so that the designations correspond to those adopted in the current (33rd) edition of *Snell*, Ch.12.

(b)   while it has been held that the right must relate to specific prop-
       erty, it is sufficient that the property in question is ascertainable;
       hence the doctrine can operate in relation to a right or benefit in
       A's residuary estate;
(c)   even though a will is inherently revocable, the doctrine can operate
       in relation to a promise to make a will in B's favour.

(2) detriment and reliance:

(a)   while the most obvious example of detriment is the expenditure of
       money, the concept is not limited to quantifiable financial detri-
       ment,[79] nor does the financial value of the detriment have to be
       substantial.[80] However, it must be more than trivial, and con-
       comitant benefit may be set off against it.[81] It may take many
       forms, among which are matters to which the court would have
       regard, as creating an obligation under s.3(1)(d), or as being
       relevant under s.3(1)(g). Examples include looking after A or his
       family without payment[82]; giving up opportunities which would
       enable B to lead an independent life, and working in A's business
       for low wages[83];
(b)   whether B in fact acted to their detriment is to be assessed by
       reference to the position at the time when A seeks to go back on
       their assurance;
(c)   once encouragement by A and detriment suffered by B have been
       established, it will be for A to prove that B did not rely on A's
       encouragement when acting to their detriment;
(d)   in the context of family relationships, it is not necessarily fatal to
       B's claim that they should have had some motive other than A's
       encouragement for acting as they did.

(3) unconscionability: here, the question is not purely whether A thought
they were acting unconscionably by going back on their assurance. While
the court has to consider whether it was unconscionable in all the circumstances for A to do so, there is no kind of general jurisdiction to enforce

---

[79]   *Gillett v Holt* [2001] Ch. 210, CA, per Robert Walker LJ, at 232.
[80]   *Pascoe v Turner* [1979] 1 W.L.R. 431, CA (£230 spent on repairs and improvements to the
       property, and other expenditure on carpets, curtains and furniture).
[81]   *Century (UK) Ltd SA v Clibbery* [2004] EWHC 1870 (Ch), at [71] where Blackburne J
       considered that the various chores undertaken by Mrs Clibbery did not amount to the degree
       of detriment necessary to establish a proprietary estoppel and that, viewed against the many
       years of her cost-free occupation, the element of detriment was not established.
[82]   *Greasley v Cooke* [1980] 1 W.L.R. 1306, CA (maidservant, originally paid, and living in
       house, remaining in occupation, after her paid employment terminated, to look after the
       owners).
[83]   *Thorner v Major* [2009] 1 W.L.R. 776, HL, reversing [2008] W.T.L.R 1289, CA, and restoring
       the order made at first instance, for which see *Thorner v Major* [2008] W.T.L.R. 155, where
       the judge had found that the claimant relied on the assurance given by the deceased by not
       pursuing other opportunities; see paras 94, 98 and 111(d) of his judgment, quoted in the
       House of Lords decision, at [15], per Lord Scott of Foscote.

assurances because it would be unfair not to do so, or to override established principles of law because their operation would be hard on the promisee. Although it is convenient for the purpose of exposition to treat those elements separately, it is important to realise, as Robert Walker LJ observed in *Gillett v Holt*[84] that the doctrine is not subdivided into watertight compartments, one per element, but that the elements of encouragement, detrimental reliance and unconscionability will generally interact.

Whereas the effect of a successful claim based on resulting or constructive **7–027** trust will be that the claimant is declared to have a beneficial interest and that interest is quantified, a successful claim based on proprietary estoppel does not necessarily lead to that result. The maximum extent of the equity is the making good, so far as is possible as between A and B, the expectation which A has encouraged; see *Griffiths v Williams*.[85] It may be that full effect will be given to B's expectation, as in *Thorner v Major*,[86] but they cannot obtain more.[87] The court may, adopting the approach of looking for the minimum equity to do justice, award them less.[88] The relief will not necessarily be in the form of an award to B of the promised or expected interest, or any interest at all in the land. Thus, in *Jennings v Rice*,[89] where the proprietary estoppel claim was to the deceased's house and contents, worth £450,000, a monetary award of £250,000 was made. It has been said that the court will not impose a liability on A which is out of all proportion to the extent of B's detriment,[90] though, as observed in *Snell*,[91] the concept of proportionality has not been defined with complete clarity. There are two approaches to the determination of the appropriate relief. One is that B's expectation is to be fully satisfied unless it is clear that that would impose a disproportionate burden on A. This in effect involves a presumption in favour of making good B's expectation which it is for A to rebut. That presumption is absent from the other approach, which is directed towards the determination of the relief which will ensure that B will suffer no detriment as a result of their reasonable reliance on A. *Snell* expresses a preference for the second approach on the ground that it:

"...gives a positive role to the need for proportionality, and defines the concept by reference to the extent of B's potential detriment, also improves on the first by providing principles that can be used to determine the extent of B's right even when it is clear that B's expectation should not be protected. It also draws an important link between

[84] *Gillett v Holt* [2001] Ch. 210 at 225.
[85] *Griffiths v Williams* (1977) 248 E.G. 947.
[86] *Thorner v Major* [2009] 1 W.L.R. 776, HL.
[87] *Griffiths v Williams* (1977) 248 E.G. 947; *Dodsworth v Dodsworth* (1973) 228 E.G. 1115; *Baker v Baker* (1993) 25 H.L.R. 408.
[88] *Baker v Baker* (1993) 25 H.L.R. 408; *Gillett v Holt* [2001] Ch. 210, C.A. at 237, where Robert Walker LJ said that the court's aim was "having identified the maximum, to form a view as to what was the minimum required to satisfy [the equity] and do justice between the parties".
[89] *Jennings v Rice* [2002] W.T.L.R. 367.
[90] *Suggitt v Suggitt* [2012] W.T.L.R. 1607, at [44], per Arden LJ.
[91] *Snell*, at para.12–048 and n.407.

the grounds on which B's right arises (the need to avoid B's being left to suffer a detriment) and the extent of that right. With one exception,[92] it is also difficult to find decisions where the result reached is inconsistent with the second approach."

7–028   Although, as remarked in relation to claims based on common-intention constructive trust,[93] the flexibility of the courts' approach may be welcome in principle, that flexibility can create a problem for the practitioner who has to advise whether the client's interests are best served by bringing a claim under this doctrine, or a 1975 Act claim, or both, since, given the wide range of ways in which the equity can be satisfied, it may be particularly difficult to predict what award the court might make in the proprietary estoppel claim.

(e) Claims to Personal Chattels and other Personal Property

7–029   All practitioners in this field will be aware of the extreme bitterness and tenacity with which claims to the ownership of personal chattels are often fought.[94] The case of *Hammond v Mitchell*,[95] in which *Lloyds Bank v Rosset* was applied, and which involved claims to the ownership of both real and personal property, is instructive. In that case, the relationship between H and M began in 1977. In 1979, shortly after the birth of their first child, H acquired a bungalow for occupation as their home. H explained to M that it would have to be put in his name because of his tax problems. It is not uncommon for excuses of this nature[96] to be made by the party who is to be the legal owner; see *Burns v Burns*[97] and *Grant v Edwards*.[98] Shortly after completion of the purchase H said to M: "Don't worry about the future because when we are married it will be half yours anyway and I'll always look after you." During the course of the relationship H acquired neighbouring land with the aid of a bank loan; the bank's representative told M that she had to execute the charge, as she had an interest in the property. The charge, which she executed, contained a covenant by M to postpone her interest to the bank's charge. H carried on various commercial activities from the property, in which M willingly participated. The relationship broke down in 1988 and M claimed an interest not only in the bungalow but in another property in Spain which H had purchased in his own name in 1985. As to this her claim failed, the necessary agreement not being proved.

7–030   However, as to the bungalow it was found that there was express discussion sufficient to amount to an understanding that the bungalow was to be shared beneficially; that the same understanding applied to the neigh-

---

[92] *Pascoe v Turner* [1979] 1 W.L.R. 431, CA; see *Snell* at para.12–048 and n.407, and para.12–048 and n.418.
[93] At para.7–023.
[94] For a very useful monograph on this topic, see Stanyer, *Personal Chattels: Law, Practice and Tax, with Precedents* (London: Sweet & Maxwell, 2009).
[95] *Hammond v Mitchell* [1992] 2 All E.R. 109.
[96] See *Lewin*, at para.9–065 on the inferences which may be drawn from such excuses in common-intention constructive trust claims.
[97] *Burns v Burns* [1984] Ch. 317.
[98] *Grant v Edwards* [1986] Ch. 638, CA.

bouring land subsequently acquired; and that M had acted to her detriment in that she gave her full support to speculative ventures which, had they turned out unfavourably, might have resulted in the bungalow having to be sold. It should be noted that the understanding expressed by way of the words quoted in the previous paragraph was not given expression until after the property had been acquired, and it is not apparent from the reports of the case that such an understanding had been reached before then. M's beneficial interest was assessed as one half, having regard to her role as mother, helper, unpaid assistant and, at times, financial supporter.

A considerable part of the hearing was taken up with a dispute about the ownership of various personal chattels. Waite J gave the following valuable guidance as to how such questions should be approached: **7–031**

(a) sorting out the ownership of chattels bought by parties who have been living together is something that the parties should be expected to achieve by themselves, without the necessity for a court hearing[99];

(b) such agreement is strongly preferable to crude acts of self-help by removing chattels from the home on the break-up of the association;

(c) while there is no English doctrine of community of property in this regard, the parties must expect the court in such cases to adhere robustly to the maxim that "equality is equity", if only in the interests of fulfilling the equally salutary maxim that it is in the public interest that there should be an end to litigation; and

(d) if it is really necessary to bring issues of disputed ownership of household chattels to adjudication, the proper way of doing it is a claim for a declaration or inquiry, supported by appropriate affidavit evidence, on lines similar to those adopted in the resolution of disputes under s.17 of the Married Women's Property Act 1882. Actions under the Torts (Interference with Goods) Act are not normally appropriate.

The question whether an intending applicant has a claim to a beneficial entitlement in personal property arises from time to time in relation to death benefits. Section 8(1) of the 1975 Act applies only to nominations in accordance with the provisions of an enactment, so it does not catch private occupational schemes or policies of life assurance. If the proceeds of an insurance policy are payable to the deceased's personal representatives, but the premiums were paid by the claimant, the application of the classical resulting trust principles discussed above leads to the conclusion that, prima facie, the proceeds are held on resulting trust for the claimant unless the presumption of advancement operates.[100]   **7–032**

---

[99] See also the comments to the same effect by Millett J in *Windeler v Whitehill* [1990] F.C.R. 268.

[100] *Re Scottish Equitable Life Assurance Society* [1902] 1 Ch. 282. It is unclear what the position will be if and when the provision by which the presumption of advancement is abolished (Equality Act 2010 s.199) comes into force.

7–033   It is suggested that claims relating to the ownership or possession of personal chattels should be dealt with separately from proceedings under the 1975 Act. In the first place, unless there are chattels of substantial value, the nature and extent of the net estate is not likely to be significantly affected by a determination of their ownership. Secondly, they are very often the subject matter of specific legacies, and it would be very unusual for the court to conclude, in deciding on the incidence of the burden of an award, that provision should be made by way of the sale of a personal chattel which has been specifically gifted; and it has no power to order that the beneficiary of such a gift should make a monetary contribution towards the provision ordered as a condition of being permitted to retain the gift. Finally, while circumstances might occur in which the making of reasonable provision involved the transfer of business chattels to the applicant, it is in the highest degree improbable that the court would consider it appropriate to make such an order in respect of personal chattels. Questions relating to the ownership of personal chattels will, therefore, very rarely arise in the context of a 1975 Act application and, given their tendency to generate more heat than light and to increase the cost of the proceedings to an extent quite disproportionate to their value, it is suggested that unless the circumstances are wholly exceptional, they should not be raised in 1975 Act proceedings.

(f) Multiple claims: An Overview

7–034   Claims under multiple heads have been made more often in the 21st century than before, and it is clear that the outcomes have rarely justified the additional costs involved. The following survey of the accessible[101] cases identifies, so far as is apparent from the reports or, as the case may be, the transcripts, the reasons for the failure of the claims, including, in some cases, both the 1975 Act claim and the other claim. The survey deals first with the relatively few cases in which there was a probate or rectification claim, and then with the more numerous cases in which there was a proprietary claim.

7–035   The earliest case of the first type was *Moody v Haselgrove*,[102] in which the applicant widow brought three probate actions seeking to have her husband's will set aside. In the last of those actions, five months after his death, the will, which disposed of an estate worth approximately £78,000, was upheld. Probate was not granted until June 1986, nearly three years later. In the 1975 Act claim, heard at first instance in May 1987, it was found that the will had failed to make reasonable provision for the applicant. By that time, all the cash in the estate had been exhausted by the probate actions and administration costs and indeed the applicant had been ordered to pay some costs personally. Falconer J made an order directing the matrimonial home to be held on trust for the applicant absolutely, subject to various provisions for raising money on it to pay costs and legacies to the deceased's three cousins who were beneficiaries under his will. The applicant was not satisfied

---

[101] Two of the cases considered are unreported decisions of the Court of Appeal and one is a so far unreported decision at first instance.
[102] *Moody v Haselgrove* unreported 16 November 1987, CA.

with this, it being her case that she should receive the entire beneficial interest in the matrimonial home. Her appeal was dismissed and the order below was varied to her disadvantage, by charging three pecuniary legacies of £1,000 on the matrimonial home instead of charging them on residue, which by then had been exhausted.

The next case, in chronological order, is *Grattan v McNaughton*.[103] This was a case in which the deceased's widow (G) claimed rectification of his will and, alternatively, provision under the 1975 Act. G and her husband, who had two children from a previous marriage, instructed a solicitor to draw up wills disposing of their respective shares in the matrimonial home separately, with a qualified right for the survivor to remain in the matrimonial home. The husband's will provided that G's right of occupation should cease on remarriage, cohabitation or ceasing to reside in the property, and there was no provision enabling it to be sold and a substitute property purchased. It was found that there was insufficient evidence to show that the will did not express his intention, but the 1975 Act claim succeeded to the extent that she was awarded the residuary estate (some £16,000 less the costs of administration) and her right to reside in the property would not be terminated by cohabitation.[104]

7–036

Pinnock v Rochester,[105] discussed in more detail above, may be a significant decision in view of the amendment to s.4 of the 1975 Act which permits claims to be made although no grant of representation has been issued. The question which arose in the case was whether a claimant who had compromised his 1975 Act claim by entering into a consent order and accepting the payment was precluded, by the doctrine of election, from challenging the will. On appeal, the decision of the trial judge to that effect was reversed. Sales J held that the two claims were conceptually different and that there was nothing inequitable or unfair in making the subsequent challenge to the validity of the will; also, there was nothing in the consent order which ruled out the possibility of a challenge to the will. It would seem, therefore, that there is now no bar to commencing a 1975 Act claim while a caveat is in force or a probate claim has already been commenced, though it is not easy to visualise circumstances in which that would be an appropriate course of action. Finally in this group of cases, the 1975 Act claim in *Watts v Watts*[106] which accompanied the probate claim did not have to be determined, as the last will of the deceased was found to be invalid as not having been executed in accordance with s.9 of the Wills Act 1837, and

7–037

---

[103] *Grattan v McNaughton* [2001] W.T.L.R. 1305.
[104] It may be, in any particular case, that a will containing conditions of this type could be seen as failing to make reasonable provision for the claimant, since the assumption underlying the inclusion of the condition is, presumably, that the person with whom the claimant cohabits will provide housing or in some other way contribute to the claimant's reasonable needs.
[105] *Pinnock v Rochester* [2011] EWHC 4049 (Ch), discussed at paras 7–005—7–006, above. There is no report of the outcome of the probate claim.
[106] *Watts v Watts* [2014] EWHC 668 (Ch), where it was found that the deceased's last will, had it been valid, would have failed to make reasonable financial provision for the claimant.

the earlier will, which was admitted to probate, had made reasonable financial provision for the claimant.

7–038   The first of the cases involving a proprietary claim and a 1975 Act claim is the unreported Court of Appeal decision in *Riggs v Lloyds Bank*.[107] There, Mrs Riggs, the daughter of the deceased, had succeeded in her 1975 Act claim at first instance; the appeal was by her brother, the second defendant to the original claim. Mrs Riggs had also made a claim, which was consolidated with the 1975 Act claim, for a transfer, on the basis of proprietary estoppel, of a strip of land adjoining the garden of her house. The award under the 1975 Act was set aside essentially on the ground that it did not represent maintenance for the applicant but was by way of provision for her minor children, which was not the way in which her case had been put. However, the appeal against the decision on the proprietary estoppel claim at first instance was dismissed. The trial judge had ordered that the disputed land be transferred to her in fee simple subject to a restrictive covenant not to erect any building on the land transferred without the consent of the owner of the retained land. It was argued in support of the appeal on that point, that the assurance given to Mrs Riggs by her father was ambiguous; and that, as she had converted the land into a garden and she liked gardening, so the garden was an amenity for her and she had to show detriment. Neither the trial judge nor Dillon LJ found the assurance relied on to be ambiguous.[108] Dillon LJ considered it to be a borderline case whether enough had been done in reliance on the assurance. He observed that:

> "Of course, in very many cases, what is done in reliance on a representation which is held to give rise to an equitable estoppel will carry elements of benefit to the persons to whom it is made, as when they put up a house on land which they are told that they will be able to have."

He went on to say that although Mrs Riggs had not done anything so extensive, it was doubtful whether she would have done so much as she did if the representation had not been made in a form which indicated that she was to have the land after the deceased's death.

7–039   *Churchill v Roach*[109] is, perhaps, the most informative case, since the proprietary claim was analysed in some depth by HH Judge Norris QC (as he then was). Dr Churchill (M) claimed a declaration that the property at 5/6 Ferry Lane, Alveston, in which she and the deceased (A) had set up home together some 16 months before his death, had passed to her by survivorship. It was argued that she had acquired an interest in that property either via a common-intention constructive trust or by the operation of the doctrine of proprietary estoppel. The 1975 Act claim was supplementary or

---

[107] *Riggs v Lloyds Bank* unreported 27 November 1992, CA.
[108] Mrs Riggs' evidence, which was accepted by the trial judge was that her father said, "I no longer need that land. I am not capable of doing it. You can take it over, tidy it up and have it as your garden". The deceased did not want her to fence it off while he was alive, but he also said, "When I am dead and gone, put your fence across and do as you like".
[109] *Churchill v Roach* [2004] 2 F.L.R. 989.

alternative to the proprietary claim. The relationship between the parties had begun in about 1991 but it was not until early 1998 (by which time A was in the process of negotiating a separation agreement under which his wife and children would be provided for) that they contemplated buying a single property for their joint occupation. The judge accepted M's evidence that when discussing this they had, in view of the difference in age between them (she being some 30 years the younger) contemplated that it would be jointly owned with a right of survivorship. However, that did not take place and 5/6 Ferry Lane, which adjoined M's property at 7 Ferry Lane, was purchased in December 1998 by A in his sole name and with his own money. 7 Ferry Lane was physically united with it in February 1999, but the two properties continued to be held under separate titles. There were some financial dealings between A and M at this time but a sum of £1,500 which M claimed as a contribution to the purchase of 5/6 Ferry Lane, was found to be a repayment of an earlier loan by A to M. There was evidence of discussions by both A and M with friends that a proposal was on foot to make a jointly owned property out of 5/6 and 7 Ferry Lane, but that never in fact took place, and the judge emphasised the dangers of treating social chitchat of the kind given in evidence[110] as equivalent to a declaration concerning the legal ownership of property. He found that immediately before his death A had intended to put the combined properties into joint names, probably as joint tenants, but his death intervened.[111]

Applying settled legal rules to the facts as he had found them, the judge   **7–040** first considered the claim, on the basis of either express agreement or by inference from conduct prior to the purchase of the property, to a beneficial interest under a constructive trust. Having cited the common-intention principle as expressed in the then current edition of *Lewin*[112] and the summary of the relevant rules by Nourse LJ in *Grant v Edwards*,[113] he first found that there was no direct evidence of an express agreement between A and M in relation to 5/6 Ferry Lane. There was no doubt that there would have been such an agreement in relation to any property purchased in joint names and jointly funded, but 5/6 Ferry Lane had been purchased in A's name with A's money. In relation to the implied agreement he adverted to the danger of treating subsequent events as proof of an earlier agreement. While that was one of the standard ways in which common-intention constructive trusts were proved, it was nevertheless to be used with care. The fact that, after the acquisition of 5/6 Ferry Lane, A agreed that it should be treated as jointly owned, did not mean that he had that intention at the time when he acquired it. That he allowed it to be joined to M's property and allowed her to undertake comparatively minor expenditure on it did not demonstrate an agreement at the time of acquisition that it should be jointly owned. Further, and crucially, it was clear that A understood the consequences of joint

---

[110] *Churchill v Roach*, at 996C–997A, e.g. "Arnold took the view that Muriel would be able to decide what to with the property if anything happened to him".
[111] *Churchill v Roach*, at 997A–998C.
[112] *Lewin* 17th edn (2000), at para.9–50.
[113] *Grant v Edwards* [1986] Ch. 638, CA at 647.

ownership and joint tenancy, but deliberately chose not to make any such arrangements. While accepting that there could be cases where an express or implied common-intention could be manifested at a later date, a mere statement of intention in relation to the legal ownership could never suffice to establish a common-intention constructive trust. On the facts as found, no common intention that M should have a beneficial interest in the property arose until about mid-1999; but there was no evidence of M having acted to her detriment on the faith of that common intention after that date. The claim based on constructive trust therefore failed.

7-041   In considering the claim based on proprietary estoppel, he began with the judgment of Robert Walker LJ in *Yaxley v Gotts*[114] which compared the concepts of constructive trust and proprietary estoppel, but pointed out the distinction that, whereas the constructive trust is concerned to focus on the parties' intentions at the time of acquisition, and the appropriate relief is to give effect without qualification to the agreement which is found to have existed, proprietary estoppel focuses on the moment at which the assurance is withdrawn and the court has a much broader range of relief available and looks to ascertain the minimum necessary to satisfy the equity. Detriment, in the context of proprietary estoppel was to be "approached as part of a broad enquiry as to whether repudiation of an assurance was unconscionable in all the circumstances".[115] The assurance relied on was that M would become a joint tenant in the joint home either from the outset or when six months of cohabitation had elapsed, but no such assurance was found to have been given; further, it would not have been unconscionable, having regard to such detriment as M had suffered through her work on the property, for A to have said (if the relationship had terminated during his lifetime) that she did not have a proprietary interest in the property. In the event, the 1975 Act claim succeeded on the basis that M was a dependant. Because of the state of relations between her and A's family, it was not thought desirable to award her a life interest in the property; instead, it was to be transferred to her absolutely subject to a charge for £65,000 representing the value of the reversionary interest to which A's family would ultimately have succeeded, together with an element representing interest for the postponement over the two years between A's death and the hearing.

7-042   The next reported case was *Negus v Bahouse*,[116] where the executors' claim for possession of the quasi-matrimonial home was met by a counterclaim for a declaration as to N's beneficial interest, under s.14 of the Trusts of Land and Appointment of Trustees Act 1996, and a 1975 Act claim. The proprietary claim was based on the same passage from *Lewin* as was considered in *Churchill v Roach*. It was disposed of very shortly on the ground that such

---

[114] *Yaxley v Gotts* [2000] Ch. 162 at 176; this aspect of the case is discussed in *Churchill v Roach* [2004] 2 F.L.R. 989 at 1002D–1004A.
[115] *Gillett v Holt* [2001] Ch. 210, CA, per Robert Walker LJ, 232D–E.
[116] *Negus v Bahouse* [2008] 1 F.L.R. 381.

assurances as the deceased may have given were equivocal[117] and insufficient to support a finding of a specific agreement, arrangement or understanding in respect of either of the two properties which they jointly occupied. No claim was established by proprietary estoppel or otherwise. Since in the 1975 Act claim N was awarded the flat in which the parties were living together at the time of the deceased's death, free of mortgage, and a substantial lump sum, the success or failure of the proprietary claim was irrelevant to the outcome.

In *Baker v Baker*[118] the deceased (B) had made a will in favour of H five   **7–043** days before he died. The will was successfully challenged by the deceased's daughter, who was the only person entitled to take on her father's death intestate. H then brought two claims, one under the 1975 Act as a cohabitant, and one in relation to the property which they had jointly occupied for some two years before his death. The facts relevant to that claim are that in about 1987 or 1988 when B and H met, they each owned their own property. As the relationship developed they spent more time together and pooled their resources to a greater extent; but they kept separate bank accounts, and when H moved out of her property to live with B she put in a tenant. Up until about 2001 H, like B, worked full time; but because of B's medical condition and short life expectancy they decided to spend as much time together as possible, and H took a part-time job. In 2003 H was diagnosed as having breast cancer. Following discussion with B she sold her property and B allayed her anxiety by saying that he would take care of her and that their assets belonged to them both.

H's proprietary estoppel claim was thus based on an alleged assurance or   **7–044** agreement by B and a reasonable expectation on her part that all his property would be hers on his death. It was found that there had been no such agreement or assurance; furthermore, she could have had no such reasonable expectation, because, among other matters, it was clear from the conversation on 21 April 2005, the day before he made his will, that he was only willing to leave his property to her if she reciprocated by doing the same, with the survivor's estate (as in his own will) going to his daughter (C) and H's daughter (N), which she did not do. That claim therefore failed.

In *Webster v Webster*[119] the 1975 Act claim was accompanied by a claim   **7–045** to a beneficial joint tenancy in the house jointly occupied by the claimant (A) and the deceased (J), and in a shareholding in a company of which he was a director. It was accepted that A was eligible to claim either as a cohabitant or as a dependant and that she had some interest in the house, but not a beneficial joint tenancy. The claim in relation to the shares failed on the basis that their acquisition was via a business opportunity personal to J; the shares were in his sole name, paid for with money borrowed by him, the loan being secured on property owned by him, in respect of which he

---

[117] N's evidence was that there was no arrangement other than that she was to be at his home and have a roof over her head; he simply made it clear to her that if anything happened, she would have a roof over her head; see *Negus v Bahouse*, at [53]–[55].

[118] *Baker v Baker* [2008] 2 F.L.R. 767.

[119] *Webster v Webster* [2009] 1 F.L.R. 1240.

was paying the mortgage; there was no evidence of any discussions between the parties as to whether A should have any interest in them. In relation to the house the judge was unable to impute an intention that A should acquire a beneficial interest in the house, but her indirect contributions to the family budget would found an inference that she had such an interest, which he would have put at 33 to 40 per cent had it been necessary to quantify it. As she was awarded the house free of mortgage in the 1975 Act claim, the partly successful proprietary claim did not improve the outcome.

7–046 In *Bye v Colvin-Scott*,[120] the litigation began with a claim by the executor for possession of a flat in which the deceased's daughter (E) had been living with her mother (S) at the date of her death. E counterclaimed on the basis of proprietary estoppel and also on a document purportedly signed by S and giving her the right to occupy the flat for her lifetime. As to the claim based on the document, there were, in fact, at least two, and possibly three versions of it. It was found (particularly since for some months previously S had wanted to sell the flat, preferably to E) that when the document was signed, S did not know what she was doing, nor did she intend to grant a life interest to E. It was clear that that idea had emanated from E and it was more likely than not that S would have repudiated the document had she seen it in her lifetime.

7–047 The judgment in relation to the proprietary estoppel claim follows the well-established analysis of assurance or representation, reliance and detriment suffered as a result of such reliance. It then considers whether in all the circumstances it would have been unconscionable for a testator to make a will giving specific property to X, if by their conduct they have already aroused an expectation in Y that they will inherit it.[121] However, unconscionability will not suffice to establish such a claim in the absence of the other elements.[122] Such disruption to E's social life, work and education as she had suffered, and such expense as she had incurred, were found to amount to only marginal detriment. Additionally, the judge concluded that even had it been substantial enough to allow E to acquire an equity in the flat, that was more than negated by her conduct towards S, which had been psychologically, emotionally and probably financially abusive. That conduct disqualified her from acquiring any interest in, or right to occupy the property. It would not be inequitable or unconscionable to disregard such assurances as had been made. The 1975 Act claim also failed as E was able to support herself and in any event, having regard to her conduct towards S, the will did not fail to make reasonable provision for her.

7–048 The next case is *Cattle v Evans*,[123] where the claimant (T) made a 1975 Act claim on the basis that she was a cohabitant, and a claim to a beneficial interest in a property under a constructive trust. The deceased (E) died intestate in April 2009, having some four months earlier acquired the property in question ("the Cross Hands property"), to the purchase of

---

[120] *Bye v Colvin-Scott* [2010] W.T.L.R. 1.
[121] *Bye v Colvin-Scott*, at [35]–[36], referring to *Uglow v Uglow* [2004] W.T.L.R. 1183.
[122] *Cobbe v Yeoman's Row Management Ltd* [2008] 1 W.L.R. 1752 at 1762.
[123] *Cattle v Evans* [2011] W.T.L.R. 947.

which T had made no contribution. On analysis of the parties' dealings with their finances and property over the course of their 18-year relationship, and of the events relating to the Cross Hands property, the proprietary claim failed. Until April 2004, five years before E's death, they had kept their property and finances completely separate. T continued to do so in respect of other property which she owned, after they had jointly purchased a property in Spain to which they did make roughly equal contributions. Had that property been sold and the proceeds used in the purchase of the Cross Hands property, as was originally contemplated, T's contention might have had some force, but that did not happen. Further, as was the case over a considerable part of the relationship in *Churchill v Roach*, the relationship was not a secure one. Finally, the wills drafted for T and E in the month before E's death clearly contemplated that E was the sole legal and beneficial owner of the Cross Hands property. The judge also commented adversely on T's evidence about the extent of her assets and the manner in which she had dealt with them. The 1975 Act claim succeeded to the extent that an order was made which would meet her housing needs, but E's sons would be the ultimate beneficiaries.

In *Suggitt v Suggitt*,[124] the primary claim, with which the judgment is exclusively concerned, was a proprietary estoppel claim by the son (J) of the deceased, in respect of that part of his estate consisting of the farm land, buildings and the business bank accounts arising out of the farming business carried on by his father (F) immediately before his death. The farm land and buildings made up some £3.8 million of F's estate of £4 million. There was also a 1975 Act claim by J and his partner (G) and two of their sons (W and A, acting by G as their litigation friend). The defendants were the executors, his daughter Caroline (C) to whom he had left his entire estate, and his accountant.   **7–049**

By his professionally drawn will F expressed the wish: **7–050**

"...(without imposing a trust) that if at any time my son John Michael Suggitt should in the absolute opinion of Caroline show himself capable of working and managing my farmland that she should transfer my farmland to him."

Although J's evidence was not considered wholly reliable, and the facts were not altogether clear cut, it was found to be more likely than not that F did make some kind of repeated promise or assurance to J that led him reasonably to expect that someday at least the farmland (and by implication, if not expressly, somewhere to live) would definitely be his following F's death. J worked on the farm in the expectation and reliance that the farm lands would be his one day. Although (as in *Riggs v Lloyds Bank*) J derived some

---

[124] *Suggitt v Suggitt* [2012] W.T.L.R. 1607, CA, where the Court of Appeal dismissed the appeal from the decision at first instance, in which only the proprietary claim was determined, as the parties had agreed for submissions on the 1975 Act claim to be deferred until after the outcome of the primary claim; see *Suggitt v Suggitt* [2011] 2 F.L.R. 875.

benefit from the work he did, there was sufficient detrimental reliance to satisfy that requirement of proprietary estoppel.

7–051　　HH Judge Kaye QC was therefore satisfied, looking at the position as at the date of F's death (the point at which the alleged promise was broken) and at matters in the round, that it would be unconscionable to deprive J of his reasonable expectations based on F's repeated assurances and indications that the farm or farm land would be his when he was gone. He was not, however, at all satisfied that F promised him everything as J suggested. In satisfaction of the equity J should have the farm land (subject to certain existing arrangements) and a house in which to live, but not the money in the business accounts or other assets beyond what might be regarded as incidental farm machinery and the farm outbuildings incidental to the farming activities. Dismissing the appeal, the Court of Appeal rejected the submissions that there was insufficient reliance or detriment, that the relief awarded was disproportionate and that it was not unconscionable for F to have made his will in the terms in which it was made. As the proprietary claim had succeeded, the 1975 Act claim did not fall to be considered.

7–052　　*Patel v Vigh*[125] is included for completeness but is mentioned only briefly as the claimant's evidence was disbelieved and his two claims, one based on resulting or constructive trust and the other, under the 1975 Act, in which the court accepted that he was eligible as a cohabitant, were both dismissed, as was his application for permission to appeal. In *Wright v Waters*[126] the claimant, who was the 64-year old daughter of the deceased, made a 1975 Act claim and a claim, based on proprietary estoppel, to two properties comprised in the estate of the deceased. In relation to one property she failed to satisfy the court that the representations on which she relied were sufficiently clear or were such as she could have reasonably relied upon, and as to the other, there was no evidence that she had acted to her detriment in reliance on any statement made by the deceased. The claim under the 1975 Act also failed as her conduct towards the deceased outweighed all the other factors in her favour.

7–053　　The above survey covers 14 cases in which there were multiple claims. Although any generalisation based on such a small amount of material has to be treated with caution, the overall indication is that the expense involved in bringing multiple claims rarely yields a commensurate benefit. Of those 14 cases, there are two[127] in which the 1975 Act claim was clearly the secondary claim and was apparently made so as to provide a fall-back position, but in the event, did not have to be determined as the primary claim succeeded. In *Riggs v Lloyds Bank*[128] the proprietary claim succeeded and the 1975 Act claim eventually failed, while in *Webster v Webster*[129] the proprietary claim

---

[125] *Patel v Vigh* [2013] EWHC 3403 (Ch); for the application for permission to appeal, see [2014] EWCA (Civ) 1825.

[126] *Wright v Waters* [2015] W.T.L.R. 353.

[127] *Watts v Watts* [2014] EWHC 668 (Ch) (probate claim); *Suggitt v Suggitt* [2012] W.T.L.R. 1607, CA (proprietary estoppel claim).

[128] *Riggs v Lloyds Bank* unreported 27 November 1992, CA.

[129] *Webster v Webster* [2009] 1 F.L.R. 1240.

would have succeeded had it been the sole claim, but in the result it did nothing to enhance the successful outcome of the 1975 Act claim which was tried together with it. However, the most frequent outcome is that the claimant failed to establish an evidential basis for the proprietary claim. Either, to the extent that the evidence was credible, it was insufficient,[130] or it was not credible.[131]

It is submitted that, small though the sample is, the range of outcomes **7–054** revealed by the above survey is very much what one would expect and that that is readily understandable when the nature of the issues which arise in the different types of claim, and of the evidence relevant to those issues, is considered. In a 1975 Act claim s.3 defines the matters to which the court must have regard in respect of all claims and of claims by particular categories of applicant. Unless there are substantial disputes relating to either the existence of an obligation within s.3(1)(d), or matters of conduct within s.3(1)(g), the primary evidence is of matters which are quantifiable or ascertainable (as in the case of disability, from professional knowledge and perhaps in relation to earning capacity, from informed opinion) and can be supported by contemporaneous documents. Thus, leaving aside issues of veracity and whether any budgets relating to the claimant's income needs are realistic, a properly prepared claim should pose few, if any, evidential problems. Those, of course, are entirely separate from the problems which arise in forming a value judgment and thereafter determining, where necessary, how the judicial discretion should be exercised. The long progress of *Ilott v Mitson*[132] through the courts testifies to those difficulties, which undoubtedly would have been reduced if more accurate information had been before District Judge Million in May 2007, but at least the decision making process is based on evidence which is for the most part, in a word, tangible.

The contrast between the decision-making process outlined in the pre- **7–055** vious paragraph and that required in determining whether a common-intention constructive trust has come into being is graphically illustrated by the list of questions to be addressed which is set out in *Lewin*.[133] The purpose of this exposition is not so much to identify the evidential difficulties of such a claim (formidable though they may be in some cases) as to draw attention to the difficulty, for the practitioner, in predicting the outcome of a claim

---

[130] *Churchill v Roach* [2004] 2 F.L.R. 989; *Negus v Bahouse* [2008] 1 F.L.R. 381; *Baker v Baker* [2008] 2 F.L.R. 767; *Wright v Waters* [2015] W.T.L.R. 353 (both claims failed). In *Grattan v McNaughton* [2001] W.T.L.R. 1305, the rectification claim failed for lack of evidence that the will failed to express the testator's intention.

[131] *Bye v Colvin-Scott* [2010] W.T.L.R. 1 (both claims failed); *Cattle v Evans* [2011] W.T.L.R. 947; *Patel v Vigh* [2013] EWHC 3403 (Ch) (both claims failed).

[132] See Ch.6, s.7(e) (ii), *Ilott v Mitson*, at paras 6–160 to 6–191.

[133] *Lewin*, at para.9–063.

based on the type of evidence which is required.[134] The questions are as follows.

(1)   Does the case fall within the domestic consumer context, such that the common-intention doctrine applies?[135]

(2)   Is there evidence of an actual common intention, in the form of an agreement, arrangement or understanding between the parties that the beneficial ownership should not follow the legal ownership, either at the date when the property was acquired or at some later date?

(3)   In the absence of such a common intention, can an agreement, arrangement or understanding to this effect be inferred[136] from the parties' conduct?

(4)   Has the claimant relied to his detriment[137] on the common intention relied on?

(5)   If there is an actual common intention, does it extend, either expressly or by inference, to the shares in which the property is to be beneficially owned?

(6)   If the common intention does not extend to the shares in which the property is to be beneficially owned, what is a fair share having regard to the whole course of the parties' dealing in relation to the property, and to both financial contributions and other factors?[138]

A judge in a common-intention constructive trust case is unlikely to have the benefit of much in the way of tangible evidence such as is adduced in 1975 Act claims, particularly when the agreement, arrangement or understanding between the parties rests on evidence of express discussion between them "however imperfectly remembered and however imprecise their terms may have been".[139] Absent this perhaps unstable evidential base, the judge is

---

[134]   Thus, it is of very little assistance to either the prospective claimant or the practitioner to know that the extent of the beneficial interest claimed is to be determined "by applying principles of law and equity which (however inadequate to meet the circumstances in which parties live together in the 21st century) must now be taken as well established"; see *James v Thomas* [2008] 1 F.L.R. 1598, at [59].

[135]   This is perhaps the one question in the list that can be answered with certainty, as one could scarcely visualise a 1975 Act claim which was not within the domestic consumer context.

[136]   "An inferred intention is, in the case of each party, the intention that was reasonably understood by the other party to be manifested by that party's words and conduct notwithstanding that he did not consciously formulate it in his own mind and even when he acted with some different intention which he did not communicate to the other party"; see *Jones v Kernott* [2012] 1 A.C. 776, at [51].

[137]   In relation to this aspect there may be tangible evidence in the form of documents relating to financial contributions to the acquisition of the property and other relevant expenditure.

[138]   *Oxley v Hiscock* [2005] Fam. 211, CA, at [69], but criticised by Lord Neuberger in *Stack v Dowden* [2007] 2 A.C. 432, at [144]. The search is for what the parties, as reasonable people, would have thought at the relevant time, and thus for what they in fact intended; *Stack v Dowden*, at [61] and *Jones v Kernott*, at [53]. The court must not abandon that search in favour of the result which itself considers fair; *Stack v Dowden*, at [61], [144]. More generally, see *Lewin*, para.9–75 under the heading "Quantifying the shares where no express agreement".

[139]   *Lloyds Bank v Rosset* [1991] 1 A.C. 107, HL at 132E–F.

required to engage in a process of inference from conduct in order to establish the common intention and a further search for "what the parties, as reasonable people, would have thought at the relevant time, and thus for what they in fact intended" in order to quantify the intended beneficial shares.

As noted above, no successful claim based on common-intention con-   **7–056** structive trust has been made in conjunction with a 1975 Act claim, but there have been successful claims based on proprietary estoppel. It may be that it is easier to make good an estoppel claim, at any rate where there is evidence relating directly to the primary facts of whether there was an assurance, whether the claimant relied on it and acted on it to his detriment, and the extent of the detriment. The outcome may also be somewhat easier to predict since the satisfaction of the claimant's expectation provides an upper limit to what is achievable by the claim; however, the lower limit of "the minimum equity to do justice" is less readily predictable, as is the extent of the relief which the court might consider proportionate.

But apart from all the evidential problems associated with proprietary   **7–057** claims, it is submitted that (with the exceptions referred to in the next paragraph) there is a more compelling reason for confining the litigation to a 1975 Act claim. The reason is that a proprietary claim, unless its purpose is to secure an outcome which will meet the claimant's housing needs or otherwise provide him with the desired support,[140] simply does not address the claimant's main objective, that is, to obtain what is reasonable, in all the circumstances by way of financial provision for him, according to the applicable standard. By far the commonest outcome of a successful 1975 Act claim is a lump sum to meet the claimant's reasonable income and/or housing needs; and housing needs are from time to time met by an order for the transfer, settlement or acquisition of specified property. There is generally little difficulty in deciding on the nature of the appropriate award, except perhaps where the choice is between an absolute or a limited interest in property. Where quantification is required, although Duxbury, Ogden or other calculations have their weaknesses, they provide a framework against which it is possible to arrive at a fairly firm idea of what is reasonable provision in the individual case, provided that the estimate of the claimant's income need is realistic.

It is therefore suggested that, as a general rule, other claims should not be   **7–058** made in conjunction with 1975 Act claims except where:

(a)   there is real doubt about the jurisdiction of the court to entertain a 1975 Act claim (though this is usually dealt with as a preliminary issue) or the claimant's eligibility to make one; or

(b)   the nature or duration of the relationship between the claimant and the deceased is likely to result in a low award; or

---

[140] As in *Suggitt v Suggitt*, where the equity arising from the estoppel was satisfied by the transfer to him of land that he could farm and a house to live in.

    (c)   if the accompanying claim is for a beneficial interest, its purpose is to obtain an order which will enable the claimant to enjoy the use and occupation of the property in question; or

    (d)   if the accompanying claim is a probate claim or a claim for rectification of a will, that claim will, if successful, entitle the claimant to all, or a substantial part of, the deceased's estate.

3.—Making a 1975 Act Claim

(a) Procedure for Bringing the Claim

(i) Rules and Practice Directions relating to the claim

7–059   The procedure for bringing a 1975 Act claim is regulated by Section IV of CPR Pt 57. The claim must be commenced by issuing a Pt 8 claim form and the prescribed form is Practice Form N208. Although 1975 Act claims usually involve a substantial dispute of fact, that circumstance is altogether irrelevant.[141] The claim form must be in practice form N208. CPR r.8.2 specifies that the claim form must state:

> "(a)   that Pt 8 applies;
> (b)   (i)   the question which the claimant is asking the court to decide; or
>   (ii) the remedy which the claimant is seeking, and the legal basis for that remedy;
> (c)   if the claim is being brought under an enactment, what the enactment is; and
> (d)   if either the claimant is claiming, or a defendant is being sued, in a representative capacity, what that capacity is."

In relation to r.8.2(b), the commentary states,[142] sensibly, that the claim form should not, in general, contain the same amount of detail as a claim form for other claims and should set out in summary form only the question or issue which the claimant wants the court to decide or the remedy that is sought, as the case may be.

7–060   What this means in practice is that the claim form should state[143]:

    (i)   under which of the provisions of s.1(1) of the Act the claimant is applying. A claim in the alternative may be made when the claimant can make out a case for eligibility under s.1(1)(ba), as a cohabitant, and under s.1(1)(e), as a dependant;

    (ii) that the claimant asks for provision to be made for them, specifying, if possible, the nature of the provision, whether by way of

---

[141] See CPR rr.8.1(2)(b) and 8.1.(6)(a).
[142] Pt 8 para.8.2.1.
[143] See App.3, Precedent 8.1.

lump sum, periodical payments, transfer or settlement of property, as the case may be, and no harm is done by adding the catch-all phrase "such further or other relief as the court thinks just" or words to that effect; and

(iii) if the claimant is applying for any orders under ss.4, 9, 10 or 11, the nature of the order sought.

It would not be inappropriate for the claim form to state that the will of the deceased or, as the case may be, the disposition of their estate on intestacy is not such as to make reasonable provision for the claimant, but those words could, alternatively, be included in the claimant's witness statement. Where an order under s.4 is sought, it is sensible to mention any relevant matters referred to in the guidelines in *Re Salmon*.[144] The judgment gives little comfort to those late applicants whose main excuse is delay in obtaining public or other funding.

CPR r.8.5(1) provides that the claimant must file any written evidence on which they intend to rely when they file their claim form, while r.8.5(2) requires them to serve that evidence on the defendant with their claim form. CPR r.22.1(1)(c) requires a witness statement to be verified by a statement of truth. The claimant may rely on the matters set out in the claim form as evidence under r.8.5 only if the claim form is verified by a statement of truth.[145] Failure to comply with the requirements of r.8.5(2) may have serious consequences, since r.8.6.(1)(b) provides that no written evidence may be relied on at the hearing of the claim unless (a) it has been served in accordance with r.8.5 or (b) the court has given permission. In the aftermath of the decision of the Court of Appeal in *Denton v T.H. White*,[146] which was critical of "the traditional approach of giving pre-eminence to the need to decide the claim on the merits", it is less likely that the court will grant as much latitude to the claimant as was the case in *Parnall v Hurst*[147] and *Hannigan v Hannigan*.[148] Rules 8.3 (acknowledgment of service) and 8.5 (filing and serving written evidence) are modified, in relation to 1975 Act claims, by CPR r.57.16(3)–(5). **7–061**

Practitioners acting for claimants may find the questionnaires contained in App.4 to be of assistance in deciding on what written evidence to adduce at this stage, but it is suggested that, as a minimum, and subject to the need to commence the proceedings within the time limit, the witness statement accompanying the claim form should deal with the following matters[149]: **7–062**

---

[144] *Re Salmon* [1981] Ch. 167.
[145] CPR r.8.5(7).
[146] *Denton v T.H. White Ltd (De Laval Ltd) (Pt 20 defendant)* [2014] 1 W.L.R. 3926, CA.
[147] *Parnall v Hurst* [2003] W.T.L.R. 997.
[148] *Hannigan v Hannigan* [2000] F.C.R. 650; [2006] W.T.L.R. 597, CA.
[149] See Appendix, Precedent 8.2.

(i)   the fact that the deceased has died, the date of their death, the date
      on which a grant of probate or letters of administration was
      made,[150] and the name(s) of the personal representative(s), exhi-
      biting a certified copy of the death certificate and of the grant;

(ii) the relationship between the claimant and the deceased, exhibiting
      (if the existence of the relationship is likely to be in dispute) a
      certified copy of any relevant birth or marriage certificate or
      document evidencing the registration of a civil partnership, and
      any relevant proof of divorce or judicial separation. If the parties
      were married or had entered into a civil partnership, or were
      cohabiting, the duration of the relationship, including any pre-
      marital or pre-partnership cohabitation, should be stated. Such
      cohabitation is not a matter to which the court is directed to have
      regard under ss.3(2) or 3(2A), but it is now common, where a
      marriage has been preceded by a period of cohabitation, for the
      court to take into account the entire duration of the relationship
      between the parties;

(iii) the nature and extent of the interest (if any) which the claimant
      takes under the deceased's will or intestacy, exhibiting a copy of
      the will in question;

(iv) a statement of the claimant's net income and outgoings, identify-
      ing the source of the income, and any relevant information about
      the claimant's employment prospects (e.g., promotion, redun-
      dancy, relocation, retirement); also any disability or other matter
      affecting the claimant's employment prospects or earning capacity.
      It is particularly important to provide accurate information about
      any tax credits or means-tested benefits which the claimant is
      receiving and it is generally helpful to obtain a pension benefit
      forecast;

(v)   a statement of the claimant's present and future capital resources
      (e.g., house, savings, investments, rights under employer's pension
      scheme, car, any particularly valuable chattels) and anticipated
      major capital expenses (e.g., repairs or improvements to house,
      purchase of new car or of major household equipment).

What is not required, in the author's view, is a lengthy disquisition about the
conduct of the deceased or anyone else, except in so far as that conduct led
(for example) to a breakdown of the relationship or amounted to a failure to
fulfil an obligation towards the claimant. In the great majority of the cases
in which conduct is a significant issue, the conduct is that of the claimant.
The case-law relating to those matters is discussed in Ch.4.[151]

7–063   The new para.3A in r.57.16 deals with the procedure for making a claim
where no grant of representation has been issued. The claimant may make a

[150] As a result of the amendment to s.4 which permits claims to be commenced before the issue
     of a grant of representation, CPR 57.16 has been amended by the insertion of new paras 3A
     and 3B, for which see para.7–063, below.
[151] Ch.4, s.4, "Obligations of the Deceased", and s.6, "Other Matters, Including Conduct".

claim without naming a defendant and may apply for directions as to the representation of the estate. Subparagraph (a) requires the claimant, in their written evidence, to explain why it has not been possible for a grant to be obtained. When the Law Commission recommended that it should be possible to make a claim before the issue of a grant of representation, the situations which it had in mind were the lack of need for a grant and the unwillingness of the person or persons entitled to a grant to apply for it. The first situation may arise when the estate or the major asset (typically the matrimonial or quasi-matrimonial home) passes by survivorship; when assets such as the proceeds of policies of life assurance or death benefits, unlocked by the death of the deceased, devolve on someone other than the personal representatives; and when assets can be released without a grant, as where the Administration of Estates (Small Payments) Act 1965 applies.[152] The second is most common where the deceased has died intestate leaving a spouse who does not wish to apply for the grant. It does not appear that the Law Commission contemplated the situation where the grant cannot be obtained because the claimant has issued a caveat, but following the decision in *Pinnock v Rochester*[153] in which it was held that a 1975 Act claim and a probate claim were conceptually different and the acceptance of a payment by way of compromise of the 1975 Act did not constitute an affirmation of the validity of the will, this state of affairs could arise.

The remainder of para.3A is concerned with the evidence which the **7–064** claimant must provide. This includes the original or a copy (if either is available) of any testamentary document in respect of which probate or letters of administration are to be granted and, as far as is known:

(i) brief details of the property comprised in the estate, with an approximate estimate of its capital value and any income derived from it;

(ii) brief details of the liabilities of the estate;

(iii) the names and addresses of the persons who are in possession of documents relating to the estate; and

(iv) the names of the beneficiaries and their respective interests in the estate.

It may well turn out, in practice, that the claimant has, or has access to, very little of this information, and, in any event, it will be supplied in compliance with the Practice Direction[154] by a defendant who is a personal representative. Paragraph 3B provides that where a claim in accordance with para.3A is made, the court may give directions as to the parties to the claim and the representation of the estate either on the claimant's application or of its own motion.

---

[152] It may be thought unlikely that a 1975 Act claim could arise in relation to an estate of this nature, but the author was once instructed to advise on a claim where the estate was almost entirely made up of such assets.

[153] *Pinnock v Rochester* [2011] EWHC 4049 (Ch).

[154] See para.7–065, below.

7–065   What the defendant has to do in response to a 1975 Act claim depends on
the capacity or capacities in which they are defending the claim. The procedure for acknowledging service in r.8.3 as modified by rr.57.16(4) and (4A)
applies to all defendants. Where a defendant who is a personal representative wishes to remain neutral in the claim, and agrees to abide by any
decision which the court may make, he should state this in Section A of the
acknowledgment of service form.[155] It is normally appropriate for a personal
representative who is not a beneficiary to adopt a neutral stance, but (as the
commentary implies), that may not be the case if the claim is not brought
within the time limit. A defendant who is a personal representative (whether
or not they are a beneficiary) must, within 21 days after service of the claim
form on them, inclusive of the day of service, file written evidence which
must include the information required by the Practice Direction.[156] As
regards the nature and estate of the net estate, figures may, at that stage, be
only roughly known; but in practice there should be no difficulty in providing a more accurate statement shortly before the hearing. As to the facts
which might affect the exercise of the court's powers, it is likely that unless
the personal representative is either a beneficiary (in which event they may
wish to oppose the application *in that capacity*) or a person who was well
acquainted with the deceased, whether socially or professionally, they may
not have very much of relevance to say.[157] The commentary in *Civil Procedure 2000* to the former RSC Ord.99 r.5 was to the effect that facts of this
nature, particularly if controversial, may in any case be omitted from the
personal representative's evidence and adduced by him at a later stage if
they appear to be relevant. *Civil Procedure 2017* does not give any such
guidance, but the inclusion of controversial matters is not compatible with
the neutral stance which (as noted above) it is normally considered appropriate for a personal representative to adopt. There are no rules which
require a person who is defending the claim only as a beneficiary to file and
serve evidence but it is obviously necessary to do so if the beneficiary wishes
to advance a defence based on need. However, if they do not disclose details
of their financial needs and resources, the court may well assume that they
have sufficient resources to support their needs without the benefit which
they stand to receive under the deceased's will or intestacy.

(ii) The Pre-Action Protocol and Practice Direction

7–066   *Civil Procedure 2017*, Section C, is devoted to this topic. At the time of
writing there are 12 protocols in force but, in line with Lord Justice Jackson's recommendations, there is no general protocol and no protocol for
Chancery litigation. However, the Practice Direction—Pre-Action Conduct
and Protocol[158] states that:

---

[155] Pt 57 para.57.16.0 and 57APD para.15.

[156] CPR r.57.16(5) and 57APD at para.16. For a precedent, see App.3, precedent 8.3.

[157] It is not uncommon for persons who do have something of relevance to say to display
considerable reluctance to say it and expose themselves to cross-examination about it.

[158] *Civil Procedure 2017*, paras C1–001 to 1–010; this version came into force in April 2015.

"2. This Practice Direction applies to disputes where no pre-action protocol has been approved by the Master of the Rolls;

3. Before commencing proceedings, the court will expect the parties to have exchanged sufficient information to—

(a) understand each other's position;

(b) make decisions about how to proceed;

(c) try to settle the issues without proceedings;

(d) consider a form of Alternative Dispute Resolution (ADR) to assist with settlement

(e) support the efficient management of those proceedings; and

(f) reduce the costs of resolving the dispute.

6. Where there is no relevant pre-action protocol, the parties should exchange correspondence and information to comply with the objectives in paragraph 3, bearing in mind that compliance should be proportionate."

Failure to comply with the Practice Direction[159] may have serious costs consequences. The court may have regard, when exercising its discretion as to costs, to the conduct of all the parties,[160] which includes, in particular, the extent to which the parties followed the Practice Direction—Pre Action Conduct.[161] Among the sanctions which the court may impose for non-compliance are orders that the party at fault pays the costs of the proceedings, or part of the costs of the other party or parties, or pays those costs on an indemnity basis. Although the ACTAPS Code[162] has never been adopted as a Pre-Action Protocol, many practitioners employ it in the conduct of 1975 Act claims. The Code, which is reproduced in App.3, addresses the matters covered by the Practice Direction, and Annexes B and C to the Code provide useful guidance as to the content of a letter of claim and requests for documents in 1975 Act claims.

(b) When the Claim May be Brought

Section 4 of the 1975 Act, as amended, provides that an application for an order under s.2 of that Act shall not, except with the permission of the court, be made after the end of the period of six months from the date on which representation to the estate of the deceased is first taken out, (but nothing prevents the making of an application before such representation is first taken out).[163] The provisions of the amended s.23, which determines the date

7–067

---

[159] For what the court may regard as failure to comply with the Practice Direction and the possible consequences of such failure, see paras 13–16 and C1–008.

[160] CPR r.44.2(4)(a).

[161] CPR r.44.2(5)(a).

[162] The full title of the Code is the ACTAPS Practice Guidance for the Resolution of Probate and Trust Disputes.

[163] Words inserted by the Inheritance and Trustees' Powers Act 2014 s.6 and Sch.2 para.6. The amendments to this provision and to s.23 apply in relation to deaths on and after 1 October 2014.

on which representation to the estate of the deceased is first taken out, have
been discussed in Ch.5.[164] When a claim is brought,[165] an official copy of the
grant of representation to the deceased's estate and of every testamentary
document admitted to proof must be exhibited to the claimant's witness
statement.[166]

7–068   Regrettably, there seems to be some uncertainty as to the date on which
the period of six months from the date on which representation with respect
to the estate of the deceased was first taken out expires. The author is of the
view, also expressed by the learned editor of *Tyler's Family Provision*[167] that
the date on which representation was first taken out is not included in the
period. The authority cited for this proposition is *Trow v Ind Coope (West
Midlands)*[168] which is not referred to in *Civil Procedure 2017*. However,
support for that view comes from the judgment of Brooke LJ in *Hannigan v
Hannigan*, in which he stated:

> "A grant of probate to Mr Hannigan's executors was made on 11
> December 1998, so that the six-month primary limitation period
> expired on 11 June 1999."

On that view, the limitation period prescribed by s.4 of the 1975 Act does
not include the day on which representation is first taken out.

(c) Death of the Claimant

7–069   The Law Reform (Miscellaneous Provisions) Act 1934 abolished the common law rule that personal actions die with the person. By s.1(1), it is
provided that:

> "Subject to the provisions of this section, on the death of any person
> after the commencement of this Act all causes of action subsisting
> against or vested in him shall survive against, or, as the case may be, for
> the benefit of, his estate."

7–070   There is no reported case on the question whether a claim under the 1938
Act would survive the applicant's death for the benefit of their estate, but it
arose in a number of matrimonial cases before the 1975 Act came into force.

---

[164] Amended by the Inheritance and Trustees' Powers Act 2014 s.6 and Sch.3 para.2. See Ch.5,
s.4(b), "When is a Grant of Representation First Taken Out?", paras 5–066 to 5–071.
[165] Other than in accordance with the new r.57.16(3A) which applies to claims made before the
issue of a grant of representation.
[166] CPR r.57.16(3).
[167] *Tyler's Family Provision*, 3rd edn (London: LexisNexis Butterworths, 1997), p.327, n.2.
[168] *Trow v Ind Coope (West Midlands)* [1967] 2 Q.B. 899. It appears from the judgment of Blain
J at first instance (with which the majority of the Court of Appeal agreed) that where the
provision determining the time limit refers to a period "beginning with" a certain date, that
date is included in the computation; but if the reference is to a period "beginning from" the
specified date, it is not included. Lord Denning, dissenting, thought that this distinction was
too subtle and that the specified date should be excluded in any event. The Act refers to "the
period of six months from the date on which representation is first taken out", so the date of
issue of the grant is excluded.

The principles on which such questions should be decided were stated by Lord Denning in *Sugden v Sugden*,[169] in which it was held that an order for unsecured maintenance for children terminated on the death of the father and did not survive against his estate except in respect of payments accrued due and unpaid at the date of his death. In his judgment, causes of action included rights enforceable by proceedings in the divorce court, provided that they were rights and not mere hopes or expectations. In that court, there were no rights until an order was made; thus, in order that the proceedings should subsist against the deceased's estate, the right must have accrued at the time of death.

Those principles were applied in *Whytte v Ticehurst*[170] where a widow **7–071** made a claim against her deceased husband's estate on 19 July 1984, and died on 11 December of that year. The registrar dismissed the personal representatives' application for an order to carry on the proceedings on behalf of her estate, and Booth J affirmed his decision. In her judgment, the wider powers of the court to grant financial relief in matrimonial proceedings did not alter the nature of the claim, holding that the principles enunciated in *Sugden v Sugden* still applied. Further, in her judgment, Parliament did not intend to create a cause of action which, in so far as it related to provision not required for maintenance, would survive for the benefit of the applicant's estate. The 1975 Act claim ceased to exist on the death of the survivor unless an order had been made on it; only then was there an enforceable cause of action which would continue to subsist for the benefit of the applicant's estate.

The question was considered again in *Re Bramwell*,[171] with the same **7–072** result. Sheldon J reviewed the cases cited in *Whytte v Ticehurst* and referred, in addition, to the then recent decision of the House of Lords in *Barder v Barder (Caluori intervening)*[172] in which those cases had apparently been accepted as correctly decided. Following *Whytte v Ticehurst*, he held that a claim under the 1975 Act, like a claim for financial provision under the Matrimonial Causes Act 1973, did not give rise to or become a cause of action for the purposes of s.1 of the Law Reform (Miscellaneous Proceedings) Act 1934 unless an order has been made in respect of it before the death of the surviving spouse or other potential claimant. The plaintiff's claim was obviously unsustainable and was struck out. These cases were followed in the Northern Ireland case of *O'Reilly v Mallon*.[173]

However, the existing case-law has been considered more recently in the **7–073** case of *Roberts v Fresco*.[174] This was a trial of two preliminary issues, one of which was whether a potential Inheritance Act claim by a surviving husband (H) against the estate of his deceased wife (W) estate abates on the death of

---

[169] *Sugden v Sugden* [1957] P. 120.
[170] *Whytte v Ticehurst* [1986] Fam. 64.
[171] *Re Bramwell* [1988] 2 F.L.R. 263.
[172] *Barder v Barder (Caluori intervening)* [1987] Fam. 24.
[173] *O'Reilly v Mallon* [1995] N.I. 1.
[174] *Roberts v Fresco* [2017] EWHC 283 (Ch), Simon Monty QC sitting as a deputy judge of the High Court.

the husband. Mr Milbour (H) and Mrs Milbour (W) had both been previously married, and on Mrs Milbour's death, which occurred on 5 January
2014, she was survived by one child of each of the previous marriages. There
were no children of their own marriage. The surviving children were H's
daughter (R), the first claimant,[175] and W's daughter (F), the defendant, who
was sued in her capacity as W's executor. The value of W's estate was over
£16 million, and under her will, made in 1993, H received a pecuniary legacy
of £150,000 and an interest in the income of £75,000. It was open to him to
make a claim under s.1(1)(a) of the 1975 Act, but he died on 20 October
2014, without having done so. His estate of £320,000 gross, including the
legacy under W's will, was left to the two claimants.

7–074   The judge observed that, having regard to what H might have expected to
receive on the "notional divorce" and the size of the estate, his claim would
have been of considerable value. However, his analysis of the decisions in
Whytte v Ticehurst and *Bramwell* led him to conclude that those cases were
correctly decided[176] and he rejected the arguments to the contrary. The first
of them was based on the Human Rights Act 1988 (HRA). Part II of HRA
includes Art.1 of Protocol 1 to the European Convention on Human Rights,
which states that:

> "Every natural or legal person is entitled to the peaceful enjoyment of
> his possessions. No one shall be deprived of his possessions except in
> the public interest and subject to the conditions provided for by law
> and by the general principles of international law."

It was argued that "possessions" includes "claims" and that any decision
which had the effect of depriving H of his claim would need to be revisited in
the light of HRA and be read in a way compatible with Art.1. This argument failed as neither H, who was deceased, nor his estate, was either a
natural or a legal person and it was impossible to argue that any Art.1 rights
could be engaged.

7–075   The second argument was concerned with the construction of the 1975
Act. The judge agreed that the wording of the 1975 Act did not, of itself,
expressly preclude a claim being brought by the estate of a person who
before his death fell within the s.1 definition of a person who could bring a
claim. In *Harb v King Fahd Bin Abdul Aziz*,[177] the Court of Appeal considered the question of whether first, a claim under the Matrimonial Causes
Act 1973 could be brought after the death of the defendant, and secondly
whether such a claim was a "cause of action" under the Law Reform
(Miscellaneous Provisions) Act 1934. In relation to the first question, Dyson
LJ said:

---

[175] The second claimant (M) was the daughter of H's son, who had died in 2004. Neither of the
claimants, nor the father of the second claimant, benefited under the will.
[176] *Roberts v Fresco*, at [16]–[18].
[177] *Harb v King Fahd Bin Abdul Aziz* [2006] 1 W.L.R. 578, CA.

"If it had been intended that all or any applications for, or in relation to, financial relief made before death by a party to the marriage should continue for or against the estate of the deceased person, one would have expected that to be stated explicitly in a statute which contains some express provisions in relation to death."

It followed that an application for an order under section 27(6) of the 1973 Act abated on the death of the party to the marriage. The court in *Harb* had been less certain about the line of authority supporting the proposition that the claim was not a cause of action, but in the instant case the judge noted that Dyson LJ in *Harb* would have followed that line of authority and would have held that the claim was a personal one which did not amount to a cause of action. The question in the instant case was whether the right to apply for an order for financial provision under the 1975 Act was a "cause of action" (which would survive the death of the applicant or potential applicant) or a mere "hope or contingency" (in which case it would not). The judge accepted the argument for the defendant that:

(i) until the trial judge carries out the s.3 exercise and decides whether or not the will does not make reasonable provision for the claimant, the claimant has nothing more than a "hope or contingency"; and

(ii) the court is required by s.3(5) to have regard to matters as they are at the date of the hearing and in various respects it is impossible to undertake the s.3 exercise; in particular, a deceased person has no financial resources or needs at the time or in the foreseeable future and their estate is merely a fund to be distributed among the beneficiaries.

As was observed in both *Whytte v Ticehurst* and *Bramwell,* the s.3 exercise would be well-nigh impossible to carry out as many of the factors were clearly based upon the fundamental assumption that one of the parties to the marriage survives at the date of the hearing. The analogy with claims under the 1973 Act was correct, and the potential claim under the 1975 Act was indeed personal to the applicant. Unless the applicant brings the claim and obtains an order, it remains a hope or contingency. H's claim did not survive his death and no proceedings by his estate under the 1975 Act should be permitted.

(d) Who Should be Parties?

CPR Pt 57 does not specify who shall be parties to an application under the 1975 Act. There may be more than one claimant as, for instance, where applications are made by a widow and adult children. If the application was issued on behalf of all of them by the same solicitor and it subsequently appears that the applicants have conflicting interests, they may appear on any hearing by separate solicitors or counsel or personally. If it appears to

7–076

the court at any stage that any applicant ought to be, but is not, separately represented, the court may adjourn the proceedings until they are.[178] This is an exception to the rule (as it used to be expressed) that "plaintiffs must speak with one voice". Under the old practice, all claimants whose interests were in conflict had to be made plaintiffs and an application had subsequently to be made, to strike out all but one as plaintiffs and join them as defendants.[179]

7–077   An applicant who is the sole executor or who is entitled to a grant of letters of administration need not, on account of that application alone, renounce probate or administration, since such an application is not an attack on the validity of the will or grant. However, it would be necessary to renounce if, in addition to the 1975 Act claim, the applicant was making a claim to be beneficially entitled to property in the name of the deceased; or, if the validity of the will or grant was to be contested. If an executor has intermeddled, the court will not accept their renunciation; but where it is not desirable to compel the executor to act, an application may be made to pass them over, although they have intermeddled, under s.116 of the Senior Courts Act 1981. Another possible solution is an application under s.50 of the Administration of Justice Act 1985 for their removal and, if necessary, for the appointment of a substitute personal representative.[180] This procedure is available in relation to an executor named in a will to whom probate has not been granted.[181] A grant to a person other than the executor will be a grant of letters of administration with the will annexed.

7–078   The defendants are normally the personal representatives of the deceased and the beneficiaries under the will or intestacy. The personal representatives who have proved are necessary parties to the action, but the action should not be constituted so that they are the only defendants, unless, also, they are the only beneficiaries. If the estate is divided between a small number of beneficiaries, they should all be joined; and it may, if there are specific or pecuniary legacies whose value is significant in relation to the value of the net estate, be advisable to join such legatees also. There will generally be no need to join legatees whose legacies are not likely to be resorted to; the notice procedure referred to in the next paragraph may be appropriate.

7–079   Where there is a large number of residuary beneficiaries, it will usually be appropriate for one (or a few of them) to be made parties, and for a representation order to be made. If a claimant wishes such an order to be made, the claim form should include a claim for a representation order. The court has power to make a representation order where the person or persons to be represented are a class of persons who have the same interest in a claim

---

[178] 57APD.17.

[179] *Dixit v Dixit* unreported 23 June 1988, CA provides an example of the difficulties that can be created by the lack of separate representation of parties with conflicting interests. In that case, the three plaintiffs were the widow and two infant daughters of the testator's second marriage and the defendants were the four adult daughters of his first marriage.

[180] CPR Pt 57 Section III and 57APD paras 12–14.

[181] *Goodman v Goodman* [2013] 3 All E.R. 190, Newey J; see 57APD para.13.1(1)(b).

and (under subpara.(ii) of that rule) where the making of such an order would further the overriding objective.[182] Paragraphs (a)–(c) of the rule apply similarly where a person or class of persons is unborn or cannot be readily found or ascertained. The court also has power to direct that notice of the claim be served on any person who is not a party thereto but who will or may be affected by any judgment given therein.[183]

(e) Children and Protected Parties

The relevant rules are contained in CPR Pt 21 (Children and Protected Parties) which does not use the term "person under a disability". A child is a person under 18; a child can also be a protected party. A protected party is a party, or intended party who lacks capacity to conduct the proceedings.[184] Section 1(1) of the Mental Capacity Act 2005 establishes a presumption of capacity and this is reinforced by s.1(2) which provides that a person is not to be treated as unable to make a decision unless all practicable means of helping them to make it have been tried without success. Further, a person is not to be treated as being unable to make a decision simply because the decision made is unwise. Section 2(1) of the Mental Capacity Act 2005 provides that for the purposes of that Act a person lacks capacity in relation to a matter if at the material time that person is unable to make a decision for themselves in relation to the matter because of an impairment of, or a disturbance in the functioning of, the mind or brain. The test of capacity is, therefore, function-specific; lack of capacity in other respects is not relevant.

7–080

Proceedings on behalf of a protected party or a child must be conducted by a litigation friend unless, in the case of a child, the court exercises its power to make an order permitting the child to conduct proceedings without a litigation friend.[185] A step taken in proceedings before a child or protected party has a litigation friend is of no effect unless the court otherwise orders, though this does not prevent a claimant from issuing or serving a claim form against a child or protected party who does not have a litigation friend, or applying for the appointment of a litigation friend.[186] CPR Pt 21 regulates who may become a litigation friend without a court order[187] and provides procedures for a person to become a litigation friend either without or with a court order.[188] If nobody has been appointed by the court or, in the case of a protected party, nobody has been appointed a deputy by the Court of Protection, a person may act as a litigation friend if he[189]:

7–081

---

[182] CPR r.19.7(2)(d). This might also be appropriate where the estate or the bulk of it is held on discretionary trusts.
[183] CPR r.19.8A(2).
[184] CPR r.21.1(2)(d). A "protected beneficiary" is defined in subpara.(e) as a protected party who lacks capacity to manage and control any money recovered by them or on their behalf or for their benefit in the proceedings.
[185] CPR r.21.2.
[186] CPR r.21.3(2)(b).
[187] CPR rr.21.4(2) (deputy) and 21.4(3) (other persons).
[188] CPR rr.21(5) and 21(6), respectively.
[189] CPR r.21.4(3)(a)–(c).

(a)   can fairly and competently conduct proceedings on behalf of the
      child or protected party;
(b)   has no interest adverse to that of the child or protected party; and
(c)   where the child or protected party is a claimant, undertakes to pay
      any costs which the child or protected party may be ordered to pay
      in the proceedings, subject to any right he may have to be repaid
      from the assets of the child or protected party.

These requirements may not be easy to satisfy in cases where claims are to
be made by a surviving spouse and also on behalf of children, and there are
no neutral family members able[190] and willing to assume the responsibility of
acting as litigation friend. The court may not appoint a litigation friend
unless it is satisfied that the person to be appointed satisfies those requirements.[191] The position in relation to compromises involving children and
protected parties is discussed in s.7(c) of this chapter.

(f) Evidence of the Right to Claim

7–082   Any claimant must, if called upon to do so, be able to prove the right to
claim, though, as to some issues, such as domicile or eligibility to claim as a
cohabitant or a dependant, proof will not be primarily by way of documentary evidence. As a general point, the common law rule whereby public
documents are admissible as evidence of the facts stated in them is preserved
by s.7(2)(b) of the Civil Evidence Act 1995. A register is evidence of the
particular transaction which it was the officer's duty to record, even if they
had no personal knowledge of the occurrence.[192] A claimant's witness
statement must therefore exhibit an official copy[193] of any relevant birth or
marriage certificate or decree, as the case may be, as well as a death certificate. Registers of birth, or certified copies thereof are, on production,
evidence of both the fact and the date of birth.[194] Independently of the
register, proof of the fact or date of birth may also be given by someone who
was present at the date of birth.[195] An entry in the Adopted Children
Register is received in evidence as if it were an entry in the register of
births.[196] Registers of marriage are evidence of the fact and date of marriage,
from which its validity may be presumed,[197] and registers of death are evidence of the fact and date of death.[198] The identity of the persons named in
the register must always be proved independently to the satisfaction of the
court, but this is most unlikely to be an issue in a 1975 Act claim.

---

[190] For instance, because they themselves benefit under the will or intestacy of the deceased and
       therefore have adverse interests.
[191] CPR r.21.6(6).
[192] *Phipson on Evidence*, 18th edn (London: Sweet & Maxwell, 2013), para.32–80.
[193] That is, a copy which has been stamped or sealed by the office which issued the original.
[194] *Phipson*, para.32–81 and n.398.
[195] *Phipson*, para.32–81 and n.408.
[196] In *Re D (An Infant)* [1959] 1 Q.B. 229, C.A. at 236.
[197] *Phipson*, para.32–84.
[198] *Phipson*, para.32–85.

4.—CASE AND COSTS MANAGEMENT

(a) Case Management Generally

As a 1975 Act claim is one in which the Pt 8 procedure must be followed, it **7–083** is automatically allocated to the multi-track. The main differences between this procedure and the Pt 7 procedure are that default judgment is not available and that no defence is required. The provisions of Pt 8 relating to acknowledgment of service and to filing and service of documents are modified by Pt 57.[199] The general provisions about management of cases allocated to the multi-track are contained in Pt 29.

A case management conference (CMC) or pre-trial review (PTR) will **7–084** normally be dealt with by a master or district judge. The Practice Direction supplementing Pt 29 deals with the approach which a court is likely to take to such hearings. Paragraph 5.3 lists the topics which the court is likely to consider at a CMC. Parties are required to endeavour to agree appropriate directions for the management of proceedings and submit agreed directions or their respective proposals to the court at least seven days before a CMC. If agreed directions are approved or if the court makes its own directions, the parties will be notified and the hearing vacated.[200] The Practice Direction states what is required in order for the directions to obtain the court's approval, and lists other matters for which provision should be made where appropriate.[201] When drafting case management directions, both the parties and the court should take as their starting point any relevant model directions and standard directions and adapt them as appropriate to the circumstances of the particular case.[202] The draft Chancery Division case management directions (amended in February 2017) are available in a short (CH 1) and an expanded version (CH 2).[203] Both versions contain an initial note stating that the court will not normally be able to make case management directions based upon an agreed order unless all costs budgets are agreed or the claim is outside the scope of costs management.

(b) Allocation and Transfer

As has been said, a 1975 Act claim will automatically be allocated to the **7–085** multi-track. Since January 2015, all cases in the Chancery Division in London have been allocated to one of four management tracks. Ordinarily, 1975 Act claims will be tried by masters[204] and allocated accordingly, though

---

[199] CPR r.57.16(2). These modifications do not affect the sanctions imposed for failing to serve and acknowledgment of service or of failing to file and serve written evidence.

[200] CPR r.29.4 and 29PD para.4.6.

[201] 29PD para.4.7.

[202] CPR r.29.1(2) .

[203] This form has some resemblance to the version of PF52 which was in use in 2011, when the previous edition of this work was published. It differs substantially from the current High Court Form PF 52, which is now entitled "Order in the Queen's Bench Division for case and costs management in the multi-track".

[204] *Civil Procedure 2017*, Vol.2, Chancery Guide, para.29.61. 1975 Act claims brought in the Family Division may be tried by district judges.

they may be transferred to the County Court for trial. The County Court has unlimited financial jurisdiction in 1975 Act cases.[205] The criteria for transfer[206] include the financial value of the claim and the amount in dispute, if different; a claim with an estimated value of £100,000 or less will normally be transferred to the County Court.[207] Another criterion is the availability of a judge specialising in the type of claim in question,[208] and the commentary to the rule warns practitioners to ensure that they should be aware not only of hearing centres with specialist lists but also of individual judges with specialist knowledge.[209] Where there are multiple claims[210] it will be appropriate to seek a direction for joint case management and trial.[211]

(c) Other Directions

7–086   The model directions contained in forms CH1 and CH2 are mostly concerned with the progress of the claim towards trial, but there are some which are specifically directed towards disposing of the claim without a trial, either by negotiation or by some other process. Alternative dispute resolution is the subject of a complete section of *Civil Procedure*.[212] The subsection which follows is concerned only with identifying the processes available and model directions for setting them in train. The topic, which was briefly surveyed in Ch.1, is discussed in greater detail in s.6 of this chapter.

(i) Settlement and ADR

7–087   One of the ways of furthering the overriding objective is the encouragement of the parties, where the court considers it appropriate, to use an alternative dispute resolution (ADR)[213] procedure and the facilitation of that process.[214] It is suggested that nearly all 1975 Act claims are suitable for resolution by ADR and that parties should have that possibility in mind from the outset. Mediation is the most frequently used procedure; it is the procedure most usually encouraged by the court and, in contrast to other methods, there is a good supply of lawyers trained and experienced both in conducting the

---

[205]   County Courts Act 1984 s.25.
[206]   CPR r.30.3(2)(a).
[207]   29PD para.2.2.
[208]   CPR r.30.3.(2)(c); see the commentary at para.30.3.4.
[209]   *Civil Procedure 2017*, Vol.2, Chancery Guide, Ch.29, "Specialist work", (2) Probate and Inheritance, paras 29.61–29.65.
[210]   See section 2(f) "Multiple Claims-an Overview", above.
[211]   For a model direction, see form CH2, "Consolidation or joint case management and trial", and the guidance in the commentary to Pt 57 at para.57.16.2 which is to make an application in an appropriate case for the claims to be tried together under CPR r.3.1(2)(h).
[212]   *Civil Procedure 2017*, Vol.2, Section 14 and Vol.2, Chancery Guide, Ch.17, "Alternative Dispute Resolution". Other texts on this topic include *The Jackson ADR Handbook*, Susan Blake, Julie Browne, Stuart Sime (eds), 2nd edn (Oxford: Oxford University Press, 2016) and Lord Justice Jackson's book, *The Reform of Civil Litigation* (London: Sweet & Maxwell, 2016), Ch.9, "Alternative Dispute Resolution". See also Ch.1, s.2(c), para.1–023.
[213]   The Glossary in *Civil Procedure 2017*, Vol.1, section E, defines Alternative Dispute Resolution as "a collective description of methods of resolving disputes otherwise than through the normal trial process".
[214]   This is an aspect of the court's duty to further the overriding objective by active case management; CPR r.1.4(1) and 1.4.(2)(e).

process and representing clients engaged in it. Other available procedures, which are less familiar, include arbitration, early neutral evaluation and financial dispute resolution, which is widely used in the matrimonial jurisdiction and a form of which has now been adopted in the Chancery Division.[215]

Arbitration, unlike the other forms of ADR discussed, is a process which results in the making of an award by which the parties agree in advance to be bound, as between themselves. It may be necessary for a court to approve the award or to enforce it. Arbitrations are conducted in accordance with the Arbitration Act 1996 and the rules of the IFLA[216] Arbitration Scheme. The scheme is designed to deal with financial and property disputes arising from relationship breakdown, and Art.2.2 states that the scheme covers (but is not limited to) claims under the specified statutes, which include the 1975 Act, TLATA 1996 and those provisions of the Civil Partnership Act 2004 which are concerned with financial relief after relationship breakdown. Article 3 specifies the applicable law as the law of England and Wales, in accordance with which the arbitrator must decide the substance of the dispute. Judicial support for the scheme has been expressed by the President of the Family Division, who, in the course of upholding the consent order giving effect to an arbitral award under the scheme, provided guidance about the proper approach of the court to applications for approval of such orders.[217]

7–088

Early neutral evaluation (ENE) is a process whereby, if all parties agree, the evaluator,[218] who is an independent party with relevant expertise, will provide a non-binding opinion about a dispute or an element of the dispute. Unlike mediation or FDR, the process is not a facilitation process; its aim is to provide an opinion based on the information supplied by the parties so that they have an informed appraisal of their positions, possibly in relation to the costs risks to which they are exposed[219] as well as the substantive issues. In addition to being consensual the process is, unless the parties agree, non-binding and without prejudice, being treated as part of the negotiations between the parties. The court ordered an ENE to be conducted in the 1975 Act case of *Seals v Williams*,[220] a claim by adult children, where mediation had failed because of the parties' differing attitudes to the issues and perceptions of the strength of their positions. It seemed plain to Norris J that the expression of provisional views, with a view to assisting the

7–089

---

[215] *Civil Procedure 2017*, Vol.2, Chancery Guide, ch.18, "Case management for settlement", paras 18.16–18.19.
[216] Institute of Family Law Arbitrators, formed in 2012. IFLA is responsible for the training and accreditation of family law arbitrators. The scheme is described in two articles by Sir Peter Singer, *Arbitration in Family Financial Proceedings: The IFLA Scheme, Part 1* [2012] Fam Law 1353, and *Part 2* [2012] Fam Law 1496. Another valuable resource is D. Sheridan, *Family Law Arbitration—A Judicially Recognised Alternative to the Family Court* (London: Law Society Publishing, 2014).
[217] *S v S* [2014] EWHC 7 (Fam); [2014] 1 W.L.R. 2299.
[218] A full-time judge, a s.9 judge, a Chancery master or a registrar.
[219] *Seals v Williams* [2015] EWHC 1829 (Ch); [2015] W.T.L.R. 1265, at [3].
[220] *Seals v Williams*, at [7]; there had already been one round of litigation on a different issue, for which see *Williams v Seals* [2015] W.T.L.R. 339.

parties, reduced the area of dispute and the general scope of the argument, was an inherent part of the judicial function. In FDR, which is also a consensual process, the role of the judge conducting the FDR is to facilitate negotiations between the parties and, if so required, to provide an opinion about the claim or any aspect of it. Again, this is a without prejudice and non-binding process and, rather like a mediation, the aim is to get the parties to agree terms but there is no power to determine the outcome.

7–090   A standard direction for ADR will include provisions for a stay while the parties try to settle, for an agreed extension, and for the submission of a draft consent order if settlement is reached or agreed directions and costs budgets if it is not. The parties will be directed to inform the court immediately if the claim or part of it is settled, whether or not it is possible to file a draft consent order to give effect to the settlement.[221] Where the court gives case management directions in cases assigned or allocated to the multi-track on its own initiative, without holding a CMC and is not aware of any steps taken by the parties other than the exchange of statements of case, those directions may include a direction such as the following (the so-called "Ungley Order")[222]:

> "The parties shall by [date] consider whether the case is capable of resolution by ADR. If any party considers the case unsuitable for resolution by ADR, that party shall be prepared to justify that decision at the conclusion of the trial, should the judge consider that such means of resolution were appropriate, when he is considering the appropriate costs order to make.
>
> The party considering the case unsuitable for ADR shall, not less than 28 days before the commencement of the trial file with the court a witness statement without prejudice save as to costs, giving reasons on which they rely for saying that the case was unsuitable."

(ii) Preparation for and conduct of trial

7–091   The first aspect of preparation for trial considered under this heading is evidence. Ideally, the witness statements of the claimant and those of the defendants who intend to defend the claim actively should address all s.3 matters relevant to their respective cases, and the necessary supporting documents should be exhibited to those statements. If that can be achieved so that there is no need to invoke the procedure under Pt 18 for obtaining further information and the parties can agree to dispense with disclosure or to limit it to defined issues,[223] a very considerable cost saving is likely to result, as it is an unfortunate feature of 1975 Act cases that, very often, costs

---

[221] See form CH1 ([2], [9]). The Chancery Guide contains specimen draft orders directing an ENE ([18.15]) or a Chancery FDR ([18.18]).
[222] 29PD.4 (directions on allocation) para.4.10(9). See also 29PD.3 (Case management—general provisions).
[223] Form CH1 ([4]), "Disclosure of documents".

are incurred on evidential matters (and particularly on disclosure) which are wholly disproportionate to the extent to which the evidence assists the court in determining the outcome of the proceedings. Filing and service of those witness statements and of the witness statement to be made by a defendant who is a personal representative is regulated by CPR r.57.16 and 57APD. There may be a need for expert evidence[224]; obvious cases are where mental or physical disability is an issue or where a valuation is required. Where expert evidence is required, time and costs will be saved if the parties can agree that such evidence should be given by a single joint expert. If there is a good reason not to make such a direction, the court may direct simultaneous or sequential exchange of experts' reports, discussions between experts and the preparation of a statement if the reports are not agreed, and a further case management conference after the date for compliance with those directions.[225]

The parties may foresee the need for further case management by way of a further case management conference or a pre-trial review, so that any further orders or directions may be made, or any applications dealt with.[226] As the court is required by s.3(5) of the 1975 Act to have regard to the facts as known to it at the date of the hearing, this provides an opportunity to apply for a direction regarding filing and service of further witness statements within a specified period before the trial date so that the court is made aware of any material changes in the parties' circumstances. A direction will be required in relation to trial bundles and skeleton arguments.[227]   **7–092**

The nature of the case and the identification of the issues will generally be the subject of a case summary.[228] This document, which, if possible, should be agreed by the parties, is normally directed to be not more than 500 words in length and should contain a brief chronology and list of issues. In a 1975 Act claim, it is very often the case that the only issue is whether the will, or, as the case may be, the law relating to intestacy, is such as to have made reasonable provision for the claimant. The other issues which may arise are domicile, proof of the relationship between the claimant and the deceased, particularly where the claim is under s.1(1)(ba), s.1(1)(d) or s.1(1)(e), and the value of the net estate. It is suggested that the chronology should set out the significant dates in the relationship between the claimant and the deceased, the date of the will in question and the dates of any other relevant testamentary dispositions, the date of death, the date of the grant of repre-   **7–093**

---

[224] Form CH1 contains provisions relating to permission to apply for directions as to expert evidence and for evidence to be given by a single expert or separate experts; see [7a]–[7c].

[225] 29PD4, para.4.8; 35PD, paras 6–9.

[226] For a direction where costs budgets have been filed and agreed, see Form CH1 ([10]), "Case and Costs Management". Form CH2 includes model directions for case management conferences and for case and costs management conferences where costs budgets have been filed and exchanged but not agreed.

[227] Form CH1, ([8]).

[228] Form CH2 includes model directions providing either for the summary to be prepared by one party and agreed by the others or for each party to prepare and file its own summary, and for definition and reduction of issues.

sentation and the date on which the possibility of a claim was first notified to the personal representative.

(d) Costs Budgeting and Costs Management

7–094   Costs management[229] is regulated by Section II of CPR Pt 3 and 3EPD, which apply to all Pt 7 multi-track cases except those specified in CPR r.3.12(1) and to any other proceedings where the court so orders. The court has a discretion, in any case where the parties are not required to file and exchange costs budgets, to make an order requiring them to do so, and it may exercise that power either on its own initiative or on the application of a party. 1975 Act claims are listed among the cases where an order for the provision of costs budgets with a view to a costs management order being made[230] may be particularly appropriate, and the commentary to CPR Pt 57 is to the effect that, in view of that specific identification, it is to be expected that in proceedings under the 1975 Act, a costs management order will often be made.[231] The sanction for failing to file a costs budget despite being required to do so is that, unless the court otherwise orders, the defaulting party will be treated as having filed a budget comprising only the applicable court fees.[232] The budget must, unless the court otherwise orders, be in the form of Precedent H annexed to Practice Direction 3E.

7–095   An additional and quite separate requirement is imposed by Practice Direction 3F which relates to Section III of Pt 3 (costs capping). Section II of Practice Direction 3F is concerned with costs capping orders in relation to trust funds, and "trust fund" is defined as including the estate of a deceased person.[233] Any party to such proceedings who intends to apply for payment of costs out of the trust fund must file and serve on all other parties written notice of that intention together with a budget of the costs likely to be incurred by that party. It would therefore appear that the provision applies whenever a party to 1975 Act proceedings intends to apply for his costs to be paid out of the estate.[234] The commentary notes that this provision does not sit easily with the provisions in Section II of CPR Pt 3 excluding 1975 Act claims from the costs budgeting requirements unless the court otherwise orders, and expresses the hope that these provisions will be revisited.[235]

---

[229] A valuable resource in this area is the now annual publication *Costs & Funding Following the Civil Justice Reforms; Questions and Answers*, by Peter Hurst, Simon Middleton and Roger Mallalieu, (London: Sweet & Maxwell, produced in conjunction with the Dispute Resolution team at Practical Law). See, in particular, Ch.4, "Case and Costs Management". The edition current at the time of writing (3rd edition, 2017) is up to date to 17 February 2017.

[230] 3EPD.1, paras 2(a), 5(d).

[231] *Civil Procedure 2017*, para.57.16.4. Anecdotal evidence and the author's own experience both indicate a lack of uniformity and predictability in relation to the exercise of the power.

[232] See CPR rr.3.12 (application of the section), 3.13 (filing and exchanging budgets) and 3.14 (failure to file a budget).

[233] 3FPD5, para.5.1.

[234] 3FPD5, para.5.4; see also the commentary at para.57.16.5.

[235] Again, in the author's experience, the provision is a source of confusion since there are practitioners who apparently believe that Section II of 3FPD imposes a requirement for costs budgeting in all 1975 Act claims.

(e) Defeating the Claim Without a Full Trial

A case may be defeated without a full trial by striking out,[236] by summary   **7–096**
judgment, or by the determination of a decisive preliminary issue in a
manner adverse to the claimant. Where the issue is whether the applicant
qualifies as a cohabitant, a person who has been treated as a child of the
family, or a dependant within the meaning of s.1(1)(e) and s.1(3), the facts
underlying those issues are generally so bound up with the other issues in the
case that little, if anything, is to be gained by trying that issue separately.
This is clearly demonstrated by the cases where applications to strike out
claims under the 1975 Act have been made. The court has power under
r.3.4(2)(a) to strike out a statement of case (which includes a claim form) if it
appears to the court that it discloses no reasonable grounds for bringing a
claim. It is difficult to see, however, that this course could ever be taken
where the claimant alleges in the claim form that they are a member of one
of the classes specified in s.1(1) of the 1975 Act. In *Jelley v Iliffe*[237] the
applicant's case was that he was being wholly or partly maintained by the
deceased as he was living in her house rent-free, though they put their
pensions into a common fund for the running of the household and he
tended the garden and did odd jobs about the house while she did the
cooking and cleaning. The defendants' application to strike out on the basis
that the facts disclosed no reasonable cause of action was granted at first
instance and on appeal to the High Court. The Court of Appeal reversed
those decisions, holding that although his prospects of success were
doubtful, the applicant had an arguable case that his contribution was less
than that of the deceased. *Jelley v Iliffe* was applied by the Court of Appeal
in *Bishop v Plumley*,[238] in which the proceedings followed a similar course.
Re Beaumont[239] was one of the relatively few successful applications to strike
out; it was found, as a fact, that the parties were simply pooling their
resources, so that the deceased never assumed responsibility for the applicant's maintenance.

Nor are the prospects of succeeding in an application for summary   **7–097**
judgment likely to be a great deal better. The court may give summary
judgment against a claimant if it considers that they have no real prospect of
succeeding on the claim or issue and that there is no other compelling reason
why the case or issue should be disposed of at a trial.[240] A claimant has to
show that they have a real prospect of success at trial; the court will disregard false, fanciful or imaginary prospects. On the other hand, the claimant does not have to show that they will probably succeed at trial. Unless

---

[236] The court has power to strike out under any of the three limbs of CPR r.3.4 and the
procedure is regulated by Practice Direction 3A.
[237] *Jelley v Iliffe* [1981] Fam. 128, CA.
[238] *Bishop v Plumley* [1991] 1 All E.R. 236, CA.
[239] *Re Beaumont* [1980] Ch. 444. The author has always contended that that decision was wrong
in principle because assumption of responsibility was not a threshold condition for eligibility under the Act; that debate has been resolved by the amendment to s.3.4 effected by
the Inheritance and Trustees' Powers Act 2014.
[240] CPR r.24.2.

it is clear that the factual assertions on which a claim to eligibility is based are without substance, it is highly unlikely that the application will succeed. As Lord Woolf said in *Swain v Hillman*[241] the proper disposal of an issue under Pt 24 does not involve the court in conducting a mini-trial. Whatever the formal difference between a striking-out application and the determination, as a preliminary issue, of the claimant's eligibility as a member of one of those classes, substantially the proceedings are directed towards the same end.

7–098   The parties may wish to consider whether it is appropriate to apply for a direction for the trial of a preliminary issue, and in doing so should have regard to the reservations about the practice of trying preliminary issues expressed by Lord Wilberforce and Lord Scarman in *Tilling v Whiteman*.[242] As Lord Scarman said, preliminary points of law are often treacherous short cuts. The court has power to direct a separate trial of any issue, and to dismiss or give judgment on a claim after a decision on a preliminary issue.[243] Suitable issues in 1975 Act cases may be whether the deceased died domiciled in England and Wales[244] and disputes about status, including paternity, the validity of a marriage or divorce, adoption and legitimation.

5.—DISPOSAL OF CLAIMS BY ADR

(a) General

7–099   Although it is not the only available form of ADR, the relative informality of the mediation process makes it particularly suitable for the resolution of family-centred disputes such as 1975 Act claims. In addition, there has been a very considerable increase in the amount of judicial attention devoted to the questions whether, and in what circumstances, parties should resort to mediation, or as the case may be, may reasonably decline to do so; and to the consequences of unreasonable refusal. The questions whether the court has, or should have, the power to compel mediation, have also been vigorously debated, perhaps because some European jurisdictions have adopted compulsory mediation.[245] Indeed, the view initially taken by the courts after CPR came into effect was that parties could be compelled to use ADR,

---

[241] *Swain v Hillman* [2001] 1 All E.R. 91, CA.
[242] *Tilling v Whiteman* [1980] A.C. 1. The warnings were against deciding the case (which was a landlord and tenant matter) on a preliminary point of law when the decision-making process would have been greatly assisted by a short investigation of the facts and it would not then have been necessary to remit it to the court of first instance.
[243] CPR r.3.1(2)(i), (l), respectively. For a model direction, see Form CH2, "Trial of issue".
[244] A complex case in which one of the issues was whether the deceased died domiciled in Belgium or England and Wales is *Morris v Davies* [2011] W.T.L.R. 1643, where the issue arose in a probate claim. The subsequent judgment on costs (*Morris v Davies* [2012] W.T.L.R. 1569) is also of interest.
[245] The criticisms of *Halsey*, which are surveyed in *Civil Procedure 2017* at para.14–9, are fortified by constant reference to compulsory mediation in other jurisdictions, a matter not addressed in *Halsey*.

the high-water mark of judicial encouragement to do so being *Dunnett v Railtrack Plc*[246] in which Brooke LJ said that:

"parties and their legal representatives should be alert to the possibility that if they 'turn down out of hand' the chance of ADR when suggested by the court, they may have to face uncomfortable costs consequences."

(b) The Decision in *Halsey*

In the landmark decision of the Court of Appeal, *Halsey v Milton Keynes General NHS Trust*,[247] the court addressed the question: **7–100**

"When should the court impose a costs sanction against a successful litigant on the grounds that he has refused to take part in an alternative dispute resolution?"

The Court of Appeal in *Halsey* was in no doubt that ADR should be a voluntary process. It was satisfied that ADR was an important and valuable resource and that legal representatives should routinely consider with their clients whether the dispute was suitable for ADR; but the court should do no more than to encourage the parties (robustly, if need be) to adopt it. It cited, with approval, the following passage from *Civil Procedure 2003*[248]:

"The hallmark of ADR procedures, and perhaps the key to their effectiveness in individual cases, is that they are processes voluntarily entered into by the parties in dispute with outcomes, if the parties so wish, which are non-binding. Consequently the court cannot direct that such methods be used but may merely encourage and facilitate."

It added that the form of encouragement might be robust.[249] In deciding whether, in circumstances when the successful party had refused to engage in ADR, there should be a departure from the normal rule that costs follow the event, the fundamental principle was that:

"...such departure is not justified unless it is shown (the burden being on the unsuccessful party) that the successful party acted unreasonably in refusing to agree to ADR."[250]

In considering what circumstances would be relevant to the decision whether the successful party had acted unreasonably, the Court accepted a submission by the Law Society that the following factors might be among

---

[246] *Dunnett v Railtrack Plc* [2002] 2 All E.R. 850, CA.
[247] *Halsey v Milton Keynes General NHS Trust* [2004] 1 W.L.R. 2002, CA.
[248] *Civil Procedure 2003*, para.1.4.11, cited in *Halsey* at [9].
[249] *Halsey*, at [11], [30].
[250] *Halsey*, at [14].

those which were relevant in a given case, viz., (a) the nature of the dispute; (b) the merits of the case; (c) the extent to which other settlement methods have been attempted; (d) whether the costs of the ADR would be disproportionately high; (e) whether any delay in setting up and attending the ADR would have been prejudicial; and (f) whether the ADR had a reasonable prospect of success.[251]

7-101   The court considered the fact that a party reasonably believes that they have a strong case as being relevant to the question whether they have acted reasonably in refusing ADR. If the position were otherwise, there would be considerable scope for a claimant to use the threat of costs sanctions to extract a settlement from the defendant even where the claim is without merit. The court did not accept at face value the statement of Lightman J in *Hurst v Leeming*[252] that "the fact that a party believes that he has a watertight case again is no justification for refusing mediation"; they might well be justified if their belief was reasonable. The fact that other methods of settlement (usually negotiation) had been unsuccessful was relevant but unlikely to be determinative; mediation often succeeded where previous attempts at settlement had failed. In any event, the court viewed this factor as being an aspect of the wider question whether the ADR had a reasonable prospect of success; and that was to be viewed in the light of the respective parties' attitudes and willingness to compromise and not solely by consideration of whether, viewed objectively, a mediation would have had a reasonable prospect of success. It also had to be acknowledged that some disputes were more intractable than others and some mediators were more skilled than others.

(c) The Cases After *Halsey*

7-102   In some cases the question has been, specifically, whether the successful party acted unreasonably in refusing to engage in ADR, but in others, that question may form part of a broader consideration of a party's conduct, in accordance with r.44.3(4)(a). The factual situations in which these questions fall to be decided are many and varied,[253] but the following survey identifies some points which might arise if the question whether a successful party should be deprived of some or all of their costs were to arise in a 1975 Act claim. The reasoning in *Halsey* has been adopted in a number of cases where mediation was never considered by the parties. In *Hickman v Blake Lapthorn*[254] it was held that the principles in *Halsey* applied to a refusal to negotiate in the same way as to a refusal to engage in ADR. In *Vale of Glamorgan Council v Roberts*[255] the court declined to apply *Halsey* in circumstances where, although the unsuccessful party had made three offers of

---

[251] *Halsey*, at [16]–[25].
[252] *Hurst v Leeming* [2003] 1 Lloyd's Rep. 379.
[253] *Civil Procedure 2017*, Vol.2, para.14–17, "Costs where ADR declined" and para.14–17A, "Disputes about costs".
[254] *Hickman v Blake Lapthorn* [2006] EWHC 12 (QB).
[255] *Vale of Glamorgan Council v Roberts* [2008] EWHC 2911 (Ch).

settlement, none of them had positively suggested mediation. In *Daniels v Commissioner of Police of the Metropolis*,[256] Ward LJ found it:

"...difficult to envisage circumstances in which it would ever be right to deprive a successful defendant of some or all of his costs solely on the grounds that he refused to accept a claimant's Pt 36 offer."

The inference to be drawn from Pts 36 and 44.3 was that (notwithstanding the terms of Pt 44.3(4)(c)) the mere fact that a successful defendant has refused a claimant's Pt 36 offer[257] cannot of itself be a sufficient reason for departing from the general rule and depriving the defendant of costs.

In *Burchell v Bullard*[258] the court analysed the defendants' refusal to **7–103** mediate by reference to the factors identified in *Halsey*. First, a small building dispute was par excellence the kind of dispute which lent itself to ADR. The merits of the case favoured mediation. Second, the defendants behaved unreasonably in believing, if they did, that their case was so watertight that they need not engage in attempts to settle. Third, the costs of ADR would have been minimal compared with the cost of the litigation. Finally, the claimant had behaved in an entirely reasonable manner throughout and had satisfied the court that mediation would have had a reasonable prospect of success. The defendants could not rely on their own obstinacy to assert that mediation had no reasonable prospect of success. Nevertheless, they were not subjected to any costs sanction,[259] but the judgment warns future defendants who obstinately and unreasonably refuse mediation of the risks of doing so.

In *The claimants appearing on the Register of the Corby Group Litigation v* **7–104** *Corby District Council (Costs)*[260] the court took into account the time at which the request for mediation was made by the claimants and the state of the evidence at the time when the request was refused. The defendants' initial response was that the decision would best be deferred until expert evidence had been exchanged and, some time after that was done, they refused to mediate on the ground that it would be highly unlikely to be productive in reaching a conclusion. Although, in the event, the defendants were wrong in their estimation of the strength of their case, the reasonableness of their stance had to be judged in the circumstances existing at the time when they made the decision to refuse mediation. They had expert

---

[256] *Daniels v Commissioner of Police of the Metropolis* [2005] EWCA Civ 1312; (2005) 102 L.S. Gaz. 30.

[257] In *Daniels*, the claimant alleged negligence and claimed damages which were agreed at £7,000. The defendant was strongly of the view that the claim had no foundation and made no Pt 36 payment or offer. The claimant made a Pt 36 offer of £4,000 which the defendant rejected and the claim was dismissed by the judge.

[258] *Burchell v Bullard* [2005] EWCA Civ 358; [2005] B.L.R. 330; (2005) 155 N.L.J. 593.

[259] However, that was largely because the litigation had been commenced in May 2001, when the law in this area was virtually undeveloped. In the light of the knowledge of the times and in the absence of legal advice, they could not be condemned as having been so unreasonable that a costs sanction should follow many years later.

[260] *The claimants appearing on the Register of the Corby Group Litigation v Corby District Council (Costs)* [2009] EWHC 2109 (TCC).

evidence supporting their stance on all material aspects of the litigation and the claimants' approach was lacking in focus; thus their view that mediation would not lead to a result was not unreasonable.

7–105   In the context of the Practice Direction—Pre-Action Conduct and Protocols, failure of compliance includes unreasonably refusing to use a form of ADR or failure to respond to an invitation to do so,[261] and the court may impose costs sanctions. It is apparently hoped that ADR will be so regularly employed that the courts will rarely feel the need to take that course, but there is an obvious danger of an increase in satellite litigation directed towards that outcome, strongly discouraged though it may have been. The review of the case-law[262] shows a wide spectrum of possible outcomes of refusal to mediate, including an award of indemnity costs against the refusing party,[263] but lesser sanctions where there have been conduct issues on both sides.[264] Refusal to mediate has resulted in disallowance of some of the successful party's costs even where it was unlikely that the mediation process would have been successful[265] or where its likely outcome was uncertain.[266] This issue has arisen in a number of contested probate cases. In *Re Rawlinson deceased*[267] (a case in which the issue was whether a will had been duly executed), David Richards J doubted whether a failure to mediate would justify a departure from the general rule that costs follow the event, and decided that in view of the (unsuccessful) defendant's conduct, a departure from the general rule would be inappropriate; his conduct meant that mediation would not have taken place on a level playing-field. In *In re McKeen*,[268] the first attempted mediation failed and the (successful) claimant was prepared to engage in a second mediation only on conditions relating to payment of costs by the defendant. HH Judge Barker QC held that the claimant's response did not justify a departure from the general rule. In *Morris v Davies*,[269] it was found that no issue had been raised which was of sufficient substance to warrant a mediation, and, in the febrile atmosphere within the family, there was little, if any, prospect of a successful mediation.

---

[261] *Civil Procedure 2017*, para.C1–008, "Compliance with this Practice Direction and the Protocols"; see the Practice Direction at paras 14(c) and 16.

[262] *Civil Procedure 2017* Vol.2, paras 14–11 ("Case management and cost sanctions"), 14–17 ("Costs where ADR declined"). See also *Cook on Costs* (London: LexisNexis, 2017), Simon Middleton and Jason Rowley (eds), Ch.21 "Costs inducements to settle—ADR".

[263] *Garrett-Critchley v Ronnan* [2014] EWHC 1774 (Ch).

[264] In *Lakehouse Contracts Ltd v UPR Services* [2014] EWHC 1223 (Ch), a company which had properly resisted a winding-up petition on the ground that the debt was genuinely disputed, was held entitled to its costs of resisting the petition on the indemnity basis but only up to the date when its own conduct became unreasonable.

[265] *Lynn v Borneos LLP (t/a Borneo Linnels)* [2015] 3 Costs L.R. 439; successful defendant denied 40 per cent of this costs.

[266] *Laporte v The Commissioner of Police of the Metropolis* [2015] EWHC 371 (QB); successful defendant awarded only two thirds of his costs.

[267] *Re Rawlinson deceased, Kayll v Rawlinson (costs)* [2010] W.T.L.R. 1479, at [13].

[268] *In re McKeen, Viva! Campaigns v Scott* [2014] W.T.L.R. 461, at [56]. The issues in the case were lack of testamentary capacity and want of knowledge and approval.

[269] *Morris v Davies* [2012] W.T.L.R. 1569. The judgment refers, at [18], to an indication by Lewison LJ that refusal to mediate is not always a trump card, but does not identify the case in which that indication was given.

The decision of the Court of Appeal in *PGF II SA v OMFS Co 1 Ltd*[270]   **7–106**
has been seen by many as a landmark decision,[271] and, as the following
discussion shows, the perils of refusing to engage with ADR can scarcely
have been more starkly pictured. The substantive claim was for breach of
repairing covenants. Both parties made Pt 36 offers and on two subsequent
occasions the claimant invited the defendant, in writing, to pursue ADR,
but the defendant did not respond. On the eve of the trial the claimant
accepted the defendant's Pt 36 offer and the claim was compromised save as
to costs. The judge found the defendant's failure to respond to those serious
invitations to be unreasonable conduct and, in exercise of his discretion
under CPR r.36.10, deprived the defendant of its costs (to which it would
otherwise have been entitled) for the period of just over eight months
between the date of its Pt 36 offer and the date of settlement, but did not
order it to pay the claimant's costs during that period. The defendant
appealed and the claimant cross-appealed, each seeking its costs during that
period; both appeals were dismissed.

Whereas *Halsey* was concerned with the consequences of a refusal to   **7–107**
mediate, the *PGF* case addresses the consequences of ignoring requests to
mediate.[272] Briggs LJ, giving the only substantive judgment,[273] said that the
time had come for the court firmly to endorse the advice given in the *Jackson
ADR Handbook*,[274] and stated that:

> "...silence in the face of an invitation to participate in ADR is, as a
> general rule, of itself unreasonable, regardless of whether an outright
> refusal, or a refusal to engage in the type of ADR requested, or to do so
> at the time requested, might have been justified by the identification of
> reasonable grounds",

and that the advice might be fairly summarised as calling for constructive
engagement with ADR rather than flat refusal, or silence. He put this forward as a general rather than an invariable rule since there might be rare
cases where ADR was so obviously inappropriate that to characterise
silence as refusal "would be sheer formalism". He rejected the submission
that the *Halsey* tests for the reasonableness of a refusal had to be assessed
objectively; the party's own perceptions had an important part in the analysis, as was apparent from the treatment in *Halsey*[275] of a party's reasonable
belief in the strength of their case. A failure to provide reasons for refusal
was destructive of the encouragement of the parties to engage in the ADR
process; reasonable objections to any particular proposal should be capable

---

[270] *PGF II SA v OMFS Co 1 Ltd* [2014] 1 W.L.R. 1386, CA.
[271] Rt. Hon Lord Justice Jackson, *The Reform of Civil Litigation* (2016), para.9–019.
[272] This issue had been addressed in *Burchell v Bullard* [2005] EWCA Civ 358, referred to
above, and in *Rolf v De Guerin* [2011] 5 Costs L.R. 892, CA.
[273] With which Maurice Kay and Beatson LJJ agreed.
[274] Susan Blake, Julie Browne, Stuart Sime (eds), *Jackson ADR Handbook*, 1st edn (Oxford:
Oxford University Press, 2013), para.11–56.
[275] *Halsey*, at [26], rejecting the objective approach employed in *Hurst v Leeming* [2003] 1
Lloyds Rep. 379.

of being addressed in other ways. Positive engagement with ADR would serve the policy of proportionality and, even if not resulting in a settlement, might save time and costs by substantially narrowing the issues. On the basis of that analysis, the defendant's silence in the face of two offers to mediate was unreasonable conduct sufficient to warrant a costs sanction. It was plain from *Halsey* and also from the reference in *SG v Hewitt*[276] to the wide discretion arising from such conduct that the proper response in any particular case might range between the disallowing of the whole, or only a modest part of, the successful party's costs. There appeared to be no recognition in *Halsey* that the court might go farther and order the otherwise successful party to pay all or part of the unsuccessful party's costs. While the court must have that power, its exercise should be reserved for the most serious and flagrant failures to engage with ADR, for example where the court had taken it upon itself to encourage the parties to do so and the encouragement had been ignored. The court's task in encouraging the more proportionate conduct of civil litigation was so important in the current economic climate that it was appropriate to emphasise that message by a sanction *pour encourager les autres*.

6.—The 1975 Act Application: The Hearing

(a) Mode of Trial

7–108   The general rule is that a hearing is to be held in public.[277] However, there are exceptions to the general rule, one of which is that a hearing, or any part of it, may be in private if it involves confidential information (including information relating to personal financial matters) and publicity would damage that confidentiality.[278] The hearings specified by the Practice Direction which shall, in the first instance, be listed by the court as hearings in private include proceedings brought under the 1975 Act.[279] Although, subject to consideration of Art.6(1) of the European Convention on Human Rights, which requires that in general court hearings are to be held in public, the default position appears to be that a 1975 Act hearing would be held in private, it is normal for such hearings to be held in public without any such representations being made to the judge as are envisaged by the Practice Direction.[280]

7–109   In any proceedings, the judgment and any summing up by the judge will be recorded, and oral evidence will normally be recorded also. The rule whereby any person (whether or not a party) may require a transcript on payment of the authorised charge does not apply where a hearing or any

---

[276] *SG v Hewitt* [2013] 1 All E.R. 1118, CA, per Arden LJ.
[277] CPR r.39.2(1)
[278] CPR r.39.2(3)(c).
[279] 39APD para.1.5(9).
[280] 39APD para.1.4.

part of it is held in private; persons who are not parties may not obtain a transcript unless the court orders that the rule shall apply.[281]

(b) Evidence at Trial

The general rule is that any fact which needs to be proved by the evidence of **7–110** witnesses at trial is to be proved by their oral evidence given in public, but this is subject to any provision to the contrary contained in the CPR or otherwise, or to any order of the court.[282] Where a witness has been called to give oral evidence, their witness statement will normally be ordered to stand as the maker's evidence in chief.[283] Nevertheless, it is open to the trial judge to require that a witness give oral evidence in chief.[284] If the court so permits, a witness giving oral evidence at trial may amplify their witness statement, and give evidence in relation to matters which have arisen since the witness statement was served on the other parties.[285] When the witness is called to give evidence at trial, they may be cross-examined on their witness statement whether or not the statement, or any part of it, was referred to during their evidence in chief.[286]

CPR Pt 33 (Miscellaneous rules about evidence) includes the rules relating **7–111** to hearsay evidence. Section 1(1) of the Civil Evidence Act 1995 provides that hearsay evidence is no longer inadmissible on the ground that it is hearsay as defined in s.1(2) of that Act.[287] Section 2(1)(a) of the 1995 Act provides that a party intending to adduce hearsay evidence in civil proceedings must notify any other party, and r.33.2 contains the provisions relating to notice of intention to rely on hearsay evidence at trial. This requirement may be excluded by agreement of the parties or waived by the person to whom notice is to be given.[288] There is a limited group of circumstances in which the duty to give notice of intention is not required; these include the situation where a party to a probate action wishes to put a statement in evidence which is alleged to have been made by the person whose estate is the subject of the proceedings.[289] Failure to give notice of intention does not render the evidence inadmissible but the court may take such failure into account in considering the exercise of its powers with respect to the course of proceedings and to costs, and as a matter adversely affecting the weight to be given to such evidence under s.4 of the 1995 Act.[290] A witness may be called for cross-examination on hearsay evidence,[291] and

---

[281] 39APD para.6.3, 6.4.
[282] CPR r.32.2(1)(a), subject to r.32.2(2).
[283] CPR r.32.5(2).
[284] *Civil Procedure 2017*, para.32.5.1.
[285] CPR r.32.5(3).
[286] CPR r.32.11.
[287] That statutory definition of "hearsay" is reproduced in CPR r.33(1)(a) and no distinction is now made between degrees of hearsay.
[288] Civil Evidence Act 1995 s.2(3); *Civil Procedure 2017*, para.33.2.1.
[289] CPR r.33.3(b)
[290] *Civil Procedure 2017*, para.33.2.3.
[291] CPR r.33.4.

r.33.5 regulates attacks on the credibility of persons making statements which are proposed to be relied on as hearsay evidence.[292]

7–112   Section 4(2) of the Civil Evidence Act 1995 specifies a series of matters to which the court is directed to have particular regard when estimating the weight (if any) to be given to hearsay evidence in civil proceedings. By s.4(2)(a), the court is required to have regard to whether it would have been reasonable and practicable for the party by whom the evidence was adduced to have produced the maker of the original statement as a witness. There is always the risk that, if the court is not satisfied that it was unreasonable or impracticable to call the witness, it may take the view that the witness would have turned out to be unreliable and discount the evidence accordingly. The common sense view that a statement made contemporaneously with the events to which it refers is more likely to be credible than one made at a significantly later stage is given effect by s.4(2)(b). The effect of s.4(2)(c) is that the distinction between first-hand and multiple hearsay is no longer relevant to admissibility, though it goes to weight. The considerations relevant to the weighing of hearsay evidence embody a certain healthy scepticism; under ss.4(2)(d)–(f) of the 1995 Act, regard may be had, inter alia, to whether any person involved has any motive to conceal or misrepresent matters; whether the original statement was an edited account, or was made in collaboration with another or for a particular purpose; and whether the circumstances in which it is adduced as hearsay are such as to suggest an attempt to prevent proper evaluation of its weight. All of these considerations may arise in relation to hearsay evidence given in 1975 Act proceedings.

7–113   In *Welsh v Stokes*[293] the Court of Appeal considered s.4 of the 1995 Act in some detail and concluded, in the instant case, that the trial judge was right to conclude that uncorroborated hearsay evidence was reliable and weight should be accorded to it. In that case, which was to do with injuries suffered by the claimant when falling off a horse, the evidence of the incident was contained in a statement made by W recounting what he had been told by an unidentified witness (X) about it. The Court of Appeal rejected the appellants' submission that hearsay evidence should not be relied on to prove the central issues in a case unless supported by other evidence and commented on some of the authorities cited in support of it. The analysis shows the dangers of relying on judicial dicta of a general nature, divorced from the facts or context of the case under consideration. To mention one such statement, Baroness Hale said in *Polanski v Conde Nast Publications Ltd*[294] "It might be grossly unjust to the other party, even contrary to his right to a fair trial under article 6 of the European Convention on Human Rights to

---

[292] CPR r.33.5(1)(c); *Civil Procedure 2017*, para.33.5.1.
[293] *Welsh v Stokes* [2008] 1 W.L.R. 1234, CA.
[294] *Polanski v Conde Nast Publications Ltd* [2005] UKHL 10; [2005] 1 W.L.R. 637, at [78]. See also the general observations made by Brandon J in *The 'Ferdinand Retzlaff'* [1972] 2 Lloyd's Rep. 120 at 126–127 (a case where the hearsay provisions of the Civil Evidence Act 1968 were under consideration) and by Leggatt J in *The 'Kilmun'* [1988] 2 Lloyd's Rep. 1 at 6, "although giving evidence by way of statements under the Civil Evidence Act 1968 was convenient, it is obvious that it is not a satisfactory way of resolving disputed issues of fact".

decide a claim principally on the untested evidence of a party who has not been subject to cross-examination of any sort". As Dyson LJ, giving the judgment of the court, observed, although there might be said to be unfairness to the defendant in having to face hearsay evidence which he cannot directly challenge, there would also be unfairness to the claimant if no weight were placed on the hearsay evidence, since without it her claim would inevitably have failed.

The admissibility and weight of statements made by the deceased are   **7–114**
governed by the provisions of the 1995 Act in the same way as any other hearsay evidence. Evidence about the deceased, as well as evidence in the form of statements by the deceased, is also sometimes relevant. The extent to which use can be made of such evidence in family provision proceedings has been considered on a number of occasions, and the following observations of Buckley J in *Re Blanch*[295] are still relevant:

(a) testamentary capacity, or the want of it, is not a matter which should be investigated in such applications;

(b) mental illness is not a reason for the deceased's dispositions, though it may be taken into account in assessing the weight of any statement in which they gave their reasons for disposing, or not disposing, of their estate in a certain way; and

(c) if the applicant cared for the deceased during a period of mental illness, evidence of the illness could be relevant in assessing the moral obligation which the deceased owed to the applicant.

7.—Compromises and Their Effects

(a) Generally

Many applications under the 1975 Act are compromised.[296] If the parties are   **7–115**
all sui juris and ascertained, the compromise, if consented to by the applicant and all the beneficiaries whose interests are affected, can be embodied in a deed of variation and family arrangement without the need for approval by the court. An order of the court may be either a consent order, or a Tomlin order under which the proceedings are stayed on the terms set out in the schedule to the order.[297] The current practice in relation to compromises of 1975 Act claims is that, when application is made for a consent order, the original grant must be produced or sent to the court for onward transmission to the Principal Registry.[298] This is the case whether or not the order is, strictly speaking, an order under the 1975 Act (e.g., where its provisions would not be within the court's powers under the Act). That might occur

---

[295] *Re Blanch* [1967] 1 W.L.R. 987
[296] *Foskett, The Law and Practice of Compromise*, 8th edn (London: Sweet & Maxwell, 2015), Ch.25, "Settlement of Inheritance Act Disputes".
[297] CPR r.40.6 applies where all parties agree the terms in which a judgment should be given or an order should be made.
[298] *Foskett*, para.25–19.

when the order is designed to dispose of one or more other claims on the same occasion as the 1975 Act claim.

7–116   The question occasionally arises in 1975 Act claims whether consent orders can be set aside on the grounds of bad legal advice.[299] It is thought that grounds similar to those available for setting aside a compromise of matrimonial ancillary relief applications would be available to set aside compromises of 1975 Act claims.[300] In *Tibbs v Beresford-Webb*[301] Miss Tibbs sought to set aside a settlement arrived at out of court on the day of the hearing and embodied in a Tomlin order, under which she and her son received, respectively, £10,000 and £5,000 out of an estate whose value was about £300,000. She was given leave to appeal against an initial refusal to set the order aside, the cases of *Edgar v Edgar*[302] and *Camm v Camm*[303] being regarded as possibly supporting the proposition that a consent order could be set aside if had been entered into as the result of bad legal advice. However, the full court dismissed her application, taking the view that those cases were concerned with the question whether an agreement in respect of which there had been bad legal advice should be enforced, not with whether it should be set aside.[304] In the matrimonial jurisdiction, the cases[305] make it clear that a consent order will not be set aside simply because bad advice was given.[306]

(b) Compromises Where a Representation Order is Made

7–117   CPR r.19.7 applies to claims about the estate of a deceased person. It empowers the court to make a representation order where the person or persons to be represented is or are unborn, or cannot easily be found or ascertained, or there is a class of persons, one or more of whom has the same interest in a claim and is unborn or cannot easily be found or ascertained. The court's approval is required to settle a claim in which a party is acting as a representative under the rule,[307] and the court may approve a settlement where it is satisfied that it is for the benefit of all interested persons.[308] Unless the court otherwise directs, any judgment or order given in a claim when a party is acting as a representative under r.19.7 is binding on all persons

---

[299] *Tibbs v Beresford-Webb* unreported 18 December 1997, CA.
[300] *Foskett*, para.25–16; see also Ch.24. "Compromise of Disputes between Husband and Wife and Civil Partners" at para.24–66 ("Agreements to which *Edgar* applies") and 24–80 ff ("Setting aside consent orders—law and practice"), particularly paras 24–94 to 24–96 ("Bad legal advice?") and 24–102 to 24–119 ("Supervening events"). See also the commentary in *Civil Procedure 2017*, para.40.6.3.
[301] Leave to appeal was also given on the ground that the order had been vitiated by mistake.
[302] *Edgar v Edgar* [1980] 3 All E.R. 887.
[303] *Camm v Camm* (1983) 4 F.L.R. 577.
[304] *Tibbs v Dick* [1998] 2 F.L.R. 1118, CA.
[305] *Harris (formerly Manahan) v Manahan* [1997] 1 F.L.R. 205; *L v L* [2008] 1 F.L.R. 26.
[306] For the practice on setting aside a compromise, see *Foskett*, Ch.12.
[307] CPR r.19.7(5)
[308] CPR r.19.7(6). The commentary in *Civil Procedure 2017*, para.19.7(5) acknowledges that difficulties may arise if, at the time when approval is sought, the persons represented remain unascertained, or are ascertained but not found, and also where the represented persons are not willing to enter into the compromise.

represented in the claim, but may not be enforced, without the court's permission, by or against a non-party.

(c) Persons Not Sui Juris: Children and Protected Parties

The relevant rules of court are CPR rr.21.10 and 21.11. Rule 21.10 is con- **7–118** cerned with the process of obtaining the approval of the court. Where a claim is made by or on behalf of a child or protected party, or against a child or protected party, no settlement, compromise or payment and no acceptance of money paid into court shall be valid, so far as it relates to the claim by, on behalf of or against the child or protected party, without the approval of the court.[309] Its operation is not confined to money claims.[310] Rule 21.11, which applies to control of money recovered by or on behalf of a child or protected party, provides that such money is to be dealt with in accordance with directions given by the court under that rule and not otherwise.[311]

It is not uncommon for 1975 Act claims to be compromised before pro- **7–119** ceedings are commenced. If an agreement is reached in a claim on behalf of, or against, a child or patient, and proceedings are commenced for the sole purpose of obtaining the court's approval of a settlement or compromise, those proceedings must be commenced using the Pt 8 procedure, and the claim must include a request to the court for approval of the settlement or compromise.[312] The commentary states that the rule provides a comprehensive code, and sets out its objects in some detail. Among those objects is the provision of means by which a defendant may obtain a valid discharge from a child's or protected party's claim.[313] It is there pointed out that, at common law, a contract of compromise out of court does not bind such a claimant unless it is proved to have been for his benefit, and no prudent defendant would wish to take a risk on the point. An order approving a settlement under the rule does bind the claimant and gives the defendant a discharge. Another object of the rule is to ensure that the interests of all dependants entitled to a possible share in the settlement are properly defined and protected; although that statement is made in the context of apportionments under the Fatal Accidents Act 1976, it serves as a reminder that the terms of the compromise of a 1975 Act claim entered into on behalf of the child or protected party should also clearly express its effect on the other persons affected by it.

The Practice Direction supplementing CPR Pt 21 sets out the practice in **7–120** relation to seeking the approval of the court. Where the claim on behalf of the child or protected party has been dealt with by agreement before the start of proceedings and only the approval of the court is sought, the claim must be made using the Pt 8 procedure. The claim must include a request for approval of the settlement or compromise, the terms of which must be set

---

[309] CPR r.21.10(1).
[310] *Civil Procedure 2017*, para.21.10.1.
[311] For the practice, see 21PD.8.
[312] CPR r.21.10(2).
[313] *Civil Procedure 2017*, para.21.10.1(b).

out in the claim or in a draft consent order (using practice form N292) attached to the claim.[314] The practice direction appears to have been produced with personal injury litigation very much in mind; thus, the information required includes details of whether and to what extent the defendant admits liability.[315] It is a requirement that, except in very clear cases, an opinion on the merits given by counsel or solicitor acting for the child or patient should be obtained, and should be supplied to the court.[316] Applications for approval will normally be heard by a master or district judge.

(d) Charities as Parties to Compromises

7–121　　It is by no means rare for the major beneficiaries, under a will which is alleged not to make reasonable financial provision for the applicant, to be charities. In both *Re Besterman*[317] (net estate roughly £1.5 million) and *Re Bunning*[318] (£237,000), the charities defended the action, though it was common ground that the will did not make reasonable financial provision for the applicant.[319] Questions about the nature and amount of any award will normally have to be resolved and, as in *Re Bunning*, where there was more than one charitable beneficiary, there will be questions as to the incidence of the burden of the provision.

7–122　　It has for over 250 years been recognised that a question relating to the interests of a charity may be compromised.[320] Where the Attorney General is a party to charity proceedings his consent to a compromise is required, and the compromise will be enforced only when that consent is obtained. It has been settled law since the early 19th century that such consent in an action binds charities who are parties, whether or not they appear.[321]

7–123　　During the 19th century, the courts developed a doctrine that it was not always necessary for the Attorney General to contend for his strict legal rights, but could act with forbearance to individuals in a proper case.[322] These authorities were relied on by Cross J in *Re Snowden*,[323] where he held that there was no inflexible rule against permitting ex gratia payments to be made out of charity funds. The power to do so was not to be exercised

---

[314] CPR r.21.10(2) and 21PD5.

[315] 21PD5 para.5.1(2); see also para.5.4 which requires the court to be satisfied that the parties have considered whether the damages should wholly or partly take the form of periodical payments. Nevertheless it should be possible to follow the general scheme of the practice direction when providing the information relevant to the compromise of a 1975 Act claim.

[316] 21PD5 para.5.2.

[317] *Re Besterman* [1984] Ch. 458.

[318] *Re Bunning* [1984] Ch. 480.

[319] Compare *Ilott v Mitson* [2012]2 F.L.R. 10, CA (net estate £486,000, which went to the charities; they did not accept that the will failed to make reasonable provision for the claimant).

[320] *Att Gen v Landerfield* (1743) 9 Mod. 286; 88 E.R. 456.

[321] *Andrew v Merchant Taylors' Company* (1802) 7 Ves. Jr. 223, 32 E.R. 90; *Andrew v Trinity Hall* (1804) 9 Ves. Jr. 525, 32 E.R. 709.

[322] *Att Gen v Brettingham* (1840) 3 Beav. 91, 49 E.R. 35; *Att Gen v Pretyman* (1841) 4 Beav. 462, 49 E.R. 418.

[323] *Re Snowden, Shackleton v Eddy, Re Henderson, Henderson v Att Gen* [1970] Ch. 700.

lightly, but only in cases where it could fairly be said that, if the charity were an individual, it would be morally wrong of them to refuse to make the payment. While this is no doubt desirable, particularly where the evidence demonstrates that the testator owed a moral obligation to the applicant, it must be remembered that, in *Re Snowden*, the circumstances in which the court authorised the charities concerned to make ex gratia payments were that, almost certainly, the charities had benefited to a greater extent than the testator had intended; whereas, ex hypothesi in 1975 Act cases, the charities benefit to the exact extent that the testator intended. However, it appears to have been accepted without argument in *Re Bates*[324] that, if a charity which is a residuary beneficiary does not wish to oppose the making of financial provision, the court may make such provision as it thinks fit.

Foskett[325] draws attention to the distinction between the power to make ex **7–124** gratia payments, discussed in the previous paragraph, and the power of charity trustees to compromise. A compromise may be effected under certain statutory powers. Thus, charitable trustees holding charitable property on trust may, in the exercise of their power under s.15(f) of the Trustee Act 1925, compromise a claim,[326] and their statutory powers are not limited or restricted in any way by reference to the consideration to be given as part of the compromise. In *Re Earl of Strafford*[327] it was held that the trustees (or, since, in that case, they had surrendered their discretion, the court) had power to accept a compromise if satisfied it was desirable and fair to all the beneficiaries and that it was not necessary for all the beneficiaries to consent before the trustee accepted the compromise. In the exercise of their power, they are subject to the statutory duty of care under the Trustee Act 2000, and must take account of the views and wishes of the beneficiaries, but the decision whether or not to compromise is theirs and they must actively exercise their discretion in making that decision.[328] In complicated cases, or cases where the trustees disagree, they may apply to the Charity Commissioners for an order under s.105 of the Charities Act 2011 sanctioning the proposed compromise.[329] The Charity Commissioners have the same power as the Attorney General to authorise ex gratia payments or to waive, to any extent on behalf of a charity, the entitlement to receive any property, in a case where, apart from that provision, they would have no power to do so, but in all the circumstances regard themselves under a moral obligation to do so. This power is clearly suitable to be exercised for the purpose of compromising a 1975 Act claim. A corporate charity may compromise a claim if its memorandum and articles of association permit it to do so.

---

[324] *Re Bates* [1953] 3 All E.R. 318.
[325] *Foskett*, at para.23–27.
[326] *Foskett*, at para.23–26.
[327] *Re Earl of Strafford* [1980] Ch. 28, C.A
[328] *Foskett*, at paras 23–20–23–23.
[329] See also Charities Act 2011 s.106, "Power to make ex gratia payments".

8.—Offers to Settle

(a) Generally

7–125   Offers to settle can be made in various ways,[330] but the Pt 36 procedure is the only method of making an offer to settle which has defined costs consequences. The procedure has undergone several substantial revisions since its first introduction in 1999 and the current version is (subject to transitional provisions) the product of the revision which took effect from 6 April 2015.[331] Nothing in the general rules applying to Pt 36 offers[332] prevents a party from making an offer to settle in any way that that party chooses, but if the offer is not made in accordance with CPR r.36.5, it will not have the consequences specified in Section I of Pt 36.[333] In exercising its discretion as to costs, the court will have regard to any admissible offer[334] that is drawn to its attention, other than one to which the costs consequences of Pt 36 apply,[335] but it will not, in doing so, make an order which invokes the Pt 36 regime directly or indirectly.[336] The most common form of admissible offer outside the Pt 36 regime is the Calderbank offer, which is an offer made "without prejudice save as to costs"[337] and which, in certain circumstances, may be thought more appropriate by the offeror.[338] The omission of the words "save as to costs" may have unfortunate consequences for the offeror since an offer so expressed could not be referred to on the question of costs between the parties.[339]

7–126   A Pt 36 offer may be made in relation to the whole, or part of, or any issue that arises in a claim, counterclaim or any additional claim, or an appeal or cross-appeal from a decision made at trial.[340] It can be made by either party[341] and at any time, including before trial.

---

[330] See, generally, *Foskett*, Pt 4, "The Settlement Process in Civil Justice"; *Cook on Costs* (London: LexisNexis, 2017), Ch.20, "Costs inducements to settle—Part 36 offers and other admissible offers".

[331] *Foskett*, at para.14–01. For the history of these revisions, see *Civil Procedure 2017*, para.36.0.2.

[332] CPR Pt 36, Section I, rr.36.1–36.23, of which rr.1–17 are potentially relevant to 1975 Act claims.

[333] CPR r.36.2(2).

[334] Apparently, including an open offer; see *HTC Corp v Yozmot 33 Ltd (Costs)* [2010] EWHC 1057 (Pat).

[335] CPR r.44.2(4)(c).

[336] *F & C Alternative Investments (Holdings) Ltd v Barthelemy* [2013] 1 W.L.R. 548, CA; and see, generally, *Cook on Costs*, para.20.38.

[337] In the context of disclosure, a Pt 36 offer will be treated as "without prejudice save as to costs"; see CPR r.36.16(1).

[338] *Cook on Costs*, para.20.37.

[339] *Reed Executive Plc v Reed Business Information Ltd* [2004] EWCA Civ 887.

[340] CPR r.36.2(3).

[341] Notwithstanding the fact that r.36.5 (form and content of a Pt 36 offer) refers at r.36.5(1)(c) to a period during which the defendant will be liable for the claimant's costs rather than referring to the parties as "offeror" and "offeree".

(b) Part 36 Offers

(i) What is a Part 36 offer?

The form and content of a Pt 36 offer is regulated by CPR r.36.5(1) which **7–127** provides that it must:

> "(a) be in writing;
> (b) make clear that it is made pursuant to Pt 36;
> (c) specify a period of not less than 21 days within which the defendant will be liable for the claimant's costs in accordance with rule 36.13 or 36.20 if the offer is accepted[342];
> (d) state whether it relates to the whole of the claim or part of it or to an issue that arises in it and if so, to which part or issue; and
> (e) state whether it takes into account any counterclaim."

(ii) Making, withdrawal and acceptance of a Part 36 offer

A Pt 36 offer is made when it is served on the offeree.[343] The offeree may **7–128** within seven days of a Pt 36 offer being made, request the offeror to clarify the offer, and if that clarification has not been provided within seven days of receipt of the request, apply for an order that the offeror do so.[344] There was, for a time, some confusion as to what constituted an effective withdrawal of a Pt 36 offer and whether a time-limited offer could be a Pt 36 offer. In *Gibbon v Manchester City Council*,[345] Moore-Bick LJ addressed the issue whether a Pt 36 offer had been superseded by another revised offer, or by a rejection. He said:

> "Rule 36.9(2)[346] is quite clear: a Part 36 offer may be accepted *at any time* unless the offeror has withdrawn the offer by serving notice of withdrawal on the offeree. Moreover, it may be accepted whether or not the offeree has subsequently made a different offer, a provision which is contrary to the general position at common law. The rules state clearly how a Part 36 offer may be made, how it may be varied and how it may be withdrawn. They do not provide for it to lapse or become incapable of acceptance on being rejected by the offeree. That would be the case at common law, but it is inconsistent with the concepts underlying Part 36, which proceeds on the footing that the offer is on the table and available for acceptance until the offeror himself chooses to withdraw it."

---

[342] This provision does not apply to offers made less than 21 days before the start of a trial; CPR r.35.5(2).
[343] CPR r.36.7(2).
[344] CPR r.36.8.
[345] *Gibbon v Manchester City Council* [2010] 1 W.L.R. 2081, CA.
[346] This was a reference to the rule as it was following the 2007 revision of Pt 36.

The Court of Appeal referred extensively to the judgment in *Gibbon* when deciding in 2011 that a time-limited offer could not be a Pt 36 offer,[347] but that decision has been nullified by a change of the regime which expressly permits the making of time-limited Pt 36 offers.[348]

7–129   The "relevant period" is a key feature of the rules relating to withdrawal and acceptance of offers. The term means, in the case of an offer made not less than 21 days before a trial, the period specified under r.36.5(1)(c) or such longer period as the parties agree, or in any other case, the period up to the end of such trial.[349] "End of trial" is not in terms defined, but a trial is "in progress" from the time when it starts until the time when judgment is given or handed down.[350] A Pt 36 offer can only be withdrawn, or its terms changed, if the offeree has not previously served notice of acceptance.[351] This is the case whether the change in terms is to the advantage or the disadvantage of the offeree, but the types of change have different consequences. Provided that the offeree has not served written notice of acceptance,[352] the offeror may:

(i)   withdraw the offer or change its terms by serving written notice of withdrawal or change of terms on the offeree, and (subject to r.36.10) the notice takes effect when it is served on the offeree[353];

(ii) after the expiry of the relevant period, withdraw the offer or change its terms without the permission of the court; or the offer may be automatically be withdrawn in accordance with its terms.[354]

Where the offeror changes the offer so as to make it more advantageous to the offeree, the improved offer is not treated as a withdrawal of the original offer but as the making of a new Pt 36 offer on the improved terms. This is an important distinction, because a withdrawn offer does not carry the costs consequences of Pt 36, nor does an offer which has been changed so that its terms are less advantageous to the offeree and the offeree has beaten the less advantageous offer.[355]

7–130   The rule discussed in the previous paragraph regulates withdrawals and changes of terms generally, but there is a further rule which applies where the offeror serves notice of withdrawal or of a change in terms of the offer which is disadvantageous to the offeree before the expiry of the relevant period. The rule contemplates two possibilities. If the offeree has not served

---

[347] *C v D* [2011] EWCA Civ 646, on appeal from *C v D* [2010] EWHC 2940 (Ch), Warren J. For commentary on the current rule relating to automatic withdrawal, see *Civil Procedure 2017*, para.36.10.3.
[348] CPR r.36.9(4)(b).
[349] CPR r.36.3 (g).
[350] CPR r.36.3 (d).
[351] CPR r.36.9(1).
[352] Acceptance is by serving written notice of acceptance on the offeror; CPR r.36.11(1).
[353] CPR rr 36.9(2), (3).
[354] CPR r.36.9(4).
[355] Specifically, CPR r.36.17(3), (4); see r.37.17(7)(a), (b).

notice of acceptance of the original offer by the expiry of the relevant period, the offeror's notice takes effect on the expiry of that period.[356] However, if the offeree has served notice of acceptance of the original offer before the expiry of the relevant period, that acceptance has effect unless the offeror applies to the court for permission to withdraw the offer or change its terms either within seven days of the offeree's notice of acceptance or, if earlier, before the first day of trial.[357] On an application under that rule, the court may give permission for the original offer to be withdrawn or its terms changed if satisfied that there has been a change of circumstances since the making of the original offer and that it is in the interests of justice to give permission.[358] There is at the time of writing no reported case which provides any guidance as to the nature of the requisite change of circumstances or the basis on which a court might conclude that the interests of justice would be served by giving permission.

(iii) Costs consequences of Part 36 offers

The general rule is that where a Pt 36 offer is accepted within the relevant **7–131** period, the claimant will be entitled to the costs of the proceedings, including recoverable pre-action costs, up to the date on which notice of acceptance was served on the offeror.[359] However, where a Pt 36 offer made less than 21 days before the start of the trial is accepted, or where a Pt 36 offer relating to the whole of the claim is accepted after the expiry of the relevant period, the liability for costs must be determined by the court unless the parties have agreed the costs.[360] In the case where the offer is accepted after the expiry of the relevant period the court must, unless it considers it unjust to do so, order that the claimant be awarded costs up to the date on which the relevant period expired, and that the offeree do pay the offeror's costs from the date of expiry of the relevant period to the date of acceptance. In considering whether it would be unjust to make those orders the court must take into account all the circumstances of the case, including the matters listed in r.36.17(5). Those matters are:

> "(a) the terms of any Part 36 offer;
> (b) the stage of the proceedings at which any Part 36 offer was made, including in particular how long before the trial the offer was made
> (c) the information available to the parties at the time when the Part 36 offer was made;
> (d) the conduct of the parties with regard to the giving of or refusal to give information for the purposes of enabling the offer to be made or evaluated; and
> (e) whether the offer was a genuine attempt to settle the proceedings."

---

[356] CPR r.36.10(2)(a).
[357] CPR r.36.10(2)(b).
[358] CPR r.36.10 (3).
[359] CPR r.36.13(1). The position where the offer relates to only part of the claim is governed by rr.36.13(2) and 36.13(4)(c).
[360] CPR r.36.13(4).

7–132   In relation to the last of those matters, the commentary[361] states that it was included to deal with the problem of claimants making very high settlement offers, often as much as 95 per cent of the value of the claim, not in a genuine attempt to settle the claim but to put the defendant at risk of indemnity costs. That situation would arise where the claimant obtained judgment against the defendant which was at least as advantageous to the claimant as the proposals contained in the claimant's Pt 36 offer.[362] The commentary refers to an unreported decision of Henderson J[363] in which he refused to make an order under what is now CPR r.36.17(4)(b) when the claimant had made a Pt 36 offer to settle for 100 per cent of the claim. He observed that any settlement must involve some genuine element of concession whereas the offer to settle for full recovery was a demand for total capitulation. Such an order was made in *Huck v Robson*[364] where the claimant had made a 95 per cent offer, though the Court of Appeal recognised the potential for abuse, holding that:

> "...if the offer was merely a tactical step designed to secure the benefit of Part 36, the court would not give effect to it."

This of course raises the question of how the court would set about characterising the offer, and the commentary is to the effect that judges would take a broad brush view largely informed by their own assessment of the strength of the case and, therefore, the extent to which the offer appeared to be a genuine effort to settle. It goes on to state that there is nothing inherently wrong with "very high claimant offers in extremely strong cases" but suggests that it would be prudent for claimants to explain in their offer letters why such a small discount was being offered for settlement.

7–133   The case of *Wharton v Bancroft*[365] also referred to in the commentary, illustrates the converse position. The claimant made a low Pt 36 offer but, as she was wholly successful, the judgment was more advantageous to her than her own offer; consequently, under what was then CPR r.36.14(1)(b), she was entitled to indemnity costs from the date on which the Pt 36 offer expired unless the court considered it unjust to make such an order. It was contended for the defendants that it would be unjust to make such an order because the offer was not a real Pt 36 offer. Norris J, in referring to the test in *Huck v Robson*, said that the concept was not an easy one to apply; all Pt

---

[361] *Civil Procedure 2017*, para.36.17.5.1. *Cook on Costs* comments at para.20.13 that this "seems to be an attempt (and one well tucked away at that) to address 'tactical offers'. However, all offers are tactical and the reality is that the provision ... is specific to the particular offer that the court is considering which, whether a genuine attempt to settle the proceedings or not, has succeeded in so doing".

[362] CPR rr.36.17(1)(b) and 36.17.4(b).

[363] *AB v CD* [2011] EWHC 602 (Ch), 7 March 2011.

[364] *Huck v Robson* [2003] 1 W.L.R. 1340, CA.

[365] *Wharton v Bancroft* [2012] W.T.L.R. 727. This is the judgment on costs; the substantive claim, which was a probate claim in which allegations of want of knowledge and approval were unsuccessfully made, is reported at [2012] W.T.L.R. 693. For whatever reason, the commentary in *Civil Procedure 2017* refers to the case as unreported.

36 offers were tactical in that they were designed to take advantage of the incentives provided by Pt 36. He went on to say:

> "A low offer in a case where the offeror considers that the offeree's position has no merit cannot be written off as self-evidently 'merely a tactical step'. But the principle has no application here. The sum to be received by each of the [defendants] was small. But the offer was not derisory."

In the event he saw no reason for it to be unjust to order indemnity costs and he also awarded interest on the costs at a rate (which he determined to be 8 per cent) such as would comfortably ensure that the claimant was not out of pocket for her expenditure on costs from and after the period when the litigation should have been brought to an end by the acceptance of the Pt 36 offer. The moral is, clearly, that Pt 36 offers should be made on the basis of a realistic assessment of the strength of the offeror's case.

The other consequences of acceptance of a Pt 36 offer[366] include a stay, on the terms of the offer; if the settlement requires the approval of the court, the stay will take effect only from the date of approval. The stay does not affect the power of the court to enforce the terms of a Pt 36 offer or to deal with any question of costs or interest on costs relating to the proceedings. If the offer that has been accepted is, or includes, an offer to pay a sum of money, the sum must be paid within 14 days unless the parties have agreed otherwise in writing, and if it is not so paid, the claimant may enter judgment for the unpaid sum.
7–134

CPR r.36.17 governs the costs consequences following judgment when either:
7–135

(a) a claimant fails to obtain a judgment more advantageous than the defendant's Pt 36 offer; or

(b) judgment against the defendant is at least as advantageous as the proposals contained in a claimant's Pt 36 offer.[367]

The uncertainty created by the decision in *Carver v BAA Plc*,[368] where the Court of Appeal held that "more advantageous" did not (as was formerly thought to have been the case) mean that the claimant had been awarded more than the sum paid into court or offered, but was "an open-textured phrase which permitted a more wide-ranging view of all the facts and circumstances of the case in deciding whether the judgment, which was the fruit of the litigation, was worth the fight".[369] However, the decision excited such widespread disapproval that a new rule, r.36.14(1A), was inserted so that, for Pt 36 offers to settle made on or after 1 October 2011 "more advantageous", in relation to any money claim or the money element of a

---

[366] CPR r.36.14.
[367] CPR r.36.17(1)(a),(b).
[368] *Carver v BAA Plc* [2009] 1 W.L.R. 113; [2008] 3 All E.R. 911, CA.
[369] *Carver*, per Ward LJ, at [40].

claim, means better in money terms by any amount, however small. The current equivalent rule adds that "at least as advantageous" shall be construed accordingly.[370]

7–136   Where a claimant fails to obtain a judgment more advantageous than the defendant's Pt 36 offer, the court must (subject to rr.36.17(7) and (8)[371]), unless it considers it unjust to do so,[372] order that the defendant is entitled to costs (including any recoverable pre-action costs) from the date on which the relevant period expired, and interest on those costs.[373] In the case where the claimant has obtained judgment against the defendant at least as advantageous as the proposals contained in a claimant's Pt 36 offer, the court must (subject to rr.36.17(7)), unless it considers it unjust to do so, order that the claimant is entitled to[374]:

(a)   interest on the whole or part of any sum of money (excluding interest) awarded, at a rate not exceeding 10 per cent above base rate for some or all of the period starting from the date on which the relevant period expired;

(b)   costs (including any recoverable pre-action costs) on the indemnity basis from the date on which the relevant period expired;

(c)   interest on those costs at a rate not exceeding 10 per cent above base rate; and

(d)   provided the case has not been decided[375] and there has not been a previous order under this subparagraph, an additional amount not exceeding £75,000.[376]

The provisions of these two rules do not apply to a Pt 36 offer which has been withdrawn or an offer which has been changed so that its terms are less advantageous to the offeree and the offeree has beaten the less advantageous offer.[377]

7–137   There are two outcomes, where Pt 36 offers are not accepted,[378] which are not provided for by the Pt 36 regime. The first is where the claimant beats the defendant's best offer (so that they are not penalised by the operation of r.36.17(1)(a)) but fails to equal or better their own offer (so that they do not receive the benefits arising from the operation of r.36.17(1)(b)). The second is where the defendant does not accept a claimant's offer but the claimant fails to equal or better their own offer (so that, again, they do not receive the benefits arising from the operation of r.36.17(1)(b)) and there is no relevant defendant's offer (so that r.36.17(1)(a) cannot come into consideration). In

---

[370] CPR r.36.17(2).
[371] This paragraph is concerned only with a specific type of personal injury claim.
[372] CPR r.36.17(5); the matters to be taken into account under that provision are listed in para.7–131, above.
[373] CPR r.36.17(3).
[374] CPR r.36.17(4).
[375] This term is defined by CPR r.36.3(e).
[376] CPR r.36.17(d) also sets out the manner in which that sum is to be calculated.
[377] CPR r.36.17(7).
[378] See *Cook on Costs*, paras 20.16–17.

either of those situations, costs will be determined in accordance with CPR r.44.2.

9.—COSTS IN 1975 ACT CLAIMS

This section surveys such case-law as there is on the costs outcomes of 1975 Act claims. In 2011, when the previous edition was published, there was little guidance to be gained from the case-law, since relatively few costs decisions were reported, and the reported decisions provided little insight into the reasons why any particular order was made. Such case-law as there was at that time did not suggest the development of a consistent approach to the making of costs orders. However, it has become more common for judgments on costs to be separately reported, either in the same set of reports as the substantive judgment[379] or in the specialist reports concerned with costs.[380] There is no doubt that this increased coverage is partly due to the necessity to provide, in some cases, reasoned judgments explaining the way in which the costs consequences of the Pt 36 regime have operated[381] and the exercise of the discretion under CPR r.44.2(2)(b) to make an order other than an order in accordance with the general rule that the unsuccessful party shall pay the costs of the successful party.   **7-138**

(a) Costs Before the CPR Regime

When the 1975 Act came into force, the general rule as to the incidence of costs[382] was as follows: **7-139**

> "If the Court in the exercise of its discretion sees fit to make any order as to the costs of any proceedings, the Court shall order the costs to follow the event, except when it appears to the Court that in the circumstances of the case, some other order should be made as to the whole or any part of the costs."

Rule 3(5) provided that r.3(3) did not apply to proceedings in the Family Division, but it is doubtful whether that led to any marked differences between the two divisions in the way in which the discretion to award costs was exercised.

There was, initially, a tendency to adopt an approach to costs similar to that encountered in certain types of probate or will construction case, where   **7-140**

---

[379] See, e.g., *Lilleyman v Lilleyman* [2013] 1 F.L.R. 47; *Lilleyman v Lilleyman (Costs)* [2013] 1 F.L.R. 69; the substantive judgment is also reported at [2013] Ch. 225.

[380] For example, the judgment on costs in *Lilleyman* is also reported at [2013] 1 Costs L.R. 25. There is also a Lower Courts supplement, Costs L.O, the costs judgment in *Wooldridge v Wooldridge*, which was heard in the County Court at Central London, is reported at [2016] 3 Costs L.O. 531. These reports are published by Class Legal.

[381] In particular, CPR r.36.13 ("Costs consequences of acceptance of a Pt 36 offer") and 36.17 ("Costs consequences following judgment").

[382] RSC Ord.62 r.3(3).

there are recognised exceptions to the general rule, such as contentious probate cases where the litigation has been caused by the conduct of the testator, in which the court may order that both parties' costs be paid out of the estate. Similarly in will construction cases, the unsuccessful party might be awarded their costs out of the estate on the footing that it was the testator's act which necessitated the litigation.[383] The practice of ordering both parties' costs to be paid out of the estate in 1975 Act cases excited the disapproval of the court in *Re Fullard*,[384] where Ormrod J said:

> "Where the estate, like this one, is small,[385] in my view the onus on an applicant of satisfying the conditions in s.2 is very heavy indeed and these applications ought not to be launched unless there is (or appears to be) a real chance of success, because the result of these proceedings simply diminishes the estate and is a great hardship on the beneficiaries if they are ultimately successful in the litigation. For that reason I would be disposed to think that judges should reconsider the practice of ordering the costs of both sides out of the estate. That is probate litigation; this is something quite different. I think judges should look very closely indeed at the merits of each application before ordering that the estate pays the applicant's costs if the applicant is unsuccessful."

In *Re Fullard*, where the application was dismissed at first instance, both parties' costs of the application were ordered to be paid out of the estate. The appeal was dismissed with costs, but the liability of the legally aided appellant was assessed as nil and an order nisi was made against the Legal Aid Fund.[386] In *Re Bunning*[387] it was ordered that the parties' costs be taxed and paid out of residue on "the usual basis".

7–141   In *Graham v Murphy*,[388] a 1975 Act application under s.1(1)(e), it was observed that, in so far as there was any usual costs order in 1975 Act applications, it was that if any provision is ordered, then in the absence of a Calderbank letter or other special circumstances, the applicant (who succeeded in the claim) should receive their costs out of the estate taxed on the standard basis. A Calderbank offer was important but not decisive. The court did not accede to the argument that a Calderbank offer should deal with the costs of the offeree. The administrators of the deceased's estate had made a Calderbank offer which the judge assessed as being extremely close to the amount which he had awarded to the applicant. In such circumstances

---

[383] See *Williams, Mortimer & Sunnucks, Executors, Administrators and Probate*, 20th edn (London: Sweet & Maxwell, 2013), Ch.39A (Court's discretion) and 39B (costs of particular parties), and the commentary in *Civil Procedure 2017*, para.44.2.10. For a review of the principles, see the judgment of Henderson J in *Kostic v Chaplin (costs)* [2008] W.T.L.R. 655.
[384] *Re Fullard* [1982] Fam. 42, CA.
[385] It was £7,100. This, if adjusted in accordance with the increase in RPI, would equate to about £25,000 at the time of writing.
[386] A similar order was made in *Re Stead* [1985] F.L.R. 16, CA, where the applicant widow failed both at first instance and in the Court of Appeal.
[387] *Re Bunning* [1984] Ch. 480.
[388] *Graham v Murphy* [1997] 1 F.L.R. 860.

any costs order was bound to have an element of rough justice; the applicant was awarded one-third of his taxed costs out of the estate. The administrators' costs, taxed on the indemnity basis, would also be paid out of the estate.

The learned editor of *Tyler's Family Provision*[389] attempted a rationalisation of costs orders in cases where the costs did not follow the event, but the number of cases in which information about costs orders was available at that time was insufficient to serve as a basis for any useful generalisations. Departures from the general rule were found where the opposition was not wholly without merit, where there was an interesting point of law involved[390] or where the interests of a person under a disability were affected.[391]   **7–142**

(b) The CPR Costs Regime: The General Rule

The general rule[392] continues to be that the unsuccessful party will be ordered to pay the costs of the successful party; but the court may make a different order.[393] In deciding what (if any) order to make about costs, the court must have regard to all the circumstances, including the conduct of all the parties,[394] whether or not a party has succeeded on part of its case, even if that party has not been wholly successful,[395] and: **7–143**

> "...any admissible offer to settle made by a party which is drawn to the Court's attention and which is not an offer to which costs consequences under Pt 36 apply."[396]

In relation to conduct, failure to observe relevant protocols, raising, contesting or pursuing issues unreasonably, and exaggeration of a claim are all liable to have adverse costs consequences.

The court has power to make issue-based costs orders,[397] but the Court of Appeal has identified difficulties of the issue-based approach and expressed the view that the additional costs incurred and time expended in adopting it may be disproportionate to the benefit gained and that a percentage order[398] may often produce a fairer result than an issue-based order. Nevertheless, the existence of the power to make issue-based costs order is a caution to litigants to be wary of raising issues which are likely to be peripheral or of making claims which are additional or alternative to the 1975 Act claim. It   **7–144**

---

[389] *Tyler*, pp.365–68.
[390] *Cameron v Treasury Solicitor* [1996] 2 F.L.R. 716.
[391] *Re Watkins* [1949] 1 All E.R. 695 (adult daughter who was a long-term patient in a mental hospital); *Re Chatterton* unreported 1 November 1978, CA (daughter, approximately six years of age at the date of the hearing at first instance). There is a note of this case in *Tyler*, p.519.
[392] CPR r.44.3(2)(a).
[393] CPR r.44.3(2)(b). For commentary on orders displacing the general rule, see *Civil Procedure 2017*, para.44.2.6.
[394] CPR r.44.2.(4)(a), and see r.44.2(5) for the matters included in "conduct of the parties".
[395] CPR r.44(2)(4)(b), and *Civil Procedure 2017*, para.44.2.10.3.
[396] CPR r.44(2)(4)(c).
[397] CPR r.44.2(6)(f) and *Civil Procedure 2017*, para.44.2.7.
[398] CPR r.44.2(6)(a).

may well be, in practice, that in the majority of 1975 Act cases there will be little scope for issue-based costs orders, because the claimant wins or loses on the basis of all the evidence relating to the matters that the court is directed to take into account; though cases might occur where the successful party has heavily canvassed an issue which is decided against them or found to be of little relevance.[399] CPR r.44.2(5)(b) is very relevant to such a situation, since it directs the court to take into account whether it was reasonable for a party to raise, pursue or contest a particular allegation or issue; the manner in which a party has pursued or defended their case on a particular issue; and whether a claimant who has succeeded in whole or part has exaggerated his claim. The conduct of the parties before[400] as well as during the proceedings, including in particular the extent to which the parties followed the Practice Direction—Pre-Action Conduct, is also relevant.

7–145   The rules relating to the basis of assessment of costs and the factors to be taken into account in deciding the amount of costs lay emphasis on proportionality and reasonableness. Thus, where costs are to be assessed on the standard basis, the court, on assessment, will only allow costs which are proportionate to the matters in issue, and will resolve any doubt as to whether they were reasonably incurred or reasonable or proportionate in favour of the paying party.[401] Where costs are ordered to be paid on the indemnity basis, any doubts whether they were reasonably incurred or reasonable in amount are to be resolved in favour of the receiving party.[402] Proportionality is a fundamental aspect of the overriding objective of enabling the court to deal with cases justly and at proportionate cost. That includes, so far as is practicable, dealing with the case in ways which are proportionate to the amount of money involved, to the importance and complexity of the case and to the financial position of each party,[403] but it is not necessarily the case that the relationship between the total of the costs incurred and the financial value of the claim will be a reliable guide in determining whether the case has been dealt with in a proportionate manner.

7–146   It is a matter for the judge's discretion whether to award indemnity costs and there are no general guidelines. There is a useful list of circumstances in which courts have traditionally awarded indemnity costs, in *Cook on Costs*

---

[399] For an example, see *Wooldridge v Wooldridge* [2016] 3 Costs L.O.531 where allegations of financial impropriety and tax evasion were raised without supporting evidence that would withstand scrutiny was a factor in the award of indemnity costs against the claimant.

[400] CPR r.44.2(5)(a). There is no relevant protocol for 1975 Act claims and, while it would usually be good practice to comply with the ACTAPS protocol so far as relevant, it is submitted that there is no power to impose a sanction simply for failure to comply with it, though such failure might attract a sanction if it was an aspect of the party's generally unreasonable conduct of the case.

[401] CPR r.44.3(2)(b).

[402] CPR r.44.3(3). Unlike r.44.3(2)(b), this rule does not use the words "reasonable and proportionate". This difference between the approach to assessing costs on the two bases is also apparent from comparison of CPR r.44.4(1)(a) and (b). For commentary on proportionality, see *Civil Procedure 2017*, paras 44.3.3, 44.4.4.

[403] CPR r.1.2(c).

under the heading "Culpability and abuse of power".[404] However, indemnity costs can be awarded in other circumstances where the litigation has been conducted with a high degree of unreasonableness. It is clear, however, that conduct which is merely wrong or misguided in hindsight is not, of itself, so unreasonable as to attract an order for indemnity costs.[405]

Costs capping orders were introduced into the CPR costs regime from 6 April 2009, but the procedure[406] has proved to be of extremely limited value. The court will make such orders only in exceptional circumstances.[407] The edition of *Cook on Costs* current at the time of writing[408] does not actually repeat the view expressed in the 2011 edition that costs capping was virtually dead in the water given the circumstances in which such orders will be made, but points out that there have been only two significant costs capping cases since March 2013 and no costs capping order was made in either of them. Such orders will be made only if (a) it is in the interests of justice to do so; (b) there is a substantial risk that without such an order, costs will be disproportionately incurred; and (c) the court is not satisfied that the risk described by (b) can be adequately controlled by case management directions and orders and detailed assessment of costs.[409] It is true that costs often get out of hand in 1975 Act cases but it should be apparent that the solution lies in sensible management by the parties in relation to the nature and number of the issues raised and the amount of oral and documentary evidence required, not in satellite litigation. **7–147**

(c) The CPR Costs Regime: Special Cases

The discussion of this aspect of the regime covers three areas, namely, awards of costs in favour of trustees or personal representatives,[410] costs where money is payable by or to a child or a protected party,[411] and the principles relevant to the making of wasted costs orders.[412] **7–148**

---

[404] *Cook on Costs*, Ch.24, "The bases of costs"; the material described under that heading is listed at para.24.9 and discussed at paras 24.10 to 24.20.

[405] *Cook on Costs*, paras 22.22–22.24 under the heading "No culpability or abuse of process". See also "Conclusions", para.22.25.

[406] See CPR rr.3.19–3.21 and PD3F. There are also separate costs capping provisions for judicial review proceedings: see CPR rr.46–16–46.19.

[407] For the procedure, see CPR r.44.19 and s.23A of the Costs Practice Direction. Applications to vary costs capping orders may be made pursuant to r.44.20 and the conditions under which such variations will be made are specified by r.44.18(7).

[408] *Cook on Costs*, Ch.17.

[409] CPR r.3.19(5) and 3FPD. It should be noted that this practice direction contains none of the detail which was required when the procedure was first introduced in 2009 as part of CPR Pt 48. *Cook on Costs* cites, at para.17.2 two cases demonstrating that the required circumstances create "virtually insuperable hurdles"; see *Barr v Biffa Waste Services Ltd* [2009] EWHC 2444 (TCC) and *Peacock v MGN Ltd* [2009] EWHC 769 (QB).

[410] CPR rr.46.3 and 44.5 (amount of costs where costs are payable under a contract).

[411] CPR r.46.4.

[412] CPR r.46.8.

(i) Matters governed by CPR 46 Section I

7–149   Where costs are payable to a trustee or personal representative who is or has been party to proceedings in that capacity, and costs are payable otherwise than pursuant to a contract other than a contract between a solicitor and their client, the general rule is that the trustee or personal representative is entitled to be paid their costs of the proceedings out of any fund held by them in their representative capacity, on an indemnity basis. The rule is supplemented by the Practice Direction—Costs-Special Cases[413] which provides that whether costs were properly incurred depends on all the circumstances of the case including whether the personal representative or the trustee ("the trustee"):

(a)   obtained directions from the court before bringing or defending the proceedings;

(b)   acted in the interests of the estate or in substance for a benefit other than that of the estate, including their own; but he is not to be taken as having so acted by reason only that he has defended a claim in which relief is sought against him personally; or

(c)   acted in some way unreasonably in bringing or defending, or in the conduct of, the proceedings.

Personal representatives are, of course, necessary parties to 1975 Act claims, so (a) does not arise; but the Practice Direction does serve to remind a personal representative who is also a beneficiary of the need to distinguish clearly between their activities in their representative and personal capacities, and to make a clear distinction between the costs incurred in those capacities. The same applies to a solicitor acting for a personal representative who is also a beneficiary, or for the personal representative who is not a beneficiary and the residuary beneficiaries (which is a sensible, economic and unobjectionable practice not involving any conflict of interest).

7–150   Where, in any proceedings, money is ordered or agreed to be paid to, or for the benefit, of a child or a protected party, or money is ordered to be paid by that party or on that party's behalf, the general rule is that the court must order a detailed assessment of the costs payable by, or out of money belonging to, any party who is a child or protected party.[414] The Practice Direction identifies the circumstances in which the court need not order a detailed assessment of costs.[415]

(ii) Matters governed by CPR 46 Section II

7–151   The jurisdiction to make orders disallowing a legal representative's costs or ordering a legal representative to meet wasted costs derives from s.51 of the

---

[413] 46PD.1.
[414] CPR rr.46(1), 46(2)(a). The rule also contains provisions for situations where detailed assessment is not required.
[415] 46PD.2.

Senior Courts Act 1981.[416] The section provides that the court may disallow costs or order a legal representative to meet part or all of any wasted costs, which are defined by s.51(7) as any costs incurred by a party:

(a) as a result of any improper, unreasonable or negligent act or omission on the part of any legal or other representative or any employee of such a representative; or

(b) which, in the light of any such act or omission after they were incurred, the court considers it unreasonable to expect the party to pay.

"Legal representative" includes a barrister, solicitor, solicitor's employee or other authorised litigator in relation to an activity which constitutes the conduct of litigation within the meaning of the Legal Services Act 2007.[417]

The principles governing the making of wasted costs orders derive mainly **7–152** from two cases, *Ridehalgh v Horsfield*[418] (a group of six appeals dealt with together) and *Tolstoy-Miloslavsky v Aldington*.[419] In *Ridehalgh v Horsfield* the three-stage test in *Re a Barrister (Wasted Costs Order) (No.1 of 1991)*[420] was referred to with approval. When a wasted costs order is contemplated, the courts should consider the following[421]:

(a) Has the legal representative whose conduct is complained of acted improperly, unreasonably or negligently?

(b) If so, did such conduct cause the applicant to incur unnecessary costs?

(c) If so, is it, in all the circumstances, just to order the legal representative to compensate the applicant for the whole or any part of the relevant costs (if so, they should be specified)?

"Improper conduct" includes, but is not confined to conduct which would **7–153** ordinarily be held to justify disbarment, striking off, suspension from practice or other serious penalty, and any significant breach of a substantial duty imposed by a relevant code of professional conduct; it also extends to conduct which would be regarded as improper according to the consensus of professional (including judicial) opinion. However, it does not, without more, extend to acting for a party who pursues a claim or defence which is bound to fail.[422] Even though it was said in *Ridehalgh v Horsfield* that they are in such circumstances entitled to the benefit of the doubt, the legal representative may need to be alive to the possibility that their conduct may

---

[416] CPR r.46.8 and 46PD.5.
[417] CPR r.2.3(1).
[418] *Ridehalgh v Horsfield* [1994] Ch. 205, CA.
[419] *Tolstoy-Miloslavsky v Aldington* [1996] 2 All E.R. 556 CA; see also the commentary in *Civil Procedure 2017*, para.46.8.17 and *Cook on Costs*, Ch.23, "Wasted costs".
[420] *Re a Barrister (Wasted Costs Order) (No.1 of 1991)* [1993] Q.B. 293.
[421] *Civil Procedure 2017*, para.46.8.3; *Cook on Costs*, paras 23.4–23.7.
[422] *Civil Procedure 2017*, para.46.8.5, "Pursuing a hopeless case".

cross the line between bona fide pursuing a hopeless case and engaging in an abuse of process of the court.

7–154   "Unreasonable" describes conduct which is vexatious, designed to harass the other side rather than advance the resolution of the case, and it makes no difference that the conduct is the product of excessive zeal and not improper motive. The test is whether the conduct permits of a reasonable explanation. "Negligence" is to be understood as failure to act with the competence reasonably expected of ordinary members of the profession. Where the order is sought on the grounds of negligence, the applicant will have to prove nothing less than they would have to prove in an action for professional negligence.

7–155   Allegations of negligence in 1975 Act cases usually relate to failure to issue the proceedings within the primary limitation period, and that issue has been discussed in connection with applications for extension of time. In the unreported case of *Murphy v Wilkinson (t/a Owenwhite) and Fulchers (A firm)*,[423] M claimed damages for alleged negligence against two firms of solicitors in relation to the commencement of proceedings by her under the 1975 Act as a dependant of the deceased (CM); there were also possession proceedings in relation to the property in which she had been living with CM, in which she counterclaimed for a declaration as to the extent of her beneficial interest. A wasted costs order was made against the first defendant during the proceedings; it is not apparent from the transcript why it was made but there was a lengthy and unjustifiable delay in applying for Legal Aid and the 1975 Act claim was not commenced within the time limit, nor was she warned that the time limit was about to expire. However, Mrs Murphy was awarded only nominal damages for her solicitors' breaches of their contractual duty of care, Rattee J finding (largely due to the unreliability of her evidence) that there was real doubt whether her claim, if launched in time, would have succeeded. He also held that her claim for damages for emotional distress failed, the contract broken not being one to provide peace of mind or freedom from distress.[424] There is, as yet, no reported decision relating to a wasted costs application in a 1975 Act case, though *Cook on Costs*[425] mentions a case in which a wasted costs order was made in family proceedings, in which it was held that the failure of one party's solicitors to seek permission of the court to extend time for directions was improper and unreasonable conduct and caused the other party to bear unnecessary costs.[426]

---

[423] *Murphy v Wilkinson (t/a Owenwhite) and Fulchers (A firm)* unreported 6 December 1999 (Rattee J); the official transcript is available on Westlaw.

[424] *Bliss v South East Thames Regional Health Authority* [1987] I.C.R. 700 at 718; *Hayes v James & Charles Dodd (A firm)* [1990] 2 All E.R. 815 at 823a–824c.

[425] *Cook on Costs*, paras 23.15–23.33 provides an interesting and valuable selection of cases in which successful and (more numerous) unsuccessful applications for wasted costs orders were made.

[426] *HU v SU* [2015] EWFC 535.

Solicitors are not necessarily protected by having taken counsel's **7–156** advice,[427] though the more specialist the nature of the advice, the more reasonable it may be for the solicitor to rely on it.[428] In *Clark v Clark (No.2)*[429] the court emphasised the duty owed by a solicitor of a legally assisted client to the Legal Aid Fund, which was as high as that owed to his client and to the court. Failure to ensure that counsel, when advising on the merits of a case, has all the relevant evidence before them may make the solicitor liable for the costs thrown away as a consequence.[430] In the cases reviewed in *Cook on Costs*[431] under the heading "Wasted costs where the solicitor places reliance on counsel" the wasted costs order, when made, has been against the solicitor, it is noted in the paragraph which follows[432] that in two cases[433] the argument that a wasted costs order could only be made against a barrister by virtue of his conduct while exercising a right of audience had been rejected. There was no reason why the expression "conducting litigation" should not extend to activities such as drafting or settling documents or advising on procedure or prospects (in other words, doing what someone conducting litigation would do). The learned authors observe that this carries a greater significance with the increasing use of direct access and the conduct of litigation by barristers authorised to do so.

(d) Case-law

(i) Cases involving Part 36 offers

The relevant provisions of the Pt 36 regime at the time of the costs judgment **7–157** in *Lilleyman v Lilleyman*[434] were contained in CPR r.36.14, the precursor of the current r.36.17. This is an extremely instructive judgment based on principles which are unaffected by the revision of the Pt 36 regime which took effect in April 2015, and is, at the time of writing, the only significant decision on the operation of the rules relating to costs consequences of Pt 36 offers.

In the claim itself, the claimant widow (W) was successful and was awarded **7–158** assets of value approximately £500,000. The history of the offers was:

(1) Pt 36 offer by W, 1 April 2011;
(2) without prejudice offer by Ds, 27 July 2011;

---

[427] And may even be exposed to liability in professional negligence by uncritical reliance on it; see *Locke v Camberwell Health Authority* (1990) 140 N.L.J. 205, where it was said that "A solicitor does not abdicate his professional responsibility when he seeks the advice of counsel. He must apply his mind to the advice received. But the more specialist the nature of the advice, the more reasonable it is likely to be for a solicitor to accept and act on it".
[428] *Davy-Chiesman v Davy-Chiesman* [1984] Fam. 48, CA.
[429] *Clark v Clark (No.2)* [1991] 1 F.L.R. 179.
[430] *Locke v Camberwell Health Authority* (1990) 140 N.L.J. 205.
[431] *Cook on Costs*, para.23.13.
[432] *Cook on Costs*, para.23.14, "Wasted costs against a barrister for his advice".
[433] *Medcalf v Mardell (Wasted Costs Order)* [2003] 1 A.C. 120, HL per Lord Bingham, at [20]; *Brown v Bennett* [2002] 1 W.L.R. 713.
[434] *Lilleyman v Lilleyman (No.2)* [2012] 1 W.L.R. 2801, also reported *sub nom. Lilleyman v Lilleyman (Costs)* [2013] 1 F.L.R. 69.

(3) Pt 36 offer by Ds, also on 27 July 2011; the time for acceptance expired on 17 August, 2011;

(4) without prejudice offers by W, 18 November and 16 December 2011;

(5) without prejudice offer by Ds, 6 January 2012;

(6) Pt 36 offer by W, 14 February 2012.

None of these offers were accepted. Following the judgment in favour of W on 4 April 2012, two issues arose in relation to costs. The first was whether the letter in which offer 5 was made[435] withdrew both offers 2 and 3 (as was contended for W) or only offer 2. That letter opened with the words "We refer to our without prejudice letter of 22 July 2011 and our clients' offer to settle your client's claim..."[436] and the second paragraph opened with the words "We are now instructed to withdraw that offer and replace it with an amended offer...". Briggs J first had to decide which offers had been withdrawn and, directing himself in accordance with the relevant passages from the judgment of Moore-Bick LJ in *Gibbon v Manchester City Council*[437] he concluded that the Pt 36 offer had not been withdrawn; the letter plainly referred to the "without prejudice" offer. He took account of the fact that the withdrawal letter had referred to the Pt 36 offer as having "expired" some time previously, but, as he said, Pt 36 offers did not expire merely because the period specified for the purposes of CPR r.36.2(2)(c)[438] had passed. They were either withdrawn by written notice as specified in CPR r.36.9(2)[439] or remained open for acceptance at any time, and continued to have the costs consequences of CPR r.36.14(2). He rejected the submission that offer 5 was a less advantageous offer to W than offer 3 (Ds' Pt 36 offer) and that W had beaten that offer; on his calculation the award fell short of offer 3 by some £50,000.

7–159   It was common ground that W should have her costs out of the estate up to 17 August 2011, that being the date of the end of the period for acceptance of offer 3. However, since she had failed to beat that offer, CPR r.36.14(2)[440] required an order to be made that the defendants were entitled to their costs from that date, and interest on those costs, unless it was unjust to make such an order. In determining whether it was unjust, the matters specified by CPR r.36.14(4)[441] were:

(a) the terms of any Pt 36 offer;

---

[435] Set out in full in the judgment at [8].

[436] The offer is made when it is served on the offeree, CPR r.36.7(2); hence the discrepancy in the dates.

[437] *Gibbon v Manchester City Council* [2010] 1 W.L.R. 2018, CA, in particular, at [4]–[6], [16]–[18], [32].

[438] That period is now the "relevant period" for the purposes of CPR r.36.5(1)(c) and references thereto in the rules governing the making and acceptance of offers and of their consequences.

[439] Which continues to be the rule, both for withdrawal of an offer and for change in its terms.

[440] The current equivalent rule is CPR r.36.17(3).

[441] The current equivalent rule is CPR r.36.17(5). There was no requirement in the then CPR r.36.14(4) to consider whether the offer was a genuine attempt to settle the proceedings.

(b)   the stage of the proceedings at which any Pt 36 offer was made, including in particular how long before the trial it was made

(c)   the information available to the parties when the Pt 36 offer was made;

(d)   the conduct of the parties with regard to the giving of or refusal to give information for the purpose of enabling the offer to be made or evaluated.

It was apparent to Briggs J that the discretion to depart from CPR r.36.14(2) was much more circumscribed than the court's broad discretion under Pt 44 and that the specified circumstances disclosed a common thread which focused the analysis of injustice on the circumstances in which the offer was made and not on the conduct of the case by the parties generally. He continued[442]:

"Nevertheless, I consider that the requirement to take into account all the circumstances of the case does enable the court to take a broader view in an appropriate case, so that it is not entirely disabled from having regard to questions of justice or injustice arising from the manner in which the offering party makes use of his costs expenditure prima facie now recoverable from the unsuccessful offeree, in the pursuit of its defence of the claim. If that were not so, then the protection of a generous Pt 36 offer would enable the offering party to conduct its part in the litigation at the offeree's potential expense without regard to the obligations and constraints which the achievement of the overriding objective now places upon civil litigants."

The potential for gaming the system by making offers which allow only a very small discount for settlement had (as noted earlier) been perceived in *Huck v Robson.*[443]

After reviewing the relevant aspects of the parties' general conduct of   **7–160** their respective cases, Briggs J concluded that it would be unjust if the strict application of CPR r.36.14(2) were to prevent the court from signifying its disapprobation of a "no-holds barred" approach to the claim by an appropriate proportionate disallowance of the costs to be recovered. Matters which particularly engaged his attention were:

(i)   the defendants' unrealistic stance, not abandoned until counsel's closing speech, that the will had made reasonable provision for W;

(ii)   the parties' approach to quantum, the defendants' approach being unrealistically low and the claimant's, unrealistically high;

(iii)   the submission that the costs burden on W resulting from her having to pay the defendants' costs from 17 August 2011 would leave her with resources insufficient for her maintenance. As to this, he said that it would be a weighty consideration were it so,

---

[442]   *Lilleyman v Lilleyman (No.2)*, at [16].
[443]   *Huck v Robson* [2003] 1 W.L.R. 1340, CA; see para.7–132, above.

but he concluded that her remaining resources would be modest, but not inadequate. However, that was not the point; the question was whether that outcome would cause her an injustice, given that it arose from her decision not to accept what had turned out to be a generous Pt 36 offer from the defendants. The unfortunate reality was that, from August 2011, she was in a high-risk venture in which she played for high stakes and, in substance, lost.

In the result he decided that the disallowance should apply only to the defendants' costs incurred after 17 August 2011 and ordered that W pay 80 per cent of those costs together with interest at the judgment rate.

7–161   At the conclusion of his judgment Briggs J addressed the disparity between the costs regimes in financial remedy cases and 1975 Act claims, both of which (at any rate in surviving spouse claims) were directed towards the same goal. The regime in the matrimonial sphere, as he understood it, emphasised the making of open offers, with limited scope for costs shifting, so that the court was able to make provision which properly reflected the parties' costs liabilities. In 1975 Act claims, as in other forms of civil litigation, without prejudice negotiation was encouraged and there was scope for very substantial costs shifting in favour of the successful party. He saw the potential for undisclosed negotiations to undermine a judge's attempt to make reasonable provision for a surviving spouse as a possible disadvantage of the costs regime currently applied to such claims, compared with the regime applicable on divorce. Whether this situation will receive the careful and anxious thought which he considered it to deserve remains to be seen, but it was not addressed, or intended to be addressed, by the introduction of qualified one-way costs shifting.[444]

7–162   In *Lewis v Warner*,[445] Mr Warner, who was the claimant in the 1975 Act claim, succeeded at trial and an order was made that Mrs Lewis (the claimant in the possession claim and the defendant in the 1975 Act claim) should pay Mr Warner's costs from 30 June, 2015 on the standard basis, to be the subject of detailed assessment if not agreed, save that she should pay only 50 per cent of his costs of a hearing on 11 November 2015, which appears to have been a hearing on costs. The date of 30 June 2015 derived from an offer made by Mr Warner on 5 June. It was contended on behalf of Mrs Lewis that the order made at trial, which permitted him to purchase the property and to live there rent-free until he did so, was less advantageous to him than offers which had been made by Mrs Lewis before the trial and the costs order was therefore wrong. The effect of the judgment at trial was that as absolute owner of Green Avon[446] he would be able to convert it for disabled use if necessary and there would be no restrictions on sharing occupation, which was important as his son (with whom Mrs Lewis was not on good terms)

---

[444]   CPR rr.44.13–17; *Cook on Costs*, paras 11.8, 20.19.

[445]   *Lewis v Warner* [2016] W.T.L.R. 1399 reports the judgment of Newey J on the appeal from the order made in the substantive claim. For the judgment on costs, see *Lewis v Warner* [2016] EWHC 1787 (Ch).

[446]   The deceased's house, in which he had lived with her for some 20 years, and was the only substantial asset of the estate.

would be able to live there so as to look after him. It was correct that an offer made by Mrs Lewis involved the transfer of title at a lower price, but it had conditions, including repairing and maintenance obligations, attached, while the offer made to let the property to him at a rent of £900 per month was on terms which did not permit him to have anyone else living there. Newey J concluded that the trial judge was entitled to take the view that these offers were less advantageous to Mr Warner than the judgment which he obtained, and dismissed the appeal against the costs order.

(ii) Other cases

The court's discretion as to costs other than in the Pt 36 regime is governed **7–163** by CPR r.44.2 and, while the general rule is that the unsuccessful party pays the successful party's costs, the court may make a different order. In deciding what order to make,[447] the court is to have regard to all the circumstances of the case, including the conduct of all the parties,[448] whether a party has been partially successful, and any admissible offer (other than a Pt 36 offer) which is drawn to the court's attention. The discretion exercisable under the rule extends to whether costs are payable by one party to another; to the amount of those costs; and to when they are to be paid,[449] but CPR r.44.2 makes no explicit reference to the basis on which costs are to be assessed, and *Civil Procedure 2017* contains no commentary on the current practice in awarding indemnity costs. It is clear from the pronouncements in a series of cases[450] that the width of the judicial discretion precludes any attempt to create a rule governing the circumstances in which indemnity costs may be awarded. *Cook on Costs*[451] states that, apart from the provisions of CPR Pt 36 and cases where a contract specifically providing for the payment of costs on an indemnity basis, indemnity costs can only be awarded by the court exercising its discretion under CPR r.44.2, which it does by reference to the overriding objective and the factors which it is obliged to consider when deciding what order to make about costs. In *Wooldridge v Wooldridge*,[452] where a surviving spouse made an unsuccessful 1975 Act claim, the question arose whether she should pay the costs of the two defendant beneficiaries, as well as those of the three representative defendants, on the indemnity basis. Lord Woolf had said in the *Excelsior*[453] case that, before an indemnity order could be made, there must be some conduct or some circumstance which took it out of the norm. The court followed the principle identified in the *Fiona Trust*[454] case

---

[447] CPR r.44.4(6) lists seven types of order which the court can make but does not limit the choice to one of the specified types.

[448] CPR r.44.2(4); conduct includes the matters specified in r.44.2(5).

[449] CPR r.44.2(1).

[450] e.g., *Excelsior Commercial and Industrial Holdings Ltd v Salisbury Hamer Aspden & Johnson (Costs)* [2002] EWCA Civ 879; [2002] C.P. Rep. 67; *Noorani v Calver* [2009] EWHC 592 (QB); *Blueco Ltd v BWAT Retail Nominee* [2014] EWCA (Civ) 154.

[451] *Cook on Costs*, para.24.7.

[452] *Wooldridge v Wooldridge* [2016] 3 Costs L.O. 531.

[453] See n.441, above.

[454] *Fiona Trust & Holding Corporation and v Yuri Privalov* [2011] EWHC 664 (Comm), Andrew Smith J.

that a claim which is "thin", "far-fetched" and "irreconcilable with the contemporaneous documents" is one where indemnity costs should be ordered. The claimant's case was found to fit that description as it had been exaggerated with respect to her lifestyle and her financial needs, she had failed to deal with sensible offers to settle in the way they ought to have been dealt with, and had had raised allegations of financial impropriety and tax evasion without evidence that would withstand scrutiny to support them.

7–164   In *Thomas v Jeffrey*,[455] the costs issue related to the claimant's failure to disclose relevant documents. He had initially made a claim for some 50 per cent of his late father's estate or a lump sum of about £100,000, as reasonable provision out of the estate of his late father and under the doctrine of proprietary estoppel. Only the 1975 Act claim was pursued at trial and he was awarded £36,475, which reflected the amount of his indebtedness due to the hire-purchase and credit card transactions which contributed to his income shortfall. That calculation was possible only because of the disclosure which the trial judge had ordered, of his own motion, during the trial. The defendants accepted that the costs of the trial should fall on the estate but argued that the claimant should pay their costs up to the start of final preparation for trial, principally because of his failure to disclose relevant documents. Referring to the judgments of the Court of Appeal in *Ford v GKR Construction*,[456] the trial judge directed himself that he had to consider whether anything different would have occurred before trial had there been disclosure, in particular whether an offer would have been made and whether the defendants would have approached the case in a different way. He had nothing concrete on which to base any such views and thus did not consider himself well placed to depart from the general rule that costs follow the event. Accordingly he ordered the executors to pay the claimant's costs out of the estate on the standard basis. That decision was reversed on appeal on the basis that *Ford* had been wrongly applied; there was no need to speculate about what might have happened to counterbalance what had actually happened, and that error of law required a fresh exercise of discretion. On the second appeal, the Court of Appeal held that *Ford* did not create a principle that any shortcoming on the part of a litigant had particular costs consequences; it simply provided a reminder of the necessity for a judge, when exercising his discretionary jurisdiction on costs, to take account of all relevant aspects of the case. The trial judge had directed himself correctly and his decision was well within the ambit of his discretion in circumstances where the defendants had not made any complaint about non-disclosure before the trial, made any request or application for further disclosure, or suggested that the evidence disclosed at a late stage of the trial changed the complexion of the case so that they needed time to consider its implications. Further, he had not relied on the evidence adduced by the late disclosure in deciding that the will had not made reasonable provision for the claimant and the claim would have succeeded without that evidence.

---

[455] *Thomas v Jeffrey* [2013] W.T.L.R. 141, CA.
[456] *Ford v GKR Construction* [2000] 1 W.L.R. 1397, CA.

Accordingly, it was wrong to have interfered with the original ruling and the trial judge's costs order was restored.

The unreported case of *Wharton v Mercer*[457] is concerned with the inci-   **7–165**
dence of costs in circumstances where the claimant had brought proceedings in which he claimed financial provision out of his wife's estate and damages for breach of trust in the handling of a joint bank account, but had died shortly before the claims had been listed for trial. *Francis*[458] suggests that:

(i)   the death does not amount to a discontinuance for the purposes of CPR Pt 38, so the rule that the discontinuing party pays the other party's costs does not apply; and

(ii)   either the costs of all parties, including the personal representatives, fall on the estate, or, if that is not correct, there must be a hearing to determine where costs fall.

That analysis was adopted in *Wharton v Mercer* and it was held that on the evidence available, the 1975 Act claim would have been bound to fail. The breach of trust claim did fail, as Mrs Wharton was entitled to take money from the joint account. It had not been created for a limited or specific purpose and her position was the same whether she spent the money or simply transferred it to her own account. The judgment is somewhat confusing as it states, at the conclusion of the part which deals with the 1975 Act claim, that the order will be for the defendant's costs to be paid out of the claimant's (that is, Mr Wharton's) estate,[459] but this is followed by a further five paragraphs relating to the unsuccessful breach of trust claim in which nothing is said about costs. One would assume that the defendant's costs of that claim would also be paid from Mr Wharton's estate.

Palmer v Lawrence[460] was a claim by a surviving spouse (W) which failed   **7–166**
as it was found that the deceased's will had made reasonable provision for her. The issue arose whether the costs of the proceedings should be taken into account when considering the resources available to W and it was submitted, for the defendants, that they should be ignored because otherwise every claim in the case of someone of modest means would become self-justifying as the means of the claimant would always be reduced by the costs. On that issue, there was no simple and universally applicable answer. However, where, as in the instant case, the will had made reasonable financial provision, it was hard to see how a self-induced costs burden could make the reasonable unreasonable.

---

[457] *Wharton v Mercer* 22 September 2011, District Judge Wright, Liverpool District Registry. Case analysis is available on Westlaw and the text of the approved judgment is available on Lawtel (20 March 2012).

[458] A. Francis, *Inheritance Act Claims, Law, Practice and Procedure*, at 5[17](3). The case is mentioned at 15[38](a).

[459] *Wharton v Mercer*, at [30].

[460] *Palmer v Lawrence* [2011] EWHC 3961 (Ch); unreported 16 November 2011, HH Judge Purle QC. The costs issue is addressed at [29]–[30] and the conclusion that the will made reasonable provision for W is set out at [44]–[46].

10.—THE ORDER

(a) Interim Orders

7–167   Section 5(1) of the 1975 Act enables the Court to make an interim order if it appears:

> (a)   that the applicant is in immediate need of financial assistance, but it is not yet possible to determine what order, if any, should be made under s.2; and
>
> (b)   that property forming part of the net estate of the deceased is or can be made available to meet the need of the applicant.

The scope of this interim relief is restricted to ordering payment of "such sum or sums ... as the court thinks reasonable". Payments may be made under an interim order until such date as the court may specify, not being later than the date on which the court makes an order under s.2 or decides not to make an order. The provision does not expressly confer jurisdiction to order that the applicant shall be permitted to reside in any house forming part of the net estate,[461,462] or that the personal representatives may purchase property for the applicant's use and occupation. Section 5(1) enables the court to impose restrictions or conditions when making an interim order, and s.5(4) specifically provides that the court may impose a condition that any sum paid under an interim order is to be regarded as paid on account of any provision made by an order under s.2.

7–168   In *Barnsley v Ward*[463] where the point was taken against the applicant that her need for financial assistance was at least in part due to the fact that she had employment but resigned from it, she gave an undertaking that she would use her best endeavours to obtain reasonable employment. The Court of Appeal affirmed the judge's decision to award her £50 per week and extended the time during which it should be paid from the date originally specified until judgment in the action or further order. Templeman LJ, giving the judgment of the Court of Appeal, observed that different considerations might prevail had there been evidence that the applicant was deliberately not taking advantage of an opportunity to obtain employment. Both he and Ormrod LJ deprecated appeals against orders for interim provision; when a judge at first instance comes to a decision that an applicant is in need of immediate financial assistance, his decision and conclusion are frustrated by the appeal. The purpose of an interim order was

---

[461]   Though a claimant who is a surviving spouse may have rights to occupy the matrimonial home, or be able to apply for an occupation order, under Pt IV of the Family Law Act 1996, and a cohabitant may also be able to apply for an occupation order.

[462]   The claim for a s.5 order in *Smith v Smith* [2012] 2 F.L.R. 230 was dismissed as the claimant failed to show that she was in immediate financial need, but Mann J added that it was not clear whether there was any jurisdiction to make on order permitting her to reside in the property in question, but if there was, it would not be exercised unless she could show a clear and immediate need or at least, a very good reason why such an order should be made.

[463]   *Barnsley v Ward* unreported 18 January 1980, CA. The case is noted in *Tyler*, p.512.

to hold the situation as reasonably as possible pending final determination, and the court would interfere with the first instance decision only in the most exceptional circumstances.

(b) Periodical Payments Orders: Commencement and Duration

For two reasons, this is a topic of considerably less importance than was formerly the case. The first is that the 1975 Act places no restriction on the power to award lump sums; the second is the general acceptance that the "clean break" principle in the matrimonial legislation should apply in family provision cases generally. Periodical payments have rarely been ordered since the 1975 Act came into operation. Under the legislation in force prior to the 1975 Act, where an order in favour of an applicant was, in the great majority of cases, for provision by way of periodical payments, the payments were usually ordered to run from the date of death; see *Re Stead*[464] (order back-dated subject to giving credit for an interim award), *Re Debenham*[465] (lump sum awarded in addition to periodical payments, to avoid back-dating the order) and *Re Farrow*[466] (periodical payments to run from the date of the order and lump sum to take account of the fact that she had received nothing from the estate since the death of her former husband seven years previously). In the first reported case under s.6, which confers power to vary orders for periodical payment, the periodical payments order was made in order to fund the claimant's further education, including the cost of a postgraduate course if he gained a place at an appropriate institution.[467] Since s.19(1) of the 1975 Act deems the order to have effect, subject to any of its provisions, from the date of the deceased's death, any periodical payments awarded should run from death subject to any order to the contrary.

7–169

(c) Orders with Suspensory Effect

Circumstances may be such that, at the date of the hearing, it is uncertain what form of provision should be ordered. This situation cannot be dealt with by making a nominal order for periodical payments and giving permission to apply. Section 2(3) of the 1975 Act forbids the setting aside, out of the estate, of any larger part than is sufficient, at the date of the order, to produce by the income thereof the amount required for the making of the payments; and the tenor of the legislation is to ensure that executors and beneficiaries should not be subjected to long periods of uncertainty as to their position.

7–170

---

[464] *Re Stead* [1985] F.L.R. 16.
[465] *Re Debenham* [1986] 1 F.L.R. 404.
[466] *Re Farrow* [1987] 1 F.L.R. 205.
[467] *Taylor v Bell* [2015] All E.R. (D) 208, Leeds County Court (HH Judge Behrens sitting as a High Court judge); see Ch.5, s.3, "Interim Orders and Variation of Orders".

(d) Termination of Orders

7–171   It follows from the decisions in *Whytte v Ticehurst*[468] and *Re Bramwell*[469] that an order for periodical payments cannot survive the death of the person in whose favour the order was made, but must then terminate, if it has not done so already.[470] Termination during the applicant's lifetime will occur on remarriage, if the applicant is a former spouse or a judicially separated spouse[471] or if the court, in the exercise of its discretion, orders that it should end on some earlier date or on the occurrence of some specified event such as, for instance, when an applicant who is a minor attains his majority or ceases to be engaged in education or in training for a trade, profession or vocation.

(e) Final Orders Generally

7–172   The form of final order most often made in recent years is a lump sum order, and occasionally, in addition to the lump sum, the income of a fund. Other types of final order made from time to time include transfer or acquisition of property orders, and orders varying shares of residue given by the deceased's will.

7–173   It may be that awards, whether of capital sums or income, will affect Social Security benefits; such effects are discussed in the next section of this chapter. Professional advisers need to consider which type of award will minimise any adverse effects on means-tested benefits or tax credits subject to an income threshold. The eventual resolution of *Ilott v Mitson*,[472] both as to whether the will had made reasonable provision for the claimant and (that issue having been decided in her favour) as to quantum was hampered by lack of a clear presentation of the effect which the award sought would affect her entitlement to those benefits and credits. An early example from the case-law is *Re Viner*[473] where the applicant was awarded a lump sum of £2,000 rather than periodical payments of £5 per week in order to ensure that her rent and rate rebates would not be affected.[474] However, the disposable capital, as well as income, limits must also be kept in mind, and not merely as they might affect the applicant. In *Rajabally v Rajabally*[475] the testator's widow applied under the 1975 Act and an order was made transferring the matrimonial home to her, subject to a legacy of £7,500 to the disabled adult son of the testator's first marriage, to be raised by a charge on the property. This was sufficient to render him ineligible for

---

[468] *Whytte v Ticehurst* [1986] Fam. 64.
[469] *Re Bramwell* [1988] 2 F.L.R. 263.
[470] It has recently been unsuccessfully argued that those cases were wrongly decided; see *Roberts v Fresco* [2017] EWHC 283 (Ch), Simon Monty QC sitting as a deputy judge of the High Court.
[471] Inheritance (Provision for Family and Dependants) Act 1975 s.19(2).
[472] See Ch.6, s.8(e)(ii), *Ilott v Mitson*, at paras 6–160–6–191.
[473] *Re Viner* [1978] C.L.Y. 3091.
[474] The position now is, broadly speaking, the other way round; it is having capital in excess of the limit that disqualifies the claimant from eligibility for means-tested benefits, though the amount may be affected by income.
[475] *Rajabally v Rajabally* [1987] 2 F.L.R. 390.

supplementary benefit without being large enough to provide an income on which he could live. However, the value of his interest under the testator's will was £13,000, so he would have been ineligible for supplementary benefit whether or not his stepmother had applied under the 1975 Act. The best solution, from his point of view, would have been for the legacy to him to have been reduced by the Court of Appeal to £6,000. In cases where a disabled claimant is in receipt of means-tested benefits, it may be possible to preserve their entitlement by setting up a discretionary trust of the sum awarded, as in *Hanbury v Hanbury*[476] and *Challinor v Challinor*[477]

Since the order takes effect from the date of the deceased's death, the **7–174** claimant is in much the same position as a legatee. Indeed, in a different context, it was held in *Re Jennery Deceased*[478] that an order declaring the plaintiff's entitlement under the 1938 Act was not an order for payment of money but had the effect of putting him in the position of a legatee, so that the proper course of enforcing it was by means of proceedings for administration of the estate, not under the provisions of the former RSC Ord.45 (enforcement of judgments and orders).[479] In *Lansforsakringar Bank AB v Wood*[480] Patten J followed *Jennery* and also the earlier case of *McDowell v Hollister*[481] in holding that the effect of an order under s.2 of the 1975 Act was simply to redistribute the estate and not to make anything equivalent to an order for payment of money that could be properly described as a debt to which r.72.2 applied.[482]

When an order for a lump sum payment is made under the 1975 Act, it **7–175** very rarely contains terms as to interest which replicate the normal rules relating to legacies. Unless there is specific provision in the will, legacies bear interest according to rules of law which differ as between one kind of legacy and another. The normal rule is that an immediate general legacy is payable at the end of the executor's year and that, therefore, it should carry interest from that date until it is paid. An exception to this rule, relevant in considering the time from which awards under the 1975 Act might bear interest, exists where the testator has given a legacy to their infant child or a child to whom they stood in loco parentis,[483] or has given a legacy to an infant, who need not be their child, but for whose maintenance they have shown an intention to provide. In such cases, the legacy carries interest from the date

---

[476] *Hanbury v Hanbury* [1999] 2 F.L.R. 255. The report of the case includes a useful precedent.
[477] *Challinor v Challinor* [2009] W.T.L.R. 931.
[478] *Re Jennery Deceased* [1967] Ch. 280.
[479] General rules about the enforcement of judgments and orders are now contained in CPR Pt 70.
[480] *Lansforsakringar Bank AB v Wood* [2007] EWHC 2419. Dr Wood had been awarded £300,000 out of the estate of his late mother and the bank were attempting to recover a judgment debt from her executors or Dr Wood personally. An interim third party debt order was made but Master Leslie refused to make it absolute and his decision was upheld by Patten J.
[481] *McDowell v Hollister* [1855] 25 L.T. 185.
[482] CPR Pt 72 (Third Party Debt orders) replaces the former provisions of the RSC and CCR relating to garnishee orders.
[483] *Wilson v Maddison* (1843) 2 Y & C Ch. Cas 372; *Re Stokes, Bowen v Davidson* [1928] Ch. 716 (also where the statutory power of maintenance applies).

of the testator's death; the court has presumed that it was intended to carry interest in order to provide for the child's maintenance, if no other provision was made for that purpose. This is a matter as to which the court can, but very rarely does, give directions, though in *Re Lewis, Lewis v Lynch*[484] the appellant was awarded further provision of £10,000 with interest from the day following judgment.

(f) Incidence of the Burden of Provision

7–176 Section 2(4) of the 1975 Act enables the court to make consequential directions for the purpose, inter alia, of securing that the order operates fairly as between one beneficiary of the estate of the deceased and another. For example, in *Re Bunning*[485] Vinelott J directed that the £60,000 ordered to be provided for the applicant widow be paid in the first instance from the 80 per cent of residue bequeathed to Cambridge University, and that any deficiency be paid rateably from the two pecuniary legacies to the University and the Royal Society for the Protection of Birds. This followed the statutory order (laid down by the Administration of Estates Act 1925 s.34 and Sch.1 Pt II) of application of assets to the payment of liabilities where the estate is solvent, save that the 20 per cent of residue divided among the individual legatees who had not been made parties was not affected. The statutory order was not followed in *Malone v Harrison*,[486] where it was plain to Hollings J that no order made in favour of the applicant should be at the expense of the beneficiary with whom the deceased had been living as husband and wife for some 20 years and by whom he had a son. It was agreed that the award be paid from the specific legacy given to the deceased's brother by his will, not out of residue.

(g) Recording of the Order

7–177 Section 19(3) of the 1975 Act provides that:

> "A copy of every order made under this Act, other than an order made under s.15(1) of this Act, shall be sent to the Principal Registry of the Family Division for entry and filing, and a memorandum of the order shall be endorsed on, or permanently annexed to, the probate or letters of administration under which the estate is being administered."

Except where CPR r.57.16(3A) applies,[487] the personal representative is required to produce the probate or grant of administration at the hearing of the claim.[488] If an order is made under the Act, the original grant, together with a sealed copy of the order, must be sent to the Principal Registry for a

---

[484] *Re Lewis, Lewis v Lynch* unreported 13 March 1980, CA; see *Tyler*, p.586.
[485] *Re Bunning* [1984] Ch. 480.
[486] *Malone v Harrison* [1979] 1 W.L.R. 1353; an application under s.1(1)(e).
[487] Inserted so as to meet the situation, created by the amendment to s.4 of the 1975 Act, where the claim is commenced before the issue of a grant of representation.
[488] 57APD.18.1.

memorandum to be endorsed on or permanently annexed to it in accordance with s.19(3).[489] Every final order embodying a compromise (whether made with or without a hearing) must contain a direction that a memorandum of the order shall be endorsed on or permanently annexed to the grant and a copy of the order shall be sent to the Principal Registry with the relevant grant for endorsement.[490]

11.—BENEFITS AND THE 1975 ACT

(a) Introduction

Many applicants under the 1975 Act are either in receipt of state benefits at the time of making the claim, or will be receiving them in the foreseeable future. It is important to consider, so far as possible, whether there is any risk that they will become ineligible, or that their entitlement will be reduced, by the change in their financial position created by the award or the settlement of their claims. This will require practitioners to keep themselves informed of the progress in the changes to the benefits system (in particular the introduction of universal credit) intended to be implemented by the Welfare Reform Act 2012. That implementation is far from complete and the situation is complicated further because there are still claimants in receipt of benefits which have long been abolished for new claims and replaced by a different benefit. There is a very useful introductory chapter in the *Child Poverty Action Group (CPAG) Welfare Benefits and Tax Credits Handbook*[491] which covers the benefit and tax credit system, the benefits and credits which it is appropriate to claim in various circumstances, and intended future changes to the system. The second chapter of the *CPAG Handbook* deals with the introduction of universal credit, which was due to have been introduced for all new claims by September 2018, followed by transfer of existing claims for the benefits which it is intended to replace, from 2019. That topic is discussed further in the part of this section which relates to means-tested benefits. The purpose of this section as a whole is to assist consideration of these aspects of a claim by providing a guide to, and commentary on, the relevant areas of the benefits and tax legislation. (Note: in the discussion of benefits and credits which follows, where the word "claimant" is used, it means a benefit claimant, not a claimant in the procedural sense. A person making a claim under the 1975 Act is referred to in this section as an applicant.)

7–178

---

[489] 57APD 18.2.
[490] 57APD 18.3.
[491] *Welfare Benefits and Tax Credits Handbook* 19th edn (London: Child Poverty Action Group, 2017–18). App.1 provides a list of useful postal addresses and websites. All references to the *CPAG Handbook* in the text and footnotes are to the 2017–18 edition.

(b) Non-Means-Tested Benefits

7–179 Entitlement to these is, of course, unaffected by the making of any award under the 1975 Act. However, such entitlements are to be taken into account in considering the financial resources of any person whose circumstances are relevant (that is to say, the applicant, any other applicant, and any beneficiary under the will or intestacy). It is necessary to know whether a benefit is taxable; a common error in presenting evidence of the applicant's financial position is to include the gross, rather than the net amount of benefits received, with the result that the income need is underestimated. Calculations of the applicant's income need may also be complicated by the fact that some benefit rates are on a sliding scale (for instance, widows' pensions between the ages of 45 and 54) or otherwise age-related (as is the case with contribution-based jobseekers' allowance, contributory employment and support allowance and, for those who are still entitled to them although they have long been abolished for new claims, incapacity benefit and severe disablement allowance).

7–180 The main alteration to the non-means-tested benefits regime before the previous edition of this book was the phasing out of incapacity benefit for claimants in receipt of it in February 2011 and its replacement by employment and support allowance (ESA), which was introduced in August 2008 and has replaced incapacity benefit and income support paid on disability grounds for new claimants from February 2011. The major change which has come into effect since the publication of the previous edition is the replacement of disability living allowance with the "personal independence payment", which has two components, a daily living component and a mobility component, each of which may be payable at a standard rate or an enhanced rate. Many of the benefits are payable for periods of one year or less and therefore will not significantly affect the applicant's financial resources; however, the longer-term benefits (retirement pension, carer's allowance, disability living allowance, attendance allowance and child benefit) will do so and will have to be taken into account under s.3(1)(a). In the case of the statutory payments it is important to ascertain whether the applicant's contract of employment provides for benefits at a higher rate or for a longer period than the statutory entitlement.

7–181 The table of non-means-tested benefits which follows[492] indicates whether the benefit is contributory, taxable, age-related or time-limited.[493] Numbers

---

[492] The author gratefully acknowledges and has adopted the broader categorisation in *Williams, Mortimer & Sunnucks*, 20th edn (London: Sweet & Maxwell, 2013), Ch.43, "Social Security Benefits and Tax Credits, para.43–16.

[493] These characteristics are indicated by Y or N in the relevant columns of the table, which are headed, respectively, CON, TAX, AR and TL. Figures in brackets in the latter two columns indicate the ages at which the amount payable changes and the number of weeks for which it is payable. SSP (28 weeks); short-term IB (52 weeks); contribution-based JSA (26 weeks); SMP, MA and SAP (39 weeks maximum); SPP (two weeks); bereavement allowance (52 weeks). It is not possible to claim for bereavement allowance and widowed parent's allowance at the same time, but bereavement allowance may be available when the entitlement to widowed parent's allowance ceases.

in square brackets refer to the end-notes to the table. Benefits are referred to in the text by the abbreviations in the second column of the table.

Non-means-tested benefits as at 6 April 2017

Benefit	Abb	CON	TAX	AR	TL
Retirement					
Retirement pension		Y	Y	Y [1]	N
State pension [2]		Y	Y	Y [1]	N
Bereavement					
Bereavement support payment [3]	BSP	Y	N	Y	Y (18m)
Bereavement payment (lump sum)	BP	Y	N	Y	
Bereavement allowance	BA	Y	Y	Y	Y (18m)
Widowed parent's allowance	WPA	Y	Y	Y	N
Disability					
Attendance allowance	AA	N	N	Y [4}	N
Disability living allowance	DLA	N	N	Y [5]	N
Incapacity benefit [6]	IB	Y	Y	Y	Y
Personal independence payment	PIP	N	N	Y	Normally [7]
Severe disablement allowance [8]	SDA	N	N	Y	N
Work-related					
Contributory employment and support allowance	CESA	Y	Y	Y[9]	N
Contribution-based job-seekers' allowance	CJSA	Y	Y	Y[10]	
Industrial injuries disablement benefit	IIDB	N	N	N	N
Care and health					
Carer's allowance	CA	N	Y	Y[11]	N
Guardian's allowance	GA	N	N	N	N
Child benefit	CB	N	Y [12]	N	N

Statutory payments [13]					
maternity	SMP	N	Y	N	Y (39 wks)
paternity	SPP	N	Y	N	Y (2 wks)
shared parenting	ShPP	N	Y	N	Y (37 wks)
adoption pay	SAP	N	Y	N	Y (39 wks)
sick pay	SSP	N	Y	N	Y (28 wks)

End-notes

[1] There is an ongoing process of equalisation of pension ages for men and women and of raising the pension age for both.[494]

[2] There are now two systems in operation, the "old" retirement pension for those who reached pension age before 6 April 2016 and the state pension for those reaching pension age on or after that date.

[3] Bereavement benefits are payable to claimants under pension age. BSP is a new benefit, available if the deceased spouse or civil partner died on or after 6 April 2017. It consists of a lump sum and monthly payments for up to 18 months. It replaces the other bereavement benefits, which are available if the deceased spouse or civil partner died before 6 April 2017. It is not permissible to claim both BA (which will be abolished from 6 April 2018) and WPA.

[4] Claimants for AA must be 65 or over.

[5] New claims for DLA can now be made only for children under 16. It has been replaced by PIP for new claimants aged 16–64.

[6] IB was abolished for new claims on 22 October 2008. It is age-related to the extent that the short-term rates are higher for claimants who have reached pension age. There are two short-term rates, for weeks 1–28 and 29–52, and a long-term rate. The shorter-rate payments for the first 28 weeks are non-taxable but the subsequent payments are taxable.

[7] PIP is available to claimants over 16 who have not reached pension age (though there exceptions to the upper age limit). It is normally awarded for a fixed period of one, two or five years; indefinite awards are reviewed periodically.

[8] SDA was abolished for new claims on 6 April 2001, and it is intended to transfer existing claimants for SDA and IB to employment support allowance.

[9] Claimants for CESA must be over 16 but under pension age.

[10] There is no lower age limit for CJSA but eligibility ceases on the claimant reaching pension age.

[11] The claimant must be over 16.

---

[494] *CPAG Handbook*, p.772 and App.12, p.1666.

[12] CB is now subject to a high income CB charge where the claimant's income in a tax year exceeds £50,000. It is possible to elect not to receive CB. [13] The claimant's contract of employment may provide for payments at a higher rate or for a longer period than the statutory rate or period.

(c) Means-Tested Benefits

(i) Generally

This area of the benefits system is in a state of transition. One of the major objectives of the Welfare Reform Act 2012[495] was to replace a number of existing means-tested benefits and tax credits by a single benefit called Universal Credit (UC). At the time of writing, UC is being introduced for certain new claimants[496] but it is planned to begin transferring claimants who are receiving any of the benefits which UC is intended to replace to the UC system from September 2019 onwards. The benefits to be replaced are income support (IS), income-related jobseekers' allowance (IRJSA), income-related employment and support allowance (IRESA), housing benefit (HB), child tax credit (CTC) and working tax credit (WTC). Council tax benefit has disappeared from the array of social security benefits and assistance with council tax payments via a local authority's council tax reduction scheme (CTR) is not subject to the rules governing means-tested benefits and tax credits.

7–182

(ii) Tax credits

CTC and WTC are non-contributory and non-taxable benefits. The rules are extremely complex but the *CPAG Handbook*[497] gives helpful worked examples of the calculation of these credits. Eligible claimants in receipt of IS, IRJSA, IRESA or pension credit (PC) are automatically entitled to the maximum amount of CTC or WTC payable. There is no capital limit above which the claimant becomes ineligible for CTC or WTC but this situation will change for current claimants when they are transferred to UC, which has the same lower and upper capital limits as the means-tested benefits which it is replacing. Claimants with capital above the upper limit of £16,000 will of course lose their entitlement to the means-tested benefits mentioned above and thus will cease to be entitled to the full amount of CTC or WTC. Both CTC and WTC payments are made up of a number of elements[498] and, where the claimant is not entitled to the maximum, the amount payable is tapered by reference to the amount by which their relevant income exceeds

7–183

---

[495] The Act received the Royal Assent on 8 March 2012 and is partially in force at the time of writing.

[496] That is, those who live in a "gateway" area and satisfy certain "gateway" conditions, and those who live in a "full service" area, who do not have to meet any such conditions. It is intended that all "gateway" areas become full service areas by September 2018.

[497] *CPAG Handbook*, Ch.59; and there is also a list of income disregards at Ch.60.

[498] See the *CPAG Handbook* at Chs 9 and 10, respectively.

the income threshold.[499] The entitlement is reduced by 41 per cent of the excess. It is therefore important, in the context of a lump sum award, to ascertain whether there will be a knock-on effect which reduces the applicant's credits because entitlement to means-tested benefits is lost.

(iii) Benefits subject to capital limits

7–184   This discussion relates only to individual claimants.[500] With the exception of pension credit, all such benefits are intended to be replaced by UC. Both UC and the three work-related benefits which are to be replaced by UC are non-contributory and, with the exception of IRJSA, non-taxable. The benefits intended to be replaced are directed at different categories of claimant. IRESA may be claimed by persons with limited capability for work because of illness or disability and are not entitled to SSP or pension credit. Eligible claimants for IS are, broadly speaking, persons who are not expected to work and who are not entitled to any form of JSA or ESA. The categories of eligible claimant include sick or disabled persons, carers, some persons who are looking after children and some pupils, students and people on training courses. Like ESA, JSA is of two types, contributory, which is not means-tested, and income-related (IRJSA), which is. Claimants for IRJSA must be fit for work and satisfy the jobseeking conditions. All three of these benefits are available only to claimants with capital of less than £16,000 and there is a tariff income deduction of £1 for each £250 or part thereof above the lower limit of £6,000.[501] Capital includes all types of property but some types of capital, and in particular, the value of the claimant's home, are disregarded. Eligibility for UC is subject to the same limits but the tariff income deduction is £4.35 for each £250 or part thereof above the lower limit.

7–185   Housing benefit is a non-contributory and non-taxable benefit for persons on a low income who pay rent. The capital limits and tariff income deduction are the same as for IS, IRESA and IRJSA for claimants under the qualifying age for pension credit, but for those over that age the tariff income deduction is £1 per week for each £500 above the lower limit.

7–186   Pension credit is not one of the benefits to be replaced by UC. It is a non-contributory and non-taxable benefit and has two components, a guarantee credit (GC) and a savings credit (SC); however, from April 2016, savings credit is being phased out; no new claims for SC can be made after that date. For those born before 6 April 1950 the qualifying age for guarantee credit is 60, and for those born after 5 December 1953 it is 65 or over.[502] There are no capital limits for GC but there is a "deemed income" reduction of £1 per

---

[499]   At the time of writing, this is £16,105 p.a. for CTC-only claimants and £6,420 for those claiming WTC only or WTC and CTC.
[500]   There are types of benefit which can be claimed jointly (joint-claim JSA) or are affected if the claimant has a partner, for example, IRESA.
[501]   The lower limit is £10,000 if the claimant lives in a care home.
[502]   The qualifying age for pension guarantee credit is being raised in line with the pension age. There is a list of qualifying ages for those born after 6 April 1950 at App.12 of the *CPAG Handbook*

week for each £500 or part thereof if the claimant has capital of over
£10,000. It is available for those whose income falls short of the standard
minimum guarantee.[503] There are additional amounts for persons with
severe disability and for carers. SC was introduced as, in effect, a reward for
thrift. It is available for to existing claimants over 65 who have qualifying
income[504] in excess of the savings credit threshold, subject to a maximum
figure,[505] which is, at the time of writing, £20.52 per week for a single claimant and £27.09 for a couple.

(iv) Common benefit rules generally

There are various rules which are common to particular aspects of the **7–187**
benefit system, including income for non-means-tested and for means-tested
benefits, and for capital. Given that nearly all monetary awards in 1975 Act
cases made nowadays are in the form of lump sums, the most important
rules in that context are those which determine how capital affects entitlement to means-tested benefits. There are some differences in the rules,
depending on whether the recipient of benefits (and their partner, if there is
one) is under or over the qualifying age for pension credit.[506]

In relation to means-tested benefits, the capital to be taken into account is **7–188**
not always simply that of the claimant. If the claimant has a "partner", and
both parties are over 16 and are:

(a) married and living in the same household; or
(b) not married but living together as husband and wife; or
(c) of the same sex, registered as civil partners and living in the same
     household; or
(d) of the same sex, not registered as civil partners but living together
     as if they were civil partners;

then the claimant and partner must claim together as a "couple" and both
parties' capital and income are taken into account in the assessment of
means-tested benefits.

(v) Tariff income

Where the claimant[507] has capital in excess of the lower limit but less than **7–189**
the upper limit, that capital is deemed to produce an income ("the tariff

---

[503] At the time of writing, £155.60 per week for single persons and £237.55 per week for
       couples.
[504] That is, all income which counts for guarantee credit except for certain state benefits and
       maintenance payments for the claimant or the claimant's partner from a former spouse.
[505] At the time of writing, the thresholds are £137.45 per week for single persons and £218.42
       for couples, and the respective maxima are £13.20 and £14.90.
[506] The rules for persons under pension credit age are discussed at paras 7–189—7–194 and the
       main differences for those over the pension credit age are summarised at para.7–196.
[507] References to a claimant in the discussion of the common benefit rules include references to
       a "couple" if the claimant and partner fall to be treated as a "couple" in accordance with
       the conditions set out in the previous paragraph.

income") of £1 per week for every £250 or part thereof above the lower limit, except in the case of pension credit, where the tariff income on capital that counts for tariff income is £1 for every £500 above the lower limit. Tariff income is taken into account in calculating the benefit payable.

(vi) Notional capital or income[508]

7–190   Claimants may be treated as having capital or income which they do not in fact possess; that is notional capital or income. The effect of having notional capital is the same as that of having actual capital except that the so-called "diminishing notional capital rule" may be applied so that the value of the notional capital is treated as decreasing over a period of time. For benefits other than UC, there are five situations in which claimants may be regarded as having notional capital. Only (a) and (e) apply in relation to UC. The situations are:

(a)   where they have deliberately deprived themselves of capital in order to claim or increase benefit;

(b)   where they have failed to apply for capital which is available to them;

(c)   where another person makes a payment to a third party on their behalf or on behalf of a member of their family;

(d)   where the claimant (or a member of their family) receives capital on behalf of a third party and uses or retains it; and

(e)   where the claimant is in business as a sole trader or a member of a partnership and the business has been registered as a limited company.

The first four of these (with "income" substituted for "capital") also apply in respect of notional income. The situations which most commonly arise in the context of family provision claims are (a) and (b), though (c) may occur because someone else is paying the applicant's bills and those bills are for items of normal living expenditure. It should be noted that there is no safe period after which it can be assumed that deprivation of capital will not be investigated. While the question is not the way in which the capital was disposed of, but the intention underlying the disposal, certain types of expenditure[509] are more likely to found an inference that the requisite intention existed. For UC, a person is not to be treated as depriving themselves of capital if it is disposed of for the purpose of reducing or paying a debt owed by that person or for purchasing goods or services that

---

[508]   The relevant regulations for capital are the Income Support (General) Regulations 1987 (IGSR) (SI 1987/1967) reg.51(1); Jobseeker's Allowance Regulations 1996 (JSAR) (SI 1996/207) reg.113(1); Employment Support and Allowance Regulations 2008 (ESAR) (SI 2008/794) reg.115(1); Housing Benefit (General) Regulations 2006 (HBR) (SI 2006/213) reg.49(1); Universal Credit Regulations 2013 (UCR) (SI 2013/376) reg.50 (1). For income they are IGSR reg.42(1); JSAR reg.105(1); ESAR reg.106(1); HBR reg.42(1).

[509]   The Handbook gives expensive holidays and putting money into trust as examples; see p.371.

were reasonable in the circumstances of that person's case.[510] A person who has deprived themselves of earned income, or whose employer has arranged for them so to be deprived, for the purpose of securing UC or an increased entitlement to UC, is to be treated as having that income.[511]

(vii) The diminishing notional capital rule[512]

The "diminishing notional capital" rule applies only to the case where   **7–191** claimants have deliberately deprived themselves of capital in order to obtain a benefit or an increase in benefit. Its function is to provide a method of determining the extent to which the claimant's notional capital is to be treated as having been reduced over time by reasonable living expenses.[513]

(viii) The "failure to apply" rule

The "failure to apply" rule[514] does not have effect, in relation to benefits   **7–192** other than UC, if the failure to apply is for capital:

(i)   from a discretionary trust;
(ii)   from a trust or fund administered by the court set up from money paid as a result of personal injury;
(iii) from a personal pension scheme or retirement or annuity contract; or
(iv)   in the form of a loan which could only be obtained by giving one's home or other disregarded capital as security.

The general position is that the "failure to apply" rule operates only in respect of capital which the claimant could obtain if they were to apply for it. Generally a claimant is treated as having the capital for which they have failed to apply as from the date on which they could have obtained it. There is a similar rule for failure to apply for income[515] and the main exceptions to its operation are in respect of income from:

(i)   a discretionary trust;
(ii)   a trust set up from money paid as a result of a personal injury;
(iii) funds administered by a court as a result of a personal injury; and
(iv)   WTC or CTC.

---

[510] UCR reg.50(2).
[511] UCR reg.60(1).
[512] The relevant regulations are IGSR reg.51A(1); JSAR reg.114(1); ESAR reg.116(1); HBR reg.49(1); UCR reg.50(3).
[513] For the operation of the rule, see the *CPAG Handbook* at 373–74.
[514] The relevant regulations are ISGR reg.51(2); JSAR reg.113(2); ESAR reg.115(2); HBR reg.49(2).
[515] The relevant regulations are ISGR reg.42(2); JSAR reg.105(2); ESAR reg.106(2); HBR reg.42(2).

For income, the failure to apply rule does operate in relation to UC but does not have effect in the case of a failure to apply for any benefit to which the claimant is entitled, other than retirement pension.[516]

7–193 As well as the home which the claimant owns and normally occupies, disregarded capital includes a house occupied as their home by the spouse of the claimant if they are still treated as living in the same household as the claimant, or by a cohabitant if the parties are still treated as living together as husband and wife; future interests in property, personal possessions (unless purchased for the purpose of depriving oneself of capital for the purposes referred to above); business assets if the claimant is self-employed and working in the business, funds held in personal pension schemes or under retirement annuity contracts, and the surrender value of any policy of life assurance, endowment policy or annuity.

(ix) Discretionary trusts

7–194 Capital from a discretionary trust is specifically excluded, in respect of means-tested benefits, from the ambit of "capital which would become available to the claimant upon application being made but which has not been acquired by him". For a case in which the court ordered a sum to be settled on the applicant on discretionary trusts which would not affect her entitlement to state benefits, see *Hanbury v Hanbury*.[517] The applicant, who was the 45-year-old daughter of the deceased and both physically and mentally disabled, was in receipt of both non-means-tested benefits (severe disablement allowance, disability living allowance and what is described in the report at 264E as "mobility allowance" and is presumably the mobility component of the DLA) and means-tested benefits (income support).

(x) Treatment of income as capital or capital as income

7–195 The regulations governing entitlement to all means-tested benefits contain such provisions. There are too many situations in which this may occur to summarise conveniently, particularly as those situations are not uniform over the range of means-tested benefits. No sum is treated, by virtue of such regulations, both as capital and income.[518, 519] The most important point in this context is that income derived from capital other than certain categories of disregarded capital is treated as capital from the date that the claimant is

---

[516] UCR reg.74.
[517] *Hanbury v Hanbury* [1999] 2 F.L.R. 255 at 275C. The settlement as approved by the court is set out at 276E–278H. A more recent case in which provision for a disabled adult child was made by way of a settlement on discretionary trusts is *Challinor v Challinor* [2009] W.T.L.R. 931.
[518] For income treated as capital, the relevant regulations are IGSR reg.48; JSAR reg.110; ESAR reg.112; HBR reg.46.
[519] For capital treated as income, see the Handbook at 293 and 337. The relevant regulations are ISGR reg. 29(2), 41(1), (2), (4), (6) and (7), and 48(2); JSAR regs 94(2) and 104 (1), (2), (5) and (6); ESAR regs 94(2) and 105 (1), (2), (4), and (5); HBR regs 33 and 41 (1), (2), (4) and (5). For UC, where a lump sum I payable by instalments, the instalments are treated as income while the claimant's capital is above £16,000 and as capital when it falls below that limit; UCR reg.46(4).

due to receive it. Income arising from such disregarded capital is treated as income.

(xi) Claimants over the pension credit qualifying age

The differences in the regime which affect such claimants relate mainly to their entitlement to pension credit and housing benefit, and to universal credit when it replaces housing benefit. The notional income rules apply if the purpose of deprivation of income is to gain benefit for the claimant or their partner.[520] The notional capital[521] and diminishing notional capital[522] rules apply as they do for those below the pension credit qualifying age, but a person above that age is not treated as having deliberately deprived himself of capital if they use it to pay off or reduce a debt or to purchase goods or services which are reasonable in their circumstances. The lower capital limit is £10,000 and the upper limit of £16,000 applies to housing benefit but not to pension guarantee credit, for which there is no upper limit. For housing benefit, tariff income is deemed to be £1 per week for every £500 between £10,000 and the upper limit of £16,000; for pension guarantee credit, the deemed tariff income applies to all capital in excess of £10,000. As for those below pension credit age, a partner's capital is taken into account, but those receiving the pension guarantee credit are entitled to housing benefit, however much capital they have.

7–196

12.—TAXATION AND THE 1975 ACT

(a) The 1975 Act and the Inheritance Tax Act 1984

The two statutory provisions which are specifically concerned with orders made under the 1975 Act are s.19(1) of the Act itself and s.146 of the Inheritance Tax Act (IHTA) 1984. Section 19(1) of the 1975 Act provides that:

7–197

> "Where an order is made under s.2 of this Act then, for all purposes, including the purposes of the enactments relating to inheritance tax, the will or the law relating to intestacy, or both the will and the law relating to intestacy, as the case may be, shall have effect and be deemed to have had effect as from the deceased's death subject to the provisions of the order."

The provisions of s.146 of IHTA 1984 most likely to require consideration in practice are subss.(1) and (8).[523] They read:

---

[520] The relevant regulations are the State Pension Credit Regulations 2002 (SPCR) (SI 2002/1792) reg.18 and the Housing Benefit (Persons Who Have Attained the Qualifying Age for State Pension Credit) Regulations (HB-SPCR) 2006 (SI 2006/214) reg.41; see regs 18(6) to 18(8B) and 41(8)–41(8BD), respectively, in relation to deprivation of income.

[521] SPCR reg.21; HB-SPCR reg.47.

[522] SPCR reg.22; HB-SPCR reg.48.

[523] The remaining subsections are largely concerned with adjustments to be made as a result of the tax implications of an order.

"(1) Where an order is made under section 2 of the Inheritance (Provision for Family and Dependants) Act 1975 ('the 1975 Act') in relation to any property forming part of the net estate of a deceased person,[524] then, without prejudice to section 19(1) of that Act, the property shall for the purposes of this Act be treated as if it had on his death devolved subject to the provisions of the order.

(8) Where an order is made staying or dismissing proceedings under the 1975 Act on terms set out in or scheduled to the order, this section shall have effect as if any of those terms which could have been included in an order under section 2 or 10 of that Act were provisions of such an order."

Since subs.(1) refers to orders affecting property which is part of the net estate, it operates in respect of property forming part of the net estate by virtue of s.8, or property ordered to be treated as part of the net estate under s.9. Orders under s.10 are dealt with by providing in s.146(2)(b) that, where a person is ordered under that section to provide money or property, the money or property is to be included in the deceased's net estate for the purpose of the transfer of value made by them on their death.

7–198 An order under s.2 may affect the entitlement of a surviving spouse or civil partner under the will or on the intestacy of the deceased, with the consequence that either more or less IHT is payable. Adjustments of the tax payable in respect of the transfer of value on the death of the deceased are dealt with by IHTA subss.146(4) and (5). Subsection (6) is concerned with the possible IHT effect of orders under the 1975 Act on settled property, and provides that:

"Anything which is done in compliance with an order under the 1975 Act or which occurs on the coming into force of such an order, and which would (apart from that sub-section) constitute an occasion on which tax is chargeable under any provision other than s.79 of this Act shall not constitute such an occasion, and where an order provides for property to be settled or for the variation of a settlement and (apart from this sub-section) tax would be charged under s.52(1) above[525] on the coming into force of the order s.52(1) shall not apply."

7–199 Unlike post-death variations which seek to take advantage of the provisions of s.142 of IHTA and s.62 of the Taxation of Chargeable Gains Act (TCGA) 1992, the order is effective for all purposes whether or not it was made within two years of the deceased's death. The edition of *McCutcheon on Inheritance Tax* current at the time of writing states[526]:

---

[524] This includes property treated as part of the net estate under ss.8 and 9 of the 1975 Act. Neither of those classes of property is covered by s.19(1) of the 1975 Act, since *donationes mortis causa*, nominated property and property held on joint tenancy do not pass by will or on intestacy.

[525] IHTA 1984 s.52(1) (charge on termination of an interest in possession).

[526] *McCutcheon on Inheritance Tax*, 7th edn (London: Sweet & Maxwell, 2016), para.8–218.

"The CGT and income tax legislation itself confers no special treatment in respect of orders under the Act. However, s.19(1) of the Act gives limited provision which would seem to cover CGT and income tax. Where an order is made under s.2 of the Act it shall have effect 'for all purposes' as from the date of the deceased's death subject to the provisions of the order. Therefore s.19(1) would not apply for example to an approved compromise agreement."

In *Re Goodchild*[527] a tax-efficient variation of the dispositions of the deceased's will for the claimant's benefit could have been achieved by the parties by agreement within the two-year period, but by the time agreement had been reached it was too late and a tax-efficient solution could only be achieved by means of an order under s.2 of the 1975 Act, so that IHTA s.146(1) applied. Morritt LJ observed that, if an order was properly within the jurisdiction of the court it was generally irrelevant that it was sought with the motive of attempting to seek a better tax position[528] but, where the effect of the order was to confer a substantial effect on the parties at the expense of the Revenue it was important that the court should be satisfied, not only that it had jurisdiction to make the order but that it was proper to make it.[529]

There is one particular arrangement which is likely to have unfavourable **7–200** tax consequences if included in an order, because of the effect of IHTA s.29A, which applies where:

(a) apart from this section the transfer of value made on the death of any person is an exempt transfer to the extent that the value transferred by it is attributable to an exempt gift; and

(b) the exempt beneficiary, in settlement of the whole or part of any claim against the deceased's estate, effects a disposition of property not derived from the transfer.

This situation is discussed in *McCutcheon*[530] under the heading "Re-routed exempt transfers" and is illustrated here by the following example[531]:

H dies, leaving his entire estate to his wife, W, so that no charge to IHT arises on his death. Z has a claim against H's estate and W settles this claim by paying Z the sum of £x from her own resources.[532] Were it not

---

[527] *Re Goodchild* [1997] 1 W.L.R. 1216, CA, affirming the decision at first instance.

[528] *Re Sainsbury's Settlement* [1967] 1 W.L.R. 476.

[529] The HMRC Inheritance Tax Manual (IHTM) at 35201–35208 is concerned with orders under the 1975 Act. Specific guidance (IHTM 35202) is that if the order creates a short-term (not exceeding five years) interest in possession for the deceased's spouse or civil partner, it should be referred for further investigation.

[530] *McCutcheon*, para.8–217. For discussion of the relevant anti-avoidance provision (IHTA 1984 s.29A), see *McCutcheon*, paras 8–86—8–93.

[531] *Mellows, Taxation for Executors and Trustees* (updated to December 2016), para.9.42.

[532] *Mellows* suggests that, arguably, there is no transfer of value because the whole arrangement is commercial (see IHTA s.10). The commentary in *McCutcheon* at paras 8–86—8–93 does not mention that argument.

for s.29A, this could be a PET and there would be no charge to IHT if
W survives for seven years. The effect of s.29A is to treat H as having
made a specific gift of £x to Z and that will reduce his nil rate band, or,
if it exceeds the NRB threshold, create a tax liability.

McCutcheon[533] expresses the view that although s.29A is rather terrifying, it
is easily sidestepped by the exempt beneficiary (W in the above example)
making the payment out of property derived from the deceased's estate.

(b) Post-death Rearrangements

7–201   It is, of course, open to parties who are sui juris to agree among themselves
at any time to rearrange the dispositions of a will or resulting from an
intestacy under which they benefit, and, additionally, a beneficiary has a
right to disclaim as a matter of general law. However, not all such rearrangements are capable of affecting the amount of tax which would be
payable on the death of the deceased. Apart from orders under the 1975 Act,
there are four types of potentially tax-efficient arrangement, regulated by
IHTA s.142 (variation or disclaimer) s.143 (precatory trust) and s.144 (two-
year discretionary trust).[534] These have the common feature that the transaction must be carried out within the period of two years after the death of
the deceased.[535] Precatory trusts and two-year discretionary trusts are outside the scope of this work and are not discussed further.

(c) Disclaimers Generally

7–202   Although variations and disclaimers are governed by the same provision,
the following points should be noted in relation to disclaimers.

> (i)   Unlike a variation, a disclaimer does not have to include the
>   statement of intent referred to in s.142(2).
> (ii)   Again, unlike a variation, a disclaimer cannot be made to operate
>   in favour of a particular person; the disclaimed property passes by
>   operation of law. The Estates of Deceased Persons (Forfeiture
>   Rule and Law of Succession) Act 2011 amended the Administra-
>   tion of Estates Act 1925 by inserting a new s.46A which provided
>   that where a person disclaims an interest to which they were
>   entitled on intestacy, they shall be treated as if they had died
>   immediately before the intestate.[536] It also amended the Wills Act

---

[533] *McCutcheon*, para.8–92.
[534] *Mellows, Taxation for Executors and Trustees*, Ch.9, "Alterations to dispositions after
death"; *McCutcheon*, Ch.8, ss.X–XIV, "Posthumous arrangements (variations, disclaimers,
two-year discretionary trusts and precatory trusts)"; *Chamberlain and Whitehouse, Trust
Taxation*, 4th edn (London: Sweet & Maxwell, 2014), Ch.45, "Deeds of variation, disclaimers and other post-death rearrangements".
[535] HMRC are believed to consider that the two-year period includes the date of the deceased's
death; see *Chamberlain and Whitehouse*, at 45.18 and n.32.
[536] Estates of Deceased Persons (Forfeiture Rule and Law of Succession) Act 2011 ss.1(1)(a)
and (2).

1837 by inserting a new s.33A which provides that where a will contains a devise or bequest to a person who disclaims it, that person is, unless a contrary intention appears by the will, to be treated for the purposes of that Act as having died immediately before the testator.

(iii) A disclaimer, being a gift made for no consideration, should be made by deed.

(iv) HMRC adopt the following principles in relation to disclaimers[537]:

    (a) the beneficiary must not have accepted any benefit from the disclaimed property;

    (b) the disclaimer must not be conditional;

    (c) the disclaimer must be of the whole of the property; however, if a beneficiary is given two separate gifts by a will, they may accept one and disclaim the other.

(v) The disclaimer must be a "real" disclaimer,[538] that is, the property ostensibly disclaimed should not soon afterwards return to the estate of the person disclaiming. HMRC guidance is that considerable care is necessary in the case of any document embodying a disclaimer that purports to be other than a simple comprehensive relinquishment of the beneficial interest of the person making it.[539]

(d) Tax Effects of Variations and Disclaimers

(i) Inheritance tax

For IHT purposes, post-death variations and disclaimers are regulated by s.142 of IHTA 1984[540] which provides that: **7–203**

"(1) Where within the period of two years after a person's death—

    (a) any of the dispositions (whether effected by will, under the law relating to intestacy or otherwise) of the property comprised in his estate immediately before his death are varied, or

    (b) the benefit conferred by any of those dispositions is disclaimed,

by an instrument in writing made by the persons or any of the persons who benefit or would benefit under the dispositions, this Act shall apply as if the variation had been effected by the deceased or, as the case may be, the disclaimed benefit had never been conferred.

(2) Subsection (1) above shall not apply to a variation unless the instrument contains a statement, made by all the relevant persons,

---

[537] *Chamberlain and Whitehouse*, para.45.64; IHTM, paras 35161–35166.
[538] *McCutcheon*, at paras 8–181–8–182.
[539] IHTM, para.35163.
[540] Subsection 7, which applies to Scotland, is omitted.

to the effect that they intend the sub-section to apply to the variation.

(2A) For the purposes of subsection (2) above the relevant persons are—

(a) the persons making the instrument, and

(b) where the variation results in additional tax being payable, the personal representatives.

Personal representatives may decline to make a statement under subsection (2) above only if no, or no sufficient, assets are held by them in that capacity for discharging the additional tax.

(3) Subsection (1) above shall not apply to a variation or disclaimer made for any consideration in money or money's worth other than consideration consisting of the making, in respect of another of the dispositions, of a variation or disclaimer to which that subsection applies.

(4) Where a variation to which subsection (1) above applies results in property being held in trust for a person for a period which ends not more than two years after the death, this Act shall apply as if the disposition of the property that takes effect at the end of the period had had effect from the beginning of the period; but this subsection shall not affect the application of this Act in relation to any distribution or application of property occurring before that disposition takes effect.

(5) For the purposes of subsection (1) above the property comprised in a person's estate includes any excluded property but not any property to which he is treated as entitled by virtue of section 49(1) above or section 102 of the Finance Act 1986.

(6) Subsection (1) above applies whether or not the administration of the estate is complete or the property concerned has been distributed in accordance with the original dispositions."

7–204   Having regard to the wording of the relevant sections of the Inheritance Tax Act 1984 and the Taxation of Chargeable Gains Act 1992, it is suggested that any order put before the court for its approval should recite, inter alia, that:

(i)   the Court is satisfied:

(a) that the will, or, as the case may be, the law relating to the distribution of the deceased's estate on intestacy, is not such as to make reasonable financial provision for the applicant, and, where appropriate,

(b) that the terms of compromise are for the benefit of the child, or protected party, or beneficiaries who are represented in accordance with the relevant provisions of CPR r.19.7, as the case may be; and

(ii)   that it is ordered pursuant to the provisions of [the relevant sections, viz. ss.2(1), 9, 10 or 11] of the Inheritance (Provision for
Family and Dependants) Act 1975 that the personal representatives of the deceased do carry the said terms of compromise into
effect.[541]

Arguably, a compromise of a 1975 Act claim is caught by the "extraneous   **7–205**
consideration" provisions (IHTA s.142(3) and TCGA s.62(8)), since the
claimant is providing consideration by giving up their right to pursue the
claim. It appears, however, that HMRC do not take this point in relation to
the operation of s.142(3) where the deceased died domiciled in the United
Kingdom. IHTM states, at para.35100 (consideration brought in from
outside the estate), that:

"These provisions[542] apply mainly where, in effect, the beneficiary under
a redirection made by a variation (or as a result of a disclaimer) pur-
chases out of his or her own pocket a benefit from the person entitled
under the deceased's Will, etc. ... A disclaimer or variation made to
avoid or compromise a claim under the Inheritance (Provision for
Family and Dependants) Act 1975 is accepted as not caught by s.142(3)
unless the deceased died domiciled outside the UK[543] ... The bar against
consideration applies only to extraneous consideration and will not
prevent a rearrangement of assets within the will."

(ii) Capital gains tax

The Taxation of Chargeable Gains Tax Act (TCGA) 1992 contains no   **7–206**
provision, such as IHTA 1984 s.146, specifically relating to the 1975 Act.
HMRC take the view that Tomlin orders or consent orders made in 1975
Act proceedings are not within s.19(1) of the 1975 Act; so the only way in
which the variation brought about by making such an order can have effect
for Capital Gains Tax purposes is by the operation of ss.62(6) and 62(7) of
the 1992 Act. Care must be taken to avoid falling foul of s.62(8), which
corresponds to s.142(3) of IHTA 1984. Section 62(9) corresponds to IHTA
s.142(6). These provisions read:

"(6) Subject to subsections (7) and (8) below, where within the period
of 2 years after a person's death any of the dispositions (whether
effected by will, under the law relating to intestacy or otherwise) of
the property of which he was competent to dispose are varied, or
the benefit conferred by any of those dispositions is disclaimed, by

---

[541]   Paragraphs CG31810–814 of the HMRC Capital Gains Tax Manual (CGTM) are concerned with the CGT implications of compromises reached and orders made in 1975 Act
claims. CG31813 states that if the order includes a positive requirement to carry out the
terms of the compromise it should be accepted as an order under s.2 of the Act.
[542]   That is to say, subss.142(1), (3).
[543]   *Lau (Executors of Lau, Deceased) v Revenue and Customs Commissioners* [2009] S.T.C.
(STD) 352.

an instrument in writing made by the persons or any of the persons who benefit or would benefit under the dispositions—

(a)   the variation or disclaimer shall not constitute a disposal for the purposes of this Act; and

(b)   this section shall apply as if the variation had been effected by the deceased or, as the case may be, the disclaimed benefit had never been conferred.

(7)   Subsection (6) above does not apply to a variation unless the instrument contains a statement by the persons making the instrument to the effect that they intend the sub-section to apply to the variation.

(8)   Subsection (6) above does not apply to a variation or disclaimer made for any consideration in money or money's worth other than consideration consisting of the making of a variation or disclaimer in respect of another of the dispositions.

(9)   Subsection (6) above applies whether or not the administration of the estate is complete or the property has been distributed in accordance with the original dispositions."

7–207   It may be possible to rely on these provisions, if the time limits are complied with, in respect of orders made under s.9 of the 1975 Act, because the property in question is property of which the deceased is, for capital gains tax purposes, competent to dispose. TCGA 1992 s.62(10) provides that references to assets of which the deceased was competent to dispose at their death include references to their severable share in any assets to which, immediately before their death, they were beneficially entitled as a joint tenant; but property falling under s.8(2) or property which is made the subject of an order under s.10 is not property of which the deceased was competent to dispose immediately before their death.

7–208   In summary, then:

(1)   an order under s.2 of the 1975 Act is immediately effective for both CGT and IHT purposes;

(2)   a consent order or a Tomlin order embodying a compromise is not regarded by the Inland Revenue as an order of the Court; but

(3)   in the case of IHT, but *not* CGT, a consent order or a Tomlin order embodying a compromise is treated as if it were a court order;

(4)   orders under ss.8, 9 or 10 are not, and cannot be regarded as, orders under s.2; they do not affect property disposed of by the deceased's will or under the laws of intestacy. Orders under s.10 are specifically dealt with in the IHT legislation;

(5)   unless the variation sought to be made is either:

(a)   ordered to be made by the court under s.2, other than as the result of a compromise; or

(b)   treated by the IHT legislation as if it were such an order,

it will not be effective for Inheritance Tax or Capital Gains Tax purposes unless, respectively, ss.142(1) and (2) of the Inheritance Tax Act 1984 and ss.62(6) and (7) of the Taxation of Chargeable Gains Act 1992 are complied with. It may be, in a particular case, that the parties wish only one of IHTA s.142 and TCGA s.62 to apply.[544]

(iii) Stamp duty land tax

Under the stamp duty regime, an instrument of variation attracted a fixed **7–209** duty of 50p unless certified as an exempt instrument.[545] Post-death variations were generally certified under categories (L) (conveyance or transfer operating as a voluntary disposition inter vivos for no consideration in money or money's worth) or (M) (conveyance or transfer of property by an instrument within s.84(1) of the Finance Act 1985 (death: varying disposition). However, the Finance Act 2003 introduced provisions similar to those in the IHT and CGT regimes. The relevant provision is para.4 of Sch.3 (Stamp duty land transactions exempt from charge) which reads:

"4. (1) A transaction following a person's death that varies a disposition (whether effected by will, under the law relating to intestacy or otherwise) of property of which the deceased was competent to dispose is exempt from charge if the following conditions are met.
(2) The conditions are—

(a)   that the transaction is carried out within the period of two years after a person's death; and
(b)   that no consideration in money or money's worth other than the making of another such disposition is given for it.

(2A) Where the condition in sub-paragraph 2(b) is not met, the chargeable consideration for the transaction is determined in accordance with paragraph 8A(2) of Schedule 4.
(3) This paragraph applies whether or not the administration of the estate is complete or the property has been distributed in accordance with the original dispositions."

---

[544] For an example of such a situation, see *Chamberlain and Whitehouse*, at para.45.53.
[545] Stamp Duty (Exempt Instruments) Regulations 1987 (SI 1987/516).

13.—APPEALS

(a) The Appeal System

7–210   The rules are contained in CPR Pt 52,[546] which is divided into seven sections
and supplemented by five Practice Directions.[547] With very few exceptions,
permission to appeal is required.[548] Section II is concerned with permission
to appeal and PD52A includes tables of destinations of appeals.[549] There is a
specific destination table for family proceedings in the principal registry of
the Family Division to which the CPR will apply, and these include 1975
Act claims and claims under TLATA 1996.[550] An application for permission
to appeal may be made in the lower court, at the hearing at which the
decision to be appealed was made, or to the appeal court in an appeal
notice.[551] Where the lower court refuses permission to appeal, a further
application for permission to appeal may be made to the appeal court, and
the order of the lower court refusing permission must specify the court to
which any further application must be made and the level of judge who
should hear the application.[552] The commentary to the rule[553] explains why a
would-be appellant would be well advised to request permission to appeal
from the lower court at the time of the judgment, and this guidance was
firmly endorsed by the Court of Appeal in *T (A child)*[554] and *P v P*.[555] The
commentary emphasises elsewhere[556] that appeals are against (as it is put,
non-technically) "results" or "outcomes" of the hearing in the lower court,
not "findings" or "reasons" given in the judgment. Section II of Pt 52 also
contains the rules relating to determination of applications for permission to
appeal[557] and the permission to appeal tests for first and second appeals.[558]

---

[546] The whole of Pt 52 was re-enacted with effect from 3 October 2016; Civil Procedure
(Amendment (No.3) Rules) 2016 (SI 2016/788).

[547] CPR r.52.2, contained in Section I ("Scope and interpretation") requires all parties to
comply with the practice directions and the commentary includes sections on directions as
to documents, skeleton arguments and citation of authorities.

[548] CPR r.52.3(1).

[549] Subject to some limited exceptions, Table 1 of 52APD identifies a regime in which the judge
who decides the appeal is from the next tier of the judiciary above the judge against whose
order the appeal is sought: *Civil Procedure 2017*, para.52.2.2.

[550] 52APD, Table 3. Any appeal from a decision of a district judge lies to a High Court judge of
the Family Division, and from a High Court judge of the Family Division to the Court of
Appeal.

[551] CPR r.52.3(2), which also refers to the rules about time limits for filing appellant's and
respondent's notices. These and other relevant procedural rules are contained in Section
IV—Additional rules. At the hearing of an appeal, a party may not rely on any matter not
contained in that party's appeal notice unless the court gives permission; CPR r.52.21(5).

[552] CPR r.52.3(3).

[553] *Civil Procedure 2017*, para.52.3.6.

[554] *T (A child)* [2002] EWCA Civ 1736; [2003] 1 F.L.R. 531, at [12]–[13].

[555] *P v P* [2015] EWCA Civ 447; [2015] W.T.L.R. 1039, at [68], now reported *sub nom. AB v
CB: Financial Remedies (Breach of Trust)* [2016] 1 F.L.R. 437, CA.

[556] *Civil Procedure 2017*, para.52.0.6, under the heading "Appeals are against orders, not
reasoned judgments".

[557] CPR r.52.4 (Permission to appeal to County Court or High Court) and 52.5 (Permission to
appeal to Court of Appeal).

[558] CPR r.52.6 (First appeals) and 52.7 (Second appeals).

(b) Circumstances in Which an Appeal Might be Entertained

(i) The permission to appeal tests

Except where r.52.7 (which governs second appeals) applies, permission to 7–211
appeal may be given only where either the court considers that the appeal
would have a real prospect of success,[559] or there is some other compelling
reason for the appeal to be heard. In *Swain v Hillman*,[560] Lord Woolf said, in
relation to that test, that the court had to consider whether there was a
realistic, as opposed to a fanciful prospect of success. It appears to be
unclear what would constitute "some other compelling reason for the appeal
to be heard". The commentary refers to *Smith v Cosworth Casting Processes*[561] in which it was said that:

> "For example, the issue may be one which the court considers should in
> the public interest be examined by this court, or, to be more specific,
> this court may take the view that the case raises an issue where the law
> needs clarifying."

The test for a second appeal is, as might be expected, more stringent; not
only must there be a real prospect of success, but, additionally, the appeal
must raise an important point of principle or practice.[562] The important
point of principle or practice must be one that has not yet been established;
an appeal concerning the correct application of an existing principle or
practice does not satisfy this requirement.[563] The alternative test is that there
must be some other compelling reason for the Court of Appeal to hear it.[564]

(ii) Hearing of appeals

In general, every appeal will be limited to a review of the decision of the 7–212
lower court, and the appeal court will not, unless it orders otherwise, receive
oral evidence or evidence which was not before the lower court. However, if
the court considers that in the circumstances of an individual appeal it
would be in the interests of justice, it may hold a re-hearing. It will allow an
appeal where the decision of the lower court was either wrong, or unjust
because of a serious procedural or other irregularity in the proceedings
before the lower court, and it may draw any inference of fact which it
considers justified on the evidence.[565]

---

[559] This is the same test as applies in relation to summary judgment; see CPR r.24.2
[560] *Swain v Hillman* [2001] 1 All E.R. 91, CA; cited by Brooke LJ in *Tanfern v Cameron Macdonald* [2000] 1 W.L.R. 1311, CA, at [32].
[561] *Smith v Cosworth Casting Processes* [1997] 1 W.L.R. 1538, CA; see the commentary at para.52.6.2.
[562] CPR r.52.7(1)(a)(ii); see the commentary at para.52.7.6.
[563] *Uphill v BRB (Residuary) Ltd* [2005] 1 W.L.R. 2070, CA. This decision is also relevant to the "some other compelling reason" test; see the commentary to r.57.7(2)(b) at para.52.7.7.
[564] See *Shared Network Services v Nextiraione UK Ltd* [2012] EWCA Civ 1171 where it was held to be in the public interest that the conflict in first instance authority on the issue should be resolved; *Civil Procedure 2017*, para.52.6.2.
[565] CPR r.52.21(1)–(4).

7–213   "Wrong" is presumed to mean that the court below (i) erred in law; or (ii) erred in fact; or (iii) erred in the exercise of its discretion.[566] Asking the wrong question, or asking the right question and answering it wrongly may fall into (i) or (ii) or both. In relation to error in the exercise of discretion it has been suggested that the appeal court should only interfere:

> "...when it considers that the judge at first instance has not merely preferred an imperfect solution which is different from an alternative imperfect solution which the Court of Appeal might or would have adopted, but has exceeded the generous ambit within which a reasonable disagreement is possible."[567]

In *Price v Price (t/a Poppyland Headware)*[568] Brooke LJ said that another helpful way of describing the appellate function in relation to judicial discretion was to be found in the judgment of Lord Woolf MR in *Phonographic Performance v AEI Rediffusion Music Ltd*[569]:

> "Before the court can interfere it must be shown that the judge has either erred in principle in his approach or has left out of account or not taken into account some feature that he should, or should not have considered, or that his decision was wholly wrong because the court is forced to the conclusion that he has not balanced the various factors fairly in the scale."

(iii) 1975 Act cases in which the appellate jurisdiction has been exercised

7–214   The questions whether the appellate jurisdiction was properly exercisable and whether, if exercised, it was correctly exercised, are particularly liable to arise in 1975 Act cases because of the nature of the decision-making process, which requires the making of value judgment followed, if the value judgment is favourable to the claimant, by the exercise of a discretion. In *Re Coventry*,[570] Buckley LJ had referred to the decision whether the disposition which the deceased had made, if any, was such as to make reasonable financial provision for the applicant as a qualitative decision, or what was sometimes called "a value judgment", and that epithet has passed into general use.

7–215   The lengthy and convoluted history of *Ilott v Mitson*[571] provides a valuable example of the pitfalls which beset the exercise of the appellate jurisdiction in 1975 Act cases. In the "value judgment" phase of the case (2007–

---

[566] *Civil Procedure 2017*, para.52.21.5.
[567] *G v G* [1985] 2 All E.R. 225, HL, per Lord Fraser of Tullybelton, adopted in *Tanfern v Cameron-MacDonald* [2000] 1 W.L.R. 1311, CA.
[568] *Price v Price* [2003] 3 All E.R. 911, CA, at 918j.
[569] *Phonographic Performance v AEI Rediffusion Music Ltd* [1999] 2 All E.R. 299, CA at 314.
[570] *Re Coventry* [1980] Ch. 461, CA at 495H; see also Goff LJ at 487A.
[571] In this discussion the case, under whatever title it was reported in the relevant judgment, is referred to for convenience simply as *Ilott v Mitson*. The case is discussed in detail in Ch.6, s.8(e)(ii), *Ilott v Mitson*, paras 6–160–6–191.

2012), Eleanor King J on the first appeal[572] reversed the decision of the district judge on the ground that he had erred in law by asking himself the wrong question. The Court of Appeal[573] considered that the district judge had identified the question correctly; that question was not whether the deceased had acted unreasonably, but whether, on an objective basis, having considered all the factors in s.3 of the Act, the resulting provision, or lack of it, was unreasonable. Thus, the conclusion that he had asked himself the wrong question was unsustainable; the district judge had both asked the right question and given the right answer. It was reiterated that a value judgment "ought not to be interfered with by us unless we are satisfied that it was plainly wrong".[574] In the "quantum" phase (2013–2017), where Mrs Ilott appealed against the district judge's award to her of £50,000, Parker J concluded on the first appeal that, doing the best that he could with the information that he had, the district judge could not be said to be wrong.[575] On the second appeal, the Court of Appeal identified two fundamental errors in the district judge's approach to the quantification of the award and exercised the discretion itself rather than remitting the matter to him.[576] On the third appeal (an event not contemplated in the Civil Procedure Rules), the Supreme Court held that the district judge had not made either of the fundamental errors which the Court of Appeal had identified and restored his award.[577]

The 1975 Act cases to date show a variety of situations in which the appellate jurisdiction has been exercised. Broadly speaking, they fall into one of four categories, which are: **7–216**

(i)   where the decision was made on a wrong basis of either fact or law;

(ii)   where the reason for the decision could not be discerned;

(iii)   where the judge had failed to take into account matters which should have been taken into account, or has ascribed undue weight to a particular matter;

(iv)   where the discretion was otherwise exercised in a manner in which no reasonable judge, properly directing himself, could have exercised it.

Cases in these categories are discussed, in that order, in the next four paragraphs.

In *Bishop v Plumley*[578] it was held that the registrar and the judge could not have arrived at the decision at which they did arrive had they had regard **7–217**

---

[572] *H v J's Personal Representatives, Blue Cross, RSPB and RSPCA* [2010] 1 F.L.R. 1613, at [63]–[70].

[573] *Ilott v Mitson* [2012] 2 F.L.R. 170, CA.

[574] *Ilott v Mitson* [2012] 2 F.L.R. 170, CA, at [52].

[575] *Ilott v Mitson* [2015] 1 F.L.R. 291.

[576] *Ilott v Mitson* [2015] 2 F.L.R. 1409, CA, at [34]–[44], [44]–[67].

[577] *Ilott v Mitson* [2017] UKSC 17; reported at [2017] 2 W.L.R. 979 as *Ilott v The Blue Cross* (on appeal from *Ilott v Mitson (No.2)*).

[578] *Bishop v Plumley* [1991] 1 W.L.R. 582, CA.

to established principles as to the test to be applied in relation to s.1(3) of the Act, while in *Moody v Stevenson*[579] it was held that the wrong test of whether the will made reasonable provision for the applicant had been applied. In both *Cameron v Treasury Solicitor*[580] and *Barrass v Harding*[581] the Court of Appeal considered that the trial judge had been led into error by sympathy for the claimant, whose financial position was precarious. In *Martin v Williams*[582] it was held that the judge at first instance had wrongly disregarded a property in which the claimant had a 50 per cent beneficial interest as a resource available to meet her needs.

7–218   In *Re J (A minor)*[583] the Court of Appeal reduced the provision of £7,500 made by the trial judge to £5,000 on that basis. In *Cunliffe v Fielden*[584] Wall LJ found the principal deficiency of the judgment at first instance to be that it lacked any kind of judicial analysis; the proper exercise of judicial discretion required the judge to explain how he had exercised it; that was the well-known "balancing exercise". He said that:

> "The judge has not only to identify the factors he has taken into account, but to explain why he has given more weight to some, rather than to others. Either a failure to undertake this exercise, or for it to be impossible to discern from the terms of the judgment that it has been undertaken, vitiates the judicial conclusion, which remains unexplained."

7–219   In *Dixit v Dixit*[585] the order of the trial judge was held to be unsustainable because he had not considered its capital gains tax implications, thereby exercising his discretion without having regard to a material factor which should have affected it. In *Re Adams*[586] it was held that the judge had given undue weight to one particular aspect of the case. He refused an application for leave to bring proceedings out of time and, in doing so, attached decisive importance to the fact that the applicant had a cast iron claim against her solicitor. The Court of Appeal had no doubt that this approach was wrong in principle and gave leave for time to be extended. In *Espinosa v Bourke*[587] the appeal against the dismissal of the claim at first instance succeeded, it being held that the trial judge had ascribed too much weight to the claimant's conduct and not enough to her precarious financial position. The

[579] *Moody v Stevenson* [1992] Ch. 486, CA.
[580] *Cameron v Treasury Solicitor* [1996] 2 F.L.R. 716, CA.
[581] *Barrass v Harding* [2001] F.L.R. 138, CA.
[582] *Martin v Williams* [2017] EWHC 491 (Ch), Marcus Smith J, allowing the appeal against the order made in *Williams v Martin* [2016] W.T.L.R. 1075.
[583] *Re J (A Minor)* unreported 9 December 1991; *Tyler*, at p.572.
[584] *Cunliffe v Fielden* [2006] Ch. 361, CA, at [22]–[23].
[585] *Dixit v Dixit* unreported 23 June 1988; *Tyler*, p.541.
[586] Originally decided by the Court of Appeal, 16 July 1981, and reported as *Adams v Schofield* [2004] W.T.L.R. 1049, CA.
[587] *Espinosa v Bourke* [1999] 1 F.L.R. 747, CA.

first instance decision attracted the comment in *Ilott v Mitson*[588] that the judge's approach to the value judgment[589] he had to make was flawed and his decision could not stand.

In *Martin v Williams*, a case falling into the first category, the appeal   **7–220** succeeded on two further grounds. One was that the relief granted to the claimant at trial was substantially in excess of what was necessary to meet those needs and the decision to grant it was a perverse decision. The other was that the trial judge had wrongly dismissed the evidence of the defendant/appellant as to her financial needs in circumstances in which her evidence had not been challenged during cross-examination

(c) Fresh Evidence

The appeal court will not, unless it orders otherwise, receive evidence which   **7–221** was not before the lower court.[590] In the appeal to the Supreme Court in *Ilott v Mitson*,[591] submissions were made as to the date at which the facts fall to be assessed. The relevant part of the judgment reads:

"The answer is given by section 3(5). Where a court has to assess whether reasonable financial provision has been made, and/or what it should be, the relevant date is the date of hearing. Of course, on an appeal, if the question is whether the trial judge made an error of principle the facts and evidence must be taken as they stood before him. And if it should fall to the appellate court to remake the decision on the merits, as ordinarily it should not, any request to adduce further evidence will have to be judged by ordinary *Ladd v Marshall* principles."

It has yet to be decided whether s.3(5) precludes the admission of fresh   **7–222** evidence relating to circumstances which existed at the date of the hearing, but as to which evidence (or all the evidence) was not adduced. On a strict reading of the section it would appear that it does so; for the court is directed to have regard to facts known to it at the hearing, and there is no provision for receiving evidence which has since become available and could not have been obtained with reasonable diligence for use at the hearing. Nevertheless, if the evidence sought to be adduced also satisfies the other two *Ladd v Marshall* conditions, namely that it would probably have an important (though not necessarily decisive) influence on the course of the trial, and that it is credible (though not incontrovertible), it may, arguably, be admitted on the basis that that it would be an affront to one's sense of fairness not to admit it. The guidance to that effect given in the commentary

---

[588] *Ilott v Mitson* [2012] 2 F.L.R. 170, CA, at [33].
[589] Arden LJ identified no less than three value judgments which the district judge made; see *Ilott v Mitson* [2012] 2 F.L.R. 170, CA, at [67].
[590] CPR r.52.21(2)(b). The commentary at para.52.21.3 states that the principles reflected in *Ladd v Marshall* [1954] 1 W.L.R. 1489, CA remain relevant and are matters which the Court of Appeal must consider in the exercise of its discretion; see *Hertfordshire Investments v Bubb* [2000] 1 W.L.R. 2318, CA, at 2325.
[591] *Ilott v Mitson* [2017] UKSC 17; [2017] 2 W.L.R. 979, at [25].

in the Supreme Court Practice 1999[592] is not reproduced in *Civil Procedure 2017*, which states that it remains the case that evidence of changed circumstances since the date of the original hearing should only be sparingly admitted.[593]

(d) Appealing a Consent Order

7–223   Much of the relevant law derives from cases in the matrimonial jurisdiction, though some basic contractual principles are also relevant.[594] Thus, it is well settled that a consent order can be set aside on the grounds of fraud or mistake.[595] However, parties who repent of the agreement arrived at and attempt to extricate themselves on the ground that they entered into a bad bargain or were given bad legal advice are unlikely to be able to do so.

7–224   In *Tibbs v Beresford-Webb*,[596] Miss Tibbs sought leave to appeal from an order made by Bennett J in Tomlin form, to which she had consented. The settlement was designed to compromise a 1975 Act claim on behalf of her and her son, out of the net estate of the late John Dick which was in the region of £300,000. Under the settlement, which was reached orally at the door of the court, she was to receive £10,000 and her son Jason, £6,750. She had been the deceased's mistress for some 30 years and Jason was the child of that relationship. When Miss Tibbs received the order from the court, drawn up from a draft minute of order, signed by counsel for herself and for her son, which was produced later, she wrote to the court stating that she did not agree that it was in full and final settlement of her claim. She sought leave to appeal on various grounds, one of which was that she consented to the order in the belief that it was an interim payment, and another that her claim had been substantially undervalued having regard to the circumstances of her relationship with the deceased.

7–225   Giving leave, the Court of Appeal considered that the cases of *Edgar v Edgar*[597] and *Camm v Camm*[598] might give some support to the proposition that a consent order could be set aside on the grounds of bad legal advice; alternatively, it might be arguable that the order made could be set aside on the ground of mistake. However, the appeal[599] was dismissed by the full court. Swinton-Thomas LJ, giving the only substantive judgment, found it difficult to accept, on reading the transcript, that Miss Tibbs and Jason had

---

[592] See, generally, the commentary to RSC Ord.59 at paras 59.10.11–159.10.9; the phrase "affront to one's sense of justice" is used at para.59.10.18(3).

[593] *Civil Procedure 2017*, para.52.21.3.

[594] See, generally, *Foskett*, Chs 4 ("Impeachment of a Compromise") covering incapacity, mistake, misrepresentation, duress and undue influence, and illegality, and 24, paras 24-080—24-119 ("Setting Aside Consent Orders"). That section relates to setting aside consent orders in matrimonial proceedings, but in Ch.25 ("Settlement of Inheritance Act Disputes") it is stated at para.25–16 that "It is thought that grounds similar to those available for setting aside a compromise of matrimonial ancillary relief applications will be available to set aside compromises of these proceedings".

[595] *De Lasala v De Lasala* [1980] A.C. 546.

[596] *Tibbs v Beresford-West* Unreported 18 December 1997, CA.

[597] *Edgar v Edgar* [1980] 1 W.L.R. 1410; [1980] 3 All E.R. 887.

[598] *Camm v Camm* (1983) 4 F.L.R. 577; (1983) 13 Fam. Law 112.

[599] Reported as *Tibbs v Dick* [1998] 2 F.L.R. 1118.

been led to believe by their advisers that the payments were interim payments; but in any event, even had she been under such a misapprehension, that would not have been a ground for setting aside the order.

Further, even if it had been clear that she had received bad or negligent **7–226** legal advice, that in itself would not be a ground for setting aside the order. *Edgar* was concerned, not with a consent order, but with the enforcement of an agreement entered into between the parties, which had not yet been embodied in an order of the court,[600] and bad advice was relevant only to the question whether the agreement should be enforced.[601] Ward LJ had arrived at a similar conclusion in *Harris v Manahan*,[602] where he said:

> "Where the vitiating factor is said to be bad advice, then I can imagine circumstances where bad advice gives rise to a mistaken belief which, if shared by the other side, may enable the underlying agreement to be attacked on the ground of mistake. I find it very difficult to envisage a cause of action in which the negligence of one's own solicitor justifies the setting aside of an agreement made with a third party."

The Court of Appeal has held, in *Scammell v Dicker*,[603] that it is theoretically possible to declare a consent order void on the ground of uncertainty, but, given that the court was always on hand to assist in the working out or clarification of its orders, it could not be a mere difficulty in interpretation or execution that could undo what, with due formality, had been entered as an order of the court in settlement of litigation before it.

14.—ADMINISTRATION AND DISTRIBUTION OF THE ESTATE

(a) Duties and Liabilities of Personal Representatives

Under the general law, personal representatives have a statutory duty to **7–227** collect and get in the real and personal estate of the deceased and administer it according to law, and that duty is to be carried out with reasonable diligence.[604] The process of administration may be regarded as being complete when all assets have been got in, and all debts and liabilities (including Inheritance Tax due on the death of the deceased) have been paid, or provision has been made for their payment, but it was held in *Harvell v Foster*[605] that, where a personal representative has in their hands assets to which another is beneficially entitled, they remain liable for them in their capacity

---

[600] As was also the case in *Camm v Camm*; see *L v L* [2008] 1 F.L.R. 26 at 43.
[601] *Camm* was not referred to in the judgment; it was a case where the wife had entered into the agreement under extreme pressure and the court considered it to be unfair and unjust that she should be held to it.
[602] *Harris v Manahan* [1997] 1 F.L.R. 205. Munby J arrived at the same conclusion in *L v L* [2008] 1 F.L.R. 26.
[603] *Scammell v Dicker* [2005] 3 All E.R. 838 at 846c per Rix LJ.
[604] Administration of Estates Act 1925 ss.9 and 25.
[605] *Harvell v Foster* [1954] 2 Q.B. 367.

as personal representative until they either obtain their discharge from liability in that capacity, or accounts for and pays them to the beneficiary.

7–228   Section 44 of the Administration of Estates Act 1925 provides that a
personal representative is not bound to distribute the estate of the deceased
before the expiry of one year from the date of death; thus, they cannot be
compelled to pay a legacy until that time has elapsed. However s.5 of the
1975 Act enables the court to make an order for interim payment, which
may well be expressed to take effect before the year has elapsed. In such
circumstances, the personal representative may not be certain whether there
are sufficient assets available out of which to make the payment ordered;
consequently s.20(2), which is discussed below, affords them a measure of
protection.

7–229   A beneficiary has no interest, legal or equitable, in any unadministered
asset of the deceased's estate; their position is that they have a chose in
action to have the estate properly administered.[606] Thus, they may follow
and recover assets which have been improperly abstracted from the estate,
but they do so on behalf of the estate, because the assets, when recovered,
are restored for use in the due administration of the estate; or they may
bring an action under CPR Pt 64 (replacing the previous RSC Ord.85) to
have the estate administered by the court. If a personal representative
commits any breach of the duties of their office, which results in a loss to the
estate, they are said to have committed a *devastavit*, that is, they have wasted
the assets; and they are personally liable to beneficiaries and creditors for
any such loss. Such breaches include failure to preserve the estate, to pay
debts with due diligence, and to distribute the estate to the persons properly
entitled under the deceased's will or intestacy.

7–230   A personal representative may also have duties in respect of the trusts of
the testator's will, and may be liable for any loss occasioned by breach of
those trusts. In respect of those potential liabilities s.61 of the Trustee Act
1925 confers on the court a discretionary power to relieve the personal
representative either wholly or in part from personal liability for any breach
of trust, or any breach of the duties incident to the office of a personal
representative, if it appears to the court that the personal representative has
acted honestly and reasonably and ought fairly to be excused from the
breach of trust and for omitting to obtain the direction of the court in the
matter in which they committed such breach. In that context, "fairly" means
in fairness to the executor and to other people who may be affected.[607] One
situation in which it might be necessary for the discretion to be invoked is
where the personal representatives have made an interim distribution
without obtaining a court order.[608]

[606] *Commissioner of Stamp Duties (Queensland) v Livingston* [1965] A.C. 694, PC.
[607] *Marsden v Regan* [1954] 1 All E.R. 475, CA, per Evershed MR.
[608] Trustees may also be faced with a problem where a 1975 Act claim is made for provision out
of an estate and the will creates a life interest trust. The trustees may well be reluctant to
constitute the trust fund while the claim is on foot but, if the claim eventually failed or the
award was such that it could have been met from assets of the estate not subject to the
trusts, they might be exposed to a claim for breach of trust in that, by failing to constitute
the trust fund, they had deprived the trust of both income and capital appreciation.

Since, by s.19(1) of the 1975 Act, any order made under s.2 has, and is   **7–231**
deemed to have, effect from the date of the deceased's death subject to any
provisions of the order, a successful applicant is in the same position as a
beneficiary under the will or intestacy, and, subject to any protection
afforded to a personal representative by the 1975 Act, has the same remedies. It has been held in *O'Brien v Seagrave*[609] that a person with a right to
make a claim for an order under s.2 of the 1975 Act had a sufficient interest
for the purpose of r.57.7(1)[610] to proceed with a probate claim. In *Randall v
Randall*[611] it was held that a creditor of a beneficiary also had a sufficient
interest, since his interest is to ensure that the beneficiary received what was
due to them under the will or intestacy. It would seem to follow, therefore,
that a creditor of a 1975 Act claimant would have a sufficient interest.

(b) Statutory Protection for Personal Representatives

Section 20 of the 1975 Act relieves personal representatives from liability in   **7–232**
certain circumstances. Section 20(1) operates in respect of a distribution of
any part of the estate of the deceased made after the end of the period of six
months from the date on which the grant of representation was first taken
out, and exempts the personal representative from liability on the ground
that they ought to have taken into account the possibility that (a) the court
might permit the making of an application under s.2 after the end of the
period, or (b) might vary, in accordance with s.6, an order made under s.2.
However, the provision does not address the situation where a claim has
been issued, but the claim form has not been served, within the time limit. It
is more prudent not to distribute until the time limited for service has
expired.

Section 20(2) operates in respect of any payment made in consequence of   **7–233**
an order under s.5 where the estate is not sufficient to make the payment,
provided that at the time of making the payment the personal representative
had no reasonable cause to believe that the estate was insufficient. Section
20(3) relates to meeting the liability of the estate under a contract to leave
property by will; and in addition s.12(4) protects the personal representative
of a donee who has received property which might be the subject of an
application under ss.10 or 11, provided they have no notice, at the time
when they distribute it, of the making of such an application. The 1975 Act
affords no protection in respect of any distribution made before the expiry
of the six-month period, so personal representatives cannot rely on the
protection afforded by advertisements under s.27 of the Trustee Act 1925 if
the notice expires within that period.

---

[609] *O'Brien v Seagrave* [2007] 1 W.L.R. 2002; [2007] 3 All E.R. 633. The claim in that case was
for revocation of a common-form grant.
[610] The claim form must contain a statement of the nature of the interest of the claimant and of
each defendant in the estate.
[611] *Randall v Randall* [2016] EWCA Civ 494; [2015] W.T.L.R. 99, CA, in which *O'Brien v
Seagrave* was approved.

(c) Preservation of Property During Litigation

7–234   Generally speaking, the court's power to preserve property during litigation is exercised under CPR Pt 25, Section I of which is concerned with interim remedies.[612] Under s.37 of the Matrimonial Causes Act 1973, the court has wide powers to make orders preventing the carrying out of any disposition of, or dealing with the property which is about to take place, provided that it is satisfied that the intended transaction is to be entered into with a view to defeating a claim for financial provision. However, there is no provision in the 1975 Act corresponding to s.37(2)(a) of the 1973 Act, which enables the court:

> "...if it is satisfied that the other party to the proceedings is, with the intention of defeating the claim for financial relief, about to make any disposition or to transfer out of the jurisdiction or otherwise deal with any property, make such order as it thinks fit for restraining the other party from so doing or otherwise for protecting the claim."

7–235   Under the 1938 Act there was no power to make orders awarding property to applicants in specie, and it was held in *Re Ferrar's Application*[613] that the court had no jurisdiction to prevent the personal representatives from selling the house in which the applicant (the former wife of the deceased) and her children were living. However, such powers do exist under the 1975 Act, since ss.2(1)(c) and (d) enable the court to make orders for the transfer or settlement of property. It was therefore said in *Re Kozdrach*[614] that the court has power to make orders preserving specific assets during an application. In *Sobesto v Farren*,[615] a claim under s.1(1)(e), the executor wished to sell a house in order to get on with the administration of the estate, but it was contended, on behalf of the applicant, that the most suitable way of making provision for her would be to transfer the house to her. An order was made restraining the sale of the house until trial; and, at the trial, which took place 17 months later, the applicant was awarded a lump sum of £19,000 on terms that if she paid the estate a further £9,000 within six months, the house should be transferred to her, presumably in satisfaction of the lump sum award.

7–236   In practice, what usually seems to happen in situations of the type described above is that the personal representatives bring possession proceedings, which are directed to be heard on the same occasion as after the 1975 Act application. Thus in *Re Coventry*, where the estate consisted, substantially, of the deceased's interest in a dwelling-house, the litigation began with an action for possession in the County Court, commenced by the beneficiary under the will. The applicant then brought proceedings under

---

[612] See the commentary in *Civil Procedure 2017*, para.25.1.25.6 (example of order to restrain disposal of assets).
[613] *Re Ferrar's Application* [1966] P. 126.
[614] *Re Kozdrach* [1981] Conv. 224.
[615] *Sobesto v Farren* unreported 9 November 1979. This was an interlocutory appeal in the case of *Kozdrach* (see previous footnote) and is noted in *Tyler*, p.652.

the 1975 Act, and the possession proceedings were transferred to the High Court and directed to be tried with the 1975 Act application.

APPENDIX 1

INHERITANCE (PROVISION FOR FAMILY AND DEPENDANTS) ACT 1975

1975 CHAPTER 63

An Act to make fresh provision for empowering the court to make orders   **A–001**
for the making out of the estate of a deceased person of provision for the
spouse, former spouse, child, child of the family or dependant of that person; and for matters connected therewith.   [12th November 1975]

1.—Application for financial provision from deceased's estate.

(1) Where after the commencement of this Act a person dies domiciled in   **A–002**
England and Wales and is survived by any of the following persons:—

    (a) the spouse or civil partner of the deceased;
    (b) a former spouse or former civil partner of the deceased, but not
         one who has formed a subsequent marriage or civil partnership;
   (ba) any person (not being a person included in paragraph (a) or (b)
         above) to whom subsection (1A) or (1B) below applies;
    (c) a child of the deceased;
    (d) any person (not being a child of the deceased) who in relation to
         any marriage or civil partnership to which the deceased was at any
         time a party, or otherwise in relation to any family in which the
         deceased at any time stood in the role of a parent, was treated by
         the deceased as a child of the family;
    (e) any person (not being a person included in the foregoing para-
         graphs of this subsection) who immediately before the death of the
         deceased was being maintained, either wholly or partly, by the
         deceased;

that person may apply to the court for an order under section 2 of this Act
on the ground that the disposition of the deceased's estate effected by his will
or the law relating to intestacy, or the combination of his will and that law,
is not such as to make reasonable financial provision for the applicant.
(1A) This subsection applies to a person if the deceased died on or after 1st
January 1996 and, during the whole of the period of two years ending
immediately before the date when the deceased died, the person was living—

    (a) in the same household as the deceased, and
    (b) as the husband or wife of the deceased.

(1B) This subsection applies to a person if for the whole of the period of two years ending immediately before the date when the deceased died the person was living—

(a) in the same household as the deceased, and
(b) as the civil partner of the deceased.

(2) In this Act "reasonable financial provision"—

(a) in the case of an application made by virtue of subsection (1)(a) above by the husband or wife of the deceased (except where the marriage with the deceased was the subject of a decree of judicial separation and at the date of death the decree was in force and the separation was continuing), means such financial provision as it would be reasonable in all the circumstances of the case for a husband or wife to receive, whether or not that provision is required for his or her maintenance;

(aa) in the case of an application made by virtue of subsection (1)(a) above by the civil partner of the deceased (except where, at the date of death, a separation order under Chapter 2 of Part 2 of the Civil Partnership Act 2004 was in force in relation to the civil partnership and the separation was continuing), means such financial provision as it would be reasonable in all the circumstances of the case for a civil partner to receive, whether or not that provision is required for his or her maintenance;

(b) in the case of any other application made by virtue of subsection (1) above, means such financial provision as it would be reasonable in all the circumstances of the case for the applicant to receive for his maintenance.

(2A) The reference in subsection (1)(d) above to a family in which the deceased stood in the role of a parent includes a family of which the deceased was the only member (apart from the applicant).

(3) For the purposes of subsection (1)(e) above, a person is to be treated as being maintained by the deceased (either wholly or partly, as the case may be) only if the deceased was making a substantial contribution in money or money's worth towards the reasonable needs of that person, other than a contribution made for full valuable consideration pursuant to an arrangement of a commercial nature.

2.—Powers of court to make orders.

A–003 (1) Subject to the provisions of this Act, where an application is made for an order under this section, the court may, if it is satisfied that the disposition of the deceased's estate effected by his will or the law relating to intestacy, or the combination of his will and that law, is not such as to make reasonable financial provision for the applicant, make any one or more of the following orders:—

(a) an order for the making to the applicant out of the net estate of the deceased of such periodical payments and for such term as may be specified in the order;

(b) an order for the payment to the applicant out of that estate of a lump sum of such amount as may be so specified;

(c) an order for the transfer to the applicant of such property comprised in that estate as may be so specified;

(d) an order for the settlement for the benefit of the applicant of such property comprised in that estate as may be so specified;

(e) an order for the acquisition out of property comprised in that estate of such property as may be so specified and for the transfer of the property so acquired to the applicant or for the settlement thereof for his benefit;

(f) an order varying any ante-nuptial or post-nuptial settlement (including such a settlement made by will) made on the parties to a marriage to which the deceased was one of the parties, the variation being for the benefit of the surviving party to that marriage, or any child of that marriage, or any person who was treated by the deceased as a child of the family in relation to that marriage;

(g) an order varying any settlement made—

(i) during the subsistence of a civil partnership formed by the deceased, or

(ii) in anticipation of the formation of a civil partnership by the deceased, on the civil partners (including such a settlement made by will), the variation being for the benefit of the surviving civil partner, or any child of both the civil partners, or any person who was treated by the deceased as a child of the family in relation to that civil partnership.

(h) an order varying for the applicant's benefit the trusts on which the deceased's estate is held (whether arising under the will, or the law relating to intestacy, or both).

(2) An order under subsection (1)(a) above providing for the making out of the net estate of the deceased of periodical payments may provide for—

(a) payments of such amount as may be specified in the order,

(b) payments equal to the whole of the income of the net estate or of such portion thereof as may be so specified,

(c) payments equal to the whole of the income of such part of the net estate as the court may direct to be set aside or appropriated for the making out of the income thereof of payments under this section,

or may provide for the amount of the payments or any of them to be determined in any other way the court thinks fit.

(3) Where an order under subsection (1)(a) above provides for the making of payments of an amount specified in the order, the order may direct that such part of the net estate as may be so specified shall be set aside or appropriated for the making out of the income thereof of those payments; but no larger part of the net estate shall be so set aside or appropriated than is sufficient, at the date of the order, to produce by the income thereof the amount required for the making of those payments.

(3A) In assessing for the purposes of an order under this section the extent (if any) to which the net estate is reduced by any debts or liabilities (including any inheritance tax paid or payable out of the estate), the court may assume that the order has already been made.

(4) An order under this section may contain such consequential and supplemental provisions as the court thinks necessary or expedient for the purpose of giving effect to the order or for the purpose of securing that the order operates fairly as between one beneficiary of the estate of the deceased and another and may, in particular, but without prejudice to the generality of this subsection—

  (a) order any person who holds any property which forms part of the net estate of the deceased to make such payment or transfer such property as may be specified in the order;

  (b) vary the disposition of the deceased's estate effected by the will or the law relating to intestacy, or by both the will and the law relating to intestacy, in such manner as the court thinks fair and reasonable having regard to the provisions of the order and all the circumstances of the case;

  (c) confer on the trustees of any property which is the subject of an order under this section such powers as appear to the court to be necessary or expedient.

3.—Matters to which court is to have regard in exercising powers under s.2.

A–004   (1) Where an application is made for an order under section 2 of this Act, the court shall, in determining whether the disposition of the deceased's estate effected by his will or the law relating to intestacy, or the combination of his will and that law, is such as to make reasonable financial provision for the applicant and, if the court considers that reasonable financial provision has not been made, in determining whether and in what manner it shall exercise its powers under that section, have regard to the following matters, that is to say—

  (a) the financial resources and financial needs which the applicant has or is likely to have in the foreseeable future;

  (b) the financial resources and financial needs which any other applicant for an order under section 2 of this Act has or is likely to have in the foreseeable future;

  (c) the financial resources and financial needs which any beneficiary of the estate of the deceased has or is likely to have in the foreseeable future;

  (d) any obligations and responsibilities which the deceased had towards any applicant for an order under the said section 2 or towards any beneficiary of the estate of the deceased;

  (e) the size and nature of the net estate of the deceased;

  (f) any physical or mental disability of any applicant for an order under the said section 2 or any beneficiary of the estate of the deceased;

  (g) any other matter, including the conduct of the applicant or any other person, which in the circumstances of the case the court may consider relevant.

(2) This subsection applies, without prejudice to the generality of paragraph (g) of subsection (1) above, where an application for an order under section

2 of this Act is made by virtue of section 1(1)(a) or (b) of this Act. The court shall, in addition to the matters specifically mentioned in paragraphs (a) to (f) of that subsection, have regard to—

 (a) the age of the applicant and the duration of the marriage or civil partnership;

 (b) the contribution made by the applicant to the welfare of the family of the deceased, including any contribution made by looking after the home or caring for the family.

In the case of an application by the wife or husband of the deceased, the court shall also, unless at the date of death a decree of judicial separation was in force and the separation was continuing, have regard to the provision which the applicant might reasonably have expected to receive if on the day on which the deceased died the marriage, instead of being terminated by death, had been terminated by a degree of divorce; but nothing requires the court to treat such provision as setting an upper or lower limit on the provision which may be made by an order under section 2.

In the case of an application by the civil partner of the deceased, the court shall also, unless at the date of the death a separation order under Chapter 2 of Part 2 of the Civil Partnership Act 2004 was in force and the separation was continuing, have regard to the provision which the applicant might reasonably have expected to receive if on the day on which the deceased died the civil partnership, instead of being terminated by death, had been terminated by a dissolution order; but nothing requires the court to treat such provision as setting an upper or lower limit on the provision which may be made by an order under section 2.

(2A) Without prejudice to the generality of paragraph (g) of subsection (1) above, where an application for an order under section 2 of this Act is made by virtue of section 1(1)(ba) of this Act, the court shall, in addition to the matters specifically mentioned in paragraphs (a) to (f) of that subsection, have regard to—

 (a) the age of the applicant and the length of the period during which the applicant lived as the husband or wife or civil partner of the deceased and in the same household as the deceased;

 (b) the contribution made by the applicant to the welfare of the family of the deceased, including any contribution made by looking after the home or caring for the family.

(3) Without prejudice to the generality of paragraph (g) of subsection (1) above, where an application for an order under section 2 of this Act is made by virtue of section 1(1)(c) or 1(1)(d) of this Act, the court shall, in addition to the matters specifically mentioned in paragraphs (a) to (f) of that subsection, have regard to the manner in which the applicant was being or in which he might expect to be educated or trained, and where the application is made by virtue of section 1(1)(d) the court shall also have regard—

 (a) to whether the deceased maintained the applicant and, if so, to the length of time for which and basis on which the deceased did so, and to the extent of the contribution made by way of maintenance;

    (aa) to whether and, if so, to what extent the deceased assumed
         responsibility for the maintenance of the applicant;
    (b) to whether in maintaining or assuming responsibility for main-
         taining the applicant the deceased did so knowing that the appli-
         cant was not his own child;
    (c) to the liability of any other person to maintain the applicant.

(4) Without prejudice to the generality of paragraph (g) of subsection (1) above, where an application for an order under section 2 of this Act is made by virtue of section 1(1)(e) of this Act, the court shall, in addition to the matters specifically mentioned in paragraphs (a) to (f) of that subsection, have regard—

    (a) to the length of time for which and basis on which the deceased
         maintained the applicant, and to the extent of the contribution
         made by way of maintenance;
    (b) to whether and, if so, to what extent the deceased assumed
         responsibility for the maintenance of the applicant.

(5) In considering the matters to which the court is required to have rd under this section, the court shall take into account the facts as known to the court at the date of the hearing.

(6) In considering the financial resources of any person for the purposes of this section the court shall take into account his earning capacity and in considering the financial needs of any person for the purposes of this section the court shall take into account his financial obligations and responsibilities.

4. Time-limit for applications.

A–005   An application for an order under section 2 of this Act shall not, except with the permission of the court, be made after the end of the period of six months from the date on which representation with respect to the estate of the deceased is first taken out (but nothing prevents the making of an application before such representation is first taken out).

5.—Interim orders.

A–006   (1) Where on an application for an order under section 2 of this Act it appears to the court—

    (a) that the applicant is in immediate need of financial assistance, but
         it is not yet possible to determine what order (if any) should be
         made under that section; and
    (b) that property forming part of the net estate of the deceased is or
         can be made available to meet the need of the applicant;

the court may order that, subject to such conditions or restrictions, if any, as the court may impose and to any further order of the court, there shall be paid to the applicant out of the net estate of the deceased such sum or sums and (if more than one) at such intervals as the court thinks reasonable; and the court may order that, subject to the provisions of this Act, such payments are to be made until such date as the court may specify, not being later than the date on which the court either makes an order under the said section 2 or decides not to exercise its powers under that section.

(2) Subsections (2), (3) and (4) of section 2 of this Act shall apply in relation to an order under this section as they apply in relation to an order under that section.

(3) In determining what order, if any, should be made under this section the court shall, so far as the urgency of the case admits, have regard to the same matters as those to which the court is required to have regard under section 3 of this Act.

(4) An order made under section 2 of this Act may provide that any sum paid to the applicant by virtue of this section shall be treated to such an extent and in such manner as may be provided by that order as having been paid on account of any payment provided for by that order.

6.—Variation, discharge etc. of orders for periodical payments.

(1) Subject to the provisions of this Act, where the court has made an order   **A–007**
under section 2(1)(a) of this Act (in this section referred to as "the original order") for the making of periodical payments to any person (in this section referred to as "the original recipient"), the court, on an application under this section, shall have power by order to vary or discharge the original order or to suspend any provision of it temporarily and to revive the operation of any provision so suspended.

(2) Without prejudice to the generality of subsection (1) above, an order made on an application for the variation of the original order may—

(a) provide for the making out of any relevant property of such periodical payments and for such term as may be specified in the order to any person who has applied, or would but for section 4 of this Act be entitled to apply, for an order under section 2 of this Act (whether or not, in the case of any application, an order was made in favour of the applicant);

(b) provide for the payment out of any relevant property of a lump sum of such amount as may be so specified to the original recipient or to any such person as is mentioned in paragraph (a) above;

(c) provide for the transfer of the relevant property, or such part thereof as may be so specified, to the original recipient or to any such person as is so mentioned.

(3) Where the original order provides that any periodical payments payable thereunder to the original recipient are to cease on the occurrence of an event specified in the order (other than the formation of a subsequent marriage or civil partnership by a former spouse or former civil partner) or on the expiration of a period so specified, then, if, before the end of the period of six months from the date of the occurrence of that event or of the expiration of that period, an application is made for an order under this section, the court shall have power to make any order which it would have had power to make if the application had been made before the date (whether in favour of the original recipient or any such person as is mentioned in subsection (2)(a) above and whether having effect from that date or from such later date as the court may specify).

(4) Any reference in this section to the original order shall include a reference to an order made under this section and any reference in this section to the original recipient shall include a reference to any person to whom periodical payments are required to be made by virtue of an order under this section.

(5) An application under this section may be made by any of the following persons, that is to say—

    (a)   any person who by virtue of section 1(1) of this Act has applied, or would but for section 4 of this Act be entitled to apply, for an order under section 2 of this Act,

    (b)   the personal representatives of the deceased,

    (c)   the trustees of any relevant property, and

    (d)   any beneficiary of the estate of the deceased.

(6) An order under this section may only affect—

    (a)   property the income of which is at the date of the order applicable wholly or in part for the making of periodical payments to any person who has applied for an order under this Act, or

    (b)   in the case of an application under subsection (3) above in respect of payments which have ceased to be payable on the occurrence of an event or the expiration of a period, property the income of which was so applicable immediately before the occurrence of that event or the expiration of that period, as the case may be,

and any such property as is mentioned in paragraph (a) or (b) above is in subsections (2) and (5) above referred to as "relevant property".

(7) In exercising the powers conferred by this section the court shall have regard to all the circumstances of the case, including any change in any of the matters to which the court was required to have regard when making the order to which the application relates.

(8) Where the court makes an order under this section, it may give such consequential directions as it thinks necessary or expedient having regard to the provisions of the order.

(9) No such order as is mentioned in sections 2(1)(d), (e) or (f), 9, 10 or 11 of this Act shall be made on an application under this section.

(10) For the avoidance of doubt it is hereby declared that, in relation to an order which provides for the making of periodical payments which are to cease on the occurrence of an event specified in the order (other than the formation of a subsequent marriage or civil partnership by a former spouse or former civil partner) or on the expiration of a period so specified, the power to vary an order includes power to provide for the making of periodical payments after the expiration that period or the occurrence of that event.

7.—Payment of lump sums by instalments.

A–008   (1) An order under section 2(1)(b) or 6(2)(b) of this Act for the payment of a lump sum may provide for the payment of that sum by instalments of such amount as may be specified in the order.

(2) Where an order is made by virtue of subsection (1) above, the court shall

have power, on an application made by the person to whom the lump sum is payable, by the personal representatives of the deceased or by the trustees of the property out of which the lump sum is payable, to vary that order by varying the number of instalments payable, the amount of any instalment and the date on which any instalment becomes payable.

Property available for financial provision

8.—Property treated as part of "net estate".

(1) Where a deceased person has in accordance with the provisions of any enactment nominated any person to receive any sum of money or other property on his death and that nomination is in force at the time of his death, that sum of money, after deducting therefrom any capital transfer tax payable in respect thereof, or that other property, to the extent of the value thereof at the date of the death of the deceased after deducting therefrom any capital transfer tax so payable, shall be treated for the purposes of this Act as part of the net estate of the deceased; but this subsection shall not render any person liable for having paid that sum or transferred that other property to the person named in the nomination in accordance with the directions given in the nomination.

A–009

(2) Where any sum of money or other property is received by any person as a *donatio mortis causa* made by a deceased person, that sum of money, after deducting therefrom any capital transfer tax payable thereon, or that other property, to the extent of the value thereof at the date of the death of the deceased after deducting therefrom any capital transfer tax so payable, shall be treated for the purposes of this Act as part of the net estate of the deceased; but this subsection shall not render any person liable for having paid that sum or transferred that other property in order to give effect to that *donatio mortis causa*.

(3) The amount of capital transfer tax to be deducted for the purposes of this section shall not exceed the amount of that tax which has been borne by the person nominated by the deceased or, as the case may be, the person who has received a sum of money or other property as a *donatio mortis causa*.

9.—Property held on a joint tenancy.

(1) Where a deceased person was immediately before his death beneficially entitled to a joint tenancy of any property, then, if an application is made for an order under section 2 of this Act, the court for the purpose of facilitating the making of financial provision for the applicant under this Act may order that the deceased's severable share of that property shall, to such extent as appears to the court to be just in all the circumstances of the case, be treated for the purposes of this Act as part of the net estate of the deceased.

A–010

(1A) Where an order is made under subsection (1) the value of the deceased's severable share of the property concerned is taken for the purposes of this Act to be the value that the share would have had at the date of the hearing of the application for an order under section 2 had the share been severed immediately before the deceased's death, unless the court orders that the share is to be valued at a different date.

(2) In determining the extent to which any severable share is to be treated as part of the net estate of the deceased by virtue of an order under subsection (1) above, the court shall have regard to any capital transfer tax payable in respect of that severable share.

(3) Where an order is made under subsection (1) above, the provisions of this section shall not render any person liable for anything done by him before the order was made.

(4) For the avoidance of doubt it is hereby declared that for the purposes of this section there may be a joint tenancy of a chose in action.

Powers of court in relation to transactions intended to defeat applications for financial provision

10.—Dispositions intended to defeat applications for financial provision.

A–011   (1) Where an application is made to the court for an order under section 2 of this Act, the applicant may, in the proceedings on that application, apply to the court for an order under subsection (2) below.

(2) Where on an application under subsection (1) above the court is satisfied—

    (a)   that, less than six years before the date of the death of the deceased, the deceased with the intention of defeating an application for financial provision under this Act made a disposition, and

    (b)   that full valuable consideration for that disposition was not given by the person to whom or for the benefit of whom the disposition was made (in this section referred to as "the donee") or by any other person, and

    (c)   that the exercise of the powers conferred by this section would facilitate the making of financial provision for the applicant under this Act,

then, subject to the provisions of this section and of sections 12 and 13 of this Act, the court may order the donee (whether or not at the date of the order he holds any interest in the property disposed of to him or for his benefit by the deceased) to provide, for the purpose of the making of that financial provision, such sum of money or other property as may be specified in the order.

(3) Where an order is made under subsection (2) above as respects any disposition made by the deceased which consisted of the payment of money to or for the benefit of the donee, the amount of any sum of money or the value of any property ordered to be provided under that subsection shall not exceed the amount of the payment made by the deceased after deducting therefrom any capital transfer tax borne by the donee in respect of that payment.

(4) Where an order is made under subsection (2) above as respects any disposition made by the deceased which consisted of the transfer of property (other than a sum of money) to or for the benefit of the donee, the amount of any sum of money or the value of any property ordered to be provided under that subsection shall not exceed the value at the date of the death of the deceased of the property disposed of by him to or for the benefit of the donee (or if that property has been disposed of by the person to whom it was

transferred by the deceased, the value at the date of that disposal thereof) after deducting therefrom any capital transfer tax borne by the donee in respect of the transfer of that property by the deceased.

(5) Where an application (in this subsection referred to as "the original application") is made for an order under subsection (2) above in relation to any disposition, then, if on an application under this subsection by the donee or by any applicant for an order under section 2 of this Act the court is satisfied—

(a) that, less than six years before the date of the death of the deceased, the deceased with the intention of defeating an application for financial provision under this Act made a disposition other than the disposition which is the subject of the original application, and

(b) that full valuable consideration for that other disposition was not given by the person to whom or for the benefit of whom that other disposition was made or by any other person,

the court may exercise in relation to the person to whom or for the benefit of whom that other disposition was made the powers which the court would have had under subsection (2) above if the original application had been made in respect of that other disposition and the court had been satisfied as to the matters set out in paragraphs (a), (b) and (c) of that subsection; and where any application is made under this subsection, any reference in this section (except in subsection (2)(b) to the donee shall include a reference to the person to whom or for the benefit of whom that other disposition was made.

(6) In determining whether and in what manner to exercise its powers under this section, the court shall have regard to the circumstances in which any disposition was made and any valuable consideration which was given therefor, the relationship, if any, of the donee to the deceased, the conduct and financial resources of the donee and all the other circumstances of the case.

(7) In this section "disposition" does not include—

(a) any provision in a will, any such nomination as is mentioned in section 8(1) of this Act or any *donatio mortis causa*, or

(b) any appointment of property made, otherwise than by will, in the exercise of a special power of appointment,

but, subject to these exceptions, includes any payment of money (including the payment of a premium under a policy of assurance) and any conveyance, assurance, appointment or gift of property of any description, whether made by an instrument or otherwise.

(8) The provisions of this section do not apply to any disposition made before the commencement of this Act.

11.—Contracts to leave property by will.

(1) Where an application is made to a court for an order under section 2 of this Act, the applicant may, in the proceedings on that application, apply to the court for an order under this section.

A–012

(2) Where on an application under subsection (1) above the court is satisfied—

    (a) that the deceased made a contract by which he agreed to leave by his will a sum of money or other property to any person or by which he agreed that a sum of money or other property would be paid or transferred to any person out of his estate, and

    (b) that the deceased made that contract with the intention of defeating an application for financial provision under this Act, and

    (c) that when the contract was made full valuable consideration for that contract was not given or promised by the person with whom or for the benefit of whom the contract was made (in this section referred to as "the donee") or by any other person, and

    (d) that the exercise of the powers conferred by this section would facilitate the making of financial provision for the applicant under this Act,

then, subject to the provisions of this section and of sections 12 and 13 of this Act, the court may make any one or more of the following orders, that is to say—

    (i) if any money has been paid or any other property has been transferred to or for the benefit of the donee in accordance with the contract, an order directing the donee to provide, for the purpose of the making of that financial provision, such sum of money or other property as may be specified in the order;

    (ii) if the money or all the money has not been paid or the property or all the property has not been transferred in accordance with the contract, an order directing the personal representatives not to make any payment or transfer any property, or not to make any further payment or transfer any further property, as the case may be, in accordance therewith or directing the personal representatives only to make such payment or transfer such property as may be specified in the order.

(3) Notwithstanding anything in subsection (2) above, the court may exercise its powers thereunder in relation to any contract made by the deceased only to the extent that the court considers that the amount of any sum of money paid or to be paid or the value of any property transferred or to be transferred in accordance with the contract exceeds the value of any valuable consideration given or to be given for that contract, and for this purpose the court shall have regard to the value of property at the date of the hearing.

(4) In determining whether and in what manner to exercise its powers under this section, the court shall have regard to the circumstances in which the contract was made, the relationship, if any, of the donee to the deceased, the conduct and financial resources of the donee and all the other circumstances of the case.

(5) Where an order has been made under subsection (2) above in relation to any contract, the rights of any person to enforce that contract or to recover damages or to obtain other relief for the breach thereof shall be subject to

any adjustment made by the court under section 12(3) of this Act and shall survive to such extent only as is consistent with giving effect to the terms of that order.

(6) The provisions of this section do not apply to a contract made before the commencement of this Act.

12.—Provisions supplementary to ss.10 and 11.

(1) Where the exercise of any of the powers conferred by section 10 or 11 of this Act is conditional on the court being satisfied that a disposition or contract was made by a deceased person with the intention of defeating an application for financial provision under this Act, that condition shall be fulfilled if the court is of the opinion that, on a balance of probabilities, the intention of the deceased (though not necessarily his sole intention) in making the disposition or contract was to prevent an order for financial provision being made under this Act or to reduce the amount of the provision which might otherwise be granted by an order thereunder.   A–013

(2) Where an application is made under section 11 of this Act with respect to any contract made by the deceased and no valuable consideration was given or promised by any person for that contract then, notwithstanding anything in subsection (1) above, it shall be presumed, unless the contrary is shown, that the deceased made that contract with the intention of defeating an application for financial provision under this Act.

(3) Where the court makes an order under section 10 or 11 of this Act it may give such consequential directions as it thinks fit (including directions requiring the making of any payment or the transfer of any property) for giving effect to the order or for securing a fair adjustment of the rights of the persons affected thereby.

(4) Any power conferred on the court by the said section 10 or 11 to order the donee, in relation to any disposition or contract, to provide any sum of money or other property shall be exercisable in like manner in relation to the personal representative of the donee, and—

(a)   any reference in section 10(4) to the disposal of property by the donee shall include a reference to disposal by the personal representative of the donee, and

(b)   any reference in section 10(5) to an application by the donee under that subsection shall include a reference to an application by the personal representative of the donee;

but the court shall not have power under the said section 10 or 11 to make an order in respect of any property forming part of the estate of the donee which has been distributed by the personal representative; and the personal representative shall not be liable for having distributed any such property before he has notice of the making of an application under the said section 10 or 11 on the ground that he ought to have taken into account the possibility that such an application would be made.

13.—Provisions as to trustees in relation to ss.10 and 11.

(1) Where an application is made for—   A–014

(a) an order under section 10 of this Act in respect of a disposition made by the deceased to any person as a trustee, or

(b) an order under section 11 of this Act in respect of any payment made or property transferred, in accordance with a contract made by the deceased, to any person as a trustee,

the powers of the court under the said section 10 or 11 to order that trustee to provide a sum of money or other property shall be subject to the following limitation (in addition, in a case of an application under section 10, to any provision regarding the deduction of capital transfer tax) namely, that the amount of any sum of money or the value of any property ordered to be provided—

(i) in the case of an application in respect of a disposition which consisted of the payment of money or an application in respect of the payment of money in accordance with a contract, shall not exceed the aggregate of so much of that money as is at the date of the order in the hands of the trustee and the value at that date of any property which represents that money or is derived therefrom and is at that date in the hands of the trustee;

(ii) in the case of an application in respect of a disposition which consisted of the transfer of property (other than a sum of money) or an application in respect of the transfer of property (other than a sum of money) in accordance with a contract, shall not exceed the aggregate of the value at the date of the order of so much of that property as is at that date in the hands of the trustee and the value at that date of any property which represents the first-mentioned property or is derived therefrom and is at that date in the hands of the trustee.

(2) Where any such application is made in respect of a disposition made to any person as a trustee or in respect of any payment made or property transferred in pursuance of a contract to any person as a trustee, the trustee shall not be liable for having distributed any money or other property on the ground that he ought to have taken into account the possibility that such an application would be made.

(3) Where any such application is made in respect of a disposition made to any person as a trustee or in respect of any payment made or property transferred in accordance with a contract to any person as a trustee, any reference in the said section 10 or 11 to the donee shall be construed as including a reference to the trustee or trustees for the time being of the trust in question and any reference in subsection (1) or (2) above to a trustee shall be construed in the same way.

14.—Provision as to cases where no financial relief was granted in divorce proceedings etc.

A–015   (1) Where, within twelve months from the date on which a decree of divorce or nullity of marriage has been made absolute or a decree of judicial separation has been granted, a party to the marriage dies and—

(a) an application for a financial provision order under section 23 of the Matrimonial Causes Act 1973 or a property adjustment order under section 24 of that Act has not been made by the other party to that marriage, or

(b) such an application has been made but the proceedings thereon have not been determined at the time of the death of the deceased,

then, if an application for an order under section 2 of this Act is made by that other party, the court shall, notwithstanding anything in section 1 or section 3 of this Act, have power, if it thinks it just to do so, to treat that party for the purposes of that application as if the decree of divorce or nullity of marriage had not been made absolute or the decree of judicial separation had not been granted, as the case may be.

(2) This section shall not apply in relation to a decree of judicial separation unless at the date of the death of the deceased the decree was in force and the separation was continuing.

14A.—Provision as to cases where no financial relief was granted in proceedings for the dissolution etc. of a civil partnership

(1) Subsection (2) below applies where–   A–016

(a) a dissolution order, nullity order, separation order or presumption of death order has been made under Chapter 2 of Part 2 of the Civil Partnership Act 2004 in relation to a civil partnership,

(b) one of the civil partners dies within twelve months from the date on which the order is made, and

(c) either—

(i) an application for a financial provision order under Part 1 of Schedule 5 to that Act or a property adjustment order under Part 2 of that Schedule has not been made by the other civil partner, or

(ii) such an application has been made but the proceedings on the application have not been determined at the time of the death of the deceased.

(2) If an application for an order under section 2 of this Act is made by the surviving civil partner, the court shall, notwithstanding anything in section 1 or section 3 of this Act, have power, if it thinks it just to do so, to treat the surviving civil partner as if the order mentioned in subsection (1)(a) above had not been made.

(3) This section shall not apply in relation to a separation order unless at the date of the death of the deceased the separation order was in force and the separation was continuing.

15.—Restriction imposed in divorce proceedings etc. on application under this Act.

(1) On the grant of a decree of divorce, a decree of nullity of marriage or a   A–017
decree of judicial separation or at any time thereafter the court, if it considers it just to do so, may, on the application of either party to the mar-

riage, order that the other party to the marriage shall not on the death of the applicant be entitled to apply for an order under section 2 of this Act.

In this subsection "the court" means the High Court or the family court.
(2) In the case of a decree of divorce or nullity of marriage an order may be made under subsection (1) above before or after the decree is made absolute, but if it is made before the decree is made absolute it shall not take effect unless the decree is made absolute.
(3) Where an order made under subsection (1) above on the grant of a decree of divorce or nullity of marriage has come into force with respect to a party to a marriage, then, on the death of the other party to that marriage, the court shall not entertain any application for an order under section 2 of this Act made by the first-mentioned party.
(4) Where an order made under subsection (1) above on the grant of a decree of judicial separation has come into force with respect to any party to a marriage, then, if the other party to that marriage dies while the decree is in force and the separation is continuing, the court shall not entertain any application for an order under section 2 of this Act made by the first-mentioned party.

15ZA.—Restriction imposed in proceedings for the dissolution etc. of a civil partnership on application under this Act

A–018 (1) On making a dissolution order, nullity order, separation order or presumption of death order under Chapter 2 of Part 2 of the Civil Partnership Act 2004, or at any time after making such an order, the court, if it considers it just to do so, may, on the application of either of the civil partners, order that the other civil partner shall not on the death of the applicant be entitled to apply for an order under section 2 of this Act.
(2) In subsection (1) above "the court" means the High Court or the family court.
(3) In the case of a dissolution order, nullity order or presumption of death order ("the main order") an order may be made under subsection (1) above before (as well as after) the main order is made final, but if made before the main order is made final it shall not take effect unless the main order is made final.
(4) Where an order under subsection (1) above made in connection with a dissolution order, nullity order or presumption of death order has come into force with respect to a civil partner, then, on the death of the other civil partner, the court shall not entertain any application for an order under section 2 of this Act made by the surviving civil partner.
(5) Where an order under subsection (1) above made in connection with a separation order has come into force with respect to a civil partner, then, if the other civil partner dies while the separation order is in force and the separation is continuing, the court shall not entertain any application for an order under section 2 of this Act made by the surviving civil partner.

15A.—Restriction imposed in proceedings under Matrimonial and Family Proceedings Act 1984 on application under this Act.

A–019 (1) On making an order under section 17 of the Matrimonial and Family Proceedings Act 1984 (orders for financial provision and property adjustment following overseas divorces, etc.) the court, if it considers it just to do so, may, on the application of either party to the marriage, order that the other party to the marriage shall not on the death of the applicant be entitled to apply for an order under section 2 of this Act.

In this subsection "the court" means the High Court or the family court.

(2) Where an order under subsection (1) above has been made with respect to a party to a marriage which has been dissolved or annulled, then, on the death of the other party to that marriage, the court shall not entertain an application under section 2 of this Act made by the first-mentioned party.

(3) Where an order under subsection (1) above has been made with respect to a party to a marriage the parties to which have been legally separated, then, if the other party to the marriage dies while the legal separation is in force, the court shall not entertain an application under section 2 of this Act made by the first-mentioned party.

15B.—Restriction imposed in proceedings under Schedule 7 to the Civil Partnership Act 2004 on application under this Act

(1) On making an order under paragraph 9 of Schedule 7 to the Civil **A–020** Partnership Act 2004 (orders for financial provision, property adjustment and pension-sharing following overseas dissolution etc. of civil partnership) the court, if it considers it just to do so, may, on the application of either of the civil partners, order that the other civil partner shall not on the death of the applicant be entitled to apply for an order under section 2 of this Act.

(2) In subsection (1) above "the court" means the High Court or the family court.

(3) Where an order under subsection (1) above has been made with respect to one of the civil partners in a case where a civil partnership has been dissolved or annulled, then, on the death of the other civil partner, the court shall not entertain an application under section 2 of this Act made by the surviving civil partner.

(4) Where an order under subsection (1) above has been made with respect to one of the civil partners in a case where civil partners have been legally separated, then, if the other civil partner dies while the legal separation is in force, the court shall not entertain an application under section 2 of this Act made by the surviving civil partner.

16.—Variation and discharge of secured periodical payments orders made under Matrimonial Causes Act 1973.

(1) Where an application for an order under section 2 of this Act is made to **A–021** the court by any person who was at the time of the death of the deceased entitled to payments from the deceased under a secured periodical payments order made under the Matrimonial Causes Act 1973 or Schedule 5 to the Civil Partnership Act 2004, then, in the proceedings on that application, the court shall have power, if an application is made under this section by that person or by the personal representative of the deceased, to vary or discharge that periodical payments order or to revive the operation of any provision thereof which has been suspended under section 31 of that Act of 1973 or Part 11 of that Schedule.

(2) In exercising the powers conferred by this section the court shall have

regard to all the circumstances of the case, including any order which the court proposes to make under section 2 or section 5 of this Act and any change (whether resulting from the death of the deceased or otherwise) in any of the matters to which the court was required to have regard when making the secured periodical payments order.

(3) The powers exercisable by the court under this section in relation to an order shall be exercisable also in relation to any instrument executed in pursuance of the order.

17.—Variation and revocation of maintenance agreements.

A–022　(1) Where an application for an order under section 2 of this Act is made to the court by any person who was at the time of the death of the deceased entitled to payments from the deceased under a maintenance agreement which provided for the continuation of payments under the agreement after the death of the deceased, then, in the proceedings on that application, the court shall have power, if an application is made under this section by that person or by the personal representative of the deceased, to vary or revoke that agreement.

(2) In exercising the powers conferred by this section the court shall have regard to all the circumstances of the case, including any order which the court proposes to make under section 2 or section 5 of this Act and any change (whether resulting from the death of the deceased or otherwise) in any of the circumstances in the light of which the agreement was made.

(3) If a maintenance agreement is varied by the court under this section the like consequences shall ensue as if the variation had been made immediately before the death of the deceased by agreement between the parties and for valuable consideration.

(4) In this section "maintenance agreement", in relation to a deceased person, means any agreement made, whether in writing or not and whether before or after the commencement of this Act, by the deceased with any person with whom he formed a marriage or civil partnership, being an agreement which contained provisions governing the rights and liabilities towards one another when living separately of the parties to that marriage or of the civil partners (whether or not the marriage or civil partnership has been dissolved or annulled) in respect of the making or securing of payments or the disposition or use of any property, including such rights and liabilities with respect to the maintenance or education of any child, whether or not a child of the deceased or a person who was treated by the deceased as a child of the family in relation to that marriage.

18.—Availability of court's powers under this Act in applications under ss. 31 and 36 of the Matrimonial Causes Act 1973.

A–023　(1) Where—

    (a)　a person against whom a secured periodical payments order was made under the Matrimonial Causes Act 1973 has died and an application is made under section 31(6) of that Act for the variation or discharge of that order or for the revival of the operation of any provision thereof which has been suspended, or

(b) a party to a maintenance agreement within the meaning of section 34 of that Act has died, the agreement being one which provides for the continuation of payments thereunder after the death of one of the parties, and an application is made under section 36(1) of that Act for the alteration of the agreement under section 35 thereof,

the court shall have power to direct that the application made under the said section 31(6) or 36(1) shall be deemed to have been accompanied by an application for an order under section 2 of this Act.

(2) Where the court gives a direction under subsection (1) above it shall have power, in the proceedings on the application under the said section 31(6) or 36(1), to make any order which the court would have had power to make under the provisions of this Act if the application under the said section 31(6) or 36(1), as the case may be, had been made jointly with an application for an order under the said section 2; and the court shall have power to give such consequential directions as may be necessary for enabling the court to exercise any of the powers available to the court under this Act in the case of an application for an order under section 2.

(3) Where an order made under section 15(1) of this Act is in force with respect to a party to a marriage, the court shall not give a direction under subsection (1) above with respect to any application made under the said section 31(6) or 36(1) by that party on the death of the other party.

18A.—Availability of court's powers under this Act in applications under paragraphs 60 and 73 of Schedule 5 to the Civil Partnership Act 2004

(1) Where—   A–024

(a) a person against whom a secured periodical payments order was made under Schedule 5 to the Civil Partnership Act 2004 has died and an application is made under paragraph 60 of that Schedule for the variation or discharge of that order or for the revival of the operation of any suspended provision of the order, or

(b) a party to a maintenance agreement within the meaning of Part 13 of that Schedule has died, the agreement being one which provides for the continuation of payments under the agreement after the death of one of the parties, and an application is made under paragraph 73 of that Schedule for the alteration of the agreement under paragraph 69 of that Schedule,

the court shall have power to direct that the application made under paragraph 60 or 73 of that Schedule shall be deemed to have been accompanied by an application for an order under section 2 of this Act.

(2) Where the court gives a direction under subsection (1) above it shall have power, in the proceedings on the application under paragraph 60 or 73 of that Schedule, to make any order which the court would have had power to make under the provisions of this Act if the application under that paragraph had been made jointly with an application for an order under section 2 of this Act; and the court shall have power to give such consequential directions as may be necessary for enabling the court to exercise any of the

powers available to the court under this Act in the case of an application for an order under section 2.

(3) Where an order made under section 15ZA(1) of this Act is in force with respect to a civil partner, the court shall not give a direction under subsection (1) above with respect to any application made under paragraph 60 or 73 of that Schedule by that civil partner on the death of the other civil partner.

Miscellaneous and supplementary provisions

19.—Effect, duration and form of orders.

A–025 (1) Where an order is made under section 2 of this Act then for all purposes, including the purposes of the enactments relating to capital transfer tax, the will or the law relating to intestacy, or both the will and the law relating to intestacy, as the case may be, shall have effect and be deemed to have had effect as from the deceased's death subject to the provisions of the order.

(2) Any order made under section 2 or 5 of this Act in favour of—

 (a) an applicant who was the former spouse or former civil partner of the deceased,

 (b) an applicant who was the husband or wife of the deceased in a case where the marriage with the deceased was the subject of a decree of judicial separation and at the date of death the decree was in force and the separation was continuing,

 (c) an applicant who was the civil partner of the deceased in a case where, at the date of death, a separation order under Chapter 2 of Part 2 of the Civil Partnership Act 2004 was in force in relation to their civil partnership and the separation was continuing,

shall, in so far as it provides for the making of periodical payments, cease to have effect on the formation by the applicant of a subsequent marriage or civil partnership, except in relation to any arrears due under the order on the date of the formation of the subsequent marriage or civil partnership.

(3) A copy of every order made under this Act other than an order made under section 15(1) or 15ZA(1) of this Act shall be sent to the principal registry of the Family Division for entry and filing, and a memorandum of the order shall be endorsed on, or permanently annexed to, the probate or letters of administration under which the estate is being administered.

20.—Provisions as to personal representatives.

A–026 (1) The provisions of this Act shall not render the personal representative of a deceased person liable for having distributed any part of the estate of the deceased, after the end of the period of six months from the date on which representation with respect to the estate of the deceased is first taken out, on the ground that he ought to have taken into account the possibility—

 (a) that the court might permit the making of an application for an order under section 2 of this Act after the end of that period, or

 (b) that, where an order has been made under the said section 2, the court might exercise in relation thereto the powers conferred on it by section 6 of this Act, but this subsection shall not prejudice any power to recover, by reason of the making of an order under this Act, any part of the estate so distributed. (2) Where the personal representative of a deceased person pays any sum directed by an order under section 5 of this Act to be paid out of the deceased's net estate, he shall not be under any liability by reason of that estate not being sufficient to make the payment, unless at the time of making the payment he has reasonable cause to believe that the estate is not sufficient. (3) Where a deceased person entered into a contract by which the agreed to leave by his will any sum of money or other property to any person or by which he agreed that a sum of money or other property would be paid or transferred to any person out of his estate, then, if the personal representative of the deceased has reason to believe that the deceased entered into the contract with the intention of defeating an application for financial provision under this Act, he may, notwithstanding anything in that contract, postpone the payment of that sum of money or the transfer of that property until the expiration of the period of six months from the date on which representation with respect to the estate of the deceased is first taken out or, if during that period an application is made for an order under section 2 of this Act, until the determination of the proceedings on that application.

21. [Repealed by the Civil Evidence Act 1995, Sch.2] A–027

22. [Repealed by the Administration of Justice Act 1982, s.75 and Sch.9, Pt I] A–028

23. Determination of date on which representation was first taken out.

(1) The following are to be left out of account when considering for the purposes of this Act when representation with respect to the estate of a deceased person was first taken out— A–029

    (a) a grant limited to settled land or to trust property,
    (b) any other grant that does not permit any of the estate to be distributed,
    (c) a grant limited to real estate or to personal estate, unless a grant limited to the remainder of the estate has previously been made or is made at the same time,
    (d) a grant, or its equivalent, made outside the United Kingdom (but see subsection (2) below).

(2) A grant sealed under section 2 of the Colonial Probates Act 1892 counts as a grant made in the United Kingdom for the purposes of this section, but is to be taken as dated on the date of sealing.

24. Effect of this Act on s.46(1)(vi) of Administration of Estates Act 1925.

Section 46(1)(vi) of the Administration of Estates Act 1925, in so far as it provides for the devolution of property on the Crown, the Duchy of Lancaster or the Duke of Cornwall as bona vacantia, shall have effect subject to the provisions of this Act. A–030

25.—Interpretation.

A–031   (1) In this Act—

"beneficiary", in relation to the estate of a deceased person, means—

    (a) a person who under the will of the deceased or under the law relating to intestacy is beneficially interested in the estate or would be so interested if an order had not been made under this Act, and

    (b) a person who has received any sum of money or other property which by virtue of section 8(1) or 8(2) of this Act is treated as part of the net estate of the deceased or would have received that sum or other property if an order had not been made under this Act;

"child" includes an illegitimate child and a child en ventre sa mère at the death of the deceased;

"the court" means unless the context otherwise requires the High Court, or where the county court has jurisdiction by virtue of section 25 of the County Courts Act 1984, the county court;

"former civil partner" means a person whose civil partnership with the deceased was during the lifetime of the deceased either—

    (a) dissolved or annulled by an order made under the law of any part of the British Islands, or

    (b) dissolved or annulled in any country or territory outside the British Islands by a dissolution or annulment which is entitled to be recognised as valid by the law of England and Wales;

"former spouse" means a person whose marriage with the deceased was during the lifetime of the deceased either—

    (a) dissolved or annulled by a decree of divorce or a decree of nullity of marriage granted under the law of any part of the British Islands, or

    (b) dissolved or annulled in any country or territory outside the British Islands by a divorce or annulment which is entitled to be recognised as valid by the law of England and Wales;

"net estate", in relation to a deceased person, means:—

    (a) all property of which the deceased had power to dispose by his will (otherwise than by virtue of a special power of appointment) less the amount of his funeral, testamentary and administration expenses, debts and liabilities, including any capital transfer tax payable out of his estate on his death;

    (b) any property in respect of which the deceased held a general power of appointment (not being a power exercisable by will) which has not been exercised;

    (c) any sum of money or other property which is treated for the purposes of this Act as part of the net estate of the deceased by virtue of section 8(1) or (2) of this Act;

(d) any property which is treated for the purposes of this Act as part of the net estate of the deceased by virtue of an order made under section 9 of the Act;

(e) any sum of money or other property which is, by reason of a disposition or contract made by the deceased, ordered under section 10 or 11 of this Act to be provided for the purpose of the making of financial provision under this Act;

"property" includes any chose in action;
"reasonable financial provision" has the meaning assigned to it by section 1 of this Act;
"valuable consideration" does not include marriage or a promise of marriage;
"will" includes codicil.

(2) For the purposes of paragraph (a) of the definition of "net estate" in subsection (1) above a person who is not of full age and capacity shall be treated as having power to dispose by will of all property of which he would have had power to dispose by will if he had been of full age and capacity.
(3) Any reference in this Act to provision out of the net estate of a deceased person includes a reference to provision extending to the whole of that estate.
(4) For the purposes of this Act any reference to a spouse, wife or husband shall be treated as including a reference to a person who in good faith entered into a void marriage with the deceased unless either—

(a) the marriage of the deceased and that person was dissolved or annulled during the lifetime of the deceased and the dissolution or annulment is recognised by the law of England and Wales, or

(b) that person has during the lifetime of the deceased formed a subsequent marriage or civil partnership.

(4A) For the purposes of this Act any reference to a civil partner shall be treated as including a reference to a person who in good faith formed a void civil partnership with the deceased unless either—

(a) the civil partnership between the deceased and that person was dissolved or annulled during the lifetime of the deceased and the dissolution or annulment is recognised by the law of England and Wales, or

(b) that person has during the lifetime of the deceased formed a subsequent civil partnership or marriage.

(5) Any reference in this Act to the formation of, or to a person who has formed, a subsequent marriage or civil partnership includes (as the case may be) a reference to the formation of, or to a person who has formed, a marriage or civil partnership which is by law void or voidable.
(5A) The formation of a marriage or civil partnership shall be treated for the purposes of this Act as the formation of a subsequent marriage or civil partnership, in relation to either of the spouses or civil partners, notwithstanding that the previous marriage or civil partnership of that spouse or civil partner was void or voidable.

(6) Any reference in this Act to an order or decree made under the Matrimonial Causes Act 1973 or under any section of that Act shall be construed as including a reference to an order or decree which is deemed to have been made under that Act or under that section thereof, as the case may be.

(6A) Any reference in this Act to an order made under, or under any provision of, the Civil Partnership Act 2004 shall be construed as including a reference to anything which is deemed to be an order made (as the case may be) under that Act or provision.

(7) Any reference in this Act to any enactment is a reference to that enactment as amended by or under any subsequent enactment.

26.—Consequential amendments, repeals and transitional provisions.

A–032 (1) [Textually amends Matrimonial Causes Act 1973 (c.18), s.36(3)(7)]

(2) [Repeals enactments specified in Sch. and textually amends Matrimonial Causes Act 1973 (c.18), Sch.2 para.5(2)]

(3) The repeal of the said enactments shall not affect their operation in relation to any application made thereunder (whether before or after the commencement of this Act) with reference to the death of any person who died before the commencement of this Act.

(4) Without prejudice to the provisions of section 38 of the Interpretation Act 1889 (which relates to the effect of repeals) nothing in any repeal made by this Act shall affect any order made or direction given under any enactment repealed by this Act, and, subject to the provisions of this Act, every such order or direction (other than an order made under section 4A of the Inheritance Family Provision Act 1938 or section 28A of the Matrimonial Causes Act 1965) shall, if it is in force at the commencement of this Act or is made by virtue of subsection (3) above, continue in force as if it had been made under section 2(1)(a) of this Act, and for the purposes of section 6(7) of this Act the court in exercising its powers under that section in relation to an order continued in force by this subsection shall be required to have regard to any change in any of the circumstances to which the court would have been required to have regard when making that order if the order had been made with reference to the death of any person who died after the commencement of this Act.

27.—Short title, commencement and extent.

A–033 (1) This Act may be cited as the Inheritance (Provision for Family and Dependants) Act 1975.

(2) This Act does not extend to Scotland or Northern Ireland.

(3) This Act shall come into force on 1st April 1976.

APPENDIX 2

INHERITANCE RIGHTS FOR COHABITANTS

1.—INTRODUCTION

(a) Overview

The purpose of this Appendix is to recount the work of the Law Commissions in considering reforms which would enhance the rights of cohabitants and children of cohabitant relationships on the breakdown of the relationship or its termination by death of the other party, and the attempts to secure the enactment of appropriate legislation. This area of the law has been considered in three Law Commission reports and, during the decade immediately before the publication of this edition of *Inheritance Act Claims*, no less than four Bills have been introduced. However, only one of those Bills progressed even as far as the Committee stage, and, for cohabitants, that state of affairs contrasts unfavourably with the position in other jurisdictions. The Scottish legislation is contained in ss.25–29 of the Family Law (Scotland) Act 2006. In the Republic of Ireland, the Civil Partnership and Certain Rights and Obligations of Cohabitants Act 2010 came into force on 1 January 2011.

B–001

At the time of writing, the Government plans for the 2017–2019 Parliamentary session do not include the introduction of any such legislation, but both Parliamentary and extra-Parliamentary attempts to further its introduction continue. On 5 July 2017, the Cohabitation Rights Bill (HL) was introduced by the Liberal Democrat peer, Lord Marks of Henley, and it was read a first time and ordered to be printed.[1] This follows the initiative which has recently been launched for reform of this area of the law; it is led by the Family Law Bar Association, and both Resolution (the Solicitors' Family Law Association) and the Chancery Bar Association are also involved. The

B–002

---

[1] Lords, *Hansard*, vol.783, 5 July 2017, recites the following preamble to the Bill (HL Bill no.34): "A Bill to provide certain protections for persons who live together as a couple or have lived together as a couple as cohabitants; to make provision about the property of deceased persons who are survived by a cohabitant; and for connected purposes." This preamble is identical with that of the Cohabitation Rights Bill (HL) which was introduced by Lord Marks during the 2012–13 session; see para.B–023.

following statement of the aims of this initiative has been provided, at the author's request, for inclusion in this Appendix.[2]

B–003   Many people in this country would be surprised at how great an effect a marriage certificate can have on their financial prospects on separation. We have no doubt that just as many will be surprised at the significance of another piece of paper to their future financial security: a will. A major argument of those who oppose reform of the law for cohabitants on separation is: if you want rights, get married. But the fact is that repeated calls over many years for "education" of the general public into these issues have broadly foundered. We at the Family Law Bar Association, supported by the Chancery Bar Association and Resolution, have taken the view that, whilst reform of the law for cohabitants both on separation and death intestate is desirable and necessary, the latter should be less politically controversial. There seems to be an obvious injustice in a situation where, when a couple have lived together for, say, 25 years and one of them dies, then even distant collateral relatives such as uncles or aunts of the half blood,[3] with whom the deceased may well have had no, or no significant contact, have succession rights which are denied to the survivor. They have no entitlement under the Administration of Estates Act 1925 and are compelled to resort, generally at considerable expense, to the uncertainties of the discretionary remedy under the 1975 Act. It is a well-known aspect of the demographic that cohabitation is increasingly an option of choice for couples in our country. We are all familiar, and the public is becoming increasingly familiar, with the problems that occur when that cohabitation breaks down. However, what of those lifelong cohabitations which remain happy? What will happen, as is likely to happen increasingly as our population ages, when those happy lifelong cohabitations end in death intestate? There is a very large, but still largely submerged, iceberg out there. We are therefore campaigning for law reform in the area of cohabitants' rights on intestacy with the aim of attempting to get the Inheritance (Cohabitants) Bill[4] onto the statute books. It is not the totality of the reform we would like in this area but, if we succeed, it would be a foot in the door. We feel sure that public opinion will increasingly be with us on this and with that in mind we are going to do our best to raise public awareness of the problems and to attract the media spotlight to them.

(b) Inheritance Rights for Cohabitants in the 20th Century

B–004   The question whether the law of intestacy should be amended so as to provide automatically for cohabitants was considered in Law Commission Report no.187, *Family Law: Distribution on Intestacy* (1989), which was item 6 of the Law Commission *Fourth Programme: Family Law* and which brought about the first reconsideration of the law of intestacy since the report of the Morton Committee in 1951.[5] Although a few consultees argued that the intestacy rules should automatically provide for cohabitants, and

---

[2] The author is grateful to John Wilson QC for preparing the statement.
[3] Administration of Estates Act 1925 s.46(3)(v).
[4] For the text of the Bill as introduced by Lord Lester of Herne Hill on 10 May 2012, see paras B–015–B–018.
[5] Report of the Morton Committee on Intestate Succession (1951) Cmnd. 8310, set up as the result of prompting by the Law Society.

that view was shared by the majority of the respondents in the public opinion survey,[6] the Law Commission did not favour that approach.[7] Their view was that:

> "To include cohabitants within the intestacy rules would mean that the simplicity and clarity of the rules would be sacrificed. There would have to be very complex provisions to determine how the property should be divided between, for example, a surviving spouse and a surviving cohabitant. As well as making the rules more complex, it would also increase the costs and cause delays in the administration of estates because disputes could easily arise as to whether a particular individual was a cohabitant."

A more popular solution among consultees was that cohabitants should **B–005** be able to apply for provision under the Inheritance (Provision for Family and Dependants) Act 1975 without the need to show dependence. It was argued that the intestacy rules did not give provision to cohabitants in need and that this defect should be remedied by creating a category of "cohabitant" under the 1975 Act. There was concern that many meritorious claims from cohabitants could not, in the then current state of the law, be pursued. The paradox was identified that the definition of "wholly or partly maintained" in s.1(3) of the Act favoured applicants who provided the deceased with little or nothing in the way of valuable services and disadvantaged those more meritorious applicants whose services amounted to full value for the contribution made by the deceased to their reasonable needs. That paradox had been recognised and was avoided in practice by judicial decisions such as that of the Court of Appeal in *Bishop v Plumley*[8] which, in effect, took the value attributable to services provided in the context of a caring and affectionate relationship out of the equation. The Law Commission's recommendation to create a new category of applicant defined in terms of the class of persons entitled to bring actions under the Fatal Accidents Act 1976 for the financial loss suffered where death had been wrongfully caused was embodied in a draft Distribution of Estates Bill[9] and was eventually implemented by the Law Reform (Succession) Act 1995, which applied to deaths on and after 1 January 1996.

---

[6] Appendix C to the Law Commission Report no.187, *Family Law: Distribution on Intestacy* (1989). Public Attitude Surveys Ltd were commissioned to conduct a survey of adults living in England and Wales in order to obtain information as to (i) what is known about the current law on intestacy and (ii) what would be thought an appropriate division of an intestate's estate in a range of different circumstances. A representative sample of 1,001 individuals was recruited from different locations to quota controls on sex, age and social class. The questionnaire which they were asked to answer was developed in consultation with the Law Commission. The Report had been preceded by Working Paper no.108, *Distribution on Intestacy*.
[7] Law Com LC no.187, at [58].
[8] *Bishop v Plumley* [1991] 1 W.L.R. 582, CA.
[9] Law Com LC no.187, App.A.

2.—THE LAW COMMISSION, 2005–2011

B–006 The Law Commission revisited this area of the law as part of its *Ninth Programme of Law Reform*,[10] and announced an important new project on cohabitation,[11] which would:

> "...focus on the financial hardship suffered by cohabitants or their children on the termination of their relationship by separation or death."

The review was to be restricted to opposite sex or same-sex couples in clearly defined relationships, which would not necessarily involve a sexual relationship, but should at the very least:

> "...involve cohabitation and bear the hallmarks of intimacy and exclusivity, giving rise to mutual trust and confidence between partners."

The review would specifically exclude from consideration blood relationships, "caring" relationships and "commercial" (landlord/tenant or lodger) relationships, and would give particular attention to:

(1) capital and income provision on relationship breakdown;
(2) capital provision where there was a dependent child or children;
(3) intestate succession and family provision on death; and
(4) the Inheritance (Provision for Family and Dependants) Act 1975.

B–007 These matters were addressed in a consultation paper[12] which was followed by the report often referred to as the "Cohabitation Report".[13] Part 8 of the report set out a list of recommendations but the report did not include a draft Bill. The general recommendation[14] was that legislation should create a scheme of general application, whereby cohabiting couples would be entitled to apply for financial relief on separation:

(1) provided they satisfy statutory eligibility criteria[15];
(2) but not where they had reached an agreement disapplying the statutory scheme ("an opt-out agreement"),[16] in which case the parties' own financial arrangements (if any) would apply.

---

[10] Law Commission Report no.293, *Ninth Programme of Law Reform* (2005).
[11] Law Commission Report no.294, *Thirty-Ninth Annual Report* (2005); the summary at para.B–004 is taken from paras 6.19–6.20.
[12] Law Commission Consultation Paper no.179, *Cohabitation: The Financial Consequences of Relationship Breakdown* (2006).
[13] Law Commission Report no.307, *Cohabitation: The Financial Consequences of Relationship Breakdown* (2007).
[14] Law Com LC 307, paras 2.94 and 8.1.
[15] Law Com LC 307, paras 3.13, 3.31, 3.84 and 8.2–8.4.
[16] Law Com LC 307, paras 5.8, 5.34, 5.56–5.60, 5.72 and 8.25–8.33.

In Pt 4 of the report,[17] the Law Commission considered the possibility of **B–008** extending or modifying the scheme of the Matrimonial Causes Act 1973 (MCA). Appendix C of the report is devoted to the discussion of this and other schemes which the Law Commission finally rejected. This option had been provisionally rejected in the consultation paper[18]; as one consultee observed:

> "Some account should be taken of the decision of the parties not to marry: it is one thing to relieve the unequal impact of the relationship, but quite another to treat the parties as if they actually had married."

The report continued with the observation that applying the MCA would impose an equivalence with marriage which many people would find inappropriate, and some consultees suggested that it was unlikely that a scheme which equated cohabitation with marriage in this way would be politically attainable. As the history of the attempts to secure enactment of the legislation demonstrates, those suggestions proved to be well-founded. The recommendations for the reform of the law of family provision[19] were expressed to be contingent upon the implementation of the scheme of financial relief on separation recommended in Pt 4 of the Report. For much the same reasons as had been given in the Law Commission's 1989 report, there were no recommendations for reform of the law of intestacy.[20] The final topic covered was jurisdiction and applicable law, and the recommendations[21] were (with some provisos) that the jurisdictional gateway should be habitual residence, not domicile, and that the applicable law should be the law of England and Wales in all cases arising in an English or Welsh court concerning financial relief on separation and opt-out agreements.

In October 2009 the Law Commission published a consultation paper (CP **B–009** 191) on the reform of the law of intestacy and family provision,[22] and the subsequent report[23] was published in December 2011. It was not possible to comment on its recommendations in the previous edition of this work, which appeared a month before the report.

CP 191 came down firmly in favour of giving intestacy rights to cohabi- **B–010** tants, observing that "the current rules are creating too many hard cases, and the number is set to rise as cohabitation becomes more prevalent".[24] The proposed definition of a cohabitant was:

> "a person who, immediately before the death of the deceased was:
>
> (1) living with the deceased as a couple[25] in a joint household; and

---

[17] For the relevant recommendations, see Law Com LC 307, paras 4.17, 4.32–4.42, 4.59, 4.127, 4.129, 4.151, 4.159 and 8.8–8.24.

[18] Law Com CP 179, para.6.239.

[19] Law Com LC 307, Pt 6; for the specific recommendations, see paras 6.26, 6.43, 6.49 and 8.34–8.38.

[20] Law Com LC 307, paras 6.5–6.10.

[21] Law Com LC 307, paras 7.15–7.16, 7.22 and 8.39–8.41.

[22] Law Commission Consultation Paper no.191, *Intestacy and Family Provision Claims on Death* (2009).

[23] Law Commission Report no.331, *Intestacy and Family Provision Claims on Death* (2011).

[24] Law Com CP 191, para.4.15.

[25] This concept appears in the definition of a de facto relationship in the law of intestacy in New Zealand and in New South Wales and was recommended as the test of cohabitation in Law Commission, *The Cohabitation Report* (2007), Law Com. No.307, paras 3.13 and 6.15.

(2) neither married to nor a civil partner of the deceased."

and it was stated that:

"...the term 'couple' is readily understood to connote an intimate relationship and to set such couples apart from flatmates, blood relatives and those in a commercial relationship."[26]

The words "joint household" emphasise the quality of interdependence which was seen as central to the cohabitation relationship. This contrasts with the existence of separate domestic economies which was fatal to the claim as a cohabitant in *Churchill v Roach*.[27]

B–011   In the previous edition of this book, the author expressed the view that if the positions of cohabitants under the law of intestacy and under the 1975 Act were brought into closer correspondence, by affording the cohabitant inheritance rights on intestacy and by defining the status of "cohabitant" in the same manner for both purposes,[28, 29] a decrease in the number of 1975 Act claims by cohabitants might be expected. On the other hand, if the proposal to afford to surviving cohabitants the higher standard of provision at present available to surviving spouses and civil partners were to gain acceptance,[30] the issue whether the claimant is a cohabitant would be contested more often, and it would no longer normally[31] be a matter of indifference whether, if the claim succeeded, it should do so on the basis that the claimant was a cohabitant rather than a dependant.

B–012   CP 191 considered in some detail the appropriate distinctions between the rights which various classes of cohabitant would have both on intestacy and under the 1975 Act. The thinking underlying the distinctions proposed was that a cohabitant who is seen to have demonstrated commitment to the relationship, either through its lasting for a significant period, or by having children with the other party, should be placed in a better position than one who is not. Thus the proposal would have disapplied the minimum duration period for a cohabitant who was a parent of a child with the deceased,[32] while the subsequent consultation question asked whether this relaxation of the eligibility conditions should operate in favour of one who was not a parent.[33]

B–013   The deliberations of the Law Commission on the reform of the law of intestacy and family provision led to a series of recommendations to which

---

[26] Law Com CP 191, para.4.56.
[27] *Churchill v Roach* [2004] 2. F.L.R. 989.
[28] The proposal would have required the amendment of ss.1(1A) and 1(1B) of the 1975 Act.
[29] Similarly, the definition of "cohabitant" proposed in Law Com LC no.307, paras 6.16, 6.34 was to be the same as that applicable in claims for financial relief on separation.
[30] Similarly proposed in Law Com LC no.307, paras 6.43, 8.37.
[31] The court is directed by s.3(2A) to have regard to the duration of the cohabitation relationship and the contribution made by the cohabitant to the welfare of the family, so a party to a long-term relationship might prefer to claim as a cohabitant; however, the length of time for which the claimant was dependent on the deceased is to be taken into account under s.3(4) and might be relevant to the quantification of an award, while the nature and extent of any services provided by a claimant who was a dependant and which conduced towards the welfare of the deceased might, in any given case, be viewed as creating an obligation for the purposes of s.3(1)(d) or as a relevant matter under s.3(1)(g).
[32] Law Com CP 191, paras 4.22, 8.18.
[33] Law Com CP 191, paras 4.23, 8.19.

legislative form was given by the two draft Bills appended (with explanatory notes) to the report, which was published on 13 December 2011, as Apps A and B. Appendix A, the draft Inheritance and Trustees' Powers Bill, implemented the recommendations made by the Law Commission in Pts 2 to 7 of its report no.331, *Intestacy and Family Provision Claims on Death* (2011). Those recommendations did not affect the position of cohabitants under either the law of intestacy or the law of family provision. The Inheritance and Trustees' Powers Act 2014, which applies to England and Wales, received the Royal Assent on 15 May 2014, and came into effect for deaths on and after 1 October 2014. It is not discussed further in this Appendix.

The draft Inheritance (Cohabitants) Bill implemented the recommenda-   **B–014**
tions made by the Law Commission in Pt 8 of its Report. The Law Commission recommended that certain "qualifying cohabitants" should be included in the list of those who benefit by default under the intestacy rules when a person dies without a will and was not married or in a civil partnership at the date of death. The Law Commission also recommended that the other parent of a child of a deceased person should be able to claim family provision if that person and the deceased were cohabiting at the date of death of the deceased, without having to show that the relationship had been ongoing for two or more years. The draft Inheritance (Cohabitants) Bill would have implemented the Law Commission's recommendation by amending existing legislation, principally the Administration of Estates Act 1925 and the Inheritance (Provision for Family and Dependants) Act 1975. It also made consequential amendments to the Intestates' Estates Act 1952, the Law Reform (Succession) Act 1995 and the Civil Partnership Act 2004.

The text of the draft Bill (omitting the title and preamble) is set out in this   **B–015**
and the following three paragraphs, together with some commentary based on the explanatory notes which accompanied it.[34] The expressed purpose of the Bill was to "Make provision about the property of deceased persons who are survived by a cohabitant". Clause 1 defines, and provides for the inclusion of, a new class of persons ("qualifying cohabitants") entitled to succeed on intestacy. Thus, a qualifying cohabitant is placed in the same position as a spouse or civil partner, but cannot supplant either of them, since the effect of cl.1(5) is that a person cannot qualify as a cohabitant for these purposes if the deceased died married or in a civil partnership. It also makes clear that the surviving spouse or civil partner of the deceased cannot also be a qualifying cohabitant.[35]

"1   Succession to estate on intestacy
(1) Section 46 of the Administration of Estates Act 1925 (succession to real and personal estate on intestacy) is amended as follows.
(2) In subsection (1)(i) (cases where the intestate leaves a spouse or civil partner)
(a)   in the words before the Table, for "or civil partner", substitute "civil partner or qualifying cohabitant", and
(b)   in the Table

---

[34] Law Com LC 331, App.B, explanatory notes, paras B5–B23.
[35] Law Com LC 331, para.B10.

(i) for the surviving spouse or civil partner, where first occurring, substitute the surviving spouse, civil partner or qualifying cohabitant ("the survivor"), and

(ii) for each subsequent occurrence of "the surviving spouse or civil partner" substitute "the survivor"

(3) In subsections (1)(ii) to (v), (2A) and (4) (which make further provision about the rights of spouses, civil partners and others on intestacy) for "or civil partner"(in each place) substitute "civil partner or qualifying cohabitant"

(4) After subsection (2A) insert.

"(2B) Where an intestate and the intestate's spouse or civil partner have died in circumstances rendering it uncertain which of them survived the other, this section has effect as if the intestate did not leave any qualifying cohabitant

(5) After subsection (4) insert

"(5) A person is a qualifying cohabitant in relation to an intestate only if—

(a) the intestate was neither married nor in a civil partnership immediately before death, and

(b) the first or second condition is met in relation to the person.

(6) The first condition is that during the whole of the period of five years ending immediately before the intestate's death the person was living as the intestate's spouse or civil partner and in the same household as the intestate.

(7) The second condition is that—

(a) the person is the other parent of a child of the intestate born on or before the date of the intestate's death,

(b) at that date the child is living in the same household as the person, and

(c) during the whole of the period of two years ending immediately before the intestate's death the person was living as the intestate's spouse or civil partner and in the same household as the intestate."

B–016   This provision, which is an essential corollary to cl.1, affords to a qualifying cohabitant the same right in respect of the family home as was already available to a surviving spouse or civil partner.[36]

"2   Intestacy: rights as respects the home

(1) Schedule 2 to the Intestates. Estates Act 1952 (rights of surviving spouse or civil partner as respects the matrimonial or civil partnership home) is amended as follows.

(2) Before paragraph 1 there is inserted:

"A1 (1) This Schedule applies where a person dies intestate and leaves a spouse, civil partner or qualifying cohabitant.

(2) In this Schedule:

"qualifying cohabitant" has the meaning given by section 46(5) of the principal Act;

---

[36] Law Com LC 331 at para.B18.

"the survivor" means the surviving spouse, civil partner or qualifying cohabitant.

(3) In paragraphs 1 to 6, for "the surviving spouse or civil partner" (in each place) there is substituted "the survivor"

(4) In paragraph 6(2) for "a surviving spouse or civil partner" there is substituted "a surviving spouse, civil partner or qualifying cohabitant"

(5) For the title there is substituted—

'RIGHTS OF SURVIVING SPOUSE, CIVIL PARTNER OR QUALIFYING COHABITANT AS RESPECTS THE HOME'."

The term "qualifying cohabitant" as defined by cl.1(5)–(7) embraced a **B–017** larger class of persons than that defined by the 1975 Act, and that extension of the class required a corresponding amendment so as to bring a cohabitant who was the other parent of a child of the deceased and satisfied the conditions of the existing subss.1(1A) or 1(1B) within its scope. "Child of the deceased" is defined by the new s.1(1C).[37]

"3 Application for financial provision from deceased's estate

In section 1 of the Inheritance (Provision for Family and Dependants) Act 1975 for subsections (1A) and (1B) (certain persons entitled to apply for provision) there is substituted—

"(1A) This subsection applies to any person who during the whole of the period of two years ending immediately before the date when the deceased died was living—

(a) as the deceased's husband or wife or civil partner, and

(b) in the same household as the deceased.

(1B) This subsection applies to a person who is the other parent of a child of the deceased if at the date when the deceased died the person was living—

(a) as the deceased's husband or wife or civil partner, and

(b) in the same household as the deceased.

(1C) The reference in subsection (1B) to a child includes—

(a) a child born alive who died before the deceased, and

(b) a child en ventre sa mere at the date of the deceased's death (whether or not the child is subsequently born alive).

(But this does not affect the generality of the definition of "child" in section 25(1))

In relation to the minor and consequential amendments it is explained **B–018** that they do not include amendment of provisions that would be repealed by the draft Inheritance and Trustees' Powers Bill, because the Inheritance (Cohabitants) Bill was drafted on the basis of the law as it would be after enactment of the Inheritance and Trustees' Powers Bill.[38]

---

[37] Law Com LC 331 at paras B19–B22.
[38] Law Com LC 331 at paras B2, B23.

"**4 Minor and consequential amendments**
The Schedule to this Act, which makes minor amendments and amendments consequential on other provisions of this Act, has effect.

5 Short title, commencement, application and extent
(1) This Act may be cited as the Inheritance (Cohabitants) Act 2011.

(2) This section comes into force on the day on which this Act is passed, but otherwise this Act comes into force on such day as the Lord Chancellor may by order made by statutory instrument appoint.

(3) An order under subsection (2) may appoint different days for different purposes.

(4) This Act applies only in relation to deaths occurring after the coming into force of this Act (apart from this section).

(5) This Act extends to England and Wales only.

SCHEDULE

Section 4(1)

MINOR AND CONSEQUENTIAL AMENDMENTS

Administration of Estates Act 1925
1(1) The Administration of Estates Act 1925 is amended as follows

(2) In section 48(2)(a) (powers of personal representative in respect of interests of surviving spouse or civil partner) for "or civil partner" substitute "civil partner or qualifying cohabitant"

(3) In section 55(1) (definitions), after paragraph (iv) there is inserted—

(iv a) "Qualifying cohabitant" has the meaning given by section 46(5)

Intestates. Estates Act 1952
2 In the Intestates. Estates Act 1952, for section 5 (rights of surviving spouse or civil partner as respects the matrimonial home) substitute—

'**5 Rights of surviving spouse, civil partner or qualifying cohabitant as respects the home**
The Second Schedule to this Act (rights of surviving spouse, civil partner or qualifying cohabitant as respects the home) has effect.

Law Reform (Succession) Act 1995
3 In consequence of the amendment made by section 3, omit section 2(3) of the Law Reform (Succession) Act 1995.

Civil Partnership Act 2004
4(1) Schedule 4 to the Civil Partnership Act 2004 is amended as follows.

(2) In consequence of the amendments made by section 2 and paragraph 2 of this Schedule, omit paragraph 13.

(3) In consequence of the amendment made by section 3, omit paragraph 15(5).

3.—THE PARLIAMENTARY HISTORY

(a) Before the Inheritance (Cohabitants) Bill: 2008–2011

As mentioned earlier, the *Cohabitation Report* did not include a draft Bill. **B–019**
On 12 December 2008, the Cohabitation Bill (HL), a bill:

> "to provide certain protections for persons who live together as a couple or have lived together as a couple; and for connected purposes"

was introduced by Lord Lester of Herne Hill. That bill established:

> "(1) ... a framework of rights and responsibilities for cohabitants, with a view to providing basic protections—
>
> (a) in the event of their ceasing to live together as a couple for a reason other than death,
> (b) in the event of the death of one of them, and
> (c) for the purpose of enabling the life of either of them to be insured by or for the benefit of the other or for the benefit of a relevant child."

The bill was mainly concerned with implementing a scheme of financial settlement orders and opt-out agreements along the lines of the *Cohabitation Report*. The protection on death was provided by creating a presumption that, for the purposes of ss.1 and 3 of the Life Insurance Act 1774, each cohabitant in a relationship had an unlimited insurable interest in the life of the other[39] and by applying s.11 of the Married Women's Property Act 1882 to a defined class of policies of assurance.[40] The Bill also amended the 1975 Act so as to bring cohabitants (as therein defined) within its scope and to entitle them to the higher standard of financial provision. There were also amendments to ss.14 and 15 which introduced provisions applying to surviving cohabitants which mirrored those already applicable to surviving spouses and civil partners. The law of intestacy was unaffected.

The Bill, having been referred to Committee, was discussed on 30 April **B–020** 2009, when cl.1 was agreed and amendments to cl.2 (definition of "cohabitant") were debated.[41] No further days of the committee stage were scheduled during that session. On 25 March 2009, leave was given under the Ten-Minute Rule procedure for the Bill to be introduced in the House of Commons as the *Cohabitation (No.2) Bill*, where it was presented by Mary Creagh (Lab. Wakefield).[42] It was ordered to be printed and read a second time on 3 July 2009, but there proved to be insufficient time for debate and it was withdrawn from further consideration.

---

[39] Cohabitation Bill (HL), cl.16
[40] Cohabitation Bill (HL), cl.17
[41] Lords, *Hansard*, 30 April 2009, cols 411–416.
[42] *Hansard*, 25 March 2009, cols 309–311.

(b) The Inheritance (Cohabitants) Bill; 2012–13

B–021 This measure[43] was introduced by Lord Lester of Herne Hill as "a bill to make provision about the property of a deceased person who is survived by a cohabitant" and received its first reading on 10 May 2012,[44] when it was ordered to be printed. The second reading debate took place on 19 October[45] and, as Lord Lester acknowledged, was a much more limited bill than the bill which he had introduced in 2008. He referred to the increased prevalence of cohabitation and the comment in the Law Commission's 2011 report that it was "no longer an insignificant minority choice, nor an unacceptable lifestyle".[46] On the one hand, it was welcomed as "part of the slow progress towards equal justice"; on the other, it was denounced as "a denial of the human rights of privacy and respect for family life".[47] Whether by chance or design, the first half of the debate after Lord Lester's introduction was taken up mainly by those who opposed the Bill and the second half by its supporters.[48] It was commented on that 40 of the 79 consultees opposed the reform and that most of those in favour were mainly organisations with a professional interest, and a substantial quantity of strongly adverse comment on social media was quoted in the debate. To some speakers, the Bill was unacceptable because it was seen as equating cohabitation with marriage, while others were unconvinced either that any such legislation was desirable or, if it was, that the Bill provided an acceptable solution. Among the views expressed by those in favour was that the proposed arrangements did not undermine or weaken the value of marriage, that for many people cohabitation was not a temporary trial-run situation but a lifetime choice and that for most intestates, and for society in general, the first priority should be given to the relationship in which the deceased was living at the time of their death. The expression of support from the Opposition benches included the following statement by Professor Elizabeth Cooke, the commissioner who led the review:

> "When a family member dies, the process of grieving and of adjustment to change can be made far worse by uncertainty and anxiety about money or belongings. It is vital that the law remains relevant and up to date, reflecting the reality of modern society and reasonable expectations of those who have been bereaved."

B–022 It was indicated by the Minister of State in his summing up that, while the Government obviously would not oppose Second Reading, it had strong reservations. The Bill was therefore read a second time and committed to a Committee of the whole House. However, as at 30 April 2013, no committee stage had yet been scheduled and it made no further progress.

---

[43] For the text, see paras B–015–B–018.
[44] Lords, *Hansard*, 10 May 2012, col.25.
[45] Lords, *Hansard*, 19 October 2012, cols 1655–1682.
[46] Law Com LC 331, para.8.123.
[47] Lords, *Hansard*, 19 October 2012, cols 1659 and 1660, respectively
[48] Lords, *Hansard*, 19 October 2012, cols 1660–1672 and 1672–1677, respectively. In his summing up, Lord McNally, the Minister of State, Ministry of Justice, commented that of the 10 speakers, five were in favour and five against.

(c) The Cohabitation Rights Bill: 2013 and after

This measure:

B–023

> "A Bill to make provisions for certain people who live together as a couple or have lived together as a couple and to make provision about the property of a deceased person who is survived by a cohabitant; and for connected purposes",

was introduced by Lord Marks of Henley-on-Thames on 9 October 2013, read a first time and ordered to be printed.[49] It made no further progress during the 2013–14 session. It was re-introduced by Lord Marks in the following session, receiving its first reading on 9 June 2014[50] and the Second Reading debate took place on 12 December 2014. The Bill was a much more comprehensive piece of legislation than the Inheritance (Cohabitants) Bill; as with the Cohabitation Bill (HL) introduced by Lord Lester, it contained provisions for financial settlement orders (Pt 2), while Pt 3 included the provisions relating to insurance and registering the death of a cohabitant which also appeared as cll.16–18 of Lord Lester's bill. However, Pt 3 also included two sections relating to the intestacy of the cohabitant, an area unaffected by Lord Lester's bill.

Clause 19 (succession to estate on intestacy), replicated cll.1(1)–(4) of the Inheritance (Cohabitants) Bill,[51] but subcl.(5), which defines "qualifying cohabitant", differs, and subcll.(6) and (7) are omitted. Subclause (5) reads:

B–024

> "(5) After subsection (4) insert—
> '(5) A person is a qualifying cohabitant in relation to an intestate only if—
> (a) the intestate was neither married nor in a civil partnership immediately before death, and
> (b) the person was immediately before the death of the intestate a cohabitant in a relationship with the intestate within the meaning of section 2 of the Cohabitation Rights Act 2014.' "

The relevant definition in cl.2 of the Bill[52] is:

> "2 'Cohabitant'
> (1) For the purposes of this Act, references to the cohabitants in a relationship are to any two people (whether of the same sex or the opposite sex) who—
> (a) live together as a couple, and
> (b) meet the first and second conditions specified in subsections (2) and (3).
> (2) The first condition is that any of the following apply to the two people ('A' and 'B') who live together as a couple—

---

[49] Lords, *Hansard*, 9 October 2013, col.81.
[50] Lords, *Hansard*, 9 June 2014, col.128.
[51] See para.B–015, above.
[52] Only subcll.2(1)–(3) are reproduced.

(a)   A and B are each treated in law as being mother, father or parent of the same minor child,

(b)   a joint residence order in favour of A and B is in force in respect of a minor child,

(c)   A and B are the natural parents of a child en ventre sa mere at the date when A and B cease to live together as a couple (whether or not that child is subsequently born alive), or

(d)   A and B have lived together as a couple for a continuous period of two years or more.[53]

(3) The second condition is that A and B—

(a)   are neither married to each other nor civil partners of each other, and

(b)   are not within prohibited degrees of relationship[54] in relation to each other."

B–025   Clause 20 (intestacy: rights as regards the home) exactly replicated cl.2 of the Inheritance (Cohabitation) Bill.[55] Clauses 21 and 22, which were concerned with financial provision for the cohabitant from the deceased's estate, read as follows:

"21 Application for financial provision from deceased's estate
In section 1 of the Inheritance (Provision for Family and Dependants) Act 1975 (c. 63) for subsections (1A) and (1B) (certain persons entitled to apply for provision) there is substituted—
'(1A) This subsection applies to any person who was immediately before the death of the deceased a cohabitant in a relationship with the deceased within the meaning of section 2 of the Cohabitation Rights Act 2014.'

22 Further provision in connection with the death of a cohabitant
(1) Schedule 2 to this Act contains additional provision—

(a)   to align with this Act certain existing statutory protections that are available to a surviving cohabitant on the death of the other cohabitant, and

(b)   to extend to the surviving cohabitant certain connected provisions.

(2) Part 1 of Schedule 2—

(a)   amends the Inheritance (Provision for Family and Dependants) Act 1975, and

(b)   includes provision setting out circumstances in which a former cohabitant who receives no reasonable financial provision from the deceased's estate may apply to the court."

B–026   Schedule 2 of the Cohabitation Rights Bill is in seven parts, which include amendments to all the statutes amended by the Schedule to the Inheritance (Cohabitants) Bill. In that Bill, the amendments to the 1975 Act were in cl.3; in the Cohabitation Rights Bill they are contained in Pt 4 of Sch.2. The text reads:

[53] Defined in accordance with subcl.2(4).
[54] Specified in cl.5.
[55] See para.B–017, above.

"PART 4
AMENDMENTS OF INHERITANCE (PROVISION FOR FAMILY AND DEPENDANTS) ACT 1975

4 In this Part of this Schedule 'the 1975 Act' means the Inheritance (Provision for Family and Dependants) Act 1975 (c. 63).

5 In section 1 of the 1975 Act (application for financial provision from the deceased's estate)—

(a) in subsection(1)(ba) omit 'or 1B';

(b) for subsection (1A) substitute—

'(1A) This subsection applies to a person if immediately before the deceased died, the person and the deceased were cohabitants within the meaning of the Cohabitants Rights Act 2014.';

(c) for subsection (1B) substitute—

'(1B) Section 14B of this Act sets out the circumstances in which a former cohabitant may apply for an order under section 2 of this Act.';

(d) after subsection (2)(aa) insert—

'(ab) in the case of an application made by virtue of subsection (1)(ba), means such financial provision as it would be reasonable in all the circumstances of the case for the surviving cohabitant to receive, whether or not that provision is required for his or her maintenance;'; and

(e) in subsection (2)(b), after 'by virtue of subsection (1) above' insert 'or section 14B below'.

6 In section 2 of the 1975 Act (power of the court to make orders), after subsection (1)(g), insert—

'(h) an order varying any settlement, including a settlement made by will—

(i) made on two persons, one of whom was the deceased, who immediately before the deceased died were cohabitants within the meaning of the Cohabitation Rights Act 2014, and

(ii) made at any time when they were cohabitants, when they were living together as a couple but before becoming cohabitants within the meaning of that Act or in anticipation of them living together as a couple, the variation being for the benefit of the surviving cohabitant, or any relevant child.'

7 In section 3 of the 1975 Act (matters to which the court is to have regard in exercising powers under section 2), for subsection (2A) substitute—

'(2A) Without prejudice to the generality of paragraph (g) of subsection (1) above, where an application for an order under section 2 of this Act is made by virtue of section 1(1)(ba) of this Act, the court shall, in addition to the matters specifically mentioned in paragraphs (a) to (f) of that subsection, have regard to—

    (a)   the age of the applicant and the length of the period during which the applicant and the deceased lived together as a couple;

    (b)   the contribution (including any contribution made by looking after the home or caring for any relevant child) which the applicant made whilst the applicant and the deceased were living together as a couple;

    (c)   any additional matter which, if the application were treated as if it had been made under Part 2 of the Cohabitation Rights Act 2014 (financial settlement orders), the court would consider relevant in determining the application.'

8 After section 14A of the 1975 Act insert—

'14B Provision as to cases where no financial settlement order was made after cohabitants ceased living together as a couple

(1) Subsection (2) below applies where—

    (a)   the cohabitants have ceased living together as a couple and, within twenty four months of ceasing to do so, one of them dies, and

    (b)   either—

        (i)   no application for a financial settlement order has been made under section 7 of the Cohabitation Rights Act 2014 or by one of the former cohabitants, or

        (ii) if such an application has been made, the proceedings on the application have not been determined at the time of death of the deceased.

(2) The former cohabitant who survives may apply to the court for an order under section 2 of this Act on the ground that the disposition of the deceased's estate by his or her will or the law relating to intestacy, or the combination of the will and that law, is not such as to make reasonable financial provision for the applicant.

(3) In subsection (2) "reasonable financial provision" means such financial provision as it would be reasonable in all the circumstances of the case for the applicant to receive for his or her maintenance.'

9 After section 15ZA of the 1975 Act, insert—

'15ZB Restriction on making an application under this Act imposed in proceedings for a financial settlement order under section 8 of the Cohabitation Rights Act 2014

(1) On making a financial settlement order under section 8 of the Cohabitation Rights Act 2014, or at any time after making such an order, the court, if it considers it just to do so, may, on the application of either of the former cohabitants, order that the other shall not on the death of the applicant be entitled to apply for an order under section 2 of this Act.

(2) In subsection (1) above "the court" has the same meaning as in the Cohabitation Rights Act 2014.

(3) Where an order under subsection (1) above made in connection with a financial settlement order has been made with respect to a former cohabitant, then, on the death of the other former cohabitant, the court shall not entertain any application

for an order under section 2 of this Act made by the former cohabitant who survives.'

10 In section 25 of the 1975 Act (interpretation), insert each of the following definitions at the appropriate place—

(a) 'cohabitants' and 'former cohabitants' have the same meaning as in the Cohabitation Rights Act 2014;";

(b) 'relevant child', in relation to cohabitants in a relationship, has the same meaning as in the Cohabitation Rights Act 2014."

The Second Reading debate in December 2014[56] exhibited as wide a **B–027** divergence of attitudes as the debate at the same stage of the Inheritance (Cohabitation) Bill had done in October 2012, but the opposition proved to be on somewhat different grounds. Opening the debate, Lord Marks of Henley drew attention to the increase in the number of people cohabiting in the UK (almost six million in 2013, with 38 per cent of cohabiting couples having children) and referred to cohabitation as a clear lifestyle choice, it being:

"...the mark of a free society that we accept and indeed embrace our freedom to choose how we live and with whom we live."

The legal status of cohabitants continued to be unclear; the myth of the "common-law marriage" persisted, and the position under the "antiquated and unwieldy law of trusts" to which parties had to resort for the ascertainment of their shares in property had not been made easier by the then recent decision in *Jones v Kernott*.[57] He emphasised that the proposals made for financial relief on separation did not equate cohabitation with marriage and that the aim of those proposals in the Bill was:

"...to address economic unfairness at the end of a relationship that has enriched one party and impoverished another in a way that demands redress",

and he referred to Lady Hale's commendation of the Scottish legislation in *Gow v Grant*.[58] He noted that the previous administration had been sympathetic to the aims of the Law Commission in 2007 but wished to see how the law was working in Scotland, and, as Lady Hale had made clear in *Gow v Grant*, it was working well.

As on the previous occasion, the opponents dominated the debate **B–028** immediately after the introduction.[59] The opening salvo of dissent was founded on a then recent Prime Ministerial announcement that all gov-

---

[56] Lords, *Hansard*, 12 December 2014, cols 2068–2092.

[57] *Jones v Kernott,* reported as *Kernott v Jones* [2011] UKSC 53; [2011] 3 W.L.R 1121; another case in which the Supreme Court had reversed the decision of the Court of Appeal which had itself reversed the decision at first instance.

[58] *Gow v Grant* [2012] UKSC 29; [2012] 3 F.C.R. 73, a case under s.28 of the Family Law (Scotland) Act 2006 which permits applications by a cohabitant for financial provision otherwise than on the death of the other party to the relationship. Mrs Gow succeeded at first instance and the reversal of that decision by the Inner House whose interlocutor was recalled by the Supreme Court and the original award restored. For the concurring judgment by Lady Hale, see [44]–[56].

[59] Lords, *Hansard*, 12 December 2014, cols 2072–2078 (three speakers).

ernment policies would be subject to a new family test, namely, the impact they would have on relationship formation and breakdown. The principal opponent of the Bill assessed it as reducing willingness to commit long-term and likely to increase greatly the stress of couple breakdown, significantly to the detriment of children. Cohabitation would become as expensive as divorce and deter even more men from providing the stability that children needed. There was no compelling reason to recognise cohabitation; the Bill ignored the human rights of privacy and respect for family life and sent a bad message to career women. Another argument was that the encouragement of cohabitation cost the country a great deal of money because of the greater instability of that living arrangement compared with marriage. Conversely, marriage was economically advantageous to the country as a whole and to the parties to it. Much emphasis was placed on the importance of a formal commitment and the stability of the relationship which flowed from it. The widespread confusion about the legal position of cohabitants might be better addressed by education rather than legislation.

B–029   Support for the Bill was essentially along the same lines as in the debate on its predecessor. It was seen as a modest adjustment to economic disadvantage suffered as a result of the relationship, and the support after death intestate was particularly welcomed, given the very high proportion of cohabitants who do not make wills. If one looked at the Bill through the eyes of an economist, its effect was to transfer some of the burden of the relationship breakdown from the state onto "irresponsible common-law husbands and fathers". The opponents of the Bill were in effect saying "Tough" to those suffering economic disadvantage on relationship breakdown and that was not good enough.

B–030   Again, the Government stance was that it would not oppose the motion to give the Bill a second reading, but continued to have reservations. The Government had consistently taken the view that major changes relating to the rights of cohabitants must be fully considered and, notwithstanding that there had been two Law Commission reports, "did not consider that proper consideration had taken place". Its current priorities were centred on improvements to the family justice system and it had already announced that the recommendations contained in the Law Commission report published in 2011 would not be implemented during that Parliament. That in fact has turned out to be the position. The Bill made no further progress during the 2014–15 session, in the 2015–16 session after its first reading on 4 June 2015, or in the 2016–17 session after its first reading on 13 June 2016. In the political situation which exists at the time of writing, the probability of it, or any similar legislation being enacted within the lifetime of this Parliament (or, if it is as short lived as some commentators are now predicting, the next) must, in the author's view, be extremely remote unless the initiative outlined earlier in this Appendix[60] gains substantial public and Parliamentary support.

---

[60] Paragraphs B–002–B–003.

APPENDIX 3

RULES, ORDERS AND FORMS

1.—CPR PART 8: ALTERNATIVE PROCEDURE FOR CLAIMS

Types of Claim in Which the Part 8 Procedure May be Followed

8.1 (1) The Part 8 procedure is the procedure set out in this Part.   **C–001**
   (2) A claimant may use the Part 8 procedure where—

   (a) he seeks the court's decision on a question which is unlikely to involve a substantial dispute of fact; or
   (b) paragraph (6) applies.

   (2A) In the County Court, a claim under the Part 8 procedure may be made at any County Court hearing centre unless an enactment, rule or practice direction provides otherwise
   (3) The court may at any stage order the claim to continue as if the claimant had not used the Part 8 procedure and, if it does so, the court may give any directions it considers appropriate.
   (4) Paragraph (2) does not apply if a practice direction provides that the Part 8 procedure may not be used in relation to the type of claim in question.
   (5) Where the claimant uses the Part 8 procedure he may not obtain default judgment under Part 12.
   (6) A rule or practice direction may, in relation to a specified type of proceedings—

   (a) require or permit the use of the Part 8 procedure; and
   (b) disapply or modify any of the rules set out in this Part as they apply to those proceedings.

(Rule 8.9 provides for other modifications to the general rules where the Part 8 procedure is being used)

Contents of the Claim Form

C–002   8.2 Where the claimant uses the Part 8 procedure the claim form must state—

(a)   that this Part applies;
(b)   (i)   the question which the claimant wants the court to decide; or

   (ii)   the remedy which the claimant is seeking and the legal basis for the claim to that remedy;

(c)   if the claim is being made under an enactment, what that enactment is;
(d)   if the claimant is claiming in a representative capacity, what that capacity is; and
(e)   if the defendant is sued in a representative capacity, what that capacity is.

(Part 22 provides for the claim form to be verified by a statement of truth.)

(Rule 7.5 provides for service of the claim form.)

Issue of Claim Form Without Naming Defendants

C–003   8.2A(1)   A practice direction may set out the circumstances in which the court may give permission for a claim form to be issued under this Part without naming a defendant.
(2)   An application for permission must be made by application notice before the claim form is issued.
(3)   The application notice for permission—

(a)   need not be served on any other person; and
(b)   must be accompanied by a copy of the claim form that the applicant proposes to issue.

(4)   Where the court gives permission it will give directions about the future management of the claim.

Acknowledgment of Service

C–004   8.3 (1) The defendant must—

(a)   file an acknowledgment of service in the relevant practice form not more than 14 days after service of the claim form; and
(b)   serve the acknowledgment of service on the claimant and any other party.

(2)   The acknowledgment of service must state—

(a)   whether the defendant contests the claim; and
(b)   if the defendant seeks a different remedy from that set out in the claim form, what that remedy is.

(3) The following rules of Part 10 (acknowledgment of service) apply—

    (a) rule 10.3(2) (exceptions to the period for filing an acknowledgment of service); and

    (b) rule 10.5 (contents of acknowledgment of service).

Consequence of Not Filing an Acknowledgment of Service

8.4 (1) This rule applies where—   **C–005**

    (a) the defendant has failed to file an acknowledgment of service; and

    (b) the time period for doing so has expired.

(2) The defendant may attend the hearing of the claim but may not take part in the hearing unless the court gives permission.

Filing and Serving Written Evidence

8.5 (1) The claimant must file any written evidence on which he intends to   **C–006**
rely when he files his claim form.

(2) The claimant's evidence must be served on the defendant with the claim form.

(3) A defendant who wishes to rely on written evidence must file it when he files his acknowledgment of service.

(4) If he does so, he must also, at the same time, serve a copy of his evidence on the other parties.

(5) The claimant may, within 14 days of service of the defendant's evidence on him, file further written evidence in reply.

(6) If he does so, he must also, within the same time limit, serve a copy of his evidence on the other parties.

(7) The claimant may rely on the matters set out in his claim form as evidence under this rule if the claim form is verified by a statement of truth.

Evidence—General

8.6 (1) No written evidence may be relied on at the hearing of the claim   **C–007**
unless—

    (a) it has been served in accordance with rule 8.5; or

    (b) the court gives permission.

(2) The court may require or permit a party to give oral evidence at the hearing.

(3) The court may give directions requiring the attendance for cross-examination$^{(GL)}$ of a witness who has given written evidence.

(Rule 32.1 contains a general power for the court to control evidence.)

Part 20 Claims

C–008   8.7 Where the Part 8 procedure is used, Part 20 (counterclaims and other additional claims) applies except that a party may not make a Part 20 claim (as defined by rule 20.2) without the court's permission.

Procedure Where Defendant Objects to the Use of the Part 8 Procedure

C–009   8.8 (1)   Where the defendant contends that the Part 8 procedure should not be used because—

(a)   there is a substantial dispute of fact; and
(b)   the use of the Part 8 procedure is not required or permitted by a rule or practice direction,

he must state his reasons when he files his acknowledgment of service.

(Rule 8.5 requires a defendant who wishes to rely on written evidence to file it when he files his acknowledgment of service.)

(2)   When the court receives the acknowledgment of service and any written evidence it will give directions as to the future management of the case.

(Rule 8.1(3) allows the court to make an order that the claim continue as if the claimant had not used the Part 8 procedure.)

Modifications to the General Rules

C–010   8.9 Where the Part 8 procedure is followed—

(a)   provision is made in this Part for the matters which must be stated in the claim form and the defendant is not required to file a defence and therefore—

(i)   Part 16 (statements of case) does not apply;
(ii)   Part 15 (defence and reply) does not apply;
(iii) any time limit in these Rules which prevents the parties from taking a step before a defence is filed does not apply;
(iv)   the requirement under rule 7.8 to serve on the defendant a form for defending the claim does not apply;

(b)   the claimant may not obtain judgment by request on an admission and therefore—

(i)   rules 14.4 to 14.7 do not apply; and
(ii)   the requirement under rule 7.8 to serve on the defendant a form for admitting the claim does not apply; and

(c)   the claim shall be treated as allocated to the multi-track and therefore Part 26 does not apply.

2.—Practice Direction 8a: Alternative Procedure for Claims

Section A: General Provisions Applicable to Part 8 Claims

[Note: Provisions of Section A which are not relevant to a 1975 Act claim have been omitted.]

Types of Claim in Which the Part 8 Procedure May be Used

3.1 The types of claim for which the Part 8 procedure may be used include: **C–011**

    (1) a claim by or against a child or protected party which has been settled before the commencement of proceedings and the sole purpose of the claim is to obtain the approval of the court to the settlement;

Issuing the Claim

4.1(1) Part 7 and Practice Direction 7A contain a number of rules and **C–012** directions applicable to all claims, including those to which Part 8 applies. Those rules and directions should be applied where appropriate.

4.2. Where a claimant uses the Part 8 procedure, the claim form (practice form N208) should be used and must state the matters set out in rule 8.2 and, if rule 8.1(6) applies, must comply with the requirements of the practice direction in question. In particular, the claim form must state that Part 8 applies; a Part 8 claim form means a claim form which so states.

Responding to the Claim

5.1 The provisions of Part 15 (defence and reply) do not apply where the **C–013** claim form is a Part 8 claim form.

5.2. Where a defendant who wishes to respond to a Part 8 claim form is required to file an acknowledgment of service, that acknowledgment of service should be in practice form N210.

Managing the Claim

6.1. The court may give directions immediately a Part 8 claim form is issued **C–014** either on the application of a party or on its own initiative. The directions may include fixing a hearing date where:

    (1) there is no dispute, such as in child and protected party settlements; or
    (2) where there may be a dispute, but a hearing date could conveniently be given.

6.2. Where the court does not fix a hearing date when the claim form is issued, it will give directions for the disposal of the claim as soon as practicable after the defendant has acknowledged service of the claim form or, as the case may be, after the period for acknowledging service has expired.

6.3. Certain applications may not require a hearing.

6.4. The court may convene a directions hearing before giving directions.

Evidence

C–015   7.1. A claimant must file the written evidence on which he relies when his Part 8 claim form is issued (unless the evidence is contained in the claim form itself).

7.2. Evidence will normally be in the form of a witness statement or an affidavit but a claimant may rely on the matters set out in his claim form provided that it has been verified by a statement of truth.

(For information about (1) statements of truth see Part 22 and Practice Direction 22, and (2) written evidence see Part 32 and Practice Direction 32.)

7.3. A defendant wishing to rely on written evidence must file it with his acknowledgment of service.

7.4. A party may apply to the court for an extension of time to serve and file evidence under Rule 8.5 or for permission to serve and file additional evidence under Rule 8.6(1).

(For information about applications see Part 23 and Practice Direction 23A.)

7.5 (1) The parties may, subject to the following provisions, agree in writing on an extension of time for serving and filing evidence under Rule 8.5(3) or Rule 8.5(5).

(2) An agreement extending time for a defendant to file evidence under Rule 8.5(3)—

(a) must be filed by the defendant at the same time as he files his acknowledgment of service; and

(b) must not extend time by more than 14 days after the defendant files his acknowledgment of service.

(3) An agreement extending time for a claimant to file evidence in reply under Rule 8.5(5) must not extend time to more than 28 days after service of the defendant's evidence on the claimant.

Hearing

C–016   8.1. The court may on the hearing date—

(1) proceed to hear the case and dispose of the claim;
(2) give case management directions.

3.—Part 57: Probate, Inheritance And Presumption Of Death

Section IV—Claims under the Inheritance (Provision for Family and Dependants) Act 1975

Scope of this Section

57.14 This Section contains rules about claims under the Inheritance (Pro-   **C–017**
vision for Family and Dependants) Act 1975 ("the Act")

Proceedings in the High Court

(1) Proceedings in the High Court under the Act shall be issued in   **C–018**
either—

(a) the Chancery Division; or
(b) the Family Division.

(2) The Civil Procedure Rules apply to proceedings under the Act
which are brought in the Family Division, except that the
provisions of the Family Proceedings Rules 2010 relating to the
drawing up and service of orders apply instead of the provisions in Part 40 and Practice Direction 40B.

Procedure for Claims Under Section 1 of the Act

(1) A claim under section 1 of the Act must be made by issuing a   **C–019**
claim form in accordance with Part 8.
(2) Rule 8.3 (acknowledgment of service) and rule 8.5 (filing and
serving written evidence) apply as modified by paragraphs (3)
to (5) of this rule.
(3) The written evidence filed and served by the claimant with the
claim form must have exhibited to it an official copy of—

(a) the grant of probate or letters of administration in respect
of the deceased's estate; and
(b) every testamentary document in respect of which probate
or letters of administration were granted.

(3A) Where no grant has been obtained, the claimant may make a
claim without naming a defendant and may apply for directions
as to the representation of the estate. The written evidence
must—

(a) explain the reasons why it has not been possible for a grant
to be obtained;
(b) be accompanied by the original or a copy (if either is
available) of the will or testamentary document in respect
of which probate or letters of administration are to be
granted
(c) contain the following information, so far as is known to
the claimant—
(i) brief details of the property comprised in the estate,

with an approximate estimate of its capital value and
any income that is received from it
(ii) brief details of the liabilities of the estate
(iii) the names and addresses of the persons who are in
possession of the documents relating to the estate;
and
(iv) the names of the beneficiaries and their respective
interests in the estate

(3B) Where a claim is made in accordance with paragraph (3A), the
court may give directions as to the parties to the claim and as to
the representation of the estate either on the claimant's application or of its own motion
(Section 4 of the Act as amended confirms that nothing prevents the making of an application under the Act before
representation with respect to the estate of the deceased person
is first taken out.)
(4) Subject to paragraph (4A), the time within which a defendant
must file and serve—

(a) an acknowledgment of service; and
(b) any written evidence,

is not more than 21 days after service of the claim form on him.
(4A) If the claim form is served out of the jurisdiction under rule
6.32 or 6.33, the period for filing an acknowledgment of service
and any written evidence is 7 days longer than the relevant
period specified in rule 6.35 or Practice Direction 6B.
(5) A defendant who is a personal representative of the deceased
must file and serve written evidence, which must include the
information required by Practice Direction 57.

4.—PRACTICE DIRECTION 57A: PROBATE

*Section IV—Claims under the Inheritance (Provision for Family and
Dependants) Act 1975*

Acknowledgment of Service by Personal Representative—Rule 57.16(4)

C–020   15 Where a defendant who is a personal representative wishes to remain
neutral in relation to the claim, and agrees to abide by any decision which
the court may make, he should state this in Section A of the acknowledgment of service form.

Written Evidence of Personal Representative—Rule 57.16(5)

C–021   16 The written evidence filed by a defendant who is a personal representative
must state to the best of that person's ability—

(1) full details of the value of the deceased's net estate, as defined in
section 25(1) of the Act;

(2) the person or classes of persons beneficially interested in the estate, and—

    (a) the names and (unless they are parties to the claim) addresses of all living beneficiaries; and

    (b) the value of their interests in the estate so far as they are known.

(3) whether any living beneficiary (and if so, naming him) is a child or a person who lacks capacity (within the meaning of the Mental Capacity Act 2005); and

(4) any facts which might affect the exercise of the court's powers under the Act.

Separate Representation of Claimants

17 If a claim is made jointly by two or more claimants, and it later appears   **C–022** that any of the claimants have a conflict of interests—

(1) any claimant may choose to be represented at any hearing by separate solicitors or counsel, or may appear in person; and

(2) if the court considers that claimants who are represented by the same solicitors or counsel ought to be separately represented, it may adjourn the application until they are.

Production of the Grant

18.1 On the hearing of a claim the personal representative must produce to   **C–023** the court the original grant of representation to the deceased's estate.

18.2 If the court makes an order under the Act, the original grant (together   **C–024** with a sealed copy of the order) must be sent to the Principal Registry of the Family Division for a memorandum of the order to be endorsed on or permanently annexed to the grant in accordance with section 19(3) of the Act.

18.3 Every final order embodying terms of compromise made in proceedings   **C–025** under the Act, whether made with or without a hearing, must contain a direction that a memorandum of the order shall be endorsed on or permanently annexed to the probate or letters of administration and a copy of the order shall be sent to the Principal Registry of the Family Division with the relevant grant of probate or letters of administration for endorsement.

5.—MODEL DIRECTIONS

[Note: High Court Form PF 52 (Order for Case Management Directions in the Multi-track (Part 29)) no longer exists in the form in which it was included in the previous edition of this work.[1] It is replaced in this section of

---

[1] This is now entitled "Order in the Queen's Bench Division for case and costs management in the multi-track (Part 29)".

the Appendix by High Court Forms CH1 and CH2,[2] which contain directions relating to the matters most likely to arise in a 1975 Act claim.]

5.1. Draft Chancery Case Management Directions CH 1 (amended, February 2017)

C–026   *This form is suitable for the most usual case management directions. Additional directions, less commonly used, are available in form CH 2.*

Claim No.

NOTE: the court will not normally be able to make case management directions based upon an agreed order unless all costs budgets are agreed or the claim is outside the scope of costs management.

IT IS ORDERED that

C–027   **1. Allocation**

(a) Allocation to Multi-Track

This Claim is allocated to the multi-track.

And

(b) Allocation to Management Track

This claim is allocated to the following management track:

    (i)   Case management by Master and trial by Judge
    (ii) Case management and trial by Judge (full docketing)
    (iii) Case management and trial by Master
    (iv) Case Management by Judge and Master and trial by Judge.

C–028   **2. Alternative dispute resolution**

(1) This claim be stayed until   *[one month]* for the parties to try to settle the dispute by alternative dispute resolution or other means. The parties shall notify the Court in writing at the end of that period whether settlement has been reached.

The parties shall at the same time lodge *either*:

    (a) (if a settlement has been reached) a draft consent order signed by all parties; *or*
    (b) (if no settlement has been reached)

        (i)   a statement of agreed directions signed by all parties or (in the absence of agreed directions) statements of the parties' respective proposed directions;
        (ii) the parties' disclosure reports; and
        (iii) the parties' costs budgets.

---

[2] Some numbering has been added to both forms for ease of reference.

(2) The parties may agree to extend the stay for the purpose granted for periods of up to three months from the date of this order without reference to the Court and shall notify the Court in writing of the expiry date of any such extension. Any request for a further extension after three months must be referred to the Court.

(3) Any party has permission to apply in relation to the extension.

3. Trial date   C–029

[for use only where it is reasonably certain that (a) the trial time estimate is unlikely to be exceeded; (b) the case will remain in the High Court in London; and (c) the listing category is clear]

(1) The trial of the claim/issue(s) take place between   *(date)*

and   *(date)* ("the trial window").

[Master to fix a 3 month window in accordance with weekly sheet from the Listing Officer].

(2). The ....*(party)* shall make an appointment to attend on the Listing Officer (The Rolls Building, 7 Rolls Buildings, Fetter Lane, London EC4A 1NL; Tel. 020 7947 6690; email rcjchancery.judgeslisting@hmcts.gsi.gov.uk) to fix a trial date within the trial window, such appointment to be not later than...........*(date)* and give notice of the appointment to all other parties and *[the trial being estimated to last more than 5 days]* to fix a date for a Pre Trial Review on......... *[a date approximately 4 weeks before the trial]* with a time estimate of half a day. (Where the trial is expected to last more than 9 days the Pre-Trial review shall if possible be held in front of the Judge who will be conducting the trial). At the Pre-Trial Review, the Court will not hear other applications unless it has proved impracticable for them to have been heard previously.

(3) The Claim be entered in the [Trial List][General List], with a listing category of [A][B][C], with a time estimate of   days/weeks to include [day(s)/hours] judge's pre-reading time and [where appropriate] an interval between close of evidence and final submissions of [day(s)] [or if *(state basis of variable)* then   days/weeks]

(4) The trial shall take place in London

[If the Master wishes the time estimate to be reviewed at a later date]

(5) The Claimant shall by   *(a date normally within 4 weeks of exchange of witness statements, but variable depending on the timetable)*, having consulted the other parties, notify the Listing Officer whether the time estimate should be varied

4. Disclosure of documents   C–030

(1) Disclosure is dispensed with; *or.*

(2) By   (date)

(i) [*party*] shall disclose the documents on which it relies and at the same time request any specific disclosure that it requires from any other party.

(ii) [Each party shall give disclosure on an issue by issue basis.]

(iii) [Each party shall disclose any documents which it is reasonable to suppose may contain information which enables that party to advance its own case or to damage that of any other party, or which leads to an inquiry which has either of those consequences.]

(iv) [[*party*] shall give standard disclosure.]; *or*

(3) [*such other order in relation to disclosure as the Court is asked to consider appropriate, including if appropriate in relation to electronic documents*] **Please set out the order proposed**

Notes:

(a) The Court will consider the disclosure reports provided by the parties and decide which of the disclosure options set out in CPR 31.5(7) should apply to this claim. Proposals put forward by the parties will be taken into account in making that decision.

*(b) **A list of issues**, preferably agreed, should be attached to the draft directions so as to assist the Court in determining any order to be made in relation to disclosure*

C–031 **5. Inspection of documents**

Any requests for inspection or copies of disclosed documents shall be made within   days after service of the list and shall be responded to within [7] days of receipt of the request.

C–032 **6. Witness statements**

(1) Each party serve on every other party the witness statement of the oral evidence which the party serving the statement intends to rely on in relation to [any issues of fact][the following issues of fact   (*define issues*) to be decided at the trial, those statements [and any notices of intention to rely on hearsay evidence] to be

(a) exchanged by   (*date*) or

(b) served by   (*party*) by   (*date*) and by   (*party*) by   (*date*)

provided that before exchange the parties shall liaise with a view to agreeing a method of identification of any documents referred to in any such witness statement.

(2) The   (*party*) has permission to serve a witness summary relating to the evidence of   (*name*)   (*address*) [on every other party by][to be served on   (*party*)/exchanged at the same time as exchange of witness Statements].

*(**Note:** The parties should consider the court's power in CPR 32.2(3)) and*

*must comply with the provisions of the Chancery Guide paragraphs 19.16–17
concerning exhibits to witness statements)*

7(a). Experts: permission to apply

C–033

(1) The parties have permission to apply for directions as to expert evidence
(if necessary).

7(b). Single expert

C–034

(1) Evidence be given by the report of a single expert in the field of
(*define field*) instructed jointly by the parties, on the
issue of   (*define issue*) [and [his][her] fees shall be limited to
£   ].

(2) If the parties are unable to agree [by   (*date*)] who that expert is to
be and about the payment of [his][her] fees any party may apply for further
directions.

(3) Unless the parties agree in writing or the Court orders otherwise, the fees
and expenses of the single expert shall be paid to [him][her] by the parties
equally.

(4) Each party give [his][her] instructions to the single expert by   (*date*).

(5) The report of the single expert be filed and served by [him][her] on the
parties by   (*date*).

(6) No party may recover from another party more than £   for the fees
and expenses of the expert.

(7) The evidence of the expert be given at the trial by [written report][oral
evidence] of the expert.

7(c). Separate experts

C–035

(1) Each party has permission to adduce [oral] expert evidence in the field of
(*specify*) to address issues relating to   (*specify*) at an estimated cost
of £   (*specify*)
[limited to   expert(s) [per party][on each side].

(2) (*where practicable*) that the experts shall be   (*specify name*) and
(*specify name*)

(3) The experts shall, before they exchange their reports, discuss and narrow
the issues between them

(4) The experts' reports shall be exchanged by   (*date*).

(5) The experts shall hold a further discussion for the purpose of:

    (a)   identifying and further narrowing the issues, if any, remaining
           between them; and
    (b)   where possible, reaching agreement on those issues.

(6) The experts shall by   [*specify date after discussion*] prepare and file a statement for the Court showing:

(a)   those issues on which they are agreed; and
(b)   those issues on which they disagree and a summary of their reasons for disagreeing.

(7) No party shall be entitled to recover by way of costs from any other party more than £   for the fees or expenses of an expert. *Note: to assist the Court in determining what order should be made in relation to expert evidence, the parties should attach a **list of issues**, preferably agreed.*

C–036   **8. Trial bundle and skeleton arguments.**

(1) No later than [4] weeks before the date fixed for trial the claimant shall send the defendant a draft bundle index for the trial bundle for the use of the Judge, in accordance with Chapter 21 of the Chancery Guide.

(2) The defendant shall send any comments on the draft index no later than [3] weeks before the trial date.

(3) The claimant shall provide the trial bundle to the defendant no later than [2] weeks before the trial date.

(4) Not earlier than 7 days or later than 3 days before the date fixed for trial the claimant shall file with the Chancery Listing Office a trial bundle for the use of the Judge,

(5) The parties shall exchange skeleton arguments and chronologies, in accordance with Chapter 21 of the Chancery Guide, [and bundles of photocopied legal authorities] 7 days before the trial date.

(6) Skeleton arguments and chronologies [and bundles of photocopied legal authorities] shall be filed not less than 2 clear days before the trial date.

Note: Where the trial is before a Master, the draft directions should be amended accordingly.

C–037   **9. Settlement**

If the Claim or part of the Claim is settled the parties must immediately inform the Court, whether or not it is then possible to file a draft Consent Order to give effect to the settlement.

C–038   **10. [Case and] costs management**

[*where budgets have been agreed*] The parties having agreed and filed budgets, the Court makes a Case and Costs Management Order which records that agreement.

(***Note****: If budgets are not agreed the Court may direct a Case and Costs Management Conference.*)

11 Extension of time limits

C–039

The parties may, where CPR rule 2.11 applies, agree to extend any time period to which the proceedings may be subject for a period or periods of up to 28 days in total without reference to the court, provided that this does not affect the date given for any case or costs management conference or pre-trial review or the date of the trial. The parties shall notify the court in writing of the expiry date of any such extension.

12. Costs The costs of this application be [costs in the case].

C–040

5.2. Draft Additional Chancery Case Management Directions CH 2 (amended February 2017)

(The most usual case management directions are available in form CH 1.)

MULTI-TRACK CLAIMS

Claim No.

IT IS ORDERED THAT

1. Transfer of claims, including transfer from Part 8

C–041

(1) The claim be transferred to:

    (a) the   Division of the High Court;
    (b) the   District Registry;
    (c) the   County Court at [Central London] (Chancery List).

(2) The issue(s) *(define issue(s))* be transferred to *(one of (a) to (c) above)* for determination.

(3) The claim be transferred to the Technology and Construction Court [*or other Specialist List*] by (date) subject to the consent of the Chancellor and the approval of the Judge of the Technology and Construction Court [*or other Specialist List*].

(4) The claim *(title and claim number)* commenced in [the County Court][the District Registry] at
, be transferred from that court to the Chancery Division of the High Court.

If the proposed trial venue is not in London,

(5) The claim be transferred, subject to the approval of [the Judge in charge of the region] to: *(Master to state transfer arrangements as appropriate]*.

Note: *the claim must be transferred to the trial venue not less than 28 days before the trial)*

(6) This claim shall continue as if commenced under Part 7 and shall be allocated to the multi-track.

C–042   **2. Probate cases only**

The   [*party*] file [his][her] witness statement or affidavit of testamentary scripts and lodge any testamentary script at Chancery Chambers, Case Management Section, The Rolls Building, 7 Rolls Buildings, Fetter Lane, London EC4A 1NL [District Registry] by   (*date*).

C–043   **3. Case summary**

[Each party][The   (*party*)] by   (*date*) prepare and serve a case summary [not exceeding   words] on all other parties, to be agreed by (*date*) and filed by   (*date*) and if it is not agreed by that date the parties shall file their own case summaries.

C–044   **4. All directions agreed.**

[If the parties have sent in a full list of agreed directions which are satisfactory, use this paragraph. A case management conference may then not be required]:

The parties having agreed directions it is by consent ordered:-

C–045   **5. Some directions agreed**

[If the parties have agreed some directions which are satisfactory, use this paragraph]:

The parties having agreed the following directions it is by consent ordered:

C–046   **6. Case management conference etc.**

(1) There be a [further] case management conference before the Master in Hearing Room...First Floor, The Rolls Building, 7 Rolls Building, Fetter Lane, London EC4A 1NL on   (*date*) at   o'clock (of   hours/ minutes duration).

(2) There shall be a case management conference (of   hours/minutes duration). In order for the court to fix a date the parties are to complete the accompanying questionnaire and file it by   (*date*).

(3) The   (*party*) apply for an appointment for a [further] case management conference by   (*date*).

(4) At the case management conference, except for urgent matters in the meantime, the court will hear any further applications for orders and any party must file an application notice for any such orders and serve it and supporting evidence (if any) by   (*date*).

C–047   **7. Where budgets have been filed and exchanged but have not been agreed in whole or in part,** *the Master is likely to make an order based on the following directions:*

(1) There be a [Case and] Costs Management Conference before the Master in Hearing Room... First Floor, The Rolls Building, 7 Rolls Building, Fetter

Lane, London EC4A 1NL on   (*date*) at   o'clock (of   hours/ minutes duration).

(2) At least 5 working days before the [Case and] Costs Management Conference the Claimant must file with the Court, and send copies to all other parties, the following documents:

(a)   a case summary and list of issues,
(b)   a one page summary of Precedent H of all parties' budgets to enable the Court to undertake comparison of the budgets, in the form set out below*

(3) (*Set out any other proposed directions with regard to budgets*)

(4) There be a Case [and Costs] Management Conference before the Master in Hearing Room...First Floor, The Rolls Building, 7 Rolls Building, Fetter Lane, London EC4A 1NL

Form of summary of Precedent H   **C–048**

PHASE	CLAIMANT	1ST DEF	2ND DEF	3RD DEF	TOTAL
Pre-action					
Issues/statements of case					
CMC					
Disclosure					
Witness Statements					
Experts' reports					
PTR					
Trial preparation					
Trial					
ADR					
Contingencies					
TOTAL					

6. Amendments to Statement of case

(1) The   (*party*) has permission to amend [his][her] statement of   **C–049** case as in the copy on the court file [initialled by the Master].

(2) The amended statement of case be verified by a statement of truth.

(3) The amended statement of case be filed by   (*date*).

(4) [The amended statement of case be served by   (*date*).] [Service of the amended Statement of case be dispensed with].

(5) Any consequential amendments to other statements of case be filed and served by   (*date*)

(6) The costs of and consequential to the amendment to the statement of case [shall be paid by   (*party*) in any event] [are assessed in the sum of £   and are to be paid by   (*party*)][within   (*time*)].

7. Addition of parties etc.

C–050   (1) The   (*party*) has permission:

  (a) to [add][substitute][remove]   (*name of party*) as a   (*party*) and
  (b) to amend [his][her] Statement of case in accordance with the copy on the Court file [initialled by the Master][attached to the application notice dated   (*date*)].

(2) The amended statement of case be verified by a statement of truth.

(3) The amended statement of case be :

  (a) filed by   (*date*);
  (b) served on   (*new party, existing parties or removed party, as appropriate*), by   (*date*).

(4) A copy of this order be served on   (*new party, existing parties or removed party, as appropriate*), by   (*date*).

(5) Any consequential amendments to other Statements of case be filed and served by   (*date*).

(6) The costs of and consequential to the amendment to the statement of case [shall be paid by the   (*party*) in any event] [are assessed in the sum of £   and are to be paid by the   (*party*)].

8. Consolidation or joint case management and trial

C–051   (1) This claim be consolidated with claim number   (*number and title*), the lead claim to be claim number   . [The title to the consolidated case shall be as set out in the schedule to this order].

(2) This claim be case managed and tried with claim(s)   (*number(s) and title(s)*

9. Definition and reduction of issues

C–052   By   (*date*) the parties list and discuss the issues in the claim [including the experts' reports and statements] and attempt to define and narrow the issues [including those issues the subject of discussion by the experts].

10. Trial of issue

C–053   The issue of   (*define issue*) be tried as follows:

  (a) with the consent of the parties, before a Master

    (i)   on   (*date*) in Hearing Room..., First Floor, The Rolls Building, 7 Rolls Building, Fetter Lane, London EC4A 1NL;

    (ii) with a time estimate of   (hours),

    (iii) with the filing of listing questionnaires dispensed with, *or*

(b) before a Judge

    (i)   with the trial of the issue to take place between   (*date*) and (*date*) ("the trial window")

    (ii) with the   (*party*) to make an appointment to attend on the Listing Officer (The Rolls Building, 7 Rolls Building, Fetter Lane, London EC4A 1NL; Tel. 020 7947 6690; email rcjchancery.judgeslisting@hmcts.gsi.gov.uk) to fix a trial date within the trial window, such appointment to be not later than   (*date*)

and to give notice of the appointment to all other parties.

    (iii) with the issue to be entered in the [Trial List][General List], with a listing category of [A][B][C], and a time estimate of days/ weeks to include [day(s)] judge's pre-reading time and [where appropriate] an interval between close of evidence and final submissions of [day(s)] and to take place in London (*or* identify venue).

11. Further information

(1) The   (*party*) provide by   (*date*) the [further information][clarification] sought in the request dated   (*date*) [initialled by the Master].   **C–054**

(2) any request for [further information][clarification] shall be served

by   [*date*].

12. Preservation of property

The   (*party*) preserve   (*give details of relevant property*) until trial of the claim or further order *or other remedy under rule 25.1(1)*.   **C–055**

13. No expert evidence

No expert evidence being necessary, [no party has permission to call or rely on expert evidence][permission to call or rely on expert evidence is refused].   **C–056**

14. Compliance with directions

The parties shall by   (*date*) notify the court in writing that they have fully complied with all directions or state: **C–057**

    (a) with which directions they have not complied;

    (b) why they have not complied; and

    (c) what steps they are taking to comply with the outstanding directions in time for the trial.

If the court does not receive such notification or if the steps proposed to comply with outstanding directions are considered by the court unsatisfactory, the court may order a hearing (and may make appropriate orders as to costs against a party in default).

6.—The ACTAPS Practice Guidance for the Resolution of Probate and Trust Disputes ("The ACTAPS Code")

C–058   Paragraph 4 of the Practice Direction on Protocols has been substantially amended. It states that "in cases not covered by any protocol, the court will expect the parties to act reasonably in exchanging information and documents relevant to their claim and in trying to avoid the necessity for the start of proceedings".

C–059   Moreover, with effect from 1 April 2003, the 30th update to the CPR imposes on all parties to a dispute (whatever its nature) an obligation to comply with specified procedures designed to avoid litigation commencing.

C–060   Practitioners will no doubt remember the dicta of the Court of Appeal in *Carlson v Townsend* [2001] 3 All E.R. 663 where it stated the use of the protocol was not limited to fast-track cases. The spirit if not the letter of the protocol was equally appropriate to some higher value claims. In accordance with the aims of the civil justice reforms, the courts expected to see the spirit of reasonable pre-action behaviour applied in all cases regardless of the existence of a specific protocol.

C–061   The Association of Contentious Trust & Probate Specialists (ACTAPS) and the Trust Law Committee have, as many practitioners will be aware, given much thought to the possibility that a special pre-action protocol ought to be developed for disputes within their area of expertise. Indeed a draft has for some time been on the ACTAPS website (www.actaps.com) and has since been the subject of extensive discussions with representatives of the judiciary concerned.

C–062   It is now clear that no special protocol will be adopted, despite a recognition that the draft contains useful elements. It will be seen that it deals in particular with the following matters:

(a)   appointment of a representative to act on behalf of beneficiaries who cannot be ascertained or traced;
(b)   requirement for a letter of claim setting out the basis of claim;
(c)   early disclosure of documents;
(d)   use of joint experts where possible;
(e)   a joint letter of request for medical records;
(f)   a joint *Larke v Nugus* letter; and
(g)   a joint letter requesting details of deceased's capacity.

C–063   In these circumstances the committee of ACTAPS has concluded that it would be useful to encourage members to have regard to The ACTAPS Code as a means of developing best practices in areas where special problems may arise, for example, the need to have representatives for persons who cannot speak for themselves in a context where others may feel that mediation would be desirable.

It is understood that the judges who have considered The ACTAPS Code   **C–064** have expressed no concerns that it is out of line with the CPR objectives or that to follow its principles would give rise to unnecessary problems in practice. In particular it is thought that CPR Rule 19.7(3)(b) gives the necessary scope for securing the appointment of representatives of those who are absent, unborn or members of a large class, as well before as after the commencement of proceedings.

It is also hoped that in the context of probate issues the common difficulty of   **C–065** medical practitioners considering that they may as a matter of professional confidence be restricted in releasing records can be overcome by joint application (and following discussions between ACTAPS and the BMA the latter has confirmed that its future guidance will facilitate disclosure in accordance with The ACTAPS Code). The ACTAPS Code contains an outline for such a letter.

In these circumstances it is suggested that practitioners in the areas of trust   **C–066** and probate law should seek to follow the approaches indicated in The ACTAPS Code, approved by the Trust Law Committee and ACTAPS, on the basis that it may serve to amplify the basic principles of the general protocols and indicate considered methods of carrying the objectives of the general protocols into effect in areas which may be found to give rise to special difficulties with which the general protocols do not grapple. In putting forward this suggestion the committee of ACTAPS believes that it has the support of all who have been concerned to consider the draft protocol; the rejection of the proposal that it be adopted as a special protocol owes nothing (so far as is known) to any perception of defects and merely reflects the belief that the public interest is best served by seeking, where possible, to avoid specific protocols and to develop best practices in areas where general protocols have to be supplemented to meet the needs of special situations.

With that in mind the committee of ACTAPS encourages members and   **C–067** other users to help move the search for best practices forward by commenting on any defects, inadequacies or other difficulties which may be found to arise in carrying the terms of The ACTAPS Code into effect. Please make any such comments to the ACTAPS Chairman's or the ACTAPS Secretary's e-mail address.

Practitioners will wish to bear in mind the need for trustees and executors to   **C–068** consider the adequacy of their powers to enter into any particular course of conduct and the possibility that they may need, e.g. Beddoes-type directions if they propose a course of conduct to which their beneficiaries might wish to raise objection (as, for example, where the trustees wish voluntarily to disclose confidential documents to third parties) or which may involve material burdens of costs (as, for example, the institution of a lengthy mediation). But of course in circumstances where the aim is to explore ways of reaching agreement or otherwise saving costs any necessary order might be expected to be forthcoming (within the appropriate limits) without difficulty on the basis that the Court would be being asked to facilitate a course of action essentially in accordance with the overriding objective.

1. INTRODUCTION

The Scope of the Code

C–069 1.1 This Code is intended to apply to disputes about:

- the devolution and administration of estates of deceased persons; and
- the devolution and administration of trust funds ("probate and trust disputes").

It is not intended to displace other protocols if in the circumstances of the case they can be seen to be more appropriate.

The main types of disputes within the ambit of this Code can be expected to be:

- challenges to the validity of a will, for example, on grounds of want of capacity or knowledge and approval, undue influence or forgery
- claims under the Inheritance (Provision for Family and Dependants) Act 1975 ("the Inheritance Act")
- actions for the removal of an administrator or executor or trustee or the appointment of a judicial trustee
- actions for the rectification of a will or other document
- disputes as to the meanings of provisions in a will or a trust
- administration actions
- allegations of breach of trust.

The ACTAPS Code may also apply to certain types of dispute where the provisions of a trust or the devolution of an estate are of the essence, for example where a claimant seeks in the alternative to set aside or overturn a trust or to take advantage of rights under a trust.

The Code has two aims; to encourage the resolution of disputes without hostile litigation; and even where litigation may be necessary to ensure that it is simplified as far as possible by maximizing the scope for the exchange of relevant information before the litigation process has commenced.

The Code is in general terms unlikely to be appropriate for disputes which involve:

- disputes as to the rights appertaining under rules of forced heirships under the law of some foreign jurisdiction
- the need for emergency injunctions
- (except in so far as concerns pre-action exchange of information) the need for a binding precedent or a declaration by the Court as to the true construction of some trust instrument or testamentary disposition.

The Code is formed in general terms to cover the broad range of trust and probate disputes; but it is recognised that the appropriate investigations and exchange of information will vary according to the circumstances of the dispute. However one of its primary purposes is to provide for a special feature of disputes in this area, namely that there may be beneficiaries who cannot speak for themselves but whose interests must be protected.

1.2 In cases where the express terms of The Code is not appropriate parties will be expected to follow the spirit of The Code and seek to achieve its aims so far as practicable in the particular case.   **C–070**

1.3 It is also to be borne in mind that there are certain cases in which a trust or probate dispute seeks to fulfil some non-contentious purpose, as for example where a question of difficulty is identified to which the parties are agreed that the best solution lies in inviting the Court to approve constructive proposals by way of compromise or where the objective is simply to find the cheapest way of protecting trustees or personal representatives against the risks involved in the existence of some theoretical doubt. In such cases The Code is unlikely to have any role to play.   **C–071**

1.4. One of the principal features of trust and probate disputes is that they may affect the interests of persons not of full capacity, as yet unborn or unascertained, or interested as members of a large class of persons who have similar beneficial interests. The Code is thus designed to make express provision for the need to find mechanisms that assist despite the absence of such persons (providing in particular an expedited process for Court approval of agreements reached in mediation). It is thus wrong in principle to regard a dispute as not amenable to the use of The Code just because there are persons concerned who cannot speak for themselves.   **C–072**

2. PRINCIPAL GUIDELINES

Parties

2.1 The parties to the probate or trust dispute will usually be trustees (or personal representatives or persons claiming to be entitled as such) and beneficiaries of the trust or estate who are of full capacity, though The Code is designed also to be capable of being used in exterior/third party disputes where appropriate.   **C–073**

2.2 In the case where interests of unascertained persons, minors, unborns, mentally incapacitated persons or members of a large class (such that it is not appropriate for all members of the class to be made parties to the dispute) will be affected, the procedure to be adopted will be an application to the Court (see Annex A) whether or not a claim has yet been instituted before the Court.   **C–074**

Status of Letters of Claim and Response

2.3 A letter of claim or of response is not intended to have the same status as pleadings. Matters may come to light as a result of investigation after the letter of claim has been sent or after the defendant has responded. These investigations could result in the pleaded case of a party differing in some respects from the case outlined in that party's letter of claim or response. It   **C–075** would not be consistent with the spirit of The Code for a party to complain about this difference provided that there was no indication of any intention to mislead.

Disclosure of Documents

C–076   2.4 The aim of the early disclosure of documents by the defendant is not to encourage "fishing expeditions" by the claimant, but to promote an early exchange of relevant information to help in clarifying or resolving issues in dispute. The claimant's solicitors can assist by identifying in the letter of claim or in a subsequent letter the particular documents or categories of documents which they consider are relevant, and by providing copies of these where appropriate.

C–077   2.5 All documents are disclosed on the basis that they are not to be disclosed to third parties (other than legal advisers) or used for any purpose other than the resolution of the dispute, unless otherwise agreed in writing or permitted by the court.

Experts

C–078   2.6 Expert evidence appropriate to probate and trust disputes may include in particular medical evidence, handwriting evidence, valuation evidence, tax-related or actuarial evidence.

C–079   2.7 The Code encourages joint selection of, and access to, experts. However, it maintains the flexibility for each party to obtain their own expert's report. It is for the court to decide whether the costs of more than one expert's report should be recoverable.

Costs

C–080   2.8 Where the Code provides for the initial cost of obtaining information or reports to be borne by one party, it shall not restrict the court's discretion in relation to ultimate liability for such costs.

Negotiations/Mediation

C–081   2.9 Parties and their legal representatives are encouraged to enter into discussions and/or negotiations prior to starting proceedings. The parties should bear in mind that the courts increasingly take the view that litigation should be a last resort, and that claims should not be issued prematurely when a settlement is in reasonable prospect. Mediation of probate and trust disputes may assist in achieving a compromise, particularly in relation to disputes between family members. The form of the mediation will be set out in the mediation agreement between the mediator and the parties.

C–082   2.10 Mediation can be used to try to achieve a compromise whenever negotiation is appropriate and can be used at any stage in a trust dispute. Typically mediation may be considered:

    (i)   before proceedings have commenced but once the issues are fairly well defined and the parties affected by them are known;
    (ii)   even after proceedings have commenced and the statements of case have been served so that the parties have a better appreciation of the issues;

(iii) at any critical stage in the litigation such as after disclosure of documents, exchange of experts' reports, exchange of witness statements and in the lead up to the trial.

The parties should seek to conclude a mediation within 42 days of the appointment of the mediator.

2.11 Since mediation negotiations are treated by the Courts as without prejudice, points disclosed during an attempt to reach a settlement will be confidential between the parties and cannot be used as evidence in subsequent Court proceedings unless expressly agreed by the party who made the disclosure. The mediator will not divulge information without consent. Also he will not pass on such information to outside parties or act for either party to the dispute in subsequent proceedings. **C–083**

2.12 A settlement reached pursuant to a mediation should be recorded in writing and signed by the parties or their authorised representative. In probate and trust disputes, if and insofar as the subject matter of the dispute requires the sanction and approval of the Court, any agreement achieved as a result of the mediation should be expressed to be subject to the approval of the Court. **C–084**

2.13 In a probate or trust dispute where the position of the Inland Revenue may have some bearing on any compromise solution which may be reached, any agreement may be made conditional upon indications of the Inland Revenue's position or adjourned to enable clarification of its position to be sought. **C–085**

3. THE CODE

Letters of Claim

3.1 The Claimant shall send a letter of claim to each of the deceased's personal representatives or to the trustees, as the case may be and, unless it is impractical (e.g. because there is a large class of beneficiaries or the beneficiaries are minors) to each beneficiary or potential beneficiary of the estate or trust fund likely to be adversely affected by the claim (referred to as "the proposed Defendants"), as soon as sufficient information is available to substantiate a realistic claim which the Claimant has decided he is prepared to pursue. **C–086**

3.2 The letter shall contain a clear summary of the claim and the facts upon which it is based and state the remedy sought by the claimant. **C–087**

3.3 Solicitors are recommended to use a standard format for the claim letter. A sample letter is set out at Annex B; this can be amended to suit the particular case. **C–088**

3.4 In claims under the Inheritance Act the claimant should give details to the best of his ability of the matters set out in Section 3 of the Inheritance Act as relevant to the exercise of the Court's discretion (see Annex B). **C–089**

3.5 Copies of documents in the claimant's possession which he wishes to rely upon or which any other party is likely to wish to rely upon should be enclosed with the letter of claim. Examples of documents likely to be rele- **C–090** vant in different types of dispute are set out at Annex C. These lists are not exhaustive. The letter of claim may specify classes of document considered relevant for early disclosure by the proposed defendants.

Letter of Response

C–091 3.6 Each of the proposed defendants should respond to the letter of claim within 21 days stating whether he admits or denies the claim, responding in outline to the matters of fact relied upon by the claimant and setting out any particular matters of fact upon which he relies. If a proposed defendant intends to make an answering claim on his own behalf, the letter of response should contain the same information and documents as a letter of claim in relation to the Part 20 claim. If a proposed defendant is unable to respond within the time limit on any particular matter, the letter of response should give the reasons for the absence of a full response and state when it will be available.

C–092 3.7 In claims under the Inheritance Act each proposed defendant should give details to the best of his ability of the matters set out in Section 3 of the Inheritance Act as relevant to the exercise of the Court's discretion (and set out in Annex B).

C–093 3.8 Copies of documents in the proposed defendant's possession which he wishes to rely upon or which any other party is likely to wish to rely upon should be enclosed with the letter of response. Examples of relevant documents in relation to different categories of disputes are set out at Annex C. These lists are not exhaustive.

Documents

C–094 3.9 In relation to the documents in Annex C, the personal representatives of the deceased (including executors named in the last alleged will of the deceased) or trustees as appropriate should provide copies of such documents (if available) to a party requesting a copy within 14 days of the date of a letter of request (or such other reasonable time as may be agreed between the parties) or, if a copy is only available from a third party with the consent of the personal representatives or trustees, provide to the party making the request written authority to the third party to provide a copy of the document to that party.

C–095 3.10 Trustees or personal representatives should not be inhibited from making full disclosure by the absence of litigation.

Applications for documents or information in control of third parties

C–096 3.11 In a probate dispute the release of medical notes may cast much light on the likely outcome and it should be assumed for the purposes of The Code that they ought to be disclosed at the outset absent special reason.

C–097 3.12 If so requested in writing by any party all parties shall (in the absence of good reason to withhold the relevant items) within 14 days of any such request (or such longer period as shall reasonably be agreed):

(1) Sign and return to the party making the request, a joint application for the provision of copies of the deceased's medical notes or

social worker's reports to all parties. The notes and/or reports should be sent separately and directly to each party. A specimen joint application is at Annex D.

(2) Sign, and return to the party making the request, a joint application for a statement by the solicitor who prepared the will of the deceased setting out all the circumstances leading up to the preparation and making of the will. A specimen joint application is at Annex E.

3.13 The party making the request for a joint application for information or documents from a third party shall: **C–098**

(1) Submit it to the third party within 7 days of receipt of the joint application completed by the other parties.

(2) On receipt of the information or documents from the third party check that they have been received by all other parties and, if not, provide them with copies within 7 days of receipt.

3.14 In cases where the mental capacity of a deceased at the date of a testamentary instrument is in issue, the party seeking to uphold the testamentary instrument should obtain a report as to the deceased's mental capacity from his GP as soon as possible after the issue is identified and send it to all other parties within 7 days of receipt. A specimen letter of request is at Annex F. **C–099**

Experts

3.15 Parties should consider the use of jointly instructed experts so far as possible. Accordingly before any prospective party (the first party) instructs an expert he should (unless of the opinion that another party will want to instruct his own expert) give the other (second) party a list of the name(s) of one or more experts in the relevant discipline whom he considers are suitable to instruct. **C–100**

3.16 Within 14 days the second party may indicate an objection to one or more of such experts and suggest alternatives. The first party should then instruct a mutually acceptable expert. **C–101**

3.17 If an expert to be jointly instructed is not agreed, the parties may then instruct experts of their own choice. It would be for the court to decide subsequently, if proceedings are issued, whether either party had acted unreasonably. No party shall be entitled to instruct an expert proposed in a list of experts for joint instructions until it is clear that joint instructions cannot be agreed and thereafter the party who submitted the list of experts shall be entitled to nominate one of the experts on this list as his own chosen expert and no other party shall instruct any expert named on the list until such nomination has taken place. **C–102**

3.18 If the second party does not object to an expert nominated, he shall not be entitled to rely on his own expert evidence within that particular discipline unless: **C–103**

(1) the court so directs, or

(2)   the first party's expert report has been amended and the first party is not prepared to disclose the original report.

C–104   3.19 Either party may send to the expert written questions on the report, relevant to the issues, via the first party's solicitors. The expert should send answers to the question separately and directly to each party.

C–105   3.20 The cost of the report from an agreed expert will usually be paid by the party first proposing that a joint expert be instructed. The costs of the expert replying to questions will usually be borne by the party asking the questions. The ultimate liability for costs will be determined by the Court.

ANNEX A

Representation in Estate or Trust Disputes of interested persons who cannot be ascertained, etc.

C–106   (1)   In any estate or trust dispute concerning:—

(a)   property comprised in an estate or subject to a trust or alleged to be subject to a trust; or
(b)   the construction of a written instrument; or
(c)   a situation where the interests of beneficiaries may require separate representation

the Court, if satisfied that it is expedient to do so, and that one or more of the conditions specified in paragraph (2) are satisfied, may appoint one or more persons to represent any person (including a person under a disability, a minor or an unborn person) or class who is or may be interested (whether presently or for any future, contingent or unascertained interest) in or affected by the dispute.

(2)   The conditions for the exercise of the power conferred by paragraph (1) are as follows:—

(a)   that the person, the class or some member of the class cannot be ascertained or cannot be readily ascertained, or is not of full capacity; or
(b)   that the person, the class or some member of the class, though ascertained, cannot be found; or
(c)   that, though the person or the class and members thereof can be ascertained and found, it appears to the Court expedient (regard being had to all the circumstances, including the amount at stake and the degree of difficulty of the point to be determined) to exercise the power for the purposes of saving expense or for any other reason.

(3)   Where, in any case to which paragraph 1 applies, the Court exercises the power conferred by that paragraph, a judgment or order of the Court given or made when the person or persons appointed in exercise of that power are before the Court shall be binding on the person or class represented by the person or persons so appointed.

(4)   Where, in any such case, a compromise is proposed and some of the persons who are interested in, or who may be affected by the

compromise have not been consulted (including persons under a disability, minors or unborn or unascertained persons) but

(a) there is some other person in the same interest before the Court who assents to the compromise or on whose behalf the Court sanctions the compromise; or

(b) the absent persons are represented by a person appointed under paragraph (1) who so assents, the Court, if satisfied that the compromise will be for the benefit of the absent persons and that it is expedient to exercise this power, may approve the compromise and order that it shall be binding on absent persons, and they shall be bound accordingly except where the order has been obtained by fraud or non-disclosure of material facts.

ANNEX B

To

C–107

Defendant

Dear

Re:

The estate of [name of deceased]/The Settlement made by [Settlor] on [date]

We are instructed on behalf of [claimant] [give details of relief sought eg to seek reasonable provision out of the estate of the above-named deceased; to set aside probate of the will of the above-named deceased dated [date]; to seek a declaration that upon a proper construction of the above settlement our client is entitled to ...]

The basis of our clients claim is: [brief outline]

The facts upon which our client relies are as follows: [set out material facts with sufficient clarity and detail for the proposed defendants to make a preliminary assessment of the claim]

The details of matters to which the Court would have regard under Section 3 of the Inheritance (Provision for Family and Dependants) Act 1975 insofar as they are known to our client are:

(a) Financial resources and needs of claimant;
(b) Financial resources and needs of any other claimant;
(c) Financial resources and needs of beneficiaries;
(d) Obligations and responsibilities of deceased towards claimants and beneficiaries;
(e) Size and nature of estate;
(f) Disabilities of claimants and beneficiaries;
(g) Any other matter; and if claimant spouse, civil partner or co-habitee,
(h) age of claimant, length of marriage/civil partnership/co-habitation and contribution to family welfare.

We enclose the following documents which are relevant to the claim:
[list documents]

In accordance with The ACTAPS Code for probate and trust disputes, we look forward to receiving a letter of response, enclosing the documents in your possession and relevant to the claim within [21] days. We believe that the following documents relevant to the claim are likely to be in your possession: (list documents)

Pursuant to The ACTAPS Code as [personal representatives of the deceased/trustees of the settlement] we invite you to furnish us within 14 days of the date of this letter with copies of the following documents or written authority, in the form enclosed, to obtain copies of such document(s): [list asterisked documents required]

We have also sent a letter of claim to (name and address) and a copy of that letter is enclosed.

Yours faithfully

ANNEX C

C–108   All documents upon which you rely or upon which the other party is likely to wish to rely including but not limited to the following categories:

1. In disputes in which the assets of an estate/trust fund or the financial resources of an individual are relevant; eg claims under the Inheritance Act, breach of trust claims:

    — The Inland Revenue Account and any Corrective Account;
    — A schedule of the capital assets (with values, estimated where appropriate) and income of the estate, trust fund or individual as appropriate;
    — Trust or Estate Accounts.

2. In disputes in which the mental capacity or medical condition of an individual is relevant, eg challenges to testamentary capacity, Inheritance Act claims where disability is alleged:

    — A copy of the medical records of the individual or, if appropriate, the written authority of the personal representatives of a deceased to obtain his medical records together with an office copy of the grant of probate or letters of administration or other proof of their status.

3. In disputes as to the validity, construction or rectification of a will or other testamentary instrument of the deceased:

    — A statement setting out details of any testamentary script (now in CPR called testamentary document) within the knowledge of the claimant or proposed defendant and details of the name and address of the person who, to the best of his knowledge, has possession or control of such script.

NB1: The provision of the statement in 3 above is of vital importance to all parties in a dispute since it ensures that the correct testamentary documents are being considered. This will prevent the problem of a dispute over a later testamentary document being allowed to overshadow the existence of an intermediate testamentary document which would be upheld if the later testamentary document fails. Also it helps identify the correct parties to the existing disputes.

NB2: Following from NB1 above, it is most important that the fullest and most exhaustive search for all testamentary documents is made. Accordingly while the following list is not exhaustive it is incumbent upon all parties to check:

(i)   with all known solicitors of the deceased as to the existence of a testamentary document;

(ii) with all attesting witnesses to testamentary documents as to the existence of testamentary documents;

(iii) with all named executors of testamentary documents as to the existence of testamentary documents;

(iv) with immediate family members (brothers, sisters, parents and children of the deceased) as to the existence of testamentary documents.

NB3: Definition of Testamentary Script (now in CPR called Testamentary document)

A will, a draft of a will, written instructions for a will made by or at the request of, or under the instructions of, the testator, and any document purporting to be evidence of the contents, or to be a copy, of a will which is alleged to have been lost or destroyed. The word "will" includes a codicil.

ANNEX D

Joint Application for Medical Notes or Social Worker's Reports

To: The medical records officer/social services   **C–109**

Dear Sir

Re: (Name) Deceased of (address), (date of birth)

We the undersigned Messrs (firm's name) (ref) of (firm's address), Solicitors for (the Executors) named in the Will of the late (deceased's name) of (deceased's address) who died on (date of death) and we, the undersigned Messrs (firm's name) of (firm's address), Solicitors for parties interested in his/her estate, hereby authorise you to forward [a full set of copies of the deceased's Medical Records] [all social workers reports and notes relating to the deceased] to each of the aforementioned firms.

We confirm that we will be responsible for your reasonable photocopying charges and your invoice in this regard should be sent to (firm's name) and marked for the attention of (ref.).

Dated [   ] 200[ ]

Signed

....

Signed

....

ANNEX E

Joint Application Letter to solicitors who prepared Will requesting Larke - v- Nugus Statement

C–110 Dear Sirs

[Name of Deceased] deceased

We, the undersigned Messrs (firm's name)(ref:) of (firm's address), solicitors for the Executors named in the Will of (deceased's name) of (deceased's address) and we, the undersigned Messrs (firm's name)(ref:) of (firm's address), solicitors for parties interested in his/her estate regret to inform you that (deceased's name) died on (date of death)

We understand that you drafted the deceased's last will dated [   ].

You may be aware that in 1959 the Law Society recommended that in circumstances such as this the testator's solicitor should make available a statement of his or her evidence regarding instructions for the preparation and execution of the will and surrounding circumstances. This recommendation was endorsed by the Court of Appeal on 21st February 1979 in Larke v Nugus.

The practice is also recommended at paragraph 24.02 of the Law Society's Guide to the Professional Conduct of Solicitors, 7th edition (page 387).

Accordingly, we hereby request and authorise you to forward to each of the aforementioned firms statements from all appropriate members of your firm on the following points:

- How long had you known the deceased?
- Who introduced you to the deceased?
- On what date did you receive instructions from the deceased?
- Did you receive instructions by letter? If so, please provide copies of any correspondence.
- If instructions were taken at a meeting, please provide copies of your contemporaneous notes of the meeting including an indication of where the meeting took place and who else was present at the meeting.
- How were the instructions expressed?
- What indication did the deceased give to you that he knew he was making a will?
- Were you informed or otherwise aware of any medical history of the deceased that might bear upon the issue of his capacity?
- Did the deceased exhibit any signs of confusion or loss of memory? If so, please give details.
- To what extent were earlier wills discussed and what attempts were made to discuss departures from his earlier will-making pattern?

What reasons, if any, did the testator give for making any such departures?

- When the will had been drafted, how were the provisions of the will explained to the deceased?
- Who, apart from the attesting witnesses, was present at the execution of the will? Where, when and how did this take place?
- Please provide copies of any other documents relating to your instructions for the preparation and execution of the will and surrounding circumstances or confirm that you have no objection to us inspecting your relevant file(s) on reasonable notice.

We confirm that we will be responsible for your reasonable photocopying charges in this connection and your invoice in this regard should be sent to (each firm's name etc) and marked for the attention of (each firm's ref.).

Dated this [ ] day of [   ] 200[ ]

Signed

....

Signed

....

ANNEX F

Letter to Deceased's GP Requesting Report as to Mental Capacity   C–111

To: Deceased's GP

Dear Dr [   ]

Re: (Name) Deceased of (address), (date of birth)

We the undersigned Messrs (firm's name) (ref) of (firm's address) are Solicitors for (the Executors) named in the Will of the late (deceased's name) of (deceased's address) who died on (date of death) and we, the undersigned Messrs (firm's name) of (firm's address), are Solicitors for parties interested in his/her estate.

We enclose a photocopy of the deceased's last Will. The clauses in the Will which cause particular concern are (clause numbers)

The question of the deceased's mental capacity at the time of the making of his/her last Will dated has now been raised.

The test of testamentary capacity remains that established in the case of Banks -v- Goodfellow where it was said:—

> "It is essential that a testator (1) shall understand the nature of the act and its effects; (2) shall understand the extent of the property of which he is disposing; and (3) shall be able to comprehend and appreciate the claims to which he ought to give effect, and; with a view to the latter object, (4) that no disorder of mind shall poison his affections, pervert his sense of right or pervert the exercise of his natural faculties; (5) that no insane delusions shall influence his mind in disposing of his property and bring about a disposal of it which if his mind had been sound,

would not have been made." (We have added numbers for convenience).

(Set out the nature of the Estate if complex).
We would therefore be grateful if you would kindly provide us with a report
setting out:—

1.   Your medical qualifications and your experience in assessing
     mental states and capacity.
2.   For how long you were the deceased's GP, how well you knew the
     deceased and a summary of his/her medical condition, insofar as it
     may have bearing upon the deceased's mental capacity.
3.   Your findings as to the deceased's mental capacity at and around
     the time of the date of his/her last will.
4.   Please also deal with any mental disorder from which the deceased
     may have been suffering at the relevant time, and any medication
     which could have affected his/her capacity as detailed above.
5.   Please also consider any issues of vulnerability or suggestibility at
     or around the date of the deceased's last Will.

We confirm that we will be responsible for your reasonable fees in the
preparation of your report which we look forward to receiving as soon as
possible.

Dated this [ ] day of [   ] 200[ ]

Signed
.... (ref:)

Signed
.... (ref:)

7.—Standing Searches and Rule 43, Non-Contentious Probate
Rules 1987

C–112   Persons who wish to make applications under the 1975 Act often enter a
caveat in order to ensure that no grant is taken out, thus guarding against
the possibility that the six-month period prescribed by s.4 of the 1975 Act
runs out before they have the opportunity to make an application. Before
the amendment of s.4,[3] which provides that nothing prevents the making of
an application under the Act before representation with respect to the estate
of the deceased person is first taken out, it was considered that no application can be brought until a grant of representation has been issued,[4] which
made the entry of a caveat a self-defeating process.[5] That amendment has
been implemented procedurally by the insertion into CPR r.57.16 of new
paras (3A) and (3B).[6] The written evidence to be filed by a claimant who

---

[3] Inheritance and Trustees' Powers Act 2014 s.6 and Sch.2 para. 6, which came into force on 1
     October 2014.
[4] *Re McBroom* [1992] 2 F.L.R. 49.
[5] *Parnall v Hurst* [2003] W.T.L.R. 997.
[6] The rule is set out in full in s.3 of this Appendix.

makes an application before representation has been granted must include an explanation of the reasons why it has not been possible for a grant to be obtained.[7] At the time of writing it remains to be seen how a court would treat the situation where it has not been possible to obtain a grant because the claimant has entered a caveat. For the purposes for which a caveat is properly entered, see, e.g. *Tristram and Coote's Probate Practice*, 31st edn (London: LexisNexis, 2015), Ch.23. It is submitted that unless the claimant wishes to challenge the validity of the will as well as making a 1975 Act claim,[8] the entry of a caveat is a misuse of the procedure and that a claimant who simply wishes to be kept informed whether a grant has been issued should apply for a standing search in accordance with NCPR r.43 and in Form 2, which are set out below. The search is effective for six months after the entry of the application, and can be renewed.

Non-Contentious Probate Rules 1987 Rule 43

43. (1) Any person who wishes to be notified of the issue of a grant may   C–113
         enter a standing search for the grant by lodging at, or sending by
         post to, any registry or sub-registry, a notice in Form 2.
    (2) A person who has entered a standing search will be sent an office
         copy of any grant which corresponds with the particulars given on
         the completed Form 2 and which—

    (a) issues not more than twelve months before the entry of the
         standing search; or
    (b) issues within a period of six months after the entry of the
         standing search.

    (3) (a) Where an applicant wishes to extend the said period of six
             months, he or his solicitor or probate practitioner may lodge
             at, or send by post to, the registry or sub-registry at which the
             standing search was entered written application for extension.
        (b) An application for extension as aforesaid must be lodged, or
             received by post, within the last month of the said period of
             six months, and the standing search shall thereupon be
             effective for an additional period of six months from the date
             on which it was due to expire.
        (c) A standing search which has been extended as above may be
             further extended by the filing of a further application for
             extension subject to the same conditions as set out in sub-
             paragraph (b) above.

Form 2   C–114

Rule 43(1)

Standing Search

In the High Court of Justice

---

[7] CPR r.57.16(3A)(a).
[8] It was held in *Pinnock v Rochester* [2011] EWHC 4049 (Ch) that the claimant was entitled both to challenge the validity of a will and to contend that, if it was valid, it did not make reasonable provision for him. The transcript is available on LexisNexis and Westlaw.

Family Division

The Principal [*or.* . . . . District Probate] Registry

I/We apply for the entry of a standing search so that there shall be sent to me/us an office copy of every grant of representation in England and Wales in the estate of—

Full name of deceased:. . . . .

Full address:. . . . .

Alternative or alias names:. . . . .

Exact date of death:. . . . .

which either has issued not more than 12 months before the entry of this application or issues within 6 months thereafter.

Signed. . . . .

Name in block letters. . . . .

Full address. . . . .

Reference No. (if any). . . . .

8.—PRECEDENTS

8.1. Claim Form [not reproduced]

C–115 In the author's view, the claim form should show on its face (1) that the court has jurisdiction to entertain the claim, and (2) that the claimant is eligible to make it. Accordingly the precedent states in relation to (1) that the deceased died domiciled within the jurisdiction and that a grant of probate or administration has been issued; and in relation to (2), the class of eligible persons of which the claimant is a member.

IN THE HIGH COURT OF JUSTICE

CHANCERY/FAMILY DIVISION

. . . . .DISTRICT REGISTRY/PRINCIPAL PROBATE REGISTRY

Or

THE COUNTY COURT AT. . . . .

Claim No. . . . .

IN THE MATTER OF THE INHERITANCE (PROVISION FOR FAMILY AND DEPENDANTS) ACT 1975

AND IN THE MATTER OF THE ESTATE OF C.D. (DECEASED)

BETWEEN:

A.B.

Claimant

and

(1) E.F
(2) G.H
(personal representatives of C.D. deceased)[9]
(3) J.K.

Defendants

Does your claim include any issues under the Human Rights Act Yes/No

Details of Claim

1. The Claimant, who was born on [date] being the [state nature of relationship] is a person entitled under sub-s.1(1)(a), (b), (ba), (c), (d) or (e)[10] of the Act to seek an order under s.2.

2. The deceased died on [date] domiciled in England and Wales.

3. Probate of the last will of the Deceased dated [date] was/ **Or** the deceased died intestate and letters of administration were granted to the First and Second Defendants on [date].

4. The value of the net estate of the deceased appears from the grant to be a sum not exceeding £[amount]. Under the will/on the death of the deceased intestate the Claimant is entitled to [amount of legacy or share of residue or specific gift] **Or** the Claimant receives no benefit.

The Claimant seeks the following relief:

1. An Order under s.2 of the Inheritance (Provision For Family And Dependants) Act 1975 ("the Act") for reasonable financial provision from the net estate of the Deceased [and if necessary][11]
2. An order under s.4 of the Act that permission be granted to commence these proceedings after the expiry of the statutory period
3. An order under s.9 of the Act that the deceased's severable share of [description of jointly owned property] be treated as part of the net estate of the deceased
4. Such further or other relief as the Court thinks just[12]
5. That provision be made for the costs of this claim.

The Part 8 procedure applies to this claim.[13]

---

[9] Where a defendant is being sued in a representative capacity, it is necessary to state that capacity. The residuary beneficiaries under the will or intestacy and any specific legatees who benefit substantially under the will should also be made defendants. If their identities are not known to the claimant at the time the claim is issued, an application should be made, when their identities are known, for a direction that they be joined.

[10] A person who is eligible to claim under any of the other subsections may not claim under s.1(1)(e), save that a person claiming under s.1(1(ba) as either an opposite-sex (subs.1(1A)) or same-sex (subs.1(1B)) cohabitant will often claim in the alternative under s.1(1)(e).

[11] Orders under ss.4 or 9 are the most common additional orders which a claimant is likely to seek but orders under s.8(1) (nominated property), s.8(2) (*donatio mortis causa*) or s.10 (transactions designed to defeat a claim for provision) may also be sought.

[12] Which will cover any consequential and supplemental provisions made under s.2(4).

[13] This statement is mandatory; CPR r.8.2(a).

Statement of Truth

I believe/the Claimant believes that the facts stated in this Claim Form are true. [I am duly authorised by the Claimant to sign this document on their behalf name of signatory and firm and position held]

(Signed)...

(Date)..

8.2. Witness Statement Of Claimant

C–116   This precedent is in skeleton form and does not attempt to provide any sort of narrative. It is designed to indicate the matters which, at a minimum, the claimant should include in the witness statement and it draws attention to the relevant questions of the questionnaire (QP) in App.4. QP should therefore be completed to the best of the claimant's ability before the proceedings are drafted. Where a paragraph in the precedent has subparagraphs [1], [2], etc., these relate to the class, as defined by s.1(1), of which the claimant is a member.

Claimant
A.B.
1st
Documents AB 1-n[14]
Date

IN THE HIGH COURT OF JUSTICE

CHANCERY/FAMILY DIVISION

.............................DISTRICT   REGISTRY/PRINCIPAL   PROBATE REGISTRY

Or

IN THE COUNTY COURT AT....................................

Claim No...

IN THE MATTER OF THE INHERITANCE (PROVISION FOR FAMILY AND DEPENDANTS) ACT 1975

AND IN THE MATTER OF THE ESTATE OF C.D. (DECEASED)
BETWEEN:

A.B.

Claimant

and

(1) E.F.

(2) G.H.

---

[14] Number of final document exhibited.

(personal representatives of C.D. deceased)[15]

(3) J.K.

Defendants

WITNESS STATEMENT OF CLAIMANT

I, A.B., of [address] [occupation or description] make this statement in support of my claim for reasonable financial provision from the estate of C.D.

1. *(Personal details and nature of relationship)*[16]

[1] I was born on [date] and am [x] years of age. At the date of the **C–117** deceased's death I was the spouse/former spouse/civil partner/ former civil partner of the deceased. We had married/ entered[17] a civil partnership on [date]. The deceased died on [date]. At the date of the deceased's death we had been married/ in a civil partnership for [y] years

Or

[2] I was born on [date] and am [x] years of age. The marriage/ civil partnership between myself and the deceased was dissolved on [date] and I have not since remarried/entered into another civil partnership

Or

[3] I was born on [date] and am [x] years of age. I lived together with the deceased in the same household at [address] as husband and wife or as his/her civil partner from [date] until his/her death on [date]

Or

[4] I am the son/daughter of the deceased. I was born on [date] and am [x] years of age

Or

[5] I am not the child of the deceased but the deceased treated me as the child of his/her [marriage to (name)] or [civil partnership with (name)] I was born on [date] and am [x] years of age and the deceased treated me as a child of his/marriage/civil partnership from [date] to (the date of his/her death on)[18] [date]

Or

[6] I was born on [date] and am [x] years of age. I was being maintained by the deceased [who was my (insert nature of relationship,

---

[15] Where a defendant is being sued in a representative capacity, it is necessary to state that capacity. The residuary beneficiaries under the will or intestacy and any specific legatees who benefit substantially under the will should also be made defendants. If their identities are not known to the claimant at the time when the claim is issued, an application should be made, when their identities are known, for a direction that they be joined.

[16] There is no need to include this and subsequent headings in the witness statement but they provide a guide to the organisation of the statement. The part of the statement relating to conduct and other relevant matters referable to the particular class of claimant is at the corresponding numbered subparagraphs of para.6.

[17] The relevant date is the date of registration.

[18] It is not necessary that the treatment was still ongoing at the date of the deceased's death; see s.1(1)(d) and compare ss.1(1A), (1B) and 1(1)(e) which do refer to circumstances existing immediately before the death of the deceased.

if any, e.g. grandparent, uncle, aunt, brother, sister)] immediately before his/her death.

(Grant and provision made by will/on intestacy)

C–118 2. I refer to the copy grant of probate/letters of administration exhibited as "AB 1" [and to the copy will exhibited as "AB 2"]. The provision made for me by the will is [description of provision, *or*, the will makes no provision for me] *or* My entitlement under the deceased's intestacy is [description of entitlement], *or* I am not entitled to take under the deceased's intestacy.

(Claimant's financial position)

C–119 3. My present financial position is as follows:

3.1 Income

My total net[19] annual/monthly income from all sources is

(Refer to QP, q.5)

My current expenditure is [*list items of expenditure as in QP, q.7*]

My annual/monthly expenditure exceeds my income by £ [amount] *or*

There is an annual/monthly surplus of income over expenditure [amount]

3.2 Capital

My own capital is £[amount] *(refer to QP, q.6)*

[but I expect to have to meet the following expenses out of capital]

(Refer to QP, q.8)[20]

C–120 4. Foreseeable changes in my financial position[21] are:

I am due to retire at age [x]/*or* I may have to retire early through disability as stated in the next paragraph. My income will then consist of [details of, e.g. occupational and/or State pension]. I refer to the statement from my employer exhibited as "AB 3" and the pension benefit forecast exhibited as "AB 4"]

My mortgage is due to be paid off in [year]. I refer to the copy redemption statement exhibited as "AB 5"

From [year] I will not have any financial responsibility for my dependent children

(Disability)—See QP, q.2—relevant medical history

C–121 5. I have suffered from [describe condition] since [date]. The effects of this condition are [describe ways in which it affects ability to carry on a normal

---

[19] Assessing the income need is much simpler if the net amount received (i.e. what the claimant actually takes home) is stated. If net amounts are not available then it should be clearly stated that the amount is gross.

[20] If it is possible to give some indication of when those expenses will need to be met, that is generally helpful.

[21] Obviously there are many other possibilities but these are the most frequent in the author's experience.

daily life and to engage in work]. I have undergone/will have to undergo [describe any surgery or other treatment] and have to take [describe medication]. The prognosis is that the condition will not get seriously worse/ is not life-threatening/ will reduce my ability to work/will reduce my life expectancy. I refer to the copy medical report(s)/letter(s)/records exhibited as "AB 6"

(Conduct and other relevant matters)[22]

6.[23] [1], [2][24] During the marriage/civil partnership I contributed to the **C–122** welfare of the family by bringing up the children *(names and dates of birth)*/ looking after the home, which involved (e.g. cleaning, cooking, shopping). I contributed financially to the household expenses *(details) or* I did not contribute financially but took on the major role in bringing up the children and looking after the home.

For other matters which might be included *(Refer to QP, q.11)*

[2] *(brief explanation, if desired, of the circumstances in which the relationship broke down)*[25]

[3] During the period when the deceased and I lived together we lived as if we were a married couple/[26]civil partners *(describe shared activities/interests/ general way of life/any event which was a public acknowledgment of the relationship).*[27] Our friends/neighbours always saw us as a married couple/as being in a permanent relationship[28]

[4], [5][29] As explained above I am in difficult financial circumstances. I am unable to support myself as I am now [x] years of age/I suffer from disability as explained above/I am still in full-time education or training which is due to be completed in [month, year]; *or*

the deceased promised me *(give details of how and when the promise was*

---

[22] It is suggested that descriptions of conduct be confined to the minimum necessary to show, for instance, why and/or in what circumstances a relationship broke down or why the claimant was treated or not treated in a certain way.

[23] Numbers in square brackets relate back to the subparagraphs of para.1.

[24] This subparagraph is designated [1], [2] because these matters are relevant to claimants under s.1(1)(a) and 1(1)(b).

[25] Applications by this class of claimant have become increasingly rare owing to the almost invariable practice, nowadays, of making s.15 (or s.15ZA, in the case of a civil partnership) orders on or after the grant of the decree which terminates the relationship. Claimants should consider carefully whether statements to the effect that the breakdown of the relationship was due to the conduct of the deceased are likely to assist their cause.

[26] If there were children of the relationship, that would be very relevant and the fact should be included.

[27] For example a housewarming party to which friends were invited to celebrate the relationship.

[28] One or two specific examples could be included here.

[29] In cases where the claimant was treated as a child of the family (s.1(1)(d)), it may not be necessary to show (as in the far commoner adult child cases) circumstances over and above the kinship, need and availability of resources in the estate to meet that need, but if there are such circumstances in the case of a claimant under s.1(1)(d), they should be referred to in the statement.

made) that if I came to live with him/looked after him/worked in his business he would provide for me in his will but he has not done so/has left me only (*state nature or amount of legacy*)[30]

(*For other matters relevant to a claim by a person who was treated as a child of the family, see QP, q.13*)

[6] The deceased was maintaining me by (e.g.) [providing me with accommodation rent-free[31] at (address)[32]/paying £[x] per week/month/year for my daily living expenses/tuition fees].
(*For other matters which might be included, see QP, q.14*)

C–123 7. For the reasons set out I believe that the dispositions made by the deceased's will/intestacy/combination of the dispositions of the will and intestacy have not been such as to make reasonable financial provision for me and I ask the court to order that provision be made for me by way of[33]:

(a) a lump sum payment;
(b) the purchase of a property for my occupation[34];
(c) transfer of the property at [address] to me; *or*
(d) settlement of the property at [address] on me for life

Except where I have indicated that they are derived from information and belief, the matters set out in this witness statement are within my own knowledge.

Statement of Truth

I believe that the facts stated in this Witness Statement are true.

Full name

Signature

Date

8.3. Witness Statement Of Personal Representative (CPR r.57.16(5))

C–124   1st Defendant.
                                                                           E.F.
                                                                           1st
                                                                           Date

---

[30] The case-law shows that these are the circumstances in which an adult child has most often succeeded or is most likely to succeed in a claim, but there is not a closed list of such circumstances.

[31] Providing accommodation at less than market rent is also considered to amount to maintenance, see *Rees v Newbery and the Institute of Cancer Research* [1998] 1 F.L.R. 1041.

[32] If the accommodation provided was in the deceased's own residence, that should be stated.

[33] These are the types of provision most commonly made. It is almost invariably the case that the claimant's income shortfall will be met by a lump sum representing its capital equivalent over an appropriate period rather than by periodical payments. The claimant's housing needs may be met by the award of an absolute or a limited interest in the residential property provided.

[34] It is not unknown for claimants to be awarded a lump sum to cover both housing and income needs, leaving them to decide how to allocate the sum between those needs; see, e.g., *Cunliffe v Fielden* [2006] Ch. 361, CA.

IN THE HIGH COURT OF JUSTICE

CHANCERY/FAMILY DIVISION

.................DISTRICT REGISTRY/PRINCIPAL PROBATE REGISTRY

Or

IN THE COUNTY COURT AT................................

Claim No...

IN THE MATTER OF THE INHERITANCE (PROVISION FOR FAMILY AND DEPENDANTS) ACT 1975

AND IN THE MATTER OF THE ESTATE OF C.D. (DECEASED)

BETWEEN:

A.B.

Claimant

and

(1) E.F.

(2) G.H.

(personal representatives of C.D. deceased)[35]

(3) J.K.

Defendants

WITNESS STATEMENT OF PERSONAL REPRESENTATIVE

I, E.F. of [address] [occupation or description] make this statement as personal representative of C.D. deceased and pursuant to CPR r.57.16(5)

1. The value of the net estate for the purposes of s.25(1) of the Inheritance Act, which comprises the following *or* is set out in the attached schedule is £[amount]

2. The following are the persons or classes of persons beneficially interested in the estate (include names and addresses where not parties to the claim)

3. So far as known the values of the interests of the beneficiaries in the estate are as follows:

[state the shares of the beneficiaries in residue and the amounts of any specific legacies]

4. To the best of my knowledge none of the beneficiaries are children or persons who lack capacity under the Mental Capacity Act 2005. *or*

The following person is a child namely X.Y. of [address] *and/or*

---

[35] Where a defendant is being sued in a representative capacity, it is necessary to state that capacity. The residuary beneficiaries under the will or intestacy and any specific legatees who benefit substantially under the will should also be made defendants. If their identities are not known to the claimant at the time when the claim is issued, an application should be made, when their identities are known, for a direction that they be joined.

The following person is a person who lacks capacity under the Mental Capacity Act 2005 namely P.Q. of [address]

5. To the best of my knowledge the only facts which might affect the exercise of the court's powers under the Inheritance (Provision for Family and Dependants) Act 1975 are[36]:

Statement of Truth

I believe that the facts stated in this witness statement are true.

Name

(Signed)

Dated

---

[36] The guidance given in the commentary to the former RSC Ord.99 was to the effect that controversial matters should not be included at this stage. Although that guidance has not been reproduced in *Civil Procedure*, the author would suggest that it should normally be followed as it is in keeping with the neutral attitude which the personal representatives acting in that capacity should adopt, though it may be appropriate to include such matters if they are known only to the personal representative and the personal representative is not also defending the claim as a beneficiary. It is suggested that personal representatives who are also defendants as beneficiaries should state these matters in the witness statement made in that capacity.

APPENDIX 4

QUESTIONNAIRES

(a) Introductory Note

(i) General

1975 Act claims are pre-eminently a type of litigation where the cost and   **D–001**
time involved can be greatly reduced by assembling all the relevant facts in a
clear and organised manner at the outset. The questionnaires are designed to
help in achieving that object by assembling sufficient information at an early
stage. It is not suggested that the questionnaires are all-embracing, or that
every question needs to be asked on every occasion when a claim is to be
made or resisted, but they are intended to draw attention to the matters
which most often arise and to those which, whether or not of frequent
occurrence, are referred to in the 1975 Act. The questionnaire relating to the
deceased (QD) is designed to be completed by personal representatives who
are defendants and in particular to facilitate the gathering of the information required by the Practice Direction 57 para.57PD.16. The other questionnaire (QP) is designed to be completed by any other party to the claim,
whether a claimant or a beneficiary who wishes to contest the claim.

Practitioners will no doubt be aware that, in many cases where the lay   **D–002**
client contemplates making an application under the 1975 Act, questions
may arise as to whether the applicant has a claim to a beneficial interest in
any of the property of the deceased, whether certain property is part of the
deceased's estate and whether there are grounds on which the validity of the
will which is claimed not to have made reasonable financial provision might
properly be challenged. The types of additional or alternative claim which
might be made are discussed briefly in Ch.1 of the main text,[1] and in greater
detail in Ch.7.[2] QP includes questions which are directed towards these
issues, although (as explained in those chapters) they will, in the majority of
cases, initially have to be raised in separate proceedings.

CPR Pt 57 and the Practice Direction specify the information to be   **D–003**
provided by the personal representatives of the deceased who are defendants,[3] which is as follows:

> "The written evidence filed by the defendant who is a personal repre-
> sentative must state to the best of that person's ability—

---

[1] Chapter 1, s.5 ("Other Proceedings Potentially Affecting the Outcome of a 1975 Act Claim").
[2] Chapter 7, s.2 ("Claims Relating to the Estates of Deceased Persons"), particularly subs.(g)
("Multiple Claims: An Overview").
[3] CPR Pt 57; see the section headed "Questionnaire relating to the Deceased".

(1) full details of the value of the deceased's net estate, as defined in section 25(1) of the Act;
(2) the person or classes of persons beneficially interested in the estate, and—
   (a) the names and (unless they are parties to the claim) addresses of all living beneficiaries; and
   (b) the value of their interests in the estate so far as they are known.
(3) whether any living beneficiary (and if so, naming him) is a child or a person who lacks capacity (within the meaning of the Mental Capacity Act 2005); and
(4) any facts which might affect the exercise of the court's powers under the Act."

There are no rules or directions which require any specific information to be provided by a claimant or by a defendant beneficiary. However, it is in the interests of all parties that relevant information is disclosed at an early stage, and the questionnaires are intended to facilitate that process.

(ii) The requirements of s.3

D–004   Subject to what is said above, the scheme of the questionnaires is largely dictated by the provisions of s.3 of the Act, which sets out in detail the matters to which the court must have regard. QD is in three parts, dealing with (A) personal details of the deceased; (B) the dispositions under the deceased's will or intestacy, and details of the grant; and (C) the financial situation of the deceased. The size and nature of the net estate, for which see s.3(1)(e), is of great importance; the personal representative is required to give full particulars of its value. The personal representative (particularly if they are a member of the deceased's family or has been the deceased's professional adviser for a substantial period) may also be aware of facts which bear on the question of obligations and responsibilities which the deceased had to any applicant or beneficiary, disabilities affecting any applicant or beneficiary, and any other relevant matter, including conduct. QP does not contain any questions specifically referring to such matters and they are usually addressed in the evidence of the parties who are making or actively defending the claim.

D–005   It is important to obtain details of all property, whether part of the net estate or not; if anyone, whether the applicant, another applicant or a beneficiary under the will or intestacy of the deceased, benefits as a result of the death of the deceased by becoming entitled to property which is not part of the net estate (such as property passing by survivorship[4] or the proceeds of insurance policies which are not caught by s.8(1) so as to be part of the net estate),[5] that person's financial resources are thereby affected and the benefit must be taken into account by the court under subss.(a), (b) or (c) of s.3(1).

D–006   The medical history of the deceased, particularly during some period immediately prior to their death, may be important in a number of ways. In

---

[4] See QD at para.D–018.
[5] See QD, q.10, para.D–018.

the first place, the conduct of the applicant or other persons during a period of the deceased's illness or disability may be relevant under s.3(1)(g).[6] A gift made during a period of illness may take effect as a *donatio mortis causa*. Also, if the will, or a grant of administration to those who would normally be first entitled, is likely to be challenged, the state of the deceased's bodily and mental health may be in issue and, where they have made a will, the circumstances of its preparation and execution will also be relevant. The medical history of an applicant or of a beneficiary may be relevant both to the question of disability under s.3(1)(f), and to the question of earning capacity under s.3(6).

QD is in four parts, which are: (A) personal details; (B) financial **D–007** resources, including earning capacity, and financial needs; (C) other types of claim; and (D) matters concerning specific classes of applicant.

Sections 3(2), 3(2A) and 3(3)[7] deal with the matters which must be taken **D–008** into account where certain relationships between the deceased and the applicant existed. It may be of assistance, having taken instructions, to construct a family tree or such part of it as is sufficient to show all the relevant relationships and the dates of the births, marriages and deaths of the persons concerned. Dates of adoption, legitimation or any event which marks the beginning of a relationship whereby the applicant claims to have been treated as a child of the family or began to cohabit with the deceased, should be included.[8]

Particular care is necessary when taking instructions for the purpose of **D–009** ascertaining the matters which the court has to consider under s.3(4).[9] It is often the case that applicants are often so concerned to present their conduct towards the deceased in a favourable light that the resulting evidence tends to demonstrate that the deceased was dependent on the applicant, rather than, as s.1(3) formerly required, that the applicant was dependent on the deceased. This is no longer a bar to the success of a claim because the amendment to s.1(3)[10] has the effect that (except in relation to arrangements of a commercial nature) there is no longer a requirement for the deceased's contribution to the claimant's reasonable needs to be "otherwise than for full valuable consideration", but the extent to which the claimant was dependent on the deceased is a relevant matter under s.3(4) and might, if quantified, be relevant to the court's assessment of the quantum of reasonable financial provision. The possibility that the applicant should be seeking a declaration as to their beneficial interest in property of the deceased rather than, or in addition to making an application under s.1(1)(e) should therefore be kept in mind.

(iii) Sections 8–13

These sections deal with property which is treated as part of the net estate **D–010** (s.8), property held on a joint tenancy which may be treated as part of the

---

[6] See QD, q.4, para.D-016.
[7] See the questions specific to parties who are members of these classes, at QP qs 11–13, para.D-023.
[8] QD, qs 2 (Marital or Other Status) and 3 (Children).
[9] QP, q.14.
[10] Inheritance and Trustees' Powers Act 2014 s.6 and Sch.2 para.2.

net estate (s.9) and certain dispositions inter vivos which may be challenged (ss.10–13).

(iv) Insurance policies and pension scheme benefits

D–011 It is advisable to ascertain whether there were any occupational pension schemes or insurance policies from which the deceased or any other person might benefit, and, if so, who has the right to nominate the beneficiary. As has been discussed in Ch.3, it may be that the proceeds of such a scheme are part of the net estate under s.8(1).

(v) Property held on a joint tenancy[11]

D–012 If the estate includes a house, enquiry should always be made as to the manner in which the beneficial interests are held. The answer may be provided by express words in the transfer or conveyance to the deceased, by a separate declaration of trust or by the form of the restriction (if any) entered on the register. The restriction will state whether the survivor is, or is not, entitled to give a receipt for capital money. However, the form of the restriction is not conclusive as to the basis of co-ownership[12]; the survivor of joint tenants is so entitled, whereas the survivor of tenants in common is not. For the law relating to bank accounts held by spouses in joint names, see *Re Bishop, National Provincial Bank v Bishop*[13]; *Re Figgis Deceased.*[14]

(vi) Gifts and contracts to leave property made by the deceased

D–013 These may fall to be considered if the gift was a *donatio mortis causa*, under s.8(2), or if it was made within six years of the date of death, when, if made with intent to defeat a claim for financial provision, it will be caught by the anti-avoidance provisions of s.10. A contract to dispose of property by will may, similarly, be attacked under s.11.

(vii) Statements made by the deceased

D–014 If the deceased has made any statement, whether orally or in writing, as to their reasons either for disposing or not disposing of his property in any particular manner, the details of such statement should be noted. It is now a recognised drafting practice to include such statements in a will. Such statements were formerly admissible under s.21 of the Act, but are now admissible under the provisions of the Civil Evidence Act 1995 relating to hearsay evidence in civil proceedings.

(b) Questionnaire Relating to the Deceased (QD)

D–015 This should be completed by a personal representative who is a defendant to a claim under the 1975 Act. The personal representative should answer all the questions relating to the estate, and such other questions which they are

---

[11] See, generally, Martyn Frost (ed), *A Practitioner's Guide to Joint Property* (London: Tottel Publishing, 2005).
[12] *Huntingford v Hobbs* [1993] 1 F.L.R. 736 (CA).
[13] *Re Bishop, National Provincial Bank v Bishop* [1965] 1 All E.R. 249.
[14] *Re Figgis Deceased* [1968] 1 All E.R. 999.

able to answer from personal knowledge. Copies of all documents referred to should be supplied with the completed questionnaire.

A. Personal Details

D–016

1. General Matters

Name and last address

Age at death

Date of death

Place of death

Domicile of deceased at death

Death certificate seen?

2. Marital[15] or Other Status

If married, name of spouse and date of marriage

If formerly married, state date and cause of termination of marriage

The like details of any previous marriages

If a party to a registered civil partnership, name of partner and date of registration of the partnership

If formerly a party to a registered civil partnership, state date and cause of termination of civil partnership

The like details of any previous civil partnership

If cohabiting, state name of cohabitant and dates during which the relationship subsisted

3. Children

If the deceased had any children, state names, ages and the identity of the other parent

If any child was adopted or legitimated by the deceased, give the name and the relevant date

If any person has been treated as a child of the family, how and when did that come about

Between what dates did that relationship subsist

4. Medical History

Cause of death

If any relevant illness or disability, describe briefly and state when the deceased suffered from it

---

[15] This now includes a marriage to which the parties are a same-sex couple.

Name of doctor/hospital treating the deceased

Brief description of treatment (medication/therapy/surgery)

D–017   B. Details of Dispositions and Grant

5. Testamentary Dispositions

If the deceased made a will, give the date (or dates if more than one). Include dates of all codicils

Do you have the original will?

If not, do you know where it is?

Have you seen it?

Has it been revoked? If so, when and by what means

Can the attesting witnesses be reached, if necessary?

Has any caveat been entered/warned or standing search applied for—if so, by whom and when?

Names and addresses of executors, and if they are professional persons, their professions

Names and addresses of beneficiaries and relationship to/connection with the deceased

Are any of the beneficiaries:

    (a) Children?
    (b) Persons lacking in mental capacity?

If the deceased died/were to have died intestate, who benefits

Summary of any statement of the deceased's reasons for making, or not making, any disposition

Details of the statement:

    (a) Whether oral or written
    (b) When made
    (c) If written, contained in what document
    (d) If oral, made to whom/in whose presence

6. Gifts and Contracts to Dispose of Property by Will

Did the deceased make any gift **either** within 6 years of his death **or** when he believed himself to be in danger of death (ignore small value Christmas/birthday presents etc). If so:

    (1) When and in what circumstances and to whom was the gift made
    (2) What was its nature and value

Did the deceased make any contract to leave any money or property to anyone else by will? If so:

(1) When and in what circumstances and in whose favour was the contract made
(2) What consideration was given by the intended beneficiary

7. Grants of Representation

Has a grant of representation (including any limited grant) been issued?

Grant seen?

Nature of grant and any limitation

Date of grant and registry out of which issued

Details of grant:

(1) Name and address of person/solicitor extracting the grant
(2) Names of grantees
(3) Relationship of grantees to the deceased
(4) Occupation of grantee if not related to the deceased

C. Financial Situation of Deceased   D–018

8. Total Value of Assets

Gross and net values of estate as stated on grant

Has an Inland Revenue account been submitted (Please obtain if possible)

9. Nature and Value of Assets

(1) Real Property

Does the realty include any residential property? If so, identify:

(a) The principal private residence of the deceased
(b) The matrimonial home, if not the above
(c) Any property used for the purposes of any business carried on by the deceased
(d) Any property owned as an investment property

In relation to each property:

Is it freehold or leasehold

If it is mortgaged, state:

(1) Name(s) of mortgagee(s)
(2) Amounts outstanding on the mortgage(s)
(3) Whether any mortgage is supported by a policy, if so with what office

If it has been valued, state:

    (1) By whom
    (2) When
    (3) At what valuation
    (4) Is such valuation on the basis of vacant possession; if not, on what basis

If any property is held on co-ownership, are the beneficial interests held as joint tenants or tenants in common?

Conveyance/transfer/declaration of trust/office copy entries/other evidence seen?

Name and relationship to/connection with the deceased of any co-owner

(2) Personal Property

Personal chattels

Any items of particular value

Has there been a valuation? If so, state in relation to the items valued:

    (1) By whom
    (2) When
    (3) Value
    (4) List seen?
    (5) Whether any dispute is foreseen as to the value/ownership of any item(s)

Bank/National Savings/Building Society/other accounts:

    (1) In whose name(s)
    (2) When started
    (3) Balance at death of deceased
    (4) Bank books/statements/other relevant documents seen?
    (5) If there are any accounts with friendly or industrial and provident societies or trade unions, has any nomination been made

Government stocks/premium bonds/national savings certificates or bonds:

    Value

Shares in quoted companies: if so, has there been a valuation (see questions on personal chattels)?

Interests in private companies/businesses carried on in partnership

    Who are directors/partners?
    Names and addresses of solicitors/accountants dealing with the company/business affairs

10. Death Benefits

Was the deceased a member of an occupational pension scheme? If so:

(1) What is the nature/value of the benefit
(2) Who are the nominated beneficiaries
(3) Who has the power to nominate
(4) Is payment of benefit mandatory or discretionary
(5) Who is the employer
(6) Is the scheme set up under any statute
(7) Copy of rules seen?

Policies of life assurance:

(1) Policy details (office, date and description of policy)
(2) What is the nature/value of the benefit
(3) Who benefits
(4) Is it written in trust? If so who are the trustees?
(5) Document seen?

11. Nature and Amount of Liabilities

Name and address of any professional adviser dealing with the deceased's financial affairs

Taxes

(1) IHT

    (a) Immediate liability
    (b) Liability payable by instalments

(2) CGT
(3) Income tax

Debts

(1) Bank overdraft (business and personal)
(2) Other business debts
(3) Personal loans
(4) Household/personal bills outstanding at death
(5) Funeral, testamentary and administration expenses
(6) Creditors (list with amounts)

In respect of any of the above, is any person (and if so whom) liable under any guarantee or charge

12. Property Passing on Death

Value of net estate for 1975 Act purposes (excluding the value of any property passing by survivorship)

Nature and value of deceased's severable share of any property passing on his death by survivorship

Value of any money or other property (identifying the property) received by any person following the death of the deceased as a result of a nomination or *donatio mortis causa*

(c) Questionnaire to be Completed by Claimant or Beneficiary (QP)

D–019   Each claimant should complete a separate questionnaire, as should each defendant beneficiary on whose behalf evidence is to be adduced. Section C relates to other claims which the claimant or defendant beneficiary may wish to bring. Section D relates to claimants only. Copies of relevant documents, particularly those which relate to financial circumstances and state of health, should be supplied so that they can be referred to and exhibited to witness statements.

D–020   **A. Personal Details**

1. General

Name

Address

DOB/age

Kinship/connection with deceased

Length and period of residence, if any, with deceased

Marital/civil partnership status

> Date of marriage or registration of civil partnership and name of spouse/civil partner
> Number of your children
> Identify children (if any) who are not children of the relationship
> Names and ages of any dependent children

If cohabiting with the deceased other than in a registered civil partnership:

> Date when cohabitation began
> Number of your children
> Identify children (if any) who are not children of the relationship
> Names and ages of any dependent children

Note: It is sometimes the case that a marriage or civil partnership is preceded by a period of cohabitation. If that is the case, give the above details in respect of each relationship

2. Relevant Medical History

Do you or does anyone dependent on you suffer from any disability?

Date of onset of condition

Likely duration of the condition

Brief description of any past/present/anticipated treatment (medication/therapy/surgery)

Does it/is it likely to affect earning capacity; if so, in what way

Name and address of doctor/hospital from or at which treatment was/is received

3. Conduct

Any relevant conduct on the part of the deceased towards (a) yourself and (b) any other party (being a claimant or beneficiary as the case may be), or of that person towards the deceased.

B. Financial Resources, Including Earning Capacity and Financial Needs   **D–021**

4. Benefit to be Taken Under Disposition (Nature and Amount, or Fractional Share)

5. Sources and Amount of Income

Employment status: employed, self-employed, unemployed or retired (delete as appropriate)

Occupation

Net annual income from occupation

Prospects of promotion/wage or salary increase

Retirement age

Is there any likelihood of early retirement; if so, for what reason

Is there any likelihood of temporary cessation of employment; if so, when, for how long and for what reasons

Income from other sources. For each, give nature/amount/frequency of payment

6. Sources and Amount of Capital

Savings and investments (nature/value)

Present value of any house owned

Is the house subject to a mortgage; if so:

> how much remains owing; and
> when is the mortgage due to be paid off

Is the house in sole or joint names; if the latter, who is/are the other co-owners

Is there any, and if so what, evidence as to the entitlement to the beneficial interest therein (For example, a conveyance, transfer, declaration of trust or restriction entered on the register)

Any other capital assets; if so, what are they and what are their values

7. Expenses of an Income Nature

In answering this question and question 8, you should include both expenses payable for yourself and expenses payable for a child or other person who is dependent on you. It is helpful if the amounts are all expressed in terms of expenditure over the same period, preferably per month or per year.

Rent/mortgage

Council tax

Water rates

Heat/light/phone/TV

Food

Clothes

Car and/or other transport expenses

Credit card/credit sale/hire purchase repayments

Holidays and leisure activities

School fees/parental contribution to grant

Dependants other than children

Insurance (other than car insurance)

Pension plan

Other major income expenses, the nature of which should be specified

Total per month (or per year)

Are any of the above expenses likely to alter significantly in the foreseeable future and if so, when and in what way

8. Expenses of a Capital Nature

Repair, improvement and upkeep of home

Cost of major household or personal items (please specify)

Other major capital expenses, the nature of which should be specified

D–022 **C. Other Types of Claim**

9. Challenges to the Will

Do you wish to claim that the will is invalid?

If so, state the facts which support your claim

Are you aware of any earlier will under which you would benefit?

If so, state the benefit

Would you benefit if the deceased had died intestate?

10. Claims to Interests in Property

Do you wish to claim that you are entitled to any property, or a share of any property, which is said to form part of the deceased's estate? If so, identify the property; and state the facts which support your claim

In particular, did the claimant make any contribution to the purchase price of the home, or make any other contribution on the basis that he or she should acquire a beneficial interest therein:

> in either case, what form did the contribution take
> in the second case, what evidence is there that the contribution was made on that basis

D. Matters Concerning Specific Classes of Claimant   D–023

11. If the Claimant is a Spouse; a Party to a Registered Civil Partnership; a Former Spouse Who Has Not Remarried; or a Former Civil Partner Who Has Not Entered into Another Civil Partnership or Married; or Lived in the Same Household as the Deceased as the Deceased's Husband or Wife or as the Deceased's Civil Partner for the Two Years Immediately Preceding the Deceased's Death

Was the claimant married to/in a civil partnership with the deceased at the date of death?

If not, when was the marriage/civil partnership dissolved?

Following the dissolution:

> Were any financial orders made?
> Did the parties enter into any agreement under which provision was made for the claimant?

Were there Matrimonial/Dissolution of Civil Partnership proceedings anticipated or ongoing at the date of death?

What was the standard of living enjoyed by the parties during the marriage, civil partnership or cohabitation relationship

During the period of any of the above relationships, did the claimant:

> contribute to the household income and if so, to what extent, with what frequency and over what periods
> look after the home and/or care for the family of the deceased, and if so, in what manner and over what periods

12. If the Claimant is a Child of the Family or a Person Who Was Treated as a Child of the Family in Relation to Any Marriage or Registered Civil Partnership

In what way or ways, for what period or periods, and with what career in mind was the child being, or intended to be, educated or trained?

13. If the Claimant Was Not a Child of the Family but is a Person Who Was Treated as a Child of the Family

Did the deceased assume responsibility for the claimant's maintenance and, if so, over what period and on what basis—that is to say, what did the deceased pay for or provide, to or for the benefit, education or maintenance of the claimant

Did the deceased know that the claimant was not his/her own child

Has anyone else any liability to maintain the claimant, and, if so, who is that person and how does the liability arise

14. If the Claimant Was a Person Maintained by the Deceased Immediately Before His Death

Did the deceased assume responsibility for the claimant's maintenance and, if so, over what period and on what basis—that is to say, what did the deceased pay for or provide, to or for the benefit, education or maintenance of the applicant

If the claimant paid any money or rendered any services to the deceased in return for what he/she received from the deceased, state the nature and amount of the money payments and/or the nature of the services rendered

APPENDIX 5

IMPORTANT CASES

In both s.1 (general topics) and s.2 (topics specific to a particular class) the topics are listed alphabetically and, within each topic, cases are listed chronologically. Section 2 follows the arrangement of App.6. Cases in which a particular word or phrase has been considered are listed in s.1 under the general heading "Words and Phrases", the words or phrases being listed alphabetically.　　E–001

Section 1—General Topics

Beneficiaries, financial circumstances of　　E–002

Re Clarke [1991] 21 Fam. Law 364

Change in circumstances between date of death and date of hearing (s.3(5))　　E–003

Re Hancock Deceased [1998] 2 F.L.R. 346, CA

Conduct of claimant, effect of　　E–004

Re Snoek Deceased [1983] 13 Fam. Law 19
Williams v Johns [1988] 2 F.L.R. 475
Espinosa v Bourke [1999] 1 F.L.R. 747, CA
Re Myers [2005] W.T.L.R. 851
Bye v Colvin-Scott [2010] W.T.L.R. 1
Wright v Waters [2015] W.T.L.R. 353

Conduct of defendant, effect of　　E–005

Stephanides v Cohen [2002] W.T.L.R. 1373

Deceased's estate, source of assets comprised in　　E–006

Re Bunning [1984] Ch. 480
Re Callaghan [1985] Fam. 1

Disability or ill-health of claimant (and see under Adult Children, s.2)　　E–007

Re Watson [1999] 1 F.L.R. 878
Moore v Holdsworth [2010] W.T.L.R. 1213
Swetenham v Walkley [2014] W.T.L.R. 845

Domicile and residence　　E–008

Cyganik v Agulian (Agulian v Cyganik) [2006] W.T.L.R. 565, CA
Holliday v Musa [2010] 2 F.L.R. 702, CA

Mark v Mark [2006] 1 A.C. 98, HL
Witkowska v Kaminski [2007] 1 F.L.R. 1547
Sylvester v Sylvester [2014] W.T.L.R. 127

E–009 Forfeiture Act 1982

Land v Land's Estate [2006] W.T.L.R. 1447

E–010 Improvident behaviour by claimant

Rhodes v Dean unreported 28 March 1996, CA
Re Farrow Deceased [1987] 1 F.L.R. 205
Robinson v Bird [2003] W.T.L.R. 1535
Cattle v Evans [2011] 2 F.L.R. 843

E–011 Lack of contact between claimant and deceased, long period of

Re Rowlands [1984] F.L.R. 813
Re Debenham [1986] 1 F.L.R. 404
Re Hancock Deceased [1998] 2 F.L.R 346
Ilott v Mitson, Land, Blue Cross, RSPB and RSPCA [2012] 2 F.L.R. 170, CA; *Ilott v Mitson* [2017] UKSC 17, reported *sub nom. Ilott v Blue Cross* [2017] 2 W.L.R. 909

E–012 Promises, unenforceable, effect of

Rajabally v Rajabally [1987] 2 F.L.R. 390; but compare *Re Snoek* (1983) 13 Fam. Law 19

E–013 Provision by way of discretionary settlement (s.2(1)(d))

Hanbury v Hanbury [1999] 2 F.L.R. 255
Challinor v Challinor [2009] W.T.L.R. 931

E–014 Provision out of property held on beneficial joint tenancy (s.9)

Re Crawford (1983) 4 F.L.R. 273.
Powell v Osbourne [1993] 1 F.L.R. 1001
Hanbury v Hanbury [1999] 2 F.L.R. 255
Dingmar v Dingmar [2007] 1 F.L.R. 210, CA

E–015 Striking out

For procedural non-compliance, whether appropriate

Hannigan v Hannigan [2000] 2 F.C.R. 650
Parnall v Hurst [2003] W.T.L.R. 997
Nesheim v Kosa [2007] W.T.L.R. 149

E–016 Statement of case disclosing no reasonable cause of action

Chekov v Fryer [2015] EWHC 1642 (Ch)

E–017 Tax issues

Dixit v Dixit, unreported 23 June 1988, CA
Re Goodchild [1997] 3 All E.R. 63, CA

Testator's reasons for making or not making provision   **E–018**

Re Rowlands [1984] F.L.R. 813 (so as to keep farm land as a unit)
Stephens v Stephens, unreported 1 July 1985, CA (assets not to go to family of wife's previous marriage)
Singer v Isaac [2001] W.T.L.R. 1045 (history of marriage)
Barrass v Harding [2001] 1 F.L.R. 138
Gold v Curtis [2005] W.T.L.R. 673 (provision made for claimant during deceased's lifetime)
Re Myers [2005] W.T.L.R. 851 (conduct of claimant)
Ilott v Mitson, Land, Blue Cross, RSPB and RSPCA [2012] 2 F.L.R. 170, CA; *Ilott v Mitson* [2017] UKSC 17, reported *sub nom. Ilott v Blue Cross* [2017] 2 W.L.R. 909 (claimant marrying person of whom testatrix disapproved)

Time limits, general guidelines for applications to commence proceedings   **E–019**
out of time (s.4)

Re Salmon, Coard v National Westminster Bank [1981] Ch. 167
Berger v Berger [2014] W.T.L.R. 35, CA (deliberate delay by claimant)

Time limits, importance of merits in applications under s.4   **E–020**

Re Dennis [1981] 2 All E.R. 140
Stock v Brown [1994] 1 F.L.R. 840
Re C (Deceased) [1995] 2 F.L.R. 24; also reported as *Re W (A minor)* [1995] 2 F.C.R. 689

Will drafting, effect of "no-contest" clause   **E–021**

Nathan v Leonard [2003] 1 W.L.R. 827

Words and phrases   **E–022**

"Immediately before death"

Gully v Dix [2004] W.T.L.R. 331
Re Watson [1999] 1 F.L.R. 878

"Maintenance"   **E–023**

Re Dennis [1981] 2 All E.R. 140
Lewis v Warner [2016] W.T.L.R. 1399 (effect of order under which provision for the claimant involved no net cost to the estate)

"Reasonable needs"   **E–024**

Malone v Harrison [1979] 1 W.L.R. 1353
Harrington v Gill [1983] 4 F.L.R. 265
Re Watson [1999] 1 F.L.R. 878
Negus v Bahouse [2008] 1 F.L.R. 381
McIntosh v McIntosh [2013] W.T.L.R. 1565

"Substantial"   **E–025**

Jelley v Iliffe [1981] Fam. 128
Re Kirby [1982] 3 F.L.R. 249, CA
Bishop v Plumley [1991] 1 All E.R. 236

Section 2—Topics Specific to a Particular Class

E–026 *Surviving spouses*

Breakdown of marriage before death of deceased

Aston v Aston [2007] W.T.L.R. 1349
Barron v Woodhead [2009] 1 F.L.R. 747

E–027 Matrimonial home, whether claimant should have absolute or life interest

Davis v Davis [1993] 1 F.L.R. 54
Re Krubert Deceased [1997] Ch. 97
Iqbal v Ahmed [2012] 1 F.L.R. 31, CA

E–028 Provision on "notional divorce", importance of (s.3(2))

Re Besterman, Besterman v Grusin [1984] Ch. 458
Re Bunning, Bunning v Salmon [1984] Ch. 480
Re Moody, Moody v Stevenson [1992] Ch. 486, CA
Re Krubert Deceased [1997] Ch. 97
Cunliffe v Fielden [2006] Ch. 361, CA
P v G, P and P (Relevance of Divorce Provision) [2006] 1 F.L.R. 431

E–029 Provision out of large estate

Re Besterman, Besterman v Grusin [1984] Ch. 458
P v G, P and P (Relevance of Divorce Provision) [2006] 1 F.L.R. 431
Lilleyman v Lilleyman [2013] Ch. 225

E–030 Separation of parties to marriage, effect of

Re Rowlands Deceased [1984] F.L.R. 813

E–031 *White v White*, when applicable

Adams v Lewis [2001] W.T.L.R. 493
Grattan v McNaughton [2001] W.T.L.R. 1305
McNulty v McNulty [2002] W.T.L.R. 737
Moorhead Deceased [2002] N.I.J.B. 83
Cunliffe v Fielden [2006] Ch. 361, CA
P v G, P and P (Relevance of Divorce Provision) [2006] 1 F.L.R. 431
Lilleyman v Lilleyman [2013] Ch. 225

E–032 *Former spouses who have not remarried*

General principles

Re Fullard Deceased [1982] Fam. 42
Cameron v Treasury Solicitor [1996] 2 F.L.R. 716
Barrass v Harding [2001] 1 F.L.R. 138

E–033 Treated as surviving spouse under s.14

Eeles v Evans unreported 6 July 1989, CA

Re Leach, Leach v Lindeman [1986] Ch. 226

E–043 *Dependants*

Assumption of responsibility for maintenance

Re Beaumont, Martin v Midland Bank Trust Co [1980] Ch. 44
Jelley v Iliffe [1981] Fam. 128
Kourgky v Lusher (1983) 4 F.L.R. 65 (responsibility ceasing shortly before death)
Bouette v Rose [2000] Ch. 662
Churchill v Roach [2004] 2 F.L.R. 989
Baynes v Hedger [2008] 2 F.L.R. 1805, affirmed on other grounds [2009] 2 F.L.R. 767, CA

E–044 Calculation of amount of reasonable provision

Malone v Harrison [1979] 1 W.L.R. 1353.
Rees v Newbery and the Institute of Cancer Research [1998] 1 F.L.R. 1041

E–045 Comparison with maintenance during deceased's lifetime

Rhodes v Dean unreported 28 March 1996, CA

E–046 Payments by Court of Protection

Bouette v Rose [2000] Ch. 662

E–047 Provision of accommodation

Jelley v Iliffe [1981] Fam. 128
Bishop v Plumley [1991] 1 All E.R. 236
Graham v Murphy [1997] 1 F.L.R. 860
Rees v Newbery and the Institute of Cancer Research [1998] 1 F.L.R. 1041

Section 3—Specific Provisions Other Than Time Limits, and Costs

E–048 Section 5 (interim orders)

Smith v Smith [2012] 2 F.L.R. 230

E–049 Section 6 (variation of periodical payments)

Taylor v Bell [2015] All E.R. (D) 208 (transcript available on Westlaw)

E–050 Section 8(1) (nominated property)

Cairnes (Deceased) Re (1983) 4 F.L.R. 228
Goenka v Goenka [2016] Ch. 267

E–051 (*Donatio mortis causa*)

King v Dubrey [2016] Ch. 221, CA, reversing [2014] W.T.L.R. 1411[1]

---

[1] This was not an application to bring the subject-matter of a *donatio mortis causa* into the net estate under s.8(2) but a claim that the deceased had made a *donatio mortis causa* of her house to the claimant; his 1975 Act claim was an alternative to that claim.

Section 9 (severable interest in chose in action)   **E–052**

Lim v Walia [2015] Ch. 375, CA

Section 10 (reviewable dispositions)   **E–053**

B v IB [2014] 2 F.L.R. 273
Dellal v Dellal [2015] EWHC 907 (Fam)[2]

Costs   **E–054**

Lilleyman v Lilleyman (Costs) [2012] 1 W.L.R. 2801 (part disallowance of costs to which defendants would otherwise have been entitled under CPR r.36.17[3])
Thomas v Jeffrey [2013] W.T.L.R. 141, CA (costs consequence of late disclosure)
Wharton v Mercer unreported 22 September 2011 (Liverpool District Registry) (incidence of costs where claimant died before the hearing). The transcript is available on LexisNexis.
Wooldridge v Wooldridge [2016] 3 Costs L.O. 531 (claimant ordered to pay beneficiaries' costs on the indemnity basis)

---

[2] This was a judgment relating to various interlocutory applications. There is no report of the case having progressed any farther.
[3] The relevant rule at that time was CPR r.36.14.

APPENDIX 6

CASE SUMMARIES

(a) Introductory Note

The summaries begin with the cases in which a substantive application has **F–001** been made under either the 1975 Act or the corresponding Northern Ireland legislation. No summaries of 1938 Act cases are included. The cases are arranged in the order in which the eligible classes are specified in s.1(1) of the 1975 Act (except that summaries of claims by infant children precede those by adult children). There are two further groups of summaries, of which the first (s.F) contains the cases on time limits. Section G has been reorganised into four parts, which summarise cases relating to domicile, specific provisions of the 1975 Act, costs, and other procedural and jurisdictional points. Cases are, as before, arranged in alphabetical order within their groups, or, in s.G, their sub-groups. In keeping with the tenor of the decisions, cases relating to male and to female applicants are listed as a whole. Where cases concern more than one class of applicant, the summary of each such case is listed under the earliest section in which it could be placed and cross-referenced to each other appropriate section; for example, the summary relating to *Re Rowlands Deceased* (surviving spouse and daughter) is found in s.A (surviving spouses and civil partners) and cross-referenced to s.C(2) (adult children). As it is quite usual for persons who claim as cohabitants to claim, in the alternative, as dependants, the relevant case summaries are placed in the cohabitant section (BA) but cross-referenced to the dependant section (E).

Case citations from the Law Reports, Vol.1 of the *Weekly Law Reports* **F–002** and the *All England Law Reports* are given where appropriate; citations from other reports and sources (which are identified in the table of abbreviations) are given only if the case has not been reported in one of the three series mentioned. In fact, during the past 10 years, relatively few reports have appeared in any of those series and the main sources of reported cases are the *Family Law Reports* (F.L.R.) (reports in which have generally been flagged up in the case reports and commentary in *Family Law*) and *Wills and Trusts Law Reports* (W.T.L.R.). Unfortunately, it is quite often the case that the reports in F.L.R. and W.T.L.R. are given different titles. In the case summaries, as in the main text, priority has been given to the F.L.R. citation but both versions will be found in the Table of Cases.

Two innovations which were introduced in the previous edition have been **F–003** retained. The availability of online information has resulted in easier access to unreported cases and also to the gradually increasing volume of Northern Ireland case law. There is also a very useful collection of case-notes at App.C of *Tyler's Family Provision*, 3rd edition (London: LexisNexis Butterworths, 1997) and those relating to cases which remain unreported are also indicated. Therefore, the first innovation is that after the citation of each such case, the following symbols indicate availability online or in *Tyler*:

- B: British and Irish Legal Information Institute (Bailii). This database holds decisions of the Northern Ireland Court of Appeal and Chancery Division from 1998 onwards, and decisions of the Northern Ireland Family Division from 2000 onwards;
- LN: LexisNexis transcript. LexisNexis holds the Northern Ireland Law Reports from 1945 and the Northern Ireland Judgments Bulletin from 1994;
- W: Westlaw. W(ca) indicates that only a case analysis is available. This includes an abstract and a list of the cases and statutory provisions cited in the judgment;
- T: followed by a page number indicates a note of the case in *Tyler's Family Provision*.

F–004   The second innovation is that, as the views of specialist practitioners about the meaning and effect of judicial decisions are often valuable, citations of articles and case comments relating to individual cases have been included. It would consume far more time than is available to attempt to list every such article or comment, so the citations are restricted almost entirely to the six journals which contain the bulk of the useful comment.[1] These are *Family Law*, the *Family Law Journal*, *Trusts and Estates Law and Tax Journal* (formerly the *Trusts and Estates Law Journal*), *Elder Law Journal*,[2] *New Law Journal* and *Private Client Business*.[3]

F–005   Although reports are not always sufficiently full for the summary to include all the information which may be thought desirable, the aim has been to include as many of the following details as possible:

The deceased:

(1)   age at death;
(2)   whether the disposition was made by will (and, if so, its date) or on intestacy;
(3)   value of net estate;
(4)   nature of estate.

Each applicant; also, any major beneficiary:

(1)   nature of relationship with deceased;

---

[1] This decision was made in accordance with Pareto's Law, which can be stated, in a generalised form, in the proposition that 80 per cent of the objectives are achieved with 20 per cent of the means of achievement. The marginal cost of achieving the remaining 20 per cent thus becomes unacceptably high. It appears that the law derives from Pareto's observation in the 1880s that 80 per cent of the land in Italy was owned by 20 per cent of the inhabitants.

[2] The first issue was published in 2011 and it appears quarterly.

[3] Note on the form of citations: citations in *Family Law*, the *New Law Journal* and *Private Client Business*, where the page numbering follows on from one issue to the next, are in the form "(year) volume, title, first page", e.g. (1990) 20 Fam. Law 337. For *Family Law Journal* and the *Trusts and Estates* journals, where the pagination in each issue (10 per year) begins from p.1, the form is "(year) title (issue) first page", e.g. (2004) 35 F.L.J. 19. Where the citation refers to a case comment rather than a journal article, the authorship has not always been attributed.

(2) length of relationship with deceased;
(3) age at the date of hearing;
(4) benefit taken (if any) under the disposition;
(5) relevant financial/personal circumstances;
(6) relevant conduct.

Award made:

(1) nature and/or value of provision ordered;
(2) beneficiary/ies affected;
(3) grounds for decision.

Other details:

(1) date of the last day of the hearing or date on which judgment
     was handed down;
(2) the composition of the court;
(3) if the report is of an appeal, details of the court appealed
     from.

Section A—Surviving Spouses and Civil Partners[4]

[Note: References to *White v White* (an ancillary relief claim under the
matrimonial jurisdiction) in this section are to the decision of the House of
Lords: [2001] 1 A.C. 596; [2001] 1 All E.R. 1; [2000] 2 F.L.R. 981.]

Adams v Lewis [2001] W.T.L.R. 493 (HH Judge Behrens, 26 January 2001).   **F–006**
The parties had been married for 54 years (with an 18-month separation
followed by a reconciliation in 1961) and there had been 12 children of the
marriage. Mr Adams died in 1991, one of his daughters having predeceased
him. By his will he left £10,000 and his household goods and personal effects
to his wife and the residue of his estate to be divided equally between his
surviving children and the children of his dead daughter. The trustees of his
will had power to apply any part of the residuary estate in providing and
keeping up a suitable residence for Mrs Adams. At the time of the hearing
she was living in the house which had been bought as the matrimonial home
in her husband's sole name and she expressed the wish to continue living
there. Mrs Adams was 86 at the time of the hearing. The judge was satisfied
that she was a good wife to Mr Adams for over 50 years and a good mother
to her children. She was not involved in her husband's business as a general
dealer and he did not contribute to the welfare of the family apart from
paying the bills and providing housekeeping money. The judge found that
the deceased owed her an obligation of the highest order. Her financial
position was that she had assets of just under £6,000 and her state pension
which was £67.75 per week at the time of the hearing. She had supplemented
her income by drawing some £2,000 from her savings over the previous six
years. The executor's account showed (in round figures) assets of £350,000,
though the value of the freehold properties needed to be adjusted upwards,
following a valuation by the court-appointed expert, by between £30,000–
£60,000. There were liabilities of £103,000 including an IHT liability of

---

[4] There is at the time of writing no report of any case in which the claimant was a surviving
civil partner.

£54,000, and legal fees to date were over £35,000. The parties' costs of the litigation were estimated at a further £52,000. Applying *White v White*, the court awarded Mrs Adams an absolute interest in the matrimonial home (valued at £173,000), while reducing the pecuniary legacy to £5,000 which, together with interest from the expiry of the executor's year, would amount to about £8,000. She thus received approximately half of the net estate.

Commentary
P. Reed, "The merry widow of Chaddock Hall" (2006) 75 T.E.L. & T.J., 8
S. Ross, "Claims by surviving spouses" (2006) 60 F.L.J. 13

F–007   *Aston v Aston* [2007] W.T.L.R. 1349 (HH Judge Reid QC, Guildford County Court). The deceased (G), whose final illness had manifested itself in 2002, died in a hospice on 7 November 2004 having duly executed his last will dated 26 November 2003. By that will he appointed his brother (J) as his sole executor and beneficiary. The value of the net estate (of which the principal asset was G's half-share in the matrimonial home) was approximately £188,000. The other half-share was owned by the deceased's wife (T), who also received a lump sum of £81,186 as the survivor under a joint life policy. The question arose whether those monies were impressed with a trust to apply them in paying off the mortgage on the matrimonial home. At the time of G's death, T's salary was £18,800 per year plus quarterly bonuses, and she was entitled to an index-linked civil service pension (£414 per month at the date of hearing) as G's widow. The provision sought by T was G's half-share in the matrimonial home together with half the cash in the estate. G was born in 1955 and T in 1961. They married in 1985 and the marriage had a troubled history. G had an affair at an early stage and the parties had a son in 1992 who died in January 2002. G had instructed solicitors to issue divorce proceedings in August 2001 but did not pursue them. His final illness became apparent shortly after the death of their son. During that illness T formed an association with another man (M) and left the matrimonial home. She did not return until G had gone into the hospice in which he died. *Held,* (1) T was not obliged to use the insurance monies to reduce the mortgage, so her claim under the 1975 Act was to that extent weakened. (2) T's financial position was better than it would have been on a divorce: she had half the equity in the house, the insurance policy proceeds and a widow's pension from the deceased's former employers; she had a satisfying job and no dependants; and if she could not make ends meet on her resources the deficiency arose almost entirely from her decision to acquire a horse (costing in the region of £4,000 per year) at a time when the marriage was dead and the deceased would never work again. However, the defendant's contention that she could reduce the deficit by taking a better-paying job was rejected as it was not unreasonable for her to continue in her current employment even though she was only required to work four days a week. (3) Despite her alleged emotional attachment to it, T did not need to continue living in the matrimonial home (a four-bedroom house which provided accommodation in excess of what was reasonable). A local house-price search showed that accommodation adequate to her needs was available in the area at a price which did not require her to take on an overburdening mortgage. Therefore, despite the length of the marriage and the fact that it was nominally in existence at the date of the deceased's death, the claim failed.

Baker v Baker [2008] 2 F.L.R. 1956 (Paul Chaisty QC sitting as a deputy **F–008** judge of the Chancery Division, 20 March 2008). Mr Baker (B) died unexpectedly on 17 November 2001, aged 61. He married the claimant, Mrs Susan Baker (W), on 8 August 1986, but they had begun to live together as man and wife in 1979, and four sons were born to them between then and 1983. Each had children from earlier relationships. W was aged 57 at the date of the hearing. The two major assets of B's estate were the matrimonial home ("Dale House") and his scrap metal and vehicle recovery business ("Whip Street Motors") and the premises from which that business operated. B had made some provision for his family outside his will, so that on his death W received some £160,000 and the sons, about £20,000 each. The material provisions of his will dated 16 July 2001 were that: (1) Dale House was left to his trustees upon trust to permit W to live there during her widowhood but to sell it with her written consent in which event the proceeds of sale were to be held on trust for such of herself and the four sons who should survive him in equal shares; (2) the goodwill, machinery, plant, stock-in-trade and effects of Whip Street Motors, and the book debts owing to him in respect of that business were left to the four sons in equal shares absolutely. The trustees were given full power to carry on the business and to postpone its sale and conversion for as long as they thought fit; and (3) the residuary estate, which included the business premises, was given to the trustees upon trust for such of W and the sons who attained the age of 21 as survived him in equal shares absolutely. It was agreed that the value of Dale House in its current state of repair was £340,000, and the value of the business premises was £150,000 in its current state of use, but £327,000 if the lapsed planning permission for residential development were reinstated. However, the parties did not agree on either the value at death or the current value of Whip Street Motors (which the sons had carried on successfully since B's death) and the learned deputy judge was in effect requested to do his best in all the circumstances with the limited information available. The possible range of figures at which he arrived was £600,000–£800,000 for the goodwill and other assets of the business which, added to the value of the business premises on the basis that they continued to be used for the business, Dale House, and the balance of funds in the estate, made up a total in the range £1.15–£1.35 million. W's claim was for Dale House to be awarded to her absolutely together with a lump sum of £550,000 which would fund a net annual income need of £30,000 and leave a further £30,000 over as a contingency fund. *Found,* the will did not make reasonable provision for W but her evidence failed to support an income need of that magnitude. The four sons had, with the encouragement of their parents, worked in the business from an early age, possibly at the expense of their formal education, and had made a significant success of it. It was self-evident that the estate's interest in the current business was inextricably mixed with it and could not easily be separated out. Having regard to s.3(5), it was necessary to consider the impact of any award on the continuation of the business. A clean break award was appropriate and the concept of equality as explained by Wall LJ in *Cunliffe v Fielden* was referred to. W was awarded Dale House absolutely together with a lump sum of £410,000, which was over half the net estate on any footing. W was left to consider whether she should trade down from Dale House and buy a smaller and less expensive home in the vicinity. However, using the Duxbury tables based on the rate of return at the date of the hearing the sum awarded would fund a net annual income need of slightly more than £25,000. It had earlier been accepted that an income of £20,000–25,000 per year would have supported the standard of living which she had previously enjoyed, but that particular circumstance was not explicitly referred to in arriving at the lump sum award.

F–009   *Barron v Woodhead* [2009] 1 F.L.R. 747 (HH Judge Behrens, Chancery Division, Newcastle District Registry, 25 June 2008). This is one of the few reported 1975 Act claims by a widower. Mrs Waite died on 3 May 2003 having made a will dated 16 October 2002 by which she appointed the two children of her previous marriage to be her executors and left her residuary estate to them. The value of the net estate was £315,000 and the will made no provision for her husband (Mr Barron). The parties cohabited from 1986 and married in September 1993. The marriage was far from peaceful as both were heavy drinkers and there were incidents of domestic violence. The parties had separated by September 2001 at the latest, before which event Mrs Waite had consulted solicitors with a view to obtaining a divorce, but no proceedings were ever commenced. The matrimonial home was originally owned by Mr Barron who purported to convey his share in it to Mrs Waite and subsequently to convey the property to his brothers and sister. His trustee in bankruptcy commenced claims against him and against Mrs Waite's personal representatives. The latter claim was compromised on the basis that her estate should receive 25 per cent of the net proceeds of sale, but at the hearing of the claim against him on 12 December 2007 both transactions were set aside and Mr Barron was ordered to give vacant possession to the trustee on 30 June 2008. In attempting the s.3(2) exercise, HH Judge Behrens found it very difficult to assess what award would have been made if the parties had divorced in May 2003, particularly in view of Mr Barron's dealings with the matrimonial home. He concluded that the court would have tried to ensure that Mr Barron had a roof over his head, but would not have been likely to award anything further if there was a risk of that further provision being claimed by Mr Barron's creditors. It was directed that a sum of up to £100,000 be applied to purchase a flat or house for his occupation, to be agreed by the parties or, in default, selected by the court. His occupation was to be rent-free for the rest of his life (he was 73 at the date of hearing) but he was to pay the outgoings. To the extent that the whole £100,000 was not used in the purchase, the balance was to be invested so as to maximise the income, which was to be paid to Mr Barron for life.

Case comment
Barron v Woodhead (2008) 38 Fam. Law 844

F–010   *Re Besterman, Besterman v Grusin* [1984] Ch. 458; [1984] 2 All E.R. 656, CA (Oliver, Fox, Robert Goff LJJ, on appeal from HH Judge Mervyn Davies QC sitting as a High Court judge). The parties married in 1958. The testator died in 1976, aged 72, when the applicant was 60. By his will dated 29 July 1973 he left a net estate of about £1.5 million, of which Oxford University was the principal beneficiary. He left he applicant his personal chattels and an income of £3,500 per year. She had a state pension of £400 per year and no other resources. An interim order was made on 21 July 1980 and increased on 31 July 1981 so as to give her aggregate capital of £259,000, amounting to one sixth of the estate. *Held*, in a case where there was a very large estate and the wife was wholly blameless and incapable of supporting herself, reasonable provision required that she should have a lump sum sufficient to relieve her of any anxiety for the future. The capital sum awarded by the judge at first instance was increased from £259,000 to £378,000. *Per curiam*: Since there is no power to vary a lump sum order, greater account should be taken of contingencies and inflation when making such an award than if a periodical payments order were made.

Commentary
J. H. McGuire and E. Frankland, "Till death us do part: Inheritance claims and the short marriage" (2006) 36 Fam. Law 374
S. Ross, "Claims by surviving spouses" (2006) 60 F.L.J. 13
G. Miller, "Provision for a surviving spouse" (2007) P.C.B. 144

Bheekhun v Williams [1999] 2 F.L.R. 229, CA (Auld, Chadwick LJJ, Sir   **F–011**
Christopher Staughton, 2 December 1988, on appeal from Raynor James QC, Clerkenwell County Court). See s.G.

Re Bunning, Bunning v Salmon [1984] Ch. 480; [1984] 3 All E.R. 1 (Vinelott   **F–012**
J, 8 February 1984). The testator died in 1982 aged 75, leaving a net estate of £237,000. The parties married in 1963, the testator's first marriage having been dissolved by divorce, but the applicant left the testator in 1978. There were no children of the marriage. He left nothing to the applicant, who was aged 55 at the date of the hearing. She had assets of some £98,000 mainly derived from gifts made to her by him during the marriage, and her annual income was some £4,800. The major beneficiary was Cambridge University, to which £100,000 plus 80 per cent of the residue of £85,000 had been left. The RSPB received £26,000 and 20 per cent of the residue. It was common ground that the will did not make reasonable financial provision for the applicant, who contended that in an application under s.25 of the Matrimonial Causes Act 1973 she would have received £90,000. *Held*, the wife would have received £36,000, but that did not limit the figure which she could receive from the estate. Having regard to the applicant's need for security during what might be a long widowhood, and on the basis that the court would not interfere with the husband's right to dispose of his assets except to make reasonable provision for his wife, £60,000 was the correct figure. That was to fall on the 80 per cent of residue given to Cambridge University and then rateably on the pecuniary legacies to the university and the RSPB.

Commentary
S. Ross, "Claims by surviving spouses" (2006) 60 F.L.J. 13

Case comment
Re Bunning (1985) 15 Fam. Law 21

Capocci v Cooke, Court of Appeal (Russell LJ, Sir Ian Glidewell, 2 February   **F–013**

1996, LN, on appeal from Mr Assistant Recorder Hyland, Newcastle-upon-Tyne County Court). The testatrix died in 1992. She and the applicant had married in 1958 and, until shortly before her death, they lived together in a house which they had bought together in 1961. The marriage deteriorated in 1990, in which year the deceased severed the beneficial joint tenancy of the home. She ceased to live with the applicant in 1991. By her will she left him a life interest in her half-share of that property, but his right to remain there depended on his not remarrying or cohabiting with anyone else; and if the property were to be sold, he was to account for the proceeds of sale to the beneficiaries of the will. The net estate was about £55,000 and consisted mainly of a half-share in the matrimonial home (£26,000), and some £24,000 in bank and building society accounts in the name of the testatrix. The applicant, who was about 58 at the date of the appeal, had an income of about £9,000 but very little capital. The application was dismissed at first instance. It was argued, on appeal, that proper regard had not been paid to s.3(2) of the 1975 Act. Dismissing the appeal, Russell LJ said that, although the section had not been specifically referred to, it was apparent from the judgment, read as a whole, that it had been properly taken into account.

F–014   *Re Clarke* [1991] 21 Fam. Law 364 (Scott Baker J, 2 November 1990). The testator died in December 1988 aged about 90, leaving a net estate of £179,501. He had married the applicant in 1976 when he was 78 and she was 71; she was 86 at the date of hearing. Both had been previously married and there were no children of the applicant's, but two children of the testator's, earlier marriage. By his will the testator left to the applicant a life interest in the matrimonial home and in a sum of £25,000, and subject thereto, his estate was left to his children and grandchildren. The parties had always kept their finances separate; the applicant had some £60,000 in two building society accounts and her monthly income was £920. *Held*, although none of the beneficiaries had advanced a positive case for maintenance out of the testator's estate, the testator was entitled to dispose of it as he pleased, subject to making reasonable financial provision for the applicant. As he had done so, the application failed.

F–015   *Cunliffe v Fielden* [2006] Ch. 361; see *Fielden v Cunliffe*.

F–016   *Davis v Davis* [1993] 1 F.L.R. 54, CA (Sir Stephen Brown P, Stuart-Smith and Mann LJJ, 15 January 1991, on appeal from Thorpe J, 25 July 1990). The testator died of cancer in April 1987. On 14 April 1987 he gave £15,000 to the applicant. By his will, which was drawn up and executed on the same day, he gave to the applicant his personal chattels absolutely (apart from two items given to the son of his previous marriage) and a life interest in the residue of his estate. The net estate amounted to £267,000, and included a house worth £70,000 purchased by the trustees of the will for the occupation of the applicant. It also included £90,000 which had not yet fallen into possession, being subject to a life interest in favour of the deceased's mother. The applicant sought the transfer to herself of the freehold of the house in which she had a life interest. On appeal it was argued that the provision made for her should have included some capital element, which would be provided by the transfer of the freehold to her. This argument was rejected and the appeal dismissed.

Re Dawkins, Dawkins v Judd [1986] 2 F.L.R. 360 (Bush J, 8 October 1985);	**F–017**
also noted in s.G. The testator died on 26 July 1982 aged 72. He and the
applicant married in November 1978, it being the second marriage of each
of the parties. By his will dated 3 February 1980 the deceased left £8,000 and
a life interest in the matrimonial home to the applicant. On 1 May 1981 he
transferred the matrimonial home for the sum of £100 to his daughter by his
first marriage. Early in 1982 the deceased said that he wanted a divorce; the
parties separated in May of that year although, when he later became ill, the
applicant cared for him in the matrimonial home. By his will dated 19 June
1982 he left his entire estate to his daughter. She and her husband were in
business, running an employment agency which was profitable. The estate
was insolvent, but the applicant claimed, under s.10 of the 1975 Act, for
provision to be made for her out of the net proceeds of sale of the matrimonial home, which amounted to £27,000 and had been kept in a separate
account to await the outcome of this application. It was conceded that, had
the matrimonial home been part of the estate, the later will would not have
made reasonable provision for the applicant. She was living in a council
house on an income of £47.78 per week. The evidence led irresistibly to the
conclusion that the disposition of the matrimonial home was made with the
intention of defeating a claim under the 1975 Act; the applicant was
awarded £10,000 and a further £426.80 for the funeral expenses.

Dingmar v Dingmar [2007] Ch. 109, CA (Ward, Jacob, Lloyd LJJ, 12 July	**F–018**
2006, on appeal from HH Judge Behrens sitting at Leeds County Court).
The deceased (H) bought a house in joint names with his first wife (W1).
There were two children of the marriage, one of whom, a son (S) was the
defendant to the claim. After W1's death, H put the house into the joint
names of himself and S by way of gift, and shortly afterwards married W2.
When the house passed by survivorship to S, on H's death in 1997, W2
continued to live there with the children of the first marriage, who were at
that time 13 and 11. H had died intestate but his estate contained no assets
of any value, so no grant of administration was made at the time. In 2004 S
claimed possession of the house. As a necessary preliminary to her claim
under the 1975 Act, W2 obtained letters of administration. Since the estate
contained no other assets, she applied under s.9 for an order that H's
severable share of the house be treated as an asset of his net estate. It was
agreed that the value of the house was £40,000 at the date of H's death and
£95,000 at the date of the hearing. The judge at trial found that reasonable
financial provision had not been made for W2, and that reasonable provision would be a half-share of the house. However, he held that under s.9 the
provision which could be made for her was limited to the value of the
severable share at H's death. In effect, he awarded her an equitable charge
over the property for £20,000. That decision gave rise to two questions on
W2's appeal, viz.: (1) could the award have been in the form of a beneficial
interest rather than a lump sum; and (2) whichever type of award was made,
was the quantum limited by the value of the property at H's death? Lloyd LJ
(with whom the other members of the court agreed on this point) held that
an order giving W2 a beneficial interest in the house could have been made
under s.2(1)(c), which gives the court power to order a transfer of such
property comprised in the estate as is specified; however, in his dissenting
judgment, he held that the award was limited by the words "at the value

thereof immediately before his death", and therefore the share to be transferred could not exceed 21 per cent, that being the percentage of the value of the house at the date of the hearing (£90,000) represented by the value of the half-share at death (£20,000). It seems that, like the trial judge, he reached this conclusion with some regret, but in his judgment, to hold otherwise would have involved treating those words as having no effect. However, for somewhat differing reasons, Jacob and Ward LJJ felt able to decide that the words did not prevent the court from awarding W2 a half-share of the property, not limited by its value at the date of death, and the trial judge's order was varied to the effect that S should hold the property upon trust for himself and W2 as tenants in common in equal shares.

Commentary
E. Exton and J. Washington, "The Inheritance (Provision for Family and Dependants) Act 1975: recent cases and developments" (2008) P.C.B. 101
A. Poulton, "The golden rule" (2006) 80 T.E.L. & T.J. 17

Case comment
R. Bailey-Harris (2006) 36 Fam. Law 1025

F–019   *Dixit v Dixit*, Court of Appeal (Sir Nicolas Browne-Wilkinson VC, Nourse, Stuart-Smith LJJ, 23 June 1988, LN, T541, on appeal from Waite J who found that reasonable provision had not been made); also listed at s.(C)(2). That finding was not in issue on the appeal, which was on behalf of the widow and infant daughters of the testator's second marriage. The testator died on 31 May 1982 aged about 63. He had five children by his first marriage; the eldest of these died in 1971. His first wife died in 1965, he remarried on 1 January 1968 and there were two children of the second marriage, born on 2 February 1972 and 28 October 1973, aged, respectively, 16 and 14 at the time of the appeal. By his will dated 11 January 1972 he made no provision for the widow or the children of the second marriage (R2 and N2). The matrimonial home (Bulstrode Road) was left equally to the second and third surviving daughters of the first marriage (T and R1) on attaining the age of 18, and the residue, some £4,000 in cash, to the four surviving children of the first marriage equally. The deceased had purchased two investment properties. One had been put into trust for the other two daughters of the first marriage (N1 and J) and, when sold after his death, realised £22,000. The second (Temple Road) was held in trusts the effect of which was to give the widow a life interest in one half, and, contingent on their attaining the age of 18, the other half for R2 and N2 during the widow's lifetime, and the capital to pass to them after her death. This property was found to be worth £65,000 at the date of the hearing, and would be worth £75,000 after being put into repair. Following the death of the deceased, the widow, N1, T, N2 and R2 were all living at Bulstrode Road, but conditions were appalling due to constant quarrelling. Waite J wished to achieve the following objects, namely (1) to give the widow, together with R2 and N2, while they were under her care, a secure home; (2) to ensure, if possible, that it be at Bulstrode Road; and (3) to strike a fair balance between the claims of the two families. He sought to achieve this (1) by giving the widow a full life interest in Temple Road and the children a vested remainder; (2) using the provisions of s.2(4) of the 1975 Act, to make the trusts of Temple Road (as varied by (1)) apply to Bulstrode Road instead, giving R1 and T, in exchange, Temple Road on trust for themselves absolutely. The order as drawn gave liberty to apply to any party who "shall be assessed to any liability for capital gains tax arising out of the terms of this order". The CGT effect of the switching of the trusts was to create a liability of some £8,500 in respect of Temple Road. The Court of Appeal did not decide whether the judge had power under s.2(1)(f) to "switch" the trusts, since it held that the order could not stand in the absence of any consideration of the tax implications. The order made was: (1) Temple Road on trust for the widow for life, remainder to such of R2 and N2 as attain the age of 18, ultimate remainder to the widow if R2 and N2 predecease her without attaining a vested interest; and (2) £15,000 to be raised out of Bulstrode Road to be applied as to £7,500 to the repair of Temple Road, as to £2,500 to the widow in repayment of her expenditure on it, and as to £5,000 to the trustee of Temple Road, £2,500 on trust for each of R2 and N2 absolutely. All parties to pay their own costs.

Eeles v Evans, Court of Appeal (Dillon, Woolf LJJ, Sir John Megaw, 6 July 1989, LN, T557, on appeal from HH Judge Boothman (Gloucester County Court, 25 October 1988)). Former spouse who had not remarried, treated as a surviving spouse under s.14 of the 1975 Act. The testator became ill in 1980 and died on 16 January 1982, having, by his will dated 20 May 1980, left his net estate, which was proved on 11 May 1982 at £159,715, to his daughter Ruby. She was born in 1934 and was the only child of the marriage, which took place in May 1933 and which broke down in 1978, when the applicant left him. In 1978 she petitioned for judicial separation and maintenance, but in March 1979 by consent she was given leave to amend the petition to pray for a divorce and full financial provision. A decree nisi was granted in August 1979 and made absolute on 14 May 1981. As less than 12 months had elapsed between the decree absolute and the death, the judge exercised his powers under s.14 of the 1975 Act and treated the applicant as if the decree of divorce had not been made absolute during the deceased's lifetime. It was common ground that reasonable provision had not been made for the applicant, who was 74 at the date of the hearing at first instance. She was not capable of living on her own and managing her own affairs and had been living in an old peoples' home since 1985. By 1986 the estate of the deceased had been greatly enhanced by the sale of land which had development potential, and the Court of Appeal put its value at some £330,000. Out of the estate, Ruby had received £177,500. Because of back trouble she had no earning capacity, and she had no assets other than the house in which she lived, the advances which she had received being mainly used in keeping down her indebtedness to her bank. The applicant had received £10,000 which was applied in payment of her own costs of the divorce proceedings. At first instance she was awarded £5,000 together with a life interest in the income of £85,000; this income would pay her nursing home fees and leave a cushion of £1,200 to £1,400 per year for other expenses. *Held*, the judge's award, though not generous, was not so plainly wrong that it should be disturbed. The appeal was dismissed with costs.

Fielden v Cunliffe, reported as *Cunliffe v Fielden* [2006] Ch. 361, CA (Wall, Mummery, Moore-Bick LJJ, 8 December 2005, on appeal from HH Judge

F–020

F–021

Howarth sitting as a judge of the Chancery Division in Manchester, 15 February 2005). The claimant was the widow of the deceased. He had engaged her as a housekeeper in April 2001, and on 25 October 2001 he made a will, expressed to be in contemplation of his marriage to her, by which he left his residuary estate (some £1.4 million) upon discretionary trusts for a class of beneficiaries of which she was a member, and which included the widow, children and remoter issue of his deceased brother. There was also £226,000 in accounts in joint names, which passed to her by survivorship. He died on 11 November 2002, aged 66; she was then 49. Probate was granted on 11 June 2003 and, shortly before the hearing, the executors made an open offer to settle the sum of £200,000 on the claimant under the terms of the will trust. That offer was rejected and at trial, HH Judge Howarth awarded her £800,000. On the executors' appeal it was agreed, in order to save the costs of a re-trial, that the Court of Appeal should provide a figure in substitution for that arrived at by the judge. The appeal was allowed (the award being reduced to £600,000), primarily on the ground that, although the judge had referred to all the statutory criteria, he had not explained how he had arrived at the figure of £800,000. That alone was sufficient to vitiate his conclusion, and, of the other seven issues raised on the appeal, the Court of Appeal considered only the application of *White v White* and the short duration of the marriage. The figure of £600,000 was arrived at on the basis that reasonable provision for alternative accommodation would be £200,000, and for income, a lump sum which would produce a net annual income of £30,000. The then current Duxbury tables gave £560,000 as the appropriate lump sum and, deducting Mrs Cunliffe's own capital resources (estimated at £150,000), that gave a lump sum of £410,000, which was rounded down to £400,000. To the extent that, on a *White v White* cross-check, this represented a departure from equality, it was justified by the brevity of, and the limited nature of her contribution to, the marriage. However, Wall LJ emphasised that there was no presumption of equality, nor that equal division should be a starting point.

Commentary
P. Reed, "The merry widow of Chaddock Hall" (2006) 75 T.E.L. & T.J. 8
G Kleiner and S. Todd, "The divorce fiction" (2006) 80 T.E.L. & T.J. 11
K. Gibson, "Extending financial provision" (2006) 59 F.L.J. 22
S. Ross, "Claims by surviving spouses" (2006) 60 F.L.J. 13
N. Francis, "If it's broken, fix it" (2006) 36 Fam. Law 104
G. Brasse, "It's payback time; *Miller, Mcfarlane* and the compensation culture" (2006) 36 Fam. Law 647
G. Miller, "Provision for a surviving spouse" (2007) P.C.B. 144
E. Exton and J. Washington, "The Inheritance (Provision for Family and Dependants) Act 1975: recent cases and developments" (2008) P.C.B. 101

Case comment
R. Bailey-Harris (2006) 36 Fam. Law 263

F–022   *Gandhi v Patel* [2002] 1 F.L.R. 603 (Park J, 31 July 2001). The claimant applied for provision out of the estate of her late husband on the footing that she was entitled to be treated as the wife of the deceased pursuant to s.25(4) of the 1975 Act. The claim failed on this point, so the merits were not considered; see s.G.

Commentary
A. Francis, "A dangerous Act to follow" (2003) 31 F.L.J. 18
G. Miller, "When 'I do' turns into 'I didn't'" (2004) 154 N.L.J. 252

Case comment
R. Bailey-Harris (2002) 32 Fam. Law 262

Goenka v Goenka [2016] Ch. 267 (HH Judge Hodge QC, Chancery Division, **F–023** Liverpool District Registry, 6 August 2014); see also s.G. Claim by the widow (V) of the deceased (N). N, who was a consultant endocrinologist, and V married on 31 August 1997 and there were three sons of the marriage, all under 18 at the date of the hearing. V petitioned for divorce on 9 May 2012 and a decree nisi was made on 12 August 2012. N made his last will, together with a letter of wishes, on 7 September 2012, supplemented by a further letter on 10 September 2012, and committed suicide on 17 September 2012. By his will N appointed his father (G) and a solicitor as executors and G, N's brother (A) and a friend as trustees. G was also the person nominated to receive the lump sum benefit (which amounted to £201,000) payable under the NHS pension scheme upon N's death. The question arose whether that sum was to be treated as forming part of the net estate by virtue of s.8(1)(a) of the 1975 Act and it was held that it should be so treated; that aspect of the case is separately summarised in s.G. The combined effect of the will and a flexible mortgage plan was that V received the personal chattels and the matrimonial home, free of mortgage. The residuary estate (not including the death in service benefit, and amounting to about £410,000 after payment of debts and provision for administrative costs and the executors' costs of the claim), was given to the trustees (subject to an overriding power of appointment) upon trust to accumulate the whole or part of the income of the trust fund and add it to the fund, but with power to pay or apply the fund for the benefit of any of the beneficiaries as they thought fit. The beneficiaries were defined as V, N's descendants and, at any time when no descendant was living, N's father and mother (G and H). In his formal letter of wishes N stated that he wished the trustees to treat his three children equally and in due course to divide the capital of the trust fund between them and pay a one-third share to each of them on reaching the age of 25, but subject to first appointing £60,000 or one quarter of the fund, whichever was less, to V. He also expressed the wish that G should transfer the death in service payment to the residuary estate but in the event G, considering himself not bound by any legal obligation, proved unwilling to do so. V's position was assessed on the basis that at the time of the divorce she had capital in the region of £25,000. Her net monthly income from her employment as a nurse, her widow's state pension and her NHS pension was £2,832.25; the court accepted the submission that the child allowance of £21,193.71 per year from the NHS should not be treated as part of her financial resources. She might also, subject to the trustees' discretion, receive the income from a sum of £60,000 and, in 14 years' time, a capital sum not exceeding £60,000. Including the death benefit, the net estate was slightly over £700,000. The divorce comparison was considered and it was found that V would not have received, on divorce, as much as she was presently receiving in income and by having a house free from mortgage. Her own financial resources would have sufficed on a maintenance basis. However, the court had to take into account what it was reasonable for V to receive in all the circumstances. She was 42 years of age, the marriage had lasted 15 years and she had made a considerable contribution to the welfare of the family by looking after the home and caring for N and their three sons. None of the defendants could be regarded as having any particular financial needs. The court was satisfied that the sum of £60,000 referred to in N's letters was his estimate of the approximate value of his savings, but they were actually somewhat greater. *Held*, in all the circumstances the will failed to make reasonable provision for V, but only to the extent the award should be of the order of £67,670 (the actual value of N's savings) and be paid out of the death in service benefit, which would also bear the costs, in the following order, of (1) the estate, properly incurred (2) the official solicitor (representing the three infant defendants) on the indemnity basis (3) V's costs on the standard basis; and, to the extent that the death in service benefit was insufficient to meet those costs, they should be borne by the estate.

F–024   *Grattan v McNaughton* [2001] W.T.L.R. 1305 (HH Judge Behrens, 20 June 2001). H and W married in 1987; there were no children of the marriage, but H had two children, aged over 30 at the time of the hearing, by his previous marriage. H died in 1996 leaving his estate to his two children subject to W's limited right of occupation of the matrimonial home. W was 69 at the date of the hearing; the marriage had lasted some nine years. As a result of H's death, W had received a lump sum of £21,551.33 and a pension of £136 per month from H's employers. She had a right to occupy the matrimonial home, the value of which was £90,000 subject to a mortgage of £3,600 which she had been paying since H's death (the current payments being £125.37 per month), and an interest in jointly owned property in France worth between £13,000 and £20,000. If the mortgage were paid off and the French property sold her income would just exceed her outgoings. The value of the net estate excluding the property in France was £79,480 of which £35,530 was in the form of liquid assets. Neither of the beneficiaries was particularly wealthy but neither was in such a position that the award which would otherwise be made to W should be reduced. *White v White* was not applied since (1) it was not possible, on the evidence, to determine what provision W might have received on divorce, and (2) the judge accepted the submission that where the means of both parties were limited it was unlikely to be decisive. The award made reflected the financial contribution made by W towards the acquisition of the matrimonial home, but not the costs incurred by W in previous unsuccessful proceedings for rectification of the will and professional negligence. The effect of the order made was that D1 and D2 (H's children) received £5,000 each and their costs not exceeding £6,000 including VAT be paid out of the estate, the mortgage was to be paid off out of the existing liquid assets and W should receive the rest of the residuary estate, which would amount to about £16,000 less the costs of administration. Her right of occupation of the matrimonial home was enlarged.

Commentary
A. Cameron, "*Grattan v McNaughton, Grattan v Brydson*—rectification of wills" (2002) P.C.B. 120
L. King, "Impact of the Civil Partnership Act 2004 on wills" (2006) P.C.B. 170
S. Ross, "Claims by surviving spouses" (2006) 60 F.L.J. 13

Hope v Knight [2011] W.T.L.R. 583 (HH Judge Purle QC, Chancery Division, Birmingham, 15 December 2010). This was a claim by a surviving spouse and adult daughter. The deceased (M) died on 8 January 2009, survived by his wife (J), and his 28-year-old daughter (L). The parties separated in 1991 and M and J entered into a separation agreement under which she received assets worth about £116,000, representing half the joint assets declared for the purpose of the agreement. L received a monthly allowance, which ceased in 2007 when M bought her a car. At the time of the agreement there was £108,000 in a bank account in the Isle of Man, controlled by M. At trial it was not ascertained what had happened to that money; at M's insistence, it had not been taken into account when the separation agreement was made, and the matter was never pursued. Following the separation, M formed a relationship with C and by his will dated 20 December 2008, which disposed of an estate of some £800,000, he appointed her sole executrix and universal legatee. The estate included the quasi-matrimonial home, worth £450,000. J, a teacher aged 57 at the date of the hearing, was found to have an earning capacity of £21,500 per year gross and a small pension income. Her property was mortgaged but the mortgage was due to be paid off within the next year, when she would have an unencumbered property worth about £120,000 at current values. Her current lifestyle was found to be comfortable, but not lavish, and capable of being supported by her existing resources. L, a care worker, was at the time living with J and her monthly income exceeded her outgoings by about £150. As a result of M's death, she stood to inherit some £45,000 from her (now deceased) paternal grandmother and also a pension of £2,000 per year. *Held*, following the separation agreement, M was entitled to conduct his affairs on the basis that it had satisfied his obligations towards J; and although he might have been more generous to L, her claims did not outweigh those of C. It was entirely reasonable for him to provide for her to the exclusion of J. In any event, J's failure to mount any further claim during the 19 years of M's lifetime after the separation agreement made it unjust for her to seek a capital adjustment after his death. Delay was a factor which diminishes, and possibly eliminates, a claim to matrimonial provision and that principle is equally applicable to cases of separation as well as divorce; *Rossi v Rossi* [2007] 1 F.L.R. 790 followed, and *Re Rowlands* [1984] F.L.R. 813, CA, also referred to. With some misgivings, both claims were dismissed.

F–025

Iqbal v Ahmed [2012] 1 F.L.R 31, CA (Pill, Jackson and Gross LJJ, 29 July 2011, on appeal from HH Judge Bidder, Cardiff County Court, 4 August 2010). The claimant (W) was the widow of the deceased (D) and the defendant (S) was his son from a previous marriage. The deceased died on 25 March 2009, leaving a net estate sworn for probate as not exceeding £178,000; it included the matrimonial home ("the Property"), valued at £115,000 and £28,000 in cash. By his will dated 28 January 2009 he

F–026

appointed S as the sole executor and S and a friend (H) as trustees. He gave W a legacy of £8,000 and the right to occupy the Property rent-free, but subject to a liability to pay for "outgoings insurance repair decoration and other matters as the Property Trustees shall from time to time consider reasonable". The property would become uninhabitable if repairs, estimated to cost about £30,000, were not carried out. The residuary estate and the Property, subject to W's right of occupation, were left to S. In a memorandum of wishes D stated that he had chosen not to make any further provision for W because of her conduct towards him. The parties had been married for 22 years and W was aged 61. She was originally from Pakistan, had poor command of English and suffered from depression. She had no history of employment in the UK. She had savings of about £3,000 and otherwise was financially dependent on state benefits and on D, who allowed her £5 per week "pocket money". She was found to have virtually no earning capacity. In regard to the criticisms made of her conduct, the trial judge found that she may not have been an easy person to live with but accepted her evidence that she had looked after D when he was ill, and during a long marriage she had looked after the house and cooked for him. Her conduct was largely irrelevant. S had received a lifetime gift of £21,500 from D; he was an independent business man with substantial resources and no immediate needs. *Held*, the will did not make reasonable provision for W. The right of occupation was precarious because of the conditions attached to it. W did not have the resources to fund the repair costs and the trustees were not obliged to fund them. If the Property became uninhabitable she would have no resources to put towards the purchase or rental of a property for her occupation. She had no share in its ownership to allow her to obtain a secured loan to cover the cost of repair. W was awarded the whole of the residuary estate and a life interest in the Property, which would be subject to a trust for sale, postponed during W's lifetime or until her agreement to a sale. There would also be an agreement by S to pay half the cost of insurance and structural repairs to the Property. The proceeds of sale would be held upon trust for W and S in equal shares. A counterclaim by S for a beneficial interest in the Property, based on proprietary estoppel or constructive trust was dismissed. S was granted permission to appeal only on the point whether the judge failed to consider adequately or at all whether reasonable provision would have been made by awarding W a life interest in the Property and its proceeds of sale and otherwise making the same orders. The appeal was dismissed. *Held*, the judge had not erred in principle and was not plainly wrong: (1) the relatively small size of the estate was the governing reality. The primary practical consideration was that the provision of a share in the capital gave W a "capital cushion" to meet whatever eventualities might occur. A life interest, as contended for on behalf of S, would be demonstrably inadequate to fund the repairs and permit W to maintain herself; (2) an award of a beneficial interest was appropriate where there had been a long marriage and that outweighed the fact that D had owned the property before his marriage to W; (3) relations between the parties were deeply hostile and a clean break would be appropriate; the award of a life interest would preclude a clean break solution.

F–027   *Jessop v Jessop* [1992] 1 F.L.R. 591, CA (Nourse, McCowan LJJ Sir John

Megaw, 11 October 1991, on appeal from Mr Michael Wheeler QC sitting as
a deputy judge of the Chancery Division). The deceased (J), a seaman,
married G in 1946 and there were three children of that marriage. Their
home was in Cleveland. In 1952, while in Portsmouth, he met D, a married
woman with three children whose marriage had broken down and was
dissolved in 1953. J, who did not initially tell D that he was married, was
able to maintain a happy domestic life in both locations, and his relationship
with D continued after he had revealed that. A daughter was born to them
in 1963. In 1964 D acquired a house in Portsmouth and in 1976 it was
conveyed to D and J as beneficial joint tenants. J died intestate in 1985 and it
was then that G learned for the first time of J's relationship with D. The
value of his estate for probate was under £2,500 but his severable share of
the property in Portsmouth was worth £21,000 and there were benefits due
to his dependants from his occupational pension with IBM, which he had
joined after leaving the Navy. The trustees had no discretion to pay the
annual pension to anyone other than G, but they decided to pay the lump
sum benefit of £39,522 to D. In 1989 when G's application for provision out
of J's estate and for his severable share of the Portsmouth property to be
treated as part of his net estate was first heard, G was 72 years of age with
net annual income of £4,686 and she was living in rented warden-controlled
accommodation. She had no capital. D, aged 67, had net annual income of
£4,392 and owned her house outright. At first instance the registrar ordered
that J's severable share of the Portsmouth property be treated, to the extent
of £10,000, as part of his net estate and that D should pay that sum to G. On
appeal, the deputy judge discharged that order, but it was restored by the
Court of Appeal. There was no reference in his judgment to the £39,522
received by D and he did not explain how he came to a conclusion contrary
to that of the registrar. The court was therefore entitled to interfere. Capital
provision against contingencies should, in accordance with the registrar's
view of the case, be made available to G and the registrar's order was
restored.

Case comment
Jessop v Jessop (1992) 32 Fam. Law 328

Jevdjovic v Milenko, Jevdjovic v Jevjdovic, CA (Dillon, Balcombe, Beldam   **F–028**
LJJ, 12 March 1990, LN, T576, on appeal from Francis Ferris QC sitting as
a deputy High Court judge, 7 October 1988). The testator (MJ) died on 14
November 1982, having made a will dated 17 May 1976. The applicant (AJ)
obtained a grant of letters of administration with the will annexed on 13
April 1984, and the court gave leave to issue the application out of time. AJ
and MJ were born in Serbia in 1904; they were married in 1942. Each had
been married previously, both former spouses being dead. There was one
son of AJ's first marriage and a son (P) and two daughters of MJ's first
marriage, but no issue of the marriage between AJ and MJ. P, who died in
1984, had a son, M. P apparently never came to England but M did so in
1974. In 1948 MJ came to England to work as a farm labourer, while AJ
remained in Yugoslavia bringing up the children of the earlier marriages. In
1960 MJ bought a freehold house (No.5) in his sole name; AJ came to
England and they occupied the house as their matrimonial home, letting
part of it. In 1975 he bought another house (No.3) in the joint names of

himself and P, to which M, in effect, succeeded. It was accepted by all parties that the effect of the will was to give AJ a life interest in No.5 and the furniture, and that this was not reasonable provision for her. There was no cash available in the estate and s.9 of the Act prevented recourse to MJ's severable share of No.3. The deputy judge ordered that No.5 be transferred to AJ absolutely. At the time of the appeal AJ had been living in Yugoslavia for 20 months, her pension was being paid to her there and there was evidence that she intended to remain there, sell No.5 and leave the money to her grandchildren. *Held*, the provision made at first instance was excessive; ordered that £50,000 be raised and paid to AJ out of the proceeds of sale of No.5, and that she have a life interest in the furniture and the remainder of the proceeds of sale. No order on the costs of the appeal save that the appellants were entitled to their costs out of the estate in due course of administration; Legal Aid taxation.

F–029   *Re Kennedy, Kennedy v Official Solicitor* [1980] C.L.Y. 2820 (HH Judge Willis, Shoreditch County Court, 22 May 1980). The testator and the applicant were married in 1941; in 1970 he deserted her and went to live with M. At some date before 29 March 1977 he made a will leaving his entire estate to M. On that date, by an assignment made in consideration of natural love and affection, he transferred his leasehold house to himself and M as joint tenants at law and in equity. On 21 April 1977, the applicant indicated her intention to apply for financial provision under the Matrimonial Causes Act 1973. The testator died before a decree nisi was granted; and M died intestate shortly afterwards. The applicant applied for an order, under s.10 of the 1975 Act, that provision be made for her out of the proceeds of sale of the leasehold property. *Held*, dismissing the application, it was not essential that the existence of the 1975 Act or its provisions were present to the deceased's mind when he made the disposition sought to be set aside; but there had to be evidence that the deceased intended to defeat a claim made after his death to his estate.

F–030   *Kusminow v Barclays Bank Trust Co, Sokolow and Sitnikowa* (1989) 19 Fam. Law 66 (Sir Stephen Brown P, 23 March 1988). The testator, who married the applicant in 1958, died in 1985. They spent their married life in England and their capital arose from their joint efforts in the way of property deals and taking in lodgers. By his will, made in 1968, he left his estate, the value of which was agreed for the purposes of the hearing to be £100,000, equally between his nephew and niece, both of whom lived in the Soviet Union in conditions of poverty. He left nothing to the applicant, who had savings of £20,000. She was 78 and suffered from arthritis. It was accepted that the will did not make reasonable provision for her. *Held*, if the matter was considered as if financial provision were being made following the dissolution of a marriage, the applicant would be entitled to at least a half-share of the family assets. She reasonably required a capital sum for her present and future provision. Having regard to the cost of administration and the fact that the other beneficiaries lived behind the Iron Curtain, a trust would be inappropriate. She was awarded a lump sum of £45,000.

Case comment
Kusminow v Barclays Bank Trust Co (1989) 19 Fam. Law 66

Re Krubert Deceased [1997] Ch. 97, CA (Nourse LJ, Cazalet J, 27 June 1996, **F–031** on appeal from Mr Recorder Curran, Caernarfon County Court). The applicant and the deceased married in 1950; there were no children of the marriage. In 1952 the deceased acquired a plot of land for £200, that money being provided by the applicant. A house was built on the land and they lived in it together until the death of the deceased, which took place in 1994. The applicant was then aged 88. The effect of the will was that the applicant received most of the personal chattels, a legacy of £10,000 and a life interest in the house and the rest of the estate, remainder to the deceased's brother and sister. The net estate of £111,676 (reduced to £77,811 by contingent and prospective liabilities) consisted of the house, worth £59,000, together with cash and securities. The effect of the order made at first instance was that the applicant took the estate absolutely, save for two specific bequests of personal property, and pecuniary legacies of £7,000 each to the brother and sister, who were the appellants. The order was varied so as to give the applicant (a) a life interest in the house, with remainder to the brother and sister equally and (b) the rest of the estate, apart from the two bequests of personal property, absolutely.

Commentary
P. Reed, "The merry widow of Chaddock Hall" (2006) 75 T.E.L. & T.J. 8
S. Ross, "Claims by surviving spouses" (2006) 60 F.L.J. 13
G. Miller, "Provision for a surviving spouse" (2007) P.C.B. 144

Case comment
Re Krubert (1996) 26 Fam. Law 785

Re Lewis, Lewis v Lynch, CA (Buckley, Shaw, Brightman LJJ, 13 March **F–032** 1980, LN, T586, on appeal from HH Judge Blackett-Ord VC, February 1979). The testator died in 1974, leaving a net estate of about £50,000. By his first marriage he had three children, one of whom had died in 1972 leaving two children who were 15 and 13 at the date of the hearing. By his marriage to the applicant, which took place in 1968, he had one child (S), aged 11 at the date of the hearing. The applicant had a 16-year-old daughter (K) by her first marriage; she herself was aged 50. By his will, made in March 1971 he left to the applicant two cars and some personal effects absolutely, and an annuity of £2,000. He also directed his trustees to expend £10,000 on the purchase of a house for her occupation during widowhood, she to pay the outgoings. He gave the residue to the four stirps of his two marriages, subject to the three stirps of the first marriage each bringing into hotchpot £20,000 advanced to them during his lifetime. The result would be that, out of the immediately distributable estate, S would take £22,850 and the other stirps £2,850 each. In fact the trustees were unable to purchase a suitable house for £10,000; the bungalow which they bought cost £18,000. Her income, including the annuity, was £3,400 per year and she also received maintenance for K and child benefit for S, totalling roughly £600 per year. At first instance it was held that the will did not make reasonable provision for the applicant; the judge ordered that she be constituted as the Settled Land Act tenant for life of the bungalow. The appeal was on the ground that, although the judge had considered the inadequacy of the provision made for the purchase of the house, he had failed to consider whether she had a sufficient income, particularly having regard to inflation. *Held*, the judge should have considered the effect of inflation on the purchasing power of the annuity. The appellant was awarded a lump sum of £10,000, to be paid with interest from the day following judgment.

F–033   *Lilleyman v Lilleyman* [2013] Ch. 225 (Briggs J, 4 April 2012); for the summary of the separate judgment on costs, see s.G. The husband (R) and wife (B) had both been previously married, there being two sons of each marriage. The parties, after a period of cohabitation beginning in 2005, married in September 2007. R died of a heart-related illness on 6 January 2010, aged 64, and leaving a net estate of approximately £6 million, of which some £5 million was represented by the value of the family business which he had created and in which both of his sons and other family members were employed. By his will dated 20 May 2008 he appointed his sons as his executors and trustees. He gave B his personal chattels not specifically bequeathed elsewhere, limited rights of occupation of the matrimonial home (Water Meadows) in which she was beneficially entitled to a half-share, and of a holiday home (Dunhome) owned in his sole name. His interest in both those properties, subject to B's rights of occupation, was given to his sons, together with the rest of the residuary estate. He had also set up a fund from which B derived a fixed annuity amounting, at then current tax rates, to £378.72 per month. At the date of hearing of her claim, B was aged 66. At the start of their relationship she was earning a modest income from two part-time jobs, but she gave up one in 2005 and the other in 2007, when his health had further deteriorated, to look after him. She also made contributions towards the renovation and purchase of Water Meadows, mainly from the proceeds of sale of her former matrimonial home (Robinson Drive) in which her son Robert had also been living. Those proceeds also partly funded the joint purchase by R and B as tenants in common in equal shares of a property (Lea Court) which was rented to Robert and which he had been given an option to purchase. *Held,* (1) it was clear that the will had failed to make reasonable provision for B and to assert otherwise was unrealistic; (2) it was a fundamental principle that marriage was an essentially equal partnership and the division of available property on breakdown should accord with that principle; nevertheless equality of treatment does not necessarily lead to equality of outcome; (3) (applying *Miller v Miller, McFarlane v McFarlane* [2006] 2 A.C. 618) the legal principles applicable to a short marriage/big money 1975 Act claim were, in summary (i) the party asserting property of either spouse to be non-matrimonial bore the onus of proving it; (ii) a matrimonial home is usually to be regarded as matrimonial and family property even if only one spouse has contributed to it; (iii) property acquired during the marriage other than by inheritance or gift is usually matrimonial property but may not be family property if it has not been acquired for family use; (iv) property pre-owned by a spouse is not so regarded unless it has been committed to family use; (v) if a spouse brings to the marriage an existing business and develops it during the marriage, its value at the beginning of the marriage may be considered as non-matrimonial, but subsequent increases may be regarded differently (*Jones v Jones* [2011] 1 F.L.R. 1723 considered); (vi) if a spouse brings a pre-existing business into the marriage it may be positively unfair to have recourse to it for the purposes of sharing, in particular if that would cripple it or seriously reduce its value. The award of £500,000 to B included outright transfers of the estate's interest in Water Meadows and in Dunhome or, at her option, its lump sum equivalent. There was also to be an outright transfer of the estate's apparent interest in Lea Court, of which B was properly to be regarded as the beneficial owner (see paras [21]–[23] and [89]).

Commentary
R. Hughes, "Spouse and cohabitee claimants under the 1975 Act; meeting in the middle" [2013] Fam. Law 43, 826–31
M. Roper, "*Lilleyman v Lilleyman*; approaching 'non-matrimonial property' under the Inheritance Act" [2012] Eld. LJ 2(4), 363–68
M. Holdsworth and L. Tatton, "Big money, short marriage" [2012] T.E.L. & T.J. 138, 4–7

Case comment
R. Bailey-Harris [2012] Fam. Law 42, 947–49
R. Hughes [2012] Eld. LJ 2(2), 140–41

McGuigan v McGuigan [1996] N.I.J.B. 47 (Kerr J, Chancery Division **F–034** (Northern Ireland), 25 March 1996, LN). The testator died in 1994 leaving a widow and three adult children. The marriage had lasted for 65 years and the applicant widow was 81 at the date of the hearing. For many years she had worked long hours on the family farm. This and another farm were the major assets of the estate. The testator left to his wife a life interest in the matrimonial home and in the family farm, with remainder to his grandson (E), who also received the other farm absolutely. The value of the net estate was found to be £95,000. It was found that the applicant's net annual income (derived from state benefits) was £5,548 and the likely level of her financial needs was between £5,000 and £5,500. She had savings of £3,448. It was held that the provision made for her in the will did not sufficiently recognise the contribution which she had made to the family and the farms, or her financial needs. It was ordered that she receive a life interest in all the deceased's lands and buildings, remainder to E, and also a lump sum of £5,000 to be realised, if necessary, by sale of part of the lands. Her costs were ordered to be paid out of the estate.

McNulty v McNulty [2002] W.T.L.R. 737 (Launcelot Henderson QC sitting **F–035** as a deputy High Court judge, 22 January 2002). In this case it was argued for the claimant that her marriage to the deceased was a long and happy one, in which she played her full part in bringing up the family, and she also assisted in the partnership business for the first seven years of the marriage by doing the clerical work, and that it was reasonable to suppose that the court would have awarded her half the family assets in the light of the guidance given in *White*. Accepting, as did Vinelott J in *Re Bunning* that it was impossible to show by any deductive process that the sum he proposed to award was the right figure, the judge in *McNulty* gave three reasons for believing that the award was pitched at about the right level:

(i)   the award, added to the value of the land comprised in the residuary estate, would produce a capital fund amply sufficient to provide an income and meet any reasonably foreseeable contingencies;

(ii) it would enable her to share in the realised value of other land comprised in the estate which had greatly increased between the date of death and the date of the hearing;

(iii) a *White v White* cross-check was carried out. This gave an amount significantly lower than the award but the discrepancy was justified because, on death, when there was only one party to provide for, it would often be appropriate under the 1975 Act to make an award greater than would have been made on the "notional divorce".

Commentary
G. Harbottle, "Tales of procrastination and pedantry" (2004) 56 T.E.L.J 4
P. Reed, "The merry widow of Chaddock Hall" (2006) 75 T.E.L. & T.J. 8
S. Ross, "Claims by surviving spouses" (2006) 60 F.L.J. 13
G. Miller, "Provision for a surviving spouse" (2007) P.C.B. 144

F–036 *Moody v Haselgrove*, CA (Purchas, Lloyd, Nolan LJJ, 16 November 1987, LN, T599 on appeal from Falconer J, 7 May 1987). The testator married the applicant on 14 March 1974 and died on 28 August 1983 leaving a net estate consisting, at the date of the hearing, of a freehold house worth £65,000 and £13,800 in cash. The cash would be almost totally absorbed by the costs of the 1975 Act proceedings and earlier proceedings in which the applicant had unsuccessfully attempted to have the will set aside, and there were also administration expenses. By his will the testator left three pecuniary legacies of £1,000 each, devised the house to trustees for sale, to permit the applicant to reside there for life and giving them power, if it was sold, to purchase another residence with the proceeds of sale and giving the applicant a life interest in the income from the proceeds if it was not sold. The remainder interest went to his three cousins and the residue of the estate to the applicant. At first instance it was held that the will failed to make reasonable provision for the applicant. The personal representatives were ordered to raise £12,000 on the house, £3,000 to be paid to each of the three cousins and the testamentary and administration expenses and costs to be paid out of the other £3,000 to the extent that they could not be met out of residue. Subject to that, the applicant was to receive the house absolutely. No provision was made for the pecuniary legatees, who had not been made parties to the action. On appeal, the judge's order was varied, using the powers under s.2(4) of the 1975 Act, so that £15,000 was to be raised on the house, enabling the pecuniary legacies to be paid from the additional £3,000.

F–037 *Re Moody, Moody v Stevenson* [1992] Ch. 486, CA (Mustill LJ, Waite J, 12 July 1991, on appeal from HH Judge Kellock, Worksop County Court, 24 January 1991). The testatrix died on 18 August 1988 leaving a net estate of approximately £45,000, consisting of the matrimonial home and about £1,000 cash. The applicant, who was 81 at the time of the hearing, married the testatrix in 1971, it being her second marriage. By her first marriage she had a daughter, aged 55 at the time of the hearing, whom she appointed her executrix and to whom, by her will dated 21 June 1985, she left her entire estate. In her will she declared that she had made no provision for the applicant as she considered that he had adequate resources of his own. From

1971 until 1984, when she became senile and had to be moved to a nursing home, the testatrix and the applicant lived on their combined pensions, together with a sum of £7,160 inherited by the testatrix from her brother in 1980. The applicant, who had savings of £6,000 and received a state pension, continued to live in the house. The respondent, who had no savings, and an income of £45 per week, lived in a council flat, her rent being paid by social security. In the County Court, the respondent applied for possession of the house and the applicant made a cross-application under the 1975 Act. A possession order was made and the cross-application dismissed. On appeal it was held that the intention of the 1975 Act was to give a surviving spouse that which corresponded as closely as possible with the inchoate rights which he enjoyed during the deceased's lifetime under the matrimonial law. Accordingly, some provision should have been made. A settlement was directed on terms which enabled the applicant to live in the house so long as he was able and willing to do so.

Commentary
S. Ross, "Claims by surviving spouses" (2006) 60 F.L.J. 13

Case comment
Re Moody (1992) 22 Fam. Law 284

Moore v Holdsworth [2010] 2 F.L.R. 1501 (Kitchin J, Chancery Division, **F–038** Birmingham District Registry, 12 March 2010). The claimant (S) and her deceased husband married in 1977. She was 55 at the date of the hearing; there were no children of the marriage. The matrimonial home, which was the major asset of the net estate, was in their joint names but in December 2004 they severed the joint tenancy. This followed S falling ill from multiple sclerosis, by which time the deceased had been suffering from a lung disease for some time. S's evidence was that they had done so because of the possibility that she might have to go into long-term residential care and, if she were to survive her husband, the whole value of the property might be used to pay care home fees and expenses. They agreed that his share of the property should be retained in his estate but that she should be able to continue living there free of charge. They made wills in similar terms which implemented that agreement but in 2007 they decided to change them. S's evidence was that she expected her husband's new will to be in the same terms as hers, but it was not. It left his half-share of the property (valued at £62,500) as to 50 per cent to SH (a friend of both of them) and as to 25 per cent to each of P and T, his nephew and niece. The residue, amounting to about £40,000, passed to S. The deceased died some two months after making the new will and S had to go into residential care as she was unable to look after herself on her own. She now wished to return home and the local authority, which had been meeting her fees, wished her to do so but would need first to assess what alterations were necessary, which could not be done until the claim was disposed of, since it might have to be sold to implement the terms of the deceased's will. Having considered the medical evidence and the assurance that the local authority supported her wish to return home and would provide an appropriate care package, Kitchin J found that her desire to return home was entirely realistic and of the utmost importance. The more difficult question was whether reasonable provision required that she be awarded an absolute interest in the entire estate, given that the order which he proposed to make would ensure that she could live in the property for the whole of her life. Factors militating against the award of an absolute interest included the unlikelihood of a change in the system of payment for the local authority's services, the wish to avoid the whole value of the property being used to pay for her care (which would have defeated her husband's testamentary wishes) and the likely outcome of the "notional divorce", under which he found that she would not have been granted an absolute interest in the property. The interest of the beneficiaries under the deceased's will was postponed to the life interest in the estate's half-share awarded to her, together with the right to employ the proceeds of sale in the purchase of another property for her occupation.

Commentary
J. Aspden, "Redressing the balance" (2010) 118 T.E.L. & T.J. 14

Case comment
R. Bailey-Harris (2010) 40 Fam. Law 701

F–039   *Moorhead Deceased* [2002] N.I.J.B. 83 (Weatherup J, 11 January 2002, LN). The deceased died aged 79 years without issue, survived by his widow (the claimant, to whom he had been married for 37 years and who was aged 80), a nephew and two nieces. The net estate was valued at approximately £600,000, two-thirds of which was represented by a farm ("the home farm") comprising a farmhouse and outbuildings together with 64 acres of land. By his will the deceased left the claimant his personal chattels and a life interest in the home farm and in two-thirds of the residue. She had some £20,000 in capital and her gross annual income (including the estimated income from the life interests) was found to be £14,000. On her marriage the claimant had given up her employment as a theatre nurse, helped on the farm thereafter, had looked after the deceased's mother for the last 10 years of her life and also cared for the deceased when his health deteriorated. Apart from making some adjustments to the rights over land comprised in the home farm, it was ordered that another farm (value £55,000) be transferred to her absolutely, together with the farm stock and machinery and that she should receive a lump sum of £40,000 absolutely out of residue. *Per curiam*, fairness in this case did not require an equal division of assets (*White v White* and *Cowan v Cowan* [2001] 2 F.L.R. 192, CA considered; *Adams v Lewis* [2001] W.T.L.R. 493 also referred to). The comparison between divorce provision and inheritance provision was necessarily inexact, as the former involves fairness between husband and wife while the latter may admit of greater flexibility as it involves the same property being available to make provision for only one spouse.

F–040   *Morrow v Morrow* [1995] N.I.J.B. 46 (Campbell J, Chancery Division (Northern Ireland), 5 April 1995, LN). The applicant, who was aged 75 at the date of the hearing, had been married to the deceased for 52 years. The marriage began to deteriorate in 1989, some four years before the death of the deceased. Throughout their marriage, of which there were three children, they lived on the family farm. In 1992, on the same day as he made his will, the testator transferred the farm to his son (J). The applicant had worked on the farm for many years as well as looking after the family. By his will, the testator left some small items to J and to one of his other children, and he left the rest of his estate to the applicant absolutely. There was therefore nothing out of which provision could be made unless an order was made under art.12 (corresponding to s.10 of the 1975 Act) in relation to the transfer of the farm, the value of which at the date of the transfer was £165,000, and which had increased to £200,000 by the date of the hearing. The applicant's resources consisted of £33,219 capital and an annual income of £5,916, though this would be reduced by £2,000 if she ceased to live in the dwelling-house on the farm. It was found that the transfer of the farm was intended (though not solely intended) to defeat a claim by the applicant for financial provision, and the applicant was awarded a lump sum of £35,000 (which would be raised by the sale of about one-fifth of the land) and an annuity of £2,500 for life, to be charged on the remaining land.

O'Neill v McPhillimy [2004] N.I. Ch. 4 (Weir J, 24 February 2004, LN). The **F–041** claim was originally made by the widow and two of the five children of the marriage, but the children's claim was withdrawn during the hearing. The deceased died aged 76; the claimant was 66 at the date of the hearing. The estate was in excess of £1 million gross, but the properties comprised in it (which included three public houses) were encumbered and the net estate was in the region of £605,000. By his will the deceased left a one-third share of his residuary estate to his widow and the other two-thirds to two of his grandchildren. This distribution could not be implemented without a sale of the businesses and the widow was concerned to keep them in being. It was common ground that the will did not make reasonable provision for the widow. During a marriage of 36 years she had made a major contribution to the welfare of the family, had brought resources of her own into the marriage and some of these were applied in the family business. It was ordered that the residuary estate after payment of debts and funeral and testamentary expenses, including the costs of the proceedings, be held upon trust for the widow absolutely and that she should also have the option to purchase for its agreed probate value of £360,000 the Queen's Arms, which was to be specifically bequeathed upon trust for the grandchildren as tenants in common in equal shares on attaining majority.

P v G, P and P (Family Provision; Relevance of Divorce Provision) [2006] 1 **F–042** F.L.R. 431 (Black J, 20 December 2004). The claimant and the deceased (Mr P) first met in 1973 when she came to act as housekeeper for him and his two infant children by his earlier marriage (S1 and D1). At that time he was in employment and owned a substantial property (Blackacre) in which there was little equity, as he was heavily in debt. She had no assets. They fairly soon commenced living together, but did not marry until shortly before the birth of their daughter (D2) in 1985. By that time, Mr P had established two successful businesses which were incorporated, and in which Mrs P worked and had a small shareholding. In about 1996 she suspected that he was having an affair with an employee and ceased to work in the business, and in 1998, after a confrontation, divorce was contemplated, but the parties continued to live at Blackacre. In July 2000, Mr P retired and began drawing his pension from the company pension fund. In October 2001, Mrs P left Blackacre, but they were both unhappy and she moved back in May of the following year. Following a fall while on holiday in Spain which resulted in injury requiring an operation, Mr P died unexpectedly on 14 August 2002. Mr P had property in Spain (disposed of by his Spanish will made on 25 July 2001 which was in favour of the children) as well as in England. By his English will made on 4 December 1998 he left his residuary estate on discretionary trusts, the beneficiaries being Mrs P, D1, S1 and D2. Blackacre was left on trust for Mrs P during her life or until remarriage, and thereafter on the trusts of the residue. The trustees, who were a solicitor (E), S1 and D1, were requested to have regard to any memorandum of wishes, and such a memorandum was signed on 24 June 1999. Probate of his English will was granted on 27 February 2003. On 7 July 2003, the trustees of the company pension fund resolved to pay pensions of £143,057 per year, backdated to 7 October 2002, to each of P and D2, and to divide the lump sum benefit of £710,220 equally between the three children in accordance with Mr P's nomination. Mrs P's 1975 Act claim was commenced on 9 August 2003. She sought to retain her pension entitlement (capitalised at £3,825,000) and to have transferred to her further property worth £3.25 million consisting partly of a cash lump sum and partly of non-pension assets. The defendants offered Blackacre (£900,000) and a lump sum of £100,000. At trial it was found that the "notional divorce" exercise would, on the facts, have resulted in an equal division of assets. On the claimant's case, the net estate was approximately £5 million; on the defendants' case it was just under £4.48 million. In the result, the claimant was awarded £2 million, to include Blackacre. Black J made the following observations in relation to the s.3(2) exercise: (1) in presenting 1975 Act claims to the court, it was inappropriate to replicate the entire fictional ancillary relief process; the court's task was simply to reach a sufficient conclusion as to the outcome of the "notional divorce" and to give due weight to that conclusion, along with the other relevant factors; (2) that exercise was simply one of the matters to which the court must have regard (*Re Besterman* [1984] followed)—there was no presumption of equality nor that equal division should be a starting point; and (3) it was probable that the difference between the termination of the marriage by death and its dissolution by divorce might often result in greater provision being ordered under the 1975 Act than would have been the case on the "notional divorce" (*Re Krubert* [1997] followed).

Commentary
S. Ross, "Claims by surviving spouses" (2006) 60 F.L.J. 13
G. Miller, "Provision for a surviving spouse" (2007) P.C.B. 144
G. Kleiner and S. Todd, "The divorce fiction" (2006) 80 T.E.L. & T.J. 11

Case comment
P v G (2006) 36 Fam. Law 178

F–043   *Palmer v Lawrence* [2011] EWHC 3961 (Ch) (LN, W(ca), HH Judge Purle QC, 16 November 2011). The deceased (P) died on 5 March 2010, survived by his wife (W) whom he had married in 2007, though their relationship began some 10 years earlier. She was 65 at the date of the hearing. By his will, made in contemplation of his marriage to her, he gave her a life interest in two properties in England with a combined value of £405,000. He gave a property in Jamaica, valued at approximately £88,000 to his sister and his residuary estate, estimated at approximately £100,000, among four of his other relatives. W's own capital resources included a property in England worth £88,600 net of mortgage, and since P's death she had also received (in round figures) £57,000 from a bond and £34,000 from an insurance policy both taken out by P, and an inheritance of £7,692 from her aunt. Those resources had been depleted by the costs of the proceedings to date (roughly £50,000), other expenses including paying off her debts, and by her giving away her inheritance from her aunt to her grandchildren. The issue arose whether the costs of the proceedings should be taken into account when considering the resources available to W and it was submitted, for the defendants, that they should be ignored because otherwise every claim in the case of modest means would become self-justifying, as the means of the claimant would always be reduced by the costs. According to a form completed 10 months before the hearing, her net monthly income from pensions and rental of the property which she owned was £2,242.83 and her monthly income shortfall was £498.36; however, her monthly expenses had been reduced by £150 since then. She was living in the larger of the two properties in which she had a life interest, and the other was producing £600 per month in rental income, which more than covered the shortfall; further, it was open to her to move to the smaller property and obtain a greater income from the other. *Held*, (1) the will did not fail to make reasonable provision for her. The divorce cross-check was not particularly helpful in this case and the court was not persuaded that it would have yielded a better outcome for W. Both P and W had acquired their capital assets before the marriage and they had always kept their financial affairs separate; (2) on the costs issue, there was no simple and universally applicable answer. However, where, as in the instant case, the will had made reasonable financial provision, it was hard to see how a self-induced costs burden could make the reasonable unreasonable.

Parish v Sharman [2001] W.T.L.R. 593, CA (Thorpe and Parker LJJ, 15 **F–044** December 2000) was an appeal by the applicant, a surviving spouse who had been separated from her husband for some 11 years prior to his death, against the dismissal on 17 January 2000 of her claim for reasonable financial provision from his estate. The facts are that the parties married in 1967 and from 1972 they lived in a property originally owned and occupied by the applicant's parents but in which the applicant had, by the end of 1979, acquired a two-thirds interest. The deceased ran a road haulage business from that property and, by 1984, the applicant had become a partner in that business. The applicant issued a divorce petition and a decree nisi was pronounced on 28 August 1985. It was never made absolute and the applicant made no application for ancillary relief. In effect, as was found, the parties went their separate ways. The applicant continued to live in the matrimonial home with the two children of the marriage, who were approximately 18 and 14 years of age at the date of the decree nisi. In 1986 the deceased bought another property as his home. In October 1988 he made a will leaving all his property (except for some business assets which he left to a friend) to S, with whom he had recently begun to cohabit. His will was made in those terms because he felt that he had already provided adequately for his family by leaving them all his property other than his business assets when he left the former matrimonial home. He died in 1996, aged 64, leaving a net estate whose value was £173,000, of which £110,000 was represented by the property in which he had been living with S. The applicant's interest in the former matrimonial home was worth £350,000 and it does not appear from the report that her total income of £251.78 per week was insufficient to meet her outgoings. At first instance the claim was dismissed. The judge concluded that, if the marriage had terminated by divorce on the day of the deceased's death, it was not likely in the circumstances that the court would have ordered any further transfer of capital to the applicant. By her delay (that is, in never applying for ancillary relief) the applicant had lulled the deceased into a false sense of security that their financial affairs had been settled once and for all. On that ground, coupled with the unreliability of her evidence on a number of material factors, the appeal was dismissed.

F–045 *Powell v Osbourne* [1993] 1 F.L.R. 1001, CA (Dillon, Simon Brown LJJ, 16 November 1992, on appeal from Mr Recorder Platt, Edmonton County Court). Mr Powell married in 1983 and separated from his wife, the applicant, in 1985. At the date of his death a decree nisi had been pronounced but not made absolute. In October 1986 he went to live with a Mrs Osbourne. In August 1988 they bought a house for £91,000, which was conveyed to them as legal and beneficial joint tenants, with the aid of a joint mortgage for £85,000 supported by a life policy on both their lives, payable on the death of the first to die (in which case the minimum payment was to be £85,000) or on survival of them both for 15 years. As the deceased's assets were exhausted by his liabilities, the applicant applied for his severable share of any jointly owned assets to be treated as part of the net estate under s.9. The trial judge awarded her £5,750, representing almost the whole of a notional equity of redemption of £6,000. In doing so, he held that the value of the life policy was nil, as it had been in force for only two months and had no sale or surrender value. He indicated that, had the house been free of mortgage, he would have awarded her £15,000. She appealed, asking that the award be increased to £15,000. The Court of Appeal held that the judge had been wrong to leave out of account the value of the life policy. In order to value the severable share immediately before death, the court had to have regard to the imminence of death. As the value of the property in question (the life policy) depended on death, its value immediately before death was effectively the value on death, and a half-share in the policy monies also formed part of the net estate. The award was increased to £15,000.

Commentary
P. Hamilton, "When is a joint right not a joint right?" (2004) 59 T.E.L. & T.J. 19

Case comment
Powell v Osbourne (1992) 22 Fam. Law 287

F–046 *Rajabally v Rajabally* [1987] 2 F.L.R. 390, CA (Sir Nicolas Browne-Wilkinson VC, Croom-Johnson, Neill LJJ, 23 February 1987, on appeal from Nicholls J, October 1985). The deceased died in 1980 aged 62, leaving a net estate, in the form of a freehold house, value £53,000–£57,000. By his first marriage he had one son, aged 35 at the date of the hearing, whose ability to work was seriously restricted by mental illness. He lived in a council flat and drew social security benefits of £34 per week. By his second marriage to the applicant, who was 45 at the date of the hearing, there were two sons, aged 26 and 23. By his will he left his estate to the widow and the three sons in equal shares. She earned £4,400 per year net and had a pension of £8 per week. At first instance the judge accepted assurances from the two sons of the second marriage that they would not seek to enforce their rights under the will; on that basis he concluded that the will made reasonable provision for the widow. *Held*, allowing the appeal, it was not permissible to arrive at that conclusion from those legally unenforceable assurances; the widow should have been given security in the house. The widow was awarded the house absolutely subject to a legacy of £7,500 to the eldest son, to be raised by a charge on the house.

Re Rowlands Deceased [1984] F.L.R. 813; (1984) 14 Fam. Law 280, CA **F–047** (Cumming-Bruce and Dunn, LJJ, Wood J, 6 April 1984, on appeal from Anthony Lincoln J, 30 November 1983; also listed at C2). Application on behalf of widow (M) and two adult daughters (W and E). The testator died on 8 June 1981, leaving a net estate approximately £96,000. He married M, who was 90 at the date of the hearing, in 1919, but they had been separated since 1938. The bulk of the estate consisted of the farmland which he had formerly worked. By his will dated 3 December 1962 he left £1,000 to each of his four children and the residue to his two sons, one of whom continued to farm the land. W, M and her husband and son were living in a cottage on the estate, with a combined income of £103 per week; the husband, a former labourer, had accumulated savings of £8,000. The cottage, described by the judge as providing "an appallingly low standard of accommodation", was let to them at £13 per year. No attempt was made by anyone to improve it. *Held*, the testator owed some small moral obligation to M in view of her age and infirmity, and her contribution towards bringing up the family, despite the long separation. She had a growing need for improved accommodation and £3,000 was a reasonable sum to award. The judge dismissed the claims of the two daughters. The only appeal was on behalf of M, and was dismissed.

Re Snoek Deceased (1983) 13 Fam. Law 19 (Wood J, 13 October 1982). The **F–048** testator died on 26 October 1980 leaving a net estate of £40,000. By his first marriage he had three children. He married the applicant in 1959, and there were four children of that marriage, of whom one was a minor. By his will he made specific bequests totalling £7,180 to the three younger children, and the residue was divided equally among all seven. The first 12 years of the marriage were happy but in 1970 the marriage began to break down because of the applicant's violent conduct, and in 1976 the deceased obtained a non-molestation injunction against her. Nevertheless from 1977 to his death she continued to subject him to violence and denied him access to the youngest child. *Held*, a reasonable man might think that in view of her atrocious and vicious conduct, it could not be said that, by leaving her nothing, the deceased had failed to make reasonable provision for her. However, this did not take into account the earlier part of the marriage, when she had managed the home and brought up the four children. Wood J also took into account that her three older children insisted that they would give their shares to their mother. She was awarded £5,000.

F–049   *Singer v Isaac* [2001] W.T.L.R. 1045 (Master Bowles, 16 March 2001). The testator, whose net estate was sworn for probate at £1,581,294 (and which did not include the matrimonial home, York Cottage, which had passed to the claimant widow by survivorship) left his widow (who was his second wife) an interest in £100,000, determinable on death, remarriage or cohabitation, but subject to the condition that the trust fund should be reduced pound for pound by the amount spent or to be spent on York Cottage as from 1 September 1999. After some small pecuniary legacies and gifts of chattels, and a legacy of £100,000 upon trust for his grandchildren, the residue (in the region of £800,000 after IHT) was given equally to the two children of his first marriage. The applicant widow was awarded £225,000. Master Bowles declined to apply *White v White* on the ground that it had not been decided in August 1999, when the deceased died, and therefore the claimant could not reasonably have expected equal division on a divorce at that time, some 14 months before the House of Lords' decision, but only a determination based on the then subsisting conventional approach to such cases.

Commentary
S. Ross, "Claims by surviving spouses" (2006) 60 F.L.J. 13

F–050   *Stead v Stead* [1985] F.L.R. 16; (1985) 15 Fam. Law 154, CA (Waller, Oliver, Purchas LJJ, 10 April 1984, on appeal from Sir John Arnold P, 10 November 1983). The testator died on 13 January 1982 aged 88, leaving a net estate valued at £64,000 at the date of the hearing, of which £30,000 was the value of the matrimonial home. The testator and the applicant, who was aged 82 at the date of the hearing, were married on 1 June 1957. Both had been married before, and there were two adult children of the testator's first marriage. By his will dated 28 May 1970 he left the estate on trust with a life interest to the applicant in (a) the matrimonial home, provided that she paid all the outgoings, and (b) a sum of £6,000. The residue was left to the two adult children. At first instance she was awarded a lump sum of £2,500, and periodical payments of £1,500 per year gross, backdated to the day after the testator's death. The trusts relating to the house were also varied, by reducing her liability for the outgoings, providing for the sale of the house and the purchase of another with her consent, and giving power to the trustees to increase the income provision for her out of any retained part of the proceeds of sale. She appealed on the grounds that the President had failed to recognise the substantial contribution which she had made during the marriage or to have regard to the provisions of s.3(2) of the Act. The appeal was dismissed.

F–051   *Stephanides v Cohen* [2002] W.T.L.R. 1373 (Mr District Judge Kenworthy-Browne, 5 March 2002). The claimant was the second wife of the deceased, the marriage having lasted for some five years. Out of a net estate of £643,000, the deceased left his personal chattels and a legacy of £25,000 to his wife, and the residue to his son by his first marriage. *Held*, the deceased had a legal obligation to make reasonable provision for his wife, but no legal obligation towards his adult child. It was also important that the wife had been a good and loyal wife, whereas the son had not been a good son and had been dependent on the deceased for much longer than he should have been due to his drug addiction. The wife's needs were to accommodate herself and to support herself, and the deceased's obligation was, so far as the resources of the estate permitted and so far as was compatible with his son's claims on his bounty, to make such provision as would satisfy those needs. The effect of the order made was that the wife received 55 per cent of the estate and the son, 45 per cent.

Commentary
S. Ross, "Claims by surviving spouses" (2006) 60 F.L.J. 13

Stephens v Stephens, CA (Sir John Donaldson MR, Parker and Balcombe LJJ, 1 July 1985, LN, T655, on appeal from HH Judge Micklem sitting as a deputy High Court Judge, 7 March 1985). The testator died in 1982, aged 85, leaving a net estate of £27,500, which consisted of the matrimonial home, valued at £23,000, and £4,500 in National Savings Certificates. The testator married the applicant on 30 July 1962. Both had been married before, and there were adult children of both marriages; their own marriage was childless. At the date of the hearing the applicant was 80 years old, had capital of £200 and an income of £2,137 per year. This left her a surplus of income over expenses of £791, but that was because her stepson and daughter-in-law paid some of the outgoings. By his will dated 11 June 1982 the testator directed his executors to permit his wife to live in the house, she being responsible for outgoings, and not to sell it without her consent; the proceeds of sale could be used to buy another residence for her, but any cash balance was to form part of residue, and she was not permitted to assign, sub-let or part with possession. The effect of this was to leave her with the house but with no money for its upkeep and no power to make any money by letting or selling it. The residue was left to his son by his first marriage and the certificates were nominated to him. The testator expressed the wish that there should be nothing in the estate which his wife would be able to pass on to her son by her previous marriage. At first instance the judge took the view that there was no-one other than the applicant with a financial claim on the estate; the marriage had lasted 20 years and she had given up her own house when they were married, on the understanding that another house would be bought in joint names. The intention of the deceased that nothing should go to his stepson did not weigh heavily with the judge. He awarded her the entire net estate absolutely. *Held*, on appeal, he had exercised his discretion wrongly in two ways: (a) by failing to have proper regard to what the applicant would have received on divorce; and (b) by not having regard to the testator's reasons for making the provision which he did. There should be a "clean break"; the house was directed to be sold, and, treating the nominated certificates as part of the net estate, she should have 60 per cent and the residuary beneficiaries, 40 per cent.

F–052

Weir v Davey [1993] 2 N.I.J.B. 45 (Kelly LJ Chancery Division (Northern Ireland), 22 January 1993, LN). The testator and the applicant married in 1972 and there was one child of the marriage, a daughter (J) aged 15 at the time of the hearing. The parties separated in 1981 but did not divorce; the applicant and the daughter left and eventually went to live in a housing executive property. In 1983 the testator began to live in the former matrimonial home with M, a married woman with three children. This rela-

F–053

tionship also did not run smoothly and he left her and went to live by himself in 1987. He committed suicide in 1988. By his will, made in 1983, he made no provision for the applicant but left whatever dwelling-house and car he might own at the date of his death to M absolutely, and the rest of his estate upon trust for J absolutely on her reaching the age of 21 years. In 1986 he bought a house and invited his widowed mother (W) to live there, and in 1988 he bought an investment bond on trust for her benefit in the event of his death, for £16,535. The net estate amounted to £77,582 of which about £34,000 consisted of liquid assets; the two houses were valued at £27,500 and £17,500 respectively. The applicant was 44 years of age at the date of the hearing. She had capital of £16,843 and a monthly income of £608. She would be in a position to return to work in the fairly near future and J's needs would not impinge on her financial position, since J's entitlement under the will amounted to over £50,000. It was found that the purchase of the investment bond for the benefit of W was intended to defeat a claim for financial provision by the applicant and she was awarded £13,000 from its proceeds.

F–054 *Winfield v Billington*, CA (Parker, Nourse LJJ, 30 July 1990, LN, T673, on appeal from HH Judge Stuart-White, Redditch County Court, 21 July 1987). The testatrix died aged 28 on 31 March 1984, having developed multiple sclerosis in 1979. The marriage, of which there were two children aged 11 and 7 at the time of the appeal, would have been terminated in undefended divorce proceedings on 31 March 1984, on the grounds of the husband's unreasonable behaviour. Her estate consisted of investments worth £9,000 and her half-share in the matrimonial home, she having severed the beneficial joint tenancy in 1983. By her will, dated 18 November 1983, she left her estate to such of her two children (B and P) as should survive her and attain the age of 18 in equal shares absolutely. The applicant remarried and there was one child of that marriage, aged 4. The former matrimonial home was sold and, by agreement, the proceeds were invested in the purchase of a house for the applicant, his wife and the three children. The applicant contended that he should receive the entire half interest in the former matrimonial home. The judge did not accept that and, having considered ss.1(2) and 3(2) of the Act, decided that B and P's presumptive share should be reduced from one fourth to one sixth, and ordered that the half-share be transferred to the applicant absolutely, conditional on his charging it with a payment of one sixth of its value to B and P at age 21. *Held*, dismissing the appeal, the judge's exercise of his discretion could not be faulted.

F–055 *Wooldridge v Wooldridge* (W, HH Judge Walden-Smith, County Court at Central London, 12 February 2016). The deceased (I) died in a helicopter accident and was survived by his widow (T), the claimant, two sons, C, aged 22 and R, aged 6, who was the child of his marriage to T, and three siblings, a brother (G), a sister (J) and a half-sister. He had been a successful businessman in the construction industry, establishing the Wooldridge Group with G in 1978, and his estate included a 33 per cent interest in a company ("Panther") and a 50 per cent interest in a partnership ("Twelve Oaks"), both of which were within that group. The value of the net estate in September 2015 was £6.8 million excluding the value of the matrimonial home (approximately £4.2 million) which had been left to T free of mortgage and was occupied by her and R. The will had raised a number of issues of construction which had been resolved with the assistance of independent counsel appointed by the parties. It provided that she should receive an annual salary of £75,000 from the company, but that provision did not take effect as independent counsel determined that it was unenforceable. Otherwise, in broad terms, the will provided that some of the insurance policies effected by I were personal and some were to be applied to discharge company debts. After discharge of the mortgage debt outstanding on the matrimonial home from the personal policies, the balance of £717,561 went to T. The will also provided that personal pensions worth about £85,000 were to be used for funding R's education until he reached the age of 18 and would then revert to T. The interests in the company and the partnership (valued, respectively, at £150,012 and £1,857,344) were left to C and R in equal shares, and a rental property valued at £139,434 was also left to R. As well as the provision made by the will, T, C and R benefited from a claim under the Fatal Accidents (Northern Ireland Order) 1977, receiving, respectively, £1.985 million, £315,000 and £200,000. T claimed that the will failed to make reasonable provision for her in that the provision made was inadequate to support her accustomed luxurious lifestyle and that her net annual income need was £372,097. In assessing what provision was reasonable for a surviving spouse, her lifestyle at the date of death was a relevant factor; see *N v F* [2011] 2 F.L.R. 533 (an ancillary relief case) and *P v G, P and P* [2004] 1 F.L.R. 431. However, evidence of I's declared income did not accord with expenditure on such a scale; while she did have a luxurious lifestyle, the highest figure at which her needs could be put was £240,000; the figure which she claimed read more like a wishlist than an accurate assessment of her needs. Her own resources had a total value of £10.5 million, of which some £5.2 million were investable; for a woman aged 50, that would provide an annual income of £210,000 calculated on a Duxbury basis. In addition, she had significant earning potential. In so far as her calculated expenditure referred to R, the benefit from the Fatal Accidents Order claim and the income of the rental property could and should be applied for his maintenance; those sums were not for providing him with capital on reaching 18. To fund T's claim in full would require an award of £5.879 million and that was not sustainable given that the value of the estate (excluding the matrimonial home) was £6.8 million. *Held*, the claim would be dismissed. The will did make reasonable provision for T. Although the evidence showed that she had had a lavish lifestyle during the marriage, it did not substantiate, but contradicted, her claimed expenditure. The liquid assets of the estate were insufficient to fund her claim. Any increase in the provision made for T was highly likely to result in the partnership assets being sold off, which would certainly be detrimental to C and, more likely than not, to R. Note, the exaggerated nature of T's claim had adverse costs consequences, for which see the summary of the subsequent costs judgment at s.G.

Section B—Former Spouses Who Have Not Remarried

F–056 *Barrass v Harding* [2001] 1 F.L.R. 138, CA (Butler-Sloss P, Thorpe LJ, 27 June 2000, on appeal from Mr Recorder Pulman, Canterbury County Court, 9 July 1999). The applicant (B) was the first wife of the deceased (D); they were married in 1939, adopted a son (R) in 1950 and were divorced in 1964. B's claims for ancillary relief were dismissed by consent but there was a separate arrangement between D and B whereby he provided her with a flat for life at a peppercorn rent, but if she vacated it she would be entitled only to half the value of the flat as it was in 1965. He also provided a flat for R. In 1985 she left her flat voluntarily, took the £1,500 and went to live with R. D remarried but his second wife predeceased him, and by his last will he left his entire estate to his second wife's sister. In a codicil, to the same effect, to his previous will, he had stated that he was not providing for B or R in view of the settlements already effected. Shortly before his death, D was to some extent reconciled with R, and this was taken into account as a special circumstance at first instance, as was the fact that the estate was £200,000. These matters, together with the fact that B was 79 and in poor financial circumstances, resulted in an award to her of £30,000 at first instance. Allowing the appeal, the Court of Appeal held that in the absence of any rapprochement between D and B, or any indication by D that he was thinking of paying her something in the future because she was old and poor, there was no basis for making provision for her out of the estate. The £200,000 was not a windfall such as occurred in *Re Hancock* due to a substantial increase in the value of the estate between the death of D and the hearing, and was not a sum such as an insurance policy which could be considered to have been "unlocked", as discussed in *Re Fullard*. The circumstances that B's ancillary relief application had been dealt with under the matrimonial law as it was before the enactment of the Matrimonial Proceedings and Property Act 1970 did not take the case out of the line of authority represented by *Re Fullard* and *Cameron v Treasury Solicitor*.

Commentary
S. Ross, "Claims under I(PFD)A" (2001) 6(3) E.C.A. 23
G. Miller, "Applications for provision by former spouses" (2001) P.C.B. 315
S. Anticoni, "Overtaken by events" (2003) 26 Fam. Law 32
S. Ross, "Surviving partners" (2006) 55 F.L.J. 10

Case comment
Barrass v Harding (2000) 30 Fam. Law 878

F–057 *Brill v Proud* (1984) 14 Fam. Law 59, CA (Sir John Arnold P, Latey J, 27 July 1983, on appeal from HH Judge Wingate, Brighton County Court). The deceased died on 12 December 1980 aged 55, having made a will by which he appointed the respondent his executrix and left her his entire estate, worth £12,000. About £10,000 of this arose from an insurance policy kept up by the deceased's employers. The parties had married in 1962. An ouster order was made against the deceased in 1978 and the marriage was dissolved three months later. A consent order was made in full and final settlement of all claims of the parties for financial provision. The applicant contended that she was no longer bound by the agreement embodied in the consent order because the insurance benefit had deliberately not been disclosed and the deceased had a legal and moral obligation to maintain her. The applicant had a flat, a car and her old age pension; the respondent had her home, a pension of £3,600 per year and capital of £6,000. The Court of Appeal affirmed the first instance decision dismissing her application. The payment of the death benefit was subject to various conditions which might have defeated it. Per Latey J:—in cases against small estates very careful consideration should be given by legal advisers and it was the duty of practitioners to inform the Law Society of the likely effect of costs on the estate.

Cameron v Treasury Solicitor [1996] 2 F.L.R. 716, CA (Butler-Sloss, Peter **F–058**
Gibson, Thorpe LJJ, 2 July 1996, on appeal from HH Judge Quentin Edwards, Ilford County Court). The applicant (C) and the deceased (R) had been married for almost 15 years; there were no children of the marriage. In 1981, a "clean break" order was made in the ancillary relief proceedings, it being ordered by consent that R pay to C the sum of £8,000 and part of her costs. The order did not contain a s.15 provision; at that time an order under s.15 of the 1975 Act could be obtained only if both parties agreed. The deceased died intestate in 1990 and his estate, the value of which was £7,677, devolved on the Crown as bona vacantia. At first instance, the applicant, who was aged 64 and in poor health and difficult financial circumstances, was awarded the entire estate. It was found that, after the dissolution of the marriage, R did not form any relationship which placed him under either a moral or a legal obligation to any other person, and that he was indifferent to the destination of his assets. C and R had remained on good terms after the dissolution of the marriage and she might well have turned to him for assistance during his lifetime. Despite the decision in *Re Fullard* [1982] Fam. 42, the fact of the "clean break" order did not preclude C from obtaining an order for provision out of the estate. The Treasury Solicitor appealed (this being in the nature of a test case). Allowing the appeal, the Court of Appeal held that:

(a) the principles set out in *Re Coventry* [1980] Ch. 461 relating to claims by adult children, were equally applicable to claims such as that made by C;

(b) applying those principles, her financial position and poor health were insufficient to found a moral claim;

(c) the fact that the estate would devolve on the Crown was neutral; and

(d) the absence of a s.15 direction did not, of itself, assist C's claim.

Commentary
S. Ross, "Claims under I(PFD)A" (2001) 6(3) E.C.A. 23
S. Ross, "*Parnall v Hurst*—A cautionary tale" (2004) 9 E.C.A. 22
M. Green, "Is a clean break the safe option?" (2004) 55 Fam. Law 2
S. Ross, "Surviving partners" (2006) 55 F.L.J. 10

Re Crawford (1983) 4 F.L.R. 273 (Eastham J, 23 February 1982). The tes- **F–059**
tator died on 23 January 1980 leaving a net estate of £30,890, which would be increased to £65,775 if his severable share of a joint account in the names

of himself and his second wife was brought in under s.9. That sum was a lump sum benefit paid to him on retirement. The applicant married the testator in 1943. There was one child of that marriage, which was terminated by divorce in 1968. By consent the deceased was ordered to pay the applicant one third of his gross salary less the mortgage and insurance on the former matrimonial home, but he did not always do so and from time to time there were court proceedings. The deceased remarried that year and there were two children of that marriage. By his will dated 5 February 1973 the deceased made no provision for the applicant. His second wife received life interests in his half-share of the matrimonial home and seven-eighths of the residue, in which his three children took various interests. As a result of his death his second wife received £72,402, plus a pension of £10,369 per year, and the children received pensions totalling £8,644 per year. The applicant, who was 59, was on supplementary benefit; she had £1,500 capital and owned the house in which she lived. *Held*, the deceased had a moral responsibility towards her; the marriage had lasted 24 years and she had clearly contributed towards the welfare of the family; and he had never expected her to work and her earning capacity was nil. She was awarded £35,000, being a sum sufficient to purchase an annuity of £4,000 per year, and that sum would be provided by treating the deceased's severable share of the lump sum retirement benefit as part of the net estate.

F–060 *Cumming-Burns v Burns*, CA (Oliver and Purchas LJJ, 4 July 1985, LN, T530, on appeal from Edward Nugee QC sitting as a deputy High Court judge, 24 May 1983). The testator died on 12 December 1979 aged 72, having by his will dated 24 July 1979 left the whole of his estate, value £64,616, to his second wife (M). The testator and the applicant (H) were married in 1929. There were four children of the marriage. During war service he formed an attachment for M, and in 1947 they began to live together as man and wife. Following his divorce from H in 1966 he entered into a maintenance agreement which was observed until his death. He married M on 22 April 1966. Using money which she had inherited, he engaged in various businesses, the last being a farm which was later sold and the proceeds used to purchase the matrimonial home. On 14 February 1969 she transferred the home to him by deed of gift. On inheriting it under his will she sold it and bought a smaller house, and the surplus was about £35,000. At the time of the hearing she was 69. Her net income was £5,300, most of which was absorbed by her outgoings. H, who was 74 at the time of the hearing, had an income of £1,890 per annum from state benefits of which £3 to £4 per week was available for "extras". She lived rent-free in a flat bought for her by two of her children but paid for minor repairs, decorations and outgoings herself. At first instance H's application was dismissed on the ground that she had failed to show that the disposition of the testator's estate did not make reasonable provision for her. The Court of Appeal declined to interfere with the judge's exercise of his discretion.

F–061 *Eeles v Evans*, CA (Dillon, Woolf LJJ, Sir John Megaw, 6 July 1989, LN, T557, on appeal from HH Judge Boothman, Gloucester County Court, 25 October 1988). Former spouse who had not remarried, treated as a surviving spouse under s.14 of the 1975 Act. See s.A.

Re Farrow Deceased [1987] 1 F.L.R. 205; (1987) 17 Fam. Law 14 (Hollings **F–062**
J, 2 May 1986). The applicant and the deceased married in 1949 and
separated in 1968. There were two sons of the marriage. A decree nisi was
granted in January 1973; on 14 June 1978 the applicant was awarded a lump
sum of £50,000 and periodical payments of £5,500 per year. Of the lump
sum, £20,000 was intended to be applied in the purchase, repair and
refurnishing of a house for her occupation and in payment of her debts; the
rest would produce an annual income of £2,280 after tax. The deceased died
intestate on 5 May 1979 and the whole of his estate passed to his two sons.
After his death the applicant received no financial support from the estate;
she had spent more than was intended on the house and she was also living
off the capital, as she had no income. Proceedings commenced in January
1980 but an application for an interim order was not pursued; this was not
the applicant's fault. By October 1981 she was £13,000 in debt to the
Midland Bank. She took in a lodger (D) who agreed, in return for board and
lodging, to obtain a mortgage for her. The house was vested in their joint
names, one third to him and two thirds to her. In late 1982 it was sold and
the entire proceeds of sale applied in paying her debts. She continued to live
with D in rented accommodation, though they ceased paying rent when
their shorthold tenancy expired in August 1984. She received a legacy of
£10,000 and D had retired on a pension. She had no income at the time of
the hearing, when she was just under 60, but would, on reaching that age, be
entitled to a state pension of £38.30 per week. *Held*, provision for her
support by way of periodical payments after his death should have been
made by the deceased; and she was entitled to some compensation for
having to draw on the original capital provision to make up for the lapsed
periodical payments order. She was awarded a lump sum of £15,000 and
£5,000 per year.

Re Fullard Deceased [1982] Fam. 42, CA (Ormrod LJ, Purchas J, 30 January **F–063**
1981, on appeal from Bush J, 17 November 1980). The testator died on 30
January 1978 leaving a net estate £7,100. The applicant and the testator
married in 1939 and the marriage was dissolved by decree absolute on 31
December 1976. Each had worked throughout the marriage and had saved
about £3,000. The applicant bought out the testator's share in the matrimonial home for £4,500. Both parties acknowledged that neither was entitled to periodical payments from the other. The testator went to live with L,
to whom, by his will dated 28 September 1978, he left his entire estate. L
owned her own home and had a pension. The applicant had a mortgage on
the former matrimonial home and she also had a pension. *Held*, (1) in view
of the financial arrangement made at the time of the divorce, there had to be
exceptional circumstances present at the date of death to show that reasonable provision had not been made for the former spouse by the agreed
settlement; (2) since the testator had no moral or legal obligation to the
applicant, it was reasonable for him to have made no provision for her;
hence the appeal would be dismissed.

Commentary
S. Ross, "Claims under I(PFD)A" (2001) 6(3) E.C.A. 23
S. Ross, "Surviving partners" (2006) 55 F.L.J. 10

F–064   *Re Legat Deceased, Legat v Ryder* (Dillon J, 2 May 1980, LN, T582). The deceased died on 20 August 1977 aged 50, leaving net estate £20,000. He married the applicant on 8 April 1955. There were no children of the marriage, which was dissolved by decree absolute in June 1968, some 18 months after the applicant had left the deceased. She never claimed maintenance from him, nor did she make a claim to a beneficial interest in the former matrimonial home. In 1970 she bought a hotel in King's Lynn, which she ran until 1976. The deceased stayed there for a while in 1973, but around Christmas of that year, he went to live with a Mrs A, whom he had met in 1967. She had left her husband in 1970 and her marriage was dissolved in December 1973. By his will dated 9 August 1977, he left nothing to the applicant, his residuary estate going to Mrs A; he had also made a will in her favour in 1976. At the date of the hearing the applicant, who was 61, owned her house, free of mortgage, together with investments of £20,000 from which she derived an income of £2,000 per year. She also had a state pension of £1,124 per year and earned £2,700 working part-time as a housekeeper in an hotel. Mrs A was 44, and the two children of her marriage, aged 14 and 13, lived with her. She also owned her home free of mortgage and had income from all sources of about £4,000 per year. Her husband paid the school fees and other expenses connected with their education. *Held*, the applicant had been independent of the deceased since 1966, she had capital which was not insubstantial, and owned her own house. Although her earning capacity could not last long, she would even then have a margin of income over expenditure and would have no difficulty finding accommodation. In all the circumstances the deceased had no obligation to provide for her; she thus failed to show that the will did not make reasonable provision for her.

F–065   *Parnall v Hurst* [2003] W.T.L.R. 987 (HH Judge Langan QC, 4 April 2003). The report relates to the application to strike out the claim by the deceased's first wife on account of procedural failures. Unusually, the claim was considered to have merits although there had been a final settlement in the divorce proceedings. This was because there was an order for periodical payments ongoing at the date of the husband's death and without those payments, the claimant's only income was the state retirement pension of £92 per week. For a summary of the procedural issues, see s.G.

Commentary
G. Harbottle, "Tales of procrastination and pedantry" (2004) 56 T.E.L.J 4
S. Ross, "*Parnall v Hurst*—A cautionary tale" (2004) 9 E.C.A. 22
S. Ross, "Playing by the rules" (2007) 70 F.L.J. 7

F–066   *Walker v Walker*, CA (Fox, Mustill LJJ, Sir Roualeyn Cumming-Bruce, 10 May 1988, LN, T661, on appeal from HH Judge Finlay). The testator died in April 1983 leaving a net estate £29,998. This derived mainly from insurance policies, the largest of which had been effected during his first marriage. By that marriage to the applicant (R) in 1947 there were three children. The marriage was dissolved by decree absolute in June 1975, and the testator married the defendant (M) the following month. By his will, made 10 days before his death, he left his residuary estate to M absolutely. In ancillary relief proceedings in 1977, it was ordered that the matrimonial home be charged in favour of R (which realised £7,899, of which £3,000 was paid to the Law Society in respect of her legal aid costs) and that she should receive £10 per week during joint lives. She also received legacies amounting to £18,000. In 1981, having initiated proceedings under MWPA relating to chattels of which she claimed the ownership, at the hearing of which she did not attend, the order for periodical payments was suspended. At some later time the testator bought another house, which passed to M by survivorship; she sold that after the testator's death and bought another house on which she spent £6,000 to put it into repair. Her income was £4,960 per year and she earned a further £1,000 per year as an auxiliary nurse. R had bought a leasehold flat, the lease expiring in 1996. She had no income except £70.61 per week from social security. *Held*, notwithstanding that R had been a good wife and that assets had been unlocked by the testator's death, the estate was modest and not sufficient to provide for R and M; the testator had to decide between them and it was reasonable to make no provision for R.

Wallace v Thorburn, CA (May, Woolf LJJ, 9 October 1987, LN, T665, on appeal from HH Judge Morrison, Mansfield County Court, 25 March 1987). The original application was on behalf of two applicants, but only the award of £7,200 to the first applicant (W), the former wife of the deceased, was challenged. The testator died on 28 May 1985 aged 58, leaving net estate £21,335, of which only £17,855 was available after deduction of the estimated costs of the hearing at first instance. By his will dated 16 May 1985 he left his estate to the respondent (T), with whom he had been friendly for some 10 years. They saw each other regularly and she helped him to find new accommodation, and with his laundry and cooking, but they did not live together as man and wife. His marriage to W, of which there were five children, took place in 1950. The marriage was dissolved by decree absolute in February 1983 and the matrimonial home was sold. In the ancillary relief proceedings, W was awarded £53 per week. As a result of the sale and the agreement that the costs be paid out of the estate, W had capital of £4,000 from that source. At the time of the hearing W, who was 58, lived on supplementary benefit in a modest flat. T, who was 54, was employed as a canteen assistant, though expecting to be made redundant, and lived in a small prefabricated house subject to a mortgage. W's application was, in effect, for a lump sum sufficient to buy a small house, which would cost £16,000. *Held*, allowing the appeal, an award of £7,200 would not be enough to put her in a position to buy the house; the approach at first instance was either wrong or could not be discerned, and the court would exercise its own discretion and increase the award to £10,000. No order as to costs was made.

F–067

Section BA—Cohabitants

Baker v Baker [2008] 2 F.L.R. 767 (Paul Girolami QC sitting as a deputy judge of the Chancery Division, 13 March 2008). Mr Baker (B) died of liver failure on 27 April 2005, having five days earlier, while in intensive care, made a will in which he appointed his brother (R) and Mrs Monica Hazel (H) executors, and left his estate (valued at £257,000) to H if she survived

F–068

him for 28 days, and if not, to his daughter Cassandra (C) and Mrs Hazel's daughter Nicola (N) in equal shares. C, who was solely entitled to take on B's intestacy, brought a claim that the will should be set aside on the grounds of lack of testamentary capacity and/or want of knowledge and approval, and for a grant of administration to her. No other will had been found. At trial H claimed a declaration as to her interest in B's house, in which they had been living before he was admitted to hospital on 7 April 2005 with his final illness; and an order under s.2 of the 1975 Act. It was found that B did not have capacity to make the will and that the claim to a beneficial interest in the house failed. As no grant of representation had been issued, no order could be made at that stage. However, the parties agreed that the deputy judge should consider and rule on the claim on the material before him. C disputed H's claim as a cohabitant but was prepared to accept that she had a claim as a dependant. *Found,* applying the test in *Re Watson,* that H and B had been living together in the same household as man and wife for considerably more than two years before his death and H was eligible to claim under s.1(1)(ba), so that s.1(1)(e) did not apply. H's principal maintenance needs were for a place to live and access to a reasonable capital sum from which she could supplement her limited income, which derived from part-time work from which she was likely to have to retire on reaching 65, and a monthly pension of £521.76. Her capital amounted to £92,000. The proposed order, which could not be implemented until C (if so entitled) had obtained a grant of administration, was that H should have a life interest in the deceased's house and its proceeds of sale, with the intent that if and when it became appropriate to sell that property, the proceeds might be applied in whole or part to the purchase of another property, or in being invested to provide further income for H. The balance of the estate would pass to C on B's intestacy.

Commentary
S. Ross, "The courts' approach" (2008) 80 F.L.J 21

F–069   *Baynes v Hedger* [2009] 2 F.L.R. 767, CA (Sir Andrew Morritt C, Longmore, Goldring LJJ, 7 May 2009, on appeal from [2008] 2 F.L.R. 1805, Lewison J, 14 July 2008). In this case the original claimant (Hetty), who was the god-daughter of the deceased (Mary), claimed on the basis that she was being wholly or partly maintained by Mary immediately before her death. Mary's will dated 6 July 1977, as amended by two codicils, included a gift of £2,500 to Hetty, a specific devise of the family home (the Dunshay Manor estate, value about £2 million) to the Landmark Trust, and a gift of residue to her friend Margaret Alice Baynes (Margot) for life, remainder to Margot's children other than Hetty who was excluded because she had already benefited. Margot, who, as a residuary beneficiary under Mary's will, was a defendant to Hetty's claim, made alternative claims under s.1(1B) on the basis that she was living in the same household as Mary and as her civil partner during the whole of the two years preceding Mary's death, and also under s.1(1)(e) on the basis that she was being wholly or partly maintained by Mary immediately before her death. This part of the case summary deals only with Margot's claim as a cohabitant; for the claims as dependants, see s.E. Lewison J found that, since the late 1970s, the settled pattern of residence was that Margot's main residence was in Kingston and Mary's at

Dunshay, and that Mary regarded the Kingston property as Margot's home, not a joint home or one in joint names; similarly, she regarded Dunshay as her home, not as the (or a) joint home of theirs. Her 1977 will left Dunshay unconditionally to charity and she never consulted Margot about her dispositions of it. For at least the last 20 years, they did not in any real sense live under the same roof; and in the last two years of Mary's life, the relevant statutory period, Margot's need for 24-hour care made it impracticable for her to go to Dunshay, while Mary was never more than a visitor to Kingston. There were two separate establishments and two separate domestic economies. That would have been sufficient to dispose of Margot's claim as a cohabitant, but, additionally, the true nature of the relationship between them was never acknowledged to the outside world. In his judgment it was not possible to establish that two people lived together as civil partners unless their relationship as a couple was an acknowledged one; consequently, her claim under s.1(1B) failed.

Commentary
S. Ross, "Terms of endearment" (2009) 90 F.L.J 22
S. Ross, "Life after death" (2009) 91 F.L.J. 17
D. Bailey, "Keeping it in the family" (2010) 118 T.E.L. & T.J. 17

Cattle v Evans [2011] W.T.L.R. 947; [2011] EWHC 945 (Ch) (Kitchin J,   **F–070** Chancery Division, Cardiff District Registry, 6 April 2011, B). In addition to the 1975 Act claim as a cohabitant, alternatively as a dependant, there was also a claim (which failed) to an interest in a dwelling-house comprised in the estate by way of constructive trust. The deceased (E) died intestate on 23 March 2009, aged 59, survived by his two sons. The claimant (T) was almost 60 at the date of the hearing and had two children. The parties met in 1990 and within a year E, who was living in rented accommodation, moved in with T, who owned a house. The relationship continued for some six years, during which E proposed marriage to T, who declined. It ceased in 1997 but was resumed some two years later. They later acquired a property in Spain in their joint names, the bulk of the purchase price being derived from the sale of E's property in Kettering. At about the same time T acquired a property in Wellingborough where her children could live until they found a home of their own and which could then be rented out. In 2008 the Spanish property was sold and the proceeds divided between E and T. There was evidence that in mid-2008 E was contemplating separating from T again but that did not happen. E had been negotiating for the purchase of a property at Cross Hands, and although by the end of July 2008 he was terminally ill with lung cancer, he completed the purchase. T did not contribute towards the price, nor did E and T make wills as they had previously intended to do. Draft wills were finally sent to them three days before E died; under E's will, the Cross Hands property worth £150,000 and his pension (worth about £35,000) would have passed to T, with the residue (cash and chattels worth £35,000) going to his sons. Kitchin J found that T was eligible as a cohabitant, having lived in the same household with E as his wife from September 2004 until his death in March 2009. At the date of the hearing she had the Wellingborough property subject to a mortgage of £15,000, a caravan worth £20,000 and cash of about £2,000. She could expect £20,000 to be repaid to her by her son in about two years' time. The rental income and a pension of £400 per year were her only sources of income though she would in due course receive a state pension. In effect she had no earning capacity. Although critical of her conduct in that (a) the purchase of the caravan in 2010 was an extravagance and (b) she had been less than frank with the court about her assets, Kitchin J considered it appropriate for her housing needs to be provided for so that she could continue to receive the rental income of the Wellingborough property. A sum of not more than £110,000 was to be provided from the estate to buy a house for her, to be held upon trust for her for life (or as long as she wished to live there) and which she was to keep comprehensively insured to its full value; and thereafter for E's sons, any property purchased in substitution for it to be held on the same trusts.

F–071   *Churchill v Roach* [2004] 2 F.L.R. 989 (HH Judge Norris, QC, Chancery Division, Birmingham District Registry, 18 July 2002). In addition to a 1975 Act claim on the footing that the claimant was either a cohabitant within s.1(1)(ba) or a dependant within s.1(1)(e) there were claims for a declaration that two properties, 5 and 6 Ferry Lane, Alveston ("the Property") purchased by the deceased in his sole name, were held for him and the claimant on a beneficial joint tenancy and that she was the survivor. This claim failed as did claims to an interest in the property based on constructive trust and proprietary estoppel. The deceased married in 1954 and, by his will dated 6 April 1979, he gave his residuary estate to his wife subject to pecuniary legacies to the two children of the marriage. The parties separated, but did not divorce. In 1987 the deceased moved to Warwick, where he acquired 42 Shakespeare Avenue. In 1989 he met the claimant, who was a professional colleague, and a friendship developed. She purchased 7 Ferry Lane, Alveston, in 1991. They became lovers in 1992 and began to live together at 42 Shakespeare Avenue, continuously for some six months and thereafter, up until December 1998, at weekends. At the beginning of 1998 the relationship between the claimant and the deceased was such that they decided to sell each of their own properties and buy a property together. He had already begun to consider the financial consequences of making a clean break with his wife, and that was achieved by way of a separation agreement made on 6 May 1998. In fact the deceased and the claimant never did buy a property together. The property 42 Shakespeare Avenue was sold first and, after the purchase of 5/6 Ferry Lane by the deceased on 14 December 1998, it was decided to convert that property, together with 7 Ferry Lane, into one property physically, but to keep them under separate titles. That was done in February 1999. The judge was in no doubt that from the time of acquisition of 5/6 Ferry Lane, the claimant and the deceased lived together in the same household as husband and wife until the death of the deceased on 15 April 2000. However, on the evidence of the state of the relationship between them before that time, he concluded that they were maintaining not only two separate properties (which would not by itself have been fatal to the claim) but (notwithstanding the time they spent together at weekends) two separate establishments with two separate domestic economies. The claim as a cohabitant thus failed as the two-year requirement had not been satisfied. On the other hand, he found that the deceased was, and had been for some time before his death, making a substantial contribution to the reasonable needs of the claimant, for less than full valuable consideration. He was providing her with accommodation in the joint home; he paid the larger share of the domestic bills and made cash advances to her to discharge her more pressing needs. This more than counterbalanced her provision of working facilities to him in her adjoining property. It was in all the circumstances not reasonable to make no financial provision for the claimant. At the time of his death they were both wholly committed to the relationship. Their properties had been physically joined and they were in the process of merging the legal titles. There was by then a common understanding that, on his death, she would be provided for. While her income was sufficient to discharge her reasonable financial needs, it did not meet her need for housing. The solution of giving her the right to live in 5/6 Ferry Lane for her life, terminable on marriage or permanent cohabitation, was not satisfactory since it would involve permanent contact with the deceased's family; the creation of the arrangement would be costly; it would be difficult to administer since there would be separate titles but united occupation; and, given that the claimant was much younger than the wife and more or less of an age with his children, it would deprive them of any real benefit from the property. The proposed solution was to transfer the property to the claimant charged with a payment to the estate of £65,000 before 30 June 2003, that sum being the approximate value of the family's reversionary interest were the claimant to have been given a life interest terminable on marriage or permanent cohabitation, and including an element of interest for the postponement of the estate's entitlement. This case is also noted in s.E.

Gully v Dix [2004] 1 F.L.R. 918, CA (Ward, Mummery, Rix LJJ, 21 February 2004, on appeal from HH Judge Weeks QC, Chancery Division, Bristol District Registry). The appeal was on a preliminary issue; see s.G. The relevant facts were that the claimant and the deceased, who was an alcoholic, had lived together for some 27 years before his death in 2001. He had suffered serious head injuries in a fall and was incontinent. On a number of occasions the claimant had left him for a short time because of the extreme squalor of their living conditions, but she invariably returned to him when he apologised and promised to reform. However, some three months before his death, she found the situation intolerable and left to live with her daughter, taking only a few clothes with her. The deceased telephoned on a number of occasions but the daughter never passed on any of the messages to her. He died intestate leaving estate worth £170,000 which passed to his brother. The claimant claimed reasonable provision both as a cohabitant under s.1(1)(ba) and as a dependant under s.1(1)(e). For the brother it was contended that as she had left to live with her daughter some three months before his death, the claimant had neither lived in the same household as the deceased as man and wife for the period of two years immediately before his death, nor was she being wholly or partly maintained by him immediately before his death. *Held*, the claimant satisfied both of those conditions, but permission to appeal was given as the claim had raised a question of interpretation of the Act. He found that the element of maintenance was satisfied by the fact that, up until the time she left him, the deceased was providing living accommodation for the claimant in his house for less than full valuable consideration. As to the word "immediately", he held that he was not confined to considering only the period of two years

F–072

ending with the death of the deceased, but was required to ascertain, by
looking also at the preceding period if necessary, the nature of the established relationship. He found as a fact that the relationship had not come to
an end and that she would have once more returned to him had he promised
her that he would reform, and the fact that her daughter had concealed the
telephone calls from her made it clear that she would have gone back to him
if asked to do so. He also found that the deceased did (contrary to the
contention of the brother) want her to come back to him. The Court of
Appeal considered the judge to have approached the matter correctly and
not to have erred in law or in fact.

Commentary
J. Piggott and M. Windram, "Cohabitants and the Inheritance Act—ex-
tending the boundaries" (2004) 34 Fam. Law 820
M. Warner, "The state of the relationship" (2004) 35 F.L.J. 19
S. Pedley, "They don't always get what they want" (2005) 155 N.L.J. 448

Case comment
R. Bailey-Harris (2004) 34 Fam. Law 334

F–073   *Guidera's Estate, Re, Bingham v Guidera* [2000] N.I. Ch. 58; [2001] N.I. 71
(Girvan J, Chancery Division (NI), 24 November 2000, B, LN, W(ca)). G
died intestate survived by his widow (M) from whom he was estranged, but
to whom he had been paying maintenance, and an adult son (D). On G's
death, M received a widow's pension from his employers and D, a lump sum
of £29,000. G had been cohabiting with the applicant (B) for nine years.
Held, the different status awarded to spouses and cohabitants by the 1979
Order recognised the special status of marriage and was consistent with
ECHR arts 8 and 12. B would be awarded the house in which she had been
living with G, subject to an index-linked charge for £25,000 in favour of M
and D and realisable on sale or B's death, marriage or further cohabitation.

F–074   *Kaur v Dhaliwal* [2014] W.T.L.R 1381 (Barling J, 17 June 2014). Appeal
from the finding of HH Judge Powles QC (Brentford County Court, 23
April 2013) on the preliminary issue whether the claimant (K), was a person
to whom s.1(1A) of the 1975 Act applied. He had found for K in an earlier
judgment (1 September 2011) but that had been successfully appealed to the
High Court, which remitted the matter to him for reconsideration in the
light of the appeal judgment and further submissions by the defendants. His
second judgment, which clarified the first judgment in some respects, was
again in favour of K. K had first met the deceased (H) in May 2005 and
they became engaged during the following month. At the hearing before
Barling J it was common ground that H was living in the same household as
K and as his wife from July to September 2006 and for the period of one
year and 49 weeks from the beginning of July 2007 until H's death on 7 June
2009. For the defendants it was submitted that the gap of eight or nine
months between the two periods of cohabitation which met the statutory
requirements precluded a finding that the statutory criteria had been satisfied in the instant case, particularly given that the trial judge had been
unable to identify any address at which they were living together during that
gap. *Held*, it was possible for the parties to be living together in the same

household at the moment of the deceased's death even if they had been living separately at that moment. The important word was "household", not "house". "Household" was a word essentially referring to people held together by a particular kind of tie, even if temporarily separated; see *Re Santos* [1972] Fam. 247, per Sachs LJ at 263. For present purposes it was sufficient to ask whether either party has demonstrated a settled acceptance or recognition that the relationship is at an end. If the relationship has irretrievably broken down the parties no longer live in the same household and the Act is not satisfied. If the interruption is transitory but the relationship is still recognised to be subsisting, then they will be living in the same household and the claim will lie. Notwithstanding that the judge was unable to make a finding that the parties were living under the same roof during the disputed period, it was open to him to conclude in the light of all the evidence that that did not matter since, once the underlying relationship had commenced in July 2006, it never came to an end but subsisted throughout. The appeal was dismissed.

Lindop v Agus [2010] 1 F.L.R. 631 (HH Judge Behrens, Chancery Division,   **F–075** Leeds District Registry, 2 July 2009). Trial of the preliminary issue whether the claimant (L) was eligible to bring a 1975 Act claim under either s.1(1A) or s.1(1)(e) of the Act. Although they accepted that there was a relationship between L and the deceased (P), his executors did not accept either that L was living with P in the same household as his wife, or that she was being maintained by him immediately before his death other than for full valuable consideration. L, who was born in 1969, was divorced; there was one child (R) of the marriage, born in 1995. Following the divorce, L and R initially went to live with L's father (B), though R had contact with her father (M) and left L to live with M in 2006. P, born in 1970, had had a number of relationships before meeting L. There was a child of one of those relationships, born in 1999. L and P met in 2001 while they were both working in the same dental practice. The relationship started some time after Christmas 2001 and in July 2002 P asked L to move in to his house, which she did gradually. Witnesses presented a consistent picture of them living together as a married couple from, at the latest, December 2003, until P's death in January 2007. They redecorated the house and bought furniture together; L bought most of the food and did most of the cooking and they shared a bedroom. Weekends were arranged so that the two children could be together. There was a considerable amount of documentary evidence showing that during the period of alleged cohabitation, L was registered at her father's address on the electoral register and that her bank statements, P60s and other official documents were sent to her there. Although there was also some documentary evidence of her living at P's address, it was argued that the relationship failed to satisfy the test of being "openly and unequivocally displayed to the outside world", since the "outside world" included public authorities. That submission was not without force, but the weight of the evidence of those who had observed the relationship pointed to their living openly together and displaying that to the outside world. Consequently, L was entitled to claim under s.1(1A) of the 1975 Act.

Commentary
M. Tringham, "What is a will?" (2009) 159 N.L.J. 1169

D. Bailey, "Keeping it in the family" (2010) 118 T.E.L. & T.J. 17

Case comment
G. Douglas (2009) 39 Fam. Law 808

F–076   *Lewis v Warner* [2016] W.T.L.R. 1399 (Newey J, 16 June 2016). Appeal from
the order of Mr Recorder Gardner QC, Gloucester and Cheltenham County
Court, 11 November 2015. The deceased (A) died on 6 May 2014. A
reconstituted will appointing her daughter (L) as her executor and leaving L
her entire estate was admitted to probate. The principal asset of the estate
was A's house ("The Property"), in which she and the claimant (W) had
lived together as husband and wife for some 20 years immediately before her
death. During that time he contributed to the household expenses, including
paying for the oil, which was one of the larger outgoings. There was no
understanding that W would have any beneficial interest in the Property or
any right to remain in or purchase it after A's death, and, at the request of L
and her husband, he had signed a declaration that he would not make any
claim to it. However, in the event, he wished to remain there; he said that he
would be very stressed and unhappy if he had to move from the house where
he had spent the happiest years of his life. He was 91 years of age and had
some medical issues, and it was particularly fortunate that his neighbour
was a doctor who, together with his wife, was able to monitor his health and
attend to him if there was an emergency. He had the means to buy the
Property or alternative accommodation and was not in any financial need. L
wished to put the Property on the market so as to realise its full value and
was willing to sell to the highest bidder, including W, if he was that person.
The parties failed to agree a price acceptable to both of them. He was
unwilling to pay the £425,000 proposed by L and she and her husband were
not content with the valuation of £340,000 made by the single joint expert
valuer. *Held*, at trial (1) there was no reason why the maintenance of a roof
over the head of an applicant for 20 years could not come within the definition of "maintenance" in s.1(2)(b) of the Act; the will did not provide for
that and therefore failed to make reasonable provision for W; (2) his age,
disabilities, the length of time for which the Property had been his home and
his contributions to the household expenses all favoured a continuance of
his remaining there. It was also right to take its location into account; it was
in the centre of the village where he had lived all his life and he had
neighbours to look after his welfare; (3) it was not reasonable for L to have
to wait for W's death in order to realise the value of the Property. However,
an alternative valuation of £385,000 obtained by L's husband was permitted
to be introduced. The solution was to give W an option for a limited period
to purchase the Property for that sum and it was ordered that L should
transfer the Property to him on payment of £385,000. Dismissing the appeal,
Newey J analysed the numerous grounds of appeal under three main heads.
The first was that the recorder had erroneously treated the claim as having
been made under s.1(1)(e). That was not so. He was making the point that
the absence of any provision in the will to allow W to remain in the Property
meant that the will had not mads reasonable provision for his maintenance
within the meaning of s.1(2)(b), to which he had specifically referred. Second, even though W had no financial needs, the recorder had not come to a
wrong conclusion in deciding that the will had not made reasonable finan-

cial provision for him. "Maintenance" was not confined to provision for a person's daily needs; it could, exceptionally, encompass an arrangement for full consideration. If a person was in want of a particular thing to sustain a reasonable quality of daily life, the provision of it could represent "maintenance" regardless of his financial means. Third, the argument that the recorder had no power to order the transfer of the Property was rejected. Section 2(4)(c) of the Act empowered the court to order the transfer of any property and since (as Newey J had held to be the case) the recorder was entitled to decide that the will did not make reasonable financial provision for W, it must have been open to him to give effect to that decision by exercising his power under s.2 to order its transfer.

Martin v Williams [2017] EWHC 491 (Ch) (Marcus Smith J, 13 March **F–077** 2017), allowing the appeal against the order made in *Williams v Martin* [2016] W.T.L.R. 1075, HH Judge Gerald, Central London County Court, 16 February 2016. Norman Martin (N) died unexpectedly on 25 June 2012, survived by his wife (M) from whom he had been separated since 1994, and the two adult children of their marriage. N moved out of the matrimonial home which he owned jointly with M, and he and the claimant (J) then lived together until N's death, the last three years being spent in a property (20 Coburg Road) purchased by J and N jointly in 2009. N had never changed the will which he had made in 1986 leaving his entire estate to M. J, who was 69 at the date of the hearing, claimed on the basis that she was a cohabitant and alternatively as a dependant. M challenged her eligibility in both categories. J sought, in particular, the transfer to her of N's half share of 20 Coburg Road and advanced no claim to any other assets of his estate. She had intended to retire in 2012 but had had to continue working in order to make ends meet. *Held*, at first instance (1) both the parties' own perceptions of their relationship and the appearance of the relationship to the outside world were highly relevant. In all material respects they were living together as husband and wife in an intimate, committed and loving relationship; (2) although the marriage between N and M was never terminated, N maintained some contact with M and contributed to the household expenses of the former matrimonial home, it was a marriage in name only, and there was no meaningful way in which N was maintaining a parallel or separate household which he shared with M. Further, there was no doubt that N and J were living in the same household as required by s.1(1A). J was eligible to claim as a cohabitant; (3) the will had plainly failed to make reasonable provision for her. Taking into account her age, the long cohabitation during which J had made a substantial contribution to the welfare of the family and her financial position, the appropriate order was to vest N's beneficial interest in 20 Coburg Road in J absolutely. *Costs*: it was submitted on behalf of M that the costs of the proceedings, which would place her in considerable financial difficulty, should be taken into account. The submission was rejected; it was not an appropriate factor to take into account when considering the merits of a 1975 Act claim. *On appeal*: permission to appeal on five grounds had been granted by Nugee J on 14 October 2016. The appeal was allowed on the following three grounds (set out in the order in which Marcus Smith J considered them):

Ground (4): That HH Judge Gerald wrongly disregarded Mrs. Williams' interest in another property known as and situated at 60 Slade Road, Bristol as an asset available to Mrs. Williams to meet her needs ([30]–[40]).

Ground (5): That HH Judge Gerald wrongly dismissed the evidence of Mrs Martin as to her financial needs in circumstances in which Mrs Martin's evidence was not challenged during cross-examination ([41]–[53]).

Ground (3): That the relief granted by HH Judge Gerald was substantially in excess of what was necessary to meet those needs and was a perverse decision ([55]).

Held, on appeal: the decision at first instance was upheld as to findings (1) (2) and (3) but the Judge's exercise of his discretion was fatally undermined by the appellant's success on the three grounds specified. In accordance with the submissions of both counsel, Marcus Smith J followed the course taken in *Cunliffe v Fielden* [2006] Ch. 361. On revisiting the exercise of the Judge's discretion he concluded that a life interest in the 50 per cent share of 20 Coburg Road that had belonged to the deceased would constitute reasonable financial provision for Mrs Williams ([58]–[64]).

F–078   *Negus v Bahouse* [2008] 1 F.L.R. 381 (HH Judge Roger Kaye QC, sitting as a judge of the Chancery Division, 23 October 2007). Oral hearing of application for permission to appeal, Mummery LJ and Munby J, 28 February 2008, [2008] EWCA Civ 1002, reported at [2012] W.T.L.R. 1117. The litigation began with a claim by the executors for possession of the property (Flat 8) in which the claimant (N) was living when the deceased (B) died. N and B had previously lived together in another property (Greenways). Those properties had been successively bought by B in his own name after the start of their relationship. N counterclaimed under s.14 of TLATA 1996 for a declaration as to the extent of her beneficial interest in Flat 8, and for an order under s.2 of the 1975 Act. The claim under TLATA failed but the 1975 Act claim succeeded. N, who was then working as a dental receptionist at a salary of £15,000 per year, met the deceased (B) in 1995. He was a fairly wealthy man who had been married and divorced twice. On 24 January 1996 B made an English will leaving £75,000 to each of his three siblings and the residue to G, his only son by his first marriage. By agreement, the value of the net estate was taken as £2.2 million for the purposes of the 1975 Act claim. B also owned a property in Spain which was left equally to N and G. In addition, they were nominated as the beneficiaries of his pension policy, valued at just under £1.15 million. The relationship between N and B became serious in late 1996; in 1997 she moved into his flat and shortly afterwards, at his request, gave up her job and became, in effect, a full-time housewife in all but name. He gave her a small allowance and they lived an expensive lifestyle with frequent foreign holidays. On one of these, in 1999, he bought her an expensive ring which N maintained was an engagement ring, though B's family did not accept that. In 2000 they began looking for a new home and, after difficulties with one property (Greenways), B acquired another (Flat 8) on a long lease in his own name, which became their home until B's death. In August 2004 B, who had been ill, developed type-2 diabetes, and also became severely depressed. The relationship became strained but HH Judge Kaye QC was satisfied that N had no intention of leaving B and that they continued to love and care for each other. On 27 March 2005 B committed suicide. N had received £459,000 from the proceeds of a Scottish Widows policy (of which she had £370,000 left at the date of the hearing), she stood to receive between £110,000 and £200,000 from her half-share of the Spanish property. The defendants contended in view of that, she did not need provision from the estate; further, she was only 50 years of age with no dependants, and could return to work and expect to earn some £15,000 per year. As for her housing needs, she could return to the type of accommodation which she had before she met B. HH Judge Kaye arrived at a figure of £38,000 per year to meet her reasonable outgoings, other than her housing needs. The remaining proceeds of the Scottish Widows policy, together with the £110,000 which was taken as the minimum value of the Spanish property, could, on a Duxbury basis, fund an income need of just over £25,000. That left an annual shortfall of £13,000 plus her housing needs to be provided for. He did not find it reasonable that she should return to accommodation of the kind which she had occupied before the relationship; it was not unreasonable that she should have a modest long leasehold or freehold flat or apartment similar to Flat 8. He concluded that the will had not made reasonable provision for N and that the correct order was for Flat 8 to be transferred to her free of mortgage (or, if that were not possible, the sum required to pay off the mortgage should be transferred to her) and a lump sum payment of £200,000 to be made to her. The application for leave to appeal was dismissed as essentially an attempt to relitigate the same facts. The judge had made a value judgment which there was no prospect of overturning.

Commentary
T. Etherton, "Constructive trusts—the search for clarity and principle" (2009) Conv 104
M. Pawlowski, "Expectations and promises" (2008) 93 T.E.L. & T.J. 4
S. Ross, "The courts' approach" (2008) 80 F.L.J 21

Case comment
C. Bridge (2008) 38 Fam. Law 208

Patel v Vigh [2013] EWHC 3403 (Ch) (LN, W, HH Judge Halpern QC,	**F–079**
Central London County Court, 11 November 2013). The claimant (P) advanced two claims. One, based on resulting or constructive trust, was for a beneficial interest in a property at 30B Mosslea Road, Whyteleafe ("30B"), registered in the sole name of his deceased partner (V) with whom he had cohabited from 1984 until her death intestate in December 2008. The other was for reasonable provision out of her estate and he claimed to be eligible both as a cohabitant and as a dependant. V was survived by a son and daughter, who were the defendants to the claims. *Found*, he was not an honest witness and his evidence was disbelieved; both claims were dismissed. He was refused permission to appeal on the papers by Gloster LJ and his oral application was dismissed by Sales LJ; see *Patel v Vigh* [2014] EWCA Civ 1825 (4 December 2014, LN). The court accepted that he was eligible as a cohabitant (*Re Watson* [1999] 1 F.L.R. 878 followed). The point of interest relates to his eligibility to claim as a dependant, based on his rent free

occupation of 30B, which he continued to occupy after V's death. *Held*, while provision of rent-free accommodation was capable of amounting to a contribution in money or money's worth, it had to be considered not in isolation, but in the round, together with other benefits given or received, as to which there had been no reliable evidence. There had been no evidence of the notional rent of 30B; in any event, the idea that he was receiving a benefit was inconsistent with his evidence that he was contributing to the mortgage payments.

F–080   *Swetenham v Walkley* [2014] W.T.L.R. 845 (HH Judge Walden-Smith, Central London County Court, 20 June 2013). Mr Alexander Bryce (B) died intestate on 12 July 2010, unmarried and without issue; there were over 30 beneficiaries entitled in various proportions to his estate. The claimant (S), who was 80 years of age, had been married and had three children. Her marriage broke down in 1975. She had met B when they were both much younger but they met again in the 1980s and a friendship developed. They began going out together and B frequently stayed overnight at S's house, where he had his own bedroom and kept his clothes; she did his washing and ironing. There were no formal financial arrangements between them but he would pay for meals when they went out. They cared for each other when the other was ill. They were invited out as a couple; he was accepted by S's children as her partner and they were perceived as a married couple. The defendants relied on the following matters as indicating that the relationship no more than one of friendship or companionship. To some extent they led separate lives; they had their own individual interests, B did not always stay in S's house and did not use her address for correspondence; he bought a property without telling her about it and he had never given her any money. When filling in a hospital admission form he described her as a "friend". There was an apparent absence of any sexual relationship. *Held*, (1) in order to find that two people lived together as husband and wife it was necessary for there to be a certain type of tie between them, both privately between themselves and publicly for others to witness—a tie which is of a mutual society or consortium whereby they give each other mutual protection and support which binds them together; (2) the fact that there were two addresses and two houses was not fatal to there being one household; (3) although individual features of their relationship might be characteristic of friendship or companionship, no one factor was utterly determinative; what was determinative was the combination of all the factors, the length of the relationship (over 30 years) and (which may be the key factor) its exclusivity (see the judgment at paras 19, 41 and 42); (4) S had a genuine claim for financial support from the estate. In the light of her "multi-difficulties" and the definition of "disability" given in s.1 of the Disability Act 1995 [sic],[5] she was a person who could properly be described as physically disabled. The support she required consisted of funding for an appropriate health care plan and a capital cushion of £3,500 per year over the period of her actuarial life expectancy (nine-and-a-half years); taking her own available resources into account, the total provision required amounted to £201,219 (see the judgment at paras 47–56).

---

[5] This appears to be a reference to the Disability Discrimination Act 1995, which has been partly repealed.

Re Watson [1999] 1 F.L.R. 878 (Neuberger J, 27 November 1998). The   **F–081**
relationship between the deceased and the applicant had existed for some 30
years but they each had elderly parents to care for, and in consequence
started living together, in the deceased's house, only some 10 years before
his death. The deceased died intestate and without surviving relatives,
leaving an estate with a value in the range £150,000–£200,000. The applicant
claimed both as a cohabitant and as a person maintained by the deceased
immediately before his death. In fact the deceased died in hospital, where he
had been for a few weeks immediately before his death, but rightly, as the
learned judge said, no point was taken on that. The applicant was 67 years
of age, had an income of less than £5,000 per year, suffered from arthritis
and her physical problems were likely to become more serious. Consequently it would be reasonable for her to require accommodation in a
bungalow or ground-floor flat and desirable for it to be in a location near to
her close friends. Her income need was assessed at £2,500 per year, and the
appropriate capital sum, in view of her age, would be £24,000. The deceased
did owe some obligation towards her and she was in need; the Crown had no
real need or moral claim. If all the circumstances of the relationship were
taken into account, she and the deceased were living together as husband
and wife. Her application therefore succeeded. The matter was adjourned to
allow the Treasury Solicitor to consider whether provision should be made
by way of periodical payments of £2,500 per year for life, or a lump sum of
£24,000 or other appropriate amount; and what amount, in addition to the
£53,000 anticipated proceeds of sale of her own house, would be necessary
to enable her to purchase, fit out and move to appropriate accommodation.

Commentary
A Meek, "Living as husband and wife" (1999) 5 T.E.L.J. 16
J. Piggott and M. Windram, "Cohabitants and the Inheritance Act-
extending the boundaries" (2004) 34 Fam. Law 820
S. Ross, "Surviving partners" (2006) 55 F.L.J. 10
S. Ross, "Terms of endearment" (2009) 90 F.L.J. 22

Case comment
Re Watson (1999) 29 Fam. Law 211

Webster v Webster [2009] 1 F.L.R. 1240 (HH Judge Behrens, Scarborough   **F–082**
County Court sitting in Leeds, 13 January 2009). The deceased (J) died
intestate on 17 December 2004, survived by five children, three by his
marriage, which took place in 1972, and broke down in 1977, and two by his
relationship with the claimant (A), who had been a friend of his since 1970
and had cohabited with him since 1978. At the date of his death, the house
in which J and A were living was in J's sole name, and J also owned 4,000
shares in a company (MKM Building Supplies) for which he worked and of
which he was a director. In the proceedings, A claimed a declaration that
both the house and the shares were held upon trust for them as beneficial
joint tenants, and in the alternative, an order under s.2 of the 1975 Act, and
it was common ground that she was eligible either under ss.1(1)(ba) and
1(1A), or s.1(1)(e). A was 54 years of age at the date of the trial. Both she
and J had worked throughout the relationship and contributed to the family
budget. At the time of J's death, he had net annual earnings of £44,000

(£20,000 of this was dividend income from MKM). A's net annual earnings as a care home manager were £13,000 and there was no occupational pension. She received two lump sum payments totalling £148,500 following J's death and at one stage she had savings of £47,000, but by the date of trial these had been reduced to £28,000. For the four years from J's death to the date of trial, A had been paying the mortgage (about £350 per month, making roughly £17,000 over that four-year period) and all other outgoings of the house. Her annual income at the date of trial was £15,609 and her expenditure, excluding holidays, entertainment and hairdressing, but including the mortgage payments, was £20,975. J's five children, who would take on his intestacy, were all over 18, in employment and none of them was suffering from any disability. To the nearest £1, the estate consisted of the house, the equity in which was £148,270, J's minority interest in MKM, which the directors had offered to buy out for £100,000, and a bank account with a credit balance of £19,495. Tax liabilities and administration costs amounted to £11,890 and the parties' costs to date were £42,800. None of the parties wished the house to be sold; if it remained unsold and the mortgage was not discharged, and the directors' offer taken up, there would be some £108,605 to pay such costs as were awarded out of the estate and to be distributed. It was not seriously disputed that the effect of the intestacy was such as not to make reasonable provision for A. There had been a long period of cohabitation during which two children were born to A and J. She clearly needed a roof over her head. Relations between A and the other three children were not good and a clean break was desirable. Apart from the poor relationship, problems would be created if A wished to effect repairs and improvements or to raise money on the property. It was not a suitable case for giving her a limited interest in the house; it should be transferred to her outright and the only question was whether there should be a further award to cover the outstanding mortgage. If the property were transferred to A free of mortgage, she would have sufficient resources to fund her present way of living other than holidays and the like, and the result of making that further award would be to reduce what remained for the beneficiaries by £2,400 each. As they were all in employment and had no demonstrated needs, it was ordered that the house be transferred to her free of mortgage.

Section C—(1) Infant Children

F–083   *Re C* (1979) 123 S.J. 35; also reported as *In the estate of McC* (1979) 9 Fam. Law 26, and as *CA v CC, The Times*, 17 November 1978 (Sir George Baker P). Claim by dependant and infant son; see s.(E). The testator, McC, had the custody of the son of his marriage which had been dissolved in 1971 by divorce on the ground of his wife's adultery. By his will, made in 1971, he left his entire estate of £25,000–£30,000 to that son on his attaining 25. In 1972 he advertised for a housekeeper and A applied for the post. A had an illegitimate child (C) whom she then had adopted at McC's request. They lived together as man and wife and he bought her clothes and other gifts. He also gave her housekeeping money but paid the outgoings himself. In 1974 they had a son and in 1976, shortly before his death, the testator considered changing his will. After his death, the son of the previous marriage returned to his mother, while A continued to look after the child of her relationship with McC. She had no resources other than social security. *Held*, she was a dependant, not a person living in the house under a contract, and both she and her child were entitled to provision. She was awarded £5,000, the remainder to be held on trust for the two children equally, each to receive his share on attaining 25.

Re Chatterton, CA (Ormrod, Waller, Brandon LJJ, 1 November 1978, T519, **F–084** on appeal from Reeve J, 11 July 1978). The original application was on behalf of the widow and infant daughter, but only that part of the order relating to the child was appealed against. The testator died on or about 2 March 1977, aged 52, leaving a net estate of about £18,000. He married in November 1971, but the marriage broke up four months later. By his will dated 23 October 1972 he left one quarter of his residuary estate on trust for his daughter, who was some five months old at the time, should she attain the age of 18, and the remainder to various charities. He made a statement in his will to the effect that he had never seen and did not anticipate ever seeing his daughter, and that the provision he had made for her was sufficient. Reeve J increased the daughter's share to one half, to be held on the trusts of the will. An application on her behalf for a larger share of the estate and for the age contingency to be deleted was dismissed with no order as to costs.

Dixit v Dixit, CA (Sir Nicolas Browne-Wilkinson VC, Nourse, Stuart-Smith **F–085** LJJ, on appeal from Waite J, 23 June 1988). Appeal on behalf of widow and infant daughters. See s.A.

Re J (A minor), CA (Donaldson MR, Balcombe and Staughton LJJ, 9 **F–086** December 1991, LN, T572, on appeal from HH Judge Matthewman, Nottingham County Court, 16 November 1990). The testator died on 11 March 1990 leaving net estate £30,000. He married twice, the applicant being the daughter of the first marriage, which was dissolved in 1976. She remained with her mother after the divorce. The applicant was 16 at the date of the hearing at first instance. From 12 May 1987, she received £10 per week maintenance under a consent order. After his death she left school and was earning £35 per week in part-time employment. By his second marriage, which took place in 1977, he had one daughter. His widow was the sole beneficiary. The matrimonial home also passed to her by survivorship and she continued to live in it with her daughter. At first instance the judge awarded her £7,500. *Held*, the widow, with a young daughter to look after, had the strongest claim; what was reasonable provision for the applicant must yield to that. The appropriate award was £5,000. Per Donaldson MR—had it not been for the presence of the younger daughter, the judge's order could not have been faulted.

Re Patton, McElveen v Patton [1986] N.I. 45 (Carswell J, LN). Claim by **F–087** illegitimate twins—daughter and son. The mother (M) of the applicants had a relationship with the deceased (P) which began in 1971 and lasted for some years. He died in 1984 leaving a net estate £46,732. M received the contents (other than cash) of his dwelling-house and the residue passed, under his will, to six named nephews and nieces. One half of a deposit of £10,000 in a joint account with one of those nephews was also treated as part of the net estate. The twins were born in 1973 and were about 12 years of age at the date of hearing. P had never shown any interest in them but had been maintaining them as a result of a series of orders made in the Magistrates' Court. M was receiving supplementary benefit and also a pension under a superannuation scheme to which P had contributed, which was payable for the support of the children until they reached the age of 17. It was held that the needs of the infant children ranked in priority to those of any of the beneficiaries, that claim was not undermined by their illegitimacy and the will had failed to make reasonable provision for them. They were awarded £10,000 each. These sums were not capital sums for them to have on reaching majority but capitalised annual maintenance payments.

F–088 *Robinson (Anne Caroline) v Robinson (Angela)* [2001] W.T.L.R. 267 (John Martin QC sitting as a deputy High Court judge, 13 February 1998). The claimants were the children, aged 15 and 12, of the deceased's first marriage, which was terminated by divorce in 1987. The deceased married the first defendant (D1) in 1990 and the second defendant was the seven-year-old child of that marriage. The deceased was killed in a road accident in 1991 and died intestate. D1 received the statutory legacy of £75,000 and a life interest in £8,000, which was half the residue. The claimants were entitled under the intestacy to £2,666 each together with the reversionary interest in a further £2,666. D1 had a house worth £104,000, bought by the deceased, and had received £132,000 from the road accident claim (her children receiving £32,000) and £65,000 from the deceased's life insurance policies. The claimants were living with their mother in a council house and had no significant resources other than the £64,000 which they had received from the road accident claim. *Held*, reasonable provision had not been made for them under the law of intestacy, their entitlement came nowhere near satisfying the deceased's obligation to them. He had a strong obligation to D1 but she was able to live in relative comfort. The claimants' needs were found to be £30,000 each, to be repaid by D1 out of the intestate estate, but they were to forgo their immediate and reversionary interests under the intestacy.

Section C—(2) Adult Children

F–089 *Re Abram* [1996] 2 F.L.R. 379 (HH Judge Roger Cooke sitting as a High Court Judge, 15 April 1996). The applicant (A), who was born in 1944, began working in the family business from 1961 until 1978. He worked long hours for very low wages. In 1972 the testatrix (T) made a will leaving substantially the whole of her estate to A. When A left the family business in 1978, T made a new will disinheriting him. They were reconciled in 1980 and, although they remained on good terms until T's death in 1985, she never revoked the 1978 will. After T's death the family company failed, as did A's own business. Substantially the only asset of T's estate was the family home. A took possession of it until the public trustee (the executors having renounced probate) obtained a possession order. It was subsequently sold and the net estate (after making provision for CGT) was some £420,000 at least. In 1992, A entered into an individual voluntary arrangement with his creditors, his indebtedness being some £200,000. At the time of hearing, A was unemployed; his wife was drawing some £150 per week from a partnership in which she traded. It was found that, A having worked in the family business for many years at low wages in the expectation that it would one day be his and having left it largely as a result of the way in which T had treated him, there were special circumstances which founded a claim to provision out of T's estate. Having regard to the terms of the IVA, a settlement in favour of A of half the estate net of everything except inheritance tax, was directed, the settlement being for life on protective trusts with remainder on the trusts of the will.

Commentary
G. Miller, "Provision for children under I(PFD)A" (1997) P.C.B. 176
A. Francis, "A dangerous Act to follow" (2003) 31 F.L.J. 18

Case comment
Re Abram (1996) 26 Fam. Law 666

Ames v Jones (W, Mr Recorder Halpern QC, County Court at Central **F–090** London, 16 August 2016). The deceased (M) died in 2013 survived by the widow of his second marriage (E, aged 63) and the daughter of his first marriage (D, aged 41). M and E had cohabited since about 1980 and married in 2001. There were no children of that relationship. By his will dated 20 December 2005 M left his entire estate to E should she survive him but if she predeceased him, 40 per cent was left to D and the remainder equally between D's two children by her partner (L) and E's two grandchildren from her previous marriage. The estate was sworn for probate at £1,049,414 net, the major assets being the matrimonial home valued at £650,000 and subject to a mortgage of £200,000, and a commercial property ("Green Lanes") jointly owned by M and E, valued at £790,000 and subject to a mortgage of £300,000. Initially, two businesses were run from Green Lanes, one a company (H & L) owned by M and the other, a partnership (the balloon business) between M and E which had ceased to trade by the date of the hearing. The residential accommodation at Green Lanes was rented out and the rent primarily applied in servicing the mortgage payments of £1,800 per month. The net estate for the purpose of s.3(1)(e) was found to consist of the matrimonial home, together with M's notional half share of Green Lanes amounting to £252,000 after taking into account 50 per cent of the surplus of rent over the mortgage payments. It was agreed that the shares in H & L were valueless and the court found the goodwill of the balloon business to be nil. In considering s.9 of the 1975 Act, which gives the court power to treat the deceased's interest in any joint tenancy immediately before their death as if it were an asset of the estate to the extent that it appears to the court to be just in all the circumstances, the court observed that there was neither guidance in the statute nor in any authority as to how the discretion conferred by that provision should be exercised. *Found*: (1) the estate was not large enough to support D and E; (2), D had not satisfied the court as to her own needs and resources; (3) D was capable of working and had failed to discharge the burden of proving that she was unable to obtain work; thus, her lack of employment was a lifestyle choice; (4) E was past working age and in poor health, though the financial consequences of her poor health were not clearly established; (5) E had at most a modest surplus of income over expenditure and required the entire capital of the estate to meet her reasonable needs. D's claim was therefore dismissed.

F–091 *Bye v Colvin-Scott* [2010] W.T.L.R. 1 (HH Judge Williams, Kingston County Court, 28 July 2009). The deceased (S) died on 26 August 2006 leaving an estate of which the only significant asset was a flat subject to two charges and in which there was an equity of about £160,000. On 15 November 2005 S had made a will appointing her brother (B) as executor and leaving her residuary estate (which included the flat) to B and her two sisters, M and K. S also had a daughter (E) who had lived at the flat since she was a child, and who continued to live in it after S had been admitted to hospital on 17 May 2004, where she remained (except for periods amounting to 33 days in all) until her death over two years later. B obtained a grant of probate on 17 November 2006 and commenced possession proceedings against E on 21 December 2007. E counterclaimed on the basis of proprietary estoppel and also on a document signed by S in 2006, some months after the making of her will, giving her the right to occupy the flat for her lifetime. She was also permitted to make a 1975 Act claim out of time, her application to do so being unopposed. The will made no provision for her other than the gift of a diamond ring. All three heads of the counterclaim failed. In relation to the 1975 Act claim, the judgment relied on a passage from *Robinson v Fernsby* [2004] W.T.L.R. 257 in which the Court of Appeal referred to the objective nature of the test of whether reasonable provision had been made and the necessity for the claimant to establish some moral claim to be maintained by the estate of the deceased beyond the mere fact of the blood relationship. S had been providing E with a home but that did not give E a moral claim to be maintained by S's estate. Further, there was evidence that S did not want to make any provision for E because of what she perceived as E's abusive treatment of her; a perception shared by other witnesses. E had, against S's wishes, taken her to a new solicitor to make a new will and execute an enduring power of attorney, and had also obtained her signature to a document purporting to give her a life interest in the flat. E was able to support herself and it was understood that she could, if she were willing and able, purchase the flat for considerably less than its market value. S had not incurred any obligation towards or responsibility for E and was providing for her against her own wishes in so far as E continued to live in her property, thereby preventing it from being sold so that sheltered accommodation could have been purchased for S. All these matters of conduct were relevant and, taking them into consideration, the will did not fail to make reasonable provision for her.

F–092 *Re Campbell* [1983] N.I. 10 (Murray J, 14 December 1981, LN). Claim by son and by grandson claiming as a person being maintained by the deceased immediately before his death; see s.(E). The son (A) was 53 and the grandson (W) was 28 at the date of hearing. A was one of 11 children of the deceased, who had died intestate leaving a net estate in the region of £70,000–£80,000 mainly represented by the family farm. A had spent almost all his life working and living on the farm. W had been brought up from early childhood by the deceased and his wife (his maternal grandparents) and had worked full-time on the farm since he was 15. It was ordered that A should have a personal and non-assignable licence to occupy the dwelling-house on the farm, rent-free for life, and that his share of the intestate estate should be increased from 1/11th to 12/66ths; that is, it was doubled. W was awarded 3/66ths of the estate. The report does not indicate any argument to have been advanced that W had given full valuable consideration for the maintenance that he had been receiving.

Challinor v Challinor [2009] W.T.L.R. 931 (Cooke J, 2 February 2009). The **F–093** deceased (G) had been married twice. The claimant (E) was the younger daughter of G's first marriage, which was dissolved in 1974. She was 49 years of age and had been diagnosed as suffering from Down's syndrome at a very early age. After the breakdown of G's marriage E lived with her mother and then with foster parents, but from 1991 onwards she lived in a residential home (Bystock). G remarried in 1974 and in January 1991 he made a will leaving his entire estate to his second wife (S). G's net estate was valued at approximately £55,000, but at the date of his death he had assets, jointly owned with S, valued at £531,191, half of which represented the severable share which could be treated as part of his estate under s.9(1). In addition to the assets passing to her by survivorship, S had assets in her own name of some £627,000 and her net income in recent years from employment and dividends had been in the region of £35,000. On G's death in March 2006, E's elder sister, subsequently her litigation friend (A), became concerned that G's will had not made reasonable provision for E. E's care home fees had been paid by a combination of benefits and a local authority top-up, and G and other members of the family contributed to the cost of her other needs. At Bystock, she had a bank account into which her personal spending allowance and cash gifts were paid, and the balance was maintained at about £3,000. She had no other resources. The only provision which G had made for E during his lifetime was a fund of National Savings Certificates initially of £10,000, worth £15,000 at the date of the hearing. He had expressed the wish that any unforeseen requirements after his death could be met as a matter of moral obligation, out of the assets passing to S. E's needs were assessed by reference to the medical evidence of the deterioration in her condition and the additional care, equipment and facilities which she might reasonably require in consequence. *Found*, E's life expectancy was unlikely to be much more than 10 years; there was no evidence to suggest when, if at all, a move from residential to nursing care might be required or, if there was a move, E's local authority funding would be adversely affected. Cooke J concluded that E's reasonable needs could be met by a fund of £100,000, which would include the £15,000 in National Savings certificates. The fund should be settled on discretionary trusts such that if it was not exhausted at E's death, the balance should revert to S. G's severable share of the jointly owned assets should be brought into the estate to the extent necessary to make that provision.

Re Christie, Christie v Keeble [1979] Ch. 168 (Vivian Price QC sitting as a **F–094** deputy High Court judge, 21 July 1978). The testatrix was a widow who died on 19 December 1976. By her will dated 23 September 1963 she devised her interest in a house in London and a house in Essex to her daughter and son respectively, and left her residuary estate equally between them. On her husband's death in 1971 she inherited a half-share in the London house (which she later transferred to her daughter by deed of gift) and the whole of the Essex house, which she later sold, purchasing a smaller house with the proceeds. The devise to the son therefore failed. The son applied for relief on the basis that "reasonable financial provision" meant the transfer of the replacement house to him as well as his receiving the half-share of residue. He was in his middle thirties with two young children, owning a house worth £14,000 subject to a £6,000 mortgage. *Held*, that "maintenance" referred to the maintenance of the way of life, wellbeing, health and financial security of the applicant and his family. The application was allowed.

F–095   *Christofides v Seddon* [2014] W.T.L.R. 215 (HH Judge Hand, County Court at Central London, 23 April 2013). The deceased (M) died on 14 May 2009 having made a will dated 27 October 2008 disposing of her property worldwide. The will appointed her daughters (P and J) as executors and left the residuary estate to them, her son (A), and her granddaughter (B, the daughter of P) in equal shares. Probate was granted on 27 May 2010 and although the claim was not issued until 31 October 2011 it was accepted that the proceedings were not out of time because there had been an "agreed standstill". The net estate included a property in London worth £420,000 at the date of the hearing and two properties in Cyprus, one of which was a house in Cyprus valued at 280,000. A substantial part of the judgment (paras [16]–[32]) was devoted to the value to be attributed to the Cyprus properties in arriving at a value for the residuary estate. Leaving the contingent cost liability out of account (*Lilleyman v Lilleyman* [2012] W.T.L.R. 1007 followed), £125,000 was a realistic estimate of the value of the quarter share of residue which each legatee stood to receive. The claimant (A) was 53 at the date of the hearing and suffered from serious health problems including diabetes, chronic kidney disease, high blood pressure and bronchial asthma; his medical records described him as morbidly obese. He had not worked since 2002 and was dependent on state benefits. The budget of £735 per week for his current care plan enabled him to engage the services of a full-time carer, who would require accommodation since A needed assistance throughout the day and night. The accommodation currently provided was in M's house. He did not want to go on living there as it was too big and expensive for him to run and was not, as he had formerly been, prepared to consider moving into council accommodation; he wished to purchase suitable accommodation for himself. All three of the defendants were in financial difficulty. P, aged 59 was a teacher but had to retire early through ill health and was in debt; part of her explanation for her indebtedness was that she had supported B. B, aged 37, was an unmarried mother with two children and was herself in debt. J was currently employed but was at risk of being made redundant; her outgoings exceeded her income. All three lived in properties subject to a mortgage; P and J owned their flats and B and her ex-partner owned 50 per cent of a property, the other 50 per cent being owned by a housing association. *Held*, (1) M had discharged her obligations and responsibilities to her adult children by giving them each an equal share; A was aggrieved by the portion given to B but M was not failing to discharge her obligations and responsibilities to him by doing so; (2) M knew that A was unwell but plainly did not regard the provision of accommodation for him as her obligation or responsibility; (3) while the test of whether reasonable provision had been made was an objective test, the deceased's wishes should count for quite a lot where there was a modest estate. Accordingly, the claim was dismissed.

Re Collins [1990] Fam. 56 (Hollings J, 12 October 1989). The application **F–096** was on behalf of a son who had been adopted by another family prior to the making of the application, and a daughter. It was held that the son was not qualified to apply. The deceased died intestate on 16 August 1980, leaving a net estate of £27,000, and letters of administration were granted to the official solicitor on 6 February 1987. The applicant, who was the illegitimate daughter of the deceased, was 19 at the time of the hearing. The deceased married in August 1978 but left her husband three months later because of his violent conduct. She obtained a decree nisi on 23 May 1980, but it was never made absolute. Consequently, her husband would have been entitled to the whole of her estate. The applicant had been employed after leaving school, but was unemployed at the date of the hearing and living with her boyfriend on social security. Their DSS benefits, including the payment of their rent, totalled roughly £340 per month. She was awarded a lump sum of £5,000 for her maintenance in times of unemployment and other needs. *Held*, an order for periodical payments was not appropriate having regard to the small size of the estate, the difficulty of assessing an appropriate amount, and the need for finality. Her receipt of payments from the DSS did not preclude her application.

Commentary
"Family provision-adoption of child after mother's death intestate" (1990) 20 Fam. Law 337

Re Coventry [1980] Ch. 461, CA (Buckley, Lane, Goff LJJ, 18 July 1979), on **F–097** appeal from Oliver J, 9 November 1978. The deceased died intestate on 10 June 1976, leaving a net estate of £7,000, to the whole of which his widow, aged 76 at the time of the hearing, was entitled. They were married in 1927 but the wife left the matrimonial home permanently soon after the applicant returned to live there in 1957, he having previously joined the Navy but not re-enlisting. She was entitled to a one-third interest in it by reason of her contribution to its acquisition. At the time of the hearing she was living on a pension in a council flat. The applicant, who was the son and only child of the marriage, was 48. He had been married from 1961 to 1975 and during that period he and his wife lived rent-free in his parents' home, where she performed the domestic duties. After the breakdown of the marriage, of which there were three children, he continued to live there, paying £12 per week maintenance out of his net earnings of £52 per week. From then until the death of his father he performed the domestic duties. Oliver J dismissed the application, holding that he could not interfere with the deceased's dispositions unless they failed to make reasonable provision for the applicant, and the mere fact that the applicant was a son of the deceased in necessitous circumstances did not create the required moral obligation on the deceased to make provision for him. This decision was affirmed by the Court of Appeal, which also held that no account could be taken of changes in the applicant's circumstances subsequent to the hearing at first instance.

Commentary

J. G. Ross Martyn, "You're on your own now, son—or are you?" (1998) 142 S.J. 576

R. Birch, "Adult children and moral obligation" (2000) 150 N.L.J. 1480

G. Harrap, "Developments in Inheritance Act claims" (2004) 9(2) E.C.A. 26

J. Wilson and R. Bailey-Harris, "Family provision: the adult child and moral obligation" (2005) Fam. Law 535

I. Johnson, "Bounty claims" (2007) 157 N.L.J. 928

D. Catchpole and L. Parker, "Charity begins at home" (2008) 93 T.E.L. & T.J. 26

F–098　　*Re Creeney* [1984] N.I. 397, Carswell J (1 January 1984, LN). The testator (W) had two children, a son (F) and a daughter (J), respectively 57 and 56 years of age at the date of the hearing. By his will, made some 13 years before his death in 1982, he left his entire estate to J. Its value was a little over £50,000. F had for many years worked in W's shoe shop for low pay in the expectation that he would succeed to the business. However, F and W fell out in 1972 and F left the business (which was not doing well) and found work in England. At the time of the hearing, J and her family were significantly better off than F and his family. It was found that F and his wife were net contributors to W's family resources in the sense that they were working, for a considerable period of time, to support what would be their inheritance. The will did not make reasonable provision for F's maintenance; he was awarded one third of the net estate. See s.(G) for the procedural issue which subsequently arose and is reported at [1988] 5 N.I.J.B. 47.

F–099　　*Re Debenham* [1986] 1 F.L.R. 404; [1986] 16 Fam. Law 101 (Ewbank J, 19 July 1985). The testatrix died in 1983 aged 78, leaving a net estate £172,000 to be divided, after a legacy of £200 to the applicant, among six charities. The applicant, aged 58 at the date of the hearing, was the child of the first of the testatrix's four marriages. Her mother did not want her and never acknowledged her; she was brought up in South Africa by her father's parents, but never formally adopted. The applicant came back to England in 1953 and settled in Bradford, where she obtained work. Between then and 1973 she had occasional contact with the testatrix, but after 1973 the testatrix refused to see her. She married in 1977 when she was 50 and her husband 58. When the testatrix heard of this, she altered her will to the applicant's disadvantage. The applicant developed epilepsy in 1978, and it had become severe by 1982, in which year they were both made redundant and moved to Cornwall. When she heard of the provisions of the will in 1984, she was upset and wrote to her mother's solicitors refusing the legacy; she was at that time unaware of the provisions of the 1975 Act. She had a pension of £500 per year from her previous employment, and they received a total of £52 per week in supplementary benefit. It was held that the testatrix owed no moral obligation to the charities and that, although she never recognised any obligation to the applicant she did, in view of her severe illness, owe her some moral obligation. The sum of £6,000 per year would have been reasonable provision for the needs of the couple but, as provision must be for the applicant only, the appropriate figure was £4,500, to be reduced when they became eligible for the old age pension. A lump sum of

£3,000 was also awarded to meet present needs and to obviate the need to backdate the order.

Commentary
C. Barton, "Stepfathers, mothers, cohabitants and uncles" (2009) 39 Fam. Law 327

Case comment
Re Debenham (1986) 16 Fam. Law 101

Espinosa v Bourke [1999] 1 F.L.R. 747, CA (Butler-Sloss, Aldous, Buxton **F–100** LJJ, 17 December 1998, on appeal from Johnson J). The testator died aged 87, leaving his entire net estate of about £196,000 to his grandson, A, aged 19. The applicant was his 55-year-old daughter (S). In 1987 S's mother was ill and made a will leaving everything to the testator. He said that if she did not change her will, he would see to it that her estate (which included a half interest in a portfolio of shares) would pass to S. At the time of his death, S had been married five times, her last marriage being to an unemployed Spanish fisherman some 20 years younger than herself. A was the child of her third marriage but had subsequently been adopted by her fourth husband; however, he had lived mainly with his grandparents since the age of eight, and, on the death of his grandmother when he was 12, with his grandfather. Shortly after that, they moved into the applicant's house, she gave up work to look after the household and the testator provided £350 per month for the upkeep of the family, paid for improvements and discharged the mortgage. He made a will in S's favour in 1988 but in December 1994, nine months before his death, he executed his last will leaving his estate to A. At this stage S was spending time in Spain and the testator was left to be looked after by A and "meals on wheels". Johnson J identified two obligations which the testator had owed to S: (i) the promise to leave to her the mother's share of the paternal grandmother's portfolio (the "promise" obligation); and (ii) the obligation arising out of her caring for him (for which purpose she had employed resources provided by him—the "conduct" obligation), but held that any obligation which the testator had to S had been discharged by her conduct. He dismissed her application. Reversing that decision, the Court of Appeal held that, while the conduct obligation might have been discharged, the "promise" obligation had not. The judge had placed too much emphasis on her conduct and given insufficient weight to her precarious financial position resulting from the lack of success of the business which she and her husband were running. She was awarded £60,000, which would pay off her business debts and leave a small amount to cover other pressing current expenses.

Commentary
G. Harrap, "Developments in Inheritance Act claims" (2004) 9(2) E.C.A. 26
J. Wilson and R. Bailey-Harris, "Family provision: the adult child and moral obligation" (2005) Fam. Law 535
K. Gibson, "Extending financial provision" (2006) 59 Fam. Law 22
J. H. McGuire and E. Frankland, "Till death us do part: Inheritance claims and the short marriage" (2006) 36 Fam. Law 374
I. Johnson, "Bounty claims" (2007) 157 N.L.J. 928

Case comment
Espinosa v Bourke (1999) 29 Fam. Law 210

F–101 *Garland v Morris* [2007] 2 F.L.R. 528 (Michael Furness QC sitting as a deputy judge of the Chancery Division, 27 January 2007). Mr Garland died on 25 February 2001, survived by the two daughters of his first marriage, the claimant (Yvette) and the second defendant (Beverley). The claimant was unmarried and had three children aged 21, 9 and 3; the second defendant was married and had two children aged 23 and 19. By his will dated 5 September 1995 and a codicil dated 17 June 1999 he left pecuniary legacies of £5,000 to each of his daughters' children who were alive at his death; there were some other small legacies, and the personal chattels and the residue of the estate (amounting to £284,361) were left to the second defendant. The claimant, who received nothing under the will and codicil, had no capital resources except for her own house, which she had bought with money inherited from her mother, and which was in a bad state of repair. Her claim at trial was for two lump sums, one of £19,000 + VAT for renovations to the house, the other of £15,000 + VAT to convert the loft into a third bedroom, which was required since her adult son was still living at home. *Found*, although the claimant was in financial need and lived in substandard housing, she had failed to establish that the will did not make reasonable provision for her. The main factors in that decision were that she had inherited all her mother's estate, which had enabled her to buy her own house; its poor condition was very largely her own fault; she bore some responsibility for her financial difficulties in that she had had three children by a man who, she must have realised, was never going to contribute to her maintenance; she had been estranged from her father for many years and he owed her no obligation, whereas her sister had had a close relationship with him and he had assumed responsibility to assist in the maintenance of her and her family, encouraged her children to undertake university education and said that he would pay for it, and there were concerns about the sister's state of health and that of her husband, and as to whether they would be able to support themselves adequately in their retirement even with the benefit of the deceased's estate.

Commentary
E. Exton and J. Washington, "The Inheritance (Provision for Family and Dependants) Act 1975: recent cases and developments" (2008) P.C.B. 101

F–102 *Gold v Curtis* [2005] W.T.L.R. 673 (Master Bowman, 4 August 2004). The deceased died, aged 80, leaving net estate £870,000. She was survived by her son (G), the claimant, aged 57, and her daughter (C), the defendant, aged 60. By her will made in 1998, some four years before her death, she left the bulk of her estate to C, who had assets of her own worth some £1.1 million. The will (which was homemade) stated that she was not leaving anything to G as "he had had enough from his parents during their lifetime and they had been very estranged these last few years". In fact he had received only two sums totalling £1,800 from her; £600 of that was a loan which he had not repaid. His position was difficult. He was married with two daughters, one of whom suffered from a psychotic condition, and he himself had had a nervous breakdown in 1996. The net joint income of G and his wife was £37,500 and their outgoings were £41,895. Their income was insufficient to meet outgoings without recourse to the capital of his pension fund and it was essential that his wife continued working. Their pensions would be inadequate when they retired in 2010 and 2006 respectively; their gross retirement income would be about £18,000. They had no capital assets other than their house, worth £380,000 net of mortgage and against which they had borrowed a further £40,000 to meet the costs of the proceedings. He was awarded £250,000, which would pay off the mortgage debt, provide for replacement of capital items and provide a cushion for contingencies. Although this would leave him substantially worse off than C, the court's jurisdiction was to relieve his financial position and not to achieve equality between him and C.

Commentary
F. Smith and H. Atkinson, "Dependent status" (2006) 73 T.E.L. & T.J. 28

Re Goodchild [1997] 1 W.L.R. 1216, CA (Leggatt, Morritt, Phillips LJJ, 2   **F–103**
May 1997); affirming [1996] 1 W.L.R. 664 (Carnwath J, 13 December 1995). The applicant (G), aged 51 at the date of hearing, was the son of D and J, who were in business together from 1966; G joined them in that business soon after. In 1988, D and J made simultaneous wills in similar form, in favour of G. J died in 1991 and some 18 months later, D married E. He made a new will in E's favour and died in January 1993 leaving an estate worth about £450,000. By that time, G was experiencing financial difficulties. Carnwath J held that the wills were not mutual wills, there being no sufficient evidence of an agreement that the wills were intended to be mutually binding. He held that as far as D's own share of the property was concerned, he was free to deal with it as he chose. However, in relation to the part of the estate which had belonged to J, it was found that she made her will on the understanding that D would give effect to what she believed to be their mutual intentions, and that gave rise to a moral (though not a legal) obligation. While E had an income sufficient for her needs, capital of some £28,000 and a property worth £43,000 (though subject to a charge in favour of the estate), G's income was scarcely sufficient for him to maintain his existing standard of life, even ignoring his business debts. It was an exceptional case and G should receive some provision. He was eventually awarded £185,000. In the Court of Appeal, Leggatt LJ reiterated the comments of that court in *Re Coventry* about the undesirability of dissipating estates of modest size by appeals against sensible judgments at first instance, and described Carnwath J's judgment as being not only sensible, but unimpeachable.

Commentary
A. Samuels, "Mutual wills; remarriage" (1997) 141 S.J. 1179
P. Hopkins, "Mutual wills" (1998) 142 S.J. 590
S. Lacey, "Tax-efficient statements and the 1975 Act" (1998) 3 E.C.A. 8
C. Davis, "Mutual wills, formalities, constructive trusts" [2003] Conv 238
J. Brown and M. Pawlowski, "Solutions for an increasingly common conundrum" (2006) 176 P.L.J. 8
K. Gibson, "Extending financial provision" (2006) 59 Fam. Law 22
J. Wilson "Death, severance and survivorship" (2007) 37 Fam. Law 1082

Case comment
Re Goodchild (1997) 27 Fam. Law 514, 660

F–104 *Hanbury v Hanbury* [1999] 2 F.L.R. 255 (HH Judge Bromley QC, Cambridge County Court, 17 July 1998). The deceased died leaving net estate £11,981, out of which he left £10,000 to the applicant, his 45-year-old daughter by his first marriage. She was both physically and mentally disabled and was looked after by her mother, but would need institutional care if she survived her mother. The deceased had lost interest in his daughter and had only with reluctance maintained her, initially at £600 per year, later increased to £900. He had taken advice as to how he might defeat a claim under the 1975 Act and had, in accordance with that advice, transferred most of his assets into the joint names of himself and his second wife, with the result that at his death she had capital (including her own sole property) of £268,477 and received net annual income of £27,625. The judge concluded that the parties intended certain of those assets to be held as beneficial joint tenants and out of the £60,000 representing the deceased's severable share, ordered that £39,000 be held on discretionary trusts, with the applicant as principal beneficiary, to fund the cost of her eventual placement in a residential home. This was a valid settlement for her benefit within s.2(1)(d) and would not affect her entitlement to income support.

Commentary
S. Watson, "Discretionary trusts and the settlement of I(PFD)A claims" (2000) 15 T.E.L.J. 14

Case comment
Hanbury v Hanbury (1999) 29 Fam. Law 447

F–105 *Re Hancock Deceased* [1998] 2 F.L.R. 346, CA (Butler-Sloss and Judge LJJ, Sir John Knox, 1 May 1998); on appeal from HH Judge Rich QC, Central London County Court. Also reported as *Snapes v Aram* [1998] 142 S.J.L.B. 167. The applicant was aged 58 at the date of her father's death, but 69 at the date of the hearing at first instance. Her application was issued in 1986, on the last day of the six-month period, but it was found that she was not in any way culpable as regards the further 10-year delay and it had not prejudiced any party. By his will the testator devised a plot of land (Plot 3), used for carrying on the family business, Hancock Brothers (HB) to HB, and the matrimonial home and the remainder of his estate, worth some £80,000, to his wife. The probate value of Plot 3 was £100,000, but as a result of subsequent events the value increased in 1989 to £663,000. The will included a clause whereby, if his wife predeceased him, the estate was to be divided between the applicant, his daughter Joan and his seven grandchildren. He also expressed the wish that his wife should provide for those persons in her will, but in fact she received only £1,000 under her mother's will, Joan receiving £2,000. HB was run by his four sons and one of his three daughters (Sally) and was at all material times a prosperous business. The applicant's financial circumstances were stringent. She had left home at the age of 19 to be married but that marriage broke down after some 20 years. From time to time she lived with various members of her family but in 1977 she began living with a Mr Pearce as (so the judge found) husband and wife.

For a period about the time of her father's death she was employed by HB at a low wage in a menial position. The judge found that there was no moral obligation or responsibility owed by the father to the applicant and that her needs were greater than they had been at the time of the application, and her prospects worse. Had there not been that substantial windfall, the estate would have been modest, and the widow's needs would have had to take precedence; but in these unusual circumstances it was appropriate to make provision for her. The judge awarded her £3,000 per year and his decision was affirmed. The judgments emphasise that a moral claim or moral obligation or other special reason is not a prerequisite to a successful application by an adult child; however, on facts similar to those in Re Coventry or where (as in Re Jennings [1994] Ch. 286), the applicant is in employment, with an earning capacity for the foreseeable future, an applicant is unlikely to succeed without some special circumstance such as a moral obligation.

Commentary
J. G. Ross Martyn, "You're on your own now, son—or are you?" (1998) 142 S.J. 576
L. King, "Family provision claim" (1998) 95 L.S. Gaz. 27
G. Harrap, "Provision for elderly children on death: what, no moral obligation?" (1998) 3(6) E.C.A. 7–9
A. Francis, "A dangerous Act to follow" (2003) 31 F.L.J. 18
G. Harrap, "Developments in Inheritance Act claims" (2004) 9(2) E.C.A. 26
J. Wilson and R. Bailey-Harris, "Family provision: the adult child and moral obligation" (2005) 35 Fam. Law 535

Case comment
Re Hancock Deceased (1998) 28 Fam. Law 438, 520

Hocking v Hocking, CA (Beldam, Millett, Otton LJJ, 12 July 1997, LN), on **F–106** appeal from HH Judge Weeks QC, Bristol District Registry. Application by the adult daughters of the deceased by his first wife. He died intestate on 27 January 1994 leaving net estate £107,850. On intestacy, the entire estate passed to his second wife, who also had the benefit of an insurance policy which discharged the mortgage on the family home and provided her with a capital sum of £20,000. At the hearing at first instance, the first wife (J) was awarded £18,000 and the two daughters, who were then aged 22 and 18, £4,000 and £8,000 respectively, the difference reflecting the longer time during which the younger daughter required maintenance. J did not appeal but for the daughters it was contended on appeal that the judge had failed to give any or any proper weight to the fact that the deceased had failed to pay any or any sufficient maintenance to the appellants. This argument was held to be contrary to the decision in Re Jennings [1994] Ch. 286; in effect, it was being argued that the obligations contemplated by s.3(1)(d) were the obligations which the deceased had had at any time, whereas they were only the obligations which he had immediately before his death. The argument that they ought to have been awarded a further lump sum to reflect the possibility that they might wish to buy their own homes at some future time, in support of which Re Callaghan and Re Leach were relied on, was also rejected; capitalising the cost of providing accommodation for the applicant in Re Callaghan in order to enable him to take advantage of the right to buy legislation constituted maintenance; providing a lump sum out of which a house might be bought in the future was not. The appeal was dismissed.

F–107   *Heather Ilott v David Mitson, Michael Land, Blue Cross, RSPB and RSPCA* [2012] 2 F.L.R. 170; [2011] 2 F.C.R. 1; [2011] W.T.L.R. 779; [2011] EWCA (Civ) 346 (Sir Nicholas Wall P, Arden and Black LJJ, 31 March 2011), allowing the appeal from the order of Eleanor King J (Family Division, 1 December 2009) in *H v J's Personal Representatives, Blue Cross, RSPB and RSPCA* [2010] 1 F.L.R. 1613, also reported as *H v M* [2010] W.T.L.R. 193. There were two sequences of hearings, the first of which was concerned with the question whether the deceased's will had made reasonable provision for the claimant. This summary relates to those hearings.

F–108   The deceased (J) died on 10 July 2006, leaving a net estate of £486,000. J's daughter H, born on 7 September 1960, was the only child of J's marriage, which was cut short when her father died in an industrial accident. In 1977 H formed a relationship with N, of whom J strongly disapproved, and this led to a profound disagreement between J and H. H left home secretly in 1978 to live with N in his parents' home, and married him in 1983. There were five children of the marriage, born between 1984 and 1996. There were three relatively brief reconciliations between J and H, but both in 1984 and in 2002 J executed wills which excluded H, accompanied by letters of wishes explaining her reasons for doing so. Under the 2002 will her residuary estate went to the three charities. H's claim for provision out of J's estate was heard by District Judge Million in May 2007. Her financial circumstances were that she, N and their four youngest children lived in a three-bedroom house rented from a housing association; she had not done any paid work since their first child was born in 1984, when she and N decided that she would be a full-time mother. N worked part-time but some 75 per cent of the family's annual income of just over £14,000 derived from state benefits; the family also received housing and council tax benefit. By an order finally perfected in December 2007, the district judge awarded H £50,000. She appealed against the amount of the award and the charities cross-appealed. Eleanor King J set aside the judgment of the district judge. She held that he had been so concerned with the rights and wrongs of the attempts at reconciliation that he asked himself the wrong question. To alter the dispositions of J's will because she had acted unreasonably was to undermine the basic premise, which applied in this jurisdiction, of freedom of testation. Looked at objectively, H had no expectation of inheriting anything from J, and the length and depth of the estrangement negatived any idea that any obligation could arise out of the relationship. Reversing that judgment and ordering that the matter be remitted to another judge of the Family Division to determine what provision should be made, the Court of Appeal unanimously held that the district judge had not erred in law. He had asked himself the right question and had found that the relevant factors, including J's unreasonable conduct, had produced an unreasonable result. In determining that the will had not made reasonable provision for H, he had arrived at a "value judgment" which was not "plainly wrong" and was therefore one with which an appellate court should not interfere.

Commentary
J. Aspden, "Redressing the balance" (2010) 118 T.E.L. & T.J. 14

J. Aspden, "Is your last will and testament worth the paper it's written on?",
The Times, 14 April 2011
R. Sime, "Code of conduct" (2010) 160 N.L.J. 525
L. Junor, "Keeping the peace" (2011) 155 S.J. 21

Case comment
C. Bridge (2010) 40 Fam. Law 343
Heather Ilott (2011) 155 S.J. 5

Ilott v Mitson [2017] UKSC 17, reported as *Ilott v Blue Cross* [2017] 2   **F–109**
W.L.R. 979 (Lord Neuberger, PSC, Baroness Hale of Richmond, DPSC,
Lord Kerr of Tonaghmore, Lord Clarke of Stone-cum-Ebony, Lord Wilson,
Lord Sumption, Lord Hughes, JJSC, 15 March 2017), allowing the appeal
from the Court of Appeal in *Ilott v Mitson* [2016] 1 All E.R. 932; [2015] 2
F.L.R. 1409, CA (Arden, Ryder LJJ, Sir Colin Rimer, 27 July 2015),
reversing *Ilott v Mitson* [2015] 1 F.L.R. 291 (Parker J). This summary,
following on from the previous case summary,[6] relates to the proceedings
following the reversal by the Court of Appeal of the judgment of Eleanor
King J and the order remitting the matter to another judge of the Family
Division to determine what provision should be made for the claimant (H).
The district judge had originally awarded her £50,000. In the appeal on
quantum, Parker J, in dismissing H's appeal, held that the district judge,
doing the best he could with the material before him, could not be said to be
manifestly wrong, or even wrong in taking the view that notwithstanding
that H and her husband and family lived in straitened circumstances, the
fact that they had done so for many years did not justify an award which
improved their circumstances. H's contention that she could only benefit
from the award if her housing needs were met could not be the right
approach because otherwise, his determination that H's lack of expectation
tempered the award would be rendered meaningless. On appeal to the Court
of Appeal, H sought funds sufficient to acquire her property together with
some capital to meet non-housing needs. The Court of Appeal set aside the
original order. *Held* (per Arden LJ at [35]–[36], [59]–[62], [67]), (1) the district judge had made two fundamental errors leading to the conclusion that
his order should be set aside. First, although he had stated that the award
should be limited because of H's lack of expectancy and her ability to live
within her means, he did not explain how he limited the award to reflect
those matters. Second, he had made a working assumption that the effect of
a large capital payment (such as the £50,000 which he did award) would
disentitle the family to most, if not all, of their state benefits, but failed to
verify it. The court could, and should, exercise its discretion afresh. (2) The
court had to balance the claims fairly. Where a claimant for whom reasonable provision needs to be made is elderly or disabled and has extra
living costs, consideration would have to be given to meeting them. The
same applied where a party had extra financial needs because she relied on
state benefits which must be preserved. The provision of housing would
enable H to receive a capitalised sum and to keep her tax credits. (3) The

---

[6] The case summary in the third edition (2011) at F–096 referred to the citations at [2011] 2
F.C.R. 1; [2011] W.T.L.R. 779, CA. At the time of writing the case had not yet been reported
in F.L.R., where it appeared at [2012] 2 F.L.R. 170. See also [2011] Fam. Law 798.

right order was to award H £143,000, the cost of acquiring the property, together with the reasonable costs of its acquisition, and an option to take a maximum sum of £20,000, exercisable in part more than once, to provide a small additional income. Agreeing, Ryder LJ observed at [69] that as a matter of public policy a court is not constrained to limit a person's reasonable financial provision as being limited to their existing state benefits, nor is the court's function substituted for by any assessment of benefits undertaken by the state. The charities appealed largely on principle because of the possible impact of the decision of the Court of Appeal on other cases. This part of the summary is concerned only with the analysis by the Supreme Court (at [32]–[47]) of the errors which the Court of Appeal held that the district judge had made. The first suggested error ([32]–[36]) was that, having stated that because of the appellant's lack of expectancy and her ability to live within her means, her award should be "limited", he had failed to show how he had limited the award to reflect those matters. The Supreme Court disagreed. There was is no warrant in the Act for requiring a process of that kind. The Act did not require the judge to fix some hypothetical standard of reasonable provision and then either add to it, or discount from it for variable factors. All the s.3 factors, which might themselves be in tension with one another, had to be considered and an assessment made in the light of all of them. The second suggested error was that he failed to verify the working assumption he had made about the effect of his award on H's entitlement to state benefits. The Supreme Court considered that the gravamen of that criticism was not so much that he had failed to verify his assumption, but that he had made an award which was of little or no value to H because of its impact on her benefits. But that was not so. At the hearing before him, H had produced a "telling list" of the equipment which needed replacement, and of elementary refurbishment required, in order to enable the household to function adequately, and he had referred to those matters in his judgment. The award was of value to her, because if a substantial part of it were spent in this way, the impact on the family's benefits would be minimised; she could put the household onto a much sounder footing without for long retaining capital beyond the £16,000 ceiling at which entitlement to Housing and Council Tax Benefits was lost. Thus he had not made the second suggested error either, and that was sufficient to require the Court to set aside the order of the Court of Appeal and restore the order of the district judge.

Commentary
B. Sloan, "Family Provision goes to the Supreme Court" [2016] Fam. Law 46, 424–26
S. Edwards, "Testamentary freedom—where next?" [2015] Eld. LJ 5(4), 434–38
S. Gore, "Inheritance provision: Ilott v Mitson" [2015] Fam. Law 45, 1136
S. Douglas, "Estranged children and their inheritance" [2016] L.Q.R. 132, 20–25
M. Allardice, "Of greatest benefit' [2015] T.E.L. & T.J. 170, 8–12
E. Hewitt, "Ilott v Mitson: round five (!)" [2015] P.C.B. 5(4), 242–47

Case comment
C. Bridge [2015] Fam. Law 45, 1196–97

R. Hughes [2015] Eld. LJ 5(4), 361–2

Re Jennings, Harlow v National Westminster Bank [1994] Ch. 286, CA   **F–110**
(Nourse, Henry LJJ, Sir John May, 13 December 1993) on appeal from
Wall J. The plaintiff (H), who was 50 at the date of hearing, was the son of J
and D. They separated in 1945, when H was two years old, and J never had
anything to do with him from then on. H was brought up by D and her
second husband, whom she married in 1948. J died in 1991. By his will,
made in November 1989, he left pecuniary legacies totalling some £170,000
and the residue equally among three charities. The estate had a value of
about £300,000 at the date of the hearing. The judge found that: there had
been no good reason for J not to support or have contact with H, and he
had therefore failed to honour his financial and moral obligations during
H's minority; none of the beneficiaries had any particular claim on J's
bounty; and H's standard of living was not extravagant or unreasonable. H
was awarded £40,000 which he reasonably required to discharge the mortgage on his house. The residuary legatees appealed, their case being that H
did not reasonably require any financial provision for his maintenance. The
appeal was allowed. It was held that s.3(1)(d) did not refer to obligations
which were long spent at the time of the deceased's death. There being no
other obligation or special circumstances, the order made was wrong in
principle. It was also held that a payment for the discharge of the mortgage
would not, in the circumstances of the case, be "maintenance"; it was not
provision which was necessary to discharge the cost of H's daily living at the
standard appropriate to him.

Commentary
C.H. Sherrin, "Succession" [1994] All E.R. Rev. 423
R. Birch, "Adult children and moral obligation" (2000) 150 N.L.J. 1480
K. Gibson, "Extending financial provision" (2006) 59 Fam. Law 22

Donald Land v The Estate of Mary Land [2007] 1 W.L.R. 1009 (HH Judge   **F–111**
Norris QC, Chancery Division, Birmingham District Registry, 29 June
2006). This is the first reported case in which the court has had to consider
the effect of s.3 of the Forfeiture Act 1982. The effect of subss.3(1) and
3(2)(a) is that the forfeiture rule shall not be taken to preclude any person
from making an application, or the making of any order, under the 1975
Act. The claimant, DL, was the executor and sole beneficiary under the will
of his mother (ML), dated 2 April 1996. DL had lived at home all his life
and had a series of labouring jobs, the last of which he gave up in 2002 at
ML's request so that he could look after her. He did this as best he could,
but after ML suffered a fall in September 2003 and refused either to go to
hospital or to permit a doctor to see her, he gradually became less able to
cope. However, he did not seek any professional help until 4 January 2004,
when she lost consciousness and he called an ambulance. She died two days
later and DL was charged with manslaughter, to which he pleaded guilty on
27 April 2004. On 21 May 2004 he was sentenced to four years' imprisonment. On 2 August 2004 he made a claim under s.2 of the Forfeiture Act
1982 ("the 1982 Act"), which was four days out of time. His legal representatives then successfully applied to amend the claim, seeking a declaration that the forfeiture rule did not apply, alternatively an order under s.2 of
the 1975 Act for reasonable provision out of ML's estate. *Held*, s.3 of the

1982 Act was to be read, so far as permissible, in a manner which enabled the court to deprive the wrongdoer of benefit when it was in the public interest to do so, but, in its discretion, to mitigate the harshness of the forfeiture rule when it was not. *Found*, the public interest would not be served by depriving the claimant of all benefit. For an adult son, the standard of provision was what was reasonable, in all the circumstances, for his maintenance. The deceased's house was ordered to be transferred to the claimant outright and he was also awarded a legacy of £1,000 to meet his immediate financial needs. The balance of the cash in the estate would pass to those entitled on intestacy.

Commentary
C. Simm, "A year in the courts" (2006) 82 T.E.L. & T.J. 26
M. Pawlowski, "Forfeiture relief" (2007) 157 N.L.J. 315
E. Exton and J. Washington, "The Inheritance (Provision for Family and Dependants) Act 1975: recent cases and developments" (2008) P.C.B. 101

Case comment
Donald Land (2006) 81 T.E.L. & T.J. 18

F–112   *Re McGarrell, Heatley v Doherty* [1983] N.I.J.B. 8 (Hutton J, 1 January 1983, LN, W(ca)). By his will, made some six months before his death, the testator (T) left his estate to three persons in equal shares. Two of these were husbands of his nieces and the other took her legacy as trustee for a religious foundation. The plaintiff (E) was his daughter. She based her claim on the housework she had done for T and her general assistance in looking after him, particularly for a period of some nine months to a year or so before he died, when he came to live with her and her family. She was married with four children aged between 12 and 20, she received £40 per week housekeeping money from her husband. She had also for some years received payment from the Social Services Board for acting as a home help for her father and her aunt who lived with him. The two older children received unemployment benefit. An argument that, as she was receiving money from her husband, anything that she received from T's estate would not be maintenance but a "bonus or enrichment" was rejected. It was held that she had established a moral claim, particularly in respect of the care she had given T while he was living in her home and she was awarded, by consent, one-fourth of the net estate.

F–113   *Re Kathleen McKernan Deceased, McKernan v McKernan* [2007] N.I. Ch. 6 (Deeny J, Chancery Division, Northern Ireland, 11 December 2007, B). The plaintiff was the third of four children of her widowed mother (K) and was 51 at the date of the hearing. K died on 26 May 2005 leaving a net estate worth £514,528, represented mainly by the family home, a new bungalow and a farm of land. By her will she gave the farm stock to her eldest son (D) and the residue to D and her youngest son (S), appointing them executors. Her second son (F) was given the right to live in the family home for life but the plaintiff (M), who had been living in the family home since 1994 and had played some part in caring for K, was given only the right to live there for a further six months. M's resources at the date of the hearing consisted of incapacity benefit of £61 per week. Deeny J commented that this was very close to the subsistence level referred to by Goff LJ in *Re Coventry*. Relying on *Re Hancock* and also two Northern Ireland decisions, *Re McGarrell* [1983] N.I.J.B. 8, and *Re Creeney* [1984] N.I. 397, he concluded that the will had not made reasonable provision for M and that although K had good grounds for preferring her sons to her daughter, provision should be made which would meet her need for a roof over her head. There were various possible options, including a right to reside in the family home, and the provision of a sum of money with which a small apartment could be bought for M. The matter was adjourned for further consideration.

Re Myers, Myers v Myers [2005] W.T.L.R. 851 (Munby J, 3 August 2004).   **F–114**
The claimant was one of the two children of the deceased's first marriage; she had had a poor relationship with him. Some years before his death the deceased had settled some shares on her and told her she could expect nothing more. *Held*, the claimant was entitled to reasonable maintenance, which was not just enough to get by on, but neither did it include anything reasonably desirable for her general benefit or welfare. Taking into account her severely straitened circumstances, the fact that her situation was due to mental fragility and awkward personality rather than indolence, that she had not behaved as badly to the deceased as he seemed to have thought, and that he had very substantial wealth, provision would be made by way of a settlement on her of a sum sufficient to buy a flat and meet her living expenses, with power for the trustees to apply capital for her maintenance.

Commentary
F. Smith and H. Atkinson, "Dependent status" (2006) 73 T.E.L. & T.J. 28

Re Pearce Deceased [1998] 2 F.L.R. 705 CA (Nourse, Peter Gibson, Buxton   **F–115**
LJJ, 25 June 1998), on appeal from HH Judge Behrens sitting as a judge of the Chancery Division. The deceased died in 1992 leaving a net estate which was worth £285,900 at the time of the hearing at first instance. By his will he appointed the defendant (E), with whom he had had a relationship since 1983, his sole executrix and universal legatee. The applicant was the only child of the deceased's marriage, which was terminated by divorce in 1985. From the age of 6 to 16 the applicant worked on a farm (Meadow Farm) which the deceased had bought, but in 1978 he left to find other employment, having been told by the deceased that he would not be paid for working on the farm. Nevertheless he kept in touch with his parents and from time to time helped on the farm, for which he was not paid. He was told by the deceased on several occasions that the farm would be his one day and he had to earn it. After a period in the army, the applicant returned to civilian life in 1990, having married in 1988. He acquired a business as owner-driver with his own JCB; the business absorbed considerable capital and provided an income of some £8,000 to £9,000 per year. At the time of the hearing he had five children between two and seven years of age, and was living in a house which required substantial repair. The trial judge found that he had substantial financial needs, whereas E had not, and that there was a moral obligation on the deceased to leave at least part of the farm and its assets to the applicant. He considered that the applicant's reasonable needs could be met by additional income of £6,000–£7,000 per year and that, applying a multiplier of 12 to 13, the appropriate capital sum would be

£85,000. Nourse LJ was in no doubt that the judge was entitled to conclude that the will did not make reasonable provision for the applicant, and was unable to say that the view taken by the judge of the applicant's needs was one to which he could not reasonably have come. The judge's decision should stand as to what was or was not reasonable unless it was clearly shown to be in error. The decision had achieved substantial justice between the parties and the appeal was dismissed.

Commentary
R. Birch, "Adult children and moral obligation" (2000) 150 N.L.J. 1480

Case comment
Re Pearce Deceased (1998) Fam. Law 588

F–116   *Re Portt, Allcorn v Harvey and Woodcock*, CA (Roskill, Brandon, Ackner LJJ, 25 March 1980, LN, T625, noted at (131) N.L.J. 242) on appeal from HH Judge Clover, 25 April 1979. The testatrix died on 24 March 1977, aged over 90, leaving a net estate of about £12,000. By her will made in 1969 she left nothing to the applicant; the major beneficiary was the granddaughter of the testatrix. The applicant, who was 71, owned her house, worth £11,000, free of any charge, though it required substantial repair. She also had cash and realisable securities of £10,698, from which, together with her pension, she derived an income of about £2,200 per year. There was evidence that the applicant was very litigious, she and the testatrix quarrelled, and that was the reason why she was cut out of the will. The granddaughter was married; she owned her house jointly with her husband and the equity in it was about £11,000. She was earning £3,000 per year, which was not likely to increase; her husband was earning £9,300 with prospects of advancement. At first instance, the judge found that neither party needed the money, and, having regard to the conduct of the applicant as well as the financial situations of the parties, concluded that the testatrix had not failed to make reasonable provision for the applicant. The Court of Appeal upheld this decision for the reasons given by the judge.

F–117   *Riggs v Lloyds Bank Plc*, CA (Dillon, Butler-Sloss, Simon Brown LJJ, 27 November 1992) on appeal from HH Judge Weeks QC sitting as a deputy High Court judge. This action involved consolidated claims by the plaintiff (H), one under the 1975 Act and the other, based on proprietary estoppel, to a strip of ground adjacent to the house in which H lived. At the date of trial H was 42 years of age, with two children aged 14 and 10 by her second marriage. H was one of the two children of the testator, who died in 1989 having made a will in 1974 by which, in the events that occurred, his entire estate passed to his son (E), who was his only other child. H's claim was based on the help and care which she had given the testator during his lifetime, both personally and in connection with the letting out of holiday chalets which he owned. It was not H's case that she was necessitous, though it was found at first instance that she lived at not much above subsistence level. Having considered the financial position of both H and E, and the actual and potential value of certain land forming part of the estate, the learned judge awarded H £20,000 payable in two instalments, from the first of which was to be deducted £6,000 which she had already had from the estate. These sums were not intended to be a legacy to H, but a commuted sum for maintenance while her children were still dependent. The appeal against the award was allowed. There was no general need for H's maintenance, and it had not been her case that she needed maintenance over the years when the children were young; that was a claim devised by the judge.

Robinson v Bird [2003] EWHC 30 (Ch) (Blackburne J, 23 January 2003). For **F–118** a summary of the report of the appeal, under the name *Robinson v Fernsby* [2004] W.T.L.R. 257, see s.G. The testatrix (E) died leaving estate undistributed at the date of the hearing amounting to £361,507, not reckoning administration costs and the costs of the proceedings. She was survived by her daughter (V), born in 1958, who was the claimant, and a grandson born in 1986 (D) to her son, who had predeceased her. V had lived with E in her home (Orchard House) until 1988 and been financially supported by her. In 1996 E left Orchard House and moved to a nursing home, where she remained until her death in 2000. The EPA executed by her in 1996 was registered in January 1997, and Orchard House was sold in September 1997. On an application to the Court of Protection it was ordered that a lifetime gift to V of the proceeds of sale (amounting to £205,306) be made on terms that it be treated as an advance made on account and in part payment of any share of the property of E to which V might be entitled under E's will or intestacy, and with V paying any IHT that might become payable in consequence of that advance. A settlement of £25,000 for the benefit of D was ordered on the same terms. On advice, V invested £165,000 of this in medium to high-risk investments so as to yield higher income, but after some three years their value had fallen to £72,000 and her other capital amounted to £14,000. It was found (using a Duxbury calculation with net rate of return 3.75 per cent, in relation to the £72,000) that, at the date of the hearing, her income from all sources amounted to £18,200, compared with the £21,000 found to be reasonable for her maintenance, given that she owned the house in which she lived outright. The judge was initially minded to award the claimant a lump sum of £60,000, representing the capital sum required (on the same Duxbury basis) to fund that shortfall. However, doubting the correctness of this approach, he invited further written submissions from counsel, as a result of which he decided to dismiss the claim because (a) substantial provision had been made for V by E during her lifetime; (b) she had decided to anticipate the major part of her inheritance by applying to the Court of Protection for a lifetime gift of the proceeds of sale of Orchard House and, though those funds could have been prudently invested to produce some £8,000 per year which, combined with her income from other sources, would have brought her in £24,000 per year, apart from any contribution made by her husband; and (c) she had chosen to adopt a way of life in which her expenditure substantially exceeded her income and to adopt a riskier investment policy. Against that background it was not unreasonable that the deceased's will failed to make provision greater than 50 per cent for her. She had not established a sufficient basis for disturbing the equal division of the deceased's estate. That conclusion was reinforced by the circumstance that the grandson, who was the only other beneficiary, would take the share that his father, the deceased's only other child, would have taken had he survived her.

Commentary
A. Francis, "A dangerous Act to follow" (2003) 31 F.L.J. 18
G. Harrap, "Developments in Inheritance Act claims" (2004) 9(2) E.C.A. 26
I. R. Scott, "Correcting drafts of undelivered judgments" (2004) 23 C.J.Q. 93
A. Taylor, "Making your mind up" (2005) 102 L.S. Gaz. 29

F–119 *Re Rowlands Deceased* [1984] F.L.R. 813; [1984] 14 Fam. Law 280, CA (Cumming-Bruce and Dunn, LJJ, Wood J, 6 April 1984), on appeal from Anthony Lincoln J, 30 November 1983. Application on behalf of widow and two adult daughters. See s.A.

F–120 *Wade v Varney* [2003] W.T.L.R. 1535, CA (Tuckey LJ 10 September 2002, on appeal from HH Judge Oliver Jones, Walsall County Court). This was an oral hearing of an application for leave to appeal on the grounds of procedural irregularity at the trial. The parties were the son and daughter of the deceased, who had died intestate on 28 February 2001, with the result that they were entitled to equal shares of her estate, whose value was £114,731. The claimant son had been living with his mother in her house, which was the main asset of the estate. He wished to remain in the house and made a claim under the 1975 Act for, in effect, the whole value of the house. Dismissing his claim, the trial judge had concluded that, objectively, there was nothing unreasonable about the estate being equally divided. His notice of appeal was filed 30 days out of time and he applied for an extension of time and permission to appeal. In relation to the 1975 Act claim, Tuckey LJ said that the judge had obviously reached the right result. It was not an exercise in sympathy for either side. The question was whether the law of intestacy made reasonable provision. Both parties were adults, both were earning. Equality was the obvious answer, equality was the result of the intestacy. The contrary was almost unarguable; the application for an extension of time and for permission to appeal would be refused.

F–121 *Williams v Johns* [1988] 2 F.L.R. 475; (1988) Fam. Law 257 (HH Judge Micklem sitting as an additional High Court judge, 23 July 1987). The testatrix died on 10 November 1985 leaving a net estate £36,000 which, by her will dated 5 October 1979, she left to her son. She made a written statement on 6 September 1984 explaining why she had excluded the applicant from her will. The applicant, who was 43 at the time of the hearing, was the adopted daughter of the deceased. She had been a juvenile delinquent and her early adult life had also caused shame and distress to her parents, though her relationship with her mother had been affectionate in later years. She had married in 1972 and divorced in 1984. She had no capital beyond the houseboat in which she lived, and, although capable of working and having been independent of her mother for some years, was unemployed and had no income. *Held*, there was no moral obligation on the testatrix to provide for the applicant and it was not unreasonable of her to make no provision.

F–122 *Re Wood Deceased* (1982) 79 L.S. Gaz. 774 (Mervyn Davies J, 2 April 1982). The deceased died intestate on 4 April 1980 leaving a net estate £26,737. Her husband (H) was entitled to the statutory legacy of £25,000 and the applicant (E), the only child of the marriage, took the residue subject to his life interest in half of it. He died on 18 January 1981, leaving his estate to his son by his previous marriage. The application on behalf of E was brought by the official solicitor on the authority of the Court of Protection. E, who was 30 at the time of the hearing, had been born mentally subnormal, with no power of speech and very limited understanding, but she had some appreciation of various comforts. Her life expectancy was a further 30 years and she had no prospect of recovery. She had capital of £3,519 and her income from all sources was £1,037 per year. The total cost of her maintenance, including such additional amenities as would be of benefit to her, such as hydrotherapy, and occasional outings or holidays, was £2,277. She was awarded £15,000 in satisfaction of her rights under the 1975 Act and under the intestacy, costs to be paid out of the estate.

Wright v Waters [2015] W.T.L.R. 353 (HH Judge Behrens, 6 November **F–123** 2014). The claimant (P), aged 64, was the daughter of the deceased (M) who died on 29 December 2010 leaving net estate valued at £138,000. By her will dated 27 September 2009 M appointed her son (D) and his wife as executors and left her residuary estate to them in equal shares. Each of their four children was left £5,000 and there were legacies totalling £7,000 to her sister-in-law and a niece. P, who was a widow, had a daughter and two grandchildren but none of them benefited under the will. By a letter written on the same day as the will, M explained that this was because P had already taken £10,000 of her savings, she had been a constant source of trouble to her for many years, there had been no contact between them for nine years and P had shown no interest in her welfare. She advanced two claims, one based on proprietary estoppel, and the other under the 1975 Act. In regard to the proprietary estoppel claim P failed to satisfy the court that there were sufficiently clear representations on which she relied, and in particular, the references by her father to the shop in which she had worked being her inheritance was not intended to be taken seriously or was one that she might reasonably have been expected to rely on (see the judgment at paras 20–31 and 94–95). In relation to the Spanish villa purchased by her father, and subsequently sold (see the judgment at paras 32–44) it may have been the case that M told her that she would be able to afford her own villa as she would be giving her half her estate. P gave evidence that she signed a document transferring her interest in the villa to M but the court was not satisfied that she had, or believed that she had, any such interest or that she had signed such a document. It could not be said that P had acted to her detriment in reliance on M's statement. In relation to the 1975 Act claim, the factors in her favour were that she was M's daughter, she had worked for a time in the family shop, she was in difficult financial circumstances, she suffered from ill-health to the extent that she was wheelchair bound, and no other beneficiary had demonstrated a need for M's bounty. Those factors had to be set against her conduct. The £10,000 referred to above, which was part of the proceeds of sale of the Spanish villa, had been paid to her to be invested on M's behalf. P paid the interest from the bond in which it had been invested for the first year but did not make any further payments to M thereafter, nor did she return the capital to M when requested to do so (see the judgment at para.88). She had also written a letter in October 2001 to M disowning her as her mother and stating that she was not fit to call herself that, and concluding by wishing her dead. If the extreme language of the letter was caused by the stress P was undergoing at the time, she had had ample opportunity to retract those words but never did so and never communicated with M again. *Held*, on taking account of all the s.3 factors, the value judgment was that P's conduct outweighed all those in her favour. In those circumstances it was objectively reasonable that M's will of January 2009 made no provision for her and the claim was dismissed.

Section D—Persons Treated as Children of the Family

F–124 *Re Callaghan (Deceased)* [1985] Fam.1 (Booth J, 12 July 1984). The deceased died intestate in September 1980, leaving net estate of £31,000, which his three sisters, all married and of modest means, would take on his intestacy. The applicant, who was born in 1937, was the stepson of the deceased, who came to live in the applicant's mother's house as a lodger in 1950. The deceased and the applicant's mother lived together as man and wife and the deceased treated the applicant as his son. The applicant married in 1960 and the two families maintained a close relationship. The deceased married the applicant's mother in 1972; she died in 1980 and the applicant and his wife cared for the deceased thereafter. The applicant and his wife lived in a council house which they intended to buy, and had a combined income of £11,750 per year. *Held*, relief under s.1(1)(d) was not restricted to infant children; also, the deceased had considerable obligations and responsibilities towards the applicant, but none towards his sisters, and the estate derived from property owned by the applicant's mother; thus it would be reasonable to make provision for the applicant and he was awarded a lump sum of £15,000.

Commentary
S. Ross, "Surviving partners" (2006) 55 F.L.J. 10

F–125 *Re Leach, Leach v Lindeman* [1986] Ch. 226, CA (O'Connor, Slade, Robert Goff LJJ, 3 April 1985) on appeal from Michael Wheeler QC sitting as a deputy High Court judge, [1984] Fam. Law 274, 8 December 1983. The deceased (M) died intestate on 7 October 1981, leaving net estate of £34,000, which on intestacy passed to her two sisters and her brother. M was the second wife of the applicant's father (B). His first wife died in 1959; B and M married in July 1960 when he was 72 and she was 52. B died in 1974, leaving his estate of £3,500 mainly to M. From 1949 to 1980 the applicant had supported herself, and did not live with B and M, but she visited them frequently and there was an affectionate relationship between her and M. A few months before M died, she told the applicant that she wished her to be one of the executors of her will and to have half of her home. The applicant assumed that M had made a will to that effect. At that time she and a friend (Miss R) were living in a flat, and following the conversation between the applicant and M, they bought a house with the aid of a mortgage. *Held*, the evidence showed that M had expressly or impliedly assumed the position of a parent towards the applicant, and her treatment of the applicant after B's death was a material consideration if that treatment arose from the marriage. There were no grounds for interfering with the finding that reasonable provision was not made for the applicant by the disposition on intestacy. However, the award of £19,000 made at first instance was reduced to £14,000, it being common ground that the net estate had, by mistake, been thought to have a value of £45,000.

Commentary
R. Oughton, "Inheritance Act—provision for adult children" (1986) 83 L.S. Gaz. 93
P. Snow, "Former spouses now 'children of the family'—an unexpected effect of *Re Leach*" (1986) 83 L.S. Gaz. 1991
C. Barton, "Second families" (2003) 33 Fam. Law 249
S. Ross, "Surviving partners" (2006) 55 F.L.J. 10

Section E—Persons Being Maintained by the Deceased Immediately Before Their Death

Re B [2000] 1 All E.R. 665, CA, also reported as *Bouette v Rose* [2000] Ch. **F–126** 662, CA (Henry, Robert Walker LJJ, Alliott J, 7 December 1999), on appeal from Jonathan Parker J, [1999] Ch. 206, 22 January 1999. The applicant was the mother of the deceased (L), who was born with severe mental and physical disabilities due to negligence at birth and died aged 14. The Court of Protection had administered the compensation and L had been looked after by B, to whom both capital and income had been paid to enable her to buy a house (held on trust as to 75 per cent for L and 25 per cent for B absolutely) and to care for L. The matter first came before the court as an application by B for leave to commence the proceedings out of time, and a strike-out application by the defendant. Master Bragge dismissed the strike-out application and exercised his discretion to give leave to proceed out of time in B's favour. Jonathan Parker J would have exercised his discretion in the same way but held that B had not been maintained by L immediately before her death. In arriving at that conclusion he was influenced by: (i) the purpose of the payments made by the Court of Protection, as evidenced by the statutory powers under which they were made; and (ii) the absence, as he saw it, of any assumption of responsibility. Reversing his decision, the Court of Appeal held that it must have been obvious to the officials of the Court of Protection that L's funds were to be used in a way that met B's financial and material needs and enabled her to look after L. There was nothing absurd in the notion of that court acting as the conscience of a patient and making provision for those to whom the patient, if of full mental capacity, would have felt an obligation; see *Re L (W.J.G.)* [1966] Ch. 135.

Commentary
S. Bridge, "For love or money? Dependent carers and family provision" (2000) 59 Camb. LJ 248
J.G. Ross Martyn, "Making provisions for carers" (2000) 14 T.E.L.J. 4
S. Ross, "Life after death" (2009) 91 F.L.J. 17
S. Ross, "Inheritance Act claims by dependants" (2010) 40 Fam. Law 490

Case comment
Re B (2000) 30 Fam. Law 316

F–127   *Baker v Bennett*, CA (Swinton Thomas, Butler-Sloss, Mummery LJJ, 4
         February 1998), on appeal from HH Judge Walker (Wandsworth County
         Court, 10 January 1997). The deceased (D) died intestate on 23 October
         1992, the sole beneficiary of the net estate of £96,000 being his son (R). The
         applicant (B) met D in 1980, when she was still married; her own marriage
         broke down in 1985 and her sexual and romantic relationship with him
         dated back to at least 1986, though she did not live with him but in her own
         flat. He made gifts of money to her from time to time and, at that date of his
         death, she had saved some £17,000 of that money; but at the time of the
         hearing she was living on income support of £78.69 per week and would
         shortly become eligible for a state pension. The judge at first instance found
         that the £17,000 did not amount to reasonable provision. She had been his
         part-time mistress for over six years; he had indeed promised to marry her,
         though it was found that he probably would not have kept that promise. R
         had not been dependent on D; he had his own home and regular job. The
         judge concluded that, had B not received any money in excess of her
         requirements from D over the years, an appropriate award would have been
         £30,000 (one-third of the net estate after allowing for the costs of admin-
         istration). He reduced that notional sum by £7,500, representing the extent
         to which he took the excess payments into account. The Court of Appeal
         found that, viewing the case in the round, there was nothing unreasonable in
         the order that he made and he was fully entitled to come to the conclusion
         that he did. The appellant (R) was ordered to pay B's costs personally, not
         out of the estate.

F–128   *Baynes v Hedger* [2009] 2 F.L.R. 767, CA (Sir Andrew Morritt C. Long-
         more, Goldring LJJ, 7 May 2009), on appeal from [2008] 2 F.L.R. 1805
         (Lewison J, 14 July 2008). Both Hetty (the original claimant) and Margot
         claimed as persons who were being maintained by Mary immediately before
         her death. The benefits which Margot received from Mary consisted of the
         house bought for her in 1978, income from a settlement made in 1972 of
         £2,000–£3,000 per year from 1996/1997 to 2003/2004, payments of about
         £8,000 per year in total for home help and grocery bills which also ceased in
         2003/2004 and when capital was advanced to Margot from the trust fund.
         On 24 August 2003, Mary consented to the capital of the settlement (then
         some £55,000) being advanced to Margot to pay for her care. Thereafter
         there were two one-off payments totalling £1,600 and a contribution of £50
         per month which did little more than cover the cost of her visits to Margot.
         There was no evidence of Mary providing in any other way for Margot's
         care thereafter. *Held*, the words "was making a substantial contribution" in
         s.1(3) of the Act suggested a continuing action on the part of the donor, not
         a one-off, completed act. Providing rent-free accommodation or allowing
         someone to live in one's property at a concessionary rent could be a con-
         tinuous provision, but an outright gift of a house 30 years previously was
         not. That contribution towards Margot's reasonable needs was made when
         the gift was made and the house became Margot's house to do as she pleased
         with. As to the advances out of the settlement, once the money had been
         settled it ceased to be Mary's money. The fact that Mary was a trustee of the
         settlement and thus a party to the exercise of the power of advancement did
         not alter that. Those contributions to Margot's maintenance came from the
         settlement, not from Mary. Thus, Margot was not being maintained by

Mary immediately before her death. In Hetty's case, from 1986 until shortly before Mary's death there was a continuous history of her getting into financial difficulties and Mary rescuing her, sometimes with gifts, and at other times with loans which were to be repaid on various terms. Lewison J identified payments of £3,000 plus a generous Christmas present in 2004, and about £8,200 in 2005, part of which were so-called "stop-gap" payments which were expected to be repaid. He concluded that, by a narrow margin, these payments were "substantial". He was also persuaded that, in so far as the sums paid by Mary were loans to Hetty, they were "soft" loans, that is, they were interest-free, would not be enforced, did not have to be repaid and were in fact unlikely to be repaid. They were therefore made for less than full valuable consideration and qualified as maintenance. Hetty was therefore eligible to make a claim as having been partly maintained by Mary immediately before her death. However, he found that the will did not fail to make reasonable provision for her and dismissed her claim. Among the factors leading to that conclusion were two particular aspects of Hetty's conduct; the way in which she had dealt with the substantial assets that Mary had given her over the years, and the pressure which she was exerting on Mary towards the end of her life to make further financial support available to her. On Hetty's appeal, it was accepted on her behalf that an assumption of responsibility for the claimant's maintenance was an essential ingredient in the qualification of a person entitled to make a claim under s.1(1)(e), though it has been generally accepted since *Jelley v Iliffe* [1981] Fam. 128 that the fact of maintenance raises at least a rebuttable presumption that responsibility had been assumed. Sir Andrew Morritt's analysis of this question was that, in order for Lewison J to conclude (as he did) that Hetty was being maintained by Mary immediately before her death, he must have considered whether Mary had assumed responsibility for Hetty's maintenance; but the facts which he found did not support such a conclusion. In his judgment, the payment of those debts was not "maintenance" for the purposes of Hetty's claim, and she knew that Mary had disclaimed any responsibility for her continuing support. Therefore, she was not being partly maintained by Mary immediately before her death. The question whether the will had failed to make reasonable provision for her did not arise, though had it done so, he would agree with Lewison J that it did not.

Commentary
S. Ross, "Terms of endearment" (2009) 90 F.L.J. 22
S. Ross, "Life after death" (2009) 91 F.L.J. 17
D. Bailey, "Keeping it in the family" (2010) 118 T.E.L. & T.J. 17

Case comment
Baynes v Hedger (2009) 39 Fam. Law 666

Re Beaumont, Martin v Midland Bank Trust Co [1980] Ch. 444 (Megarry J, **F–129** 25 May 1979). The applicant, who was aged 77 at the date of hearing, and the testatrix, who died aged 79, lived together in her house as man and wife from 1940 until her death in 1976. By her will, made in 1974, she made no provision for the applicant but left her net estate of £17,000 to her three sisters. In 1975 she nominated savings certificates worth £550 to him. The applicant, who received a state pension after his retirement in 1964, together with earnings from part-time employment, had paid for his accommodation since 1945, had contributed towards the household expenses and did work around the house. The application was dismissed, it being held that the applicant was not a person maintained by the deceased but that they were two persons of independent means who had chosen to pool their resources and live together without either undertaking responsibility for maintaining the other.

Commentary
M. Warner, "The state of the relationship" (2004) 35 F.L.J. 19
S. Ross, "Life after death" (2009) 91 F. L.J. 17
S. Ross, "Inheritance Act claims by dependants" (2010) 40 Fam. Law 490

F–130   *Bishop v Plumley* [1991] 1 W.L.R. 582, CA (Purchas and Butler-Sloss LJJ, Sir Patrick O'Connor, 28 June 1990) on appeal from HH Judge Fallon QC sitting as a High Court judge. The testator died in November 1984, having by his will, made in 1974, left his entire estate (no details of which are reported) to his son and daughter. He and the applicant, who were each married to other people, lived together from 1973, with a short break in 1974 during which they returned to their respective spouses, until his death in November 1984, aged 49. In January 1984, as a result of receiving a legacy from an uncle, the deceased bought a house in which the applicant lived rent-free with him until his death. It was found by the judge, and accepted by the Court of Appeal, that the applicant was dependent on the deceased only during the period in 1984 when she was living rent-free in his house. During that time she nursed him devotedly during his illness. Both the registrar and the judge had taken the view that her contribution to his needs by looking after him at least balanced, if not outweighed, the benefit that she obtained from living rent-free. The Court of Appeal rejected this approach and held that the care provided by the applicant had to be looked at in the context of the relationship as a whole. He had made a substantial contribution to her reasonable needs by providing that accommodation. The case was remitted to the registrar to consider whether an order for financial provision should be made.

Commentary
S. Bridge, "Money for nothing? Family provision in dire straits" (1991) 50 Camb. LJ 42
F. Bates, "Housekeepers, companions and family provision—a comparative interlude" [1993] Conv. 270
S. Ross, "Inheritance Act claim by dependants" (2010) 40 Fam. Law 490

Case comment
Bishop v Plumley (1991) 21 Fam. Law 61

F–131   *Re C* (1979) 123 S.J. 35; also reported as *In the estate of McC* (1979) 9 Fam. Law 26 and as *CA v CC, The Times*, 17 November 1978. Application by illegitimate infant son, and by his mother as a dependant. See s.C(1).

F–132   *Re Campbell* [1983] N.I. 10 (Murray J). Claim by son and by grandson claiming as a person being maintained by the deceased immediately before his death. See s.C(1).

Cattle v Evans [2011] W.T.L.R. 947; [2011] EWHC 945 (Ch) (Kitchin J,   F–133
Chancery Division, Cardiff District Registry, 6 April 2011, B). 1975 Act claim on the alternative bases that the claimant was either a cohabitant within s.1(1)(ba) or a dependant within s.1(1)(e). The claimant succeeded on her claim as a cohabitant. See s.BA.

Churchill v Roach [2004] 2 F.L.R. 989. 1975 Act claim on the alternative   F–134
bases that the claimant was either a cohabitant within s.1(1)(ba) or a dependant within s.1(1)(e). The claim as a cohabitant failed but the claim as a dependant succeeded. For the full summary, see s.BA.

Clark v Jones, CA (Robert Goff and Dillon LJJ, 2 December 1985, LN,   F–135
T523) on appeal from HH Judge Mott (Wolverhampton County Court, 8 July 1985). The application at first instance was on behalf of the deceased's widow and the present respondent, Mrs Clark. Only the award to the latter was challenged on appeal. The deceased died intestate on 7 December 1983, aged 58, leaving net estate of some £34,000. On his intestacy his four married sisters were entitled to his estate. At first instance the widow was awarded £11,000 and Mrs Clark £6,000. Mrs Clark's weekly income was approximately £63 from all sources. Her association with the deceased had lasted some three years and Judge Mott took the view that it was likely to have been long-lasting. For the appellant it was said that the award was too high as Mrs Clark had been dependent on the deceased to the extent of only £500 per year rather than the amount in excess of £1,000 at which the judge had arrived. For the respondent it was said that the award was too low, the dependency being £2,004 per year. Per Dillon LJ the approach of calculating a dependency and a multiplier may be convenient in such cases but there was no hard and fast rule. There was no basis for interfering with the judge's conclusion and the appeal was dismissed, costs to be paid from the estate.

Graham v Murphy [1997] 1 F.L.R. 860 (Robert Walker J, 25 June 1996). The   F–136
applicant (G) and the deceased (M) had lived together from 1976 until her death in 1994 and for the last nine years of that period they had lived in houses owned by M. She died intestate and her estate (about £240,000 after discharge of her liabilities and of Inheritance Tax) passed to her parents, who were not in any financial need. During the last few years of the relationship M's health deteriorated and G cared for her to some extent. G was 54 at the date of the hearing, and was taking home about £200 per week, some £30 per week less than his expenditure. He had savings of £3,000 but an overdraft of £5,000 incurred for the purpose of funding the litigation. It was found that M was de facto maintaining G for the last nine years of the relationship by providing him with free accommodation and the good things of a consumer society. Having regard to that, to the absence of any other dependency or strong moral claim, the length of the relationship, and such care as he gave her, the distribution of her estate on intestacy was not such as to make reasonable financial provision for him. He was awarded £35,000 and a three-quarters interest in a Discovery motor vehicle whose value was £10,000, making a total of £42,500. The Calderbank offer made to him was

"too close to call" to the value of the award, so G was awarded one third of his costs on the standard basis.

Commentary
J. Piggott and M. Windram, "Cohabitants and the Inheritance Act-extending the boundaries" (2004) 34 Fam. Law 820

Case comment
Graham v Murphy (1997) 27 Fam. Law 393

F–137 *Gully v Dix* [2004] 1 F.L.R. 918, CA (Ward, Mummery, Rix LJJ, 21 January 2004), on appeal from HH Judge Weeks QC, Bristol District Registry. Claim as cohabitant and as dependant, summarised in s.BA and also noted in s.G as there was a preliminary issue. This case was considered in *Kotke v Saffarini* [2005] EWCA Civ 221, a dependency claim under the Fatal Accidents Act 1976, in which the issue was whether the claimant had been living as the wife of the deceased and in the same household for a period of two years before his death, as is required by s.1(3)(b) of that Act in order to establish a dependency claim. See also *Pounder v London Underground Ltd* [1995] P.I.Q.R. 217.

Commentary
J. Piggott and M. Windram, "Cohabitants and the Inheritance Act—extending the boundaries" (2004) 34 Fam. Law 820
M. Warner, "The state of the relationship" (2004) 35 F.L.J. 19
S. Pedley, "They don't always get what they want" (2005) 155 N.L.J. 448

Case comment
R. Bailey-Harris (2004) 34 Fam. Law 334

F–138 *Re Haig, Powers v Haig* [1979] 129 N.L.J. 420 (Browne-Wilkinson J, 22 February 1979). The testator died leaving a net estate £57,000 to his son. The applicant, who was 73, had lived with him for the three years preceding his death. She had moved most of her furniture to the new house which he had bought and had looked after him when he became ill. *Held*, the will did not make reasonable provision for her. As her assets were sufficient if she could live rent-free, the house should be sold and the proceeds applied to the purchase of a new house for her. Since the son lived nearby and the two were on bad terms, it would not be appropriate to provide for her by giving her permission to remain in the testator's house.

F–139 *Harrington v Gill* (1983) 4 F.L.R. 265, CA (Ormrod, Dunn LJJ, Waterhouse J, 3 June 1981) on appeal from Hollings J, 5 November 1980. The deceased, aged 77, died intestate in July 1977 leaving net estate £65,000, which passed to his sister. The applicant and the deceased, each of whom had been married before, had lived together in his house as husband and wife for a little under six years, though she retained the tenancy of her council flat. During that time she performed the duties of a housewife and he paid all the outgoings. The applicant, who was 74 at the date of hearing, had capital of £1,400 and a state pension of £27 per week. She continued to live in the deceased's house and gave up the tenancy of her council flat in April 1980.

At first instance she was awarded £5,000 together with the income of a further £5,000. The applicant appealed on the ground that the order did not make reasonable provision for her accommodation and the defendant cross-appealed against the finding that she had been maintained by the deceased. The cross-appeal was dismissed and the appeal was allowed, the court ordering that the house be settled on her for life.

Jelley v Iliffe [1981] Fam. 128, CA (Stephenson, Cumming-Bruce, Griffiths   **F–140**
LJJ, 16 December 1980) on appeal from Bush J, 12 June 1980. The deceased died on 8 April 1979 leaving net estate of about £18,700, the principal asset being the house in which she lived. She was the widow of the applicant's brother-in-law. In 1972 she made a will leaving her estate to her children. They had been entitled to the house under their father's will, but had conveyed it to her on the understanding that she would leave it to them. From 1971 she and the applicant lived together. He paid no rent; they pooled their old age pensions, he did household and gardening jobs, she cooked and washed for him. The registrar struck out the application on the ground that the evidence disclosed no reasonable cause of action and Bush J dismissed the applicant's appeal from that decision. *Held*, allowing the appeal, the provision of rent-free accommodation was a substantial benefit and, unless the applicant's contributions equalled or outweighed that, there was an arguable case that he was being maintained by her. The provision of the accommodation for eight years amounted to an assumption of responsibility for his maintenance. The application to strike out ought not to have been granted and the matter should proceed to trial.

Commentary
F. Bates, "Housekeepers, companions and family provision—a comparative interlude" [1993] Conv. 270
J. Piggott and M. Windram, "Cohabitants and the Inheritance Act—extending the boundaries" (2004) 34 Fam. Law 820
M. Warner, "The state of the relationship" (2004) 35 F.L.J. 19
S. Ross, "Life after death" (2009) 91 F.L.J 17
S. Ross, "Inheritance Act claims by dependants" (2010) 40 Fam. Law 490

King v Dubrey [2016] Ch. 221, *sub nom. King v The Chiltern Dog Rescue*   **F–141**
[2015] W.T.L.R. 1225, CA (Jackson, Patten, Sales LJJ, 9 June 2015) affirming in part [2014] W.T.L.R. 1411 (Charles Hollander QC sitting as a deputy High Court judge, 1 July 2014). See also s.G. The claimant (K) claimed in the alternative for a declaration that his deceased aunt (J) had made a valid *donatio mortis causa* of her house in his favour, and for financial provision out of her estate as a dependant. The relevant parts of the judgments are paras 53–67 of the judgment at first instance and paras 77–82 of Jackson LJ's judgment on the appeal, in which the parties requested the Court of Appeal to determine the issue of quantum rather than to remit it for reconsideration. At first instance it was concluded, on the basis of the following findings of fact, that he was a dependant within the meaning of s.1(1)(e): (1) he moved into J's house in 2007 for the purpose of caring for her, which he did until her death in 2011; (2) in return, he received board and lodging, expenses and small sums of money; (3) that arrangement involved an assumption of responsibility on both sides; (4) with minor

exceptions, K did not work during that period, nor could he realistically could he have done so. He had not worked since J's death and was unable to maintain himself. Following the approach in *Jelley v Iliffe* [1981] Fam. 128, CA, a realistic analysis of the dependency would be that there was maintenance in money and money's worth for a lengthy period and an assumption of responsibility for such maintenance by J to a considerable extent and on a settled basis. Matters relevant to the assessment of quantum were that K, aged 58, was unlikely to get much further employment and had no significant assets nor a home, other than J's property; that the property, valued at £350,000, was the only significant asset of the estate; that the benefit in money and money's worth which he received was modest and was received over a period of only four years; that there were no other claimants under the Act and it was not suggested that the charities had relevant financial needs. For K it was submitted that an appropriate award might be a sum of £100,000–£150,000 which would enable him to purchase a small flat in the area, but this was considered to overstate the dependency under the Act. K was awarded £75,000. On appeal it was argued for the charities that the judgment was not properly reasoned and that £40,000, which would provide K with support for two years at £20,000 per year, was the most that could be justified. It was again argued for K that £150,000 would be a proper award. Jackson LJ considered that both parties were wrong and the judge was right. He had taken into account all relevant factors and their evaluation was a matter for him. The appellate court would interfere only if there had been an error of law or the award had been outside the permissible bracket. Accordingly, it was upheld.

F–142   *Kourgky v Lusher* [1983] 4 F.L.R. 65; [1982] 12 Fam. Law 86 (Wood J, 8 December 1981). The deceased died intestate on 7 August 1979 leaving net estate £1,975; his severable share of the joint tenancy of the matrimonial home was valued at £27,500. The deceased and the defendant, his widow, were married in 1939. The applicant and the deceased met in 1963, and in 1969 the deceased left his wife and went to live with her. The relationship continued intermittently for 10 years, towards the end of which he became increasingly reluctant to support her. By the beginning of 1979 it could be inferred that he had divested himself of permanent financial responsibility for the applicant. In the last month of his life he went on holiday with his wife and did not cohabit with the applicant again. *Held* (a) the discretion under s.9 would not be exercised; (b) the applicant was not being maintained by the deceased immediately prior to his death; she had a half interest in a house worth £25,000, she had other, undisclosed sources of income and could seek financial support from her family, while the defendant owned the matrimonial home and had an income of £4,800; and (c) in view of the above matters and the fact that the net estate was only £1,975, the applicant had failed to show that reasonable financial provision had not been made for her.

F–143   *Re Kozdrach, Sobesto v Szczepanska and Farren* Conv. [1981] 224 (Ewbank J, 7 April 1981, LN, T654). There had been an interlocutory appeal (heard by Denning MR and Donaldson LJ on 9 November 1979) from HH Judge Dow, sitting as a High Court judge. The deceased, a doctor in his 60s, who had been practising in England for 30 years, died intestate on 6 August 1978, his only known relative being a sister in Poland of a similar age to himself. The estate was £52,000 subject to payment of capital transfer tax. The applicant, a woman in her early 30s, and the deceased, had lived together as man and wife for some four or five years. She was able to earn her own living and there was nothing to stop them marrying. She was awarded £19,000 and, if she paid £9,000 to the estate within six months, the deceased's house, valued at £28,000 at the date of the hearing, was to be transferred to her. All parties' costs to be paid out of the estate, up to £3,000 on the common fund basis, the remainder on the party and party basis.

Malone v Harrison [1979] 1 W.L.R. 1353 (Hollings J, 25 May 1979). The **F–144** testator died on 25 July 1977, aged 71, leaving net estate £480,563. The deceased's marriage, of which there was one child, had broken down in 1939, but the deceased maintained her during the rest of his life. In 1958 he formed a relationship with CM, who brought her four-year-old son with her. They lived as man and wife and CM became known as CH, eventually changing her name to Harrison by deed poll in 1973. The deceased met the applicant in 1965 and in October 1965 they went abroad for a holiday, after which he maintained her for the rest of his life. During the 12 years of the relationship he gave her shares worth £15,000, a flat in Malta and a flat in Sutton Coldfield, a car, furs and jewellery. The total value of the assets was £34,320, plus £500 per year with interest remittable from Malta. At the time of the hearing she was 38 and earning £23 per week looking after old people. There were seven beneficiaries under his will, the most substantial being his brother, RH, who received shares worth £192,000. *Held*, (a) the deceased had fully maintained the deceased for 12 years on the basis that she would not be left unprovided for after his death; (b) any order made should be on the basis that the applicant would have to resort to capital as well as income, but the value of her home should not be treated as expendable capital; and (c) she should receive £4,000 per year in total. She was awarded a lump sum of £19,000 calculated on a multiplier/multiplicand basis, the award representing the difference between the £42,000 so calculated and her free capital of £23,000.

McIntosh v McIntosh [2013] W.T.L.R. 1565 (Lindsay Davies, Luton CC, 19 **F–145** August 2013). The deceased (K) died unexpectedly on 13 September 2010, aged 34, intestate, leaving net estate £333,564. He was a member of two pension schemes. He was survived by his estranged wife (A), his mother and two siblings, a sister and a brother (B), eight years younger, who was the claimant. A was nominated to receive 100 per cent of the benefits under one scheme and 70 per cent under the other; B received £4,316.45, which was 10 per cent of the benefits under that scheme. Following the death of his father in 1997 when B was aged 13, he had become entitled to a dependant's pension, which his mother had put into a savings account; however, he had spent most of the £15,000 thus accumulated before K's death and had never claimed any state benefits. B had never led any independent existence or obtained any but occasional work. He had suffered a major, but treatable, depressive disorder, but had never undergone treatment for it. B's case was that since his father's death, K had taken on a fatherly role towards him. He had given him £200 per month since he was 16, except during his periods of employment, and had paid for his clothes, car, car insurance and an annual

holiday. B had spent that money on cigarettes, alcohol, petrol and socialising. Food and lodging, towards which he made no contribution, had been
provided by his mother but it was not envisaged that that would continue.
Held, the money given by K to B was not given for full valuable consideration but it was not a substantial contribution to his reasonable needs;
those needs did not include smoking, drinking and socialising. B had not
satisfied the court that K had assumed responsibility for his maintenance or
that there was a relationship of dependency accepted by him and K, *Baynes
v Hedger* [2008] 2 F.L.R. 1805 applied. On the contrary, the arrangement
subsisted only for as long as K allowed it, and neither party saw it as a
continuing or long-term obligation. It followed that B was not a person
being maintained by K for the purposes of s.1(1)(e) and his claim was
dismissed.

Case comment
H. Cumber [2014] Eld. LJ 4(1), 31

F–146   *Musa v Holliday* [2013] 1 F.L.R. 806, CA (Sir Nicholas Wall P, Lloyd and
Sullivan LJJ, 15 October 2012). Ramadan Guney (R), who was born in
Cyprus, had died intestate in November 2006, survived by D, with whom he
had had a relationship, their teenage son (H), and the six adult children of
his marriage. Claims for provision out of his estate, as dependants, were
made by D, H, and K, the adult son of D's previous marriage. At first
instance HH Judge Kushner QC found that R had died domiciled in England and Wales. He had assets within the jurisdiction (the value of which the
judge estimated at £2 million) and in Northern Cyprus. After allowing for
potential liabilities and administration costs Judge Kushner valued the net
estate within the jurisdiction at about £1 million. The principal assets were
shares in a cemetery company (Brookwood) and associated property rights,
the family home, a rented property (60 Green Lanes) and a share in another
property (58 Green Lanes) forming part of the estate of R's deceased wife.
The award to D included provision for the schooling and long-term edu-
cational needs of H. The effect of the judge's order was that D received the
shares in Brookwood (but assuming the risk of satisfying any outstanding
tax liabilities of Brookwood) and the family home free of mortgage, the
mortgage being discharged so far as possible from the estate's share of 58
Green Lanes and the shortfall from the proceeds of sale of 60 Green Lanes.
The children of the marriage appealed in relation to the finding on domicile
and that appeal was dismissed; see *Holliday v Musa* [2010] 2 F.L.R. 702, CA,
summarised in s.G. They also sought leave to appeal the order made in
favour of D; she cross-appealed by respondent's notice in relation to the
effect of the judge's order on the incidence of liabilities (including administration costs) of R's estate. Leave to appeal was granted and the appeal
was dismissed. The respondent's notice was also dismissed but the judge's
order was varied in order to clarify the liability for administration costs.
Held, per Wall P at [26]–[34]: (1) the judge was exercising a judicial discretion in difficult circumstances and had not erred in law or principle; if (which
was not accepted) the decision to award her the bulk of the English estate
was harsh on the family, they had only themselves to blame for the manner
in which they conducted the litigation; (2) if the judge concluded that the
transfer of the principal asset (the shares) was necessary to achieve the

statutory objective there could be no objection in principle to it (see also Lloyd LJ at [54]); (3) the case was one which cried out for a clean break and on the facts presented to the judge an outright transfer of the family home was not an inappropriate decision (see also Lloyd LJ at [52]–[53]); (4) it was common ground that the deceased did not make reasonable provision for D and their son and the proposition that the court should interfere as little as possible with the deceased's dispositions had to yield to the facts of the case; (5) per Lloyd LJ at [58]–[62], the respondent's notice would be dismissed but the judge's order would be varied to make it clear that the proceeds of sale of 60 Green Lanes were not subject to the burden of testamentary and administration expenses, which were to be borne in the first instance by the assets awarded to D.

Rhodes v Dean, CA (Nourse, Ward, Schiemann LJJ, 28 March 1996, LN, W(ca), T639) on appeal from HH Judge Micklem, sitting as a High Court judge. The testator (D) died in 1989, by which time he had been living with the applicant (R) for about four years. By his will, made in 1986, he divided his estate (roughly £100,000 net) equally between his son, his daughter and his two granddaughters. R received nothing. It was found that R was substantially dependent on D before his death and that, at that time, she had capital of £35,869 in a joint account with D and a pension of £26.60 per week. She was not in a position to earn her own living. At first instance it was found that D had assumed responsibility for providing accommodation for R but not for the rest of her maintenance needs. She had enjoyed a high standard of living while she was with R but keeping up that standard was not the measure of her need. She had spent about three quarters of the money in the joint account in the 13 months after R's death. That money could have been used either to provide her with accommodation suitable to her needs or to enhance her income. It was, therefore, reasonable for D to have made no provision for her out of the estate. The Court of Appeal held that the judge was perfectly entitled to come to that conclusion and dismissed the appeal.

F–147

Rees v Newbery and the Institute of Cancer Research [1998] 1 F.L.R. 1041 (HH Judge Gilliland QC sitting as a judge of the Chancery Division, 30 July 1997). The deceased (L) died at the end of 1993 aged 79, unmarried and without issue. By his will dated 3 May 1979 he left his residuary estate, consisting of some £250,000 in cash, and residential property valued at £485,000, among three charities and a benevolent fund. The applicant (R) and L had met in 1960. While L was in the business of buying and letting out property, he also worked as an actor, and it was in that way that he met and became a close friend of R, an impecunious actor. In 1984, R moved into a flat in premises owned by L, paying rent of £200 per month. In October 1993, L gave instructions for a will to be drawn up whereby the premises would be devised to the Royal Opera House Covent Garden Benevolent Fund ("the Fund") subject to R's right to remain in the flat for life at the same rent adjusted to take account of inflation, the remainder to go to charities. However, he died before the draft will had been finalised and the 1979 will was proved. R's application was on the basis that, as a person paying rent substantially below the market rent, he was being wholly or partly maintained by L, and that the will did not make reasonable provision

F–148

for his maintenance. He sought to be allowed to stay in the flat, as L had intended that he should. It was held that since it was clear that L had intended that R should continue living in the flat for as long as he wished at a rent substantially below the market rent, both s.1(3) and s.3(4) were satisfied. Although there was a tenancy agreement, the relationship was one of friendship rather than of landlord and tenant. Where the competition was between those whom the testator wished to benefit but who in fact had not benefited, and those whom he wished to, and who did, benefit, his wishes could be given greater weight than would normally be the case. However, since in the circumstances the premises would have to be sold if the residuary beneficiaries were to receive their shares within a reasonable time, the appropriate order was to make a payment to R which took account of the capitalised value of the difference between the open market rent and the rent payable by R. Using the Ogden tables, the difference of £4,650 between those two figures would be capitalised, on the basis of a yield of 4.5 per cent, at £65,565 for a man aged 50. After some minor adjustments R was awarded £64,000, to be treated as a pecuniary legacy and carry interest from the date of handing down the judgment.

F–149   *Re Viner, Kreeger v Cooper* [1978] C.L.Y. 3091 (Master Chamberlain, 25 January 1978, W(ca)). The testator died in April 1976, leaving net estate £44,202 subject to capital transfer tax. He had two sisters, one of whom, aged 71, was the applicant. She had been widowed a year before the testator's death and was in difficult financial circumstances. For some time he had been paying his other sister £10 per week. He was reluctantly persuaded by her to maintain the applicant, which he did for six months before his death by dividing the £10 equally between them. By his will dated 7 March 1975, he gave the other sister an annuity of £520 per year, but left the applicant nothing. *Held*, that as she had been maintained grudgingly, provision should be restricted to what she had received during the testator's lifetime; as a weekly payment of £5 would affect her rent and rate rebates, she was awarded a lump sum of £2,000.

F–150   *Re Wilkinson, Neale v Newell* [1978] Fam. 22 (Arnold J, 5 May 1977). The testatrix died on 23 May 1975, leaving £5,000 and such furniture and household articles as she should choose, to her sister, the applicant, and the residue of her estate to the respondent. The respondent appealed against the registrar's decision that the applicant was a person entitled, within s.1(1)(e) of the Act, to apply for reasonable financial provision out of her sister's estate. The applicant was 68 at the time of the hearing. She had been living with the testatrix for some seven years. The whole of the household expenses were paid by the testatrix; the applicant did some housework and cooking. *Held*, it was irrelevant whether there was a contract under which those services had been provided; and (with uncertainty) that they did not constitute full valuable consideration for the benefits received by the applicant. Accordingly, the appeal would be dismissed.

F–151   *Williams v Roberts* [1986] 1 F.L.R. 349; [1984] Fam. Law 210 (Wood J, 9 February 1984). The testator died on 12 March 1981 leaving gross estate of £110,000–£120,000, which, by his will dated, 16 January 1962, he left to be divided equally between his twin sisters. The applicant, who was 68 at the time of hearing, was widowed in 1946, there being two children of her marriage. The applicant and the testator met and became friendly in 1969. He moved into a guesthouse run by the applicant. From 1971 they lived together as man and wife. He helped in the running of the guesthouse, made weekly payments for board and lodging as well as lump sum contributions, and bought clothing and furniture for the applicant. In 1975 they bought land intending to build a retirement home, which was conveyed into his name; in 1977 they became engaged. The applicant had a house which would be worth £23,000 after renovation, £1,000 in the bank, and £60 per week derived from her pension and the rent of flats into which the guest-house had been converted. The two defendants each had a pension of £33 per week, capital of about £2,000 and a half-share in the house where they lived, worth £10,000. *Held*, there was no doubt that the applicant was a dependant of the deceased; he would have continued to make regular pay-ments to her if he had survived; she was awarded £20,000 and her costs out of the estate.

Wright-Gordon v Legister, reported *sub. nom Gordon v Legister* [2014] **F–152** W.T.L.R. 1675 (Master Bowles, 20 June 2014). *Note*: This case was decided before the coming into force of the Inheritance and Trustees' Powers Act 2014 and the judgment at paras 23–25 relating to assumption of responsi-bility, at paras 26–32 relating to maintenance, and at paras 52–57 in relation to full valuable consideration, should now be read in the light of the amendment to s.3(4) of the 1975 Act by Sch.2 para.5 and to s.1(3) by Sch.2 para.3, of the 2014 Act. The deceased (AL) died intestate on 1 February 2012 and letters of administration were granted to his brother (IL). The principal asset of AL's estate was a four-bedroom property in south-east London ("The Property") worth about £285,000, in which IL had lived with his brother since 1993. The claimant (A) moved into the Property in 2004 and lived with AL until 2008, when she married a Mr G. However, she returned when that marriage broke down in 2010 and was living with AL at the date of his death. It was conceded that her relationship with AL did not fulfil the requirements of s.1(1A); her claim was as a dependant under s.1(1)(e); nevertheless the nature of the relationship was relevant when considering whether AL had assumed any responsibility for A's main-tenance. The settled arrangement subsisting at the date of AL's death was that he had been providing A with rent-free accommodation, and the household tasks including cooking, cleaning and washing carried out by A as a member of the household, quasi-family member and friend did not amount to full valuable consideration. AL's provision of free, or cheap, accommodation for A for an extended time also demonstrated his assumption of responsibility. *Held* (1) on that footing, AL owed an obli-gation to A to ensure that, after his death, she was sufficiently provided for to resettle herself in suitable accommodation. The dispositions on his intestacy did not meet that obligation; (2) the yardstick for reasonable provision in this case was the cost to A of living in a shared home, which was currently £6,600 per year. Reasonable provision should also include some support while she was resettling herself and a modest amount for the expenses occasioned by her having to find a new home. A proper allowance would be two years' rent together with that support and contribution to expenses. She was awarded a lump sum payment of £16,500.

Section F—Time Limits

F–153   *A v C* [2009] N.I. Ch. 10 (Deeny J, Chancery Division, Northern Ireland, 16
November 2009, B). Application by former cohabitant, on behalf of herself
and her infant son (AD) by the deceased (D), to commence proceedings out
of time. At the date of his death, D was paying maintenance for AD. The
period of cohabitation was for about two years at some time in the 1990s.
A's solicitors wrote a letter shortly after D's death, explaining that she was
the mother of D's child, AD, and inquiring about an endowment policy but
not intimating a claim. There was no reply and A did not pursue the matter
before probate was granted on 14 March 2008. The claim was issued on 10
July 2009, some 10 months out of time. It was found that she was in
employment, married to a man who was also in employment, had no further
children and was not in a position of need or dependence. There was a
degree of prejudice to E with whom D was cohabiting at the date of his
death; the estate had been administered and the personal representatives
were entitled to some finality. A's application on her own behalf was
refused. However, AD was in a different position. Although approaching
maturity, he was still a minor. He might be entitled to some pension benefits
which might require the assistance of the court and would have to be taken
into account. He could not be blamed for inactivity on the part of A or
anyone else. The application to proceed on his behalf was allowed.

F–154   *Adams v Schofield* [2004] W.T.L.R. 1049, CA (Ormrod and Dunn LJJ, Sir
Stanley Rees, 22 July 1981), on appeal from Reeve J, 23 June 1981. Claim by
widow, issued 19 days after expiry of the six-month period; leave to commence proceedings out of time refused by Reeve J. The court treated her
application for leave to appeal as the hearing of the appeal. Reeve J considered the guidelines in *Re Salmon* and found in her favour on all but one
of them; since the delay had been entirely the fault of the applicant's solicitor, she had a clear case against him and on that ground he refused leave.
Dunn LJ was not prepared to consider the existence of that remedy irrelevant, but in a case where the delay had been so short, the estate had not been
distributed, the executors and their solicitors had known from an early stage
that a claim would be made, and the applicant would be seriously prejudiced
if her claim were barred, he had no doubt that the decision below was wrong
in principle. Ormrod LJ considered that in a case where the prejudice to the
defendants was purely formal, in the sense that they have simply lost the
protection of s.4, the existence of the remedy was of little weight and to
confine the applicant to that remedy would be a bonus for the defendants,
as:

> "...the claim would be transferred to the shoulders of the solicitor's
> insurers, unnecessarily and quite contrary to the justice of the case."

Further, the remedy in damages would be difficult to assess. The appeal was
allowed.

Commentary
S. Ross, "Playing by the rules" (2007) 70 F.L.J. 7

Berger v Berger [2014] W.T.L.R 35, CA (Moses, Black, Gloster LJJ, 29   **F–155**
October 2013), dismissing the appeal from the order of HH Judge Hayward-
Smith QC on 5 February 2013 refusing permission to the claimant widow
(W) to commence her claim out of time. W and the deceased (H), both of
whom had been previously married, had lived together since 1969 and were
married in 1983. H died on 26 June 2005 and probate was granted on 27
January 2006. The major assets of the estate, which had a total value of
between £7–7.5 million were the matrimonial home (£2.5 million), a half
share in a property in Arizona (£467,000), three properties in London (£1.66
million in total) and the deceased's majority shareholding in a property
company (£2.89 million). The will provided for the matrimonial home to be
held upon trust for sale so as to enable W to live in it for as long as she
wished or to request that it be sold and an alternative property purchased
for her occupation. There were specific gifts of two of the London properties, to H's sons and to W's daughter by their respective previous marriages.
The income of the residuary estate was directed to be held upon trust for W
for life with power to advance capital to her and thereafter for H's children
and grandchildren. W expressed concern about her income position within a
few months of H's death, her central complaint being that she was dependent on H's sons (who managed the properties from which the trust income
was derived) for her income and she never received either enough for her
needs or what was intended by the deceased (see the judgment at [62]). She
consulted a series of solicitors, but it does not appear that she was ever
advised at that time about the existence of the 1975 Act or of any possible
claims which she might have under it, and she is recorded at that time as
wishing to avoid litigation or disputes with other family members or the
executors. She did not seek any further advice until about August 2011 and
had not entirely overcome her reluctance to take proceedings by the end of
March 2012. There was then a delay because she had a heart attack at the
beginning of April and proceedings under the 1975 Act were finally brought
on 15 June 2012, almost six years out of time. At first instance the judge
considered that the absence of negotiations within the time limit, the position as to the administration of the estate and the position with regard to
alternative remedies did not point irresistibly to the dismissal of the claim.
He also thought that W did not have an arguable case on the merits, but the
factor which pointed inexorably to the dismissal of the claim was the failure
to act promptly. The lengthy delay without any good reason was fatal to the
claim. *Held*, on appeal (per Black LJ): (1) the judge's conclusion on the
merits of the claim was vitiated by his approach to a material factor, namely
what W might reasonably have expected to receive on divorce; (2) the fact
that the estate had not been fully distributed and the residue was sufficient to
fund any provision that might be made for W was important but not
determinative; (3) the judge was right to focus on the very significant delay
in commencing proceedings (citing the passage in *Re Salmon* [1981] Ch. 167
at 175, which emphasised that s.4 was a substantive, not a procedural
provision); (4) the history of the claim, as well as the very substantial delay,
was relevant; the circumstances giving rise to the claim had not been
brought about by a particular event (cf. *Stock v Brown* [1994] 1 F.L.R. 840
and *McNulty v McNulty* [2002] W.T.L.R. 737 where there had been such
events giving rise to claims long out of time). W had shown from the outset
that she was able to pursue her interests but for years she took no steps to do

so. In such circumstances it would not be appropriate for her to be permitted to make her claim six years out of time.

Commentary
H. Cumber, *Berger v Berger—How late is too late?* P.C.B. 2014 1, 32–36

Case comment
R. Hughes, Eld. LJ, 2014, 4(1), 29–30

F–156   *Budd v Fowler* [1999] C.L.Y. 4635 (HH Judge Morrell, Peterborough County Court, 3 December 1998). Application by husband (B) to commence proceedings out of time. His wife had excluded him from her will on the grounds of his unreasonable behaviour. B accepted £700 from the executors (F) in full and final settlement of all claims against the estate, including any 1975 Act claim, and executed a disclaimer to that effect. After the limitation period had expired, he notified the executors of his intention to make a claim under the 1975 Act. *Held*, (inter alia): (1) applying *Re Salmon*, there were no grounds for the delay. The appropriate test was whether B had reasonable grounds for making a claim and leave should only be refused if it was clear that there was no substantial issue to be tried; (2) B was bound by the disclaimer; agreements for value to compromise rights prior to the precipitating event could be distinguished from agreements to settle claims concerning statutory rights where the precipitating event had occurred and the claims were immediate; *Hyman v Hyman* and *Edgar v Edgar* distinguished. The application was dismissed on those and other grounds.

F–157   *Re Dennis* [1981] 2 All E.R. 140 (Browne-Wilkinson J, 10 November 1980). Application made on 22 February 1980 under s.4, for leave to bring proceedings out of time. The testator died on 21 November 1977 leaving a net estate of about £2.5 million. Probate of his will was granted on 14 January 1978. He had been married twice, the applicant, who was 38 at the time of the hearing, being the son and only child of the first marriage. The applicant had been given £90,000 during the testator's lifetime. By the will he was left £10,000, and £30,000 was left to the trustees of the will on protective trusts for him, the capital to go to his two children. The bulk of the estate went to the children of the second marriage subject to the second wife's life interest in the residue. No provision had been made for the first wife, who had made an application within the time limited by s.4 of the 1975 Act. The son's application had not been made until 19 months after the expiry of that time limit. It was specifically for a sum of £45,000–£50,000 to meet the capital transfer tax payable on the lifetime gift. *Held*, the application was not for maintenance, which connotes only payments that, directly or indirectly, enable the applicant to discharge the cost of his daily living at whatever standard is appropriate to him. The payment of debts may in some circumstances amount to maintenance, but the payment of this tax liability would not, directly or indirectly, contribute to his future cost of living. As the applicant had no arguable prospect of success and there had been a long delay, part of which was inexcusable, the application for leave to proceed out of time would be dismissed.

Commentary
M. Skinner, "Keeping it in the family" (2009) 159 N.L.J. 822

Escritt v Escritt (1982) 3 F.L.R. 280, CA (Ormrod and Oliver LJJ, Purchas **F–158**
J, 15 October 1981), on appeal from Sir John Arnold P. Application made
some three years out of time. The applicant widow had been advised, during
the six-month period, that she had a claim against her husband's estate
which was likely to succeed. She did not apply in time because she was afraid
of causing dissension within the family, and only did so after her health and
her financial position had deteriorated. At the time of the application, the
estate had not been distributed apart from one specific legacy of a parcel of
shares. *Held*, when a person entitled to apply fails to do so within the time
limit and afterwards repents that decision and applies out of time, and the
only point in her favour is that there has been no distribution, the case is not
strong enough to warrant giving permission to apply out of time. In such
circumstances the guidelines in *Re Salmon* (q.v.) have very little relevance.

Re Longley, Longley v Longley [1981] C.L.Y. 2885 (Judge Blackett-Ord, 19 **F–159**
November 1980, W(ca)). L died survived by his widow (D) with whom he
lived until his death, and a mistress (P) by whom he had a daughter. By his
will he left the house occupied by P to her and appointed her as executor.
The rest of his estate, some £24,000, was undisposed of and passed to D on
L's intestacy. P renounced probate in favour of D in order to make a claim
but although there was some correspondence, no claim was made by P until
14 months after a distribution had been made to D; however, the cash in the
estate remained as an identifiable fund in a building society. *Held*, applying
Re Salmon: (1) the court's discretion was unfettered; (2) D was aware of the
claim but no offer or prospect of a settlement was ever held out; (3) the cash
was still available and the court could make an order out of that fund; (4)
P's daughter, who was also a claimant, had a good case against her solicitors
and it was not the duty of the court to protect negligent solicitors. Given the
long delay before the claim was formulated and the existence of that remedy,
it was not appropriate to extend the time limit.

Commentary
G. Harbottle, "Tales of procrastination and pedantry" (2004) 56 T.E.L.J. 4

Moffat v Moffat [2016] N.I. Ch 17 (Horner J, 23 November 2016). The **F–160**
plaintiff, an adult child (whose age is not given in the report) brought claims
for provision out of the estates of her father (F) and mother (M). F died on 9
March 1994 and probate was granted on 7 June 1994. His will, dated 29 July
1983, recorded that he was not making any provision for the plaintiff or for
his son James, as they were not in need of any provision from him and
would not expect such provision. M, who had inherited a life interest in a
farm owned by F, and his residuary estate, under his will, died intestate on
11 October 2007 and letters of administration were granted to the defendant
(L), the other son of the marriage, on 14 June 2009. The proceedings were
commenced in December 2012. The relevant provision of the Inheritance
(Provision for Family and Dependants) (Northern Ireland) Order 1979 is
art.6 and in its application the Northern Ireland Court of Appeal has
commended the guidelines laid down in *Re Salmon* and *Re Dennis*; see

Campbell v Campbell [1982] 18. N.I.J.B. In the instant case the court acknowledged that if a claim was meritorious, or that it was brought about by unforeseen circumstances, those factors could outweigh a substantial delay (*Stock v Brown* [1994] 1 F.L.R. 840 and *Re C (deceased)* [1995] 2 F.L.R. 24 considered) but the merits of the claim were not decisive (*Berger v Berger* EWCA Civ 1305; [2014] W.T.L.R. 45, CA, considered). The plaintiff was a qualified teacher and there was no evidence of her being dependent on F at the time of his death. It was true that she had not seen the will until 1999 but eleven years had elapsed before she brought the proceedings, during which there had been no negotiations. The estate had long since been distributed and the delay, even if brought about by bad legal advice (which the court was not in a position to determine) was gross and inordinate. In those circumstances and following the guidelines, it was not a claim for which time should be extended. Her claim against M's estate was weak; it was difficult to see how, in the circumstances, the law of intestacy failed to make reasonable provision for her. The delay of three and a half years before bringing the claim was unexplained. Permission to bring that claim was also refused.

F–161   *Nesheim v Kosa* [2007] W.T.L.R. 149 (Briggs J, 4 October 2006), on appeal from Master Price. This case is concerned with the principles relevant to a grant of retrospective permission to amend defective service and the principal facts are summarised in s.G. The result of the procedural irregularities was that the 1975 Act proceedings had not been commenced in time. On that aspect of the case, Briggs J considered that the principles laid down in *Re Salmon* [1981] Ch. 167 were called into play where the remedy of a defect in service would deprive the defendant of the benefit of the limitation period under the 1975 Act, being plainly relevant to the question of the extent to which a defendant might be prejudiced by remedying the defect. However, he considered that prejudice to be at a very low level, because it was inevitable that an application under s.4 to commence proceedings out of time would be made and, given that there was an early intimation of the claim, sensible requests for information had been made and discussion had taken place, there was a clear indication that the claim had been issued on 5 July 2005 and the estate had not been distributed, the *Re Salmon* criteria would tend to favour that application. As to the availability of a remedy against K's solicitors, Briggs J observed that the relief sought in the claim was principally the transfer of the matrimonial home to him, or a grant of a life interest or other right to reside in it. A financial remedy would be of little use to an elderly man in poor health who had lived in the matrimonial home for many years and wished to go on doing so. For guidance on the weight to be attached to the existence of a remedy against the claimant's solicitor (which was not considered in *Nesheim v Kosa*), see *Adams v Schofield* [2004] W.T.L.R. 1049.[7] In that case it was held that, having found in favour of the claimant on all the other *Re Salmon* guidelines, the judge at first instance should not have decided against her solely on the ground that she had a remedy against her solicitor.

---

[7] Judgment was given on 16 July 1981 but the case remained unreported until resurrected by publication in W.T.L.R.

Re Salmon, Coard v National Westminster Bank [1981] Ch. 167 (Megarry   **F–162**
VC, 27 June 1980). The testator died on 11 October 1978, aged 83. By his
will, made on 16 June 1961, he left his net estate of about £75,000 to his
sister and two elderly lady friends. The parties were married on 12 April
1932. The marriage was unhappy and the applicant finally left the testator in
1944 and never saw him again, though the marriage was never dissolved.
She formed a stable relationship with a Mr Coard in 1953 and they lived
together as man and wife until his death in 1974. Probate was granted on 15
December 1978 and after an informal approach to the executors on behalf
of the applicant had been rejected, legal aid was applied for on 24 April
1979. The time limit passed without the applicant's solicitor noticing the
fact, and legal aid was not granted until 30 July 1979. After various further
delays, the originating summons was issued on 27 November 1979, nearly
six months out of time. During the period between the expiry of the time
limit and the issue of the summons, most of the estate had been distributed.
The application to issue proceedings out of time was refused for the following reasons (i) there had been a substantial delay, and the executors had
not been warned of the proposed proceedings until over four months after
the time limit had passed; (ii) the fault was entirely on the applicant's side;
(iii) the explanations for the delay were not adequate; and (iv) during the
period of delay, almost all the estate had been distributed. The time limit
was substantive, not procedural, and the applicant, on whom the burden
lay, had failed to make out a case for extending it.

Commentary
G. Harbottle, "Tales of procrastination and pedantry" (2004) 56 T.E.L.J. 4
S. Ross, "Playing by the rules" (2007) 70 F.L.J. 7
M. Skinner, "Keeping it in the family" (2009) 159 N.L.J. 822

Wade v Varney [2003] W.T.L.R. 1535; see s.C(2). The summary deals with   **F–163**
the result of the hearing at first instance and the refusal of the single Lord
Justice to give permission to appeal out of time.

Zarrinkhat v Kamal [2013] W.T.L.R. 1477, Master Marsh, 16 July 2013.   **F–164**
This was an application under s.4 and a claim for reasonable financial
provision by H, the 51-year-old daughter of the testatrix (T). T died on 18
February 2009 leaving a net estate £573,000. By her will dated 29 October
2007 she left pecuniary legacies of £50,000 to H, £40,000 to her niece (Y) the
first defendant, and £10,000 to her son (F), the fourth defendant, who also
received her flat in London, worth £240,000. Residue was divided between Y
and F equally. T had given H approximately £16,000 during her lifetime and
F had received much more. Probate of the will was granted on 11 March
2011, but H did not issue her claim until 20 June 2012, some nine months
out of time. In practice it was not possible to separate the s.4 application
from the substantive claim, because the strength of the claim is relevant to
the s.4 application. H had lived in Germany for many years and German
was her primary language, though she had some command of English. She
sought to justify the delay on the basis that she was not fluent in English and
had difficulty in finding a German-speaking solicitor to assist her, and the
solicitors whom she had first instructed in 2009 (and disinstructed on 24
January 2010) did not advise her of the possibility of making a claim. She

also said that she had been constantly trying to negotiate with F in the hope that they could reach a fair agreement. *Found*: (1) the limitations of her English language skills had not put her at a significant disadvantage in taking advice about a claim or bringing a claim; (2) there was no satisfactory explanation for the delay of over 18 months between disinstructing her first solicitors and instructing new solicitors or for the further delay of nine months before the claim was issued; (3) her conversations with F could not be properly characterised as negotiations in relation to her claim; (4) the claim for provision was a weak claim (see the judgment at paras 23–32); she would receive a substantial legacy of £50,000 as matters stood and on the balance of probabilities she was likely to receive a substantial sum from her father's estate. *Held*: (1) the onus was on H to show sufficient grounds for the delay and she had failed to do so; (2) had the substantive claim been brought, no provision would have been made for H. The s.4 application was refused and the claim dismissed.

Section G—Jurisdiction and Procedure

G(1)—Domicile and Residence

F–165 *Agulian v Cyganik* [2006] W.T.L.R. 565, CA (Mummery, Longmore LJJ, Lewison J, 24 February 2006), reversing *Cyganik v Agulian* [2005] W.T.L.R. 1049 (Nicholas Davidson QC sitting as a deputy High Court judge, 13 March 2005). Determination of the preliminary issue whether the testator, Mr Andreas Nathanael (N), who was born in Cyprus in 1939, was domiciled in England and Wales on 17 February 2003, the date of his death. His net estate was sworn for probate at £6,527,362. N lived in Cyprus until about 1958; he then came to London, where he lived until 1972. After some two years of living in Cyprus, he returned to London in 1974 (the year of the Turkish invasion) and lived there for the rest of his life, returning to Cyprus only for visits which became less frequent as time went on. From 1974 onwards he built up a hotel business in London, but remained emotionally very strongly attached to Cyprus and spoke frequently of buying or building property there. From 1996 onward he built up a substantial balance in his bank account in Cyprus, which stood at £1.3 million at his death; and during his last significant visit to Cyprus in 2001–2002, he told his bank manager of his intention to retire to Cyprus and asked for his help in finding a property, though nothing came of that in the end. The claimant, Miss Cyganik (C) had come to England in 1992 on a student visa and was an illegal overstayer. She found work in a hotel owned by N, eventually attaining a responsible position, and a stable relationship developed between them. Her case was that on her 27th birthday, in 1999, they agreed to marry, and that the preparations made during 2002 would have culminated in a marriage at Easter 2003. The trial judge found as a fact, and the Court of Appeal upheld the finding, that the parties would have married had N not died unexpectedly. At trial, the judge concluded that at some time between 1995 when N made his will (under which C, to whom he left £50,000, was the only non-family beneficiary) and 1999, when she understood that she had obtained a commitment to marriage, N had formed the intention to reside in England and Wales "permanently or indefinitely", and declared accordingly. The Court of Appeal unanimously allowed the appeal. Mummery LJ, giving the leading judgment, held that in order to decide whether the deceased had acquired a domicile of choice at the date of his death, the court had to look at:

"...the whole of [his] life, at what he had done with his life, at what life had done to him, and at what were his inferred intentions...",

and that special care had to be taken in regard to the analysis of evidence about isolating individual factors present over time and treating a particular factor as decisive. He concluded that had the judge taken into account all the connecting factors with Cyprus and England over the whole of the deceased's life, he would have found that the evidence was not sufficiently cogent and convincing to establish such a serious matter as a change of domicile. As Longmore LJ put it in his analysis of the trial judge's judgment, the question was not so much whether the deceased intended to return permanently to Cyprus, as whether it had been shown that, by the date of his death, he had formed the intention permanently to reside in England. The crucial point was that he had a domicile of origin in Cyprus until it was proved that he intended to reside permanently or indefinitely in England.

Bheekhun v Williams [1999] 2 F.L.R. 229, CA (Auld, Chadwick LJJ, Sir   **F–166** Christopher Staughton, 2 December 1988) on appeal from Raynor James QC, Clerkenwell County Court. See s.A. The testator, who was born in Mauritius, died in 1993, aged 62, leaving an estate in England worth £72,000 and in Mauritius worth about £88,000. By his will he left his entire estate to his niece. The applicant had left the testator in 1975 and commenced divorce proceedings in 1977, but the decree nisi was not pronounced until 1990 and was never made absolute, nor had the applicant's financial claims in the divorce proceedings been resolved at the date of death. On appeal, it was held that the court was entitled to have regard to the whole estate and, having regard to the existence of the Mauritian property, the judge was entitled to award the applicant almost the whole of the English estate. His finding that the testator had acquired a domicile of choice in England was upheld.

Commentary
P. Stibbard, "Nationality as a (possible) passport to domicile" (1999) P.C.B. 360
J. Woolf, "A change of domicile" (2000) 5 T.E.L.J. 4
G. Miller, "The international dimension in family provision" (2001) I.F.L. 135
S. St John, "A wolf in sheep's clothing" (2009) 105 T.E.L. & T.J. 24

Case comment
Bheekhun v Williams (1999) 29 Fam. Law 379

Holliday v Musa [2010] 2 F.L.R. 702, CA (Waller, Rix, Wilson LJJ, 30   **F–167** March 2010), appeal relating to the finding on domicile. For the case summary of the judgment of the Court of Appeal in *Musa v Holliday* [2013] 1 F.L.R. 806, CA (Sir Nicholas Wall P, Lloyd and Sullivan LJJ, 15 October

2012), relating to the provision ordered at first instance, see s.E. Ramadan Guney (R), who was born in Cyprus, had died intestate in November 2006, survived by D, with whom he had had a relationship, their teenage son (H), and the six adult children of his marriage. Claims for provision out of his estate, as dependants, were made by D, H, and K, the adult son of D's previous marriage. The outcome of the substantive claim is summarised in s.E. This summary relates to the appeal against the finding of HH Judge Kushner QC that R had died domiciled in England and Wales. The detailed chronology set out by Waller LJ at [25]–[62] recounts the material facts. R was born in southern Cyprus to Turkish parents and in 1958 moved to England with his wife and two children to escape the sectarian conflict in Cyprus. Between then and his death in 2006 he purchased property including a home and a shop in England, and four more children of his marriage were born there between 1959 and 1967. He acquired residential properties as family homes and as investment properties, and after purchasing 55 burial plots in Brookwood cemetery (where his wife was buried in 1992) he bought shares in the cemetery company, Brookwood Park Limited. In 2000, some two years after their relationship began, he purchased a home for D, their child and the children of her previous marriage. During this period he did not entirely sever his ties with Cyprus. He bought a property there in 1992 which was let out to tenants, and maintained another property which he sometimes used himself. At about the same time he applied to the Inland Revenue for non-domiciliary status, giving his domicile as Northern Cyprus and stating an intention to retire there, though he never actually did so. In 2000 he declared his intention to stand for the presidency of Northern Cyprus, but this was not pursued as (inter alia, because he was not resident there) he was not qualified to hold the office. He maintained bank accounts in Northern Cyprus, to one of which £550,000 was transferred in 2004. He spent time in Northern Cyprus every year from 1996 to 2006, though much of the time between 2004 and 2006 was taken up by litigation there, and although he and D made holiday visits, he never set up a permanent home there and his diary entries referred to *living* in England and *visiting* Cyprus (emphasis as in the judgment). Also in 2006 he had wanted the vault in the mausoleum at Brookwood to be completed, as a final burial place for him, his wife and all the family. The appeal was dismissed. *Held*: (1) the issue was whether the court could infer that at any stage of R's residence in England, he had formed the intention to settle in England indefinitely and to abandon his domicile of origin, and the onus of establishing that was on those alleging it; (2) in considering that issue it was necessary to look at the whole of his life (*Cyganik v Agulian* [2006] 1 F.C.R. 406, CA, applied); it was common sense that the longer the residence, the stronger would be the inference of intention to reside permanently. However, it was important to balance that against any continued connection with his domicile of origin and the court had to be satisfied that R had simply not made up his mind, for, in that case, the domicile of origin would be retained; (3) on the evidence, R's permanent home had been in England for many years; importantly, it had been the home of both his families. His intention to return to Cyprus had been vague for some years and was never fulfilled. The indications were that he wished to end his days in England and be buried there.

F–168　*Kebbeh v Farmer* [2016] W.T.L.R. 1011 (HH Judge Purle QC, 23 December

2014). Trial of preliminary issue whether the deceased (M) died domiciled in England and Wales or in The Gambia, where he died on 26 September 2011. By his will dated 5 May 2006 he divided his residuary estate equally between his three daughters, two of whom were the children of his first marriage, which was dissolved in 1994, and the other (Jennifer), who was the child of his marriage in 2000 to the claimant (K). His will made no provision for K. M had an English domicile of origin but moved to Gambia in 1994 where he built himself a "rather splendid" home. There was much evidence from those who were close to him that he had expressed the intention to live indefinitely or permanently in Gambia and the desire to be buried there. It was not decisive that he did not obtain Gambian citizenship or that he retained a number of connections with England. Jennifer was born in England on 25 October 2001 and M had a property there in which he lived with her and K for a short time. She had obtained indefinite leave to remain in August 2001 but M returned to Gambia, with Jennifer, in late 2003. There was evidence that he intended her to be educated and brought up there. Although he had had business interests in England, he had ceased to take any active part in running the business by, at latest, 2000. He did make a will in English form with an English executor and beneficiaries in 2006, and in 2010 or 2011 he purchased two investment properties in England which formed part of his residuary estate. Neither of these matters was of importance in determining his domicile. He purported to divorce K in Gambia and he registered it there but it was found as a fact that he never served the papers on her. It might be said that as he had married a Gambian wife who had gone to the trouble of obtaining UK citizenship, that showed he remained domiciled in England. That might have been a powerful point had there been a conventional marriage, but even assuming that the parties were, as a matter of law, still married, it did not take anything away from the totality of the evidence demonstrating M's intentions. *Held*, M had died domiciled in The Gambia and accordingly K's claim must be dismissed.

Sylvester v Sylvester [2014] W.T.L.R. 127 (Master Marsh, 13 July 2012). The **F–169** deceased (S), a widow, died on 18 February 2008, survived by her four adult children, one of whom (T) made a claim for reasonable financial provision out of her estate. S was born in Carriacou, a dependency of Granada, on 20 July 1925, and was married in Trinidad in 1953. She came to live in England, where her husband (Sh) had already obtained employment, in 1957, and she also obtained employment, continuing to work until about the time when Sh retired, in 1986. Their two younger children were born in London, in 1959 and 1965, respectively. They purchased a house in Kilburn in 1962 and occupied it as the matrimonial home; Sh died in 2004 and S continued to occupy it until her death. The question whether she had acquired a domicile of choice in England and Wales was ordered to be tried as a preliminary issue. In addition to the family history summarised above, other significant factors were (1) S had strong family connections with England and Wales—all four of her children and her 10 grandchildren were living within the jurisdiction, but there were also family ties with Carriacou; (2) both S (in 1983) and Sh (in 1989) became naturalised as British citizens, but also maintained their citizenship of Grenada—S was on the electoral roll at the Kilburn address from 1980 until her death; (3) in 1981 a caution was registered on behalf of S recording her rights under the Matrimonial Homes

Act 1967 and at about the same time Sh decided to have a house built at Grand Bay, Carriacou. It was almost certainly built by the end of 1988 and was a substantial property capable of use as a permanent, not merely a holiday home; in 1989, about the time of Sh's retirement, the couple moved a good deal of their personal possessions there from their London home; (4) S thereafter spent much of her time in Carriacou but made frequent visits to London for medical treatment; (5) S's mother became ill and from 1996 until her death in June 1998 S was caring for her at her house at Mount Royal, Carriacou, which she later had rebuilt at a cost of some £20,000; (6) from about 2001 Sh's medical conditions necessitated longer and more frequent visits to London; in 2001 Sh was informed that he had terminal cancer and from September 2001 until his death in 2004 they lived together in the Kilburn house; (7) after Sh's death S went to Carriacou only twice more, once in connexion with his burial there and once for a short visit in early 2006. In September 2006 she was diagnosed with renal failure and it became impracticable for her to return to Carriacou had she wished to do so. *Held*: (1) cogent and clear evidence is required to show that a domicile of choice has been acquired; (2) the evidence of S's intentions up to the late 1980s was not sufficiently clear to show that she had rejected her domicile of origin; (3) although it was clear that Sh retained his domicile of origin until his death, S's position was different; (4) S was not in a position to make a choice during the period of Sh's illness but after his death, she could have returned to Carriacou and remained there. Her return to England after the brief trip in early 2006 was not forced upon her by ill health (see *Udny v Udny* [1869] L.R.1 Sc and Div. 441 for the importance of the choice not being dictated by external pressures such as illness, cited at para.63 of the judgment); she had a substantial home in Carriacou and the resources to obtain treatment there, but she chose to return to London; (6) the evidence pointed firmly to her then state of mind being that she intended to remain permanently in England and Wales for the rest of her life. The requisite intention had been formed by early 2006 at the latest. It follows that the court had jurisdiction to entertain T's claim, but there is no reported indication of its outcome.

F–170   *Witkowska v Kaminski* [2007] 1 F.L.R. 1547 (Blackburne J, 25 July 2006), on appeal from HH Judge Cowell, Central London County Court. Mrs Witkowska (W)'s claim for financial provision out of the intestate estate of the deceased was on the alternative bases that she was eligible as a cohabitant under subss.1(1)(ba) and 1(1A), or a dependant under subs.1(1)(e). The deceased died on 6 October 2002 and letters of administration were granted to the defendant (K), his son, who was the person solely entitled on intestacy. A particular issue was whether her claim could succeed, having regard to her illegal presence in England during the period of her cohabitation with and/or dependence on the deceased. W succeeded at trial but was given permission to appeal on the basis that that the trial judge had recognised that the award of maintenance at the rate of approximately £2,600 per year which he had made was inadequate to meet her needs if she were to continue to live in England, where she had, by the date of the hearing, been living for eight years. K was given permission to cross-appeal in relation to the question whether W was precluded from making a claim under the 1975 Act because her presence in the United Kingdom was illegal. Both the appeal and the cross-appeal failed. As to W's appeal, Blackburne J did not accept that the decision as to the level of maintenance assumed that W's residence in England continued to be unlawful. On the cross-appeal, he rejected the argument that her unlawful presence in England during the period while she was being maintained by and/or cohabiting with the deceased barred her from making a 1975 Act claim.

G(2)—Specific Provisions of the 1975 Act

Section 5 (interim orders)

Smith v Smith [2012] 2 F.L.R. 230 (Mann J, 8 July 2011). The claimant **F–171** widow (O) had married the deceased (T) in 1991, but the marriage broke down and in 2003 she returned to her native country, Russia, where she had a flat, and thereafter returned to England only for short periods, during which she stayed with T in the property which had been the matrimonial home ("the Property"). In 1992 T had made a will under which O was the principal beneficiary, but in 2005 he executed a further will, in favour of various relatives, and under which O took no benefit. T died on 23 July 2009 leaving a net estate consisting of the Property, worth £350,000 and other assets amounting to £175,000. On 20 January 2010 O commenced a probate claim challenging the 2005 will for lack of testamentary capacity and propounding the 1992 will, and, if that claim failed, making a claim under the 1975 Act. On 14 February 2011 she made a claim for interim relief under s.5, seeking a sum of £25,000 and (although she still lived mainly in her flat in Moscow and made occasional visits to England) an order that she be permitted to live in the Property. She stated that she needed the money in order to repay loans made to her by friends. *Held*, dismissing both limbs of the application: (1) she had failed to meet the requirement laid down by s.5(1)(a) of showing that she was in immediate financial need. She had not satisfactorily explained how she had managed between 2003 and 2009 and the historic pattern of her bank accounts raised serious questions as to what assets she had and has, and what she was living on. The need to repay loans made by friends which had been outstanding for many years did not amount to an immediate financial need, at least not in the absence of indications that they were seriously pressing for repayment; (2) it was not clear whether there was any jurisdiction to make on order permitting O to reside in the Property. On the assumption that there was, such an order would be made only if O could demonstrate a clear and immediate need or at least a very good reason why she should have that right of residence now. She had failed to do so; she had no family in England and there was no evidence that she wanted to move away from her family and social circle in Russia or make her home in the Property.

Case comment
R. Bailey-Harris [2011] Fam. Law 1200
R. Hughes [2011] Eld. LJ 1(4), 362

Section 6 (variation of periodical payments)

F–172   *Taylor v Bell* [2015] All E.R. (D.) 208 (LN, W, HH Judge Behrens sitting as
a High Court judge, Leeds, 16 February 2015). The claimant (T) was the son
of the deceased (G) who died on 18 December 2006 leaving a net estate of
approximately £2 million. G's will made no provision for him; it gave
pecuniary legacies to two charities and the residue to trustees as an accretion
to a discretionary trust created on the same day as the will. The beneficiaries
of the trust included G's other son (L) and remoter issue, but T was
excluded. T, who was aged about 17 at the time of G's death, made a claim
for reasonable financial provision out of G's estate, which was eventually
compromised by a consent order made on or about 27 May 2008 which
provided for periodical payments up to a maximum of £210,000 in total, so
as to provide maintenance for him during his education at sixth form college
and University. T was a talented singer and wished to train for a career in
music. The payments were to cease on 31 August 2014. Partly due to T's
learning difficulties and partly to his being seriously injured in a road traffic
accident shortly before the order was made, the anticipated timetable was
not met. In August 2014 he applied to vary the terms of the consent order so
as to cover the remainder of his undergraduate career, up till August 2015,
and a further two-year postgraduate course. At that stage he had received
payments amounting to £112,443.21; he claimed a further £90,000. By then,
it had become apparent to the executors that the full amount was not going
to be claimed; distributions had been made to other beneficiaries of the trust
with the result that the amount available was £38,479. For the executors it
was submitted that T bore a heavy onus in seeking to set aside the consent
order, that a variation should only be made if the circumstances set out in
Barder v Caluori [1988] A.C. 20 were made out. Reliance was also placed on
the importance of holding the parties to their agreement unless there were
good and substantial grounds to conclude that it would be unjust to do so;
see *X v X* [2002] 1 F.L.R. 508 at para.103. The court derived little assistance
from these and other authorities, which concerned matters within the
matrimonial jurisdiction, not applications to vary periodical payments
under the 1975 Act. *Held*: (1) the application was not to set aside the consent
order but to vary the periodical payments specified by the order under the
express power in the Act. There were no specific hurdles for T to overcome
and the discretion to exercise that power was unfettered; (2) in all the circumstances (see para.40 of the judgment), this was an appropriate case for
the exercise of the power conferred by s.6. The expressed purpose of the
order was to provide maintenance for T until the end of his postgraduate
studies and the fact that the timetable anticipated when the order was made
had proved inaccurate was not due to any failure by T to apply himself to
his studies. The application had been made within the period specified by
s.6(2) and the court had power, under s.6(10), to provide for the making of
periodical payments after the expiration of the period specified in the original order. T was awarded £6,500 for the final year of his undergraduate
studies and a further £7,500 for each of the following two years, conditional
on his attending a full-time course of postgraduate training.

Commentary
R. Selwyn Sharpe "Lesson plan" [2015] T.E.L. & T.J. (167), 26

Section 8(1)—Nominated property

Cairnes (deceased) Re, Howard v Cairnes (1983) 4 F.L.R. 225 (Anthony   **F–173**
Lincoln J, 18 March 1982). This was the trial of the preliminary issue
whether the death benefit under the pension scheme of which the deceased
was a member should be treated as part of the net estate pursuant to s.8(1)
of the 1975 Act. If that was not the case, the value of the net estate would be
very small. In this case, the defendant (C) was the former wife of the
deceased, whom she had married in 1954 and divorced in 1976, and the
applicant was the woman (H) with whom he had formed a relationship. The
deceased lived with each of H and C for varying periods after the divorce
and he continued voluntarily to provide financial support for C until his
death in January 1980. The deceased, who was employed by TWA as a
baggage handler, was a member of the TWA pension scheme, and the rules
which came into effect on 1 April 1960 required that he should nominate a
beneficiary who was either (a) his wife or (b) any person who immediately
before his death either in receipt of any regular payment from him or was
wholly or partly dependent on him for the ordinary necessities of life. If the
member left no widow and made no nomination, the benefit was payable to
his legal personal representatives. On 23 October 1968, he nominated C as
the beneficiary, using the form specially provided for in the rules, and that
nomination received the consent of the scheme trustees, which was necessary
to make it effective. It was submitted for H that the proper time of determining whether an alleged beneficiary fell within the designated class was
the time of the member's death, not the time of the nomination. Assuming
for the purposes of the hearing that that was correct, Anthony Lincoln J
found, on the evidence before him, that at that date C satisfied the
description of the second class of eligible beneficiary since the deceased was
contributing voluntarily to her support up until the time of his death. The
nomination of C was therefore, on any footing, effective. *Held*, the nomination was not made in accordance with the provisions of any enactment. It
was the case that the word "enactment" had on occasion been applied to
regulations made in pursuance of an enactment, but there was nothing in the
authorities to suggest that the meaning of the word could be widened to
include "a mere trust deed which is the creature of a contract between
employer and employee", nor any dictionary meaning which would support
such a wide construction. The words of s.8(1) were very plain and Parliament appeared to have stopped short of extending its protection to such
schemes.

Goenka v Goenka [2016] Ch. 267 (HH Judge Hodge QC, Chancery Division,   **F–174**
Liverpool District Registry, 6 August 2014). For the summary of the facts
and the award made, see s.A. On the death of the deceased (N), a death in
service benefit was payable pursuant to the provisions of the NHS Pension
Scheme Regulations. N had nominated his father (G), who was also an
executor and trustee of his will, as the person to whom the benefit should be
paid, and a sum of £201,000 was paid to G accordingly. This raised the issue

whether that sum should be treated as part of the net estate by virtue of s,8(1) of the 1975 Act, which provides, so far is relevant, that:

> "...where a deceased person has in accordance with the provisions of any enactment nominated any person to receive any sum of money ... on his death and that nomination is in force at the time of his death, that sum of money ... shall be treated for the purposes of this Act as part of the net estate of the deceased."

It was common ground that the applicable regulations were the National Health Service Regulations 1995 (SI 1995/300). Those regulations were made under powers conferred by ss.10 and 12 of, and Sch.3 to, the Superannuation Act 1972. It was submitted on behalf of G (as the statutory nominee) that the nomination was not caught by s.8(1) because the relevant regulations were not primary legislation. *Held*, although it was possible to give meaning and content to s.8(1) by construing "any enactment" as limited to primary legislation by way of Act of Parliament, there was no good reason to do so. There was nothing in the 1975 Act which would justify such a limitation to the scope of that section. It could be that the context indicated, in a particular case, that "enactment" was to be construed as not including subordinate legislation; see *Rathbone v Bundock* [1962] Q.B. 260. However, and consistently with the view expressed in *Re Cairnes* (1983) 4 F.L.R. 225, at 231–232, the nomination in the instant case, which was made pursuant to rules made by way of statutory instrument which itself was made under a power conferred by a statute, should, within the meaning of s.8(1), be regarded as "made in accordance with the provisions of any enactment". Accordingly, the death in service benefit fell to be treated as part of the net estate; see the judgment at paras 45–59, especially the concluding paragraph.

Section 8(2)—Donatio mortis causa

F–175   *King v Dubrey* [2016] Ch. 221, *sub nom. King v The Chiltern Dog Rescue* [2015] W.T.L.R. 1225, CA (Jackson, Patten, Sales LJJ, 9 June 2015) reversing in part [2014] W.T.L.R. 1411 (Charles Hollander QC sitting as a deputy High Court judge, 1 July 2014). See also s.E. [Note: This case is concerned with the question whether the gift of the deceased's house was a valid *donatio mortis causa*, not with whether (if it were such) it should be treated as part of the net estate. It is included here for convenience.] The main issue in the case was whether the deceased had made an effective *donatio mortis causa* (DMC), but the question whether the subject matter of the DMC fell to be treated as part of the deceased's net estate by virtue of s.8(2) of the 1975 Act did not arise. The claimant (K) claimed a declaration that his aunt (J), who died on 10 April 2011, had transferred her house to him by way of DMC and, in the alternative, that her will made in March 1998 did not make reasonable provision for him. At first instance the judge granted the declaration, holding that: (1) the gift had been made expressly in contemplation of death at a time when J was increasingly occupied with impending death. The contemplation of death within five months was contemplation of impending death; (2) the gift had not been revoked by subsequent attempts to perfect it by making a will; (3) J had parted with physical possession. K had placed the title deeds in a wardrobe in his room in the house, in a place known only to him and which was part of the property used only by him. The terms of his conversation with J indicated that she intended to part with dominion over the property. Her continued enjoyment of the property was not incompatible with an intention to make a gift which was effective on her death. *Vallee v Birchwood* [2013] W.T.L.R. 1095 was followed in relation to (1) and (3); see the judgment at paras 46 and 49. The evidence in relation to J's capacity to make a DMC came nowhere near justifying a conclusion that she did not have capacity to do so. He also found that, had the transfer not taken place, K, as a dependant of his aunt, would have been entitled to the sum of £75,000 as reasonable provision. The charities who were legatees appealed on five grounds, four of which were to do with the validity of the DMC, the other being that the award under the 1975 Act was excessive. By a respondent's notice K cross-appealed in respect of the quantum of the award, which he contended should have been £150,000. *Held,* (allowing the appeal in relation to the DMC) such gifts were anomalies and the doctrine ought not to be extended beyond its proper bounds. The requirements for the making of a valid DMC (see the judgment of Jackson LJ at paras 66–74) were that: (1) the deceased should be contemplating impending death—*Vallee v Birchwood* had been wrongly decided on this point; (2) the gift would take effect only if the contemplated death of the donor occurs and will otherwise revert to him; (3) the donor should deliver dominion over the subject matter of the gift to the recipient; that would include the means of accessing the subject matter or documents evidencing entitlement to the subject matter. On the facts of the case, the first requirement had not been met. Contemplation of impending death meant that the deceased should be contemplating death in the near future for a specific reason, though the contemplated death did not need to be inevitable. In the instant case, the relevant conversation had taken place at a time when J was not suffering from a fatal illness, nor was she about to undergo a dangerous operation or set out on a dangerous journey. Further, the words "this will be yours when I go" were more consistent with a statement of testamentary intent than a gift which was conditional on J's death within a limited period of time, and the parties subsequently acted as if the conversation had constituted a statement of testamentary intent. Thus, the second requirement was not satisfied. The appeal and cross-appeal against the alternative award under the 1975 Act were dismissed (see the judgment of Jackson LJ at 77–82).

Section 9—Severable share of chose in action

Lim v Walia [2015] Ch. 375, CA (Arden, McFarlane, McCombe LJJ, 29 July   **F–176**
2014). Appeal from HH Judge Hodge QC, sitting as a High Court judge, on the trial of a preliminary issue. On 21 May 2002 the deceased (J) and Mr Walia (W) took out a policy of fixed-term life assurance on their joint lives ("The Policy"). They married on 18 July 2003, lived together in a property in Lancashire, and their daughter (E) was born on 8 November 2004. The marriage broke down and when the parties separated, J went to live in the Philippines, where she formed a relationship with a Mr Lim (L). Their son, Philip (P) was born on 20 July 2009. In February 2011 J was diagnosed with

terminal cancer and she died intestate on 15 March 2011. By that time W had commenced divorce proceedings but the marriage had not yet been dissolved. Letters of administration were granted to him on 1 April 2011 and he inherited J's entire estate. As to the Policy, the obligation to pay arose (1) on the death of the first of the insured to die or (2) on satisfactory proof that one of the lives insured was suffering from a terminal illness; a claim of that nature had to be notified to the insurers. Only one claim would be paid in respect of the Policy. No terminal illness claim was made and the death benefit of £113,000 was paid to W on 19 May 2011. 1975 Act claims were commenced on behalf of P on 21 September 2011 and later that month by L, on his own behalf and on that of E. The preliminary issue was whether J, immediately before her death, was beneficially entitled to a joint tenancy of the right under the Policy (1) to benefit from her death before that of W, and/or (2) to benefit from her (assumed) terminal illness before her death. *Held*, at first instance, J was, immediately before her death, beneficially entitled to a joint tenancy of the right under the Policy to benefit from her (assumed) terminal illness before her death. The Court of Appeal unanimously held that that was correct. However, in order to facilitate the making of financial provision under s.9 of the Act, the court was required to determine the value of the severable share immediately before the death of the deceased. At that stage their views diverged. McCombe LJ, dissenting, concluded that the trial judge had been correct to look at the position immediately before J's death and to treat the proportionate share of the jointly held property as forming part of the net estate (as he had effectively done by ordering W to pay half the death benefit into court). The appeal was allowed, the majority (Arden and MacFarlane LJJ) holding that the Policy had to be valued taking into account that under the terms of the Policy, J's severable interest in the terminable illness benefit would cease on her death if that event occurred without a claim having been made. No claim for the terminal illness benefit having been made before J's death, the value of that interest immediately before death was nil. The judge was wrong in ordering W to pay half the death benefit into court; there was no interest of any value to be brought into the net estate under s.9(1).

Case comment
R. Bailey-Harris [2014] Fam. Law 1517

F–177   *Murphy v Holland* [2003] EWCA Civ 1862 (Court of Appeal, Pill, Chadwick, Thomas LJJ, 19 December 2003), on appeal from HH Judge Hywel Moseley QC. The issue was whether the proceeds of a policy of life insurance effected by the deceased and his then wife, which became payable (inter alia) on the death of the first to die, was property out of which financial provision could be made under s.9(1) of the 1975 Act. It was common ground that, by virtue of ss.9(4) and 25(1) of the Act there could be a beneficial joint tenancy of the policy. The trial judge found that immediately before the death of the deceased the policy was jointly held and the benefit of severance was built into it. Per Thomas LJ, the plain inference to be drawn was that the death benefit was intended by the parties to be payable to the survivor of them for his or her exclusive benefit. That was the ordinary inference where life insurance is effected for a fixed sum without profits, without a surrender value and without an endowment element. The appeal was allowed by the majority, Chadwick LJ dissenting.

Section 10 (reviewable dispositions)

B v IB [2014] 2 F.L.R. 273 (Parker J, 29 November 2013). H and W married **F–178** in 1984. There were three children of H's previous marriage, one of whom was his son (IB). Between 2002 and 2006, H transferred three sums of money to IB. The last of these, in the sum of £1.75 million, was made in 2006, five years before H died. In 2009 W filed for divorce and applied under s.37 of MCA 1973 to set aside the transfers. The district judge ordered the 2006 transfer to be set aside but IB successfully appealed that order. A retrial was directed and notice was given on behalf of W that she would seek an order under s.423 of the Insolvency Act 1986 as well as an order under s.37. H died before the retrial was concluded, leaving a net estate of about £2 million, and his will made no provision for W. She intended to commence 1975 Act proceedings but at the date of the hearing she had not been able to do so, as no grant of probate had been made. The issue at the hearing was whether she could pursue the s.423 remedy concurrently with the 1975 Act claim, in which she could apply for an order under s.10. *Held*, (1) the s.423 remedy was additional to the remedy under s.10 of the 1975 Act and was available even if there was no formal insolvency; (2) an applicant for an order under s.10 was required to prove that a disposition was made for the purpose of defeating an application for financial provision, whereas in a s.423 application, proof of a more general purpose to put assets beyond reach or prejudice interests was required. That was a wider test than the s.10 test and s.423 provided a wider remedy. Under s.10 the beneficiary of the disposition could be ordered to provide, for the purpose of making financial provision, such sum of money or other property as the court specified, whereas the effect of s.423 was to set aside the impugned transaction. In such a situation the principle in *Richards v Richards* [1984] A.C. 174 (per Lord Hailsham LC at 199) did not apply. The existence of the s.10 remedy did not preclude an application under s.423.

Case comment:
G. Douglas, (2014) 44 Fam. Law 287

Re Dawkins, Dawkins v Judd [1986] 2 F.L.R. 360 (Bush J, 8 October 1985). **F–179** Application by a surviving spouse, also noted in s.A. The testator died on 26 July 1982 aged 72. He and the applicant married in November 1978, it being the second marriage of each of the parties. By his will dated 3 February 1980 the deceased left £8,000 and a life interest in the matrimonial home to the applicant. On 1 May 1981 he transferred the matrimonial home for the sum of £100 to his daughter by his first marriage. Early in 1982 the deceased said that he wanted a divorce; the parties separated in May of that year although, when he later became ill, the applicant cared for him in the matrimonial home. By his will dated 19 June 1982 he left his entire estate to his daughter. She and her husband were in business, running an employment agency which was profitable. The estate was insolvent, but the applicant claimed, under s.10 of the 1975 Act, for provision to be made for her out of the net proceeds of sale of the matrimonial home, which amounted to £27,000 and had been kept in a separate account to await the outcome of this application. It was conceded that, had the matrimonial home been part of the estate, the later will would not have made reasonable provision for the applicant. She was living in a council house on an income of £47.78 per week. The evidence led irresistibly to the conclusion that the disposition of the matrimonial home was made with the intention of defeating a claim under the 1975 Act; the applicant was awarded £10,000 and a further £426.80 for the funeral expenses.

F–180 *Dellal v Dellal* [2015] W.T.L.R. 1137 (Mostyn J, 1 April 2015). J, described as a "legendary property dealer", died on 28 October 2012 survived by his widow (R), eight children (including two from his marriage with R) and a sister aged 96. J and R had married in 1997 following 10 years' cohabitation. By his will dated 15 November 2006 he left his entire estate to R, but the disclosed assets of the estate amounted to only £15.4 million. In her claim, commenced on 10 March 2014, R sought orders under ss.10 and 13, alleging that J's wealth had shrunk to such an extent that he must have given it away to the family members who were the defendants to the claim. The defendants applied to terminate the claim for an order under s.10 either by striking out the statement of case under CPR r.3.4(2) or by way of summary judgment in accordance with CPR r.24.2. In that regard they contended that: (1) R had not identified any disposition in favour of a defendant in the six years before J's death; (2) R had not identified any matters which could prove the necessary motive (i.e., that dispositions were made with the intention of defeating a claim for financial provision) and (3) given the scale of her assets, amounting to £41.5 million, R had no prospect of persuading the court to award her more (in which case there would be no room to exercise its discretion under s.10). For D2 and D7 it was also argued that ex parte orders granting leave to serve the claim form out of the jurisdiction (in New York and Switzerland respectively) should be set aside as being flawed by the breach of the duty of candour, and D7 also argued that the claim was abusive as R had commenced actions in Nyon and Geneva against her which were inconsistent with the English claims. *Held*: (1) the application to strike out did not in any respect meet the standards specified in CPR r.3.4(2) and would be dismissed. The power to strike out under para.(a) of that rule was limited to a claim which was not legally recognisable (*Wyatt v Vince* [2015] 1 F.L.R. 972 applied), and R's s.10 claim could not be so characterised. Nor was the claim an abuse of process within the meaning of para.(b); a claimant could plead a case in a laconic or protean way in anticipation of particularisation following disclosure, and that was what R had done (*Arsenal Football Club Plc v Elite Sports Distribution Ltd (No.1)* [2002] EWHC 3057 (Ch); [2003] F.S.R. 26 applied). Nor was it abusive, at any rate at that stage, for her to proceed against a defendant on different grounds in different places (*Clarke v Marlborough Fine Art (London) Ltd (Amendments)* [2002] 1 W.L.R. 1731 applied); (2) the application for summary judgment would be adjourned with liberty to restore and there should be specific disclosure pursuant to CPR r.31.12. Disclosure would be limited to all documents in the custody, possession or power of any defendant evidencing any individual transfer whose value was £10,000 or more to or for them during the six-year period ending on the date of J's death which derived from him or an entity over which he had de jure or de facto control. Summary judgment would be given where the claimant or defendant had no real prospect of success and there was no other compelling reason why the case or issue should be disposed of at a trial. R had put up a strong prima facie case that at his death the deceased had access to very considerable resources. The evidence was, however, thin as to (a) how those resources were held and (b) that outright dispositions were made to family members during the six-year period. It was a reasonable inference that most of those resources were held in trusts. In relation to dispositions and the existence of the required motive R's case was almost entirely inferential. However, although it was weak, it was not merely a speculative punt. It would be fundamentally unjust to terminate her application before there had been a scrutiny of the underlying documents which would prove conclusively whether or not the averrals by the family members that there had been no relevant dispositions in their favour were true or false; (3) the challenge based on service out of the jurisdiction was dismissed. Leave to serve out would definitely have been granted if the relevant matters had been disclosed.

Section 15 (bar to making 1975 Act claim)

Chekov v Fryer [2015] All E.R. (D.) 303; [2015] EWHC 1642 (Ch) (Master **F–181** Matthews, 23 June 2015). Antony Fryer (AF) died on 14 December 2014 survived by his two sons, who were the executors and sole beneficiaries of his will dated 17 January 1980. The claimant (C) was his former wife, their marriage having been terminated by divorce on 5 January 1981. The subsequent consent order for financial provision, as varied, stated (as provided by s.15(1) of the Act) that:

> "Neither party shall be permitted to claim against the estate of the other under the Inheritance (Provision for Family and Dependants) Act 1975 unless the parties shall remarry."

At that time an order under s.15(1) could only be made with the consent of both parties. The parties did not remarry but it was common ground that at the time of AF's death they were living under the same roof. C made a claim on the basis that she was a cohabitant within the meaning of ss.1(1A) and 1(1)(ba) of the Act; the defendant sons did not accept that. They applied to strike out the claim on the basis that the statement of case disclosed no reasonable cause of action. They contended that: (1) s.15(3) of the Act, which provides, so far as relevant, that where an order made under s.15(1) has come into force with respect to a party to the marriage, the court shall not entertain any application for an order under s.2 by that party, should be construed literally; and (2) that as the class of persons entitled to apply under s.1(1)(ba) was defined so as to exclude persons included in classes 1(1)(a) and 1(1)(b), a cohabitant who was a former spouse was not entitled to apply for an order under s.2. *Held,* (1) s.15(3) had no rational function except to implement s.15(1). The application which under s.15(3) was not to be made was one which otherwise would have been made by a person who was formerly a party to a marriage with the deceased. At the time of the divorce the only such person would have been one within s.1(1)(b). Thus the reference in s.15(1) in the Act as originally enacted to "being entitled to apply" was a reference only to entitlement arising under s.1(1)(b). There was nothing to indicate that that reference had been changed or expanded when s.1 was amended in 1996 to include claims by cohabitants. The application to strike out would therefore be dismissed; (2) the claimant's alternative argument that the consent order should be treated, by analogy with pre-nuptial agreements, as not binding in all circumstances, was rejected. A consent order embodies the agreement between the parties but is none the less an order of the court. The parties' mere agreement did not have the force of an order.

Commentary
C. Roberts, "He loves me... he loves me not", T.E.L & T.J (2015) 171, 20–23

Section 25(4) "Void marriage entered into in good faith"

F–182 *Gandhi v Patel* [2002] 1 F.L.R. 603 (Park J, 20 July 2001). The claimant applied for provision out of the estate of her late husband on the footing that she was entitled to be treated as the wife of the deceased pursuant to s.25(4) of the 1975 Act, which provides that "wife" includes a person who in good faith had entered into a void marriage with the deceased. Her claim failed on two grounds, the first being that the so-called "marriage" was not a void marriage, but a non-marriage; the second was that she did not enter into it in good faith. The distinction between a void marriage and a non-marriage appears from the authorities, in particular *A-M v A-M* [2001] 2 F.L.R. 6, which was treated as decisive. In *Gandhi*, the parties went through a Hindu ceremony of marriage in an Indian restaurant in London. The celebrant's evidence that the full requirements of Hinduism were met was accepted, and he also confirmed that nothing was done to comply with the requirements of English law for a lawful marriage in this country. English law recognises the validity of a marriage conducted in an overseas jurisdiction if the ceremony complies with the requirements of that jurisdiction, but it will not recognise a ceremony conducted in England which does not comply with the formal requirements of English law as giving rise to a marriage at all. The judge held that a void marriage meant the same thing in the context of s.25(4) of the Inheritance Act as it did in s.11 of the Matrimonial Causes Act 1973 and that the ceremony which the parties went through was not a void marriage within s.11; it was a non-marriage. The judge expressed the view that (questions of conduct aside) the provision made by the will was not reasonable. The deceased was a prosperous man; the parties had lived together for the last nine years of his life, and she had borne him two children. The only provision made for her was the right to reside in one of his houses, which had been left to a son, for life or until remarriage or cohabitation. Had she claimed in the alternative as a cohabitant under s.1(1)(ba) or a dependant under s.1(1)(e), he would have had to consider whether any award should be reduced by reason of her conduct but as there was no alternative application, the question did not arise.

Commentary
A. Francis, "A dangerous Act to follow" (2003) 31 F.L.J. 18
G. Miller, "When 'I do' turns into 'I didn't'" (2004) 154 N.L.J. 252

Case comment
R. Bailey-Harris (2002) 32 Fam. Law 262

G(3)—Costs

Lilleyman v Lilleyman (costs) [2012] 1 W.L.R. 2801 (Briggs J, 26 April   **F–183**
2012). Determination of costs after a successful claim by the widow (W) of
the deceased, resulting in her being awarded assets of total value £500,000.
Both W and the defendants (D) had made Pt 36 offers. On 27 July 2011 D
made both a Pt 36 offer and a without prejudice offer; the 21-day period for
acceptance of the Pt 36 offer expired on 17 August 2011. W did not accept
either offer. On 6 January 2012 D made a further without prejudice offer
withdrawing the previous without prejudice offer; the letter described the Pt
36 offer as having "expired". In the event the award to W was less advantageous to her than either the July 2011 Pt 36 offer or the January 2012
without prejudice offer. Two issues arose. The first was whether D's January
2012 offer had withdrawn the July 2011 Pt 36 offer; *held*, it had not done so.
The subject matter of that letter was clearly expressed to be the July 2011
without prejudice offer. Part 36 offers do not expire simply because the date
specified for acceptance for the purposes of r.36.2(2)(c) had passed; they
remain open for acceptance unless withdrawn by notice pursuant to
r.36.9(2) and continue to attract the costs consequences specified in
r.36.14(2), subject to the exception in para.(6). The second was whether, as
W had failed to obtain a judgment more advantageous than the July 2011 Pt
36 offer, it would be unjust to order that D should be entitled to their costs
and interest thereon as provided by r.36.14(2); *held,* it would not be unjust to
do so. The offer had been made long before trial and within a reasonable
time after an unsuccessful mediation, and there was no suggestion that W
had been adversely affected by any lack of relevant information or by the
conduct of D in relation to the giving of such information. It was common
ground that W should be entitled to her costs up to 17 August 2011 but it
was submitted that the full application of r.36.14(2) in relation to the subsequent period would leave her with insufficient resources for her maintenance. On a broad brush calculation she would be left with capital of
£380,000 excluding her home, which would be £145,000 more than the
Duxbury figure required to meet her income shortfall. That provision would
be modest but not obviously inadequate (see para.[20] of the judgment) and
there was little injustice in allowing the provisions of r.36.14(2) to take their
course. Nevertheless there was an injustice in allowing the parties to obtain a
full recovery of costs incurred in pursuing the litigation in the "no-holds
barred" way in which it was pursued, in particular Ds' refusal to concede
until the last moment that the will had not made reasonable provision for
W. It would be unjust if the strict application of those provisions were to
prevent the court from signifying its disapprobation of the "no-holds barred" approach adopted by an appropriate proportionate disallowance of the
costs to be recovered. Most of the responsibility for that approach, which
was not at all appropriate in claims under the Inheritance Act, lay with D
(see paras [22]–[24]). It was ordered that W's costs up to 17 August 2011 be
paid out of the estate and that she should pay 80 per cent of D's costs after
that date together with interest at the judgment rate.

Commentary
A. Francis, "Family Provision; what is the trouble with modern 1975 Act disputes?" [2012] Fam. Law 42, 1246–53
M. Holdsworth and L. Tatton, "Big money, short marriage" [2012] T.E.L. & T.J. 138, 4–7.

Case comment
R. Bailey-Harris [2012] Fam. Law 42, 949–50

F–184   *Thomas v Jeffrey* [2013] W.T.L.R. 141, CA (Laws, Rimer, Patten LJJ, 31 May 2012). Second appeal relating to a costs order. In the original proceedings, R had initially made a claim for some 50 per cent of his late father's estate or a lump sum of about £100,000, as reasonable provision out of the estate of his late father and under the doctrine of proprietary estoppel. Originally, only the executors were named as defendants, but the residuary beneficiary was joined at a later stage. The estoppel claim was not pursued at trial but the 1975 Act claim succeeded and R was awarded £36,475. His witness statement had provided very little information about his financial circumstances but disclosed that he had no capital and an income shortfall of roughly £200 per month. It referred to hire-purchase and credit card debts but did not specify his total indebtedness. The award of £36,475 made by Mr Recorder Wood at trial reflected the amount of his indebtedness, which was only ascertained from disclosure ordered by the recorder during the trial, of his own motion. The defendants argued that the costs of the trial should fall on the estate but that R should pay their costs up to the start of final preparation for trial, their principal ground being his failure to disclose relevant documents.. In his ruling on costs the recorder referred to the judgments of the Court of Appeal in *Ford v GKR Construction* [2000] 1 W.L.R. 1397. He directed himself that he had to consider whether anything different would have occurred before trial had there been disclosure, in particular whether an offer would have been made and whether the defendants would have approached the case in a different way. He had nothing concrete on which to base any such views and thus did not consider himself well placed to depart from the general rule that costs follow the event. Accordingly he ordered the executors to pay R's costs out of the estate on the standard basis. On the first appeal, HH Judge McCahill QC reversed the recorder's decision and ordered R to pay the costs of the claim. In his view, *Ford* had been wrongly applied by the recorder; there was no need to speculate about what might have happened to counterbalance what had actually happened. He considered that that error of law required him to exercise his own discretion afresh. *Held*, on the second appeal, *Ford* did not create a principle that any shortcoming on the part of a litigant had particular costs consequences; it simply provided a reminder of the necessity for a judge, when exercising his discretionary jurisdiction on costs, to take account of all relevant aspects of the case. The recorder had directed himself correctly and his decision was well within the ambit of his discretion in circumstances where the defendants had not made any complaint about non-disclosure before the trial, made any request or application for further disclosure, or suggested that the evidence disclosed at a late stage of the trial changed the complexion of the case so that they needed time to consider its implications. Further, he had not relied on the evidence adduced by the late disclosure in deciding that the will had not made reasonable provision for R and the claim would have succeeded without that evidence (see the judgment at paras 30–36). Accordingly, the judge was wrong to interfere with the original ruling and the recorder's costs order was restored.

Wharton v Mercer, Lawtel (12 March 2012, W(ca), District Judge Wright, Liverpool District Registry, 22 September 2011). The case is concerned with the incidence of costs in circumstances where the claimant (W) had brought proceedings in which he claimed financial provision out of his wife's estate and damages for breach of trust in the handling of a joint bank account, but had died shortly before the claims had been listed for trial. The parties had married in 1975, each of them having children of their previous marriages. By his will made in 1977, W left his estate to his wife and, if she failed to survive him, equally between his children and her son (M), the defendant. In 1980, they bought a house ("the Property") as beneficial joint tenants and in 1994 the wife made a will leaving her interest in the property to M. She explained in a note that she was making no provision for her husband because if he survived her, the Property would become his by survivorship. In 2005 W was admitted to hospital and then moved to a nursing home, where he remained until his death on 7 February 2011. On 30 June 2005 he had granted an EPA, which was registered on 15 August 2007. On 27 July 2005 he made a new will entitling his wife to live in the Property or to enjoy the income until her death or remarriage, upon which his share would pass to his children; if she did not survive him, it would go to them directly. On 2 August 2005 he served a notice of severance in respect of the Property and, eight days later, his wife served a similar notice. On her death on 11 October 2008, her half share of the property passed to M in accordance with her 1994 will. They had also maintained two joint accounts which at or about the time the time of her death held a combined balance of about £6,200. The Property was sold in April 2010 and W received approximately £88,000. For W it was submitted that: (1) while it might have been reasonable for his wife to leave her half share as she did, it was unreasonable for her not to ensure that the income should go to him during his final illness, whether he needed it or not, so he had some prospect of success in the 1975 Act claim; and (2) she had committed a breach of trust by putting money drawn from the joint account into an account in her sole name rather than purchasing an asset with it. *Held*, (1) the 1975 Act claim fell away as a result of W's death, but that was not a discontinuance in relation to costs; (2) there was no evidence that W's financial resources might become inadequate to meet his needs. He did not require the whole of his income in order to meet the cost of his care and additional extras, and he had capital of about £90,000, which would have been sufficient to top up his income, if required, during the short period of his remaining life expectancy, so the claim was bound to fail; (3) there was no breach of trust (*Re Bishop* [1965] Ch. 450 applied). Mrs Wharton was entitled to take money from the joint account. It had not been created for a limited or specific purpose and her position was the same whether she spent the money or simply transferred it to her own account; (4) as the 1975 Act claim would have failed, the defendant's costs would be paid out of W's estate. The judgment does not explicitly refer to the costs of the breach of trust claim.

F–185

F–186   *Wooldridge v Wooldridge* [2016] 3 Costs L.O. 531 (HH Judge Karen Walden-Smith, County Court at Central London, 25 May 2016). Costs judgment following the dismissal of the surviving spouse's claim (see the
summary at s.A). There were five defendants to the claim. D1–D3 were the
executors, D4 was the deceased's adult son (R) and D5 was the infant son of
the claimant's marriage to the deceased. The claimant accepted that she
should pay the costs of D1–D3 on the indemnity basis and those of D4 and
D5 on the standard basis, but it was argued for D4 and D5 that she should
pay their costs on the indemnity basis. There are no firm principles governing the basis on which indemnity costs should be awarded save that it
must be "out of the norm"; see *Excelsior Commercial and Industrial Holdings Ltd v Salisbury Hamer Aspden & Johnson (Costs)* [2002] EWCA Civ
879. It is not a basis for awarding indemnity costs merely that one party lost
resoundingly or that the case was unlikely to succeed or failed in fact; see the
judgment at para.12. However, the claim fell within the principle identified
in *Fiona Trust & Holding Corporation v Yuri Privalov* [2011] EWHC 664 by
Andrew Smith J that a claim which is "thin", "far-fetched" and "irreconcilable with the contemporaneous documents" is one where indemnity
costs should be ordered. T's claim was outside the norm because of its
weakness and the manner in which it was conducted. It had been exaggerated with respect to her lifestyle and her financial needs. As to conduct, T
had failed to deal with sensible offers to settle in the way that they ought to
be dealt with and had raised allegations of financial impropriety and tax
evasion without evidence that would withstand scrutiny to support them.
Accordingly T was ordered to pay the costs of D4 and D5 on the indemnity
basis.

G(4)—Other Procedural and Jurisdictional Matters

F–187   *Barker v Casserley* unreported, 23 October 2000 (Johnson J). The issue was
whether proceedings had been served within four months of issue as
required by CPR r.7.5. The power under r.7.6 to extend time for service is
not referred to in Pt 8; however, the district judge extended the validity of
the claim form. *Held,* the object of the CPR was to achieve justice; the
defendants who contested the extended validity must have known of the
existence and nature of the claim and their position was to seek to evade the
issue by recourse to procedural technicalities. CPR Practice Direction 8
confirmed that Pt 7 contained rules and directions applicable to all claims. It
would be extraordinary and contrary to the claimant's rights under the
European Convention on Human Rights for there to be no power to extend
time for service. The district judge had acted entirely in accordance with the
overriding objective.

F–188   *Burnard v Burnard* [2014] EWHC 340 (Ch) (W, HH Judge Behrens, Leeds
Chancery District Registry, 24 January 2014). G died on 15 September 2007
survived by the widow of his second marriage (S) and the three sons of his
first marriage. By his will dated 4 September 2007 he appointed S and the
partners in a firm of solicitors to be his executors. Probate was granted to S
on 29 December 2008. Her claim for reasonable financial provision was
made out of time, as was the claim by the sons for rectification of the will,
which was made on 22 December 2010. An order for the trial of preliminary

issues was made on 27 March 2013. The rectification claim was dealt with, at the court's suggestion, as a matter of construction. However, the court observed that there was a powerful argument that the will contained a clerical error and, given that S would require an extension of time in order to bring her claim, it would have been difficult to envisage circumstances where time would be extended for her claim and not for the rectification claim (para.66). Other issues included the validity of a declaration of trust (both whether it was a sham and whether it had been duly executed) and whether a TR1 had been duly executed, whether the deceased had had capacity to execute those documents and whether the execution of the TR1 had been procured by undue influence. *Found*, both the declaration of trust and the TR1 were valid documents. There was also an issue relating to the ownership of shares in a company (Grangeway) which was decided in favour of S on the ground that there was no reliable evidence of her ever having transferred the shares back to G, who had transferred them to her in 1993. Finally, the court referred to the vast amount of costs that had been incurred and urged the parties to put their heads together and achieve some sensible solution so as to avoid the whole estate vanishing in costs.

Gully v Dix [2004] 1 F.L.R. 918, CA. The substantive decision at first instance is summarised in s.BA. The case is also noted in s.E. The appeal was on the preliminary issue whether the claimant had cohabited with the deceased for the two years immediately before his death and/or was being maintained by him immediately before his death. The trial judge found in favour of the claimant on both issues and the Court of Appeal considered that he had approached the matter correctly and had not erred in law or in fact. **F–189**

Hannigan v Hannigan [2000] F.C.R. 650, CA (Peter Gibson, Brooke, Robert Walker LJJ, 18 May 2000). Claim by surviving spouse, struck out by the district judge for procedural irregularities; decision upheld by the circuit judge. Probate was granted on 11 December 1998, so that the six-month primary limitation period expired on 11 June 1999. The proceedings were issued on 10 June 1999, but, presumably as a result of a misunderstanding, they were issued not on the form N208 under the CPR, but on the old County Court form N208. In addition to that error, the statement of case was not verified by a statement of truth; there was no Royal Coat of Arms; a party was incorrectly named; no acknowledgment of service form was served on the defendants; and there were four things wrong with the claimant's witness statement, which were that it was signed in the name of her solicitors; it omitted the requisite legend in the top right-hand corner; there were no marginal notes and no 3.5cm margin. The exhibit was also defective, having no legend, no front page setting out a list of documents and their dates, and the documents were not paginated. The district judge concluded that the petition was not a statement of case as defined by CPR Pt 2 r.2.3, and added that, if he were wrong about that, he would in the exercise of his discretion refuse to allow any amendment, the proceedings being fundamentally flawed. On appeal, where an order was sought for relief under CPR Pt 3 r.3.9, and for permission to reinstate or amend the proceedings and witness statement in accordance with the CPR, the circuit judge considered the factors mentioned in CPR r.3.9(1) and, although he **F–190** was conscious of the effect that a refusal of relief would have on the claimant, he did not consider that he had power to rectify serious omissions; he referred to the fact that the proceedings were wrongly drawn even under the pre-CPR rules. There was too much wrong with the proceedings to exercise discretion in the appellant's favour. In the Court of Appeal, it was common ground that the circuit judge did have discretion under CPR rr.3.9 and 3.10 to grant relief from the district judge's order. The important factors were the interests of the administration of justice; whether there was a good explanation of the failure, and the effect that the granting of relief would have on each party. However, the petition, although in the wrong form, contained all the information the defendants needed to know in order to understand what was being claimed; they were told that CPR Pt 8 applied; and they were told that the claimant relied on the evidence in her witness statement filed with the claim. Although strongly critical of the way in which the claimant's solicitor had conducted her case, the Court of Appeal allowed the appeal as the sanction of striking out the claim would, in all the circumstances, have been disproportionate.

Commentary
M. Walker, "Latest CPR-and sloppy work by solicitors" (2000) 97 L.S. Gaz. 44
G. Harbottle, "Tales of procrastination and pedantry" (2004) 56 T.E.L.J. 4
S. Ross, "*Parnall v Hurst*—A cautionary tale" (2004) 9 E.C.A. 22
M. Iller, "Parting shot—The overriding objective at the sharp end" (2005) 39 P.I.L.J. 21
M. Iller, "Bending the rules—Part 3" (2005) 149 S.J. 1380
S. Ross, "Playing by the rules" (2007) 70 F.L.J. 7

F–191   *Lansforsakringar Bank AB v Wood* [2007] EWHC 2419 (QB) (Patten, J, 17 July 2007). In proceedings under the 1975 Act (neutral citation [2006] EWHC 929 (Ch)) Patten J had awarded the claimant, Dr Malcolm Wood, the sum of £300,000 out of the residuary estate of his late mother. Lansforsakringar Bank AB ("the Bank") were attempting to recover from Mrs Wood's executors or Dr Wood a judgment debt plus interest, amounting to some 1.25 million Swedish Krona (approximately £97,000). The Bank obtained an interim third party debt order under CPR r.72(4) but Master Leslie refused to make that order a final order under r.72.2(1)(a), and Patten J upheld the Master's decision. He held that the sum of £300,000 was not "a debt accruing due to the judgment debtor" (Dr Wood) "from the third party" (the executors of Mrs Wood's estate). Third party debt orders were introduced, as from 25 March 2002, by way of CPR Pt 72, and have replaced the method of enforcement formerly known as garnishee proceedings, which was regulated by RSC Ord.49. *McDowell v Hollister* was clear authority for the proposition that the interest of a beneficiary in a pecuniary legacy under a will could not be the subject of a garnishee order. In *Re Jennery (Deceased)* the Court of Appeal had held that an order for a lump sum payment under the Inheritance (Family Provision) Act 1938 was not an order for a payment of a sum of money which would enable the court to exercise its powers under the then applicable RSC Ord.42. Following these authorities, Patten J held that the effect of an order under s.2 of the 1975 Act was simply to re-order the provisions of the deceased's will and not to make anything equivalent to an order for payment of money that could properly be described as a debt under r.72.2.

Nathan v Leonard [2003] 1 W.L.R. 827 (Mr John Martin QC sitting as a deputy judge of the Chancery Division, 28 May 2002). The questions were: (a) whether a clause in a will excluding a beneficiary if he disputed the will was triggered by a 1975 Act application; and (b) whether clauses of this nature were void as being contrary to public policy. There are no English decisions relating to (a) but in two Commonwealth decisions (*In the Will of Gaynor* [1960] V.R. 640, an application under Pt IV of the Administration and Probate Act 1958 (Victoria); *Re Kent* (1982) D.L.R. (d) 382, an application under the Wills Variation Act 1979 (British Columbia)) it was held that such an application did bring the clause into operation. Contrary to those decisions, but in accordance with two 19th-century decisions in this jurisdiction (*Cooke v Turner* (1847) 15 M. & W. 727; 153 E.R. 1044, approved by the Judicial Committee of the Privy Council in the case of *Evanturel v Evanturel* (1874) L.R. 6 P.C. 1) it was held that such clauses do not offend against public policy.

F–192

Commentary
L. King, "No-contest clauses" (2002) 99 L.S. Gaz. 32
J. Pickering, "Where there's a will, is there a way?" (2002) 41 T.E.L.J. 10
C. I. Howells, "Will drafts" (2003) 153 N.L.J. 977
S. Ross, "Forfeiture clauses in wills" (2003) 1 T.Q.R. 7
G. Harrap, "Developments in Inheritance Act claims" (2004) 9(2) E.C.A. 26
E. Exton and J. Washington, "The Inheritance (Provision for Family and Dependants) Act 1975: recent cases and developments" (2008) P.C.B. 101

Nesheim v Kosa [2007] W.T.L.R. 149 (Briggs J, 4 October 2006, on appeal from Master Price). Diana Kosa died on 24 October 2003 and probate was granted to N, who lived in Norway, on 7 January 2005. The report of the case does not state the nature and extent of the net estate, but K's claim was for the transfer to him of his wife's share of the matrimonial home, alternatively, a grant to him of a life interest or other right to reside in it. The claim was intimated to N's English solicitors in correspondence which began on 9 February 2005, and the claim form was issued on 5 July of that year. N's English solicitors informed K's solicitors that they had no instructions to accept service, and on July 7 reminded them of the need to obtain permission to serve out of the jurisdiction. On 14 November K's solicitors had the claim form resealed for service in Norway and it appears that they considered that permission was not necessary because it was a claim which could be served under the Lugano Convention without permission. On December 30 (six days before the time limit for serving out of the jurisdiction would have expired), a copy of the proceedings and a translation into Norwegian were purportedly served on N in Norway. In the course of the copying, the original date stamp of 5 July 2005 was omitted, so that on its face the claim form was stamped with the date of re-sealing. Since the four-month limit for service within the jurisdiction had by that date expired, N's English solicitors, when acknowledging service on 18 January 2006 stated that they intended to dispute jurisdiction on that ground. On 15 February a copy of the original claim form bearing the 5 July 2005 date

F–193

stamp was faxed to them and on 17 February they first took the point that the service in Norway was invalid, since permission to serve out had not been obtained and Inheritance Act claims were outside the scope of the Lugano Convention. On 20 February Master Price granted retrospective permission to serve out; on 1 March N applied to set that permission aside and on 20 March K made a fresh application, on notice, for retrospective permission. Dealing with those applications de novo on the merits, Briggs J identified a tension between two competing principles, viz.: (1) CPR r.3.10 (an important purpose of the overriding objective and the CPR was to avoid, as far as possible, long, costly and arid warfare over procedural matters, and to focus on resolving the underlying issues); and (2) rules governing the commencement and service of originating process were there to be obeyed and were likely to be strictly enforced. In Briggs J's judgment, the principal objection to the grant of retrospective permission was the seriousness of the failure to seek permission to serve out, even where (as in the instant case) it would have been granted if sought. Such relief would be given sparingly and only after very serious consideration of its appropriateness. The situation had been brought about by the errors of K's lawyers in adopting the view that permission was not required and their inactivity in that respect once they had been notified that N's English solicitors would not accept service. He therefore considered that (as in *Hannigan*) the overriding objective was a speedy and economic trial of the issue where there was a bona fide and arguable case, and was therefore directly opposed to a focus on essentially procedural matters. To refuse retrospective permission would be to put the need to discipline lawyers for a genuine mistake ahead of the clear interests of doing justice between the parties. The order made by Master Price was therefore affirmed, the defendant's appeal was dismissed and her application to set aside the order was refused. Permission to appeal was also refused.

F–194 *O'Brien v Seagrave* [2007] 1 W.L.R. 2002 (HH Judge Mackie QC sitting as a judge of the Chancery Division, 4 April 2007), on appeal from Master Price. The case concerns the right of a claimant for an order under the 1975 Act, who has no interest under the deceased's will or on his intestacy, to commence a probate action. CPR r.57.5(1) requires that the claim form in a probate action must state the interest of each party in the estate. The claim form issued by C, who had lived with the deceased for the last 12 years of his life, disclosed no such interest, and Master Price granted the application to strike it out but gave permission to appeal. Judge Mackie held that he was not bound by any authority; however, C had a clear and accepted financial interest in the outcome of the dispute and one would expect her to have the right to bring such an action. Were the case to have been decided in the context of the CPR generally, rather than in the probate jurisdiction, he would expect her to have a sufficient interest to seek a declaration. The facts of the case were unusual and that of itself made it improbable that a decision favourable to C would "open the floodgates"; and if such cases became more common, the importance of removing a potentially unjust obstacle would be emphasised. Accordingly he held that C's right to bring a claim under the 1975 Act was a sufficient interest to permit her to proceed as a claimant under CPR r.57.

O'Reily v Mallon [1995] N.I. 1 (Campbell J, Chancery Division, Northern   **F–195**
Ireland, 10 March 1995, LN, T612). O died on 20 November 1987 and the
main beneficiaries under his will were two of his three sons. His widow (E)
and the other son (R) brought claims under the 1979 Order. At a hearing on
12 June 1991 it was found that E was in need of immediate assistance and an
order was made under art.7 (corresponding to s.5 of the 1979 Act) for O's
executor to make payments to E in respect of certain specified expenses. E
died on 1 January 1992 and R contended that E's claim survived her death
as a cause of action subsisting against or vesting in her in accordance with
s.14 of the Law Reform (Miscellaneous Provisions) (Northern Ireland) Act
1937. *Held*, applying *Whytte v Ticehurst* [1986] Fam. Law 64 at 69 and
Bramwell v Tobin [1988] 2 F.L.R. 263, E's claim was personal to her and did
not enure for the benefit of her estate; R's only cause of action was in respect
of any payments that might be outstanding under the order of 12 June 1991.

Re Parker's Estate, Parker v Gibson [1999] N.I. 315 (Girvan J, Chancery   **F–196**
Division, NI, 28 September 1999, LN, W(ca)). By his will, A left his estate to
his executors on trust for his wife, C, for life and after her death for G, his
daughter by an earlier marriage. Before he died, he transferred the family
home to G. C applied for an order under art.12 of the 1979 Order (corresponding to s.10 of the 1975 Act) on the basis that the transfer had been
made without her knowledge and was not for full valuable consideration.
On the preliminary point raised by G that C's application was premature, as
no grant had been taken out, Girvan J distinguished *Re McBroom* [1992] 2
F.L.R. 49 on the ground that in the instant case it made sense to have the
question whether the transfer was a transaction intended to defeat an
application for financial provision resolved at an early stage, as there was
little else of any value in the estate.

Parnall v Hurst [2003] W.T.L.R. 997 (HH Judge Langan QC). Application   **F–197**
to strike out for non-compliance with procedural requirements and/or as an
abuse of process. *Found*, (a) there was only one breach of the rules, that
being the failure to comply with CPR r.8.5, which requires a claimant in Pt 8
proceedings to serve their evidence with the claim form; but (b) she was also
in breach of para.4 of the Practice Direction Protocols, in that she did not
act reasonably in exchanging information before proceedings were commenced; indeed, an offer of settlement was made on her behalf although she
had at the time of the offer provided no financial information. The judge
was also critical of the issue of a caveat by her solicitors, the delay in service
of the proceedings until almost the end of the four-month period, the service
of particulars of claim (which are, of course, inappropriate to a Pt 8 claim)
and the failure to serve the witness statement until many months after it had
been signed. *Held*, to strike out the claim would be a drastic remedy for the
breach which had been established. If the court could deal justly with the
case by the imposition of some penalty less than striking out the claim, it
should do so. Relief from sanctions would be granted because: (a) the claim
had merit; (b) the court should be reluctant to dispose of a claim such as this
at an early stage and without a substantive hearing; (c) the case was not one
of wholesale disregard or repeated breaches of court rules and procedures;
(d) the real fault lay not with the claimant but with her solicitors; and (e) it
was possible to deal with the default by an appropriate costs order. Relief

from the sanction imposed by CPR r.8.6 (that is, permission for the claimant to rely on her witness statement notwithstanding that it had not been served with the claim form) was therefore granted on terms that:

(i)   none of the costs incurred on her behalf up to the date of publication of the judgment should be recoverable from the defendants; and

(ii) the defence costs from the date of entry of the caveat to the date of publication of the judgment should be paid by the claimant in any event.

It was further ordered that, at the conclusion of the litigation, the claimant's solicitors should show cause why a wasted costs order should not be made, so as to render irrecoverable by them some or all of the claimant's costs referred to in (i) above, and to make payable by them some or all of the defence costs referred to in (ii) above.

Commentary
G. Harbottle, "Tales of procrastination and pedantry" (2004) 56 T.E.L.J. 4
S. Ross, "Parnall v Hurst—A cautionary tale" (2004) 9(2) E.C.A. 22
S. Ross, "Playing by the rules" (2007) 70 F.L.J. 7

F–198   *Pinnock v Rochester* [2011] EWHC 4049 (Ch) (LN, W, Sales J, 15 November 2011), on appeal from the order of Mr Recorder Thomas QC, Central London County Court. The deceased (S) died on 24 December 2005, three days after making a will naming the defendant (R), who was his sister, as his sole executor and universal legatee. Probate of the will was granted to R on 3 April 2006. The claimant (P), the son of the deceased, had been born on 29 December 1988; thus, the time limited by s.4 would have expired before his 18th birthday and the claim was brought by his mother as litigation friend. His paternity was challenged but confirmed on 2 July 2007 in the report of a DNA test. In subsequent correspondence P's solicitors initially and throughout stated that P reserved his right to challenge the validity of the will, even after the conclusion of the 1975 Act proceedings. On 1 April 2008 a consent order was made under which P accepted a payment of £27,500 (and costs of £21,500) in full and final settlement of his 1975 Act claim. On 27 November 2008 P issued a probate claim and on 1 September 2009 R applied to strike it out on the basis that, having brought the 1975 Act proceedings and accepted a payment in full and final settlement, he had affirmed the validity of the will and it would be inequitable and/or an abuse of process for him now to dispute it. In holding that it would be inequitable to allow the probate claim to proceed, the recorder adopted the analysis of s.3(1) of the Inheritance (Family Provision) Act 1938 (a provision in identical terms, so far as is relevant, with s.19(1) of the 1975 Act) by Wynn-Parry J in *Re Pointer* [1946] Ch. 324, at 326, and concluded that the effect of the compromise of the 1975 Act claim was that he was to be treated for all purposes as a beneficiary of the will, leading to the further conclusion that by so doing, he had asserted the validity of the will (see paras 8–10 of the judgment of Sales J setting out the relevant passages). *Held*, (allowing the appeal against the striking out of the probate claim); (1) a 1975 Act claim is a claim for proper financial provision to be made for the claimant out of the estate and is conceptually independent of the existence or otherwise of a valid will. There was no inconsistency or illogicality involved in a claimant saying that an existing will is invalid, but, if it is valid, it does not make reasonable provision for him; (2) if, as in the instant case, a claimant would have a claim to the estate or part of it if the will is set aside, he would have to bring that into account in the subsequent administration of the estate; (3) s.19 did not have the effect that a person who seeks an order under the 1975 Act is to be taken as necessarily affirming the will; it was concerned with stipulating when certain events are deemed to have occurred, in particular, in the context of the incidence of capital taxes. That analysis was not undermined by anything said in *Re Pointer*; (4) on its proper construction, the consent order contained nothing to rule out the possibility of a later challenge to the will; in its own terms it was simply an order in respect of P's 1975 Act claim and said nothing about any other claim which he might properly have brought.

Commentary
S. Hodgson, "Reserving the right" [2014] T.E.L. & T.J., 153, 26

Roberts v Fresco [2017] EWHC 283 (Ch) (Simon Monty QC sitting as **F–199** deputy judge of the Chancery Division, 17 February 2017). This case summary deals only with the issue whether a potential Inheritance Act claim by a surviving husband against his deceased wife's estate abates on the death of the husband. Mr and Mrs Milbour married in 1973. Mr Milbour (H) had a son (who predeceased him) and a daughter from his first marriage, and Mrs Milbour (W), had a daughter from hers. Originally, the first claimant (LR) had claimed provision out of W's estate as a child of her family, alternatively as a person being wholly or partly maintained by her immediately before her death, and the second claimant (FM), the daughter of H's son who had predeceased him, as a person being wholly or partly maintained by her immediately before her death. W died on 5 January 2014, leaving a net estate of £16,776,054. By her will, dated 29 October 1993, she left H a pecuniary legacy of £150,000 and an interest in the income of £75,000. Neither LR nor FM's father benefited under that will. H died on 20 October 2014, without having brought a claim for provision out of W's estate. The claimants applied to amend the claim form so as to make the claim which H could have made under s.1(1)(a) of the 1975 Act. However, there are two decisions of the High Court in which it was held that a claim under the 1975 Act, like a claim for financial provision in matrimonial proceedings, does not survive the death of the applicant. In *Whytte v Ticehurst* [1986] Fam 64, Booth J held that a surviving widow, who applied under the 1975 Act but had died before the substantive hearing, had no enforceable right against the deceased's estate and hence no cause of action that could survive her death and be enforced by her personal representatives. That decision was followed in *Re Bramwell deceased* [1988] 2 F.L.R. 263, where Sheldon J reached the same conclusion, holding it to be clear from the authorities that in matrimonial proceedings a claim for financial provision neither gave rise to nor became a cause of action unless an order had been made in respect of it before the death of the deceased; until that time, it remained a mere hope or contingency which survives neither against nor for the benefit of the deceased's estate. Similarly, a claim under the 1975

Act was not a cause of action within s.1(1) of the Law Reform (Miscellaneous Provisions) Act 1934 ("the 1934 Act") unless an order had been made before the death of the surviving spouse; until then it remained a hope or contingency of no surviving value to a deceased claimant's estate. For the claimants it was contended on two grounds that those cases were wrongly decided and should not be followed. (1) Before his death, H had a reasonable expectation of succeeding in his 1975 Act claim, and that expectation was a possession within the meaning of Art.1 of Protocol I of the European Convention on Human Rights, which appears at Pt II of the Human Rights Act 1988 and provides that "Every natural or legal person is entitled to the peaceful enjoyment of his possessions". This argument failed; H was now deceased, and his estate was neither a natural or legal person. There was no scope for arguing that Art.1 rights were engaged in the present case. (2) On a true construction of the 1975 Act, there was nothing in its wording to suggest that claims could not, in principle, be brought after the applicant's death, particularly in the case of a claim by a spouse which is not limited to reasonable financial provision for his maintenance. However, *Harb v King Fahd Bin Abdul Aziz* [2006] 1 W.L.R. 578, CA was clear authority for the proposition that a claim under the Matrimonial Causes Act 1973 ("the 1973 Act") for financial provision does not survive the death of both spouses. Dyson LJ had said in *Harb* that had it been intended that a claim under the 1973 Act should survive for the benefit of the estate of a potential claimant, the statute would have expressly so provided. It seemed to the judge that a similar point could be made in respect of claims under the 1975 Act; the 1975 Act does not expressly provide for such claims to enure for the benefit of a deceased's estate. *Held*, the 1975 Act gave a personal right to bring a claim, but that right was not itself a cause of action; it was a hope or contingency which fell short of being a cause of action in the sense of "a state of facts which if true enable the applicant to get a remedy from the court" (Lord Diplock's definition in *Letang v Cooper* [1965] 1 Q.B. 232, 242–3, considered). The facts were not determined until the court has carried out the s.3 exercise; until that point, the claim remained a hope. In the present case, there was no enforceable right at the time of death (*Sugden v Sugden* [1957] P. 120, per Denning LJ at 134–5 considered) and thus no cause of action. The claim abated on H's death. The test for whether permission should be given for an amendment to a claim form under CPR r.17.3 is summarised at para.17.3.6 of *Civil Procedure 2017* as being the same as under Pt 24 (Summary Judgment) viz., whether there was a real rather than a fanciful prospect of the claim succeeding. The application to amend the claim form to enable the claim which H had had before his death had no real prospect of succeeding and should be dismissed.

F–200 *Seals v Williams* [2015] W.T.L.R. 1265 (Norris J, Manchester District Registry, 16 April 2015). There had previously been litigation between the parties (*Williams v Seals* [2015] W.T.L.R. 339, David Richards J) in which Mrs Williams, as executrix of the estate of the late Arnold William Seals, had successfully sought an order that the chief land registrar be directed forthwith to cancel a caution against first registration of a farm property (Wallands Farm) in Derbyshire. She was also the sole beneficiary under Mr Seals' will and his estate included a 50 per cent interest in Wallands Farm. He also wrote a letter of wishes explaining that he had made no provision for his three adult children (the respondents to Mrs Williams' application) because they had not been in contact with him since his wife died and he preferred to leave his estate to someone who had been a very good friend to him. The letter was to be produced if a claim was made under the 1975 Act or otherwise. The respondents contested the truth of the letter and intimated challenges to the will on the grounds of undue influence and lack of testamentary capacity. They also asserted a claim to an interest in Wallands Farm on the basis of proprietary estoppel. The hearing before Richards J began on 24 October 2014 and at that date the only claim issued by any of the respondents was a 1975 Act claim by the deceased's two sons. The judgment records that the parties had given serious consideration to mediation and that Richards J considered mediation to be virtually essential. Proceedings were directed to be transferred from the High Court to the Manchester District Registry of the Chancery Division as all the witnesses lived in Derbyshire. However, the mediation process stalled because of differing perceptions of the issues in dispute and the strength of the respective arguments. At the hearing before Norris J the parties proposed that the court should undertake an early neutral evaluation (ENE) of the case. Norris J welcomed this course as being highly commendable and observed that it was being adopted in both the Birmingham and Manchester District Registries. *Held*, the advantage of ENE over mediation was that a judge would evaluate the parties' cases in a direct way and might provide an authoritative (albeit provisional) view of the legal issues and an experienced valuation of the evidence available to be deployed in addressing them. The expression of provisional views, with a view to assisting the parties reduced the areas of dispute and the general scope of the argument was not dependent on the consent of the parties but was simply part of the judge's inherent jurisdiction to control proceedings before them. If the parties asked a judge to express provisional views on particular hypotheses then it was part of the judge's judicial function to accede to doing so. In the instant case, the directions were carefully crafted so as to afford the settlement judge the opportunity to make non-binding recommendations as to the outcome and to state short reasons for doing so without in any sense attempting a provisional judgment. The directions also provided that in the light of the recommendations, the parties may agree a consent order, and they would be bound, not by the outcome of the ENE, but by their consent to the making of the order.

Commentary
D. Houghton, "Is early neutral evaluation the start of a new way of resolving probate disputes?" [2016] Eld. LJ 6(1), 25–28.

Tibbs v Beresford-Webb, finally disposed of in the Court of Appeal, reported   **F–201**
as *Tibbs v Dick* (1998) 2 F.L.R. 1118 (Stuart-Smith, Swinton Thomas, Aldous LJJ, 25 June 1998). Initially, a 1975 Act claim by Miss Tibbs and her son Jason was compromised out of court, on the day of the hearing, on terms that they would receive, respectively, £10,000 and £6,250 out of the deceased's estate, out of which their costs would also be paid. The value of the estate, which passed under the deceased's will to his nephews and nieces, was in the region of £300,000. The compromise was embodied in a Tomlin order. When Miss Tibbs received the order from the court, she did not

accept that those payments were in full and final settlement of her claim, but thought that they were interim payments. She contended that she would not have accepted it but had no alternative because there was a bankruptcy order against her. Her application for leave to appeal was heard by Morritt and Thorpe LJJ, and was granted, the cases of *Edgar v Edgar* [1980] 3 All E.R. 887 and *Camm v Camm* (1983) 4 F.L.R. 577 being regarded as possibly supporting the proposition that a consent order could be set aside if had been entered into as the result of bad legal advice. It was also thought arguable that it could be set aside for mistake. On the hearing before the full court, it was found that (a) Miss Tibbs and Jason were not led to believe that the payments were interim payments; and (b) there were various good reasons why counsel might have advised the acceptance of a relatively low offer. It was held that even if she had received bad or negligent advice from her lawyers, that was not a ground for setting aside the order. A consent order would be set aside for fraud or mistake, but not because of bad advice. *Edgar v Edgar* was concerned, not with a consent order, but with the enforcement of an agreement entered into between the parties, and bad advice was relevant only to the question whether the agreement should be enforced. Similar considerations applied to *Camm v Camm*. The appeal was dismissed.

INDEX